TANGANYI
A
SIA
NYASALAND
L. Nyasa
ort
on
Zomba
Blantyre
ambezi
MOZAMBIQUE
INDIAN OCEAN
tali
Beira
FEDERATION OF
RHODESIA AND NYASALAND
Boundary of the Federation
Boundaries of other States
Railways
100 0 100 200
MILES
D. SCHAFER

The Welensky Papers

The Rt. Hon. Sir Roy Welensky, K.C.M.G.

The Welensky Papers

A History of the Federation of Rhodesia and Nyasaland

J. R. T. WOOD

GRAHAM PUBLISHING
DURBAN

To Carole

The Graham Publishing Company (Pty) Ltd
P.O. Box 37387, Overport 4067, Durban

First published 1983

Standard Hardcover Edition ISBN 0 620 06410 2
De Luxe Limited Edition ISBN 0 620 06411 0

Printed by Printpak (Cape) Ltd
Dacres Avenue, Epping 3, 7460 Cape

Contents

List of Illustrations

Author's Preface

THE inspiration for this book came from Sir Albert Robinson who was anxious that the vast and rich collection of manuscripts, memoranda, minutes and correspondence of the Federal era possessed by Sir Roy Welensky should be exploited while the Federation of Rhodesia and Nyasaland was still fresh in the minds of its participants. Sir Albert sought the assistance of Mr Harry Oppenheimer who readily suggested that The Ernest Oppenheimer Memorial Trust might help with the project and this it has done with unstinting generosity. The University College of Rhodesia (now the University of Zimbabwe) accepted the commission in 1969 and I was appointed in 1970 as a Research Fellow to assist Professor R. S. Roberts in the task of cataloguing the Welensky Papers (now lodged in the Bodleian Library, Oxford). In 1973 I was given complete charge of the project under the guidance of Lord Blake.

The purpose of the project was to exploit fully a unique and otherwise closed collection of papers. As this collection comprised, in the main, most of the papers which found their way into the Federal Prime Minister's office, it very soon became apparent that the main theme was the history of the Federal and territorial constitutional relationships with Britain. I concentrated on this because it provides the framework on which future studies will hang. There is much more to be won from the Papers and they will provide a fertile field for research into a wide range of Federal activities and life in the Rhodesias and Nyasaland from 1938 to 1963. The strength of my account is that it is based on material which will not be generally available for a decade or more.

My greatest debts are owed to The Ernest Oppenheimer Memorial Trust for its most generous sponsorship, to Sir Albert Robinson for his ready encouragement and advice, to Lord Blake for his guidance, and especially to Sir Roy Welensky who not only gave me access to his Papers, but provided me with an office and everything which goes with it. His daughter and secretary, Mrs Joan Bridge, made me and my assistants welcome and guided and counselled all of us. The pleasant atmosphere of her office made our task all the more enjoyable. In addition to providing me with office accommodation, Sir Roy read my drafts and submitted to innumerable interviews. He corrected many mistakes of fact but never censored me and I am deeply grateful for the time which he gave to the project. I am also grateful to Mr P. G. Henwood, Secretary to The Ernest Oppenheimer Memorial Trust until early 1980, and to his successor, Mr G. R. H. King, for their efficient and good-humoured assistance.

In researching the book, I have been greatly assisted by the hard-working Kathleen Greenburg, Pam Burke, George Gibbons, Jenny Briscoe, Lyn Purves and Ann Campbell. Without their accurate, painstaking research, persistence and encouragement, for which Lyn Purves deserves particular mention, the book would have taken longer than the decade of its gestation. My wife, Carole, had the arduous task of typing the 700 000 words of the first draft and did so with unfailing accuracy and good humour. Pam Flint, Fiona Whitfield, Shirley and Deborah Graham, Shelly Bolton and Enos Majoka matched Carole's accomplishment with the second draft. I am particularly grateful to Mr Gordon Graham, my publisher, for his tireless, meticulous and merciless attention.

Nothing gets done in the field of academic research without the assistance of librarians and archivists, and I was truly well served by Mr E. E. Burke and Mr R. W. S. Turner of the National Archives of Rhodesia (now the National Archives of Zimbabwe) and their staff. The Librarians of the Library of the Parliament of Rhodesia (now the Library of the Parliament of Zimbabwe), Mr G. Dellar and his successor, Mr E. E. Burke, and their staff were particularly helpful. Rhodes House and the Bodleian and the University of Zimbabwe Libraries provided me with efficient and speedy service.

The Principals of the University of Zimbabwe, Professor Robert Craig and Professor L. J. Lewis, counselled and guided me, while their Registrars and Bursars administered the project with unfailing efficiency. Charter Consolidated of London, through the good offices of Major H. St L. Grenfell and Mr John Richardson, not only provided me with a base in London but afforded me the services of Ruth Cook who spent many hours on the telephone arranging dozens of interviews. She found addresses for me and the trains and buses to get to them.

There are many others who contributed to the success of the project. The University of Zimbabwe Principals' secretaries, Mrs Rhodes and Mrs Penfold, and the History Department's secretary, the late Mrs Pat Thompson, had much to do. Enid Cocksedge of the Bursar's Department dealt good-humouredly with a multitude of requests. Val Shaw attempted to keep me tidy.

In writing this History, I am indebted to the work of others: in particular to Sir Roy Welensky, Dr H. I. Wetherell for his study of Amalgamation, to Lord Blake, the Hon J. M. Greenfield who also read my drafts, Professors L. H. Gann and R. I. Rotberg, Lord Birkenhead, Sir Nigel Fisher, the Rt Hon Harold Macmillan, the late Lord Butler, Lord Alport, and the others whose works provided the basis on which to build. In addition I had hundreds of conversations with people in all walks of life, with Prime Ministers, Secretaries of State, Governors, senior civil servants, leading politicians, as well as men in the street. Particularly helpful to me were Lord Alport, the Rt Hon Julian Amery, Sir Robert Armitage, the late Sir Malcolm Barrow, the late Sir Hugh Beadle, Sir Arthur Benson, the late Mr Colin Black, Mr J. F. Bowles, the Rt Hon Lord Boyd, the late Mr W. V. Brelsford, Lord Brockway, Sir Cecil Burney, Mr R. Burns, Mr R. P. Bush, the late the Rt Hon Lord Butler, Sir John Caldicott, the late Mr E. D. Campbell, Mr Chad Chipunza, the Hon James Clark, Mr T. P. M. Cochran, the late Mr Ian Colvin, the late Mr Stanley Cooke, the Rt Hon Lord Colyton, the late Sir Colin Coote, the Rt Hon Lord Dalhousie, Mr A. C. W. Dixon, the late the Hon Clifford Dupont, the Hon Geoffrey Ellman-Brown, Sir Athol Evans, the late Sir Patrick Fletcher, Sir Charles Footman, Sir John Foster, the late Mr W. D. Gale, Prince Yurka Galitzine, the Hon Benjamin Goldberg, Sir William Gorell-Barnes, the Hon Julian Greenfield, Major H. St L. Grenfell, the late the Rt Hon James Griffiths, the late Sir Ernest Guest, Lord Hale, Mr J. Hennessy, the Rt Hon Lord Home of Hirsel, the late Sir Evelyn Hone, the late Mr F. S. Joelson, Sir Glyn Jones, Mr A. R. Kemp, Sir Richard Luyt, Mr J. P. MacDonagh, the late Sir Donald Macintyre, Sir Ian Maclennan, the Rt Hon Harold Macmillan, the late the Rt Hon Reginald Maudling, Mr H. J. Millar, the late Mr Charles Mzingeli, Mr W. S. Parker, Sir Hugh Parry, Mr and Mrs Stanley Pegrum, Mr J. Pollock, the late Sir Charles Ponsonby, Sir Ronald Prain, the late Sir Gilbert Rennie, Sir Kenneth Roberts-Wray, Sir Albert Robinson, Lord Salisbury, the late Mr S. Sawyer, the Hon. I. D. Smith, Colonel B. G. Spurling, Mr B. St Quinton, Sir Robert Stanley, Colonel D. Stirling, the late Sir Andrew Strachan, the late the Hon. A. R. W. Stumbles, Mr J. W. Swan, Mr D. Taylor, Sir Robert Taylor, the late Sir Robert Tredgold, Mr G. F. van Eeden, Mr T. R. Wade, the late Sir Kenneth Wheare, Sir Peveril William-Powlett, Mr S. E. R. Wynne and Mr K. Young. The Rt Hon Harold Macmillan assisted me even further by not only sending me a proof copy of the final volume of his memoirs, *At the End of the Day*, but by allowing me, in conjunction with his publishers, Macmillan Limited of London, to quote extensively from both the latter volume and his penultimate one, *Pointing the Way, 1959-61.*

Salisbury, Zimbabwe J. R. T. WOOD
March 1982.

Foreword by Lord Blake

THE Federation of Rhodesia and Nyasaland, like the Crusader Kingdom of Jerusalem, now looks like an aberration of history — a curious deviation from the inevitable course of events, a backward eddy in the river of time. It lasted only ten years. It began with a 19-gun salute when its first Governor-General, Lord Llewellin, steamed into Salisbury station on a heavy overcast day on 4 September 1953. It faded out at midnight on 31 December 1963. Lord Malvern (Godfrey Huggins), one of its architects and its first Prime Minister, was asked earlier that day whether he was distressed at its end. "No," he replied, "I shall have my usual whisky with dinner. Then I shall go to bed and allow the Federation to pass away in my sleep."

The story of the origins, history and end of the Federation are set out in full by Dr Richard Wood in this major work - the first to be based on full documentation from the Federal side. The British Foreign and Colonial Office documents are closed till 1983–93 under the thirty-years' rule, but one cannot wait for ever, and it is possible to gain much valuable information from published sources and private interviews. Nobody can be sure, but it seems unlikely that researchers are going to gain startling new insights when these archives are opened up. No doubt some "t's" will be crossed and some "i's" dotted, and a certain amount of detail hitherto unknown will emerge. It would be surprising, however, if this will fundamentally alter the history which Dr Wood has written.

The attack which is most likely to be launched against his book is that he has based himself mainly on European rather than African sources, and that his narrative is essentially the history of what white men did rather than black men. This would be an unfair and basically anachronistic criticism - which of course will not stop it being made. The fact is that the history of the Federation of Rhodesia and Nyasaland must be primarily an account of the political, commercial and administrative decisions of Europeans because the system was such that they were the only people in a position to decide. It can be argued that this was a bad thing, that the white monopoly of power went on far too long, and that the Africans ought to have been given a share of it, perhaps all of it, many years earlier. But the history of a period deals with what happened, not what ought to have happened, or with what actually happened several years later. Dr Wood's book is largely based on the papers of Sir Roy Welensky, the other architect of the Federation and its second and last Prime Minister. The fate of the Federation did not depend only upon him and his colleagues. It depended also upon another set of Europeans in Whitehall and Westminster, as the book makes clear. But it did not depend on African attitudes except in a very general sense — the repercussions of their unquestionable misgivings, doubts and downright hostility upon the outlook of those who in the end made the final decisions.

One can see now that if a union between Northern and Southern Rhodesia was to have any chance of lasting, it ought to have been made much earlier, and it ought not to have been complicated by the addition of Nyasaland, a protectorate which had no common history with the other two and was historically, economically and racially quite different. Things might have been otherwise. Rhodes had intended Nyasaland to be a part of his gigantic empire, like many other areas which he never in the end acquired — Katanga, Moçambique, Bechuanaland. But his efforts were frustrated by the tenacity of the Commissioner of Nyasaland, Sir Harry Johnston, his former protegé, but later bitter enemy. By a curious and still inexplicable intervention from the Foreign Office, which suddenly produced the necessary funds to keep Nyasaland going, Johnston was saved from the take-over bid which Rhodes was planning. In 1894 Nyasaland slipped away from the clutches of Rhodes's British South Africa Company (the Chartered Company), never to return.

Union between Northern and Southern Rhodesia was frequently mooted from an early stage. The Chartered Company, which had vast interests in both territories, was in favour of it. Leander Starr Jameson, who was president of the Company, was a strong advocate and so was Drummond Chaplin, the Administrator of Southern Rhodesia. In 1917 the Southern Rhodesian Legislative Council actually carried a resolution in favour of amalgamation with the North. But the majority was only made possible by the "official" or nominated Members. The elected Members were against it by eight to four, and the Company decided not to pursue the matter. The snag was that the settlers on both sides of the Zambezi River were hostile to amalgamation, though for different reasons. The Northern Rhodesian settlers, who only numbered about 3000, thought that Livingstone would become a mere backwater and that their own representation on an enlarged Legislative Council in Salisbury would be no compensation. The Southern Rhodesian settlers who wanted "responsible government" for themselves thought that their chances of extracting it from Whitehall would be damaged if the ratio of white men to black men went down from 1 in 27 to 1 in 60, as would be the case if the two territories were united. Whether they would have pressed this argument if they had known of the immense mineral wealth in the Copperbelt is another matter, but the technological change which made possible the exploitation of the low-grade sulphide ores in that region did not occur for another ten years. The conventions which governed relations between Whitehall and the elected Members of a Colonial legislative assembly were such that the Colonial Office would not lightly force through a major constitutional change over their heads, even though the Secretary of State had the legal power to do so.

There matters stood for eleven years till the setting up of the Hilton Young Commission to consider the future of all the British possessions in East and Central Africa. By now European opinion in Southern Rhodesia was in favour of amalgamation with the North, and, if the Southern Rhodesian Prime Minister, H. U. Moffat could have had his way, it would have been carried over 20 years before the Federation of Rhodesia and Nyasaland came into being. The Hilton Young Report issued in 1929 was divided. The Commission was unanimously in favour of federating Kenya, Uganda and Tanganyika, but excluding both Nyasaland and Northern Rhodesia. The Chairman himself considered that the "railway belt" (the central strip comprising the line of rail from Lusaka to Katanga) should be amalgamated with Southern Rhodesia, that North Eastern Northern Rhodesia should be joined to Nyasaland as a Crown Colony, while, in the west, Barotseland would become a native reserve governed as a separate protectorate. There would be a central authority to co-ordinate defence, tariffs and communications under the authority of the Governor of Southern Rhodesia acting as High Commissioner for the other territories and taking over the supervisory powers of Whitehall in respect of African and imperial policy. This arrangement would have suited Salisbury admirably. Southern Rhodesia would now have direct rule over the most prosperous area of the North, without having to take responsibility for the impoverished remainder.

The other Commissioners favoured leaving the *status quo* unaltered as regards Northern Rhodesia and Nyasaland, and this was the view taken by the British Government. In fact it is very doubtful, given what happened to the Commission's recommendations about Uganda, Kenya and Tanganyika, whether even unanimous support for Sir Edward Hilton Young's plan would have carried the day. This is for two reasons. First, copper had become a key strategic metal, and it was much easier to control the Copperbelt through the machinery of a Crown Colony governed directly by the Colonial Office, than one governed for all internal purposes by a settler legislature. Second, the doctrine of "paramountcy", promulgated under the signature of the Duke of Devonshire in 1923, stated that native interests should be regarded as paramount over those of immigrant communities. The context was the status of Indians in Kenya, but the doctrine could obviously have a wider implication. It did not apply directly to Southern Rhodesia with "responsible government", but it could certainly be regarded as relevant to Northern Rhodesia and used as an argument against subordinating Africans north of the Zambezi to a settler government in Salisbury. There were other sources of opposition. The British South Africa Company which had been pro-amalgamation in 1917 had now become hostile, and the Northern Rhodesian settlers remained for the most part on the same side.

Both the strategic and the "trustee" arguments were powerful, but in retrospect one can see that the chance of creating a prosperous multi-racial

Central African state had been missed. Of course it might not have worked anyway, but a unitary state set up in the 1930s possibly could have succeeded where a federation set up 20 years later was to fail. At any rate some of the major difficulties encountered by those who ruled the Federation of Rhodesia and Nyasaland would not have been so serious or damaging then as they were to be later. Obviously a unitary state might have become a mere appanage of South Africa with the same dogmatic commitment to total white ascendancy. But the population ratio was so different that the accommodations and compromises needed to create a mixed racial, social and political order might have been easier to achieve. The sceptics would say that the chances were slim. They were to be even slimmer in the 1950s.

The whole question was to arise again before the Second World War. The amalgamationists had not given up. From 1933 onwards the majority of the Northern Rhodesian settlers were in favour of a union. Their most conspicuous opponent, Leopold Moore, went over to the other side. The settlers were by now alarmed lest they should be merged with the East African protectorates where African interests were bound to be paramount. The Governors of both Northern and Southern Rhodesia, Sir Hubert Young and Sir Herbert Stanley, supported amalgamation. The British South Africa Company under Sir Henry Birchenough had reverted to the attitude of Jameson and Chaplin in 1917. Sir Ernest Oppenheimer, whose companies controlled the larger part of the Copperbelt, took the same view. Under these pressures the British Government in 1938 set up another Commission to investigate the situation in Central Africa. The Chairman was Lord Bledisloe, a former Governor-General of New Zealand. An immense amount of evidence was taken — far more than by any previous investigative body. Some of it is highly significant in the light of later events, particularly the evidence of the various African organisations in the two Rhodesias and Nyasaland. They were uniformly hostile to amalgamation which they saw as an extension of Southern Rhodesian settler power and ideology into the paternalistic sphere of Colonial Office administration. In an appendix to the Report there was an interesting comment which at the time surprised Godfrey Huggins (later Sir Godfrey and then Lord Malvern), the Southern Rhodesian Prime Minister, and also made him think. The African, it said, "possesses a knowledge and shrewdness in matters affecting his welfare, with which he is not always credited. It would be wrong to assume that his opposition is based, to a very large extent, on ignorance or prejudice or an instinctive fear of change".

The Commission came out against amalgamation of the Rhodesias, with or without Nyasaland; the reason was largely the discrepancy between the "native" policies of the three territories which were less discriminatory in the North but also less successful in terms of material welfare. The Southern Rhodesian African was better off than his northern brother but he was more of a stranger in his own land, the subject of a conquest which left an indelible impression on his whole way of life. The Commission was not prepared to go beyond recommending an inter-territorial council to co-ordinate fiscal policy, transport, development and administration. Nothing further occurred. The war swept considerations of constitution making away for the time being, and all that resulted from the Bledisloe Report was the setting up in 1944 of the recommended inter-territorial council. It was christened "the Central African Council". It was only to be advisory and it had no effective powers. Amalgamation was not even on the horizon. There had, however, been debates in 1939 of some importance in both Houses of Parliament on the Report. Lord Bledisloe made the case for Southern Rhodesian native policy, but Lord Lugard, a name with which to conjure, came down heavily on the other side. He was and always will be associated with the policy of "indirect rule", i. e. rule through traditional African offices or institutions. From his point of view it seemed that in Southern Rhodesia these had been deliberately or accidentally destroyed. He vigorously opposed any form of political union with the North. He carried with him almost the whole of the academic and intellectual Africanist world, A. B. Keith, E. A. Walker, Margery Perham and many others. The lines were drawn for the political battle that was to rage after the war. It was that element in British society which was to criticise the creation and policies of the Federation most strongly and to welcome its dissolution most eagerly.

The prospects for closer union of Southern and Northern Rhodesia did not seem at all promising on the eve of war. Ten years later the scene had changed. The reader must follow the detailed course of Dr Wood's narrative to understand why this transformation occurred, but one or two features can be singled out. The turning point was the year 1948 in which three crucial elections took place in Africa. The first was on 28 May in the Union of South Africa. A majority of the popular vote supported Smuts but the vagaries of the first-past-the-post system gave a parliamentary majority to Dr Malan's National Party, the supporters of *apartheid.* This result was a disagreeable shock to the British Government. The South African situation had long been one of doubt and anxiety. The personal position of Smuts, however, had masked the realities. His reputation as an imperial statesman and member of the British War Cabinet in 1917–18, and his close relations with Churchill in the Second World War gave the impression that he both symbolised and spoke for his country. He appeared to move in a sphere high above parochial politics. His defeat and the victory of the Nationalists caused a silent, peaceful but conclusive change in South Africa. The Afrikaner leaders were hostile towards Britain. Many of them had been positively in favour of the Nazis, with whose racial doctrines, transposed into African terms, they had some sympathy. This new situation resulted in a major revision of British policy towards South Africa.

The South African general election was followed almost at once by two others equally significant. On 27 August Roy Welensky, a strong supporter of amalgamation, won the day, insofar as it could be won by an electoral process, in Northern Rhodesia. On 16 September Huggins, whose political position had been precarious ever since his narrow escape from defeat in 1946, obtained an overwhelming majority in the Legislative Assembly. Both the Rhodesias were now led by powerful personalities deeply committed to amalgamation in some form or other, and the victory of Malan was bound to make the British Government more sympathetic towards their case. The need for a counterpoise to South African power had always been a part of the case for a Central African state. This need seemed stronger than ever, now that power in the Union had fallen from the hands of the friendly Smuts into those of a political party with a very different outlook.

The importance of the changed course in South Africa deserves strong emphasis, for it affected just those elements in Britain which were naturally least inclined to support amalgamation – Labour and Liberal MPs and their sympathisers in the academic and administrative world. Their instinct was to oppose amalgamation on the grounds that articulate African opinion in Northern Rhodesia and Nyasaland disliked the whole concept. It was easy to suspect the movement as a sort of Southern Rhodesian sub-imperialism, an attempt by the most deeply entrenched of the settler communities north of the Limpopo River to acquire the wealth of the Copperbelt, and consolidate their entrenchment. Labour was in power in Britain with an overwhelming majority, and the climate of opinion was adverse to the plans of Huggins and Welensky. But the South African election made many people of the Labour Party think again. Anyone who had studied the mentality of the Nationalists in South Africa knew that their leaders meant business. *Apartheid* was not a mere piece of rhetorical electioneering. Its supporters were ideologues and fanatics, with a surge of opinion behind them; it was not at all likely that the election result would be soon reversed. In fact the Nationalists have been in power from that day to this. The case for a powerful Central African state, based on the hope of achieving a multi-racial system, became far stronger than ever before in the eyes of the Left. Not all were convinced but enough were, to make the notion at least a subject for serious consideration. On two points, however, the whole of British official opinion was clear. There was to be no question of a unitary state. It had to be a federal system which reserved African affairs for the component territories and retained their direct links with the Colonial Office. The second was that Nyasaland had to be included, for this was the only way in which the Colonial Office could rid itself of financial responsibility for that impoverished, backward, debt-ridden protectorate.

Both Huggins and Welensky paid visits to London in October 1948, hoping to strike while the iron was hot, in the aftermath of the three southern African elections. They soon found that amalgamation in the sense of a unitary state was not on. Nor was there any chance of playing off one political party in Britain against the other. Oliver Stanley, the Conservative "shadow" for the Colonies, made it clear to Welensky that, on this issue at least, the major Parties pursued a bi-partisan policy. It was federation or nothing and, what was more, federation which gave very substantial powers to its component parts. No British Government, whatever its political colour, would put the four million Africans of Northern Rhodesia and Nyasaland under the direct rule of a settler-type regime of the sort prevailing at Salisbury. It was also made clear that even if a federation was agreed – which was by no means certain in the late 1940s – there would be a price to pay, namely the inclusion of Nyasaland. On both these major conditions successive British Governments remained adamant during the next five years.

At this stage one is bound to wonder whether the two conditions were not in themselves fatal for the success of the central African state. The inclusion of Nyasaland, a country with a tiny white population and one far better suited to direct "colonial" rule than to responsible government, was a major disadvantage. African advancement there was sure to lead to a demand for secession, and, if there is one feature which is essential for the success of a federation, it is that the regions not only should not have the right to secede but also that they should not be perpetually clamouring for that right. Secession, more than slavery, was what the American civil war was about. When Western Australia petitioned the British Government to secede from the Australian Federation, the petition was rightly turned down flat, and there has been no trouble since. Much of the trouble in modern Canada stems from the quasi-secessionist attitude of an influential Party in Quebec. The European political establishment in Southern and Northern Rhodesia would in some ways have been only too glad to see the last of Nyasaland. It was the precedent that was so damaging, for if Nyasaland could secede, why not Northern Rhodesia? And this was of course what happened.

The other question is whether a federal system should have been adopted at all. It is interesting that not only were Huggins and Welensky against it, but also two of the leading contemporary constitutional lawyers, Sir Kenneth Wheare, who was an Oxonian Australian of the highest academic eminence, author of the standard work on federalism, and Sir Robert Tredgold, Chief Justice of Southern Rhodesia, later of the Federation. Wheare who was consulted in 1949 by Huggins's Minister of Justice, Sir Hugh Beadle, saw great difficulties in creating a federation out of territories at such different levels of constitutional development as Nyasaland at one end and Southern Rhodesia at the other. One could not easily elevate the former or depress the latter, but without some such movement he did not believe that federation would work. A unitary state would be a better answer.

Sir Robert Tredgold in 1951 was equally clear that this was a preferable alternative. In a memorandum which he showed to the Governor of Southern Rhodesia, Sir John Kennedy, and to Patrick Gordon Walker, Dominion Secretary, after seeing the Report of the Conference of Officials he wrote:

> "It took one of the bitterest civil wars in history to prove what should have been obvious from the beginning, that a problem, the concern of the whole union could not be settled in one state and another way in other states.
>
> This to my mind is the fatal defect in the proposals in the Report. They seek to avoid an issue which is unavoidable. They endeavour to postpone a decision which can only be made vastly more difficult by delay."

There can be little doubt that the criticism was justified. Native policy was to be the rock on which the Federation was destined to founder, and the distribution of power was such that federalism exacerbated the situation. What should have been done? Tredgold's solution was a unitary state with a second chamber constituted to protect African rights, and provision for a veto by the UK Government in the last resort. He did not spell out how the second chamber would be elected or appointed — a crucial question by no means easy to solve. Nor did he say how the Africans were to be persuaded of the virtues of a unitary state, especially since it was usually advocated by the exponents of settler supremacy and not by people like Tredgold. Still, the idea had its advantages. It certainly would have been more economical and less complicated than the system enacted. There would have been one Governor, a single civil service, and two legislatures instead of four of each — quite a saving.

Among the advocates of a Central African state two stood out head and shoulders above the others. But for Sir Godfrey Huggins and Sir Roy Welensky the Federation would never have come into being. It is true that neither wanted it in the particular form that it eventually took. Indeed they much preferred amalgamation of the Rhodesias to a Federation which embraced Nyasaland as well. But it is equally true that no form of closer union would have been achieved at all if these two influential political figures had not thrown their full weight behind it.

For Huggins it was the closing episode in a long career which he began as a successful surgeon and ended as Prime Minister of the Federation, Privy Councillor and Viscount Malvern. When he retired in 1956 no Prime Minister in the history of the British Empire had served the Crown continuously for so long, not even Sir Robert Walpole. Huggins first became Prime Minister of Southern Rhodesia in 1933 and held that post for the next 20 years. He then moved up to be the first Federal Prime Minister, making way three years later for Welensky. He was a very English figure. He came from an upper middle class family in Kent, went to school at Malvern College (hence his title), qualified as a doctor at St Thomas's, and emigrated to Salisbury in 1911 at the age of 28. He always referred to England as "home" and he spoke with the ordinary English accent of his class and none of the flat vowels which distinguish the Rhodesian and South African way of speech. He had the imperturbable temperament, the geniality and the good health which are so helpful to a Prime Minister. His one physical defect was deafness but he put even this to good use, e.g. by ostentatiously taking off his deaf aid and putting it on the table when a well-known bore had been addressing the Assembly for long enough. He was not a man of original ideas. He was a pragmatist who always moved just a little ahead of the generality of settler opinions; he has been described as "a consummate politician", and certainly his success in retaining power justifies the phrase. He was a skilful negotiator and in Britain felt none of that slight inferiority complex which some "colonials" evince in dealings with Whitehall.

Welensky, although at one with Huggins on the question of a Central African state, was a very different personality. He had come up the hard way and he did not have a drop of British blood, despite his strong identification with a British Empire that was vanishing, even as he rose to power within it. He was born in 1907. His father was a Lithuanian Jew, his mother an Afrikaner who died when he was eleven. He was their thirteenth child, and he lived alone for several years with an aged father who, after making and losing money all over the world, had come to Bulawayo in 1894 as a loser and was never to recoup his fortunes. Welensky had to earn his living at the age of 14 after a primary education. He worked as a storeman, a bartender, an auctioneer's assistant, and at 17 joined the railways, moving upwards through the powerful railway union, that most exclusive of white artisan elites, into politics. He was self-educated, a voracious reader fascinated by the history of politics and politicians. He was large and formidable, and he was a heavy weight boxer of no mean ability. People paid their union dues when he asked for them and avoided anti-semitic jokes in his presence. He played a major part in the Wankie strike of 1929, which may have been the cause of his virtual banishment to Broken Hill. This diverted his career from Southern to Northern Rhodesia. In 1938 he became Member for Broken Hill, and seven years later leader of the elected "unofficials" in the Legislative Council. He was a strong believer in amalgamation and a unitary state for the reasons set out by Dr Wood. But although he regarded federation as a fall-back position, he was prepared to go all out for the second best, once it was clear that the best was unobtainable. His dream was of a multi-racial partnership in Central Africa. He believed that this was more likely to come about if the economy boomed, and that the economy was more likely to boom if the Rhodesias ceased to be separate colonies and came under a common government.

It is fair to say that the partnership envisaged by Welensky and Malvern was one in which the Europeans were the senior and the Africans very much the junior partners. The possibility of complete equality in the political status of the two races, which of course implied African domination, was envisaged as something no doubt ultimately inevitable, but in practice inconceivable for very many years to come. If this may seem in the 1980s to be a blinkered attitude, one must make that effort of imagination which historians have to attempt, and project oneself back into a very different world. In 1950 the advance of indigenous nationalism all over Asia was obvious. European rule had crumbled or was crumbling everywhere. But Africa seemed very differently placed. There had been nothing comparable to the Japanese conquests which — transitory though they were — had shown that the Europeans could be defeated and humiliated. Despite the subsequent reversal of Japanese fortunes, the impression on Asia of European decline was indelible. In Africa, however, there had been no such collapse of white ascendancy. The system seemed well established and likely to last for the lifetime of those concerned. The attitude of Malvern, Welensky and their many supporters in the Rhodesias and in Britain was not as anachronistic as it now seems. There were few who predicted the speed with which the whole situation was to change in the course of the next 15 years.

In the history of politics, personalities should never be forgotten. If Malvern and Welensky had not been so determined, articulate and able, the Federation, essentially a settler initiative, might never have got off the ground. Personalities mattered also in London. The Secretary of State for the Colonies till 1950 was Arthur Creech Jones. He had a long history of hostility to white rule. He was, as it was once said, "the principal voice of the House of Commons' conscience on colonies". He was in close contact with African opinion and well aware of its hostility to federation. But he lost his seat in the election of 1950 which nearly brought the Labour Government to an end. His successor, James Griffiths, had not such close connexion with African affairs and he was a member of a Cabinet whose tenure was now highly precarious. In November 1950 the new Colonial Secretary made an important decision. He agreed to convene a conference of officials from the four Governments involved to meet in London and examine the feasibility of federation.

The federationists had gained a major victory. The Labour Government might declare in emphatic terms that it was not committed to federation, but the chances that the officials would declare it to be impossible were remote, and if it was recognised as feasible, those who thought it positively beneficial would be greatly reinforced. Why did a Labour administration, naturally unfriendly toward a settler initiative, agree to this step at all? The reason was not the economic advantages so frequently pressed by Europeans in the two Rhodesias. These were speculative anyway, and London was not much interested. The reason was increasing awareness of the possibility that Southern Rhodesia might move into the South African orbit, that its already segregationist racial policy might be reinforced by a form of *apartheid*, and that it would *de facto* if not *de jure* become a fifth province of the Union.

There is no means of assessing the reality of this threat. There had been a good deal of Afrikaner immigration into Southern Rhodesia. The language and slogans twelve years later of the Rhodesian Front, which were not invented overnight, suggest that there may well have been sympathy for the Nationalist attitude towards Africans in some settler circles in the late 1940s. On the other hand there is little evidence to suggest that Malan and Strydom were expansionists. Smuts after the First World War had a powerful reason for trying to incorporate Southern Rhodesia in the Union, for the balance of political power would have been tipped in his favour. But the Nationalist leaders after the Second World War had every reason to avoid the addition of a large number of predominantly English-speaking voters to their electorate for the effect might well have been to tip the balance against them. The Boer War was still a vivid memory. It is doubtful whether there was really much danger of political incorporation. However, if matters were left as they were, Southern Rhodesian racial attitudes would at best not be liberalised and at worst might move nearer to the South African pattern. Federation by bringing the more relaxed and liberal attitude of the northern protectorates to Southern Rhodesia might create a strong multi-racial Central African state which would act as a barrier to the advance of *apartheid* and perhaps as a magnet to attract liberal opinion in South Africa itself.

This argument had a powerful influence on the most powerful official in the Colonial Office, Sir Andrew Cohen, who in 1947 under the aegis of Creech Jones had become Assistant Under-Secretary in charge of African affairs at the early age of 38. He was a man of vast size and great ability. He was well to the left of centre, and was as near to being a political civil servant as anyone can be under the British system. If Labour had won the 1951 election, it is highly likely that he would have received an even more startling promotion and become Permanent Under-Secretary at the Colonial Office. Cohen was a strong sympathiser with the Africans and regarded white segregationist attitudes with acute distaste. He came, however, to take the view that federation would make the South liberal rather than the North segregationist. His conversion was a potent element in bringing official opinion in London over to the side of federation, and it was official opinion that mattered, unless the Secretary of State had a strong view of his own. Public opinion in Britain was of no significance about a subject in which the public took little interest. It was a feature of the history of the origins, course and demise of the Federation that the ultimate decisions were all taken in London, capital of a country which by and large was bored stiff by the whole business. There were of course one or two pressure groups on each side, and they made from time to time a display of anger or enthusiasm, but the effect was like striking a match in a foggy night. It was infuriating for those who lived 6 000 miles away and to whom Whitehall's policy was of vital importance to know that it was made in this sort of atmosphere; but that is a characteristic — and perhaps a condemnation — of colonial rule all down history.

The detailed process of committees, compromises, debates and referenda, by which the Federation was brought into being, is described with meticulous care by Dr Wood. It is a complicated story which can only be touched upon here. It is enough to say that the Officials Conference came down in favour of federation despite African objections which were recognised but largely discounted. The ground was that African opinion did not discriminate between amalgamation which would in practice probably have meant white Southern Rhodesian domination and federation with all the checks and balances designed to protect African rights and interests. The Conference committed none of the Governments, and its Report made this point clear. Nevertheless, an important hurdle had been jumped. Business and commercial opinion in the two Rhodesias, already in favour of federation, received a new fillip. There was, it is true, a minority white view on the other side. Later, when the whole business went sour, a section argued that Huggins in 1950–51 had missed a golden chance of getting dominion status for Southern Rhodesia, and later still there grew up the myth that federation had been "imposed" by Britain. There is no truth in either of these propositions. It is most unlikely that dominion status would have been granted at any time after the war to Southern Rhodesia unless the deal had included irreversible provisions for African advancement, which would have been anathema to the European electorate. As for "imposition" it may be true that the Conservatives who came into power in October 1951 were rather more favourable to federation than Labour, but neither Party would have dreamed of forcing it on to a reluctant settler community. The initiative came from the settlers and nowhere else. The only general points on which London did insist was that Nyasaland should be included and that the system must be federal, not unitary.

Changes in the pattern of British politics were of great importance in the creation of the Federation of Rhodesia and Nyasaland. It was not that the subject aroused any great interest in either Party. Colonial affairs had just about the lowest priority in the series of Conservative Party statements from 1945 to 1949; and a Transport House pamphlet, *Facing Facts in the Colonies* written in 1965 by John Hatch (Lord Hatch of Lusby), elicited only one reply from over 600, despite numerous requests for reactions from local Party organisations. As Mr David Goldsworthy observes, this "cast an ironic hindsight on the pamphlet's confident assertion that 'in sharp contrast to the Tories we in the Labour Party are specially sensitive to the needs and aspirations of colonial peoples'".[1] Moreover the question of a central African state was only one of many colonial issues, some of which in the late 1940s and early 1950s seemed equally important, e.g. the Seretse Khama affair, the war in Malaysia, the Mau Mau revolt and the British Guiana crisis.

What mattered was not public interest in colonial policy but the attitudes of leading politicians towards it. Until 1951 there had been a largely bi-partisan approach to colonial affairs. This had not been the case with other overseas possessions. The granting of self-government to India and Pakistan aroused bitter passions. But the colonies as such — mainly situated in Africa and the Caribbean — did not enter much into the area of political debate. The question of the central African federation was the first major issue to bring this bi-partisanship to an end. Until October 1951 the two British Parties followed an apparently very similar line, and at the Victoria Falls Conference of September 1951 Griffiths and Gordon Walker, who was Commonwealth Secretary, endorsed "the principle of federation so far presented and examined". The Conference was immediately followed by the general election of October which gave the Conservatives a slender majority over the other two Parties. The new Colonial Secretary, Oliver Lyttelton, was a business man who thought in terms of financial and commercial development; he accepted the arguments of Huggins and Welensky that a central African state would pave the way to racial partnership through economic growth. He also accepted the argument of the Colonial Office that Nyasaland should be thrown in to save money for the Treasury.

At an early stage Labour spokesmen began to express doubts about the concept of federation. They were of course accused of reneging for partisan purposes, placating the wild men of the Left, exploiting governmental difficulties, etc. — the usual small change of parliamentary debate. But it was not as simple as that, nor was Labour united. The key to the Party divide was the view taken of the attitude of the Africans. Griffiths was of course well aware of the hostility of the articulate and educated Africans in all three territories to the notion of federation, and it could be fairly said that he had endorsed the principle with his eyes open. But there was nothing inconsistent in regarding federation as a sensible and desirable answer, if the reasons for African dislike could be removed. This came near to saying that federation should only be enacted if African consent could be obtained, although it still left an important question mark. How was African opinion to be ascertained — not only educated and articulate, but uneducated and inarticulate? This question, however, did not arise since the new Government was not prepared to hold up federation until African consent had been obtained.

Here was a real dividing line between Parties. Lyttelton and the Conservatives believed that the British Government was a guardian for the Africans.

[1] D. Goldsworthy, *Colonial Issues in British Politics 1945–61* (Oxford, 1971), p. 334.

A guardian or trustee is entitled to overrule the wishes of his ward when he deems it to be in the ward's best interest to do so. If the ward can be persuaded of his wisdom so much the better, and every effort should be made to convince him, but in the end the decision lies with the guardian. A small group of Labour figures accepted this view — Gordon Walker, George Brown, Richard Stokes and others — and abstained on some important divisions. They believed that multi-racialism might work, that the Europeans of the territories meant what they said and that a real partnership would counteract the consequences of the National Party's victory in South Africa. And so federation went ahead. It was not a bi-partisan decision, but Attlee promised to do his best to support a *fait accompli.* This is a measure of the change of the last 50 years. A modern Labour leader would proclaim his intention to repeal the Act at the first opportunity.

The details of the federal system, ultimately confirmed in 1953, were set out in a White Paper of June 1952. It was a draft, but there were few subsequent changes. Something very like it was at this stage sure to go through Parliament and was bound to be accepted by the two northern protectorates which were ruled from Whitehall, whatever the misgivings of the indigenous inhabitants.

In Southern Rhodesia, however, the issue went to a referendum, as Huggins had promised. The electorate was almost exclusively European but it did not follow that federation would win the day. In June 1952 during the debate in the Legislative Assembly on the White Paper and the holding of a referendum, and again during the referendum campaign itself in April 1953, Huggins and Welensky faced a major propaganda dilemma. They could use arguments to reassure the Europeans or to reassure the Africans but not both, for those which encouraged the former alarmed the latter and vice versa. It was, however, the white vote which actually mattered. Inevitably their emphasis was on the senior partnership of the Europeans. Equally inevitably doubts in African opinion were confirmed and consolidated. For example Huggins described the African Affairs Board (a piece of proposed constitutional machinery intended to safeguard African rights) as "a frightful waste of money and manpower" and later as "a little piece of Gilbert and Sullivan" which would make no difference at all. Federation gained the day by 25 570 votes to 14 729. This was a conclusive victory but its circumstances weakened the prospect of lasting success.

The Federation of Rhodesia and Nyasaland was one of the most complicated systems of government ever established, rivalled only by that of the Netherlands in the seventeenth century and the universities of Oxford and Cambridge today. Five different governments had overlapping and interlocking responsibilities for its affairs. There was the British Government in London, theoretically united but divided for practical purposes into two by no means friendly or united departments, the Commonwealth Office which dealt with the Federal and the Southern Rhodesian Governments through separate sets of High Commissioners in Salisbury and London, and the Colonial Office which dealt with the two northern protectorates through their respective Governors who possessed very wide powers. There was also a Governor-General of the Federation and a Governor of Southern Rhodesia, both of whom, unlike their northern analogues, were constitutional monarchs acting on the advice of their prime ministers.

In all British-based systems of government the civil service is the most important and usually the least noticed or studied component. The Federation had six sets of civil servants to deal with. Two were locally based, the Federal and the Southern Rhodesian. Four were in the end based on London. Two, those of Northern Rhodesia and Nyasaland, were part of the Colonial Service as a whole and could be posted anywhere in the colonies. The officials in the Colonial Office itself and in the Commonwealth (formerly Dominions) Office were a part of the Home Civil Service and could be moved to other departments, although this seldom happened in practice. It is no criticism of the integrity, ability and conscientiousness of the officials concerned to say that compartmentation of this sort was a serious disadvantage. The attitude of locally-based civil servants was bound to be different from that of civil servants whose postings and promotions were made in London as part of a wider Colonial or, as it was later called, Overseas Civil Service; and in Whitehall itself there was a conflict between the Colonial Office with its long tradition of paternalistic trusteeship, and the Commonwealth Office which had in many ways more in common with the Foreign Office, dealing as it did largely with what were for all practical purposes independent sovereign states.

Huggins and Welensky, whose aim was dominion status for the Federation, repeatedly pressed for a unified and locally-based civil service as in Canada or South Africa. From their point of view they were quite right, and, if one believes that the Federation had a chance of ultimate success, there can be little doubt that the chance was diminished by the existence of London-based colonial officials in the northern protectorates with other loyalties and in some cases with no great desire to make the Federation work. Another change which might have helped, and which was strongly pressed by Welensky in 1957 after he had succeeded Huggins as Federal Prime Minister, was the creation of a Central African department in Whitehall to avoid, as he put it on 15 February to Lord Home, then Commonwealth Secretary, "the anomaly of two departments, with two outlooks and two policies, controlling our relations with the United Kingdom Government". Nothing came of either of these proposals, and one can easily see why. The Colonial Service was not lightly going to give up Northern Rhodesia and Nyasaland to settler-based civil servants, and neither the Colonial nor Commonwealth Office was anxious to see one of the most important areas of their jurisdiction, however much disputed, go to a new geographically-demarcated department. It is true that a Central African department was in the end created, but for a very different purpose from that sought by Welensky. It was set up in 1962 under R. A. Butler not to preserve but to liquidate the Federation.

Neither a unified civil service nor a Central African department, however desirable, was politically feasible in 1957. Nor, given the determination of the British Government to keep African affairs in the territories under the control of the Colonial Office, is it easy to see how the Federal Constitution could have been much modified. Within the limits of what they regarded as a second best solution to the question of closer association, Huggins and

Welensky got most of the things that they could reasonably expect. There was perhaps one exception. Huggins attached great importance to law and order being a function of the Federal Government rather than the territories. There was no strong reason why this should not have been done, and some of the riots which occurred in the North might have been better handled by a Federal than a territorial police force.

Why did the Federation fail? Dr Wood traces its rise, decline and fall in a wealth of detail. There are many episodes which might have turned out differently, decisions which went marginally wrong, avoidable errors that were made. This is not the place to discuss those. But there are some broad questions which inevitably arise. Was it a reasonable proposal in the first place, or was it foredoomed from the start? The answer surely is that there was nothing foolish, absurd or impracticable about the notion. The principal objection at the time was the hostility of the African spokesmen in Northern Rhodesia and Nyasaland, and to a lesser extent in Southern Rhodesia. This was not ignored, but one has to think back into the much more "paternalistic" attitude in those days of even enlightened Europeans towards the Africans in their colonial empires. It was not unreasonable to hope that once the Federation had come into being and its expected material advantages had been realised, African opinion would come round. And, in any case, there was the question, mentioned earlier, of what African opinion really was. Whose opinion and how could one find out? It is true that the British politicians were divided on the issue, and it is probable, though not certain, that if Labour had won the 1951 election, federation would have been postponed until in the end it would never have been enacted. But the Conservatives were not behaving unreasonably or recklessly in carrying a measure which their predecessors had come very near to endorsing, and which the ruling minority in the two Rhodesias strongly supported on what at least appeared to be impeccably enlightened grounds. Political decisions have to be taken on the balance of probability. No one could argue that success was so improbable as to make the venture hopeless or ridiculous. The arguments for a counter to Afrikanerdom and for economic growth were respectable and rational.

What of the attitude of the white Rhodesians? But for them the project would never have been conceived. Theirs was the initiative, and, far more than the British Government, they had the real, as opposed to the formal legal, responsibility for the creation of the Federation. Here too it is difficult to censure the motives or purposes of the settlers. There was a mixture of multi-racial idealism and commercial opportunism, but the former certainly existed, and a real effort was made, though perhaps not very successfully, to bring Africans a little more than hitherto into social and political life. It may have been an error to make Salisbury the Federal capital. If the money could have been found it would have been better to create a capital *de novo* like Canberra. Alternatively, Livingstone or Lusaka might have been politically more suitable. In Salisbury the segregationist policy of Southern Rhodesia, enshrined in the Land Apportionment Act, was omni-present. Exceptions were made for Africans in the Federal Government, but that did not make those excepted feel that they were accepted. It was always an uneasy situation. There is no reason to doubt that a large number of the Europeans in the Federation believed in partnership quite genuinely. It was the time scale which they failed to appreciate. And time was to be crucial.

What was it that went wrong in their estimate? We can now see that sub-Saharan Africa was about to explode into the Balkanised condition familiar today; the European colonial powers would cut their political losses and retire from the scene not in despair or despondency, but reckoning that with any luck trade would not follow the flag backwards. Their retreat, however, would leave the white settlers stranded unless they too adapted themselves to a new world. If the Federation was to develop into a genuine multi-racial state, movement had to be quick, but this was a very difficult matter for a dug-in settler community. Given 25 years it might have worked. The Federation was to have less than ten.

Yet this was not obvious in its early years. Huggins, resigning from the premiership of Southern Rhodesia, took on that of the Federation, and did not retire till 1956. During those three years, prosperity was the order of the day, and the early stages of adaptation to the complexities of the Constitution went smoothly enough. There were no major external or internal crises, and the Prime Minister was on excellent terms with the Governor-General, Lord Llewellin, who had a long experience of British politics. At the end of October 1956 Huggins, full of years and honours, bowed himself out. Roy Welensky was his inevitable successor, and there seemed no reason why he should not continue along the same lines. But quite suddenly the whole tempo of change in Africa quickened. For years and years time on that continent had been flowing slowly and torpidly as if on the meandering bends of one of those giant African rivers, the Congo or the Zambezi. Now it suddenly reached a series of precipitous rapids, bubbling, foaming and turbulent. Welensky was unlucky enough to have to pilot his ship of state in these dangerous waters which ultimately proved fatal. There is no reason to think that any other captain could have steered more successfully.

Welensky had no sooner taken office than the Suez crisis occurred. An episode thousands of miles away and wholly unconnected with the affairs of southern and central Africa might seem irrelevant. But its indirect significance was at once noted in Salisbury. British withdrawal was symbolic of Britain's decline as a major power. Julian Greenfield, Welensky's Minister of Justice, came to believe that it marked a turning point in the fortunes of the Federation. It was not so much the question of British power which had been put to the test as that of willpower. Militarily Egyptian nationalism could have been crushed, and so could emergent African nationalism in the Federation. But it was one thing to have the means, another to believe that it was right or expedient to use them.

The problem was the more acute because African nationalism suddenly "took off". Precisely why, it is difficult to say. Perhaps the question is unanswerable, just as no one really knows exactly what caused the revolutions of 1848 in Europe. No doubt the sentiment had long been smouldering beneath the surface of affairs. It may have been helped by the grant of independence to the Gold Coast (Ghana) one of Britain's oldest African colonies, which occurred in 1957. This was the upshot of a long, slow and carefully-prepared process. The same background was true for Nigeria which secured its independence three years later. These, however, were the last colonies to achieve their new status in this leisurely, cautious, step-by-step manner. Everywhere else in the colonial field a sudden sense of urgency appeared. The process of transition from colonialism to independence was abruptly hastened. Now that African colonies on the west coast had gained independence, what was there to hinder a similar transition in the rest of Africa? And why should the process go on being as slow as it had been in West Africa? In 1959 any British observer who thought about the matter would have expected at least ten years or more to elapse before Tanganyika and Uganda achieved independence. In fact they did so in 1961 and 1962 respectively.

British Colonial Africa was not the only part of the continent to be affected. In 1960 the Belgians abruptly abandoned their rule in the Congo. Between 1958 and 1960 de Gaulle granted independence to the whole of Francophone Africa. Included among the "liberated" territories was Algeria — an ominous portent, for it was theoretically a part of metropolitan France and contained a European settler population, the *pieds noirs*, almost as large as that of the Union of South Africa and far larger than the Federation. The difference of course was that Belgium ruled the Congo and France ruled Algeria, whereas Britain ruled neither South Africa nor in practice the principal European bastion of the Federation, Southern Rhodesia. But Whitehall did rule the northern protectorates, and the Federation was created by a British Act of Parliament which, whatever might be said about betrayal of pledges, could in the end be repealed in Westminster, and in the end it was.

The detailed process of the break-up of the Federation, the complicated constitutional changes, the role of the police and the armed services, the interminable negotiations between Salisbury and London, Lusaka and Blantyre, are analysed in Dr Wood's chapters. In the exchanges between Welensky and Macleod and Macmillan one can see the gulf between the British and Federal Governments widening, and appreciate the conflicts and misunderstandings. Strong feelings were aroused. The historian can feel sympathy for both sides - for Macmillan and Macleod tormented by the intricacies of A rolls and B rolls, for Welensky and Greenfield infuriated by the remote *insouciance* with which, as it seemed to them (unfairly no doubt), decisions of vital importance to Central Africa were being taken in distant London.

Over and above these irritants there was a major problem that would not go away. The Africans in the North saw Federation as an insuperable barrier to their own ambitions for national self-determination, and it is difficult to see how any amount of tinkering with the Federal Constitution could have changed their attitude. A radical change in the franchise was the only step that might have reconciled them to the continuation of the Federation, but it would have had to be really radical. Perhaps it could have stopped short of one man, one vote, but nothing less than a measure giving an early and irreversible prospect of an African majority in the electorate would have satisfied Kaunda and Banda. One only has to look at the Federal Electoral Act of January 1958 which actually *reduced* the proportion of Africans elected by Africans in the legislature to see the vast gap between the two sides.

Failing the rapid and radical change in the franchise which was the key to everything else, Whitehall would be faced by an interminable sequence of riots and revolts. Britain had not become so feeble militarily as to be incapable of suppressing them, but that had been equally true of her situation in Ireland after 1918. It was not a matter of power. It was a matter of the inclination to exercise that power against the overwhelming majority of the inhabitants of the northern territories. No British Government wanted to cope with a series of African Irelands. It was probably also true that the whole concept of empire and commonwealth was beginning to lose its appeal in Britain. The Prime Minister was thinking more and more in terms of Europe, and, although Macmillan's attempt to enter the EEC was to be temporarily blocked by de Gaulle's veto, the policy continued to be the guide to his successors after de Gaulle's resignation, until it was finally settled by the referendum of 1975. Britain's economic interests in the Federation, though substantial, were not immense, and the most important of all, the Copperbelt, seemed safer under a well-disposed autonomous black regime than a settler-ruled state constantly beset by turbulent nationalist agitation.

Britain was neither prepared to abandon her trusteeship of the Africans in the North nor to sustain Federal rule by force of arms. In the circumstances only one outcome was possible, unless, as seems to have been occasionally contemplated in Salisbury, there had been a Federal unilateral declaration of independence. The Federation was bound to be dissolved. Whatever the reasons, it had not succeeded in reconciling African opinion to its continuance. By the end of 1962 secession had been granted in principle to Nyasaland. On 28 March 1963 the British Cabinet agreed that Northern Rhodesia too could secede. Of course the process led inevitably to charges of bad faith. The rights and wrongs of those charges are discussed in the book. In one sense they were justified. The Ministers in London who were responsible for the creation of the Federation in 1953 never contemplated dissolution, and there was no right of secession written into the Constitution. Moreover Lyttelton had said in 1953 that all four Central African Governments would have to agree to the Federation's liquidation and its continuation had been guaranteed in the Declaration of 1957 and a statement by Lord Home in 1960. The extreme bitterness of Welensky, Greenfield and other Federal Ministers, who had committed their political lives to the new state, is fully comprehensible. On the other hand the British Parliament is sovereign. What it can enact it can repeal. The truth is that the promises which had undoubtedly been made had simply become obsolete, and by 1962–63 there was no way of preserving the Federation except at a cost that no British Government was willing to pay. The world had changed far more quickly than anyone could have predicted ten years earlier. When Macmillan in 1960 referred to the wind of change he was not, as many white South Africans and Rhodesians alleged, stirring up trouble or encouraging agitation. He was simply commenting on an undoubted fact — a fact which was to be fatal to the Federation.

One cannot end without a word about Sir Roy Welensky, the symbol and embodiment of the Federal regime. He was a statesman of great ability, much charm and immense determination. Within the constitutional framework which he inherited he did all that could practicably have been done to make the new state work. It has been suggested above that the only step which might have saved the Federation was a drastic change in the franchise. This he did not attempt, but, even if he had believed in it himself, he could hardly have achieved it within the electoral system set up by the original Act. No such measure had a chance of being passed in an overwhelmingly European-dominated legislature. The only hope was a change of heart in the electorate, and prime ministers, being in a sense the creation of the electorate, are ill-placed to change its heart.

Roy Welensky lacked luck, the quality Napoleon most prized in his marshalls. The undoubted economic achievements of the Federation, for which he was largely responsible, could not counter-balance the growing passion for national self-determination which suddenly swept through Africa almost as soon as he became Prime Minister. It was the tragedy of his career to be caught up in a process which he could neither lead nor appease nor reverse. It may be some consolation to him, though perhaps not much, to know now that no one else would have been likely to cope any better with the tides that swept the Federation away, and its Prime Minister with it.

The Queen's College, Oxford ROBERT BLAKE
March 1982.

CHAPTER ONE

The Prospect of Amalgamation

The Idea of Closer Association between the Territories of British Central Africa, 1894–1939

THE founding of the Federation of Rhodesia and Nyasaland on 4 September 1953, was the culmination of a sustained effort — albeit by different people and agencies at different times — since the turn of the century to persuade the British Government first to unify the two Rhodesias and, later, all three territories of British Central Africa. There are some who argue that, to the contrary, the British Government promoted Southern Rhodesia to self-governing status in 1923 and created the Federation 30 years later as liberal counterpoises to rampant, expansionist Afrikaner nationalism in South Africa.[1] However, it would seem that, far from realising such a long-term strategy, the British Government reacted in an *ad hoc* manner to the pressure of the local Europeans and the logic of the situation while always remembering its role as protector of Northern Rhodesia and Nyasaland. The result was a federation with a fatal flaw in its constitution because, although the control of African affairs was crucial to its success, its Government was denied any contact with the day-to-day affairs of the Africans in the territories and the northern protectorates in particular. This was because, conscious of its protective duties, the Colonial Office from the beginning would not countenance the transfer of the control of the northern African to the local European in any circumstances.

The Federation in fact inherited the situation in which the British South Africa Company of Cecil John Rhodes found itself in 1894 after having conquered the Ndebele. The Company had thereby added control of Matabeleland to that of Mashonaland while it administered what subsequently became Northern Rhodesia, later Zambia. In addition, it subsidised the new

[1] M. Chanock, *Unconsummated Union, Britain, Rhodesia and South Africa, 1900–45* (Manchester, 1977), p. 110; see also a review article: H. I. Wetherell, "Britain and Rhodesian Expansionism: Imperial Collusion or Empirical Carelessness?" in *Rhodesian History* (Salisbury, 1977), Vol. 8, p. 115 f.

British protectorate of Nyasaland. As the area was surrounded by Portuguese, Belgian and German possessions, its unification was an obvious step. Rhodes was to terminate his Nyasaland subsidy the next year, but the Colonial Office intended to give the Company the administration of the "Railway Strip" in Bechuanaland, together with the areas there which had not been designated as native reserves.[2] The Jameson Raid of 1895–6 and the rebellions in Matabeleland and Mashonaland abruptly changed the British mind about entrusting the Company with anything more than the administration of the Rhodesias. An Order in Council which provided for Northern Rhodesia and Bechuanaland to become the responsibility of the Company Administrator in Salisbury, Southern Rhodesia, was therefore cancelled. Thereafter, Northern Rhodesia continued to be administered by the Company but under the direct supervision of the British High Commissioner in South Africa and not via Salisbury. The best chance for a durable union had been lost.

If the unification had been effected, the crippling consequences of the divergence of policies and political philosophies between the Colonial Office and the Southern Rhodesian Government, from which the ill-fated Federation would suffer, would have been avoided. Never again would conditions so favour unification. Instead, with regard to Southern Rhodesia, the Company was shackled from 1898 by an Order in Council which provided not only Imperial control but a legislative role for the local Europeans. The latter were given a minority of seats in a legislative council and would soon gain a majority. They were not, however, given an executive role. Mashonaland and Matabeleland each had a Company Administrator until the posts were merged in 1901, but an Imperial Resident Commissioner would be appointed and be paid by the Colonial Office. He would be an *ex officio* Member of the Legislative and Executive Councils but without the power to vote. As he was directly responsible to the High Commissioner in South Africa, his task was to advise the latter on the allowance and disallowance of legislation. The command of the military and police henceforth came under a Commandant-General who was also directly responsible to the High Commissioner. In practice, the Resident Commissioner and the Commandant-General were often the same man. In addition, all resolutions of the Company would be scrutinised by the Colonial Office and could be disallowed or amended by the Secretary of State who could also remove from office the directors and officials of the Company. In the event, the Company's Administrators were hardly hampered by these provisions and retained much power.

In 1899 Northern Rhodesia had two separate administrations established by Orders in Council. The first was in North Western Rhodesia and the second in North Eastern Rhodesia. A third was established in Barotseland in 1900 when a final treaty was signed with the Lozi Paramount Chief, Lewanika, who had first sought British protection in 1890. As has been said, the Company continued to provide the administration for the whole area but at the behest of the High Commissioner. There were no legislative councils, but

[2] H. I. Wetherell, *The Rhodesias and Amalgamation: Settler Sub-Imperialism and the Imperial Response, 1914–48* (unpublished D. Phil. thesis, University of Rhodesia, 1977), p. 1, citing C. Palley, *The Constitutional History and Law of Southern Rhodesia, 1888–1965* (Oxford, 1966), p. 126.

then there was only a handful of European settlers. Nyasaland, now Malawi, had been divorced from the rest of British Central Africa in 1895 to become a separate protectorate under the aegis of the British Foreign Office. Nonetheless, its recent association with Rhodes, its isolation from British East Africa and its close trade, tribal and other relationships with North Eastern Rhodesia, meant that it continued to play a role in the area.

Perhaps more important for the prospects of unification was the victory of the Colonial Office with regard to the philosophical approach to the area's development. The Colonial Office had objected, unsuccessfully, to the Letters Patent of 1889 allowing the Company *carte blanche* north of the Limpopo River. It had wanted the Zambezi River to be declared the limit of white domination. Nine years later, in 1898, however, Lord Salisbury, the Prime Minister and Foreign Secretary, proclaimed — albeit privately — that the Zambezi would be the frontier for the whites, and in 1899 Lord Milner, the High Commissioner, advised the Colonial Office to consider the river as the dividing line between the white-ruled territories which would be self-governing and those which would be developed as "Native" protectorates.[3] The Colonial Office would adhere to this concept throughout subsequent history until the end of the Federation.

A further considerable obstacle to unification was the introduction of English Law in Northern Rhodesia in contrast to Southern Rhodesia which had, in 1891, adopted the laws of the Cape Colony and thus the Roman-Dutch Code. A lesser hindrance was the employment of English-trained officials in the northern territories, often fresh from British universities, when Southern Rhodesia used Cape-trained and schooled men. Soon the feeling grew that the northern officials regarded themselves as superior.

The cancellation of the Order in Council in 1896 did not mean that the idea of unification was forgotten, and proposals for it began to emerge from various quarters. In 1907, the Native Commissioner for the Sebungwe in Southern Rhodesia suggested that, as his Tonga people lived on both banks of the Zambezi, the two Rhodesias should be amalgamated.[4] The same year, Lord Selborne, the current High Commissioner, suggested a federation of British states stretching from the Cape to the northern frontier of North Eastern Rhodesia.[5] If this was impossible, he thought that at least North Western Rhodesia — the "Railway Belt" — and Southern Rhodesia should be joined together as they were already linked by rail. He intended that the remaining African areas should continue to be protected while North Eastern Rhodesia be amalgamated with Nyasaland because its lines of communication were established through there to the Moçambique port of Beira. An additional reason was that North Eastern Rhodesia was copying the Nyasaland practice of "Native development" and was already employing Africans as clerks and telegraphers. Thus Lord Selborne was the author of the idea which Sir Stewart Gore-Browne, Guy van Eeden, Sir Edgar Whitehead and many

[3] Wetherell, *The Rhodesias and Amalgamation, op. cit.*, p. 2.
[4] *Ibid.*, p. 3.
[5] Palley, *The Constitutional History and Law, op. cit.*, p. 325; J. B. Stabler, "The British South Africa Company Proposal for Amalgamation of the Rhodesias, 1915–17: Northern Rhodesian Reaction", *African Social Research*, 7 (Lusaka, 1969), p. 499.

others were to resuscitate in the forthcoming years. However, the Colonial Secretary, Lord Elgin, disapproved and did not think that the South Africans, if Rhodesia ever joined them, would welcome the addition of the large black populations of the northern territories.

By 1909, unification was a popular subject of discussion in public and Company circles. One reason for the Company's enthusiasm was that it had never paid a dividend and was anxious to pare costs. To this end, it had merged the Mashonaland and Matabeleland administrations in Southern Rhodesia and, in 1911, it created Northern Rhodesia from its two territories there, choosing Livingstone for the administrative capital. Moreover, since 1900, it had sought to achieve a uniformity of administrative policies in all its territories even though the High Commissioner reminded it that, as a result, the northern administration could not be subordinated to that of Southern Rhodesia. The Northern Rhodesian merger encouraged the directors to think of doing likewise with the new territory and Southern Rhodesia. On 9 August 1912, one of them, Lord Grey, publicly endorsed it but the Europeans in Northern Rhodesia were more anxious to secure representative government and to persuade the Company to liberalise its land policies to allow further white settlement. The resistance of the Company to these demands, led the local Europeans and, in particular, Leopold Moore (later Sir Leopold), a chemist and the crusty editor of the *Livingstone Mail*, to prefer Colonial Office rule because it would not have to satisfy shareholders.

The first hint of the Company's thinking on amalgamation was given in Northern Rhodesia in December 1913 by the Company's president, Sir Leander Starr Jameson. At a public meeting in Lusaka, he rejected a claim for representation on the grounds that the European population was too small, but implied that it could be secured by joining Southern Rhodesia. He gave the Northern Rhodesians the choice of doing that or of developing their own government. The meeting favoured the latter course. A second meeting confirmed this rejection unless a Northern Rhodesian legislative council was granted first. The Southern Rhodesians were more receptive. At a crowded meeting in Salisbury on 23 December 1913, Jameson said he looked forward to the day when the Company could hand over to a fully responsible Southern Rhodesian government and immediately struck a chord with his audience. He won further applause by referring to recent South African statements on the settlement of impoverished Afrikaners in Southern Rhodesia and by declaring his opposition to the incorporation of the latter in South Africa for which the Act of Union of 1910 had provided. Then he proposed, amid applause, the amalgamation of the two Rhodesias to form a single Rhodesia, which might include Bechuanaland as "a fitting monument to our founder".[6]

The Colonial Office, however, could not believe that the Southern Rhodesian Legislative Council would welcome the Northern Rhodesian deficit.

Jameson continued to enjoy some success because, in December 1914, the shareholders warmly welcomed the idea. It also attracted Drummond Chaplin (later Sir Drummond), the Administrator of Southern Rhodesia, because, as a South African Progressive, he saw a Greater Rhodesia as a liberal

[6] Wetherell, *The Rhodesias and Amalgamation*, *op. cit.*, p. 9.

counterpoise to South Africa. He did not fear a threat to the European domination of the new state because the franchise proposed for it was qualified and of such a standard that no Africans would yet secure it.

The elections of that year, 1914, encouraged the Company because the electors filled 14 out of the 15 seats with men who advocated the continuance of Company rule. In fact, they endorsed the renewal of the Charter because the alternatives were Crown Colony status or incorporation in South Africa. They did not consider the third course because responsible government appeared unattainable without sources of capital other than those of the Company.[7] However, not all the directors were convinced that Southern Rhodesians should gain a voice in the administration of Northern Rhodesia. An administrative union was preferred, but Chaplin doubted that the Southern Rhodesians would happily pay for services over which they would have no control. For the reasons already given, he continued to favour a legislative union even though he did not expect there to be any savings at the outset. He thought that, combined, the two Rhodesias would have a greater influence on the future course of events and would stand a better chance of sharing in the spoils of the anticipated peace settlement following the World War — a British victory was confidently predicted.

The directors sympathised with Chaplin's pro-British and anti-Afrikaner attitude and knew that the creation of a Greater Rhodesia with its large African population would not encourage the South African Government to exercise its option of absorption. In any case, they knew that the Colonial Office would probably resist the handover of that population to the South Africans. They were probably also anxious to secure a favourable settlement with the British Government because they knew that the life of the Charter was limited. Chaplin believed that the Northern Rhodesians would be attracted to amalgamation, but Moore, in the *Livingstone Mail*, promptly attacked the idea because he thought that it could be a step towards a wider South African union which would bring the disadvantages of bilingualism and Roman-Dutch Law. He welcomed the prospects of thereby obtaining representative government as well as a flood of immigrants, but he warned that not only would Livingstone decline, but Northern Rhodesia would be neglected by Pretoria. He counselled delay until the war ended because then there might be the possibility of an association with Belgium's Katanga and British and German East Africa. This was preferable to becoming South Africa's forgotten province.

The Company intended to reveal its ideas during a tour of the Rhodesias by Jameson and his fellow director, D. O. Malcolm (later Sir Dougal), in late December 1915. However, the local Press guessed this intention. On 1 December, *The Bulawayo Chronicle* claimed that the decision to amalgamate was the prerogative of the Rhodesians. This, of course, was not true because of the power which the British Government retained. Simultaneously, in the *Livingstone Mail* and two days later at a public meeting, Moore declared that the Company wished to push through amalgamation in the absence of the servicemen at the war because it feared that it would be left with the dubious

[7] Stabler, "The British South Africa Company Proposal for Amalgamation", *op. cit.*, p. 499.

asset of Northern Rhodesia after Southern Rhodesia had joined South Africa. Fears were voiced at the meeting about Southern Rhodesian competition in the export of agricultural produce to Katanga, but the Company was told that only the curious had been present and that Moore's support had been confined to those who had a stake in Livingstone.

On 24 December, Jameson proposed a simple amalgamation which would extend the services provided in Southern Rhodesia to the North. He argued that this was logical because already the two territories shared defence, police and education. He did not expect there to be any savings, but he believed that amalgamation would increase efficiency and offer the civil servants better prospects of promotion. Northern Rhodesia would gain representative government and more revenue would be available for development. Rhodesia would be more attractive to the post-war immigrant and would have a greater chance of influencing the peace settlement. To woo the Southern Rhodesians, Jameson promised that the Company would meet the Northern Rhodesian deficit at amalgamation and forecast prosperity from the lifting of trade restrictions and the improvement in communications. He believed that the prospect of gaining responsible government would not be affected because it was unlikely while Southern Rhodesia had such a small white population and lacked finance. Amalgamation would attract immigrants and thereby boost the economy and, if the electorate wished to join South Africa, it would ensure a reasonable representation in the Union Parliament while protecting the Rhodesian identity. Like *The Bulawayo Chronicle*, Jameson and Malcolm said they were confident that the Rhodesians had only to indicate their choice for the British Government to sanction it.

This provoked the Colonial Secretary, Andrew Bonar Law, to remind Jameson that, when they had last met, he had indicated only that his Government would consider the issue with an open mind. Lord Buxton, the High Commissioner, hastened to add that, while he might have given Jameson the impression that he favoured amalgamation, he was duty bound to consult the Colonial Office first. Jameson responded by claiming that he had only predicted the likely attitude of the British Government in the event of a Rhodesian public acceptance of the proposal. Bonar Law replied that it would, of course, receive sympathetic consideration.

Nevertheless, the Colonial Office criticised Buxton because he had failed to mention the intention that Northern Rhodesia should not be dominated by the whites. It also questioned the statement about the Rhodesians speaking with one voice in the post-war settlement and thought that inadequate reasons had been given for raising the matter in wartime. It suspected that the Company was seeking to strengthen its position in Central Africa and thereby to postpone the absorption of Southern Rhodesia by the Union. The Colonial Office wanted the Southern Rhodesian option kept open in case the loyalist position in South Africa was rendered precarious by the representatives of South West Africa joining forces with the Afrikaner nationalists.

The Colonial Office's Permanent Secretary, Sir John Anderson, irritated by the reluctance of the Company to meet the cost of the war in Northern Rhodesia, had little sympathy for amalgamation because he could not see what the northern territory would gain. Indeed, he foresaw only friction between the British and Rhodesian Governments over the latter's administration of the vast African areas in Northern Rhodesia. He doubted if the Rhodesian legislature would be fit for that task and reminded his Government of its role as protector of the Africans. He preferred Northern Rhodesia to relinquish North Eastern Rhodesia to Nyasaland but knew that the fate of German East Africa had first to be settled.[8]

In any case, the Northern Rhodesians showed little interest in amalgamation when Jameson and Malcolm toured. They were anxious to secure representative government. However, Jameson gathered that the opposition was chiefly represented by Moore and a few of his fellow Livingstonians. Moore, in pungent editorials and at meetings, did not disappoint him. After alleging that the real purpose of the Company was to retain its hold on both territories in order not to be left with impoverished Northern Rhodesia, Moore suggested that Britain might divide its possessions into European- and Indian-dominated states along a line drawn across Africa from Lobito Bay to the northern border of Tanganyika.

The result of the impression given to Jameson was that he would inform the British Government that the Northern Rhodesians really favoured amalgamation. This was not confirmed by Herbert Stanley (later Sir Herbert), the British Resident Commissioner in Salisbury, when he visited Northern Rhodesia in January 1916. Stanley was an advocate of amalgamation but he reported honestly that the opposition to it was widespread and that it was underlain with a thorough dislike for the Company. He found that the Europeans hoped for British intervention to improve their situation and that they would prefer to join Nyasaland. Stanley's opinion would be confirmed at meetings in the next two months at which the North Eastern Rhodesians spoke of joining Nyasaland even though they would lose their current markets for their coffee and tobacco which were provided through the South African Customs Union. They hoped instead to obtain an Imperial preference to compensate for that loss.

Even the Southern Rhodesians had not considered amalgamation as seriously as Jameson thought and, in the main, believed that only the Company would gain anything from the post-war settlement. Malcolm sounded the opinions of the Members of the Legislative Council and found that the majority were unenthusiastic but not opposed to amalgamation. Nevertheless, Jameson thought that even those who wished to join South Africa would be won round by the arguments of efficiency and economy. In fact, there was already a considerable group of Southern Rhodesians who feared that amalgamation would delay the advent of self-rule. Jameson was sufficiently encouraged by his discovery, and by the sympathetic attitude of Bonar Law, to order the drafting of an amalgamation bill.

Simultaneously, Chaplin and his Northern Rhodesian counterpart, L. A. Wallace, devised a scheme of amalgamation. They excluded Barotseland because they thought that it should continue to be governed by the High Commissioner, and for the remainder chose Salisbury as the administrative and judicial capital. Any redundant civil servants would be placated with

[8] Chanock, *Unconsummated Union, op. cit.*, p. 110.

compensation and Fort Jameson, the capital of North Eastern Rhodesia, would be offered the sop of the acquisition of postal communications. Roman-Dutch Law and the Southern Rhodesian ordinances, including its electoral law, would apply throughout. Three seats in the Legislative Council would be given to Northern Rhodesia to represent the areas of settlement around Livingstone, Broken Hill and Fort Jameson. The Northern Rhodesian African would be represented by two nominated Members and, in all, the Legislative Council would have a membership of seven nominated and 15 elected Members. The scheme provided for the maintenance of the ratio of representation between Northern and Southern Rhodesia of one to two whenever the House was enlarged.

However, before anything was revealed, the Rhodesian Agricultural Union, when meeting in March 1916, almost unanimously opposed amalgamation. The debate uncovered a suspicion that the Company wished to entrench its position, and the farmers disliked the Company because it seemed to put the interests of its shareholders first in the matters of land and profits. The farmers found allies in the commercial sector. Farming, of course, was the major occupation in Southern Rhodesia and the farmers were emerging as a major political force which would endure throughout the history of the territory. The elected Members of the Legislative Council had by then been given a majority in the House and, although their leader, Charles Coghlan (later Sir Charles), a Bulawayo lawyer, was not yet totally opposed to amalgamation, he feared that it might delay the attainment of responsible government. Moreover, he wished to strengthen the British character of the European settlement in Southern Rhodesia before it joined the Union of South Africa. Accordingly, he marshalled support against taking a decision on amalgamation. Thus it transpired that Jameson had erred in not unveiling his ideas before opposition was rallied against amalgamation. A visit by the High Commissioner, Lord Buxton, did little for the Company's cause even though he openly advocated amalgamation and declared that he believed that his Government would not oppose it.

The Company delivered its first draft of the amalgamation bill in May and the final one in June, but the elected Members reacted by deciding in Caucus that any decision should be postponed until a conference could be convened at the end of the war. They set a precondition for the conference which was that first the Privy Council would have to issue a ruling on the ownership of unalienated land which the Company claimed. This was hotly debated because local opinion held that the concessions gained by the Company did not entitle it to claim that ownership. There was a further setback for the Company because Bonar Law corrected Buxton on the impression which he had given that local opinion would decide the fate of amalgamation. He acknowledged that it would be taken into account, but he reminded Buxton that the opinion of the large and unrepresented African population would have to be heard. The Colonial Office added that Buxton should not have blessed the scheme because there could be dangers in settler control of African affairs. It took this approach because in Natal, under responsible government, the Africans had been provoked into rebellion. Buxton was told that a line had to be drawn between the territories which would gain responsible government and those which would become Crown Colonies. That line would be the Zambezi River. However, this had to be done subtly because there was no desire to provoke the Rhodesians to the extent that the Imperial veto would have to be used.

Somewhat disappointed, Malcolm suggested a merger of the offices of the two Company Administrators when Wallace retired shortly. Otherwise, he thought that the Company should wait until the local protagonists of amalgamation, led by a Colonel Raleigh Grey, were victorious. Grey and Chaplin currently believed that a period for reflection would undo the opposition and this seemed to be confirmed by Grey's public meetings. A debate in the Legislative Council, in April 1917, was forced after an attempt to win over Coghlan failed. It was preceded by a vigorous public campaign, but, despite the airing of the argument for a strong voice in the post-war peace settlement, the earlier informal rejection was confirmed by the Council. Telling arguments were that the British Government would not relinquish control over so large an African population as that of Northern Rhodesia, and that the northern policy of advancing Africans in clerical and other fields could result in the swamping of the white vote. Buxton supported the idea of unifying the administrations, but the British Government had already rejected it in the previous month in order to remain free to decide the future of Northern Rhodesia. The British Government would not side with the Company against the Rhodesians because it wanted to retain their confidence, and Coghlan and his followers were opposed to the administrative union. Coghlan, in fact, was steadily becoming more convinced that responsible government had to be secured before anything else happened.

The Northern Rhodesians gained from the debate because a delegation to London had extracted a promise that a limited form of representative government would be introduced if the Southern Rhodesians rejected amalgamation. An Advisory Council was established in 1918 and, although it could only discuss matters which affected the Europeans, it allowed an expression of their feelings. Its franchise was effectively reserved for Europeans because the vote could only be obtained by British subjects, and the Northern Rhodesian Africans, unlike their southern counterparts, were British Protected Persons. The voter was also required to have an annual income of £150 or to possess property worth £150.

The surprise of the first Northern Rhodesian election was that the voluble Northern Rhodesian Farmers' Association failed to gain a single seat. Yet it was from the farmers that the next proposal on amalgamation came. In 1919, the farmers in the Kafue and Mazabuka areas declared that they looked forward to amalgamation in the expectation of profiting from the proposed rail link between Kafue and Sinoia. However, their colleagues in North Eastern Rhodesia still preferred a link with Nyasaland, and the commercial interests in Northern Rhodesia were equally unenthusiastic. Moore then concentrated on ridding Northern Rhodesia of the Company and was so successful in his agitation that amalgamation became a side issue. Backed by the farmers in his area, he advocated transformation into a Crown Colony with an elective legislative council which could only deal with internal matters. He was attracted to this idea by the level of aid which was being given to

Nyasaland under Imperial administration. He gathered so much support that, in June 1921, the Advisory Council rejected a further proposal on the merger of the administrations and demanded real representation in return for increased taxation. It voted against absorption by Southern Rhodesia.[9]

In 1918, the decision of the Privy Council on unalienated land in Southern Rhodesia resulted in demands for constitutional change. It ruled that the land did not belong to the Company in its commercial capacity and could only be sold to defray administrative expenses. The Company reacted by refusing further capital expenditure on behalf of the settlers. This was not just spite as the Company was anxious to rid itself of the administrative burden. As such capital was required, it was therefore necessary to change the system of government. The Southern Rhodesians had no need for budgetary assistance because of the Company's good management, and thus were not interested in Crown Colony status. In any case, distracted by problems in the Near East and Ireland, Britain would probably not have welcomed an increase in her colonial burden. The choice lay between joining South Africa or acquiring responsible government. Opinion within the Company had changed on the question of joining South Africa. In 1909, it had resisted incorporation into the proposed union because it felt that postponement would allow the value of its assets to improve through the development of Southern Rhodesia. This would mean better compensation for the shareholders when they were ultimately paid out by the South African Government. It had also preferred to wait for the political influence of the Afrikaner to wane. A decade later, in 1919, Malcolm enthused over the political change wrought by the new South African Prime Minister, General Jan Smuts. Even Chaplin, whose political past had made him dislike the Afrikaner, was converted when Smuts brought the moderates to power.

More important than the support of the Company was the enthusiasm of the current Colonial Secretary, Lord Milner, for incorporation. He felt that responsible government was inappropriate but that he could not force Crown Colony status on Southern Rhodesia. So he thought that Southern and, perhaps, North Western Rhodesia should join South Africa. An enlarged protectorate would then be created comprising North Eastern Rhodesia, Nyasaland, Tanganyika, Kenya and Uganda. In suggesting this, he was echoing proposals advanced in 1917 by the Reverend Alexander Hetherwick of Nyasaland and in 1918 by a Northern Rhodesian civil servant, F. H. Melland. However, Melland proposed to include the Belgian territory of Ruanda-Urundi.[10]

Moore answered Milner in the *Livingstone Mail* by alleging that all that joining South Africa would bring would be higher taxes as there would be little South African capital available for development. He expressed dislike for the native policies of the Union and thought that the Northern Rhodesian

[9] R. I. Rotberg, *The Rise of Nationalism in Central Africa: The Making of Malawi and Zambia, 1873–1964* (London, 1965), p. 97.

[10] L. H. Gann, *A History of Northern Rhodesia: Early Days to 1953* (London, 1964), pp. 184–186; Rev. A. Hetherwick, "Nyasaland Today and Tomorrow", *Journal of the African Society* (London, 1917), Vol. 17, No. 66, pp. 11–19; F. H. Melland, "A Central African Confederation by Africanus", *Journal of the African Society* (London, 1918), Vol. 18, No. 67, p. 267.

civil servants would be reluctant to join the South African service. He dismissed Milner's protectorate as impracticable because none of its territories was self-sufficient. Thus they would be unable to find the funds for development.

The Southern Rhodesians who favoured union with South Africa gladdened Milner's heart by arguing that it would strengthen the loyalist cause against the republic-minded Afrikaner nationalists. They claimed that only South Africa had the resources to purchase the assets of the Company and its mineral and railway rights. If a Southern Rhodesian government attempted to do that unaided, it would have to resort to confiscation which would provoke a flight of capital and result in ruin. By contrast, the advocates of responsible government talked of patriotism while the European workers expressed fears about the Union's anti-strike legislation. The railwaymen were concerned about the lower rates of pay in South Africa and the miners feared the introduction of the practice of using black labour *en masse* which reduced the need for white skills. The civil servant was worried by his inability to speak Dutch, and the farmers were concerned about competition for labour and the possibility of a land grab. Some businessmen were fearful of the effect of the South African protectionist policies because Southern Rhodesia had to encourage both exports and an inflow of capital while keeping the cost of living down by low tariffs. Missionaries and others with the well-being of the Africans at heart joined the Indians and Coloureds in rejecting the South African racial policies.

The appointment of Milner led the Company to make its second bid for the unification of the administrations and provoked the Colonial Office to remind it that the destinies of the two Rhodesias differed. The Under-Secretary of State, Leopold Amery, agreed, but the Company was supported by Milner who telegraphed the High Commissioner to permit the merger provided that there was no local objection. The Advisory Council in Northern Rhodesia voted against the idea but, as Coghlan had no objection, Chaplin was given the additional post of Administrator of Northern Rhodesia in January 1921.[11]

The return of twelve supporters of responsible government in the Southern Rhodesian general election of 1920 prompted Milner to indicate that his Government would consider granting it. The Company, predictably, had other ideas and proposed the addition of North Western Rhodesia — the "Railway Belt" — to the suggested incorporation of Southern Rhodesia in the Union of South Africa. It argued that North Eastern Rhodesia's natural and established outlet was Nyasaland and that the two territories should be unified and directly administered by Britain. Barotseland and adjacent areas would then join Bechuanaland, leaving the "Railway Belt", which was dominated by European settlers, most of whom had come from the South, to share Southern Rhodesia's fate. In recommending this partition, the Company advised the British Government to ignore the protests of the 4 000 Northern Rhodesian Europeans because they lacked political experience.

True to form, these Northern Rhodesians rejected this proposal as well as another which suggested Northern Rhodesia's incorporation in an amal-

[11] Wetherell, *The Rhodesias and Amalgamation, op. cit.*, p. 69.

gamation of East Africa. The British Government responded by appointing a Commission under Lord Buxton to report on the future government of the Rhodesias. This recommended a referendum in Southern Rhodesia on responsible government and greater settler involvement in the governing of Northern Rhodesia through minority representation in a legislative council.[12] The Commission also suggested that the Privy Council should rule on the Company's claims to the ownership of land and mineral rights in Northern Rhodesia. The Company accepted the verdict on Southern Rhodesia but rejected the proposed Northern Rhodesian legislative council as an unnecessary luxury. The Colonial Office replied by offering to assume responsibility for the administration in return for land and mineral rights.

Knowing the strength of its position, the Company refused this offer, and warned that, if anything more was said, it would ask the Privy Council to decide the future of Northern Rhodesia and that, in the interim, it would meet only its single formal obligation which was to pay the costs of the administration of African affairs. This meant that the local Europeans would have to pay for all other services. As the main supplier of capital, the Company was in as strong a position in Southern Rhodesia. It could call in Land Bank loans and control the supply of labour from Northern Rhodesia. Nevertheless, the Southern Rhodesians decided their own course by choosing responsible government in the referendum of 1922. In so doing, they destroyed the hopes of those who sought to create a great dominion of Southern Africa which was loyal to the Crown, and which would halt the expansion of the Union of South Africa.[13] They also decided the fate of Northern Rhodesia because the winning faction, led by Coghlan, was opposed to amalgamation and the Company was no longer willing to meet the annual Northern Rhodesian deficit of some £157 000 a year.

The current Colonial Secretary, the Duke of Devonshire, and his Under-Secretary, W. G. A. Ormsby-Gore, believed that the British Government had treated the Company harshly and should now be generous. Ormsby-Gore, in fact, favoured the incorporation of Southern Rhodesia in South Africa and wished Northern Rhodesia to amalgamate with East Africa, but was not unsympathetic to the idea of unifying North Western Rhodesia with Southern Rhodesia. His friendly attitude, however, did not induce the Company to yield entirely on the issue of land in Northern Rhodesia but it is reflected in the agreements of 1923.

In September 1923, Southern Rhodesia was formally annexed to the Crown to become a self-governing colony. The Company retained its mineral rights there and was guaranteed against the confiscation of its railway assets. It was paid £3 750 000 by the Crown for its accumulated administrative debts, and the Southern Rhodesian Government bought the unalienated land for £2 300 000. The war debt of £2 000 000 was waived. Northern Rhodesia remained a protectorate but its administration was transferred to the Colonial Office on 1 April 1924. The Company relinquished its ownership of public buildings and its land rights to allow the Northern Rhodesian Government to

[12] Gann, *A History of Northern Rhodesia, op. cit.*, p. 189; *First Report of the Committee Appointed to Consider Certain Questions Relating to Rhodesia,* Command 1273 (London, 1921).

[13] R. Hyam, *The Failure of South African Expansion, 1908–48* (London, 1972), p. 1.

administer these in the public interest. In return the Company would receive half the proceeds of the sale of land until 1965. It retained three freehold areas given to it under the "certificates of claim" issued by Harry Johnston but the Crown reserved the right to establish native reserves in the concession area of the North Charterland Exploration Company in North Eastern Rhodesia. The mineral rights remained the property of the Company.

If this settlement appears generous, it should be remembered that the great copper deposits were yet to be uncovered and, in fact, the Company thought that it had been ill-treated. However, it was able to pay its first dividend of sixpence in the pound.

Ignoring amalgamation for the moment, the Southern Rhodesians revived their claims to Bechuanaland and suggested the building of a railway line through it to Walvis Bay. Britain, however, was reluctant to provoke South Africa on the issue of its rights to Bechuanaland in terms of the Act of Union. The unification of the British possessions in sub-Saharan Africa continued to attract British attention despite the Southern Rhodesian attitude. In 1919, Amery had suggested a scheme of unification for East Africa and, even though it was rejected,[14] Ormsby-Gore, ruling out partition, thought in 1923 that Northern Rhodesia should be more closely allied to Nyasaland and the East African territories. Consequently, when Herbert Stanley was appointed Governor of Northern Rhodesia in 1924, he was ordered to do nothing which would conflict with the policies being adopted in East Africa. However, he was also asked to examine the consequences of partition. Before he could report, his counterpart in Southern Rhodesia, Sir John Chancellor, suggested partition as a means to avoid any difficulties which would arise if Southern Rhodesia took over its portion of the railway from the Company. Coghlan indicated that he would support this idea if the British Government provided some short-term financial assistance. The British Government did not respond favourably. In fact, the Southern Rhodesian Government was also anxious that Northern Rhodesia should not drift into the East African sphere of influence and its fears were deepened by the Devonshire Declaration of 1923 which ruled that Kenya was an African-dominated territory and that therefore the interests of the African population were paramount when in conflict with those of the immigrants.[15] This was a telling blow to those East African Europeans who aspired to self-government. Indeed, it dashed those hopes by claiming that the current system of government was the only method of ensuring that the Imperial trusteeship was fulfilled.

The outbursts provoked by the Declaration induced the incoming British Labour Government, in 1924, to re-examine the idea of unification in East Africa, and a Commission chaired by Ormsby-Gore was dispatched to the area. This Commission found little enthusiasm for the idea except in official circles in Northern Rhodesia and Nyasaland, but it did recommend governmental co-operation and the establishment of a permanent body to run common services which could provide the nucleus of a future federal administration. It demanded improvements in communications and trade between

[14] R. I. Rotberg, "The Federation Movement in British East and Central Africa, 1889–1953", *Journal of Commonwealth Political Studies* (Leicester, 1964), Vol. II, p. 143.
[15] *Memorandum concerning Indians in Kenya,* Command 1922 (London, 1923).

East and Central Africa but discounted the idea of unifying North Eastern Rhodesia and Nyasaland.[16] The report was unanimous but later one of the members recanted. Writing in *The Times* on 13 December 1925, A. G. Church advocated the partition of Northern Rhodesia, with North Western Rhodesia being given to Southern Rhodesia and North Eastern Rhodesia to Nyasaland. He was ignored and his Commission's recommendations were implemented to the extent that the Governors of East and Central Africa, the Civil Secretary of the Sudan, and the Resident of Zanzibar met in Nairobi in 1926 and agreed to create a permanent secretariat and to meet annually to co-ordinate policy. In the event, they met infrequently and only technical information was exchanged. There was no standardisation of matters such as land tenure. Their action was paralleled by the Legislative Councils of East and Central Africa which met together annually for three years. While they called for increased white immigration, for the annexure of their protectorates to the Crown, and for the guarantee of white interests in any future federation, they evinced little enthusiasm for unification. The Northern Rhodesians, in particular, found their problems very different from those of the others because their territory was closely linked with the South in the fields of trade, communications and finance, whilst Nyasaland and East Africa depended on Britain for everything including markets. Indeed, in 1926, the Legislative Councils decided that federation was impracticable. In 1927, when meeting in Nairobi, the Northern Rhodesians made it even more unlikely by insisting that Southern Rhodesia should be included. They rejected any idea of participation and expressed fears of ultimate African domination.

In the meantime, Coghlan had done a *volte face* to become an advocate of amalgamation. He was prompted to embrace the cause by the current discontent over the high railway rates charged by the Company, and thought that nationalisation of the railway system would only be effective under a single government. He was determined, however, that the assets of the Company would also be acquired and that land would not be left in the hands of the Africans which was the system prevailing in Northern Rhodesia.

However, the Northern Rhodesian Government did not view the railway issue in the same light and feared a Southern Rhodesian bid for the Katangan markets. In any case, it welcomed the new outlet to the sea which the railway being built from Lobito Bay in Angola would provide. It considered that, as the Company had invested in local industries, it was unlikely to harm their interests. The Northern Rhodesian Government rejected partition because it would sever the new mines from their labour supply and the African areas from their source of wealth.

The opinion of the Northern Rhodesian Europeans divided on the issue. The farmers welcomed the prospect of sharing the excellent Southern Rhodesian agricultural and veterinarian services and hoped that, if the Southern Rhodesian land settlement policies were adopted, the price of land would rise. Typically, however, Moore and the Livingstonians hoped that Northern Rhodesia would become a dominion on its own. They feared competition in trade and the decline of their town if it ceased to be the capital. The civil servants

[16] *Report of the East African Commission,* Command 2387 (London, 1925).

disliked the Southern Rhodesian conditions of service, and the mining companies doubted the ability of the Southern Rhodesian Government to deal with the financial problems which the exploitation of copper would bring.

Coghlan was rebuffed by the current Colonial Secretary, Leopold Amery, but this did not deter the protagonists of amalgamation. Immediately, three unofficial Members of the Northern Rhodesian Legislative Council met the Southern Rhodesian Cabinet to devise a scheme of amalgamation. They rejected partition and suggested that Northern Rhodesia should be fully represented in the Cabinet and the new Legislative Assembly. The Southern Rhodesian policy of land settlement would be adopted and the land rights of the Company would be purchased. The legal codes would be unified and the Southern Rhodesian mining laws applied throughout. The Southern Rhodesians agreed to reduce their recruitment of labour in the North. However, no action followed their planning, and in 1926 the railway issue was resolved by the creation of an inter-territorial commission.

Amalgamation continued to be discussed and, in 1927, the Progressive Party in Southern Rhodesia proposed a "Greater Rhodesian Dominion" which would secure a west coast port as well as absorbing Bechuanaland north of latitude 20° 40 South.[17] Coghlan also raised the subject with Amery when he visited Southern Rhodesia that year, but Amery showed little interest because he was preoccupied with the possibilities of an East African federation. This preoccupation led the British Government to refuse to allow the Rhodesians to meet to discuss amalgamation later in the year.

Amery had been ignoring the public apathy in East Africa towards unification and, to promote it, he had appointed Governors in Uganda and Kenya, Sir William Gowers and Sir Edward Grigg, who were sympathetic to federation. He was, however, somewhat frustrated in his aim by Sir Donald Cameron, the previous Labour Government's appointee in Tanganyika, who was opposed to the idea as well as being antagonistic towards his fellow Governors. Determined to resist policies which favoured the white settler, Cameron opposed Grigg's ideas on the unification of transport, customs, defence and research under a federal council. Grigg ignored him and drew up a plan for closer union to avoid the wastage of money on parallel projects. In 1927, Amery made a declaration in favour of the unification of East Africa, but was thwarted by pressure from the African Rights lobby led by Dr J. H. Oldham and Lord Lugard. All he could do was to dispatch another Commission, under the leadership of Sir Edward Hilton Young, to East Africa.[18]

In 1929, the Commission reported in favour of federation in East Africa, although it did not include Northern Rhodesia and Nyasaland in it because they had so little in common with the other territories.[19] However, it did examine the question of unifying the two Rhodesias and Nyasaland and attempted to assess public opinion. It found that the northern Africans had reservations about the idea while, generally, the Europeans welcomed it.

[17] M. C. Steele, *The Challenge of Rhodesia to European Liberal Thought* (unpublished M. Litt. thesis, University of Edinburgh, 1968), p. 340.

[18] *Future Policy in Regard to East Africa,* Command 2904 (London, 1927).

[19] *Report of the Commission on Closer Union of the Dependencies in Eastern and Central Africa,* Command 3234 (London, 1929).

Hilton Young alone advocated the unification of the three Central African territories and revived the idea of partition. Accordingly, he proposed a self-governing colony comprising Southern Rhodesia and Central Northern Rhodesia. There would be a Crown Colony of North Eastern Rhodesia and Nyasaland, and a protectorate in Barotseland. A central authority would be established, presided over by the Governor of Southern Rhodesia as High Commissioner who would be invested with the current supervisory powers over the Imperial and African interests which the Colonial Secretary possessed. The purpose of the central authority would be to co-ordinate policies on defence, communications and customs and excise.

The three other members of the Commission, Sir Reginald Mant, Sir George Schuster and Dr J. H. Oldham, were unwilling to allow the Southern Rhodesians to extend their influence over further African populations until they had shown themselves capable of solving their existing problems. They believed that a future union of the northern territories with East Africa was desirable and thus argued that nothing should be done with regard to establishing links with Southern Rhodesia. They were also anxious to preserve the independence of the protectorates in order to safeguard African rights.

The Colonial Office was pleased with the Report, and Hilton Young's idea drew support only from the Southern Rhodesian Government. Sir James Maxwell, the Governor of Northern Rhodesia, protested that partition would divorce the copper mines from their sources of labour. The African centres of population, likewise, would lose their source of income. He wanted nothing to be done until the economic effect of the railway line from Lobito Bay could be gauged. The British Government stressed its obligations as the protecting power with regard to the Africans, and objected to the separation of the agricultural areas from the mining towns. However, privately it indicated to Southern Rhodesia that it might cede to it the land between the Kafue and the Zambezi Rivers. For the moment, local support for amalgamation waned and the idea was rejected in 1928 by a majority of the unofficial Members of the Northern Rhodesian Legislative Council when they discussed it again with the Southern Rhodesian Cabinet. In August 1929, the new Labour Colonial Secretary, Lord Passfield, informed the Southern Rhodesians that he would permit amalgamation if they would concede to him greater control of policy with regard to the African. As this proposed a diminution of the hard-won self-governing status of Southern Rhodesia, it could hardly have encouraged the amalgamationists.[20]

In mid-1930, however, Passfield would be responsible for a renewed interest in amalgamation in Northern Rhodesia when he issued his *Memorandum on Native Policy in East Africa.* In this he re-stated the policy with regard to the protectorates and the paramountcy of African interests and extended it to Northern Rhodesia.[21] In addition, the continual refusal of the British Government to allow further constitutional advance in Northern Rhodesia won Moore and his cohorts to the amalgamation cause.[22]

[20] Palley, *The Constitutional History and Law, op. cit.*, p. 328, fn. 2.
[21] *Memorandum on Native Policy in East Africa*, Command 3573 (London, 1930); Rotberg, "The Federation Movement", *op. cit.*, p. 151.
[22] Wetherell, *The Rhodesias and Amalgamation, op. cit.*, p. 132.

The Governor of Northern Rhodesia was wise enough to see the need to subdue the local reaction to the Memorandum, and claimed that it was of academic interest only, because it contained no departure from established policy. He felt that matters of colour would not be the foundation of decisions on the constitutional future of Northern Rhodesia and that Passfield had not precluded the Europeans from securing greater control over their own affairs. He forecast that there would be no African membership of the Legislative Council within the next 20 years.[23] However, he failed to quieten the fears of his unofficial Members who called for and held a Conference at the Victoria Falls with the Southern Rhodesian parliamentarians in September 1930. Indeed, far from being a tempering influence, Sir James Maxwell deliberately tried to divide the Conference by commenting that the Southern Rhodesians had only become interested in amalgamation since Northern Rhodesia had become a "rich young lady". He provoked the Southern Rhodesian Prime Minister, H. U. Moffat, to reply angrily that the issue had first been discussed when Northern Rhodesia suffered a yearly deficit.

The delegates at the Victoria Falls rejected the Memorandum and decided to meet regularly. In addition, they demanded a conference on amalgamation in London, but the British Government would not agree to convene it because there were too few Europeans in Northern Rhodesia and because the Africans were not as yet sufficiently advanced. Professor Palley has revealed that this was what the British Government said officially and that, privately, as he had done in August 1929, Passfield offered such unacceptable terms that Moffat realised that a conference would be pointless.[24]

The British Government remained outwardly intransigent but, in fact, a Cabinet committee which included Conservative and Liberal representatives examined the possibility of partition. It proposed that nothing more than the area south of the Kafue River — which contained the farmers who were the bulk of the protagonists of amalgamation — could be ceded to Southern Rhodesia because the Copperbelt and the areas which supplied it with food and labour had to be retained in Imperial hands as copper was such a vital commodity to the Empire both in peace and war.[25] However, Sir Herbert Stanley, currently High Commissioner for South Africa, thought that this idea would not appeal to either the Southern or Northern Rhodesians, and he suggested a federation of the Rhodesias and Nyasaland. The Colonial and Dominions Offices had suggested the secession of the southern Kafue area but remained as adamantly opposed as ever to amalgamation and — to bolster the anti-amalgamation argument — added to the Cabinet committee's recommendation the comment that, amongst other matters, the copper wealth could not be effectively managed by a "farmers'" government.[26]

However, in July 1931, Passfield did suggest that there should be greater

[23] Steele, *The Challenge of Rhodesia*, *op. cit.*, p. 346.

[24] Palley, *The Constitutional History and Law*, *op. cit.*, p. 328, fn. 2.

[25] K. N. Mufuka, "Britain and Amalgamation of the Rhodesias, 1937–41", *Rhodesian History* (Salisbury, 1977), Vol. 7, p. 89.

[26] Wetherell, *The Rhodesias and Amalgamation*, *op. cit.*, pp. 153–161; H. I. Wetherell, "Settler Expansionism in Central Africa: The Imperial Response of 1931 and Subsequent Implications", *African Affairs* (London, April 1979), Vol. 78, pp. 219–221.

co-operation between the Rhodesias even though he would not consider amalgamation in the current circumstances. He conceded that there might be a future possibility of amalgamation and hinted that, if there were, Northern Rhodesia might be partitioned.[27] His successor, J. H. Thomas of the "National" Government, was just as firm and stated that, before the question of amalgamation could be resuscitated, definite proposals for African welfare and development would have to be forthcoming. Dr Wetherell notes that Passfield and Thomas had thus kept the hope of amalgamation alive, and maintains that they had done so when they could, indeed should, have ruled it out for all time by totally discouraging the Southern Rhodesians through setting equal political and economic opportunities for Africans as prerequisites to amalgamation.[28] The Southern Rhodesians were never totally converted to the idea of closer association and might well have given up the game. However, the necessities of war after 1939 would have still demanded inter-territorial co-operation in a wide variety of fields and might well have revived the clamour for closer association.

When Moffat sought to re-open the discussion on amalgamation in 1932, he received no encouragement, but the British Government did re-define "paramountcy" as a result of an examination of closer association in East Africa by a joint select committee of Parliament which construed it to mean that the interests of the overwhelming majority of the natives should not be subordinated to those of the immigrant minorities. For the moment, this seemed to satisfy the Europeans and brought Moore back into the anti-amalgamation camp.

Moffat was not entirely discouraged and he and others remained convinced that amalgamation was inevitable. The effect in 1933 of the Depression on Northern Rhodesia would make self-government seem unattainable and brought new life to the amalgamation issue. Active support came from those most directly affected by the economic plight of the country — the artisans, farmers and white-collar workers. Remaining opposed were the bulk of the missionaries who feared the loss of the Imperial trusteeship and the illiberal rule of Salisbury. The civil servants also had no desire to lose their conditions of service under the Colonial service or their promotion prospects therein. The lawyers opposed any change in the legal codes, and the senior mining men continued to doubt the ability of the Southern Rhodesian Government in the financial field. Opposition was expressed by African associations in Livingstone and Ndola. These "Welfare Societies" recognised the economic advantages of joining Southern Rhodesia, but did not think that these outweighed the lack of an official colour bar in Northern Rhodesia which provided them with greater employment opportunities. They also disliked the Southern Rhodesian imposition of grazing fees and timber royalties.[29]

Moore changed sides again and voted in favour of a motion on amalgamation which was carried through the Legislative Council. Then he and C. S. Knight, junior Member for Livingstone, sought support from the Southern

[27] Steele, *The Challenge of Rhodesia*, *op. cit.*, p. 346.

[28] Wetherell, *The Rhodesias and Amalgamation*, *op. cit.*, p. 336.

[29] Gann, *A History of Northern Rhodesia*, *op. cit.*, pp. 269–270; Palley, *The Constitutional History and Law*, *op. cit.*, p. 329.

Rhodesian Government, urging haste lest Northern Rhodesia be drawn into an East African union. Moore feared that his territory was destined to become a purely African state. He also wished to limit the activities of the British capitalists, of whom he had a deep suspicion. However, Moore and Knight were partly concerned to save Northern Rhodesia the unnecessary expense, in their view, of the transfer of the capital to Lusaka. The Southern Rhodesian Government responded favourably and, in addition, its Governor, Sir Cecil Rodwell, was won round. The Southern Rhodesians joined the Northern Rhodesians in pressing the British Government for amalgamation.[30]

The idea of unification drew wider support, and *The Nyasaland Times* called for it on the grounds of administrative efficiency and savings. In 1933, an unofficial delegation from Nyasaland and the two Rhodesias called on the Colonial Office. Although the delegates mentioned a need to contain the spread of Afrikaner nationalism, their arguments for union concentrated on its economic advantages. They claimed that the Imperial Tobacco Company and other tobacco dealers had come to regard the Rhodesias and Nyasaland as a single economic unit. It was therefore logical to unite and there was a need, in the light of this, to secure a common approach to tariffs. Nyasaland, they argued, had won the right to be included in any scheme of unification by virtue of her position as supplier of 80 per cent of the agricultural labour in Southern Rhodesia. In the interests of economy and efficiency, they proposed that there should be a common court of appeal and common services embracing research, customs and excise, communications, mining, non-African education, and defence. Political change in Southern Rhodesia in 1934 won the amalgamation cause a powerful ally, the British South Africa Company. In 1933, Godfrey Martin Huggins, a local surgeon and already a politician of some note, and his Reform Party, with the support of the white artisans and farmers, had edged Moffat's Rhodesia Party out of power. Huggins had thus begun what was to be the longest premiership in British and Commonwealth history, characterised by a rare ability to survive changing circumstances despite his abrasive character which was compounded by deafness.

However, the Reform Party had lacked the cohesion to survive, and in 1934 Huggins abandoned it to form a coalition of the conservative elements of the Rhodesia and Reform Parties. This strengthening of his position encouraged a *volte face* by the Company. Hitherto, the Company had expressed much reserve about the amateurism of the Southern Rhodesian Government. However, it had sold its mineral rights to that Government in the previous year for £2 000 000 to provide capital for investment and now, in 1934, Sir Henry Birchenough, the chairman of the Company, pointed to Southern Rhodesia's history of industrial peace, expressed confidence in Huggins and suggested to the Colonial Office that a British bloc should be formed in Central Africa by combining the two Rhodesias with Nyasaland and perhaps Tanganyika.

In that year, 1934, Huggins also pressed the British Government on amalgamation, proposing the partition of Northern Rhodesia with the "Railway Belt", including the copper mines, joining Southern Rhodesia to create an area in which the interests of the whites would predominate. The re-

[30] Gann, *A History of Northern Rhodesia, op. cit.*, pp. 267–269; Wetherell, *The Rhodesias and Amalgamation, op. cit.*, p. 179.

mainder of Northern Rhodesia would become African areas, administered by the Colonial Office, which would provide employment opportunities for the growing output of the African schools in Southern Rhodesia. He thought that in these areas it should be possible for Africans to rise to the highest levels. As Dr Chanock points out, Huggins, like the Afrikaner nationalists in South Africa, was searching for an alternative policy to that formulated by Rhodes, which implied the ultimate political equality of the races.[31] Believing that this would be unacceptable to his electorate, Huggins sought an alternative outlet for the Africans' political aspirations. However, the Colonial Office rejected the idea, and Moore would not hear of the partition of Northern Rhodesia.[32]

The continuing effects of the slump, the termination of the customs arrangement with South Africa, and the African industrial riots on the Copperbelt in 1935 were fuel to the unification cause. The Southern Rhodesians looked to the North for markets, while the Northern Rhodesians made vociferous demands for union with Southern Rhodesia where industrial peace reigned and more was done for the welfare of the African than in the neighbouring countries. In part, the northerners attributed the success of Southern Rhodesia to the permanent nature of its civil service which contrasted with the North's shifting population of civil servants who stayed briefly in their passage from colony to colony up the promotional ladder.

The Northern Rhodesians might thus attack their civil servants but, in fact, they had found allies amongst them and, most significantly, in the Governors of the three territories.

Sir Harold Kittermaster, the Governor of Nyasaland, saw the administrative and economic advantages of a union between his territory and Northern Rhodesia. His view, however, was not shared by the Colonial Secretary, Malcolm MacDonald, who rejected it on the grounds that, as Zomba would not be the capital of the new state, Nyasaland was more likely to suffer from administrative neglect. He saw no economic reason for union because there was little trade between the territories and, in any case, the northern part of Northern Rhodesia fell within the Free Trade Area of the Congo Basin Treaties of 1885, thereby ruling out the possibility of a customs union. MacDonald added that, as Northern Rhodesia would be saddled with Nyasaland's annual deficit, the local Europeans would not support this union unless it was a step towards amalgamation with Southern Rhodesia. Amalgamation, however, was repugnant to MacDonald because he was determined to preserve Britain's role as protector of the northern African.

The situation in Central Africa nonetheless prompted the new Governor of Northern Rhodesia, Sir Hubert Young, to propose a greater measure of co-operation. In so doing, he interpreted the current policy of "Indirect Rule" by the Colonial Office through Native Authorities as merely providing training for Africans in government and not as implying that, in time, they would achieve political domination. Impressed by their achievements, he thought that the local Europeans had won a permanent place in the country and that they should be given greater political power. In addition, he admired the readiness of Huggins to put the interests of the whole area before those of

[31] Chanock, *Unconsummated Union*, *op. cit.*, p. 217.
[32] Gann, *A History of Northern Rhodesia*, *op. cit.*, p. 270.

Southern Rhodesia. Thus Young proposed an association of the territories which would be called British Central Africa. It would come under a single high commissioner, and a customs union would be established to encourage secondary industries. Young hoped to see a textile industry created which would compete with the Japanese for cheapness by using African labour and skilled unemployed workers from Britain. Transport would be co-ordinated, and the links with East Africa would be severed because Young thought that they were artificial.

Young claimed that his scheme would halt the Southern Rhodesian drift into the South African orbit. The new Governor of Southern Rhodesia, Sir Herbert Stanley, echoed this sentiment in a memorandum submitted to the Colonial Office in which he advocated a Central African union of the two Rhodesias to balance the Afrikaner-dominated Union of South Africa.[33] Young and Stanley were rebuffed by the Colonial Office which warned them that they should not promote the cause of unification. However, they ignored the Colonial Office and met Kittermaster informally aboard a train travelling between Bulawayo and Salisbury in January 1935. The result was a formal meeting with Huggins to discuss the provision of common services which included research, customs and excise, education, communications, defence and publicity. The meeting wanted trade representation in London, a common court of appeal, consultation in mining law, and the avoidance of the double taxation of Africans. There was regular consultation thereafter with the result that, in 1939, an Inter-Territorial Court of Appeal was created under the presidency of the Chief Justice of Southern Rhodesia.[34] An Inter-Territorial Communications Board, an Inter-Territorial Labour Conference with a standing committee, and a common currency were established. The Colonial Office, however, had forbidden in 1935 the use of "British Central Africa" as a title in order not to encourage the amalgamationists.[35]

In 1935, South Africa provided encouragement for the unification of Central Africa by lifting its ban on the recruitment of foreign Africans, thereby beginning to compete with Southern Rhodesia for Nyasaland labour. It also imposed unfavourable tariffs. Accordingly, Huggins suggested a loose federation which would strengthen the Southern Rhodesian economy and bolster the British position in Central Africa. He did not propose to standardise African policies because he thought that they could be made complementary. He would keep political control in white hands on the Southern Rhodesian pattern which was to train Africans to serve the growing needs of their people and not to replace Europeans.[36]

A fear that Adolf Hitler might acquire the reversion of Tanganyika to Germany, through British appeasement, led Moore to call for the immediate amalgamation of the Rhodesias.[37] Hitler did not trouble the Nyasalanders,

[33] *Ibid.*, pp. 270–271.

[34] Welensky Papers, 17/46, ff. 109–110, Sir Hubert Young to G. M. Huggins, 20 July 1937; Gann, *A History of Northern Rhodesia, op. cit.*, pp. 271–272; Palley, *The Constitutional History and Law, op. cit.*, p. 329, fn. 4.

[35] Wetherell, *The Rhodesias and Amalgamation, op. cit.*, p. 202.

[36] Gann, *A History of Northern Rhodesia, op. cit.*, p. 269.

[37] Author's interview with Sir Roy Welensky; Rotberg, *The Rise of Nationalism, op. cit.*, p. 109.

but economic stagnation did, and they formed a "Greater Rhodesia League" to achieve a federation of the Rhodesias and Nyasaland. By ending the Colonial Office's opposition to white settlement, the Nyasalanders hoped to encourage development. As the congress of Huggins's United Party in 1935 fully supported the amalgamation of the three territories, it is not surprising that Huggins responded to an approach by Moore by calling for an unoffical conference at the Victoria Falls in early 1936. In doing so, he assured Moore, who had doubted their eagerness, that the Southern Rhodesians were "red-hot amalgamationists". Nonetheless, Huggins suggested the propagation of a rumour that Northern Rhodesia intended to join South Africa to excite Southern Rhodesian enthusiasm for amalgamation. The disclosure of this suggestion to the British Government brought a strong protest.[38]

At the Victoria Falls, the delegates — seven unofficial Members of the Northern Rhodesian Legislative Council and 30 representatives of the political parties of Southern Rhodesia — unanimously chose amalgamation. They proposed the adoption of the Southern Rhodesian Constitution for the unified territory and the pursuit of dominion status. The new legislative assembly would contain nominated and elected members with three appointed to represent African interests. For the moment, the territories would retain their separate legal codes but ultimately there would be a single high court in the capital, Salisbury.[39]

On 7 May 1936, the Southern Rhodesian Legislative Assembly recorded its approval of the decision of the Conference.[40] In Northern Rhodesia, however, dissension appeared in the ranks of the unofficial Members. Two of them, Lieutenant-Colonels A. Stephenson and Sir Stewart Gore-Browne, were aware of the extent of the African opposition, and agreed that amalgamation would not serve the interests of the African, and that it was therefore incompatible with the Imperial trusteeship. Gore-Browne, in particular, was confident that the British Government would not sanction amalgamation, and proposed as an alternative a federation composed of a "white" state in which the interests of the Europeans would be paramount, and two "black" states in which the Africans' interests would dominate. The "white" state would comprise the "Railway Belt" and Southern Rhodesia, and the "black" states would be North Western Rhodesia and a union of North Eastern Rhodesia and Nyasaland. The "black" states would continue to be administered by the Colonial Office. Gore-Browne was critical of the Colonial administration, nonetheless, and thought that the concept of trusteeship was impractical unless Britain was prepared to return the territories to the Africans. However, he did not want to see the latter happen. Yet he rejected repression, and thought that segregation without an element of self-government would be unworkable. His answer would be echoed later in the Verwoerdian solution for South Africa. It was a partnership between the races in

[38] Wetherell, *The Rhodesias and Amalgamation*, *op. cit.*, p. 207; R. I. Rotberg, *Black Heart: Gore-Browne and the Politics of Multiracial Zambia* (Berkeley, 1977), p. 192.

[39] Rotberg, "The Federation Movement", *op. cit.*, p. 152; Gann, *A History of Northern Rhodesia*, *op. cit.*, p. 272.

[40] S[outhern] R[hodesia] *Debates* [*of the Legislative Assembly*] (Salisbury), Vol. 16, Col. 1560, 7 May 1936.

which their particular interests could be developed in their own areas. Thus European standards would be maintained by their political autonomy in their territory, while African standards would improve from an increase in social services and from experience in learning to govern their areas. He rejected social intercourse between the races and consigned the African to a permanent junior role in the partnership.[41]

This proposal was greeted with some enthusiasm but, for the moment, the British Government did not shift its ground. Ormsby-Gore, the current Colonial Secretary, proclaimed that nothing had happened to warrant a change since Passfield's statement rejecting amalgamation in 1931.[42] Huggins, who preferred amalgamation to Gore-Browne's federation, however, was not discouraged. He felt that there was no time to be lost as the policies being applied in the Rhodesias were beginning to diverge to the extent that soon unification would be impossible. He had also gained significant support — even amongst the missionaries. In addition, Sir Ernest Oppenheimer, the Southern African mining magnate, encouraged him, despite the fear of the mining houses in Northern Rhodesia that the introduction of the formalised Southern Rhodesian colour bar practices would significantly affect labour costs.[43] The Southern Rhodesian Governor, Sir Herbert Stanley, called for immediate fusion and claimed that the territories would gain from settler control because in Southern Rhodesia the African policies had proved to be excellent, and its development had outstripped that of the Colonial Office-controlled Northern Rhodesia.

As 1936 wore on, the opposition to unification abroad fell away. In South Africa, Smuts and the nationalist, Oswald Pirow, declared that they no longer opposed it. Indeed, Smuts said that he had erred in seeking to unite Southern Rhodesia with South Africa. Moreover, Huggins had begun to win allies amongst the British civil servants, particularly at the Dominions Office, even though generally the British civil service was even more critical of the Southern Rhodesian policies. Even at ministerial level there was a mellowing, and Ormsby-Gore, although opposed to amalgamation, expressed a willingness to consider a suggestion for a federation from Sir Hubert Young.[44]

A threat from Huggins to join South Africa prompted a meeting between the Dominions and Colonial Secretaries and their senior officials. They agreed to a formal examination of the unification issue. Ormsby-Gore proposed consideration of a loose federation to co-ordinate economic affairs, defence and the judiciary. He thought that some technical departments might be amalgamated, but he would not allow the Colonial Office to relinquish its absolute control of African affairs. However, he would not convene the conference which Huggins wanted, but censured Young for a premature disclosure, in October 1936, of the British rejection of amalgamation.

[41] Gann, *A History of Northern Rhodesia*, *op. cit.*, p. 272; Sir Stewart Gore-Browne, "The Federated States of Rhodesia", *Journal of the African Society* (London, 1937), pp. 2–7; Rotberg, *Black Heart*, *op. cit.*, pp. 194–195.

[42] Rotberg, *The Rise of Nationalism*, *op. cit.*, p. 109.

[43] Gann, *A History of Northern Rhodesia*, *op. cit.*, p. 273; L. H. Gann and M. Gelfand, *Huggins of Rhodesia* (London, 1964), p. 117; Palley, *The Constitutional History and Law*, *op. cit.*, p. 329, fn. 1.

[44] Gann, *A History of Northern Rhodesia*, *op. cit.*, p. 273.

At a further meeting, during the Coronation celebrations in 1937, the Dominions and Colonial Secretaries explained to Huggins, Gore-Browne and the three territorial Governors that amalgamation could not be considered and that the British had responsibilities for the well-being of the African. If the Colonial Office kept its control of African affairs in the northern territories, the British Ministers thought that a form of closer association would be possible. This, of course, was the form which the subsequent Federation would take and which would condemn it to an early demise. As Dr Wetherell notes, the significance of this decision, which was the product of an official memorandum, was the crystallisation of the British approach to unification. The control of "Native" policy in the North would not be relinquished, but henceforth in other fields the Dominions and Colonial Offices could respond to the demands of Southern Rhodesia.[45] Huggins and the Secretaries of State reflected further and accepted a suggestion from Stanley for the appointment of a commission to enquire into the question of closer association.[46]

Huggins was aware that the British Government would be free to accept or reject the commission's recommendations, but thought it important that the commission should consider the merits of amalgamation, and he applied pressure for its inclusion in the terms of reference. Ultimately amalgamation was not specifically mentioned, but the commission was required to discover whether any form of closer association between the territories was desirable or practicable while bearing in mind the British responsibilities to the African.

The Commission was chaired by a former Governor-General of New Zealand, Viscount Bledisloe, who had proven expertise in agriculture and administration. Serving with him were: Thomas Fitzgerald, a former Postmaster General of the amalgamated services of Kenya, Uganda and Tanganyika; Patrick Ashley-Cooper, a director of the Bank of England; Ian Leslie Orr-Ewing, Conservative MP for Weston-super-Mare; Ernest Evans KC, Liberal MP for the University of Wales; and William Henry Mainwaring, Labour MP for the East Rhondda.[47] The Commissioners would tour the territories in 1938 and would record that the Africans to whom they spoke had an imperfect understanding of the issues involved and, indeed, were generally incapable of comprehending them. Nonetheless, they found the northern Africans almost unanimous in their opposition to amalgamation because they disliked the policies of the Southern Rhodesian Government and wished to remain under British protection. They feared that the Southern Rhodesians might tax marriages, the collection of firewood, and even children. They thought that there might also be expropriation of land. They criticised the Southern Rhodesian pass laws, native reserves, racial attitudes and the denial of opportunities to African clerks and traders. They decried the lesser role which the Chiefs played in the Southern Rhodesian system of government. Another contributing factor to the rejection was an airing of the ideas of Colonel C. L. Carbutt, the Chief Native Commissioner of Southern Rhodesia, which envisaged the settlement of Africans in the northern terri-

[45] Wetherell, "Britain and Rhodesian Expansionism", *op. cit.*, pp. 124–125.

[46] Gann, *A History of Northern Rhodesia*, *op. cit.*, pp. 273–274; Rotberg, *The Rise of Nationalism*, *op. cit.*, p. 111.

[47] *Rhodesia-Nyasaland Commission Report*, Command 5949 (London, 1939).

tories in order that Southern Rhodesia could become a white state. Huggins hastened to correct Carbutt, but the damage was done.[48]

The Commission found that the Europeans in the North mostly saw amalgamation as a means of ridding themselves of rule by the Colonial Office. The African support for amalgamation, by contrast, was based on a variety of reasons. The Lovale tribe was prepared to accept it if it meant that they would not have to share the same province with the Lozis. Some Africans sought a uniformity of taxes, while others hoped that Northern Rhodesians would cease to be regarded as foreigners in Southern Rhodesia in order to share the better schooling there and be paid as much as the Southern Rhodesians.[49]

The reasons for opposition to amalgamation amongst the Africans in Southern Rhodesia were markedly different. The Southern Rhodesian Bantu Congress and the Bantu Community Association thought that their progress would be impeded by the backwardness of the northern African. These bodies were in favour of Huggins's theories of parallel development and stressed that Africans were better paid in Southern Rhodesia. There was one delegation which preferred incorporation in the Union of South Africa because of its better living conditions. It argued that amalgamation with the North was a retrograde step on the road to civilisation.

The Commission reported in March 1939, and acknowledged the need for co-operation between the three territories. Indeed, it proposed machinery to realise it. Federation was considered and rejected because it would be rendered unworkable by the wide disparity in the constitutional and economic development of the territories. Immediate amalgamation was ruled out by the Commission even though it believed that the territories would, through their common interest, inevitably unite. It urged the British Government to endorse this view publicly and thereby remove Central African anxieties about the future. Such a statement, the Commissioners felt, would be a fitting tribute to the progress made by Southern Rhodesia in 15 years of self-government. It would encourage the Southern Rhodesian Government to co-operate with the North, increase the sense of responsibility amongst the Europeans towards the Africans and help to develop the mutual interests of all races.

Heading the list of reasons for postponing amalgamation were the differing approaches to the administration of the affairs of the African in Northern and Southern Rhodesia. The Commission acknowledged both policies were still in the experimental stage and that it was too early to judge them. However, as Southern Rhodesians would inevitably dominate a union, it was particularly necessary to give their policy of "Parallel Development" time to prove itself and to mellow. Northern Rhodesia would have to match Southern Rhodesia's social and development services. However, Southern Rhodesia would have to modify its restrictive practices in regard to African employment such as those enshrined in its Industrial Conciliation Act of 1934 which was the product of the lean years of the Depression during which the informal colour bar had been ignored in order to employ Africans as cheaper labour. With their

48 Wetherell, *The Rhodesias and Amalgamation*, *op. cit.*, p. 259.
49 Command 5949, *op. cit.*, p. 218.

position thus undermined, the white workers had successfully demanded statutory protection. The Africans were effectively kept out by "natives" being excluded from the definition of "employees". The Commission thought that the European population needed more experience in the responsibilities of government before it could assume control of the enlarged area and of its 4 000 000 Africans. It acknowledged that the Southern Rhodesians had gained some such experience, but the same could not be said for the northern Europeans who should be given more responsibility in the field of government.

As the Commission found that the Africans in the northern territories unanimously opposed amalgamation, it concluded that their resistance would make it unworkable. Nonetheless, it believed that the passage of time would make amalgamation appear more attractive to the Africans. The final reason for rejection was that the financial resources of the area were insufficient to provide services immediately at the standard set by Southern Rhodesia.

The Commission decided that it would be premature to recommend a constitution for the ultimately amalgamated territory, but felt that it was essential to continue the Southern Rhodesian practice of entrusting the Governor with powers to reserve his assent to certain classes of legislation as a measure of protection for the African. It also sought to maintain the established northern practice of European nominated Members to represent Africans. Indeed, the Commission developed this idea to propose a means by which the African could be brought in to represent his own interests. This was adopted by the Northern Rhodesian Government in the latter days of the war when it established African Provincial Councils which nominated Members for an African Representative Council. The Provincial Councils provided the Governor with a list of candidates from which to draw the African representatives in the Legislative Council.

The Commission urged that the special position of Barotseland should be respected, and warned finally that, if a bi-cameral system were adopted, both houses would have to be representative of African interests or they would divide over racial matters.

Another recommendation which was to be implemented in the war dealt with inter-territorial co-operation. The Commission noted the efforts already made in this direction, but was aware that there were no means of implementing the decisions of the inter-territorial meetings. It proposed a standing inter-territorial council to examine existing services and to ensure co-ordination. This council would survey the territorial economies and plan development. Membership would include the Prime Minister of Southern Rhodesia and the two northern Governors, and all three would be responsible for the implementation of the decisions of the council. Associated with them would be three Southern Rhodesian representatives, two Northern Rhodesians and two Nyasalanders. The Governor of Southern Rhodesia would take the chair, and to assist the council there would be a joint appeal court and a measure of uniformity in the legal systems. Co-operation would be effected in education, agriculture, research, defence, transport, roads and publicity. A single department to deal with the supply of African labour was thought to be a possibility.

The Commission prophesied that this experience in the handling of mutual problems would produce the modifications of policy which would facilitate amalgamation, and to this end it proposed periodical reviews of progress. To complement this co-operation between the territories, the Commission recommended the establishment of a combined agency of the Dominions and Colonial Offices to handle the affairs of the territories exclusively. This was to be effected, but only in 1962, and by then it was too late for it to have an influence on the course of events.

The Commissioners not only urged the constitutional development of the northern territories, but recommended the changes which should be made. The Northern Rhodesian Legislative Council currently comprised seven elected Members and one nominated Member representing African interests, with parity of representation secured by the presence of eight official Members. The Commissioners preferred an unofficial majority and proposed the addition of a second nominated Member to represent the Africans and another elected Member for the Europeans.

Nyasaland had possessed a nominated Legislative Council since 1907 and the Commissioners agreed that the racial imbalance of the population continued to preclude the introduction of an electoral system. They advised, however, that this matter should be kept under review and that the unofficial element should be strengthened to balance the influence of the official membership. Moreover, to give the Europeans of both northern territories experience in government, the Commission proposed that the Executive Councils should comprise three official and three unofficial Members, including a representative of African interests. The Commission also felt that the Colonial Office should allow the Governors and their staffs greater autonomy.

Although they proposed these constitutional changes, it seemed to the Commissioners that there was no reason why there should not be an immediate amalgamation of Northern Rhodesia and Nyasaland. They had found identical interests, policies and territorial boundaries which divided tribes and argued that amalgamation would save the duplication of services and would assist in co-ordinating them with Southern Rhodesia. The merging of the European populations would justify the introduction of an electoral system in Nyasaland.

Although they signed the Report, the Commissioners considered it necessary to append their personal observations. Lord Bledisloe and Ashley-Cooper praised the progress of Southern Rhodesia and called for the creation of a British bloc in Central Africa. They endorsed the rejection of immediate amalgamation, but thought that the posts of the northern Governors could be combined with that of Southern Rhodesia. Orr-Ewing thought that, while desirable, amalgamation was not inevitable. Fitzgerald urged the British Government not to make the recommended statement on the desirability of ultimate amalgamation until the Southern Rhodesian policies with regard to the African had been reformed. Mainwaring opposed any transfer of the control of the affairs of the Africans to the local Europeans. He ignored the Northern Rhodesian mineral wealth, and claimed that the economic progress of Southern Rhodesia could be explained by its greater natural resources. However, Dr Wetherell thinks that he was referring to the higher level of revenue collected in Southern Rhodesia.[50] The final minority report was from Evans who pressed for the expansion of the social services in the northern territories.

Gore-Browne reacted to the Report by stating that it had "funked the issue" on all essentials.[51] Moore resigned and sought a new mandate from his electors. The Governor of Nyasaland, Sir Donald Mackenzie-Kennedy, echoed the comment of the Luanshya branch of the European Protection League when he said that only when the Africans were capable of an intelligent assessment of amalgamation should their opinions be considered. He did not praise, as did the League, the Southern Rhodesian African policy or claim that clearly the local European could not be trusted to administer the African's affairs justly. Indeed, in contrast to the Report, he could not find any striking difference between the Colonial Office approach and that of Southern Rhodesia. At least, he claimed, the differences were capable of reconciliation. He maintained that unification with Southern Rhodesia was necessary if Nyasaland were to obtain the development capital which it needed.[52]

The Governor of Northern Rhodesia, Sir John Maybin, thought that there was great significance in the almost unanimous rejection by the northern Africans of amalgamation. This rejection seemed more emphatic as it had been forthcoming without influence in either direction by the Colonial Office. As the Africans, however, were accustomed to being given a lead by the district officers in political matters, it is not surprising that they should have reacted conservatively towards political change. Maybin acknowledged the economic arguments in favour of amalgamation but felt that the differences in the policies with regard to the Africans were crucial. He believed that these would have to be eliminated before amalgamation could be accepted even in principle. He aired his dislike for the Southern Rhodesian policy of "Parallel Development" with its separate areas and its discrimination in employment. Yet he was confident that Southern Rhodesians could be persuaded to reform. He also opposed the recommendation of the amalgamation of the northern territories on the grounds that they had only a slight trading relationship and had differently based economies, with Nyasaland's being founded on agriculture and Northern Rhodesia's on mining. The result would be that Northern Rhodesia would have to subsidise Nyasaland. He said that the distances involved would make administration difficult and expensive. He dismissed the proposed inter-territorial council as an unnecessary expense and a waste of the time of the senior staff. As the unofficial element would dominate, he feared that the Colonial Office's policy of "Indirect Rule" for Africans would be threatened and that, in any case, an irretrievable step would have been taken towards amalgamation.[53]

Sir Herbert Stanley shared the acute Southern Rhodesian disappointment as he had always favoured amalgamation and saw little justification for an indefinite period of half measures. He was convinced that the personalities of

[50] Wetherell, *The Rhodesias and Amalgamation*, *op. cit.*, p. 271, fn. 2.
[51] Gann, *A History of Northern Rhodesia*, *op. cit.*, p. 276.
[52] Rotberg, *The Rise of Nationalism*, *op. cit.*, pp. 113–114.
[53] Gann, *A History of Northern Rhodesia*, *op. cit.*, pp. 277–278.

the Commissioners had militated against unanimity for immediate amalgamation. Yet the Report gave him some satisfaction because, if its proposals were adopted, there would be an improvement in the *status quo*. He thought that the annexures by the individual members had weakened the Report, although Bledisloe and Ashley-Cooper had reinforced the closer union cause and he was confident that their opinion would carry the greatest weight in official circles in London. He was particularly impressed by Bledisloe's suggestion of a single governorship for the three territories.[54] In fact, from the manner in which he harped on it, it would seem that he saw himself in that role.[55]

Stanley advised Huggins — who had departed for London to negotiate on a range of subjects including the Report — that he should not at first concede that immediate amalgamation was impossible. He should not allow the Report to be seen as conclusive, and should claim that the differences in the African policies were slight and could be reconciled. Indeed, Stanley hoped that aspects of the Southern Rhodesian policy could be adopted in the North. Thus he advised Huggins to portray the fears of the African witnesses as being unfounded or, at least, grossly exaggerated. Finally, he should threaten that an indefinite postponement of amalgamation would lead to a piecemeal absorption of the territories by South Africa.

Stanley knew that this pressure was unlikely to persuade the British Government to yield on amalgamation but its consequence might be the all-important statement accepting the principle of amalgamation. Flowing from that would be the single governorship which would smooth the path to amalgamation as would the unification of Northern Rhodesia and Nyasaland. As the machinery of co-operation would have a similar effect, Stanley urged that the inter-territorial council should be accepted on any terms even though he thought that, without the single governorship, the council would be little more than a debating society. He warned that Southern Rhodesia should not be committed to anything other than ultimate amalgamation.

In mid-July 1939, Huggins, having dealt first with aviation and defence took up the matter of the Report. Before he did, he wrote to Stanley in typical fashion. He said: "The youth and beauty at the D[ominions] O[ffice] say that after Palestine our problem is the thing that troubles the Government most and in their opinion there is not a hope of the I[mperial] G[overnment] accepting the principle [*sic*] if that is so then all talks will be off." Huggins said he had been in contact with Maybin and was to dine with the members of the Bledisloe Commission. Of Bledisloe himself, Huggins reported that "if something is not done he will be in an asylum [*sic*] he is explaining the matter all the time".[56] There was no respite for Bledisloe because he would have to explain himself further as Lord Elibank had put down a question in the Lords to be debated on 25 July.

In the Lords, Bledisloe defended the Southern Rhodesians. He depicted them as trying only to develop the country and improve the health and education of the African. He contrasted this with the Northern Rhodesian

[54] Rhodes House MSS, Af.S. 1250, f. 60, Sir Herbert Stanley to Huggins, 1 May 1939.
[55] *Ibid.*, f. 113, Stanley to Huggins, 30 June 1939.
[56] *Ibid.*, f. 175, Hughes to Stanley, 12 July 1939.

failures in these fields. Baron Lugard of Arbinger acknowledged the progress which had been made in Southern Rhodesia, but harped on the racial discrimination there which he believed would produce increasing discontent and frustration as more Africans became educated. He knew that union with the northern territories might reform Southern Rhodesia, but he argued that a loose economic association could have the same effect. Lugard won support in academic circles. Margery Perham, who was to become a doughty opponent of closer association, rejected amalgamation because it would entrench the white minority in power. A. B. Keith, the eminent editor of Dicey's *Conflict of Laws*, and Professor E. A. Walker, the historian of South Africa, supported her.[57]

Huggins made contact with Perham and Lugard and found the latter to be very old but interesting and Perham completely academic on the subject of Africans. Huggins did not hear the Lords debate, but the report in *Hansard* led him to protest to the Dominions and Colonial Secretaries, Sir Thomas Inskip and Malcolm MacDonald, that the references to him had been overdone. It was unfair to portray him as different from other Rhodesians because, he argued, a prime minister represented the spirit of the people. Inskip and MacDonald agreed that he did.[58]

That, however, was all that the British Ministers would concede. By the date of the Lords debate, they had held two discussions with Huggins on amalgamation in which Inskip had shown little interest or knowledge, had taken the chair and had left MacDonald to make the running. MacDonald was fully *au fait* with the problem, but it soon appeared that he sought only a formula which would placate Huggins and yet avoid a British commitment to act. His tactic was to concentrate on the effects of amalgamation on the Africans and, when the discussion became heated, to switch to the subject of the inter-territorial council. The rest of the Report was not discussed. MacDonald agreed with Huggins that amalgamation was in the interests of all in Central Africa but said that he could not wear it politically.[59] One of Huggins's aides wrote: "Malcolm knows very well the advantages of amalgamation both to the European and the native, but all he is concerned with is finding the formula which will either enable him to pigeon-hole the report or accept it, he does not mind which, provided there are no political repercussions. He is the embodiment of all that is bad in the professional politician."[60]

MacDonald claimed that, unless the political future of the Africans was assured, amalgamation would be resisted within and without the British Parliament. The Rhodesians were not convinced as the MPs whom they met — Huggins addressed groups at the Commons — had expressed little interest and had indicated that they would have followed any lead which was given to them. In fact, many said that they could not understand why amalgamation could not be allowed. Huggins took tea with members of the Anti-Slavery and Aborigines Protection Society and heard them admit that their greatest fear was that Southern Rhodesia would join South Africa. He made good use

[57] Gann, *A History of Northern Rhodesia*, *op. cit.*, p. 278.
[58] Rhodes House MSS, *op. cit.*, f. 179, Huggins to Stanley, 5 August 1939.
[59] *Ibid.*, f. 177, Huggins to Stanley, 25 July 1939.
[60] *Ibid.*, Lawrence Smith to Sir Herbert Stanley, 27 July 1939.

of the moment to terrify them further on this prospect.[61] As a result, he was confident that they would not oppose amalgamation. Staff members of *The Times, The Daily Telegraph* and the *Evening News* led Huggins to believe that there would be no opposition from the British Press. The British public, the Rhodesians thought, as the international scene darkened, were likely to welcome with acclamation any move to strengthen the Empire.[62]

On 27 July, Inskip gave Huggins the chance to strike out. The opportunity came at a luncheon in Huggins's honour as, in the course of proposing the toast, Inskip said that the Bledisloe Commission had performed an exploratory operation and that, for the moment, it was improper to say anything more. Huggins, in reply, said that he had been waiting for Inskip to say something which he would have to answer in order to have a chance to vent his feelings. He went on:

> "I should like to refer to this exploratory operation. It is this. That certain people met and discussed a disease. They decided that a major operation was necessary, but owing to some of the consultants not being quite satisfied, the whole lot lost their nerve, the operation was not performed, and the patient died."[63]

The audience roared with laughter. Inskip's reaction is not recorded, but MacDonald is supposed to have looked uncomfortable when Huggins went on to threaten to run a political campaign in Britain. He said that he might have to do this because Southern Rhodesia, not being fully independent, came under the tutelage of the House of Commons and thus could not criticise it nor defend itself when its detractors were given the full run of the field.[64]

Through August Huggins continued his campaign — addressing MPs, dining with Bledisloe[65] — but without success. MacDonald made it clear that Southern Rhodesian ideas could not be allowed to spread and Africans had to be permitted to aspire and rise to any position. He warned that the Africans would not be content to allow the European minority to dominate the legislature. All he would concede was that the Report's conclusion, that the major obstacle to amalgamation was the policy of Southern Rhodesia, should be re-examined by an independant expert, Lord Hailey.

Sir Cosmo Parkinson, of the Colonial Office, made it plain to Huggins that, before the question of amalgamation could be re-opened, the British Government had to be able to claim that real efforts had been made to reconcile the territorial policies.[66] To Stanley, Huggins muttered darkly about the lack of co-operation from the British Government on all issues. When he asked for

[61] *Ibid.*, f. 177, Huggins to Stanley, 25 July 1939.
[62] *Ibid.*, Lawrence Smith to Stanley, 27 July 1939.
[63] *East Africa and Rhodesia* (London), 27 July 1939; D. Taylor, *The Rhodesian: The Life of Sir Roy Welensky* (London, 1955), p. 51.
[64] Rhodes House MSS, *op. cit.*, Lawrence Smith to Stanley, 27 July 1939.
[65] *Ibid.*, f. 182, Huggins to Stanley, 11 August 1939; f. 184, same to same, 15 August 1939; f. 185, same to same, 29 August 1939.
[66] Rotberg, *The Rise of Nationalism*, *op. cit.*, p. 114.

information, he was told that he was not entitled to receive it because Southern Rhodesia was not a dominion. Huggins sounded a note of warning: Southern Rhodesians "can be just as nasty as S[outhern] Ireland or S[outh] Africa if they force us to be".[67]

He sailed home in early September. The war intruded, and twelve years were to pass before the British Government could be induced to consider seriously again the question of the unification of its Central African territories.

[67] Rhodes House MSS, *op. cit.*, f. 185, Huggins to Stanley, 29 August 1939.

CHAPTER TWO

Amalgamation in Wartime

The Continuing Struggle for the Unification of British Central Africa, 1939–44

HUGGINS returned home to direct his country's war effort. The only concession which he had been able to wring from the British was that Lord Hailey would examine the degree of difference between the policies relating to the African in the three territories. The circumstances of the hour had led Huggins to promise in return that the issue of unification would not be raised during wartime in order that there should be no distraction from the main task of defeating the Axis powers. It did not mean that the issue was forgotten even if its supporters had to hold themselves in check. Indeed, the war, in stimulating demand for the area's products (copper, chrome, tobacco, asbestos, mica, lead, zinc) highlighted the need for close co-operation and the pooling of resources, particularly manpower. The problem of developing a war economy led the northern Governors to concentrate on the extension of existing links with Southern Rhodesia. It was a logical consequence of their efforts, since 1935, to rationalise the administration of the terroritories. Their co-operation had produced a common court of appeal, an inter-territorial labour conference with a standing committee, an inter-territorial communications board and northern representatives had been given seats on the Southern Rhodesian Currency Board. The practicalities of their situation led them to decline, at the East African Governors' Conference in 1940, to participate in the East African Economic Council. This Conference then decided that the war effort in the Rhodesias and Nyasaland should be directed by a local conference with a permanent secretariat. This related only to the economic effort. Northern Rhodesian and Nyasaland troops continued to serve under East Africa Command. Southern Rhodesia wished to preserve its link with the Dominions Office and not to be mistaken at any level for a colony administered by the Colonial Office. Therefore it chose to be associated with the South African High Command. At a practical level, bearing in mind communications and other aspects, it was a logical step.

The proposed inter-territorial conference seemed most necessary to Sir John Maybin and Sir Donald Mackenzie-Kennedy. They felt that it need not affect the political issue of amalgamation. Professor R. I. Rotberg, however, claims that in fact the Conference was abused by being used to advance the cause of unification.[1] Huggins accepted the proposal and magnanimously indicated that he would even approve the staffing of the secretariat by the Colonial Office. Kenya's Governor, Sir Henry Moore, advocated it as a counterbalance to the increasing South African influence in Central and East Africa and the Dominions Office happily concurred. However, the Colonial Office opposed it because it seemed a definite step towards amalgamation.

Mackenzie-Kennedy was particularly worried about the effect of the war on Nyasaland's economy. He refused to accept the Colonial Office's decision as irreversible. He knew that Southern Rhodesia was about to establish a war supplies committee and wanted Nyasaland to be associated with it. He dismissed association with East Africa because Nyasaland had no economic ties with it. Furthermore, he argued, the existing machinery — the Inter-Territorial Labour Conference and Communications Board — was ineffective. Co-ordination was needed in many matters: agriculture, transport, import control, exports and the use of the common port, Beira. These arguments were persuasive and the Colonial Office agreed, provided that the Conference was an experiment to improve the war effort and not to implement the Bledisloe Commission's recommendations. When the war ended it would be reviewed. In 1941 a permanent secretariat was established in Salisbury under K. L Hall, Nyasaland's current Chief Secretary. The existing boards became redundant and the needs of the whole area were reviewed while the territories re-organised their individual contributions.[2]

In an address in June 1940 to the Northern Rhodesian Legislative Council, Maybin welcomed the recent visit of Lord Hailey and looked forward to his assessment of the territories' African policies.[3] At that time, Sir Stewart Gore-Browne, the nominated Member for Native Interests, was leader of the Council's unofficial Members in succession to Sir Leopold Moore (he was knighted in 1937). Moore had lost his leadership when he resigned his seat in 1939 in protest over the Bledisloe Report. The Livingstone electorate returned him to the Council in the subsequent by-election, but he never regained leadership. His gesture was needlessly empty because if he had informed his colleagues of his intention, they would undoubtedly have resigned with him.[4] Politics in Northern Rhodesia had been enlivened in 1935 by the advent of Sir Hubert Young as Governor because he had paid attention to local settler opinion. The threat of resignation *en masse* was twice used by the elected Members against him. It was threatened in 1935 over the amalgamation issue and again in 1936[5] when, thwarted over amalgamation,

[1] R. I. Rotberg, *The Rise of Nationalism in Central Africa: The Making of Malawi and Zambia, 1873–1964* (London, 1965), p. 215.

[2] L. H. Gann, *A History of Northern Rhodesia: Early Days to 1953* (London, 1964), pp. 352–354.

[3] N[orthern] R[hodesia] *Debates* [*of the Legislative Council*] (Lusaka), p. 5, 1 June 1940.

[4] Author's interview with Sir Roy Welensky.

[5] M. C. Steele, *The Challenge of Rhodesia to European Liberal Thought* (unpublished M. Litt. thesis, University of Edinburgh, 1968), p. 348.

the unofficial Members had demanded parity of seats with the official Members in the Legislative Council. This demand for parity has relevance to the amalgamation issue because the British response to it gave Roy Welensky, then a prominent trade unionist, an opportunity to enter politics.

Young recommended that the Colonial Secretary should grant parity to lessen settler disappointment over the refusal to allow amalgamation. In 1937, Moore and Gore-Browne visited London to ask for equal unofficial representation in the Executive Council - four unofficials, four officials, with the Governor presiding. One of these unofficials would be chosen by the Governor from the elected Members to represent African interests. They sought parity in the Legislative Council and the diminution of the Governor's role so that his veto would be used only on specific reserved subjects. Furthermore, the official Members would be free to vote as they thought fit except on certain issues. Africans would be given parallel representative institutions but the races would not share the same Council. Moore and Gore-Browne were partially successful. Young established a tradition of the Governor acting as Speaker, except at the committee stage, to allow uninhibited discussion. Moreover, the Colonial Secretary, W. G. A. Ormsby-Gore, gave them parity by removing one official Member and allowing for the appointment of an unofficial representative of African interests who would be chosen by the Governor from outside the Legislative Council. The Council was to consist of seven elected, one nominated and eight official Members with the Governor as President.[6] In the 1938 election, Gore-Browne vacated his seat at Broken Hill to accept the Governor's nomination as the first representative of Native Interests. The vacancy was filled by Welensky.

When Gore-Browne had warned Welensky of his intention to accept the Governor's nomination, it had not occurred to Welensky that he might be Gore-Browne's successor as the representative of Broken Hill.[7] Yet, considering Welensky's activities since his arrival in Broken Hill in 1933, it was a logical step. Although Welensky was only 31 in 1938, he had been interested in politics since the days of the campaign for responsible government in Southern Rhodesia when, as a boy of 14, he heard, among other speakers, South Africa's General Jan Smuts. His family voted against incorporation in South Africa. At 17 he joined the railways and in 1929, during the Wankie strike, he was drawn into the affairs of the Rhodesia Railways Workers' Union. He had opposed the strike because he thought that it would achieve little but, when it came, he fought to keep the strikers together. His brother, Ben, hit a "scab" at Dett and was suspended without pay for 30 days, and the part Welensky played earned him removal to Salisbury and he was not promoted from shunting driver until 1936. If his transfer to Broken Hill in 1933 was meant to be a banishment, it must be acknowledged that the railway company took a long time to do it. The move was significant, for what Welensky found in Broken Hill drove him into union, then civic and finally national affairs.

Finding the Broken Hill branch of the union almost non-existent, Welensky set about re-building it. He became chairman almost immediately. His

[6] J. W. Davidson, *The Legislative Council of Northern Rhodesia*, (London, 1948), p. 35.
[7] Author's interview with Sir Roy Welensky.

physical size and the reputation of his recent successes in the boxing ring, where he became Rhodesian heavyweight champion, were assets when collecting union dues as well as countering the anti-Semitism of the mid-thirties — to be found particularly amongst the Afrikaner working class in Northern Rhodesia. He also assisted in the re-organization of the local branch of the Northern Rhodesia European Mineworkers' Union. This prompted the Broken Hill Mine management to try to persuade the railway company to transfer him. He built up recreational facilities in Broken Hill for the railwaymen, becoming chairman of their club. He became a member of the Broken Hill Town Management Board. From these activities Welensky acquired the training in organization and the experience in debate which he would need in his political life. His duty to speak for his union members in disciplinary enquiries assisted in developing fluency of speech.

The circumstances of Welensky's childhood were calculated to breed an aggressive, self-reliant man. His father, Michael, was 64 when Roy, the thirteenth and last child, was born. Michael's prosperous days were then behind him. Since leaving Vilna in Lithuania as a young man, he had made and spent fortunes in Sweden, the United States and South Africa. Arriving in Southern Rhodesia in 1894, his flair for making money had deserted him in what were lean times for everyone. After failing as a trader and as a hotelier he was forced to rely upon what employment the Jewish community could offer him, upon the energy of his wife, Leah, the Afrikaner girl he had married in the Cape, and upon the contributions of his sons.

Leah died in 1918 leaving Roy, aged eleven, to live alone with his 75-year-old father. If Roy lacked shoes, and if they ate badly, he gained much from the old man's wide knowledge of the Bible, his philosophical ramblings and his vast experience of life. The need to earn to eat forced Welensky to leave school at 14 with only primary education behind him. However, he could read, and through reading he educated himself. He served in trading stores, acted as a barman and assisted an auctioneer. The last allowed him to read the books which came in provided that he returned them before the sale. The *Everyman's* book series, being cheap, was the basis of his education. He read widely in politics, literature and history. Later he built up the library of the Railway Club in Broken Hill and read most of its books. After he became a mainline driver in 1936, he broke the rules by reading on the footplate as he drove through the night from Broken Hill to Ndola. Once he had been elected to the Legislative Council, he gained access to its library.

Although Welensky had been denied a formal education, he did not lack tutors in life and he was quick to learn from them. His brothers had preceded him into the trade union movement. The use of cutlery and other domestic niceties were taught him by his wife whom he had met in the cafe of Donald Macintyre (later the Federal Minister of Finance, and knighted) in Bulawayo where she was a waitress. Like him, her genial manner belied an iron will, the product of as harsh a childhood as his. Born of Scots and Afrikaner parents, Elizabeth Henderson had become a crack shot through the need to shoot for the pot. Welensky made friends with William Watson, a Scottish metallurgist employed by the Broken Hill Mine, who influenced and assisted him. Welensky's union secretary in Broken Hill, Mrs Lou Easton, helped him to compose his letters and assisted him in the deep preparation which underlay all his public utterances. In politics, Welensky's mentor was Lieutenant-Colonel Sir Stewart Gore-Browne, the Member from 1935–38 for the Northern Electoral Area which included Broken Hill. The dissimilar characteristics of the members of this political partnership have been commented upon — the young, burly trade unionist with his purely Rhodesian background, and the slender, middle-aged "Establishment" colonel from Harrow and the Royal Military Academy, Woolwich. Their friendship was rooted in the 1935 Legislative Council election. Welensky had given his support initially to Arthur Davison, a railwayman, Gore-Browne's opponent, but soon withdrew it. He and Gore-Browne shared a desire to see the two Rhodesias amalgamated and it was as an amalgamationist that Gore-Browne won the seat.

At first Welensky followed Gore-Browne's political lead. In 1936 he supported Gore-Browne's idea of unifying the "Railway Belt" with Southern Rhodesia. However, their political thinking began to diverge on the question of amalgamation and by 1938 Welensky had rejected the "Railway Belt" idea in favour of total amalgamation. Nevertheless, this independence of thought did not damage their relationship and it was from Gore-Browne that Welensky learned the fundamentals of politics. Gore-Browne found Welensky to be possessed of a natural political aptitude. Indeed, Welensky would become the scourge of the official Members of the Legislative Council who came to dread his ability to detect the weaknesses of the material which they were presenting to the Council. Gore-Browne, in the changed atmosphere in the Council under Sir Hubert Young, brought a new standard to the debates. He wrought further improvements when he took over the leadership of the unofficial Members from Moore in 1939. He retained this leadership until the war's end when he relinquished it to Welensky because he felt he could not continue to lead the unofficials who supported amalgamation when he represented Africans, who opposed it.

When the Broken Hill political interests in 1938 cast around for candidates to replace Gore-Browne, Welensky was away on a first family holiday, in Cape Town. While there, he received, pondered on and accepted his union branch's suggestion that he should stand. There were other candidates but they soon lost heart and Welensky was returned unopposed. He would represent Broken Hill for the next 25 years — in the Northern Rhodesian Legislative Council until 1954, and in the Federal Assembly until 1963.

In the first session of the new Council in 1938, Welensky made his mark with carefully considered, positive contributions to the debates on the issues of the day. In the 1939 debate on the Bledisloe Report, he was deeply disappointed that immediate amalgamation had not been recommended.[8] He felt, however, that the recommendations in the Report contained some good advice for the Northern Rhodesians. He doubted the wisdom of Huggins's promise of a referendum on amalgamation because he was sure that the Southern Rhodesian voter would not wish to burden the amalgamated government with the expense of purchasing the Northern Rhodesian mineral rights. Yet he felt those rights could not be left in the hands of the British

[8] NR *Debates* (Lusaka), p. 247, 6 June 1939.

South Africa Company. He agreed that the Southern Rhodesian policy towards the Africans was incompatible with that of the northern territories and thought that any Southern Rhodesian Government would founder if it proposed to adopt the northern policy. He promised to support the recommended inter-territorial council if it was to be a declared step towards amalgamation. Other Members did not agree with him over the degree of difference between the two African policies, but Gore-Browne did. Gore-Browne thought that, though practically the differences were small, theoretically they were fundamental.[9] He felt that, if a referendum in the three territories favoured amalgamation and if a common African policy could be formulated, the British Government should make the recommended declaration in support of ultimate amalgamation.

Welensky's background and his trade union activities would be reflected in his frequent statements that he was a socialist and in his efforts to secure compulsory education for the Europeans, pensions and social security schemes. He fought for silicosis legislation and his long-term aim was to wrest the mineral rights from the British South Africa Company but the war swept all that aside for the moment. Yet, though inter-governmental discussion on amalgamation was postponed, the officials — as has been seen — persuaded the British Government to agree to the founding of the Inter-Territorial Conference in 1941.

The war brought the unofficial Members into government for the first time. Major H. K. McKee became the Director of Civil Supplies, T. S. Page the Price Controller, and Gore-Browne the Director of War Evacuees. The unofficials were made members of a committee to assist in drafting the budget. In September 1940, a manpower committee was established, served by the Attorney-General, Gore-Browne and Welensky. In 1941, Welensky was appointed as full-time Director of Manpower. The unofficials, Gore-Browne, Moore and Colonel A. Stephenson, gained seats on the Executive Council. In 1942 an "inner cabinet", called the War Committee, was formed comprising the Governor, the Chief Secretary, the Financial Secretary, Gore-Browne and Welensky. The first wartime election in 1941 prompted Welensky to found the Northern Rhodesia Labour Party which contested and won five of the eight elective seats — an extra electoral district had been created on the Copperbelt, balanced by the appointment of another official to the Legislative Council to maintain parity. Welensky wished to ensure the protection of the interests of the white workers in Northern Rhodesia and to introduce party politics into the Council to which hitherto all unofficial Members had been elected as independents. Moore's resignation over the Bledisloe Report, without informing his fellow unofficials, convinced Welensky of the need for solidarity amongst the unofficials. Bred in Southern Rhodesian ways, Welensky found the unfettered Colonial administration unbelievably arrogant and dictatorial. On the broader plane, a fundamental aim of his Party was to achieve amalgamation with Southern Rhodesia and thereby rid itself of the influence of the Colonial Office.[10]

[9] *Ibid.*, p. 228, 6 June 1939.

[10] Author's interview with Sir Roy Welensky; Welensky Papers, WE 7, Un-numbered Series NRLP 1943–6, NRLP questionnaire (undated).

Huggins (by then Sir Godfrey) also had not forgotten amalgamation. There were various immediate reasons why he favoured it. He was founding government-run major industries, such as the Rhodesia Iron and Steel Corporation which he established in 1942, and argued that investors would be more impressed by "Greater Rhodesia" than Southern Rhodesia alone, because of the larger internal market. He thought that it would attract better recruits to the civil service, thereby solving his staffing problem. Always an imperialist at heart, Huggins, with some foresight, felt that a British bloc in Central Africa would be needed to counterbalance the South African Republic which he felt the Afrikaner nationalists would form a decade after Smuts's fall, which he believed was imminent. Southern Rhodesia, he argued, could not then continue to stand alone and would be forced to join South Africa if amalgamation were not allowed. He saw no particular danger to the continuing domination of politics by his United Party even though the Northern and Southern Rhodesian Labour Parties were likely to co-operate, because the number of seats that the Northern Rhodesians would gain was not likely to affect the situation radically. Moreover, perhaps affected by British objections as well as the practicalities of the hour, Huggins was changing his ideas on his policy towards the Africans. In his Statement on Native Affairs in June 1941, he spoke no longer of parallel development but of the parallel lines eventually meeting when Europeans and Africans would enjoy the same status.[11]

In Northern Rhodesia, amalgamation had continued to be discussed. In the 1941 debates in the Legislative Council on the provision of the extra elected seat, on African representation, and on the possibility of an elected majority, quite naturally the issue of amalgamation was raised. Welensky expressed reluctance to support a majority if it meant a postponement of amalgamation. The annexation of Northern Rhodesia to the Crown as an interim step was proposed but Welensky thought this unnecessary because it would be a natural consequence of amalgamation.[12] T. S. Page asked, in July 1941, that the Colonial Secretary be informed that the unofficials wished to form a committee with the Southern Rhodesian Government to consider points of difference and to formulate a policy which would be acceptable to an amalgamated Rhodesia.

This suggestion was taken up on 5 August 1941 by Huggins when he threw down a challenge to the Imperial Government.[13] Recounting the recent history of the struggle for amalgamation at a United Party congress, Huggins said that he and the British Government had agreed to defer discussion on amalgamation for the duration of the war. In the interim, Lord Hailey was to have examined the degree of difference between the African policies which Huggins claimed could be explained by differing local conditions because the theoretical objectives were identical. Lord Hailey had visited the territories but no result had been forthcoming, and Huggins surmised that Hailey had not yet written his report or it had been pigeonholed. The needs of war had

[11] Gann, *A History of Northern Rhodesia*, *op. cit.*, p. 355; SR *Debates* (Salisbury), Vol. 21, Part I, Col. 1527 f., 19 June 1941.
[12] NR *Debates* (Lusaka), p. 35 f., 12 March 1941; p. 172 f., 19 March 1941.
[13] *The Rhodesia Herald*, 6 August 1941.

finally convinced the British Government of the necessity for inter-territorial co-operation in the form of the Inter-Territorial Conference and the post-war problems, Huggins claimed, would make amalgamation imperative. He warned that he could not be fobbed off with excuses of difficulties with the Commons as he saw no reason why the more enlightened who had emigrated to the Commonwealth should be dictated to by the insularity of those who had stayed behind. He proposed an inter-territorial conference on amalgamation.

The British reaction was hostile and through the Press, Professor A. B. Keith warned that British trusteeship would be betrayed if amalgamation were allowed,[14] while Professor E. A. Walker likened Huggins's African policy to the South African segregation policy and claimed that the Africans would only be used to further white ends.[15] He felt that Huggins wanted to secure control of the Northern Rhodesian section of the railway before it passed into black hands. The London journal, *South Africa*, questioned Huggins's sense of urgency and his undiplomatic language which must have startled the British people when obviously the British Government had more pressing problems.[16] This journal, however, regretted the lost opportunity of the British Government to declare itself in favour of amalgamation in the pre-war period. It predicted that pressure from the Rhodesians on amalgamation would be resisted because the wartime working agreement between the Conservative and Labour Parties required substantial unanimity for action. The Fabian and Labour MP, Arthur Creech Jones, noting that Huggins proposed to work out a constitution embracing Northern Rhodesia, declared that, even if Britain had virtually renounced her responsibilities in Southern Rhodesia, she must not do so in Northern Rhodesia. He alleged that Huggins had steadily implemented his segregation policy without protest from the Dominions Office and was now concentrating on amalgamation. The Inter-Territorial Conference constituted a further step towards the closer association of the territories when the Africans remained implacably opposed to amalgamation and would be grossly betrayed if it were permitted. Yet Creech Jones was concerned that there should be a positive alternative given to the Rhodesians in the form of a vigorous social and economic reconstruction of Northern Rhodesia.[17]

In Southern Rhodesia, opposition elements claimed that Huggins was trying to induce a state of mind in which not the desirability of amalgamation but its timing was the issue. Welensky welcomed the proposed conference[18] and *The Rhodesia Herald* thought that Huggins was right to protest over the inordinate delay in the production of the Hailey Report. It felt that it was logical to raise the issue of amalgamation in view of the recent dispatch from Lord Moyne, the Colonial Secretary, to all colonies asking them to forward to London their post-war development plans. For Southern Rhodesia to co-operate, the British attitude on amalgamation had to be declared. In fact there

[14] *Manchester Guardian*, 9 August 1941.
[15] *The Times*, 12 August 1941.
[16] *South Africa*, 9 August 1941.
[17] *New Statesman and Nation*, 23 August 1941.
[18] Davidson, *The Legislative Council*, *op. cit.*, p. 110.

should be ministerial discussion on the subject before the war ended because, in the flurry of post-war reconstruction, there would be a hundred reasons for postponing such consideration and a decade would pass before it was renewed.[19]

Huggins drew support from a long-standing protagonist of closer association, the British journalist, F. S. Joelson, who specialised in East African and Rhodesian affairs. Joelson depicted the proposed conference as an open condemnation of British dilatoriness. The further suggestion by Huggins, that the resultant constitution should be sent to Whitehall for acceptance and not consideration, was a warning that Rhodesian patience was not inexhaustible. Joelson decried the years in which the British Government had played for time and yet had not found time to study the problem properly. The Bledisloe Commission had only been appointed when frustrations had become explosive and its Report had been full of misunderstandings, contradictions and futilities. It had only bought time and currently the Rhodesians were being further irritated by having Lord Hailey's findings kept from them. Patriotism had led the Rhodesians to make a magnificent contribution to the war effort in men, money and materials, and as amalgamation would strengthen the Empire, the same patriotism would lead them to challenge the Imperial Government on it. Joelson warned that British colonial history showed that Britishers were not content to wait when they had a sound case for action. Huggins had given a friendly signal that temporising would no longer serve.[20]

Support for Huggins was declared in the Salisbury Chamber of Industries on 27 September 1941. It wanted amalgamation before the war ended so that the post-war industrial and commercial situation could be exploited by having an enlarged territorial unit. Amalgamation would create new markets in which new industries could be founded. The Chamber was confident that there was public support for amalgamation and that compromise was possible on the differing territorial African policies. On the latter, however, the Chamber misunderstood the nature of British objections to the Southern Rhodesian policy. It thought that the British were concerned about the welfare of the African when this was a field in which Southern Rhodesia outdid its neighbours.[21]

Huggins's outspokenness was partially vindicated in early October when the Colonial Secretary announced that Hailey's Report was being published and would be sent to the three territorial Governments.[22] Simultaneously the Northern Rhodesian unofficial Members telegraphed Huggins to accept his invitation to the conference. *The Rhodesia Herald* thought that the conference would be opportune because there was much work to be done before a final scheme would be ready. The formulation of the plan could take place in wartime even if a decision was postponed until peace.[23]

A Northern Rhodesian delegation visited Salisbury in late October and

[19] *The Rhodesia Herald*, 6 August 1941.
[20] *Ibid.*, 22 September 1941.
[21] *Ibid.*, 27 & 29 September 1941.
[22] *Ibid.*, 3 October 1941.
[23] *Ibid.*, 14 October 1941.

Welensky found Huggins to be as keen an amalgamationist as himself. Indeed, Welensky was sufficiently encouraged to believe that amalgamation was nearer reality than it had ever been. Yet the strength of the opposition convinced him that a propaganda campaign was necessary to persuade the Southern Rhodesian public on the need for unification. He was sure that the Southern Rhodesia Labour Party, in particular, would not welcome amalgamation.[24] He was proved correct by its leader, Donald Macintyre, stating at an "informal" Labour congress on 26 October that his Party's acceptance of amalgamation was conditional on total British surrender of control of African policy. He could not accept the northern policy of the paramountcy of African interests as it threatened the position of the white worker.

Hailey's Report — which was restricted to governments only — reinforced the Bledisloe conclusion that the differences in the territories' African policies were obstacles to amalgamation. Moreover, Gore-Browne's contact with the Northern Rhodesian Africans revealed an implacable opposition to amalgamation. Speaking on this in the Legislative Council, Gore-Browne also revealed that the unofficial Members had decided not to ask for a debate on amalgamation as their official counterparts could not contribute. However, Gore-Browne felt that he should say something on the issue as both sides of the argument were currently being overstated. He, like the Bledisloe Commission, was convinced of the advantages of amalgamation to all parties. In his view the problem of the differing African policies had to be solved and merited greater inter-governmental discussion. He accepted that 90 or 95 per cent of the unofficial (non-civil servant) white population of Northern Rhodesia favoured amalgamation and would forfeit their self-interests to obtain it. He acknowledged every Briton felt that self-government was part of his birthright and that it was, perhaps, dangerous to frustrate this desire. However, there were only 14 000 whites and Gore-Browne had, as the representative of the 1 400 000 Africans, to reveal that most of the latter opposed amalgamation. He knew it would be said that the Africans were unable to judge the issue and certainly a great number of them were content with the current system. However, tens of thousands had worked in Southern Rhodesia and qualified to have an opinion. There was, too, a small minority which was capable of assessing problems and should not be brushed aside. The Africans could not see what benefits amalgamation would bring them and Gore-Browne thought that a good propaganda campaign could enlighten them. Nevertheless, seeing Southern Rhodesia as a country which repressed Africans for the white man's benefit, they did not want to join it. This opinion was only confirmed by the local Europeans writing to the Press about amalgamation putting Africans in their place. Equally, the British liberals had a similar effect through their half-truths and distortions about Central African affairs. The existence of the pass laws, even though Huggins described them as a passing phase, only added substance to African fears. The northern Africans suspected that the Southern Rhodesian land policy would be applied throughout the unified territory. More important was the African view of the

[24] Welensky Papers, 23/60, f. 225, Welensky to Sir Godfrey Huggins, 23 October 1941; f. 224, Welensky to H. Bertin, 23 October 1941; f. 220, Welensky to F. Sinclair, 24 October 1941; f. 214, Welensky to W. Watson, 24 October 1941.

Southern Rhodesian Industrial Conciliation Act. Gore-Browne saw the merit of this Act and thought that Northern Rhodesia should similarly provide the white worker with minimum wage levels, better conditions of work, and conciliation machinery to settle disputes. However, in doing this, he felt the Act went too far and prevented the African from getting his fair share of semi-skilled work. Thus, if amalgamation was to be acceptable, the white worker, in particular, would have to be generous.[25]

Huggins's proposed unofficial conference continued to alarm the opponents of amalgamation. The *Economist* warned of the possibility of a "Munich in Africa",[26] while in the Commons Creech Jones called for the prohibition of the conference on the grounds that it infringed Britain's prerogatives and was calculated to create disaffection and disturbance in her territories.[27] Geoffrey Shakespeare, the Under-Secretary of State for Dominion Affairs, in reply, stressed that, though his Government was jealous of its prerogatives, the conference was merely an unofficial attempt to devise constitutional, financial and administrative arrangements for a scheme of amalgamation. George Hall, the Colonial Under-Secretary, questioned by Creech Jones the following day, underlined Shakespeare's statement by stating that there would be no Colonial officials at the conference. Creech Jones asked Hall to scrutinise any developments and the latter replied that he was confident that Creech Jones would do this for him. In fact, there was no need for Creech Jones to comply because the Rhodesians bowed to pressure not to distract the sorely-tried British Government and abandoned the conference.

Even though privately he felt that the chance to amalgamate might be lost through delay, Welensky co-operated in not pressing the issue until the war improved.[28] Amalgamation, however, remained a topic of conversation. In April 1942, the Mlanje Native Association claimed that Nyasaland Africans were invariably alarmed by the raising of the amalgamation issue.[29] In September, Gore-Browne exhorted Southern Rhodesia to reform its industrial legislation to enhance the prospects of unification.[30] In October the chairman of the Luanshya branch of the Northern Rhodesia Labour Party spoke of an ultimate aim of a unified Southern Africa.[31] In the Legislative Council in December it was suggested that the possible development of the hydro-electric potential of the Kafue River would enhance the prospects of amalgamation.[32]

The Northern Rhodesian unofficial Members, however, did not entirely stay their hands. In March 1942, they attacked the Inter-Territorial Conference for its inadequate distribution of available supplies in the Rhodesias. Welensky, in November, reiterated the need for an unofficial majority in the

[25] NR *Debates* (Lusaka), p. 18 f., 9 December 1941; *The Nyasaland Times*, 19 January 1942.
[26] *Economist*, 29 November 1941.
[27] House of Commons *Hansard* (London), Vol. 376, Col. 1379, 9 December 1941.
[28] NR *Debates* (Lusaka), p. 17, 14 September 1942.
[29] P. Short, *Banda* (London, 1974), p. 43.
[30] NR *Debates* (Lusaka), p. 17, 14 September 1942.
[31] Welensky Papers, WE 7, Un-numbered Series NRLP 1943–6, R. Robertson to Welensky, 21 October 1942.
[32] NR *Debates* (Lusaka), p. 130, 9 December 1942.

Legislative Council to involve the Northern Rhodesians in their country's affairs. This was not, he said, an alternative to amalgamation but a step towards it.[33] Gore-Browne was unhappy with his role as the sole representative of over a million Africans and sought to broaden the involvement of the urban African with the administration. In 1938, Native Urban Advisory Councils had been set up on the Copperbelt to advise the local district commissioners and, in September 1942, Gore-Browne proposed that this system should be applied to all towns. He thought that these Councils and the existing Native Authorities in the rural areas should send delegates to regional councils to provide a grounding in politics. He envisaged them taking their rightful place ultimately in the Legislative Council. The official Members and Welensky supported Gore-Browne and the motion was carried.[34] This was implemented in 1943.

Although the Rhodesians had been asked to refrain from raising the matter of amalgamation, the future of the colonies had become a subject of international discussion. Since the weaning of the United States of America from "isolationism" and her assumption of a dominant role in the Allied war effort, imperialism had come under attack from a new quarter. Both Franklin D. Roosevelt and his Republican rival in the 1940 presidential election, Wendell Willkie, shared an antipathy to the existence of colonies. Roosevelt was restrained by the need to avoid disrupting the military alliance from sympathising too openly with, for example, the aspirations of the Indian nationalists. Willkie was not. As part of his effort in the congressional election campaign in 1942, he embarked on a world tour during which he attacked isolationism, colonialism and racial hatred, and demanded that the United States face its post-war obligations, especially that of maintaining peace through an international organisation.[35] In Chungking, he made his views plain, stating:

> "We believe that this war must mean an end to the empire of nations over other nations . . . We believe that it is the world's job to find some system for helping colonial peoples who join the United Nations' cause to become free independent nations . . . We must establish ironclad guarantees, administered by all the United Nations jointly, that they shall not slip back into the colonial status."[36]

Willkie drew a response from Britain where the House of Lords debated whether there was a need for a "Colonial Charter" which would embody the principles of the Atlantic Charter. It acknowledged that, as the United States was assuming a major role in recovering the Pacific colonies, her views were important. Lords Faringdon and Samuel wished that they could welcome the idea of an international authority assuming the supervision of all colonial possessions but experience had proved that international bodies were in-

[33] Welensky Papers, WE 7, Un-numbered Series NRLP 1943–6, Minutes of a Public Meeting, Mufulira, 5 November 1942.
[34] NR *Debates* (Lusaka), pp. 74 & 78, 17 September 1942.
[35] J. M. Burns, *Roosevelt the Soldier of Freedom 1940–5* (London, 1971), pp. 274 & 608.
[36] House of Lords *Hansard* (London), Vol. 125, Col. 374 f., 3 December 1942.

adequate and inefficient in such a role. Viscount Cranborne (later Lord Salisbury), who had just been replaced as Colonial Secretary by Colonel Oliver Stanley, put the Government's view so convincingly that the motion was withdrawn. He disputed the need for innovations. He defended the record of the Colonial Office and stated that the colonies were progressing in the right direction in harmony with the principles of the Atlantic Charter. He argued that a Colonial Charter was unnecessary and irrelevant because the individuality of the colonies militated against blanket legislation.[37]

Oliver Stanley, himself, dealt with the suggestion for the internationalisation of the colonies in a speech at Oxford. He affirmed that Britain would retain control of the destinies of her colonies despite pressure from the United States. He, too, was cynical about the efficacy of international bodies.[38] The British Labour Party accused Stanley of displaying truculence, but Winston Churchill defended him and, in rejecting a condominion, stated that one should be as wary of sounding truculent as of appearing to grovel.[39]

The British Labour Party was not convinced that colonial affairs could continue along established lines. On 7 April 1943, it published "The Future of the Colonies: Statement of Labour Views" which would be submitted to the Labour Conference. This dealt with post-war policy in the African and Pacific colonies and favoured the Crown Colony system as it permitted a gradual transition to responsible government but felt that the latter should be withheld from colonies which had European minorities until the native could be enfranchised on the same basis as the European because all colonies were held in trust by Britain for the native inhabitants. It was specifically stated that territories such as Northern Rhodesia and Nyasaland should remain responsibilities of the Imperial Parliament unless the Africans desired change, in which case their social and political equality with the minorities had to be completely assured.

The Labour Party thought that world peace would continue to be menaced by the existing monopoly of colonial possessions and that to safeguard it the strategic and economic advantages of colonial possession would have to be removed. The strategic advantages could only be neutralised by the establishment of a general international system from which the constant threat and fear of war had been eliminated. The economic advantages could be removed by putting all states on an economic equality in regard to access to raw materials, markets and capital investment. It was determined that the "colour bar" in all British colonies would be abolished and felt that the economic development of the colonies should make the interests of the Africans paramount. The aim should be to increase wealth and equitably distribute it. There should also be adequate planning of health and educational services. This expansion would call for a considerable increase in governmental expenditure, and international funds might be forthcoming if Britain placed herself at the head of an international movement to develop the African territories and promote the well-being of the inhabitants.[40]

[37] *Ibid.*

[38] *The Times*, 6 March 1943.

[39] *Ibid.*, 18 March 1943.

[40] *The Times*, Weekly Edition, 7 April 1943.

The postal difficulties of wartime could explain the lack of an immediate response in Northern Rhodesia. In the Legislative Council debate in May, only the idea of placing colonies under an international authority drew comment and Gore-Browne merely expressed relief that Churchill had firmly dismissed the idea. He urged all Northern Rhodesians to emulate the arch-realist of the day, Joseph Stalin, and face squarely every possible feature of Northern Rhodesia's situation. The effect of the climate on the European had to be considered when post-war immigration drives were contemplated. The African's place in the economy had to be improved and he had to be politically educated. As for Northern Rhodesia itself, Gore-Browne was convinced that it could not stand alone and he proposed, but did not elaborate upon, a federal solution.[41] Page, too, welcomed the British Government's dismissal of the proposal to internationalise the colonies but he worried lest the frequent changes of Colonial Secretaries would affect the position.[42]

On 24 June, a copy of the British Labour Party's statement at last reached Welensky. He distributed it to the unions and to his Party, describing it as "shocking". He calculated that, if the circumstances for change would be dependent upon political and social equality between the races, it would mean "no constitutional reform for at least a couple of hundred years".[43] Welensky was alarmed because he was convinced that the British Labour Party would win the first general election after the war. Thus it was imperative to secure amalgamation or at least a measure of self-government before that happened. He called the statement disheartening and frightening to any man who thought of Northern Rhodesia as home. Welensky's aim was to create a sense of security for the European and he proposed to use the statement as the basis of a motion calling for amalgamation in the next session of the Legislative Council. He would ask if the European was merely to be used for as long as he was needed or if he would be permitted to have a stake in Northern Rhodesia.

The Northern Rhodesia Labour Party congress at Nkana on 11 July supported this intention with a call for immediate amalgamation under a constitution similar to that of Southern Rhodesia. It was also proposed that a British Labour Party delegation be invited to examine conditions in Northern Rhodesia with the proviso that it took a year so to do.[44]

A public platform was provided for Welensky to comment upon the British Labour statement by the Southern African Labour Conference in Johannesburg in mid-July 1943. Welensky was elected to the chair because he had instigated the Conference with the idea of establishing an identity of interests among the Labour parties and unions in South Africa, the Rhodesias and the Belgian Congo. In his speech, Welensky concentrated upon the particular problems of Northern Rhodesia. He said he had proposed the Conference in an effort to organise the working classes to see that the experiences of the last

[41] NR *Debates* (Lusaka), pp. 16–17, 27 May 1943.
[42] *Ibid.*, p. 17.
[43] Welensky Papers, WE 7, Un-numbered Series NRLP 1943–6, Welensky to F. B. Robertson, 24 June 1943; Welensky to Secretary, Northern Rhodesia European Mineworkers' Union, 30 June 1943; Welensky to Chairman, Northern Rhodesia Labour Party, Broken Hill branch, 2 July 1943; Welensky to Chairman, Rhodesia Railways Workers' Union, 9 July 1943.
[44] *Ibid.*, NRLP Congress, Nkana, 11 July 1943.

25 years were not repeated — to be ready for the fight after the war. The obligation to the men fighting was to give them decent conditions to which to return, to create a world in which the profit motive had been eliminated. Northern Rhodesia was suffering at the hands of the profit-maker. The single industry, copper mining, was currently producing an income of £12 000 000 a year. However, £400 000 of this was paid to the British South Africa Company as mineral royalties and over £5 000 000 went to the copper companies' directors and shareholders in the form of fees and dividends. Northern Rhodesians feared for copper in the post-war markets and Welensky thought it was essential to secure state ownership of the mines.

He said that equally serious a problem was Northern Rhodesia's political future on which the British Labour Party's statement had raised doubts. The statement had displayed a complete lack of understanding of Northern Rhodesia where the African lagged about 600 years behind the European culture and civilisation and did not speak English or have even an elementary understanding of politics despite the efforts of the Northern Rhodesian Government to educate him. The British Labour Party had expressed favour for international control of the colonies and his Party would resist. After all, Welensky noted, if an influential section of British opinion had been heeded, Germany's former colonies would have been returned to her before the war. He thought that the British Labour Party should devote itself to eliminating exploitation, to seeing, in particular, that the mineral royalties stayed in Northern Rhodesia for the benefit of all races. He hoped that the British Labour Party would send out a delegation and discover that his Party was concerned with the future of every man irrespective of colour or creed. Welensky declared his purpose was to secure the amalgamation of the Rhodesias as a prelude to a federation of Southern African states.[45]

Welensky was in fact echoing ideas of the South African Prime Minister, General Smuts, who, earlier in the year, by speaking of a Southern African federation, had caused some consternation at the Colonial Office because it felt that inevitably discussion on the Rhodesian amalgamation would be regenerated.[46] Smuts was anxious also to secure co-operation and collaboration on an Africa-wide scale with a permanent conference established to promote common approaches to policy in subjects such as communications, trade, African affairs, veterinary research and a mutual foreign policy. British fears were realised, to a degree, when in October 1943, Huggins expressed a need for amalgamation to reduce the number of states in Africa, in order to make an African federation feasible. However, Huggins made it plain that his agreement with the Dominions Office, not to embarrass the British Parliament by raising the amalgamation issue, still stood and thus nothing could be done immediately.[47]

Welensky, though, pressed ahead with his efforts to secure amalgamation. In his correspondence he continued to attack the British Labour Party's document, wondering where in the British Empire political and social equa-

[45] *Ibid.*, p. 82, Minutes of the Southern African Labour Conference, 17 & 18 July 1943; Senator C. L. Henderson to Welensky, 25 September 1942; Welensky to Henderson, 30 September 1942.
[46] R. Hyam, *The Failure of South African Expansion, 1908–48* (London, 1972), p. 175.
[47] *The Nyasaland Times*, 21 October 1943.

lity was to be found as it was certainly not a feature of life in Britain herself. He feared that British exhaustion would allow the United States to dominate any peace conference. Thus, if by the end of the war Northern Rhodesia were not annexed to the Crown through amalgamation, the threat of it becoming a mandated territory was very real. One of his correspondents, however, welcomed such a proposal, hoping that Russia would be the mandatory power because the Russians would give the Africans education, culture and a sense of responsibility in record time. The African would never be free under the capitalist who would only exploit him.[48]

In late July 1943, an opportunity came for Welensky to have discussions with the senior official at the Colonial Office when Sir Cosmo Parkinson visited Northern Rhodesia. At their meeting, Welensky pressed for an unofficial elected majority in the Legislative Council because the existing system of government had to meet the needs of the industrialisation of Northern Rhodesia. He acknowledged that the population was too small to sustain self-government and to staff a civil service. He proposed that the Legislative Council would not be able to sanction expenditure of more than £50 000 without the consent of the Governor. Furthermore, the Governor would have the right to veto legislation involving African interests. The Africans would be given another nominated representative to assist Gore-Browne. On the issue of the colour bar, Welensky claimed that the trade unions were duty bound to seek to maintain existing standards and therefore to protect the white worker. He thought that the colour bar would be best removed by a declaration in the form of a "guarantee to both races", rather than by legislation. He informed Parkinson that he had not abandoned amalgamation as a goal but was seeking a "half-way house" towards it. Parkinson listened without commenting.[49] Later in the year, Welensky sought to broaden this contact by inviting Stanley, the Colonial Secretary, to extend a visit to East Africa to Northern Rhodesia[50] but he could not comply.

Welensky spent the months before the next Legislative Council session in November 1943 preparing his Party for the elections in 1944. The Northern Rhodesia Labour Party had never been a particularly cohesive unit and was currently in some disarray. The Livingstone branch was moribund and in Lusaka the Afrikaner farmer element had taken exception to the left-wingers and had shied away. Welensky's political campaign met with some success in September when, at his invitation, Duncan Burnside, a South African Labour Party MP, toured Northern Rhodesia speaking on behalf of Labour.[51]

In the Legislative Council the first comment on the unification issue came from Gore-Browne when he called again for a federation to end Northern Rhodesia's isolation.[52] Welensky then proposed immediate amalgamation under a constitution similar to that enjoyed by Southern Rhodesia. He knew, nevertheless, that he did not possess Gore-Browne's support because African

[48] Welensky Papers, WE 7, Un-numbered Series NRLP 1943–6, Major A. W. Edwardes Jordan to Welensky, 3 October 1943.

[49] *Ibid.*, Welensky to F. B. Robertson, 29 July 1943.

[50] *Ibid.*, Welensky to Chief Secretary, Northern Rhodesia Government, 29 September 1943.

[51] *Ibid.*, Minutes of a Public Meeting, Broken Hill, September 1943.

[52] NR *Debates* (Lusaka), p. 26, 23 November 1943.

opinion — which Welensky could not evaluate — was opposed to amalgamation. Welensky claimed that the prospects of victory had improved sufficiently to allow the Imperial Government to examine the question. He sought to discover the feelings of the European population which had last been assessed in 1936. He could speak for his Labour colleagues but he hoped to attract the support of the independent Members.

Welensky, pressing for constitutional change, decried the use of the Council as only an indicator of public opinion. His Party's solution was amalgamation though it would accept a "half-way house" to it. Believing that a post-war slump was likely, he wanted the closest collaboration between Government and people. Noting how Northern Rhodesia lagged behind Southern Rhodesia in development, he blamed the outflow of the copper revenues. As the life of the mines was limited, it was clearly advantageous to join Southern Rhodesia.

Turning to the political advantages of amalgamation, Welensky recalled ominously how strong the call had been before the war for Tanganyika to be handed back to Germany. He remembered also that significant support had been gained in the Commons in 1938 for a motion, albeit unsuccessful, urging the extension of the mandate system to all colonies not yet considered ripe for self-government. This might be proposed again after the war. Moreover, the United States was taking an interest in Africa, perhaps regarding it as the last continent ripe for exploitation. Certainly the British Labour Party was interested in the internationalisation of the colonies. Thus the best prospect for Northern Rhodesia, black and white, was to join Southern Rhodesia as the European population of 14 000 was too small to sustain self-government. He argued that the differences in the African policies need not be a permanent obstacle to unification because, in a rapidly changing world, policies were only valid for a decade. He did not expect significant resistance to amalgamation in the Commons because colonial affairs attracted so little interest that one debate was attended only by 14 Members. As a rider to this call for amalgamation, Welensky said that he had given little thought to a wider Southern African union.[53]

The official reply was that the British Government was the best judge of whether or not the motion was timely. However, other unofficials merely regretted Huggins's gentleman's agreement with the Dominions Office and sought again to have Northern Rhodesia annexed as a first step to amalgamation. Gore-Browne responded with an additional reason for the African rejection of amalgamation, which was a fear that the Chiefs would lose their power and authority. Gore-Browne conceded that amalgamation was the logical destiny of the three territories as it would solve their administrative and economic problems, but the difficulty remained the African resistance. It was not, as the British public appeared to believe, that Southern Rhodesia was a black man's hell any more than Northern Rhodesia could claim to be a black man's paradise. Yet no one could deny that the application of Southern Rhodesia's Industrial Conciliation Act would accentuate the existing colour bar in Northern Rhodesia.

[53] *Ibid.*, p. 76 f., 25 November 1943.

Other unofficials noted a morbid American interest in the future of the British colonies, while Major McKee rued the Bledisloe rejection of a federal solution. He proposed an amendment which deleted the call for the amalgamated constitution to be similar to that of Southern Rhodesia because he lacked a mandate from his constituents on it. In fact he thought that it would harm the prospects for amalgamation. Welensky replied by calling the amendment a red herring because the constitution was a vital part of the proposal as the Southern Rhodesians would not contemplate surrendering their constitution. The amendment was defeated but the motion itself was, of course, foredoomed to failure. The official Members and Gore-Browne voted against it, McKee and one other abstained, and the motion was lost by six votes to ten.

Page was more successful in securing total unofficial support on 30 November when he proposed that the unofficials be given a greater share in the responsibilities of government. His ultimate aim, he said, was to join Southern Rhodesia and he believed in taking small steps in that direction. He acknowledged that Northern Rhodesia was not ready for responsible government. Therefore he proposed that, instead of the current system of parity of representation with the Governor, as president, having the casting vote, there should be an unofficial majority with the Governor retaining a veto.[54] Gore-Browne seconded the motion and Welensky gave it his Party's support although his prime objective was amalgamation. The official verdict was that this could only be decided by the Imperial Government and, accordingly, the official Members would have to vote against it. However, the unofficials were undeterred and the Governor had to use his casting vote to defeat it.

Welensky was not entirely discouraged by his failure to win the unanimous support of his colleagues. When the Ndola branch of the Northern Rhodesia Labour Party asked him if the Party should continue to support the current farcical and undemocratic system, he replied that constitutional reform would be achieved by a display of solidarity. Much depended on strengthening the Party's representation in the Council in the elections of 1944. If this was done he was confident that there would be a change in the Colonial Office's attitude towards the unofficials.[55] The Northern Rhodesian Farmers' Union was more impatient than Welensky and asked the Colonial Secretary on 30 December 1943 for an immediate and straightforward statement on Northern Rhodesia's constitutional future.[56]

Colonel J. B. Brady, Southern Rhodesia's Minister of Education, complimented Welensky on his speech on amalgamation.[57] In thanking Brady, Welensky took the opportunity to complain about Southern Rhodesia's failure to consult the North on industrial development and petrol rationing. He noted also the lack of interest in Southern Rhodesia in amalgamation. Huggins, he felt, should have consulted the Northern Rhodesians over his decision

[54] *Ibid.*, p. 154, 30 November 1943.

[55] Welensky Papers, WE 7, Un-numbered Series NRLP 1943–6, Welensky to Mrs L. Davies, 14 December 1943.

[56] *Ibid.*, WE 7, Un-numbered Series NRLP 1944–5, NRFU Memorandum to Secretary of State for Colonies, 30 December 1943.

[57] *Ibid.*, WE 7, Un-numbered Series NRLP 1943–6, J. B. Brady to Welensky, 11 December 1943.

to agree to let the amalgamation question lie dormant until the war ended. It was imperative, in Welensky's view, to induce the Colonial Office to accept amalgamation in principle before hostilities ceased as he was "scared stiff about the influence that America will have at the Peace Conference, and if you were as close to the Belgian Congo as I am, you would realise the interest that they are taking in this part of Africa".[58]

The debate on the amalgamation motion drew comment in the Copperbelt Regional Council from Harry Nkumbula, a schoolmaster and a representative of the Kitwe Urban Advisory Board. Speaking on 20 December 1943, Nkumbula confirmed that the African objections to amalgamation recorded by the Bledisloe Commission were still valid. In particular, he stressed the fear that the land problem in Northern Rhodesia would be aggravated by an influx of Africans from Southern Rhodesia where they had been squatting on European land. Nkumbula alleged that Southern Rhodesia had adopted the South African native policy of economic and political discrimination and racial segregation. Huggins, he said, had made it clear that Southern Rhodesia was a white man's country where the black would remain as a servant, if not a slave, in contrast to the Northern Rhodesian policy of giving the African a prominent place in society. The Chiefs had gained wide administrative powers, and educated Africans were now playing a significant role in the civil service, in mining and in commerce. Moreover, health and educational services were not run on a racial basis as in Southern Rhodesia. Nkumbula questioned whether, if amalgamation were permitted, Huggins would drop his African policy in favour of that of the northern territories. He claimed that if the British Government signed an agreement, which would require the approval of the Northern Rhodesian Africans, with Southern Rhodesia to the effect that the existing African policy in Northern Rhodesia would not be altered, then the support of the northern Africans would be forthcoming for the unification of the territories. However, if Northern Rhodesia and Nyasaland were handed to Southern Rhodesia without that agreement, Britain would lose the confidence of all Africans living in East Africa. He concluded by urging those capitalists, who found that the current territorial divisions hampered them, to depart and leave the African in peace. The Council responded by voting against amalgamation.[59]

No one seems to have thought it necessary to correct Nkumbula's misrepresentations, particularly on the lack of racial approach to health and educational matters. Welensky had departed on leave and only on his return in early February did he try to engender the feeling that it was "now or never".[60] By then Brady had discovered reasons for the lack of inter-territorial co-operation, of which Welensky had complained, and ascribed it to the hurried decisions of wartime. He reported to Welensky that he had asked Huggins about amalgamation. Huggins had answered that his remarks, in 1941, about Northern and Southern Rhodesia settling the matter between themselves, had so embarrassed the British Government that he had been

[58] *Ibid.*, Welensky to J. B. Brady, 14 December 1943.
[59] Davidson, *The Legislative Council*, *op. cit.*, p. 113.
[60] Welensky Papers, WE 7, Un-numbered Series NRLP 1943–6, Welensky to E. Evans, 3 February 1944; Welensky to F. B. Robertson, same date.

forced to say nothing more. Huggins felt, however, that he had not fettered Northern Rhodesia but thought that it would be tactically wrong at that moment for Southern Rhodesia to take the lead in the fight for amalgamation because its opponents would merely claim that it was aggressively attempting to enlarge its territory. Huggins argued that an active campaign for amalgamation was untimely because Churchill had revealed that the biggest and bloodiest battles of the war were about to be fought, and the men the Rhodesians sought to influence would be preoccupied with decisions which would brook no delay. The current task was to keep the issue alive and to educate the electorates about its advantages. He was expecting to attend the Dominions Prime Ministers' Conference later in that year, 1944, and proposed to use the opportunity to do some spadework for amalgamation in London.[61]

Welensky, however, remained impatient. His sense of urgency was sharpened by a fall in the demand for copper and a consequent cut in production. He warned Brady that some of his colleagues in the Legislative Council were at best lukewarm on amalgamation. His contacts in the British trade unions and the Labour Party indicated that a more sympathetic view was being taken of the European in Northern Rhodesia, but he was still convinced that change had to be effected before the Labour Party was returned.[62]

In March 1944, the Governors of Northern Rhodesia and Nyasaland were recalled to London for consultation, and Gore-Browne, as leader of the unofficials, went with them. Huggins followed later in May promising Welensky that he would raise the matter of amalgamation.[63] Welensky, feeling that change was imminent, briefed Gore-Browne on the Northern Rhodesia Labour Party view on amalgamation and provided him with a memorandum for the Colonial Secretary together with a request to read the *Hansard* of the amalgamation debate.[64] Welensky's optimism was partially justified in April, when, in announcing the appointment of a development adviser to Northern Rhodesia and Nyasaland, the Colonial Office proposed to involve the unofficial Members in both territories in post-war planning.[65]

While the outcome of the London discussions was awaited, the electoral campaign continued in Northern Rhodesia. At Broken Hill on 22 June, Welensky publicly referred to his sensing of imminent change. He agreed that change was necessary and, if social security and economic development would be possible, it had to be towards self-government. It was also vital to secure the mineral rights for the state. He noted an announcement that the Seychelles' constitution would be reformed at the end of the war to allow parity of unofficial and official representation, and the appointment in Kenya of an African to its legislature to represent African interests. However, he believed that it would be a tragic error to copy the latter step in Northern Rhodesia because, while there were Africans capable of contributing to the work of the

[61] *Ibid.*, J. B. Brady to Welensky, 16 February 1944.
[62] *Ibid.*, Welensky to J. B. Brady, 23 February 1944.
[63] *Ibid.*, 23/1, f. 65, Welensky to T. H. Grey, 6 May 1944.
[64] *Ibid.*, WE 7, Un-numbered Series NRLP 1943–6, Welensky to E. H. Cholmondley, 15 March 1944; Welensky to J. Purvis, 20 March 1944.
[65] *East Africa and Rhodesia* (London), 6 April 1944.

Legislative Council, they represented only a very small section of the African population and in fact would not gain the support of the masses for many reasons, such as tribal differences and station in life. He felt instead that Gore-Browne, being impartial, could more accurately reflect African opinion and should continue to do so. Turning to self-government, Welensky maintained it should be achieved through amalgamation. He proposed to influence the British Government by means of a petition which would establish the precise feelings of the Europeans on the issue. This was particularly necessary as it had been suggested in the Press that support for amalgamation was declining. Welensky did not pretend that amalgamation would solve all problems, but claimed that recent experience had proved the resilience of the larger unit and that the existing system would only deny Northern Rhodesia the opportunity to progress. He was aware that many Southern Rhodesians opposed unification, but he was confident that there were enough of the enlightened there to persuade them.[66]

If the Northern Rhodesians expected to hear in the August session of the Legislative Council why the Governor had been summoned to London in March, they would be disappointed. In his opening speech, Sir John Waddington merely revealed proposed legislation and welcomed the opportunity for the wider political contact presented by an impending visit of a British parliamentary delegation under the auspices of the Dominions Parliamentary Association.[67]

However, Gore-Browne reported that, when they met in London, the Colonial Secretary had welcomed direct contact with a Northern Rhodesian and hoped soon to discuss industrial matters with Welensky. Gore-Browne had pressed for a decision on the political future because everything depended upon it. In so doing, he had claimed that 95 per cent of the Europeans favoured amalgamation as a method of securing self-government and of ridding themselves of the Colonial Office's native policy. However, he said he had warned that 99,9 per cent of the African population opposed amalgamation because they feared the policies of South Africa and Southern Rhodesia. Gore-Browne stated that, while he supported most of the arguments for amalgamation, he could not subscribe to the Southern Rhodesian policy even though it did more for the African than was done in Northern Rhodesia. Yet, impelled by the necessity for Northern Rhodesia to be part of a larger unit, because of its sole dependency on copper, Gore-Browne had proposed its fusion with Nyasaland and Southern Tanganyika which would also give access to the port at Linde. Otherwise, he had discussed increasing the number of nominated Members to represent African interests, as well as a number of other subjects such as education and mining royalties. He had addressed the Parliamentary Labour and Conservative Parties but had found them preoccupied with West African affairs. He had spoken also to the Anti-Slavery and Fabian Societies.[68]

Welensky, in his turn, agreed that an early decision on the constitution was

[66] Welensky Papers, WE 7, Un-numbered Series NRLP 1943–6, Notes of a Public Meeting, Broken Hill, 22 June 1944.
[67] NR *Debates* (Lusaka), p. 1 f., 4 August 1944.
[68] *Ibid.*, p. 16 f., 4 August 1944.

vital, particularly as the current white unease about the territory's future had been sharpened by the recent cut in copper production. His solution was amalgamation. He took the opportunity to reiterate his opposition to following the Kenyan precedent of nominating an African to represent African interests. Page favoured immediate amalgamation with Southern Rhodesia and felt that experience in co-operation should be gained before incorporating Nyasaland. In any case, there remained the problem of Nyasaland's large external debt. Other Members suggested gradual amalgamation, department by department, and wondered why Northern Rhodesian Africans sought work in Southern Rhodesia if they found it so repugnant.

The question of the representation of African interests was discussed again a few days later, during a debate on a motion to secure the vote for Coloureds. Many Coloureds, because of their mixed parentage, were denied British citizenship and therefore the vote. It was proposed that if a British Protected Person possessed the necessary financial, educational and residential qualifications, he should be enfranchised. Welensky was sympathetic towards the Coloureds but he was concerned that some Africans would thereby obtain the vote. As a Southern Rhodesian he was not opposed to this in principle but maintained that enfranchising Africans in Southern Rhodesia had been an empty gesture as only 85 had registered in 25 years of responsible government. Consequently, he felt that the African had more to gain from the current system of councils. He preferred that these should be improved by the introduction of electoral machinery to give practical political experience and ultimately he wanted the Africans to elect their representatives in the Legislative Council. Gore-Browne supported the motion but it was overwhelmingly rejected.[69]

Welensky used the opportunity of a meeting with the British parliamentary delegation in mid-August to press again for amalgamation. He argued that it was essential for the defence of the Empire to create a British dominion in Central Africa. Lauding Southern Rhodesia's progress, he spoke of the difficulties of establishing secondary industries and of the drain of resources through the payment of the mineral royalties. The delegation, in its turn, attempted to reassure him on the Labour Party's attitude, claiming that it had changed since 1938.[70]

As part of the election campaign and to secure support for his petition, Welensky issued on 14 August a pamphlet on amalgamation. This proclaimed that the Southern Rhodesians could not be expected to accept less than their current constitution and that existing government contracts, particularly those with civil servants, would be honoured. Amalgamation would rid Northern Rhodesia of the system under which the elected Members could merely advise, while the Governor made the decisions, and the Colonial Office dictated on major issues. Northern Rhodesians paid taxes and should have a say as to how they were spent. Northern Rhodesia depended upon Southern Rhodesia for supplies and it was anomalous that two British states

[69] *Ibid.*, p. 89, 9 August 1944.

[70] Welensky Papers, WE 7, Un-numbered Series NRLP 1944–5, Welensky to G. S. Rankin, 14 August 1944; Notes of a Meeting with the British parliamentary delegation, Broken Hill, 18 August 1944.

should share a common boundary and yet erect a customs barrier. Unification would improve communications, marketing and administration. The growth of secondary industry, which was vital in view of the cut in copper production, would be encouraged. Indeed, without amalgamation it was likely that secondary industry would be stunted by the British seeking markets for their vital export trade. Amalgamation would avoid the danger of Northern Rhodesia being internationalised, just as it would frustrate the British Labour Party's intentions to establish political and social equality. The Bledisloe Commission had recommended the recognition of amalgamation as the ultimate destiny of the territories, and the Northern Rhodesia Labour Party wanted it effected immediately.

As for the place of the African in amalgamated Rhodesia, the Party thought that, if Northern Rhodesia was to develop, the African had to progress, but not at the expense of the European. Under the capitalist system the African would be exploited to the detriment of the European, thus the Party favoured Southern Rhodesia's "Parallel Development" policy with each race developing to its full capacity in its own areas. The need for this policy would cease at the "socialist" stage when the danger of the African being used to the disadvantage of the European would have fallen away. The African would gain from contact with Southern Rhodesian practices, and the Party believed in promoting an African economy and culture rather than forcing on the African a veneer of European ways. In conclusion, the pamphlet promised to forward the petition to the Colonial Secretary, and to keep the issue of amalgamation in the forefront of local politics. The Party would endeavour to show the Southern Rhodesians that their advantage lay in amalgamating, and it wanted Northern Rhodesians to be free to choose their government and to manage their own affairs with due consideration to classes, creeds and colours.[71]

Despite energy expended by Welensky, and although it had no rival organization and only independents with whom to compete, the Northern Rhodesia Labour Party, however, made little headway with the electorate. It had an impressive legislative record, including securing the Workmen's Compensation and Apprenticeship Acts, an amendment to the Shop Assistants' Act and had dealt with many other social and economic aspects. However, conflicts within the Party did not assist, and in the end the personalities of the candidates standing in each constituency were of more importance than Party affiliations and achievements.

In the general election at the end of September only one Labour candidate, Hedley Priest of Livingstone, was elected. Welensky was returned unopposed and he could count on the support of Brian Goodwin who had won the Nkana-Chingola seat as an independent Labour candidate, defeating the official Labour nominee. Although Welensky would fail to secure a decision on the amalgamation of the Rhodesias before a post-war election in Britain, his instinct that change was in the offing was proved correct in the next month, October, by a statement in the British Parliament.

[71] *Ibid.*, 23/1, f. 264, *A Case for Amalgamation* by Roy Welensky, 14 August 1944.

CHAPTER THREE

The Death-Knell of Amalgamation

The Founding of the Central African Council and British Rejection of Territorial Fusion, 1944–48

ON 18 October 1944, Oliver Stanley, the Colonial Secretary, announced changes in Northern Rhodesia's constitution and an intention to implement the Bledisloe Commission's recommendation to establish a permanent inter-territorial council to co-ordinate policy in the three territories. This latter move was the outcome of British attempts to resolve the future association of the territories which had begun in 1942 when Lord Cranborne, who favoured a loose association rather than amalgamation, had succeeded Lord Moyne as Colonial Secretary. Moyne had been totally opposed to any form of unification in Central Africa. Cranborne chaired a meeting in the Colonial Office which decided that, as the territories formed a natural economic bloc, the co-operation as established by the Inter-Territorial Conference in Salisbury should be continued after the war. To regain the initiative from the Rhodesians, Cranborne asked for the drawing up of a scheme of union which would answer the economic needs of the area and satisfy the aspirations of all races.

The scheme, which was consequently produced, proposed that the Governor of Southern Rhodesia be given an additional role as High Commissioner of the northern territories so that he could chair an inter-territorial council to co-ordinate policy. An inter-territorial commission would be responsible for all development and welfare plans, and for allocating to the northern territories finance provided by the Colonial Development Fund. However, African policy would remain the responsibility of the individual governments.

The authors of the scheme noted that their proposal was in accordance with the general Imperial policy of encouraging larger territorial groupings, and claimed that a strong Central African unit was necessary to resist the northward spread of South African ideas. They rejected amalgamation because they objected to Southern Rhodesia's African policy, and cast doubts upon the efficacy of the method of safeguarding African interests by reserving legislation for the Dominions Secretary's approval. In any case, they believed that the wrath of the British Parliament would be incurred if the surrender of African policy into local hands was proposed. A federation would be unworkable because of differences in the territories' levels of constitutional advancement, and thus the inter-territorial council was the only solution.

The opinions of the northern Governors were sought but, in contrast to Sir John Waddington, Sir Edmund Richards, Nyasaland's Governor, showed little enthusiasm for the proposal. Although he disliked Southern Rhodesian colour practices, Waddington saw closer association as inevitable because of the economic needs of the area and the lack of alternative links with East Africa. He thought that the European desire for amalgamation stemmed from fears of the consequences of the Colonial Office's African policy which were enhanced by the possibility of a British Labour victory at the next election. The inter-territorial council was to him a workable compromise.

Oliver Stanley, Cranborne's successor, and his officials agreed with Waddington. They would not allow amalgamation. However, they were anxious not to lose Southern Rhodesia to South Africa and thereby stifle the former's growing liberalism, subject its Africans to the Union's policies and delay economic growth. Furthermore, Britain would lose a valuable source of raw materials. As the Southern Rhodesians had lately proved their loyalty, and the unofficials in Northern Rhodesia had worked willingly with the officials, both had to be answered positively. The best alternative was the inter-territorial council because it did not infringe upon Britain's responsibilities as the protecting power yet it could effectively co-ordinate policy. Local co-operation could be secured by ensuring that the unofficial Members of the legislatures served upon the council's standing and *ad hoc* committees.

The British Cabinet concurred and the proposal was revealed to Huggins during his visit to London in 1944. He was told that amalgamation could not be considered and that the inter-territorial council, to be known as the Central African Council, was all that could be offered. Huggins replied this was a mere sop to Rhodesian opinion. As the council's powers were to be advisory, he remained convinced of the need for amalgamation, but agreed to co-operate. His Cabinet hesitated but was won over by the prospect of the northern territories being lost to East Africa, leaving South Africa as the only potential partner. It was prompted also by the need to win back the political support of organised commerce and industry which had been alienated by the wartime economic measures and controls. Co-operation with the North in the council offered more accessible markets there.[1]

On 18 October 1944, the British Government publicly outlined the scheme. It claimed that the Central African Council's consultative and advisory nature would ensure the closest possible co-operation in the administrative and technical services of the three territorial Governments. The involvement of the unofficial Members of the northern legislatures in the working of the Council was emphasised, while the Southern Rhodesian qualification, that amalgamation remained the best course, was noted. However, the British Government ruled, without giving reasons, that amalgamation was impracticable in existing circumstances. The statement expressed

[1] L. H. Gann, *A History of Northern Rhodesia: Early Days to 1953* (London, 1964), pp. 357-358.

confidence that this scheme would make an important contribution to the future prosperity of the three territories.

There was also a surprise for the Northern Rhodesians as it was announced that they would be granted an unofficial majority in the Legislative Council through an increase in the number of nominated unofficial Members from one to five. Two of the new Members would join Gore-Browne in representing African interests but the tasks of the other two were not specified. Furthermore, it was stated that as soon as possible Africans would replace the European nominated Members to represent African interests. To this end it was intended that a territorial African Representative Council would be established. Its members would be drawn from the recently-established African Provincial Councils and ultimately, when the Governor saw fit, African representatives would be selected from the African Representative Council to sit in the Legislative Council.[2]

The British announcement took the Rhodesians by surprise and left Welensky wondering why the unofficial Members could not have been consulted.[3] Huggins, as a party to the proposal, was questioned in his legislature on his failure to reveal anything. He explained that, on his return, his Cabinet had accepted the proposal because it fell within the United Party's aims on amalgamation, although it was not what the Cabinet had hoped to gain. Parliament was free to reject the decision but the Cabinet felt that the spurning of the offer would forfeit the co-operation of the northerners and sound the death-knell of amalgamation. Huggins added that he had been unaware of the proposal to increase the number of Northern Rhodesian nominated Members which created, in effect, a senate without a lower chamber. Yet, he argued: "Had we known that, I believe we should still have favoured clinging to the straw offered us."[4]

Huggins, in fact, dissuaded Welensky from rejecting the Central African Council as a useless innovation. He argued that it could be exploited to demonstrate the need for unity. If it failed, they would be in a better position to demand something more effective.[5] This attitude of acceptance of half the loaf typified the general reaction in the territories. However, there was no slackening in the determination to achieve amalgamation. Sir Ernest Guest, the Southern Rhodesian Minister of Internal Affairs, for example viewed the CAC as a step towards amalgamation.[6]

Welensky and the other Northern Rhodesian unofficial Members agreed. Publicly he welcomed the CAC, calling it the "only bright spot" in the announcement. He declared that he would give it his support because it left the door to amalgamation slightly ajar. He stated that the Colonial Office was mistaken in viewing Southern Rhodesia's policies as too reactionary to permit amalgamation. Yet he acknowledged that the amalgamationists had mistakenly ignored the need to influence the African and should strive to win his

[2] Nyasaland Government *Gazette Extraordinary, 1146* (Zomba), Vol. LI, No. 28, 18 October 1944; House of Commons *Hansard* (London), Vol. 403, Cols. 2364–2368, 18 October 1944.
[3] *The Rhodesia Herald*, 20 October 1944.
[4] SR *Debates* (Salisbury), Vol. 24, Col. 2448, 22 November 1944.
[5] D. Taylor, *The Rhodesian: The Life of Sir Roy Welensky* (London, 1955), p. 72.
[6] *East Africa and Rhodesia* (London), 11 January 1945.

support.[7] Gore-Browne thought that much good could flow from the CAC if it was operated properly, but remained convinced that amalgamation could not be allowed while the African policies remained incompatible.[8] Sir William Tait-Bowie, the leader of the Nyasaland unofficial Members, accepted the CAC as a first step to unification but felt that it would have to gain some executive powers to be effective.[9] The Bulawayo Chamber of Industries saw the advantage in inter-territorial planning, but felt that any opportunity to amalgamate should be grasped and believed that, in fact, the European would continue to work for amalgamation.[10]

There were some, of course, who disapproved. The Bulawayo Chamber of Commerce saw the CAC as an example of over-organisation and expected little from it.[11] J. H. Smit, the leader of Southern Rhodesia's main opposition party, the Liberal Party, claimed that the British refusal on amalgamation was a retrograde, but not wholly unexpected, step which was a consequence of the dominant feeling in Britain that the European's main aim was to exploit the African. What the British Government failed to appreciate, he said, was the real benefit which the African would gain from European administration under self-government. He urged Southern Rhodesians to forget amalgamation for the moment and concentrate on developing their territory to strengthen its bargaining position. Given time, they could demonstrate the superiority of their African policies.[12]

In Northern Rhodesia most of the dissatisfaction centred on the proposed constitutional changes. In the Press in October and in the Legislative Council in January 1945, Welensky declared that the British Government sought only to divide and rule. It tried to prevent unanimity among the unofficials by adding to their number the four new nominated Members. He did not object to the increase in the number of Members representing African interests *per se*, but regretted that the Africans would not elect their own representatives. He rejected the two extra nominated unofficials to represent non-African interests as superfluous because the elected Members did just that. His fellow unofficials agreed with him. The elected Members, he felt, should have been given at least numerical equality with the official Members. The unofficial majority, in any case, did not give Northern Rhodesia responsible government, the "half-way house" to amalgamation which he had been seeking, because the Governor retained his blanket veto and thus could nullify the influence of the unofficials.[13]

The local Press warned that the innovation of Africans representing African interests in the Northern Rhodesian Legislative Council might be the death-blow to amalgamation because Southern Rhodesia could not unify with Northern Rhodesia under such conditions. It could signal the end of European settlement in the North.[14] *The Rhodesia Herald* concurred with Joelson's

[7] Taylor, *The Rhodesian*, *op. cit.*, p. 107.
[8] NR *Debates* (Lusaka), p. 136, 18 January 1945.
[9] Ny[asaland Legislative Council] *Debates* (Zomba), p. 18, 5 December 1944.
[10] *The Sunday Mail*, 22 October 1944. [11] *Ibid.*
[12] *The Rhodesia Herald*, 20 October 1944.
[13] *Ibid.*; NR *Debates* (Lusaka), p. 94, 16 January 1945.
[14] *The Rhodesia Herald*, 20 October 1944; *The Sunday Mail*, 22 October 1944.

East Africa and Rhodesia that a decision on amalgamation had merely been postponed again but both papers felt that the Central African Council could be used to salvage something for the unification cause.[15] *The Sunday News* of Bulawayo thought that the CAC would be a stillborn hope, promising much and realising nothing. The *Kenya Weekly News* saw it as a glorified Governors' Conference. *The Sunday Mail* of Salisbury advised that, as Southern Rhodesia could not contemplate the alternative of becoming enmeshed in the internal strife of South Africa, it should exploit its own considerable resources and stand alone, while using the CAC to strengthen its economy. However, it predicted that the CAC would be enfeebled by the northern territories having to refer every decision to Whitehall for confirmation. With amalgamation indefinitely postponed, the newspaper suggested federation because it would allow the territories to realise most of their aspirations while they continued to manage their own affairs. It was, it said, a practical solution which might be the logical outcome of the new situation.

Welensky continued to press publicly for amalgamation. On 8 February 1945, he revealed that he had discussed the matter with Africans and was confident of success.[16] However, in the end, overworked as he was with political, trade union and governmental work crowding his day, he never found time to undertake a campaign to secure African support and lost an opportunity which never occurred again. He would have undoubtedly faced resistance from the Colonial Office because he would have intruded into its arena. However, this resistance would have been overcome had he accepted Gore-Browne's invitation to accompany him when he toured Northern Rhodesia speaking to Africans.[17] By that time, Welensky had already addressed African trade unionists on the Copperbelt and in Lusaka with considerable success, and had he toured with Gore-Browne it is possible that he could have allayed the fears of the Africans and won their support before African nationalism gathered the strength it did in the post-war era.

More immediately, the Northern Rhodesian unofficial Members strove to ensure that their new numerical majority could be used to influence the Government. Led by Gore-Browne and Welensky, they formed the Unofficials' Association with Gore-Browne as chairman so that they would be able to speak with one voice.[18]

The British Government's view of the Central African Council was clearly defined on 24 April 1945 by Admiral Sir Campbell Tait, the Governor of Southern Rhodesia, when he chaired the inaugural meeting of the CAC in Salisbury. With what was described as "nautical bluntness",[19] he stated that he should establish at the outset the exact nature of the CAC. He explained:

[15] *East Africa and Rhodesia* (London), 26 October 1944.

[16] Welensky Papers, WE 7, Un-numbered Series NRLP 1944–5, Notes of a Public Meeting, Broken Hill, 8 February (1945).

[17] Taylor, *The Rhodesian*, *op. cit.*, p. 70.

[18] Welensky Papers, WE 7, Un-numbered Series NRLP 1944–5, "Note on Unofficial Unity", 30 January 1945; "Comments . . ." by Welensky, 5 February 1945; "Notes . . ." (February 1945); "Comments . . ." (1945); Memorandum by Sir Stewart Gore-Browne, 20 February 1945; G. Beckett to (Gore-Browne), 3 May 1945.

[19] *Livingstone Mail*, 4 May 1945.

> "The Southern Rhodesia Government adhere to their view that the three territories should be amalgamated, but His Majesty's Government in the United Kingdom have come to the conclusion that in existing circumstances amalgamation is not practicable. With this difference of opinion, therefore, this Council cannot be regarded as a half-way house towards amalgamation, but it can and should be a foundation so firm as to support any edifice, amalgamation not excluded, that experience may show to be desirable."[20]

The CAC, Tait said, would be consultative in character and its general function would be to promote the closest co-operation between the three Governments. There would be no joint services, but standing committees would be appointed and full co-ordination would extend below the level of governor and prime minister to the heads of departments and the technical officers. Tait suggested the immediate appointment of standing committees on communications, European education, health and the supply of African labour.

Sir John Waddington agreed in substance with Tait, welcomed the presence of the unofficial Members, and proposed the addition of African housing and road research to the list of subjects for review. The Nyasaland Governor, Sir Edmund Richards, stressed that Nyasaland was not the poor relation as it had the largest population, a fertile countryside and administrative and technical expertise.

Huggins was not as welcoming, reiterating the Southern Rhodesian view that amalgamation was the simplest method of effecting co-operation to develop the area. Men were not given much time on earth and he would always choose the simpler method. He continued:

> "However, the Powers-that-be in London have decided otherwise and presented us with a scheme which is certainly better than nothing, but which belongs to the difficult rather than the easy from the point of view of achieving much in regard to our desire. Although difficulties are a challenge to human ingenuity, this Council can in no way replace amalgamation but I hope and believe that with goodwill we may progress along the right path."

He claimed that trivial differences in African policies had been cited as reasons for not sanctioning amalgamation. Nonetheless, Southern Rhodesia would continue to promote African well-being by its traditional method of trial and error as policies had always to be in a state of flux to meet changing conditions. He felt that the African would have to be considerably better educated before he would fully understand where his best interest lay. However, Southern Rhodesia would work to make the CAC a success even if he had not been "very fulsome in my welcome to the Council because I am genuinely disappointed at the action of the people in London".

Indeed, he continued, to ensure that there would be continuity of support for the CAC, in case of possible ill-fortune for his United Party in a future

[20] Welensky Papers, 23/31, ff. 83–122, Report of the Inaugural Meeting of the CAC, Government House, Salisbury, 24–26 April 1945.

election, he had included in his delegation the Leader of the Opposition, Donald Macintyre.

Gore-Browne made a like commitment even though the majority of Northern Rhodesian Europeans would have preferred amalgamation. Co-operation was necessary in the modern world and he hoped that the CAC would provide the machinery for it.

Welensky confessed to have been extremely disappointed when amalgamation was shelved, and found it necessary to explain that he was at the meeting because he believed that the CAC could "be used as a yardstick to judge the co-operation that can exist between the territories; and if it is a success, it can be the beginning, or foundation, of amalgamation".

M. P. Barrow (later Sir Malcolm), a taciturn old Malvernian tea planter, of the Nyasaland delegation, agreed. He was sure that, if co-operation were possible, it would inevitably lead to the closer association of the territories. His colleague, Sir William Tait-Bowie, concurred, though he felt that amalgamation could not have been pressed on an unwilling — if perhaps misinformed — mass of Africans.

The last to speak was M. Danziger, the Southern Rhodesian Minister of Finance, who expressed a hope that the territories would be regarded as equals because inevitably they would be partners in a great Central African dominion.

Then the delegates turned their attention to a draft of the proposed constitution of the CAC, the appointment of a secretary, and finally the standing committees.[21]

By July 1945, a draft constitution was in being and W. A. W. Clark, an experienced British civil servant, had been named as Chief Secretary of the CAC. Standing committees, served by unofficial appointees including Gore-Browne and Welensky, were at work on health questions, the centralising of the archives and civil aviation, and on research into African housing.[22] In September, at Welensky's suggestion, a committee met to discuss the distribution of goods, common industrial problems and the publication of statistics.[23] In October a civil aviation bill was being drafted, a migrant labour bill was under discussion, and the co-ordination of European education was being studied.[24] A study of the hydro-electric potential of the Zambezi and the Kafue rivers was undertaken in 1946.

Involved as he was in the fortunes of the CAC, Welensky did not waste any opportunity to re-affirm his determination on amalgamation. In the Legislative Council in June 1945, he proclaimed that amalgamation was the only solution for Northern Rhodesia.[25] In the August session he proposed that, as administration by the Colonial Office did not offer the best means of developing primary and secondary industries to improve the standard of living, the Rhodesias should be amalgamated under a constitution similar to Sou-

[21] *Ibid.*

[22] Nyasaland Government *Gazette 1172* (Zomba), Vol. CXI, No. 20, 27 June 1945; *East Africa and Rhodesia* (London), 28 June 1945.

[23] Welensky Papers, 23/31, ff. 20–24, Minutes of a CAC Meeting, Salisbury, 19 September 1945.

[24] *Ibid.*, Copy of CAC Migrant Labour Agreement, 17 October 1945.

[25] NR *Debates* (Lusaka), p. 21, 21 June 1945.

thern Rhodesia's. His arguments had a familiar ring. He acknowledged that the representatives of African interests would not be able to vote with him but he doubted whether anyone knew the true opinion of the African masses. He was sure that the adherence of the Colonial Office to its dictum of paramountcy of African interests would lead to the European's expulsion from Northern Rhodesia. Thus he sought to protect European interests without impeding African advancement. There was, he warned, a very real possibility that Britain's new Labour Government would implement the policy contained in their Party's statement of 1943. He described the impressive development of Southern Rhodesia under self-government: it had been supplied with power through the establishment of the Electricity Supply Commission, an iron and steel industry had been created as had leather and dehydrated food industries, chrome was being mined and citrus was being exported to Europe. Southern Rhodesia had superior health and mental health services. It trained African nurses, had expanded education and paid higher wages. By contrast Northern Rhodesia's development was hampered by constant change in government personnel.

To open the way to amalgamation, Welensky proposed that the industrial colour bar could be rendered unnecessary by providing protection for European wage levels. This could be effected by an insistence that, when an African replaced a European, he should be paid the same as the European.

In the debate, Welensky drew support from his elected colleagues and from one of the nominated Members for unspecified interests, Geoffrey Beckett, a forthright farmer from Mazabuka who would soon become one of Welensky's closest allies. Like Welensky, the unofficial Members doubted the quality of African opinion. They felt that the African did not truly fear amalgamation but saw, in the continuation of Colonial Office rule, his best chance to achieve equality with the European. The economic advantages of amalgamation were emphasised and it was hoped that the British Labour Government, being composed of practical men, would sanction amalgamation once it understood the true situation. Beckett demanded union whether it was called federation or amalgamation. He called the formation of the Central African Council a bluff, a typical example of British vacillation.

Gore-Browne thought Welensky was seeking to draw from the British Government a clear statement on Northern Rhodesia's political future. He agreed that it was imperative that this question should be answered because the 1931 statement on the paramountcy of African interests no longer sufficed. He argued that he and his colleagues representing African interests could not support the motion because of the strength of African opinion against it, but thought that it was necessary to explain why they were so confident that they knew how the African felt. They had the published expressions of opinion by Africans to the Hilton Young and Bledisloe Commissions and the statements made in the African Provincial Councils. Furthermore, he said, over the past seven years he had built an unofficial organisation to tap African opinion on a variety of subjects. He had recently travelled the country, meeting Africans privately in their homes and publicly at large gatherings. He had been to Southern Rhodesia to speak to Northern Rhodesian Africans working there, and everywhere had found a total rejection of amalgamation for the oft-stated reasons. He agreed with Welensky that the Colonial Office administration inhibited Northern Rhodesia's economic growth, but he would not accept the introduction of Southern Rhodesia's race policies though he did not want the Africans advanced as fast as those in West Africa.[26]

Although the Northern Rhodesian Africans were content for the moment with the system of Provincial Councils and the representation of their interests in the Legislative Council by nominated Europeans, the Nyasaland African intelligentsia were becoming convinced that they needed direct representation in their Legislative Council. There was a feeling that something more effective than the various African associations was needed to voice African opinion. The Nyasaland Government had established Provincial Councils from which, in time, a central protectorate council would be chosen, but it did so only in 1945. It had already occurred to one Nyasalander, J. F. Sangala, when the Bledisloe Commission had visited Nyasaland, that the Africans should organise to defend their political interests and to ensure their advancement. The war intervened and only in October 1943 did he propose the formation of the unofficial African National Council — under governmental pressure he later changed the name to the Nyasaland African Association to avoid confusion with the established councils. With official concurrence, his proposal was published and was warmly received at home and abroad by Nyasaland Africans and their European sympathisers. One particular enthusiast was Dr Hastings Banda, Nyasaland's first African physician, who was then practising in Britain. In January 1944, the Association called for better education, equality of pay and opportunity in the civil service, and for the restoration to the African of unoccupied European-owned land. It also demanded that Africans should form the majority of the appointees to the country's boards and be directly represented in the Legislative Council. Later the Association met Bishop F. O. Thorne, the nominated Member for African interests, and told him that African progress was being retarded by the appointment of missionaries to represent them. They also warned that they would not consider unification with the Rhodesias "until we have been given at least 99 per cent of the rights we are entitled to enjoy in the administration of our country".[27]

In October 1944, the Association, re-named the African National Congress, held its first conference. By then it had gained the support of 17 native associations and had formed a branch in Johannesburg. Its first president-general was Levi Mumba, a founder member of the North Nyasaland Native Association in 1912. Other committee members were drawn from associations such as the Blantyre Native Association. The treasurer-general, I. M. Lawrence, was a close friend of Clements Kadalie who, in 1919, had founded South Africa's first African trade union, the Industrial and Commercial Workers' Union. The conference called on the Government to provide free schooling for all, thereby ousting the missionaries. It suggested, too, that it should elect the members of the newly-formed African Provincial Councils.

The Nyasaland Government rejected these demands while conceding that

[26] *Ibid.*, Col. 55 f., 28 August 1945.
[27] P. Short, *Banda* (London, 1974), p. 44.

the Congress represented the African associations in the territory. The Congress was largely ignored but, at its second conference in October 1945, the protagonists of amalgamation were given a preview of events to come when a British assurance was demanded that the Central African Council would not lead to any amalgamation "without adequate consultation with the Africans themselves through . . . the Congress".[28]

In Southern Rhodesia, too, in the latter part of 1945, a political pattern — this time of the immediate future — was emerging in which the politicians would leave the struggle for unification to the leaders of commerce and industry. In November 1945, at the Empire Commerce Conference in London, the Southern Rhodesian delegation proposed the unification of northern Bechuanaland, Southern and Northern Rhodesia, Nyasaland, Tanganyika, Kenya and Uganda to create a sufficient internal market to ensure the economic growth of the area.[29] By contrast, in the previous month, the United Party had clearly indicated that amalgamation would not be the foremost issue in the election due in 1946 because it no longer interested the electorate. Though amalgamation remained one of the stated aims of the Party, there was talk of securing dominion status for Southern Rhodesia alone. Although disappointed, *The Bulawayo Chronicle* acknowledged that the prospects for amalgamation had been considerably dimmed by the outcome of the British election. However, it wondered if dominion status was a vital issue because the reserved powers had never been used and Huggins and Danziger had recently been treated in London as if they came from a dominion.[30]

The United Party seemed more concerned about a potential threat to the European's political position from the African within Southern Rhodesia. Consequently, its congress in 1945 resolved that no more Africans should be registered as voters, and that alternative machinery should be devised to give them parliamentary representation. In the debate, T. H. W. Beadle (later Sir Hugh), a leading advocate and Parliamentary Secretary to the Prime Minister, declared that the rights of the existing African voters could not be interfered with, but agreed that no more should be enrolled. Huggins argued that a means of giving the African adequate parliamentary representation had to be found because the northern territories would soon have Africans in their legislatures and Southern Rhodesia had to keep abreast of the times. The election of representatives through the native councils had been examined but those chosen could hold the balance of power in the Assembly and he did not feel that perhaps two representatives adequately compensated the Africans for the privileges which they would lose by being disenfranchised.[31]

The Southern Rhodesian Cabinet was not, however, entirely silent on amalgamation. In April 1946, Huggins published an article on the need for co-operation in Africa, claiming that the best way to achieve this was to amalgamate the Rhodesias to create a large internal market to attract foreign capital, technical assistance and immigrants. The Central African Council

[28] *Ibid.*, p. 48.
[29] *The Rhodesia Herald*, 29 November 1945.
[30] *The Bulawayo Chronicle*, 26 October 1945.
[31] *Ibid.*

would indicate how far co-operation could be developed, but, he felt, only the utmost goodwill would make it effective.[32] Earlier, in January, it had seemed to the CAC's secretary, W. A. W. Clark, that his appointment would be shorter than anticipated, if Sir Ernest Guest, the Minister of Internal Affairs, was not exaggerating in reporting on his recent discussions at the Dominions Office. Clark noted dourly, however, that Guest was prone to over-enthuse. Guest claimed that the Dominions Secretary, Viscount Addison, had said that he was wholeheartedly in favour of amalgamation because it was the obvious and logical solution for the problems of the area. He had added that too much notice should not be taken of African wishes because they were incapable of judging the issue. Consequently, in a referendum on amalgamation, only the opinions of the European settlers would be sought. When evaluating African policies, Addison felt that the criterion should not be the long-termed objective but the current practice and plans. If Guest had recalled the conversation accurately, it seemed to Clark that all that was necessary was to devise a constitution to put before the two electorates in a referendum. Clark was delighted that a Secretary of State might be so sympathetic to the ultimate objective, but he had found the path to unification strewn with obstacles. Clark said he had the utmost difficulty in co-ordinating subjects as uncontroversial as European education. He agreed that long-termed objectives should not be over-stressed as events might overtake them and acknowledged it was true that there were many practical aspects of Southern Rhodesian policy which were worthy of praise. If Huggins were returned to power in the general election in April, the continuance of enlightened government would be assured. Yet illiberal forces were abroad with the white workers determined to keep the "kaffir" out of their closed shop. Thus there was wisdom in persisting with the CAC to ensure co-operation and create an atmosphere of combined endeavour which would lead to the blending of policies through collective experience.[33]

Guest must have exaggerated, and in any case the United Party lost its overall majority in the election. It won 13 seats; the Liberal Party, which was hostile to both the CAC and to amalgamation, gained twelve; and the Rhodesia Labour Party with three seats and the Southern Rhodesia Labour Party with two found themselves holding the balance of power. This situation forced Huggins to concentrate on more parochial issues and to leave the amalgamation campaign to Welensky and his supporters.

Welensky had been variously occupied. He had sought an unequivocal reply from London on the definition of the paramountcy of African interests, and was referred to the British Government's 1931 statement on the subject.[34] In December 1945, he had won, with the assistance of the nominated Members, a debate on mineral rights. In this he had pointed to the £2 000 000 which the British South Africa Company had gained in ten years, and argued that, while the Government taxed profits, the royalties were in effect a tax on the far greater value of gross production. He sought to have the legality of the Company's possession of the royalties questioned on the premise that the

[32] *The Rhodesia Herald*, 6 April 1946.
[33] Welensky Papers, 14/1, f. 55, W. A. W. (Clark) to Sir Eric Machtig, 4 January 1946.
[34] NR *Debates* (Lusaka), Col. 154 f., 11 December 1945.

Copperbelt had been outside Paramount Chief Lewanika's possessions and not his to give away. Welensky's preference was that the rights should be expropriated, but he was willing to see the Northern Rhodesian Government make overtures to buy them. He proposed that a purchase price could be calculated on the basis of the last 20 years' profits or the Company could retain the royalties until 1950 when they would revert to the people of Northern Rhodesia. If the royalties were bought, the British Government should find the money because it had profited by taxing the royalties over the years. In any case Britain, as trustee, should never have signed away the royalties in perpetuity.[35]

In that month, December, Welensky and Gore-Browne were invited to accompany the Governor, Sir John Waddington, to London in the New Year to discuss constitutional, financial and other matters with the Colonial Secretary.[36] In partnership with others — he had a 75 per cent holding — Welensky bought the defunct *Northern News* to acquire an additional means of influencing the electorate.[37] In February 1946, at an arbitration hearing in Bulawayo, he succeeded, as a union representative, in winning for his colleagues on the railways a 46-hour working week and a twelve per cent rise in pay. In Bulawayo, he pressed publicly in favour of the re-unification of the Southern Rhodesian Labour Parties and used the opportunity to call for a change of attitude towards Africans.[38] However, the pressures of his many activities and the emotional strain of being Director of Manpower, in a small community where he had inevitably known the men he sent to war, overwhelmed him physically. He was unconscious for several days and spent weeks in bed recuperating.

By May, Welensky was well enough to travel and *en route* to London he sought to promote the idea of amalgamation in Southern Rhodesia, revealing that he intended to discuss it with the Colonial Secretary, George (later Viscount) Hall. Amalgamation, he felt, was not merely an alternative to Southern Rhodesia joining South Africa, but a necessary step towards the wider federation of British territories which many Southern Rhodesians favoured. He regretted that Gore-Browne would not support him in this matter as he would have preferred to have shown Hall a united unofficial front.[39]

In London Welensky accompanied the Governor and Gore-Browne to meet Hall. He and Gore-Browne addressed meetings of the Empire Parliamentary Association and the Royal Empire and Royal African Societies. Gore-Browne introduced him to Dr Banda, whom Welensky found amiable but excitable.[40] Being the leader of a colonial Labour party proved to be an asset at that particular moment as Welensky was invited to meet the Cabinet,

[35] *Ibid.*, Col. 183 f., 11 December 1945.
[36] Welensky Papers, 23/1, f. 20, Welensky to T. H. Grey, 14 December 1945; WE 7, Unnumbered Series NRLP 1944–5, Welensky to H. H. Davies, 21 December 1945.
[37] *Ibid.*, WE 7, Un-numbered Series NRLP 1944–5 [*sic*], Welensky to C. Legum, 21 January 1946; Welensky to C. L. Henderson, 22 January 1946.
[38] *Ibid.*, Welensky to C. Legum, 26 February 1946; Welensky to M. Visagie, 27 February 1946.
[39] *The Bulawayo Chronicle*, 17 May 1946.
[40] Short, *Banda*, *op. cit.*, p. 47.

Labour Party and trade union officials. He broadcast on the BBC, making an impressive debut with British audiences, revealing a breadth of mind and an unexpected flexibility of attitude. In turn, he was surprised by the apathy he found, particularly amongst MPs, towards the Empire.[41]

Welensky succeeded in persuading the British Government to examine the issue of the mineral royalties by arguing that it could hardly do otherwise when it was itself nationalising the British coal mines.[42] The British Government, in its turn, revealed that in 1948 the two nominated Members for unspecified interests would be replaced by two elected Members. Simultaneously, the number of nominated Members representing African interests would be increased to four, two being Africans. Welensky doubted whether the African was ready for the experiment but he did not reject the proposal because the Europeans would gain two more seats and, furthermore, the Governor would be replaced in the Legislative Council by a Speaker. Indeed, he felt that this was a modest step towards self-government. He demanded amalgamation, but Hall replied that, as African opinion was opposed and as the Southern Rhodesian African policy was still objectionable, the British Government could not sanction it.[43] Oliver Stanley, for the Conservatives, was as adamant in rejecting amalgamation but suggested that the Rhodesians might examine federation as an alternative.[44]

Welensky returned determined to re-vitalise the campaign by convincing the Africans of the advantages of amalgamation. He believed that if he failed Northern Rhodesia would share West Africa's fate, where Britain was introducing self-government with power devolving into black hands. He told his constituents that it was unfortunate that the British generally did not understand that the average African was not just an Englishman with a black skin. He said it was premature to involve the Africans directly in national politics because they had still not gained sufficient experience in the Provincial Councils, and the African Representative Council had not yet been appointed. He conceded that, while political maturity and not the counting of heads was the true fundamental of democracy, the Africans would be justified if they protested at the anomaly that 1 500 000 of them were represented by two, whereas 15 000 whites had ten representatives. As the constitutional change was a *fait accompli* he urged its acceptance. Nevertheless, he said he would speak again on amalgamation in the Legislative Council and proposed that Southern Rhodesian MPs should be invited to examine the difficulties with the unofficials.[45]

However, before Welensky could speak in the Legislative Council, much of what Gore-Browne had been saying about African opinion was confirmed on 14 November at the first meeting of the African Representative Council. From Welensky's point of view, this opinion was not as bleak as it might have

[41] Taylor, *The Rhodesian*, *op. cit.*, p. 83.

[42] *Ibid.*, p. 82; Welensky Papers, WE 7, Un-numbered Series NRLP 1944–5 [*sic*], Notes of a Public Meeting, Broken Hill, 11 October 1946.

[43] NR *Debates* (Lusaka), Col. 52 f., 3 December 1946.

[44] Welensky Papers, 24/73, Gore-Browne to Welensky, 18 June 1946.

[45] *Ibid.*, WE 7, Un-numbered Series NRLP 1944–5 [*sic*], Notes of a Public Meeting, Broken Hill, 11 October 1946.

been, as discussion on amalgamation arose during a successful debate on a motion for the dispatch of two Africans to investigate conditions in Southern Rhodesia. The speakers, nonetheless, depicted Southern Rhodesia as a "white man's" country where Africans were ordered about like dogs. They stated that Northern Rhodesian Africans had gained considerable experience of the Southern Rhodesian ways when working there and they did not want the adoption of the pass laws by Northern Rhodesia nor did they wish their Chiefs to lose their powers. Indeed, the speakers threatened serious labour trouble if amalgamation was imposed. Gore-Browne attempted to reassure them by reading from a letter from the Colonial Secretary in response to a request from the Western Provincial Council that Africans be consulted before a decision was taken on amalgamation. The reply was that no change would be allowed until the opinion of all inhabitants had been sought.[46]

Welensky's personal political position was enhanced a week later when he became chairman of the Unofficials' Association on the resignation of Gore-Browne over the Association's support for amalgamation. In fact, Gore-Browne had lost the sympathy of the elected Members. Earlier in the year, in the Legislative Council, he had annoyed the electorate by speaking about the worsening race relations and had done so late in the day, giving no opportunity for a reply. Furthermore, he had broken the Association's rules by not informing the Members in advance of what he intended to say. In the subsequent debate in early May, he drew considerable fire and Welensky had to dissuade him from resigning. By November, the estrangement was such that Gore-Browne could not continue.[47] His resignation, however, did not affect his relationship with Welensky and they continued to be warm friends, working together and sharing confidences.

In November, Welensky was invited to speak in Salisbury and took the opportunity to educate the Southern Rhodesian public on amalgamation. He emphasised that the Northern Rhodesians did not come cap in hand: Northern Rhodesia was prosperous with copper earning £11 000 000 a year, with Government revenue rising in 20 years from £200 000 a year to £4 000 000, and currently financed its own development. Amalgamation was needed to strengthen the Empire after the recent British withdrawal from Egypt and, although the Colonial Office would not agree to the application of the Southern Rhodesian Industrial Conciliation Act to Northern Rhodesia, Welensky was confident that the two territories could amalgamate and yet retain different approaches to such matters as the pass laws and the status of Chiefs. This would reassure African opinion and, he stressed, little had been done to influence the African on amalgamation.[48]

The Legislative Council opened on 30 November 1946, with the Governor, Sir John Waddington, formally revealing its new composition of a president, nine official Members, ten European elected Members and four nominated representatives of African interests — two of whom would be Africans. Waddington said that a general election was due in 1947 but that, at the suggestion

[46] African Representative Council *Proceedings* (Lusaka), p. 15 f., 14 November 1946.
[47] Welensky Papers, WE 7, Un-numbered Series NRLP 1944–5 [*sic*], Welensky to C. Legum, 2 December 1946.
[48] *The Rhodesia Herald*, 25 November 1946.

of Welensky and Gore-Browne, he would postpone it to 1948 so that it would be held under the new constitution. Welensky and Gore-Browne had also suggested the appointment of a Speaker and he said it was being considered. Furthermore, at their request, unofficials would be allowed for the first time to introduce financial motions, provided that they were for the general welfare of the territory. As chairman of the unofficials, Welensky welcomed the changes and, though he thought that the introduction of Africans into the Council was premature, he accepted it as a *fait accompli*.[49]

On 11 December, in the Council, Welensky proposed again amalgamation as soon as practicable. He predicted that, if the current pattern of development was maintained, there would be an African majority in the Council by 1968 and if this was the British intention, he demanded that it should be declared. In his view it would be tragic if the Africans would be denied the 50 to 100 years they needed to develop. He questioned again the representative nature of African opinion on amalgamation because the Africans were mostly incapable of judging such issues. With amalgamation likely to bring tremendous economic advantages, Welensky said he was not convinced that the African would wish to starve and enjoy political rights. He doubted that Northern Rhodesia could develop on its own because it was run by civil servants who lacked a sense of urgency. He was convinced that all the African objections could be met by compromise and safeguards. Thus, he proposed a conference of Northern and Southern Rhodesian parliamentarians to examine and eliminate the difficulties. He wanted the new Colonial Secretary, Arthur Creech Jones, his opponent of old, to take the chair to gain first-hand knowledge of local circumstances. If the conference was not permitted, Welensky declared he was ready to resign and would ask the elected Members to follow suit; however, first it was necessary for the Southern Rhodesian Government to express its opinion on amalgamation in order that the British Government might be persuaded to act.

Predictably, the elected Members supported Welensky, while the representatives of African interests opposed him. The latter noted a statement by the African Representative Council on African contentment with the current system of government. Welensky replied that the system was the invention of the unofficial Members and not the Colonial Office. He found it curious that the Africans rejected just as strongly union with Nyasaland where similar systems prevailed and the Colonial Office ruled. As the official Members were still bound by the British statement on amalgamation of 1944, the motion was defeated.[50]

There was no response from Southern Rhodesian political circles, but at least *The Bulawayo Chronicle* believed that Welensky was entitled to ask for Southern Rhodesia's verdict on amalgamation. However, the newspaper noted, with nearly half the seats in the Legislative Assembly held by the Liberal Party, which was opposed to immediate amalgamation, there seemed little point in Welensky's proposed conference.[51]

Welensky then resigned from the Executive Council on 21 December to

[49] NR *Debates* (Lusaka), Col. 3 f., 30 November 1946.
[50] *Ibid.*, Col. 275 f., 11 December 1946.
[51] *The Bulawayo Chronicle*, 13 December 1946.

free himself from identification with the Government and thus be able to lead the unofficial Members as an effective opposition in the Legislative Council. His newspaper, the *Northern News*, interpreted this as heralding a period of militancy and suggested Welensky's unofficial colleagues in the Executive Council, Page and Gore-Browne, should follow suit. It began calling Welensky "the Leader of the Opposition".[52] Some support was forthcoming from the Northern Rhodesian public, the warmth of which was noticed by *The Rhodesia Herald* when it demanded, in February 1947, a vigorous propaganda campaign to rouse the Southern Rhodesians on amalgamation.[53]

Welensky demanded again Southern Rhodesia's verdict on amalgamation on 27 April 1947 at a meeting in Lusaka. As copper was selling at £120 per ton, and consequently the mining industry had earned £2 500 000 in a single month, the prospects of development, he said, would be bright if it were not for the dead hand of the Colonial Office at the helm. Local initiative was needed, but he proposed to do no more towards securing amalgamation until the Southern Rhodesians answered. He rejected the British belief that amalgamation was impracticable because all the African objections could be met. He warned the Colonial Office that the Europeans would not tamely allow Northern Rhodesia to share the fate of the West African colonies. It was tragic to him that the British Government should think that in slightly more than a generation it could impose a Westminster parliamentary model which had taken a thousand years to evolve on the basis of compromise and toleration. He threatened active opposition, perhaps even passive resistance, if the pressure for amalgamation was ignored after Southern Rhodesia declared its support for it.[54]

The Southern Rhodesian Press had continued to urge that the amalgamation campaign should be revitalised, and noted the current Nyasaland dissatisfaction with the Central African Council because it was felt there that individual government departments would function more efficiently and economically. Thus, the Press warned, the CAC could not be relied upon to bring about amalgamation, and suggested a vigorous campaign to compel the British Government to realise it could no longer ignore the public demand for amalgamation.

However, it was only in May that Huggins was drawn to comment on amalgamation when his Government had been forced by the Liberal Party to defend the CAC. This was not surprising (given the Liberal Party's antagonism towards amalgamation and the CAC) because in January 1947 the Chief Secretary, when outlining the progress made by the CAC, had publicly claimed that quiet advances were being made towards achieving amalgamation and the ultimate Central African dominion.[55] In March, the CAC had met and, amid a flurry of signing agreements of collaboration between the three territories, announced that a special committee, on which Welensky would serve, was to be set up to study unification.[56]

[52] *Northern News*, 9 January 1947.
[53] *The Rhodesia Herald*, 21 February 1947.
[54] *Northern News*, 27 April 1947.
[55] *The Bulawayo Chronicle*, 28 March 1947.
[56] *The Rhodesia Herald*, 17 March 1947.

The Liberal Party's attack was led by A. R. W. Stumbles, a Salisbury lawyer, when the Southern Rhodesian House considered, on 12 May, an increase of £3 000 to £18 000 in its annual grant to the CAC. He asked if the appointment of a sub-committee to frame a Press communiqué by the CAC meant that its proceedings were secret. He noted that education would be unified and asked how it would be done. He also commented that the CAC's constitution had never been submitted to Parliament so that it could be accorded official recognition, and that the £18 000 was to be paid for an ostensibly terrestrial body which seemed to function on a celestial plane. He wondered if there was a ceiling for contributions. Because his Party opposed amalgamation, he asked if the CAC was the foundation of amalgamation and, if so, what action was it taking towards that end. It appeared to him that the CAC exercised a great deal of authority without responsibility.[57]

Huggins explained that the purpose of the CAC was to further co-operation and that it could only recommend policy. He explained that before the recent election Southern Rhodesia had been represented in the CAC by three United Party Ministers and the then Leader of the Opposition. He suggested that the new Opposition, the Liberal Party, would have been better informed if its Leader, J. H. Smit, had not refused his CAC seat. Furthermore, the CAC's minutes had lain on the table in the House and, Huggins claimed, there was nothing abnormal in the issuing of the Press communiqué because the minutes took time to be completed. He promised that the CAC's constitution would be placed before the House later in the year. The education issue, he felt, arose simply because the other territories admired the Southern Rhodesian system and wished to share it. The CAC had served a useful purpose: it had secured Southern Rhodesia's African labour supply; and, with Northern Rhodesia sharing the cost, the Central African Airways had been created; the hydro-electric power potential of the Zambezi was being investigated, and a distinguished scientist would advise upon research. The CAC, he believed, was a way of realising projects which would be beyond the means of the individual territories and that £18 000 was a moderate price to pay.

The Liberal Party countered that it only approved of international bodies which had defined limitations. It concluded that, as the CAC was considering the establishment of joint services, it was really evolving a policy of amalgamation. The Party warned that, if it was not reassured on the real purpose of the CAC, it could not support its continuation. Smit explained that he had refused to serve on the CAC because he would always be out-voted and yet be identified with its decisions. He felt that only the northern territories would benefit, while Southern Rhodesia might have to contribute as much as £50 000 to the CAC in the next year without having any option. He charged that Huggins had already committed Southern Rhodesia in the CAC on other occasions without even consulting his own Party. Should he do this again, Smit threatened that Huggins would be forced to bring it before the House and that the Liberal Party would make it a matter of confidence.[58]

On 16 May the Government won the debate after Huggins had again

[57] SR *Debates* (Salisbury), Vol. 27, Part 1, Col. 627 f., 12 May 1947.
[58] *Ibid.*, Col. 718 f., 12 May 1947.

decried Smit's refusal to serve. Huggins claimed that it was fallacious to argue that joint services would lead to amalgamation, when East Africa, for example, had enjoyed them for years without unifying. There was a great gulf, he said, between the United Party's approach to African affairs and the Liberal Party's mid-Victorian attitude. The Liberal Party were unconcerned about events in Nyasaland provided that the labour supply was forthcoming and the inference, that the CAC operated without restraint, showed a lack of understanding that every action had to be approved by Parliament.

Huggins then broke his silence on amalgamation, explaining why he had not even raised it when in London that year. The reason, he explained, was that Creech Jones had rendered such a discussion pointless by saying in the Commons in February that he was prepared to discuss matters of common interest with Huggins, but would adhere to the statement on amalgamation of 1944. Huggins added that, within the CAC, only he and Welensky supported amalgamation: the Nyasaland unofficial representatives, Barrow and Tait-Bowie, said nothing and had to be assumed to be neutral, while the opposition to amalgamation came from Gore-Browne and the northern Governors and their official Members who were bound to support the British attitude. Huggins concluded that what concerned him was the prospect of acquiring a black-dominated state as a neighbour, should amalgamation be resisted.

Stumbles proclaimed that, while the CAC continued to act on party lines, his Party could not support it. He challenged Huggins to fight an election on amalgamation and the continuing existence of the CAC. Smit stated that the CAC decided on the spending of money before Southern Rhodesia had agreed to supply it, and sought a cut of £7 000 to avoid wastage on a film unit. The Rhodesia and Southern Rhodesia Labour Parties declared that, as they did not oppose the CAC, they would not attempt to defeat the Government on it. However they both felt that the House should be supplied with the relevant financial details.[59]

The Rhodesia Herald reported Huggins as saying only that the balance of opinion within the CAC was against amalgamation,[60] and Welensky felt impelled to explain to his Legislative Council, on 10 June, what Huggins had said. Welensky claimed that, as Beckett had recently replaced Gore-Browne in the CAC, the position of the amalgamationists had slightly improved. The *Herald* report, he said, had caused considerable alarm in Northern Rhodesia and he was grateful that Huggins had informed the Press that:

> "The amalgamation of Northern and Southern Rhodesia may be brought about unexpectedly by economic factors. Amalgamation would be popular with the Southern Rhodesian who believed that the present British Government's attitude to the Colony is unfortunate."

Welensky endorsed this statement and lectured the British Labour Party on the mineral royalties, which were currently earning the BSA Company some £2 000 000 a year. He felt that the British should stop talking about placing Africans in high administrative posts and instead do all the inhabi-

[59] *Ibid.*, Col. 839 f., 16 May 1947.
[60] *The Rhodesia Herald*, 16 May 1947.

tants a good turn by promoting the economic welfare of the Africans. Returning to amalgamation, Welensky claimed that, since his proposal of a conference, the initiative had lain with the Southern Rhodesians and he appealed to them to confirm his belief that most of them wanted amalgamation and that the vocal Liberal Party did not represent their views. He believed that Southern Rhodesians recognised the importance of the position the amalgamated Rhodesia would occupy in Africa and the Empire. Those who stood in the way were doing the Empire a grave disservice.[61]

A week later, in a further attempt to secure Southern Rhodesian support, Welensky and Beckett proposed to tour that country to win the support of the man-in-the-street in order to convince the Colonial Office of the need for action. Thus, opined *The Bulawayo Chronicle*, the wheel had turned full circle. In the past Southern Rhodesians used to lecture the Northerners on amalgamation. Now a Northern Rhodesian delegation would tour to explain the need for it. The *Chronicle* agreed that the moment for amalgamation was opportune and that the Southern Rhodesian public needed awakening. Amalgamation was, it felt, the first step to the United States of Africa. However, though it welcomed their visit, the newspaper warned Welensky and Beckett to steer clear of involvement in Southern Rhodesia's domestic politics. Furthermore, the great obstacle was African opinion of amalgamation and the African's fears had to be allayed. The suggested visit by the African delegation from Northern Rhodesia might assist, but the promoters of amalgamation had to find a less one-sided method of presenting their case.[62]

To avoid any misunderstanding in Southern Rhodesia, Welensky felt it was necessary to explain publicly that he and Beckett had no intention of interfering in Southern Rhodesian party politics. As a Southern Rhodesian by birth, he said, he hoped for the utmost progress for that country and he would not promote amalgamation if this would adversely affect its interests. Northern Rhodesia had to wrest control of its economy from the Colonial Office because the latter would be incapable of handling it once the post-war boom fell away. It was necessary, he concluded, for the Northern Rhodesians to know at once whether Southern Rhodesia supported amalgamation because, if it did not, they would need to make alternative plans.[63]

No comment was forthcoming from Southern Rhodesia nor did Welensky and Beckett visit that country. Consequently, in the next session of the Northern Rhodesian Legislative Council, the unofficial Members revealed proposals for responsible government. However, the Southern Rhodesians were not entirely idle as their Government sponsored a goodwill and trade mission to the Belgian Congo, Northern Rhodesia, Nyasaland and the British East African territories, taking the opportunity to speak on the advantages of unification everywhere it went. In Blantyre, on 17 August, the leader of the mission, G. A. Davenport (later Sir George), the Southern Rhodesian Minister of Mines, Commerce and Industry, said that Southern Rhodesians considered they were peculiarly well situated to be the leaders of a future

[61] NR *Debates* (Lusaka), Cols. 159 & 174, 10 June 1947.
[62] *The Bulawayo Chronicle*, 17 & 20 June 1947.
[63] *The Rhodesia Herald*, 11 July 1947.

Central and East African federation and a bulwark of the British Empire against future world trouble.[64]

One enthusiastic delegate, Stanley Cooke, a sugar refiner, on his return to Bulawayo chose to circularise the delegation and the people they had met, urging them to remain in contact. However, he suggested nothing radically new, proposing the immediate amalgamation of the Central African territories, followed by the freeing of East Africa from the Colonial Office, and, finally, an invitation to South Africa to join a great African federation. Cooke felt that the Europeans of the territories should strive to secure unification whilst they were politically dominant, and promised to form a strong amalgamationist committee in Southern Rhodesia.[65]

He did not do so until February 1948, and any interim comment on amalgamation came from Northern Rhodesia. On 20 September 1947, H. St L. Grenfell, the secretary of the BSA Company in Northern Rhodesia, expressed the view that he thought amalgamation would be the product of economic necessity rather than political agitation.[66] On 18 November, in the Northern Rhodesian Legislative Council, a bellicose Welensky re-entered the lists to offer the Government the choice of either conceding amalgamation or granting the unofficial Members more power. He told how the supporters of amalgamation believed that a Central African dominion had a great role to play in the Empire, which the British Labour Party was beginning to appreciate. He hoped that the mistake made in India, of trying to impose from above a Westminster type of government, presumably with full adult suffrage, would not be repeated in Northern Rhodesia.[67]

Later, on 7 January 1948, Welensky criticised the Financial Secretary, G. M. Thornton, for conducting important negotiations in London without the assistance of an unofficial Member. Demanding change, he threatened that, if the unofficial Members were not given a significant role, they would obstruct the Government. He hoped that a solution could be found because he could not believe that the Government was satisfied with the current system. He proposed that the Colonial Secretary be invited to attend the March meeting of the CAC to acquaint himself with local circumstances. He also warned that he would create trouble if there was no action on the mineral royalties.

The unofficials, to a man, supported Welensky on the demand for responsible government. They acknowledged that 1 500 000 Africans could not be handed over without adequate safeguards, but maintained that government by bureaucracy could no longer endure and that the executive had to be responsible to the legislature. Gore-Browne disclosed that his fellow unofficials had constitutional proposals, which they would reveal in due course, and which took cognisance of the Northern Rhodesians' lack of political experience and numbers. He said he supported these proposals because they provided adequate representation of African interests. He asked Creech Jones to visit Northern Rhodesia in March, or alternatively to allow one or more unofficials to travel to London to discuss the proposals with him.

[64] *The Nyasaland Times*, 18 August 1947.
[65] Circular letter in the possession of the late S. Cooke, 1 September 1947.
[66] *The Rhodesia Herald*, 21 September 1947.
[67] NR *Debates* (Lusaka), Col. 68 f., 18 November 1947.

Thornton, for the Government, would not comment on the need for change, but opined that some of the Members regarded self-government as no more than a prelude to amalgamation. Gore-Browne retorted that this was reading too much into his statement.[68]

In Southern Rhodesia, questions of amalgamation or dominion status were raised when, on 22 January 1948, Huggins chose to debate a motion of confidence. As dominion status was a goal which every Southern Rhodesian political party had set itself, Huggins favoured it. However, because the Liberal Party demanded this in preference to amalgamation, he warned that external representation would be expensive and a larger bi-cameral legislature to meet the increased responsibilities would be needed. Amalgamation, he observed, was the more likely prospect, particularly as large companies wishing to invest in the Rhodesias supported it.[69]

On 28 January, Huggins's minority Government survived a further "no confidence" motion concerning alleged irregularities over shipping charges. This encouraged Huggins the next day to state confidently that he would not contemplate an election until after the budget for 1948/9 had been presented.[70] Then, on 11 February, Stanley Cooke chaired a small meeting of influential people in Bulawayo convened by the Southern Rhodesian Goodwill Mission. After he had argued that a Central African dominion could rank with any other, a committee to promote unification was formed. He said his dominion would be a federation of self-governing territories, taking in the six British Central and East African colonies and northern Bechuanaland, but that there would be many difficulties "and the Beecher's Brook of our Grand National will probably be the Colonial Office". However, he felt, Rhodesians would relish a difficult course. Action was needed to secure markets against South African competition.

The Northern Rhodesians present at the meeting, notably Beckett, urged the Southern Rhodesians to shake off their lethargic attitude towards amalgamation as "we must be rescued from the shackles of the Colonial Office".[71]

On 20 February, Captain F. E. Harris, a former Southern Rhodesian Cabinet Minister whom Huggins had asked to assist Cooke, met the Northern Rhodesian unofficials in Lusaka to explain that an all-party committee was being formed to promote amalgamation. The unofficials welcomed this, and Welensky informed the Press that Harris's visit was an encouraging sign that there was public support for amalgamation in the South.

Welensky chose this moment to reveal the unofficial Members' constitutional proposals which would be placed before the new Northern Rhodesian Governor, Sir Gilbert Rennie, for transmission to London. In these, the Executive Council or Cabinet would be responsible to the Legislative Council. It would have an unofficial majority and the leader of the unofficials, as prime minister, would be in the chair. The Governor, however, would retain his veto. Unofficial Members would be given portfolios as ministers and, in particular, the European representative of African interests would be Minister

[68] *Ibid.*, Col. 683 f., 7 January 1948.
[69] SR *Debates* (Salisbury), Vol. 27, Part 2, Cols. 2675, 2687 & 2695, 22 January 1948.
[70] *Ibid.*, Col. 2929, 29 January 1948.
[71] *The Rhodesia Herald*, 12 February 1948.

for African Affairs. There would be an unofficial majority, which would include six African representatives, in the Legislative Council. Welensky said he wanted Gore-Browne to tour Northern Rhodesia immediately to explain the scheme to the Africans and hoped that the British Government would consider it urgently.[72]

Gore-Browne toured, but met with little success despite his arguments that responsible government in this form would place the Africans in the position where they could resist white domination and amalgamation. Part of the reason for the African resistance was that Godwin Mbikusita Lewanika (a member of the ruling house in Barotseland who, since 1933 had been involved in the emergent African nationalist movements) seized upon Thornton's comments on the motives behind the proposals. Before Welensky could release the details, Lewanika put two resolutions to a well-attended meeting of the Kitwe African Society. These were accepted and Lewanika asked for their immediate transmission to London.[73] The resolutions read:

> "Although the unofficial members deny that their proposal does lead to amalgamation with Southern Rhodesia, all Africans agree with Mr Thornton that it is a way to amalgamation, and that is why the Africans have been on the alert."

And:

> "Under responsible government Africans will be treated exactly as Southern Rhodesian Africans and the chiefs will not only lose much of their power but also much of their land and will be on the same footing as the Southern Rhodesian chiefs. The country will be a white man's home like Southern Rhodesia and there will be no difficulties in amalgamating the two Rhodesias together. The interests of Africans will cease to be paramount. The Africans foresee a grave danger in this move, and, therefore, in order to safeguard their rights and precious land, they are all opposed to this demand and they crave for the existence of the present Government under colonial rule."[74]

The Society also called on Gore-Browne and his colleagues to resign or oppose the scheme. These resolutions received wide publicity, and across the country African societies and councils joined in condemnation of the demand for responsible government. The partition of Northern Rhodesia was even suggested as a method of avoiding amalgamation but, mostly, the demand was for the continuation of Colonial Office rule.

The Africans were not alone in rejecting the proposals. A Press survey on the Copperbelt in early March revealed that an overwhelming majority of Europeans preferred amalgamation to self-government and were puzzled why this demand had suddenly been made. They would, however, support any

[72] *Ibid.*, 20 & 21 February 1948.
[73] R. I. Rotberg, *The Rise of Nationalism in Central Africa: The Making of Malawi and Zambia, 1873–1964* (London, 1965), p. 215.
[74] NR *Debates* (Lusaka), Col. 135, 12 March 1948.

move to oppose the Colonial Office. The commercial sector disliked the increased number of African seats and there was general criticism of the lack of provision for an opposition. The greatest doubt centred on the capacity of a European population of 19 000 to provide men with sufficient time, ability and ideas to govern. The demand for self-government was expected to fail, particularly as Gore-Browne had been unsuccessful in securing African support. The survey concluded that the outlook for unification had never been better, though it was likely to be on federal lines which would leave local affairs in local hands. It was rumoured that senior Northern Rhodesian civil servants had been won round. Moreover, the possibility of economic development of Africa was receiving such world-wide publicity that it was probable that events had marched ahead of the politicians.[75]

The Northern Rhodesian Legislative Council met on 6 March, for the first time under the presidency of Sir Gilbert Rennie, in an atmosphere of seething discontent. Rennie, a somewhat dour Scot, drew fire immediately by stating that all interests in Northern Rhodesia would be consulted before a decision was taken on the constitutional proposals. Welensky at once asked if he implied that the unofficial Members did not represent their communities. Thornton was lashed by the unofficials for his comment on the proposal for self-government being a prelude to amalgamation. Speaker after speaker denied implying anything like that. They swore that they might continue to favour amalgamation but that, because the British Government had ruled it out of consideration for the moment, they had given their support to the demand for self-government. They suggested that the Government, through Thornton, had deliberately sought to sow discord among them; to implant the idea in African minds that the proposals were amalgamation in disguise; and, later, to mislead the Colonial Secretary by failing to inform him that Lewanika had not seen the proposals before he had protested.

Gore-Browne requested that a special session of the African Representative Council be convened, but the Secretary of Native Affairs, R. S. Hudson, refused because, in terms of Rennie's statement, the proposals had to be placed before the lower councils first. Gore-Browne was disappointed for, he claimed, the Africans on the councils were incapable of comprehending the proposals and would reject them, correctly, because they did not understand them. The African, he said, was always suspicious of change. For his oft-stated reasons, Gore-Browne explained that he remained opposed to amalgamation but that, after years of searching, he and the other representatives of the African had discovered a method of safeguarding African interests and had found to their great surprise that the elected Members were prepared to accept it. They had thought that they would show the rest of the Empire how African and European rights could be safeguarded and self-government achieved. However, he claimed that, before it had seen the proposals, the Kitwe African Society had expressed an opinion which had received great publicity. The Society had achieved some prestige because their resolutions were immediately transmitted by the Northern Rhodesian Government to London. Consequently, he revealed, in the nine meetings which he had held

[75] *The Rhodesia Herald*, 3 & 4 March 1948.

across Northern Rhodesia, Lewanika's arguments had been flung at him and the people for whom the constitution had been devised had thrown it away in ignorance. To him, it was a great tragedy.[76]

The unofficials were not entirely united. The Bishop of Northern Rhodesia, the Right Reverend R. Selby Taylor, a representative of African interests, declared that he supported the proposals but would not join a militant opposition if they were rejected.

The Reverend E. G. Nightingale, another representative of African interests, proclaimed his support but then launched into a rambling attack on amalgamation, in which he rejected Southern Rhodesia's method of representing Africans in Parliament, and called attention to the failure of the elected Members to fulfil their promise of 1945 to educate and influence the African on amalgamation. He provoked Welensky to decry his comments as inaccurate and insulting to a friendly neighbour.

Welensky explained why so little had been done to put amalgamation across to the Africans. At the single meeting which he had held, he said he had found that his inability to express himself in the vernacular had rendered the task impossible. The elected Members agreed with him. However, he proposed to remedy this by publishing an African newspaper. He reaffirmed his faith in amalgamation and warned that he would introduce a further motion on it in June. The Government might be content to have divided the unofficials, but he vowed that opposition would continue and expected that, when the African sat in the House and realised that he was powerless, he would promptly join it. Welensky said he felt heartily frustrated because he knew that the constitutional proposals were doomed.

Lewanika's demand for the maintenance of Colonial Office rule to perpetuate the policy of the paramountcy of African interests, brought renewed calls from Members for a precise definition of the policy. This prompted Welensky to state that he had never accepted it because the European was in Northern Rhodesia to stay. He called on the British Government to inform the Africans that there would be a racial partnership lest the racial troubles which were besetting the Gold Coast be mirrored in Northern Rhodesia. Nightingale and the officials retorted that the African acknowledged the permanency of European settlement, and they noted that Lewanika had emphasised how vital it was that the European should stay. Welensky recalled, however, that, when last he had asked, he had been told by the Government that European interests were inviolate unless they clashed with those of the African. He recalled being referred to the statement of 1931 and the subsequent debates, and claimed that, when he and Beckett replied that the question had not been answered, the Attorney-General and the Chief Secretary had made play with the word "subordinate" as opposed to "dominate". Welensky told the Council he remained dissatisfied and would take the matter up with the Colonial Secretary together with that of the mineral royalties.[77]

Gore-Browne closed the debate by suggesting that the next step should be amalgamation with Nyasaland to give the area a balanced economy. There-

[76] NR *Debates* (Lusaka), Col. 19 f., 6 March 1948.
[77] *Ibid.*, Col. 141, 12 March 1948.

after Northern Rhodesia and Nyasaland could federate with Southern Rhodesia. Federation, he alleged, would be very different from amalgamation as each territory would control its domestic affairs and the federal government would be charged only with external relations and common problems such as communications. Thus, he felt, the African fears would be allayed and their rights would be guaranteed. He asked for this proposal to be transmitted to Whitehall.[78]

Simultaneously with the Northern Rhodesian debate, the encouragement given to F. E. Harris in Lusaka had led him to call his meeting in Bulawayo to promote amalgamation. The result of the meeting was an agreement to create a non-partisan organisation to reinforce the efforts of the Northern Rhodesians. Accordingly, on 31 March, the formation of the United Central Africa Association, with Harris as president, was announced. Its objects were the amalgamation of the Rhodesias, to be followed by the creation of a federation in Central Africa which would have dominion status, and the establishment of the closest possible links with neighbouring territories. The Association would be based in Bulawayo and branches would be formed throughout the country. It would advise the Government on the strength of public feeling on the unification issue.[79]

Harris was confident that sufficient pressure would achieve amalgamation. He spurned an offer to merge with the Salisbury organisation, the Federal Union Capricorn Africa, which had been formed in July 1947, because its objective was the federation of the territories and not amalgamation.[80] One of Welensky's correspondents thought that Harris's Association should achieve the quick results which were necessary because Northern Rhodesia's rapid advancement of the African would soon render amalgamation, under terms acceptable to the white population, impossible.[81]

The subject of unification was again raised in public in Bulawayo a week later when Major-General Sir Francis de Guingand, Lord Montgomery's former Chief of Staff, addressing a public meeting, said that some action on amalgamation had to be taken soon because "this idea of running territories which have so much in common, and which are economically so inter-woven, through a committee such as the Central African Council is absolutely wrong." He favoured the gradual formation of a federation of Africa.

The Bulawayo Chronicle agreed that amalgamation was the first vital step towards the unification of Africa. It felt that:

> "The particular danger of the Central African Council from Southern Rhodesia's standpoint is that it deals with countries standing at different stages of political and constitutional development. The inevitable pull is away from full parliamentary control such as is essential in [Southern] Rhodesia, while the inevitable pace is that of the least developed or least progressive of the territories."[82]

[78] *Ibid.*, Col. 377, 22 March 1948
[79] *The Rhodesia Herald*, 13 March & 1 April 1948.
[80] Welensky Papers, WE 7, P/C/F/49, Memorandum by C. T. C. Taylor, 25 November 1948.
[81] *Ibid.*, 23/1A, T. H. Grey to Welensky, 1 April 1948.
[82] *The Bulawayo Chronicle*, 9 April 1948.

M. P. Barrow of Nyasaland was prompted to comment that, while the form of the association of the Rhodesias was their domestic matter, amalgamation was for Nyasaland an irretraceable step which should not be hastily taken. Thus he preferred federation.[83] Simultaneously, however, speaking at an Empire Day banquet, Huggins rejected federation because the territories lacked the manpower to serve three state parliaments as well as a federal legislature. He preferred the pattern adopted in South Africa, under which the provinces could keep their different laws and customs and yet maintain a common treasury and services. Once established the whole unit could be properly developed without endless discussions between three semi-dependent sovereign states. He, like de Guingand, Cooke and others, said he looked forward to an African federation, preceded by a smaller British unit of South, Central and East Africa. The foundation of the Western European Union, he believed, would enable the French, Belgian and other colonies to join the British territories in a greater African federation.[84]

Four days later, on 28 May, Dr D. F. Malan's National Party won a narrow victory in South Africa over Smuts's United Party. This had a direct, though not immediate, effect on the campaign to unify the Central African territories because it resurrected fears of Afrikaner expansionism in British Labour and Liberal circles. The Southern Rhodesians were soon to use this to advantage, but Welensky was the first to comment. It was imperative, he felt, for the Rhodesias to review their position as South Africa was likely to switch from defending the pound sterling to using its gold to purchase its requirements from America. Furthermore, though the Afrikaner nationalists had taken recently a more tolerant attitude towards everything British, they preached republicanism. Thus a counterpoise was needed and the economic, political, and strategic value of unity in Central Africa became more obvious. He added that he had never given much thought to union with East Africa, but the new situation made it pertinent.[85]

Welensky was immediately reminded by Charles Olley, a journalist and former mayor of Salisbury, that the nationalists had dropped republicanism as an election issue and that they had been in power for years between the wars without troubling the rest of Africa. In his view, no advantage was to be derived from amalgamating with Northern Rhodesia which depended entirely on the fortunes of copper, and whose policy had African self-government as its final objective.[86]

Then the Southern Rhodesian Liberal Party made a determined bid to avert any prospect of immediate amalgamation by proposing in Parliament that an all-party delegation be sent to Britain to secure dominion status for Southern Rhodesia. It claimed that the territory had earned this status by an ample demonstration of its capabilities in government and service to the Empire since 1923. The danger was that the opportunity to secure it would be lost if Southern Rhodesia waited for Northern Rhodesia to achieve a constitutional status to match its own which was the prerequisite to amalgamation.

[83] *Ibid.*, 24 May 1948.
[84] Welensky Papers, 23/1A, T. H. Grey to Welensky, 1 April 1948.
[85] *The Rhodesia Herald*, 7 June 1948.
[86] *Ibid.*, 8 June 1948.

A Northern Rhodesian delegation was going to London, the Party noted, seeking a measure of self-government, but time would pass before it was implemented. Moreover, amalgamation would only increase the black to white population ratio from 18:1 to 28:1. Stumbles, the proposer, urged Huggins to match the achievement of self-government by Sir Charles Coghlan by securing dominion status for Southern Rhodesia.

The United Party sought an amendment for the examination of the possibilities of attaining dominion status by a select committee. It felt this would ensure that, if the committee approved of the visit, the all-party delegation would be fully supported by the House. The amendment was accepted after Huggins had said that, if there was a serious interest in the higher status, and as the decision should be postponed for a few years, the committee was a good idea. He still felt that it was too soon to think of becoming a dominion because Southern Rhodesia still lacked the men and resources to succeed. He did not want it to become another Newfoundland. He rejected the concept of an all-party delegation, maintaining that, if a delegation were to go, it would have to be from the executive which had a mandate to govern. He felt the Rhodesias should unite before dominion status was sought because, otherwise, unification would never take place.[87]

The session of the Northern Rhodesian Legislative Council in June began peacefully enough with Rennie announcing that a delegation, including one or two Africans chosen by the African Representative Council, would shortly travel to Britain to discuss the constitutional proposals with the Colonial Secretary. Welensky was grateful that this would occur before the Northern Rhodesian general election in August because the electorate would have a chance to accept or reject any changes which might result. He warned that he would raise the matters of the mineral royalties and of federation.[88] This was the first indication that he had been weaned from the idea of amalgamation and was responding to pressure from Gore-Browne who, for the past year, had been urging that such an alternative to amalgamation had to be found if Britain would ever sanction the unification of the Rhodesias.

The session ended with the Government being castigated by the unofficials for Thornton's allegation in January, that they sought amalgamation through self-government, which led to the African rejection of Gore-Browne's constitution. Gore-Browne confessed that he had erred in not releasing the details of the proposals in January. His reason was that he had thought it was necessary to delay until Rennie arrived in Lusaka in February. Nevertheless, he criticised the Secretary for Native Affairs for not correcting Thornton even though he knew the details of the proposals because Gore-Browne and Welensky had discussed them with him in late 1947. Gore-Browne claimed also that the officials had prevented the Provincial Councils from debating motions in favour of the proposals while allowing debates against them. He urged the Government to correct the wilder statements within the Councils because, if they went unchallenged, they would mislead Creech Jones.[89]

The unofficial Members had been preparing their case for the negotiations

[87] SR *Debates* (Salisbury), Vol. 28, Col. 1345 f., 23 June 1948; Col. 1481 f., 28 June 1948.
[88] NR *Debates* (Lusaka), Col. 21, 8 June 1948.
[89] *Ibid.*, Col. 392 f., 24 June 1948.

in London in July. On 28 April, Gore-Browne had written to Rennie to explain his motives. He had attempted in his constitution to meet a demand from the unofficials to make the Government responsible to the people of Northern Rhodesia. He had aimed also at associating the Africans with the Government before, and not after, they had reached the stage of frustration and discontent common in many parts of Africa. It was necessary that Northern Rhodesia should be thus reformed before it joined Southern Rhodesia in a federation which was vital for the development and security of Central Africa. He said the unofficials wanted to stress that they differentiated between federation and amalgamation because the latter was anathema to the Africans and they recognised that, in many aspects of government, particularly in African policy, the two territories would have to continue to work on different lines.

Gore-Browne alleged: "It is necessary to make this point because one of the main reasons for the opposition to our proposals expressed by Africans, long before they knew what the proposals were, was the fact that they had been led to believe they were a preliminary to amalgamation with Southern Rhodesia under its present form of government." He knew, he continued, that Northern Rhodesia was not ready for self-government, but believed it was necessary to advance constitutionally in preparation for the envisaged development. He explained that his constitution was a compromise between Crown Colony administration and responsible government, and that there was every intention of retaining the African Representative Council and its subordinate bodies, as these were playing the useful role of educating the Africans in government at the lower level. Within the legislature, the six African representatives would be in a stronger position than originally planned. They would hold the balance of power through the minister of African affairs in the cabinet and their votes would have a decisive influence on the election of the chairman of the Executive Council whenever there were two parties in the legislature which was likely to be the rule rather than the exception.[90]

In July, the unofficial Members defined their concept of the constitution. They proposed that communications with the Colonial Secretary would be effected through the Governor who would retain his veto for use when the public interest demanded it. In turn, contact between the Governor and the Executive Council or "Cabinet" would be made through the Chief Secretary who would have the right to attend its meetings. The membership of the Executive Council would comprise the chairman of the unofficials, two elected Members, one nominated European representative of African interests, the Attorney-General, the Financial Secretary and one other official Member. The chairman of the unofficials would be the president or chairman of the Executive Council. He and the other two elected Members would be entrusted with portfolios, and the representative of African interests would be the minister of African affairs. The Legislative Council would be chaired by a Speaker and would have a membership of 20, consisting of ten European elected Members, three European representatives of African interests, two

[90] Welensky Papers, WE 7, Un-numbered Series V–W "England 1948", Gore-Browne to Sir Gilbert Rennie, 28 April 1948.

Africans elected by the African Representative Council, one African representative from Barotseland, the Attorney-General, the Financial Secretary, the Director of Medical Services, and one other official. The unofficial Members, both European and African, would elect their own chairman who would submit the names to the Governor of the other unofficial Members to serve on the Executive Council. If a vote of no confidence in the chairman of the unofficials was carried in the Legislative Council, the Governor would dissolve the Council and call for elections.

However, the unofficials were aware that, even if pressed, the British Government would not accept their proposals because of the African attitude towards them.[91] Accordingly, they armed themselves with alternative proposals which suggested that the Governor should retain his current constitutional position and powers. He would chair the Executive Council, the membership of which would be the Chief Secretary and four other officials, an elected Member as minister of agriculture, another as minister of internal affairs, and two elected Members without portfolios. The Legislative Council would retain the form it would take in August, after the general election, when the two African Members would take their seats for the first time. The Standing Finance Committee and the Development Authority would still have unofficial majorities. The Native Affairs Committee would continue to be chaired by the Secretary of Native Affairs but its membership would include at least one nominated and one elected unofficial Member. They proposed also to discuss with the Colonial Secretary the doctrine of paramountcy and the formation of a federation with Southern Rhodesia. They would endeavour to persuade him to agree to pronounce that the establishment of a federation, with the status of a dominion, was acceptable in principle to the British Government if the existing rights of the Northern Rhodesian Africans were guaranteed. If the Southern Rhodesian Government concurred, a Royal Commission would be appointed to draw up a detailed scheme. The unofficials would also demand that, if serious racial trouble were to be avoided, it was essential for the Colonial Secretary to declare unequivocally that the declaration on the paramountcy of African interests was no longer relevant. Furthermore, he should state clearly that the African colonies and protectorates which had "plural" communities were not automatically destined to remain under direct Colonial Office rule until the African populations were ready to take over government. A statement to this effect, they claimed, was as much the right of the African as the European population in Northern Rhodesia and was of the utmost importance.[92]

In Salisbury, the Central African Council's acting Chief Secretary, H. N. Parry (later Sir Hugh), was similarly occupied. After a year's work, he had become convinced that the CAC could achieve little more. This, he has since claimed, was due in part to Huggins's deliberate policy of not allowing the CAC to be over-successful lest it weakened the case for amalgamation. Indeed, Huggins had admitted as much when Parry taxed him on it. The success of the CAC was also limited by the persistent feeling in Southern Rhodesia that it would intrude into fields in which the Southern Rhodesian

[91] *Ibid.*, Gore-Browne to Rennie, 11 July 1948.
[92] *Ibid.*, Gore-Browne to Rennie, 28 April 1948.

Government had been independent for years. A political unification of the three territories would overcome these obstacles, but Colonial Office policy had been evolving in such a way that Parry knew amalgamation would never be allowed.[93]

On 29 June, having discussed the matter with a visiting British official, Parry wrote to J. H. Wallace of the Colonial Office noting that the Southern Rhodesians were threatening to raise the issue of dominion status in London in the near future, and that a Northern Rhodesian delegation would be arriving in July to discuss responsible government. He felt that it would be a pity if both ideas were considered in isolation on an *ad hoc* basis and not in the context of the unification of the three territories. Parry was convinced that the moment to unify had arrived and that, like W. A. W. Clark before him, there should be a federation.

Parry argued that federation would avoid the obstacles on which amalgamation foundered. If the northern legislatures retained control over African affairs, and if this was properly explained, the African objections would fall away. The federal solution was comparatively new and was free of preconceived notions and party pronouncements. It was gathering support. He noted that Welensky had recently spoken in favour of it and the United Central Africa Association had decided to drop amalgamation for it.

Parry defended the CAC but agreed that it was too cumbersome to solve current problems efficiently. In his letter he apologised to Wallace for inflicting his views on him but felt that a speedy decision was necessary.[94]

Parry believed the issue was important enough to persist and, on 12 July, circulated a memorandum on federation to all members of the CAC. In this he alluded to the contemplated Western European Union as an example of the need to enlarge the boundary of the political unit to correspond with the underlying economic structure. Union would secure prosperity, orderly development and greater influence in external affairs. The strength derived from unity would ensure the attainment of independence. The territories had to unite and ultimately, perhaps, join East Africa. Historically, he claimed, economic inducement had always been a most important influence behind unification.

The problem then was not whether to unite but how to achieve an effective union. The answer, he argued, was surely federation which offered a middle path between the two extremes of separatist disunity and the complete absorption of independent entities by one state. Federation implied unity in certain directions combined with freedom and independence in all others. It provided an effective solution to the problem of how to unite sovereign communities so that they might achieve security, stability and prosperity without the necessity of surrendering the independence which they might value above these goals. The alternatives were a loose and more or less useless form of consultative co-ordination through an inter-territorial advisory body without executive or legislative power; or a confederation which would be a diluted form of federation or, finally, amalgamation which implied the surrender of sovereignty to a central legislature and executive, leaving the

[93] Letter from Sir Hugh Parry to author, 5 January 1973.

[94] Welensky Papers, 14/3, f. 195, H. N. Parry to J. H. Wallace, 29 June 1948.

constituent parts with limited responsibility for local affairs. He felt that absorption by Southern Rhodesia was unlikely to appeal to any section of the Northern Rhodesian population.

Parry listed the advantages of federation. Its constitution could not be changed unilaterally by itself or by one of the constituent states, and would have a supreme court to arbitrate in inter-state disputes. It was necessary to define only the powers ceded to the federal government, but the latter would need financial independence to permit it to operate effectively and control such central subjects as external affairs, defence and communications. There were, he acknowledged, considerable difficulties to be surmounted. The British Government could, perhaps, place each territory on an equal footing by granting them limited self-government. More significant was the problem of the responsibility for African affairs which most certainly should be left as a territorial responsibility. At the federal level, African interests could be safeguarded by the appointment of nominated European representatives to the federal upper house. If Switzerland could unite, despite her religious, racial and language problems, Parry concluded, it should be possible to do likewise in Central Africa.[95]

Three days after Parry had issued his memorandum, it was, seemingly, demonstrated that the CAC had reached the limit of its usefulness. Huggins contrived to be defeated in the Southern Rhodesian Legislative Assembly by forcing a vote of confidence on an issue involving a decision of the CAC.[96] His other motives were various. He was ridding himself of the irritation of trying to govern without a majority in Parliament. He acted also to save the sugar industry in Southern Rhodesia. The growing of a thousand acres of cane on the Triangle estate in the Lowveld, due to heavy financial loss, had come under increasing criticism, particularly from a Select Committee on Public Accounts which included, incidentally, R. O. Stockil (later Sir Raymond) of the Liberal Party who would play a leading role in the development of the sugar industry. The Select Committee called for the termination of the sugar experiment and the sale of the land to private farmers. Bent on saving it, a senior civil servant persuaded Sir Ernest Guest, then Minister of Finance and one of the waverers in the Cabinet, to inspect the cane. Guest went, and returned brimming with enthusiasm. He secured the Cabinet's support for the project, and the parliamentary defeat was staged on the next day, leaving the Government free to continue the experiment.[97]

The defeat was occasioned by the rejection of the Coinage Amendment Bill designed to implement a CAC decision to use the funds of the Currency Board for the erection of a building to provide it with offices and storage. In the second reading, the Liberal and Labour MPs claimed that building materials could not be diverted from the current effort to meet the shortage of housing, schools and hospitals. They rejected the Bill by 14 votes to twelve.

To their surprise, on 15 July, Huggins suddenly demanded that the Bill be restored. He wondered if the MPs understood that they had breached an international agreement which had involved, among others, the Dominions

[95] Memorandum dated 12 July 1948 given to the author by Sir Hugh Parry.
[96] SR *Debates* (Salisbury), Vol. 28, Col. 2016, 15 July 1948.
[97] Author's interview with the late Sir Andrew Strachan.

Secretary. The Press had aggravated the situation by calling this a minor defeat for the Government when, in fact, he claimed, it was a major defeat with international consequences.

Guest railed at the Opposition, scorning their arguments and daring them to defeat the Government. Huggins, he said, was at last giving them an opportunity to outvote him. However, he predicted that the Liberal and Labour Parties would have difficulty in convincing the electorate that it was necessary as there was no doubt that the Currency Board needed new premises. The Opposition refused to restore the Bill, the Government was defeated by one vote, and Huggins announced that Parliament would be dissolved.[98] The consequent election in September was to prove Guest right, and it put Huggins in a position where he was free to work with Welensky on the unification issue.

The Northern Rhodesian delegation met Creech Jones on 27 July, and Gore-Browne and Welensky immediately gave notice that they were withdrawing their proposals for constitutional change because of African resistance. They regretted this as the Africans had lost a great opportunity to advance. Nonetheless, they argued, there was still need for reform because the current Constitution had proved unworkable. Their remedy was to bring the unofficial Members into the Government in more than an advisory capacity but, as the African Members had not yet had the necessary experience, a European would have to represent them in the Executive Council. Creech Jones, by contrast, thought that the psychological advantage was such that it would be worth having an African in the Executive Council immediately.

Rennie then revealed that the Government intended to offer four seats in the Executive Council to the unofficial Members with one representing African interests, two responsible for government departments and the last without portfolio. The appointees would remain Members of the Legislative Council and the Governor would retain his reserved powers. As this was precisely what the unofficial Members had been hoping to gain as an alternative to their ill-fated proposals, it is not surprising that Welensky welcomed it. He said that the scheme could work and he hoped that the unofficial Members would be given charge of the departments which dealt directly with the affairs of the European population. The African representatives present, E. S. Chileshye and E. Mubitana, agreed with Welensky[99] and on 15 August it was publicly announced that the four seats had been offered and accepted by the Northern Rhodesian delegation.

Federation in Central Africa does not seem to have been discussed with Creech Jones. However, and inevitably, the Colonial Office had received a copy of Parry's memorandum. Parry was reprimanded by the head of the department dealing with Northern Rhodesia and Nyasaland, C. E. Lambert, and was told that the British Government was not prepared to contemplate federating the three territories and that he was not employed to make political proposals. A few weeks later Lambert softened and, though he told Parry to

[98] SR *Debates* (Salisbury), Vol. 28, Col. 2016 f., 15 July 1948.
[99] Welensky Papers, WE 7, Un-numbered Series V–W "England 1948", Record of a Meeting in the Colonial Office, 27 July 1948.

do nothing to promote it, he revealed that the British Government was studying the idea.[100] Then, during the Northern Rhodesian constitutional discussions, Creech Jones told Welensky that the British Government had come to regard federation as the possible political destiny of the Central African territories.[101] At last, though the idea of amalgamating was lost, the British Government had been brought to consider a form of unification.

[100] Letter from Sir Hugh Parry to author, 5 January 1973.

[101] Welensky Papers, *op. cit.*, "England 1948", Welensky to S. Cooke, 19 August 1948.

CHAPTER FOUR

First Steps towards Federation

British Encouragement and an Attempt at formulating a Federal Constitution, 1948–49

WELENSKY'S immediate task upon his return to Northern Rhodesia was to secure, in the polling on 27 August 1948, the election of men sympathetic to his ideas. Huggins, too, had to strive to win his election on 16 September. Both were successful, and *The Rhodesia Herald* hailed the northern results "as a triumph for Mr Welensky". Huggins's United Party matched this by extricating itself from its previous precarious situation by winning 24 of the 30 seats, leaving the Liberal Party with five, and Labour with one. As Huggins could now ignore the Liberal Party's anti-unification attitude, Welensky had next to draw him into a more active role in the effort to unify the Rhodesias and to woo him finally from amalgamation as the method by which it should be effected. Once Huggins was convinced that the British Government would only consider federation, the Rhodesians then had to tempt it to implement its promise to examine the possibility of federation.

The importance of the Southern Rhodesian election to Welensky's plans is revealed in his letter to Stanley Cooke on 19 August 1948. He told how Arthur Creech Jones, the Colonial Secretary, had said that the Central African Council had outlived its usefulness and that he recognised the tremendous advantages of the closer association of the territories, provided that the rights of the indigenous peoples were protected. However, Creech Jones had made it plain that he was not yet speaking for his Government as the matter had not been considered by the Cabinet. Thus Welensky proposed that "should Huggins be returned I will make an approach requesting him to lead the three territories here in an approach to the United Kingdom Government for an examination of this problem". Everything, therefore, hinged upon the return of a non-parochial Southern Rhodesian Government capable of thinking in Central African terms.[1]

[1] Welensky Papers, WE 7, Un-numbered Series V–W "England 1948", Welensky to S. Cooke, 19 August 1948.

In fact, Creech Jones had so encouraged Welensky that on the same day, 19 August, he said publicly that "the stage has arrived when the dream of a great British Central African Dominion can become a reality . . . If the two Rhodesias and Nyasaland were to make an approach to the British Government on the question of Federation, I believe they would not go unheeded".[2]

Huggins, in turn, on the morrow of his electoral success, 17 September, was sufficiently elated to announce that he would take the opportunity, while attending the Dominions Prime Ministers' and Commonwealth Parliamentary Conferences in London in October, to discuss with the British Government the "marriage of the Rhodesias". The first step would be the unification of the Rhodesias, then Nyasaland would join them to form a Central African dominion, and there would follow a partnership with South Africa. The ultimate aim was a United States of Africa. He envisaged little initial difficulty as the CAC could provide most of the co-ordinating machinery needed for amalgamation. If there were to be any opposition, he said, it would not come, as might be expected, from the Afrikaner nationalists in South Africa, but from the Colonial Office.

Two days later, the reaction to this statement was such that Huggins felt it was necessary to qualify it by calling the United States of Africa "a vision of the future, how far distant none can say". The immediate step would be the amalgamation or the federation of the Rhodesias and would have to be sanctioned by the Colonial Office and a referendum.

Welensky and Huggins were joined in calling for British consideration of a federation in Central Africa by the Federated Chambers of Commerce of the British Empire which, at its congress in late September, argued that thereby conditions most favourable for the economic development of the area would be created.

Before departing for London, Huggins used, on 2 October, the opportunity of a radio broadcast on the 25th anniversary of responsible government in Southern Rhodesia to speak again of the creation of a Central African dominion, giving as a further reason that "we do not want our grandchildren to have as a neighbour a state such as Liberia which has no European guidance".

Welensky was already in London as a delegate to the "African Conference" at Lancaster House from 29 September to 9 October, held to discuss the problems of the ten African colonies which came under the aegis of the Colonial Office. Welensky made full use of his time within and without the Conference. Outside it, he would convince Huggins that he would have to pursue the idea of federating rather than amalgamating; within it, he even succeeded in drawing from Creech Jones a public hint of his conversion on the issue of unifying the Central African territories.

Welensky's initial contribution was to air his grievances on the mineral royalties. He soon grew impatient with the long-winded monologues, and by the concluding day he was in an aggressive mood. Creech Jones gave the final speech from the platform. He thought that the Conference had been useful because it had given glimpses of the problems besetting Africa. However, he

[2] D. Taylor, *The Rhodesian: The Life of Sir Roy Welensky* (London, 1955), p. 100.

had been dismayed at colonial cynicism towards the Colonial Office and denied that it was cold and impersonal, and promised that it would strive sincerely to meet the aspirations of the colonies. The British goal in Africa was to build up the sense of responsibility in the communities and to create conditions of nationhood. The British Government would assist in political advancement, establish sound local government, spread democratic ideals, and ultimately grant self-government. There would be, he said, scope for regional co-operation in some areas of Africa. There would be, too, a wider co-operation with the other powers which had interests in Africa.

Welensky was one of two delegates chosen to reply. Bluntly critical, he said that the Conference had heard too many platitudes and too many speeches from officials. There should have been an unofficial Member from one of the colonies in the chair, for, in his opinion, Creech Jones had proved to be far too indulgent. The only purpose which the Conference had served was to afford the delegates the chance to get to know one another. As regards the interest taken in the problems of Africa, he decried the continuing failure of the successive Colonial Secretaries, or even their Under-Secretaries, to find the time to visit Northern Rhodesia. However, he welcomed the proposal that there should be regional conferences in Africa. He was also pleased that the Colonial Office's political objective had been revealed so that planning could be adjusted accordingly. Recalling that Creech Jones had spoken of the possibility of creating greater units in Africa, Welensky said he was "most anxious . . . to see the creation of a Central African body with some very loose form of political link".[3]

After the Conference, Welensky sought a final confirmation of the British verdict on amalgamation, and Creech Jones firmly reiterated that it was a lost cause as no British Government, whether Labour or Conservative, would relinquish control of the affairs of the 4 000 000 Africans in Northern Rhodesia and Nyasaland. The Conservative Shadow Colonial Secretary, Oliver Stanley, confirmed this verdict. He wondered why the Rhodesians did not make better use of the CAC. When Welensky replied that they had done what they could with it to the extent that Huggins had been defeated in Parliament, Stanley suggested that they should consider federation. Welensky conveyed these findings to Huggins at his hotel and they decided that they should concentrate on securing a federation of the three territories. They agreed that a conference of the northern unofficial Members and the Southern Rhodesian politicians should be convened shortly to evolve a constitutional formula as a basis of negotiation. The parlous state of Southern Rhodesian finances, as a massive immigration drive began to drain resources, was undoubtedly a major influence on Huggins in deciding at last to take positive action.

Their plans were revealed in London on 27 October by Huggins who told the assembled journalists that, though the British Government had blocked every attempt to unify, he was confident that "it cannot go on resisting it forever unless it wants to damn Africa in perpetuity".

When the Press sought Welensky's opinion two days later, he called Huggins's announcement "a red letter day in Rhodesian history". In fact, he

[3] Minutes of Sessions 1–12 of the African Conference, London, 29 September–9 October 1948 (African No. 1176).

hoped it would be known as the day on which the eighth dominion was founded. He was confident that he spoke for all Rhodesians when saying that the hour had come to rationalise the boundaries in Africa, and give the territories some political objectives. He went on: "Like Sir Godfrey I also believe in the amalgamation of the two territories but I am afraid straight-out amalgamation of the Rhodesias would meet with considerable opposition from the African people — whereas the varying political privileges and rights now enjoyed by the natives can most definitely be enjoyed under federation." He claimed that through federation — into which Nyasaland would eventually come — the chances of securing dominion status would be immediately improved, and the creation of a large dominion in the centre of Africa was not only vital to the Commonwealth but to the peace of the world. Creech Jones, Welensky said, had not been able to commit the British Government on the question of federation, but any proposals would be carefully examined.[4]

Huggins did not think that it was necessary to say anything to his Legislative Assembly on the unification issue beyond denying, when taxed by R. O. Stockil, that he had discussed it with the British Government. He said he had reviewed it informally with the Northern Rhodesians. He added, erroneously: "The last time I discussed amalgamation with the Secretary of State was in 1939 when I asked for a loaf and was given a crumb — the Central African Council."[5]

Welensky, however, gave his Legislative Council a full report. He hoped, he said, that the conference on federation would be held early in the New Year, not later than February or March. Having accounted for his final abandonment of amalgamation, he pleaded for the Government's assistance to avoid a repetition of the fiasco which had occurred over Gore-Browne's self-government proposals. He wanted the Government to influence the Africans to give federation a fair hearing and not to equate it with amalgamation before its case had been presented. Gore-Browne and the retiring Secretary for Native Affairs, R. S. Hudson, echoed this appeal.[6]

It could not yet be assessed whether Welensky in his London Press statement had actually expressed the hopes of the Rhodesians, but the organisations in Southern Rhodesia, the United Central Africa Association in Bulawayo and the Federal Union in Salisbury, busied themselves with the task of influencing them. Both bodies produced pamphlets, and on 22 and 23 November the Federal Union held discussions with Huggins, his Finance Minister, E. C. F. Whitehead (later Sir Edgar), the future Prime Minister of Southern Rhodesia; H. F. Eckstein of the Kenyan Electors' Union; Major-General Sir Francis de Guingand; Colonel David Stirling, the founder of the Special Air Service Regiment, and currently a Southern Rhodesian businessman; A. M. Bentley of the United Central Africa Association; and G. G. S. J. Hadlow, the chairman of the Nyasaland Convention of Associations. All agreed that British policy had to be steered away from its direction because its lack of understanding of the African's mentality and his real needs was leading them to disaster. They discussed tactics, accepting that they should

[4] Taylor, *The Rhodesian*, *op. cit.*, p. 103.
[5] SR *Debates* (Salisbury), Vol. 29, Col. 234, 24 November 1948.
[6] NR *Debates* (Lusaka), Col. 55 f., 12 November 1948.

not suggest incorporating South Africa, except as a bargaining counter, in any future association of territories because its political ideas were so abhorrent to the British. Whitehead recalled that it was unofficial pressure which had nudged the British Government into appointing the Bledisloe Commission, and the meeting agreed that, though Southern Rhodesia should make the initial approach, it should not be made at governmental level. What was needed, therefore, was an expression of opinion from the representatives of the three territories. There would have to be a fusing of the organisations, they felt, promoting federation and a considerable effort was needed to stir the apathetic Southern Rhodesian public.[7]

On 20 December 1948, Welensky announced that the Conference would be held at the Victoria Falls in mid-February. Each territory would be represented by four delegates who would be supported by observers and advisers, and he hoped that Stockil, the Leader of the Southern Rhodesian Opposition, would be there and that the Governments of the northern territories would send observers. He used this opportunity to accuse the CAC of retarding the development of the area because every decision, however unimportant, had to be referred back to the legislatures for approval.[8] This criticism was mild compared with that which Huggins had levelled at the CAC and its members during its meeting in December. Northern Rhodesia was a particular target when an argument of some magnitude had arisen over the congestion of the railways and the allocation of the coal supplies. Huggins had tersely stated: "Northern Rhodesia actually started this row — as if we were filling our cellars here and starving Northern Rhodesia. The time Northern Rhodesia was making the biggest noise we had no more than two days' supply of coal and brickmakers had to stop making bricks." Huggins had decried the overuse of the title "Central Africa" for the common services because it was geographically incorrect and therefore misleading. He rejected a suggestion that Southern Rhodesia should give up its independent military status to join the northern territories under the East African Command. He also criticised the CAC's broadcasting arrangements because he believed that the Lusaka radio station, which provided the African service for the three territories, was ignoring the Southern Rhodesian Africans.[9]

Welensky's announcement excited interest in Bechuanaland, and his preparations for the Conference were interrupted by pleas from L. S. Glover of Gaberones for advice on a suggestion he would make in the Bechuanaland European Advisory Council, in March 1949, for union with a neighbouring territory for the survival of the economy. Glover preferred to join Central, rather than South, Africa.[10]

[7] Welensky Papers, WE 7, P/C/F/49, C. T. C. Taylor to Welensky, 25 November 1948; Memorandum by Taylor of the same date

[8] *Ibid.*, Welensky to the unofficial Members, 20 December 1948; *The Rhodesia Herald*, 21 December 1948.

[9] Welensky Papers, WE 7, "Minutes and Memos.", Vol. 3, 8th Meeting of the CAC, 16 & 17 December 1948.

[10] *Ibid.*, P/C/F/49, L. S. Glover to J. H. N. Hobday, 16 January 1949; Hobday to Glover, 5 February 1949; Welensky to Glover, (9 February 1949); same to same, 12 February 1949; Glover to Welensky, 14 February 1949.

The Northern Rhodesian delegation examined the case for federation. Gore-Browne acknowledged that its advantages in regard to defence, communications, research, supplies and similar subjects were self-evident. However, he felt it was important to realise that the Northern Rhodesian Africans, with very few exceptions, would not appreciate these advantages and had a deep-rooted suspicion of anything remotely resembling amalgamation with Southern Rhodesia. Their attitude would profoundly affect the British Government. There was no point, he said, in discussing this attitude but it could not be ignored as everything depended on it. The Africans had taken his advice to refrain from discussing federation publicly and were awaiting the proposals but, he warned, they would only commit themselves in favour of federation if the administration of their affairs would remain the direct responsibility of the Colonial Office until such time that they agreed, through their Councils, to it being transferred to the federal government. They would also require: the security of African land under the current tenure; non-interference with the powers of the Chiefs; African representation in the Northern Rhodesian Legislative Council and, eventually, representation in the federal legislature. Although Gore-Browne confessed that he was guessing, as no African had yet made a public statement on the subject, he knew that the idea had been received with great suspicion, and urged that the proposals be presented to influential Africans as soon as possible.[11]

Huggins's conversion to federation had not been as final as it might have been. Indeed, such were his plans that Major C. T. C. Taylor of Banket thought that it was important to warn Welensky of them. Taylor wrote that, at a preparatory meeting of the Southern Rhodesian delegation to the Conference, in late January 1949, he had asked Huggins what form he envisaged the federation would take, and Huggins had replied that he did not approve "of the milk-and-water ideas of the Stanley Cooke bunch in Bulawayo . . ."

Cooke's ideas on federation were akin to those of H. N. Parry of the CAC and centralised economic and other non-controversial subjects, but left African affairs to the territories. However, Taylor reported Huggins as saying that he wanted amalgamation "but failing that, a real federation".

Taylor reported that he had suggested at a previous meeting a small federal parliament with the territorial legislatures kept at their current strength, but Huggins now maintained that the populations were too small to afford territorial as well as federal governments. He thought that the Southern and Northern Rhodesian legislatures would have to be combined (he made no mention of Nyasaland) to act in defence, communications, finance, currency, taxation, immigration and African affairs. The territories would be served by small provincial councils. The extinction of the Southern Rhodesian Parliament would be acceptable to its Members because they would be able to stand for election to the federal legislature in their same constituencies. This copy of the South African system had not been well-received by the meeting, and Taylor believed that in any case it would be difficult to disguise that it was, in fact, amalgamation.

Taylor revealed that Stockil and the Liberal Party were refusing to take the

[11] *Ibid.*, "Notes on Federation as it affects Africans", (February 1949).

two places in the Southern Rhodesian delegation which had been offered to them. Stockil had been invited to the meeting and had not even replied. His spokesman had said, Taylor reported, that the Liberal Party could not attend the Conference because Huggins had snubbed them when they had protested that the recent trade agreement with South Africa would tie Southern Rhodesia to South Africa politically as well as financially and thereby prevent the federation with the North which, curiously enough, they now claimed to favour. As five United Party delegates could hardly commit Southern Rhodesia to any course of action, Taylor, in particular, was anxious that a cross-section of Rhodesian opinion should be represented at the Conference.[12] In the end, Stockil did attend the Conference, but only as an observer.

The Conference was held at the Victoria Falls Hotel on 16 and 17 February.[13] Southern Rhodesia was representated by Huggins, Whitehead, Cooke and Harris; Northern Rhodesia by Welensky, G. Beckett, J. F. Morris and A. A. Davies; and Nyasaland by M. P. Barrow, Hadlow and J. Marshall. Among the observers present were Gore-Browne, L. J. W. Keller and, of course, Stockil. Sir Miles Thomas, then Southern Rhodesia's development adviser, spoke first as chairman. Maintaining that in the modern world only the larger units would survive, he claimed that realism demanded that political considerations had to be influenced by economic factors and thus inter-territorial co-operation had to be more efficient. Therefore, any new co-ordinating body would need executive powers. Speaking in business terms, he claimed that everyone would benefit if the overhead administrative charges in the three territories could be reduced. There would be difficulties in devising a system because the territories had been separately administered but, he urged, these had to be overcome as the Conference should not be accused by posterity of failing to recognise the need for unification. He fervently hoped that the delegates would disprove the critics' claims that the Conference would produce only superficial and abstract results.

Huggins declared that he wanted to make it clear that, as he had favoured amalgamation when the Southern Rhodesian Legislative Council had rejected it in 1917, he would not accept the accusation that he was "chasing copper profits". He recalled the history of the efforts to unify and how the previous conference, in 1936, had resulted in the appointment of the Bledisloe Commission which, in turn, had suggested the Central African Council. The CAC had been useful, but it was "proving what was found in America — that you cannot divorce financial control from political control".

Common services, he said, had to be controlled by one government, and in a federation the central government would be responsible for matters of mutual concern while the territorial governments took care of their domestic affairs. The federal constitution would be designed to work for the benefit of all and not for sectional interests. The Conference, he felt, should emulate the Australian colonies and draw up a constitution in as much detail as possible, designed to meet all possible objections so that the British Government would have difficulty in disagreeing with it. Before the constitution was

[12] *Ibid.*, P/C/F/49, C. T. C. Taylor to Welensky, 3 February 1949.
[13] *Ibid.*, 17/24, Report of the Conference of Delegates from Northern and Southern Rhodesia and Nyasaland, Victoria Falls, 16 & 17 February 1949 (typescript).

referred to London, a referendum could establish the support of the people. The task, he said, would have been immeasurably easier if amalgamation, rather than federation, was being considered, but he knew that the Northern Rhodesians and the Nyasalanders thought it worthless to discuss amalgamation "on account of the propaganda that has been done among the indigenous Africans, and, therefore, that Native policy, or rather Native administration must loom large in our discussions".

Just as Taylor had predicted, Huggins claimed that the burden of providing for a federal and three state parliaments and governments would be beyond the federation's manpower and financial resources. On the premise that the greater the number of services which were made federal, the cheaper government would be, Huggins argued that, if most functions were centralised, a commission made up of elected and nominated members could be appointed to deal with African affairs on a provincial basis. As the federal government would be responsible for internal as well as external security, it would have overall control of all policy except in regard to the African's domestic affairs, but there was no reason why the law might not differ in the territories. He denied, however, that there had ever been an African policy, as distinct from a European policy, because "you cannot have a policy for individual human beings; you might think that you have one but, if there was much in it, you could never carry it out in the constant change of human relationship". What was usually meant, he explained, was the utilisation of the land by Africans, as employment in industry involved the European far more than the African.

Huggins found that, apart from a small elite, the Africans were incapable of using the vote and would remain so for some time. Thus any system had to be flexible to meet constantly changing conditions but, for the moment, the African would have to be ruled by a benevolent aristocracy as had happened in Britain while progress was made towards full democracy. The African should be grounded in local government to discover what role he could play in federal politics. All the territories would be developed but some could be more Africanised than others. Time would reveal the capabilities of the races, but experience had shown that the African could not be advanced too quickly. In the interim, Africa could not be left to waste in the hands of the indigenous and, as this part could not be allowed to be added to the desert, the African would have to be compelled to conserve the soil.

Concluding, Huggins echoed Parry by claiming that, even in Europe, the political area would have to be related to that in which the economic forces operated. In Central Africa an effective union was required for the full development of its potentialities. Central Africa, he maintained, was fortunate not to be inhibited by an internal race problem, and the races had only to go forward as partners. However, if they did not do so Western civilisation would fail, and the territories would become vassals of an Eastern Communist state. He expected objections from selfish, hypersensitive race-conscious people, but fortunately they were few in number. There would be other objections, as inevitably everyone would have to sacrifice something, but Southern Rhodesians would cheerfully accept the inconvenience of having to consider others. As Northern Rhodesia already had nominated African Members in its Legislative Council, there would have to be Africans in the federal upper house. Huggins said, however, he would not contemplate their election as, under current conditions, it would be a farce and the federal constitution had to be based on realism. To avoid discrimination, he proposed that all members of the upper house should be nominated.

He closed by saying that Welensky would propose federation, with his full support.

Welensky endorsed Huggins's statement and said he would accept Africans in the upper house even though Europeans could represent African interests more effectively. He confessed that at heart he remained an amalgamationist, but he was also a realist and knew that it was a lost cause. Amalgamation was out of the question because, whether the expressed African opinion was truly representative or of any value, it counted with the British Government. Nonetheless, there were still great advantages to be gained from unification. He had wanted to resist the introduction of the CAC, but Huggins had advised him to accept it and had been right because the experiment had proved the need for inter-territorial co-operation. Welensky then moved:

> "That this Conference advocates the Federation of Southern Rhodesia, Northern Rhodesia and Nyasaland under a constitution which will create a Federal Parliament, with such powers as are surrendered to it and which will not affect the other powers of government of the member states."

He proposed that the Conference should immediately vote on the resolution and thereafter produce a document embodying a federal constitution which Gore-Browne could place before the Africans.

However, Barrow had yet to speak. Barrow explained that the Nyasaland delegation was not as well prepared as the others because the first he had known of the Conference was when he had read the announcement in *The Rhodesia Herald*, and thus had had no time to sound public opinion. The Nyasaland Convention of Associations and the Chamber of Commerce had been consulted and had accepted Huggins's suggestion in his invitation that the Conference should merely explore the possibilities. As the Members of the Nyasaland Legislative Council were nominated by public bodies, they were bound by this decision. He promised full co-operation, but warned that he and his colleagues would have to keep open minds and would reserve their decision until the will of their people was known, as federation was impossible without African support. However, he was confident that they could secure that support.

Thomas invited others to speak before the vote on the motion was taken, and Harris took the opportunity to recount the reasons for the formation of the United Central Africa Association.

Whitehead said that everything would depend on what powers were surrendered to the federal government as, given insufficient, it would fail. In the financial field, in particular, it had to have greater powers than those currently enjoyed by the Southern Rhodesian Government, whether dominion status was granted or not. The problem of finding the men and the money for the federal government, the three state parliaments, governments and governors had also to be resolved. Southern Rhodesians, he affirmed, knew that they would have to sacrifice more of their powers than any other territory but had no doubt that federation was an absolute economic necessity. There could be no delay as economic plans had to be finalised. Whitehead thought that "what we have to prove to the United Kingdom is that they, themselves, will simply be holding up the whole development of Central Africa if they refuse to allow this movement to proceed and that holding up the economic development of any area cannot be for the benefit of the African inhabitants". It was imperative, too, to build up the European population to create the basis of a dominion or the "forces which have resulted in Europeans leaving the Continent of Asia will come here". He could not see why agreement on federation should not be reached that year.

After the motion was carried unanimously, Welensky suggested that the Conference should next consider a list of non-controversial subjects which could be given to the federal government. He read aloud an excerpt from the *Encyclopaedia Britannica* which listed the powers held by the Australian Federal Government. Amongst these were: internal and external trade and commerce; some taxation, as the Federal Government had to finance the services which it was providing; the power to borrow money; posts and telegraphs; defence; census and statistics; currency, and a range of financial and social measures. Welensky asked for the Conference's reactions before he continued, reminding it that Gore-Browne had to have something to sell to the Africans.

Huggins appreciated the Northern Rhodesian difficulties, and accepted that the Australian model was probably the most suitable and certainly better than the Canadian. However, in view of the difference in functions of the existing three territorial Governments, he felt that the transfer of certain powers to the federal government, leaving everything else to the states, "is going to leave too much in the air".

He agreed that the Conference could accept a list of subjects to be transferred, but warned that sufficient power had to be given for the financial and manpower resources to be able to support the new structure. Important, too, was that "if you have half in half — if the federal government has half the powers and leaves the other half to the States everybody will be trying to get into the Federal Parliament because it sounds grander and you will have trouble in getting members to sit in the local Parliament. It may be a farce".

To conserve resources, he had a suggestion to make, which he claimed he had written down while flying up that morning, and he repeated that the bulk of the powers should be given to the federal government and the residue to partially elected and nominated local commissions. He believed something novel was required and could be condoned if the principles of parliamentary government were preserved at federal level.

No one commented that his scheme could hardly be called a federation and was truly amalgamation in thin disguise. Instead the Conference proceeded to hold what Huggins described as an auction sale of subjects which could be transferred.

Working through Welensky's list and one supplied by Huggins, the delegates paused to consider the difficulties of offering to the civil servants as good conditions as those of the Colonial Service. There was, too, the difficulty of whether the two existing legal systems could co-exist.

When "Land: alienation and re-distribution of land" came under review, Gore-Browne pronounced it to be the most delicate problem of all. He said he had learnt this to his cost when he had alarmed the Africans by his responsible government proposals in the previous year. Barrow agreed that it would prove very difficult to devise a formula which would win African co-operation and enable the British Government to accept federation.

It was a complex question because, in the northern territories, land was only sold on a leasehold basis, while in Southern Rhodesia it was freehold. In Southern Rhodesia, too, apart from African reserves and European-owned land, there were areas set aside for future expansion, designated as Crown Land. In contrast, in the North the bulk of the land was held as Native Trust Land, and Native Reserves with the Colonial Secretary as trustee. To alienate any of this land, the permission of the relevant Native Authority was required as well as the consent of the Colonial Secretary.

As, in Nyasaland in particular, the Native Authorities had been of late resisting applications on the most frivolous of grounds, the Conference was anxious to introduce some machinery whereby land for development could be acquired when it was in the interests of the Africans or the federation as a whole. Huggins thought that the Conference could offer the safeguard of writing African rights into the constitution and providing that any alienation of their land would have to be sanctioned by the consent of two-thirds of the federal parliament. However, Gore-Browne warned that he did "not believe we have a chance of getting either the acceptance of the African or the acceptance of the Imperial Government unless we stick exactly to what we have got now, which vests land in the Secretary of State, with those provisions for alteration. I regard that as fundamental".

To clarify their ideas, the chairman asked the delegates if land was to be a federal or a state subject, and it was accepted as the latter. However, Whitehead pointed to the anomaly that the states would refer directly to the Secretary of State on questions of land and not to the federal government when the latter, being the possessor of dominion status, would be entirely independent of the British Government. The Conference thereupon decided to refer the issue to a sub-committee.

Likewise, in the afternoon, "Justice" and "Social Services" were left to sub-committees. "Social Services" in particular presented difficulties as it seemed necessary to avoid centralising them so as not to lose close contact with the people being served. Yet the level of services would have to be equalised in the federation and would be more costly than that currently provided.

Continuing, the delegates decided that "Police" and "Mental Health" should be federal subjects. Then the chairman asked if there was anything that the delegates wished to raise, and Welensky responded, saying it was necessary to issue a statement which would reassure the northern Africans that their rights would be guaranteed. He wanted, if possible, to secure African support because it would greatly assist the federal cause. The chairman agreed that this was necessary if the sanction of the British Government was ever to be obtained, but Huggins pointed out that they had agreed to go as far as they could on the question of African rights while not forging unbreakable chains. He felt there was no need for detail on a method of guaranteeing the rights, as a simple statement of intention would suffice. Southern Rhodesians, he averred, had thought of reviewing only one of the privileges which their Africans enjoyed.

He explained that his Party proposed "that no more natives should be put on the Voters' Roll for fifteen years and during that time we shall push on with local native government and then Parliament can consider what is the best way of getting more direct native representation. As I have told the natives over and over again, I don't mind natives who really represent natives coming to see me and taking part in the Government but until there is a tremendous change in the native people in this country, we have not the slightest intention of handing over the administration to them. That is we shall never give them a majority in the local Parliament. I cannot see what the end will be". Thus he did not want to say that there would never be any interference, although it seemed that the northern policy on land was acceptable.

Welensky wondered how they could express this. He said he was a realist and he knew that they had to declare that they were prepared to honour the existing guarantees of African rights. Huggins replied that they could say that they had no intention of interfering at local level, but Beckett felt that this was an overstatement because a categorical declaration was needed that the guarantees made to Africans would be honoured until the local governments, on which the Africans would be represented, decided that change was necessary. Gore-Browne thought that this was suitable as the African was fundamentally concerned about the prospect of any adjustment of the *status quo* regarding his land, the position of the Chiefs, the introduction of pass laws or an industrial colour bar. However, Huggins argued that they had to look to when there might be policies which they would want to apply overall. Welensky replied that the safeguard then was that the state government would have to decide to implement the policies and, if it did, the African would have to concur. The observers suggested that a commission composed of equal numbers of Europeans and Africans could be appointed to sit in judgment on any proposals for change. Huggins rejected this because he had never succeeded in persuading the few capable Africans to take an interest in public affairs, and predicted that those who would come forward would be useless and would only make the commission's task impossible. The delegates returned to Beckett's suggestion, and proposed to make a statement to that effect upon the morrow.

The chairman asked if any issue had been ignored, and provoked Huggins to claim that the Conference had been avoiding the important question of whether it was desirable to seek dominion status for the federation. He assumed that to satisfy everyone the Conference would have to ask the British Government for that status, although he preferred the status of Southern Rhodesia until the federation was ready to become a dominion. Whitehead agreed, and pointed out how expensive it would be if the federation had not only to be responsible for the conduct of its external relations but for its defence, in addition to contributing to the defence of the Empire. Huggins was anxious, however, for the machinery for change in the federal constitution to be similar to that in the North America Act. Neither Welensky nor Barrow viewed the issue as "burning", though they hoped that federation would mean a lessening of their contact with the Colonial Secretary. The meeting accepted that dominion status should be a long-term objective because, as Whitehead pointed out, "the reservations of the Constitution will never be effective. We are bound to prevail if it came to a showdown. The only sanctions which could be imposed would be financial ones".

They discussed next the question of timing: whether the referendum should be held before the British Government was approached, or whether there should be constitutional negotiations first so that a finalised scheme could be presented to the people. Huggins preferred the former because "then it would be a very grave responsibility for Whitehall to take [*sic*] to thwart the wishes of the three territories".

The holding of a referendum, however, was deemed to be impossible in Northern Rhodesia because the Africans were not enfranchised, and in Nyasaland because there was no elective system. While Barrow offered no solution for Nyasaland, Welensky thought that a referendum could be held while African opinion was sounded through their Councils.

They returned to the federal constitution and agreed immediately on a bi-cameral legislature with the upper house containing both elected and nominated members, including Africans. After some debate, they accepted Huggins's suggestion that the lower house should seat approximately 50 European elected members, but had some difficulty in deciding on the territorial allocation of seats. Welensky proposed that Nyasaland should be given five seats to accord with the ratio of territorial populations. Hadlow preferred that they used a basic ratio of Southern Rhodesia having ten seats when Northern Rhodesia was given seven and Nyasaland three. Cooke suggested the Australian formula of giving one seat for every 3 000 head of population, which he calculated would give Southern Rhodesia 35 seats, Northern Rhodesia 15, and Nyasaland five. Whitehead agreed because he maintained that Southern Rhodesia should have at least 35 members as it had 47 000 registered voters and Northern Rhodesia only 7 000. He would allow Northern Rhodesia twelve to 15 seats and Nyasaland five.

This ratio, 35:15:5, proved to be acceptable to Welensky. Barrow hesitated because he wanted Nyasaland to be strongly represented at federal level, yet he wondered if it had sufficient men of calibre to serve its own legislature. Moreover, though the Conference generally agreed that the dominance of the federal lower house by Southern Rhodesia was of no significance as men would be elected on party not territorial affiliations, Barrow warned that the Imperial Government would reject this ratio on the grounds that Nyasaland had the largest African population. Furthermore, the British Government would maintain "that they are handing over two and a half million natives to Southern Rhodesia, and that is, in fact, what will be happening".

Huggins thought that the northern territories could well be offered two ministers without portfolio who would reside in Northern Rhodesia and Nyasaland and only come south for meetings and parliamentary sessions. The

Conference agreed that a sub-committee should examine the constitution using, as a basis for territorial representation, the ratio of 35:15:5.

The next question was what role would the state legislatures play, but Huggins felt that they should wait for the sub-committees to report because everything depended on what powers were given to the federal government. The result might be that the states would need little more than a chairman. Barrow disagreed, arguing that, as Nyasaland's representation in the federal parliament was small despite the size of its population, considerable powers would have to be left in state hands if federation was to be possible. The African had been given an increasing say in local affairs and would never agree to exchange it for nominated representation in the federal upper house.

L. M. N. Hodson from Southern Rhodesia then raised an issue, which was to be hotly debated on the next day, by asking what would be the role of the Secretary of State in local government if the territorial legislatures were left unreformed. Welensky could see no difficulties as the Secretary of State, like the territorial Governments themselves, would surrender those powers which would be allocated to the federal government. Then, in answer to Huggins's oft-repeated claim that they would not be able to afford the maintenance of the territorial Governments as well as the federal government, Welensky revealed that, in fact, the Northern Rhodesian Legislative Council only cost the taxpayer £17 000 a year.

The subject was pursued no further that day and the proceedings terminated with the appointment of sub-committees to examine the problems posed by the social services and taxation, the land rights of Europeans and Africans in the three territories, the judiciary, and the composition of the federal upper and lower houses.

On the morrow, 17 February, the conference considered the Report of the Constitutional and Judicial Sub-Committee. R. J. Morton, Southern Rhodesia's Attorney-General, the Sub-Committee's chairman, reported that the Australian Constitution had been chosen as a model, and accordingly the legislative power would be vested in the King, represented by a governor-general, a senate, and a house of representatives. The senate would seat 15 members, five from each of the territories, and the latter would decide whether their senators would be elected or nominated. The federal parliament would be able to increase or reduce the size of the senate, provided the basic ratio of 5:5:5 remained constant. The senators would serve for six years, with half of them retiring mid-way through the session. The senate would be able to return bills to the house of representatives for amendment, though, in the case of money bills, it could only suggest amendment. There was a provision for joint sessions of the houses in the event of disagreement. The royal assent would be given or withheld or the legislation could be reserved for the King's pleasure.

In regard to the size of the lower house, the Sub-Committee had concluded that 100 Africans should equal one European, which would yield a ratio for the division of seats, between the territories, of five for Southern Rhodesia, two for Northern Rhodesia and one for Nyasaland. There was no recommendation of a precise number of seats but, as Southern Rhodesia would want at least 30, the ratio of 5:2:1 would give a total membership of 48. Some of the

Sub-Committee thought this would waste manpower and make the federal parliament too costly. There had been no time to discuss electoral qualifications or those needed for MPs, but advantage was seen in having a separate federal electoral roll. Common citizenship might also be considered.

The lack of time meant also that there were only general recommendations on the judiciary. Indeed, the Sub-Committee did not disturb the *status quo*, and their federal supreme court hardly differed from the existing Rhodesia and Nyasaland Court of Appeal. Judicial power in the federation would be vested in a supreme court. The federal parliament would prescribe the number of judges who would be appointed by the governor-general. The supreme court would have original jurisdiction on the interpretation of constitutional and federal law, with appeal to the Privy Council. It would serve as a court of appeal — the Privy Council being the final one — in all criminal cases, and in civil cases in Northern Rhodesia and Nyasaland. For the moment, until reviewed by the federal parliament, Southern Rhodesian civil cases would continue to be referred to the South African Appellate Division.

Asked for his opinion, Huggins claimed he could say little until he knew what powers would be given to the federal government. Southern Rhodesia was intending to increase the size of its legislature to 40 seats and, if most functions were given to the federal parliament, it would want to be represented there by 40 members. He warned that, unless the federal government was given considerable powers, the Southern Rhodesians would reject the scheme.

Welensky agreed that everything would turn on the allocation of functions, but he was disappointed to hear Huggins reiterate that the scheme would founder unless the central government dominated. He called on the Conference to face the realities. He would dearly love to see amalgamation, but that was impossible. Though he knew they would not get all they were hoping for when federating, they would get something and, however limited it might be, they should grasp it. As the Conference's time was limited and the question complex, he suggested that they should appoint a standing committee to work on the constitution. The resolution, however, could be passed.

Barrow and Sir Miles Thomas agreed with Welensky but, when Thomas asked Morton to propose the adoption of the Report, Huggins interrupted with an outburst directed at the northern delegates: "If you are frightened of the Colonial Office we are frightened of our electors."

Welensky retorted that he had amply demonstrated in the past year how little he feared the Colonial Office and indeed he viewed the Conference as an opportunity to devise machinery to rid the northern territories ultimately of it. However, he asked: "Do I understand the Prime Minister, in fact, to say that if we can't get the whole loaf we throw three-quarters of it away?"

Huggins replied that he meant that the loaf had to be big enough to tempt the Southern Rhodesian electorate. This, Welensky averred, they could provide, but real progress was dependent on establishing the precise functions of the federal government.

When one of the observers questioned again whether it was advisable for the federation to have constituent states controlled by the Colonial Office,

Welensky remarked that it appeared that the delegates had not seemed to realise that the subject under discussion was not amalgamation. In a federation, he explained, common services would be established but everything else would be left to the states, and they would not interfere with each other. The northern territories were anxious to supplant the Colonial Office, and federation was a step in that direction. However, they had to carry their African populations with them and that, he warned, implied caution. Moreover, in practice, the Secretary of State interfered little in the daily administration of the territories. He would surrender control of the services which became federal, but otherwise the structures of the northern Governments would remain as they were. The services run by the federal and state governments would be entirely divorced from each other.

Welensky's concern about practicalities and the possible reactions of the British Government and the northern Africans, dismayed some of the Southern Rhodesians who thought it was groundless. One of them, C. M. Newman, claimed he had discussed Central African affairs with a member of the British Government who had "simply barked back at me, 'In matters of this kind the Colonial Office will do as it is told'". The Conference had forgotten that it had sympathisers in Britain and had tended "to see how we can whittle down our just desires and our aims to placate the Secretary of State. I suggest we give him a nice, juicy joint — not the bare bones, because he will get his sandpaper out and polish it still further".

The Rhodesians, therefore, Newman argued, should merely transmit their own and not African opinion to the British Government. They should use their friends in the British Parliament and not over-estimate the influence of the Secretary of State as this opportunity might not re-occur.

Although the chairman wished to move on, Welensky chose to reply to Newman. He noted that Newman had said that he did not care a fig for the Secretary of State, neither did he, but he and others had responsibilities which Newman did not have. Newman, he alleged, had given the impression that if amalgamation were unobtainable, the attempt to unify should be abandoned. Newman interjected to deny this. Continuing, Welensky turned to the question of whether the African loomed too large in the thoughts of the northern delegates. He was well aware of the value of African opinion and he knew, too, that "if the Colonial Office wanted amalgamation the African would be told it was a good thing and the next thing they would want it but the United Kingdom has persistently refused any suggestion of amalgamation, and that is what you are advocating".

He questioned the value of their British friends because they had left Huggins and himself to keep the issue alive. The Rhodesians had to take the initiative and he hoped that "by being provocative we are going to get great advantages. I believe we can bring about the first stages. I believe the thing is inevitable, that we will get what we want, but don't let us spoil it".

Beckett concurred, and argued that it was imperative to devise a formula which would not evoke a protest from the Africans and an adverse reaction from the British Government.

Hodson came to Newman's defence and said that they should not be too pessimistic about British attitudes because it was likely that they would accept that the basic motive for unification was efficiency, even though a federation of a self-governing colony and two protectorates was unique.

The chairman intervened to propose the adoption of the Report on the constitution and Welensky responded by moving it. They acted in vain because Huggins insisted that it could not be accepted until they knew the precise powers and size of the federal parliament. He returned to the question of the reserved legislation as he had understood Welensky to say, with Barrow's support, that this would be the responsibility of the states over whom the Secretary of State would retain the power of veto. He believed that the British Government would prefer to deal with the federal government with regard to the reservations because it would represent a fusion of the interests of the three territories which would exert a moderating influence on each other. All Southern Rhodesia wanted was that the Commonwealth Relations Office — the successor to the Dominions Office — and not the Colonial Office should be responsible for the reserved legislation. He felt that the British Government would favour a federal veto over state legislation, but he doubted the feasibility of federation because, though the federal government would be responsible for both external and internal security, the state governments would be subordinate not to it but to the Secretary of State 6 000 miles away. Thus it was necessary to know the powers of the federal government.

Welensky doubted the need to be pessimistic as he believed they could achieve enough to justify the establishment of a federation. He reminded Huggins that they had discussed the powers of the federal government on the previous day.

To avoid stalemate, Huggins suggested that they should interrupt the debate to hear the reports of the other sub-committees. Welensky and Barrow agreed. Whitehead produced the Report of the Sub-Committee on Taxation and Social Services, warning that the Sub-Committee had not been entirely accurate because it, too, needed to know the precise functions of the federal government. It was obvious, however, that the federal government would be expected to finance the governor-general, the federal parliament, the cabinet office, and the high commission in London. Native affairs, embracing African administration, education and agriculture — including the Southern Rhodesian Department of Native Engineering — would be a state responsibility, though, as the federal government would be charged with internal security, there would be general federal supervision. The federal government would provide the inspectorate of African labour. The poll tax should be collected by the federal government, but it was noted that the northern delegates thought that the African would prefer that it should continue to be a state function. The treasury would obviously be a federal department. Pensions would be a federal responsibility except in regard to those of state employees. The raising and servicing of loans would likewise be federal, though the states would be responsible for those relating to their assets. When refunds of revenue became necessary, the federal government would return them to the taxpayers in respect of its taxes, and the state governments would do likewise.

To be effective, the control of the cost of living would have to be federal and the audit, too, would have to be centralised. The posts and telegraph service and the central mechanical engineering department would be federal provided that the *status quo* was maintained in the northern territories where they had been considerably Africanised. Customs and excise, statistics, price control, printing and stationery, transport, archives, public relations, mining, public works, surveys, irrigation, defence and civil aviation would all be financed by the federal treasury.

The states would pay for the district courts but the federation would meet the expense of the administration of justice, the prisons, and the police, because it was responsible for internal security. The federal government would co-ordinate local government at national level but would leave the states to deal directly with the municipalities and town management boards. The federal government would support the hospitals, and the states the clinics and dispensaries. Likewise, it would maintain and build the trunk roads, and the states the remainder. European education would be entrusted to the federal government, and African education to the state in order not to alarm the northern Africans. Land and agriculture would be entirely state responsibilities for the same reason, except that the federal government would providc the research service. The public service board would only be a federal responsibility in as far as federal civil service affairs were affected.

To finance these services, the federal government would need the revenue from income tax, cutsoms and excise, petrol tax and company registration. The state governments would have the income from the poll and vehicle taxes, the general dealers and other licences and stamps. Interest on loans would accrue to the lender, whether it be the federal or state governments. In years of poor return, the federation would subsidise the state on a population basis. Whitehead calculated that thus Southern Rhodesia would be left with a yearly income of £1 500 000, and Northern Rhodesia £375 000.

Whitehead was praised for this report and, indeed, Welensky rued that they had not heard it earlier and thereby saved much time in debate. Then Welensky was asked for his wording of the statement to be made on African rights and land appropriation. He read:

> "It is agreed that all existing rights now enjoyed by Africans in Northern Rhodesia and Nyasaland shall be guaranteed by the Federal Government, and that any change affecting such rights can be effected only with the consent of the local legislature concerned."

This, Welensky claimed, put across their intention and yet did not interfere with Southern Rhodesia's position.

Huggins, however, was not satisfied. He objected to the omission of mention of Southern Rhodesia and to the specification that the consent of the local legislature would be needed. Thus the delegates found themselves back in the midst of the earlier controversy as Huggins went on to repeat that he wanted reserved bills to proceed from the state legislature to the federal parliament for approval and, if necessary, the federal government would fight it out with the British Government. He maintained that the federal government had to dominate because it was not feasible to have a federation in which the state governments were not responsible to the central government but to the far-distant Secretary of State. Welensky was grateful to know Huggins's precise attitude and proposed to agree so as not to wreck the Conference. It was important, he claimed, that they should at least agree within the Conference, even though they might achieve nothing outside it.

Huggins then contributed a form of words produced by Whitehead:

> "That legislation of a reserved nature could only arise in the State Parliament, but must pass all its stages in the Federal Parliament before transmission to the Secretary of State."

This, Huggins stated, emphasised his earlier point, and he was still confident that a federal request to alter reserved legislation would carry more weight than a provincial one. Barrow interrupted to say, and the chairman confirmed, that the Secretary of State's veto would then pass to the federal government. Huggins maintained, though, that this made the constitution less of a Heath Robinson one because within the federation the Secretary of State would not be the supreme power. At this point the debate was suspended, the Constitutional Report was accepted, and the Conference adjourned for lunch.

In the afternoon, Barrow sought further clarification — whether the power to veto and to reserve legislation would lie with the federal government. Huggins confirmed that it would, but he wondered if they were talking at cross-purposes. As far as the Southern Rhodesian delegation was concerned, he said, the only significant piece of reserved legislation was a law which imposed a disability on an African but not on a European. Such a law would be subjected to far greater scrutiny by a federal parliament with its responsibilities to its electorate, than by a Secretary of State. Answering Welensky, Huggins said that there was no intention of giving the federal government a veto over territorial affairs outside the reserved legislation.

At last, Welensky said, he understood Huggins's view on this crucial point. Huggins maintained, however, that it was unnatural to expect the federal government to stand entirely aloof from an argument between a state and the Secretary of State. He expected that African rights would be written into the constitution, and to alter them a state would have to make an application to the federal government which would accept it or refuse it.

Welensky thought it was timely to warn the Conference again about harming their cause by reaching for the unattainable. He would be guided by wiser men but he did not want to risk rejection of the scheme in Northern Rhodesia. He doubted claims that the British Government favoured federation as it had remained silent on the issue. He warned: "We will have to screw it out of them . . . I was in England four months ago and I talked to the Secretary of State for the Colonies and other Ministers, and I saw no anxiety on their part to meet us in federation. I believe we will have to fight them every inch."

Gore-Browne confirmed that Creech Jones had refused to express an opinion on federation. As for the scheme as it now stood, Gore-Browne pleaded for time to consider it, as it represented "a considerable spring-round from what I understood was implied by federation". Thus he would tell the

Northern Rhodesian Africans to keep quiet, to think the question over, and to ask for all the information possible on the proposals. He affirmed that the Northern Rhodesian delegation was not frightened of African opinion. If he was convinced that federation was in the interests of the Africans, he would assist in realising it, however much the Africans disapproved. Nonetheless, he claimed that the Northern Rhodesians and Nyasalanders knew that for success "we must leave no stone unturned to make things as clear as we can to the limited intelligence of the African, and if possible to get him in to help us with the show".

The Conference looked again at the question of finance, and Whitehead was asked how the states would be supported. The exact allocation of revenue, he explained, would depend upon what services the states had to provide, but they would be given enough to live upon, and the federal government would be empowered to make grants to meet extraordinary expenditure. He proposed that they should take a pragmatic view: deficits would be met as they arose, and development plans would be shared. He reassured the Northern Rhodesians that existing reserves would be allocated to support plans which had already been formulated, and accordingly most of Northern Rhodesia's reserves would not be touched. The most important immediate step was to pool their major external finances to improve their standing in the London market.

When Whitehead had finished speaking, but before his report was accepted, Welensky produced two paragraphs from the Australian Act:

> Paragraph 99, "The Commonwealth shall not, by any law or regulation of trade, commerce or revenue, give preference to one state or any part thereof."

And:

> Paragraph 101, "There shall be an Inter-State Commission with such powers of adjudication and administration as Parliament deems necessary for the execution and maintenance, within the Commonwealth, of the provision of this Constitution relating to trade and commerce, and of all the laws made thereunder."

The Conference agreed to adopt both these paragraphs and the Report of the Sub-Committee on Finance.

F. E. Harris produced the last of the Sub-Committees' reports, that on "Land and Agriculture". In doing so, he warned that he, the chairman, did not agree with his Committee's findings. The Report recommended that the federal constitution should reaffirm and accept all existing guarantees of tenure of land by Africans and Europeans. Agriculture would ultimately be a federal subject, but at first all its aspects except research should remain under state control. There should be, however, a federal board to effect coordination between the states. Harris accepted the recommendation on land as being necessary, lest there be African unrest. Indeed, he wanted to ensure that the guarantees extended to the Southern Rhodesian Africans. However, he and several other Southern Rhodesians wanted European agriculture to be centralised because it was Southern Rhodesia's major industry, and therefore the farmers were politically most important.

Whitehead explained that Southern Rhodesia had twin departments of agriculture because the African needed more supervision than the European farmer would tolerate, and an attempt was being made to turn the African into an efficient agriculturist to meet the needs of the growing population. Whitehead argued that, as agriculture was ultimately to be a federal responsibility, there was no reason why European agriculture at least might not be federalised. Becket explained that the Sub-Committee had not wished to prejudice the Conference's aims. Hadlow, in support, pointed out that in Nyasaland the Europeans occupied five per cent of the land, and the federal scheme had to be sold to 2 500 000 highly suspicious Africans whose opinion would influence the Imperial Government.

The delegates decided that this and other outstanding matters should be examined after the Conference and, when they met again at the April meeting of the CAC, a steering committee should be set up to direct the campaign for federation. They briefly considered the question of the Barotse, whose rights they acknowledged would have to be recognised. Huggins hoped that the federation might be given a mandate over Barotseland for reasons of soil-conservation alone. Finally, there was agreement on the need for a propaganda campaign among the Africans.

Thomas praised the delegates for their workmanlike effort in achieving a *modus operandi* and in turn was complimented by Huggins, Welensky and Barrow on his able display as chairman. Barrow promised to give Nyasaland a fair report on federation, and the Conference thereupon concluded.

Nothing was published after the Conference — the minutes were circulated privately to the delegates and to the Secretaries of State — which left the public with only two Press statements from which to glean the delegates' intentions. Furthermore, these statements were made to seem curious by the decision to debate in secret after the opening speeches and the preliminary debate. The initial survey of federal subjects was given in full, together with a resumé of the speeches which quoted Huggins's rejection of the concept of a policy for Africans distinct from that for the other inhabitants, and his and Welensky's ideas of having only nominated African representation in the upper house and none in the lower. The second statement gave no details of the later debates, and merely revealed that, in the final session, the Conference had laid down the steps to secure federation. It announced that a committee of technical experts would be appointed to frame the constitution and to plan the financial arrangements. When this committee had reported, a further conference would be convened to consider its findings. There would follow a referendum in the three territories, and a further meeting to decide upon the method of approach to the British Government. The statement revealed that, in agreeing to this, the Conference had unanimously agreed that the rights of the civil servants in the three territories would be fully protected, that all existing land rights enjoyed by Africans in Northern Rhodesia and Nyasaland would be guaranteed by the federal government, and that any change affecting those rights would require the consent of the territorial legislature concerned. Agricultural research and major development would be a federal responsibility, and the name to be adopted for the federation and the position of Barotseland in the overall scheme would be further considered.

After the Conference, Sir Miles Thomas repeated his admiration for the pragmatic approach of the delegates and their efficiency in producing a plan. He spoke in admiration of the team-work which Huggins and Welensky had displayed, the latter the perfect complement to the former. His exaggeration was undoubtedly aimed at promoting the cause.[14] Indeed, on 6 March, he published an article entitled "The Dominion of Capricornia" in which he stressed the need for effective inter-territorial co-operation so that the region's vast mineral resources could be exploited.[15]

By contrast, Gore-Browne was brutally accurate when he wrote, some time after the event: "Almost every mistake possible was made. Welensky was certainly not to blame — indeed, he was the only person present who came down to the meeting with a clear idea of what was wanted." Gore-Browne criticised Huggins for making a public speech which was liable to frighten any African who read it. The Conference compounded this error by immediately going into secret session, and thus "the suspicions of the Africans were raised to fever-heat — no difficult matter when racial politics are concerned. From then onwards the harm was done".[16]

Another fatal error, in Gore-Browne's estimation, was not to include Africans in the territorial delegations when it would have been easy to bring the two Northern Rhodesian African Members of the Legislative Council to the Victoria Falls.

In fact, the potentially most hostile element to federation, the Northern Rhodesian African National Congress, had sought in January a place at the Conference on the grounds that "we are scared of the European threats and we must know our position before we decide whether for or against the federation issue".[17]

This, and a similar request from a Coloured organisation called the Eurafrican Federation of Central Africa,[18] was addressed to the Northern Rhodesian Government which, arguing that it was uninvited, passed the requests to Welensky. Welensky had asked Huggins, who was convening the Conference and was therefore the host, if he intended to include Africans in his delegation. Huggins had replied that the Conference was limited to the leaders of the established political parties in the territories and, moreover, it was unnecessary to make any special arrangement for the representation of Africans, as in Southern Rhodesia they were free to join any political party. Welensky, who rightly recalls in his *4 000 Days* that, in any case, what the Conference could have achieved was limited by its unofficial nature, acknowledges that perhaps it would have been wiser to have included "a direct

[14] Taylor, *The Rhodesian*, *op. cit.*, p. 108.
[15] L. H. Gann, *A History of Northern Rhodesia: Early Days to 1953* (London, 1964), p. 398.
[16] Taylor, *The Rhodesian*, *op. cit.*, p. 109.
[17] R. Hall, *Zambia* (London, 1965), pp. 146-147.
[18] Welensky Papers, WE 7, P/C/F/49, R. A. D. Snapper to Chief Secretary, Northern Rhodesia Government, 12 March 1949.

expression of African opinion". He had thought so at the time but had only been able to persuade Huggins to allow Gore-Browne to represent the African, which he did ably.[19]

Given the northern Africans' unswerving resistance to date to every proposal on unification with Southern Rhodesia, no one should have been surprised when in early March Sam K. K. Mwase, who had succeeded Charles Matinga as president of the Nyasaland African Congress, rejected federation in colourful terms, claiming that thereby pass laws would be introduced, the Africans' economic life would be crippled and their family ties broken.[20]

In Northern Rhodesia, Gore-Browne toured explaining the Conference, and returned conscious of an unyielding hostility to the idea of federation.[21] He had taken with him the two African Members of the Legislative Council, and together they had proclaimed that they had not yet reached a personal decision on the merits of the scheme. However, as Richard Hall has revealed, their audiences had. At a meeting in Chingola, discussion lasted five hours, and in the end federation had been unanimously rejected.[22] However, in the Legislative Council on 17 March, Gore-Browne claimed that the Africans had generally responded to his plea to refrain from public comment until they were confident that they understood the proposals. He acknowledged that there had been some intemperate statements and that some — what he termed "thinking" — Africans had questioned the need for change when the current system so adequately met their aspirations. He asked the Government to assist him in pleading for moderation. Furthermore, he felt that it would assist if the Government would proclaim its attitude to federation, as there were three territories and great issues involved.[23]

On the previous day, however, the Governor, Sir Gilbert Rennie, had already adopted a neutral line in his opening speech to the Legislative Council: he claimed it was too early for him to comment, and was clearly reserving that task for Creech Jones who would visit in April.[24] Welensky, welcoming the opportunity to discuss the federal issue with Creech Jones, argued a case for federation on economic grounds and asked the Africans to consider the future seriously. He insisted that the soundest possible guarantees had been offered with regard to African rights, and promised that every effort would be made to consult African opinion. He proposed to consult Huggins about the technical committee which would examine the constitution.[25] He reserved, however, his comments on African opposition for Cooke and Huggins. Blaming the Government, he said: "African opinion is hardening against Federation . . . merely because the Government have not indicated a line. If the Secretary of State would have the guts to say that Federation is good, the natives here would welcome it with open arms. The

[19] Sir Roy Welensky, *Welensky's 4 000 Days* (London, 1964), p. 27.
[20] P. Short, *Banda* (London, 1974), p. 57.
[21] Taylor, *The Rhodesian*, *op. cit.*, p. 109.
[22] Hall, *Zambia*, *op. cit.*, p. 147.
[23] NR *Debates* (Lusaka), Col. 43, 17 March 1949.
[24] *Ibid.*, Col. 6, 16 March 1949.
[25] *Ibid.*, Col. 21 f., 17 March 1949.

fact ... is, the African, because there is a lack of direction, assumes the United Kingdom Government don't want it."[26]

Welensky revealed, too, to Huggins that there were some reservations about the federal plan in European political circles in Northern Rhodesia, but he was confident that these would disappear in the course of the referendum campaign.[27] In fact, in Southern Rhodesia, the United Central Africa Association was already busying itself with that campaign.[28] Welensky noted that in Britain, despite an attack by Dr Rita Hinden, there had been some favourable comments.[29] Indeed, Monica Wingate, chairman of the National Council for Federal Union, and John Boyd-Orr, president of the World Movement for World Federal Government, welcomed the proposal. The Conservative Party's Joint East and Central Africa Board claimed that federation was the key to the area's security and social and economic advance, and felt that the uncomprehending Africans and the constitutional difficulties should not be allowed to affect the welfare of all. The Board believed that for the foreseeable future European leadership was required, and that the devolution of power to Africans could not be attempted yet.[30] Although Creech Jones stated in the Commons on 1 March that he could not comment on an unofficial conference, the minutes of which he had not seen,[31] he viewed the Conference's conclusion sufficiently seriously to visit Central Africa.

Welensky did not yet know that, on 28 February, a small group of Africans living in Britain, including Harry Nkumbula who was then studying at the London School of Economics with the assistance of the Northern Rhodesian Government, met at Dr Hastings Banda's house in Brondesbury Park and decided that, as federation was not in the Africans' interest, it had to be rejected. Banda and Nkumbula were delegated the task of framing a memorandum on the case against federation, which would prove significant in the moulding of African opinion.[32]

After the Conference, Welensky kept in close correspondence with Huggins, learning that the Southern Rhodesian Government would take over the federal campaign from the unofficial bodies some six weeks before the referendum. Huggins and Welensky decided to meet Creech Jones together.[33] Welensky's other correspondent of the moment was L. S. Glover of Gaberones who, as promised, proposed in the Bechuanaland European Advisory Council that the possibilities of joining the Rhodesias should be explored, and had been nominated to meet the Rhodesians.[34] Welensky welcomed this, but

[26] Welensky Papers, WE 7, P/C/104/F, Welensky to S. Cooke, 27 March 1949; same to Sir Godfrey Huggins, same date.
[27] *Ibid.*, Welensky to Huggins, 5 March 1949.
[28] *Ibid.*, P/C/F/49, Circular letter by A. S. Bright, 28 February 1949; (S. Cooke) to Welensky, 2 March 1949; Cooke to Welensky, 14 March 1949.
[29] *Ibid.*, Welensky to Huggins, 27 March 1949.
[30] *Ibid.*, P/C/104/F, Chairman, JE & CA Board to Welensky, 2 March 1949.
[31] House of Commons *Hansard* (London), Vol. 462, Written Answers, Col. 38, 1 March 1949; G. B. Jones, *Britain and Nyasaland* (London, 1964), p. 127.
[32] Short, *Banda, op. cit.*, p. 57.
[33] Welensky Papers, WE 7, P/C/104/F, Welensky to Huggins, 5 March 1949; P/C/F/49, Huggins to Welensky, 15 March 1949.
[34] *Ibid.*, P/C/F/49, L. S. Glover to Welensky, 14 March 1949.

warned Glover that, because of South Africa's claim to Bechuanaland in the Act of Union, Huggins might have to handle this issue delicately.[35]

Welensky's main preoccupation, however, was not the federal issue. In late 1948 he had given notice of a motion which would seek to have a tax imposed on the mineral royalties. This provoked the British South Africa Company's chairman, Sir Dougal Malcolm, to accuse Welensky publicly on 4 March 1949 of being motivated by envy of the hard-won prosperity of others. He drew Welensky's attention to a British confirmation in 1939 on the validity of the Company's possession of the royalties. Welensky took up the challenge in the Legislative Council on 24 March, questioning the validity of the British judgment, and establishing that his motive was to ensure that Northern Rhodesia's development would not be hampered by a lack of finance. The motion was seconded by the Reverend H. Kasokolo, and the Council decided by 13 votes to one to tax the royalties.[36]

The shareholders' reaction was such that Malcolm was forced to meet Welensky in Bulawayo in April to seek an alternative solution. The discussions were renewed in London in late July under the chairmanship of A. B. Cohen (later Sir Andrew), a senior official in the Colonial Office who was soon to play a significant role in securing British acquiescence to federation in Central Africa. The Company's case rested on its possession of the mineral concessions, and Welensky did not believe that the suzerainty of the conceder, Paramount Chief Lewanika, had extended over the whole of what became Northern Rhodesia. Welensky was gambling as he claimed to have the full backing of the unofficial Members when, in fact, he had only their qualified support. His bluff was not called, and he won. On 9 August, it was announced that the Company's mineral rights would revert to the people of Northern Rhodesia in 1986, and until then the Company would contribute 20 per cent of its net earnings from the royalties to the Northern Rhodesian Government. In return the Company would be exempt from any special tax of any variety.[37] Some £30 000 000 accrued to the Government before President Kaunda of Zambia terminated the agreement.

Although Welensky had not entirely neglected the federal cause, little progress was being made. Creech Jones arrived in April and, though the Rhodesian leaders expected to gain little from their negotiations with him, his abrasive presence at least brought some of the waverers to their side. He had arrived in a suspicious mood as he had been asked if he would object to the Attorney-Generals of the three territories examining the proposal to identify any constitutional obstacles, and had interpreted this as an attempt to commit him to federation. Thus he had allowed them to do so informally on the clear understanding that this could not be seen as a step towards the federal goal.

He met Huggins and Welensky in Lusaka on 9 April and heard their case that, because the CAC had failed, federation was a necessity. Welensky, playing the more aggressive role, had demanded that the British Government take the initiative by convening an official conference. Creech Jones resisted,

[35] *Ibid.*, Welensky to L. S. Glover, (March 1949).
[36] NR *Debates* (Lusaka), Col. 198 f., 24 March 1949.
[37] G. Allighan, *The Welensky Story* (London, 1962), pp. 161–186; Welensky, *4 000 Days, op. cit.*, pp. 31–32.

arguing that he could hardly persuade his Cabinet to act if he could not produce proof of the CAC's shortcomings. He talked of the necessity to maintain the integrity of the protectorates and of the need to defend African interests, and convinced Huggins and Welensky that he would be decisively swayed by African opinion. Huggins believed that Creech Jones would demand direct African representation in the federal lower house — which would be premature in Huggins's opinion — if he ever allowed discussion on the issue. Creech Jones, in turn, gathered the impression that Huggins and Welensky were determined to impede the CAC and, indeed, would be quite unscrupulous in their efforts to outmanoeuvre the British Government. Their meeting ended indecisively.[38]

A consequence of the secrecy of the proceedings at the Victoria Falls manifested itself during Creech Jones's visit, causing Welensky to deliver a public admonishment. He stated that the majority of the Europeans favoured federation, but he knew that there were rumour-mongers at work attempting to alienate them by circulating completely inaccurate and highly coloured versions of the Conference — in particular, that Southern Rhodesia had demanded "back-breaking" terms.[39]

Creech Jones also commented publicly that, as he had not received any definite proposals on federation, he could not remark on it. He added on 28 April that, however, it might be wise to consider alternative methods of ensuring inter-territorial co-ordination to the CAC but without affecting the British commitments and assurances to the Africans. His tour of Northern Rhodesia and Nyasaland, he claimed, had revealed a considerable African apprehension about unification, and he was anxious that political developments should not interfere with social and economic progress, as it was important that both territories should enjoy a period of constructive work in these fields. Permanent white settlement, he proclaimed, would have to be controlled because Northern Rhodesia was a protectorate guaranteeing certain inherent rights to the African. This meant that in agriculture, in particular, the role that the European could play was limited. Nevertheless, he maintained that, for the country's social and economic health, the European must have a permanent place and consequently British policy had been, while safeguarding African interests, to encourage a degree of European development.[40]

A storm of protest ensued in Northern Rhodesia, with the result that Creech Jones would claim to have been mis-reported by the Press, as all he had meant to say was that an uncontrolled influx of settlers could not be allowed. He was confident that Welensky had understood this and thus had misrepresented him when replying. Spurred on by a unanimous meeting in Livingstone, Welensky, on 30 April, rejected Creech Jones's statement as completely unacceptable. He recalled that, in August 1948, it had been announced that the policy of partnership had superseded that of the paramountcy of African interests. As Creech Jones had chosen to reverse that decision, Welensky proposed to seek the support of the Southern Rhodesians,

[38] Taylor, *The Rhodesian*, *op. cit.*, p. 119–120.
[39] *The Rhodesia Herald*, 17 April 1949.
[40] *Ibid.*, 29 April 1949.

the Kenyans and the South Africans if the British Government persisted in this vein. He said he would also cable Lord Winterton, a sympathiser and former Conservative Cabinet Minister, to ask him to challenge Creech Jones in the British Parliament.[41]

Creech Jones countered in a local radio broadcast on 2 May. He stated that, in fact, British policy, as far as the European settler was concerned, had not changed and that the European had a most important role to play in the economic development of the territories. Yet, he said, he was anxious to reassure the African that his rights would be safeguarded, and thus promised that the British Government would bear this in mind when any proposals for federation were forthcoming. A federal scheme would be examined carefully but he would not predict the likely British attitude towards it before seeing it.[42]

In this atmosphere of conflict, he departed for Britain. The prospects for unification seemed bleak, the hope engendered by the British Government's encouragement of the idea of federation, as an alternative to amalgamation, in late 1948 had dissipated. Yet, as Welensky recalls, at least they had learnt "without confusion or equivocation, what the differences were between our ideal and the policy of the British Government".[43]

[41] Welensky, *4 000 Days*, *op. cit.*, p. 34; *The Rhodesia Herald*, 1 May 1949.
[42] *The Rhodesia Herald*, 3 May 1949.
[43] Welensky, *4 000 Days*, *op. cit.*, p. 34.

CHAPTER FIVE

The First Victory

The Persuasion of the New Colonial Secretary to examine the Federal Solution, 1949

ALTHOUGH the Rhodesian leaders would continue their efforts to formulate a plan for federation which could be laid before their electorates and the British Government, relations with Creech Jones would deteriorate even further. Indeed, the moment would come when Huggins and Welensky would be close to despair. However, albeit inadvertently, the British electorate would come to their assistance in the general election of February 1950 by failing to return Creech Jones to the Commons. He would be replaced at the Colonial Office by a more malleable man, James Griffiths, a veteran trade unionist.

Even though their discussions with Creech Jones were fruitless, the determination of the protagonists of federation to achieve their goal was unshaken. Huggins and Welensky continued to devise terms of reference for the committee on which the Attorney-Generals and their financial advisers would serve. On 18 May 1949, Huggins informed his Parliament that a conference would be held, this time in public, once a constitutional plan was ready.[1]

Within the immediate circle of the leadership, the campaign was reviewed. It was felt that Creech Jones intended to do no more than give the Central African Council some executive powers. This was seen as a retrograde step as it would bring Southern Rhodesia, to an extent, under the aegis of the Colonial Office. Thus Creech Jones stood accused of empire-building, and an inter-departmental conflict between the Commonwealth Relations Office and the Colonial Office was thought possible. It was decided that he might be persuaded to shift his ground if the bogey of Afrikaner expansionism was further exploited. The pro-federal editor of *The Rhodesia Herald* had already co-operated during Creech Jones's visit by playing on the fear that Southern Rhodesia might be drawn into the South African orbit. Currently, and

[1] *The Rhodesia Herald*, 19 May 1949.

fortuitously, the Dutch Reformed Church had demanded that Afrikaans be taught in Southern Rhodesian schools by right, threatening that, if the Government did not comply, it would influence its congregations in the Rhodesias to strive for union with South Africa. Welensky surmised that the Afrikaner nationalists, being very astute, opposed the creation of a new dominion because it would swing the focus of development from Southern to Central Africa.[2]

This fear of Afrikaner nationalism found a place in a memorandum which Welensky sent in May to Lord Winterton for reference when campaigning for federation in the House of Lords. Welensky apprised Winterton of recent developments, expressing confidence that Creech Jones's visit had won the federal cause much European support. However, he said the Africans were opposed to federation and he thought it would be tragic if they prevented it.[3]

As if to confirm this, Dr Hastings Banda wrote to Welensky on 29 May saying that he had read of the Victoria Falls Conference with interest and alarm. He noted that the Press had claimed that the people of the three territories unanimously supported federation, and he asked who had given the delegates their mandates to discuss it. He recalled earlier correspondence with Welensky in which they had agreed to differ and he stated that "while you and, perhaps, most of the Europeans desire federation, I and most of my people certainly do not". Sharing this opinion, the Africans living in Britain had asked him and Nkumbula to express their rejection in a memorandum, a copy of which he enclosed. He expected Welensky to reject their reasons but claimed they were as valid as Welensky's.[4] Later Banda would tell Gore-Browne that he had not been prepared to wait for the full details of the scheme because he feared a trap.[5]

The core of Banda's argument was that Southern Rhodesia would dominate the federation, and thus its racial policies and attitudes would be adopted throughout, to the detriment of the African's progress and, indeed, his very existence. When it circulated in Northern Rhodesia and Nyasaland, the effect of the memorandum was so marked that Sir Gilbert Rennie would claim, in 1958, that it was largely responsible for northern African opposition to federation. Indeed, so important did he consider it, that he took the trouble to dissect the memorandum in the African Representative Council in late 1951 in order to point out its inaccurate, misleading and, in places, untruthful statements on the consequences of federation.[6]

The memorandum maintained that federation would sever the northern African's direct political and cultural ties with Britain and terminate the current British policy of educating the African towards the ultimate goal of self-government. The Africans would lose their Provincial and Representative Councils, their educational opportunities abroad, and even their right to claim British citizenship and the vote. The memorandum depicted the British people and their Government as regarding Africans as human beings

[2] Welensky Papers, WE 7, P/C/158/52, "Federation Summary", 3 May 1949.
[3] *Ibid.*, P/C/F/49, Welensky to Lord Winterton, (undated).
[4] *Ibid.*, 42/15/J, f. 1, Dr H. K. Banda to Welensky, 29 May 1949.
[5] P. Short, *Banda* (London, 1974), p. 61.
[6] Welensky Papers, 42/15, f. 94, Sir Gilbert Rennie to Welensky, 27 June 1958.

with full rights "to a dignified and refined existence". This attitude had produced the representative institutions for Africans and the appearance of Africans in the northern legislatures. Education had been improved and Africans had been found places at British institutions. The British allowed Africans to become full British citizens and, as Banda himself had done, they could join professions and even vote in British elections. By contrast, the Southern Rhodesian Europeans were portrayed in the memorandum as racialists who followed the disproved theory of racial inferiority. Huggins's recent comments were cited as evidence that the Southern Rhodesians were determined not only to discourage the African from enrolling as a voter, but were bent on denying him the vote altogether. Furthermore, Huggins and his followers were likely to allow only whites to become British subjects. In addition, it was alleged that the Southern Rhodesian Government did not allow the Africans to study overseas to prevent them from discovering the fallacy of inferiority.

The memorandum predicted that it was inevitable that Southern Rhodesia would dominate federal affairs as it was likely that federal parliamentary seats would be allocated on the basis of the ratio of territorial European populations. Thus it was likely that, as in Southern Rhodesia, though entitled to federal votes, the Africans would be dissuaded from claiming them and would be left with two nominated representatives in the upper house. (In fact, the question of the number of African seats had not been raised at the Conference.) Likewise, the memorandum claimed, the other rights of the Africans would be threatened. The Southern Rhodesian Europeans had never forgotten that they had conquered the Africans and therefore would expect them to be servile and would treat them arrogantly and contemptuously. All African advancement would be halted. The African could expect to be beaten or kicked and have no recourse to the protection of the law because magisterial attitudes would reflect those of the Southern Rhodesians. Therefore, the memorandum alleged, the African would exchange his status as a ward of the British Government for that of a slave of the Southern Rhodesian Government. As Huggins had built his political career on the Urban Areas Act, the Natives Registration Act and the Industrial Conciliation Act, it was likely that these would be adopted by the federal legislature. Europeans would be advanced in all spheres to the detriment of Africans, and the current British policy of abolishing discrimination wherever it existed was doomed.

The memorandum fastened onto recent statements by Huggins and Welensky to prove that they were unrepentant amalgamationists who had been driven by failure to adopt federation as a method of achieving their ambition. It argued that federation, too, was the only means by which the Southern Rhodesians could secure dominion status as their country was too small to claim it. They hoped to gain thereby, as had the South Africans, "an imperium over the destiny of the Africans", free of the critical influence of the British.

For these reasons, the memorandum maintained, the African refused to discuss federation. Southern Rhodesia would have to reform radically before Africans could consider federation, and the argument that African rights could be safeguarded was rejected as worthless because, once dominion status had been achieved, they would be a prey to Southern Rhodesian intentions. It was noted in this context that, at the Victoria Falls, Huggins and Welensky had expressed intentions of securing for the European the role of master while relegating the African to that of slave. Huggins, the memorandum alleged, had not even tried to conceal his contempt for Africans, doubting whether they were of the same human family (Huggins, in fact, had said that they shared a common ancestry), and claiming that they needed to be ruled by a benevolent aristocracy. There had been hope that the European attitude had changed since the Second World War, but the Conference had shown that it had not. Africans, the memorandum declared, were neither primitive nor ignorant, and should have a voice in national affairs. They were not hostile towards Europeans, and were anxious only to avoid servitude. They would join the Europeans as equal executive partners and not the juniors of the firm. Only when the northern Africans felt they were capable of playing an active and effective part in government, would they contemplate federation, and then only on the basis of universal African suffrage, common citizenship and representation. Moreover, the right to secede at any moment — when the majority of the people in any territory felt that federation was curbing their political, social or cultural progress — had to be established. Finally, the memorandum demanded the immediate union of Northern Rhodesia and Nyasaland to rejoin tribes and to benefit both territories politically, economically and socially.[7]

Welensky replied to Banda but did not bother to rebut his allegations.[8] Indeed, soon an inertia seemed to grip the promoters of federation to the relief of their opponents, both black and white. Nevertheless, opposition mounted among the northern Africans and the Southern Rhodesian whites, and in September the Liberal Party resolved that unification could not be contemplated before Southern Rhodesia had been granted dominion status.[9]

By late October the Attorneys-General had made so little progress that Huggins decided to dispatch his Minister of Justice, T. H. W. Beadle, and the Attorney-General to London to discuss the legal questions confronting them because only the British Government could answer them. Beadle had to make it plain that Southern Rhodesia would not accept a substitute for federation on the pattern of the East African High Commission which Creech Jones was believed to favour. Huggins insisted that the federation would have to possess a higher constitutional status than Southern Rhodesia, or the Southern Rhodesians would not surrender any powers to it, and the latter would only allow the Commonwealth Relations Office, and not the Colonial Office, to administer the British right to reserve certain legislation.[10]

To A. E. T. Benson (later Sir Arthur), the former Chief Secretary of Nigeria and the new Chief Secretary of the CAC, it seemed that the Rhodesians had the best chance of creating a state in which the races could happily co-exist. However, he told a Colonial Office colleague that "they are

[7] *Ibid.*, 42/15/J 5, "Federation in Central Africa", Memorandum by H. K. Banda and H. Nkumbula, 1 May 1949.
[8] *Ibid.*, 42/15/J 3, Welensky to Banda, 11 July 1949.
[9] *The Rhodesia Herald*, 8 September 1949.
[10] Welensky Papers, WE 7, P/C/100/50, Sir Godfrey Huggins to Welensky, 27 October 1949.

so ham-handed and divided among themselves on major political questions, e.g. Federation, that they will probably make a mess of it even now".[11]

In Northern Rhodesia the unofficial Members had refrained from commenting until the legal committee had produced a formal proposal on federation. They had also agreed to allow 30 months to pass before demanding a re-examination of the Northern Rhodesian Constitution. However, they used the mid-year session of the Legislative Council to reiterate the ambiguities in current British statements on the doctrine of the paramountcy of African interests and the concept of a racial partnership. Their pressure undoubtedly underlay the British pronouncement in November by Lord Listowel, the Minister of State for Colonial Affairs, on the need for differing policies in Africa. Unlike West Africa, Listowel noted, East and Central Africa had considerable settled immigrant communities, and the achievement of responsible government in these areas had to accommodate them as well as the Africans in a mutually beneficial partnership.[12]

In the November session all restraint fell away, and on 24 November, the day after Beadle began his negotiations in London, Welensky proclaimed that the moment was opportune for the British Government to take the initiative in creating a federation of the Rhodesias and Nyasaland.[13] Welensky had decided to broaden the front so as not to leave the entire effort to the Southern Rhodesians because he knew that opposition to federation within the British Labour Party was hardening, and he feared that, as Creech Jones was bent on making a success of the CAC, deadlock was near.[14]

In an earlier debate, Welensky had pointed out that the British Government had just granted the literate minority in the Gold Coast a constitution very similar to Southern Rhodesia's while it continued to refuse to do likewise for Northern Rhodesia.[15] Now he drew attention to the constitutional developments in the West Indies where the Colonial Office was seeking to federate the British islands. Creech Jones had chaired the West Indian Conference in September 1948, and had thereafter produced a blueprint for a constitution which was almost tailor-made for British Central Africa. Pointing this out, Welensky argued that, in an era of declining British prestige, the strategic and economic advantages of a Central African federation would assist a British recovery. Tracing the history of the unification effort, he acknowledged the blunders and the existence of massive African opposition. He knew that delay was assisting his opponents, and he regretted the existence of the feeling that only the British Government would give the Africans a square deal despite the long history of local European efforts to advance the African. He called on the British to act in their own interests before the situation further deteriorated.

G. E. Thornton, the Acting Chief Secretary, asked why British initiative was being sought when the understanding was that a proposal would be forthcoming from unofficial sources, and that it was for this reason that

[11] *Ibid.*, 14/3, f. 141, A. E. T. Benson to K. G. Bradley, 19 October 1949.

[12] House of Lords *Hansard* (London), Vol. 165, Col. 1117, 30 November 1949.

[13] NR *Debates* (Lusaka), Col. 322 f., 24 November 1949.

[14] D. Taylor, *The Rhodesian: The Life of Sir Roy Welensky* (London, 1955), p. 124.

[15] NR *Debates* (Lusaka), Col. 105, 23 November 1949.

Beadle was in London. Creech Jones, he said, had made a statement to this effect on 29 July and had also indicated that his mind was not closed but that no tangible evidence of the failure of the CAC had been produced. Thorton warned that the officials would abstain from the debate because they did not want the Africans to think that the Government was repudiating its guarantees. He hastened to add that the Africans, through their Councils, would be consulted in the event of the British Government changing its mind on federation.

Gore-Browne and the other African representatives argued against the motion, dwelling on African suspicions and claiming that the un-reformed Southern Rhodesian African policy remained an insurmountable obstacle to unification. The unofficials said that the Europeans were not being sufficiently consulted, and that the Southern Rhodesians were being allowed to lead and would dominate the federation to the detriment of northern interests.[16]

The debate was won by four votes, with the officials abstaining, but Welensky believed that their abstention "was as near a death-blow as our campaign suffered; and I don't believe that whatever propaganda was put out afterwards gave us a snowball's chance in hell of wiping out the harm that had been done". The Africans in the main had a child-like faith in the British Colonial Government and totally accepted its guidance. He was convinced, therefore, that if the officials had voted for the motion, the Africans would have accepted federation. Thereafter every opponent of federation could claim that if federation were a good idea it would have received official support in that debate.[17]

Beadle's first meeting in London was not with the British Government but with T. P. Patterson, chairman of the Tati Concession Company of Bechuanaland. L. S. Glover had maintained his pressure on Welensky for the inclusion of Bechuanaland in any scheme of federation in Central Africa, and Patterson sought Beadle's assistance in pressing the British Government to incorporate in Southern Rhodesia the Tati Concession area which was adjacent to the border and had ethnic, social and economic links with that territory. In any case, the concession had been gained from Lobengula and not Bechuanaland's Khama. A reason for Patterson's, and indeed for Glover's, agitation was that on 26 October 1949 the South African Prime Minister, Dr D. F. Malan, had publicly proclaimed his intention to have Bechuanaland, Basutoland and Swaziland incorporated in South Africa in terms of the 1909 Act of Union. Beadle revealed to Patterson that, if there was a prospect of a change in Bechuanaland's status, Southern Rhodesia would bid for the territory north of latitude 22° South. He warned, however, that the Tati Company would have to present powerful arguments to persuade the British Government to separate its lands from Bechuanaland.[18]

The future of Bechuanaland was not, of course, foremost in the minds of Beadle and the Colonial and Commonwealth Secretaries, Creech Jones and P. J. Noel-Baker, when they met on 23 November 1949. Beadle merely stated

[16] *Ibid.*, Col. 404 f., 24 November 1949.

[17] Sir Roy Welensky, *Welensky's 4 000 Days* (London, 1964), pp. 35–36.

[18] Welensky Papers, WE 7, Minutes and Meetings "Federation", Minutes of a Meeting, Rhodesia House, London, 18 November 1949.

Southern Rhodesia's interest in Northern Bechuanaland should Malan press his claim. Noel-Baker was confident that Malan would drop the issue because the public reaction in Bechuanaland had been hostile. Noel-Baker proposed that the British and Southern Rhodesian Governments should compare their views on the future of the protectorate.

Beadle explained the reason for his visit was that, while the Victoria Falls Conference had favoured federation, it had not produced a blueprint and, in the aftermath when the drafting of a constitution was being attempted, it was found necessary to discover precisely what the British Government felt because, if it was totally opposed, there was little point in proceeding. If the British Government had an open mind, the Rhodesians would proceed to formulate their arguments and to submit proposals to London. He foresaw difficulties arising out of the differing levels of constitutional advancement in the three territories, and warned that Southern Rhodesia would not surrender any power to an inter-territorial body patterned on the East African High Commission but would accept an extension of the current system of reserving legislation relating to African affairs for the sanction of the British Government.

However, it was immediately apparent that Creech Jones, who dominated the British delegation, was intending to develop the CAC along the East African lines and was unimpressed by Beadle's arguments against the CAC because the Colonial Office was pleased with its achievements. Beadle claimed that the CAC was objectionable because, firstly, it lacked executive powers and, secondly, the Southern Rhodesian legislature resented decisions being made in the CAC and presented for sanction as *faits accomplis.* Creech Jones retorted that surely the Southern Rhodesian Ministers saw the CAC's minutes and agenda before its meetings and thus could argue within it with a fair knowledge of what the Legislative Assembly would accept. Both he and P. C. Gordon Walker, the Commonwealth Parliamentary Under-Secretary (later Lord Gordon Walker) pointed out that, in a federation, Southern Rhodesia would surrender many more of its powers to a central government. Thus it appeared that Southern Rhodesia wished to dominate any resultant inter-territorial organisation despite the considerable contributions that the other territories would make towards it.

Creech Jones added that the Colonial Office feared that Nyasaland's development would be neglected in a federation. He warned that Britain took her responsibilities to the Africans seriously and would not agree to the mere reservation of legislation as sufficient protection. He also knew that the northern Africans would not accept a system in which they had no rights or say. Representation for them in the upper house would not be sufficient because the lower house would continue to deal with matters affecting them. However, while warning that he was not committing himself to any course of action, he offered British legal facilities to the search for a solution. Indeed, he claimed that his Government would favourably consider any scheme for unification which would still allow it to meet its responsibilities in the area. It was Britain's intention to advance all her colonies towards self-government but, in the process, she could not in all conscience grant absolute self-government to the Europeans in Northern Rhodesia and Nyasaland. Questions by Beadle revealed that Creech Jones regarded direct African representation in the central legislature as fundamental to any solution.

Seeking a *modus operandi,* Beadle proposed that his Government should show why the CAC was inadequate, why it was essential to have closer economic association and why this was only possible through political integration.

The Secretaries of State agreed that their Government might be thus swayed if the solution made allowance for the British commitments. They thought perhaps some looser form of association might prove to be more manageable. It might be possible to decide on the central representation of the territories on the basis of their total populations. Cohen, the Colonial Assistant Under-Secretary, stressed the economic and strategic needs for unification and wondered whether a federal government with strictly limited powers might not serve. The delegations agreed to meet again.[19]

Before the next meeting on 25 November, N. R. Bertram, a Southern Rhodesian official, prepared papers for British perusal on the claim to Northern Bechuanaland and the reasons for the dissatisfaction with the CAC. He recalled that it had been originally suggested by the Bledisloe Commission as a means of promoting an eventual economic and political union. However, it had merely provided a means for exchanging views, and it was thought that this would be better done at a lower level on an *ad hoc* basis which would obviate the need for the expensive CAC secretariat.[20]

In conference on 29 November, Beadle referred to Bertram's paper and claimed that everything achieved under the CAC would have been perfectly possible without it. It was, he said, the fifth wheel in the coach and did not warrant the money spent on it. The Southern Rhodesians remained convinced that economic integration was impossible without political association.

However, though Creech Jones acknowledged that everyone present favoured a political structure, he claimed that the practical obstacles rendered it impossible for some considerable time. The chief obstacle was that the British Government could not surrender its powers in the northern territories to a federal government which, without these powers, would be little better than the CAC. The alternative could well be the latter which, he noted, Bertram had maligned by ignoring its achievements in setting up the Central African Airways, the archives and the Rhodesia and Nyasaland Court of Appeal, and for being responsible for co-operation in public health, broadcasting, the regulation of migrant labour, currency matters, and the floating of local loans. The CAC could serve current needs, and he asked if Southern Rhodesia sought to dominate the inter-territorial association.

Denying this, Beadle claimed that Southern Rhodesia merely wanted to have the central authority made directly responsible to the people of the territories. Southern Rhodesia would have preferred amalgamation to federation, but knew that it was unacceptable in the North. The Southern Rhodesians, he said, objected to the CAC because it cut across parliamentary tradition by making decisions outside their House. Thus they would only preserve the CAC if it would be a stepping stone to federation. Beadle

[19] *Ibid.*, Minutes of a Meeting at the Commonwealth Relations Office, 23 November 1949.

[20] *Ibid.*, N. R. Bertram to J. S. Gandee, 25 November 1949; same to same, 28 November 1949.

reminded the British Ministers that he sought their attitude towards federation in order that plans could be framed accordingly.

Creech Jones, anxious to avert any hasty action, urged the retention of the CAC while the problem of a political association was being resolved. He found that there were major questions to be answered on the powers to be possessed by the political authority, on the structure of government, the financial implications, and on the issue of representation. He claimed that his Government did not really understand the alleged difficulties and demanded further explanation as to why the CAC was not functioning satisfactorily, and why it could not have its powers extended. He sought, too, Southern Rhodesian views on political integration, including their ideas on the division of powers between the federal and state governments. In particular, he wished to know how African interests would be represented and how the standing British undertakings to the African would be implemented. He said his Government feared that the northern territories would be denied adequate federal seats, that there would be no direct African representation and that African interests would not be adequately safeguarded. These fears, he demanded, would have to be dispelled. He and Noel-Baker accepted in conclusion, however, a suggestion by Beadle that, once Southern Rhodesia had answered these questions, a conference of territorial representatives should be convened in London to explore ways of overcoming the difficulties and to consider the form of a possible inter-territorial association.[21]

The discussions were postponed for a week. In the meantime, Beadle sought expert advice from K. C. Wheare (later Sir Kenneth), the Gladstone Professor of Government at Oxford. Wheare, drawing on his studies of the federal form of government, had little comfort to offer. He told of the difficulties being experienced in the West Indies over the drafting of a federal constitution for colonies which did not share the same privileges of self-government. He felt that Southern Rhodesia would have to sacrifice much of its political autonomy as it was inconceivable that Nyasaland could be elevated to enjoy the status that Southern Rhodesia currently possessed. Furthermore, it was unlikely that the British Government would surrender control of African policy and, as this affected directly or indirectly all legislative activity, the federal government would be left with such limited powers that it might not justify the expense of its existence. If the Colonial Office applied an African policy in the northern territories which ran counter to that in Southern Rhodesia, the resultant friction might incapacitate the federation. Thus, Wheare concluded that only a unitary solution was appropriate.[22]

Having set Southern Rhodesia the task of answering their questions, the British Ministers had only to frame with Beadle a joint statement on their talks. They had still to discuss the future of Bechuanaland and, in addition, Beadle was seeking their opinion on proposed legislation regarding Asiatic land tenure in Southern Rhodesia. However, before they could meet again, Huggins made an unexpected intrusion. Angered by Beadle's reports that the

[21] *Ibid.*, Minutes of a Meeting at the Commonwealth Relations Office, 29 November 1949; "Mr Beadle's Notes on some Statements made at a Meeting with Creech Jones and Noel-Baker", 29 November 1949.

[22] *Ibid.*, Notes of a Meeting between Beadle and K. C. Wheare, 1 December 1949.

British would not allow African affairs to be a federal responsibility, and perhaps employing the time-honoured tactic of attacking the British Government when his United Party's popularity was slumping, Huggins used the opportunity of the St Andrew's Night Dinner of the Gatooma and District Caledonian Society to indicate that there was little point in pursuing the federal goal.

Huggins began by apologising for reading his speech, but said it was necessary because "when one is making calculated indiscretions one must be certain to get the actual wording right".[23]

He recalled the British rejection of amalgamation even though, through it, the Rhodesias would have acquired the economic strength to survive in the hurly-burly of international politics. The reason was that, in contrast with the Southern Rhodesian belief in an evolutionary process which would ensure the European a place in the future society, the British Government was determined to implement its policy of trusteeship under which the trustee would retire as soon as the ward had grown up. The sop offered had been the CAC which had shown the desirability of closer association but had not been a stepping stone towards it. Its expense, he claimed, was widely regarded as unnecessary, but the Labour Government was even more intransigent on unification than its predecessor. It was clear that this Government did not consider the Southern Rhodesians fit to be entrusted with the destinies of the Africans in the three territories. In this, of course, the Labour Cabinet was surrendering to the ill-informed faction within its Party which found nothing absurd in the suggestion that the African people, who until recently had known no other form of government than that of a military despot and his train of wizards, should now grasp the full complexity of the Westminster system of government.

With amalgamation a dead letter, Huggins went on, federation was considered and the Victoria Falls Conference found that an examination thereof was justified. The immediate problem was to find a place for the African, to guarantee his rights and to arrange for his full participation in the system without allowing him to control it completely. The solution, he proposed, was to adopt the Southern Rhodesian formula of reserving legislation affecting the African for the British Government. However, the northern Africans were convinced that the British Government would give them a better deal, and it was determined they should have direct representation at the outset, although there were not yet enough Africans capable of using the vote responsibly to fill a single constituency. Thus, he said, the development of Central Africa had to be delayed until sufficient numbers were politically prepared, and until then it was pointless being impatient. It was regrettable, nonetheless, that the scheme should founder on opinions based on dogma rather than realities.

As federation was therefore dead, Huggins examined the alternatives. He rejected the British idea of developing the CAC along East African lines because this meant a senate without a lower house. As union with South Africa was unpalatable to Rhodesians, there remained the difficult task of

[23] *Ibid.*, 14/3, f. 124, (A. E. T. Benson) to C. E. Lambert, 7 December 1949.

fitting Southern Rhodesia to become a dominion. Referring to Northern Rhodesia, he remarked that he did not relish as a neighbour an African state condemned to perpetual backwardness and likely to revert to type. The only difference would be that, in the place of the autocratic Chief, there would be a dictator and his friends. If the continent would ever play its true role in world affairs, Huggins maintained, there would have to be a United States of Africa.[24]

When Beadle arrived at the Commonwealth Relations Office on 6 December, he knew nothing of what Huggins had said. The British Ministers, however, had received a cabled report from the CAC Secretariat in Salisbury, and Beadle instantly gathered from their hostile countenances that something was amiss. He was immediately accused of being party to the speech, and he could only reply lamely that he could not comment until he knew its contents. After being "brow-beaten" for 15 minutes, he learnt what Huggins had said, and laughingly asked: "Did he say that? Isn't that just Huggie all over?"

Only partially mollified, the British Ministers declared that, as Huggins had intimated publicly that he was dissatisfied with the talks, confidences had been betrayed and protocol breached. (Beadle subsequently found that, in some circles in Britain, Huggins's speech was interpreted as a veiled threat of a unilateral declaration of independence if Southern Rhodesia was not allowed to control its political destiny. With hindsight, he believes that "as such this speech may perhaps be regarded as one of the earliest rumblings of UDI".)

Beadle and K. M. Goodenough, the Southern Rhodesian High Commissioner in London, answered the British Ministers by claiming that grave concern about the future in Southern Rhodesia, with South Africa exerting pressure, had prompted Huggins to speak as he did. (In a lengthy cable after the meeting, Beadle declared to Huggins that the speech had been ill-timed, and he had suffered embarrassment as a result. Unrepentant, Huggins merely replied that the embarrassment had not been acute enough to prevent Beadle accompanying Noel-Baker to Twickenham for the Oxford and Cambridge rugby match that afternoon.)

The meeting agreed that the statements to the Press and in the Commons would be subject to mutual approval, and then it turned its attention to the Southern Rhodesian paper on Bechuanaland. Beadle reiterated that the Southern Rhodesian Government was seeking no more than a reassurance that, if change were contemplated, its claim would be entertained. Noel-Baker and Gordon Walker replied that they thought that such action was unlikely and that, in any case, the Act of Union had also provided for the absorption of Southern Rhodesia. This had not happened and thereby had weakened South Africa's case. British policy was as declared in the White Paper of 1935: that it was not yet opportune to seek the opinion of the inhabitants of Bechuanaland on their future.

The severance of the Tati Concession area was considered to be premature as it would provoke a crisis in South Africa. Noel-Baker said he was in correspondence with Patterson and would reply in that vein. He was happy to

[24] *The Rhodesia Herald*, 3 December 1949.

reassure the Southern Rhodesians on their claim but would not do so publicly for fear of inflaming South African opinion, and it was agreed that it would be announced that the British Government had merely noted Beadle's reminder.[25] In the event, the joint statement issued after the final meeting on 12 December served only to provoke Malan who publicly protested at Southern Rhodesia's intrusion into the solemn agreement of 1909 that only Britain and South Africa would decide on the disposal of the protectorates.[26] Noel-Baker replied to Malan that, though Southern Rhodesia's comments would be heard, he was correct, and that the ultimate decision would be an Anglo-South African one. Huggins promptly reminded Noel-Baker of the 1935 British ruling that Southern Rhodesia's change of status since 1909 did affect the issue.[27]

Complementing what Huggins had said, Welensky also interfered in the negotiations by stating on 6 December that the federal cause was hopeless and that thus the Northern Rhodesians were faced with either accepting the continuance of Colonial Office rule with all its consequences, or of struggling to secure self-government. He said he would not accept the limited federation with Nyasaland, and was confident that the swelling tide of immigration would render the call for self-government irresistible.[28] He was ignored in London, and Beadle told the Press the next day that the prospects were not so bleak as deadlock had been avoided and Southern Rhodesia had been entrusted with the task of drawing up fuller proposals.[29] Noel-Baker confirmed this in the Commons on 15 December, explaining that Southern Rhodesia had been asked to re-examine its ideas and their alternatives, as the practical difficulties facing the CAC were formidable. He said that he and Creech Jones had emphasised the British obligations to the Africans, the Africans' objection to political integration, and the radical differences in the constitutional status of each territory.[30]

When the Northern Rhodesian Government received a copy of this statement, it was found that Creech Jones had appended an order for the northern territories to produce a parallel expression of views. In the spirit of this, in late January 1950, Welensky was briefed by Beadle who told him that, though the British were not closing the door, they were not being particularly helpful. The Southern Rhodesians, he revealed, had resented the suggestion that, not only should the African have direct representation in the federal legislature, but that the Southern Rhodesian House should be thus reformed. He said his Government thought that Nyasaland and Barotseland, being true protectorates, should be excluded from the scheme. Welensky disagreed but

[25] Old Rhodian Union, "How we could succeed where Rhodes failed", the Second Cecil Rhodes Commemoration Lecture by the Rt. Hon. Sir Hugh Beadle, *Rhodes Newsletter* (Rhodes University, Grahamstown, December 1971), Vol. 11, No. 2, p. 8; Welensky Papers, WE 7, Minutes and Meetings "Federation", Minutes of a Meeting at the Commonwealth Relations Office, 6 December 1949.

[26] *The Rhodesia Herald*, 22 December 1949.

[27] Welensky Papers, WE 7, Minutes and Meetings "Federation", Draft Dispatch to Secretary of State of Commonwealth Relations, (undated).

[28] *The Rhodesia Herald*, 7 December 1949.

[29] *Ibid.*, 8 December 1949.

[30] House of Commons *Hansard* (London), Vol. 470, Col. 207, 15 December 1949.

said he would condone their exclusion if Creech Jones wished it. He agreed, at Beadle's request, to furnish his ideas, on what powers a federal government might have, before Southern Rhodesia drafted a constitution for submission to London by April. Welensky added that these powers should be strictly limited in order to justify the expense of federation.[31]

The Southern Rhodesians maintained their attack on the CAC, and at its meeting on 26 January they submitted an acid memorandum demanding its dissolution. The grounds given were that, as it had been formed to serve as a step towards unification, and as both amalgamation and federation were now out of reach, the CAC's continued existence was pointless. The memorandum declared that it was entirely impracticable to suggest closer economic ties without a political merger because politics and economics could not be divorced. To illustrate this, it pointed out that Northern Rhodesia, and the Copperbelt in particular, would be drastically affected if Southern Rhodesia curtailed its railway development, the production of coal and the provision of services in order to meet the housing and other needs of the current influx of immigrants. If there would be no political union, there was little point in retaining the cumbersome CAC which became merely a second post office when co-operation could be better effected through direct inter-governmental contact. As matters were routed through the CAC, Governments had tended to wait for its recommendations before considering them. However, as anyone could make suggestions to the CAC, issues before it had often not been sufficiently investigated, and therefore could not be finalised. As the high-ranking members of the CAC could not be expected to concern themselves with detail, and yet much of the detail had to be handled inter-territorially, it was obvious that a less august body would serve.

Furthermore, the memorandum averred, Southern Rhodesia could not agree to the CAC acquiring executive powers because the majority of its members were Colonial officials who took their instructions from London and could not be removed by any local legislature. The need for the northern Governments to have the Colonial Secretary's sanction occasioned further delay and, in practice, the CAC was inclined to ignore important but controversial matters and to concentrate on what could be easily achieved. The memorandum maintained that the joint services under the CAC tended to be neglected because no Government administered them. Yet if Southern Rhodesia took charge, it faced the possibility that, in time, the northern territories would develop their own services, and Southern Rhodesia's staff would face redundancy. This, and the likelihood of transfer to the North in the course of duty, would make it difficult to attract recruits. Finally, the memorandum stated that the CAC was never more than a forum. It declared that, although each Government fully examined any problem before it was submitted to the CAC, action by the latter required unanimity from the three Governments — a single dissension producing impotence.[32]

The Southern Rhodesian delegates, Huggins, Whitehead and Stockil, claimed that the dislike of the CAC within their territory was so intense that

[31] Welensky Papers, WE 7, Un-numbered Series P–R "Rail Link", Welensky to unofficial Members, 30 January 1950.

[32] *Ibid.*, Minutes and Memoranda "CAC Committees", Memorandum, (undated).

the Government dared not defend it. Even within the Government, the Ministers who were not CAC delegates resented the interference with their portfolios and, because decisions rather than advice emanated from the CAC, United Party MPs felt ignored and estranged. Huggins and Whitehead added that their Government also resented the tendency of the British Government to route correspondence via the CAC.[33] (Certainly, the CAC's files for the years 1949-50 show its secretariat caught in a cross-fire on this issue.[34])

Huggins and Whitehead acknowledged the need for continuing inter-territorial co-operation but thought that there was little more that the CAC, as constituted, could exploit. A lower-keyed organisation, they felt, was required so that departmental heads would feel free to criticise.

Welensky emphasised that the will to make it work underlay the success of any organisation. He regretted the Southern Rhodesian attitude because the CAC had done good work and thus should be defended. Northern Rhodesia had not shared the feeling that its legislature's rights had been violated. He agreed, however, that there was a limit to economic co-operation without political unity but, until federation was a reality, machinery was needed.

Barrow used a harsher tone in the CAC's defence: the will to make it work was crucial, and the clash with Southern Rhodesia was the product, not of failure, but of success. He recalled that, though never entirely happy with it, the Southern Rhodesian delegates had co-operated within the CAC in the first year. However, they had become jealous of the CAC's intrusion into their preserves, and had become increasingly obstructive. The meeting concluded that it should appoint a committee to review the current structure and its alternatives, and that in the meantime the CAC be retained.

Welensky's immediate task was to formulate his ideas on a federal structure. In early 1950 it seemed that, of the protagonists of federation, only Welensky strove to keep it alive and before the public eye. Certainly, he took every opportunity to speak on federation and related matters. After the CAC meeting in January, it was he who announced that the pursuit of the federal goal would continue. In March he took the British Government to task for its equivocal attitude on partnership, and the African Provincial Council for the Western Area for accepting the "parrot-cry" that federation would harm African interests.[35] Huggins, by contrast, seemed to be adhering to the position that nothing more could be done to achieve federation, and this encouraged Stockil to offer him the Liberal Party's support in the pursuit of dominion status for Southern Rhodesia.[36] It seemed that the nadir of the federal campaign had been reached.

However, though not immediately apparent, the prospects for unification were brighter because, on 24 February, the British Labour Party had won the closest general election to date, and Creech Jones was among the casualties. He was replaced as Colonial Secretary by James Griffiths, while Patrick

[33] *Ibid.*, Secret Paper MCAC/2/50 by A. E. T. Benson, CAC Chief Secretary, 20 February 1950.
[34] *Ibid.*, 14/3, f. 168, (H. N. Parry) to C. E. Lambert, 6 January 1949; f. 167, Lambert to Parry, 12 February 1949; f. 156, Benson to Lambert, 28 June 1949; f. 138, Benson to T. G. Gisborne, 28 October 1949; f. 111, Benson to Lambert, 8 February 1950.
[35] *The Rhodesia Herald*, 7 March 1950.
[36] *Ibid.*, 11 March 1950.

Gordon Walker was promoted to Secretary of State for Commonwealth Relations, and both men would prove to be less obstructive than their predecessors. As important, perhaps, Cohen of the Colonial Office was now willing to admit privately that he favoured a federal solution.[37] Furthermore, Huggins was prepared to tell a visiting Kenyan delegation that, while he sympathised with their predicament, he could do little more than attempt to impress upon the British Government that the African needed economic before political advance, because he did not wish to harm the prospects of federating the three Central African territories.[38]

The Kenyan visit had been prompted by contact with Welensky in Nairobi in January and by a recent change of policy in Tanganyika. Spurred by the Trusteeship Committee of the United Nations to fulfil the objects of its Charter, which ordained that mandated territories should be advanced as quickly as possible to self-government and — if the people wished — independence, the British Government had announced a reform of Tanganyika's provincial government on a democratic basis. The whites there feared a total loss of political power, and the Kenyan whites, who aspired to join the federation in Central Africa, feared that they would be cut off by a black state.

To assist him in devising a federal constitution, Welensky had a memorandum written in the previous year as a guide to the three Central African Attorneys-General.[39] Aided by this, he was ready to circulate his proposals on 30 March. In these, he began by claiming that, though a substitute for amalgamation, federation was in fact a better solution because it preserved the territories' individualities. It allowed African rights to continue to be safeguarded in traditional ways and thereby answered British anxiety about African fears. He proposed that there should be a governor-general and a bi-cameral legislature (he gave no hint of its size), the lower house of which would seat elected Europeans while the upper held elected or nominated senators according to the individual territorial whim. Voting would be by secret ballot, and constituencies would be delimited on a population or geographical basis. The franchise should be devised by a commission on the assumption that there should not be fewer voters than currently, nor should the qualifications be higher.

Welensky suggested that, whilst the senate would possess delaying powers only, it might be allowed to initiate legislation. The governor-general would appoint the leader of the majority party as prime minister and he, in turn, would draw his cabinet from within the ranks of the assembly. The size of the cabinet would depend on the number of federal departments. The governor-general would be appointed by the King on the advice of the federal prime minister transmitted through the Commonwealth Secretary who could not veto the choice. Federal government powers would be specifically defined

[37] Author's interview with Sir Arthur Benson.

[38] Welensky Papers, WE 7, P/C/169/52, Minutes of a Meeting between Huggins and Representatives of the Kenyan European Elected Members' Organisation, 13 March 1950; Secret Report of a (later) Meeting (between the same), 15 March 1950; *The Rhodesia Herald*, 16 March 1950.

[39] Welensky Papers, 14/22, f. 36 f., "Suggested Federation of the Rhodesias and Nyasaland", (undated).

with everything else, including African affairs, remaining in territorial hands. Should any federal legislation impinge on African affairs, it should be reserved for consideration by the British Government. The federal government would be responsible for Commonwealth relations, foreign affairs, defence, communications, customs and excise, currency, meteorological services, research, broadcasting, and possibly health. As there could be no barriers between the states, the Congo Basin Treaties would need to be abrogated. Social and industrial matters would remain territorial subjects, though a high level of inter-territorial co-ordination would be established.

Welensky suggested three methods of financing the federal government. It could receive all taxes and subsidise the states, which would hardly be popular, or the states could gather the revenue and make grants for the maintenance of the federal government, but this would weaken the federation. The best solution would be for the federal government to have limited taxation powers, and be subsidised by the states if necessary. Welensky warned that it might be necessary to exclude Nyasaland and Barotseland because of their sparse European populations, and their tardy political development might create difficulties that could cause the rejection of the whole scheme.

As the 30-month trial period for the Northern Rhodesian Constitution was almost at an end, and as Welensky was shortly going to Britain to review it, he chose to discuss it in this memorandum. He said he expected that the territorial governments, though shorn of those functions assumed by the federal government, would continue otherwise unchanged, with their constitutional advancement unimpeded. He felt that the Northern Rhodesian Legislative Council need only be broadened to encompass a future flow of immigrants. It was the Executive Council which required immediate reform as it had to become the chief instrument of policy and had to be responsible to the Legislative Council. The Executive Council should be chaired by the Governor and have three official and five unofficial Members, including a nominated European Member representing African interests. The four elected unofficial Members would be made departmental heads. All Members would have a vote, and would vote by conscience. Decisions would require a majority vote, with the Governor having a casting vote. The Governor's veto, however, would be retained for use when he considered it necessary in the interests of good government. He could reserve legislation for certification by the Colonial Secretary.[40]

The reactions of Welensky's Legislative Council colleagues to his proposals are not recorded, but to Colonel David Stirling it seemed to be a particularly effective example of the "thin edge of the wedge" approach. Stirling was confident that, if adopted, the federation would soon become a dominion. His only criticism was that Welensky was prepared to allow the Colonial Office to continue its mismanagement of African affairs by his proposal that the subject be left in territorial hands. Northern Rhodesia, Stirling thought, would be advised to adopt the Southern Rhodesian African policy.[41]

[40] *Ibid.*, WE 7, P/C/100/52, Welensky to unofficial Members, 30 March 1950; Circular, "The Federation of Rhodesia and Nyasaland", (undated).

[41] *Ibid.*, Un-numbered Series "UK Trip, April–May 1950", D. Stirling to Welensky, 12 April 1950.

A. E. T. Benson asserted that, if it had been practicable, he would have preferred amalgamation. He proposed that the federal senate should be given an absolute veto to prevent one state passing legislation which the others opposed. Provision, too, had to be made for machinery for the interpretation of the constitution, and it was vital for the federal government to have absolute control over finance so that it should not be hamstrung by a state withholding its contribution. He predicted that the British Government would take exception to the legislative assembly consisting entirely of Europeans. The African, Benson said, would not be ready for at least five generations to take part in state affairs, but that Creech Jones and his ilk favoured African advancement as quickly as possible "so that he can play at politics and get himself established in them before the white man is numerous enough in Central Africa to hold the fort". The only valid argument on the African side was that of numerical strength and for this reason, he felt, European immigration should be fostered. However, the immediate problem was to win British co-operation, and the door had to be left open to allow the African the opportunity of acquiring a share of political rights — though no more than his fit share. Apart from the problem of the African, there was the political threat from the immigrant Afrikaner who might soon dominate politics. To combat this, Benson suggested that the franchise qualifications might well have to be raised.[42]

This problem worried F. S. Joelson who, commenting on the memorandum, warned Welensky that a predominance of Afrikaners in most Northern Rhodesian constituencies might cause the British and the Southern Rhodesians to shy away from the idea of federating.[43]

When Welensky's federal plan was circulated, Huggins was away in London but, when he commented, his verdict was curt: "I am afraid it would make no appeal here." He said it amounted to little more than setting up a government with a bi-cameral legislature to take over matters already handled by the CAC with the addition of defence and customs and excise. Unless the federal government took over finance and justice, its expense could not be justified. He thought that the states should control little more than education, public health and certain African matters. He felt "we shall get nowhere until what is *called* Native opinion is ignored [*sic*] they are quite incapable (that is the natives) of understanding what it is all about".[44]

Though a statement by Huggins in London that he was thinking of retiring from politics prompted Cohen to say that he, at least, wanted Huggins to be the first federal prime minister,[45] Huggins advised Welensky that he had found the Labour Government to be unyielding on the federal issue, and concluded that it did not wish to upset its left wing. He had been encouraged by Conservative attitudes, but believed that nothing could be achieved at present. He said his remark that, if the problem of the Africans was the obstacle, then the Europeans should be allowed to unite and Britain should look after the Africans, had not been any better received than it had been by

[42] *Ibid.*, Benson to Welensky, 12 April 1950.
[43] *Ibid.*, F. S. Joelson to Welensky, 13 April 1950.
[44] *Ibid.*, Huggins to Welensky, 19 April 1950.
[45] Author's interview with Major M. N. C. St. Quintin.

Welensky. Huggins felt that "the only thing to do . . . is for you to improve your set-up but do not take any more natives at present or the whole issue will be killed stone-dead. Good luck to you".

On 4 May 1950, when in London with Rennie and Gore-Browne to discuss the Northern Rhodesian Constitution, Welensky also sought the British reaction to his federal proposals. He confessed to Griffiths, the Colonial Secretary, that Huggins had found them top-heavy. Welensky said that, while he appreciated the British desire to protect the African, if development was held to the pace of the African, nothing would be realised and Northern Rhodesia might fall prey to a flood of Asiatic immigrants.

Gore-Browne, however, said that he agreed with Huggins's verdict. He thought that there had to be provision for eventual advancement by Africans and a guarantee of their rights if their whole-hearted opposition were to be avoided. He opined that both the Africans and the Southern Rhodesians were being unreasonable in their demands. Griffiths would not comment beyond noting that the Southern Rhodesians wanted more than Welensky had conceded. Rennie added that, at heart, the Southern Rhodesians remained amalgamationists who wanted a federation in which the states would be little more than provinces. Welensky did not rise to the defence of the Southern Rhodesians but acknowledged the difference in approach in the Rhodesias and thought that it could be resolved in a conference.

Griffiths was as non-committal about the reform of the Northern Rhodesian Constitution. He ignored questions on the possibilities of enhancing the role of the unofficial Members, but did say that any change would require a *quid pro quo* for the Africans. In doing so, he ignored Welensky's statements that African advancement had been too rapid and that he could not answer for a possible adverse European reaction.[46]

On 12 May, the meeting was reconvened with Gordon Walker and other representatives of the Commonwealth Relations Office. Welensky asked for a reassurance that any proposals for federation produced by Huggins would not be rejected out of hand and would be considered as the basis for a meeting of the three territorial Governments under a British chairman. He acknowledged that Huggins was an amalgamationist but, as the Northern Rhodesians would not accept absorption, the meeting would serve to resolve such differences. Griffiths, in turn, insisted that there would have to be a limit placed on discussion as Britain could not debate her responsibilities towards the Africans. However, if an acceptable agenda was forthcoming, he could see no reason for refusing to convene a conference. Welensky agreed to convey to Huggins the message that Southern Rhodesia was expected to produce a plan as the basis of a meeting, and asked whether development would be set to the pace of the African, because, if European opinion would be ignored, the European should be told. Griffiths denied that British policy had ever implied this, but maintained that Britain had to safeguard African interests, and this had to be absolutely understood before any agenda could be considered.[47]

On his return to Lusaka, Welensky gave the Legislative Council the gist of

[46] *Ibid.*, 14/22, f. 5, Minutes of a Meeting, Colonial Office, 4 May 1950.
[47] *Ibid.*, f. 1, Minutes of a Meeting, Colonial Office, 12 May 1950.

his discussions in London before going to see Huggins in Southern Rhodesia. Huggins had not apparently shifted his ground since his speech in Gatooma. Indeed, in April, he had told a meeting that amalgamation was the only possible method of unifying the territories.[48]

Stockil attempted to exploit the situation by moving that the Legislative Assembly appoint a select committee to report on the necessary steps for amending the Southern Rhodesian Constitution to remove the British right of reserving certain categories of legislation. On the receipt of this report an all-party delegation would be dispatched to secure the change. Stockil said he was convinced that dominion status was Southern Rhodesia's for the asking.[49] Indeed, Southern Rhodesians have since generally believed that an opportunity was lost. However, given the British Government's attitude to Southern Rhodesia's African policies in particular, it seems doubtful that there was any prospect of success. In the event, to Stockil's dismay, Huggins's Party would support the establishment of the select committee and not the dispatch of the delegation.

In late June, this committee recommended the setting up of a second chamber even if the power to reserve legislation remained in British hands. The committee ruled that the membership of the existing Assembly should be increased from 30 to 40.[50] This latter recommendation was debated in January 1951, but by then Huggins had secured a vital advance towards the federal objective.

Huggins did not pursue a further inter-territorial meeting. Instead, in August he suggested to the British Government that, hitherto, the problem had been discussed at too high a level. He proposed, therefore, that the issue should be examined in London by civil servants of the four Governments to see if federation was feasible. Alarmed by the threat of Afrikaner expansionism implied by the influx of South African immigrants into the Rhodesias, Clement Attlee, the British Prime Minister (acting for Gordon Walker), and Griffiths accepted this suggestion.[51] Professor P. S. Gupta maintains that the real reason was a consequence of the decision to develop an independent British nuclear bomb after the Klaus Fuchs affair had damaged Anglo-American collaboration in this field. Chrome was an essential ingredient in the nuclear process and, therefore, the Labour Government had to woo Southern Rhodesia because of its extensive chrome deposits.[52] On 8 November 1950, Griffiths announced the British decision in the Commons, stressing the purely exploratory nature of the civil servants' task. He promised that African opinion would not be ignored.[53]

Griffiths faced a storm of questioning from all sides of the House. His most

[48] L. H. Gann and M. Gelfand, *Huggins of Rhodesia* (London, 1964), p. 218.

[49] *The Rhodesia Herald*, 26 April 1950.

[50] SR *Debates* (Salisbury), Vol. 31, Part 2, Col. 2770, 23 June 1950.

[51] Taylor, *The Rhodesian*, *op. cit.*, p. 128; J. Griffiths, *Pages from Memory* (London, 1969), p. 113. Despite Professor Rotberg's claim – Rotberg, *The Rise of Nationalism*, *op. cit.*, p. 231, fn. 37 – that A. B. Cohen persuaded Griffiths to agree to this conference, I have accepted D. Taylor's version on the strength of a letter to Taylor from Huggins in Welensky Papers, 6/42, f. 138, Huggins to Taylor, 5 October 1954. — JRTW.

[52] P. S. Gupta, *Imperialism and the British Labour Movement, 1914–64* (London, 1975), pp. 339–340.

[53] Welensky Papers, WE 7, P/C/169/52, Press Communiqué No. 706, 9 November 1950.

bitter critic, however, was his predecessor, Creech Jones, who accused him of being hoodwinked by Huggins and Welensky into "selling the pass".[54] Since his electoral defeat, Creech Jones had condemned the federal campaign, finding that it had resulted in widespread African apprehension because it seemed to the African to dam his political progress, to limit his responsibilities and his freedom, and to disregard treaty obligations. Creech Jones said that the attack on the CAC had worsened the position, and he was adamant that, despite the local Europeans' opinion of the Colonial Office, British responsibilities could not be transferred without a breech of trust and considerable African resentment. He pointed to the Southern Rhodesian African policy as evidence of what would happen if the British withdrew. He warned that the further Britain departed from her established policy, the more embittered the African would become.[55]

As if to support Creech Jones, on the same day that he published his views, *The Rhodesia Herald* discovered that the Northern Rhodesian Africans had viewed the official abstention from voting in the recent federal debate in the Legislative Council as confirmation that their Government was moving towards a compromise on unification.[56] Godwin Lewanika, president of the African National Congress, confirmed this in July when addressing the British Labour Party's Colonial Affairs Group.[57] It seemed to Creech Jones that Griffiths had been manoeuvred by the Rhodesians into agreeing to an official examination of the problem and had thus accorded formal recognition to the idea of federating. Griffiths, however, held a different view: if the African would consent and effective British control could be maintained, he did not want to lose the opportunity to federate. He believed, unlike Creech Jones, that there was no time to lose. He maintained that he and Creech Jones differed only over timing.[58]

[54] Taylor, *The Rhodesian*, *op. cit.*, p. 128.
[55] *Spectator*, 6 April 1950.
[56] *The Rhodesia Herald*, 6 April 1950.
[57] *Ibid.*, 26 July 1950.
[58] Taylor, *The Rhodesian*, *op. cit.*, pp. 128-129.

CHAPTER SIX

The Blueprint for Federation

The Officials' Conference and its Evolution of the Basis of the Federal Constitution, March 1951

IN the immediate aftermath of Griffiths's announcement, the civil servants of the three territories would set to work to produce the basic documents needed for the Officials' Conference. They would not be briefed by the local politicians, but their efforts would be co-ordinated by the Central African Council. Though the passage of their conference would not be entirely smooth, they would produce a unanimous report which recommended federation as an urgent necessity, and provided the blueprint on which the Federation of Rhodesia and Nyasaland was built.

Predictably, Griffiths's action drew statements of total opposition from the African Representative Council in Northern Rhodesia, the Protectorate Council in Nyasaland, and the African National Congresses in both territories. In London, Banda reacted by having copies of his memorandum of 1949 printed and distributed. He added a preface which called on both Congresses to become truly mass movements to attract the support of the Chiefs and the educated and uneducated populations in the fight against federation.[1] Later, during the Conference, Banda tried to lobby support to influence its outcome, but without success.

Huggins's actions in the months of preparation for the Conference served to assist the officials. Although he reassured his electorate that the promise of a referendum still held good,[2] he proclaimed his Government's anxiety to develop Southern Rhodesia on the basis of a racial partnership in which colour would not be a test of a man's ability and culture.[3]

Welensky, too, spoke in favour of partnership but thought it necessary to stress that the European's dominant role would have to be recognised. He was not, however, in an accommodating mood and, in the Legislative Council in

[1] P. Short, *Banda* (London, 1974), p. 64.

[2] *The Rhodesia Herald*, 9 November 1950.

[3] *Comparative Survey of Native Policy: Northern Rhodesia, Nyasaland and Southern Rhodesia*, PAC I, Central African Council, Salisbury, 5 February 1951, p. 5.

November, he accused the British Labour Government, its Party and "the long-haired men and the short-haired women of the Fabian Society" of stirring up racialism in Africa. He was referring to a claim by Creech Jones that the Europeans were seeking to secure political dominance of Northern Rhodesia. He noted that Fenner Brockway, a Labour MP (later Lord Brockway), after a week's visit to the Sudan, had proclaimed that it was ready for immediate independence. John Dugdale, another Labour MP, had spoken in Tanganyika against the European settlers there, and Ernest Bevin, the current Foreign Secretary and a man whom Welensky had admired, had stated that Britain was not exploiting her colonies but was guiding them to the road down which India had travelled. Welensky said he would summon up all possible resistance to any proposal to copy the precedent of the Gold Coast by handing Northern Rhodesia to a minority of semi-literate Africans. He challenged the British Government to prove that the Europeans had not advanced the Africans politically and economically.[4]

In January 1951, Welensky's negotiations on the constitutional development of Northern Rhodesia reached deadlock when Griffiths insisted that the leader of the unofficials should hold a portfolio, which would limit his ability to criticise the Government, and would not allow any increase in the membership of either the Executive or Legislative Councils. Griffiths was also adamant that any change would require the sanction of both races and be accepted by the African Representative Council. However, he and Welensky agreed that they should meet in London later in the year and, in fact, both sides were hanging fire in anticipation of what the Officials' Conference would produce.[5]

The four civil service delegations met at the Commonwealth Relations Office on 5 March under the chairmanship of G. H. Baxter, the Commonwealth Assistant Under-Secretary.[6] Of the 15 memoranda before them, the Southern Rhodesians had been responsible for nine, covering the unification of government services, the cost of government, and the economic implications of closer association. The CAC provided perhaps the most crucial preparatory document, the "Comparative Survey of Native Policy".

This document was considered first by the Conference, and a sub-committee was immediately appointed to study it. In the event, the Conference accepted the document's conclusions and annexed a summary of them to its Report, thereby making public the vital comment that in all the territories:

> "... the ultimate aim of policy ... is to advance the African to a stage where he is in all respects a full partner exercising all the rights and accepting all the responsibilities of citizenship."[7]

[4] NR *Debates* (Lusaka), Cols. 41–53, 10 November 1950.

[5] Welensky Papers, 7/10, f. 83, Northern Rhodesia Government Statement, 6 January 1951; 5/95, f. 475, Welensky to Rev. E. G. Nightingale, 9 February 1951; 7/10, f. 99, Welensky to Sir Gilbert Rennie, 10 February 1951.

[6] Conference on Closer Association in Central Africa, London, "Volume II – Minutes and Conference Papers", March 1951.

[7] *Ibid.*, "Volume III – Report of the Conference", Annex. II, March 1951, published as *Report of the Conference on Closer Association in Central Africa*, Command 8233 (London, June 1951).

In addition, because all the territories were concerned with the social and economic advance of the African, their policies were seen to be even more compatible: there was parallel development of local government institutions, native courts, authorities, treasuries and matching policies in education, health and agriculture.

It was acknowledged that there were differences in the African policies but largely of timing. Yet these differences were important enough to be dealt with in full. Foremost were the constitutional realities for, while in the northern territories the Colonial Secretary had special responsibilities for the protection and advancement of the Africans and was answerable to the British Parliament, in Southern Rhodesia full power was vested in the Legislative Assembly, limited only by the British reserved powers. There was in the North some *de facto* geographical separation of the races, but it was established legally only in the case of the exclusive Native Reserves. In contrast, in Southern Rhodesia the Land Apportionment Act defined special European and African areas. The Report recorded that the northern territories believed that, to prepare the African for full partnership in the community, he had to be induced to participate fully in the politics and administration of his own area and to take a direct role in national affairs. It was argued that political education would spur the African's material and economic development. Southern Rhodesia believed that the African needed to match the European's health, prosperity and education before he could play a full political and administrative role in his own area, let alone in the whole territory. This divergence of approach illustrated that the essential difference was one of timing. In the North, the Report continued, the native courts had extensive civil and criminal jurisdiction, while those in Southern Rhodesia had only civil powers. The northern African involvement in local government was certainly greater. Moreover, the Africans had been given direct representation in the legislatures unlike their southern cousins who, sharing a common roll with Europeans, had not yet gained a place in the Legislative Assembly. The northern Africans, however, did not possess the vote automatically because they were British Protected Persons.

There were differences, too, in attitudes to exclusively African trade unions as Southern Rhodesia was only prepared to give them *de facto* recognition. There were, nevertheless, in existence in that country, African works committees and Native Labour Boards. The Rhodesia Railways African Employees' Association had been given official sanction. Unlike Nyasaland, both Rhodesias possessed an industrial colour bar, a product of certain wage agreements, which only in Southern Rhodesia had received statutory recognition through the Industrial Conciliation Act. While the pass laws in the Rhodesias were similar, Nyasaland had only night passes in urban areas, though non-indigenous Africans had to register on entering the territory. Because of inter-territorial migrant labour agreements, and for reasons of good order, Southern Rhodesia applied more stringent pass laws to African immigrants than to her own population. The northerners had no legal or administrative obstacles to the employment of Africans in any government post if they were suitably qualified, and Africans were more widely employed than in Southern Rhodesia where the Public Services Act reserved most occupations for Europeans. However, greater opportunities for Africans were being created in Southern Rhodesia.

Only Southern Rhodesia provided separate services for the races; in Northern Rhodesia the European and African education departments came under the same Secretary. Southern Rhodesia, on the other hand, spent more on its African population than did the northern territories, but the latter did not separate their services, and contributions from the private sector, particularly from the mining companies, could not be ignored.

In its second plenary session, on 6 March, the Conference turned its attention next to Southern Rhodesian arguments in favour of unification, and accepted that a single major unit, rather than three small ones, would be better able to defend itself and the Commonwealth. It would have more influence abroad and could resist the expansionist aims of South Africa. The British pattern had been to devolve responsibility, and a greater Central African state would be more fitted to receive it.

E. I. G. Unsworth, the Northern Rhodesian Attorney-General, interjected that the Africans were likely to protest at any move to withdraw British protection but his views were merely noted. It was acknowledged that the unified state would offer greater incentives to people to enter public life. Shared experience in other fields, it was felt, would bring about a closer alignment of African policies. The range of climatic conditions could be exploited to achieve self-sufficiency in food. Large internal markets, the common exploitation of hydro-electric power potentialities, the more efficient use of labour, financial and mineral resources, and transport systems would spur economic development and attract foreign investment. The larger pool of internal savings would encourage the growth of local financial institutions. In fact, the three economies were already so linked that centralised planning was essential and many administrative advantages would flow from bulk buying and combined higher education, health and research institutions. The conclusion was that the economic, political and strategic strength would benefit all, particularly the Africans.

The Northern Rhodesians supplied a counter-argument, fastening upon the differences in the internal political structures and the place of the African within them. The Conference's adviser, Professor K. C. Wheare, replied that the difficulty of adjusting these was not sufficient grounds for a refusal to unify if the other reasons were overwhelming. He suggested, and the meeting agreed, that perhaps entirely new systems would probably have to be devised. The Northern Rhodesians then pointed to the African objection to any form of closer association, while the Southern Rhodesians commented that their Africans were indifferent to it. The latter considered that the northern Africans confused South Africa's policies with theirs. The Northern Rhodesians nevertheless remarked that, though their district administration had been ordered to persuade the Africans to keep an open mind until formal proposals were forthcoming, the African Representative Council had recently petitioned the Colonial Secretary protesting against the Conference and any suggestion of closer association. It was acknowledged that the ARC was not a truly representative body but its opinion was indicative of the depth of African feeling against unification. The meeting accepted that, although Africans were always opposed to change, due weight had to be given to African opinion. Moreover, it was recognised that, should unification be recommended, consideration would have to be given to methods of correcting African misconceptions.

The Europeans in all three territories, the Conference found, would support bold proposals for unification, though the Northern Rhodesians would not accept total absorption by Southern Rhodesia. Within Britain, the only opposition was expected to come from the small but vocal Fabian group, but this it felt would be counter-balanced by more right-wing elements. No real hostility was anticipated from the British Press. The Conference postponed discussion on difficulties raised concerning the differing constitutional status of the territories. It did likewise with the financial implications when the Northern Rhodesians expressed fears for the fate of their development plan. The Southern Rhodesian answer was that Northern Rhodesian prosperity might not endure, and the broad-based Southern Rhodesian economy could cushion a fall in mineral prices. No comment was forthcoming on Northern Rhodesian claims that the geographical situation of the territories might make daily administration difficult, or that the existing terms of service of the northern civil servants, both black and white, constituted a most serious argument against unifying.

It was thought to be premature to discuss, on 7 March, the question of partitioning Northern Rhodesia which Gore-Browne had recently revived in a fit of despair over current political trends in that country.[8] Logically the next document to be considered was the Southern Rhodesian "Unification of Departments and Services of the Governments of the Central African Territories". This examined the territorial services on the basis that, even if a central legislature were not established, the unification of departments would be practicable. The memorandum's findings were based on information obtained from the territorial Governments and, in making their recommendations, the authors assumed that staffing difficulties, both European and African, could be overcome, that differences in civil service pay could be reconciled, and that standards would be maintained. It was presumed that closer association would not sever links with the Colonial Development Corporation. There was confidence that modern communications could solve the problems of distance. Dwelling only on broad principles and long-term advantages, the authors believed certain general benefits would flow from unification. Appreciable economies could be achieved in bulk buying and standardisation of equipment. Less manpower would be needed and facilities could be pooled. The basis of their examination had been a concern for the welfare and the prosperity of all. They were particularly perturbed about the African's fear of unification and had only recommended it when they felt that it was to the positive advantage, both in theory and practice, of the indigenous people. The African administration, for example, was a service which the three territories had to provide and therefore its unification had to be considered because there were insufficient reasons against it.

They did not include, however, African administration in the 27 depart-

[8] Welensky Papers, WE 7, P/C/100/52, Memorandum by Sir Stewart Gore-Browne, 16 September 1950.

ments whose merger seemed to them to be desirable and immediately practicable. They chose customs and excise, printing and stationery, income tax, census and statistics, posts and telegraphs, broadcasting, prisons, defence, police, immigration, national parks, town planning, archives, public relations, health, education, geological survey, roads, civil aviation, meteorological services, veterinary, surveyor-general, forestry, irrigation, research and specialist services, conservation and extension, and trade and industrial development.

Taking these departments in turn, the memorandum examined first the problem of unifying the customs services which was complicated by the existence of the Congo Basin Treaties affecting Nyasaland and North Eastern Rhodesia. The Treaties were the Berlin Act of 1885, which regulated trade within the defined area; the Brussels Act of 1890, which imposed a duty not exceeding ten per cent *ad valorem* on imports into the Congo Basin and reaffirmed that no differential rate or transit duty could be established; and the Convention of St Germain of 1919, which ratified that there could be no differential treatment within the area of the trade of all nations. This had necessitated an internal customs barrier in Northern Rhodesia which would have to be considered when a single customs unit was being formed. Nevertheless, the memorandum maintained, a customs union would enhance the domestic market and minimise the duplication of industry. A single headquarters would mean a better handling of imports and a reduction in staff. As Southern Rhodesia was already employing African clerks within its customs department, there would be no difficulty over unification.

In the debate, the Southern Rhodesians stressed these recommendations while acknowledging that existing trade agreements would have to be renegotiated and that current policies differed because Southern Rhodesia attempted to keep the cost of living down to protect its Africans. A single administration and the greater domestic market would be worthwhile assets, and the service could easily handle the three territorial variations of law. Professor Wheare felt that with great difficulty there could be, if necessary, a unified service without a customs union, but warned that if there were separate territorial laws, there would be little point in merging as the central body would merely become a clearing house.

The Northern Rhodesians acknowledged the benefit of a customs union but claimed that the existing trade agreements with Southern Rhodesia and South Africa precluded its immediate formation. It was impractical, in their view, to have one service administering separate laws and there would be no advantage if these laws survived. There would have to be a tariff advisory board but they doubted whether suitable persons could be found to serve on it. They pointed out that the basis of income tax in the Rhodesias differed: Northern Rhodesia tried to tax as many people as possible, while Southern Rhodesia preferred higher rates of import duty. The Northern Rhodesians claimed that the Congo Basin Treaties had worked in favour of their mining industry. There would be difficulties over the distribution of revenue and over Africans in the service. The Northern Rhodesians sought postponement of this discussion until the form which closer association would take was known.

The Nyasalanders thought that the revocation of the Congo Basin Treaties would be very difficult. Moreover, as Nyasaland alone taxed the import of cotton piece goods and the export of tea and tobacco, it would lose much revenue if made to conform to Rhodesian practice. G. H. Baxter, summing up, suggested a fiscal commission might examine the case for a customs union. He claimed that the economic advantages of unification were highly desirable and that the obstacles in its path were not insuperable. Discussion on excise was postponed until the financial arrangements were known.

In like manner, with the Southern Rhodesians urging unification and the northerners dragging their feet, the Conference continued to examine the list, item by item, and in four meetings agreed that 17 departments were most suitable for unification. These were: census and statistics, broadcasting, defence, immigration, national parks, town planning, archives, public relations, geological and trigonometrical survey, civil aviation, meteorology, research, higher education, inter-territorial roads, patents, and weights and measures and assays. Looking at the statutory bodies, it was found that Central African Airways was already an inter-territorial service, and that the unification of the Electricity Supply Commission, railways, Land Bank and Currency Board was desirable. Further consideration by a working party was felt to be needed in the cases of the Cold Storage Commission, Natural Resources Board, Cotton Research and Industry Board, and the National Building and Housing Board.

It was agreed that there would be no advantage to be gained from unifying the mining departments or, because there were two different systems of law, those of justice. Agreement on the merger of income tax departments was, however, never reached. The Southern Rhodesians maintained that, even if three separate laws were retained, a single organisation could administer them and at the same time reap the benefit of not needing double tax agreements between the territories, lessening the work of assessing, increasing the interchange of information and the ability to decentralise and thereby achieving closer contact with the taxpayer. Benson told how the East African High Commission had gained from having a single tax department. Professor Wheare supported the Southern Rhodesians, but the Northern Rhodesians and the Nyasalanders stated that the full current and expected income would be needed by their territories, and that their legislatures were jealous of their powers to tax. Thus only the administrative advantages of centralisation could be discussed, and the northerners doubted whether there were any. In their view, there was little point in surrendering the administration of a department and not the control of policy.

When discussing a unified police force, the Southern Rhodesian memorandum acknowledged that in the northern police forces the lowest European rank was that of assistant-inspector who received a short period of training in Britain before being placed on strength. In Southern Rhodesia the European joined as a constable and had prolonged initial training. His force, the British South Africa Police, had also a military role. The Southern Rhodesian Native Department had only a minor police role, but the northern district administrations were totally responsible for policing the rural areas, with the police forces confining themselves to the developed areas. (There was, in fact, a police presence in some rural districts.) The advantages of unification would be that there would be no territorial boundaries across which criminals could escape, and thus no need for extradition. Areas could be quickly reinforced. There would be better intelligence coverage, and centralised training would be of great benefit. Immigration was a police subject in all three territories and much could be gained from a central bureau of criminal records and fingerprints. There would be no problem in aligning African terms of service.

The northerners, unmoved, argued that the territories should be responsible for their own police forces, particularly while the territorial legislatures retained a preponderance of powers. A common training, they felt, would benefit only senior officers, but there might be advantages in having a central force as a reserve — in the past the BSAP had several times served in neighbouring territories. Professor Wheare commented that in the United States and Australia, police was a state function and, in Canada, where there was a federal force, some of the provinces employed it while others raised their own. He thought that, as the police dealt with local affairs, they should be responsible to the state but should co-operate closely with other forces. The meeting decided that only services such as finger-printing would benefit from unification. The centralisation of the prison services was, by contrast, recognised as desirable but impracticable on psychological grounds because of the likely reaction of the northern African population.

As the three territories formed broadly a homogeneous ecological unit, the Southern Rhodesians proclaimed that there was much to be gained from pooling research and experience in forestry. The members of the Colonial forestry service were transferred throughout the Empire and thus, it was argued, unification would ensure that men who had local experience were retained. The Nyasalanders, however, were anxious for conservation reasons to keep local control. The Northern Rhodesians commented that if amalgamation were permissible — and the chairman interrupted to say that it was not — then unification would be the forestry service's fate. They demanded that it remained a territorial subject because the fruits of the forest were an integral part of the African's economy, and anything involved with the African's daily life could not be centralised. They wanted to be entitled to use facilities such as the Imperial Forestry Institute and remain members of the Colonial service with its world-wide promotional prospects. The Conference responded by immediately appointing a working party to examine conditions of service for the civil servants. Yet the Northern Rhodesians still demanded recognition of their objections because they had co-operated so well in agreeing to the unification of 17 departments. In the event, the Conference decided that only the research aspect of forestry could be combined.

In the debate on printing and stationery, the difficulty raised by the Northern Rhodesians was that their African employees were doing more advanced work than their southern counterparts which made it awkward to assimilate them. The Southern Rhodesians confirmed that their department was staffed entirely by Europeans, but claimed the employment of Africans was being considered.

The same Northern Rhodesian objection was raised over employment in the postal service because, unlike Southern Rhodesia, Northern Rhodesia had a racially mixed staff, while Nyasaland employed mainly Africans. The Southern Rhodesians, however, proposed that established systems could continue under unification. The Northern Rhodesian delegates jibbed because the Association of Post Office Officials in Southern Rhodesia objected to Africans being employed in certain skilled posts. They sought to avoid having this attitude imported into their territory as had happened with the railways. The Southern Rhodesians acknowledged that it was unlikely that this Association would change its mind but, they argued, unification remained feasible because, when a man accepted inter-territorial transfer, he would have to accept conditions as he found them. In any case, the position in Southern Rhodesia was under review, and training schools to fit the Africans for more advanced positions were being established. Accordingly, the Conference appointed a working party to examine the question of safeguards for Africans in government employment in the event of unification.

A common irrigation service was resisted, fruitlessly, by the Northern Rhodesians because it would affect African rural life. By Thursday, 8 March, Southern Rhodesian patience was beginning to fray. In an inconclusive debate on the merger of the health services, the Northern Rhodesians conceded that it was highly desirable but claimed that it was impossible, beyond employing a common staff, because their Government had directly involved the district administration in certain health matters. Furthermore, funds had already been set aside for the expansion of health facilities in their development plan. They cautioned that great care would have to be taken in recommending services for unification because there was still a good chance that the African would accept the plan if reassured that his day to day life would be unaffected. The proposals had to be bold to attract Southern Rhodesian Europeans but, if they were too ambitious, they were doomed and should not be hazarded over a combined health service. In any case, before a decision could be taken, the view of the three territorial medical directors would be needed. The Nyasaland delegation supported these views.

Replying, the leader of the Southern Rhodesian delegation, A. H. Strachan (later Sir Andrew), emphasised that the economic benefit of closer association was the vital consideration. Health, he maintained, was a subject peculiarly suited to unification. He did not take seriously the likelihood of African objection because only the administrative structure would be changed and the African would continue to attend the same hospital as before. Southern Rhodesia had earmarked funds for development but would be prepared to revise its plans if any proposals were forthcoming from the Conference. He rejected the consultation of the medical directors because each delegation should have been fully briefed by its Government.

His deputy, and Secretary for Internal Affairs, A. D. Evans (later Sir Athol), was less restrained, confessing to being bewildered by the lack of objectivity or realism being displayed. He said he had come to the Conference believing that the task was to consider objectively closer association in all its aspects on the basis of its desirability and practicality. He had to judge the issue dispassionately and come to his own conclusion, bearing in mind the total situation in Central Africa and the Commonwealth. There were, he acknowledged, tremendous problems to be overcome and if they were insuperable the Governments would have to be told. He defended the Southern Rhodesian document as a genuine attempt to state the advantages and difficulties of unification. The Southern Rhodesians were aware of the intensity of the northern African opposition, but felt that it should not inhibit free discussion of every problem.

Benson thought that, as all were agreed on the economic and administrative advantages of unification, the Conference, in making its recommendations, should draw attention to the African opposition and suggest ways of overcoming it. He did not, however, convince the Northern Rhodesians who argued that they wanted the Conference's recommendations to have a chance of being accepted and thus African prejudice would have to be evaluated. They believed that the unification of the health services should not be proposed because of the likely African rejection. The meeting, in fact, took no decision.

In the debate on the next subject, the Northern Rhodesians alone objected to the unification of the European education departments because they were planning to expand their own system and a merger could disrupt their plans. This provoked the Southern Rhodesians to comment that there was a disturbing note in the Northern Rhodesians' objections, which was that their development plan might be affected. The Southern Rhodesians knew, too, that their plans would be disrupted but thought it was most undesirable to consider matters from a parochial point of view. The Northern Rhodesian defence was that reference to their development programme would reveal what capital was available. However, on the next day, without debate, it was agreed that the European education departments were most suitable for unification.

Although a number of subjects was likewise accepted that day, Friday 9 March, the Southern Rhodesians were close to despair. The final debate of the day concerned trade and industrial development which the Southern Rhodesians had wanted to be centrally controlled as a logical consequence of the common use of Beira and the railway system. They argued that the territories, in any case, had almost identical policies, although Southern Rhodesia was not subject to British control and had recently relaxed some import restrictions. They felt that the advantages of centralisation were the co-ordination of planning and the development of economic resources and transport. It would give the area greater external bargaining power.

The northerners were not to be persuaded: the Nyasalanders wished to control their own economy, and the Northern Rhodesians wanted their Government to retain its role, through the development plan, of sponsor of industry. The Northern Rhodesians had recently established a trade, transport and industrial development department and they were loathe to lose it. They suggested the formation of an advisory inter-territorial production and supply council.

The Southern Rhodesians, standing their ground, rejected this council, calling it anaemic because it would lack executive power. They reminded the Northern Rhodesians that they also had a department with similar functions. They claimed that the maximum benefit to the overall economy would be obtained from this merger and they felt that the Northern Rhodesians should not assume that the centralised department would adopt Southern Rhodesian practices and policies. The avoidance of duplication would mean that development capital would not be wasted. The territories already shared the currency, the southerners noted, and their economies were closely interlinked.

Professor Wheare counselled that all existing federations had experienced difficulties with the division of control of this subject as the functions of trade and industry could not be divorced entirely from either the federal or the state governments without weakening their structures. Usually the federal government handled external trade and left the internal to the states. Price control was a federal subject in most cases to secure uniformity. The chairman then adjourned the discussion for the weekend.

The Southern Rhodesians took a desperate view: it was a depressingly cold and wet March and they decided that, unless there was a radical change in the Conference's attitude, they would endure one further week of negotiations before throwing in their hand. This they revealed to Benson who, being a personal friend of Cohen, thought he could persuade him to bring the northerners to heel. That evening, Friday, 9 March, Benson visited Cohen at his Hampstead home where he had spent the week with influenza. Cohen agreed to discuss the situation with Strachan on the following afternoon.

Strachan told Cohen of the dismay of his delegation at the negative and destructive criticism encountered to date. Cohen, though hardly recovered, responded by promising to attend Monday's plenary session to remedy matters.[9] He was as good as his word.

On Monday, 12 March, discussion was renewed on trade and development. The Northern Rhodesians were just as intransigent. They had decided that, at least until the form of closer association was known, they could not change their attitude and, unless the territories were amalgamated, they would not relinquish control of this subject. They were anxious to retain the British direction of Northern Rhodesia's external trade relations to avoid any conflict with British interests. They were prepared, however, to abandon their proposed production and supply council for a central advisory committee on economic policy which could assist in the task of co-ordination in the early stages. They argued that their Legislative Council would not allow them to make any greater concession.

The Nyasaland delegation supported this stand, but the Southern Rhodesians warned that they regarded this matter as one of fundamental importance because the chief aim of the Conference was to lay the foundation of a great British Central African state which could not be done by unifying a few services of little significance. In a world recession the central government would have to act quickly which the United States President had been unable to do in the Great Slump. They maintained that the retention of control of economic policy by the territories would render the customs union unworkable, particularly because Northern Rhodesia would continue to negotiate tariffs with British guidance. An advisory council could not act to prevent over-capitalisation which could have serious results in a depression. Furthermore, there would be little point in having a common statistics department if

[9] Author's interviews with the late Sir Andrew Strachan and Sir Athol Evans.

it would not serve a central economic organisation. The Southern Rhodesian delegation doubted the efficacy of purely consultative bodies in the light of the experience of the Central African Council, because when public opinion ran against them they were powerless to influence policies.

Provoked, Benson interjected that not enough ground had yet been covered for the Conference to judge this issue. However, he recalled a similar advisory committee of the CAC had been emasculated by a Southern Rhodesian refusal to allow it executive power. The current discussion showed to him, at least, a mellowing of the Southern Rhodesians. He believed that, in the last three years, the lack of economic co-ordination had been the principle cause of dissension within the CAC. He agreed that advisory bodies were only successful when they had public support and felt that, if closer association was to succeed, there would have to be central control of some of the economic functions.

Cohen sided with Benson: he stated there would have to be some effective common machinery to deal with economic matters if closer association were to be achieved, as planning and control were the keys to success of inter-territorial organisations. He suggested, and the Conference agreed, that a sub-committee should examine this problem. The Southern Rhodesians, when questioned, reassured the Conference that their Government would not again refuse to surrender control of economic matters, provided the central body was responsible to the peoples of the territories.

Cohen had wrought such a change that, by the early afternoon, the Conference had decided whether or not to recommend the unification of mining, justice, higher education and the statutory bodies. This was done with such speed that the Southern Rhodesians had to confess that they were unprepared when the chairman proposed the examination of the form of closer association. The Northern Rhodesian delegation, however, was ready to speak and outlined the possible formulae: amalgamation, federation or confederation. The last, they proposed, would have a central legislature to deal with the unified services, while the territorial legislatures would be responsible for the residue. A fourth possibility was to unify services without establishing a central legislature.

Rejecting amalgamation, the Northern Rhodesians noted that there was a large number of services which the Conference had agreed could not be unified. These would need separate legislatures to control them as would the administration of African policies. There was, too, no possibility of persuading the northern Africans, the Europeans or the British public to accept or condone amalgamation. Furthermore, harping on their established theme, they maintained that, as Northern Rhodesia had embarked on an elaborate development plan, its Legislative Council was unlikely to surrender it at this stage. The unification of services without a central legislature would be impossibly difficult as departments had to be responsible to a higher authority for policy, and the territories had already experienced considerable problems in enacting parallel legislation. What the Northern Rhodesians did favour was federation or confederation because then powers would be defined and each government would be independent within its own sphere. Experience elsewhere had proved federation to be a worthwhile practical solution. It provided a body to legislate for common services but left the territories free to deal with African affairs and departments which could not be unified. It would allow a large measure of Colonial Office control, particularly of African affairs, to be maintained.

The Nyasaland delegation agreed that unified services had to be responsible to a legislative authority. It was important, too, that the federal representatives should feel responsible for the interests of their territories. Thus the territorial legislatures should be used as electoral colleges for the federal parliament, selecting the members on an inter-racial basis.

Benson, seeking to simplify the issue and winning Cohen's support, argued that a central legislature could be established but it need not function fully on a federal pattern. It was generally felt that it was most important to avoid the use of the word "federation" because of the political significance it had already acquired.

Wheare thought that the title "Central Africa" would suffice. He stated that there was a number of different suitable governmental forms. He understood that public opinion was more likely to accept the surrender of more functions to an organisation which appeared to have powers delegated to it than one which seemed to take over powers from the three Governments. It was difficult to say yet which form of government would be the most appropriate, and he thought it should be remembered that, under the unitary system, a great deal of decentralisation was possible. Benson's suggestion was not, in Wheare's opinion, as clear cut as federation, but it could take several forms. The central legislature could be tied to the territorial legislatures and its bills require the assent of the territorial Governors. Some of the British protective functions could well be assumed by the "African Affairs Board" which the Working Party on Safeguards for African Employees would propose to the Conference.

Cohen said that, at the outset, the existing Governments should recognise that closer association would bring some limitation of their powers.

Before adjourning for the day, the meeting considered again the partition of Northern Rhodesia. Benson rejected it because the African areas would be cut off from their source of development finance, the mines, and could bankrupt the Rhodesias by withholding their labour. The chairman chose to play the Devil's advocate and argued that, as the line of rail territory was similar to Southern Rhodesia in that it contained a significant European population, the unified territory would be more cohesive than if it included the northern territories in their current form. The British Government could assume financial responsibility for the excluded areas or force Greater Rhodesia to do so as part of the price of unification.

The Northern Rhodesian delegation noted that the most vocal opponents of unification lived along the line of rail, and claimed that partition would stunt growth. To Cohen, partition was the worst of the solutions offered because inherent parts of Northern Rhodesia would be lopped off, severing the industrial areas from their sources of labour. It was a form of *apartheid* which would undermine the concept of partnership when the African realised that the area in which he lived would be excluded.

On the following morning, 13 March, the Southern Rhodesians were ready to speak on closer association. Evans, who was leading the delegation in the absence of Strachan, who had been stricken by influenza, spoke first and called on the Conference to be realistic, objective, honest and determined in seeking a solution which would be of enduring benefit to Central Africa and the Commonwealth. The ideal formula should be advanced so that its obstacles should be identified and the way round them discovered. He believed the Conference had recognised the advantages of closer association in the social, strategic and political fields, and knew that there was an urgent need to establish a British bloc capable of resisting dangerous outside influences. The Conference had accepted the advantages of unifying services yet would only condone it where no major issues of policy arose. Thus there would have to be a greater measure of agreement before closer association became possible. In particular, the alignment of African policies would have to be more closely studied. These difficulties aside, Evans was confident that the discussions had pointed to a single ideal solution, namely the union of the three territories under one sovereign government.

Evans acknowledged, however, that the Conference would not recommend amalgamation unless it could find a method of overcoming African opposition. Unitary government was, of course, the most efficient method and there were substantial objections to the federal alternative. The essence of federation was a contract between the states, and there was always a great deal of constitutional wrangling. A great disadvantage was the power of the judiciary to declare legislation invalid which led to confusion of the legal and judicial branches of government. Roosevelt's New Deal had been hindered by the United States' judges, and in Australia there was discontent over the power of the judiciary to override the wishes of the electorate. Federal government was costly in terms of manpower and money, and there would be difficulties over citizenship. It was a rigid system and the difficulties of amending it were notorious. The Northern Rhodesians had suggested federation as a step towards unity, but experience elsewhere had proved to the contrary. The Africans, Evans thought, would not understand the federal system and might see it as an attempt to minimise their political standing and aspirations.

The main principle of federation, Evans argued, was that the central government should tackle problems which were common to all the territories and the African population could only be governed successfully if a common policy was pursued throughout. The need for a common native policy had turned convinced federationists in South Africa into unionists in 1909. Friction was inevitable if the Colonial Office retained control of African affairs in the northern territories and applied a different policy from that of Southern Rhodesia. A division of functions on a racial basis was undesirable and it would be difficult to divorce African affairs from other aspects of government. If the territories retained control of African policies, it would be difficult to justify direct African representation in the central parliament and this could constitute a serious objection to federation.

Evans recalled that it had been recognised that the amalgamation of the Rhodesias was the ultimate objective and even the Northern Rhodesians present had proposed federation as a step to ultimate union. He was not, however, blind to the objections to amalgamation. He knew that the northern Africans disliked Southern Rhodesia's pass and de-stocking laws and that they feared the loss of their political rights. However, the Conference had found little difference between the two Rhodesias' pass laws and a unified state could apply different laws to meet local circumstances. De-stocking had been effected on pragmatic grounds to meet a local problem and need not apply elsewhere. It would have to be established at the outset that there could be no retreat on African political rights.

Evans appealed for a bold, imaginative approach. Union was the ideal solution and the Southern Rhodesians would recommend to their Government direct African representation as part of the price. They would propose six African members, two from each territory. It was likely that the Southern Rhodesians would accept this, if Huggins recommended it, because they were worried about the increasing influence of South Africa. It might be necessary to introduce the common roll in the North and nominated African members might then be gradually replaced by elected Africans. The protection of African rights in local government, too, might be made a pre-condition of amalgamation. If there was an upper house it could contain nominated members specially charged with the care of African interests and they could be associated with the working party's proposed African affairs board. The continuance of development plans could also be made a condition of amalgamation if the territories felt that their parliamentary representatives could not offer them sufficient defence. Evans acknowledged that the annexation of the northern territories might set a precedent for South Africa to acquire the High Commission Territories, but then she would have to agree to direct African representation in her parliament. Evans also expected Britain to be attacked on this subject in the General Assembly of the United Nations but was confident that she could withstand it.

Evans's colleagues supported him, stressing that any proposals had to be of real substance. They were confident that the Africans could be persuaded to accept change. They had not, however, won Cohen round. He explained that those who rejected amalgamation were, nevertheless, aware of the benefits of closer association. They realised that this could be the last chance and thus were loath to waste it by proposing something which had little hope of being accepted in Britain. Cohen acknowledged that there were many British misconceptions, that the Southern Rhodesian African policy was often confused with South Africa's, but the British Parliament was being asked to surrender its responsibility for government in the northern territories and would not accept the mere reservation of certain legislation as had happened in Southern Rhodesia. Yet the latter's electorate had to be won over, and decisions had to be taken on the form of government and which services could be centrally administered. He wanted to hear Southern Rhodesia's views and thought that the disadvantages of federation had been overstated, while the advantages of amalgamation had been exaggerated.

W. L. Dale, Professor Wheare's fellow legal adviser, immediately dismissed annexation as an obstacle to federation because protectorates had been absorbed without it in Kenya, the Gold Coast, Sierra Leone and Malaya. The territorial constitutional differences did raise the problem of federal citizenship but this, to him, was not of prime importance, and the best compromise was to have an internal status without external effect.

The northern delegations supported Cohen and warned that closer association could not be imposed on a reluctant people, either black or white. In their opinion, federation would create the desired strong British bloc. It was certainly feasible because they had agreed to centralise everything except police, prisons, agriculture, veterinary services and forestry, and a compromise might yet be found on health. The federal government would administer the railways, the airways and the roads which represented a capital expenditure of several millions. The Southern Rhodesians then drily noted that the last-named services were the functions of the established statutory commissions.

The Southern Rhodesians were unconvinced and in the following week would raise again the desirability of amalgamating in order to be able to resist the militancy and aggressiveness of South Africa. They provoked further lengthy expositions by Cohen, the chairman, and the northern delegations on its impracticability in the face of African and British opposition. They were told the choice lay between confederation or federation and, on 19 March, the chairman ordered the Conference to concentrate on a federal solution. The Southern Rhodesians thereupon accepted federation as the better alternative. The Conference responded by allowing the Southern Rhodesian viewpoint on amalgamation to be recorded in their confidential, but not their public, report.

Before this decision was taken, the Conference had examined a document on a federal structure written by the Northern Rhodesians in response to a Southern Rhodesian suggestion that they should abandon their negative attitude towards unification. In the midst of discussion on this, the problem of safeguarding African interests was considered and it was recognised that the mere reservation of certain categories of legislation would not satisfy the British Government and would remove from the British Parliament its right to debate the northern territories' affairs. One solution was to place the power of assent to federal legislation in the hands of the territorial Governors, thus effectively leaving the existing machinery intact. If this were adopted, the British Government would have to proclaim that this power would not be used except in circumstances when African interests seemed seriously threatened. The same convention would have to apply to the Southern Rhodesian Governor because constitutionally he could only act on the advice of the Southern Rhodesian Government. Another method, the Northern Rhodesians said, was to use the proposed African affairs board to review legislation. If this board found the legislation to be detrimental to African interests then it would be reserved for His Majesty's pleasure.

The African affairs board was the invention of R. S. Hudson, head of the Colonial Office's African Studies Department and the late Secretary for Native Affairs in Northern Rhodesia. He had proposed it from the chair of the Working Party on Safeguards for African Civil Servants when it had met on 8 March. He envisaged a board served by the three Secretaries for Native Affairs, three European members chosen by each of the territorial legislatures, and three Africans drawn from the Legislative Councils or the

African Representative and Protectorate Councils. The board, Hudson thought, should examine any proposed legislation regarding the unified services and report on it, if African interests were affected, to whichever legislature was enacting it. This would have a moral effect and provide a strong safeguard, particularly if the board's opinion was published along with the draft bill. The board would also have a watching brief over the administration of the combined departments and would be empowered to hear representations from any aggrieved African.

The working party and, in particular, the three Secretaries for Native Affairs serving on it, greeted this as the germ of a commendable idea. The British representatives and their legal advisers in the plenary session on 14 March saw it as a method of establishing links between the federal and British Governments. Wheare and Dale suggested that the board's chairman should be an *ex-officio* member of the federal cabinet and legislature and be appointed and dismissed directly by the relevant Secretary of State or indirectly through the governor-general. The chairman would be responsible for initiating all discussion on matters affecting African interests. The federal ministers would not have the power to influence the governor-general in the appointment of the chairman. Rather than give the chairman the power to disrupt the working of the Cabinet, Wheare and Dale proposed that he should report to the governor-general to whom would be entrusted the veto. Cohen, though demanding careful definition of the functions of the board, welcomed this as a means to make the abdication of power more palatable to the British Parliament. Baxter agreed, remarking that an upper house would not serve as an alternative because it would contain a majority of European members.

Predictably, the opposition to aspects of this suggestion came from the Southern Rhodesian delegation because they feared that some of these could result in the total rejection of the federal scheme by their electorate. Southern Rhodesians well understood parliamentary and cabinet systems and might object to the chairman of the African affairs board having a seat in the cabinet when he was not responsible to the electorate but was capable of rendering government impossible by provoking crises which resulted in mass resignations of ministers. Cohen answered that, therefore, the chairman and the governor-general would have to take great care. Wheare agreed that the chairman's position would be anomalous yet this was, in his opinion, the best solution. Cohen thought that the connection with the Secretary of State could be made less obvious by allowing the governor-general to use his discretion in appointing the chairman. The Conference entrusted Dale with the task of formulating a definite proposal.

He had done so by 19 March and his proposal was substantially adopted after considerable debate. One adjustment that was made was to accommodate the Southern Rhodesians who conceded the placing of the chairman in the cabinet but demanded that he be chosen from the ranks of the federal legislature. The Southern Rhodesians were driven to co-operate by the feeling that the unanimity of the Conference was important and that issues such as the African affairs board could be re-examined by their politicians in subsequent negotiations.

Thus the Conference's subsequent report proposed that, apart from a chairman, each territory be represented on the board by three members: its Secretary for Native Affairs, a nominated or elected unofficial Member of its legislature, and an African — the last two being appointees of the territorial Governor. Before publication, the board would examine proposed principal and subsidiary legislation and report on it to the federal government. If the board reported that the legislation would be, in its opinion, detrimental to African interests, the federal government could introduce it, but the governor-general would have to reserve it for the Secretary of State. The board would generally watch over African interests and in particular consider and report on any representations made to it by any recognised body concerning African interests and the administration of the unified services. The third objective was to promote liaison between the territorial departments dealing with African affairs, a task made all the easier by the presence of the three Secretaries for Native Affairs within the membership of the board. The chairman and his board, however, would be powerless to intervene in subjects outside the federal compass, such as the internal workings of the territorial Governments.

The chairman, having a seat in the cabinet, would be called the minister for African interests and would be appointed by the governor-general from amongst the members representing African interests in the federal legislature. Though the governor-general would use his discretion in making or terminating this appointment, he would need confirmation by the Secretary of State. The chairman would propose, within the cabinet, measures needed to serve African interests and to ensure that his fellow ministers' proposals were not detrimental to Africans. It was expected that discussion would resolve most difficulties. If it did not, and the chairman was confident that African interests were endangered, he would have to report on the proposed action to the governor-general. The governor-general would certify this opinion, transmit it to the Secretary of State, and action would be suspended until it was known whether the latter would give or withhold his approval. If the federal prime minister demanded action on the grounds of urgent public necessity, the governor-general could use his discretion to sanction it but would still have to report thereafter to the Secretary of State.

Imbued with this spirit of constructive compromise, the Conference worked through the remaining days of March to produce its unanimous Report which recommended the federation of the three territories. The Report was prefaced with a recollection of Griffiths's statement of 8 November 1950 that the delegates' work would be exploratory and that their Governments were free to accept or reject their findings provided that public opinion was consulted first. Following the established form of such reports, it reviewed the area's geography and history and detailed its physical resources, national income, industrial development and constitutional status. It recalled that the Bledisloe Commission had predicted increasing inter-dependence but had jibbed at recommending immediate amalgamation because of the experimental nature of the African policies, the existing African opposition, the smallness and inexperience of the European population, the difficulties presented by the differing constitutional status of the territories, and the financial weakness of the northern territories. The Bledisloe Commission had rejected a federal solution without, in the Conference's opinion, a sufficient examination. Instead the Bledisloe recommendation had been the creation of the Central African Council.

When conditions had permitted it, the CAC had been established with some success. However, it had reached the limit of its usefulness in promoting closer collaboration because it lacked executive powers and, since the Bledisloe Report, substantial changes had occurred in the area. The Conference's examination of current African policies had discovered a greater degree of similarity, rather than of difference, in the three Governments' concepts and practices. There was no difference in policy in education, agriculture, animal health and forestry as far as they affected Africans. Southern Rhodesia continued to spend more on services for the Africans but the northern territories had encouraged a greater participation of Africans in local government. Southern Rhodesia was, however, making amends in this field. There were acknowledged differences in political development, particularly in the direct representation of Africans in territorial politics, in land allocation, certain aspects of employment, and the recognition of trade unions. The differences largely related to timing and method, for the common goal was the political, social and economic advancement of the Africans in partnership with the Europeans. The differences, the Conference reported, no longer constituted a valid objection to closer association, provided a suitable scheme could be evolved. Indeed, closer association was likely to stimulate the alignment of African policies.

The opposition of African opinion to unification was a serious obstacle, yet the delegates were convinced that the Africans would ultimately judge any proposal for closer association on its merits, taking note of its form and the range of subjects within the competence of the central government. Africans might recognise the substantial advantages of closer association if their representation was adequate and their interests protected, and if services directly affecting their daily lives were not administered centrally. Northern and Southern Rhodesian Europeans would be attracted by the establishment of a strong central government. Constitutional advances since the Bledisloe Report, the Conference explained, made it possible to devise a plan which would take into account the still differing constitutional status of the territories and yet provide effective common services. The northern territories, and Northern Rhodesia in particular, had grown in financial strength and had sufficient resources to participate in closer association.

The experience of the last decade, the Conference maintained, had shown the need for inter-territorial co-ordination of policy and action in economic development. A single economic unit would exert greater influence in external economic relations, and recessions would be better worn by the diversity of the combined economy. In addition, local and Commonwealth defence and communications would be improved, and services such as higher education for all races, which currently could not be provided by the individual territories, could be established. Moral and social aspects were not being ignored, for quickening economic expansion would bring greater prosperity and development for the African in particular. Indeed, the Conference claimed, a crucial stage had been reached as African political consciousness — a product of expansion of social and economic services — was growing, and the thoughtful elements of both races were anxious about developments in South Africa. All three territorial Governments recognised that partnership was the only policy likely to succeed and the benefits of closer association would provide the basis for extending partnership without fear of outside interference. Inter-territorial institutions would promote in all races a common outlook, and the nature of the population could be determined by a mutual immigration policy.

The recommendation for closer association was urgent but not without qualification, as any scheme would have to encompass Southern Rhodesia's self-governing status and British responsibilities in Northern Rhodesia and Nyasaland. The African's welfare, political advancement and place within government and political institutions had to be guaranteed at least until he was in a position to compete on equal terms with the European. Lastly, the central government had to be economically self-sufficient and autonomous in the field of finance.

The Conference Report examined the form of closer association on the premise that it should promote the well-being of the territories and their inhabitants and be acceptable to the governments and legislatures concerned. Amalgamation and the partition of Northern Rhodesia were rejected as impracticable, unacceptable solutions which would only engender African hostility. The solution was a true federal system which would permit effective common action when necessary but leave territorial authority and British obligations largely unimpaired. The name of the federation would be British Central Africa.

The federal authority would be responsible for specific matters, particularly external economic relations, leaving the territories, their constitutions and their relations with the British Government otherwise unchanged. In their own fields, however, the federal government and its legislature would reign supreme. Matters affecting the daily life of the African, such as education, health, agriculture, land, settlement and African administration generally would remain territorial responsibilities. Where African interests were affected by federal legislation, protection would be provided by the direct representation of Africans in the federal parliament and through an African affairs board and its chairman who, though a cabinet minister, would be appointed by the governor-general under the direction of the British Government. For harmony and efficiency, consultative machinery would be established.

This, the Conference claimed, was not a compromise because the delegates were united in believing it to be in the interests of all and consistent with British responsibilities. The proposed new institutions, the African affairs board and a Central African loans council, could be of inestimable value. Giving the federal government external and inter-territorial affairs, the Conference proposed that defence, rail, trunk road and air communications, posts and telegraphs, external and some aspects of internal trade, customs and medium- and long-termed research should be federal functions. The territories would administer local government for all races, African affairs, African primary and secondary education, health, agriculture, animal health, forestry, game and police. Thus African fears about the effects of closer association should be answered and African advancement in national politics and local government could continue along current lines. Territorial constitutional status would be unaffected, Southern Rhodesia would continue to be self-governing and Northern Rhodesia and Nyasaland would remain responsible to the British Government. The federation itself would have a fully responsible government and legislature with a cabinet system, subject only to the safeguards preserving British responsibilities.

The functions of the African affairs board were detailed together with the methods of appointing and dismissing the chairman and his responsibilities. These arrangements, the Conference stated, would have several advantages. The chairman would be a local man and the board would operate in Central Africa. The members would be men of practical experience in the territories and the presence of Africans would ensure that their peoples' views would be known. The British governmental and parliamentary position would be safeguarded by having British sanction for any legislation suspected of being contrary to African interests. The Conference expected, however, that this power would be little used. A further advantage was the sense of security which these arrangements could be expected to induce in the African.

Turning to the economic aspects of closer association, the Conference proposed to exploit existing territorial development programmes by co-ordinating them through a development commission composed of representatives of the federal and territorial Governments and legislatures. In close co-operation with them would be a central planning staff, forming part of a federal ministry. Both bodies, in reviewing and co-ordinating development, would take into account the existing territorial plans which must continue. The planning staff, working closely with the territorial Governments, could calculate the whole area's needs for finance, personnel and supplies. The responsibility for the execution of development programmes would lie with the federal and territorial ministries.

Persisting in this theme, the Conference proposed the establishment, on the Australian model, of a Central African loans council to assess all the loan requirements of the federal and territorial Governments and to control all external borrowing. The members of the council would be of ministerial or equivalent rank and it would be empowered to take final decisions on federal and territorial priorities and the size of the loan programme, subject to consultation with the British Government before access was sought to the London market. The Conference believed that, through this council, co-ordination of development throughout Central Africa could be best effected by the development commission and the tariff and economic advisory committees. It was the best way to harness the resources for the benefit of all, particularly if attention was paid to encouraging the more backward areas to play their full part in the economy.

Taking up the questions of the apportionment of functions between the four governments, the federal constitution, its legislature, ministerial offices and relationship with the British Government, the Conference thought it necessary to state that, if the advantages of federation would be realised, the federal government would have to possess sufficient authority and prestige to attract not only loyalty above local and territorial influences, but men of calibre to serve it in the difficult formative period. Thus it had to have a wide range of activities and executive responsibilities and financial independence even though it had to be excluded from matters relating to the daily life of the African. In framing their proposals, the delegates had borne in mind that the major advantages of unification lay in the economic field, had acknowledged that some services were better administered on a regional basis, and had dwelt only on the subjects to be federalised as it was outside their competence to make recommendations for the territories.

An outline of the division of functions was provided. The federal list contained: external affairs, defence, federal income tax, federal borrowing, immigration and aliens, customs, external trade (including import and export control and promotion and the negotiation of trade treaties), exchange control, certain inter-territorial trade matters, census and statistics, currency, company legislation, insurance, banks and land bank, bills of exchange and promissory notes, bankruptcy and insolvency, copyright, patents, trade marks and designs, economic planning and development (including general industrial development), medium- and long-term research, major water development, electricity supply and distribution, civil aviation, meteorological services, railways, trunk roads, posts and telegraphs, broadcasting, films and tourism, European primary and secondary education, higher education, certain specific health services, geological, trigonometrical and topographical surveys, national parks, town planning, factory inspection, certain specialised police services, weights and measures, archives and legal proceedings by and against the federal government.

The federal government would obviously also have the power to set up its own treasury, audit, public services commission, public works department and other necessary organs of government. This left the territories with: provincial and African administration, territorial income tax, agriculture, forestry, veterinary services, game, fisheries, co-operative societies, marketing, health, African primary and secondary education, labour, mines, local government, police, prisons, territorial public works, roads and irrigation.

Dwelling on this list, the Conference assumed that, like Southern Rhodesia, the federal government would be allowed to conduct certain international negotiations, particularly of a commercial nature. The questions of customs and tariffs were complicated by existing differing structures, industrial needs and the Congo Basin Treaties which forbade discriminatory tariffs within the conventional zone. These problems were soluble in the Conference's opinion and it proposed that there should be a tariff advisory committee which would be representative of the four governments and empowered to make recommendations on tariff matters. This would work in conjunction with the development commission, the loans council and the central planning staff. An economic advisory committee, likewise representative of the federal and territorial Governments, would assist the federal government in co-ordinating marketing, price stability, expansion of production, wages, rents and building control, all of which would remain in territorial hands.

The Conference examined next the structure of government and proposed the appointment of a governor-general who would assent to the acts of the federal legislature, subject to His Majesty's usual power of disallowance. This appointment, it was expected, would do much to promote a common loyalty. There was, however, no thought for the moment of supplanting the territorial Governors. A bi-cameral legislature was thought to be inappropriate because of the expected difficulty in finding men of calibre to serve it in addition to the territorial legislatures. As it was undesirable for any one territory's representatives to outnumber the combined forces of the other two, the Conference proposed that the federal parliament should have 35 seats, with 17 allocated to Southern Rhodesia, eleven to Northern Rhodesia and seven to Nyasaland. Three members from each territory would be specially chosen to represent African interests, and in the case of the northern members two of these would be Africans. A uniform franchise for the whole area was neither desirable nor possible because of the differing stages of political development.

The governor-general would reserve for His Majesty's pleasure any bill reported by the African affairs board to be detrimental to African interests. Furthermore, the Royal Instructions would require the governor-general to refer to the Secretary of State before assenting to certain classes of legislation such as those inconsistent with treaty obligations or those affecting currency. The governor-general would invite the member of the legislature most likely to command the support of the majority of the representatives to form a government. This member would submit to the governor-general a proposed list of ministers. A convention would be established that there should be at least one member of the cabinet from each territory. All ministers, except for the minister for African interests, would be responsible to the legislature. The prime minister would decide on the size of his cabinet, but the Conference suggested that the most appropriate number of ministers would be six, including the minister for African interests.

The Conference recommended that the federal government should have its own civil service. It proposed that the Rhodesia and Nyasaland Court of Appeal should become the supreme judicature and would be responsible for deciding questions on the respective powers of the federal and territorial Governments. The Conference did not expect that any difficulties would arise out of the existence of differing systems of law. There was a need for separate sources of finance for the individual governments and it was estimated that the federal government would require £10 000 000 per annum for the services it would provide. This would be found from customs and postal revenue which currently earned £4 500 000 and £1 500 000 per annum respectively, and from federal income tax. Before federating, the territories would arrive at a financial settlement.

A common federal citizenship was found to be desirable, but the current territorial constitutional differences led the Conference to recommend postponement of its consideration. Finally, the Conference expressed its pleasure at reaching a unanimous conclusion. It acknowledged that it had omitted to include a specific provision for amendment of the federal constitution. It did not regard the structure as immutable but considered that the governments should indicate that there should be no major changes in the first five years.

Thereafter a review might be necessary but the governments should not commit themselves to any specific time for this. The Conference was confident that it had found an effective form of closer association.

The detail of the Conference's recommendations was largely reserved for the annexures to the Report. These surveyed the differences between the existing African policies. The functions of the African affairs board and the minister of African interests were discussed. The federal services were listed and the economic and financial arrangements were given in detail, as were the conditions of membership of the federal legislature and of service in the federal departments. The problem of federal citizenship was aired again.

The Conference, however, had more to say and appended to its Report a confidential minute. It assumed that the British and territorial Governments would wish to publish the Report and rather than give offence to the South African Government, because delegates had been influenced by certain considerations, it had chosen to reveal some of its findings under a confidential cover. The delegates had, too, discussed a variety of proposals for unification and the publication of this would only serve to confuse the public and divert its attention from the recommended solution. They had sought also to provide a document which could be easily read and could be sold at a low price.

The advantages of the closer association of the territories, the Conference noted, were clear and the arguments for it had been valid for some time. Its current urgency arose from a threat of an extension of South African influences over the Rhodesias. The expansionist aims of certain Union politicians were well known and, combined with a recent alarming increase in Afrikaner immigration, endangered the independent existence of Northern and Southern Rhodesia.

The Conference acknowledged that economic ambition and love of adventure played a large part in this northward movement. However, the immigration flow from South Africa now greatly exceeded that from Britain. Ties of blood and nationalist sympathies would make these immigrants responsive to intrigue and pressures from South Africa. Very few among them would be assimilated into the British way of life which characterised the European population. If this flow were not stemmed, the Afrikaner would predominate, particularly in Northern Rhodesia, and halt African advancement thereby prejudicing race relations.

This would inevitably lead to absorption into the Union and, in that event, Nyasaland's future too would be jeopardised. South Africa was well placed, through geographical situation and communication links, to apply economic pressure which, in the event of a slump, might prove fatal. The situation was grave, and only a larger unit could provide the strength to resist. Overall control of immigration and other aspects was needed. If African and British opinion only knew the extent of the danger, there would be little difficulty in securing support for closer association. Delay could be fatal and thus the Conference urged that "the opportunity of commending such a scheme to Southern Rhodesian opinion should now be taken under the leadership of Sir Godfrey Huggins".

The Conference revealed in this confidential minute the arguments which had been advanced for amalgamation and other forms of closer association, and explained how the arguments for federation had prevailed. Its recommendations, the Conference believed, offered a solid framework and would serve the best interests of the peoples of Central Africa. The Conference found:

> "It is of great significance that they [the proposals] have been unanimously agreed to by responsible officials of the three territories who will have the duty of operating them if the new constitution is brought into being, and some of whom will be called upon to explain and commend them to the African inhabitants."

The delegates hoped that the scheme would be simultaneously published as soon as possible with the recommendation of their Governments. They believed in particular that "nothing is better calculated to secure favourable reception of the Report by Africans than to have this measure of support from His Majesty's Government and we trust that their support may readily be made known". The British Government, the delegates acknowledged, was bound like the others to consult the peoples concerned before taking a final decision, but this did not debar it from commending the Report. The Report was in being by 31 March, but the plea for its immediate publication was ignored and it was only released in mid-June.

CHAPTER SEVEN

Marking Time under Labour

The Fourth Victoria Falls Conference and the Undermining of the Federal Cause, September 1951

ALTHOUGH the Officials' Conference had recommended federation as an urgent necessity, little was done towards achieving it in the seven months of life left to Clement Attlee's Labour Government in Britain. Eventually the Rhodesians believed that James Griffiths, the Colonial Secretary, was "sitting on the fence". The Officials' Report was published on 13 June 1951, and a Conference was held at the Victoria Falls in September. However, this Conference was undermined by disruptive elements within it and by Attlee's announcement, on its second day, of a British general election in October. Griffiths committed himself in principle to the federating of the three territories but real progress had to await the Conservatives' victory at the polls. Even then federation was delayed for two years.

After deadlock had been reached in correspondence concerning the unofficial Members' demands for a greater role in governing Northern Rhodesia, an invitation from Griffiths arrived in early February 1951 to meet him in London in April. Therefore, while the civil servants conferred in London on closer association, Welensky sought to marshal support for the secondary goal of self-government for Northern Rhodesia. Solely to achieve this, he attempted to weld together all European political groupings into a single party. He failed despite a meeting in Broken Hill which endorsed his plan, and the formation in Chingola of the Central Africa Independence Association with self-government for Northern Rhodesia as one of its aims. Welensky made the point that Southern Rhodesia had obtained self-government with an annual income of little more than £1 000 000. Northern Rhodesia's was currently £15 000 000, matching South Africa's at the time of the Union.[1] He told the Press that, while the British view of democracy was the counting of

[1] *The Rhodesia Herald*, 18 & 19 February 1951; Welensky Papers, 5/95, ff. 447–449, G. van Eeden to Welensky, 14 March 1951; f. 446, Welensky to van Eeden, 30 March 1951; 5/61, ff. 15–17, Chairman, C.A. Independence Association to Welensky, April 1951.

heads, he wanted a reasonably qualified electorate. Echoing Cecil John Rhodes, he said that partnership would achieve the enjoyment of equal rights by all civilised men. The European, through his drive, initiative and capital, would of course be the senior partner.

Welensky argued that suppression was no answer, nor was the British idea of break-neck advancement because 80 per cent of the Africans were illiterate and had no tradition of liberalism. Northern Rhodesia would be better served by steady progress. He stressed that the demand for self-government had no anti-African connotation because it was intended that the African should play the part in government for which he was fitted. Government from afar had not succeeded in Northern Rhodesia and, indeed, the country had only progressed since attaining an unofficial majority in the Legislative Council.[2]

Before Welensky left for Britain with the Northern Rhodesian delegation in late April, Huggins had been obliged to stave off an Opposition attempt to secure the alternative to federation, namely dominion status for Southern Rhodesia. The final report of the Select Committee on the Amendment of the Constitution was debated on 19 April. However, Stockil, the chairman of the Select Committee, succeeded only in detailing the proposals (a 13-man senate and the removal of the constitutional restrictions) before Huggins moved for adjournment until the Officials' Report had been published. The House overwhelmingly, to Stockil's fury, agreed.[3]

Before this debate, Huggins had written twice to give Welensky his initial reactions to the Report. Both found several unacceptable recommendations and there were aspects of federation which Welensky favoured but Huggins disliked. However, many of these could in time be adjusted and the others Huggins would accept because the federal government would be strong and, most important of all, the administration of the whole federal area would be locally-based. This was a structure on which they could build. It would serve, too, to keep "Krugerism" out of Southern Rhodesia and avoid absorption by the Union. Northern Rhodesia would also be preserved from the fate of becoming a black dominion, and in so saying Huggins showed that, unlike Griffiths, he did not expect Afrikaner expansionism to threaten the northern protectorate.[4]

On 19 April Huggins revealed that his Cabinet had agreed to the publication of the Officials' Report and that he and some of his colleagues thought that his proposed referendum on federation would be the greatest event in Southern Rhodesia's history. He remained adamant that adjustments would be necessary before the Southern Rhodesians would accept the scheme. That would be true, too, he predicted, in Northern Rhodesia if there was not a concerted effort there towards self-government. He was still convinced that failure would mean absorption by South Africa. Northern Rhodesia, once self-governing, could come to Southern Rhodesia's rescue but, if denied

[2] *Die Burger*, 18 March 1951; *The Rhodesia Herald*, 11 April 1951; Sir Roy Welensky, *Welensky's 4 000 Days* (London, 1964), p. 38.
[3] SR *Debates* (Salisbury), Vol. 32, Part 1, Col. 290 f., 19 April 1951.
[4] Welensky Papers, WE 7, Un-numbered Series "UK Correspondence, April 1951", Sir Godfrey Huggins to Welensky, 17 April 1951.

self-government, would fall to black domination. Failure in the referendum, he warned, would hasten his retirement from public life.[5]

The initial meeting in London with Griffiths on self-government was postponed to 24 April by the British Cabinet crisis which culminated on the previous day in the resignation of Aneurin Bevan and Harold Wilson (the future British Prime Minister and later knighted). The Northern Rhodesian demand which confronted Griffiths had its origin in 1950 when the elected Members had proposed the addition of two more portfolios in the Executive Council to the two they already held. Compromise, however, had been necessary to secure the support of both African and European nominated Members representing African interests, and it was agreed that one of the new portfolios should be given to one of these nominated Members while the other went to an elected Member.

After this agreement, however, H. Kasokolo and N. Nalumango were succeeded by P. Sokota and D. L. Yamba as African representatives. Sokota and Yamba appeared at first to confirm the agreement but later, to the annoyance of the elected Members, they rejected it. They explained to Griffiths on 24 April that, as the elected Members had gained two portfolios in 1948, the two additional portfolios should be given to the African representatives to place them on an equal footing, within the Executive Council, with the European Members. They demanded that no further power be granted to the elected Members until the African was ready to participate in the government. G. Beckett, Welensky's fellow elected Member, interjected that the change would merely make the Executive Council more responsible to the Legislative Council and would not affect the balance of power between the races. Sokota and Yamba were unheeding and warned that the Africans would not support any demand for self-government while they were excluded from major offices in government and industry. Colonial rule, they urged, should continue in its current form so that the Colonial Office could guide development.[6] There is no doubt that Yamba and Sokota were responding to pressure from the African National Congress to have nothing to do with the proposal or with self-government, partition or any other solution. The president of the ANC, G. Lewanika, had telegraphed them to this effect and had suggested that they ask for equal representation for Africans. He had also asked them to take advice from Dr Hastings Banda and others in London.[7]

Griffiths thereupon decided that, as they seemed irreconcilable, he should meet the Africans and Europeans separately. He did so and, on 30 April, reported to Welensky and Beckett that the African delegates had twice rejected the compromise because it would weaken Colonial Office control which they considered a vital safeguard of African interests until the Africans themselves were ready to participate in government at all levels. Griffiths believed, therefore, that African opinion would evaluate the Officials' Report on the extent to which African interests were safeguarded and whether the Colonial Office administration would continue. As he announced that the

[5] *Ibid.*, Huggins to Welensky, 19 April 1951.
[6] *Ibid.*, Welensky to Huggins, 24 April 1951; 7/10, f. 189, Minutes of a Meeting, Colonial Office, 24 April 1951.
[7] *Ibid.*, 39/45, f. 37, G. Lewanika to D. L. Yamba and P. Sokota, 16 April 1951.

publication of the Report was imminent and that he would visit the territories later in the year to discuss closer association, he proposed that this discussion should be postponed to await the fate of the federal issue. He avowed that, had the delegation been unanimous, he would have acted differently.

His listeners' reaction was savage: Welensky retorted that this was an affront to the Legislative Council because all parties had accepted the compromise. Griffiths had simply allowed himself to be influenced by two ignorant Africans. The Legislative Council, itself, had done much to build up African representative institutions but it had to be understood that they were as yet in their early stages of development.[8]

The heated discussion overflowed into the following day. Griffiths and his Assistant Under-Secretary, A. B. Cohen, repeatedly stressed that consideration of the issue was only being postponed, but Welensky and Beckett would do no more than promise to consult their colleagues on their return.[9] (In fact, these colleagues would persuade them not to provoke a crisis before the publication of the Report by resigning from the Executive Council.[10]) Welensky told Griffiths that this postponement was pointless because he was sure that African opinion would condemn closer association without examining the Report. The Governor, Sir Gilbert Rennie, decried such pessimism and promised to urge the African Members to consider the federal proposals on their merit and to take a reasonable view. He maintained that, if indeed the Africans rejected the scheme without examination, the value of African opinion would be shown in its true light. Welensky was unconvinced. He was sure that nothing anyone could say would sway African opinion and he feared that, if the Africans opposed it, closer association would not become reality because "it now appeared that His Majesty's Government would always bow to African opinion".

Welensky's trip to London was not entirely wasted. He had been converted earlier, through his dealings with Griffiths and his predecessor, Arthur Creech Jones, to the view that a Conservative Government might prove helpful to Europeans in Central Africa.[11] Perhaps sensing the impending political change, he made use of an introduction from F. Crawford (later Sir Frederick), a recent Financial Secretary in the Northern Rhodesian Government and currently Governor of the Seychelles, to meet Alan Lennox-Boyd (later Lord Boyd) who would be the Minister of State for the Colonies in the next Conservative Government.[12] Through Huggins's good offices, Welensky also met other influential Conservatives, Lords Altrincham and Swinton, and Anthony Eden (later knighted and Lord Avon), soon to be Prime Minister.[13] Welensky laid a foundation of friendship which would serve the federal cause well.

[8] *Ibid.*, 7/10, f. 184, Minutes of a Meeting, Colonial Office, 30 April 1951.

[9] *Ibid.*, f. 181, Minutes of a Meeting, Colonial Office, 1 May 1951.

[10] *Ibid.*, 5/95, f. 439, Welensky to H. K. McKee, 11 May 1951.

[11] *Ibid.*, 5/93, f. 58, Welensky to A. Pugh, 1 March 1951.

[12] *Ibid.*, 5/95, ff. 450–454, Welensky to F. Crawford, March 1951; WE 7, Un-numbered Series "UK Correspondence, April 1951", Welensky to A. Lennox-Boyd, 8 May 1951.

[13] *Ibid.*, WE 7, *op. cit.*, Huggins to Welensky, 19 April 1951; Welensky to Huggins, 24 April 1951; same to same, 8 May 1951.

Griffiths's promise of the early publication of the Report could not be kept due to the difficulty of printing sufficient copies for simultaneous release in Britain and the three territories.[14] The delay did not serve the federal interest as it was soon apparent that African opposition was hardening. Lennox-Boyd, on a visit to an overseas students' hostel in London, found the northern Africans opposed to federation.[15] Gore-Browne agreed with Welensky's prediction that the African reaction would be severe. He was surprised to hear the Colonial officials thought otherwise.[16] Welensky, however, was comforted on his return from London to find Huggins prepared to advise him to accept the scheme. He amused Welensky by taking a similar line to that which he had adopted in 1944 over the Central African Council, namely that, if the proposed federal constitution would not work, it would provide the best argument for altering it.[17]

By 13 June, all was ready and the simultaneous announcements were made. Griffiths stated that his Government would adhere to the established policy of advancing all colonies to self-governing status within the Commonwealth but would make proper provision for the rights of all. It welcomed the Officials' endorsement that partnership was the only possible policy. He announced that he and the Commonwealth Secretary, Patrick Gordon Walker, would visit the territories to sound opinion there and recommended, without commitment, careful consideration of the Report which seemed to be constructive.

The Conservatives welcomed the Report and, noting that there was no commitment, hoped that the Government would be ready to act once the Central African people had indicated their acceptance. Labour MPs stressed that African opinion had to be fully consulted.[18] The Fabian Colonial Bureau tended to side with Huggins on one point, that it would be politically unrealistic to plant the proposed minister for African interests, who was responsible to the Secretary of State, within the federal cabinet which was answerable to its legislative assembly.[19]

Welensky was pleased that so much progress had been made even though failure remained possible. He was confident, however, that the federal argument would win the day. Both he and Huggins deferred any debate on the issue to give their electorates time to digest the implications. Huggins added the reassurance that his promise of a referendum on the issue still stood.[20]

In Northern Rhodesia, if there was any opposition to the proposal amongst the Europeans it was silent. This did not apply in Southern Rhodesia where prominent political figures such as R. O. Stockil, Sir Ernest Guest and Sir Robert Tredgold, the Chief Justice and former Cabinet Minister, issued

[14] SR *Debates* (Salisbury), Vol. 32, Part 1, Col. 1331, 11 May 1951.

[15] Welensky Papers, 39/116, ff. 88–89, Lennox-Boyd to Welensky, 16 May 1951.

[16] *Ibid.*, 5/95, f. 425, Sir Stewart Gore-Browne to Welensky, 25 May 1951.

[17] *Ibid.*, f. 434, Welensky to C. E. Lambert, 28 May 1951.

[18] House of Commons *Hansard* (London), Vol. 488, Col. 2315 f., 13 June 1951; House of Lords *Hansard* (London), Vol. 172, Col. 51, 13 June 1951.

[19] C. Leys and C. Pratt, *A New Deal in Central Africa* (London, 1960), p. 52.

[20] NR *Debates* (Lusaka), Cols. 58–59, 13 June 1951; SR *Debates* (Salisbury), Vol. 32, Part 2, Col. 2541 f., 13 June 1951.

public and private condemnations. Guest warned through the Press that federation would hasten African political advance and, perhaps, even subject the Southern Rhodesian Native Department to domination by the Colonial Office.[21] Acting in his capacity as legal adviser to the Governor which was one of the roles of his office, Tredgold concluded that the Report contained a fatal weakness. He believed that the differences in the policies towards the Africans were fundamental and was sure that the federal constitution would be unworkable if subjects common to the constituent parts, such as African affairs, were dealt with separately by the territorial Governments. Huggins acknowledged this most pertinent judgment to be true but was not shaken from his course because Southern Rhodesia stood to gain so much economically.[22]

Griffiths had commended the Report and, accordingly, the three Secretaries for Native Affairs decided that the territorial Governments could, when explaining it to their Africans, point out that it was signed by senior officials. Furthermore, the British Government, which had African interests at heart, had accepted that the proposals would be of lasting benefit to all. In the July meeting of the African Representative Council, the Governor and the Chief Secretary did just this. Indeed, the warmth of their tone contrasted with their statement that the Government was not committed to the Report's recommendations and did little to allay suspicions that opposition would be ignored.[23] Just as Welensky and Gore-Browne had expected, the northern Africans were not in a receptive mood and hostility towards any suggestion of closer association was already well-rooted.

African suspicions had been aroused at the outset when the African National Congress's demands for representation at the Officials' Conference had been — quite reasonably — refused.[24] With regard to explanations to be offered at district level, the three territories accepted British guidance. Griffiths was anxious that he and Gordon Walker should be responsible for selling the idea and that district officials should be neutral.[25] Thus, as in 1938, these officials were ordered to explain but not to advocate the scheme. In fact, more than one district official in Northern Rhodesia advised Africans to reject it.[26] This decision has been heartily criticised and has been depicted as a reason for African hostility then and throughout the life of the Federation. In retrospect, many of those involved, including Griffiths, have acknowledged that this was a mistake, for the African had traditionally looked to the district officer for advice on political matters and, suddenly, on this most important issue, the officer was muzzled: he could explain the ramifications but could not recommend it.[27] In the event, it would seem that any chance of swaying the northern African was lost.

[21] *The Rhodesia Herald*, 20 June 1951.

[22] Sir Robert Tredgold, *The Rhodesia that was my Life* (London, 1968), p. 194; Author's interview with the late Sir Robert Tredgold.

[23] D. C. Mulford, *Zambia: The Politics of Independence, 1957–1964* (London, 1967), p. 27.

[24] Welensky Papers, 39/114, f. 93, R. P. Bush to Welensky, 8 February 1951.

[25] House of Commons *Hansard* (London), Vol. 680, Col. 1460, 11 July 1963.

[26] Author's confidential interview.

[27] Author's interviews with the late the Rt. Hon. James Griffiths, Lord Brockway and R. P. Bush.

The territorial Governments' anxiety to be impartial is illustrated by their reaction when given an opportunity to suppress, by ignoring, a telegram from Banda to the Southern Rhodesian Government publication, the *African Weekly*, calling for rejection of the federal proposals and for a meeting of the Congresses of Northern Rhodesia and Nyasaland. It was published because the Governments did not want to be accused of applying censorship.[28] In any case, Banda had also cabled the *Bantu Mirror* which published his call on 23 June.

There were some crumbs of comfort for the protagonists of federation in the Africans' immediate reaction to the proposals. On 27 June the *African Weekly* reported a swing in favour of federation and an acceptance of partnership. In early July school teachers in the Chibi Reserve in Southern Rhodesia welcomed the federal scheme.[29] However, more typical were the reported views of B. Zulu of the Salisbury branch of the Northern Rhodesian ANC who cited his organisation's resistance since 1948 to any moves to unify and recalled the walk-out of the official Members from the federal debate in Lusaka in 1949.[30] Letters in a similar vein (with the writers fearing for African land and rights) began to appear in the Press, and it was soon clear that the federal proposals would be overwhelmingly rejected by the Africans.

Welensky and Beckett only heard the initial African protests because, in early July, they returned to London to attend a Commonwealth Conference which coincided with the Festival of Britain. The Conference was addressed by leading British Cabinet Ministers and by public figures such as the Chief of the Imperial General Staff, Sir William Slim. Welensky judged the Conference a failure as it degenerated into an anti-South African tirade and thereby served only to heighten racial antagonism.[31]

Although he was a guest at the Festival, Welensky had no time to enjoy the cultural feast for he spent the three weeks either in the Conference or seeking out British politicians, particularly the Conservatives. He would record that he had seen everyone in the Conservative Party from Churchill downwards. Developing the contacts which he had made during his previous visit, on 19 July he lunched with Lords Altrincham and Swinton and persuaded them to raise the question of federation in the House of Lords. Because Griffiths was hanging fire, Welensky considered promoting a debate in the Commons but was advised against it by Lennox-Boyd and others because the Labour Party's left wing would exploit it. Welensky had hoped that Lord Salisbury would be the main speaker. However, he was ill and Lord Swinton, a veteran parliamentarian whose long ministerial experience included that of Colonial Secretary from 1931–5, was an adequate substitute. Welensky primed him with memoranda, stressing the need for constructive criticism of the federal proposals and emphasising that the most vocal African opposition need not be the most representative. He suggested that weight should be given to the

[28] Welensky Papers, 39/118, f. 40, H. N. Parry to Chief Secretaries, Lusaka and Zomba, 20 June 1951.

[29] *Bantu Mirror*, 7 July 1951.

[30] *African Weekly*, 27 June 1951.

[31] Welensky Papers, 39/119, f. 269, Welensky to Gore-Browne, 27 July 1951; 39/114, f. 68, Welensky to J. S. Moffat, 31 July 1951.

opinion of the experienced official. Praising Southern Rhodesia, he noted that Britain's reserved powers had never had to be used because of the wisdom of the administration there. Furthermore, the Southern Rhodesian Africans were better off and better served than their northern cousins.[32]

Thus the hand of Welensky is discernible in the speech which Swinton made in the Lords on 1 August, drawing attention to the Officials' Report and asking for information on the forthcoming visits to the territories of the Secretaries of State. Convinced of the need for closer association for economic and other reasons, Swinton depicted the officials as wise, unbiased men and warned that African opinion, if it existed at all, would be difficult to assess accurately. Swinton saw the unanimity of the officials, on a subject over which opinions had divided so sharply, as a tremendous step forward. Federation would extend and reinforce the policy of partnership without fear of outside influence. Referring to the Report, Swinton claimed to be nauseated by current "false, malicious and bilious propaganda issued by persons who had not taken the trouble even to read the proposals and whose sole object appears to be to stir up racial hatred". Swinton's own criticism of the Report was that it would have been better to define the powers of the territorial Governments and to leave every other function to the federal government. However, he knew that every constitution was a compromise and assured the Labour Government of Conservative support.

Lord Lucan, the Commonwealth Parliamentary Under-Secretary, thought it inappropriate to discuss the Report and gave only the details of the dates of Griffiths's visit. Lord Altrincham called for an act of faith, such as that of 1923 when Southern Rhodesia was granted self-government, if moderation was to survive when nationalism was rampant in West and South Africa. He praised Southern Rhodesia for its enlightened policies and claimed the choice of Huggins illustrated the quality of the electorate's judgment. The current volume of criticism was of little value as it emanated from students, itinerant professors and politicians. He hoped for an all-party agreement on closer association. The only dissenting voice came from Lord Hailey who, though he thought a form of closer association was desirable, believed that there were significant differences in the territorial African policies. He was sure that the whites were seeking supremacy and was not convinced by the argument that Southern Rhodesia might be drawn into South Africa.

Lord De La Warr noted that it was only Hailey who thought that the African policies constituted a barrier to closer association. Lord Salisbury expected that the territories would align their African policies. Finally, Lord Ogmore thought that Welensky and Huggins were men of great distinction. When Huggins heard of this, he concluded that Ogmore, the late Minister of State for the Colonies and currently the Minister for Civil Aviation, must have been courting "the sack" from the Socialists.[33]

[32] *Ibid.*, 5/98, ff. 404–405, Welensky to Crawford, 20 August 1951; 39/112, f. 141, Welensky to R. C. S. Stanley, 1 August 1951; f. 143, Welensky to NR unofficial Members, 24 July 1951; 39/114, f. 66, Welensky to Huggins, 25 July 1951; f. 65, Welensky to Lord Altrincham, 25 July 1951; 39/116, ff. 81–82, Welensky to Lord Swinton, 23 July 1951.

[33] House of Lords *Hansard* (London), Vol. 173, Col. 170 f., 1 August 1951; Welensky Papers, 39/119, f. 213, Huggins to Welensky, 24 August 1951.

Welensky was pleased with the debate and bought many copies of its *Hansard* to circulate in Central Africa. Furthermore, Lennox-Boyd and Lords Altrincham, Harlech, Salisbury and Winterton proposed to form a committee to promote the federal cause in Britain.[34] However, Welensky was not over-confident because, although Gordon Walker seemed to be won over, Griffiths avoided contact with the visiting Northern Rhodesians and seemed to be "sitting on the fence". Welensky gathered that the British Government was generally influenced by the Fabian view that "everything black is good, everything white is evil", which was the consequence of the failure in the last two decades of that Government to emphasize the role of the white man in the territory.[35]

At that moment, Welensky's relationship with British and Northern Rhodesian officials was strained because they had failed to give him prior information of the details of Griffiths's visit and had sent the wrong official, the Financial Secretary, and no unofficial Members, to a regional defence conference in Nairobi. Grudgingly, Welensky agreed to an extension of 30 months to his membership of the Executive Council (his appointment was without portfolio, as leader of the unofficial Members) provided that a constitutional change was effected within that time.[36]

Welensky journeyed to Cape Town by sea in early August and spent the remainder of the month on holiday there. The volume of his correspondence, however, shows that he cannot have had much rest as he strove to engender support for the federal cause and to combat African opposition. He sought to encourage all the communities to come forward to give evidence to the visiting Secretaries of State[37] and, when seeking a means to influence Africans, thought again of purchasing an African newspaper.[38]

His concern was wholly justified because, in his absence, African opposition had deepened. The need for federation had been questioned and the scheme had been depicted as merely promoting racialism. The use of the district officers to explain the terms was decried because they were thought to be agents of white supremacy. The motives of the promoters of the scheme were described as evil because Africans had been excluded from the Officials' Conference and because the proceedings at the Victoria Falls Conference had been kept secret. A warning was issued not to share the fate of the Africans of the Cape Colony whose rights had been eroded after Union.[39] Southern

[34] Welensky Papers, 39/116, f. 64, Lord Winterton to Welensky, 4 August 1951; 39/114, f. 56, Welensky to Winterton, 22 August 1951.

[35] *Ibid.*, 39/112, f. 141, Welensky to Stanley, 1 August 1951; f. 143, Welensky to NR unofficial Members, 24 July 1951; 39/116, ff. 70–71, Welensky to Rennie, 31 July 1951; 39/119, f. 261, Welensky to R. Smith, 1 August 1951.

[36] *Ibid.*, 23/4, ff. 39 & 32, Welensky to Stanley, 26 July & 17 August 1951; ff. 38 & 33, Stanley to Welensky, 27 July & 7 August 1951; 5/83, f. 19, Stanley to Welensky, 5 August 1951; f. 17, G. Beckett to Welensky, 2 August 1951; ff. 15–16, Welensky to Beckett, 17 August 1951; 39/114, f. 61, Welensky to E. M. Wilson, 31 July 1951.

[37] *Ibid.*, 39/119, f. 224, Welensky to D. Cole, 18 August 1951; 23/4, f. 8, Welensky to M. Went, 29 August 1951.

[38] *Ibid.*, 5/96, f. 72. C. A. G. Paver to Welensky, 23 October 1951.

[39] *Ibid.*, 39/119, ff. 179–183, H. B. Phiri to *African Weekly* and *Central African Post*, 2 August 1951; *Bantu Mirror*, 14 July & 18 August 1951.

Rhodesian Africans were unwilling to see their country's repressive laws implemented in the North.[40]

A steady flow of letters rejecting federation was received by the African Press. In the northern territories, Chiefs, District and Provincial Councils declared their opposition. The Fort Jameson District Council gave its support but withdrew it after a visit from one of the African Members of the Legislative Council.[41] In Southern Rhodesia opposition was expressed by the Southern Rhodesian ANC and the Federation of African Welfare Societies.[42] In Nyasaland and Northern Rhodesia the Congress branches expressed total opposition. Speakers were generally unrestrained in their comments, but the Northern Rhodesian Government became alarmed when, on 22 July, at an ANC meeting in Lusaka, violent, seditious speeches drew the longest applause.[43]

At that meeting the moderate Lewanika was ousted from the presidency and replaced by Harry Nkumbula who had returned home having lost his government bursary through failing his university examinations. A more virulent and uncompromising tone would be heard henceforth and, for the first time, the organisational activities of Simon Ber Zukas, an engineer employed by the Ndola Municipality, and the encouragement of Commander Thomas Fox-Pitt, a provincial commissioner on the verge of retirement, was noticed in European political circles. As African crowds began to attend meetings wearing black and red anti-federal badges designed by Zukas, attention soon focused upon him.

Zukas, a young man in his twenties, was the son of *émigré* Lithuanian parents who had settled in Northern Rhodesia before the Second World War. He had become unhappy with the concept of colonialism when dealing with civil commotion in Uganda in 1945 as a sergeant in the King's African Rifles. Then at Cape Town University, he had rejected, like many others, South Africa's segregationalist policies. In 1948 he and James Chikerema, a Southern Rhodesian African nationalist, produced the clandestine *Rhodesia Study Club Newsletter* which took an anti-colonial line, often with Marxist overtones. In 1950 he returned to Ndola and, together with Justin Chimba, Reuben Kamanga and Edward Munongi, produced the *Freedom Newsletter*, demanding equal rights for Africans. They formed, too, the Anti-Federation Committee.

It was Lewanika who drew the attention of the police to Zukas's activities and paid the price by losing his office. Zukas had suspected that Lewanika was in contact with the authorities and when Lewanika made a moderate speech at the July meeting of the African National Congress he presented Zukas and his cohorts with their opportunity. They succeeded, too, in drawing into their ranks the two African Members of the Legislative Council. D.

[40] *The Rhodesia Herald*, 25 August 1951.

[41] *African Weekly*, 22 August 1951; *The Rhodesia Herald*, 24 August 1951; Welensky Papers, 5/95, f. 137, Welensky to C. R. R. Dawson, 27 September 1951.

[42] *The Rhodesia Herald*, 22 & 24 August & 4 September 1951; *Bantu Mirror*, 25 August 1951.

[43] Welensky Papers, 23/4, f. 42, Rennie to A. B. Cohen, 24 July 1951; f. 43, NRG Liaison to Welensky, 25 July 1951; 39/116, ff. 72–74, Rennie to Welensky, 25 July 1951; 39/114, f. 69, J. S. Moffat to Welensky, 25 July 1951; 39/112, f. 142, R. C. S. Stanley to Welensky, 25 July 1951.

L. Yamba was elected vice-president of the ANC. This meant that the established system had been overturned because Yamba and P. Sokota looked henceforth to the ANC, and not to the African Representative Council, for guidance. Soon that Council itself followed the ANC line — to the distress of J. S. Moffat (later Sir John) who, as Gore-Browne's successor as a representative of African interests, strove to get the Africans at least to consider the issues at stake. With a weight of evidence before it suggesting a Communist agent at work, the Executive Council considered action against Zukas. However, to the disgust of the unofficial Members, it decided that, with Griffiths's visit in the offing, the moment was inopportune.[44]

Despite the African opposition, the hopes of the supporters of federation were undiminished and further support for their cause was forthcoming when a British delegation of the Commonwealth Parliamentary Association visited the territories in August. Moreover, the briefing by Griffiths of this delegation on the advantages of federation belied any impression that he was "sitting on the fence". At meetings with African organisations, the delegates (Stanley Evans of the Labour Party, Julian Amery and A. E. Baldwin of the Conservative Party, and William Coldrick of the Liberal Party) were presented with memoranda and heard protests against the federal concept and the current conduct of the Governments. Zukas's Anti-Federation Committee threatened to protest to the International Court at The Hague or to the United Nations.

The delegation was plainly unimpressed and its public utterances were restrained and conciliatory.[45] On their return to Britain on 2 September, Evans, as leader, gave a clear indication that they would recommend the federating of the territories as it was the fastest way to develop them. He argued that Britain's purpose was to develop Africa for the benefit of the Commonwealth and the world, and federation would make this possible. Britain also had to safeguard African interests and to consider if African opposition to federation was justified. He was satisfied it was not.[46]

In their report to the Commonwealth Parliamentary Association, the delegates gave first their findings on Northern Rhodesia. The Europeans seemed generally to favour closer association and, though they would have preferred to amalgamate, they saw federation as a step in the right direction. There were important economic reasons for their opinion as their territory's economy depended solely on copper. Moreover, the delegates found that the territories were already inter-related, with Northern Rhodesia needing Southern Rhodesia's coal, and both using labour from Nyasaland. The development of Kariba called for combined action and federation would make international credit easier to find, and certain anomalies arising out of the

[44] R. I. Rotberg, "The Federation Movement in British East and Central Africa, 1889–1953", *Journal of Commonwealth Political Studies* (Leicester, 1964), Vol. II, pp. 234–235; Welensky Papers, 5/79, f. 153, R. Hungerford to Welensky, 1 August 1951; f. 135, Welensky to Hungerford, 17 August 1951; 39/114, f. 58–59, J. S. Moffat to Welensky, 11 August 1951; f. 57, Welensky to Moffat, 18 August 1951; 39/119, f. 237, D. Cole to Welensky, 20 August 1951; f. 233, Welensky to W. Warden, 23 August 1951; f. 236, Welensky to Cole, 28 August 1951.
[45] *African Weekly*, 15 August 1951.
[46] *The Rhodesia Herald*, 3 September 1951.

Congo Basin Treaties would be removed. A strong British bloc would be created and, because the federal government would control immigration, the fears that an influx of Afrikaners would divide the white community would not be realised. The area would be immune, too, from the northward spread of *apartheid* or the transposition from West Africa of the Colonial Office policy being applied there.

The delegation found that the great majority of Northern Rhodesian Africans was ignorant of the federal proposals and was disinterested in them. The delegates had met the Paramount Chief of Barotseland and other Chiefs, leaders of the ANC, trade unionists and others of the intelligentsia and had found them moderately or violently but unanimously opposed to federation. The delegates diagnosed the African opposition to be based on a natural deep aversion to change, heightened by a fear of losing British protection. There might also be less money available to spend on African development, and increased European immigration would threaten African land. Southern Rhodesia might dominate the federation and impose its African policies throughout to the disadvantage, in particular, of the Chiefs and the intellegentsia. Nevertheless, the delegates noted, the Northern Rhodesian Africans were not disinclined to seek work in the South.

By contrast, the delegation discovered that most officials working in African administration, together with the clergy and the missionaries, favoured the federal proposals, believing that, if they were not implemented, racial tension would increase. The Coloured population supported the Europeans, but the Indians wanted their interests safeguarded and to be allowed to move freely between the territories.

Except for the Afrikaner element, which favoured joining South Africa, Southern Rhodesia's Europeans appeared also to favour closer association. They chose, however, amalgamation because they feared that the Colonial Office might be able to impose its African policy. Exception was taken to the proposed inclusion of nominated members in the federal legislature. Many preferred the exclusion of Nyasaland because its "irresponsible" or "Whitehall-picked" nominated members would be dealing with Southern Rhodesian affairs. There was also strong opposition to the proposed minister for African interests within the cabinet who would be neither appointed by the prime minister nor responsible to him. The delegates found that, though African opinion was not as vehement as in the North, the Chiefs and intelligentsia were mostly opposed. They had a sense of solidarity with the northern leaders and, like them, feared pressure on their land from an influx of European immigrants. However, they also wished to avoid an inrush of northern Africans into Southern Rhodesia, thereby depressing wages.

The Nyasaland Europeans favoured federation but felt that the African had to be won over before any action was taken. The proposal to have nominated members in the legislature was seen by the Europeans to be undemocratic. Vocal African opinion was overwhelmingly against federation. The strongest opposition which the delegation met on its tour came from the meeting of the Nyasaland African Congress in Lilongwe which feared that any lessening of the Colonial Office's influence would stunt their political and social aspirations. It was found that the Indians would support the proposals if their interests were safeguarded and if movement between the territories was allowed. The delegates thought that the federal plan fitted Lord Lugard's concept of the "Dual Mandate" as it would develop Central Africa for the benefit of the Commonwealth and the world, but would not endanger African interests. Indeed, association with the North was likely to reform Southern Rhodesia's policies. Federation would certainly advance all the interests of the African populations. The delegates found that race relations were worse in Northern than Southern Rhodesia, because government by officials kept the races apart. The Europeans thought that the Colonial Office pampered the Africans, while the Africans saw it as protecting them from their European enemies. In Southern Rhodesia, by contrast, direct contact had made the European recognise and live up to his responsibilities.

The delegates gave *apartheid* little chance of gaining ground while the British element predominated, and thought that a balanced immigration policy, to achieve a European population of 250 000 in ten years, could allay fears of an Asian and Afrikaner influx. The delegates believed "therefore, that while everything should be done to safeguard African interests . . . African opposition should not be allowed to stand in the way of the Federation of the three territories".

Care would have to be exercised in further negotiations to avoid arousing Southern Rhodesian suspicions of Colonial Office encroachment. However, the Rhodesians were loyal and were led by wise men who understood their dependence on Britain for defence and capital investment. It would, thus, be right to meet their reasonable demands though they, too, should make concessions — perhaps to allow direct African representation in the federal legislature and to recognise African trade unions.

The delegates recorded their belief "that the achievement of a Central African Federation is both urgent and important. There is good reason to believe that this may well be the last chance of building up a strong Central Africa under British influence and leadership . . . such a Central Africa may well hold out the best hope of developing a genuine partnership between Europeans and Africans — a partnership which could do more than anything else by its example to relax the existing racial tensions throughout the African Continent".[47] Although they dismissed the African opposition, the delegates provided their readers with a sample of the memoranda which were submitted to them. It was, of course, the fervent hope of the protagonists of federation that the Africans would overstate their case.[48]

The sample document was signed by H. Nkumbula, D. L. Yamba, S. H. Chileshi and A. K. Kanike and gave 24 reasons for rejecting federation. Closer association with Southern Rhodesia was depicted simply as a postponement of the day when the African would take his proper place in the administration. With Southern Rhodesia likely to dominate, African political advancement, rights to form trade unions and co-operatives, and to grow any crop they wished, would all be at risk. The Southern Rhodesian Subversive Bill, which would restrict freedom of speech, might be applied throughout.

[47] Welensky Papers, WE 7, P/C/149/52, Report of the Delegation from the UK Branch of the Commonwealth Parliamentary Association, September 1951.
[48] *Ibid.*, 39/116, ff. 70–71, Welensky to Rennie, 31 July 1951.

Southern Rhodesia, too, had just raised the monetary franchise qualification to curb African political strength. The federation would become a dominion thereby terminating Colonial Office control and rendering the safeguards useless. The Officials' Report on Closer Association, they claimed, had not dismissed this possibility, having only said that the *status quo* had to be maintained for five years. The influence of the Colonial Office would wane before the change of status as the officials sought to please their future masters, and the clamour against the Colonial Office would increase if it continued its liberal policies in education, land and labour issues, or if it defended African interests. The federal legislature would be predominantly European, and Europeans had already demonstrated in Northern Rhodesia how portfolios could be used unfairly as had happened when Africans had sought to be allowed to grow flue-cured tobacco.

Nkumbula and his colleagues claimed that it was very unlikely that Africans would gain portfolios. The British reserved powers had never been used in Southern Rhodesia even though discriminatory legislation had been promulgated, and it was, thus, unlikely that the proposed minister for African interests and the African affairs board would report on legislation to the governor-general. At best the threat of such action might deter the federal government. The governor-general, and not the Africans, would appoint this minister and the latter would have to be acceptable to the prime minister. If the minister acted, he could cause delay, annoy the cabinet and place his appointment in danger. The African affairs board, too, would not be chosen by Africans and therefore the appointees were unlikely to be champions of African interests. The Secretary of State, to whom the governor-general would report on discriminatory legislation, had not been named and, if he was the Commonwealth Relations Secretary, he would have to take into account South African views.

Nkumbula and his co-authors believed that the federal government, being charged with higher education, would ensure that the Africans would not fairly share it. The control of defence would give the federal government the power to conscript Africans for service anywhere when they did not wish to leave their own territories. The conclusions of the Officials' Report were based on the Survey of Native Policies and other erroneous documents. The figures given for African education in Southern Rhodesia were false, and doubt was cast on the unanimity of the Report. For example, it had not been able to agree on which Secretary of State should be made responsible for federal affairs. Africans were puzzled by the Northern Rhodesian Government's support for the scheme when Griffiths had refused to go any further than to say that the proposals offered a "constructive approach". Africans were not convinced of the urgency of the need, or the need itself, for closer association as in the spirit of the Commonwealth all difficulties between the territories were soluble. Africans recognised the danger of South African expansionism but could see no determination in Southern Rhodesia to resist it. Finally, Nkumbula and his colleagues recalled that pressure by the Northern Rhodesian officials on the African Representative Council to accept the federal scheme had led to some members refusing to attend a tea-party at Government House.

Griffiths would take notice of African opinion on his tour. On arrival in Nyasaland, on 24 August, he was alerted by the local Europeans to the totality of African opposition. They alleged that events in West Africa, and the Gold Coast in particular, had aroused in the Nyasaland African ambitions which rendered the total acceptance of federation impossible. Federation, in the Europeans' opinion, should have been imposed without the lengthy consultations and explanations.[49]

Four days later, at a Press conference, Griffiths confirmed that discussion with the Northern Province African Provincial Council had revealed a firm, unanimous opposition to federation. He had striven without success to allay their fears, pointing out that, as the federal government would deal only with subjects such as transport and defence, their daily lives would be unaffected. The British Government, he had averred, would see that land settlement remained in the hands of the territorial Governments. He had found that the missionaries considered the proposals constructive, but the safeguards inadequate. When they proposed that the Central African Council could be developed, Griffiths had disagreed because it lacked executive powers. He reported that the Nyasaland African Congress refused to attend any conferences. It rejected the policy of partnership because it was never implemented in practice. Orton Chirwa, the Congress spokesman, had proclaimed that Nyasaland had no need to federate when all that was required was hard work and greater co-operation between the Government and the people. Chirwa had dismissed the federation as a means whereby Southern Rhodesia would acquire dominion status. Nonetheless, Griffiths told the Press conference that he had tried to impress on the Congress that the British Government had not yet committed itself to federation and had only recommended the federal scheme as constructive and therefore worth consideration.[50]

At a meeting with the Convention of Associations of Nyasaland, Griffiths was told by its chairman, O. Shelford, that African fears had to be allayed and federation introduced without disturbing Nyasaland's social harmony. Griffiths agreed that, only in this way, could the policy of partnership prosper. The British Government, he alleged, was wedded to the concept of partnership and recognised that the growth of nationalism could not be curtailed but had to be developed along constructive lines. When attacked by the meeting on the policy being implemented in the Gold Coast, he defended it as a great experiment in democracy.[51]

On 1 September, Griffiths addressed the Nyasaland Protectorate Council, telling its members that he was satisfied that they expressed the opinion of the Nyasaland African. He explained he was gathering such opinions for his Government to equip it to judge the federal issue. He reiterated that many of the Africans' fears were groundless, that their daily life would be unaffected and that their political progress would be inviolate. The federal government would be unable to tamper with any of the safeguards. He believed that development was necessary to meet the needs of the rising populations and that inter-territorial co-operation had already benefited the Africans even

[49] *The Rhodesia Herald*, 25 August 1951.
[50] *Ibid.*, 29 August 1951.
[51] *Ibid.*, 31 August 1951.

though they had been unaware of it. He invited the Council to send two delegates to a conference later that month at the Victoria Falls.[52] It refused but later accepted, after he promised that federation would only be discussed and that no decisions would be taken.[53]

When Griffiths moved to Northern Rhodesia on 3 September he found, similarly, that the Africans rejected federation while the Europeans welcomed it. The difference was that the Europeans generally — perhaps because there were more of them — were not conscious of a need to carry the African with them. Griffiths rebuffed an attempt by a meeting of management board officials to convince him that African opinion was entirely worthless. On the contrary, he told them, the Africans' fears were very real to them even though, in fact, many were groundless. He was distressed, in particular, by the racial attitudes of the white trade unionists.[54]

Again Griffiths attempted to persuade the Africans at least to consider the proposals. On 11 September he pointed out to the African Representative Council the contradiction that, though they claimed to distrust the European, they had confidence in the officials who were, after all, Europeans. However, the ARC rejected federation as unnecessary and thought it merely a means to attain European supremacy. It was unnecessary because economic progress was being made and two world wars had demonstrated how effective inter-territorial co-operation could be without unification. The fate of safeguards in South Africa led the ARC to doubt their value. It predicted that only lip-service would be paid to partnership.

On 12 September, the elected Members put their case to Griffiths. They viewed the proposals, Welensky proclaimed, as a basis for discussion because they rejected, for example, the proposed minister for African interests because his appointment and responsibilities cut across the principles of cabinet government. A bi-cameral legislature might well serve as an alternative safeguard. Federation was urgent for economic and strategic reasons — the area's possession of strategic minerals was reason enough — and because of the threats posed by rampant nationalism in West and South Africa. Time in which to achieve something was short, Welensky thought that two to three years at the most were left. If federation were not implemented, Southern Rhodesia, which was experiencing economic difficulties, would turn south, taking the High Commission Territories with it. The elected Members, proclaiming themselves liberal men believing in partnership, warned that race relations were already deteriorating, that, though the Government had not realised it, Communist agents were already at work. The African did not appreciate the urgency of the need for federation and feared change, but was not being asked to step into the complete unknown.

Griffiths revealed to the elected Members that, as he favoured federation, he wished to avoid having to place before his Government the stark fact of total African rejection. Consideration of federation, he thought, should be

[52] Welensky Papers, 39/112, ff. 136–140, Griffith's speech to the Nyasaland Protectorate Council, 1 September 1951.

[53] *The Rhodesia Herald*, 4 September 1951.

[54] J. Griffiths, *Pages from Memory* (London, 1969), p. 115; *The Rhodesia Herald*, 7 September 1951.

postponed for six months, and the Victoria Falls Conference that month could then be reconvened in the calmer atmosphere of London. Even if time was short, the intervening period could be usefully employed in swaying African opinion. Furthermore, because the Conference would be reconvened, there would be no call for a debate on his return to London when African hostility would be at its height. Because of the difficulties he had experienced in persuading the Nyasaland Africans to attend the Conference, and because they were likely only to expound on their objections to federation, he would merely seek to avoid a breakdown and work to secure an adjournment.

Griffiths did not dismiss African objections as being of no consequence. The African, he found, approached the problem at a personal level, largely ignoring the issues at stake. Chief Mwase, for example, a member of both the Central Province African Provincial Council and the Protectorate Council, had told him that he feared for his position as Chief because he had travelled to Southern Rhodesia in 1947 to meet the King and had seen how Chiefs were treated there.

Griffiths acknowledged to the elected Members that the Kremlin, having been stalemated in Europe, would seek to exploit racial conflict in Africa. Nevertheless, as trustee, Britain had to give full weight to African opinion, and at the Victoria Falls Griffiths would attempt to reassure it. If adjournment could be secured, he was in favour of using the device of a round-table meeting on the next occasion. What Griffiths did not mention — but Welensky suspected — was that there was a likelihood of an imminent British general election which was reason enough for seeking an adjournment.[55]

Simultaneously, Gordon Walker, the Commonwealth Secretary, had been visiting Southern Rhodesia and found the picture less clear-cut. The Rhodesia Railways Workers' Union had debated federation that month and, while accepting it in principle, had expressed dissatisfaction with the details of the proposals.[56] The Bulawayo Indian Association asked for an end to all discrimination towards Indians before implementing federation. A Coloured organisation petitioned for a federal minister to be charged specifically with the care of Coloured interests.[57] On 9 September, in a move which Griffiths in particular found to be sinister, the Association of Afrikaners dissolved to form the new Democratic Party. The Party's philosophy was racial separation based on the assumption that Europeans would control Southern Rhodesia's affairs for all time. There would be laws against miscegenation and the African would be allowed to advance only in his own areas.[58]

The Africans had given federation a mixed reception. The Southern Rhodesian African National Congress and the Federation of African Welfare Societies were opposed, as were the Mashonaland and Manicaland Chiefs who claimed to have nothing in common with the northern Africans and thought that Southern Rhodesian Africans should first have direct parliamentary representation to give them equality with their northern cousins.

[55] Welensky Papers, 39/120, f. 133, Notes of a Meeting between the Colonial Secretary and NR elected Members, Lusaka, 12 September 1951; Leys and Pratt, *A New Deal*, *op. cit.*, p. 29.
[56] Welensky Papers, 39/112, ff. 107–116, Minutes of RRWU, September 1951.
[57] *The Rhodesia Herald*, 1 & 11 September 1951.
[58] *Ibid.*, 10 September 1951; Griffiths, *Pages*, *op. cit.*, p. 113.

These Chiefs demanded that, before anything else happened, there should be a meeting of Africans from the three territories. The Southern Rhodesian African Association, by contrast, did not object to federating provided that, as a consequence, Southern Rhodesia's policies became more enlightened. Urban Africans in Bulawayo, however, rejected federation, while the Matabeleland and Midlands Chiefs asked for more information.[59]

Though Nyasaland chose its delegation to the Victoria Falls Conference from a number of organisations including its Legislative Council, the Rhodesias selected only Members of their legislatures. To stave off overseas criticism, the Northern Rhodesian delegation comprised an equal number of representatives of African and European interests.[60]

The Southern Rhodesian delegation represented the three Parties in Parliament. Unaware of Griffiths's intentions and expecting that there would be a detailed examination of the federal proposals, the Parties (the United, the Rhodesia, and the Rhodesia Labour Parties) met to formulate a common approach. They rejected the proposed single chamber legislature in favour of a bi-cameral one with a lower house of 30 members (17 Southern Rhodesians, eleven Northern Rhodesians and two Nyasalanders). If that ratio were unacceptable, they would settle for 15 : 11 : 4. The Southern Rhodesians would be elected on the existing territorial franchise while the Northern Rhodesians would be free to use theirs or adopt the Southern Rhodesian model. The two Nyasalanders would be nominated by their Governor from a panel of candidates supplied by the Convention of Associations. Any constitutional amendment would require the sanction of two-thirds of this house.

The upper house would have 18 members, giving the territories the equal representation of 6 : 6 : 6. Three of these members, one from each of the territories, would be nominated by their respective Governors to represent African interests. In Southern Rhodesia's case this would be done by Governor-in-Council after bodies believed to be representative of African interests had been consulted. The northern territories would follow their established procedures in selecting such representatives. The remaining five Southern Rhodesian members of the upper house could be selected by the governing and opposition parties on a 2 : 1 basis or elected by the voters using Southern Rhodesia as a single constituency. Northern Rhodesia's five remaining members would be elected by the elected Members of the Legislative Council. (Nyasaland, of course, had no elective system and thus its five remaining members would be nominated by its Governor.) The lives of the two houses would run concurrently.

The upper house could not alter money bills but could make recommendations on them. Otherwise, if a bill was passed twice by the lower house and twice rejected by the upper, the governor-general would be empowered to assent to it if it was certified by the federal government as being urgent and necessary. The federal constitution could be amended if the territorial legislatures agreed.

Within the federal cabinet there would be a minister for African interests who would be appointed by the prime minister from either of the houses. The

[59] *The Rhodesia Herald*, 14 September 1951.
[60] Welensky Papers, 23/4, ff. 10–12, G. Beckett to Welensky, 28 August 1951.

African affairs board would not exist but the Southern Rhodesian system of the reservation of legislation would be adopted as a safeguard for African interests. The Central African loans council would be responsible for the raising of foreign loans on behalf of the federal and territorial Governments. The federal government would control immigration from without the area, but inter-state immigration would be a territorial subject and the territories would be empowered to prevent the entry of any person.

The Congo Basin Treaties would be terminated. The franchise and constitutions of the territories could be altered only with the consent of the federal parliament. All the governments would be responsible to the Commonwealth, and not to the Colonial, Secretary. Southern Rhodesia would be given the right to secede from the federation after ten years. The referendum in Southern Rhodesia would have to be held within three months of the publication of the proposals. No suggestions were forthcoming on the division of power between the Governments and it was felt that this could be discussed at a later conference.[61]

No details of this agreement were furnished to the public but nothing was expected because Huggins, in August, had warned that his hand could not be disclosed before negotiating. The intransigent tone of this agreement is not surprising when one knows that Huggins had told the Matabeleland executive of the United Party in July: "Once the Imperial Government have granted this constitution they have lost all control, don't forget that." Of constitutional reservations, he had said that they "are not worth the paper they were written on". This assertion had been confirmed by a conversation with Creech Jones before the war when Huggins had said — and Creech Jones had agreed — that, if the British Government withheld consent on legislation, he would hold a general election and proceed to implement it, and the British Government would be powerless to prevent him.[62]

The Southern Rhodesian delegation had thus prepared itself by early September, but when he realised how Griffiths had been received in the northern territories and the course he proposed to follow, Huggins tried to persuade the British Government that the Conference would be abortive and should be postponed. Griffiths agreed and cabled Gordon Walker who, however, would not accept a postponement, arguing that they could not now withdraw.[63]

At the Victoria Falls, on 18 September, welcoming the Secretaries of State and the delegates, Sir John Kennedy, Governor of Southern Rhodesia and chairman of the Conference, warned that the complexity of the problem before them could be measured by the number of years during which it had been under discussion. This Conference, being one of deliberation and not decision, was a step in the process of establishing the degree to which the territories could draw closer together. The Officials' Conference had recommended federation as an urgent necessity. The three territorial Governments,

[61] *Ibid.*, 39/112, ff. 133–135, Record of a Meeting between the United, the Rhodesia, and the Rhodesia Labour Parties, Salisbury, 3 September 1951; ff. 127–132, Report to the Executive Council of the RLP, (undated).

[62] Leys and Pratt, *A New Deal*, *op. cit.*, pp. 28–29.

[63] Author's interview with Mr Charles Footman.

Kennedy claimed, had endorsed this finding and had subjected the scheme to close examination. The Conference should, therefore, clear the air and define the issues.

Speaking first, Huggins noted that, despite 30 years of discussion, this was the first official conference to be held on the subject of closer association in Africa. He warned that federation was necessary to prevent Southern Rhodesia falling victim to South African expansionism — a fate which Northern Rhodesia possibly could share. In any case, Southern Rhodesia had always sought to realise Rhodes's dream of a British Central African state. Quite erroneously, Huggins stated that it had only recently been understood that Nyasaland should be included for economic and other reasons — one being that it was entitled to enjoy the fruits of its migrant workers' efforts.

Huggins reiterated the strategic and economic advantages of federation, the urgency of which, quite unprompted by their Governments, the officials had recognised. He felt that the Conference had to understand the vital role played by the European in development. The African had too recently emerged from barbarism for his potentialities to have been realised. Accordingly, an efficient civil service was greatly dependent upon a high proportion of European recruitment, and progress was conditional upon that service having strong local roots. These conditions appertained in Southern Rhodesia but then it had a larger European population. He claimed that the African was not being neglected, however, and employment opportunities were being found for him. Unlike the northern territories, Southern Rhodesia had always paid for its own development and one way to continue was to attract more settlers and increase the number of taxpayers.

Huggins pointed out that, in the proposals, the Southern Rhodesians would be making the greatest sacrifices of their hard-won political gains. He was determined that the northern Africans should not be given any advantages over the Southern Rhodesian Africans who had the vote and were British citizens. He advocated his territory's democratic system of a non-racial common roll franchise as being most suitable for multi-racial societies. This franchise was, admittedly, qualified but that was not uncommon in political systems, and he hoped that Southern Rhodesians would agree that the educational qualification was more important than the financial one. He disliked the northern system of representation by nomination, and defended the absence of Africans in his delegation, claiming that, as the vote was open to everyone of all races who qualified, his delegates being elected Members represented all races. He revealed that the African voters were beginning to influence elections in a number of constituencies.

Huggins avowed federation would hardly change daily life in the territories, as it would be some time before any benefit was apparent. His Europeans would welcome federation if it was practicable and not too reliant on goodwill, and the majority of Southern Rhodesian Africans would agree if a concrete, detailed and recommended scheme were placed before them. All people in the area had an intense local patriotism and wanted to see the federation develop as part of the Commonwealth. There was, however, some impatience and Huggins urged the British Ministers not to allow pure politics to obstruct closer association.

E. C. F. Whitehead, Huggins's Finance Minister, provided a broad outline of the economic advantages of federating. The three territories currently co-operated in the use of a single port, Beira, and two of them used a common railway system. Each territory assisted the other but there were occasions when territorial interests were put first and, in any case, each had its own development plans with differing targets, and congestion was inevitable and a complete breakdown possible. The dependence of the two Rhodesias upon a single source of coal, Wankie, led to similar difficulties, and the moment might arrive when Southern Rhodesia would feel that it could no longer starve its industries. The territories had also been supplying each other with food in drought years. Such *ad hoc* co-operation was not a substitute for centralised government, planning, development and pooling of resources. The populations would double in the next 25 years and food production and industry had not only to meet their requirements but also to support rising living standards. Integration of the economies would give them great resilience in a depression. Hydro-electric resources could be more easily developed together than if the territories had to compete for capital. As economic co-operation was the key to prosperity, Whitehead urged the Conference to ensure that it took a step in this direction.

Stockil, Leader of the Southern Rhodesian Opposition, and L. J. W. Keller, the veteran trade unionist and Rhodesia Labour Party parliamentarian, stressed that the Southern Rhodesian delegation was united and that it represented its entire community. They were confident of a reasonable compromise.

M. P. Barrow, the first Nyasalander to speak, questioned Huggins's assertion that Nyasaland had been considered only recently as a partner. Huggins had also ignored the positive contributions which would be forthcoming from Nyasaland's Europeans and from the territory itself. These Europeans, Barrow warned, would not associate themselves with Huggins's disparaging remarks about Africans and their ability to progress. Nevertheless, the non-African communities in Nyasaland favoured federation though they disliked some of the proposals. As there had been a vigorous propaganda campaign conducted amongst the African population (at the instigation of Banda whose opinions were believed to be out of date because he had not been in Nyasaland for 20 years) and, as the future depended on mutual trust between the races, a pre-condition to federation was, unavoidably, the winning of African support.

C. R. Kumbikano spoke for the Nyasaland Africans, all of whom he claimed to represent as a member of the Protectorate Council. In a rambling speech he stated that the Nyasaland Africans rejected federation and said he was only at the Conference because he had been reassured that no decisions would be taken and that the British Government had not yet examined the proposals. He was grateful, nonetheless, for the invitation but alleged that the Africans would have preferred a conference in London because there the British Government would have predominated. They were not being anti-European in their stand against change as they were loyal to the Crown and wished to retain Colonial Office administration because it understood the pace at which they should progress. To Africans, Kumbikano alleged, the Officials' Report (even though it rejected amalgamation) was the thin edge of the amalgamation wedge because men and governments could be influenced by the European communities and could change their minds when the British Government was powerless to stop them. African policies, which experience had shown to be very different in each territory, might be affected. An influx of non-African immigrants could lead to a struggle for existing wealth, and the intensive development recommended by the Report might prejudice African interests. The British Government, he said, would have failed Africans if it allowed federation to become a reality.

Welensky repeated much of what he had already said to Griffiths. As federation was in the interests of all, Northern Rhodesians would consider the Report as a basis for discussion even though they rejected some of its recommendations. Indeed, it was possible to improve the officials' arguments for federation. The three territories were already using common services such as rail and air transport and currency. Welensky wondered if any African understood just how dependent Northern Rhodesian prosperity was upon coal and that life, as they currently knew it, could not continue much longer without federation. The disruptive influence of nationalism, rampant amongst the Africans in West Africa, the whites in South Africa and the Indians in East Africa would soon reach Central Africa. In any case, government from afar was becoming increasingly ineffective and there would have to be a transference to local hands. Thus, he advised the British Government to examine the contribution of the local Europeans in 40 years as proof of their ability to govern. The choice was not, as the Africans believed, between federation or the continuance of the current system. Southern Rhodesia, denied federation, would choose isolation or a merger with South Africa — the latter action would seal the fate of the Southern African Protectorates. Northern Rhodesia would be isolated and its whites would seek self-government through a struggle which would be predictably bitter. Development capital was Central Africa's greatest need but political instability would drive the investor away. In an effort to soften African rejection, Welensky demanded a clear indication that any African who attained European standards should be made an equal partner in the government.

J. S. Moffat, the nominated Member for African interests, said that he would confine himself to describing African reaction to the Report and would answer Huggins's assertions later. He had discussed the proposals at all levels in Northern Rhodesia and had found a unanimous African rejection. Thus if federation were imposed, he warned, the Africans' trust in the British Government would be destroyed and race relations would deteriorate. In the face of this, he claimed the delegates representing African interests felt that, as alteration of the scheme would be pointless at this stage, discussions on federation should be suspended until the principles of partnership had been defined and implemented. D. L. Yamba was blunter, declaring that the Africans rejected domination by one race and would not discuss federation until they had been advanced politically to take a full part in the government of Northern Rhodesia.

Griffiths in his turn said little that was new. As usual, he explained that he and Gordon Walker were consulting the Central African populations before debating the issue in Britain. His Government had not committed itself but recognised the economic advantages and the threat of engulfment by Afrikaners. He and Gordon Walker would report that the Europeans generally favoured federation but with some reservations, the Nyasalanders, in particular, being anxious to preserve racial harmony. All the Africans he had consulted had rejected the proposal because they feared for their protected status, that federation could lead to amalgamation, that current systems of administration could be upset and that their political advancement and land would be jeopardised. He claimed that partnership was the only possible policy to apply because the local multi-racial society was very different from the homogeneity of the Gold Coast. He was glad that Welensky agreed with him and that Moffat had revealed that the Africans did likewise. Griffiths proposed that the meeting be adjourned to allow time for informal discussion before resuming on the morrow.

Gordon Walker said he wanted all to understand that they would have to make sacrifices if anything would be achieved. Events would not stand still and Central Africa was exposed to dangers from Krugerism and economic weakness, and the first would exploit the latter. His interpretation of the Report was that it hoped to leave the territories fundamentally unchanged while providing a means for joint action. He had found the Europeans concerned about the contents of the Report while the Africans ignored them and feared its omissions. He felt that it should be understood that it would be perfectly possible to absolutely exclude certain matters from federal control. This had in fact been done in the case of land settlement and should quieten African fears. It was to the African's advantage to have federal control of immigration to preserve the British character of the European population. Federation would make higher education available to a greater number. The concept of the minister for African interests was quite practicable because the federal government would have little to do with the African, and African issues would rarely arise. When they did, tolerance alone was needed for the system to work. The Conference then adjourned.[64]

The day's events had not surprised Welensky and he thought that the adjournment to London which Griffiths was seeking would be the likely outcome. He suspected, however, that if there was an adjournment he would have to deal with a new Colonial Secretary as he had received a hint that a British general election was in the offing.[65] He was still taken by surprise as he had not expected Attlee to make his announcement of that election the following day, 19 September. Welensky wondered if either Griffiths or Gordon Walker had known of Attlee's decision before they arrived. He recalls that "it was certainly a shock to realise that, within twenty-four hours of its opening, the conference which we thought was to take us a long way nearer our goal was turned into a sham and a showpiece, powerless to take any effective decisions; and the interest of Griffiths and Gordon Walker . . . was obviously concentrated on their constituencies, six thousand miles to the northward. Though I admit that the Conference was, to a certain degree, a success from our point of view, I was very browned off about the whole

[64] Welensky Papers, 17/11/1, Minutes of the Conference on the Closer Association of the Central African Territories, Victoria Falls, 18–21 September 1951.
[65] *Ibid.*, 5/96, f. 145, Welensky to W. Watson, 18 September 1951.

episode".[66] Huggins too was furious, but both men could console themselves that they might soon be dealing with the Conservatives.

Attlee's action together with the positions adopted in the Conference, and fruitless private discussions with the Secretaries of State, nearly occasioned the withdrawal of the Southern Rhodesian delegation. Huggins, however, advised his colleagues to stay to see if an accommodation with Northern Rhodesia at least could be reached.[67]

Nevertheless, he was in a bitter mood when the Conference met again on 20 September. Again speaking first, he pointed out that his alone of the delegations had come to the Conference prepared unreservedly to discuss closer association. Because part of the Nyasaland delegation had totally rejected federation while a portion of the Northern Rhodesian delegation had refused to discuss it until their territorial constitution had been revised, he wondered if the subject should be aired in current company. The Southern Rhodesians, he revealed, were most reluctant to show their hand in these circumstances. The Conference could, perhaps, only consider a limited union of the Rhodesias, excluding Nyasaland. He was annoyed at finding himself in this position when he had twice offered advice on the Conference and had been ignored. He felt that Colonial Office attitudes towards Africans were being allowed to dominate. In his case, he and his delegation were responsible for the interests of the Southern Rhodesian Africans because they were not sufficiently advanced to evaluate the proposals. He hoped that another Conference could be convened later on a more realistic basis.

When one knows that Welensky thought that Griffiths "leaned over backwards trying to placate the African representatives", and that "it is a sad fact but true that James Griffiths and I grated on one another from the outset",[68] it is not surprising to find Welensky supporting Huggins. The Northern Rhodesian elected Members, Welensky alleged, wondered whether the Conference could continue in the face of the total rejection of federation by part of the Nyasaland delegation. He called on Barrow to clarify whether Nyasaland's unofficial delegates would only approve of federation if it was accepted by the Nyasaland Africans.

Barrow could not reply immediately because Griffiths could not contain himself. No one, he interjected angrily, had come to the Conference labouring under any misapprehensions. It had been made perfectly clear at the outset that there was to be merely an exchange of views. Huggins had certainly understood this. Griffiths took personal responsibility for the presence of the Africans and would not remain if they left.

Gordon Walker backed him, but in more measured tones. He regretted Huggins's and Welensky's statements because the Conference could not proceed by way of ultimatum or by refusals to discuss particular points in front of certain delegates. Everyone had known that the problems were not instantly soluble. Furthermore, as Griffiths had said, all had understood that no decisions would be taken at this Conference. Yet Huggins had virtually retracted that agreement. Nonetheless, Gordon Walker felt that issues could

[66] Sir Roy Welensky, *Welensky's 4 000 Days* (London, 1964), p. 41.
[67] Welensky Papers, WE 7, P/C/104/52, Report of UP Congress, Umtali, 5 October 1951.
[68] Welensky, *4 000 Days*, *op. cit.*, pp. 41–42.

still be clarified and broad principles discussed. The pre-condition to federation was that African opinion had to be satisfied. The details could be considered at a later conference.

Huggins was not deterred and objected again to the presence of delegates who were pledged to oppose the object of the Conference. Gordon Walker replied that the African point of view had been well known and, if Huggins wished to change the nature of the Conference, the British delegation would have to reconsider its attendance. If the Conference broke up as a consequence, it would be plain who had been responsible. Huggins retorted that he was willing to accept that responsibility.

Welensky pointed out that the delegates had known that they would not commit themselves and yet the Nyasaland Africans had come to the Conference already pledged to reject federation. This provoked Griffiths to repeat that he was responsible for the Africans' presence. They had not wanted to come but he had persuaded them to, guaranteeing that there would be a full and frank exchange of views but no committal.

Beckett knew that both British Ministers appreciated the reasons for federation and, assuming that they had attended the Conference to clear away difficulties, asked if they would be prepared to show the Africans that federation was not only necessary but justified. Griffiths snapped back that Beckett should recall his speech on the opening day as he would only discuss matters on that basis. Again, Gordon Walker was less curt and more helpful. It was true, he said, that he and Griffiths recognised the substantial advantages but they felt African opinion had to be won round. The Conference's objective, he repeated, was to find common ground. Beckett agreed that the Conference could be used to identify the basic principles. However, he argued at length that the Secretaries of State should give a lead.

At last Barrow could speak. He said he was surprised at Huggins's ultimatum and answered Welensky's question by saying that the Nyasaland European population was too small to resist determined African opposition. However, it was possible for the Africans to change their minds as they were not fools and would listen to reason. The Nyasaland Europeans, therefore, would not stay if their African colleagues were excluded. The great mistake of the previous Conference at the Victoria Falls was that Africans were not present. The African delegates had come to the Conference unwillingly and the only mandate which they had was to oppose federation. They could not, and to their credit, would not change their views but they might leave the Conference with new ideas. He appealed to Huggins to reconsider the question of the inclusion of Nyasaland as everyone would have to make sacrifices when federating. The Nyasaland Europeans, he averred, still believed federation to be possible but only if it was discussed openly.

Moffat agreed with Barrow but, when claiming that the doubts expressed by the African delegates were insufficient reason for their being expelled, the chairman forced him to withdraw the word "expelled".

The Conference decided that it could continue if it discussed general problems such as guaranteeing the Africans' protected status, their political advancement and their land. However, Huggins further upset Griffiths by asking for an adjournment until the afternoon to allow private discussions with the British Ministers. Griffiths repeated that he was responsible for the presence of the Africans. Then he said he would agree to Huggins's request but only if the plenary session, when resumed, would consider the broad principles alone. Huggins agreed if discussion was frank.

The meeting was thus adjourned but not before Yamba had claimed, piteously, that the northern Africans had been reluctant to attend the Conference because they were sure that they would not be welcome. They had only come in response to pressure from Griffiths and regretted that, in fact, their presence had caused difficulties just when they felt that they were about to get somewhere and that Africans and Europeans could work together to establish racial harmony.

When the plenary session was reconvened that afternoon, it concentrated on African fears, and Huggins later commented that the Conference had "degenerated into a native benefit society, led by the Secretary of State".[69] Given the Southern Rhodesian delegation's preparations for the Conference and their expectations, it must have been a cruel disappointment not to discuss anything directly relating to the Report's proposals.

The questions of the future of the northern Africans' protected status under federation and whether federation would be a step towards amalgamation were discussed first. The Africans who spoke, P. Sokota, E. K. Gondwe and Yamba, pointed to the fate of constitutional safeguards in other countries such as South Africa, and recalled local European demands for the severance of the link with the Colonial Office, and public utterances that federation was indeed a step towards amalgamation.

The Conference accepted these fears as reasonable and, as Griffiths emphasised, that it was necessary to remove them or nothing durable could be built. Moffat, however, was confident that there was a large body of Northern Rhodesian African opinion which would accept the British Government's reassurances on the federal proposals which themselves envisaged the continuance of the relationship with the Colonial Office and the maintenance of the protected status. It was acknowledged that guarantees could not be expected to endure for all time and the Africans were urged to take note of a reassurance which was forthcoming from Huggins — with endorsement by Welensky — that there could be no change until it was the expressed wish of the majority of the inhabitants. African fears for their land were similarly answered: the existing Orders in Council would remain in force and thus only the King, advised by the British Government, could adjust the allocation of land in Northern Rhodesia and Nyasaland. Moffat stressed that Huggins's declaration was of the utmost importance in this context, but Yamba wondered how it could be implemented in practice. Huggins answered that a general election in Southern Rhodesia would suffice, and in the northern territories opinion could be gathered as it had been before this Conference.

The remainder of the discussion centred on the Africans' prospects of political advancement and on the implementation of the policy of partnership. Kumbikano stated that the Nyasaland Africans were content with their current political system even though it was not as advanced as that of their

[69] D. Taylor, *The Rhodesian: The Life of Sir Roy Welensky* (London, 1955), p. 139.

neighbours. The difference was in fact, he claimed, a reason for not federating.

Little, indeed, was said on the federal government's potential threat to African advancement beyond Sokota imputing that the great federal influence upon the territorial governments would mean political retardation for Africans. Griffiths replied that the federal government would be powerless in this field and that it was the British Government's avowed intention to see that all colonial possessions ultimately gained self-government.

Most of the comment centred on current constitutions and Northern Rhodesia's in particular. The African delegates demanded that they be given a greater share of political power. Welensky retorted that in the same breath they called for protection and greater representation which implied political maturity. Griffiths expressed willingness when it was suggested that the suspended Northern Rhodesian constitutional negotiations should be renewed after the Conference. With regard to partnership, the Conference agreed that there was a general need for a definition of it. Welensky suggested that the British Government should supply it, but Griffiths wanted the territories to discover a formula and to refer it to him for approval. Huggins closed the proceedings with the comment that he had already defined partnership as the "antithesis of *apartheid*".

Informal discussion occupied most of the next day, 21 September, and the plenary session was only resumed at 5.30 p.m. Because there had been Press reports of Southern Rhodesian demands for the expulsion of the African delegates, a categorical denial of them was deemed necessary. Discussion then centred on what the delegates could reveal of the Conference on their return home, and it was decided that discretion should be used.

The final matter was to compose the Press communiqué which was released that evening. This recalled the urgent recommendation of federation by the Officials' Report and stated that this current Conference had never been intended to do more than to discuss the problems of federation. In these discussions it had become apparent that adjournment was necessary to allow further discussions and exchanges between the four Governments. The Conference would re-assemble in London in mid-1952. With the exception of the African delegates, the Conference had favoured federation. In addition, the Northern Rhodesian African representatives had expressed a willingness to consider it, once the policy of partnership had been defined and progressively implemented in their territory.

The Conference recognised that partnership was the only basis on which the federation could be founded. Alluding to Afrikaner and other nationalisms, grave concern was expressed of the dangers of weakening the British connection and tradition. The Conference recognised the advantages of common handling of problems, given adequate safeguards, but knew that the main obstacle was the apprehensions of the northern Africans. Thus it was agreed that any scheme would have to acknowledge that the protectorate status of the northern territories should be preserved and thus, unless desired by a majority of the inhabitants of the three territories, the consideration of amalgamation was inadmissible. Land and land settlement questions had to remain the responsibility of the territorial Governments and their legislatures. African land rights in Northern Rhodesia and Nyasaland had still to be secured in accord with existing Orders in Council. Likewise, the political advancement of the people would be a territorial responsibility. These provisos would be enshrined in any federal constitution. It was recorded finally that, in looking forward to the next Conference, the delegates reserved their positions on issues other than protected status, African interests, political advancement, land and land settlement.

Though Stockil would call the Conference "a dismal failure", neither Huggins nor Welensky was quite as pessimistic.[70] Privately, and afterwards publicly, Welensky decried Griffiths's emotional, sentimental but uncompromising attitude. He acknowledged, though, that Griffiths had been exhausted by the time he had reached the Victoria Falls. He was annoyed that Griffiths had not found the time, in Northern Rhodesia, to see people like himself and Gore-Browne privately. Welensky considered Gordon Walker, though inclined to dither, to be shrewder and more realistic than Griffiths. However, disappointing though the Conference might have been, Welensky felt that some progress had been made and more was likely if the Conservatives won the election. Nevertheless, he did not think that the Conservatives would ride roughshod over African opinion, but the delay would give time for the northern Governments to attempt to sway African opinion just as it would give the African time to read and understand the proposals, thereby lessening the influence of the extremists.[71] Huggins (to whom Welensky had felt impelled to write to urge him not to be too harsh[72]) in turn pointed out that at least the British Labour Government had been associated with the statement that the Conference was in favour of federation, and thus a commitment had been secured.

Huggins made this point when explaining the ramifications of the Conference to the United Party congress at Umtali on 5 October. He did not agree, however, with Welensky that delay could serve the unification cause because experience had shown that the difficulties only increased with time. It would have been easy to unify in 1938. He explained that little had been said before the Conference because the Southern Rhodesian Government had not wanted to prejudice the negotiations. He had tried but failed to secure an adjournment of the Conference when he realised (from the reception accorded to Griffiths in the northern territories) that his advice to the British Government, to give a lead on federation to the Africans, had been ignored. It seemed that the British Government was unable to do this. Huggins felt that the Colonial Office had, in fact, made the "pace too hot" and had given backward people ideas too advanced for them. The Nyasaland Africans had come to the Conference instructed to vote against federation at all costs and, consequently, Southern Rhodesia would insist that at any future conference only representatives should be present and not delegates bound by mandates.

[70] *The Rhodesia Herald*, 4 October 1951.

[71] Welensky, *4 000 Days*, *op. cit.*, p. 41; Welensky Papers, 5/96, f. 141, Welensky to W. F. Willis, 27 September 1951; 5/95, f. 136, Welensky to S. H. Veats, 27 September 1951; WE 7, P/C/141/52, F. S. Joelson to Welensky, 8 October 1951; 39/119, f. 174, Welensky to Mrs Silby-Warne, 18 October 1951; 5/95, f. 385, Welensky to Lennox-Boyd, 18 October 1951.

[72] Welensky Papers, 5/96, f. 107, Welensky to A. B. Cohen, 10 October 1951.

Huggins said that the Southern Rhodesians had hoped that something positive would be produced by the Conference as they were anxious to improve aspects of the Officials' scheme. In particular, they felt that the federal government should have some involvement with African affairs, but the Conference had never progressed beyond discussing African fears. Nevertheless, Huggins asked Southern Rhodesians to brace themselves because recently he had shocked people by stating that there would be Africans in the Southern Rhodesian Legislative Assembly within 25 years. Henceforth, they would have to accept that there would be direct African representation in the federal parliament from the outset, and Southern Rhodesian Africans could not be denied the opportunity. R. S. G. Todd, a New Zealand missionary, one of the congress members and the future Prime Minister of Southern Rhodesia, protested at this and urged the introduction of the common roll to avoid racial polarisation. Huggins maintained that he had tried to do this but that the Southern Rhodesians would have to accept nominated members from the North for some time. There would be an effort, nonetheless, to prevent the African members from being cast as a permanent Opposition.

Huggins claimed to have surprised the Africans at the Conference by his declaration against amalgamation. On the whole, however, he concluded that the Conference had been a bitter and expensive disappointment and that as much could have been achieved by an exchange of letters. He and his delegation had not been surprised at the result as "the antics of Mr. Griffiths in the Northern territories had led them to believe this might happen". Huggins concluded by saying that the onus was thus on the two Rhodesias to devise a plan for presentation to the British Government, and he thought that Northern Rhodesia and perhaps Nyasaland could have a similar relationship to Southern Rhodesia as Northern Ireland had to the British Parliament.[73]

The alternative methods of unifying were being reviewed, and Welensky, who was being pressed by Gore-Browne to reconsider the partition of Northern Rhodesia,[74] found this idea being bandied about, when he visited Bulawayo in mid-October, to such an extent that he thought it necessary to warn publicly that few Northern Rhodesians would support it.[75] Amalgamation was proposed by Stockil, and by some of Huggins's United Party at their congress. However, on 12 October, when meeting Advocate J. M. Greenfield of the United Party to discuss the fusion of their Parties, which was impossible because no common ground could be found, and federation, which most of his Rhodesia Party opposed, Stockil changed his mind and abandoned amalgamation for the variation of the Northern Ireland Constitution.[76]

Huggins, Greenfield and Welensky discussed the idea and, on 24 October, Greenfield sent Welensky a memorandum entitled "United Rhodesia: A plan for the closer association of the two Rhodesias". This envisaged Southern Rhodesia continuing to be a self-governing colony and Northern Rhodesia remaining a protectorate. However, Southern Rhodesia's legislature would

[73] *Ibid.*, WE 7, P/C/104/52, Report of UP Congress, Umtali, 5 October 1951.
[74] *Ibid.*, P/C/109/52, Gore-Browne to Welensky, 9 October 1951.
[75] *Ibid.*, Welensky to Gore-Browne, 24 October 1951; *The Rhodesia Herald*, 20 October 1951.
[76] Welensky Papers, WE 7, P/C/100/50, J. M. Greenfield to Huggins, 13 October 1951.

become the federal parliament with complete control of Southern Rhodesia and of certain aspects of Northern Rhodesia's affairs. If this house were uni-cameral, its membership would be based on the current number of voters in the two territories, giving Southern Rhodesia 40 seats and Northern Rhodesia ten. Southern Rhodesia's franchise would apply throughout except that, in the North, the voter would not need to be a British subject. Northern Rhodesia would be compensated for the disparity in numbers by providing the prime minister or, at least, a cabinet minister. Direct African representation was envisaged with each territory having two African members who, in Southern Rhodesia's case, would represent Matabeleland and Mashonaland and would be elected by the voters on the ordinary roll. There would be no Africans in the lower house if a bi-cameral system was allowed. The upper house would be modelled on the current proposal for Southern Rhodesia made by its Select Committee on the Constitution, except that Northern Rhodesia would be given one seat for every two allocated to Southern Rhodesia. Britain's reserved powers with regard to Southern Rhodesia would be transferred to the federal parliament. The Northern Rhodesian constitution would only be affected by the transfer of some powers, unspecified at this stage, and its legislature would continue to be responsible for land, law and local government.[77]

However, Welensky felt that it was impossible to plan until the British election result was known, but he was unimpressed with Stockil's claim that most of the Rhodesia Party opposed federation, because he was confident that, given reasonable proposals, he and Huggins campaigning together could win the support of the Rhodesians. Welensky avowed that he would only be party to the dismemberment of Northern Rhodesia when the federal issue was finally dead and then it would be his last political act. He told Huggins, Lennox-Boyd and others that he did not expect the Conservatives to trample African opinion underfoot but thought they would provide a lead which, with some persuasion, could win the Africans round. He let Lennox-Boyd know, too, of his despair at current British policies at home and abroad.[78] He informed Gore-Browne that he was particularly distressed by the British withdrawal from Persia, that Egypt was about to chase "us" out of the Canal Zone, and that the Greeks wanted Cyprus and Malan the Protectorates. He asked: ". . . so what hope have we got if we have to depend on a spineless gutless crowd such as control the destinies of England these days." Other worries clouding his horizon were "that dear little James Griffiths left me a pair of bouncing twins to nurse . . .".[79] He was alluding to the tasks of defining partnership and resolving the question of Northern Rhodesia's constitution. These thoughts, together with the fear of the success which Zukas was enjoying in rendering the African opposition more militant, crowded Welensky's mind as he awaited the British result.

[77] *Ibid.*, 39/112, f. 102, Greenfield to Welensky, 24 October 1951; ff. 103–106, Memorandum by J. M. Greenfield, 24 October 1951.
[78] *Ibid.*, WE 7, P/C/100/50, Welensky to Huggins, 25 October 1951; 5/95, f. 385, Welensky to Lennox-Boyd, 18 October 1951.
[79] *Ibid.*, WE 7, P/C/109/52, Welensky to Gore-Browne, 14 October 1951.

CHAPTER EIGHT

A Positive Decision

British Government Action and Preparations for the Next Conference, November 1951-April 1952

THE fate of the federal issue seemed to hinge so much upon the outcome of the British election that Welensky recalls he felt as involved as any of the contestants. The election result emboldened him to declare on 27 October 1951: "The prospects of federation in Central Africa are a good deal better at this moment than they were twenty-four hours ago. If we can create here in Central Africa a British Dominion strong enough to protect its own interests, to tell people to keep off the grass, I believe we can build a society that will demonstrate to the world that we can live side by side in a multiracial society."[1]

Nevertheless, the Conservative victory was narrow enough — an overall majority of seven — for the Rhodesians to remain apprehensive because Winston Churchill, now back in power, seemed to care little for Africa. Welensky had failed to interest Churchill in federation and, if a forceful ally would not be found in his appointee to the Colonial Office portfolio, it seemed unlikely that Churchill would risk a passage of arms over this issue with the still powerful and determined Labour Opposition.[2] Such fears were proved groundless when Oliver Lyttelton (later Lord Chandos) was named as Colonial Secretary. Although Lyttelton was never entirely at home in a commons debate, he was experienced, capable, intelligent and even ruthless, and would soon be convinced of the need for federation. Given such an ally, the federal campaign quickly gathered momentum.

Confident of British support, the protagonists of federation now felt that the most serious problem was finally to win over the Southern Rhodesian Government and electorate. Considerable pressure was being exerted on that Government by Stockil's Rhodesia Party and others to consider the alternatives. To outflank this lobby, Welensky and Beckett travelled to Salisbury

[1] Sir Roy Welensky, *Welensky's 4 000 Days* (London, 1964), p. 43.
[2] D. Taylor, *The Rhodesian: The Life of Sir Roy Welensky* (London, 1955), pp. 140–141.

on 2 November. Their warning that their elected colleagues would not contemplate the dismemberment of Northern Rhodesia persuaded the Southern Rhodesian Cabinet to accept federation as its goal. The Cabinet then appointed a ministerial committee to examine its objections to the federal plan and to suggest alternatives. Welensky also secured Huggins's agreement to discuss the federal campaign with the Northern Rhodesian unofficial Members when visiting Ndola in early December.[3]

Because the European delegates insisted that African sanction for closer association was crucial, the effect of the Victoria Falls Conference in Nyasaland had been to improve race relations for the moment.[4] The converse was true in Northern Rhodesia but was not immediately apparent, for J. S. Moffat had been well received, particularly in Kitwe. He had gone from the Conference to hold a series of meetings on the Copperbelt to explain the insistence of the representatives of African interests that the definition and implementation of partnership should precede African consideration of federation.[5] In early October, in accordance with an Executive Council decision,[6] Moffat and W. F. Stubbs, the acting Secretary of Native Affairs, spoke again in the major centres to the members of the African Urban Advisory Councils and other organisations. Their purpose was to secure African participation in the task of defining partnership. Again, except in Luanshya, they were well received. In Luanshya, however, support from P. Sokota was fruitless and Moffat's actions were condemned. The meeting rejected Moffat's preliminary definition of partnership as being incompatible with the concept of trusteeship and claimed that he had possessed no mandate for his action at the Conference.

Ignoring Moffat's plea for quiet contemplation of the issue, 21 members of the African Urban Advisory Councils, the African trade unions, the African National Congress and one member of the Legislative Council (Sokota) met in Kitwe on 8 November. Sokota, in fact, tried to influence the meeting to accept the Victoria Falls statement but finally was party to a unanimous condemnation of it because it was not supported by any African organisation. Without dissension, too, the British Government was condemned for betraying the Africans' protected status by adopting the policy of partnership without consulting them. This policy, it was claimed, would lead to a severance of the direct link with the Colonial Office and would be responsible for all land becoming common property. Partnership was a ploy to induce the Africans to accept federation and prevent the introduction of the democratic principle of rule by the majority. It would bring an increasing influx of white immigrants. As Moffat had failed to suggest ways to implement the recent Dalgleish Commission's recommendations on removing racial discrimination in skilled trades, the meeting concluded that economic equality would not be

[3] Welensky Papers, WE 7, Un-numbered Series "Legco November 1951", Welensky to unofficial Members, 4 November 1951; 5/96, f. 59, Welensky to G. G. S. G. Hadlow, 6 November 1951; 5/95, f. 380, Welensky to Sir Stewart Gore-Browne, 7 November 1951; 39/116, f. 59, H. N. Parry to Welensky, 10 November 1951.

[4] *Ibid.*, 5/96, f. 81, Hadlow to Welensky, 10 October 1951.

[5] *Ibid.*, 39/112, f. 98, Memorandum by J. S. Moffat, (undated).

[6] D. C. Mulford, *Zambia: The Politics of Independence, 1957–1964* (London, 1967), p. 29.

an aspect of partnership. The final resolution stated that partnership would also frustrate the Africans' desire to become a nation within the Commonwealth — meaning presumably an African-dominated dominion. Sokota was ordered to ensure that the Legislative Council did not debate partnership. Furthermore, he and D. L. Yamba were forbidden to speak within the Council without instructions from the African organisations.[7]

Determined that the definition of partnership was an essential prerequisite of a full campaign for federation, Sir Gilbert Rennie ignored the Kitwe resolutions and convened a meeting of the African Representative Council in early December to secure its co-operation. Welensky commented that the Kitwe meeting confirmed that the Africans were only interested in political domination.[8] He dissected the Kitwe resolutions during the debate in the Legislative Council on the Governor's speech on 14 November, questioning how representative of African opinion the Kitwe meeting had been. The Africans, he felt, were being misled into believing that their opinion on partnership was being sought when in fact Britain, as trustee, had adopted the policy, as was its right, without consulting any of the inhabitants. It was nonsensical to speak of partnership severing the direct link with the Colonial Office when the latter, as the agent of the Colonial Secretary, was implementing the policy. Likewise, the Africans should have known that the statement on land was untrue, and it ignored the affirmations by successive Colonial Secretaries of the British guarantee as well as the statements by the Legislative Council, the Prime Minister of Southern Rhodesia and himself. He warned that the Europeans, who had accepted partnership, would resist African domination and would reject recent African demands for a majority in the Legislative Council and for universal suffrage. He questioned whether more than three per cent of the African population could define universal suffrage and announced he would resume the suspended constitutional negotiations. Then, as a believer in Rhodes's dictum of equal rights for civilised men, he defended the existing racial discrimination as a necessary temporary protection of standards and warned Africans to beware of those who fished in troubled waters. They should take care to retain the services of Moffat as they had displayed their inability to represent their own interest.[9]

Moffat, in turn, reserved most of his comments for the forthcoming meeting of the African Representative Council but maintained he and his colleagues had obtained the sanction of this body and of the ANC before going to the Victoria Falls. Two members of the Kitwe meeting had acknowledged this, another had been party to the Victoria Falls statement but the remaining 18 had not been present and therefore were not qualified to comment. Moffat recalled that Africans, within and without the ARC, had previously endorsed the policy of partnership. He favoured partnership and avowed that he would work for its implementation. He warned the Africans that they would do their cause great harm if they repudiated agreements, freely made, just to satisfy a few extremists. His fellow European represent-

[7] Welensky Papers, 39/112, f. 99, Report of the Joint Conference of African Members of the African Urban Advisory Councils and Members of other organisations, (undated).
[8] *The Rhodesia Herald*, 9 November 1951.
[9] NR *Debates* (Lusaka), Col. 46 f., 14 November 1951.

ative, E. G. Nightingale, supported him, but Yamba and Sokota refused to comment until the ARC had instructed them on the true African opinion.

Aware that Lyttelton would soon make a pronouncement, Welensky said little more on federation than to urge inter-governmental discussion.[10]

Huggins was even more reluctant to comment but was forced to by a debate in the Southern Rhodesian Assembly instigated by Stockil to compel him to give priority to the acquisition of dominion status because the late Conference had done nothing more than stimulate the fanatic and give Africans a false sense of their importance. Stockil was confident that the economic benefits could be obtained without a political union.[11]

Other speakers agreed that the two goals were quite compatible and depressed Welensky with their lack of understanding of the issues involved. Pressed, Huggins agreed to go to London but proposed to discuss only federation with Lyttelton because to suggest amalgamation, despite its merits, was to cry for the moon. He dismissed dominion status as too ambitious for Southern Rhodesia's resources. It would merely endanger its external credit. He proposed to accept the Officials' Report as the basis of negotiation because it envisaged a strong federal government. He praised partnership as fitting the Churchillian concept of a Commonwealth which outlawed discrimination on the grounds of colour, race or creed. He stressed that there would be no threat to the northern protected status or to land which would remain a territorial subject. He cut Griffiths to the quick, however, when he agreed that Griffiths's visit had done little more than provoke the Africans. Griffiths, he said, had not understood the innate conservatism of the Africans or appreciated the pressure being exerted by the extremists among them.[12]

Two days later, on 21 November, Lyttelton announced in the Commons that his Government was convinced of the urgent need for closer association and that federation was the only appropriate method of achieving it in the circumstances. The basis of discussion would be the Officials' Report because it provided effective machinery for the executive and the legislature, and provided protection for African interests. As he believed that the assurances given at the Victoria Falls Conference and the expected economic benefits would win the African round, he took care to repeat these assurances, stating that land, land settlement and political advancement would remain in territorial hands. Protectorate status would be unaffected, and amalgamation would be allowed only if desired by a majority of the inhabitants of the three territories. All this would be specified in the constitution including that social and economic partnership would be the foundation of all federal policy. Lyttelton proposed to adhere to the decision of the Conference to reconvene in London in mid-1952, and to that end he would begin preliminary discussions with the representatives of the three territories.

Griffiths was not directly critical of Lyttelton, but warned that he was speaking for a great section of his Party in saying that there should be no action in the face of African opposition. Moreover, because Huggins had made damaging remarks about himself and the Africans, Griffiths demanded

[10] *Ibid.*, Col. 73 f., 14 November 1951.

[11] SR *Debates* (Salisbury), Vol. 32, Part 2, Col. 3323 f., 14 November 1951.

[12] *Ibid.*, Col. 3535, 19 November 1951.

an early debate on federation. He defended the Africans because they made a positive contribution to the Conference by suggesting that partnership be defined. Furthermore, because the question of closer association had been bedevilled by their exclusion, Griffiths also insisted that Huggins should not be allowed to come to London unless accompanied by African representatives. Lyttelton replied that debates were matters for the Leader of the House and that Huggins did not need permission to visit London. He promised, however, to impress upon Huggins that the presence of Africans at the next conference would assure success.[13]

Huggins attempted to placate Griffiths in his speech at Ndola on 1 December, but without success, and Lyttelton only agitated Griffiths further by ordering the district officers to advocate federation.[14] Welensky and his unofficial colleagues used their meeting in Lusaka with Huggins on 2 December to ensure that he went to London clearly understanding their view of the federal plan. Huggins agreed that the safeguards were too elaborate when African affairs would be in territorial hands. Also, there would be too many nominated members when a method of electing many of them could be devised. He was particularly anxious that the federal parliament should not divide on racial lines and wanted Africans to join parties for political and not racial reasons. He warned of a growing opposition to federation in Southern Rhodesia where there were doubts about the inclusion of Nyasaland and the retention of the northern protected status. Huggins was not, however, suggesting the abandonment of the Officials' Report as the basis of negotiation. If the current effort to secure closer association failed, he promised to support a bid to obtain representative government for Northern Rhodesia.

The elected Members urged Huggins to paint as black a picture as possible in London of the consequences of failure. They felt, however, that the Southern Rhodesians were overly concerned about protected status and tended to exaggerate the influence of the Colonial Office. Not entirely convinced, Huggins pointed out that the elected Members had been powerless to prevent the introduction, against their wishes, of two African Members into their Legislative Council. He accepted that a statement of Northern Rhodesian aims in African advancement might assist him but warned that policies should not be projected too far into the future because, for example, one problem of implementing partnership was to avoid African domination. The meeting agreed that Huggins's Government should immediately supply the Northern Rhodesian Government with a note on its proposed modifications of the federal plan and arrange a meeting at ministerial level to secure a common approach to the problem. Thereafter Nyasaland would be consulted. The meeting also decided that the presentation of a common front in London would be greatly assisted by finding an excuse for Welensky to be present to support Huggins.[15]

[13] House of Commons *Hansard* (London), Vol. 494, Col. 392 f., 21 November 1951.

[14] Welensky Papers, 39/116, f. 51, D. Dodds-Parker to Welensky, 1 December 1951; f. 52, Welensky to G. Sayers, 4 December 1951; 39/119, f. 158, Welensky to Gore-Browne, 4 December 1951.

[15] *Ibid.*, 39/120, ff. 10–12, Notes of Meeting between Sir Godfrey Huggins and NR elected Members, Lusaka, 2 December 1951.

If progress was now being made towards federation, the reverse was true with the attempt in Northern Rhodesia to define partnership. On 3 December, Rennie delivered a speech in the African Representative Council which had been written with the assistance of Moffat and Welensky.[16] Rennie strove to answer the Kitwe charges. He reminded the ARC that partnership had been an established policy since 1946 and had been approved by the African delegates in constitutional discussions ever since. Partnership, he maintained, was consistent with protected status and did not weaken the link with the Colonial Office or jeopardise land rights, which remained secured by Orders in Council. It had already brought enormous benefit to Africans. It was best described as a way of life, an attitude of mind based on the recognition of co-operation and the resolve of all sections of the community to assist each other. This meant that the Africans would experience steady progress in all aspects of national life until they were able to play the role of full partners. There would be no subordination of the interests of one community to another. Though Moffat (whom Yamba and Sokota tried to exclude from attending) spoke in support of Rennie, the ARC went into committee and no result was forthcoming that day.[17]

When the ARC met again on 5 December, it resisted two attempts by Yamba and Sokota to involve it in the partnership discussions. It preferred that the Northern Rhodesian Government should produce the definition and, even then, would not consider it until it had been submitted to the subordinate bodies, the Native Authority, Urban Advisory and Provincial Councils. A second motion expressed concern at Lyttelton's pronouncement on federation and claimed that it was premature. A third motion, seeking to confirm the statement of the African representatives at the Victoria Falls, was narrowly defeated because it was felt that federation would be a consequence of partnership.

That evening at an informal meeting, after some difficulty, R. P. Bush, the Secretary for Native Affairs, succeeded in persuading the ARC to withdraw the replacement motion which condemned the action at the Victoria Falls. The ARC, however, would not confirm Moffat's statement at the Victoria Falls unless it read that the African "might", instead of "would", be willing to consider federation after partnership had been defined and implemented. At least total rejection had been avoided.[18]

Welensky spoke in the Legislative Council two days later on federation but reserved his comments on the ARC until 19 December. The federal issue seemed more important because a Commons debate on it was scheduled for that day. (In fact, the debate had been postponed because the Labour Party wanted it to be longer than an hour and a half.) Welensky welcomed Lyttelton's statement because at last the British Government had given a lead,

[16] David C. Mulford finds it extraordinary – Mulford, *Zambia, op. cit.*, p. 30 & p. 30, fn. 5 – that Welensky should have been involved because he assumes that Welensky was not on the Executive Council when, in fact, he was, as leader of the unofficials, a member without portfolio. – JRTW.

[17] *The Rhodesia Herald*, 3 December 1951; Welensky Papers, 39/119, f. 158, Welensky to Gore-Browne, 4 December 1951.

[18] Mulford, *Zambia, op. cit.*, p. 31.

although Lyttelton had done little more than endorse the Victoria Falls communiqué and declare that federation would serve all interests. However, the initiative had thereby passed to the Rhodesians. Declaring that such action was a year late, Welensky criticised Griffiths for making federation a Party issue and maintained that this was the first time a section of the Commons had tried to drive a wedge between the races. The Labour Party insinuated that they alone cared for the African's future when, in reality, the Conservatives had done and would do more for the African while not being ashamed of the Empire. Griffiths had also tried to interfere with the right of a prime minister of a self-governing colony to consult freely with his Secretary of State, and furthermore had spoken of the exclusion of Africans, thereby ignoring Gore-Browne's presence at the 1949 Conference as an observer representing African interests and his subsequent activities in reporting to Africans throughout Northern Rhodesia. At the recent Victoria Falls Conference, Griffiths had not found time to confer with the elected Members though he had frequently met the African delegates. Ruling the Commons debate to be untimely, Welensky appealed to the British politicians to guard their tongues for fear of strengthening the opposition in Southern Rhodesia. He urged the Southern Rhodesians to have faith in their Government and not to complicate the situation by advancing alternative solutions to federation.[19]

Yamba told the familiar tale of Griffiths inducing Africans to attend the Conference with the promise that there would only be an exchange of views. Thus the statement at the end had taken the African delegates by surprise. Yamba was asked if he would deny that he and Sokota had signed it, and he replied that the only perfect understanding was that the Conference was being adjourned to mid-1952. Otherwise confusion had reigned amongst Africans, and the ARC had managed only partially to dispel it. Lyttelton's statement had been just as unexpected because partnership had not yet been defined. He and Sokota, Yamba said, were now being accused by the Africans of having accepted federation in addition to prematurely supporting Moffat.[20]

Privately, Welensky acknowledged that Huggins had provoked Griffiths. However, he excused his own outburst as the product of Griffiths's irresponsibility when out of office in leading the Africans into excesses. He added that Zukas had been at work and there had been considerable intimidation. In addition, the ARC had sanctioned Moffat's statement but would not endorse it in public.[21] Welensky said as much in the Legislative Council on 19 December and wondered, even though he was a founder of it, if there was any point in retaining the ARC. It had not only reneged on its agreement with Moffat and emasculated the Conference's statement, but had failed to learn yet to grasp the difference between a representative and a delegate. The definition of partnership consequently became a government task and there should be no delay. Moffat concurred. Defining partnership as a way of life, he asked the Africans to appreciate that it was perfectly possible to have partnership without federation and federation with partnership.[22]

[19] NR *Debates* (Lusaka), Col. 530, 7 December 1951. [20] *Ibid.*, Col. 543, 10 December 1951.
[21] Welensky Papers, 5/95, f. 350, Welensky to Gore-Browne, 12 December 1951; f. 349, Welensky to F. S. Joelson, 12 December 1951.
[22] NR *Debates* (Lusaka), Col. 900, 19 December 1951.

H. Nkumbula, president of the ANC, was inspired by these debates to issue a pamphlet which claimed that racial tension was reaching a peak through illegal Afrikaner immigration — illegal because Northern Rhodesia was not a "full part" of the Empire, through white encroachment on the land and the proposals for amalgamation, federation, responsible government and partnership. Lyttelton's efforts would fail, it said, because the African would not be convinced that federation would not merely enrich Britain and the local white colonists. Furthermore, partnership did not exist when there were separate institutions, more was spent on European education, African representation was limited to two members of the legislature and equal pay for equal work was denied.

The pamphlet supplied a host of other examples and argued that the African Representative Council had been right to refuse to define a fiction. Africans had to tell Europeans that they no longer trusted them and demand "Home Rule" which, while protecting the rights of the minorities, would give the Africans the final say on the form of government.[23]

Welensky, of course, had not neglected the federal issue and in mid-December had briefed Sir Geoffrey Colby, the Governor of Nyasaland, and M. P. Barrow on current plans.[24] The exasperation engendered by the Nyasalanders' attitude at the recent Conference lingered, however, and relations with Barrow, in particular, remained strained.[25]

Huggins had wasted little time after his visit to the North and on 14 December could cable his Government's criticisms of the federal plan to Lord Ismay, the Commonwealth Secretary, in preparation for their meeting in London in January. Huggins made it plain that the Southern Rhodesians still thought that the reasons for refusing the best solution, amalgamation, were insufficient. Welensky and others concluded that Huggins knew he would be rebuffed and was merely seeking to convince his followers that he had tried and could do no more. Huggins warned that his people would insist that cabinet government was made possible by the appointment of the minister for African interests by the prime minister. The African affairs board, too, would have to be reduced to an advisory body, providing liaison between the territorial Governments on African matters. The question of nominated members needed examination because the proposed numbers could prevent the development of the party system and hold the balance of power within the assembly when it was possible, for example, to devise a method of election for the Nyasaland members. A common franchise might be necessary and there might have to be an extension of British citizenship to the Protected Persons. There was a danger of creating racial politics. Furthermore, there was insufficient protection for non-African inhabitants when it could be arranged that any territorial legislation which infringed their interests would have to have federal sanction. To ensure smooth functioning of government, the Indian constitutional example could be followed thereby

[23] Welensky Papers, 39/112, ff. 67–69, Address by H. Nkumbula, Kitwe, 25 December 1951. (As only three people turned up, Nkumbula did not deliver the address but issued it to the Press as a pamphlet.)
[24] *Ibid.*, ff. 85, Welensky to Huggins, 14 December 1951.
[25] *Ibid.*, WE 7, P/C/100/50, Welensky to Huggins, 24 December 1951.

creating a category of territorial legislation designated concurrent so that the central government could supervise it to ensure uniformity in important matters.[26]

Welensky's diagnosis was proved correct when Huggins asked Ismay on 22 December for a clear British ministerial statement, on the reasons why amalgamation was impossible, to assist him in selling the federal idea at a referendum.

The very success of Southern Rhodesian self-government, Huggins explained, had made amalgamation so attractive and was responsible for the depth of criticism of the federal proposals. The forthcoming reconvened Conference, too, would have to provide him with an acceptable constitution for the referendum. He reiterated that his electorate would insist on normal cabinet and party government and suggested that, in lieu of a common voters' roll, a temporary secondary roll could be used for new voters, or the various African representative councils could nominate candidates for election. British citizenship for all was most desirable. A concurrent list of legislation — in other words a list of subjects for which the federal government was ultimately responsible but on which the territorial Governments could legislate — seemed undesirable but unavoidable. The alternative of giving the central government an inclusive list and leaving all matters affecting Africans to the state legislatures might result in important divergencies which the federal government could be powerless to correct.

Drawing on Malayan and Canadian examples, Huggins proposed that the concurrent list should contain legislation designed to protect civil rights, ensure law and order, and control wages and marketing. A safeguard requiring federal endorsement of changes in territorial electoral law could be adapted from the Swiss Constitution. A declaration in the federal constitution of the right of all races to permanent residence would please the Southern Rhodesians as would the provision for a federal veto of territorial legislation with regard to the interests of the non-African population. To avoid excessive litigation, Huggins favoured the Swiss practice of declaring territorial legislation void if it clashed with federal law. There should also be provision for the transfer of powers to the federal government at the request of a state government. Concluding, Huggins declared that these proposals would be laid before a meeting in Salisbury of the three territorial Governments and hoped that, after his visit to London, work could begin in earnest on a draft constitution.[27]

A Central African Council meeting in Salisbury on 28 December provided the opportunity for Huggins to secure broad agreement on his proposals from the northern Governors and their official and unofficial delegations. Furthermore, the meeting felt that federation was truly urgent and that, as the Africans were unlikely to waver in their opposition, they could not be allowed to render any more conferences abortive and thereby increase racial tensions. Thus the British Government had to be persuaded to commit itself firmly to

[26] *Ibid.*, 39/112, ff. 87–89, Huggins to Lord Ismay, 14 December 1951; 39/114, ff. 40–42, R. C. S. Stanley to Welensky, 15 December 1951; WE 7, P/C/109/52, Welensky to Gore-Browne, 21 December 1951.

[27] *Ibid.*, 39/112, ff. 79-84, Huggins to Ismay, 22 December 1951.

the federal plan and ignore the Africans. The date of the forthcoming reconvened Conference should be advanced and the British should make it plain to all attending that only the plan, and not federation itself, would be under discussion.[28]

On 3 January 1952, the Northern Rhodesian Executive Council ratified the inter-governmental decisions and instructed Rennie to act accordingly.[29] The elected Members had intended that Welensky should be in London with Huggins. Consequently, Welensky approached Rennie for permission to go but was refused. He persisted, suggesting that either he should go on the pretext of raising finance for African housing, or in a private capacity representing the Capricorn Africa Society. Rennie was adamant, however, that Welensky's presence would only embarrass the British Government by arousing the Labour Party's suspicions on the purposes of Huggins's visit. The British Government, Rennie maintained, was well-disposed towards federation but would wish to avoid a public clamour. Welensky was not entirely disappointed as he was tired, but he did not trust Huggins completely.[30]

When Lyttelton confirmed Rennie's decision, Welensky demanded that Rennie should go in his stead to protect Northern Rhodesia's interests. Somewhat to Rennie's dismay, Lyttelton and Ismay agreed and consequently Huggins's discussions were upgraded (rather illogically) to a full-blown inter-governmental meeting attended by both Secretaries of State and the two northern Governors.[31] Any fear of Labour Party clamour was forgotten.

Huggins and Welensky arranged to confer at Livingstone on 15 January, when Huggins would be *en route* for London, to establish finally what they were seeking. Huggins wanted a written statement of Northern Rhodesian views and, to that end, sent Welensky a series of questions.[32] He irritated Welensky by asking whether the Northern Rhodesians would agree to amalgamation if all else failed because he believed that the British would be powerless to prevent the Rhodesians from acting.[33] In his reply, Welensky reiterated the imperfections of the federal plan and, true to his word, stated that, while amalgamation was the simplest and best method of unifying, no British government would agree to it.[34]

When they met, however, they decided to object only to the dual loyalty of

[28] *Ibid.*, 23/33, ff. 1–2, CAC Draft Press Communiqué, 12th Meeting and Agenda, 28 December 1951; WE 7, P/C/100/50, Welensky to Dodds-Parker, 29 December 1951; Welensky to unofficial Members, 29 December 1951; 39/116, ff. 46–47, Welensky to F. S. Joelson, 29 December 1951.

[29] *Ibid.*, 39/112, ff. 72–74, Welensky to Chief Secretary, NRG, 3 January 1952.

[30] *Ibid.*, 39/114, f. 44, Welensky to H. St L. Grenfell, 14 December 1951; ff. 40–42, R. C. S. Stanley to Welensky, 15 December 1951; 5/48, f. 265, Welensky to D. Stirling, 14 December 1951; 39/112, f. 85, Welensky to Huggins, 14 December 1951; 39/119, f. 153, Welensky to H. T. Low, 18 December 1951; WE 7, P/C/109/52, Welensky to Gore-Browne, 21 December 1951; same to same, 24 December 1951.

[31] *Ibid.*, 39/112, f. 75, G. Beckett to Welensky, 29 December 1951; ff. 72–74, Welensky to Chief Secretary, NRG, 3 January 1952; WE 7, P/C/109/52, Welensky to Gore-Browne, 5 & 12 January 1952; P/C/135/52, Welensky to F. Crawford, 5 January 1952; 39/114, f. 33, R. C. S. Stanley to Welensky, 9 January 1952; f. 34, Welensky to Stanley, 10 January 1952.

[32] *Ibid.*, 39/112, f. 66, Huggins to Welensky, 5 January 1952.

[33] *Ibid.*, WE 7, P/C/109/52, Welensky to Gore-Browne, 12 January 1952.

[34] *Ibid.*, 39/112, ff. 64–65, Welensky to Huggins, 12 January 1952.

the minister for African interests, to demand the partial elimination of the nominated members (by introducing a method of election such as that employed in Northern Rhodesia for the two African representatives), and to ensure some control of the amendment of the franchise so that the states could not unilaterally alter the basis of the federation. There would also have to be a guarantee of non-African rights.[35]

One task which befell Welensky in Huggins's absence in London was to attempt to curb the impetuosity of Colonel David Stirling of the Capricorn Africa Society, who, quite as much as Huggins and Welensky, had looked forward to the change of regime at Westminster and had lost no time in seeking to win Lyttelton to his version of unification. Stirling had written to Lyttelton urging him to embrace the federal cause, assuring him that African resistance would fall away if the grim alternatives were revealed. However, Stirling had gone on to argue that, as the three territorial economies were not sufficiently diverse and the territories themselves were landlocked, there was a need for an eight-fold federation of the three Central African territories, the three East African, Zanzibar and Northern Bechuanaland. He listed the dangers confronting the area as being: Asian infiltration, Communist subversion, the absorption of Southern Rhodesia by a neo-Nazi state (South Africa), and extreme African nationalism. Copies of this letter were sent to Churchill, Lords Salisbury and Ismay and certain Conservative backbenchers but to no avail as Lyttelton ignored it.[36] Undaunted, Stirling toured Central and East Africa and Britain in December and January, urging support for a conference of settlers from British colonies south of the Sahara to be held in Salisbury before the reconvened federal Conference. He planned to draw a parallel with the Philadelphia Convention of 1774 and call his conference the "Salisbury Convention". He proposed to issue its agenda as the "Salisbury Declarations".

There is no doubt that Stirling fired many imaginations, but he overestimated his support. Certainly his reports on the reception given to his scheme by the territorial leaders never quite matched their comments in their correspondence. He never won round Michael Blundell (later knighted) of Kenya, and both Welensky and Huggins treated him with reserve because they would brook no distractions from their aim. They refused to be directly involved with Stirling's Convention but, reluctant to lose the support of his followers, they agreed to speak as guests. A conference of settlers, they felt, would only serve to agitate the left wing.[37]

Events overtook Stirling because, on 19 January, Welensky called for the postponement of the Convention as he expected the date of the federal Conference to be advanced. On 28 January, it was announced that the Conference would be held in April and Welensky then insisted that the Convention should not meet in mid-March. He repeated this demand on 5 February but, in the event, it was unnecessary because Huggins had met

[35] *Ibid.*, 39/119, f. 136, Welensky to Gore-Browne, 17 January 1952.
[36] *Ibid.*, 5/48, f. 267, D. Stirling to O. Lyttelton, 1 November 1951; f. 26, R. Byrne to Welensky, 9 November 1951.
[37] *Ibid.*, f. 243, M. Blundell to Welensky, 2 January 1952; f. 242, Welensky to Blundell, 8 January 1952; f. 220, Stirling to Welensky, 8 January 1952.

Stirling in London and had persuaded him to postpone the Convention tc mid-June.[38]

Douglas Dodds-Parker, a former Colonial civil servant and currently a British MP, had told Welensky how keen the Conservatives as a body were on the idea of federation, and Huggins found this to be true when, in the opening session of his talks with the British Government on 22 January, Ismay declared their intention to have the territories federated if at all possible. Lennox-Boyd proclaimed this in public on 27 January.[39]

Despite Welensky's warnings to the British of Huggins's angry mood,[40] Huggins appeared jaunty on arrival in London, and his only public jibe was directed at the Labour Party when, referring to the turning of the federal issue into a party matter, he claimed that it was "a very terrible thing that people elected to look after the drains in Shoreditch should have control over huge areas of Africa".[41]

On 24 January, Huggins gave the Royal Africa and Empire Societies some idea of the adjustments he would seek to the federal plan, mentioning the excessive numbers of nominated members and hinting at the need for a locally-based civil service.[42] However, he did not reveal that, quite unrepentant, he and Whitehead had resuscitated the question of amalgamation, claiming that their electorate would demand more convincing arguments than had hitherto been given by the British Government as to why amalgamation, the most logical and economical solution to closer association, was impossible. The British answer was that amalgamation, unlike federation, was irreconcilable with their standing treaties with the Africans and that, in any case, the last Labour Government had ruled it out in the Victoria Falls statement.[43]

In the course of seven further sessions of the inter-governmental talks, not only was the federal Conference's date advanced and a declaration in favour of federation forthcoming, but Lyttelton and Ismay accepted the Southern Rhodesians' rejection of the proposed minister for African interests because he would render cabinet government unworkable. It was agreed that this minister's functions could be assumed by the chairman of the African affairs board who would communicate with the cabinet and the government through the prime minister. The meeting felt that, as the governor-general would rely on the advice of his prime minister in all matters, he could not play an intermediary role in this except to certify legislation as being necessary in an emergency even though the African affairs board had lodged an objection to it because it was detrimental to African interests. The Southern Rhodesians

[38] *Ibid.*, f. 218, Welensky to Stirling, 19 January 1952; f. 211, Stirling to Welensky, 19 January 1952; f. 210, Welensky to Stirling, 28 January 1952; f. 200, same to same, 5 February 1952; f. 192, Stirling to Welensky, 11 February 1952; 39/116, f. 27, F. S. Joelson to Welensky, 6 February 1952.

[39] *Ibid.*, WE 7, P/C/100/50, Dodds-Parker to Welensky, 20 January 1952; 39/120, f. 9, CA (52) Minutes of 1st Meeting, London, 22 January 1952; WE 7, P/C/109/52, Welensky to Gore-Browne, 28 January 1952; *The Bulawayo Chronicle*, 28 January 1952.

[40] Welensky Papers, WE 7, P/C/100/50, Welensky to Dodds-Parker, 29 December 1951.

[41] Taylor, *The Rhodesian*, *op. cit.*, pp. 145–146.

[42] *The Rhodesia Herald*, 25 January 1952.

[43] Welensky Papers, 39/120, f. 9, CA (52) Minutes of 1st Meeting, London, 22 January 1952; f. 8, CA (52) Minutes of 2nd Meeting, London, 23 January 1952.

were anxious that the federal parliament, and not the board, should sit in judgment on all legislation. It was pointed out, however, that the board could only object to protect African interests and otherwise would remain silent.

The British Ministers thought that the board's membership could be reduced to a chairman and three European and three African representatives shared equally between the territories. The chairman and members would be extra-parliamentary appointments but, at the insistence of the northern Governors, it was thought it was necessary to allay African fears by having the governor-general appoint the territorial representatives on the nomination of the territorial Governors. The provision for a decision by a two-thirds majority within the board, it was hoped, would prevent any irresponsible action. Ismay and Lyttelton agreed with Huggins that civil servants should never be in a position to criticise policy and over-rode Colby's and Rennie's objections to the exclusion of the three Secretaries for Native Affairs from the board's membership. Their expertise could still be available to the board.[44]

The question of the nine nominated members in the federal parliament remained unsolved though it was accepted in principle that their number should be reduced because they could radically affect the power balance within the 36-member assembly. It was acknowledged that a method of electing the African members could be found, perhaps using in the North the system currently employed in Northern Rhodesia, and, in Southern Rhodesia, allowing the electorate to chose from a panel of nominees. A Southern Rhodesian proposal to abandon a special category of African representative and merely to have members elected in the normal way was resisted on the grounds that the Commons would not accept it. Colby pointed out that it would be difficult in Nyasaland to have an elective system for the federal representatives when the territorial Members were chosen by nomination. It was felt that, for the time being, the territorial system could not be overturned. As far as possible, the meeting agreed, the federal franchise would be written into the constitution and any amendment would require a two-thirds majority of the federal assembly and the sanction of the Secretary of State.[45]

The apportionment of the financial resources between the Governments, it was felt, needed to be examined by a fiscal commission. The Southern Rhodesians argued that European agriculture, being a major industry, should be a federal subject, but the meeting would not allow anything more than the specialist services to be transferred.[46]

To avoid excessive litigation, the meeting proposed that the federal list of subjects be kept as short as possible and that this and the concurrent list should be carefully defined. Inter-state migration was raised because the Southern Rhodesians, in particular, were anxious to avoid an influx of Asians from Nyasaland but, as this would cause embarrassment, it was agreed that this subject should not be listed and therefore remain in territorial control. However, immigration from external areas would be a federal matter. The

[44] *Ibid.*, f. 8, CA (52) Minutes of 2nd Meeting, London, 23 January 1952; f. 7, CA (52) Minutes of 3rd Meeting, London, 24 January 1952.

[45] *Ibid.*, f. 4, CA (52) Minutes of 6th Meeting, London, 29 January 1952.

[46] *Ibid.*, f. 2, CA (52) Minutes of 8th Meeting, London, 1 February 1952.

issue of a locally-based civil service to staff the federal and territorial administrations was not resolved because the existing promotional opportunities in the world-wide Colonial service would be affected, and the northern Governors doubted whether their needs could be met effectively by federal personnel.[47]

On immediate action before the forthcoming Conference, the final meeting decided that it had to be made clear to any Africans attending that discussion would be confined to the existing framework provided by the Officials' Report. Rennie, however, regretted the necessity to make such a ruling because, he announced, an African delegation would be coming to London to see Lyttelton and if it stayed for the Conference it would expect to be able to discuss anything. Huggins, by contrast, wondered if there was any point in inviting Africans. To avoid any suspicion that there had been a full constitutional conference behind the backs, so to speak, of both the African and European, the meeting decided that its public communiqué should only announce the new date for the Conference, make clear the intention merely to revise the plan and to state that, to this end, the Governments had been asked for their proposals on the federal structure.[48]

Accordingly, before the Conference, the three territorial Governments reviewed the federal scheme and reached a wide measure of agreement. There was not, however, complete accord and an inter-territorial meeting in Salisbury on 27 February was marred by Huggins's truculence and Rennie's caustic response.[49] Each Government communicated directly with its Secretaries of State and no joint paper was produced.

Nothing more was said on the subject of the African affairs board until the Northern Rhodesian delegation met in London on 22 April, on the eve of the Conference, to review its tactics, and Moffat expressed dissatisfaction, in particular, with the dilution of the board's powers. He thought that all legislation, both principal and subsidiary, should be submitted to the board before publication. He also wanted Members of the territorial legislatures and territorial civil servants to serve on it. The delegation moderated these demands to suggestions that the Secretaries of Native Affairs should be associate non-voting members and that, where practicable, the board should be given the opportunity to review legislation before the committee stage. At this meeting, too, for the first time the provision for the amendment of the constitution was questioned. E. I. G. Unsworth (later Sir Edgar), the Northern Rhodesian Attorney-General, accepted the requirement to secure the approval of two-thirds of the federal parliament and the Secretary of State's sanction as quite adequate to protect African interests in practice but doubted that the British opponents of federation would agree.[50]

The Northern Rhodesian despatches reveal a willingness to allow the Conference to allocate revenue and divide governmental services on constitutional and administrative grounds and to leave the financial implications to be resolved by the proposed fiscal commission. The Nyasaland Government

[47] *Ibid.*, f. 3, CA (52) Minutes of 7th Meeting, London, 31 January 1952.
[48] *Ibid.*, f. 2, CA (52) Minutes of 8th Meeting, London, 1 February 1952.
[49] *Ibid.*, 39/114, f. 23, Welensky to H. N. Parry, 29 February 1952.
[50] *Ibid.*, 39/113, ff. 87–92, Notes of a Meeting, London, 22 April 1952.

concurred but felt that it was necessary to stress the realities of its financial situation and warned that only a token contribution to federal funds could be expected from Nyasaland. Indeed, such was the Nyasaland concern, that its Government called for reconsideration of the sources of federal finance. If Nyasaland would remain capable of sustaining its development programme, it could not afford to lose revenue from customs duty and export taxes on tea and tobacco because little more could be extracted from the tiny tax-paying population, and nothing more from the Africans. It suggested that perhaps recognition of the contribution of its labour to the development of the Rhodesias could serve in lieu of actual contribution.

The Southern Rhodesian Government remained anxious that European agriculture, along with other expensive services such as police, prisons and public health should become federal. It argued that European agriculture was, after all, its major industry and thus its farmers were politically most important and should not feel neglected. The northern Governments were unsympathetic. They maintained that, in an administrative sense, their services were indivisible and feared, in any case, that their European farmers, being few in number and far from Salisbury, would be neglected when competing for attention with the sophisticated, well-established Southern Rhodesian agricultural industry. There would be advantage, however, in centralising research.

The northern Governments resisted also the federalisation of the police because they would remain responsible for law and order and would need the services of territorially-based forces as local contact was essential. They would accept the creation of a federal police force for purely federal functions, but saw it as an extravagance. Benefit could be gained, they acknowledged, from centralising finger-printing, intelligence and signals.

The Nyasaland Government recognised that the federal government could provide a more comprehensive health service than its own, but felt that change would be premature. Northern Rhodesia, on the other hand, thought that only Nyasaland would gain. Centralisation, it was acknowledged, would cut overhead costs but there would have to be regional control of health which would limit the saving. There would be, too, a long-term levelling of standards and less delay in implementing policies affecting the whole area. However, the Northern Rhodesians claimed, the aims of their service differed from Southern Rhodesia's in seeking to involve the Africans directly and there could be conflict with federal intentions which would lose the African goodwill upon which the service depended. The federal government would not have the resources to replace the expertise and information supplied by the Colonial medical service, and the existing staff would resent the ending of their world-wide promotional prospects. Recruitment, too, would be difficult and centralisation on Salisbury would draw the best of the northern territories' staff south.

Much of this argument was repeated in the northern rejection of the Southern Rhodesian proposal for a federally-based civil service to serve the four Governments. Aside from promotional opportunities, the northern Governments were adamant that they, and not even an independent civil service commission, should have full control of their employees. Welensky, mindful of African concern for the retention of the link with the Colonial Office, was prompted by civil service fears to propose that the whole question of employment in the federal government be referred to an independent commission. The idea that service should be locally-based found a place, too, in a demand from the Southern Rhodesian judiciary for the federalisation of all High Courts which henceforth would sit in three divisions and be served by judges appointed by the federal government. The Southern Rhodesian motive was to seek to acquire, for the federation, permanent populations by terminating the Colonial Office practice of employing "birds of passage" on the Bench and in the civil service.

J. M. Greenfield concurred with this and with the suggestion of a federal supreme court because the existing Rhodesia and Nyasaland Appeal Court was not competent to judge constitutional cases. He did not accept the further proposal that the South African Appeal Court should continue to be used for civil cases in Southern Rhodesia once the federal supreme court was in being. Nyasaland suggested that litigation could be reduced to a minimum if potentially controversial legislation had to lie for a specified period on the tables of the territorial legislatures, thereby open to objection. The Southern Rhodesian Government, however, thought that the Swiss precedent on ruling that the courts could not declare federal law unconstitutional should be considered.

The Southern Rhodesians continued obstinately to demand a British declaration on the reasons for refusing amalgamation, while the Nyasalanders insisted that the constitution declare that amalgamation would be impossible without the sanction of the majority of the inhabitants of the federation. The Southern Rhodesian contention that nominated members of the federal legislature had to be reduced to a minimum was not questioned, but the Nyasalanders were anxious that, as the introduction of universal suffrage into their territory was impossible for the moment, if the federal franchise, which would vary from territory to territory, was written into the constitution, provision should be made for change in accordance with political advancement. The Nyasaland Government argued, too, about the necessity to discuss inter-state migration when the existing controls of land, land settlement and the recruitment of labour would be territorial. Finally, no harm was seen by the northern Governments in the proposal to have a federal citizenship for the purposes of engendering loyalty to the federation because they did not envisage that it would confer British citizenship upon their Africans thereby changing their protected status.[51]

Perusal of the minutes of the London meetings, and briefings from

[51]*Ibid.*, 39/112, ff. 46–47, Note on points raised by Whitehead on finance of closer association, London, 31 January & 23 February 1952; ff. 34–35, Comment on Huggins wanting all agriculture to be federal, 25 February 1952; ff. 48–56, Comments of Nyasaland Government on the Report of the Conference on Closer Association, February 1952; ff. 57–58, SRG to Commonwealth Secretary, February 1952; ff. 42–45, Federalisation of Health Services – Arguments for and against, February 1952; ff. 36–41, Notes by NR Attorney-General on Inter-State Migration, Police and Citizenship, February 1952; WE 7, P/C/100/50, Welensky to Huggins, 20 February 1952; 39/113, ff. 93–97, Two Papers on Federal Judiciary by J. M. Greenfield, 10 April 1952.

Huggins and Rennie convinced Welensky that at last he could feel confident the federation would become a reality.[52] He knew that there was little chance of winning the African round but it seemed that the Conservatives would ignore African protests and implement federation.[53] Griffiths shared this belief and, on 4 March, expressed alarm in the Commons at the Government's apparent intentions with regard to federation. He was careful enough, though, to preface his comments with a lengthy defence of his role in the promotion of federation, claiming that he would not have contemplated acting without African consent. There had been no Africans at the recent London talks and he wondered if the advancement of the mid-year Conference to April was evidence that federation was being "rail-roaded" through. Certainly the Africans believed it was and he knew that they were forming action committees and were contemplating the withdrawal of labour. He had been confident that the proposed safeguards for African interests would have been effective but he chose to quote Margery Perham's warning that day in *The Times* that the Imperial Government would be unable to intervene once power had been transferred into the hands of the local settlers. Griffiths urged that the Conference be postponed. Clement Davies, the Liberal leader, was not surprised at African suspicions when a partnership was proposed in which the senior partners represented only 0,1 per cent of the population.

Amidst a barrage of questions and interruptions, Lyttelton defended his Government's record. He pointed out that the Africans had refused to become involved in the definition of partnership and that the discussions in February had been pre-ordained by Griffiths who had proposed that there should be further inter-governmental contact before the next Conference. These discussions had been held to establish the agenda of the Conference and the territorial Governments were now analysing their objections to the details of the Officials' Report. Africans had not been present in London as these had been purely high-level inter-governmental meetings. However, he said, nothing was secret and Africans would be present at the Conference and able to suggest amendments. Indeed, Africans from the northern territorial representative institutions had been invited to come to London ten days before the Conference to discuss their fears with him. On the question of the date of the reconvened Conference, Lyttelton noted that Griffiths had not specified anything more than the middle of the year and April was nearly there and was convenient to all parties. However, Lyttelton had always thought that a single conference (meaning the reconvened Conference) would not suffice. A second conference was needed to review and revise the scheme in the light of public reaction. He had consulted Huggins (hurriedly by cable that day) who had agreed to this. To belie any impression of haste, Lyttelton was prepared to make a firm commitment to the convening of a second conference in July. He was seeking to preserve the non-partisan aspect of the issue, for, after all, the previous Labour Government had accepted the principle of federation. He failed and the House divided.

[52] *Ibid.*, WE 7, P/C/109/52, Welensky to Gore-Browne, 11 February 1952; P/C/100/50, Welensky to Huggins, 20 February 1952.
[53] *Ibid.*, P/C/100/50, Welensky to Dodds-Parker, 26 January 1952.

The Government, of course, was not defeated, securing a majority of 18, and was heartened by two Labour MPs, W. Coldrick and S. N. Evans, abstaining from voting.[54] However, much to their chagrin, the Central Africans had gained an extra conference, and federation was henceforth a party issue in British politics. The attainment of federation would be postponed to the extent that the Southern Rhodesian referendum, scheduled for mid-1952, was only held in March 1953 and federation ratified in June that year.

Welensky was understandably annoyed to discover from a BBC broadcast that Lyttelton, after consulting only Huggins, had committed himself to a second conference.[55] Aside from the dislocation of his plans (he had already begun to deal with the next obstacle, the Southern Rhodesian referendum, and had launched a private and successful appeal for funds), he was having what he described as a "grim time". The irrepressible Stirling wished to publish his "Salisbury Declarations" because he was sure that they, with their supposed appeal to all races and factions, would ensure success in the referendum. Welensky disagreed but was loathe to lose the support of Stirling and his followers at a time when opposition to federation in Southern Rhodesia was coalescing. Huggins was being characteristically awkward and Welensky found himself playing the unfamiliar role of mediator at the sour inter-governmental meeting on 27 February. His union, the Rhodesia Railways Workers' Union, was proving a distraction, too, through conflict within it over its leadership. In Cape Town, there had been a United Party parliamentary motion calling for the incorporation of the Rhodesias into South Africa but, as Welensky predicted, Dr D. F. Malan, the Prime Minister, merely replied that any initiative had to come from the Rhodesians. However, Welensky feared that this could be the clarion call to the pro-Unionists in Southern Rhodesia where the new Democratic Party was active and the Rhodesia Party, never really convinced, was turning its back on federation.[56]

Welensky was also annoyed that the elected Members' claims for more seats in the Legislative Council and two additional portfolios had apparently been forgotten by the British Government. He and his colleagues thought of withdrawing from the Executive Council but were asked to desist from agitating by the Chief Secretary as the moment was awkward for Lyttelton.[57] Welensky had no intention of remaining in territorial politics if the federation became a reality and offered his services to Huggins both in the referendum campaign and in the federal house.[58] Nevertheless, it remained imperative to

[54] House of Commons *Hansard* (London), Vol. 497, Col. 208, 4 March 1952.

[55] Welensky Papers, 39/112, f. 25, Welensky to A. T. Williams, 5 March 1952.

[56] *Ibid.*, WE 7, P/C/109/52, Welensky to Gore-Browne, 15 March 1952; 5/48, f. 192, Stirling to Welensky, 11 February 1952; f. 186, Stirling to J. Baines, 11 February 1952; f. 181, Stirling to Welensky, 25 February 1952; 39/116, f. 26, Welensky to F. S. Joelson, 22 February 1952; 39/114, f. 23, Welensky to H. N. Parry, 29 February 1952; WE 7, P/C/100/50, RRWU Minutes, 26 February 1952; *The Sunday News*, 20 January 1952; 39/116, f. 41, Welensky to Joelson, 23 January 1952; WE 7, P/C/109/52, Welensky to Gore-Browne, 28 January 1952; *The Rhodesia Herald*, 5 March 1952.

[57] Welensky Papers, 7/10, f. 198, Welensky to Rennie, 8 February 1952; f. 200, R. C. S. Stanley to Welensky, 25 February 1952; WE 7, P/C/109/52, Welensky to Gore-Browne, 11 & 24 February 1952.

[58] *Ibid.*, WE 7, P/C/100/50, Welensky to Huggins, 20 February 1952.

him, particularly if federation were rejected, to strengthen the unofficials' hold on the Northern Rhodesian legislature.

Welensky could not have been entirely dissatisfied with his Government's reaction when the ANC called for industrial action to combat federation. The Attorney-General read Yamba and Sokota a lesson on sedition and the illegality of strikes for political motives, and warned that the ANC had to act within the law.[59] The guiding hand of Zukas, now a vice-president of the ANC, was detected behind the ANC's agitation, and action was contemplated to still it.[60] Lyttelton, too, ruled that the African delegations to London from the northern territories could not contain members who were not from the representative institutions.[61] In fact, the actions of the ANC were not successful, little money was forthcoming, and few urban Africans responded to pressure to withdraw themselves and their families to their tribal villages. However, there were strikes of an apparently political flavour, and violence flared during industrial unrest in Broken Hill. The racial situation was tense enough for Welensky to claim that Lyttelton's unilateral decision on a second conference would only exacerbate it by embarrassing the Northern Rhodesian Government because it would be unable to furnish any justification as it did not even know what Lyttelton had said. Why, Welensky protested, had it been necessary to spring a second conference upon the Northern Rhodesians when time had been found to consult Huggins by cable? Lyttelton denied that there had been any opportunity to do so, and Welensky, not wishing to prejudice his relationship with him, let the matter rest though he pointed out to the officials that there would have been little difficulty in simultaneously copying to Lusaka the cable to Huggins.[62]

Welensky's correspondence is full of acid comments on the partisanship of Griffiths and the futility of Lyttelton's gesture. He was given the opportunity to comment publicly when the Press sought his reaction to further remarks made by Griffiths to the Fabian Colonial Bureau on 19 March. Griffiths described his attack in the Commons as deliberate because, though he accepted the desirability of federation, he was sure that it would fail with grave consequences if it was imposed without the consent of the Africans. He criticised the exclusion of Africans from the February inter-governmental talks in London, the failure to define partnership and the advancement of the reconvened Conference. He was anxious about African advancement in the mining industry and demanded the abolition of all racial barriers. He wanted a more direct African involvement in politics.

Welensky replied through the Press that Griffiths was again merely seeking to make political capital because his Party was fundamentally hostile to the

[59] *Ibid.*, 39/112, ff. 29–30, Report by Attorney-General, 26 February 1952.

[60] *Ibid.*, 39/116, f. 25, Welensky to F. S. Joelson, 26 February 1952; 39/114, f. 18, Interview by *Northern News* with Welensky, 6 March 1952; P/C/141/52, Welensky to Joelson, 15 March 1952.

[61] *Ibid.*, 39/112, f. 28, R. P. Bush to General Secretary, NR African National Congress, 25 February 1952.

[62] *Ibid.*, WE 7, P/C/135/52/K, Welensky to Sir John Kennedy, 8 March 1952; P/C/100/50, Welensky to Huggins, 8 March 1952; P/C/109/52, Welensky to Gore-Browne, 15 March 1952; 39/112, f. 25, Welensky to A. T. Williams, 5 March 1952; f. 22, Williams to Welensky, 15 March 1952; f. 21, Welensky to Williams, 17 March 1952.

European in Africa. However, Welensky pointed out that it was the African who had proved unco-operative over the defining of partnership. Furthermore, there was nothing sinister about the reconvened Conference in April as its purpose was to produce something concrete for the Central African inhabitants to examine.[63]

Huggins and Welensky had not, in fact, been diverted from their preparations for the referendum campaign. Welensky successfully raised money while Huggins took advantage of an offer of unstinting help from Stirling to merge the Southern Rhodesian branch of the Capricorn Africa Society with the United Central Africa Association — adopting the latter title — under his presidency. The new UCAA set up a headquarters in Salisbury, cast around for an executive secretary, and began to plan publicity campaigns and the formation of country-wide branches. Welensky provided the first of a series of donations from his campaign funds, accepted a vice-presidency and looked for suitable candidates to represent Northern Rhodesia on the new association. Huggins formally launched the new UCAA on 3 April.[64]

Although Huggins and Welensky were concentrating on securing the Southern Rhodesian Europeans' vote, they were not entirely neglectful of the African. Huggins, after some pressure from Welensky among others, added two Africans — Jasper Savanhu, a journalist, and Joshua Nkomo, a trade unionist — to his delegation to the Conference. Huggins was confident that these two would make a positive contribution, and 17 African organisations, though adamantly opposing federation, agreed with him. However, Huggins feared that in London they would be depicted as "stooges",[65] and this was exactly the epithet used by jeering Labour MPs on the eve of the Conference when Lyttelton justified holding it in the face of the refusal of the northern Africans to attend because the Southern Rhodesian delegation at least was multi-racial.[66] In the Conference, Savanhu and Nkomo would prove the falsity of this sneer. Welensky for his part laid plans for informal meetings with leading Africans.[67]

The Africans were able to claim that the Commons debate showed that half of its Members supported them, but in general their response in Northern Rhodesia to the ANC's campaign was apathetic and the ANC itself was divided over tactics. The Paramount Chief of Barotseland contributed to the ANC's disarray by ordering the Barotse to stay within the law, when opposing federation, and to avoid involvement in politically-motivated strikes.[68]

The Northern Rhodesian Government's contribution was to take the

[63] *Daily Herald*, 20 March 1952; *The Rhodesia Herald*, 24 March 1952.

[64] *The Rhodesia Herald*, 4 April 1952; N[ational] A[rchives] [of] Z[imbabwe], Hist. MSS, UN 1/3/1, Minutes of Joint Meeting of UCAA and CAS, 26 March 1952.

[65] Welensky Papers, 39/112, ff. 14–15, Huggins to Welensky, 24 March 1952; f. 16, Welensky to H. N. Parry, 28 March 1952; f. 8, Huggins to Welensky, 31 March 1952; WE 7, P/C/100/50, Huggins to Welensky, 4 April 1952; *The Rhodesia Herald*, 16 April 1952.

[66] House of Commons *Hansard* (London), Vol. 499, Cols. 403-413, 23 April 1952.

[67] Welensky Papers, 39/112, f. 13, Welensky to Dr A. Scott, 28 March 1952; f. 7, Welensky to Huggins, (?) April 1952.

[68] *Ibid.*, 39/116, f. 22, Welensky to Joelson, 11 March 1952; 39/114, f. 8, Welensky to H. K. McKee, 11 March 1952; WE 7, P/C/141/52, Welensky to Joelson, 15 March 1952; 39/112, f. 12, Welensky to Huggins, 31 March 1952; *The Rhodesia Herald*, 3 April 1952.

action which it had long contemplated and deport Zukas on the grounds that he had deliberately sought to excite the impressionable Africans by publicly extolling the virtues of violence, suggesting mass protests and political strikes, and by vilifying the British and Northern Rhodesian Governments in his *Freedom Newsletter*. A search of Zukas's home uncovered seditious material advocating the seizure of power by the proletariat to create a classless society in Northern Rhodesia. A judicial hearing before the Chief Justice, A. W. Lewey, upheld the deportation order. Zukas compounded the charge and was fined £50 for contempt when he became dissatisfied with his legal counsel and telegraphed the ANC demanding that it organise a public demonstration if the hearing was not postponed. This proved to the Chief Justice that Zukas believed that anything could be achieved by public protest. The ANC did not react, but two of Zukas's lieutenants, Reuben Kamanga and Noah Sambona, were arrested and fined for showing disrespect to the Chief Justice by sending telegrams alleging that Zukas was being denied legal representation. The *Livingstone Mail* was fined £10 for publishing matters which were *sub-judice*. Welensky was relieved at the Government's action but was privately sarcastic about the length of the delay resulting from official timidity with regard to Griffiths's reaction when, in August, there had been sufficient reason to act.[69]

The Northern Rhodesian Government then published its view of partnership. The ultimate constitutional aim, it proclaimed, was self-government for the territory within the Commonwealth and thus there had to be full cognizance and provision for the rights of Africans. Partnership was the only way to effect this and would ensure the African's social, political and economic advance to full equality within the community. However, such progress would entail the acceptance of responsibility as well as privilege. There would be no subordination of the interests of one section to another's and each would have to recognise the right of the other to a permanent home in Northern Rhodesia. Ultimately there would be equality of representation and towards this end the Africans would be given more seats in the next Legislative Council. Likewise, everyone should be allowed to rise to the level of his ability, energy and qualifications, consequently Africans would be given more responsible employment and improved training facilities. There were long-term plans to improve education at all levels, thereby eradicating illiteracy. Africans were to participate more effectively in rural administration and their membership of the African affairs sub-committees of the municipal councils and town management boards would be extended. It was too early, the Government maintained, to remove differential legislation as it largely protected African interests, but this would be done as it became unnecessary. Discriminatory practices were acknowledged to be incompatible with partnership but these were falling away rapidly as Europeans and Africans recognised each others' needs. It was important, it concluded, that this should continue.[70]

[69] *The Rhodesia Herald*, 5, 6, 9 & 10 April 1952; L. H. Gann, *A History of Northern Rhodesia: Early Days to 1953* (London, 1964), p. 430; R. Hall, *Zambia* (London, 1965), p. 154; Welensky Papers, 8/6, f. 5, Note of telephone report from *Northern News*, 4 April 1952; 39/112, f. 12, Welensky to Huggins, 31 March 1952; WE 7, Un-numbered Series, Memorandum on Communism in Northern Rhodesia, 1952; 39/116, f. 16, Welensky to Joelson, 1 April 1952.
[70] *The Rhodesia Herald*, 7 April 1952.

If the Northern Rhodesian ANC was not being entirely effective, Banda in Britain was enjoying considerable success. In late February and early March he was given opportunities to address meetings in London, Edinburgh and Glasgow. In London he spoke to a small meeting of the Institute of International Affairs at Chatham House. He alleged that, though he had not been home for 20 years, he could put the African's case better than anyone else.[71] In Edinburgh he addressed the World Church Group, which included prominent churchmen and laity, and secured a resolution that federation should not be implemented against African wishes. He scored another success in Glasgow at a similar gathering sponsored by the Iona Community of the Church of Scotland. These meetings triggered off debates in the presbyteries of Scotland and a volume of correspondence in the Scottish Press as eminent churchmen, in particular, urged the British Government to stay its hand.[72]

Pressure from Banda, too, contributed to the Nyasaland and Northern Rhodesian African delegations' refusal to attend the Conference.[73] They met Lyttelton on 18 April, but were deaf to his advocacy of federation as a means to curb Afrikaner expansionism because the territorial Governments could merely end Afrikaner immigration. They ignored Lyttelton's claims that only federation could produce the level of economic expansion to maintain advancement, and argued that, in the light of experience in South Africa, the value of any safeguard was dubious. They could see no point in attending the Conference, even as observers, because their minds were made up. Lyttelton's arguments that, as his Government would still consider any alternatives, the Africans should attend and, perhaps, sign a minority report, were without effect.[74]

Yet the African victory was hollow, for Lyttelton was prepared to ignore both them and hostile Press comments like the claim of the *New Statesman and Nation,* on 22 April, that the white agitation for federation was nothing more than a desire to be rid of certain obligations to Africans. Indeed, his sympathy for white aspirations was revealed to Welensky and Beckett in discussion on the Northern Rhodesian Constitution on 18 April when he indicated that he would concede to their demands.[75] No postponement was forthcoming and the reconvened federal Conference met at Lancaster House on 23 April as planned.

[71] Welensky Papers, 39/114, ff. 10–11, H. K. McKee to Welensky, 29 February 1952.
[72] *The Scotsman*, 28 February 1952; *Glasgow Herald*, 10, 11 & 12 March 1952.
[73] P. Short, *Banda* (London, 1974), p. 69.
[74] Welensky Papers, 14/16, f. 2, Note of a Meeting, Colonial Office, 18 April 1952.
[75] *Ibid.*, f. 11, Minutes of a Meeting, Colonial Office, 18 April 1952.

CHAPTER NINE

Constitutional Accord

The Lancaster House Conference and Agreement on the Basis of Federation, April 1952

UNDETERRED by the African refusal to attend, the delegates to the reconvened Conference met in plenary session at Lancaster House, London, in the afternoon of 23 April 1952. This Conference, unlike its predecessor at the Victoria Falls, would achieve its objective in that sufficient agreement was reached to enable a draft scheme to be published in the form of a White Paper. However, it was to be felt that there was need for expert guidance before certain decisions could be taken, with the result that the second and final Conference had to be postponed to await the findings of commissions appointed to examine questions relating to the judicial, fiscal and administrative aspects of the federal plan.

The chairman, Lord Salisbury, the new Commonwealth Secretary, welcoming the delegates, regretted the absence of the northern Africans but was confident that much could be achieved. He felt the territories were so interdependent that unification was necessary. He acknowledged that federation would provide the increased prosperity for partnership to be firmly established. Thus the Conference, using the practical basis of the Officials' Report, would seek to discover a formula for a prosperous racial partnership. Success, he claimed, could have a wide effect in Africa but failure would leave the weak and divided territories prey to external influences under which the Africans in particular would suffer. There would be no further opportunity to unify.[1]

Huggins, endorsing what Salisbury had said, particularly with regard to the dire consequences of failure, felt that, while benefiting Central Africa, federation would be "a chance for the United Kingdom itself, if it so desires, to retain an Empire, to get a strong bloc of people essentially wedded to the

[1] Conference on the Proposed Federation of Southern Rhodesia, Northern Rhodesia and Nyasaland, London, April–May 1952, "Volume III – Verbatim Record of Proceedings", ACM (52) 1st Meeting, p. 1 f.

British tradition who are not likely to wander from the true path and leave the old country". He understood African fears on constitutional safeguards because of events elsewhere, but reassured them that they were dealing with people of British stock who would not betray them. He regretted that there were not more Africans at the Conference.

Colby and Lyttelton echoed this last sentiment, while Rennie fiercely avowed that, nevertheless, his delegation would play its full part in the Conference. The two Southern Rhodesian Africans, Savanhu and Nkomo, also regretted the absence of their northern African colleagues, but warned that similarly they had no mandate to support federation because their people felt they had been excluded from their country's prosperity and that federation would make no change. Savanhu suggested that a Royal Commission should be dispatched to Central Africa to study the issue. Both thought that they would have to reconsider their decision to attend the Conference but were reassured by Lyttelton that no committal to the federal plan was expected. They stayed to the end despite pressure — including abusive letters — to withdraw.

Outside the Conference, the northern African delegations were joined by Nkumbula who had brought with him a party of Northern Rhodesian Africans who were avowedly anti-federal. One of these, Chief Chitimukulu, was summoned by Lyttelton but refused to see him unless an African witness was present. Lyttelton was not amused, and they did not meet.[2] On 24 April, coincidental with the second plenary session of the Conference, the northern Africans held a Press conference to explain their refusal to attend. They revealed that the Nyasaland delegation had been prepared to appear as observers but had been dissuaded by the Northern Rhodesians and others. The main reason for their refusal was that the Conference would be confidential which would prevent them from discussing its proceedings with people outside it. They had asked to see the agenda but were told that it was also confidential. Thus, Yamba commented, it was to be handed to them at the door "like a ticket to a theatre". In any case, they maintained, they had only come to Britain to express the total African rejection of federation and therefore could not be present at a conference which would only discuss modifications to the federal plan. Furthermore, they claimed that "Africans found it most embarrassing to attend the London Conference which was arranged in a private way between the Secretary of State for the Colonies and the Governors of Northern Rhodesia and Nyasaland, as well as the Prime Minister of Southern Rhodesia, thus being a repudiation of the Victoria Falls Conference".[3]

The remaining question was whether the northern African delegations would have to return home immediately. On 23 April, the Labour Party demanded in the Commons that they should stay to give it an opportunity to meet them. However, Lennox-Boyd, the Minister of State for the Colonies, replied that they would have to go because many of them were civil servants and were needed at their posts. Consequently, on 24 April, the Africans hinted darkly that the British Government wished to be rid of their embarras-

[2] Welensky Papers, 5/95, f. 287, Welensky to Sir Stewart Gore-Browne, 26 April 1952.

[3] *Manchester Guardian*, 24 April 1952.

sing presence but this was promptly denied and they stayed. The Africa Bureau immediately arranged a public meeting for them. This body had been recently formed under the chairmanship of Lady Pakenham, with the Reverend Michael Scott as honorary director, to preserve what was best in the traditional British policy dealing with the African and to provide better understanding between the races.

Welensky found the manner in which the British condoned the African delegates' behaviour galling and the uncritical reaction of the British Press particularly annoying. He was surprised by the degree of hostility shown towards the European in Central and South Africa. The British reaction, too, depressed Huggins who realised that he would have to deal with people who were not interested in Central Africa but merely in the reaction of the Commons. Welensky had a heated late-night discussion with Greenfield and Huggins at their hotel on 23 April when he urged the necessity of securing a draft constitution lest the Africans claim a considerable victory.[4]

The question of the Africans' attendance was raised by Griffiths in the Commons on 29 April. He blamed Lyttelton's mishandling for the African decision because he could easily have secured them as observers despite their anxiety to avoid being implicated in the acceptance of the federal plan, particularly as they believed that the British Government had already decided to implement federation. Griffiths found that their attitudes had hardened since the Victoria Falls Conference when the Northern Rhodesians had at least been prepared to consider federation if they were given a working definition of partnership. However, nothing had been done about partnership in the interim. Griffiths continued to favour closer association in some form, and thus was concerned that the fate of the whole issue should not hinge on the acceptability of federation. He wanted the African Representative Council's acceptance as well as that of the territorial legislatures and the Southern Rhodesian electorate. He feared the tense racial situation in Northern Rhodesia and thought that the return of the African delegates, embittered by their rebuff, would only aggravate it. (In fact, there was an African railway strike, ostensibly for industrial reasons, but a call for a stoppage of work on the mines over the deportation of Zukas was ignored.)

Griffiths thought that the African delegations should remain in London until the Conference was over so that Lyttelton could brief them on its proceedings. Thereafter, Lyttelton should visit the territories to explain any changes to the Officials' Report. Above all, Griffiths wished to remind the Commons that the ultimate decision was its prerogative and, in a rare display of parliamentary bad manners, to emphasise this point, he turned as he spoke to face Welensky sitting in the Strangers' Gallery.

Lyttelton, ignoring this last gesture, congratulated Griffiths on managing to couch his speech in non-controversial terms. He explained how he had tried to persuade the African delegates to attend the Conference and confirmed that the Nyasalanders had agreed to be observers until they realised that the Press would be excluded. The purpose of the Conference, he re-

[4] Welensky Papers, 17/40, f. 62, Welensky to D. Dodds-Parker, 24 April 1952; ff. 71-72, Welensky to W. Watson, 24 April 1952; 39/115, f. 188, Welensky to unofficial Members, 24 April 1952.

peated, was to formulate a plan which would not be binding on the delegates and he had offered the Africans a written guarantee on this. As the federal scheme was not yet in being, the Africans' letter in *The Times* that day was irrelevant because they could not judge the value of the safeguards before they were disclosed. Questioned by Griffiths, Lyttelton acknowledged that this letter was at least correct in alleging that the idea of having a minister for African interests had been dropped. However, he maintained that only the potential effectiveness of the safeguards was in question. He maintained that his decision to hold the current Conference without the Africans was correct, because otherwise he would be granting them a power of veto. Finally, answering Griffiths's erroneous criticism, he pointed out that it had been the Northern Rhodesian Africans' refusal to co-operate in the matter of defining partnership which had caused the delay.

The debate did not entirely run Griffiths's way, because 20 Labour MPs supported S. N. Evans who had toured the territories in the previous August as a delegate of the Commonwealth Parliamentary Association, and who, speaking in favour of federation, demanded that it should not be used as a "political football". He maintained that, if African rejection were the only obstacle, it should be ignored because he had found that 95 per cent of the Africans were not politically conscious and neither understood nor cared about federation. Development could not be held to the pace of African advancement. He drew cries of "shame" from members of Griffiths's faction.

The debate was concluded by Lennox-Boyd who dwelt on the difficulties of explaining the concept of federation when the African languages did not have alternative words for "federation" and "amalgamation". It was impossible, too, to hold a round-table discussion on partnership when one party refused to attend, and thus the Northern Rhodesian Government had been obliged to act unilaterally in producing a definition. It was Britain's duty as trustee to consult the inhabitants but it had also to indicate what should be done. Before Lennox-Boyd had spoken, Mrs Eirene White had summed up for the Labour Party saying that the debate had been most opportune because it had allowed the Conference's delegates to see the level at which their affairs were debated. There must have been some wry smiles in the Strangers' Gallery.[5]

In the plenary session of the Conference on 23 April, work had begun immediately on the evolution of a federal constitution which could be published as a White Paper for public evaluation in Britain and the three territories. The basis of discussion was the Officials' Report, as amended by subsequent negotiations. The draft constitution comprised a preamble and nine chapters describing the federation, its legislature and its functions. The preamble was the product of an *ad hoc* sub-committee set up under the chairmanship of Lennox-Boyd to find a form of words to express the ideas of the Conference on the underlying principles of the scheme. It was hoped that, without being too specific on matters such as land and land settlement, both African and European fears would be answered. Without much debate, the Conference accepted the sub-committee's recommendation which read:

[5] House of Commons *Hansard* (London), Vol. 499, Col. 1233 f., 29 April 1952; Welensky Papers, 39/115, f. 178, Welensky to unofficial Members, 30 April 1952.

"Whereas the Colony of Southern Rhodesia is part of Her Majesty's dominions and Northern Rhodesia and Nyasaland are territories under Her Majesty's protection:

And whereas the said territories are the rightful home of all lawful inhabitants thereof, whatever their origin:

And whereas the association of the said territories in a Federation under Her Majesty's sovereignty would conduce to the security, advancement, and welfare of all their inhabitants:

And whereas the Colony of Southern Rhodesia should continue to enjoy self-government as a member of such a Federation:

And whereas Northern Rhodesia and Nyasaland should continue to enjoy separate Governments, responsible for local and territorial political advancement, under the special protection of Her Majesty, so long as their respective peoples so desire:

It is accordingly desirable that provision should be made for such a Federation under Her Majesty's sovereignty and for the establishment of a Federal Government charged, to the extent of its functions, with promoting the security, advancement and welfare of all lawful inhabitants of the said territories."

"Chapter I: The Federation" was brief and stated that a federation should be established, that it should be called "The Federation of Rhodesia and Nyasaland", and that the seat of government would be at a place chosen by a majority of the federal assembly. Huggins proposed the substitution of "Kingdom" for "Federation" to short-circuit African rejection, but its use was without precedent in the British Commonwealth and the Conference thought that it would be inappropriate.

The siting of the federal capital occasioned some debate and, when the Africans' fears of domination by Southern Rhodesia are borne in mind, this was a curious omission from all the previous discussions. Huggins, however, was aware that the Africans would equate the federal with the Southern Rhodesian Government if they shared Salisbury which was the obvious choice because of its size and existing facilities. He proposed, therefore, that it should be clear that the federal capital need not necessarily be in Salisbury or even in Southern Rhodesia. The Conference agreed but felt that nothing more was needed than a statement to that effect in a Press bulletin. Huggins thought that the Australian pattern of a separate federal state might be fitting, but the Conference did not welcome the purely civil service atmosphere of a "Canberra" and agreed that it would be a waste of finance not to exploit the existence of water and power supplies and other services in one of the established towns. Lord Salisbury and Welensky advanced Bulawayo as a suitable site but Huggins was adamant that the capital had to be near the geographical centre of the federation. The Conference was unwilling to make a choice and left the matter to the federal assembly.

"Chapter II: The Federal Legislature" described its powers, functions and membership. The legislative power was vested in the legislature which would consist of a governor-general, representing the Monarch, and a federal assembly. The governor-general, however, would merely assent to bills and would not preside over or belong to the assembly. Care was taken to define precisely the exclusive federal list of legislative subjects and the concurrent list.

To emphasise that, aside from the services to be administered centrally, the powers of the territorial Governments would not be disturbed, it was specifically stated that all other subjects would be exclusively territorial. This was necessary because of the fundamental British criterion that the federal government would not be allowed to have any involvement with the daily life of the African. A consequence of the particular assurance that the African rights in land would not be disturbed was that the federal government's power, to acquire property for its installations in Native Trust or Native Reserve Land in the northern territories, was made subject to the provisions of the existing Orders in Council. In the case of Southern Rhodesia the power was limited in the Native Reserves, the Native Area and the Special Native Area by the provision of the Southern Rhodesia Constitution Letters Patent, 1923 and the Land Apportionment Act, 1941.

This was accepted despite spirited resistance by the Southern Rhodesians who argued that, on the grounds of propriety and efficiency, the federal government should not have to acquire land through the agency of the territorial Governments. Moreover, the territorial Governors could grant 100 acres at their discretion but had to refer to the Colonial Secretary when larger areas were required. The Southern Rhodesians maintained that the Orders in Council would have to be amended to include the federal government in the definition of "government" and that the opportunity should be taken to empower the governor-general to refer directly to the Secretary of State. They were anxious that federal development should not be subject to territorial whim and claimed that the guarantees on land at the Victoria Falls Conference had referred only to broad areas.

Huggins, in particular, was vehement. He conceded that the governor-general should be compelled to consult the territorial Governors over the acquisition of land but was insistent "if you are going to try and please a lot of natives who will not even come to a conference we cannot have the thing made ridiculous by that". He was adamant that the territorial Governments could not be used as "post offices" and concluded that the northern delegations were motivated in this matter purely by suspicions of a government not yet in being. However, the British and northern Governments refused to be brow-beaten. They declined to tamper with the Orders in Council because of the existing guarantee and the Conference had to accept the *status quo*.

The rigid delineation of federal powers was illustrated by a further clause in the first part of Chapter II which, despite the federalisation of "External Affairs", prevented the federal legislature making any laws relating to international treaties which involved matters not designated either federal or concurrent. Yet the Conference was concerned about future difficulties and made provision to facilitate the federal assumption of power by allowing the governor-general to prescribe dates when the territorial Governments would lose their ability to legislate on matters in the federal list.

Furthermore, there was an attempt to impart some flexibility into the constitution by the device of delegation. The federal legislature would be allowed complete freedom to delegate legislative power to the territorial Governments over matters within its purview. The territorial Governments' power to delegate, however, was strictly limited and defined. They could delegate authority over a non-federal subject where there was need for a corporate or similar body to provide an inter-territorial service such as the regulation of veterinary research. The territorial legislature could also delegate authority to its federal counterpart when non-federal matters were closely related to subjects to be found in the federal or concurrent lists. This was also closely controlled because the federal assembly could only legislate on the delegated item when doing likewise for the federal subject. The delegating legislature would retain the power to reverse its action, would be able to continue to make laws in that field and, where there was any inconsistency, its authority would prevail.

The Conference inserted this power to delegate in response to pressure from the Southern Rhodesians who thought it an unnecessary complication to have to amend the constitution if a territory lacked the finance for a new service but could persuade the federal government to provide it. Delegation would also lessen the volume of litigation for which federations were notorious. However, the British and northern delegates adamantly refused to allow the territories unlimited freedom of delegation, thereby providing a loop-hole, "a back door to amalgamation", which would arouse African hostility. Because, they argued, without African goodwill, federation would fail. They claimed also that it was possible Southern Rhodesia would use the device to rid itself of expensive services which in effect would force the Northern Rhodesians to pay for them. Welensky, while favouring flexibility, pleaded with the southerners to appreciate northern difficulties. Lord Salisbury endorsed his appeal, and the restrictions on territorial delegation were accepted on the understanding that the issue could be reviewed at the next Conference.

The second part of Chapter II listed the subjects designated federal or concurrent. This had been the first task of the delegates when they began work on 23 April but it was not easily completed and, indeed, there were subjects which had to be reserved for expert examination by a fiscal commission after the Conference. The delegates reduced the federal or "Exclusive" list in the Officials' Report from 43 subjects to 32. It now contained: external affairs; extradition; defence; immigration; aliens; citizenship of the federation; import and export control; exchange control and the promotion of exports; control of the distribution and the wholesale and retail price of such manufactured or unmanufactured commodities specified from time to time by the governor-general; customs and excise; currency, coinage and legal tender; companies and corporations; insurance; bills of exchange and promissory notes; copyright, patents, trade marks and designs; trunk or inter-territorial roads; railways and ancillary services; aviation, aerodromes and ancillary services; meteorology; posts and telecommunications; broadcasting; the supply of electricity; radio-active minerals and the generation of atomic energy; primary and secondary education of non-Africans; higher education for all races; weights and measures; archives; the federal public service; audit of federal public accounts; the federal supreme court; establishment and constitution of any federal courts other than the supreme court; legal proceedings between the federal government and territorial Governments or between territorial Governments; and legal proceedings by and against the federal government.

Although the selection of these subjects was achieved without controversy, the same was not true of the compilation of the concurrent list. It finally read: deportation; movements of persons from one territory to another; purchase and sale of commodities by governments; marketing boards; development of industries; banks and banking (subject to examination by the proposed fiscal commission); bankruptcy and insolvency; hire purchase; roads other than trunk roads; road-rail crossings; regulation of road traffic; water supply, storage, power, irrigation and riparian rights; electricity distribution; scientific and industrial research, other than veterinary and tsetse research; the service and execution in any territory of civil and criminal processes and judgments of the courts of any other territory; prisons; care and protection of minors; European police recruitment, European police training, police force central reserve, criminal investigation department and records; health; tourism; national parks; town planning; geological, trigonometrical, topographical and cadastral surveys; production and distribution of government films; census and statistics; and jurisdiction of the federal courts.

The inclusion of inter-territorial migration in the legislative lists was a hotly-contested triumph for the Southern Rhodesian delegates, both European and African, who maintained that their populations would reject federation if the Asians living in Nyasaland were allowed to migrate freely to Southern Rhodesia. Greenfield had raised this issue on the first day of the Conference when the federal list, and "Immigration and Aliens" in particular, was being reviewed. Lord Salisbury, as chairman, pointed out that this was an irrelevancy when external migration was being considered, but Welensky was all too willing to fight and Salisbury was ignored. Greenfield claimed, in mitigation, that in any case there would have to be inter-territorial deportation of criminals and that, eventually, a shortage of land and the over-burdening of the social services would necessitate a curb on the mass migration of Africans. Barrow, for Nyasaland, joined Welensky in proclaiming that the ability to move within federations was a fundamental freedom which should not be denied to all just because approximately 2 000 Asians who could migrate would not be welcome in Southern Rhodesia. Such an innovation would make it difficult to engender loyalty to the federation and would complicate immigration. Lennox-Boyd and Salisbury agreed that it was unnecessarily vindictive towards a minority and would be distasteful to world opinion and the Indian Government in particular. Professor Wheare, present as an adviser, pointed out more subtle methods of achieving the same end such as withholding trading licences. Barrow thought that the Southern Rhodesian requirement that business records had to be kept in English constituted a sufficient barrier. However, the Southern Rhodesians stood fast through three plenary sessions and, in the end, the Conference conceded that the Southern Rhodesian referendum could not be hazarded and "Inter-Territorial Movement" was included in the concurrent list.

The Conference wondered whether income tax and other revenues should be collected and distributed by the federal government or whether these duties should be shared with the territorial Governments. The Finance Sub-Committee favoured wide powers for the federal government as a collector and distributor of revenues, but neither this Sub-Committee nor the Conference felt competent to judge the issue and it was referred to the proposed fiscal commission. The same attitude was adopted with regard to governmental borrowing. The fiscal commission, when formed, would also be asked to review the Conference's decision to make "Banks and Banking" a concurrent subject to allow such activity in the territorial sphere.

The question of "Industrial Conciliation" was passed by the Conference to its Legal Sub-Committee which, in turn, found contradictions it could not resolve because, for example, the federal government would control the railways and should have the power to conciliate labour disputes. Yet this involved the Africans' daily life and thus had to be a territorial responsibility. When the matter was reviewed in plenary session, E. I. G. Unsworth, the Northern Rhodesian Attorney-General, insisted that all industrial conciliation had to be territorial because the northern Africans feared that the federal government would copy Southern Rhodesia by not recognising African trade unions. He and Rennie thought that the current system of managing a common railway with differing territorial industrial laws was quite adequate.

Lyttelton and others agreed that a system which worked should not be disturbed and that future friction might produce a solution. Huggins and Whitehead, however, wondered how long it would continue to work when there could be two different arbitration awards in two different territories. Welensky supported them, confessing that during the Second World War he had, as a trade unionist, used Northern Rhodesian law to put pressure on the Southern Rhodesian Government. He felt that the system had to be changed. Rennie thought that the answer could be to align southern with northern law, but Whitehead pointed out that the dilemma of a higher arbitration award in the North would remain. Deadlock was reached because Unsworth, nevertheless, maintained that African sensitivity would not allow federal involvement in this field, while Whitehead could not understand why the federal government should not just deal solely with its own employees.

When the matter was debated for the third time (in the tenth meeting on 5 May), Lord Salisbury proposed an arrangement whereby the territorial Governments would implement federal law. However, Whitehead would not shift his ground. When Lyttelton said that the African unions might be disenfranchised, Huggins lost his patience. Whitehead was right, he proclaimed, the railways would have to have their own conciliation machinery because "to be bound by Mr Griffiths's trade union laws in the North, to upset a Federal thing, I think is absurd. We have nearly had a boiling row over it already".

Although Whitehead pointed out that the African affairs board would never condone the disenfranchising of African unions, Unsworth continued to harp on this fear and the Conference decided that the concurrent list should have an appendix stating that the power to make laws relating to trade unions and industrial conciliation would remain territorial. A note was added to the appendix stating that this was necessary as an interim measure in view of the differences in existing territorial law. The three territories were urged to align their industrial legislation.

The debate on the exclusion of "African Primary and Secondary Education" from the concurrent list produced some surprises. W. Gorell Barnes (later Sir William) of the Colonial Office explained that the drafters had taken the advice of an educational expert and had made African education concurrent because it would have to be dovetailed with higher education which would be a federal responsibility. Moffat dissented because the commitment on the Africans' daily life would be infringed. Lyttelton then concluded that the Conference would agree. The Southern Rhodesian Government delegates said nothing because, though they were happy to pass expensive departments into federal hands, the federalisation of all education had political ramifications which were likely to upset their electorate in that, if it happened, the ultimate fate of racial segregation in schools, in the light of the partnership policy, was sealed.[6]

Somewhat to their horror and to the surprise of the British delegates, Savanhu demanded that all education be federal in accordance with the goal of the partnership policy of working towards a community of interests. He explained that "the feeling of the Southern [Rhodesian] Africans is that they are in a position in which they would perhaps have little influence in determining whether they should go into a Federation or not, therefore, we are determined to get all we can get out of this scheme". He was emphatic that the Southern Rhodesian Africans did not share the northerners' desire to continue education by the territorial Government.

Nkomo was more restrained and merely said that he was concerned with ensuring that Africans could gain qualifications enabling them to enter public service. This, Lord Salisbury and Lyttelton argued, vindicated the drafters' decision to make African education concurrent. However, Rennie warned that Northern Rhodesian Africans would never agree because non-interference with the African's daily life was fundamental to their agreement. Moreover, Lennox-Boyd reminded the Conference that the reassurance on the effect of federation on the Africans had been given in the Commons and that to ignore it was to hazard the support of both sides of the House.

When Rennie opposed Huggins's proposal of an additional legislative list in which the federal government could act only with the permission of the territorial Governments, the Conference referred it to an *ad hoc* sub-committee. This sub-committee supported Moffat's and Rennie's conclusion and argued that the territorial Governments would be forced to co-ordinate their policies with the federal government because the latter would control higher education. The Conference concurred. African education was designated territorial, and provision was made, through delegation, for special schools for the blind and others.

Health, too, though clearly affecting the African directly, had initially been made a federal subject. Predictably, however, the northern official delegates and Moffat refused to condone it, arguing that the commitment to the Africans had been made and that, if efficiency was the criterion, amalgama-

[6] Author's interview with the Hon. J. M. Greenfield.

tion should be allowed. The Southern Rhodesians claimed that only the federal government could improve current systems and that, indeed, the Nyasaland Government would be unable to provide an adequate service. They knew that the northern system more directly involved the African administration but felt that local adjustments could be made because the service would have to be de-centralised. They believed that the African would not even notice the change and, because disease knew no bounds, it had to be combated federally.

Beckett agreed that the African would be unaware of the change, and Savanhu thought that there was nothing to be gained from making health a territorial subject. Nkomo, characteristically, was concerned that Africans should have promotional opportunities within the service. Huggins thought that it was opportune to make the point that, unless some "big-spending departments" were made federal, Southern Rhodesia was unlikely to accept the scheme. Certainly, he warned, there would be few Southern Rhodesian civil servants who could be spared for federal departments.

Lennox-Boyd accepted this but reminded the Conference of the position within the Commons, and Rennie argued that, if the principle of "big-spending departments" was accepted, the African reassurance was irrevelant and the additions to the federal list would be limitless. However, Lyttelton ruled that Rennie was raising a wider issue than the federalisation of health, and the Conference agreed that the service should be made concurrent.

The debate on whether there should be more than the centralisation of certain aspects of the police services was long and hard-fought through four plenary sessions and was referred twice to specialised sub-committees. The Conference readily accepted the idea of having common criminal investigation and records departments and the need for a reserve force because, in recent years, Southern Rhodesia's British South Africa Police had been called upon to reinforce neighbouring territories when it was clearly better to use policemen than soldiers to quell civil commotion. The federal capital would need policing and justified a federal force. There were, too, obvious savings to be made if training could be combined, and it was desirable that the territories should not compete for recruits.

However, the questions of recruiting, training and indeed inter-service transfer were complicated by the rank structure of the forces. The BSAP recruited Europeans as constables, and all its officers were drawn from the ranks and were not commissioned until they had served for seven years. The Northern Rhodesia Police and the Nyasaland Police recruits joined as sub-inspectors and the lower ranks were entirely African. Consequently, the northern territories employed proportionately more Africans than Southern Rhodesia: the ratios were one European to seven Africans in the North, and one to three in the South. The promotional prospects also differed because, unlike the Southern Rhodesian, the northerner could seek promotion in the world-wide Colonial Police Force. When Unsworth declared this last aspect to be fundamental, because the loss of it would unsettle the current force, he earned a rebuke from Welensky who questioned the value of policemen who allowed themselves to be disturbed by a political decision.

It was agreed that inter-service transfer should be allowed at a high level but the question of centralised training proved more difficult to resolve. It was acknowledged that a federal depot could provide a reserve force in an emergency. However, the difficulties of training constables and sub-inspectors together were enhanced by Roman-Dutch Law in Southern Rhodesia and English Law in the northern territories. The Northern Rhodesian unofficial delegates, together with Lyttelton and Salisbury, believed that syllabi could be adjusted, but Greenfield questioned whether this was practicable and the northern officials were convinced that their Africans would object to officers being drawn from the common pool. Furthermore, Rennie was anxious about the fate of his new training depot.

Unsworth suggested that the matter be deferred so that advice from the territorial police commissioners could be secured. In response, the Colonial Office summoned its Inspector-General of Police, W. C. Johnson, but he proved a hostile witness for the northern system by finding merit only in Southern Rhodesia's training and promotional methods. The northern officials countered by claiming that federal law could be enforced by the territorial police and that, as the territorial Governments were responsible for internal security, they should control the police. They maintained that, to be successful, the police forces had to retain their local character and, moreover, that the Africans would be sensitive to any change in the *status quo*.

The Southern Rhodesians, in turn, although unconcerned about the local identity of the police, argued that the territorial Governments could have full control of the police and still prevent the duplication of training. The necessity of having territorial commissioners and their headquarters' staff could be removed by applying the Canadian system whereby a federal force would be available on hire to the territories. Even if this were unacceptable to the Conference, Southern Rhodesia would transfer the BSAP to the federal government by delegation to effect considerable savings. Whitehead argued that the northern territories could not reasonably object to this move because Southern Rhodesia would pay for the services rendered by the federal force. He did not convince Rennie who concluded that this would merely mean that the federal taxpayer living outside Southern Rhodesia would have to share the burden of the expense. The question of such a use of the power to delegate was referred to the Legal Sub-Committee which recommended its rejection. The Conference concurred and, after Lyttelton had argued that Sandhurst had set a successful precedent for the basic training of divergent forces, agreed that police training should be a concurrent subject.

In the debate on the Report of the Economic Sub-Committee in the seventh plenary session on 1 May, the Southern Rhodesians, as they had done in the negotiations in January, made a strong bid for the federalisation of agriculture on grounds of efficiency and economy. Huggins later admitted that, as agriculture was Southern Rhodesia's major industry, it was politically important that it should be federal. He was prepared to allow African agriculture to be a territorial subject. The northerners, however, found that European and African agriculture in their territories were so integrated, and specialised staff so few in number, that division was impossible. Beckett, in particular, as elected Member holding the portfolio of agriculture, was adamant on this point even though he, as a farmer, would welcome the federalisation of agriculture. He thought that, as marketing and price-fixing would be federal subjects, farmers would be interested in federal politics. He saw in this suggestion a danger that the federal government would become identified with European interests only while the territorial Governments would deal exclusively with the African which would be the antithesis of partnership.

The Southern Rhodesians abandoned their attempt but not before they had ridiculed the suggestion by the Officials' Report that the function of research should be federal while its application should be territorial. They argued that the laboratory worker could not be divorced from the field. An *ad hoc* sub-committee found that land allocation, forestry and fisheries should be territorial, and that agricultural, veterinary and tsetse research, cadastral survey and irrigation should be concurrent to allow flexibility in federal and territorial involvement. Veterinary, animal husbandry and conservation extension services constituted a problem because these intruded into the African's daily life. The sub-committee thought that these services should perhaps be made concurrent so that the territorial Governments could apply federal policies.

In the Conference, the Southern Rhodesians said that it was ludicrous to hamper research by dividing animal health from animal husbandry and to allow the federal government to administer the health service whilst being unable to deal with the tsetse fly-borne disease, trypanosomiasis. The northerners, however, said they would not allow federal officers to work on animal husbandry in African areas. A compromise was suggested by Lord Salisbury and it was accepted that research in animal health and the tsetse should be territorial but that it would be possible to delegate it to the federal government. Irrigation and cadastral survey were made concurrent and everything else relating to agriculture and the veterinary services would remain in territorial hands.

The third part of Chapter II detailed the composition of the federal assembly, but before it was discussed, Stockil and W. H. Eastwood of Southern Rhodesia had raised, in the first plenary session, the possibility of a bi-cameral legislature because this was the overwhelming desire of the Southern Rhodesian electorate. Nominated members, they argued, should be in an upper house and not in a lower where legislation was initiated. The Africans, Stockil claimed, harping on a popular Southern Rhodesian theme, were not ready for an electoral system and should be educated first through their councils while an upper house, a reviewing body with powers of delay, offered them protection for their interests and a forum for debate.

In order that this proposal could be properly evaluated, Lord Salisbury asked for a written submission, and Stockil and Eastwood prepared a memorandum for the second plenary session, on 24 April. Salisbury warned that the delegates had not had time to read it, but Huggins was the exception because he immediately recognised it as the document to which the three Southern Rhodesian political parties had agreed before the Victoria Falls Conference. He maintained, and Welensky agreed, that there was no point in discussing it further because the northern territories had rejected it as impracticable. Eastwood, however, thought that at least the Conference should provide, in the constitution, for an ultimate bi-cameral system. Huggins agreed because this would avoid the necessity for a constitutional amendment when it was opportune to have an upper house which would serve all races by ensuring that no sectional interest was ignored.

Salisbury and Lyttelton reminded the Conference that, since the Officials' Report, the number of nominated members had been reduced from nine to two and, as this provision could be regarded as weakening the constitutional safeguards, the possible reactions of the Africans and the British Parliament should be borne in mind. The second chamber, they maintained, was inherent in the constitution and it would be simple enough to effect an amendment when it became necessary. Welensky supported them and appealed to the Southern Rhodesians not to create difficulties in order to avoid stirring up the "lunatic fringe" in Britain. The Conference concurred.

When agreement was sought on the membership of the assembly, Savanhu proposed that, because Africans would have little influence on the election of the 26 ordinary members, the Conference should ensure that a single group within the assembly should be capable of making decisions where racial interests were at stake. Lyttelton replied that safeguards would be discussed later and that Savanhu should not assume that the 26 would act together as they would come from different territories. Savanhu, nevertheless, was concerned about the effect of the combination of the white supremacists in Northern and Southern Rhodesia because he thought that the safeguards were inadequate. He did not pursue the issue after Welensky had dwelt on the likelihood of the emergence of a party system in which the African members could hold the balance of power. Welensky doubted whether any party would be able to govern without African support and expected parties to seek the allegiance of African candidates in the general election. Thereafter, the Conference agreed that the assembly should consist of 35 members, comprising 26 elected members, and seven elected and two appointed members for African interests. The speaker and his deputy would be chosen by the assembly from its membership or, in the case of the speaker only, from outside the assembly. The territorial division of the 26 elected seats would be 14 for Southern Rhodesia, eight for Northern Rhodesia and four for Nyasaland.

After the first general election, which would be held in accordance with the standing territorial regulations, the federal legislature would be empowered to prescribe the qualifications and disqualifications for the election of the 26 members, the circumstances in which seats could be vacated, electoral qualifications and registration. It would pronounce on the holding of elections, the delimitation of electoral districts and the relevant offences and penalties. Provision could be made for different methods of election in different territories and also for different methods of election within the same territory. Bills to implement these powers would be passed by two-thirds of the total membership of the assembly and would be reserved for the signification of the Monarch's pleasure.

For the purposes of the first general election, the governor-general would be empowered to make regulations delimiting the federal electoral districts. If a Member of a territorial legislature was elected to the federal assembly, he would not be able to take his seat there until he resigned his territorial seat. As

Nyasaland had no electoral system and as its delegates stressed that they wished to control its introduction, the Conference decided that the federal legislature would not be able to legislate on electoral matters for Nyasaland until the Nyasaland legislature resolved that it could. Until that legislature signified its assent, the governor-general would have to consult the Nyasaland Governor before he made electoral regulations.

Of the seven elected seats for African interests, Southern Rhodesia would have three and Northern Rhodesia and Nyasaland two each. At Greenfield's insistence, the Conference laid down that no one could stand for election to represent African interests in Southern Rhodesia unless he was a Southern Rhodesian citizen. In the North, he would have to be a British citizen or a British Protected Person. Otherwise, the candidate could not owe allegiance to a foreign power, be an undischarged bankrupt, an unpardoned criminal or be insane. The Southern Rhodesian Governor would prescribe the electoral regulations for the three Southern Rhodesian members — one of whom would be a European. The northern Governors would do likewise for their candidates. The prescription for the method of election in the northern territories reflected Rennie's fear that the African Representative Council might refuse to co-operate. Thus the two Northern Rhodesian and the two Nyasaland members would be elected by such bodies as their Governors designated to be representative of the African populations. The Conference detailed the reasons for disqualifying these members and Huggins succeeded in getting it to agree to have any appeals directed to the federal supreme court and not the territorial Governors. The two appointed members for African interests from the northern territories would be selected by their Governors and would be subject to similar qualifications and disqualifications.

"Chapter III: Legislation and Procedure" dealt with quorums, gave the speaker a casting, not original vote, and empowered the federal assembly to make its standing orders. The governor-general's powers of assent were described and he could not, without reference to the Secretary of State, assent to bills which were inconsistent with the constitution, to which the African affairs board had objected, which were contrary to international agreements, or contained the provisions of a bill which had previously been disallowed. The Monarch could disallow a bill within twelve months of the governor-general giving his consent. The federal assembly had to be summoned once every twelve months but the governor-general would have the power to prorogue it. The life of parliament would be five years.

In "Chapter IV: The Executive" it was stated that the governor-general would always act on the advice of his ministers except when he had to use his discretion, in which event he would be responsible to the Secretary of State. The governor-general would be able, with the consent of the territorial Governor, to entrust that Governor or any other territorial officer or authority with federal functions. The federal assembly would be able to make a like delegation. Such power would be given effect by announcement in the territorial gazette by the territorial Governor. Similar provision was made for delegation by the territories to the federal authority within the defined limits. The governor-general could appoint a prime minister and ministers and would be assisted by an executive council in which they would serve. A minister would have to become a member of the federal assembly within four months of his appointment and would cease to be one the moment he was no longer a member. Lennox-Boyd found great merit in this innovation because Britain, in the Second World War, had been denied the services of able men who had not been in Parliament. Otherwise, normal constitutional conventions would be followed. Finally, the governor-general was entrusted with the prerogative of pardon with respect to federal law.

When "Chapter V: The African Affairs Board" was discussed in the third plenary session on 25 April, Savanhu demanded its deletion because it supposed that there was a difference between the races and was thus incompatible with the policy of partnership. He argued that it was unnecessary if ways were found for Africans to influence every federal constituency. In Southern Rhodesia this would mean the broadening of the franchise. Eastwood agreed, but Lord Salisbury regarded the board as a fundamental of the constitution, and the northern Governors were convinced that their Africans would not accept its deletion. Welensky agreed with Savanhu in principle but also felt that it would be inexpedient. Savanhu, undeterred, warned that the board, like the South African Natives Representative Council, would face extinction unless it was powerful enough to influence the legislature. The Conference, however, felt that this safeguard was necessary for the moment but that it would be rendered obsolete by African advancement. Nkomo agreed but was anxious to ensure that the parliamentarians did not shelve their responsibilities to Africans because of the safeguard.

The Conference accepted without demur that the membership of the African affairs board should consist of a chairman and six members, none of whom would also be a member of the federal assembly or the territorial legislatures or be a public officer. The draft before the Conference provided that the chairman would be appointed by the governor-general with the approval of the Secretary of State but did not specify whether the governor-general would be empowered so to act on his own discretion or in council. Huggins strove hard for the latter provision because he was convinced that the Southern Rhodesians would insist that the governor-general should act as a constitutional monarch. He argued that the Conference could not reasonably object because the Secretary of State would have to sanction the choice and the governor-general would not be prevented from privately indicating that he disagreed with his cabinet. It was important to bear in mind, with regard to the fate of the referendum, that "the more grandmotherly things that are put in the Constitution, the more violently our Europeans are going to react".

His warning was to no avail because the British Ministers were convinced that the Commons and the Africans would demand that the African affairs board should be entirely independent of the cabinet, and the Conference accepted that the governor-general should use his discretion. There was, however, no argument about the method of appointing the members of the board, who would be nominated by their territorial Governors — an African and a European for each territory — and appointed by the governor-general. The governor-general was given the power to dismiss the chairman or a member of the board.

Great care was taken in defining the functions of the African affairs board in an attempt to avoid it incurring public displeasure. The board would be empowered to protest — to the prime minister — if it considered that a bill or a subordinate law was a differentiating measure by which Africans suffered disadvantages which Europeans did not. As late intervention could incur public wrath, it was provided that a copy of all proposed legislation should be sent to the board before it was introduced in the federal assembly. This would happen automatically unless the governor-general intervened to certify, in writing, that the nature of the legislation was such that its publication before its introduction in the assembly was undesirable, or was too urgent to await the board's evaluation. In this manner, provision was made for the preservation of secrecy in matters such as the budget.

The Conference ensured, too, that there would be opportunity for informal solution of disputes by substituting "may" for "shall" when describing the manner in which the board would formally protest to the prime minister. A written notice of objection would be sent to the prime minister as soon as practicable and certainly before the bill was presented to the governor-general for assent. In the case of an objectionable subordinate law, however, protest had to be lodged within 30 days of its publication. To facilitate informal conciliation, the board was empowered to withdraw its notice of objection. On receipt of the board's notice, the prime minister would table it in the assembly when the bill was introduced or, if the bill was already under discussion, as soon as possible. If the bill was passed by the assembly despite the objection, or if the latter was received too late, the board's notice would be laid before the governor-general when the bill was presented for assent. Thereupon, the governor-general would reserve the bill for the Monarch's pleasure and dispatch it and the notice of objection to the Secretary of State.

The governor-general, however, could assent to the bill if he considered that it was not differentiating or if he accepted the prime minister's recommendation that it was in the public interest. In the case of a protest on a subordinate law, the prime minister would pass it to the governor-general with his comments. The governor-general would transmit the protest and the comments to the Secretary of State who could, within twelve months, express disapproval and upon which the governor-general would act by publishing a revocation of the law in the federal gazette.

To ensure the independence of the board, the governor-general was made responsible for framing its regulations on terms of service, methods of working, quorums and other matters. The Conference decided that the board would arrive at a decision by a simple majority, with the chairman's casting vote only being used to keep an issue alive. If the board was not unanimous, this fact would be made known to the governor-general to assist him in his evaluation of the issue. The African affairs board would not, however, be entirely confined to the defence of African interests, and provision was made for it to furnish advice to the territorial Governments.

With regard to "Chapter VI: Finance", the Conference confessed that it needed expert advice and decided that a fiscal commission would be appointed. The commission would recommend financial arrangements and estimate the effect of the transfer of services to the federal government on the territorial economies. It would examine the question of collecting revenues without endangering the financial autonomy of the territories. The Conference, itself, having examined existing federations, favoured the centralisation of the assessment and collection of all taxes on income, but would expect advice on this, on the most suitable forms of taxation and on the establishment of a customs union. Whatever else the commission recommended, the revenues from customs and excise, postal and telecommunication services and the fees earned by federal departments would accrue to the federal government. Furthermore, the commission would be instructed that all revenue should be received in a consolidated revenue fund to which would be charged the emoluments of the governor-general, the chief justice, the judges of the federal supreme court and the chairman and members of the African affairs board. The commission's advice would be sought also on the question of borrowing. It was thought that perhaps the Australian Loans Council, on which federal and territorial representatives sat, could be copied.

The intention to appoint a civil service preparatory commission, proclaimed in "Chapter VII: The Federal Public Service", was the product of unresolved arguments on civil service matters. Welensky had suggested the commission in the pre-Conference arguments at governmental level, and Whitehead echoed him after Huggins had clashed with the Nyasaland official delegates over their demand for a statement in the constitution to protect the jobs of their Asian civil servants. Huggins accepted that the federal civil service would be open to all but warned that a specific reference to Asians could adversely affect the Southern Rhodesian referendum. The Conference, in any case, felt unqualified to pronounce upon the intricacies of the establishment of a new civil service and welcomed Whitehead's suggestion.

The Conference specified that the commission should suggest arrangements for the transfer of federal functions by the territorial Governments, devise the organisation and structure of the federal public service and formulate the terms and conditions of service of federal employees. It would arrange the transfer to the federal service of territorial employees but would bear in mind the need to preserve the existing rights and avenues of advancement of these personnel. Those whose offices were becoming federal, but who refused transfer, would be offered abolition of office terms. The commission would suggest ways of achieving uniformity in the terms and conditions of service in the federal and territorial Governments. The definition of a "Federal Public Officer" would not include judges. It was the Conference's intention that the governor-general should be given the power, to use at his discretion, to appoint, dismiss and discipline federal officers. He would be advised by a public service commission, the membership of which would be entirely independent of the federal and territorial legislatures. The federal assembly, however, would legislate to establish the commission and to define its powers.

The Conference found itself incompetent to prescribe the technicalities of the establishment of a federal supreme court and recommended the appointment of a judicial commission to study and report upon the matter. Thus the definition to be found in "Chapter VIII: The Federal Judicature" would be subject to the commission's findings. The Conference prescribed that the supreme court would consist of a president and as many other judges as the governor-general found to be necessary. The removal of judges from office would be solely the prerogative of the governor-general, and the federal assembly would be able to do no more than to submit an address to the governor-general suggesting the dismissal of a judge on the grounds of misbehaviour, incapacity or infirmity of body or mind. The supreme court would provide interpretation of the constitution for other courts. It would have original jurisdiction in proceedings between the territorial Governments or between the federal government and a territorial Government and in such other matters as might be prescribed. The federal supreme court would hear and determine appeals from its own side, where appeals were provided for in federal law, as well as appeals from territorial courts on matters arising in territorial or federal law. The territorial courts would apply federal law unless they were explicitly excluded from so doing.

The final "Chapter IX: Miscellaneous" covered five subjects which, though important, did not warrant separate presentation. The first paragraph provided that, in the interim period before the federal government was in being, the governor-general would be empowered to adapt, if necessary, territorial laws for subjects designated federal. Rights reserved under the Lewanika Concessions would be preserved by adopting section 41 of the Northern Rhodesia Order in Council, 1924 — under which territory reserved for prospecting, as conceded by Lewanika on 17 October 1900 and 11 August 1909, could not be alienated without the consent of the Barotse Chief and the approval of the Secretary of State. All existing rights given under these concessions would be honoured.

The third paragraph laid down a fine of £20 per day for knowingly sitting or voting in the federal assembly when not qualified so to do. The fourth paragraph sought to reduce constitutional litigation for which federations are infamous. The device adopted would allow the federal assembly to order the tabling of a federal law in the territorial legislatures for a six-month period during which these bodies could resolve that more than just federal matters would be affected. If there was no objection, the courts would be powerless to question the validity of the law on these grounds.

The final paragraph dealt with the controversial subject of the amendment of the federal constitution. The Conference adopted a compromise formula under which the amendment would have to be passed by two-thirds of the total membership of the federal assembly excluding the speaker and would be reserved by the governor-general for Her Majesty's pleasure. An order in council would be necessary as a means of signifying the Monarch's assent to the amendment if any of the territorial legislatures objected, by resolution, to the bill or any of its provisions within 60 days of its passage through the federal assembly or if the African affairs board submitted a notice of objection to the governor-general. A draft of the order in council would be tabled in the British Houses of Parliament and would lie there for 40 days. Thereafter, if no objection was raised to it, the order in council would be presented for assent. If there were no territorial or African affairs board objection to an amendment, an order in council would be unnecessary and the Secretary of State would merely signify assent after 65 days had elapsed. The process could be shortened by the territorial legislatures indicating that they would not lodge objections to the amendment.

The British Government had, in fact, proposed that all constitutional amendments should lie before its Houses of Parliament because it felt that this would encourage the Commons to support federation. The northerners accepted this happily as it would allay African fears on the safeguards. Moffat thought that perhaps the suggestion of the Officials' Report, that all constitutional amendments should be frozen for an initial period, should be adopted, but the British Ministers thought it impracticable.

The Southern Rhodesians, however, were not so co-operative. As their territorial Constitution could be altered simply and without consulting the Secretary of State except when African interests were involved, and even then the bill did not lie before the British Parliament, they rejected the British proposal because it was likely to be unacceptable to the Southern Rhodesian electorate. They insisted that the process of change be smooth, quick and protected from petty interference by people of ill-will. Thus it was with much reluctance that the Southern Rhodesian delegates conceded that the opinion of the territorial legislatures and the African affairs board should be taken into account and accepted the compromise formula.

Although the Conference was prepared to add a sentence to the final chapter allowing the power to amend the constitution to include the ability to establish a second chamber of the federal legislature, it would not include Stockil's other demand for a clause which would permit secession. When Stockil made this suggestion in the final plenary session on 5 May he was sufficiently attuned to the mood of the Conference not to expect its acceptance. Nevertheless, he thought that the Conference should consider providing machinery for Southern Rhodesia to leave the federation, perhaps after ten years, if it became unhappy with the experiment. He foresaw the weakening of British control in Africa leading to the Southern Rhodesians wishing to defend their way of life and having to withdraw from the federation so to do. This, he predicted, would be a significant factor in the referendum campaign.

Stockil's suggestion reminded Welensky of the first words of the Burial Service, "... in the midst of life we are in death", and he, Beckett, and Shelford of Nyasaland sought to convince Stockil that this provision was unnecessary. They echoed Lyttelton's reasoning that it would always be constitutionally possible to secede even without this clause which would weaken the federal cause because who, he asked, would be attracted to a federation which was under a perpetual sentence of death. Lord Salisbury agreed that a secession clause would make the federation's demise inevitable because there would never be any public confidence in the experiment. It would be a grave error to insert this clause particularly in the White Paper. Savanhu thought that what Stockil really feared was the inevitability of racial equality under federation, and Stockil gained only a single ally, Eastwood, and even he feared for the effect on the federation's ability to borrow. Stockil bowed to *force majeure*, saying that what he feared most was the effect of a change of government in Britain in the light of the colonial retreat under Labour. Thus he wanted his views recorded "because I do feel the time will come when we shall have to consider this before very long". Salisbury acknowledged that it had been an important debate.

The Conference ended that day, 5 May, with what Lyttelton called the "Third Reading" speeches. Huggins merely expressed appreciation for the assistance given by the British officials and for the opportunity to confer. Nkomo counted himself fortunate to have been present because the Conference had proved his suspicions to be false. He avowed that he would explain to the Southern Rhodesian Africans what had happened but was not confident that he could win them to the federal cause. Southern Rhodesian Africans, he explained, recognised that benefits would flow from federation but they wondered which racial group would enjoy them. It would greatly assist the federal case if racial discrimination could be relaxed so that Africans could see that everyone would gain. The key to success, he thought, would be the attitude of the ruling class and it would have to be one of patience, understanding and honesty.

Eastwood agreed that the fate of federation lay in European hands. Rennie promised that the Northern Rhodesian Government would do its best to secure the acceptance of the federal plan and urged the British Government to make a similar effort in the United Kingdom. Welensky depicted the Conference as a positive gain in what had been a long struggle because at last they had concrete proposals to lay before their people and the Africans in particular. The next year, he predicted, would set the pattern of race relations in Central Africa and it could be an example to the world.

Barrow confessed that he had not been a proponent of federation but now saw federation as the only safe course to follow. He was confident that federation stood a fair chance of being adopted. The British Ministers agreed. Lyttelton promised to visit Central Africa if necessary and urged the implementation of partnership in an enlightened spirit. Lord Salisbury thought that the Conference had brought them closer to the federal goal and closed the proceedings by proposing to convey to the Queen, the delegates' loyal address.

Lyttelton's last task was to brief the northern African delegates, telling them, the next day, that he had readily accepted Griffiths's suggestion to speak to them. However, he regretted that they had not attended the Conference as observers and wondered at their temerity in criticising the safeguards, in *The Times*, when they knew nothing about them. The intention of the Conference, he avowed, had not been to seal the fate of Central Africa but to produce proposals for a constitution to be published in the form of a White Paper for public perusal. Thereafter, he explained, discussion would continue and, once three expert commissions had reported on particular problems, a further conference would be convened to produce a formal proposal to be submitted to the territorial legislatures and the Southern Rhodesian electorate. If the legislatures and the Southern Rhodesians concurred, the British Government would decide whether or not to implement the scheme.

As the White Paper was not yet at hand, Lyttelton briefly described its contents to the northern African delegates, stressing that only subjects which would benefit from being centralised and which would not affect the daily life of the African would become federal. He claimed that, though the idea of having a minister for African interests had proved impracticable, the safeguards had been strengthened. The African affairs board had been made more effective, and the constitution could not be amended without the santion of the board and the territorial legislatures. He closed by proclaiming that his Government saw the policy of partnership as the only possible method of political evolution.

There was no debate, however, and K. E. Mposa of Nyasaland, the only delegate to speak, merely reiterated that he and his colleagues had no mandate to discuss federation. He warned that, as African opinion had not changed in the last 20 years, the White Paper was fated to be rejected. Lyttelton replied that he could not believe that Africans could be so unreasonable as to refuse even to consider the proposals.[7]

Welensky confessed to his correspondents that he had found the Conference exhausting because he had combined lobbying the federal cause with his work in plenary session and in the sub-committees. The difficulties, too, of the Conference had been enhanced for him by having often to play the disagreeable role of mediator. Nonetheless, he was pleased with the progress made even though the White Paper would not appeal to those who sought either black domination or the imposition of *apartheid*. He was surprised and perturbed, however, when Huggins told the Press, and Whitehead informed Beckett, that the Conference had been disappointing from the Southern Rhodesian point of view.[8]

P. B. Fletcher (later Sir Patrick), the Southern Rhodesian Minister of Native Affairs, explained later that they felt that the constitution was untidy and could have been made more effective without endangering the safeguards. He thought that, if agriculture, veterinary services and education did not become federal subjects, development would be retarded. He felt better use should be made of the concurrent list. Less surprising were Stockil's comments to a Press conference that the proposals were unworkable and would not serve the interests of any section of the population. He urged that Southern Rhodesia should seek to be completely independent under the Crown and that closer association should only be contemplated when Northern Rhodesia had responsible government, and then only in the form of amalgamation.[9]

Welensky, Beckett and Unsworth stayed on in London to discuss purely Northern Rhodesian affairs with the Colonial Office and for Welensky and Beckett to continue their lobbying. They met Lyttelton on 7 May to review the questions of loans for hydro-electric development, the need for effective measures to control the influx of Asians and Afrikaners, and the transfer of the domicile of the copper companies to Northern Rhodesia.[10] On 8 May, Welensky asked Lyttelton to reduce the number of official Members of the Executive Council by transferring two more portfolios to the elected Mem-

[7] Welensky Papers, 14/16, f. 13, Record of a Meeting in the House of Commons, 6 May 1952.

[8] *Ibid.*, 39/155, f. 177, Welensky to unofficial Members, 5 May 1952; f. 176, Welensky to Huggins, 7 May 1952; 17/40, f. 32, Welensky to A. T. Williams, 7 May 1952; f. 35, Welensky to Lennox-Boyd, 6 May 1952; 5/95, ff. 282–283, Welensky to Gore-Browne, 7 May 1952; *The Rhodesia Herald*, 7 May 1952.

[9] *The Rhodesia Herald*, 11 May 1952; Welensky Papers, 39/113, f. 82, Reuter Report, Salisbury, 15 May 1952.

[10] Welensky Papers, 14/16, f. 6, Minutes of a Meeting, Colonial Office, 7 May 1952.

bers. He rejected out of hand any question of a *quid pro quo* being made to the Africans or the suggestion that any decision of the Legislative Council should be referred to the African Representative Council for ratification. Lyttelton listened with apparent sympathy and suggested that they should have further discussions in the presence of Africans.[11]

Welensky sought to exploit the advantage gained by the decision of the federal Conference, and of being in London. He revised an article on federation which he had written for the North American journal *Foreign Affairs*, arranged a wider distribution of Joelson's *East Africa and Rhodesia* in the Rhodesias, and sought out journalists such as Patrick O'Donovan of the *Observer* and Oliver Woods of *The Times*, telling the latter that it seemed to him that the only way to obtain reasonable Press interest was for himself or Huggins to become involved in "a good sexy murder".[12] Welensky pressed Lyttelton to undertake a propaganda campaign in favour of federation.[13] When Lennox-Boyd (Welensky's most valued ally at the Colonial Office) was promoted to the Transport and Civil Aviation portfolio, Welensky had the impudence to protest in writing to Churchill. He received a polite reply.[14]

Welensky wooed his British opponents, addressing both the Fabians and the Parliamentary Labour Party on 8 May. Griffiths took the chair at the three-hour long meeting of the Parliamentary Labour Party. Both Welensky and Beckett spoke on federation and the consequences of the failure to implement it, and were well received. However, in "question time" Welensky clashed with Griffiths over his decision to divide the Commons in the March debate on federation. Griffiths explained that he had done so because the British Government had failed to ensure that African representatives were present at the inter-governmental talks in late January. Welensky retorted that no European representatives had been invited and that Rennie had only gone to London because of pressure from the unofficial Members. Furthermore, it was pitiable, in his opinion, that the Labour Opposition should question the right of the Colonial Secretary to consult one of his Governors on the affairs of his territory, particularly a Governor appointed by the last Labour administration. Griffiths made no reply, but when he closed the proceedings he warned that British Church and public opinion was still opposed to the imposition of federation.[15]

Exploiting the division on federation in Labour ranks, Welensky met S. N. Evans, T. Reid and W. Coldrick and, through the good offices of George Hall, dined with Clement Attlee, using the opportunity to invite him

[11] *Ibid.*, 39/115, ff. 174–175, Welensky to unofficial Members, 8 May 1952.

[12] *Ibid.*, 39/115, ff. 159-163, Welensky to the Editor, *Foreign Affairs*, New York, 5 May 1952; f. 176, Welensky to Huggins, 7 May 1952; 34/12, f. 408, Welensky to F. S. Joelson, 16 May 1952; f. 400, Joelson to Welensky, 16 May 1952; 17/14, f. 19, Welensky to P. O'Donovan, 14 May 1952; f. 7, Welensky to O. Woods, 16 May 1952.

[13] *Ibid.*, 17/40, f. 1, H. Fraser to Welensky, 15 May 1952.

[14] *Ibid.*, 5/95, ff. 282–283, Welensky to Gore-Browne, 7 May 1952; f. 275, Welensky to W. S. Churchill, 13 May 1952; D. Taylor, *The Rhodesian: The Life of Sir Roy Welensky* (London, 1955), p. 151.

[15] Welensky Papers, 17/40, f. 4, Welensky to Gore-Browne, 9 May 1952; 39/119, ff. 285–290, Correspondence between Welensky and H. Nicholson, 2–12 May 1952; f. 173, Welensky to unofficial Members, 12 May 1952.

to visit Northern Rhodesia. After some reflection, Attlee, unlike Clement Davies, the Liberal leader, agreed to go.[16]

The meeting with Attlee was particularly memorable because of an incident in a corridor of the House of Commons. After dinner, *en route* to Attlee's office, he and Welensky met an eminent member of the Labour Party, who caught Attlee's eye, nodded deferentially, and said, "Good evening, sir." Attlee stopped and gazed after him, asking, "Who's that?" Welensky, the visitor, had to enlighten him. This would be paralleled almost exactly on another occasion when Welensky had to identify a leading Conservative for Churchill. Attlee would surprise and amuse Welensky even more when they reached his office. Attlee asked what was to be discussed first, and Welensky replied that he was particularly disturbed about a current petition in the Commons, signed by 20 Labour MPs, demanding the release of Zukas. Attlee asked who Zukas was and, after Welenksy had explained, enquired whose name headed the petition. Welensky named a prominent member of the Labour Left and was taken aback when Attlee muttered "that white baboon would sign anything".[17]

Finally, Welensky developed an idea suggested by Prince Yurka Galitzine, a London public relations expert, and convened a meeting of interested persons with the purpose of forming a committee to combat the gross misrepresentation of the federal case in Britain. At the meeting, on 14 May, Galitzine was elected chairman and J. H. Wallace, recently retired from the Colonial service, became the full-time secretary. The meeting decided that the talents of F. S. Joelson and Colonel L. van der Post (later Sir Laurens) should be tapped.

Welensky was not present at the first executive meeting of the new committee on 16 May but Beckett deputised for him. The name, the London Committee of the United Central Africa Association, was adopted and plans were laid to attract a distinguished membership from outside the ranks of the serving politicians to avoid the taint of party politics. Sir John Waddington, the former Governor of Northern Rhodesia, was thought to be a suitable recruit. Three sub-committees were projected to work in the fields of parliamentary lobbying, public relations and research. A close alliance with the Capricorn Africa Society would be sought, a subscription to a Press-cutting service would be taken, secretarial assistance found and the executive would meet every Friday at Queen Anne's Lodge. Such was the calibre of the men who would serve this committee that it would wage the most efficient and effective publicity campaign that Galitzine can recall.[18] Welensky and Beckett had every reason to be satisfied with their accomplishments in London as they journeyed home on 18 May.

[16] *Ibid.*, 34/12, f. 410, C. Davies to Welensky, 12 May 1952; 17/40, f. 10, T. Reid to Welensky, 13 May 1952; f. 22, Welensky to C. Attlee, 14 May 1952; 39/115, f. 172, Welensky to Huggins, 14 May 1952.

[17] *Ibid.*, 39/115, f. 171, Welensky to Sir John Kennedy, 14 May 1952; Author's interview with Sir Roy Welensky.

[18] Welensky Papers, 34/12, ff. 412–413, Y. Galitzine to Welensky, 9 May 1952; 39/84, f. 99, Minutes of a Meeting, London, 14 May 1952; WE 7, P/C/158/52, Agenda of 1st Meeting, London Committee, UCAA, 16 May 1952; Author's interview with Prince Yurka Galitzine.

CHAPTER TEN

The Federation Campaign

The Effort to secure Public Acceptance of the Proposed Federal Constitution, May-July 1952

HUGGINS and Welensky returned home convinced that they had reached the last lap because there remained only the final Conference in October after which the federal plan could be laid before the Southern Rhodesian electorate in the referendum in November. Against a background of mounting unrest in other parts of Africa (there were racial riots in South Africa and Bechuanaland and, later in the year, the Mau Mau struck in Kenya), the contestants would fling themselves into the struggle to convince the Southern Rhodesians. Their campaign, however, would be upset by a postponement of the Conference to January 1953, and the referendum to April.

It was Welensky's expressed intention — proclaimed as he departed from London — to postpone further action until the complete federal scheme was published in a White Paper in mid-June.[1] His decision was supported by the pro-federal delegates to the Conference, but in no way restrained their opponents. The Northern Rhodesian ANC and the Nyasaland African Congress parties stayed on in Britain until late May in a sustained effort to woo the Churches, the Labour and Liberal Parties. They won considerable support, particularly in Scotland, but not sufficient to divert the British Government from its chosen path.

In fact, 1952 was not a year of distinction for the Northern Rhodesian ANC, and financial mismanagement and lack of integrity was to lead to a number of resignations.[2] Nevertheless, it was forming the branches which in later years would be the basis of a formidable and effective organisation. Kenneth Kaunda, a young teacher, was already playing his part in the building of this structure. It was difficult, too, in 1952, as Welensky would discover to find a significant number of Africans who disagreed with the ANC opposition to federation.

[1] *The Bulawayo Chronicle*, 19 May 1952.
[2] L. H. Gann, *A History of Northern Rhodesia: Early Days to 1953* (London, 1964), pp. 424–425.

Moreover, in May the representatives of the two northern African Congresses were being lionised in Britain. The two visitors to Scotland, L. C. Katilungu of the Northern Rhodesian ANC and president of the Northern Rhodesian African Trades Union Congress, and O. E. Chirwa of Nyasaland won the sympathy of Church, trade unionist and political groups by stressing the value of Scottish resistance and the strong bond which Africans felt they had with Scotland.[3] The highlight of their tour was the recognition accorded Katilungu when, at the May Day demonstration in Queen's Park, Glasgow, he walked with Clement Attlee and was given a seat on the rostrum.

In England, Nkumbula and J. R. N. Chinyama of Nyasaland were so eloquent, yet moderate, in giving their views that the *News Chronicle* concluded on 9 May that they should be heeded. They claimed that pledges on land and immigration had been broken and that Southern Rhodesia would be given a dominant position in the federal legislature. They rejected federation and called for the return of alienated land. Their alternative was a programme to introduce reforms giving equal pay for equal work, a common roll franchise open to all inhabitants, the encouragement of the growing of cash crops and the provision for more technical education and wider social services.

The London Committee of the United Central Africa Association entered the fray almost immediately upon its formation when, in late May, these arguments were repeated by Nkumbula, Sokota and Chief Chitimukulu of the Bemba tribe at a meeting convened by the Africa Bureau. F. S. Joelson, speaking for the UCAA, divined that the Africans present really sought to dominate the northern territories which, in his opinion, was an impractical aim because the economies were already sufficiently sophisticated to require the presence of Europeans. He was confident that partnership offered the only way forward, but was continually interrupted as he spoke and had not finished his argument when the chairman forced him to make way for other speakers.[4]

In Northern Rhodesia, after Welensky's return, Simon A. Kaluwa, general secretary of the African Mineworkers' Union, published his reasons for rejecting federation in the *Northern News* on 20 May. Professor Rotberg commends Kaluwa for displaying "considerable prescience" in detailing African fears and the possible ways in which the proposals would adversely affect their interests.[5] Kaluwa acknowledged that most Africans, being illiterate and ignorant, did not understand the proposals (which had not yet been published), but he maintained that at least they knew, disliked and feared Southern Rhodesia because there Africans were denied work in towns, the pass laws were more difficult to understand and were more rigorously enforced. Trade unions were prohibited and the African felt that he did not have a rightful place in society. The provision of land for African reserves was inadequate which limited the numbers of cattle and consequently denied the land manure. The structure of family life had been weakened and the Chiefs were not respected.

[3] *The Scotsman* and the *Glasgow Herald*, 5 May 1952; *Greenock Telegraph*, 6 May 1952.
[4] *Northern News*, 24 May 1952.
[5] R. I. Rotberg, *The Rise of Nationalism in Central Africa: The Making of Malawi and Zambia, 1873–1964* (London, 1965), p. 242.

AMALGAMATION 1894-1938

1 Founder of the Rhodesias: Cecil John Rhodes (left) with his chief lieutenant, Dr Leander Starr Jameson, at Groote Schuur, Cape Town, in the early 1890s. They intended that the two Rhodesias form a single unit of their planned British Africa.

2 Nyasaland's principal architect: Sir Harry Johnston distrusted Rhodes and steered Nyasaland away from the BSA Company.

3 The first to suggest federation: Lord Selborne, British High Commissioner (front), with Sir Charles Coghlan, S. Rhodesia's first Prime Minister (peering over his left shoulder). Coghlan resisted amalgamation until he had achieved self-government for his country. (*Picture: St George's College.*)

4 First bid for amalgamation: Jameson (left, on a stoep in Shamva) in 1915, as president of the BSA Company, assisted by his fellow director, D. O. Malcolm (front), attempted to sell amalgamation to the Rhodesians. (*Pictures: National Archives of Zimbabwe.*)

AMALGAMATION 1894-1938

5 Keen amalgamationists: Lord Buxton, British High Commissioner (seated), visits Paramount Chief Lewanika of the Barotse in company with Sir Herbert Stanley (extreme right), who would serve as Governor of Northern and then of Southern Rhodesia.

6 Unanimous endorsement of amalgamation: The Victoria Falls Conference in 1936 attended by the unofficial Members of the Northern Rhodesian Legislative Council and representatives of Southern Rhodesia's political parties. Leopold Moore is in the front row (left, in white suit and bow tie) with Donald Macintyre, the future Federal Minister of Finance (extreme right). L. J. W. Keller is in the middle of the second row, E. C. F. Whitehead, future Southern Rhodesian Prime Minister, is in the fourth row (extreme right, in white jacket, standing almost between the pillars). Right at the back, in the middle, is the young Robert Tredgold, the future Chief Justice of Southern Rhodesia and then of the Federation.

7 The Bledisloe Commission: In the Matopos outside Bulawayo in 1938, Lord Bledisloe is in the front row in dark suit and bow tie. His Commission was appointed in response to agitation for amalgamation from the Europeans of both the Rhodesias, but it was to disappoint them by recommending nothing more than immediate inter-territorial co-operation. (*Pictures: National Archives of Zimbabwe.*)

THE MAKING OF THE FEDERATION 1945-1953

8 The first British concession towards unification: The inauguration of the Central African Council in 1945. Front row (left to right): Sir Ernest Guest, Southern Rhodesian Minister of Internal Affairs; Sir Godfrey Huggins, Prime Minister of Southern Rhodesia; Sir John Waddington, Governor of Northern Rhodesia; Sir Campbell Tait, Governor of Southern Rhodesia; Sir Edmund Richards, Governor of Nyasaland; Sir Stewart Gore-Browne; Max Danziger, Southern Rhodesian Minister of Finance. Third from the left in the second row is the young Roy Welensky, and third from the right is Malcolm Barrow. (*Picture: National Archives of Zimbabwe.*)

9 Doughty champion of the African: Arthur Creech Jones, Colonial Secretary, 1945-1950. Creech Jones (left) sits in conference with Ernest Bevin, Foreign Secretary, and the man Welensky admired most in the Attlee Government. Although Creech Jones encouraged the contemplation of federation, he never sanctioned it because he believed it did not accommodate the aspirations of the African. (*Picture: BBC Hulton Picture Library.*)

10 A step towards federation: After Sir Godfrey Huggins visited London in March 1950, Clement Attlee's Government agreed to examine the possibilities of federation. At London Airport, anchoring his hat, Huggins walks from the aircraft with Patrick Gordon Walker, the new Commonwealth Secretary, who was to prove to be a staunch ally of the Federation. (*Picture: Sports & General Press Agency Ltd., and National Archives of Zimbabwe.*)

THE MAKING OF THE FEDERATION 1945-1953

11 Marking time: The almost fruitless Conference at the Victoria Falls in September 1951. However, the Colonial Secretary, James Griffiths, committed the British Government to a further conference in London in 1952. The incoming Conservative Colonial Secretary, Oliver Lyttelton, would exploit this to found the Federation.

Front row (left to right): Huggins, Patrick Gordon Walker, Maj-Gen Sir John Kennedy, chairman of the Conference and Governor of Southern Rhodesia; James Griffiths; Sir Gilbert Rennie, Governor of Northern Rhodesia; Sir Geoffrey Colby, Governor of Nyasaland.

Second row (left to right): P. Sokota (NR); P. B. Fletcher, E. C. F. Whitehead and L. J. W. Keller (SR); K. O. Shelford, C. W. F. Footman, J. Marshall, Chief Mwase, M. P. Barrow and G. G. S. J. Hadlow (Ny.).

Third row (left to right): D. L. Yamba (NR); Sir Archibald James and R. O. Stockil (SR); G. B. Beckett, Lt Col E. M. Wilson, Welensky and R. C. S. Stanley (NR); C. R. Kumbikano, J. A. G. Corrie and E. K. Gondwe (Ny.).

Fourth row (left to right): W. E. Arnold and A. R. W. Stumbles (SR); G. M. Thornton (NR); J. N. R. MacLennan (UK); L. Powys-Jones (SR); W. F. Stubbs (NR); A. D. Evans and V. L. Robinson (SR); G. H. Baxter (UK); J. M. Greenfield (SR).

Fifth row (left to right): L. F. G. Anthony (NR); J. R. H. Shaul, A. H. Strachan and T. G. G. Gisborne (SR); E. I. G. Unsworth (NR); R. G. Feltham (SR); D. J. King (UK); J. S. Moffat (NR); V. Fox-Strangways (Ny.).

Sixth row (left to right): G. B. S. Clarke (SR); N. A. Gibbon (Central African Council); J. S. Gandee (UK); W. F. Nicholas (SR); H. J. Bewg and A. B. Cohen (UK); Maj R. T. Hungerford (NR); K. J. Knaggs and Cmndr J. P. P. Michell (CAC); A. M. Macintosh (UK); and H. N. Parry (CAC).

(Picture: National Archives of Zimbabwe.)

THE MAKING OF THE FEDERATION 1945-1953

12 Attempt at influencing: In 1952 Welensky invited Clement Attlee, then Leader of the British Opposition, to visit Northern Rhodesia. A year later, once the Federation was a reality, Attlee committed his Labour Party to its support. Here Attlee (centre) confers with the unofficial Members in Lusaka. He is flanked by Welensky (left) and Geoffrey Beckett (right). On the extreme left is Rex L'Ange, future Federal Minister of Works. (*Picture: NR Information Dept., in the possession of Mrs Joan Bridge.*)

13, 14 and 15 The architects of federation: (Left) Oliver Lyttelton (Lord Chandos), Colonial Secretary, promoted federation in 1951 and saw it through to fruition;
(Centre) Lord Salisbury, Commonwealth Secretary in 1952, assisted in the founding of the Federation and remained its staunchest British supporter;
(Right) Lord Swinton, the new Commonwealth Secretary in 1952, helped Lyttelton to frame the Federal Constitution. (*Pictures: BBC Hulton Picture Library.*)

16 The first day of the Federation: A beaming Sir Roy and Lady Welensky greet the Governor-General Designate, Lord Llewellin, at Salisbury Station on 4 September 1953. In the background are Sir Godfrey Huggins and Sir Robert Tredgold, who performed the swearing-in ceremony. (*Picture:* The Herald, *in the possession of Mrs Joan Bridge.*)

17 The reality: The Governor-General and territorial Governors pose on the lawn of Downing House, Salisbury, after Lord Llewellin had taken his oaths of office on 4 September. L. to r.: Sir John Kennedy (SR), Llewellin, Sir Gilbert Rennie (NR) and J. C. Talbot Edwards for Sir Geoffrey Colby (Ny.). (*Picture: National Archives of Zimbabwe.*)

THE HALCYON YEARS 1953–1958

18 The Federation's greatest material achievement: Kariba. Welensky inspects progress in company with its engineer, Henry Olivier (left) and Duncan Anderson (right), the chairman of the Federal Power Board. (*Picture: Federal Information Department, in the possession of Mrs Joan Bridge.*)

19 The end of an era: Lord Malvern retires on 31 October 1956 after 23 years as Prime Minister, first of Southern Rhodesia and latterly of the Federation. He is photographed in his office. (*Picture: H. M. Crane, Federal Information Dept., in the possession of Mrs Joan Bridge.*)

20 First day in office: Welensky addresses his first Press conference as Prime Minster on 1 November 1956. (*Picture: Federal Information Dept., in the possession of Mrs Joan Bridge.*)

THE HALCYON YEARS 1953-1958

21 Gubernatorial elegance: The Governor-General and his sister, Miss Mary Llewellin, entertain the territorial Governors and their ladies. Left to right: Lady Colby, Sir Geoffrey Colby of Nyasaland, Miss Llewellin, Lord Llewellin, Lady William-Powlett, Sir Peveril William-Powlett of Southern Rhodesia, Sir Arthur Benson of Northern Rhodesia and Lady Benson. *(Picture: R.D.K. Hadden, Federal Information Dept.)*

22 An architect of the Federation: The Colonial Secretary, Alan Lennox-Boyd meets Welensky and the Federal Cabinet in Salisbury in January 1957. Left to right: F. S. Owen (Commerce and Industry), J. M. Greenfield (Law and Education), Sir Malcolm Barrow (Home Affairs and Power), Welensky, Lennox-Boyd, D. Macintyre (Finance), J. M. Caldicott (Agriculture, Health and Public Service) and W. H. Eastwood (Transport and Works). *(Picture: R. D. K. Hadden, Federal Information Dept.)*

THE HALCYON YEARS 1953–1958

23 A Federal supporter: The Commonwealth Secretary, Lord Home, and Welensky meet in London in November 1958. Eighteen months earlier with Lennox-Boyd, Home had reached constitutional accord with Welensky, the high point of Anglo-Federal relations. (*Picture: Sport & General Press Agency Ltd., in the possession of Mrs Joan Bridge.*)

24 Before the revolt: The Southern Rhodesian Cabinet pose for a photograph. Left to right: G. Ellman-Brown, P. B. Fletcher, R. S. G. Todd, C. J. Hatty and A. R. W. Stumbles. In January 1958, the four Ministers would revolt against Todd. (*Picture: National Archives of Zimbabwe.*)

Kaluwa criticised the suggested federal control of economic affairs. He claimed that the Africans would be inadequately represented in the legislature and that the safeguards were valueless because they could be circumvented by the prime minister using the threat or act of resignation to coerce the Secretary of State. He found support in a statement by Lord Lugard in his *Dual Mandate* that the Imperial Government became powerless in colonies once executive power passed into local hands. Universal suffrage, Kaluwa insisted, was the only true safeguard. He predicted that the federal government would deny Africans adequate training through its control of higher education. It would use its departments to influence the territorial Governments to further European interests exclusively and would refuse loans in order to hinder the African trade unions. Indeed, it was likely to prevent any economic or other development in the North until the Governments there agreed to give land to immigrants. In any case, Southern Rhodesia's better climate and urban growth would facilitate its greater development. Finally, Kaluwa believed that, in the event of a war or any other emergency, Africans would be conscripted to serve as labour on Southern Rhodesian farms with the inevitable result of food shortages in the North.

Welensky did not comment on Kaluwa's article but was critical of the editorial objective of the *Northern News*, particularly as it seemed to be supporting Gore-Browne's plea for partition which it had published at the beginning of May.[6] Indeed, so powerful did the threat of partition seem that Welensky issued a statement dismissing it.[7] He did so in *The Bulawayo Chronicle* possibly because it had carried, on 1 May, a report on the resignation of L. J. W. Keller from the Rhodesia Labour Party and his call for the rejection of federation and the adoption of an ambiguous amalgamation of Southern Rhodesia and "White interests in the North".

In fact, Welensky intended to keep silent until the publication of the White Paper but was forced again to comment on 13 June after Stockil had succeeded in generating fears which threatened the federal concept. Even then Welensky's comment was mild as he reassured the white worker that he had little to fear from the African in open competition. He acknowledged the growth of African nationalism but claimed that it could be directed, and stated that African advancement in the federal arena would be governed entirely by African performance.[8]

In Southern Rhodesia, however, where Charles Olley, the inveterate opponent of federation, had begun an anti-federal pamphlet war, not even the parliamentarians matched Welensky's reticence. As has been seen, Keller, Stockil, Eastwood, Huggins and Fletcher had all commented on the proposals in some detail while Welensky was still in Britain. Huggins later made soothing noises, as far as the British critics were concerned, saying that no minority could expect to dominate for ever, observing that although the African should not be advanced too fast, it would be fatal to go too slowly.[9] However, Eastwood, in a fit of enthusiasm for federation, gave a meeting in

[6] Welensky Papers, 34/12, f. 368, Welensky to D. Cole, 21 June 1952; *Northern News*, 1 May 1952.
[7] *The Bulawayo Chronicle*, 24 May 1952.
[8] Welensky Papers, 5/45, f. 311, Welensky to J. H. Wallace, 14 June 1952.
[9] *The Bulawayo Chronicle*, 22 May 1952.

Salisbury on 15 May a detailed description of the proposals. He defended this action by claiming to have secured permission from Huggins provided the attitudes of the delegates remained secret. He did not convince Welensky, who protested privately to Huggins. Stockil demanded an immediate debate, perhaps in secret session, because the gentleman's agreement had been broken. Huggins would not concede the necessity for this, nor was his Government shaken by a "no confidence" debate on 29 May, on a motion by Stockil, in which all the Government's failings were paraded.

Stockil attacked the recent controversial budget and the consequent curb on immigration. The Government, he said, had failed to secure a West Coast port; it had promised at the 1948 election to secure dominion status and end the enrolment of Africans but, in fact, by mishandling the federal negotiations, had contrived to have Southern Rhodesia menaced by interference from the Colonial Office. One United Party MP, J. R. Dendy Young, threatened to cross the floor, but, unmoved, Huggins fought off the challenge and the motion was soundly defeated.[10] Stockil, however, was equally undeterred and continued to attack the federal plan. He claimed that there was nothing to prevent Africans, in time, capturing all the federal seats.[11] Nkomo and Savanhu, likewise unrestrained, were increasingly critical of the inadequacies of the partnership policy.

Characteristically, Welensky was not idle in these weeks before the publication of the White Paper. He planned a series of speaking engagements in both the Rhodesias. He dispatched money to the London Committee of the UCAA which was attempting to improve its public image by recruiting prominent men, while continuing to combat the efforts of the African nationalists, Banda in particular, and their allies. It also strove to win over the British Press. At the request of this committee, Welensky provided money, anonymously, for a study tour of the territories by the distinguished British historian, Professor W. M. Macmillan, to collect material for a series of pro-federal articles.[12] Coincidentally, the federal campaign was considerably assisted by an article by Professor Wheare who described the scheme as viable and spoke in praise of the delegates' efforts to answer the fears of the Africans.[13]

Welensky employed a full time organiser, J. D. Phillips, to assist the small UCAA committee in Northern Rhodesia. Welensky attended UCAA meetings in Southern Rhodesia, assisted its campaign, and conferred with Huggins. He also urged Lord Salisbury, as Commonwealth Secretary, to undertake an active campaign, assisted if possible by Churchill, to turn the tide in Southern Rhodesia. In addition, Welensky employed two Africans to work in

[10] *Ibid.*, 4 June 1952; Welensky Papers, 5/95, f. 270, T. H. Grey to Welensky, 22 May 1952; 39/113, f. 66, Welensky to Huggins, 6 June 1952; SR *Debates* (Salisbury), Vol. 33, Part 1, Col. 1503 & Col. 1553 f., 29 May 1952.

[11] *The Bulawayo Chronicle*, 7 June 1952; *Observer*, 8 June 1952.

[12] Welensky Papers, WE 7, P/C/158/52/G, Welensky to Y. Galitzine, 22 & 30 May 1952; 39/84, f. 91, Minutes of 3rd Meeting, London Committee, UCAA, 22 May 1952; f. 88, Minutes of 4th Meeting, London Committee, UCAA, 28 May 1952; 34/12, f. 404, F. S. Joelson to Welensky, 22 May 1952; f. 405, Joelson to Huggins, 22 May 1952; WE 7, P/C/161/52, Huggins to Welensky, 26 May 1952.

[13] *Northern News*, 5 June 1952.

African areas in Northern Rhodesia but neither particularly distinguished himself.[14]

On 18 June Lyttelton announced in the Commons the publication of the White Paper, simultaneously giving notice of the intention to appoint judicial, fiscal and public service commissions, and reminding the House that there would be a further conference later in the year, possibly in October. He described the recent Conference and maintained that, despite the regrettable absence of the northern Africans, their interests had been fully safeguarded, and the criteria of the Victoria Falls communiqué had been met. He explained carefully the new form of the proposed African affairs board and the manner in which the constitution could be amended.

His explanations did not satisfy Griffiths who confessed, nevertheless, that he needed to read the White Paper. Griffiths warned that the lack of a minister for African interests was setting a precedent in the Empire because, in all colonies, the indigenous people were directly represented in the executive councils. He wondered if the chairman of the African affairs board would have that minister's direct access to the governor-general, and thus to the Secretary of State. If he did not, there had been a fundamental change. He asked if all legislation would come before the board and whether it would be empowered to cause delay while the Secretary of State considered it.

Lyttelton replied that the Conference had found the concept of the minister for African interests to be constitutionally unsound with regard to cabinet government. However, the chairman and the board itself would have direct access to the prime minister and, when objecting, would delay legislation for consideration by the governor-general and then the Secretary of State. Lyttelton avowed that every step would be taken to consult African opinion and, under pressure from Griffiths, agreed that he or his Minister of State would tour the territories. When Fenner Brockway asked whether the sanction of the territories, including Southern Rhodesia, was needed if the meagre number of African members of the federal assembly were to be increased, Lyttelton suggested that he should read the White Paper.[15]

Two days later, undoubtedly responding to the requests for positive gestures in favour of the scheme, Lyttelton broadcast to the territories on the BBC, stressing the benefits which would accrue to all inhabitants and the strength of the safeguards. He asked for careful consideration of the details and for his audience to remember that there would be a further conference, at which he hoped there would be African delegates, before any decision was taken.[16] Shortly after the broadcast, the Colonial Office announced that its Minister of State, H. L. d'A. Hopkinson (later Lord Colyton), would visit the territories in the near future.[17]

The day before the publication of the White Paper on 17 June, the London Committee of the UCAA had held an inaugural Press conference to announce

[14] Welensky Papers, 5/45, f. 317, Welensky to J. D. Phillips, 6 June 1952; WE 7, P/C/158/52/S, Welensky to Lord Salisbury, 14 June 1952; P/C/158/52/J, Welensky to Joelson, 28 June 1952; 34/12, f. 394, M. C. Mwale to Welensky, 30 May 1952; f. 393, Welensky to Mwale, 6 June 1952.
[15] House of Commons *Hansard* (London), Vol. 502, Col. 1200 f., 18 June 1952.
[16] Welensky Papers, 39/113, ff. 57–58, BBC transcript, 20 June 1952.
[17] *Observer*, 22 June 1952.

its formation and to issue its first pamphlet, which claimed that, above all, federation would create conditions favourable to the propagation of partnership, which was the only conceivable solution to racial confrontation. The Committee was pleased by the reception accorded it and the White Paper by the British Press.[18]

The initial Southern Rhodesian reaction was cautious. *The Rhodesia Herald*, hitherto a staunch advocate of federation, depicted on 24 June the African affairs board as a backward step because all matters, including those of Southern Rhodesia, were being placed in the hands of "a Secretary of State". It saw this as a vote of no confidence in Southern Rhodesia despite its record of having done more for the mass of its population than any other state in Africa. Otherwise, it seemed that the Southern Rhodesians were waiting to see how the battle would develop in their Legislative Assembly, and Nkomo was alone amongst public figures in making a pronouncement when, on 21 June in the Bulawayo Location, he said: "The Europeans must be told now that we are not willing to wait as junior partners. We are only willing to accept partnership that does not give seniority to one group." He demanded that all talk of scientific advancement and superior skill should cease because the fruits of that skill belonged to the whole human race. Africans were perfectly capable of holding public office and should be given that opportunity immediately.[19]

On 23 June, Huggins opened the debate on the White Paper in the Legislative Assembly with what was adjudged one of the finest speeches of his career. He claimed that everyone accepted the need for larger units in modern times, for defence and, more particularly, for the attraction of development capital, and thus he regretted that public discussion had begun and minds had been made up before the facts contained in the White Paper were available. He commended federation, citing the United States of America as an example of how successful this system could be. This particular scheme left the individual constitutional status of the territories unchanged — Southern Rhodesia would continue to be self-governing — yet it provided great flexibility to avoid excessive constitutional litigation and to allow change. He described the workings of the African affairs board without reference to his earlier hints about its inadequacies. This and other safeguards existed but might prove unnecessary and disappear through disuse. Federation was a means of ultimately acquiring dominion status but Rhodesians would have to demonstrate their fitness to be thus rewarded.

Turning to electoral matters, Huggins felt no need to defend government by a minority when even the West African nationalists recognised control by the intelligent, educated minority. This was exactly the position in Southern Rhodesia where skill, education, civilisation and certain hereditary factors, and not colour, were the criteria for the possession of power. As there was no evidence that these attributes were the exclusive characteristics of white men, it was in the interests of all that others be encouraged to attain them to build a society which would be a bulwark against Communism. He warned, too, that

[18] Welensky Papers, WE 7, P/C/158/52/J, Joelson to Welensky, 19 June 1952; P/C/158/52/W, J. H. Wallace to Welensky, 19 June 1952; *The Times, et al*, 19 June 1952.
[19] *The Bulawayo Chronicle*, 23 June 1952.

the partially educated Africans could not be ignored because, historically, it had been the "noisy boys" who had begun the great British trade union movement. Then, characteristically, Huggins succumbed to the temptation to be provocative and stated that out of this movement had grown the socialist governments which were wrecking Britain.[20] His further remark, that some members of the Labour Party took orders from Moscow, was no doubt gleefully received by his audience but antagonised the very men, the pro-federal elements of that Party, whom Welensky was carefully cultivating.[21]

Huggins asked Rhodesians to ignore their unctuous critics in Britain. He revealed that the Southern Rhodesian delegates at the recent Conference had rejected the nomination of any of the Southern Rhodesian federal representatives in the first parliament because they were wedded to the principle of the common roll. He clearly hoped that the federal assembly would adopt the common roll because he warned the Africans that if they misused this opportunity and did not co-operate, his descendants would disenfranchise them.

Huggins specified that the Secretary of State for Commonwealth Relations would be responsible for federal affairs. Land rights had been guaranteed but this only meant that Southern Rhodesia's policy would still be exclusively its affair. He explained "delegation" and other details and alleged that the statement in the preamble, that the territories were the rightful home of all their inhabitants, dashed the hopes of the African nationalists for domination. Africa, he maintained, stood at the crossroads with African nationalism rampant in West Africa while in the northern territories the Europeans sought more control of their destiny. Partnership offered the solution, and if federation succeeded in demonstrating this, it would offer hope for the rest of the continent. He concluded by commending federation and by claiming to have reminded the British of the consequences of the American precedent of making federation a party issue.

The debate which followed occupied two further sessions, as every MP chose to speak, and was privately described by Huggins as "a mass display of ignorance".[22] Nevertheless, Huggins was rewarded by 20 of the 28 MPs receiving the White Paper with enthusiasm — albeit in varying degrees. However, almost to a man, they demanded further adjustment to the African affairs board because they knew that, as it stood, it would be rejected by the electorate. Dendy Young gained much support for his constructive criticism of this proposal. He found that almost any law could be construed as "differentiating". He thought that it was necessary to prevent outside interference by ensuring that the members of the board were local residents and suggested that their objection to legislation should be passed to the federal high court, with a final appeal to the Secretary of State for consideration and resolution.

[20] SR *Debates* (Salisbury), Vol. 33, Part 2, Col. 2621 f., 23 June 1952; NAZ, Hist. MSS, UN 1/1/5, A. F. Hopkinson to J. H. Wallace, 24 June 1952; Welensky Papers, 34/12, f. 363, Welensky to S. H. Veats, 25 June 1952; 5/48, f. 74, Welensky to L. van der Post, 28 June 1952; WE 7, P/C/158/52/S, Salisbury to Welensky, 8 July 1952.

[21] House of Commons *Hansard* (London), Vol. 504, Col. 774 f., 24 July 1952.

[22] Welensky Papers, 39/113, f. 56, Huggins to Welensky, 29 June 1952.

J. M. Greenfield took this further and maintained that the high court should replace the African affairs board as there were sufficient "watch-dogs" for African interests in the persons of the African representatives. Moreover, if the board failed, it would provide an argument for its elimination. W. H. Eastwood alone believed that the board should be accepted as it stood, but only because it was unlikely ever to be used. Whitehead agreed but thought that it could be improved.

R. S. G. Todd declared it was imperative that the common roll principle be preserved as a means of avoiding racial representation which would inevitably lead to racial conflict. He and others diagnosed the actions of Nkomo and Savanhu since the Conference as merely manoeuvres to gain concessions. Furthermore, it was the general opinion of the House that, as the African *en masse* would not have any worthwhile opinion on the issue and seemed to prefer to be led, federation should be imposed if the Europeans accepted it.

Those who rejected the White Paper were not as cohesive in their aims. One MP wanted amalgamation, while others sought unification with the Northern Rhodesian "Railway Belt". Fears were expressed for the European and it was believed that amalgamation could yet be forced through. I. D. Smith, of the Rhodesia Party and future prime minister, favoured federation but thought the White Paper should be cast aside and fresh negotiations initiated. Stockil and the remainder of the Rhodesia Party preferred that Southern Rhodesia should pursue its own destiny.

Replying to Huggins, Stockil agreed that federation would have an Africa-wide effect and, if it succeeded in braking the spread of the "Gold Coast" policy, it would serve everyone. However, the counter effect was possible. He doubted, in fact, that a federation with two protectorates could be viable, warning that the copper price could drop, leaving the Southern Rhodesian taxpayer to bear the federal burden when federal government was by nature expensive. Unlike R. F. Halsted of the United Party, who wondered whether there would be any economic advantages, Stockil thought there would be in the long term but doubted that his son would be present to enjoy them. Southern Rhodesia was proposing to sacrifice her self-governing status, and would be so stripped of power as to be imperilled if a Fabian government were returned in Britain. In the federal assembly, Stockil concluded, Southern Rhodesia would be under-represented and there was nothing to prevent all its representatives being Africans, a position which could not be reversed because the African affairs board would intervene. Smith concurred and made this last point his reason for demanding a revision.

When Huggins summed up, on 27 June, he did not spare his critics, berating them for failing to understand that the negotiations were continuing, that the White Paper was not final. Dealing with the points raised and Stockil's arguments in particular, he said that, in view of the constant changes of Secretaries of State, it had been necessary to use the device of the preamble to state certain fundamentals. One of these was that Southern Rhodesia would be self-governing, which "torpedoed" most of Stockil's arguments. Huggins confessed that he had never been over-enthusiastic about closer association but had been converted when he became aware that Rhodesia was being squeezed between the forces of African and Afrikaner nationalism. The

Opposition, however, had misled the public into believing that the United Party had made dominion status an immediate objective instead of an ultimate goal. Federation made inter-racial advancement possible and could lead to a "United Africa". Huggins said that Southern Rhodesia was not alone in surrending powers and, in any case, he had hoped for an even more powerful central government. His years of experience of working under the Southern Rhodesian reservations had led him to believe that there would be little difficulty with the federal constitution as any competent prime minister could prevent "blow-ups". He maintained that, criticising, Stockil had ignored the limitations imposed on the African affairs board itself because it could not initiate legislation and its chairman would not be a minister.

It pleased Huggins that the *Manchester Guardian* had been forced to admit ruefully that the board would be effective, which it could be, with one amendment on which he did not elaborate. He still thought, however, that it was a "frightful" waste of men and money but it was a concession to the British who were relinquishing so much. He liked Dendy Young's suggested amendment and thought it would be acceptable to the other Governments. It would prevent the African affairs board being facetious. The safeguards were not indicative of mistrust of Southern Rhodesia but were the consequence of the federal government being new and unknown. It was an unprecedented compliment, in fact, for so small a community to be entrusted with the care of six million Africans. He was sure the British would not be disappointed.

Dismissing Stockil's claims that Africans could dominate the federal assembly, Huggins reiterated that it would devise its own franchise and that thereafter a two-thirds majority would be required to change it. In time Africans would gain more seats but by then the assembly would have been enlarged and might have acquired a second chamber. It was a pity, Huggins claimed, that the Colonial Office had made the mistake of introducing separate racial representation in the northern territories, but it was an even greater pity that Stockil and his ilk had not waited until they had seen the White Paper before raising alarm. Nevertheless, Southern Rhodesia would retain her common roll thereby facilitating the development of mutli-racial politics. It was pertinent to warn again on complacency about race relations as the Europeans in India and Indonesia had learned to their cost. Huggins was determined to ensure that the civil services would be locally based and concluded by saying: "The scheme in front of us now is for the emancipation of Northern Rhodesia and Nyasaland and the preservation of Southern Rhodesia."[23]

In Nyasaland, where the European remained reluctant to make a public stand on federation because of African opposition, the White Paper was not discussed in the Legislative Council until December. The Government, however, published and distributed a summary of the White Paper in the vernacular. A Press survey discovered, nonetheless, that the White Paper was welcomed by all the Europeans and rejected by the Asians and Africans. The mass of the population seemed content with the current method of administration and could not see any advantage in change. The few thousand intelli-

[23] SR *Debates* (Salisbury), Vol. 33, Part 2, Col. 2939 f., 27 June 1952.

gentsia favoured the tactic of rejection in the hope that they would instead be granted "Gold Coast" style self-government.[24]

Although Welensky gained almost unanimous support at meetings immediately after the publication of the White Paper, he reported to his correspondents that it had been given a mixed reception in Northern Rhodesia. He was confident, however, of carrying the day. The situation in Southern Rhodesia worried him more but the public response to Huggins's speeches soon eased his anxiety.[25] There were also encouraging strains within the African ranks.[26] When G. M. Lewanika and Safeli Chileshi publicly proposed a conference between Africans and Europeans in Northern Rhodesia, they provoked a call, at an ANC meeting in Lusaka in early July, for Lewanika's expulsion for failing to toe the ANC's line.[27] Welensky was made aware of the ANC's current methods when Northern Rhodesian security officials warned him, as he revealed to J. H. Wallace, that "the African Congress have decided to liquidate me . . . it shows how politics have changed in this country".[28] Welensky was no stranger to acts and threats of personal violence. The *Ossewa Brandwag*, the pro-Nazi Afrikaner organisation, had loosened the nuts of one of the wheels of his car during the war but the wheel had come off at low speed and Welensky had escaped injury. The police now asked him to avoid being punctual in his daily travel to make ambush difficult.[29]

Nkumbula revealed the ANC attitude to the White Paper at a meeting in Lusaka on 26 June. He mixed half-truths with distortion. He explained that, as the intention of the recent Conference was not to discuss the concept but the plan itself, and, as the Africans were totally opposed to federation, the African delegates could not attend. The British Labour Party had demanded that the Conference should not be held without the Africans but the European and Conservative Party delegates had proceeded to produce a draft constitution which would realise their aims of domination and exploitation of the Africans. In saying this, Nkumbula proved Huggins to be correct in predicting that the provision in the preamble, making the federation the rightful home of all its inhabitants, bothered the African nationalists excessively. Nkumbula claimed that the architects of federation were Huggins, who was an Imperialist, and "Roy Welensky — a man of continental origin who is leading the feeble-minded British people in Northern Rhodesia". Therefore, Nkumbula claimed, Welensky had deliberately secured the provision in the preamble to create an opening for all "continentals". How did this tally, Nkumbula asked, with the British obligations to Africans? It surely belied the oft-stated claim that federation was necessary to stem the influx of Afrikaner nationalists.

[24] *The Rhodesia Herald*, 19 June 1952.

[25] *The Bulawayo Chronicle*, 21 June 1952; Welensky Papers, WE 7, P/C/158/52/W, Welensky to J. H. Wallace, 21 June 1952; 39/115, f. 118, Welensky to Lord Altrincham, 24 June 1952; f. 116, Welensky to G. Sayers, 27 June 1952.

[26] Welensky Papers, 39/119, f. 103, Mpangula to Welensky, 21 June 1952; 34/12, f. 357, Welensky to Huggins, 28 June 1952.

[27] *Central African Post*, 26 June 1952; *Bantu Mirror*, 5 July 1952; *African Weekly*, 9 July 1952.

[28] Welensky Papers, 5/48, f. 73, Welensky to Wallace, 28 June 1952.

[29] Author's interview with Sir Roy Welensky.

If federation was imposed, he warned, the six million Africans would make life impossible for the whites. He claimed that the northern legislatures would be stripped of power, that African land would be affected by matters on the federal and concurrent lists, that federal law would prevail, and that the territories could delegate their powers to the federal government — he did not say that this last ability was strictly limited. The federal assembly, he averred, would be dominated by whites who would use their ability to constitute a two-thirds majority without the African members to achieve their real aims of amalgamation or of securing dominion status. He doubted the efficacy of the African affairs board as a safeguard because its members, not being elected and responsible to the Africans, would be merely "stooges" of the governor-general and would only object to legislation when the latter agreed. The board could not consult African organisations or outside bodies, like the United Nations, without the governor-general's consent. In any case, the board would be thwarted and sabotaged by the federal assembly. Moreover, there had never been a progressive governor. The Africans would not have any method of appealing directly to the House of Commons. Thus, Nkumbula concluded, he had to "say the one thing I have always avoided . . . the best government for the Black people is government fully manned and run by the Black people of Africa. This is also true of any race . . . I do not accept Welensky's or Huggins's Governments. They are to me foreign and foreign they shall remain".[30]

The Legislative Council session in early July provided Welensky with an opportunity to debate the issue directly with Africans. However, he spoke first on more immediate matters such as the coal shortage and a recent railway strike. Indeed, when he mentioned his recent negotiations in Britain, he referred first to the question of the Northern Rhodesian Constitution in order that the public should not think that he had forgotten it. He told how Lyttelton had listened but wanted Africans to be present before he expressed an opinion. Nevertheless, Welensky had asked for the reduction of the membership of the Executive Council to eight — four official and three unofficial Members and a Member representing African interests — and for the introduction of the cabinet practice of the will of the majority prevailing, except when the Governor found it necessary to use his reserve powers. The Members, too, should be given the title of "Minister". He had asked for an increase in the unofficial representation in the Legislative Council to be matched by a decrease in the official membership. The current anomaly of a powerless majority would have to be changed.

When Welensky asked if it was intended that the African Representative Council should be a parallel legislature, on *apartheid* lines, or perhaps become a second chamber with a power of veto, R. P. Bush, the Secretary of Native Affairs, denied either intention. Yamba offered a solution in which the ARC would become unnecessary by reinforcing the two overworked African Members with eight new African Members representing the provinces and the urban areas. By this means the African would learn the practice as well as the

[30] Welensky Papers, 34/10, ff. 303–307, Nkumbula's Statement at an ANC Meeting, Lusaka, 26 June 1952; F. Macpherson, *Kenneth Kaunda of Zambia: The Times and the Man* (Lusaka, 1974), p. 112.

theory. Sokota added a demand that an African should be appointed to the Executive Council.

Welensky retorted that, since the war, African representation had been increased by 300 per cent while the more sophisticated Europeans had gained only 25 per cent. In any case, the limits of African knowledge of democracy and freedom of speech were well illustrated by the motions of no confidence in Lewanika and Chileshi passed at the recent ANC meeting for daring to suggest a conference with Europeans. Moreover, Welensky claimed, there had been attempts to prevent Africans from meeting him. The demand for parity, it seemed, was based on a fear of European intentions and Welensky resented it because the European had a proud record as a legislator for the African. The hand of friendship, he declared, was being spurned.[31]

Then on 3 July, Welensky recalled the history of closer association and reminded the House that the federal scheme in the White Paper was not final. He favoured the suggested concurrent list because it was a device to reduce federal power to a minimum to leave the daily life of the territories unaffected. He described how Northern Rhodesia had gained eight representatives for a European population of 41 000 when Southern Rhodesia with 160 000 Europeans had only 14. Federal representation was not a matter of counting heads, and Northern Rhodesia was making an important contribution to federation.

Examining other details, Welensky acknowledged that the African affairs board was a peculiar instrument designed to answer African fears and that it was causing a great deal of "heartburn" in Southern Rhodesia where it was seen as a critical commentary of Government policy. It was right to have qualms about anyone being able to interfere with the actions of an elected parliament, but everyone was aware of how South Africa evaded its constitutional safeguards. Thus he, like Huggins, would not refuse half the loaf and would accept the board, perhaps with Dendy Young's amendment, because he was confident that, in time, Rhodesians would demonstrate their ability and earn a higher constitutional status.

Welensky found that the current railway congestion was an argument in itself for federation. Borrowing was crucial and, while he did not decry African demands for political advancement, he did criticise their call for the nationalisation of the copper mines because it frightened off the investor. It was important that everyone understood that the choice was stagnation or progress.

To the Europeans, who baulked at Southern Rhodesia's seemingly insolvent state, Welensky said that the Southern Rhodesian national debt of £111 000 000 was nothing to be ashamed of because it represented an investment in railways, electricity, steel, land banks, buildings, housing, cold storage, communications and heavy plant. Furthermore, Southern Rhodesia bore a greater share of the common defence burden. He wished that Northern Rhodesia had as good hospitals or roads. Northern Rhodesia, with its external trade of £100 000 000, its £8 000 000 reserve and its small public debt of £13 400 000, was prosperous but had not always been so. He knew that, in

[31] NR *Debates* (Lusaka), Col. 45, 1 July 1952.

turn, the Southern Rhodesians feared that Northern Rhodesia would fall to black domination. He was determined that it would not. White domination was equally undesirable because it would have to be maintained by force. Federation, he was sure, was the way to ensure political and economic stability.

Welensky also dwelt on current white apprehensions about having to face social equality with other races, and even miscegenation. He had experienced inter-racial friendships and had never found his dignity had been lowered and, in any case, the whole matter was governed by economic standing. Miscegenation was a matter for social attitude and not legislation. Under the federal scheme, the African could aspire to capture white seats but would have to learn democratic ways and, in the federal parliament, would have to join the parties, which would evolve, to have any influence. The European could not ignore the rising tide of African nationalism and would have to take the African with him, as a friend, but it was a fact of life that, in this partnership, there would be senior and junior partners for a long time ahead. While immigrants were required, if Northern Rhodesia was not to be coveted by the over-populated nations, African interests had to be protected. It was tragic that the antagonists of federation chose to ignore the attempts of the communists to exploit African nationalism, just as it was to be regretted that racial politics had recently appeared, because politics had to be based on economic considerations to ensure peace and prosperity. He felt that race relations, however, were still good and thus a system which recognised the aspirations of both races had to be found. It was interesting to find that the communists combined with fascists and nationalists to resist federation.

The unofficial Members echoed Welensky's words, while the officials wondered what further reassurance could be given to the Africans. Unsworth, however, ruled that Dendy Young's amendment was impracticable because not all the issues before the African affairs board would be questions of legality. E. G. Nightingale favoured a "moderate form" of federation but was perturbed that the uneasiness engendered by the 1949 Victoria Falls Conference had never been allowed to subside. He felt that Lyttelton had not assisted by failing to confirm the partnership declaration of the 1951 Victoria Falls Conference. However, the federal scheme carefully defended African interests, and the African affairs board, in particular, was a very adequate safeguard. There were matters of concern, such as the future of the northern employment of Africans in posts which in Southern Rhodesia were filled by Europeans, but the greatest obstacle in the federal path, Nightingale maintained, was that at heart the Southern Rhodesians remained amalgamationists. As Southern Rhodesia was unlikely to join South Africa, where nationalism was rampant, there seemed no urgency to Nightingale, and thus patience could be exercised with the African population. Even though the African mass could not absorb the details of the White Paper, its opposition could not just be ignored. The future would be most unhappy if federation were imposed.

Moffat agreed that it was unwise to hurry, but felt that no permanent damage would be done if federation was forced through so long as it was wisely administered thereafter. He recognised that such action would provide ammunition for the Africans who were already preaching racialism, but reassured the Africans that the officials at the Conference had taken great pains to protect their interests. The White Paper had successfully combined the protection of African interests with the desire to federate. Yet the scheme was not perfect, and at the next conference he would ensure that the power of the territories to delegate anything to the federal government would be strictly limited to prevent Southern Rhodesia ridding itself of expensive services. (This was a curious demand from a delegate to the Conference because precisely that limitation had already been placed.) Moffat also felt that the federal assembly should not be able to amend its constitution without territorial sanction, and that he would insist that every such amendment should first secure the support of two-thirds, or at least a bare majority, of each territorial legislature. To allay some of the Africans' suspicions, Moffat proposed to arrange a meeting with prominent Africans and asked if Welensky and the Chief Secretary would attend. Both agreed.

Yamba and Sokota confirmed the solidarity of African opinion on federation, citing the sums raised throughout the country to send the ANC representatives to Britain to voice their opposition. Sokota decried the current European effort to divide Africans by sending amongst them African agents from Southern Rhodesia. These agents bore circulars for the Chiefs to sign, but fortunately most of the Chiefs could not understand English. In familiar vein, Sokota spoke of African fears of amalgamation with all its ramifications for chiefly status and the possession of land. The Africans wanted to secure the vote and retain their protected status, but it seemed that the European wished to establish himself in power before they advanced. Furthermore, the Colonial Office policy of leading Northern Rhodesia to self-government within the Commonwealth would be displaced by federation before the African was capable of protecting himself. The whites would use their two-thirds majority in the federal assembly to exclude the Colonial Office by securing dominion status. Sokota and Yamba demanded that Britain reject federation and adhere to the commitment of 1931 to the paramountcy of African interests.

These comments provoked the Chief Secretary, A. T. Williams, to remind the House that, since the statement in the Commons on 22 September 1948 by Creech Jones, partnership and not paramountcy had been official policy. Welensky was undoubtedly grateful, but did not spare the Government for its failings in his wide-ranging reply. The task of persuading the innately conservative Africans, Welensky maintained, would have been immeasurably easier if the Government had declared at the outset that federation was a good idea. He criticised the Church of Scotland for intervening before it understood the facts. It would have been better if Nightingale had left many of his comments unsaid as they were inaccurate and negative. Lyttelton, for example, had certainly pronounced on partnership, and it should not be presumed that the federal government would adopt Southern Rhodesian practices when employing Africans, because the proposed civil service preparatory commission was bound to preserve existing opportunities and, moreover, the African affairs board would intervene. There had been little difficulty in 1948, when the population was much smaller, in finding men to serve the enlarged Legislative Council, and a large British state would be a powerful draw in the recruitment of civil servants. Sokota had spoken of the Europeans' possession of more than two-thirds of the federal seats without mentioning the safeguards which were designed to prevent its abuse. Welensky asked Moffat what the point was of further hobbling the federal assembly when these safeguards appeared adequate. A powerless legislature was useless, and it was surely a negation of democracy to elect federal representatives only to make them dependant upon the sanction of the territorial legislatures. He reminded Moffat that the power to delegate was already specifically limited, and stated that, moreover, the federal assembly had no obligation to accept a delegation of power.

Welensky reminded Yamba, as he had asked why he was denied hotel facilities, that the African, unlike the European, did not pay income tax, yet possessed 97 per cent of the land and could become a voter even though he was specially represented in the legislature and had a government specifically charged to protect him. Moreover, the European was still waiting to discuss partnership. The African aspired to parity of representation, yet demanded the paramountcy of African interests and protection in the same breath. The African needed to learn the basics of democracy and, more specifically, the difference in the roles of the representative and the delegate. It was particularly annoying for Welensky to be continually thwarted in his efforts to speak to Africans. Were the African leaders, Welensky asked, afraid that he could dispel the fears of the normal, reasonable African? Nevertheless, he did have the names of leading Africans, including two Chiefs, who were willing to support federation. However, he would not reveal any names, despite pressure from Yamba, particularly that of an African who had complained to him that Yamba had failed to explain the White Paper at a meeting specifically called for that purpose. Yamba retorted that he had not done so because he had only read the White Paper once and did not want to mislead his audience.

Welensky alleged that the fears of amalgamation, of Huggins's intentions, of Southern Rhodesia's policies and attitudes, and of Northern Rhodesia's constitutional future had been answered *ad nauseam*. There was no question of the European minority in Northern Rhodesia imposing its will because Britain was the trustee. However, if offered a choice of racial dominance, the European would see that it would be his. Welensky reviewed the debate on federation in the Lords, which had ended on the previous day, noting in particular that Lord Salisbury had spoken in favour of federation. In general, Welensky found, there had been wide differences in the Lords' opinions. He was confident that delay would only hurt the prospects of federation because Southern Rhodesia could not be expected to continue for much longer to put the interests of the Northern Rhodesian copper industry first, yet deny coal to its manufacturers. If African interests were adequately protected, federation should be imposed in order to provide an opportunity for the European to use his peculiar talents for the benefit of all. The choice otherwise was black or white domination.[32]

Welensky ignored the argument of Lord Ogmore and John Dugdale, in the Commons on 25 June, that the British Parliament was the final authority and

[32] *Ibid.*, Col. 148 f., 3 July 1952.

had an ancient historic right to amend as well as to accept or reject the final constitution. They claimed that to act otherwise would be a denial of democracy. Lyttelton, however, would not allow Parliament to interfere with the final product of the four Governments after they had signified their acceptance. Parliament would be merely asked to pass an enabling bill to permit an order in council to be laid before the Queen. However, Lyttelton did promise Dugdale a further debate before the Governments accepted the final formula.[33]

Welensky had, in fact, had an influence on the Lords debate because the London Committee of the UCAA had briefed some of the speakers.[34] The Committee, with mixed success, had sought the patronage of prominent persons of the calibre of Lords Tedder, Rennell of Rodd, Brabazon of Tara, Tweedsmuir, and Altrincham, Lady Baden-Powell, Leopold Amery and Lionel Curtis. J. W. Wallace and other committee members wrote to the Press, answering such critics as Michael Scott and Creech Jones. They briefed Professor Macmillan, employed a firm which specialised in political promotion, set up regional committees in England and Wales, and attempted to do so in South West Scotland. They sought to influence the Churches and the Press by seeking out prominent members and editors, and continued the public debate with Banda and others.[35]

Considerable ire was aroused in the federal camp when David Stirling's privately circulated memorandum, "The Central African Federation and the Capricorn Declarations", fell into the hands of the London *Daily Worker* which claimed to have discovered thereby a capitalist plot. Though the British Press ignored this revelation, Welensky, with Blundell and Havelock of Kenya following suit, withdrew his signature on 2 August from the Declarations. Stirling explained to Welensky that what had happened had been risked by Huggins when he agreed to the limited circulation. Stirling hoped that Welensky would be pleased with his efforts in getting the rest of the British Press to ignore the *Daily Worker*, and with his own announcement that the Declarations would be published with the signatures of the members of the Capricorn Africa Society and their African supporters only. However, Stirling was aggrieved to discover from Huggins that the early publication of the Declarations was likely to harm the federal cause. His followers were equally discouraged to hear this, for they had invested much effort and £1 000 in the federal campaign, seeking in particular to influence the British Labour Party. They found it difficult to reconcile Welensky's unfriendly attitude with their steady support.[36]

When the Commons debated the White Paper on 24 July, Gordon Walker

[33] House of Commons *Hansard* (London), Vol. 502, Col. 182, Written Answer, 25 June 1952; House of Lords *Hansard* (London), Vol. 177, Col. 590 f., 7 June 1952.

[34] Welensky Papers, 39/84, f. 77, Minutes of 10th Meeting, London Committee, UCAA, 20 June 1952; f. 71, Minutes of 11th Meeting, London Committee, UCAA, 27 June 1952.

[35] *Ibid.*, WE 7, P/C/158/52/J, Joelson to Welensky, 20 June 1952; P/C/158/52/W, Wallace to Welensky, 25, 27 & 30 June & 10 July 1952; 5/45, f. 256, Wallace to Welensky, 15 July 1952; *The Times*, 3 & 11 July 1952.

[36] *Daily Worker*, 18 July 1952; Welensky Papers, WE 7, P/C/161/52, Welensky to Stirling, 2 August 1952; 5/48, f. 63, Stirling to Welensky, 19 August 1952.

claimed that the fundamental problem was that of colour. Just as it had fallen to Britain to solve the problem of nationalism in India and West Africa, so had she to resolve this one. He did not under-estimate the difficulties, but had always favoured federation as a means to achieve a genuine partnership. It would develop Central Africa economically, make higher education possible, and assist Britain in ridding herself of her "dollar dependence". It would prevent Southern Rhodesia being drawn into South Africa against the wishes of the Africans. Nevertheless, he was not entirely happy with the current proposals, and wondered what constructive role the African affairs board could play when it was excluded from the executive field. Furthermore, the governor-general could ignore it, despite elaborate procedures, and not just in emergencies. The only possible assumption was that the members of the board, though appointees of the territorial Governors, might be expected to be frivolous. The question of constitutional amendment presented a dilemma, for there had to be the greatest protection against undesirable change, and yet provision had to be made for African advancement, and in this Britain had to retain the initiative. African advancement in the northern territories was assured by the retention of protected status, but parallel progress in the federal field was not assured because the Europeans would have a two-thirds majority in the assembly.

Thus Gordon Walker proposed that there should be a review of the constitution after five but before ten years had elapsed. Furthermore, as in the United States of America, the territories should control the federal franchise. This could happen in the existing scheme in Nyasaland, as the Governor there could postpone indefinitely his relinquishment of power in this matter, but Northern and Southern Rhodesia, however, should have a similar opportunity.

Gordon Walker was critical of Government failings on the partnership discussions in Northern Rhodesia and in giving the impression of urgency by advancing the mid-year federal Conference to April. The objective was to federate with consent, and a further effort should be made to secure African support. He declared that Lyttelton should postpone the October Conference and tour Central Africa.

Lyttelton replied that Hopkinson would tour the territories in August, and announced that the next conference was indeed being postponed to January 1953 to accommodate the commitments of the British Ministers and Huggins. This postponement was welcome, too, because it allowed time for careful study of the reports of the three commissions. After Griffiths had interjected, Lyttelton ridiculed any accusation of undue haste when, in fact, the final conference would be held seven months after the date prescribed by the previous Labour administration. Moreover, defending his actions, he maintained that it was better to attempt to assess opinion on something definite although it would be a fruitless task even in Britain despite universal suffrage and literacy. He was not, therefore, surprised by reports of mass disinterest from the officials who were explaining the proposals.

Under fire from Mrs Eirene White, Lyttelton declared that the district officers were doing no more than their normal duty in explaining Government intentions. If they stressed the advantages, it was because the Government favoured federation. They had found that Africans preferred to be told which choice to make and, though the representative institutions were opposed, there was evidence that there were Africans who favoured federation. However, these Africans were afraid to proclaim public support, and it was clear that the northern African Congresses had been attempting to prevent even the examination of the White Paper. To substantiate this, Lyttelton read a telegram from the Governor of Nyasaland which described African fears and the widespread intimidation. However, the Nyasaland African Congress had recently been asking Africans to study the proposals. It seemed to Lyttelton, from the evidence, that much of the phraseology of African resistance emanated from Britain. When Dugdale asked if the Government was committed to federation, Lyttelton replied that there had been repeated reassurances that the matter was still under consideration.

Lyttelton insisted that the African affairs board had been improved. It would, he acknowledged, affect legislation in its "adolescence" rather than its "infancy", but it had been given the role of the minister for African interests to draw attention to African considerations in legislative and executive policy. The nature of the appointment of the minister, as the Fabian pamphlet of September 1951 had pointed out, would have destroyed the principle of collective responsibility. The membership of the board had been reduced to six, but the African membership of three had been kept constant, and the chairman was charged to use his casting vote to keep discussion open. It was true that the governor-general would use his discretion if the government and the board were deadlocked, but Gordon Walker had omitted to say that the governor-general's action could be disallowed by the Secretary of State. There would, Lyttelton maintained, have to be overwhelming reasons for the governor-general to use this power. The ability of the African affairs board to object to constitutional amendments strengthened the safeguards. It was regrettable that the process of constitutional amendment had to be so difficult because change would be necessary with the development of partnership. In conclusion, Lyttelton noted the inconsistency of African demands for both protection and advancement, repeated that decisions would be taken later, and re-affirmed that partnership, and not European dominance, was the governing principle.

Hopkinson, who seemed to have no illusions about his task, promised to test opinion. He would, however, indicate to the northern territories that the British Government wanted them to federate. Federation, he felt, could herald in a new era in Central Africa. Other Conservatives thought that if Gordon Walker wanted a constitutional review within ten years, he must favour federation. However, they thought that such a provision would only produce instability in the new state. They concluded that the safeguards were little changed since they were proposed by the Labour Government, but would be strengthened by Dendy Young's amendment.

T. Reid and W. Coldrick, federation's Labour supporters, remained steadfastly loyal even though they expressed their annoyance at the comments of Huggins. The Liberal leader, Clement Davies, by contrast, made use of Southern Rhodesian statements in his criticism of the effort to federate. He noted Greenfield's remarks that the African affairs board was an unnecessary safeguard and that there would never be a black majority in the federal assembly. Davies welcomed a further debate, questioned the need to hurry, and urged that federation should not be imposed on an unwilling mass. Immediate steps should be taken, he felt, to eradicate humiliating discrimination.

Mrs White agreed there was unnecessary haste. She was sure, too, that the safeguards could be rendered useless by the European majority in the federal assembly threatening to resign. Griffiths welcomed the conference's postponement and the further debate. He agreed that African consent, and the ability of the safeguards to ensure political and social advance, was fundamental. Just as important, was the retention of adequate power to carry out British responsibilities. The reasons for not having a minister for African interests were understandable, but the South African experience of safeguards should not be forgotten. Furthermore, Lord Hailey had recently declared that African interests were more likely to be affected by administrative and executive action than by legislation. Griffiths said that the removal of the minister left the Secretary of State without anyone on whom he could rely in the federal cabinet. His replacement, the chairman of the African affairs board, would be outside political life and unable to veto cabinet action. The African would have only nine members in the assembly, and would be denied the services of the Secretaries of Native Affairs on the board although they were allowed to sit in the territorial Legislative Councils. In addition, legislation could be detrimental to the African without being "differential".

Lyttelton interjected that, nevertheless, Lord Hailey had said that the safeguards had been made stronger. Griffiths replied that he disagreed with Hailey on this, and noted that the federal assembly was empowered to set up a second chamber, and that there was no provision for change except at the whim of the elected European members. The Secretary of State could ensure political advancement in the protectorates, but had no influence in this direction at federal level. Griffiths noted that Huggins had confirmed that the European would control the allocation of seats to Africans and would only increase their numbers when there was a bigger parliament. The European should understand that the African would advance. Thus colour discrimination should be terminated and discussion on partnership begun. Griffiths would not commend the proposals as they stood.[37]

[37] House of Commons *Hansard* (London), Vol. 504, Col. 774 f., 24 July 1952.

CHAPTER ELEVEN

The Continuing Campaign

Sustained Efforts to sell Federation, and the Reports of the Preparatory Commissions, July–December 1952

THE postponement of the final federal Conference would, in the event, be justified because the Fiscal Commission was not ready to report until late October. The delay, however, would present opportunities for exploitation by the opposition and would occasion some anxious moments for the proponents of federation.

Huggins had already announced in early July that the referendum could not be held until 23 March 1953,[1] and consequently Welensky was already planning a reduction in the tempo of the federal campaign when Lyttelton postponed the Conference. Nevertheless Welensky continued to speak in public in both the Rhodesias. He also planned a Press campaign which included an effort to influence the Afrikaner community through Martin Visagie, a former elected Member for Nkana and a prominent trade unionist, who joined G. F. M. van Eeden in writing in support of federation in the widely-read *Die Huisgenoot*.[2]

Welensky's criticism in the Legislative Council of the lack of African understanding of democracy provoked Nkumbula to explain that if he agreed to discuss federation with Europeans he would give the impression of weakening. Yet he was anxious not to appear unreasonable, and proposed to debate the idea of such a meeting — at which Attlee might be present during his forthcoming visit to Northern Rhodesia — when the ANC met on 21 August. In the meantime, he advised Africans to say nothing more on the subject.[3]

Ignoring Nkumbula's final remark, Welensky asked the Secretary for Native Affairs to convene a meeting with G. M. Lewanika and S. H. Chileshi,

[1] Welensky Papers, 39/113, f. 54, Huggins to Welensky, 2 July 1952; 5/45, f. 263, Welensky to J. H. Wallace, 16 July 1952.
[2] *Ibid.*, 5/45, f. 269, Welensky to C. D. Dryden, 11 July 1952; 5/95, f. 231, M. Visagie to Welensky, 17 June 1952; 5/53, ff. 24–25, G. van Eeden to Welensky, 5 July 1952.
[3] *Central African Post*, 10 July 1952.

both of whom the Bulawayo branch of the Northern Rhodesian ANC wanted banned for life and removed from the urban areas lest they do further harm.[4]

In Broken Hill, on 18 July, the Provincial Commissioner, J. Murray, held a meeting lasting two hours with the Africans who had refused to meet Welensky earlier in the month. Murray explained the White Paper and urged them to rescind their decision. Although he tried to dispel any impression of Welensky being illiberal, the majority refused to meet not only Welensky but H. L. d'A. Hopkinson, the Minister of State, and all members of the Colonial administration. The Africans at the meeting informed Murray that all negotiations should be with their leaders, Yamba and Nkumbula. They were, however, prepared to speak to Attlee. Murray thereupon warned them that Attlee, like other current British parliamentarians, would expect to hear a reasonable explanation for their opposition and not just a blunt "No". In reply, they reiterated the ANC slogan that unity was strength, and that Lewanika was a traitor. Murray concluded that they were beyond persuasion, and advised Welensky to pursue the matter no further. In accepting this advice, Welensky replied that he thought that Attlee — whose tour he was arranging — should meet only the representative bodies.[5]

In Southern Rhodesia, too, Huggins and his Cabinet had not been idle, with Huggins, Greenfield and Whitehead to the fore. They were reinforced by Eastwood and Welensky. In opposition, Stockil likewise aired his views, while L. J. W. Keller attacked Eastwood and worried the proponents of federation by raising fears that the existence of the white skilled worker was threatened by the implementation of partnership.[6]

Huggins scored against Stockil when, in late June, he strengthened the national executive of the United Central Africa Association which had been suffering from internal discord, resulting partly from friction between old established Rhodesians and new immigrants, many of whom were also members of the Capricorn Africa Society. He recruited a number of prominent men and women, including J. M. Caldicott (later Sir John, and a Federal Cabinet Minister), his Minister for Agriculture, Sir Ellis Robins of the British South Africa Company, Sir Harold Cartmel-Robinson, a former Northern Rhodesian Chief Secretary, and, perhaps of greater significance, T. P. M. Cochran, the chairman of Stockil's Rhodesia Party.[7]

At the Rhodesia Party congress on 18 July in Gwelo, Cochran advocated federation and the majority of the delegates concurred. He urged the Rhodesia Party not to deepen the impression that it opposed federation simply because Stockil did so in performing his duty as Leader of the Opposition. If the public continued to think this when voting in favour of federation at the referendum, the Rhodesia Party would be discredited. The rejection of

[4] Welensky Papers, 34/10, f. 332, G. M. Lewanika to R. P. Bush, (undated); f. 331, Bush to Lewanika, 17 July 1952; ff. 329–330, Welensky to Dr A. Scott, 18 July 1952; f. 322, Bush to Welensky, 19 July 1952; *Bantu Mirror*, 19 July 1952.

[5] Welensky Papers, 34/10, f. 327, J. Murray to Welensky, 19 July 1952; f. 326, Welensky to Murray, (undated).

[6] *The Rhodesia Herald*, 28 June & 1 July 1952; *The Bulawayo Chronicle*, 9 & 10 July 1952.

[7] Welensky Papers, 5/45, f. 274, C. D. Dryden to Welensky, 1 July 1952; f. 277, Dryden to R. M. Cleveland, 2 July 1952.

federation would be a pyrrhic victory because Southern Rhodesia could not stand alone (the majority of the congress demurred on this point) and would be drawn into the future Republic of South Africa. Cochran was anxious that the chance of federating should not be lost through Southern Rhodesia being inflexible. The Rhodesia Party, he thought, would find itself in an unholy alliance with the Left and the nationalists.

Stockil and Stumbles sought the re-opening of all-party negotiations with Huggins because the White Paper, being the British terms for federation, was unfit to be presented to the electorate at the referendum. They hoped for the revival of the plan devised with the Rhodesia Labour Party and the United Party in September 1951, because, if the current proposals were not significantly adjusted, they would have no other option than to oppose, making federation a party issue.[8]

On 29 July, Hopkinson embarked on his three-week journey through the territories during which he addressed more than 60 meetings. Simultaneously, Welensky went to Southern Rhodesia three times to reinforce the effort to sell federation. The main burden of the campaign continued to fall, obviously, on Huggins, his Cabinet and his supporters. One of them, A. E. Abrahamson, president of the Bulawayo Chamber of Commerce, in his enthusiasm, however, did little for the cause in Northern Rhodesia when he welcomed federation as an opportunity to spread the burden of the Southern Rhodesian National Debt.[9]

The United Party congress in early August gave Dendy Young another opportunity to air his misgivings. This time he sought reassurance that the final constitution could be amended, in time, to eliminate the African affairs board by enlarging the legislature so that the federation should not continue to be inferior in status to Southern Rhodesia. Huggins replied that the federation would not be inferior, and warned that the British would not allow anything more than an adjustment of the African affairs board. The existence of the board did not worry Huggins because it would, he predicted, have little to do as African policy was a territorial matter.[10]

This last fact had been decried by Sir Ernest Guest on 1 August, when he claimed that thereby a unique opportunity to formulate a common African policy was being lost — a chance to ensure inter-racial harmony and prosperity. The only alternative he saw was to merge Southern Rhodesia with the Northern Rhodesian "Railway Belt" to create the strong British bloc needed to replace South Africa when it became a republic. Stumbles added that the board was being used as a smoke-screen to obscure the under-representation of European interests in the federal assembly where, if one party gained 18 seats, the nine African representatives would hold the balance of power. By contrast, Huggins claimed that the African representatives would have to join the party system if they were to have any influence. Stumbles and Stockil again urged Southern Rhodesians to present their minimum terms for federating because they were likely to be accepted. Stockil said this on 14 August

[8] *The Bulawayo Chronicle*, 19 July 1952.
[9] *Ibid.*, 15 & 23 August 1952; *The Rhodesia Herald*, 29 July 1952; Welensky Papers, 5/95, f. 227, Welensky to Sir Stewart Gore-Browne, 31 July 1952; *Northern News*, 27 & 29 July 1952.
[10] *The Rhodesia Herald*, 5 August 1952.

even though an all-party meeting had just failed to find any common ground on federation. Huggins concluded that what Stockil feared was Africans in Parliament.[11]

African opposition was voiced by Nkomo on 24 July. The Africans, he stated, had sought to know what they would gain from federation and had found very little. The Africans were also very discontented with their current circumstances. The remedy was the abolition of all forms of discrimination to allow Africans to earn a place in society on merit. However, the Chief Native Commissioner, L. Powys-Jones, in his annual report issued at the end of July, claimed that the vast majority of the population would accept the lead of their native commissioners. Opposition, he claimed, was confined to a small, vocal group which was critical of what seemed to be repressive legislation which, in fact, was often for their protection. A larger body of opinion feared a general reduction of standards and wages to northern levels. The latter, Powys-Jones maintained, was, however, capable of being reassured and would accept federation, perhaps without enthusiasm.[12]

Welensky and Huggins concluded, by mid-August, that they were making good progress in Southern Rhodesia and that the report of the Fiscal Commission, which was bound to favour that territory, would cap their efforts and ensure success. Welensky was anxious, nevertheless, that something should be done to ensure that all voters were enrolled. He was also confident that there was no significant European opposition in the North, and his contacts with the Africans revealed some dissension in their ranks. Certainly, Africans were joining the Capricorn Africa Association, and Lewanika and others remained willing to meet Welensky. The Secretary for Native Affairs, however, took care to point out that inter-tribal tensions, particularly directed against the dominance of the Bemba, should not be misinterpreted as support.[13]

With regard to Nyasaland, Welensky and other federal proponents were concerned about the seeming lack of enthusiasm there, noting that the Legislative Council had not found the time in its mid-year session even to mention the White Paper. Indeed, a report was received in Salisbury which claimed that the officials (including the Governor) and the Europeans were lukewarm about federation because their territory was in such financial straits that it would have little to offer. Consequently, Welensky was under pressure from the United Central Africa Association to secure some positive response from the Nyasalanders.

This report, however, had revealed a general lethargy, for the African Congress was not being particularly successful in recruiting members despite

[11] *Ibid.*, 2, 8 & 15 August 1952; Welensky Papers, 5/53, ff. 13–14, Huggins to Welensky, 14 August 1952.

[12] *The Bulawayo Chronicle*, 25 & 31 July 1952.

[13] Welensky Papers, 39/113, f. 46, Welensky to Huggins, 17 August 1952; 5/45, f. 225, Welensky to H. Williams, 6 August 1952; f. 222, Welensky to Huggins, 8 August 1952; 5/53, ff. 13–14, Huggins to Welensky, 14 August 1952; WE 7, P/C/158/52/W, Welensky to J. H. Wallace, 9 August 1952; P/C/158/52, Minutes of 19th Meeting, London Committee, UCAA, 26 August 1952; 34/12, f. 274, Welensky to R. Reynolds, 13 August 1952; 34/10, f. 278, Welensky to R. P. Bush, 16 August 1952; f. 291, Bush to Welensky, 31 July 1952; f. 290, Welensky to Bush, 2 August 1952.

its lowering of its subscription from five shillings to three pence. The mildness of the opposition led to the conclusion in pro-federal ranks that there would be little reaction to the imposition of federation.[14]

Accordingly, on 2 August, Welensky wrote to Barrow and asked for the names of two prominent Nyasalanders to be elected as vice-presidents of the UCAA. He suggested, if possible, G. G. S. J. Hadlow and Barrow himself, and must have been surprised by Barrow's resentful reply. Barrow claimed that, in typical fashion, the Southern Rhodesians had neglected Nyasaland, had not kept the supporters there informed of the activities and intentions of the UCAA, and now, at the last minute, were trying to secure their affiliation. This was not strictly true, because it was not the first time that Nyasaland affiliation had been sought. On the other hand, though, the Salisbury committee of the UCAA had suffered of late from internal strife.

To compound this, Barrow complained that F. S. Joelson had incorrectly named him, in his *East Africa and Rhodesia*, as a vice-president of the UCAA. Thus Barrow felt that he would appear to be opposed to federation if he issued a correction. He favoured federation but believed he was the best judge of appropriate tactics, and knew that a further declaration of support from Hadlow and himself would only deepen African resentment while failing to influence the British Government because the European population was so small. This was why the Nyasaland unofficial Members had contented themselves with nothing more than a simple expression in favour of federation. Furthermore, the enthusiasm of the Nyasalanders had been dampened by the derogatory remarks of the Southern Rhodesians. However, Barrow promised to take a firmer line once the African opposition showed signs of weakening, and there were already indications that the Nyasaland Congress had overstated its case. The Nyasaland Government had not been entirely supine as its district officers had been explaining the White Paper and distributing pamphlets in the vernacular, including one written by the London Committee of the UCAA.[15] (Hopkinson, the Minister of State, would reinforce this effort.)

Welensky found that Hopkinson's visit "was an important . . . one. He has been bitterly attacked ever since because he had the courage to declare himself in favour of federation; the wisdom not to be hoodwinked or frightened; the shrewdness to discover for himself the content and the manner of African opposition; the statesmanship to reaffirm, every time he spoke to Africans, the strength of the safeguards . . . and the independence of mind to declare openly that Europeans had the right to remain in the country built up by their efforts and enterprise".[16]

It was certainly true that Hopkinson intended that no one should misunderstand him, and even before he left Britain he carefully defined his purpose to a public meeting on 21 July and three days later in the Commons.

[14] *Ibid.*, WE 7, P/C/158/52/G, Welensky to Y. Galitzine, 4 August 1952; *Northern News*, 27 July 1952; NAZ Hist. MSS, UN 1/1/1, R. Hood to Sir Harold Cartmel-Robinson, 25 July 1952.

[15] Welensky Papers, 5/45, f. 242, Welensky to M. P. Barrow, 2 August 1952; 17/41, ff. 29–30, Barrow to Welensky, 11 August 1952; WE 7, P/C/158/52/W, J. H. Wallace to A. F. Hopkinson, 28 July 1952; P/C/158/52, Minutes of 15th Meeting, London Committee, UCAA, 1 August 1952.

[16] Sir Roy Welensky, *Welensky's 4 000 Days* (London, 1964), p. 57.

His Government, he explained, in rejecting racial domination, was satisfied that federation was the only way to create a truly multi-racial society within a state which, unlike any of its constituent territories, could provide its rapidly growing population with political stability and advancement, and supply its material needs. He later told his Central African audiences that federation also offered a means of inducing change in South Africa through example. He promised to make his Government's view plain to the Africans when assessing their opinions. He would seek also to convince them of the adequacy of the proposed safeguards. He was aware of the African opposition but knew that much could be attributed to ignorance and misconception, and that the latter was, in part, a product of the fundamental error of the former Labour Government in insisting that the district officers remain neutral when explaining federation. Hopkinson, in the light of events, now considers this to have been a fatal error.[17]

Thus there should have been no surprise in the northern territories when he told his audiences that his Government totally supported the effort to federate and that the safeguards seemed perfectly adequate. Final decisions depended on the outcome of the Southern Rhodesian referendum and the debates in the British and territorial legislatures but he was confident that federation would be achieved. Indeed, in Mongu where he praised the Litunga, Mwanawina III, for telling the Barotse to eschew violence and strikes for political ends, Hopkinson stated that the federation would come into being in the latter half of 1953.[18]

Hopkinson impressed the Northern Rhodesians with his firm but patient manner as he listened to and answered the standard African questions. As he travelled he soon found evidence of intimidation in the villages. (In fact, the Nyasaland Government later furnished him with the names of Congress officials who were moving ahead of him.[19]) In Ndola, Hopkinson informed leading Africans that he was aware that intimidation was preventing people from expressing support for federation. The impression he gained on his travels was that most of the population had not even heard of federation (or feigned not to have) but, as he revealed in Broken Hill, would welcome it.[20]

Although the Northern Rhodesian ANC merely stated that it was tired of saying "No" to visiting ministers, Yamba attempted to enlighten Hopkinson on African opinion. He believed Hopkinson neglected the rural areas and behaved like Stanley Evans who had visited a few towns in 1951 and then had returned to Britain to claim that the African leaders represented less than five per cent of the population. Maintaining this was not true, Yamba drew on his knowledge of the Chiefs, councillors and "the humble", and claimed that the rural African rejected federation for the oft-stated reasons. He asserted that the pro-federal Africans had lied to Hopkinson, leading the latter to believe that there was some tacit support. Yamba added that African suspicions of Government intentions with regard to land and, more particularly, the grant-

[17] *The Times*, 19 July 1952; House of Commons *Hansard* (London), Vol. 504, Col. 804 f., 24 July 1952; Author's interview with Lord Colyton.
[18] *The Rhodesia Herald*, 1 August 1952; *The Bulawayo Chronicle*, 5 August 1952.
[19] Author's interview with Lord Colyton.
[20] *Northern News*, 9 August 1952; *The Bulawayo Chronicle*, 5 August 1952.

ing of dominion status to the new state to ensure white domination, had been aroused by the federal proposals. Hopkinson's statement that the British Government totally supported federation had only aggravated the situation. If federation was imposed, Yamba warned, the future would be bleak. The solution was to adopt the Tanganyikan racial parity proposals in Northern Rhodesia and Nyasaland.[21]

Hopkinson, nevertheless, before leaving Northern Rhodesia on 11 August 1952, stated that federation had many African supporters who were afraid to reveal themselves. He remained confident, too, that 90 per cent of the population knew nothing of federation. He had not heard any arguments which shook his belief in federation and found it had become, in fact, "the whipping boy" for matters unrelated to it. The African, emotionally disturbed by events in West Africa and elsewhere, was anxious to advance politically and economically and, in his frustration, rejected federation. He reassured the Africans that the safeguards, particularly the African affairs board, would be inviolate.[22]

Hopkinson then toured Nyasaland and, in Lilongwe, fell ill from bursitis. He recalls with amusement that there was a rumour that he was a victim of a witch-doctor.[23] He was ill enough to seek hospital treatment in Blantyre. He continued, however, to meet people including the Press from his bed. To answer African claims that Britain was obliged to transfer power to them, Hopkinson displayed at his meetings the original treaty signed on 15 August 1892.[24] This said no more than:

> "... Her Majesty and Her Government have learnt ... with much satisfaction of the friendly relations which exist between Jumbe and Mr. Johnston, the Representative of Her Majesty's Government in Nyasaland ... It is the wish of the Queen and Her Government that this state of things should continue, and that the Chiefs of Nyasaland may always be guided in peace and prosperity by the advice which they may receive from Her Majesty's Representative."

Consequently Philip Short maintains it was a telling enough blow for Banda to succumb "to blank impotent fury".[25]

In Blantyre on 18 August, Hopkinson, while stressing the urgent desirability of federation, acknowledged that there was considerable if misguided African opposition. He noted that the Congress failed to understand that there was no question of racial domination because any government had to represent all races. African opinion, not approval, was being sought because Britain, as trustee, would act as she thought fit. So seriously did Hopkinson view the incidence of political intimidation that he provided Attlee with a dossier on it when he arrived on the morrow.[26]

[21] Welensky Papers, 34/10, ff. 284–287, D. L. Yamba to H. L. d'A. Hopkinson, 8 August 1952.
[22] *The Rhodesia Herald*, 11 August 1952.
[23] Author's interview with Lord Colyton.
[24] D. Taylor, *The Rhodesian: The Life of Sir Roy Welensky* (London, 1955), p. 158.
[25] P. Short, *Banda* (London, 1974), p. 70.
[26] *The Rhodesia Herald*, 19 August 1952; *Northern News*, 21 August 1952.

Hopkinson reiterated these points in Salisbury on 26 August and in London three days later. In Salisbury, however, he tailored his speech to his audience, stressing the European's permanent place in the future state and dismissing any idea of Colonial Office influence on Southern Rhodesian affairs. He concluded that much of the opposition would fall away once federation was in being.[27]

His report led the British Cabinet to decide immediately before the final conference, to commit itself to federation.[28] A more immediate result was that Sir Geoffrey Colby, the Nyasaland Governor, bestirred himself to counter the intimidation and propaganda of the Congress. Urging the African Protectorate Council, on 28 August, to value free speech and lead its people responsibly, Colby questioned the logic of the Africans placing their entire trust in the British Government and rejecting federation when that Government recommended it. He warned that there was no prospect of African domination and claimed there was nothing in the Jumbe Treaty to suggest there ever had been. Nyasaland would be advanced constitutionally to a form of self-government in which all races would participate.[29]

Attlee, in turn, endured a crowded twelve days in the Rhodesias. His trip was marred by tragedy when Welensky's official private secretary, A. S. Campbell, assigned to assist Attlee, depressed it seems by personal financial problems, excused himself from the dinner table of the Provincial Commissioner in Fort Jameson, took a pistol from a drawer and killed himself.

It is a pity that Attlee saw fit only to record, in his autobiography that "I had not been in that part of Africa before and was glad to learn something of the problems from the people on the spot, for undoubtedly one of the gravest problems facing the world is the relationship between people of different colours residing in the same territory",[30] because he proved to be as forthright as, and perhaps less patient than, Hopkinson. In Lusaka Attlee brusquely interrupted a long-winded dissertation by a delegation of 13 Chiefs and Yamba and Sokota to ask if they would accept or reject federation. They chose rejection but their pronouncement that they would rather die than see federation imposed aroused little sympathy. In Kitwe Attlee rejected as erroneous a memorandum by the African Trades Union Congress, which criticised the federal proposals and the policy of choosing reactionary governors. He warned that it could invalidate all other African statements. At Livingstone he lectured Nkumbula on politics, telling him that there were no short cuts on the long road to political maturity.[31]

The northern Africans clearly thought that they would find Attlee more sympathetic to their cause than previous visitors with the exception, perhaps, of James Griffiths. The Ndola Urban Advisory Council thanked him for

[27] *The Rhodesia Herald*, 27 August 1952.
[28] Author's interview with Lord Colyton.
[29] NAZ Hist. MSS, UN 1/1/6, Address by the Governor, African Protectorate Council, Zomba, 28 August 1952.
[30] C. R. Attlee, *As it Happened* (London, 1954), pp. 215–216.
[31] *Northern News*, *Daily Express*, 21 August 1952; F. Macpherson, *Kenneth Kaunda of Zambia: The Times and the Man* (Lusaka, 1964), p. 112; *The Bulawayo Chronicle*, 23 August 1952; *The Rhodesia Herald*, 1 September 1952; Welensky, *4 000 Days*, *op. cit.*, p. 58.

coming to hear its "bitter" opposition to federation which it had constantly made known to the unsympathetic British and Northern Rhodesian Governments. It was anxious to prevent Attlee being deceived by a handful of Europeans who claimed to know how the African thought but never bothered to listen to him. It said that the Government was equally guilty of deception by arranging "beautiful tea-parties" for visitors at which the races pretended to mix, when, in reality, there was discrimination at every level. If the British Government indeed totally supported federation, it had broken its trust and, consequently, the African would be at "war" with it. There would be no peace, the Council warned, if federation were imposed.[32]

Nkumbula, as he had promised, held an ANC meeting in Lusaka from 21 to 24 August, at the beginning of Attlee's visit, warning that internal strife would continue until control passed into African hands. There was no intention of driving the Europeans out, he said, but they had to understand that "the country is ours". Nkumbula rejected the charge of intimidation because it was not part of his organisation's policy. This meeting was attended by a large number of Chiefs and was, he pointed out, the first time that the Chiefs and "commoners" had discussed federation together. The Chiefs were the legitimate rulers and they would have to accept or reject federation and Nkumbula avowed the ANC had no desire to intimidate them.

He was somewhat let down by his followers when one apparently dissenting chief, Chief Musokotwane, was assaulted after a session of this meeting. Nkumbula blamed the Capricorn Africa Society for spreading the lies about intimidation and claimed that the Government was attempting to overawe the population with a show of military force in all provinces by bringing in from Kenya 27 armoured cars, seven of which, supported by one Spitfire, had been sent to Fort Jameson. The Government responded immediately by acknowledging that six armoured cars had come from Kenya, but simply to participate in a display at a sports meeting. It added that there were no Spitfires in the territory.[33]

At the suggestion of the Fabian Colonial Bureau, and partly to placate European fears, Nkumbula proposed a four-stage plan to achieve self-government as an alternative to federation. The first step would be to give the Africans parity of representation with the Europeans, the African members being elected on a special voters' roll. The official members — some of whom would be Africans — would continue to represent Britain as the protector in the house and would hold the balance of power. The European unofficials would surrender their portfolios to Africans. The second stage would be a consequence of more Africans qualifying for the common roll and capturing European seats. The official members, however, would hold the balance of power. In the third stage, a bi-cameral parliament would be established, the lower house of which would initiate legislation and provide the cabinet, while the upper house possessed a veto. The lower house would be elected on a common roll open to all British citizens and British Protected Persons who earned more than £100 p.a. The existing provinces would become constituencies, each represented by two European, one Asian and five African

[32] Welensky Papers, 42/14, f. 18, Ndola Urban Advisory Council Memorandum, 24 August 1952.
[33] *Northern News*, 21 August 1952.

members. An additional constituency would be created to represent the Copperbelt and the larger towns. The upper chamber would have 20 African, ten European, and ten Asian and Coloured members. Ten of these African members would be elected by the Chiefs and the other ten by the African electorate. The other members would be elected by the European, Asian and Coloured voters. Nkumbula had not worked out the details of the final step, but promised a truly multi-racial democracy based on a common roll and no racial differentiation in either chamber.[34]

Attlee was invited to the ANC meeting. He declined (his itinerary was so full that it was impossible for him to accept) but he saw the delegation of Chiefs. Welensky also refused an invitation because of the imminence of his departure to Canada, and the presence of Attlee as his guest did not allow him the time.[35]

Attlee made it plain to all his audiences that, while he was seeking opinion, his Party was committed in principle to federation. It would not become a party issue. He understood that Central Africa, with its settled non-indigenous populations, was very different from West Africa and he sought a just solution for all races.

Attlee published his findings in the *Daily Herald* on 8 September, stating that the whites were justly proud of their achievements and the Africans, to their credit, acknowledged them even though they resented the discrimination. The African had much to learn before he could match European standards, skill and experience but a start had been made and the African had already been brought into local government in both the Rhodesias. He said there was a strong economic and political case for federation, and the creation of a strong bloc to preserve the British way of life was most desirable. However, he believed that the majority of Africans opposed federation and, indeed, only a handful were prepared to support it publicly. Nonetheless, most who opposed it did not understand what federation meant and were suspicious of all change. He knew, too, that some of the leaders were motivated by personal ambition and unrealistic dreams of black domination. It was interesting that fear of black domination accounted for much of the European opposition to federation. Attlee noted that recent South African Government actions had cast doubt on the value of any constitutional safeguard but he did not repeat here his comment on tour that the African affairs board might be strengthened. He described the advocates of federation as liberal, forward-looking men who saw partnership as the solution to the racial problem, albeit with the European as the senior partner for some time to come. Nevertheless, Attlee found that the British Government faced a dilemma because it was dangerous to impose federation, yet to abandon it at this stage could have disastrous results and would damage, in particular, race relations which he had found to be good.

Welensky was in Canada by the time Attlee returned to Britain, but his

[34] R. I. Rotberg, *The Rise of Nationalism in Central Africa: The Making of Malawi and Zambia, 1873–1964* (London, 1965), p. 246, fn. 75; *The Rhodesia Herald*, 26 August 1952.

[35] Welensky Papers, 34/10, f. 274, General-Secretary, Lusaka branch of the ANC, to Welensky, 19 August 1952; f. 273, G. Beckett to the General-Secretary, Lusaka branch of the ANC, 21 August 1952.

decision to invite the Labour leader seemed to the unofficial Members to have been vindicated by his "no nonsense" attitude. Attlee also earned laurels from the British Press for his objective search for the truth, and his personal victory in a "lion's den" of conservatism (European Rhodesia) where Churchill was held in total affection.[36]

Attlee, however, had not committed himself to support federation and thus Welensky took care to meet him in London when returning from Canada. At their meeting on 26 September, Attlee dwelt on the British dilemma, arguing that the imposition of federation could adversely affect Britain's standing *vis à vis* the world's non-white population and could set a precedent for the South Africans to demand the incorporation of the High Commission Territories (Bechuanaland, Basutoland and Swaziland) into the Union. Yet he feared violent consequences if the federal effort were abandoned. He would not make any personal commitment until he had discussed the matter with his Party. Sketching for Welensky his impressions, Attlee believed the Europeans on the Copperbelt were only really interested in their high incomes, and the African trade unionists there were more preoccupied with politics than with unionism. The northern African at large seemed to him backward in comparison with his Southern Rhodesian counterpart. Welensky concluded that Attlee was an honest man in a difficult position and was anxious that the pro-federal elements of the Labour Party should gain his ear rather than Griffiths's who, Welensky suspected, believed "that every African was a Welsh miner with a black skin".[37]

The London Committee of the UCAA had been developing its contacts within the Labour Party with considerable help from David Stirling. It secured, in particular, the assistance of Gordon Walker who, by mid-August, indicated that he had won the outright allegiance of 20 MPs to federation, and the support of 100 others even though the Party generally discouraged such discussion within its ranks.[38] Nevertheless, Gordon Walker, T. Reid, S. N. Evans and the others were powerless to prevent a reverse of fortune at the Labour Party Conference at Morecambe on 1 October when, after Griffiths had depicted 1953 as a year of crisis, a five-point resolution was passed to the National Executive without a vote. This embraced the whole Southern African question, proclaiming that the High Commission Territories should not be incorporated in the Union of South Africa unless it was the wish — democratically expressed — of their African populations. Likewise, federation should not be imposed without the consent of the Rhodesian and Nyasaland Africans. To assist all these territories, as well as the Rhodesias, towards self-government, constitutions modelled on the Gold Coast should be rapidly and progressively introduced. The segregation policy of South Africa was condemned and the British Government was urged to initiate discussion thereon in the Assembly of the United Nations. The smearing of the federal issue with the odium of South African affairs angered Welensky at

[36] *Ibid.*, 39/115, f. 69, Beckett to Welensky, 2 September 1952; *Daily Mail*, 2 September 1952; *Daily Herald*, 1 September 1952.

[37] Welensky Papers, 39/115, ff. 67–68, Welensky to Lord Salisbury, 26 September 1952.

[38] *Ibid.*, WE 7, P/C/158/52/G, Y. Galitzine to Welensky, 6 August 1952; 39/84, f. 47, Minutes of 17th Meeting, London Committee, UCAA, 15 August 1952.

a moment when he was most concerned at the ground being lost in Britain and Southern Rhodesia.[39]

As the London Committee of the UCAA, despite its unflagging energy, seemed to face an uphill battle because the opposition had gained an ascendancy in the Press, the chance to be in London twice within a month was most welcome to Welensky. He met the Press on his way to Canada, and was favourably received. Yet he refused to debate the federal issue on radio with Professor Arthur Lewis on the grounds that Lewis was a West Indian and would know nothing of Central Africa. However, Welensky submitted to a televised confrontation with journalists — including Colin Legum, of the *Observer*, and Peter Abrahams, a South African Coloured author and free-lance reporter. Again Welensky gave a good account of himself. He spoke also to the Chamber of Commerce in London on 22 September. Meanwhile, the London Committee continued its vigorous campaign, using the Reverend Percy Ibbotson, the Methodist minister from Southern Rhodesia with great experience of African affairs. The Committee sought also personal contact with editors and members of newspaper boards. Its chairman, Prince Galitzine met the Reverend Michael Scott and discovered that they shared some common aims.[40]

This effort had, however, little noticeable effect. The opposition of the British Churches was particularly worrying because it persisted even after churchmen in Central Africa had indicated their willingness to accept federation provided that partnership was implemented. Welensky's reassurance that the African affairs board was a *sine qua non* of the federal proposals was an assistance to F. S. Joelson when he attempted to calm the fears, in mid-September, of visiting Northern Rhodesian missionaries who were prepared to support federation if the Southern Rhodesians dropped their demands for alteration to the African affairs board.[41]

To correct the attitude of the British Churches, Welensky and the London Committee's secretary, J. H. Wallace met the Reverend L. G. Greaves, the Africa secretary of the Conference of British Missionary Societies on 25 September. They protested at the damage being done by the resolution of the Conference, when it met in Belfast in April, that federation should not be imposed without African consent. Welensky was particularly annoyed about an erroneous pamphlet, entitled "African Nationalist Movements", which was being circulated by the Conference. He warned that, as the moderate African was already being intimidated, the danger of violence was very real if the federal campaign failed and the liberal leaders were consequently discredited. Greaves was surprised that this pamphlet was in circulation as it had

[39] *Ibid.*, 39/115, f. 84, Welensky to J. Amery, 2 October 1952; *The Bulawayo Chronicle*, 2 October 1952.

[40] Welensky Papers, 17/41, f. 18, Welensky to Sir Gilbert Rennie, 27 August 1952; f. 16, Welensky to Rennie, 19 September 1952; 38/36, f. 104, Welensky to M. Worsley, 28 August 1952; 5/95, f. 202, Welensky to Gore-Browne, 20 September 1952; WE 7, P/C/158/52, Minutes of 22nd Meeting, London Committee, UCAA, 19 September 1952; *The Daily Telegraph*, 26 August 1952; *The Bulawayo Chronicle*, 19 August 1952.

[41] Welensky Papers, WE 7, P/C/158/52, Minutes of 18th, 21st, 22nd & 24th Meetings, London Committee, UCAA, 22 August, and 12, 19 & 26 September 1952.

been produced in 1948 in the context of the unrest in the Gold Coast. He promised to recommend its withdrawal. Greaves asked if federation would encourage South Africa to demand the High Commission Territories. Welensky, though, dismissed any similarity between the two issues because the federal scheme was progressive in contrast with current South African moves to end the direct representation of its Coloureds. Greaves suggested that the federal case would be considerably strengthened if a prominent African would pronounce in its favour. Welensky agreed.[42]

Welensky was concerned to make the London Committee more effective and proposed, while not denigrating Galitzine's efforts, that a man of national standing should replace him as chairman. To avoid confusing the public, Welensky also ordered the severance of links with the Capricorn Africa Society.[43]

Unconnected with the progress of the campaign itself, but significant nevertheless, was the sole product of Welensky's discussions with the British ministers. He discovered that J. L. Foster (later Sir John), the Under-Secretary of State for Commonwealth Relations, could not travel to Africa, and advised Huggins to accept London as the venue for the January conference. Huggins happily agreed because he was concerned about the problems of accommodation, of serving liquor to the African delegates, and of the excitement which would be engendered. With the referendum in mind, Welensky asked the British ministers to ensure that the Southern Rhodesian Opposition delegates should not be antagonised by British parliamentarians while in London.[44]

Welensky immediately warned the Rhodesians on his return that opposition in Britain had grown to the point that the federal issue was "in the melting pot". The British Government, he claimed, had not wavered and opposition was based on ignorance and emotion over colour. However, he believed that the Conservatives did not relish a bitter struggle in Parliament over an issue which should be non-partisan. Griffiths and Creech Jones were leading the opposition with Griffiths particularly uninhibited. Their status as former Colonial Secretaries, Welensky said, gave them an air of authority amongst people with little real knowledge of Africa.[45]

This warning was given credence by the resolution at the Labour Party Conference at Morecambe two days later. Hopkinson, however, immediately protested privately to Welensky that, in attempting to influence the Europeans, he had undermined his (Hopkinson's) efforts to convince the Africans that Britain was determined to achieve federation. It was dangerous, Hopkinson argued, to give the Africans the impression that their demonstrations and threats might have had an effect. Welensky explained that he had acted thus because, on his return, he had found the Southern Rhodesians convinced

[42] *Ibid.*, P/C/158/52/W, Welensky to L. B. Greaves, 26 September 1952; P/C/158/52, Minutes of 24th Meeting, London Committee, UCAA, 26 September 1952.

[43] *Ibid.*, P/C/158/52, Minutes of 25th & 26th Meetings, London Committee, UCAA, 3 & 10 October 1952.

[44] *Ibid.*, P/C/161/52, H. N. Parry to Huggins, 7 August 1952; 5/60, f. 32, Welensky to Huggins, 28 August 1952.

[45] *The Rhodesia Herald*, 30 September 1952.

that the British Government was so anxious to effect federation that it would accept radical alteration of the plan.[46]

This idea that major concessions were possible was not new for the Southern Rhodesian Opposition had continued to believe that Britain would even find it difficult to resist a demand for dominion status. What was surprising was that some of the Salisbury members of the UCAA national executive agreed with their deputy chairman, T. P. M. Cochran, when he publicly proclaimed on 11 September that, while federation was essential, the referendum gave Southern Rhodesia the whip hand and made radical adjustment easy to achieve. He felt that Southern Rhodesia should press for better terms at the January conference. Southern Rhodesia was under-represented in the federal assembly and should demand 20 seats to gain a majority.[47]

This drew a demand to Huggins that UCAA members should adhere to the bounds laid down in the UCAA's *Speaker's Handbook*.[48] In response, Huggins warned the UCAA's secretary that he would deal with Cochran's speech at their standing committee meeting on 26 September. It was proper to strive for amendments but, he maintained, it was quite another matter to oppose the whole scheme until concessions were forthcoming. "There is a tendency to forget that the proposed constitution was fought out at the meeting in January, and there we had our showdown, and that was when I said Southern Rhodesia would never agree to this, that and the other. To the extent I could not get any way, [*sic*] I gave in private. Otherwise the April Conference would not have taken place. We expect amendments in January but not ones of obvious major importance although of considerable importance in fact."[49] There would be amendments to embrace the recommendations of the three Commissions and Lord Salisbury had indicated that he had others to suggest, but Huggins was mystified by the claims that Southern Rhodesia was in a strong bargaining position.

At the standing committee meeting, Cochran apologised but denied any intention of embarrassing the UCAA. He tendered his resignation which Huggins and the committee rejected. It was agreed that henceforth speakers would adhere to the guidelines. The only person to resign was the secretary, A. F. Hopkinson, who did so when the campaign in general — which was being widely criticised — came under fire.[50]

However, before the UCAA had mended its fences, Stockil and Sir Ernest Guest had struck telling blows by echoing Cochran's words. Guest was in fact taking the first step towards unifying the opposition into the Rhodesia League, the formation of which he announced on 30 October. He discounted any need for urgency for closer association because both H. L. d'A. Hop-

[46] Welensky Papers, 39/113, f. 42, Hopkinson to Welensky, 1 October 1952; f. 35, Welensky to Hopkinson, 9 October 1952.

[47] *The Rhodesia Herald*, 13 September 1952.

[48] Welensky Papers, 5/45, ff. 178–180, N. H. Wilson to Huggins, 20 September 1952.

[49] NAZ Hist. MSS, UN 1/1/1, Huggins to A. F. Hopkinson, 22 September 1952.

[50] *Ibid.*, UN 1/1/3, A. F. Hopkinson to S. Cooke, 29 September 1952; UN 1/1/1, A. F. Hopkinson to T. P. M. Cochran, 30 September 1952; Welensky Papers, WE 7, P/C/161/52, Minutes of a Meeting of UCAA Standing Committee, Salisbury, 26 September 1952; 5/45, f. 173, N. H. Wilson to Welensky, 30 September 1952; f. 189, Sir Harold Cartmel-Robinson to Welensky, 2 October 1952.

kinson and Attlee had dismissed any prospect of black domination in the North. Moreover, Southern Rhodesia could not be forced to join South Africa and, in any case, its English-speaking electorate was unlikely to be welcomed by the ruling Afrikaner nationalists. Guest believed that Southern Rhodesia would survive in the interim as its economic difficulties were only temporary and the three territories might come together naturally for social, economic and political reasons which Britain would be unable to reject. He favoured federation but not the current proposals because each territory was surrendering its sovereign rights, and the reward had to be commensurate with the sacrifice. Increased prosperity should be the outcome and the next conference should work to achieve this goal rather than waste energy in trying to force upon the electors a scheme which was universally recognised as unacceptable. The minimum requirements of the Rhodesians should be discovered and placed before the British Government. Permanent prosperity depended on good race relations, a field in which Southern Rhodesia led the rest of Southern Africa, yet there would be separate control of the territorial African policies which would lead to divergence and friction. To Guest, it was fundamental that there should be overall central control of African affairs.

He was in distinguished company in making this point, for the Chief Justice, Sir Robert Tredgold, had already diagnosed it as the scheme's fatal weakness. Guest claimed that the Africans had not understood the reasons for federation and had become suspicious, falling prey to the ambitions of the intelligentsia who seized the opportunity to demand privileges and political equality which, lacking in responsibility, they were unfitted to enjoy. He maintained that the fatal defects in the British strategy had been their method of consultation, which Attlee and Hopkinson had since tried to correct, the falsity of their argument that the White Paper should not be accepted on its merit but on the consequences of its rejection, and their insistence that the acceptance or rejection should be decisive.[51]

The resolution at the British Labour Party Conference at least corrected the impression given by Guest and Stockil that there was no need to hurry to achieve federation while the Conservatives were in power. It certainly made people realise that the prospect of a "Black North" was very real and that the reconciliation of the Africans to federation was most unlikely.

This latter point was made forcibly by Huggins and Welensky when they commented on the resolution. Both, however, urged the Rhodesians not to attach too much importance to it because, even if it were adopted by the Labour Party executive, many Labour MPs still favoured federation, and it was the British Parliament which would decide its fate. Welensky warned, nevertheless, that it was clearly possible that federation might become a British political "football". He was annoyed that the Labour Party, which might soon be in power, should tie the federal issue to South African affairs. Such action, he felt, showed how little thought lay behind the resolution, and the proposal to give Northern Rhodesia a "Gold Coast" constitution completely ignored the facts. The territory had a virile, growing European population which was prepared to give the African a fair opportunity in govern-

[51] *The Rhodesia Herald*, 30 October 1952.

ment but would never accept a subordinate position. Huggins predicted that, if more African-dominated states were created before the African had gained sufficient experience, the white man would be driven out. The British, Welensky said, needed to remember how much they depended on Central Africa's resources for their economic recovery and on federation to retain an influence in Africa.[52]

The British opponents of federation, such as the United Nations Association and the Africa Bureau, immediately exploited the linking of federation with South African issues, but the Kenyan Mau Mau attacks that month distracted public attention. Seemingly unnoticed was the allegation in the General Assembly of the United Nations by the member for Byelorussia that federation would contravene the Charter.[53] In Southern Rhodesia the publication of the reports of the Judicial, Fiscal and Civil Service Commissions at the end of October restored the federal campaign to a slightly more even keel, but until then the opposition enjoyed ascendancy.

Welensky was well received in Salisbury on 10 October, but simultaneously Huggins had to endure a rowdy reception at an Umtali cinema after white women had to sit on the floor while seats in the two front rows were occupied by 26 African men. The uproar continued until the chairman persuaded the Africans to vacate their chairs. Most of these remained unoccupied and the humiliated Africans must have wondered why they were the target of abuse when they were specifically invited and had been seated by the organisers in the front two rows which, in the manner of the segregation of cinemas of the time, were normally reserved for Coloureds and Asians. When able to speak, Huggins reviewed the White Paper and stressed the urgency of securing federation before there was a change of government in Britain. However, his statement that the African affairs board would be abolished, if it proved to be unnecessary, provoked the Archbishop of Canterbury to comment publicly that thereby African fears had been substantiated.[54]

Two meetings addressed by Charles Olley, on 14 and 22 October, in Salisbury and Gwelo, voted for dominion status for Southern Rhodesia first and, on 16 October, the National Affairs Debating Society accepted a motion: "That if the White Paper terms are the best we can get, we should reject Federation." On 30 October, Guest announced the formation of his Rhodesia League. However, the reports of the Commissions had been favourably received when released on the previous day. Furthermore, Huggins had again re-organised and strengthened the UCAA, although he did not accept the advice of Welensky and others to hand over the premiership to Caldicott and assume direct command of the federal campaign.[55]

Welensky, who had spent a day in bed in London through exhaustion and who was to suffer in the coming weeks from a number of ailments, was not

[52] *Ibid.*, 3 October 1952; *Northern News*, 4 October 1952.

[53] *The Amrita Bazar Patrika* (Calcutta), 30 October 1952.

[54] *The Rhodesia Herald*, 11 October 1952; Welensky Papers, 39/115, ff. 61–62, Welensky to Joelson, 16 October 1952; WE 7, P/C/161/52, Welensky to Lord Salisbury, 12 October 1952.

[55] *The Rhodesia Herald*, 14 & 17 October 1952; *The Bulawayo Chronicle*, 23 October 1952; Welensky Papers, 5/45, f. 193, R. Byone to Welensky, 30 September 1952; 34/12, f. 226, Welensky to S. H. Veats, 15 October 1952.

given a moment's respite. Finding on the day of his return that the unofficial Members, for various reasons, had been neglecting the legislative session, he went immediately into the Chamber.[56] A feature of the debates in late 1952 was the presence of Nkumbula in the Strangers' Gallery whenever the African Members spoke.[57] Welensky might have been fully extended but Northern Rhodesia caused little worry and he was received with acclamation when he toured the Copperbelt in late October.[58] There was an industrial strike on the copper mines over a refused pay increase for African workers, but there was no violence.[59] Although the ANC was currently eschewing a public role, the claim by Capricorn Africa Society agents that Nkumbula was at heart a federal supporter was clearly so erroneous that they were dismissed in November but not before Nkumbula had complained formally that, despite these agents' misrepresentations and allegedly drunken misbehaviour, the Government gave credence to their reports of pro-federal African support.[60]

Because he was in Switzerland attending a Moral Rearmament conference, Lewanika had failed to appear at the August meeting arranged for himself and Chileshi with Beckett who substituted for Welensky. Yet Lewanika remained expressedly willing to confer with Europeans. Indeed, he declared that he would apply Moral Rearmament principles to the federal discussions to avoid racial antagonism. In London, on 16 October, he declared that Moral Rearmament had given him new hope and had led him to apologise to Welensky (who was finding his elusiveness most irritating) for the bitterness of the past and to propose a round-table discussion between all the races before the constitutional conference. He acknowledged that other Africans believed in non-co-operation, but pleaded that African opinion should be heard and evaluated in the light of the European desire for federation. He was grateful for the frankness of Hopkinson and Attlee but denied that there had been any intimidation because he had never met an intelligent African who supported federation. He maintained that the African did not aspire to dominate but was fearful of European intentions and thought the proposed safeguards were inadequate. There were, in fact, sufficient leading Africans prepared to join Lewanika, for he and Welensky were able to meet on 20 November to discuss an agenda for a conference on 15 December.[61]

In both northern territories, the district officers, in their task to explain the

[56] Welensky Papers, WE 7, P/C/109/52, Welensky to Gore-Browne, 3 October 1952; Papers of Mrs N. Pegrum, Mrs L. Easton to Mrs N. Pegrum, 1 October 1952.
[57] Welensky Papers, 34/12, f. 156, Welensky to Veats, 14 November 1952.
[58] *Ibid.*, P/C/158/52/J, Welensky to Joelson, 1 November 1952; *The Rhodesia Herald*, 30 October 1952.
[59] *Observer*, 19 October 1952; Welensky Papers, WE 7, P/C/109/52, Welensky to Gore-Browne, 25 October 1952.
[60] Welensky Papers, 34/10, f. 255, A. Nyirenda to Welensky, 4 October 1952; ff. 180–181, N. H. Wilson to Nyirenda, 26 October 1952; f. 240, Wilson to W. S. Parker, 25 October 1952; f. 225, H. Nkumbula to Wilson, 27 October 1952.
[61] *Ibid.*, 17/41, ff. 14–15, Welensky to Beckett, 11 September 1952; 34/10, ff. 201–202, Press Release, 10 September 1952; f. 213, W. S. Parker to R. P. Bush, 22 November 1952; f. 186, Circular letter by J. S. Moffat to Africans, 24 November 1952; *Central African Post*, 18 September 1952; *The Rhodesia Herald*, 17 October 1952.

White Paper, had continued to represent the Colonial Office's main effort to counter African nationalist propaganda. Both northern Governments sought, as Professor Rotberg has discovered, to lessen the opportunities for contrary discussion by limiting the number of meetings of the representative councils.[62] The Church of Scotland in Nyasaland, however, concluded: "Discussions on Federation have increased racial antagonism to such a degree that there is not a chance of attaining that measure of racial partnership which is necessary to make Federation workable." Thus the Church demanded that federation be delayed to allow the validity of partnership to be proved. If this was done the African would be willing to discuss federation. Hopkinson, the Colonial Under-Secretary, had been wrong, the Church maintained, to claim that opposition was confined to a minority because the missionaries were surprised by the depth of African knowledge on the subject. However, Africans were not concerned about the detail when they rejected the principle. The African, the Church argued, was emotionally aroused and opposition was becoming a mass movement, but the absence of prosecution by the police was evidence enough of the falsity of the claims of intimidation. In fact, the Church alleged, such allegations had been preceded by reports of pressure and bribery by the supporters of federation.[63]

Nevertheless, three Africans were prepared to write to *The Nyasaland Times* on 14 October criticising the African Congress for refusing to discuss the White Paper. The editor confirmed that this was the view of many intelligent Africans and, in late October, at the request of Africans, round-table discussions on the White Paper were held in Cholo and Limbe, attended by the Secretary of Native Affairs, the provincial commissioners, Barrow, senior Chiefs and others.[64] On 29 October, the Governor summoned the president and vice-president of Congress, J. R. N. Chinyama and C. Chinula, to lecture them on the dangers of agitation, warning that it could get out of control. The ultimate goal was self-government but not domination by one race and they were assured that if federation was not in the interests of all, the Nyasaland Government would not advocate it.[65]

The possession of the reports of the three Commissions in late October enabled Huggins and his Cabinet to invite Welensky and Beckett to review their strategy for the forthcoming conference. Huggins made the most significant suggestion which was that the African affairs board should be brought into the parliamentary structure as a select committee. Its membership would then be drawn from the African representatives. This would be more acceptable to the public and would make the board a more effective safeguard because its members would be able to initiate discussion directly in the legislature on everything affecting Africans.[66]

The Judicial Commission, chaired by a former chief justice of Southern Rhodesia, Sir Robert Hudson, and served by the three current territorial

[62] Rotberg, *The Rise of Nationalism*, *op. cit.*, p. 243.
[63] *The Rhodesia Herald*, 9 October 1952.
[64] *Ibid.*, 27 October 1952.
[65] Rotberg, *The Rise of Nationalism*, *op. cit.*, p. 246.
[66] *The Rhodesia Herald*, 1 November 1952; Welensky Papers, WE 7, P/C/158/52/J, Welensky to Joelson, 1 November 1952.

chief justices, Sir Robert Tredgold, Mr Justice Lewey and Sir Enoch Jenkins of Nyasaland, ruled that the proposed federal supreme court would be competent to deal with all questions of English and Roman-Dutch and constitutional law. Final appeals would be made to the Judicial Committee of the Privy Council. There would be three permanent judges with the territorial chief justices co-opted when necessary.[67]

Sir William Douglas, a senior retired British civil servant, chaired the Civil Service Preparatory Commission, the membership of which comprised A. G. Cowling, a former Southern Rhodesian secretary for internal affairs, Sir Geoffrey Follows of the Northern Rhodesian Government and A. C. Talbot Edwards, Nyasaland's Chief Secretary. They examined the federal civil service, concluding that it would require the transfer of 15 600 civil servants of all races from the three territorial services which currently employed 42 600. 6 500 of the 15 600 would be Europeans which was slightly less than half of those serving the three territories. The Commission detailed the federal departments and recommended that the federal cabinet should consist of a prime minister, five ministers with portfolios and one without. It stressed the need for inter-governmental co-operation, particularly in the matters of civil service transfers and conditions of employment. These recommendations, because the Southern Rhodesian civil servants would vote in the referendum, were regarded as crucial and were greeted with some relief.[68]

The Fiscal Commission's recommendations, of course, would influence the whole Southern Rhodesian electorate. Sir Jeremy Raisman, a distinguished British banker, was the chairman and the members were two current financial secretaries, A. H. Strachan of Southern Rhodesia and K. W. Simmonds of Nyasaland; a former financial secretary, G. M. Thornton of Northern Rhodesia; three territorial parliamentarians, Macintyre, van Eeden and Barrow. They dealt with the transfer of assets to the federal government, the portions of the public debts relating to those assets and like matters. They recommended that the four governments should adopt the same financial year, that all customs and excise duties (with the exception of those relating to petroleum products) should be federal but should be divisible between the four governments on the same basis as income tax. The latter would be assessed and collected by the federal government and distributed so that it would retain 60 per cent and give Southern and Northern Rhodesia 17 per cent each and Nyasaland six per cent. The territorial governments would also be able to impose a surcharge on income tax which the federal government would assess and collect for them. The federal government, itself, could only impose a surcharge for defence expenditure in times of emergency. Three years after the inauguration of federation and every five years thenceforth, a commission would be appointed to review the distribution of income tax and loan funds. The federal government would be empowered to make grants-in-aid to the territories. Two-thirds of taxes on sales and income would go to the territorial governments.

A loans council would be established and would be solely responsible for raising external loans. The federal treasury would be responsible for the

[67] *Report of the Judicial Commission*, Command 8671 (London, October 1952).

[68] *Report of the Civil Service Preparatory Commission*, Command 8673 (London, October 1952).

management of all existing and future debts of the four governments. A customs union would be created in the first year of federation to establish free trade in the products of the three territories. External goods would be subject to a uniform tariff scale of preferences in Southern Rhodesia and Western Northern Rhodesia, the territories outside the area of the Congo Basin Treaties. A tariff commission would draw up the tariff scale and until that was done the existing tariffs would apply. Territorial customs arrangements with the Union of South Africa would be re-negotiated.

Finally the Fiscal Commission recommended that the federal exclusive list be enlarged to include: customs and excise, except for duty on motor spirit; taxes on incomes, except for territorial surcharges; old age pensions paid to persons other than Africans; national monuments; banks and banking, excluding the control of credit; and taxes on the sale of goods and turnover, provided that not more than a third of the net revenue be allocated to the federal government. It was made plain that, while the federal government was likely to cost £350 000 more than previously estimated, there would be substantial relief for Southern Rhodesian consumers and taxpayers.[69]

In November and December, the months remaining before the constitutional Conference, the Governments made their final preparations. Huggins included Keller in his delegation to make it more representative of the electorate but confined his invitations to parliamentarians, thereby excluding any Africans. He explained, privately, that there was little point in repeating the unsuccessful experiment of inviting Africans. The northern Governments invited their African Members of the Legislative Councils but, true to form, they declined.[70]

The federal campaign continued on established lines, with Olley and Guest more prominent in opposition than Stockil. Umtali was in a receptive, friendly mood when Welensky spoke there on 22 November[71] but there were indications of hardening African opposition in Southern Rhodesia. Indeed, the Capricorn Africa Society became concerned for the safety of their agents when Chief Mangwende warned Africans to beware.[72] The London Committee of the UCAA welcomed the acceptance of its chair by Lord Milverton, a former governor of Nigeria and colonial administrator of wide experience, and was relieved that the storm which it feared did not materialise when Stirling published his re-written Declarations in early December. The illness of Lord Woolton, the Lord President of the Council, dealt a blow, however, for Churchill reshuffled his Cabinet and moved Lord Salisbury from the Commonwealth Relations Office. The blow was softened by Salisbury being replaced by Lord Swinton, a man of considerable ministerial experience of

[69] *Report of the Fiscal Commission*, Command 8672 (London, October 1952).

[70] Welensky Papers, 5/52, f. 28, Welensky to L. J. W. Keller, 15 October 1952; 39/113, ff. 32–33, Huggins to Welensky, 20 October 1952; *Northern News*, 20 December 1952.

[71] Welensky Papers, 34/12, f. 133, Welensky to S. H. Veats, 26 November 1952; 34/10, f. 176, Welensky to N. H. Wilson, 26 November 1952.

[72] *Ibid.*, 34/10, ff. 177–178, Wilson to Welensky, 18 November 1952; *African Weekly*, 1 November 1952; curiously, in the Commons in October, Foster denied that there were paid Capricorn Africa agents at work in the territories and the London Committee believed him — Welensky Papers, 5/45, f. 113, Minutes of 29th Meeting, London Committee, UCAA, 31 October 1952.

the Empire, and by Churchill agreeing to allow Salisbury to attend the January Conference.[73]

On 8 December, the Nyasaland Legislative Council at last debated the White Paper and the reports of the Commissions, claiming that the debate had been deferred to allow time for consideration because the Council had never been confronted by a more important question. Barrow began by denying the allegation of *East Africa and Rhodesia* in October that Nyasaland had always obstructed the moves towards closer association. He dismissed black domination as a path to disaster, simply because Africans could not be given responsibilities for which they were not yet fitted. Federation was the way to improve the lot of all Nyasalanders. The Fiscal Commission had shown what advantages would accrue, but the majority of the Africans knew nothing of this and only wished to be left undisturbed. Barrow could reassure them that federation would not affect their daily lives. He recognised that it was difficult for the Government to explain these complex proposals, while it was easy for the African Congress to play on fears for land and of the malign influence of the Southern Rhodesians. Land, in reality, would remain secure and there was none available to accommodate a vast influx of European immigrants. Pass laws were matters of domestic policy. Africans in Nyasaland had queried the need for the African affairs board, asking why Africans should be treated differently from other races. Barrow agreed that the board probably was unnecessary and noted that its abolition would certainly please the Southern Rhodesians. He asked that it should be remembered that it was the British and not the Southern Rhodesians who had insisted that Nyasaland be included in the scheme.

Barrow claimed that Africans had been given plenty of time to evaluate the proposals but still he met with a blank refusal to discuss them. Yet, he asserted, on the few occasions he had managed to do so, the Africans present had been enthusiastic about the advantages. Because the African believed that if he said "no" the matter would be pursued no farther, it had clearly been a mistake to consult him. Barrow was confident that the Africans would find federation beneficial just as they had all other innovations which their innate conservatism had led them to refuse. It was the duty of all Nyasalanders, he concluded, to examine the White Paper without personal interest or prejudice.

The Financial Secretary explained how Nyasaland would gain financially from federation. He, like Barrow, was applauded by the Members with the exception of the African representatives, E. A. Muwamba and A. B. Doig. Muwamba claimed that, though the Africans were kept well-informed on the subject by the Government, they nevertheless rejected federation for the very good reason that they believed that the Europeans were seeking perpetual political dominance. Disputing the existence of any intimidation, he asked why African leaders should even attempt to persuade their people to accept

[73] Welensky Papers, 5/45, f. 127, Welensky to Lord Salisbury, 7 November 1952; 39/84, f. 25, Minutes of 34th Meeting, London Committee, UCAA, 25 November 1952; WE 7, P/C/158/52/W, J. H. Wallace to Welensky, 10 December 1952; 39/115, f. 10, Welensky to Lord Salisbury, 27 November 1952; 39/113, ff. 3–5, Salisbury to Welensky, 3 December 1952; *The Rhodesia Herald*, 25 November 1952; *The Times, Manchester Guardian*, 8 December 1952.

proposals which they knew they rejected. He read out the resolutions of a recent meeting of Chiefs and councillors at Lilongwe which denied any intimidation apart from that of the Government towards its own servants, denounced the Government's efforts to persuade the Africans to accept federation and praised the effort of the Church of Scotland to try to explain the African point of view. Muwamba also read out the demands of the Council of Chiefs for African members of the representative councils at all levels including the Protectorate Council, to be elected by the Africans and presided over by African chairmen. The Chiefs insisted there should also be 18 Members of the Legislative Council elected by Africans, and Africans in the Executive Council. Muwamba listed Nyasaland's resources to prove that federation was unnecessary.

To Doig the economic advantages were undeniable, and he agreed that there should be some form of closer association when the territories grew towards each other. He called for an objective acknowledgment that, as none of the conditions of the Hilton Young and Bledisloe Commissions had been met, federation was not practicable. He cast doubt on the value of the safeguards, claiming that events in Southern Rhodesia and South Africa proved the claim of Hilton Young that, once power had been transferred to a local legislature, that body could not resist the will of its electorate, leaving the metropolitan power with only the choice of using force to ensure the preservation of the safeguard. Doig maintained that there was substance in the Africans' fears and that Huggins's speech in Umtali had only offered confirmation of it. Doig was convinced that the proponents of federation intended to seek dominion status for it in order thereafter to amalgamate the three territories. He reminded them that all the conferences and royal commissions had pronounced that amalgamation should only be possible when all the inhabitants of the territories desired it. Doig warned the Government not to be misled by the African's habit of feigning ignorance when he did not wish to discuss something. A lack of education did not mean that there was no public opinion and he had been surprised, in fact, at the depth of understanding of the scheme. Furthermore, the African rejection could not just be explained as the product of foreign influences, and federation would not survive without the support of the majority of the inhabitants.

Doig urged that nothing should be done which might harm race relations. If necessary the two northern territories should be unified and Southern Rhodesia brought in later when African fears had been proved to be groundless. Or, perhaps the idea of a parallel organisation to the East Africa High Commission should be re-examined.

The Secretary for Native Affairs, V. Fox-Strangways, dismissed the claim that the federal motive was white domination, as a "most malignant lie" which would be merely ludicrous if it were not believed by thousands. The Governments had sought opinion and had been rebuffed. If the Africans had been prepared to discuss federation, it might have taken a different form. Instead the scheme and its safeguards had been devised to suit what were thought to be the African requirements. Even so, there was no doubt that the safeguards were the soundest which could have been devised. Whatever Doig said, Fox-Strangways argued, the questions asked by Africans showed clearly that the proposals were not understood. Nevertheless, the territories had arrived at the point where their economies would have to be combined. Federation, in any case, would increase the strength of the Commonwealth's position in the world and lighten Britain's burden. Federation would serve everyone's interests and should be supported lest it be doomed from the outset. To this end, Fox-Strangways sought to reassure the Africans on Southern Rhodesian intentions and policies which, he claimed, were being progressively modified and would be increasingly so when affected by the moderating influence of the federation.

C. W. F. Footman, the Chief Secretary, agreed that the White Paper had not received a fair hearing. He dismissed Muwamba's speech as largely irrelevant and sought to make it plain to the African civil servants, in particular, that their employment and prospects of advancement would be secure. He reminded the Africans that the scheme was supported by both the Nyasaland and British Governments.

Barrow, closing the debate, said that the economic advantages could not be ignored because there could be no political advance if the country stayed poor. He also believed that the African did not understand and cited one Chief who had said so in the Protectorate Council on 4 December. Barrow was confident that all obstacles could be surmounted and deplored, in conclusion, the refusal of the African delegates to attend the Conference in January.[74]

The depth of African confusion over the federal proposals was revealed at the round-table conference in Lusaka on 15 December at which Welensky, Beckett and other unofficial Members met Lewanika, Chileshi and other prominent Africans. Both sides would conclude that the exchange had been valuable and that further meetings should be held. Although the arguments of the Africans were often mystifying and somewhat irritating, it was quite clear that they distrusted, indeed, even feared, European intentions. Nothing would dissuade them from the belief that federation would only place them at a greater disadvantage. Although federal citizenship seemed irrelevant to Lewanika, because there was no purely federal territory, nevertheless it seemed to threaten African interests. Somehow he concluded that the existence of this citizenship would allow the European to gain dominion status for the federation and sever the link with Britain which the Africans treasured. By an equally curious process of thought, Lewanika arrived at the conclusion that federal citizenship would allow the federal government to assume the trusteeship of the northern territories. Bemused by these arguments, Welensky and the other unofficials could only reply that Britain was not abandoning her role, that neither the protected status nor African land was endangered, and that the future role of the Chiefs was a matter of British, not federal, decision. The Africans, in turn, taxed Welensky on his public statements on getting rid of Colonial Office control and he could only reply that he had meant to the extent that it affected European affairs. Lewanika was convinced that the Europeans were seeking a paramount position, while Welensky maintained that paramountcy of any variety was no longer contemplated as partnership was the official policy.

[74] Ny *Debates* (Zomba), p. 42, 8 December 1952.

When Welensky stated that partnership would secure African advancement in all fields, he was told that the African did not care for the pursuit of wealth but preferred the possession of land and the happiness of rural life. The value of the African affairs board was questioned. Federal control of immigration was again depicted as a threat to African land, and questions were asked as to why Southern Rhodesia, a poor country, should be given such a dominating position. Much time was spent decrying the current colour policies and it was alleged that, as they were unlikely to be reformed under federation, they constituted a major reason as to why the Africans were not attracted by the scheme.

In answer, the unofficials could only claim that the colour bars would diminish as they lost their *raison d'être* which was the vast cultural gap between the races. The Africans were clearly unimpressed and Lewanika maintained that, despite the pronouncements on partnership, men who had attained the highest standards, like Yamba, never received anything but disgraceful treatment. Lewanika could not, thus, see any real difference between the Northern Rhodesian and South African policies on race and, in fact, he preferred the more open South African approach. Welensky wondered why Africans were then so anxious to maintain the link with the Colonial Office which not only condoned but enforced the colour bars.[75]

With this meeting accomplished, Welensky left for London to join Huggins who had been attending the Commonwealth Prime Ministers' Conference. However, before Welensky departed, he was again made aware of another aspect of the African nationalists' campaign against federation — a level of crudity in propaganda which the European was at a loss to combat. Two African civil servants, and members of the ANC, were charged with the misuse of the Government Information Department's machinery by using it to print pamphlets which alleged that Welensky had returned from Canada with sugar containing a substance which would render African males sterile.[76]

There had been many such stories. Earlier in the year the condensation trail of a high-flying aircraft had been depicted as a trick by Welensky to "sell" federation.[77] The songs sung by Kenneth Kaunda, in particular, likened the European to a vulture hovering over the land of the African. Huggins and Welensky were supposed to covet a metal to be found in the Mwinilunga area which enabled aircraft to fly. Vampire-men were said to be abroad, sucking their victims and rendering them powerless to resist the persuasion of the advocates of federation. Such was the effect of this campaign that a soap factory had its free samples spurned for fear that they might have been contaminated. Welensky, however, felt only contempt for such tactics and had other matters on his mind as he journeyed to London.

[75] Welensky Papers, 14/7, ff. 104–124, Draft Minutes of a Meeting, Lusaka, 15 December 1952; 34/10, ff. 143–147, G. Lewanika to Welensky, 20 November 1952; f. 138, Welensky to Lewanika, (undated).

[76] *Ibid.*, 5/95, ff. 121–122, Welensky to R. C. S. Stanley, 17 December 1952; L. H. Gann, *A History of Northern Rhodesia: Early Days to 1953* (London, 1964), pp. 426–427.

[77] Welensky commented (Welensky Papers, WE 7, P/C/109/52, Welensky to Gore-Browne, 2 June 1952), "You will agree, Stewart, I am a marvellous fellow in more ways than one. I shall probably persuade the Lord to write "Federation" across the African skies in the near future."

CHAPTER TWELVE

The Final Conference

Argument and Decision on the Structure of the Federal Constitution, London, January 1953

ON 1 January 1953, at Number 10, Carlton House Terrace, London, Viscount Swinton, as Commonwealth Relations Secretary, welcomed the delegates to what he called the last lap in a long course. Nevertheless, in this conference, battles would be re-fought with some rancour but compromises would be found, and by the end of the month an explanatory White Paper and a draft constitution would be accepted by the delegations for publication in early February. A final offer could at last be laid before the British and Central African populations, and the Southern Rhodesian electorate in particular.

The Conference, of course, did not open without a prelude and fanfare by the British Press. The newspapers of the Right hailed federation as a great opportunity to strengthen the Commonwealth. The left-wing Press highlighted the northern African refusal to attend the Conference and announced the impending arrival of parties of Chiefs and Congress officials to campaign against federation. These newspapers urged that federation should not be imposed on the unwilling masses but predicted that it would be. Welensky contributed to the debate by informing *The Times* that one concession which would be sought would placate the Southern Rhodesians by bringing the African affairs board within the federal parliamentary structure as a select committee. This idea was endorsed by the Church and Nation Committee of the Church of Scotland which, otherwise, rejected the plan as premature until partnership had been fully and willingly implemented.[1]

In the Conference, on 1 January, Swinton stated that the purpose of the meeting was to evolve the final formula for ratification by the Southern Rhodesian electorate, the northern legislatures and the British Parliament.[2]

[1] *The Times*, 27 December 1952; *Glasgow Herald*, 31 December 1952.
[2] Conference on the Federation of Southern Rhodesia, Northern Rhodesia and Nyasaland, London, "Volume III — Verbatim Record of Proceedings", January 1953.

Then he invited Huggins to speak first, but Huggins ceded that honour to R. O. Stockil who proclaimed his Rhodesia Party's enthusiasm for a workable scheme and warned that the best laid plans would founder in Southern Rhodesia if not given all-party support. He felt it was unfortunate, therefore, that the United Party had not bothered to apprise his Party, until the previous day, of developments since April. He maintained that the United Party did not know that all the previous negotiations had merely served to exacerbate public feelings as scant regard was being paid to the proud Southern Rhodesian record of self-government and, unless more power was placed in local hands and confidence displayed in local integrity, the electorate would reject federation. There was still, however, no doubt that amalgamation would be eagerly received, even if it excluded Nyasaland, and Stockil would support it because it would create a better and more stable state which would improve everyone's lot and assure the continuance of the British way of life. However, he accepted that the Conference would concentrate on the hitherto unresolved aspects of the April proposals. He hoped, nevertheless, that certain ambiguities would be clarified because how, for example, could eventual dominion status be promised when protected status would be maintained?

The Conference heard the whole range of Southern Rhodesian opposition views because Stockil was followed by Keller, Eastwood and George Munro. With his eye undoubtedly on his rival, W. H. Eastwood, L. J. W. Keller claimed to represent the white worker and then aligned the latter with a memorandum supplied by the Rhodesia League which called for either radical alteration of the proposals or the postponement of federation. Neither the white worker, Keller maintained, nor the League was opposed to the concept of unification, but both believed that the proposed constitution would be ineffective and clumsy. This criticism, he felt, could vitally affect the outcome of the referendum.

Keller said the white worker also agreed with the League's bitter rejection of the safeguards as unjustifiable slurs on the integrity of the European population. The African affairs board was inconsistent with the concept of democratic, responsible government and would embarrass, hinder and undermine the federal assembly. In addition it would encourage Africans to believe that the board and not the federal members of parliament was concerned with their affairs. The board was seen to be unnecessary when a second chamber could adequately protect African interests. The League thought the failure to centralise African affairs, the most crucial aspect of government, would condemn the federation to be short-lived. It opposed the introduction of nominated members as repugnant and dangerous in a small legislature where they could hold the balance of power.

Keller explained that the provision for the continuing protection of the northern Africans had particularly irritated the Southern Rhodesians and a large meeting in Bulawayo had asked him to have it replaced by a provision for a more effective form of unification such as the amalgamation of the Rhodesias or of Southern Rhodesia and the "Railway Belt". The lack of provision for advancement to dominion status and an escape or secession clause was also resented. The white worker was specifically anxious about industrial legislation remaining in territorial hands because it would produce differential wage rates, cheaper labour and competition in vital services. This, Keller concluded, was a recipe for friction and chaos.

Eastwood wondered about the unexplained fate of the Southern Rhodesian all-party accord of September 1951, mentioning it because, like Keller, he favoured a bi-cameral legislature. He thought that the lower house should contain 15 elected Southern Rhodesian members, eleven Northern Rhodesian and four Nyasalanders. The upper chamber should have nine African and nine European nominated senators. This would replace the African affairs board and please the Southern Rhodesians and the British Parliament.

George Munro, the chairman of the Rhodesia Party, wondered why the northern territories should not be raised to Southern Rhodesia's self-governing status. He was a veteran amalgamationist, having attended the 1936 Victoria Falls Conference, and still questioned the need to accept the second prize, federation. He expected federation to be rejected at the referendum.

Huggins delivered a speech which Welensky described later as being more rabid than those of Keller and Eastwood and which risked terminating the Conference in its opening session.[3] In a fierce uncompromising mood, Huggins revealed why he had declined to speak first. The British delegates, he said, should understand how intensely unpopular was the African affairs board. He confessed he had been so pleased to be rid of the minister for African interests that he had accepted a hybrid body which was half in and half out of parliament. However, he had not expected the uproar which greeted the proposal on his return but then the emphasis laid on this safeguard in the British Parliament had been most provocative. The Southern Rhodesians rejected the board because their legislative freedom had never been hampered by anything more than their constitutional reservations. The board had to be brought within the parliamentary structure or federation would not survive the referendum.

The British, Huggins felt, had also failed to understand how difficult it was for the Southern Rhodesians, with their parliamentary tradition, to accept the presence at this moment of Africans in the federal assembly. The Southern Rhodesian philosophy was that Africans had to earn their place in parliament, in contrast with the policy in the northern territories where "your system is your particular form of *apartheid* . . ." under which Africans were specially nominated because there was no electoral system for them and they were mostly unfit for parliament. This was not to say that only Africans were unfit for legislative service, but the northern system had only been evolved in response to British left-wing agitation. The Southern Rhodesians had been shocked by British policies since 1945 "of treating the African more as a performing animal than a backward human being . . ." Herein, he said, lay an explanation of the extreme Afrikaner nationalist reaction in South Africa. The northern system cut across the Southern Rhodesian policy of trying to get the races to co-operate politically.

Huggins acknowledged current sneers, the comments on the length of time

[3] Welensky Papers, 17/38, f. 126, Welensky to T. H. Grey, 1 January 1953.

it would take to produce an African member of parliament under the Southern Rhodesian system, and pointed out that already many constituencies could be affected significantly by the African vote. He claimed that, nevertheless, the Southern Rhodesians would have accepted nominated Africans "if you had not then proceeded to graft this sort of wart [the African affairs board] . . . on to the parliamentary structure . . ." A second chamber would not resolve the problem because the British Ministers were determined to have Africans in the lower house, and he acknowledged that the British had to keep the support of some 60 Labour MPs to secure federation a safe passage through the Commons. Nonetheless, it would be a pity to lose federation through failing to amend a body which in reality would have little to do.

Huggins had not finished, however, because he revealed a second pitfall which was that the electorate would not allow the governor-general "to run riot on his own until we can have an election". There had to be an interim government.

Sir Gilbert Rennie, speaking as leader of the Northern Rhodesian delegation, and stunned, perhaps, by Huggins's bluntness, thought that it was too early to say anything. John Moffat, however, warned that as the Africans in Northern Rhodesia remained totally opposed to federation, any amendment seemed crucial. After Barrow had pleaded that discussion should be raised above parochialism, Swinton adjourned the Conference until the morrow to allow the British delegation time to compose a considered reply.

Although the fate of the federation seemed to be in the balance, Welensky remained confident that good sense would prevail. He told his correspondents that Huggins was, perhaps, attempting to influence the opposition elements in his own delegation.[4]

The next morning, 2 January, Oliver Lyttelton, the Colonial Secretary, spoke first, as chairman, but gave little more than a broad outline of British attitudes. It is probable that he sought to avoid controversy to get the Conference and its sub-committees working on matters on which they could agree, before risking a confrontation with the Southern Rhodesians. In the event, the African affairs board was only first discussed in detail four days later.

Lyttelton asserted that his Government had not and would not flinch from unpopular decisions and would not be deterred by its narrow parliamentary majority. Nevertheless, he considered it vital to win the support of British moderate opinion outside the Commons, for to lose it would cost the federation its best chance of success. He claimed that any secretary of state would pause before answering even remarks "of a rather acidulated character" if they emanated from Southern Rhodesia because of the success of that territory in the field of African affairs. However, he was sure that, while British policy might not be right, it was at least coherent and deliberate. The introduction of nominated Members in the Legislative Councils, he explained, had not been a response to left-wing pressure, but was a long-established method of providing an interim representation while the people were being politically educated. This was done because Britain had no choice

[4] *Ibid.*, 17/38, f. 126, Welensky to T. H. Grey, 1 January 1953; f. 153, Welensky to C. J. M. Alport, 2 January 1953.

but to attempt to govern by goodwill when it lacked the forces to do otherwise. The presence of nominated members in the federal assembly and the other safeguards were necessary because the mass of the inhabitants would not be enfranchised. Lyttelton, personally, recoiled "from the idea of primitive Africans having a sufficiently large franchise to make safeguards unnecessary" because the European was so necessary for development that his position should not be endangered. Southern Rhodesians, Lyttelton claimed, need not fear the attitudes of future British governments because the federal constitution only allowed them powers of delay. He concluded by dismissing amalgamation as impossible because the British Government was committed to preserving the northern protected status.

Swinton expounded on three specific issues. The first was a provision for secession which he was certain would not be found in any existing federal constitution. It certainly was an odd way to begin; after all, Swinton argued, marriage was not founded on the prospect of divorce. Its effect on potential investors alone ruled it out of consideration. Swinton had something to offer, however, with regard to the second issue, the eventual attainment of dominion status. He asserted that his Government would allow the insertion of a clause providing for this once partnership was fully developed. His third assertion was to deny that federation in any way belittled Southern Rhodesia's status because the latter's constitutional reservations remained. He closed by reminding the delegates of the reasons for federation and urging them not to waste this last opportunity.

Lyttelton asked if there were any other specific problems. Eastwood demanded reconsideration of a bi-cameral parliament but Swinton dismissed it as impracticable because of the shortage of suitable manpower. Swinton wondered if thereby Eastwood sought to exclude Africans from the lower house, but the latter replied that he only wanted it to be composed of members elected on existing franchises. It would be a grave error, Swinton countered, to confine African representation to nominated seats in an upper chamber which possessed a legislative veto. Much strife would be avoided if Africans were in the lower house where legislation was forged.

Stockil regretted that the opportunity to discuss this had come so late. He was anxious that it be understood that the fundamental of this demand was the Southern Rhodesian fear of African domination through the progressive broadening of the franchise when the growth of the European population would never match that of the African. This fear had led people to consider segregation or union with South Africa. They certainly distrusted partnership, which would be better named "co-operation" and, if the federal scheme was not radically altered, it would be rejected.

However, Stockil had not convinced G. Beckett that there was any other option than that of racial co-operation, or partnership. Welensky closed these preliminary remarks by pleading for a more objective approach, a positive search for solutions, with an acceptance that it was a fact of life that franchises would broaden.

The Conference turned its attention to the production of an acceptable constitution and an explanation thereof which would appear in February as Command Papers 8753 and 8754. The preamble had been re-drawn in a manner which satisfied many of the delegates but not the Southern Rhodesians. The Conference ignored a plea by Keller that the preamble should recognise a future possibility of an amalgamation but accepted that it should not imply that the Southern Rhodesian constitutional reservations were permanent or that the federation was inferior in status to Southern Rhodesia. It was agreed:

"The preamble . . . will contain recitals to the effect that:-

a. the Colony of Southern Rhodesia is part of Her Majesty's dominions and Northern Rhodesia and Nyasaland are Territories under Her Majesty's protection;
b. the three Territories are the rightful home of all lawful inhabitants thereof, whatever their origin;
c. the Colony of Southern Rhodesia should continue to enjoy responsible government in accordance with its constitution;
d. Northern Rhodesia and Nyasaland should continue, under the special protection of Her Majesty, to enjoy separate Governments for so long as their respective peoples so desire, the said Governments remaining responsible (subject to the ultimate authority of Her Majesty's Government in the United Kingdom) for, in particular, the control of land in those Territories, and for the local and Territorial political advancement of the peoples thereof;
e. the association of the three Territories in a Federation under Her Majesty's sovereignty, enjoying responsible government in accordance with the Constitution hereinafter set forth, would conduce to the security, advancement and welfare of all the inhabitants; and in particular would foster partnership and co-operation between their inhabitants and enable the Federation, when the inhabitants of the Territories so desire, to go forward with confidence towards the attainment of full membership of the Commonwealth;
f. it is accordingly desirable that provision be made for such a Federation and for the establishment of a Federal Government."

In "Chapter I: The Federation", the Conference decided that the first paragraph should read:

"Unless and until it is otherwise provided by Federal law, the Federation will be known as the Federation of Rhodesia and Nyasaland"

in order that the electorate could change the name if it so wished. This was a compromise after J. M. Caldicott and others objected to "Rhodesia and Nyasaland". Huggins had favoured "Rhodesland", while E. C. F. Whitehead preferred the short title "Rhodesia", but Barrow argued that these would be viewed by the Africans as confirmation of amalgamation. A similar formula was adopted for "the seat of the Federal Government" which would be at Salisbury until decided otherwise by federal law. Provision was made for the future acquisition of land by the federal government for a capital over which the jurisdiction of the federal assembly would apply. This legislature would decide how far territorial law would prevail in the capital.

The Conference accepted much of "Chapter II: The Federal Legislature" without change. The legislature and the federal exclusive and concurrent lists were defined. (The exclusive list contained powers for which the federal government would be solely responsible, and the concurrent had powers which could be handled by any of the governments but for which the federal government would be responsible.) The federal power to acquire land for its installations continued to be limited by the Orders in Council and other enactments relating to African land. As a further sop to African opinion, this limitation was extended to land to be acquired for immigrants. Southern Rhodesian pressure resulted in the appending of a footnote to the clause limiting the federal power to acquire land. At the previous Conference the Southern Rhodesians had sought to prevent the federal government having to secure land through a territorial Government. Defeated but undeterred, they had suggested before this Conference that the federal government should be able to acquire land for railways and canals if it secured a two-thirds majority in the federal house. However, the drafting party ruled that, in terms of the territorial Orders in Council, it would be impossible to transfer to the federal legislature any of the powers of the Colonial Secretary over northern land, because land there was vested in him and not in the legislatures. In Southern Rhodesia, by contrast, the Commonwealth Secretary had only limited powers in terms of the Land Apportionment Act. The draftsmen disputed any need for change because secretaries of state were unlikely to refuse to allow the transfer of land to the federal government unless there was a territorial objection on the grounds of infringement of African interests and land rights.

In the tenth plenary session on 16 January, J. M. Greenfield explained that the Southern Rhodesians had sought to provide for railway development and would, in fact, accept something less than the acquisition of land as there could be servitudes or easements. In Southern Rhodesia the Postmaster-General would put up his poles and acquire servitude, which was not ownership but a right of way. Greenfield wished to avoid having to refer every federal demand for land to the territorial Governor or the Secretary of State in terms of the Orders in Council. He acknowledged that the railways would thereby acquire virtual ownership of the land and knew that the Northern Rhodesians feared the African reaction but asked them to remember that the railway would benefit the community. Moreover, this situation already existed and the advent of the federal government would make little difference.

E. I. G. Unsworth, the Northern Rhodesian Attorney-General, maintained that difficulties remained but, because they were close to agreement, he proposed an examination by the Legal Committee. This Committee reported that the Orders in Council would have to be adjusted anyway to recognise the existence and the rights of the federal government and that this matter should be dealt with when it arose. Thus the Conference adopted the footnote provided by the draftsmen:

"In view of the provisions of the Orders in Council mentioned in this paragraph and of Her Majesty's Government's undertakings to the Northern Territories in respect of African lands, it is not possible to transfer to the Federation control of the compulsory acquisition of such lands (including interests in or rights over such lands) for public purposes of the Federation. It would not, however, be reasonable to refuse the Federal Government permission to acquire land, or interests in or rights over land, for public purposes which would be in the general interests of the community as a whole unless African interests would be adversely affected to a disproportionate extent, and the Secretary of State, who would have the final decision on this matter, would not normally do so. The Federal Government would be entitled to state their views direct to the Secretary of State on any proposal for the acquisition of African lands for public purposes."

This first part of Chapter II continued to forbid the federal assembly to interfere, except with the consent of the relevant territorial government, with international agreements relating to matters not included in the federal exclusive or concurrent lists. The governor-general would, as before, prescribe dates on which the territorial legislatures would cease to legislate regarding matters in the exclusive list.

Little changed, too, was the power of delegation. The federal government could delegate any of its powers in contrast to the territorial legislatures which could only do so in relation to corporate or like bodies which provided inter-territorial services, special schools or the control of tsetse fly. However, veterinary research and animal health which were included in this list in April were now excluded. These subjects were, of course, part of the larger question of whether or not to centralise agriculture. As will be seen, this Conference placed Southern Rhodesian European agriculture and the research, veterinary and animal health services in that territory on the exclusive list and gave the northern territories the option of declaring their services to be concurrent subjects. Therefore there was no need to confer on the territories the power to delegate these subjects. However, before this had been decided, Huggins sarcastically remarked that: "The position arises that we discussed at the last Conference where the Territorial cow could not be inoculated by a Federal syringe."

The territorial legislatures also retained their power to delegate authority over subjects which were closely related to some which were found in the exclusive and concurrent lists. However, they could reverse such action and could continue to legislate, concurrently with the federal assembly, for the delegated subject. In the case of any inconsistency, territorial law would prevail.

In accordance with the pattern established in April, the federal legislative lists were described in "Chapter II, Part 2: Definition of Federal Legislative Powers". The exclusive list grew from 35 subjects to 42. It contained: external affairs; defence; immigration and emigration; aliens; citizenship of the federation; banks and banking; control of imports and exports and exchange control; promotion of exports; the distribution, purchase and sale of certain specified goods; customs and excise, including export duties; taxes on income, profits and sales; currency, coinage and legal tender; guarantee of loans; incorporated companies; insurance other than insurance undertaken by a territorial government; bills of exchange, cheques and promissory notes; copyright, patents, trade marks, designs and merchandise marks; inter-territorial roads; railways and ancillary services; shipping and harbours; aviation; meteorology; agriculture in Southern Rhodesia; animal health and diseases in Southern Rhodesia; plant pests and diseases in Southern Rhodesia; posts, telegraphs, telephones, wireless and post office savings banks; major irrigation and water works; atomic power; primary and secondary education of persons other than Africans; higher education (of all races); weights and measures; the federal public service; federal public relations; audit of federal public accounts; federal police; federal courts other than the federal supreme court; legal proceedings between the federation and a territory or between territories; legal proceedings by or against the federation other than proceedings against or by a territory; professional qualifications; old age pensions paid by the federal government; national parks; national monuments; and any other matter, whether or not otherwise within the exclusive legislative competence of the federal legislature, with respect to which for thc time being a power to make laws was expressly conferred by or under any other provisions of the constitution on the federal, and not a territorial, legislature.

Some of these subjects were accepted in this list without comment, others merited some discussion and a few provoked heated debate. The problem which arose in the course of the examination of the first subject, "External Affairs", was the question of the Congo Basin Treaties. "This nauseating receptacle — the Congo Basin," commented Swinton, confessing that he had never understood these treaties in all the years in which he had administered or dealt with them when President of the Board of Trade or Colonial Secretary. He doubted whether anyone understood them but was convinced that it was enough to say that the federal government would be bound by existing treaties. The Conference agreed to make such a general reference to permit matters to be dealt with as they arose. It included in the definition of "External Affairs" the implementation of treaties, conventions and agreements with other countries and organisations, and the extradition of fugitive offenders and the removal of prisoners.

The internal security aspects of the second subject, "Defence," drew the delegates into a considerable debate on the question of centralising the police forces. With regard to "Defence" itself, Huggins insisted that the federation should inherit the autonomy and financial responsibility currently enjoyed by Southern Rhodesia lest the new state be a long way from attaining dominion status. The British hoped that the existing forces would continue to constitute a reserve for their Middle-East Command, while the northerners expressed fears of increased costs. Huggins was confident, however, that economies could be made by a reduction in manpower and, in any case, the Finance Committee of the Conference found that any extra costs would not be as high as feared and there would be no need to adjust the pattern of the distribution of revenue.

"Immigration into and Emigration from the Federation" provoked an argument as to whether these were matters to be administered by the police. "Aliens" and "Citizenship of the Federation" were non-controversial. "Banks and Banking, other than Land Banks as defined in item 49 (in the Concurrent List); control of capital issues" was a compromise between the recommendations of the Fiscal Commission, which wanted this subject to be in the exclusive list, and the drafting party who sought to have it made concurrent because of the difficulties of leaving the land banks in territorial hands. The Conference accepted the advice of its Finance Committee and left "Banks" in the exclusive list and inserted "Land Banks" in the concurrent to encourage agriculture in the federal and territorial spheres. This would enable the land banks also to continue to provide finance for housing. While the "Control of imports into and exports from the Federation: exchange control" and "Promotion of exports from the Federation" were accepted without comment, there was some argument over "The distribution, purchase and sale of such manufactured and un-manufactured commodities as the Governor-General may from time to time specify, the control of their wholesale and retail price and the payment from the revenues of the Federation of subsidies in respect of commodities so specified".

There was an established practice, particularly in Nyasaland and Southern Rhodesia, of paying the African farmer a lower price than the European farmer and using the balance for the development of the African areas. The premise was that, while African production costs were lower than those of the European, African districts always lagged in development. The Conference agreed that the territories should continue to raise levies from source, and excised from the concurrent list the "Purchase and Sale of Commodities by Governments" and "Marketing Boards", which had been placed there in April, to ensure total territorial control.

"Guarantees by the Federal Government of loans", which was new, was inserted to allow borrowing by the territorial Governments which was sanctioned by the loans council. "Railways and ancillary services, including ancillary transport services", were readily accepted as exclusively federal but, as will be seen, featured in a considerable debate on trade unionism.

As could be expected, the resolution of the question of centralising agriculture, or at least aspects of it, was hard fought. Prior to the Conference, the Southern Rhodesian Government, still anxious to be rid of this, suggested that European agriculture together with animal health should be concurrent and that African agriculture and tsetse fly control should be capable of upward delegation by the territories. Alternatively, "Agriculture other than the supervision of Agriculture in areas occupied by Africans" could be made concurrent. The drafting party, in turn, reminded the Conference that its predecessor had decided to leave agriculture entirely in territorial control because the Northern Rhodesian and Nyasaland agricultural departments were indivisible and, in any case, agriculture closely affected the daily life of the Africans. Moreover, the drafting party found difficulty in defining European and African agriculture because it was likely that a member of one race would want to provide capital for a member of another. This latter likelihood, it was acknowledged, was not a problem if the second Southern Rhodesian suggestion were adopted.

In the Conference, Caldicott pointed out that, in the White Paper, agriculture had remained a divided subject because import and export control and the control of prices had been placed in the exclusive list, and the marketing boards in the concurrent list, despite all other aspects remaining territorial. The Southern Rhodesian motive, Caldicott claimed, was only to make the federation self-sufficient in food which required centralised planning. Southern Rhodesia, he was confident, had the right system, modelled on that in Britain and South Africa, which ensured that all agricultural matters came under one portfolio. The flaw in the Northern Rhodesian system was that the Member for Agriculture did not direct marketing or price control. The real anxiety in the North was that African agriculture should not become federal. As Southern Rhodesia agreed with this, there was no reason why all European agriculture and its supporting services should not be gradually transferred through being made concurrent. Beckett, the Northern Rhodesian Member for Agriculture, though warning that he did not have the support of his delegation, agreed. He felt, however, that, as the dissection of the northern departments would be difficult, the tempo of transfer would have to be slow. He proposed that tsetse and veterinary research should join the other agricultural research topics already in the concurrent list.

On 5 January, Caldicott suggested that agriculture should remain under territorial control until the territories asked to be relieved of their departments. Thus Southern Rhodesia could transfer its departments immediately and its share of revenue could be accordingly adjusted to avoid any additional burden on the other territories. The amount in question was about £2 000 000.

Rennie, the first to reply, ignored this suggestion and merely revealed that some of his delegation felt that the current staff shortages would render the division of the departments impossible. Swinton and Welensky, however preferred agriculture to be concurrent to avoid the difficulties of a constitutional amendment when federalisation was required. Sir Geoffrey Colby, Governor of Nyasaland, disagreed because agriculture then became ultimately a federal responsibility. He suggested upward delegation and won over some of the British representatives, including Swinton. Caldicott then accepted agriculture as concurrent with the reservation that it could only become federal with the permission of the territorial Governors.

After Beckett suggested that they should return to the first idea, Barrow declared that they were making heavy weather of this when logic demanded that agriculture be concurrent so that it would remain territorial but could easily become federal. Argument then ensued over the definition of "concurrent". The matter was passed to the Legal and Finance Committees but not before Lyttelton and Welensky had remarked on the necessity to exclude African agriculture or greatly damage the cause.

The Legal Committee proposed, and the Conference accepted, that Southern Rhodesian European agriculture be placed in the exclusive list. Consequently, the Finance Committee suggested that Southern Rhodesia's share of revenue should be reduced, and the federal share increased, by four per cent.

Accordingly, "Item 24. Animal health and diseases in Southern Rhodesia" and "Item 25. Plant pests and diseases in Southern Rhodesia" were included in this list. Likewise a provision was made in the description of the concurrent list allowing the northern legislatures to declare non-African agriculture, animal health and the control of animal and plant pests, excluding the tsetse fly (the control of which could be delegated), to be concurrent. The definition of agriculture specifically omitted forestry and irrigation. A footnote prescribed the necessary adjustment to the federal revenues.

Inevitably, similar arguments arose over the control of irrigation. The Conference in April had placed "Water, including canals and other inland waters, catchment areas, water supply and storage, water power, irrigation, drainage and embankments, control of silt, and riparian rights" in the concurrent list. However, the Northern Rhodesian delegation now demanded that this item should be re-drawn to read: "Such irrigation and water works as the Governor-General may designate as major irrigation or water works and as works ancillary thereto", and be transferred to the exclusive list. The Southern Rhodesians in the drafting party, and Caldicott in the debate on 7 January, however, resisted any change. Considerable argument ensued because catchment areas were involved and were mainly to be found in African areas which, in the northern view, could not be affected by federal legislation. Southern Rhodesian arguments on the conservation of entire river systems were to no avail, and on 14 January the Northern Rhodesian prescription was adopted.

In the April 1952 Conference the governor-general had been entrusted to decide whether an institution could be described as one providing higher education. The Southern Rhodesian delegation were now, however, anxious to prevent any friction between the governor-general and the legislature, and insisted that this provision be removed from Item 30. The Conference concurred that it should read: "Higher education (including higher education of Africans), that is to say, institutions or other bodies offering courses of a university, technological or professional character."

Pressure by the Southern Rhodesians also affected the degree of centralisation of the police forces. In the course of the discussion on "Defence", reference was made to a Southern Rhodesian proposal to include "Internal Security" in the concurrent list, while all other matters relating to law and order remained in territorial hands. Huggins explained that his Government favoured an organisation like the American FBI to deal with insurgencies such as Mau Mau on a federation-wide basis. However, with the exception of a fingerprint bureau, certain aspects of criminal investigation and the gathering of intelligence, Swinton would not allow any centralisation of the police forces. Unsworth agreed, and Lyttelton sought confirmation from the Conference, but Huggins was not yet satisfied because, in certain types of emergency, police, rather than military, reinforcement was appropriate.

Greenfield declared that he still favoured the Canadian system and noted that the Civil Service Preparatory Commission saw the appointment of the inspector-general as a step towards unification. He felt that the complexities of the problem should not be disregarded as the army would be involved in internal security, and there were matters of treason, subversion and the promotion of racial hatred which should be legislated against federally. Rennie maintained that subversion could be adequately dealt with by the territories, but Greenfield disagreed because it was an aspect of defence. Swinton could not see the relevance of subversion to the control of the police and, with the support of Salisbury, sought agreement on the centralisation only of the collection of intelligence, leaving the territorial forces to co-operate on their traditional *ad hoc* basis. The delegates disagreed, and the argument rambled on inconclusively until Lyttelton closed the morning's proceedings.

Undeterred, Greenfield raised the question again during the afternoon, repeating his contention that the last Conference had been mistaken, and drawing attention again to the provision of the Civil Service Preparatory Commission for the eventual merger. He noted that this Commission had condemned as pointless the inclusion in the concurrent list of European police recruitment, central reserve and criminal investigation and records. It had only recommended the transfer of fingerprint records and immigration by upward delegation. Greenfield preferred civilian control of immigration and found the value of a central intelligence unit in an internal crisis, uniformity, economy and efficiency, all reasons to federalise the police. The Canadian system, he said, remained the most suitable method.

Predictably, the main resistance to Greenfield came from Unsworth who, remarking that this subject had been exhaustively debated in April, reminded the Conference that the Canadian system had not been universally adopted in Canada. He objected to "Police" being concurrent as the federation would thereby acquire ultimate responsibility, and he thought that there would be little difficulty arising out of territorial control. Immigration was currently handled only by the police on an agency basis and, when the army was called in to restore order, it, and not the police, decided on the degree of force to be used.

Swinton concluded that the Conference was close to accepting a provision for eventual centralisation, but Colonel E. M. Wilson of Northern Rhodesia wanted the eventual adoption of the Canadian system. Greenfield supported Wilson, while Welensky could not see why the Canadian system could not be adopted immediately.

After Professor K. C. Wheare had doubted the need to say anything specific, the matter was passed for comment to the Legal and Finance Committees. Wheare, on request, wrote a paper on states of emergency in which he found that the powers granted under "Defence" met all contingencies.

The Conference adopted the formula devised by the Legal and Finance Committees which placed in the exclusive list, as "Item 35. The establishment, training, maintenance and administration of a Federal police force for service in the employment of any Territory or use in any Territory at the request of the Governor of that Territory in addition to or in substitution for the police force of that Territory: and the conditions (including conditions as to payment by the Territory) on which the Federation will make such police available for such use or employment". A footnote provided that "unless and until the Federal Police are employed by all three Territories the charge made to any Territory for the services or use of the Federal Police (other than occasional use for emergency purposes) will include a proportionate share of the cost of Headquarters and training". In the concurrent list appeared "Item

61. Fingerprints, Identification and Criminal Records", and "Item 62. Security information".

There was no further difficulty with the remaining eight items of the exclusive list and much accord in the discussions on the "Second Part — The Concurrent List" which contained: deportation; naturalisation; inter-territorial migration; control of movement of goods between territories; industrial development; land banks; co-operative societies with objects connected with agriculture except where a majority of the members are African; hire purchase; roads other than inter-territorial roads; road-rail crossings; regulation of road traffic; electricity; scientific and industrial research; the service and execution in any territory of the civil and criminal processes, judgments, decrees, orders and decisions of the courts of any other country and the attendance of persons from any territory at the courts of any other country; prisons and other institutions for treating offenders against the law; care and protection of minors; fingerprints, identification and criminal records; security information; health (other than silicosis in Northern Rhodesia); tourism; town planning; geological, trigonometrical, topographical and cadastral surveys; government films, broadcasting and television; archives; census and statistics; indemnity for acts or omissions in breach of a territorial law within the exclusive legislative competence of a territorial legislature; registration of births and deaths; registration and record of printed publications; commissions of inquiry; any other matter, whether or not otherwise within the legislative competence of the federal assembly or, as the case may be, of a territorial legislature, with respect to which, for the time being, a power to make laws was expressly conferred by or under any other provision of this scheme on both the federal assembly and a territorial legislature.

There was little that was extraordinary in this list. The inclusion of migration between territories reflected Southern Rhodesian fears of an Asian influx from the northern territories. The control of the movement of goods would allow a levelling of prices and prevent unreasonable territorial restrictions on the flow of trade. Silicosis was excluded from "Health" because the Northern Rhodesian Government and the copper industry, which would be a territorial responsibility, had worked and would work so closely together on this matter that there would be little role for the federal government to play.

In the notes attached to this list there was the Conference's provision for the possible transfer of the Northern Rhodesian and Nyasaland non-African agriculture. The second note dealt with the controversial control of the trade unions. A footnote in the White Paper had expressed the hope that, ultimately, unified conciliation machinery would be devised, but the drafting party proposed that a note be included after the description of the concurrent list which merely acknowledged the exclusive right of the territories to legislate in the matters of trade union affairs and the settlement of disputes arising out of employment. The federal government would deal with its own employees but not with those of the statutory corporations. Keller, in the first plenary session, it will be recalled, had entered a plea for the incorporation of the control of the unions in the exclusive list to avoid the growth of differential wage structures and other sources of friction. Later he interrupted Swinton to repeat this demand and added that he wished all negotiations concerning employment on the railways to be based on Southern Rhodesia's Industrial Conciliation Act. After much discussion, no progress had been made and Welensky was asked to seek an accommodation with Keller in private. The stubborn refusal by the Southern Rhodesians not to allow civil servants, as opposed to the employees of state corporations, to belong to trade unions, led, in the tenth plenary session, to the setting up of an *ad hoc* committee under Hopkinson.

The *Ad Hoc* Committee sensibly separated the question of civil servants and trade unions from the problem of fulfilling the undertakings which had been given to the railway workers when the Rhodesia Railways had been nationalised in 1947. The Committee, using the formula of the working party, produced wording adopted by the Conference which gave the territories exclusive power to legislate for the trade unions and like associations and to settle disputes between employers and employees, with the exception of those involving federal government employees. The federal government would exclusively deal with disputes with and among its own employees and civil servants, and could recognise any of their associations. The Committee and the Conference were guided by Keller and Welensky, and appended a footnote to the exclusive list which proclaimed that the territorial legislatures would retain the power to amend the existing legislation relating to the trade unions and industrial conciliation on the railways. This would in particular apply to the laws giving legal effect to the assurances given at the time of the nationalisation of the railways.

The third note to the concurrent list provided that the federal legislature could legislate on incidental matters arising out of its powers and could appoint officers to enforce the resultant law. The territorial Governments would have like powers with respect to their own legislation.

The Conference made some changes in "Part 3. The Federal Assembly". The total membership remained at 35 and, as before, comprised 26 elected members and nine representatives of African interests. In the latter category, adjustments had been made and the seven elected and two appointed members had been replaced by six "Specially Elected African Members" and three Europeans, one of whom, from Southern Rhodesia, would be "Specially Elected" while the others, representing Northern Rhodesia and Nyasaland, would be "Specially Appointed". Although the speaker could be chosen from within or without the assembly, the deputy speaker would be one of the members. The territorial allocation of the 26 elected seats was unchanged with Southern Rhodesia receiving 14, Northern Rhodesia eight and Nyasaland four.

After the first general election, the federal assembly would decide on the qualifications of its members and on all matters relating to their election. However, as such legislation was politically important, it would require the sanction of two-thirds of the total membership of the house and would be reserved for the Monarch's pleasure. A member of a territorial legislature standing for federal election would have to resign his territorial seat before assuming the federal seat. The reverse procedure would apply to federal MPs standing in territorial elections. The first federal general election would be held under existing regulations in Northern and Southern Rhodesia with the exception that the governor-general would delimit the electoral districts. As Nyasaland did not possess an electoral system, it had been decided in April that, for the first federal general election, the governor-general, adopting whichever method seemed appropriate, direct or indirect election, would make the necessary regulations with the agreement of the Governor and the sanction of the Secretary of State. These regulations would exist until the Nyasaland Legislative Council decided that federal electoral law could apply and thereby relinquished control to the federal assembly. Prior to the Conference, the Southern Rhodesian Government wished to know what regulations were likely to be applied, and the drafting party suggested a five year limit on the power of the Nyasaland Legislative Council to delay. In the Conference, however, Barrow rejected any further discussion and warned that the imposition on Nyasaland of any advanced electoral system could result in Asians capturing all four of the Nyasaland federal seats. Huggins explained that his delegation merely wished to reduce the possibility of friction between the governor-general and the federal government. The Conference decided that the safest course was not to amend this provision.

The two African and the one European specially elected representatives of African interests from Southern Rhodesia had to be British citizens, while those from Northern Rhodesia and Nyasaland could also be British Protected Persons. These members could not owe allegiance to foreign powers, hold offices of emolument under the Crown, be bankrupts, criminals, or insane, or be disqualified from election to the federal assembly. The Southern Rhodesians would be elected in accordance with regulations made by their Governor, and the two Northern Rhodesian and two Nyasaland members would be elected by bodies designated by their Governors as representative. Here again a Southern Rhodesian innovation was rejected which sought to ensure that these members should be drawn into the party system and should not stand purely as representatives of one race, elected, perhaps, for their anti-white stance. The Southern Rhodesians also proposed multi-racial electoral colleges so that all races would have a voice in the election of these members. Barrow, however, thought that, given the current African frame of mind, this would be disastrous. Welensky, though sympathetic with the Southern Rhodesian objective, agreed and the Conference decided against amendment because, at least, the system would enable the northern Governors to find African representatives even if the existing territorial representative bodies refused to elect them.

The specially elected and appointed representatives would retain their seats until the dissolution of the federal assembly, their death, resignation, bankruptcy or insanity. The federal supreme court would resolve any question of their right to membership. The two specially appointed members would be chosen by the Governors of Northern Rhodesia and Nyasaland.

This third part of Chapter II described also the election and tenure of the speaker and his deputy. It prescribed that the quorum of the assembly would be twelve members and penalties were established for knowingly sitting and voting in the house when not entitled so to do. The privileges of membership would be defined by federal law but would not exceed those of the Commons. The initial provisions for immunities would be made by the governor-general.

In "Chapter III: Legislation and Procedure" no adjustment was made to the requirement that members would swear oaths of allegiance. Decisions in the house would depend on a majority of the votes of members present. The assembly would make its own standing orders but the governor-general would prescribe them for the purposes of the first meeting of the house. No vote, resolution, address or bill for the appropriation of any part of the revenues or other funds could be passed unless it had been recommended in the same session in a message to the house by the governor-general. Bills, having been passed by the assembly, would be presented to the governor-general who would be empowered to assent to them or reserve them for Her Majesty's pleasure. He would have to reserve any bill which revoked or amended any provision of the federal constitution or which was repugnant to or inconsistent with the provisions of that constitution. He would have to do likewise with any bill to which the African affairs board objected, with bills relating to the electoral regulations of the assembly, and where there appeared to be an inconsistency with Her Majesty's obligations under any international agreement. He would also have to reserve bills which granted him land, money or any other donation, or which contained provisions which had already been refused Her Majesty's assent or which had been totally disallowed by her. She would be able to disallow a federal law within twelve months of its being assented to by the governor-general. The federal assembly had to meet at least once a year, and twelve months could not pass between its meetings. The governor-general could prorogue or dissolve the federal assembly at any time, and would have to dissolve it five years after the first day of the first meeting after a general election. General elections would be held within three months of dissolution.

It was provided in "Chapter IV: The Executive" that the latter would be headed by a governor-general or an acting governor-general who would act on the advice of his ministers except in the circumstances where he was empowered to use his own discretion, when he would be ultimately responsible to the Secretary of State. The executive authority of the federation would extend to all matters on which its assembly was empowered to legislate. The current arrangements between the Southern Rhodesian and British Governments would be adopted to enable the latter to conclude trade and other agreements on behalf of the federation. The governor-general would be able, with the consent of a territorial Governor, to entrust that Governor or other territorial authority with any matter over which the authority of the federal assembly extended. He could likewise delegate some of his personal powers to the territorial Governors. Provisions of federal law relating to any territory would not have effect until the territorial Governor had declared so in his gazette. The executive authority of the territories would be unaffected by federation except with regard to subjects on the exclusive list. The federation and the territories would share control over subjects on the concurrent list. A territorial Governor, with the consent of the governor-general, could entrust the federal government with any subject which he felt was ancillary or closely related to any matter included in the exclusive or concurrent lists.

The governor-general would appoint a prime minister and other ministers and assign their departments to them. A minister would hold office during Her Majesty's pleasure but would not retain his office unless, within four months of his appointment, he became a member of the federal assembly. A minister could not hold a federal and a territorial portfolio simultaneously. The governor-general would be assisted by an executive council comprising the prime minister and such ministers whom he recommended. The council members would take the normal oaths of allegiance and, unless there was a specific reference to this discretion, the governor-general would act in accordance with their advice. Finally, the governor-general was given the prerogative of pardon for offences against federal law.

The debate on "Chapter V: The African Affairs Board" absorbed much of the Conference's time. Huggins, it will be recalled, had made this the subject of his ultimatum on the opening day because the result of the referendum depended on it. Speaking in the plenary session on 6 January, he revealed that the first Southern Rhodesian demand after the April Conference had been for the removal of the board, but it was realised that the British Government would not concur, and the alternative of bringing the board into the parliamentary structure was advanced. If the board became a select committee, it would at least, Huggins claimed, answer a hitherto unnoticed criticism that the board would have little to do and consequently its members would seem overpaid and would be resented. By contrast, the select committee would be MPs having plenty with which to occupy themselves, and the board itself would be an inexpensive instrument because the staff of the legislature would provide secretarial and other services. Huggins declared he would use this argument to advantage in the referendum campaign. The Southern Rhodesians proposed that a European representative of African interests should be chairman and could be chosen by a majority of the federal assembly, or by three European members for African interests or by all nine representatives of African interests. The board, the Southern Rhodesians thought, should comprise the three African members, the remaining two European representatives of African interests and one ordinary elected member. This amendment would soften the dislike of the Southern Rhodesians for the special representation of Africans.

Although the Southern Rhodesian Opposition delegates acknowledged that the board would be improved, they warned that the Southern Rhodesians wanted its abolition and would reject even this amendment because they already possessed a more advanced system of safeguards and were, in any case, being asked to accept the special representation of Africans. Welensky confessed that he would prefer the abandonment of the board but knew that this would be asking too much of the British Government. Rennie reminded the Southern Rhodesians that the federal government would not merely be a projection of their Government but also had to take into account northern views. Unsworth found some substance in Huggins's proposal yet warned that, if a party system came into being, the select committee could be governed by party dictates. Equally undesirable would be the result of a failure to develop political parties because then there would be in parliament a body of men who were interested only in the affairs of one racial group instead of the nation as a whole. Furthermore, it would be anomalous that a select committee should be able to impede the work of parliament by having bills reserved. He found accord with Stockil who claimed that a select committee should never be more than an instrument of review.

Swinton and Lyttelton thereupon pointed out that the African affairs board would not interrupt the flow of business within parliament and, moreover, that despite an objection by the board, the governor-general would be free to assent to a bill if he did not think that it was a differentiating measure or if it was in the public interest to implement it despite its racial bias. Hopkinson wondered why Stockil had seemingly changed his mind, because during his visit in August 1952, Hopkinson had questioned two prominent Rhodesia Party members — one of whom was Winston Field, the future Prime Minister of Southern Rhodesia — and they had said that the African affairs board was no longer an obstacle with regard to their acceptance of federation. Stockil replied that this merely illustrated that federation was not a party issue in Southern Rhodesia. He would not accept, however, that Field had purported to speak for him.

Huggins, joining the debate, agreed that Southern Rhodesians could not comprehend why anything more than their well-proven system of safeguards was needed. Whitehead claimed that the probable lack of expertise of the board would worry the Southern Rhodesian public, but its merit as a select committee was that, if it was too idle, it would be easier to disband than a statutory body.

Eastwood raised again the alternative of a bi-cameral parliament, but the British Ministers warned that Africans had to be, at the outset, in the lower house which, if it were entirely elective, would force a considerable lowering of the existing qualifications which currently disenfranchised 97 per cent of the population. As this would end the dominance of the literate minority, it was unacceptable to the British Government. However, the majority could not be entirely neglected, and as a result Britain was irrevocably committed to the principle of special representation.

Moffat confirmed that the board, as a safeguard, would mean something to the Africans even though it would not seem as important to them as those preventing undesirable constitutional amendments. He would therefore support the amendment if it would make the African affairs board more acceptable to the British public and the Southern Rhodesian electorate. Welensky concurred and reminded the Conference that they were balancing the fate of the board with that of the federation. Lord Salisbury recognised this to be so and sought time to consider the issues. He could see that the select committee might be an improvement, and answered Unsworth by saying that any party political pressure within it would be counteracted by the responsibilities of the members to the African population. Safeguards, he reminded the Conference, were fundamental, and justice had to be seen to be done. Lyttelton agreed that the issue of the African affairs board was "the key point of the whole Conference" over which they needed a night's reflection.

The next day, 7 January, the British Ministers agreed that the select committee would avoid duplicating the functions of the African MPs by an independent body. The title, the "African Affairs Board", would, however, have to be retained if the change were to be accepted in Britain. They proposed a reduction of members by one so that there would be a chairman and five members, drawn only from and chosen by the nine representatives of African interests. The six members would comprise three Africans and three Europeans from whom the governor-general would choose a chairman who would have a casting as well as an original vote. After Rennie had regretted that the members, with the pressure of all their other parliamentary duties, would not have the time to become experts in the complexities of African affairs, this proposal was passed to the Legal Committee for re-drafting and thereafter through several plenary sessions, whence it emerged as the formula adopted by the Conference. The board's function remained to make representations to the prime minister, or through the prime minister to the executive council, on anything it felt would advance African interests. It would also assist the territorial Governments in the study of matters affecting Africans. A particular function was to draw attention to any bill or other instrument of law which had been introduced into the federal assembly and which seemed to be of a differentiating nature. A differentiating measure meant one which subjected Africans to any disadvantageous conditions, restrictions or disabilities, but did not do likewise to the Europeans.

This definition was the product of lengthy debate, as was the decision whether or not a select committee should be so privileged as to receive any bill before it was introduced into the assembly. It was eventually decided that, to fulfil its role, this would have to happen unless the governor-general, in his discretion, certified in writing that the proposed bill was of such a nature that it was not in the public interest that it should be publicised before its introduction in the assembly, or was so urgent that it was not in the public interest to delay its introduction while a copy was sent to the African affairs board. An outside body could not have interfered with the workings of the federal assembly, but now that the African affairs board would be part of the parliamentary structure, it became possible to empower it, at any stage of the passage of a bill through the assembly, to table a report in the house stating that it found the bill or one of its clauses to be a differentiating measure. If its objections were then met, it would signify its acceptance of the revised bill to the assembly. If, nevertheless, a seemingly objectionable bill was passed, the board would signify, in writing, to the speaker that it wished the bill to be reserved for the Monarch's pleasure. The speaker would deliver this request to the governor-general when the bill was presented for assent. Thereupon the governor-general would withhold the assent and send the bill and the verdict of the board to the Secretary of State. As the Southern Rhodesians feared that Africans could be elected to the federal parliament on an "anti-white ticket" and could, when absenteeism weakened the board, force through their views, it was provided, however, that the governor-general could use his discretion and give his assent if he was satisfied that the bill did not differentiate between the races and that the objections of the board were irrelevant or frivolous. He could do likewise if convinced by the prime minister that it was essential in the public interest that the bill be brought into law. If the governor-general did take such action, he would have to furnish the Secretary of State with the bill, the board's objection and a statement on his reasons for assenting.

With regard to subordinate legislation the board would report to the prime minister, within 30 days of its publication, giving reasons why it considered this legislation to be differentiating. The prime minister would send the board's report and his comments thereon to the governor-general who would transmit them to the Secretary of State. The Secretary of State would have twelve months in which to express his disapproval of this legislation. If he disapproved, he would inform the governor-general who would appoint a day after which that legislation would be deemed to be revoked. This action would not prejudice anything already done under this legislation or the making of new legislation.

The recommendations of the Fiscal Commission were, in the main, incorporated in "Chapter VI: Finance". The revenues of the federation would consist of its share of the taxes on income and profits, the yield of customs and excise duties, earnings from postage, telephones and telecommunications, a proportion of sales tax, fees on services rendered by the federation and such other revenues which might accrue from matters under federal jurisdiction. All revenues would be paid into one consolidated revenue fund. First charges against this fund would be the cost of collection, its management, the emoluments of the governor-general and the salaries or allowances of the chief justice of the federation and the judges of the supreme court. Money could only be withdrawn from the consolidated revenue fund under an appropriation made in terms of federal law. The federation could make grants-in-aid to any territory and could supply, on request, the services of the auditor-general whose duties were described.

The second part of this Chapter empowered the governor-general to name a date when territorial laws would cease to apply with regard to the free movement of goods. Taxes on exports would be divided between the Governments on the same ratio as income tax but sales tax would be distributed as described by federal law with the proviso that not more than a third should go to the federation. Motor spirit was the exception and would be totally exempt from federal tax.

In the third part of the Chapter, "Taxes on Income", "income" was interpreted to include profits. It was laid down that, after the cost of collection had been deducted, the proceeds of income tax would be distributed in accordance with the ratio established by the Fiscal Commission but adjusted by the Conference to cover the cost of the federal administration of European agriculture in Southern Rhodesia. Thus the federal share was increased by four per cent to 64 per cent, while Southern Rhodesia's was reduced to 13 per cent. Northern Rhodesia kept its 17 per cent and Nyasaland its six per cent. The territories would be able to charge a surcharge on income tax but the federal legislature could only do so in times of internal emergency or external war. The territorial legislatures could authorise the federation to levy and collect surcharges on the incomes of persons and corporate bodies. A surcharge could not, however, exceed 20 per cent of the income tax paid by an individual in a year, and a body corporate's surcharge would be a levy on every pound which was liable to income tax and would not exceed a fifth of the income tax rate.

In order to review the proportions of the inter-governmental distribution of revenue after the first three years of federation, the governor-general, after consulting the territorial Governors, would appoint a commission of inquiry. Thereafter such commissions would be appointed every five years. Governments would be able to tax each other's property and, finally, the governor-general and the territorial Governors were instructed to co-ordinate the distribution of incomes from taxes in the transitory period and the governor-general would furnish the necessary regulations.

"Part 4. Borrowing" established that there would be a loans council consisting of a federal minister nominated by the governor-general and one representative of each territory appointed by its Governor. When the voting within the council was equally divided, the federal member would have a casting vote. The loans council would require the federal and territorial Governments to submit external loan programmes which would include amounts which the statutory corporations required. Any loan raised by the federal assembly in an emergency would be outside the jurisdiction of the loans council but, otherwise, it would have to approve the borrowing requirements and could decide on lower aggregate amounts when it felt that the programmes conflicted with the economic interests of the federation. If the aggregate figure was lowered, the money raised would be distributed on the same ratio as the proceeds of income tax. The Governments would have to abide by the decision of the council, but the governor-general would require the loans council to re-examine the proportions of its loan distribution and lay an explanation before the federal assembly. The Governments would not have to take up the full amounts of the loans assigned to them by the council and the federal government would be empowered to guarantee loans raised by the territorial Governments. The federal government would bear the costs of the loans council but the expenses incidental to the raising of a loan would accrue to the body raising it. None of these regulations would apply to money advanced by the British Government to the federal or territorial Governments.

In the fifth and final part of this Chapter, the governor-general was instructed to appoint an apportionment commission to effect the transfer of assets and liabilities. The membership of this commission would be five, comprising a chairman and one member appointed by the governor-general and three nominees of the territorial Governments. It was intended that the commission would complete its work within a year of its appointment, and the governor-general would make the regulations for the conduct of its business and to effect its decisions with regard to the transfer of assets and liabilities which would include portions of the public debts of the territories, representing loans relating to assets to be adopted. The amount of the responsibility for public debts to be assumed would, in the case of Southern Rhodesia, be not less than £60 000 000, Northern Rhodesia £17 000 000 and Nyasaland £7 000 000.

The final form of the provisions of "Chapter VII: The Federal Public Service" was the product of a considerable struggle. The Public Service Sub-Committee of the Conference would meet six times over the question of inter-service transfer alone. One inherent danger was that, if too much was written into the constitution, a constitutional amendment would be needed and a two-thirds majority would have to be secured every time a minor adjustment was required. Before the Conference, there had been fundamental differences of opinion. The Southern Rhodesian Government had thought that transfer and secondment to the federal public service should be compulsory, in contrast to the view of the British and northern territorial Governments. The Civil Service Preparatory Commission had strongly recommended that a powerful independent public service commission be on hand at the outset to advise the governor-general on matters of pay, conditions of service, posts to be created, the organisation of government and the recruitment of men.

The British and northern territorial Governments supported this contention, but the Southern Rhodesian Government felt that only an interim body was needed, but it also proposed that there should be an interim ministry assisting the governor-general. The interim commission would be composed of representatives of the northern Establishment Boards and of the Southern Rhodesian Public Service Commission. It would act under the interim ministry whose advice the governor-general would be bound to accept. Once the federal assembly was established, the permanent federal public service commission could be created by federal law. The British Government contended that the delicacy and complexity of its work meant that the initial body would have to be called the public service commission and that it would have to be in existence for at least three years before being replaced by a permanent body. The Southern Rhodesians had replied that they would accept this if an interim ministry were allowed. However, in the Conference on 8 January, Greenfield explained that the Southern Rhodesians really preferred that the federal assembly should have the task of framing the legislation for the permanent commission. The temporary commission could make preliminary arrangements on the understanding that the powers of the interim ministry should be strictly limited.

The Conference accepted this as a means of avoiding the inflexibility which would result from prescribing the establishment of the public service commission in the federal constitution, obviating the need for a constitutional amendment for every minor change. The Legal Committee confirmed that placing "The Federal Public Service" in the exclusive list conferred sufficient power for its establishment. Thus "Part I" of this Chapter said little more than that the governor-general could establish, before the first meeting of the federal assembly, the interim public service commission to advise him on matters relating to the public service. He would prescribe the powers and duties of the commission. Its membership would comprise a chairman appointed by the governor-general and three members nominated by the territorial Governors. The regulations of the governor-general would remain in force until revoked or amended by the federal assembly.

The Civil Service Preparatory Commission found the compulsory transfer of civil servants, who were domiciled outside the territories, objectionable and recommended that the terms and conditions of service should be so attractive as to induce men to volunteer. To give these men time to evaluate their decision, the Commission proposed that they should have the option of secondment, so that, if they decided to refuse, they could claim "abolition of office" terms in accordance with the pension laws. The terms sufficient to tempt were thought to be those of the Southern Rhodesian Civil Service with, in the case of the northern officers, cash equivalents of their free passages, housing and non-contributory pension schemes.

The British and northern territorial Governments concurred, but the Southern Rhodesian Government felt that, if secondment were compulsory but for a limited period, the careers of the officers involved would not be affected and they would remain eligible for promotion within their own services. The underlying fear was that a key group of officials in Southern Rhodesia might take advantage of the advent of federation to demand "abolition of office" terms thereby denying the new government the most essential men. Thus compulsory transfer was as important as secondment.

In the debate, Lyttelton felt that this arrangement was only appropriate while the interim commission existed. Rennie and Greenfield disagreed, stating that two or three years of duration was necessary. Rennie did not favour compulsion but acknowledged that it was the only way that staff would be secured. The Conference accepted compulsory secondment of officers for two years beginning from the date of the first general election, because thereafter the federal government would start taking over its departments. The Conference, however, rejected the idea of compulsory transfer.

Thus "Part 2. The Employment of Territorial Public Service Officers in the Federal Public Service" gave the governor-general the power to name a day when any department or office, over which the federal government had executive authority, could be transferred, and every territorial officer employed therein would be seconded for five years. Other personnel could be acquired by the territorial Governor agreeing to their transfer. The conditions of secondment provided that the officer would remain a territorial employee entitled to territorial conditions of service. He would continue to perform the same duties unless he agreed to a change. He did not have to serve outside his territory and his period of secondment would end when he accepted transfer to the federal government. Secondment would only be compulsory for two years. Abolition and pension terms for seconded officers were described.

Finally, "Part 3. Eligibility for Employment in the Service of the Federal Government" proclaimed that race alone would not make a person, otherwise qualified, ineligible for federal government service. Competence, experience, suitability and the circumstances of the locality where a person was to be employed would govern his selection.

There was little comment on "Chapter VIII: The Federal Judicature". The supreme court would consist of a chief justice and, unless the federal assembly sanctioned an increase, not less than two, and not more than six judges. The judges would be appointed by the governor-general under the public seal of the federation. This Chapter prescribed the qualifications of the judges, their tenure of office, salaries, precedence, oaths, and stated that the court would sit at a place designated by the governor-general. The expenses of the court and the emoluments of the judges would be charged to the consolidated revenue fund into which would be paid any fees earned. The federal supreme court would have original jurisdiction in any dispute between the federation and a territory, or between territories over the existence of a legal right. It could determine the right of any person to be or remain a member of the federal assembly, and any matter in which a writ or order of *mandamus* or prohibition or an injunction or interdict was sought against a federal officer.

The federal court would exclusively decide questions of interpretation of the federal constitution, or federal or territorial law referred by a lower court for decision. It would have exclusive appellate jurisdiction on interpretation of the federal or territorial constitutions. The federal legislature would be able to confer on the federal court the power to hear appeals on non-constitutional matters, and its decision would be final if the issue did not fall within the exclusive competence of a territorial legislature. The federal supreme court could be empowered with non-appellant jurisdiction by the federal and territorial legislatures with regard to affairs within their competence, though not with regard to criminal law or territorial law unless the sanction of the federal assembly was given. This court was given the ability to enforce its orders and the power to formulate its rules. Provision was made for appeals to the Privy Council when prescribed in federal law, except where the decisions of the federal supreme court or the territorial High Courts were deemed to be final. In the transitional period before the federal supreme court was in being, the practice of using the Rhodesia and Nyasaland Court of Appeal or the Appellate Division of the Supreme Court of the Union of South Africa would continue.

The first statement of "Part 1" of "Chapter IX: Miscellaneous" was a compromise between the Southern and Northern Rhodesian desire for a stronger statement and Lyttelton's view that nothing should be said, and urged that whenever practicable the federal and territorial Governments should consult together on all matters of common interest and concern. The second provision stated that the official language would be English. The third was that the rights under the Lewanika Concessions would be preserved. Finally, the federal government would adopt the British obligations, within its legal competence, with regard to agreements entered into on behalf of the territories before federation. Omitted was the provision in the April White Paper for federal legislation to have to lie on the tables of the territorial legislatures.

"Part 2. General Provisions as to the Interim Period" contained arrangements for the setting up of an interim government. It will be recalled that, as a rider to his ultimatum on the reform of the African affairs board, Huggins, in the first plenary session, had claimed that the Southern Rhodesians would not entrust the task of setting up the federal structure to the governor-general alone. The problem was discussed again on 5 January when a memorandum of the drafting party was laid before the Conference stating that, at first, it had been assumed that the governor-general would act in this matter in his own discretion. However, the Southern Rhodesian Government had pointed to the precedents in Australia and South Africa and had suggested that there should be an interim ministry to advise the governor-general, but had forgotten the matters of British protection in the North and the lack of dominion status. The Southern Rhodesian representatives on the drafting party had gone further and insisted that the interim cabinet should have executive power. The rest of the drafting party disagreed but would allow a convention under which, though the governor-general would act in his discretion, he would consult his ministers on all matters, and if he did not accept their advice he would have to inform the Secretary of State of his reasons. The drafting party thought that the interim ministry should comprise four representatives from Southern Rhodesia, three from Northern Rhodesia and two from Nyasaland.

In the Conference, Huggins again warned that the Southern Rhodesians would not accept an autocratic governor-general. Welensky suggested that a sub-committee should consider an interim ministry served by the delegates present at this Conference and headed by the man whom the governor-general thought would lead the first federal government. It would obviously be difficult to finance the interim body as it could not immediately take over the income tax receipts, but the sub-committee should suggest what functions could be performed by this ministry, what assistance it would need and how long it should exist. The Conference appointed the sub-committee, but rejected the Southern Rhodesian view and was determined that the temporary ministry should have only an advisory role.

The sub-committee reported on 14 January that the role of the temporary ministry would be to deal with the preparation of the territories for the first federal general election and thereafter form the skeleton of the future government. The general election was expected after January 1954, even though the rainy season would create difficulties for polling, because the federal order in council was unlikely to be ready before mid-1953. Thus it was thought that the interim period could be six months.

The Conference accepted thereupon that the order in council establishing the federation would authorise the immediate appointment of a governor-general and would allow him to choose a temporary ministry to advise him. To avoid unnecessary by-elections, it was agreed that service with the temporary ministry would not disqualify a person from membership of a territorial legislature. The governor-general, of course, would have full executive and legislative powers until the first meeting of the federal assembly. He would use his discretion but would seek the advice of his temporary ministers and, if it was unacceptable, obtain the views of the Secretary of State and act according to his instructions.

The review of "Part 3. Amendment of Constitution" resulted in the sharpest exchange in the Conference. Unsworth and Moffat laid a memorandum before the eighth plenary session which noted that this constitution was easier to amend than those of the existing federations. They accepted that it gave laudable flexibility but maintained that, because of the undertakings given, African land should not be affected by a constitutional bill. Furthermore, the territories would be autonomous and any bill which altered the legislative lists should require the support of two-thirds of each of the territorial legislatures. In the Drafting Committee, the Northern Rhodesians and the Nyasalanders had agreed to "freeze" the legislative lists, but the Southern Rhodesians had not. The British had then suggested that perhaps the African affairs board could be empowered to object to any alteration of the legislative lists.

Although in the Conference, Unsworth declared that there was little more to say, Swinton insisted on a full explanation of what was a radical change and a criticism of existing safeguards. Obliging, Unsworth, restating his appreciation of flexibility, explained that he was only seeking to secure the fundamental basis of the federation. Part of this was that African land would remain a territorial responsibility, secured by the existing Orders in Council, and that the territories would be autonomous and in no sense subordinate to the federation. As the Africans had been assured that the federal assembly could not interfere with their land, there would be the most serious consequences if the federal house sought to amend the constitution with regard to land rights. The British Government could veto any bill but only after its passage through the federal legislature. Therefore, land rights could not be mentioned in constitutional bills. Swinton warned that such was the nature of parliaments that nothing was permanent, but Unsworth was adamant that African land rights should only be capable of amendment through an order in council.

Turning to his second point, Unsworth still feared that the federal parliament could, through a constitutional bill, take away the autonomy of a territory even though the federation itself was a creation of the territories. Warming to his task, he maintained that the British veto would be inadequate protection because he had found firstly "that Southern Rhodesia does not really accept or agree with Federation. It is their view, . . . that it ought to be amalgamated, and that is the view not only of Southern Rhodesia but quite a number of people". He expected, at a comparatively early stage, the appearance of a bill to amend the constitution to remove the territorial functions and powers. As it was also clear "that the self-governing Federation will not . . . take kindly to interference by Her Majesty's Government in the United Kingdom", Unsworth could not see how the British Government would be able to prevent the gradual take-over of territorial powers. The only secure method was to copy the procedures of the existing federations and require constitutional amendments to be sanctioned by two-third majorities in the federal and territorial houses.

Swinton reminded Unsworth that the procedure was not merely a veto: it provided that a constitutional amendment, when objected to by the African affairs board or a territorial legislature, could not be approved by the British Government before it had won the acceptance of both Houses of the British Parliament. This was very different from a mere veto. Be that as it may, Unsworth argued, it was a negative power and it did not avert the possibility of a "head-on" collision with the self-governing federation which could have dangerous consequences.

Angrily Welensky reminded Unsworth that he, Huggins, and the Northern Rhodesian elected Members had given up amalgamation because the British Government would not accept it. "It is, to say the least, unfair to suggest that because we have now accepted the possibilities of Federation we are going to aim to twist the Federation into an amalgamation . . ." This was a most unjustified allegation, Welensky continued, because if Unsworth was right, the safeguards would be pointless and, "We have been completely dishonest right up to now because the whole value of the African Affairs Board is that it can have direct access to Her Majesty's Government and ask that their views should be presented to the Government of the United Kingdom before any action is taken." He might be mistaken, Welensky said, but it appeared very difficult to him to secure a two-thirds majority in the federal house because the representatives of two territories at least would have to agree. Out of the 35 members, 24 would have to vote for the amendment, and the moment that it appeared to be discriminatory the African affairs board would intervene. The provision that, if the African affairs board objected, the bill would have to lie on the tables of the British Parliament alone disproved Unsworth's claim that the safeguards would be nugatory. Nothing more was needed because in Canada, for example, the states were not consulted on constitutional change, the federal legislature passed it and the British Government was obliged to effect it. Unsworth interjected that this merely illustrated his contention that Britain was hamstrung when a territory was self-governing. Wheare agreed but corrected Welensky on Canadian procedure, for there was a convention regarding adjustment of the division of powers which required, in fact, provincial assent.

Welensky continued: if Unsworth's suggestion were adopted, the Secretary of State could ensure through the official Members that the two northern legislatures denied the amendment the necessary two-thirds majorities. He wondered if Unsworth was trying merely to shield the British Government from confrontation with the federation. He remained convinced of the value of the proposed, if derided, safeguards which, if they did nothing else, would promote a spirit of compromise. In the circumstances where the territories differed so widely in their levels of constitutional advancement it was advisable that an impartial body, like the British Government, should express its views on anything arising.

Moffat felt, however, that Welensky had not answered Unsworth. He noted that, despite the response to African opposition and the British obligations which had produced compromises like the concurrent list, the federation had been given wider powers than normal even though the vast majority of the people rejected it. The power of the federal parliament to amend anything in its constitution was particularly dangerous. Moffat conceded that, once practical experience had been gained, the non-controversial aspects of the constitution should be capable of amendment and for this the proposed process was suitable and, indeed, could be simplified. However, when the federal parliament sought to alter the carefully contrived balance of power between itself and the territorial legislatures, the latter were entitled to a say. The specially-reserved subjects had to be incapable of amendment until the African no longer objected and normal conventions could be adopted. The assurances given to Africans might not have been wise but they had been given and this was an opportunity to reassure the doubters. There would not be much more than a clamour if federation was imposed but, Moffat predicted, there would be serious trouble if the Africans discovered that the guarantees were not what they seemed and the embargoed subjects could be debated in the federal assembly.

Welensky interjected that he was not prevented from raising the question of land in the Northern Rhodesian Legislative Council, but Moffat replied that the difference was that the Africans feared the federal government to a far greater extent than the Northern Rhodesians. Moreover, it had been stated all along that the federal assembly would not be able to debate the subject of land, so why allow it to do so when a feeling of security could be induced?

The next day, 9 January, Lyttelton reminded the Conference of his pledge in the Commons on 21 November 1951 that protected status would be preserved and that amalgamation would be excluded until the majority of the inhabitants of the three territories desired it. However, he could not see how to answer the fears of Moffat and Unsworth of a dishonest federal government, a rigged majority in the federal assembly, a lightweight Secretary of State and a complacent British Parliament. He found the issue to be purely psychological because Moffat and Unsworth had acknowledged that the safeguards were adequate.

Unsworth disagreed because the legislative powers could be taken by stealth. Huggins, however, believed that the safeguards on land would be secure because to amend them the federal government would first consult the Secretary of State who would seek the opinion of the territorial Governments which were likely to reject it. There would be little point, then, in the federal assembly wasting its time debating something which the Secretary of State would veto. However, he suspected that the northern Africans had been told that the land laws could never be altered which was unfortunate because development would be stultified. He was confident that the safeguards were "cast-iron" simply because a Secretary of State would never be cowed by the federal government. He reminded the Conference of the difficulties in getting the Southern Rhodesians to accept the safeguards because they felt that they should be better rewarded. Any increase was certain to occasion a defeat at the referendum.

Prompted by Lyttelton, Unsworth and Moffat confessed they were trying to ensure that land could not even be debated because of the damage which would result. Wheare reminded them that in parliaments, whatever the strictures, anything could be raised in debate. Argument then ensued over the Orders in Council themselves and whether a federal constitutional amendment could affect them. Sir Kenneth Roberts-Wray, a British legal adviser, confirmed that an ordinary constitutional amendment could remove from Chapter II the specific provision which made the federal power to acquire land subject to the Orders in Council. However, Welensky added that the Secretary of State would nevertheless have the last word.

Wheare, seeking Southern Rhodesian opinion, drew attention to the division of powers, as normally in federations the states, as contracting powers, had some say in the alteration of this. In terms of the White Paper the territories could object to federal intentions but could not prevent a bill from reaching London. It was surely better to settle matters locally and avoid a direct confrontation with London when, in fact, if the federal and territorial Governments were agreed on a change a secretary of state could hardly resist them. Therefore he suggested that a constitutional amendment should require a two-thirds majority in the federal house and bare majorities in the territorial legislatures. Such an arrangement would be necessary, in any case, when the federation became a dominion.

Beckett warned Wheare that the referendum was being endangered. He concluded that Moffat and Unsworth were seeking to prevent federation, and certainly their statement on amalgamation seemed to confirm this, because they knew that their proposal would be unacceptable to the Southern Rhodesian electorate.

Unsworth replied that he sought a *quid pro quo* for the radical alteration to the African affairs board obtained by Southern Rhodesia. The Conference had to realise, he claimed, that misled or ignorant, perhaps, African opposition was total. Fox-Strangways, the Nyasaland Secretary for Native Affairs, and Welensky disagreed that it was. Unsworth then maintained that the internal situation in Northern Rhodesia was explosive. Beckett called this gross exaggeration. Barrow, too, was confident that the vast majority of Africans was so ignorant of the issues as to hold no opinion. Hopkinson agreed because he had found the opposition to be confined to the literate minority.

Welensky and Huggins suggested that this amendment would be more appropriate once all the territories had achieved self-government, but Unsworth felt that it would then be impossible to introduce. J. L. Foster, the Under-Secretary of State for Commonwealth Relations, proposed a preface in which the question of African land ownership, at least, could be mentioned to reinforce the preamble and the reference in Chapter II. Huggins was prepared to consider this but Welensky commented acidly that perhaps they should provide each federal MP with a muzzle to inhibit discussion. Rennie wondered why the Victoria Falls communiqué had not been specifically mentioned in the preamble. Foster replied that its commitments were in the safeguards but that a preface could emphasise that fact.

Foster won an ally in Swinton. However, Lyttelton had one more card to play. He revealed that the British Ministers felt that there should be a constitutional review after a number of years. He thought that a decade was appropriate and that any constitution needed periodic review. He provoked Huggins who was considerably annoyed that this should be sprung on the Conference without warning, giving no time for consideration. Nevertheless, Huggins did not wish to impede discussion and, with his impishness reasserting itself, said "However, I will consider anything — even murder if it is necessary." After further haggling over Wheare's idea, which he now thought could be introduced five years after federation, Lyttelton closed the discussion.

On 12 January, Swinton asked Moffat for his reaction to Wheare's proposal and received the reply that the sanction of the territories should be required for the amendment of the legislative lists until the constitutional review by which time, through practical demonstration, African fears of federation should have been proved groundless. Swinton then sought to have this adopted but Welensky opposed him and the Conference turned its attention to other matters.

Two days later, with the support of Wheare, the British Ministers formally proposed that the legislative lists should be frozen for ten years until a constitutional review, except when there was accord between the federation and the territories over the necessity for change. This would prevent the exploitation of African fears by the opponents of federation. Huggins agreed but thought a seven year limit was more appropriate. Welensky did likewise because, otherwise, the review would coincide with the third general election due at that time. Lyttelton replied that he and his colleagues had only suggested the ten year period to deter people from "finessing for position" and to avoid affecting the power of the federation to borrow. Moffat and Rennie would accept the compromise as reasonable but Barrow insisted that a decade was too long. Lyttelton then suggested a minimum of seven and a maximum of ten years should elapse before the review. After Whitehead had said that the review should be complete by the ninth year, the matter was referred to the Legal Committee.

The Legal Committee produced the formula which the Conference adopted. Thus "Part 3. Amendment of Constitution" provided that a bill for the amendment of the constitution would require an affirmative vote of two-thirds of the total membership of the federal assembly, excluding the speaker. The governor-general would not assent to the bill but would reserve it for Her Majesty's pleasure. Bills would also be reserved if objected to, *in toto* or in part, by resolution of a territorial legislature within 60 days of their acceptance by the federal assembly or if the African affairs board found them to be differentiating measures. No draft of an order in council signifying Her Majesty's assent to a constitutional bill would be laid before the Monarch unless it had lain on the tables of the British Parliament and, within 40 days of that action, neither House had resolved that the draft should not be presented for assent. If Her Majesty's assent to a constitutional bill did not require an order in council it would be signified through a secretary of state but not sooner than 65 days after it had passed through the federal assembly unless, within that time, all three of the territorial legislatures had resolved not to object to the bill or to any part of it. The power to amend the constitution by federal law was still to include the provision permitting the establishment of a second chamber. No bill purporting to amend the legislative lists could be introduced into the federal assembly for ten years after federation, unless a draft of it had been laid before the three territorial legislatures and each had resolved that its introduction would not be objectionable. Finally, it was provided that in not less than seven and not more than nine years from the date of federation coming into force there would be a conference consisting of delegates from the federation, the three territories and Britain to review the federal constitution.

The debate, however, had not ended and the subsequent verbatim record would be unearthed and quoted in the exchanges in 1960 over Lord Monckton's Review Commission and its findings, one of which was that the territories should have the right to secede. In the plenary session on 19 January, Eastwood asked whether the provision for the review could be interpreted as offering a loophole for secession or a voluntary liquidation because the financial world might assume this impression. Lyttelton thought that this was unlikely as this was a review and he did "not think you can review a constitution off the map". The review did not mean voluntary liquidation. This reassurance did not satisfy Welensky who felt the review could "envisage the complete break-up of the Federation". Unsworth disagreed because only the practicality of the provisions of the constitution would be examined. However, Lyttelton conceded, "You might knock them out one by one."

Swinton discounted this possibility as any subsequent alteration would require a constitutional amendment and, in reality, only adjustments could be made. Lyttelton reversed his position and agreed there was no danger because all four Central African governments would have to agree to the liquidation. Lyttelton felt, perhaps, that it should be specified that only the constitution would be reviewed. Whitehead obstinately feared for the credit of the federation and thought that some sort of idea should be given of what alterations were likely. Lyttelton, however, was confident that financiers were informed people and careful wording would make it clear that liquidation would depend on the unanimous decision of four governments. Welensky, clearly uneasy, remained convinced that any aspect, and not just the division of powers, could be reviewed and Lyttelton reminded him that, even so, it could not be altered without agreement. This Greenfield acknowledged to be true, because certainly, "you could not do so constitutionally without the intervention of Her Majesty's Government here".

Swinton could see that there was "a risk you always run in a sense that it would be possible I suppose for Her Majesty's Government if they could persuade Parliament to do it to pass an Act of Parliament tomorrow morning to take away the whole of responsible government from Southern Rhodesia and the whole of the functions which would be given to the Federation. You cannot legislate against the United Kingdom Parliament going off its head".

These words would have an ironic ring when they were remembered when Welensky was fighting to convince the Government of Harold Macmillan of the necessity to preserve the Federation. Lyttelton, thinking Swinton had misunderstood Greenfield, explained that the latter had meant that as long as the intervention of the British Government was required, the lender's investment was secure. However, Lyttelton added: "Nobody is safe from the Sovereign Government repudiating its obligations. In this case there would have to be four people to do it." Greenfield mused somewhat sarcastically, "In this case it is 'The Lord giveth and the Lord taketh away.'"

Sir Kenneth Roberts-Wray began to outline possible new wording but Lyttelton impatiently interrupted him to say that nothing new was needed as all he sought was an assurance from the lawyers that "with the concurrence of each and all the Governments concerned, major alterations could take place in the Constitution". Somewhat affronted, Roberts-Wray did not continue and the Conference adjourned for the day.[5]

On 23 January, though various versions were aired, no adjustment was made to these provisions which would have such important consequences when the African nationalists gained the ascendancy in the northern territories at the same time as the British Government decided to end its colonial role in Africa.

The last task of the Conference was to devise the explanatory *Report by the Conference on Federation*, Command 8753. This was prefaced by a statement by the three senior British Ministers present: Swinton, Lyttelton and Salis-

[5] Author's interview with Sir Kenneth Roberts-Wray.

bury, and by Huggins and the two northern Governors. It told of the previous Conference and how the current one had reached agreement on all aspects of the scheme. The opportunity was taken to proclaim the reason for federation as being the need to develop the resources of the three territories to the full so that they could reach their proper station in the world.

They dwelt on the complementary natures of the territorial economies and how the experience of the Central African Council had proved that political association was the only way to secure an effective combination to provide for the development of the area's resources to meet the needs of its growing population. Only a well-balanced and co-ordinated unit would attract development capital on a scale to realise the potentialities of the three territories. All the inhabitants would benefit if an effective central authority could take major economic decisions in the interests of the whole area. Amalgamation could have created a single territorial unit but it was incompatible with Britain's special responsibilities in the northern territories. A structure like the East Africa High Commission would not give sufficient financial and economic authority to achieve the essential objects.

The solution was a federation which would strengthen the co-operation and partnership between the races and the territories and alone would secure a full measure of contentment. The proposed scheme described in Command 8754, the signatories claimed, was a true federation with the necessary strong central authority. The territories would be autonomous within their spheres, and to ensure this the federal powers had been clearly defined. In particular, the territories would remain responsible for matters affecting the daily life of the African and would discharge their special obligations with regard to land and territorial political advancement.

A short description was given of the preamble and the changes in the structure of the African affairs board. Confidence was expressed in the marked improvement of the board, for not only would its European members be highly qualified but the Africans would have the opportunity to select the best of the African members. As the board's primary function was to watch and safeguard African interests it could obviously best be done within the legislature. There could no longer be the accusation that the board merely duplicated the duties of the representatives of African interests.

To build confidence in the federation amongst its peoples and to give it time to establish itself, there would be no adjustment of the division of power between the territories and the federation except with the consent of the territorial legislatures. Towards the end of the first decade, the five governments would review the constitution.

The penultimate paragraph of this statement recorded a question asked in the Conference — by Huggins on 20 January — as to the likely attitude of the British Government if the scheme of federation were rejected. The reply was that the British Government would not then consider the amalgamation of all or part of the territories. Federation, it was maintained, had been revealed by the past two years of intensive study to be the best and most practical solution. If the scheme were rejected there would be no prospect of reopening the subject in the foreseeable future.

In the debate, after Lyttelton had furnished this reply, Huggins could not resist the quip, *vis à vis* amalgamation, "That means we must rely on the Labour Party then."

Swinton answered, "I am sorry, Prime Minister, that you contemplate that our successors will be of that complexion. What they should do, should they unfortunately succeed us — perhaps I should not use that adjective [*sic*] — should they succeed us, can be anybody's guess round this table. I do not think it would be either amalgamation or Federation."

In the final paragraph the signatories claimed that the moment for decision had been reached and they chose federation as the means to secure the future and the well-being and contentment of all their peoples. It was a sound and fair scheme, they added, which would promote the essential interests of all the inhabitants of the territories and should be carried through.

This White Paper, Command 8753, then reviewed in greater detail than its preface the history of the closer association movement, and summarised the preamble and the chapters of the constitution. Particular care was taken to emphasise again that not only were the assurances on protected status, African land and African political advancement to be upheld, but that subjects closely related to the daily life of the African would remain responsibilities of the territorial legislatures.

The summary of "Chapter IX: Miscellaneous" is of interest because it included a statement which would be referred to by Welensky as being ignored when a new constitution was devised for Northern Rhodesia in 1958. This was:

> "As regards amendments of the Territorial Constitutions, the existing machinery and the responsibility of Her Majesty's Ministers in the United Kingdom remain unchanged but Her Majesty's Ministers would naturally seek the views of the Federal Government before advising Her Majesty."

In fact, prior to the Conference, the Southern Rhodesian Government had suggested that such amendments should only be made with the approval of the federal government and had suggested that this be written into the constitution.

In discussion, however, the Southern Rhodesians in the drafting party had admitted that they had not intended that the federal government should be invited to approve all territorial constitutional amendments. Furthermore, the majority of the drafting party had taken the view that a federal veto on territorial amendments was not consistent with the undertakings at the Victoria Falls Conference on territorial political advancement. It was thought that it would be embarrassing to the territorial and British Governments to include such a provision in the constitution. It appeared obvious to the drafting party that the British Government would always consult the federal government on such changes. If, to satisfy the Southern Rhodesians, anything had to be said, the drafting party suggested that a resolution be passed by the Conference and included in the constitution as a footnote. The drafting party produced the basis of the formula which the Conference amended and adopted. At the suggestion of the Steering Committee of the Conference this provision was included in the explanatory White Paper, Command 8753.

The summary of Chapter IX also recorded that the provision in the draft scheme that federal laws could be laid on the tables of the territorial legislatures for a fixed period after which their validity could not be questioned in any court, was rejected by the Conference because it would not have the desired effect of reducing litigation as, in any case, uncertainty would arise when amendments to federal law were subsequently introduced. This provision was accordingly omitted.

The last section of this White Paper was used to reveal other conclusions of the Conference which were not included in the draft scheme but were, nonetheless, important. It told how the Fiscal Commission had reported that a satisfactory financial framework could be created and how the Conference had endorsed the Commission's findings and recommended the adoption of its suggestions on income tax, customs and other matters. The Fiscal Commission suggested, and the Conference agreed, that the Apportionment Commission should decide how much compensation should be paid to the Southern Rhodesian Government for expenses incurred in the siting of the federal capital in Salisbury, and should assist in raising the money. With regard to defence, the federal government would acquire the powers currently enjoyed by Southern Rhodesia. It was recommended that the federal and territorial Governments should align their financial years so that they began on 1 July. The Fiscal Commission had suggested that the federal government should guarantee all loans approved by the loans council but the Conference thought that such a mandatory provision would unduly tie the hands of the federal assembly. Instead, a convention would be established under which a federal guarantee would be forthcoming for territorial loans approved by the loans council. The Conference decided that the governments of the federation should be able to tax each other's property. It laid down that the governor-general should receive £250 000 as an initial grant for the interim period, of which Southern Rhodesia would contribute 52 per cent, Northern Rhodesia 36 per cent, and Nyasaland twelve per cent. Further sums would be negotiated by the temporary ministry with the territorial Governments. After the federal government had been established it would secure short-term loans locally or in London. The governor-general would set dates for the assumption by the federal government of financial responsibility for the subjects it was assigned. Arrangements would be made for the adjustment of accounts for services provided for the federation by the territorial Governments.

The Conference also considered the Report of the Civil Service Preparatory Commission and its detailed recommendations on the organisation of the federal civil service. It chose to prescribe here the functions of the interim public service commission, including the staffing of the temporary ministry, the drafting of the federal public service bill, the terms and conditions of service for federal employees, examining housing and other building requirements and advising on the establishment needed for the federal departments. The Conference decided that there should be close liaison between the Colonial Office and the federal government in recruiting men who would be working closely with federal departments. This would particularly apply to men who would work in departments concerned with subjects set down in the concurrent list.

Finally, the Conference decided that, despite the recommendations of the Report, the administrative arrangements of government would be a matter for the federal government alone. Its last action was to append to this White Paper a copy, procured by Welensky, of a letter from Huggins to the Rhodesia Railways Workers' Union on 19 June 1947, guaranteeing the privileges of the Union's members on the nationalisation of the railways. This letter had been referred to in the footnote dealing with the rights of the railway workers which was appended to the exclusive list.

Their work done, those delegates who remained in London — many of the Southern Rhodesians had already returned home — met for the last time at 12 noon on 29 January. Their closing speeches were unusually terse. Swinton thanked the secretaries and the legal advisers. Lyttelton praised the harmony of the Conference, the foresight of the delegates from Africa and expressed the belief that the whole future development of the continent depended on the success of the federation. Huggins likewise expressed his gratitude. He was relieved that the Conference was over and believed that, if it was not for public annoyance with his Government over coal and meat shortages, the federal scheme would be well received. Rennie followed, and having thanked the delegates for their co-operation, expressed the hope that the sunshine that day would be a good omen. Colby endorsed this sentiment.

Then the heads of the delegations signed the Conference document and recorded a loyal message to the Queen. Having taken the last step on a long road, the delegates dispersed. All that remained to be done was to secure public acceptance of the plan.

CHAPTER THIRTEEN

The Ratification of Federation

Southern Rhodesia's Referendum and British and Northern Approval, February-September 1953

ONCE the proposed constitution was in being, the campaign to secure the acceptance of federation could enter its final phase. The advocates of federation had firstly to persuade the Southern Rhodesian electorate to endorse it in the referendum in April and then to convince the northern legislatures and the British Parliament to do likewise and thus make it possible for the necessary order in council to become law. The anti-federal lobby did not give ground easily.

Clearly, while the outcome of the Conference in January 1953 was awaited, there was little active campaigning to be done. However, although Huggins and Welensky refused to give a formal Press conference in London in late December 1952, they did not entirely neglect the opportunity to influence British opinion.

On arrival Welensky told *The Times* of the proposed amendment of the African affairs board, and on 31 December Huggins addressed a meeting at the House of Lords and warned that the result of the Southern Rhodesian referendum was by no means certain. Welensky, when reviewing progress with the UCAA in London two days previously, had said the same but had felt that concessions such as bringing the African affairs board into parliament could tip the balance. Yet he felt all could be lost through delay and thus the final White Paper had to be published as soon as possible so that the campaign could begin. Reviewing northern affairs, Welensky was dismayed at how little Lewanika and Chileshi had understood of federation. He credited Attlee with doing much to reduce federal opposition but believed his efforts had since been undermined by delay and intimidation.[1]

Later in January, Welensky, Caldicott and Whitehead addressed public

[1] *The Times*, 26 December 1952; Welensky Papers, 17/38, f. 154, C. J. M. Alport to Welensky, 31 December 1952; 14/7, f. 90, Minutes of 39th Meeting, London Committee, UCAA, 29 December 1952.

meetings in Britain. At Reading on 23 January, Welensky stressed the economic potential of the federation and claimed that the new state could prove to be the exception in the Commonwealth because it could produce a society in which people of different colours would be able to live together. African opinion, he said, could not be ignored but should not be allowed to stop this great experiment. There should be no delay in implementation. Indeed, such were the dangers inherent in the current uncertainty that he warned he would advocate the dropping of the proposal entirely if the British Government sought a postponement.[2]

Despite issuing regular communiqués on the negotiations, the British Government chose to treat the matter as *sub-judice* and Lyttelton refused, even on 28 January, when questioned in the Commons, to divulge any details. The BBC co-operated and cancelled a televised debate.[3]

The British opponents of federation naturally did not fail to present their case when public attention was thus focussed on the subject. Organisations such as the Africa Bureau and the Opposition and Church newspapers pointed out the dangers and futility of imposing federation. Arthur Creech Jones *et al* wrote to the Press and addressed meetings. A memorandum was presented to Churchill.[4]

Counter statements were issued by the London Committee of the UCAA and by such pro-federal stalwarts as S. N. Evans and C. J. M. Alport (later Lord Alport). However, the opposition was reinforced by the arrival in early January of Nkumbula, Nkomo and, from Nyasaland, Chiefs Gomani, Maganga, and M'Mbelwa accompanied by Orton Chirwa and B. W. Matthews Phiri of the African Congress. Later in the month, Yamba and Sokota flew in to join discussions between the Northern Rhodesian representatives and Lyttelton on constitutional change. These were, however, again postponed until the federal issue had been resolved.[5]

Nkomo, on arrival, delivered to Huggins a memorandum from the Southern Rhodesia African National Congress which demanded the introduction of partnership before any further consideration of federation and depicted the safeguards as mere sops to British liberal opinion which would be amended as soon as they threatened white supremacy. This was the substance of the speech by Nkomo at a meeting in London a week later. He told other audiences that the African would even return to savagery in his struggle to resist the imposition of federation.[6]

Banda, who provided the Nyasa Chiefs with winter clothing and paid their accommodation expenses, arranged that they should meet the Press immediately in the company of the Reverend Michael Scott. The Press highlighted

[2] *Daily Herald*, 14 January 1953; *Oxford Mail*, 22 January 1953; *The Sunday News*, 25 January 1953.

[3] House of Commons *Hansard* (London), Vol. 510, Cols. 116–117, 28 January 1953; *News Chronicle*, 6 January 1953.

[4] *Daily Herald*, 10 January 1953.

[5] Welensky Papers, 7/10, f. 213, Note of a Meeting in the Colonial Secretary's Room, House of Commons, 29 January 1953.

[6] *The Bulawayo Chronicle*, 10 January 1953; R. I. Rotberg, *The Rise of Nationalism in Central Africa: The Making of Malawi and Zambia, 1873–1964* (London, 1965), p. 248; *The Scotsman*, 19 January 1953; *The Sunday News*, 25 January 1953.

the Chiefs' theme that they had been sent by popular subscription by their impoverished tribesmen to affirm their preference for freedom to material prosperity. This had been made plain to the territorial and British Governments but, having been ignored, the Chiefs said they now wished to explain their grievances to their "Great Mother", the Queen, and the British people. They reaffirmed their loyalty to the Crown but claimed that they no longer trusted the British Government. Finally, they played on the menace of Southern Rhodesia's policies. Scott's contribution was an allegation that the British Government had always been evasive on the nature of the safeguards.[7]

At their request, Lyttelton met the Chiefs who delivered a memorandum drafted by Banda which rejected federation, demanded self-government and asked for the dismissal of the Nyasaland Governor and his senior officials. Thereafter they departed on a tour of England and Scotland, during which Banda denounced the British Government for its "cold, calculated, callous and cynical betrayal of a trusting, loyal people". He claimed that the Nyasaland Africans had the right to be ruled in accordance with the Atlantic Charter which guaranteed the right of any people to choose the form of government under which they would live. The Chiefs warned that they would have to be bombed into submission.[8]

They sought an audience with the Queen but Lyttelton would not allow them to embroil her in a political argument. Instead they, Banda and the Northern Rhodesian Africans wrote to *The Times* on 5 February, the day of the publication of the White Papers, explaining the African rejection of federation as the fear of the adoption of Southern Rhodesia's policies which were identical to those of South Africa. They denied that the African population had no opinion on the issue because the Bledisloe Commission had been struck by the totality of African opposition to amalgamation and because, since 1951, the White Paper had been translated and universally discussed. Furthermore, they claimed, the northern Governments had failed to reverse the verdict of rejection. However, they did not reiterate their demands for immediate self-government and the dismissal of the Nyasaland Governor and his administration. To the contrary, purporting to speak for all Africans, they acknowledged that the majority of them were not politically advanced enough to forego the protection afforded by the impartial British officials. This should be retained until they were ready for self-government. They warned that they would regard any transfer of power to the local Europeans without their consent as illegal. Such action would destroy confidence in the British administration and embitter race relations. They would resist the imposition of federation with all the means at their disposal.

The question of resistance had, in fact, divided the Nyasaland Congress leadership in January, after Mikeka Mkandawira of the militant Blantyre faction had cabled Banda proposing non-violent resistance. While Banda, an admirer of Ghandi, would have approved, the president of the Congress, J. R. N. Chinyama, publicly rebuked Mkandawira. Unrepentant, the Chiefs reasserted in London their determination to resist. Their final blow on their

[7] P. Short, *Banda* (London, 1974), p. 71; *The Rhodesia Herald*, 2 & 4 January 1953; *The Times*, 9 January 1953.

[8] Short, *Banda*, *op. cit.*, p. 71; Rotberg, *The Rise of Nationalism*, *op. cit.*, p. 248.

departure was to castigate Lyttelton for his rude, threatening attitude and, in particular, for his refusal to listen to their complaints about Government intimidation.[9]

Although Huggins, before leaving London, upbraided the Labour MP, John Dugdale, for claiming to the World Church Group that they would witness the largest sale of Africans since the end of the slave-trade, his British and African federal opponents did not succeed in distracting him or his cohorts from the problem of winning the referendum. This time no one waited for the publication of the White Papers. Indeed, Stockil, Munro and Keller returned home during the Conference to declare their rejection of the proposals.

Stockil was quick to exploit a move by Huggins earlier in the month when he had persuaded Barrow and a somewhat reluctant Welensky that a federal party was necessary in the three territories. Huggins's reasoning was that the federal campaign should not be burdened with the current unpopularity of his United Party because it had failed to curb inflation. He hoped this move would attract the pro-federal sympathisers who would not associate themselves with the United Party. When, in the latter stages of the Conference, this intention was announced Stockil immediately claimed this as evidence that federation was a party issue.[10] This forced Huggins and Welensky to postpone the formation of a federal party and to continue with the UCAA until the referendum.

The UCAA, which had been hard at work, planning, canvassing and urging voters to register, had, in fact, won the allegiance of further federal sympathisers in Stockil's Party. Geoffrey Ellman-Brown, a chartered accountant, on the threshold of a political career, was a notable example. In an effort to belie further Stockil's allegation, Huggins resigned the presidency of the UCAA and persuaded the former Chief Justice, Sir Robert Hudson, to assume it.[11]

Stockil immediately declared that the postponement of the formation of the federal party was meaningless because it already existed in the guise of the UCAA. Huggins then tried to use this controversy to advantage when he returned from London on 1 February. The whole campaign, he claimed, had been bedevilled by detail which the Southern Rhodesians had to ignore when deciding whether to create a strong British bloc in Central Africa which the Africans and Europeans could develop fully and thereby contribute not only to the Empire but to the world.[12]

Stockil was unimpressed. Referring to pending visits by Welensky and Guy van Eeden, he protested at such outside interference when the choice at

[9] Short, *Banda*, *op. cit.*, p. 71; *News Chronicle*, 6 February 1953.

[10] *The Rhodesia Herald*, 23 & 30 January 1953; *Central African Post*, 20 January 1953; *The Bulawayo Chronicle*, 20 & 23 January 1953; *South Africa* (London), 24 January 1953; *South China Sunday Post* (Hong Kong), 1 February 1953; Welensky Papers, 14/7, f. 90, Minutes of 39th Meeting, London Committee, UCAA, 29 December 1952; 17/29, f. 163, Welensky to J. Easton, 31 December 1952; 17/38, f. 153, Welensky to Alport, 2 January 1953.

[11] Welensky Papers, WE 7, P/C/161/31, Welensky to M. P. Barrow, 7 February 1953; *The Rhodesia Herald*, 8 February 1953; NAZ Hist. MSS, UN 1/3/1, Minutes of a Meeting, National Executive Committee, UCAA, Salisbury, 11 February 1953.

[12] *The Rhodesia Herald*, 2 & 10 February 1953.

the referendum would be made by the Southern Rhodesians alone. Moreover, on these grounds, Stockil and other MPs refused an invitation from Welensky to visit Northern Rhodesia to see development there. Stockil decried the introduction of racialism when he discovered that van Eeden was being brought to Southern Rhodesia to appeal to the Afrikaner community. Stockil's supporters asked why the electorate could not have the final federal constitution laid before them instead of the White Paper which merely described the scheme. They demanded also that the referendum should be decided by a two-thirds, and not a bare, majority.[13] Having survived a censure motion on 4 February over the current shortage of coal,[14] Huggins had to answer these questions when the Southern Rhodesian Assembly debated the Federal Polling Bill on 10 February.

Opening the debate Greenfield said his Government did not intend to discuss the federal issue but merely to provide the machinery for the referendum which would be held on 9 April. He recalled, as precedents, the referenda in 1922 and 1923 on the questions of responsible government and state lotteries, and Stockil's insistence on a referendum in 1951 on the federal question. A two-thirds majority was unwarranted, Greenfield argued, because the Southern Rhodesian Constitution was not seriously affected and normal democratic practice demanded nothing more than a bare majority.[15] His opponents, however, replied that they would not only discuss federation but would contest every aspect of the Polling Bill and they prolonged this debate until 20 February, severely trying Huggins's patience.

Stockil repeatedly described the governing Party's attitude, to the most important issue since Rhodes's decision to dispatch the Pioneer Column, as flippant. He and his Rhodesia Party representatives, reinforced by Keller and J. R. Dendy Young, who was now an independent MP, pressed for the total re-negotiation of the terms of federation. If that was impossible, they argued, the House should at least debate the issue as there would be no other opportunity before the referendum. Serious concern was expressed over the changes which might be made by the legal draftsmen when interpreting the White Paper. Grounds for this were seen in a misleading statement on the African affairs board by Lyttelton five days previously when he announced the publication of the White Papers. This to them was reason enough for the electorate to be presented with the final constitution before the referendum. They still demanded that the referendum should be decided by a two-thirds majority. Dendy Young preferred a bare majority but thought that the decision should be ratified by a two-thirds majority in the Legislative Assembly because the Southern Rhodesian Constitution would be altered. Keller felt that the voters ought to be compelled to vote, while Stockil thought that a minimum poll of 70 per cent should be demanded. The Opposition persisted with its theme that federation was being treated as a party issue, and Keller, in particular, was convinced that vested interests supported the UCAA.

[13] *Ibid.*, 10 February 1953; *Northern News*, 12 February 1953; Welensky Papers, 34/13, f. 352, R. O. Stockil and others to Welensky, 17 February 1953; ff. 418–419, N. H. Wilson to Welensky, 2 February 1953.

[14] SR *Debates* (Salisbury), Vol. 33, Part 2, Col. 3718 f., 4 February 1953.

[15] *Ibid.*, Col. 3953 f., 10 February 1953.

Stockil vowed that his imminent Party congress would eschew a party approach.

The likely detrimental effects of the federation were paraded, including interference by the Colonial Office and the disturbing effect of the turbulent North on Southern Rhodesia's tranquil race relations. Keller feared for the livelihood of the white worker. George Munro proposed amalgamation. Dendy Young claimed that wherever integration had been practised, inevitably whites had been forced to leave. He prophesied with some accuracy that the federation would fail because it lacked the essential similarity between the constituent states, freedom from outside interference and acceptance by the Africans. He blamed the Colonial Office for the African rejection, suggesting that, for the highest humanitarian ideals, the British assisted those who wished to destroy Britain's work overseas.

Huggins and others dismissed the party issue allegation and pointed out that the earlier referenda had been decided by simple majorities. They wondered why Stockil distrusted legal draftsmen who were competent writers of English, and urged that the opportunity to federate should be grasped while the Conservatives were in power. Federation, to them, was the only secure way to achieve dominion status without having black power blocs as neighbours.

Greenfield summed up, expressing surprise at the demand for a debate on federation when the issue would be so thoroughly discussed at public meetings. He reviewed the questions of decision by majority, the non-party nature of the campaign, and the production of the final constitution which, in reality, he said, would be nothing more than the White Paper phrased in legal terminology. He maintained that the Colonial Office would be stripped of much power and claimed that the reservations would not embarrass the federal government.

These replies did not deter the Opposition from exploiting the committee stage of the Bill to the full, with Stockil proposing an amendment to have the final constitution published before the referendum because he still feared that the British could change the constitution when framing it. Dendy Young, Munro, Smit and Keller supported him in the protracted debate.

Huggins, Greenfield and Fletcher replied, avowing that the legal draftsmen would be assisted by Southern Rhodesian law officers. Huggins, who wondered what people who could not understand the White Paper would make of the constitution, likened the agreement to federate to a treaty signed by the four Governments which would be ratified or rejected, but not altered, by their legislatures. He pointed out that the Commons itself would merely vote on a bill enabling the Queen to sign an order in council. It seemed to him a considerable waste of time and effort to undertake the lengthy task of drafting the constitution when federation might still be rejected. As to the details, there seemed little point, to him, in becoming agitated about the African affairs board when it was likely to disappear in a decade once the federation had proved its trustworthiness. When all the reservations fell away, there would be no impediment to advancement towards dominion status. If the three African members of the board proved to be unnecessarily obstructive, there was provision for disregarding their action as frivolous.

Greenfield answered further points on the progression to self-government for the territories, secession, integration and the federalisation of agriculture. Fletcher responded to a requested definition of partnership by saying it was nothing more than co-operation between the races. He reminded the Rhodesia Party that Nyasaland did not yet possess an electoral system; that the Commonwealth Secretary would be concerned with federal affairs; and prophesied that when the federal and the three territorial Governments asked together for dominion status, the British Government would be unable to resist them.

Stockil and Dendy Young continued to insist that the constitution should be published before the referendum. Consequently, on the third day of the debate, 13 February, Huggins, to his intense irritation (he told Welensky that even Greenfield, by being conscientious, was annoying him[16]) had to repeat his assertion that prior publication was unnecessary. In fact, he was forced to ask for confirmation of this from London. By 18 February, when the debate resumed, Stockil and Dendy Young sought not only the publication of the final constitution but the postponement of the referendum to October to allow for more leisured consideration. Such was their pressure that Huggins had to reiterate that the British Government had informed him that the principles of the agreement were unalterable and that the constitution would only be formally set out in the draft order in council to be tabled in the British Parliament for ratification. There could be no delay because the whole process of acceptance of the federation began, not with the final drafting of the constitution, but with the result of the referendum. Even the British Parliament, he explained, would not see the actual constitution before debating the order in council. Greenfield wondered why the Opposition had made this demand at such a late stage as the Federal Polling Bill had been published on 24 December 1952, a week before the Conference.

On 19 February, the Assembly rejected overwhelmingly three amendments to the Bill providing for the prior publication of the final constitution, the postponement until October and the ratification of the result of the referendum by a two-thirds majority of the House.

As Stockil and Dendy Young continued to demand the final constitution and the other points which they had raised in the debate, Huggins and Cochran of the UCAA felt impelled to repeat publicly the British Government's verdict that the terms of the final agreement were unalterable. In fact, on 27 February, Huggins revealed that he had received a second message from the British Government confirming the first. Indeed, Swinton, leaving nothing to chance, took care to ensure that Welensky also understood that the authorisation of the British Parliament, in the form of an enabling bill, was required before the constitution could be drafted.

The speaking programmes of both camps had not been disrupted by the protracted debate in the House, but Stockil's support had been weakened by the defection of Sir Ernest Guest to the pro-federal lobby when on 16 February he resigned from the Rhodesia League. Guest thereafter gave the UCAA the benefit of his advice. The federal effort had been further enhanced

[16] Welensky Papers, 34/13, ff. 311–313, Huggins to Welensky, 14 February 1953.

by the presence of Welensky during the debate who denied that he was interfering because not only did federation affect everyone in Central Africa but he had been born in Southern Rhodesia and had a father who had fought in the rebellions. On 18 February he addressed three meetings in Salisbury and was warmly received.[17]

Later in the month, van Eeden arrived to tour the areas where the Afrikaners predominated. By stressing the economic case, he persuaded many of his audiences, including one in Fort Victoria, Stockil's constituency, to vote for federation.[18] Van Eeden's tactics, however, coupled with acidic comments in the Press by C. D. Burney (later Sir Cecil) of Ndola, forced Huggins to defend the strength of Southern Rhodesia's economy. Van Eeden had exploited, as an illustration, a recent reverse on the London Market when the underwriters had been forced to take up 78 per cent of a £10 000 000 loan being floated by Southern Rhodesia. Burney had commented on this and on a World Bank refusal of railway finance for Southern Rhodesia, but not for Northern Rhodesia. He also drew attention to a recent Southern Rhodesian request for a grant from Northern Rhodesia of £300 000 to meet the deficit on Southern Rhodesia's defence expenditure. Huggins replied that keeping the economy sound had cost him considerable popularity. Contradicting Burney, he explained that the World Bank had limited funds, that Southern Rhodesia had already received money from it for electricity and thus it had been thought it would be more expedient for Northern Rhodesia to make the approach. Southern Rhodesia had secured the £10 000 000 because the underwriters had judged it to be worth the risk. The Market itself had been badly affected the day before the flotation by adverse weather conditions in England which had caused extensive flood damage. The money for defence was not to meet Southern Rhodesia's current expenditure but to provide extra capability in which Northern Rhodesia had been invited to share.[19]

However, Huggins did not reveal, as Whitehead would in the Legislative Assembly on 21 April, that the Imperial defence authorities had told him that, without jet aircraft, the Southern Rhodesian Air Force was useless for their purposes and should be disbanded. Huggins, short of £200 000 to meet the bill, discussed with Welensky in mid-February the possibility of a contribution from Northern Rhodesia. Welensky spoke to Rennie and the money was forthcoming. Huggins must have known that the Northen Rhodesian Government, itself lacking an air force, would not happily see the SRAF disbanded and would understand that re-equipment was inevitable and that, once the federation was in being, the Northern Rhodesians would have to bear their proportion of the cost.[20]

[17] *The Rhodesia Herald*, 16, 17, 19, 21, 23 & 28 February 1953; Welensky Papers, 34/13, ff. 56–57, Lord Swinton to Welensky, 5 March 1953; f. 58, Welensky to H. D. Wightwick, 20 February 1953.

[18] *The Rhodesia Herald*, 23 February 1953; *Northern News*, 25 February 1953; Welensky Papers, WE 7, P/C/161/52, Welensky to C. Goosen, 8 March 1953.

[19] *The Rhodesia Herald*, 4 March 1952.

[20] SR *Debates* (Salisbury), Vol. 34, Cols. 112–113, 21 April 1953; Welensky Papers, 34/13, ff. 311–313, Huggins to Welensky, 14 February 1953; f. 264, same to same, 1 March 1953; Author's interview with Sir Roy Welensky.

From mid-March Welensky toured Southern Rhodesia for a month to complement the efforts of Huggins, his Cabinet, the UCAA and other federal enthusiasts who were also travelling widely. Part of his task was to nullify any effect Keller might have on the white workers.

The federal opposition enjoyed some success, but neither threats by Stockil to refer any decision to impose federation to the International Court at The Hague or the United Nations, nor the stock arguments on secession, Southern Rhodesia's loss of status, black domination and others, had the desired effect and a swing in favour of federation soon became apparent. When van Eeden publicly debated the federal issue with Dendy Young in Salisbury on 22 March, the audience's overwhelming verdict was two to one in favour of federation.[21]

In early February Welensky had asked the UCAA London Committee to curb its expenditure because of his need to conserve his resources for the campaign in Southern Rhodesia. The Committee complied but was confronted with an undiminishing effort by its opponents. Accordingly, it continued to address meetings and to write to the Press. It was supported by Stanley Evans of the Labour Party who spoke publicly on the need for federation, and by Lord Bledisloe who wrote to *The Times*. Lyttelton made a party political broadcast and fended off Opposition questioners in the House, while J. L. Foster, the Commonwealth Under-Secretary, addressed two meetings in early March.[22]

Although three prominent Church newspapers, the *Church Times*, the *Methodist Recorder* and the *Tablet*, favoured federation or at least were neutral on the subject, the *Church of England* and the *British Weekly* endorsed the opposition which was being proclaimed by some churchmen and organisations such as the London Missionary Society and the Church and Nation and Foreign Missionary Committees of the Church of Scotland. The *British Weekly*'s comment that it was the Christian's duty to oppose federation provoked R. E. F. Paget, Bishop of Mashonaland, to declare that the Anglican Church would not attempt to influence the voter. The Reverend Kennedy Grant of the Presbyterian Church in Southern Rhodesia did likewise. Knowing that the Archbishop of Canterbury had told Welensky in January that he favoured federation, the UCAA London Committee promptly induced Leopold Amery to persuade the Archbishop to make a similar statement to Paget's. Moreover, after the Reverend Michael Scott and his cohorts announced a plan to induce British Churches to hold days of prayer and protest to coincide with the debate on the Enabling Bill, the Archbishop spoke out again. On 10 March, he decried the polarisation of the Press, in particular, because Christians could hardly take sides when any of the courses, federal or otherwise, were clearly equally fraught with dangers and difficulties. Two days later the Reverend L. B. Greaves, the Africa Secretary of the Conference

[21] *The Rhodesia Herald*, 4, 21 & 23 March 1953.

[22] Welensky Papers, 5/46, f. 97, Welensky to J. H. Wallace, 5 February 1953; 34/13, f. 338, L. Hastings to Welensky, 12 February 1953; *The Bulawayo Chronicle*, 6 February 1953; *The Times*, 5 February & 2 March 1953; *The Rhodesia Herald*, 25 February & 5 March 1953; House of Commons *Hansard* (London), Vol. 511, Col. 2085, 25 February 1953; Vol. 512, Cols. 373–375, 4 March 1953; *The Listener*, 12 March 1953.

of British Missionary Societies issued a statement in support of the Archbishop.[23]

If the Archbishop had occasioned something of a reverse for the opponents of federation within the Church, the advocates of federation lacked as potent an ally in other fields. At the international level, Russia objected in the United Nations Assembly to federation. The appointment by Russia of an attaché specialising in African affairs to her embassy in London in January had been indicative of her new and increasing interest in Africa.[24]

In Britain, the Trades Union Congress called for a year's postponement while the Union of University Liberal Associations rejected federation outright. The Liberal Party itself issued a call for a national protest. Dingle (later Sir Dingle) and Michael Foot, Margery Perham, Creech Jones, Lady Pakenham and others wrote to *The Times*. Dugdale, in the Commons, not only maintained pressure on Lyttelton but attacked the colour bar in the Empire generally.[25] Within the Parliamentary Labour Party, the faction in the Commonwealth and Colonial Group supporting Griffiths out-voted those sympathising with the views of Gordon Walker and Stanley Evans in a series of debates on federation in mid-February. The consequence was that, contrary to the intention of the authors of federation, the Labour Party secured another debate on it before the scheduled debate on the Enabling Bill and, more important, before the Southern Rhodesian referendum.[26]

Welensky and Huggins were highly displeased when the debate was granted and the date fixed for 24 March. Both called it irresponsible, and Welensky pointed to the ludicrous possibility of the British Parliament rejecting federation when thereafter the Southern Rhodesian electorate at the referendum might accept it.[27]

Griffiths, however, gained little from the debate because he failed to dissuade the pro-federal faction within the Labour Party from abstaining. This gave the Conservatives a comfortable majority after he had forced a division on a motion which, while recognising the advantages of federation, rejected the proposed scheme because it provided insufficient protection for African interests. Lyttelton, defending the scheme, explained that the specified constitutional review, to be held within the first decade, would only decide how the federal constitution could be adjusted in the light of experience. The review could not consider the abolition of the federation.[28]

[23] *The British Weekly*, 19 February 1953; Welensky Papers, 5/46, f. 84, Wallace to Welensky, 2 March 1953; 17/38, f. 148, Welensky to Sir Geoffrey Follows, 10 January 1953; WE 7, P/C/161/52, Minutes of 50th Meeting, London Committee, UCAA, 13 March 1953; *The Bulawayo Chronicle*, 3 March 1953; *The Rhodesia Herald*, 3 & 5 March 1953; *The Times*, 11 March 1953.

[24] *The Rhodesia Herald*, 19 February 1953; NAZ Hist. MSS, UN 1/1/5, Wallace to Sir Harold Cartmel-Robinson, 6 February 1953.

[25] *The Times*, 26 February 1953; *Manchester Guardian*, 23 February 1953; *News Chronicle*, 23 March 1953; *Cape Times*, 5 March 1953.

[26] *The Rhodesia Herald*, 16 & 18 February 1953; Welensky Papers, 5/95, ff. 87–89, T. Reid to Welensky, 17 February 1953; *The Times*, 5 March 1953.

[27] *The Bulawayo Chronicle*, 17 March 1953; Welensky Papers, WE 7, P/C/141/52, Welensky to Joelson, 21 March 1953.

[28] House of Commons *Hansard* (London), Vol. 513, Col. 658 f., 24 March 1953.

(This statement, together with those on the subject of the review, at the recent Conference, would be recalled with bitterness in the fight to prevent Lyttelton's successors from dissolving the Federation.)

Little that was new was said but much ignorance was displayed in the protracted debate and in its lengthy counterpart in the Lords on 1 and 2 April. There was, however, a contrast because supporting the Labour opponents of federation in the Lords was a Conservative peer, Lord Hemingford, the former rector of Achimota Training College in the Gold Coast and currently a vice-president of the Africa Bureau. The advocates of federation, though, were powerfully reinforced by Lord Hailey, who crossed the floor on this issue, Lord Bledisloe and the Archbishop of Canterbury.[29]

The size of the vote for federation in the Commons, 44 instead of the normal 17, came as a relief to Welensky while he travelled through Southern Rhodesia fulfilling an exhausting itinerary of three speeches a day. Henceforth, he could tell his audiences that it only remained for them to vote "Yes". The activities of the African opposition had nothing like the effect of those of its British sympathisers and was largely ignored by the campaigners. There was, however, some alarm over African agitation in the rural areas of Southern Rhodesia in early February, particularly when the BBC, whose midday news broadcast was relayed over the local radio, reported a possible "Native Uprising" if federation were implemented. The Southern Rhodesian Government quietly took security precautions and, as the BBC could not be censored, the UCAA decided to say nothing. There can have been little substance to the report because it was not repeated. The outcome of a mass meeting of Africans called by the Industrial and Commercial Workers' Union in Salisbury's Harare township seems hardly to have worried the electorate. Its subject of discussion was the proposed gatherings at the Northern Mashonaland Native Commissioner's office to explain the White Paper. One speaker preferred that the Native Commissioner should address the public *en masse* but the other three speakers were so adamant in their rejection of federation that they would not hear of the White Paper being discussed. The meeting recorded a vote in favour of boycotting the Native Commissioner's office. Nkomo thereafter formed a committee to fight federation. He argued that it could not be considered until Southern Rhodesian law provided a radical improvement in the economic and political position of the African.[30]

Unrest in February in its Northern Province caused some concern in Northern Rhodesia but was ignored in Southern Rhodesia. Gore-Browne reported that sugar was still not being bought, and agitation over game and fish laws in Luapula led to arrests and the dismissal of one Chief and the suspension of two others. On the Copperbelt, European allegations of intimidation were somewhat borne out when a prominent African trade unionist was goaled for issuing death threats against supporters of federation. Nkumbula decried current government action in Luapula when speaking in Lusaka

[29] House of Lords *Hansard* (London), Vol. 181, Col. 457 f., 1 April 1953.

[30] Welensky Papers, 39/85, f. 28, Minutes of a Special Meeting, UCAA, Salisbury, 6 February 1953; f. 19, Minutes of a Special Meeting, UCAA, Salisbury, 13 February 1953; NAZ Hist. MSS, UN 1/1/5, H. D. Sutherns to Wallace, 16 February 1953; *The Rhodesia Herald*, 18 & 20 February 1953; *Bantu Mirror*, 21 February 1953.

on 23 March. He claimed that the continuing European domination of the territorial legislatures as well as the proposed federal assembly was proof that amalgamation with dominion status would follow federation. He burned the White Paper and announced that the trade union leaders would co-operate in paralysing industry in two "days of prayer" on 1 and 2 April. This action would coincide with the debate in the Lords.[31]

The Government promptly warned the trade unions that political strikes were illegal and when the two "days of prayer" were poorly supported, Lawrence Katilungu and other trade union leaders claimed that they had not been consulted and blamed the failure on the ANC's poor organisation. Only the workers at the Mufulira mine, the Chilanga cement factory and some civil and domestic servants in Lusaka went on strike. Katilungu, however, warned that, if any of the strikers were dismissed, a general strike would follow, and he persuaded the mining companies against punitive action beyond a loss of pay. The Government was more resolute and, as it had warned, dismissed those of its employees who had gone on strike.

This decision was confirmed at a meeting on 4 April between the Governor, Bush, Unsworth, Welensky and Beckett. The meeting decried the weakness of the mining companies as setting an unhealthy precedent and decided to ask them to prevent ANC spokesmen from addressing their employees on their property and to issue warnings about the consequences of political strikes. The Government would review its industrial legislation in the light of Nkumbula's action who, as Professor Rotberg has noted, had introduced a new weapon into the ANC's armoury. Nkumbula denounced the action of the Government as intimidation and warned that the labour force would bleed the federation to death.[32]

A measure of co-ordination was attempted on 31 March when, in Fort Jameson, Joshua Nkomo, C. C. Ngcebetsha, D. B. Ntuli and Stanlake Samkange (later Professor) from Southern Rhodesia met Nkumbula, Yamba, Sokota, Dixon Konkola, president of the African Railway Workers' Union, and Adamson Musukwa, president of the General Workers' Union. They agreed to ensure that no African stood as a federal MP. They wanted the Central African Council to continue to effect any inter-territorial co-operation, and reform of the territorial constitutions to give the Africans their rightful share of power. A policy of non-co-operation was adopted and it was decided that a joint delegation would lobby the British Parliament when it debated the Enabling Bill. Taking up Stockil's idea, they agreed, also, that this delegation should present their case to the International Court of Justice at The Hague and to the Privy Council.

[31] *The Times*, 29 January 1953; Welensky Papers, WE 7, P/C/109/52, Gore-Browne to Welensky, 18 February 1953; Welensky to Gore-Browne, 28 February 1953; 5/98, ff. 215–216, Welensky to D. Welensky, 20 February 1953; House of Commons *Hansard* (London), Vol. 515, Col. 407, 6 May 1953; Rotberg, *The Rise of Nationalism*, *op. cit.*, p. 249; F. Macpherson, *Kenneth Kaunda of Zambia: The Times and the Man* (Lusaka, 1974), p. 120.

[32] *Northern News*, 28 March 1958; Welensky Papers, 5/83, f. 9, O. B. Bennett to ?, 30 March 1953; f. 8, Notes of a Meeting with L. Katilungu, Kitwe, 1 April 1953; ff. 6–7, Minutes of a Meeting, Government House, Lusaka, 4 April 1953; *The Rhodesia Herald*, 3 April 1953; *The Times*, 6 April 1953; Rotberg, *The Rise of Nationalism*, *op. cit.*, p. 250; Macpherson, *Kenneth Kaunda*, *op. cit.*, p. 122.

Thereafter at a public meeting, Nkomo proclaimed the Southern Rhodesian Africans' rejection of federation and support for Nkumbula who pronounced federation to be a disease which must be fought. Yamba demanded parity in the Northern Rhodesian Legislative Council with what he called "Welensky's Party". The meeting supported Nkumbula after he claimed to have a plan of action if the federation became a reality.[33]

The campaigners in Southern Rhodesia also ignored the events in Nyasaland where the Congress was enjoying increasing success in the rural areas. After meeting at Lilongwe on 14 and 15 March, the Council of Chiefs cabled the Colonial Office claiming that all Nyasalanders opposed federation. It protested at intimidation by the Government and expressed deep disappointment that the delegation of Chiefs had been denied an audience with the Queen. The Council resolved to resist the imposition of federation. On 5 April, the Reverend Michael Scott arrived from Britain with instructions from Banda to initiate a campaign of civil disobedience and immediately proposed a series of nation-wide strikes, the non-payment of taxes and the boycott of European-owned stores. Like the delegates at Fort Jameson, Scott suggested an approach to the International Court and an appeal to the United Nations. He secured agreement that the Congress should work with the Council of Chiefs to direct the Nyasaland resistance.[34]

Although Welensky publicly warned Dugdale that remarks such as his in the Commons had been responsible for tea floating in harbours, the advocates of federation continued to ignore their opponents while explaining the constitution and dwelling on the prospects of development and on how the advantages of federating would outweigh any disadvantages. Despite Welensky's momentary worry that Huggins might have blundered by declaring that only madmen or cowards would reject federation, and despite Churchill's refusal to provide an eve-of-poll message, there was nothing to fear. On 9 April, 82,84 per cent of the electorate polled their votes, and approximately 62 per cent of them supported federation, with only four constituencies, Fort Victoria, Selukwe, Gatooma and Charter, favouring rejection.[35]

The first goal had been achieved; Southern Rhodesia had ratified the agreement and, while the congratulations flowed in, calling the result a victory for moderation, attention quickly focussed on securing the sanction of the Northern Rhodesian and Nyasaland Legislative Councils. The African opposition was not prepared to accept the verdict of the electorate, and Nkomo warned that no African candidates would be forthcoming for the federal seats. In Nyasaland, Paramount Chief Mwase and the Reverend Michael Scott addressed a meeting of Chiefs and the Congress in Blantyre on 12 April and reiterated that Nyasaland should not be handed over and that instead the Africans should be trained in preparation for self-government. Resistance was imperative. In Northern Rhodesia, however, the strains within the leadership were more apparent than the continuing effort against

[33] *Central African Post*, 31 March 1953.

[34] Short, *Banda, op. cit.*, p. 72; House of Commons *Hansard* (London), Vol. 514, Col. 11, 15 April 1953; *The Rhodesia Herald*, 8 April 1953.

[35] *The Rhodesia Herald*, 3, 11 & 26 April 1953; Welensky Papers, 34/13, f. 66, Welensky to V. Bartlett, 8 April 1953; WE 7, P/C/158/52/W, Welensky to Wallace, 4 April 1953.

federation. Nkumbula merely berated Yamba, Sokota and the trade union leaders for failing to support him during the "days of prayer". Yamba called a meeting of miners in Mufulira but then only spoke of his intention to secure a reform of the Northern Rhodesian Constitution.[36]

The Northern Rhodesian ratification was, of course, expected to be a foregone conclusion and explains why Welensky and Huggins immediately turned their attention to forming a federal party to ensure success in the first federal general election at the year's end.[37] The Northern Rhodesian Governor, in any case, took a hard line on African opposition when he opened the Legislative Council on 16 April. Having decried irresponsible and irregular methods of attempting to influence the federal decision, he warned that the flouting of the law would not be tolerated and, later in the session, made it a crime to incite violence at a public meeting. He acknowledged the considerable African opposition but argued that, while some of it was the product of genuine misunderstanding, most of it could be attributed to deliberate misleading of the ignorant. Moreover, he had just returned from discussing federation with the Paramount Chief and Council of Barotseland and had reached a common understanding, issued as a joint statement: "If Her Majesty's Government in the United Kingdom decide to proceed with the federation of Southern Rhodesia, Northern Rhodesia and Nyasaland, the Paramount Chief and Council of Barotseland will raise no objection so far as Barotseland is concerned, provided, firstly, that the rights reserved under the Lewanika Concessions are preserved by an appropriate provision in the Federal Constitution as stated in paragraph 139 of the Federal scheme, and, secondly, that that part of Northern Rhodesia known as Barotseland is declared or styled by Order-in-Council the Barotseland Protectorate." This would not mean, of course, that Barotseland was being removed from Northern Rhodesia.[38]

The federal debate in the Northern Rhodesian Legislative Council on the following day, 17 April, like its predecessors and its British and Southern Rhodesian counterparts, merely aired again the standard arguments. Although the result was a foregone conclusion, Moffat divided the House because the irrevocable nature of the proposal allowed no prospect of African reconciliation without which the federation would fail. Welensky retorted that Moffat himself had played a role in London in achieving the compromise on federation.

As they had done with the Southern Rhodesian referendum, the African opponents of federation ignored the ratification by the Northern Rhodesian Legislative Council. On 19 April, Yamba, Sokota and Nkumbula cabled the British Government to delay the consideration of the Enabling Bill as they had an alternative which might prove acceptable to everyone. They added that the African leaders of the three territories would meet within two weeks and would then release the details. Thereafter they would seek to meet the

[36] *Daily Worker*, 16 April 1953; Short, *Banda, op. cit.*, p. 73; *Central African Post*, 14 April 1953; *The Times*, 13 & 15 April 1953; *The Rhodesia Herald*, 13 & 15 April 1953.

[37] Welensky Papers, WE 7, P/C/143/52, Welensky to H. K. McKee, 10 April 1953; 17/32, f. 147, Welensky to Gore-Browne, 14 April 1953.

[38] NR *Debates* (Lusaka), Col. 1 f., 16 April 1953.

three territorial Governments before approaching the British Government. They were confident that they would not be ignored and appealed to the Africans to remain calm. That day, however, there was a noisy demonstration, led by Dixon Konkola, at the Broken Hill post office against its colour bar.[39] Moreover, the British Government did not respond to the cable.

These actions had no effect on the third step in the process of ratification as the scheduled debate in the Nyasaland Legislative Council took place on the next day, 20 April. K. W. Simmonds, as Acting Chief Secretary, moved a motion in favour of Command 8754, and Barrow seconded it. As in Northern Rhodesia, opposition to the motion came from the European representative of African interests, the Reverend A. B. Doig, and the two African Members, joined by the Asian representative, P. Dayram. As before, the result was obvious, despite an African walk out, and nothing new was said.[40]

On the morrow, 21 April, the *Report of the Commission on Higher Education for Africans in Central Africa* was published. The Commission had examined the problem in the previous November and its Report had been completed in March but, in deference to the wishes of the Southern Rhodesian Government, it had been withheld until the result of the referendum was known. This action considerably irritated the chairman, Sir Alexander Carr-Saunders, director of the London School of Economics and chairman of the Inter-University Council for Higher Education in the Colonies. He and the majority of his Commission, namely Dr A. V. Hill of London and Dr F. G. Young of Cambridge Universities, recommended the early establishment of a multiracial university college in Salisbury. The third member of the Commission, Dr Alexander Kerr, the former principal of the South African Native College at Fort Hare, in the light of his experience, expressed a preference for a separate college for Africans to avoid the unnecessary racial tensions which would arise from the different backgrounds of the students.[41]

Neither the recommendation of this Commission nor the warnings of K. G. Bennett, the Acting Nyasaland Attorney-General, that cases could not be brought before the International Court *et al* by private individuals, deterred Paramount Chief Mwase and J. R. N. Chinyama from acting on behalf of 20 Nyasa Chiefs in despatching petitions to the United Nations and to the British Parliament. The UN was requested to prevent the imposition of federation until its legality had been tested at The Hague, while the British Parliament was asked to receive a delegation at its Bar. Chinyama and Mwase explained that, as every other method had failed, they were forced to appeal directly to Parliament to prevent a violation not only of justice and honour but of the treaties. If this request was refused, they threatened to petition to appear before a joint select committee of Parliament. In their appeal to the UN, they claimed that they had not been represented in the referendum or in the debates in the Legislative Councils.[42]

[39] *The Rhodesia Herald*, 20 April 1953; *Manchester Guardian*, 19 April 1953.
[40] Ny *Debates* (Zomba), p. 7 f., 20 April 1953.
[41] *Report of the Commission on Higher Education For Africans in Central Africa*, Central African Council (Salisbury, 1953); Welensky Papers, 14/6, f. 92, Chief Secretary CAC to Colonial Secretary, 23 February 1953; f. 86, same to same, 3 March 1953.
[42] Short, *Banda*, *op. cit.*, p. 73; *The Scotsman*, 22 April 1953.

Nkumbula, Yamba and Gore-Browne, at the meeting of the Northern Rhodesian and Nyasaland Congresses, the Nyasaland Council of Chiefs and the Southern Rhodesian All African Convention in Lusaka on 27 April, revealed their promised alternative to federation. The confusion in the ranks of the African leadership, however, was amply illustrated by a statement to the Press by Yamba only four days previously that he would accept federation if the Northern Rhodesian Legislative Council was reformed to include 13 African elected Members while the European elected membership was reduced to three and the official to seven. The alternative plan was the one so often proposed by Gore-Browne, namely to partition Northern Rhodesia into two black states while the existing European areas along the line-of-rail, including the Copperbelt, would be absorbed into Southern Rhodesia. It was received with hostility by the meeting but the decision on its acceptance was deferred.[43]

The next day, Scott arrived from Nyasaland amidst great acclaim. He explained that the purpose of the Nyasaland petition to the British Parliament was to awaken the British conscience as Britain had still a major role to play even though he would prefer that the northern territories were placed under UN trusteeship. Denouncing federation as designed to ensure white domination, Scott again advocated non-violent resistance. He did not mention partition, but when Gore-Browne explained it and Nkumbula proposed that the resulting black states should be UN trusteeship territories, the delegates remained unremittingly hostile. Moffat, who was also present, rejected partition as did the two Southern Rhodesian delegates and the meeting itself on the third day. Instead, the delegates promised the British Government that, if it abandoned the existing federal plan, the African organisations of the three territories would co-operate in drawing up a constitution which would eschew racial segregation or the supposition of racial superiority.[44]

One immediate reaction was that the Bishop of Nyasaland publicly dissociated himself from the actions of his fellow Anglican, Michael Scott.[45] By contrast, in Britain, determined to fight federation with any means, Griffiths immediately exploited the opportunity presented by the petition. In the Commons on 29 April, he asked what the petition was about and what action would be taken.

Lyttelton replied that it was a request that an African delegation be allowed to plead at the Bar of the Commons or to appear before a select committee of the House or a joint select committee of both Houses. He had not seen the petitions to the United Nations or to the International Court but promised to ensure that the Africans understood that those bodies were not competent to hear their appeals. The Speaker found that the rules of the House permitted only MPs, the Lord Mayor and the Sheriffs of London to petition Parliament.[46] Time did not allow an MP so to do before the Enabling Bill was debated on 6 May, but Griffiths was determined that the Africans should not be disappointed. He persuaded Attlee to sponsor a motion which was debated

[43] *Central African Post*, 24 & 28 April 1953; Rotberg, *The Rise of Nationalism*, *op. cit.*, p. 251.
[44] *Northern News*, 29 April 1953; *The Rhodesia Herald*, 1 May 1953.
[45] *The Scotsman*, 22 April 1953.
[46] House of Commons *Hansard* (London), Vol. 514, Col. 2125, 29 April 1953.

on 4 May calling for addresses to the Government, the Speaker and the Lord Chancellor on behalf of the Chiefs and other representatives of the Africans against federation to be referred to a select committee. The motion also called for an opportunity to be given to the signatories to appear before this committee.

Justifying this, Griffiths claimed that the process of ratifying federation had been unrepresentative of African wishes. In Southern Rhodesia only some 400 African voters were registered, and in the northern territories there had been only seven representatives of African interests to protest against what had been a foregone conclusion. As African vocal opinion had hitherto been opposed, Griffiths did not intend to debate federation but to give the Africans an opportunity to put their case. For the enlightenment of the House, Griffiths read the petition and was promptly ruled out of order by the Speaker on the grounds that only ministers could lay documents before the House. Griffiths answered that this should have been done by Lyttelton who had received the documents. (There were, in fact, two petitions, as the Northern Rhodesians had sent an identical one to that of the Nyasas.)

The matter was crucial, Griffiths maintained, because fear was its sole basis and the signatories, many of whom he had met, were responsible men who played a vital role in the administration of their territories. Alport interjected that the Paramount Chief of the Barotse had accepted federation. When Griffiths then claimed that the Barotse had been given special privileges which had not been revealed in the published scheme, Lyttelton showed him the relevant provision in the White Paper in Chapter IX, Part 1. The atmosphere of mistrust, Griffiths claimed, had only been intensified by statements made by van Eeden and even Huggins, provoking responsible people in the territories and in Britain to call for practical demonstrations of partnership to belie African fears. Thus it was surely right to allow a select committee to hear the African case and would only slightly delay the final order in council. He concluded that a few months would not be wasted if the consequence, otherwise, was the irrevocable loss of the trust of the Africans.

Griffiths provoked a tirade from Lyttelton, who found it difficult to believe that Attlee could have sponsored such "an unhappy piece of Parliamentary tactics", which, if successful, would nullify the ancient usage of only allowing MPs to present petitions in Parliament. Lyttelton recalled how often he had invited Africans to participate, and defended his refusal to allow the Nyasa Chiefs to meet the Queen. To illustrate the falsity of the claim in the petitions on the abrogation of the original treaties, he read aloud the Barotse treaty and reiterated that, therefore, Griffiths was simply indulging in an "unhappy" manoeuvre as Parliament had debated federation four times since March 1952, and had accepted it on 24 March 1953. He found it curious that Griffiths, a distinguished parliamentarian and the author and architect of the federation, should descend to this.

Griffiths interjected that his hand had been forced by the impending debate on the Enabling Bill, implying that the motion would have little point after it. Whereupon Lyttelton wondered what would happen if the Commons appointed the select committee but, nevertheless, passed the Enabling Bill. Or, he asked, was the intention to force postponement at unreasonably short notice? This did not accord with the gravity and importance of the federal question but supported Scott and others in attempting to impede the implementation of the will of the territorial legislatures and the British Parliament. Among the untutored Africans, Lyttelton claimed, the success of this motion would only engender a spirit of resistance which would mar the early days of the federation. He found no precedent for the appointment of a select committee to examine "high" policy which, by Wednesday (6 May), would have been debated five times. It was merely an inappropriate imitation of the Senate committees of the United States which could set a precedent for pressure groups and could have, in particular, unimaginable effects on financial bills. To him, it was clearly also a "creaking device" to win back the dissident Labour faction which had abstained from voting in the last debate. The false assumption, that African representations had not been considered, was being promoted. It was true that they had been rejected, but there were always moments when the trustee was at variance with his wards even though he was acting in their best interests. There were few matters of policy, he asserted, which had been so exhaustively examined, and thus to expect to raise new arguments two days before the debate on the Enabling Bill was to ignore the whole history of the affair. Therefore, Lyttelton could not believe that the underlying motive was anything more than an effort to restore party unity, but warned that the outcome would be tantamount to killing one's own child, not because one disliked it, but because other people did not like it.

Lyttelton's diagnosis was strenuously denied by the Opposition, but was somewhat exonerated by James Hudson, who had abstained from voting in March, now favouring the motion. Griffiths was defended by his supporters who claimed that the Labour Party could not be accused of wanting to kill its own child as it had always insisted on African consent as a basic criterion. Lyttelton had failed, they claimed, to understand that the problem was not one of economics but of race because no economic benefits were possible without racial co-operation and, as there was strong African opposition, the Labour Party sought to avoid the serious consequences of pressing forward despite it. After all, Nkumbula had indicated that he would consider proposals which were not based on the concept of racial superiority. An argument ensued with Lyttelton over whether Moffat had accepted federation before voting against it, but a Conservative, Niall Macpherson, noted that Moffat had declared in the Legislative Council that he would vote to reflect African opinion, an action which surely made his apparent change of heart less significant. Then the Labour MPs pointed to the widespread concern in Britain, particularly in Scotland, which transcended partisan considerations. An example, it announced, would be revealed on the morrow when a petition against the imposition, signed by 27 000 Scots, would be presented at Buckingham Palace. Macpherson interjected that 27 000 was hardly a significant figure. The Opposition disagreed because the signatories mainly represented Church congregations. Furthermore, when Queen Victoria had been petitioned on the need for a protectorate over Nyasaland in 1889, 11 006 signatures had been deemed sufficient and, as the consent of the Chiefs had then been sought with regard to protection, it was only right to do so again. It was essential for the success of the federation to get to the roots of the opposition immediately and delay was justified because Parliament bore the heavy responsibility of taking a most fateful decision on behalf of millions of people without the vote.

Although the Government spokesman declared that federation should be implemented immediately, the Labour MPs continued to call for delay because, however late in the day, the Africans had at last expressed a desire to discuss the issue and should be listened to because then at least they would feel that they had been heard.

Dugdale asked Lyttelton what the Chiefs would make of comments like "unhappy tactics", and claimed that much could have been gained from allowing them to see the Queen. Sir Frank Soskice summed up for the Opposition, finding that the reason for the last debate was to examine the adequacy of the safeguards, and that the current purpose was to plumb the depth of the African opposition and to discover whether the Chiefs had been intimidated. As there had been no relaxation of tension since the last debate, there would be no harm in hearing the African case. Soskice claimed that the world's coloured population waited to see how the Africans would be treated, and the motion could rescue the Government from error and save harmonious race relations. The select committee would reveal to Parliament the true African opinion with which to reconsider the federal scheme.

The Conservatives, however, remained convinced that the motion was merely an attempt to heal the split in the Labour Party. They feared a select committee would lead to a lengthy examination which would be made difficult by Labour intransigence, and by the time the committee reported and Parliament had debated the issue again, the chance to federate might well be lost. The moment for decision had arrived, and the agreement in January meant that the federal plan could not be re-examined without being re-negotiated. The existence of African opposition was acknowledged but its depth was questioned in the light of the poor support for the "days of prayer". The Commons was reminded that the objective of Nkumbula and his ilk was black domination. It was felt that it was unlikely that the Chiefs would admit to having been intimidated, and experience had shown that they would refuse to discuss federation. Foster, who concluded the debate, thought it pertinent to quote a statement by Huggins that the fundamentals of partnership were merit and civilisation and not the colour of skin. The debate ended in sound defeat for Griffiths and the Labour Party.[47]

The refusal of admission to Buckingham Palace the next day, 5 May, of the delegation bearing the Scottish petition, which included Miss Margaret Herbison, G. M. Thomson and Sir Richard Acland of the Labour Party,[48] meant that the second reading of the Enabling Bill was not delayed. Before examining the Bill itself, on 6 May, Lyttelton, by way of encouragement, revealed that Huggins wanted the new university college to adopt British entrance standards and therefore be multi-racial. Higher education would be a federal subject and, although Huggins could not commit a non-existent government, Lyttelton was confident that such an endorsement was tantamount to a commitment. In addition, the Roan Antelope and Mufulira copper mines

[47] *Ibid.*, Vol. 515, Col. 37 f., 4 May 1953.
[48] *The Rhodesia Herald*, 6 May 1953.

would negotiate the advancement of their African workers with the Northern Rhodesian European Mineworkers' Union. As this was essentially a dispute between the European and African unions, interference by the employer obviously incurred the risk of strikes, but Lyttelton was hopeful that a successful outcome would be one of the first fruits of federation. The Government remained convinced that, although most of the educated Africans rejected federation, the bulk of the population remained unaware of it. Lyttelton condemned the Labour Party for using phrases like "the overwhelming weight of African opinion" when opposed but responsible Africans did not. Recounting the events of the "days of prayer", he revealed that the ANC leaders had sat under a banner at the Lusaka meeting which had read "self-government the only ultimate objective". He dismissed the need for a select committee to discover that there was a hard core of resistance, but believed that most Africans were waiting to judge federation in practice.

The Enabling Bill was by nature short, and Lyttelton hoped that the Opposition would deal with it fairly. He absolved the Labour Party from any responsibility. However, he asked Attlee and Griffiths to emulate Stockil and do everything to make the federation prosper as it was an issue of the greatest gravity which could be a turning point in race relations, establishing partnership as the foundation on which the future should rest.

Attlee explained that there were those who considered federation to be a most dangerous experiment, and their concern was responsible for Monday's (4 May) debate and not political manoeuvre. He had gathered, on his Central African visit, a broad impression of African opposition which subsequently seemed to have hardened. It might be innate conservatism but Moffat and Hopkinson had attributed it to fear which gave the federation a most inauspicious start. Despite constant African harping on the South African experience, Attlee observed that the Government had sought only to influence the European and had thus kept the safeguards to the minimum. He welcomed the statement on the university, and admitted that Welensky and Huggins were without doubt liberal-minded men. However, he warned, everyone had to understand that statesmanship was required. As great patience was needed with the Africans as well as time for a concrete demonstration of a new relationship, he refused to support the Bill because it was being rushed through, giving the federation a poor start when it was, in fact, totally dependent for success upon the goodwill of its people. Events in the federation, after all, could affect the whole of Africa. Lyttelton, Attlee concluded, "knows perfectly well that if this becomes the law it is the duty of all of us to try to make it work to the best of our ability, but even at this eleventh hour I urge that it is worthwhile delaying so that we may get some tangible proof of a new relationship which will bring the Africans into harmony with the scheme".

The issue was, of course, stale and those who were opposed merely again reiterated the points which had so often been raised, and drew the standard defence. Nevertheless, Clement Davies, Griffiths and Dugdale wished the federation well if it became a reality, even though they aired again their views on its defects. Gordon Walker joined the Conservatives in urging implementation of federation and in demanding implementation by Huggins of the changes which had been promised, to build, for example, the university college and not just to talk about it.

Foster, concluding the debate, thought federation offered the best chance of creating a multi-racial society. Griffiths had claimed again that the excision of the minister for African interests had weakened the safeguards, but Foster called the proposal an abnormality and reminded the House that it would be the responsibility of the four contracting Governments, including the British, and not the two-thirds majority of the federal house, to ensure that the necessary changes were made at the review. The second reading of the Enabling Bill was accepted by a majority of 26 votes, with four former ministers, Gordon Walker, Sir Hartley Shawcross (later Lord Shawcross), the former Attorney-General, R. S. Stokes, the former Minister of Materials, and Morris Webb, the former Minister of Food, amongst those who abstained. Welensky, however, found the majority to be disappointingly small.[49]

Having won the referendum, Huggins had asked for British goodwill, and the commitments of Attlee, Griffiths and Dugdale to assist the federation were in a sense a response. Nevertheless, despite a public appeal after the second reading from Welensky to Attlee to end the campaign against federation, the British Opposition would still exploit every opportunity presented by the legislative process. Aware that this would happen, the UCAA London Committee immediately pressed Welensky to retain its services in order not to leave the field to their opponents. Welensky managed to find the money they required. However, he responded half-heartedly when the Committee suggested establishing a permanent organisation to serve as a counter-weight to the Fabian Society and its adjuncts, and to defend the role of the European in the Empire and in East and Central Africa in particular. An *ad hoc* committee, chaired by Leopold Amery, met its Kenyan counterpart and both concluded that such an organisation was most desirable. They estimated that they would need to raise a capital sum of £500 000, but Welensky warned that he would not be able to contribute any money and could not see how any of the Governments could be directly associated with the proposed organisation.

The idea was only explored and, of course, when the federation became a reality, the *raison d'être* of the UCAA fell away. Although J. H. Wallace became Northern Rhodesian Commissioner in London in June 1953, the rump of the UCAA London Committee was prepared to continue to support the federation publicly. However, because the UCAA in Southern Rhodesia had not distinguished itself in fund-raising, Welensky had to meet the costs of the referendum and then to support the Federal Party and had nothing to spare for external private propaganda.[50] Huggins, in any case, was content to use the information service provided by Rhodesia House in London. Conse-

[49] House of Commons *Hansard* (London), Vol. 515, Col. 407 f., 6 May 1953; Welensky Papers, 39/83, f. 1, Welensky to Huggins, 7 May 1953.

[50] *The Rhodesia Herald*, 11 May 1953; Welensky Papers, WE 7, P/C/141/52, Joelson to Welensky, 24 April 1953; same to same, 11 May 1953; P/C/158/52, Wallace to Welensky, 13 May 1953; Welensky to Wallace, 16 May 1953; 39/84, f. 11, Minutes of 58th Meeting, London Committee, UCAA, 8 May 1953; f. 8, Minutes of 59th Meeting, London Committee, UCAA, 29 May 1953; f. 5, Minutes of 60th Meeting, London Committee, UCAA, 24 June 1953; 5/46, f. 27, W. S. Parker to Y. Galitzine, 27 August 1953.

quently, the London Committee of the UCAA was disbanded. To have concentrated exclusively on the erection of the new state and to have neglected to defend it externally was a mistake which was belatedly recognised by Welensky when, in his premiership, he established a similar organisation to the London Committee of the UCAA and later employed the London publicity firm, Voice and Vision. Until then, in the first vital years, the British public was left to the mercy of the opponents of federation.

Immediately after the referendum, Huggins and Welensky turned their attention to the recruitment of an interim cabinet to be ready for formal appointment, when the governor-general arrived in September, so that there should be no delay in beginning the preparatory work for the establishment of the federal government early in the New Year, immediately after the federal general election in January 1954. Huggins and Welensky conferred in Salisbury on 16 April, and Huggins, the automatic choice as interim prime minister, offered Welensky the deputy premiership and the portfolio of finance. Welensky accepted the former, but chose a porfolio closer to his heart, that of transport.[51]

In May the territorial legislatures extended their lives until after the federal general election, for clearly many of their current Members would seek federal seats and there was little point in holding the territorial elections until the federal results were known. Huggins and Welensky also decided to form a quite separate Federal Party. The idea that the UCAA, with its United Party overtones, should become the Federal Party was fiercely attacked by Stockil who, while favouring the principle of opposition in an established parliament, felt that party politics were undesirable in the formative period. In time, he felt, natural cleavages of interests would appear and parties would form. Welensky, who was resisting pressures to form a purely Northern Rhodesian party or an idea that he should lead a progressive party to oppose the conservatism of Huggins, was inclined to agree with Stockil.[52]

Huggins, Welensky and Barrow floated the new Party, and by the end of May, Welensky had formed branches in Kitwe, Ndola and Lusaka, and in Southern Rhodesia an inaugural meeting on 29 April, attended by Stockil, Stumbles and I. D. Smith amongst others, chose Cochran as interim chairman. A divisional meeting on 4 June elected Greenfield as its chairman. The enlistment of members, the raising of finance and the formation of branches began immediately. An inaugural congress was planned for 7 and 8 August to elect officers and to adopt a constitution, a name and a policy. Considerable public support was forthcoming, though Dendy Young expressed a need for party politics in the federal assembly, and the Democratic Party attempted to persuade Stockil to lead an opposition. The resistance to the Federal Party in Northern Rhodesia amongst the Afrikaner community was sufficient to worry van Eeden and to prompt Welensky to denounce in late May any attempt to divide the electorate on racial grounds. Furthermore, David Stirling threatened again to distract the public mid-way through the electoral campaign by

[51] Welensky Papers, WE 7, P/C/141/52, Welensky to Joelson, 19 & 24 April 1954.
[52] *The Rhodesia Herald*, 21 April & 14 May 1953; Welensky Papers, 17/32, f. 147, Welensky to Gore-Browne, 14 April 1953; 5/95, f. 75, Welensky to T. Reid, 23 April 1953; WE 7, P/C/161/52, N. H. Wilson to Welensky, 15 May 1953.

proposing to hold an inter-racial conference to discuss a wider union in October. Welensky and Huggins again had to attempt to dissuade him.[53]

The otherwise harmonious relationship between the Northern and Southern Rhodesians was somewhat ruffled in early May by Welensky announcing that he was going to Johannesburg to confer with Sir Ernest Oppenheimer on the raising of £27 000 000 with which to build the Kafue hydro-electric scheme. Immediately, questions were asked in the Southern Rhodesian Parliament about a Northern Rhodesian attempt to commit the future federal government to a project about which considerable doubts had been expressed and which possessed a formidable rival in the proposed Kariba scheme.[54] The evaluation of the power potential of the Kafue and Kariba gorges was a product of the need in the immediate post-war years to discover an alternative to thermal power. In 1947 the Hydro-Electric Power Commission of the Central African Council was entrusted with the study of the feasibility of both sites. Accordingly, it appointed a committee of experts, known as the "Panel", under the chairmanship of Sir William Halcrow. The "Panel" reported in July 1951 in favour of Kariba because, not only was the Kafue hydrological and other data too scanty to evaluate, but the expected power output would only meet immediate needs. This meant that the construction of the Kariba dam might have to begin before the Kafue dam was complete. It recommended, however, that the Kafue investigations should continue.

There was a public outcry in Northern Rhodesia, and the Northern Rhodesian Government disagreed with the "Panel" because an eminent hydrologist, Brigadier Hawes, who was re-examining the possibilities, indicated that the Kafue power output would exceed that predicted by Halcrow. The cost of the first stage of the Kariba project was expected to be £50 000 000, to produce some 380 megawatts, at a time when money was difficult to raise. By contrast, Kafue would produce between 200 and 300 megawatts while costing between £14 000 000 and £20 000 000. Moreover, for several reasons, including terrain, it would be quicker to build than the first stage of Kariba. This was important because the transport crisis was not only hampering development but was forcing the copper mines to burn wood to supplement their inadequate coal supply.

In October 1951, the "Panel" was asked to examine the new data, and confirmed, in late 1952, that Kafue would be quicker and cheaper to build and could produce some 258 megawatts. Consequently, the Northern Rhodesian Government and its Legislative Council decided to implement the scheme even if the Southern Rhodesians were unenthusiastic because the cost of the transmission of power would be high. It was argued that the saving in coal would be a million tons a year and would benefit both territories.

[53] *The Rhodesia Herald*, 30 April, 1, 23 & 28 May, 5 June 1953; *Central African Post*, 1 May 1953; *The Bulawayo Chronicle*, 8 May 1953; *Northern News*, 23 May 1953; Welensky Papers, WE 7, P/C/109/52, Welensky to Gore-Browne, 10 May 1953; P/C/161/52, Welensky to N. H. Wilson, 21 May 1953; 14/26, Circular by H. D. Sutherns, 11 May 1953; 5/95, f. 19, Huggins to Welensky, 9 May 1953; 5/46, f. 55, Welensky to Galitzine, 30 April 1953; 39/83, f. 1, Welensky to Huggins, 7 May 1953; WE 7, P/C/141/52, Joelson to Welensky, 1 May 1953; Welensky to Joelson, 10 May 1953.

[54] *The Rhodesia Herald*, 11 & 12 May 1953.

In February 1953, R. A. Nicholson, the Economic Secretary, sought and received enthusiastic, indeed unanimous, support from the Legislative Council to raise the necessary finance, some £30 000 000, and to begin the preparatory work. Nicholson acknowledged that power and the raising of loans would soon be federal responsibilities, but felt time was the essence because it would be a year or more before the federal government considered hydro-electric power. Southern Rhodesia, he was confident, would welcome the release of railway trucks for other purposes.[55]

On 9 May, however, having read in the Press of Welensky's intention to raise the money, Huggins wrote to him asking him to remember the federal aspects of the question. They met on 15 May on Welensky's return from Johannesburg where Oppenheimer indicated that the initial £10 000 000 would be forthcoming. Investigative and preparatory work had, of course, been continuing at the Kariba site and, while Huggins and Whitehead received Welensky's news without antagonism, some of the other Southern Rhodesian Ministers did not. Welensky, confident that Kafue could be producing power by 1958, nevertheless remained determined to proceed. He was, however, aware of the possibility of crisis if Northern Rhodesia had to secure the remaining £20 000 000 on the London Market because then it could be argued that the ability of the federation to borrow would be drastically affected.[56] For the moment, feelings were not running high and, in May 1953, other preoccupations abounded.

Although, on 6 May, Lewanika, Nalumango, Chileshi and other Africans discussed federation and partnership with Unsworth, Welensky, Beckett and other unofficials and officials, the Africans otherwise remained intractable. Welensky feared that they would not be encouraged to reverse their position by a visit from Apa B. Pant, the Indian Commissioner in Kenya, who gave a dinner for the nationalist leaders in Lusaka and spoke, albeit privately, on non-violent resistance. Statements from Welensky that the Northern Rhodesian colour bar was not legal, and that, as African nationalism had to be guided and not confronted, the objections of the Africans should be listened to, had no apparent effect on African attitudes.[57]

In Southern Rhodesia a meeting of the All African Convention, representing the ANC, the unions and several other organisations, again adopted a policy of non-co-operation which would include a refusal of nomination for election to federal seats. Care was taken, however, to state that the objection was against the federation, because it was not democratic, and not against the European *per se*.[58]

In Nyasaland, in early May, the Council of Chiefs made an unsuccessful

[55] NR *Debates* (Lusaka), Col. 207 f., 20 February 1953; F. Clements, *The Struggle with the River God* (London, 1959), pp. 41–42; Welensky Papers, 17/39, f. 54, R. L'Ange to Sir William Halcrow, 11 April 1952.

[56] Welensky Papers, 5/95, f. 19, Huggins to Welensky, 9 May 1953; WE 7, P/C/141/52, Welensky to Joelson, 16 May 1953; P/C/109/52, Welensky to Gore-Browne, 16 May 1953.

[57] *Ibid.*, 34/10, ff. 23–26, Minutes of a Meeting, Lusaka, 6 May 1953; WE 7, P/C/161/52, N. H. Wilson to Welensky, 15 May 1953; *The Bulawayo Chronicle*, 8 May 1953; *Northern News*, 22 May 1953.

[58] *The Rhodesia Herald*, 12 May 1953; *African Weekly*, 13 May 1953.

application to the High Court to have federation declared *ultra vires*, and success did not attend the other attempts at expressing opposition. A "non-co-operation" strike planned for 6 May failed to materialise, and later in the month it was reported that leading Africans were ignoring the call of the Council of Chiefs to boycott the regional councils. A number of Chiefs ordered their people to ignore agricultural regulations and to refuse to pay taxes, resulting in the deposition of the Paramount Chief of the Ncheu Angoni, Philip Gomani, one of the delegation to Britain in January. The enforcement of the deposition led to a minor riot and the flight of Gomani into Moçambique in the company of his two sons and the Reverend Michael Scott. The Portuguese authorities arrested the party and returned it to Nyasaland where Gomani was deported from his tribal area, while Scott was declared a prohibited immigrant. Paramount Chief Mwase refused to represent Nyasaland at the Queen's Coronation in London but was replaced by the Yao Chief, Kawinga. The northern African Congresses, however, enjoyed some success in disrupting the local Coronation celebrations. There were attempts to break the colour bar in the European canteens and cafes in Kitwe but the presence of the police reserve prevented any racial violence.[59]

After the Coronation, at which it was announced that Welensky and Barrow would be knighted, the British Enabling Bill reached its committee stage which the Opposition attempted to exploit fully with a string of amendments which Lyttelton refused to entertain because adjustment was impossible without re-negotiation. The Conservative majority and the Labour abstainers defeated all these attempts which included delaying implementation by a year, seeking a ruling from the International Court on the abrogation of protection, the reintroduction of the minister for African interests, and an enlarged federal assembly. On secession, Lyttelton commented that no marriage contract had a divorce clause.

Finally Lyttelton could move the acceptance of the third reading, noting even more wearily that the issue had now been debated on eleven separate occasions. He had been attacked by R. T. Paget MP who had whipped himself into a lather, patronised by the *Manchester Guardian*, and lectured by *The Times*. Nevertheless, Lyttelton hoped that the Opposition would assist this experiment which aimed at inducing the races to develop Central Africa together. As the decision was such a momentous one, Griffiths demanded in his conclusion that tangible evidence of the implementation of partnership be furnished before the order in council was presented to Parliament. He said that he and his Party would oppose the third reading because the safeguards had been weakened.

The third reading was accepted by 188 votes to 165. The Enabling Bill had still to pass through the House of Lords and, while its debates, which began on 2 July, were not as protracted as those in the Commons, the peers who supported Griffiths were as obstructive.[60]

[59] *Observer*, 10 May 1953; *The Rhodesia Herald*, 7, 22 & 29 May, 3 & 4 June 1953; Short, *Banda*, *op. cit.*, pp.73–74; Welensky Papers, 5/81, f. 9, Mrs L. Easton to Welensky, 26 May 1953; 17/30, R. L'Ange to Welensky, 5 June 1953.

[60] House of Commons *Hansard* (London), Vol. 516, Col. 37 f., 9 June 1953; House of Lords *Hansard* (London), Vol. 183, Col. 189 f., 6 July 1953.

In the interim, since the referendum, the British drafting team, in consultation with the territorial legal experts, had been at work on the constitution and, on 27 July, the moment arrived when Lyttelton could move in the Commons: "That an humble Address be presented to Her Majesty praying that the Federation of Rhodesia and Nyasaland (Constitutional) Order in Council 1953 be made in terms of the Draft laid before this House on 14 July." He reviewed, for the last time, the whole concept of federation: its advantages, its safeguards and its limitations. Perhaps in anticipation of criticism, he drew attention to the omission of the provision for the reservation of legislation by the governor-general explaining that its place was in the governor-general's instructions.

Griffiths replied that he had to continue to protest because, while the economic advantages were clear, there was inadequate provision for the protection of the interests of the African and for his social, economic and political advancement. Griffiths was concerned that apparently a suspended sentence within the last five years could preclude a person from standing for the federal parliament and that a specially appointed member would vacate his seat on dissolution. He asked why it was necessary for Article 29, in paragraph 6, to provide for variations of the law to apply in the different parts of the federation. Furthermore, he suspected that there had been further negotiations because the final constitution seemed to differ from the White Paper. If this were true, he asked why the amendments of the British Parliament could not have been allowed.

Attlee had made a commitment to making a success of the federation, but Griffiths asked the House to remember also the demand for tangible proof of the intention to implement partnership. The announcement on the university and the initiative taken by the copper mining companies were welcome, but the federal government should take the opportunity to declare at the outset that it would use the African affairs board to the full to belie the recent denigration of the board. When devising its franchise, the federal government should also make certain that it embodied the principles of partnership. Moreover, no matter how late the hour, the anxiety in Nyasaland should be acknowledged by writing into the constitution similar protection to that which had been provided for Barotseland. The Northern Rhodesian constitutional discussions were to be held in London in September and, Griffiths believed, presented an opportunity to advance the Africans radically in the spirit of partnership, and to prove the effectiveness of the territorial Government and the European elected Members in safeguarding African interests. The partnership proposals of the previous year should also be implemented. Griffiths warned that his Party would expect the federal review to produce democratic progress and, in conclusion, he hoped that the federation would be equal to the challenge with which it had been presented.

Other Labour MPs indulged themselves in lengthy and familiar dissertations on the undesirability of federation, while the Conservatives, in their turn, despised Labour timidity, their failure to recognise that progressive action was already being taken, and that the Federal Party was attracting African membership. They claimed the division of the House in this debate would serve only to give the federation a poor start.

Foster closed the debate, opining that the Labour Party would have done better to give the federation a good start instead of airing its misgivings. He denied that there had been any further negotiations; the White Paper had merely been translated into legal language. As the Opposition had no sensible amendments, it could not have expected them to be considered. Answering Sir Lynn Ungoed-Thomas and Griffiths, Foster explained that only actual detention, rather than conviction, would disqualify a federal member and, in confirming that the territorial police would administer federal law, he suggested that Ungoed-Thomas surely did not want the establishment of a federal police force. Britain, Foster avowed, would do her duty if the African affairs board protested, but he did not expect any need to resort to the veto. The Africans were not being betrayed, and federation was a great experiment. He welcomed Labour's intention to make federation work even though they would vote against it. The vote at the division, he said, would reveal the extent of the rift in Labour's ranks over the issue. The House divided and 288 MPs voted for federation, while 242 rejected it.[61]

While the final stages of the British legislative process were being completed — the Order in Council became law on 16 August — the Rhodesians and Nyasalanders continued to prepare themselves for federation. Since the referendum, a co-ordinating committee of civil servants, chaired by A. D. Evans, had been at work building an embryo administrative structure to support the interim government when it came into existence after the arrival of the governor-general. By early August it had sub-committees examining likely development, tariffs, the federal parliament and public service.[62]

Such activity was matched in the political field, and the Federal Party had continued to formulate its structure, constitution and policy. Huggins's idea that, in Southern Rhodesia at least, there should be separate federal and territorial governing parties was endorsed by Stockil and was accepted by the nucleus of the Federal Party after Whitehead had urged that notice should be taken of Robert Menzies's maxim that Australian federal and state politics did not mix. This meant that the United Party would continue its separate existence, but would obviously lose many men, including Huggins, to the federal arena. By contrast, in the northern territories, the shortage of manpower meant that the Federal Party would have to become involved in territorial politics.[63]

Any hope that party politics would not develop in the formative period was dashed in late July when the Democratic Party transformed itself into the Confederate Party, under the leadership of Dendy Young, to fight the federal election on the basis of racial segregation. Dendy Young campaigned in Northern Rhodesia with some success. The Federal and Confederate Parties both planned to hold inaugural congresses in August. Amongst the supporters of federation, the cordiality of inter-territorial relations was enhanced when Whitehead announced in Lusaka on 29 July that he expected the Kafue

[61] House of Commons *Hansard* (London), Vol. 518, Col. 899 f., 27 July 1953.
[62] Welensky Papers, 14/6, f. 38, Chief Secretary, CAC, to the Governors of Northern Rhodesia and Nyasaland, 7 May 1953.
[63] *Ibid.*, 14/26, f. 10, Minutes of 2nd Divisional Committee Meeting, 17 June 1953; *The Rhodesia Herald*, 22 June & 1 July 1953.

project to be a priority in the first federal development plan, along with the necessary improvement of the railway system.[64]

The two-day inaugural congress of the Federal Party was opened by Huggins in Salisbury on 7 August, with Greenfield in the chair, and attended by 105 Southern Rhodesians, 28 Northern Rhodesians and 15 Nyasalanders. Huggins said that he had hoped that the first federal government could tackle its enormous administrative task without distraction but their opponents would not allow this and there would be a political "scrap". He dealt with criticisms of the federal scheme and of his recent statements, including that on the university. He explained that he had opted for a multi-racial institution because, when separate African colleges had been established elsewhere, particularly in South Africa, they had proved to be merely forcing houses of anti-European sentiments. He referred also to Article 29 (7) of the federal constitution,[65] which stated: "Nothing in this Constitution shall affect any power to make laws for the Federation or any of the Territories conferred on Her Majesty by any Act of the Parliament of the United Kingdom."

The constitutional theory of the sovereignty of the British Parliament held that, as there was no defined British Constitution, there were no constraints on Parliament with regard to the subject matter of legislation. Thus the British Parliament could unilaterally act for its own and subject territories and only full independence placed the latter beyond its reach. This applied to Southern Rhodesia, even though there was no parallel provision to Article 29 (7) in its constitution, but few people there realised that it applied or even knew anything of constitutional theory. As the British Parliament possessed this power, Article 29 (7) was unnecessary and had not been included in the White Paper. The legal draftsmen had insisted, however, that it was needed for constitutional tidiness and the Rhodesians had not resisted them. Its inclusion was spotted and publicised by N. H. Wilson in his journal *New Rhodesia*, prompting Dendy Young, in May, to lay down a parliamentary question on it.

Neither Huggins's explanation of the law at the Federal Party congress nor his claim that nevertheless no British Government would ever act without the agreement of the federal and territorial Governments, satisfied Dendy Young. In September, Article 29 (7) was the subject of a most acrimonious debate in the Southern Rhodesian Legislative Assembly when Dendy Young claimed that thereby the federation was inferior to Southern Rhodesia. To placate Dendy Young, if he could not convince him of the realities of British power, Greenfield agreed to secure an exchange of letters with Britain on the subject. Consequently this, together with matters such as the unresolved federal franchise, formed the substance of the Anglo-Federal negotiations which produced the Accord of 1957 which included the convention that the British Parliament would not legislate unilaterally for the Federation.

A parallel situation arose in 1961 when, despite a warning from Greenfield, Whitehead was careless enough to allow the inclusion of a like provision in

[64] *The Rhodesia Herald*, 25 & 27 June & 30 July 1953; *Northern News*, 13 July 1953; Welensky Papers, WE 7, P/C/109/52, Welensky to Gore-Browne, (July) 1953.

[65] *The Rhodesia Herald*, 8 August 1953; Welensky Papers, 14/26, f. 22, Minutes of the Inaugural Congress, Federal Party, Salisbury, 7 & 8 August 1953.

the new Southern Rhodesian Constitution when it had not appeared in the White Paper on which the 1961 referendum had been fought. Whitehead's opponents claimed then and since that he had signed away Southern Rhodesia's quasi-dominion status, that it was less independent than it had been.[66] It is an abiding myth.

Having dealt with the constitution and its ramifications, Huggins asked the Federal Party congress to adhere to it and to remember that many of its aspects were merely designed to placate the Africans. Welensky's address was short. He proposed that, as partnership defied written formulation, they should adopt a pragmatic approach and deal with problems as they arose. It would greatly assist them if the British Labour Party abandoned its campaign against federation. He proposed a drive to attract immigrants. Barrow, in turn, reminded the congress that Nyasaland had yet to experience party politics.

From the floor, van Eeden suggested that it was necessary to provide speakers with an outline of partnership, related to the terms of the preamble, for their reference when asked questions. He was concerned that such a statement should describe a system in which the races could live in harmony. It would recognise the European as the senior partner who would guide and reward his junior partner. Privileges, political rights and the disadvantages of higher status, such as income tax, would be possessed by those who had attained civilised standards. The traditional desire of the races to remain socially separated would be recognised and, consequently, he suggested that the necessary facilities had to be provided. R. S. G. Todd disliked the emphasis on the term "junior partner" and, later in the Northern Rhodesian Legislative Council, Moffat expressed disquiet over van Eeden's ideas. G. T. Thornicroft, the Southern Rhodesian Coloured leader, thought that partnership was too difficult to define at that moment.

The congress, however, agreed with van Eeden and delegated Huggins, Welensky, Barrow, van Eeden, Greenfield, Todd and Stanlake Samkange to compose the statement. Three weeks later they announced that they recognised that the races had distinct and complementary roles to play and that there was a desire to continue to develop on traditional lines. The policy to be adopted would gradually extend political rights and privileges to those who had attained civilised standards of behaviour and culture. This, they believed, would lead to the diminution of the need for special representation.[67]

The congress went on to discuss its constitution, the raising of finance and the functions of its branches. Huggins was elected president, Welensky and Barrow its vice-presidents, and Cochran its chairman.

At its congress on 10 August, the Confederate Party expressed its confidence that only its policy could foster racial harmony because it was based on segregation which protected the European's future and consequently promoted stability and prosperity. It claimed that segregation was the traditional British policy in Africa and gave the African the security of the possession of his land and the right to follow his own path of self-development. It claimed

[66] Author's interview with the Hon. J. M. Greenfield; SR *Debates* (Salisbury), Vol. 34, Col. 1610, 23 September 1953; Col. 1878, 30 September 1953.

[67] *The Rhodesia Herald*, 28 August 1953.

that it was a realistic policy because it avoided frustrating the enlightened, educated African, who, otherwise, would have to compete with the European. The African would work with the European for his living but would realise his political ambitions in his own areas. As they did not intend to segregate the races any more than at present, the Confederates argued that their policy could not be called *apartheid*.[68]

The United Party at its congress in Bulawayo on 14 August decried this attempt to introduce racial politics, and called on all the other Southern Rhodesian Parties to unite with them to fight off this challenge. The central issue at this congress was, of course, the leadership. For several months, members had been dwelling on the problem of finding a successor to Huggins. It was apparent that there was no suitable candidate within his Cabinet. The obvious choice to many was Whitehead, but he was being forced to retire from politics because of failing eyesight. G. A. Davenport, the Minister of Mines and Transport, had earned disfavour in the coal crisis. P. B. Fletcher did not seem to be suitable, D. Macintyre had been assigned the federal portfolio of finance, and Caldicott and Greenfield aspired to federal posts. Amongst the backbenchers, it seemed to Greenfield that the most likely man was Todd and, accordingly, he sucessfully sought support for Todd's candidature from the influential Action Group of Bulawayo. However, other factions then proposed Greenfield himself, and he reluctantly agreed. Davenport was also nominated, but withdrew from the contest. When the congress voted, the result was a tie. Greenfield thereupon withdrew and the leadership passed to Todd who, though possessed of considerable personal qualities, had as yet no experience of government and, with regard to federal affairs, had no intimate knowledge of the arguments on which the federation had been founded because he had not attended the Conferences. When Greenfield and Caldicott departed for the Federal Parliament, Todd was left with a Cabinet whose members, apart from Fletcher, were as ignorant as he of the behind-the-scenes intricacies of federal history.[69] This did not help the federal cause.

At this congress, Huggins delivered his valedictory address to the Party which he had led for 20 years. He paid tribute to Whitehead, his close associate for many of those years. Then he urged the Party not to yield to pressure to define its African policy as one could not be dogmatic about human affairs. Situations should be met as they arose and the Party, in any case, was set on the right course. Partnership, Huggins noted, had been dragged into the federal arena where his formula of "all working together in the common cause and developing the country for the benefit of all its inhabitants" had been dismissed as nebulous. He urged the United Party to continue on its civilising course even if it proved unpopular with the more ignorant voters. It had to stand firm on the dictum of equal rights for civilised men. Civilised men, he felt, had to have a sense of duty and responsibility and be industrious and capable. It would be necessary to reserve areas for the races to develop their own social life, but the frustration of the African, as well as the elimination of the European, had to be avoided. Confession, he admitted, was good for the soul, and there had been a time, when he was

[68] *Ibid.*, 11 August 1953.
[69] *Ibid.*, 14 August 1953; Author's interview with the Hon. J. M. Greenfield.

young and green, when he had honestly thought that his "twin-pyramid" policy would provide the answer even though it contained no provision for the African to rise to the top. He accepted he had been mistaken.

Examining his opponents' ideas, Huggins diagnosed fear as the motivation of the Confederates. He felt that "Confederate" itself was an unhappy choice of name because it was the Confederates in the United States of America who had fought to keep their slaves. In conclusion, he appealed to the electorate to return reasonable men to the Southern Rhodesian Legislative Assembly so that the federation would be given the support it would need to succeed.

In this spirit, Todd sought to encourage an all-party grouping to fight off the challenge of the Confederates. He vowed also that his Government would do all it could to assist the federation.[70] The result was that, on 2 September, Sir Ernest Guest chaired a meeting at which Todd, Greenfield, Caldicott, Macintyre and others of the United Party met Stockil, Robert Halsted, I. D. Smith, Stumbles, G. W. Rudland, R. Hawkins and R. Williamson of the Rhodesia Party. They agreed to merge their Parties to form the United Rhodesia Party under the leadership of Todd.[71]

At last the preparations for the new era were complete. The Governor-General Designate, Lord Llewellin, a wartime British Cabinet Minister and a distinguished and veteran parliamentarian, arrived in Salisbury from Cape Town by train at 10 a.m. on 4 September. The same morning he was sworn in by the President of the Rhodesia and Nyasaland Court of Appeal, Sir Robert Tredgold. The long struggle was over. The Federation of Rhodesia and Nyasaland was a reality.

[70] *The Bulawayo Chronicle*, 16 August 1953.
[71] *The Rhodesia Herald*, 3 September 1953.

CHAPTER FOURTEEN

The Interim Government

Preparation for Power and the First Federal Elections, September 1953 – February 1954

THE primary task of the Interim Federal Government was to frame the regulations under which the first Federal general election would be held in mid-December. It would be the function of the new Federal Assembly to translate the Federal Constitution into legislative reality, but obviously for reasons of speed and efficiency much of the planning and drafting of the relevant legislation would be done in the interim period. Although Huggins, Welensky and Barrow, the initial members of the Interim Government, could have been fully occupied in this field alone, they had to ensure that the Federal Party secured sufficient seats in the Federal general election to have a working majority. It was important, too, that the territorial general elections in January and February 1954, should produce legislatures which would be sympathetic to the Federal cause and assistance would have to be furnished to achieve this end. In Southern Rhodesia, the parliamentarians who had gained Federal seats had merely to be replaced, but in Northern Rhodesia the oft-postponed constitutional negotiations had to be concluded before a general election could be held. The resolution of the Northern Rhodesian question would provoke the first bitter confrontation between Welensky and the British Government in the Federal era.

The Interim Federal Cabinet had in fact met for the first time — albeit informally — a week before the arrival of the Governor-General and, of course, the civil service preparatory committees had been hard at work for some time.[1] However, just as the Federal Parliament would open in early February 1954 in an atmosphere of industrial and civil unrest in Southern Rhodesia, the Interim Government began its task, in September 1953, to the accompaniment of daily reports from Nyasaland of intimidation, stone-throwing, baton charges and the like. The trouble stemmed from an incident in

[1] Welensky Papers, 14/26, f. 39, Report of a Meeting, Salisbury, 27 August 1953.

Cholo on the evening of 17 August when a car-load of Europeans arrested two African thieves. African bystanders rescued the thieves, and in the confusion thought others had been murdered. Consequently, a crowd of a thousand attacked the Tennent Estate the next day. In a skirmish with the police, an accidentally discharged rifle killed a rioter. Strikes and sabotage followed, and gangs of Africans armed with primitive weapons roamed the area. The unrest spread to other centres in the Southern Province, and to suppress it the Nyasaland Government had to be reinforced from neighbouring territories. It took a month to restore order.

By dint of brow-beating, the Nyasaland Governor induced the president of the Nyasaland African Congress, J. R. N. Chinyama, to tour the area appealing for calm. He also influenced his Congress to dissociate itself from the violence and terminate its non-co-operation campaign. On 7 September, the Nyasaland Council of Chiefs followed suit. It seemed that the resistance was over and that the days of the Congress were numbered. Shortly afterwards, a schism occurred with the new Nyasaland African Progressive Association emerging as a rival to the Congress. Chinyama resigned and was succeeded by a graduate of South Africa's Fort Hare University College, Wellington Manoah Chirwa. The riots, which cost eleven lives and 72 injuries, could be attributed to land pressure, squatters' rents and other local issues, but there is no doubt that the widespread suspicion of federation, exacerbated by the activities of the Congress and, in particular, the recent visit of the Reverend Michael Scott and its consequences, had heightened tension.[2]

In Northern Rhodesia, similar manifestations of resistance appeared in September and October in the Northern and Southern Provinces in the form of localised lawlessness. In the towns, the campaign against the colour bar practices continued. It was at this time that Kenneth Kaunda came to the forefront of the African National Congress leadership. The African Mineworkers' Union took the opportunity to press its long-standing claims for the advancement of its members. However, of more immediate importance was the unresolved constitutional issue, and a delegation comprising the Governor, Sir Gilbert Rennie, Welensky, Beckett, Moffat, Sokota and Yamba left for Britain after the formal installation of the Federal Governor-General.[3]

Review of the Northern Rhodesian Constitution had been promised after 30 months of its reform in 1948 and, as 60 months had passed, Lyttelton had promised it as soon as the Federation was a reality. The imminence of the next Northern Rhodesian general election was an added incentive. However, it is surprising that Lyttelton should have courted a confrontation with the Northern Rhodesian delegates of both races when the Federation was less than a week old. When deadlock was reached almost immediately, it is difficult to see why he could not have suspended the negotiations, as he was urged to do, and give the Federation at least a year's respite. Welensky certainly would not have opposed this, but Lyttelton chose to accept the advice of W. L. Gorell Barnes, the Assistant Under-Secretary of State for the

[2] R. I. Rotberg, *The Rise of Nationalism in Central Africa: The Making of Malawi and Zambia, 1873–1964* (London, 1965), pp. 262–263; P. Short, *Banda* (London, 1974), p. 77; daily reports in *The Rhodesia Herald* and other newspapers.
[3] *The Rhodesia Herald*, 9 September 1953.

Colonies, that a solution should be imposed without delay. This was the first indication that the Colonial Office would not be diverted from its objective of achieving self-determination for all the subject peoples of the Empire as soon as practicable. In Central Africa, the European never succeeded in shaking the will of the Colonial Office to prosecute this policy, and the inevitable consequence was the devolution of power into the hands of the African nationalists who had so strenuously opposed federation. This was partly responsible for the premature demolition of the Federation.

The changes proposed by Welensky were that there should be one less official Member in the Legislative Council and two or three new elected Members, and that one European representative of African interests might step down for an African, or that another African seat should be created. If the elected Members were reinforced by three, the officials reduced to eight while African representation remained constant, the resultant ratio of 13:8:4 would mean that the elected Members would have a majority of one every time the African representatives sided with the officials at a division. If the officials were reduced to eight, but only two elected Members were added, while the African representative strength was increased by one, the result at least would be parity in a division.

Welensky and Beckett were also seeking to have the Executive Council consist of four officials, three elected Members and a European representative of African interests. All would hold portfolios and sit in the Legislative Council as a "Front Bench". The Governor's powers would remain intact but the practice of treating the elected Members as juniors would cease. Beckett, who held the portfolio of agriculture, particularly resented this practice.

The difference between European and African aspirations was emphatically illustrated by the African ideas, as Yamba and Sokota had been instructed by the ANC and the African Representative Council to demand nothing less than parity of racial representation in the Legislative Council. Thus, if the elected Members secured two more seats, the Africans would be given eight. They wanted all portfolios removed from unofficial hands, but would allow one to be held by a European representative of African interests. The African delegates wanted also to influence the elections by securing the vote for British Protected Persons who otherwise qualified for the franchise.

Thus it is not surprising that Lyttelton found it impossible to secure agreement in the course of two weeks of negotiations. Deadlock was made all the more likely when the African delegates declared at the outset that they had no mandate to depart from their brief. Their demands had to be accepted or rejected.[4]

Welensky wanted to settle the issue and had limited his demands to the two additional portfolios as a means to avoid an impasse. Lyttelton appeared pleased, but Gorell Barnes found it unacceptable. Understandably, Welensky was somewhat amazed by this naked display of the influence of the senior civil servant. In any case, he was incensed by the tone in which he had been addressed and the manner in which he had been treated, feeling that he

[4] Welensky Papers, 20/4, f. 320, H. Smedley to Huggins, 16 September 1953; 42/52, f. 416, Welensky to D. Cole, 14 September 1953; 17/45, f. 535, Welensky to Gore-Browne, 18 September 1953; *The Rhodesia Herald*, 9 September 1953.

should be accorded a little more respect than Yamba and Sokota who neither matched his length of service nor his achievements. Furthermore, his confidence in Lyttelton had been shaken when the latter had asked him to consider the enfranchisement of British Protected Persons. Welensky had had no warning of this, but opposed it because it threatened the very basis of a qualitative franchise. He and his colleagues were determined that anyone obtaining the vote should share both its disadvantages and advantages. Currently only British subjects who possessed the income and property qualifications had the vote but they alone were subject to income tax and conscription. It cost £5 to register as a British subject, and Welensky had been prepared to have that fee reduced, or to have Northern Rhodesia annexed to the Crown, which would immediately make every inhabitant a British subject. Annexation would smooth the path to dominion status, but the termination of protection would open to question the reservation of 97 per cent of the land for the African.[5]

On 16 September, tiring of the fruitless argument, Lyttelton informed the delegates that he would add two European and two African Members to the Legislative Council immediately. Moreover, he was considering replacing one of the European representatives of African interests with an African, thereby increasing the Africans in the Legislative Council to five. His purpose was to temper some of the British parliamentary criticism. He proposed to announce his final decision on 18 September but was obliged by the Federal agreement to discuss any territorial constitutional alterations with the Federal Government, and he immediately cabled the draft of his announcement to Salisbury. He asked Huggins if he would prefer the retention of two European representatives of African interests.[6]

The draft stated bluntly that agreement between the parties had proved unattainable. It revealed that the long-term British objective was to reduce the need for separate racial representation to a point where a democratic system was possible with a widened franchise. However, until then the official Members had to hold the balance to prevent either racial group from dictating policy. The aim was to achieve, by stages, an equality of racial representation, and it was undesirable that the Africans should be able to influence the election of the unofficial Members while nomination existed. If, in due course, a common roll could be devised which achieved a balanced representation, then the need for special arrangements to fill the African seats would fall away. This point was not immediately important because the number of Africans who were British subjects was negligible and few of them had the vote. The next Legislative Council would comprise twelve elected Members, five African and one European representative of African interests, and nine officials. The number of officials was likely to be reduced as the Federal assumption of power would perhaps make the post of Financial

[5] NR *Debates* (Lusaka), Col. 127 f., 12 November 1953; Welensky Papers, 24/151, f. 434, Welensky to F. S. Joelson, 21 November 1953; WE 7, P/C/160/52, Welensky to C. J. M. Alport, 2 November 1953; 43/*Malvern*, Welensky to Huggins, 12 September 1953; 39/45, Welensky to unofficial Members, 14 September 1953.

[6] Welensky Papers, 20/4, f. 320, H. Smedley to Huggins, 16 September 1953; f. 324, same to same, 8 September 1953.

Secretary redundant. In the Executive Council all nine members would hold portfolios and would constitute a front bench. Five of these would be officials, three elected Members, and the last the European representative of African interests. Nothing was said about treating the latter four as equals.[7]

Huggins immediately referred Lyttelton to Welensky because he was better qualified to answer. Barrow endorsed this reply when he and Huggins met later that day, 16 September. Together they composed a formal reply rejecting the reference to the objectives of British policy because it would affect the Federal electorate drastically and endanger the chances of the Federal Party of forming the first Federal Government. Lyttelton accepted this argument but nevertheless felt that it was imperative to state the British intention clearly, and proposed to do so during his contemplated visit to Northern Rhodesia in 1954. Huggins agreed.[8]

However, Lyttelton refused to discuss the appointment of the fifth African with Welensky because he was not negotiating in his capacity as a member of the Interim Federal Cabinet. Instead, Lyttelton and Rennie devised a formula which anticipated an adverse reaction in Northern Rhodesia to the fifth African, but kept the option open because the advance towards racial parity had to be continued. Accordingly the communiqué was re-drafted to include the comment that, in the long term, the British Government looked forward to the day when racial considerations fell away, when it would be possible to move towards a system based on a widened franchise with no separate racial representation. On the franchise, Lyttelton would note that the African delegates had asked for the vote for the British Protected Persons on the same terms as the British subjects. He would acknowledge that this raised the questions of whether Northern Rhodesia should develop politically on the basis of the existing system of separate racial representation until the long-term objective was reached, or whether it would be possible and desirable at some earlier stage to adopt a form of common roll which would give the degree of African representation appropriate at the time. The communiqué said that careful consideration was needed and that Lyttelton would re-examine the problem when he visited Northern Rhodesia in 1954.[9]

The release of the revised communiqué was delayed until Lyttelton, Rennie and Welensky met on 21 September. Welensky furiously rejected the constitutional award outright and warned that the European would interpret it as evidence that the British Government would not do anything which might be unpopular with Africans. Lyttelton retorted that Yamba and Sokota had already accused him of completely surrendering to European demands. It seemed to him that, if the award were interpreted purely as a concession to the African, it was difficult to escape the conclusion that the Europeans were, in fact, seeking domination. Welensky, however, bluntly warned that, if the award were published unaltered, he would resist its implementation with

[7] *Ibid.*, f. 322, Draft Communiqué from the Colonial Secretary, 16 September 1953.
[8] *Ibid.*, f. 319, Huggins to H. Smedley, 16 September 1953; FGC (53), 1st Meeting, Minute 1, Federal Cabinet, 16 September 1953; 20/4, f. 315, H. Smedley to Huggins, 19 September 1953.
[9] *Ibid.*, 20/4, f. 315, Smedley to Huggins, 19 September 1953; 7/10, f. 232, Draft Communiqué, 18 September 1953; 20/4, f. 316, Statement by the Colonial Secretary, 19 September 1953; f. 313, Smedley to Huggins, 23 September 1953.

everything at his disposal. He wondered whether this was an attempt to win African support for the Federation through appeasement, because, if so, it would fail. Lyttelton replied that, as the Federation was a reality, he had indeed decided that it was essential to demonstrate that Africans could advance in the territorial sphere. He pleaded with Welensky not to carry out a consequent threat to remain in territorial politics as his guidance was essential to the Federation in its formative years. At least, he urged, Welensky should consult Huggins before acting.[10]

Welensky immediately informed his colleagues in Northern Rhodesia that he would expect them to cease to co-operate with the Government by resigning their portfolios and appointments. On the next day, 22 September, when Lyttelton formally announced his decision, Welensky warned Huggins that he might leave the Interim Federal Government to lead the territorial Opposition. He informed the Press that neither he nor Beckett could accept the constitutional award and would decide with their colleagues in Lusaka on 25 September what action should be taken.

Yamba and Sokota, in the name of the African people of Northern Rhodesia, rejected the award because it merely enhanced European power while virtually ignoring African demands. They revealed that they had rejected the system of nominating the African representatives and had sought to enfranchise 5 000 Africans by lowering the qualifications from an income of £250 p.a., or the possession of fixed property of that worth, to £100 of income or property. Africans, they felt, should not have to become British subjects to qualify. Despite their rebuff, they remained confident that British Protected Persons would be enfranchised in the life of the next Legislative Council because the British Government knew that only this would regain the confidence of the African.[11]

While the Rhodesian Press urged caution because the Federation was so new, and *The Times* consoled Lyttelton that there was little else he could have done in the face of deadlock, the British left-wing Press inevitably sided with Yamba and Sokota. Against this background, the elected Members met Welensky and Beckett on 25 September and heard how Lyttelton had refused or deferred every suggestion. The high-handed manner of the British delegation had been particularly galling. It was quite clear, Welensky and Beckett claimed, that the African delegates' Fabian advisers had convinced them that they only had to be vociferous to obtain power. The meeting decided that Welensky should continue to lead the unofficials until the Federal general election when Beckett would take over. Hitherto, Beckett had intended to seek a Federal seat. The constitutional award was rejected, and Rennie was asked to secure its suspension and to invite Lyttelton to visit Northern Rhodesia as soon as possible to discuss the impasse.[12]

[10] *Ibid.*, 7/10, f. 251, Minutes of a Meeting, Colonial Office, 21 September 1953.

[11] *Ibid.*, 39/45, f. 350, Welensky to E. W. Sergeant, 21 September 1953; 20/4, f. 314, Smedley to Huggins, 22 September 1953; *The Rhodesia Herald*, 23 September 1953.

[12] *The Rhodesia Herald*, 23 September 1953; *The Times*, 23 September 1953; *New Statesman and Nation*, 26 September 1953; *Tribune*, 25 September 1953; Welensky Papers, 7/10, f. 270, Minutes of a Meeting of elected Members, Lusaka, 25 September 1953; f. 271, Welensky to Rennie, 25 September 1953; *Northern News*, 26 September 1953.

In support, Huggins requested the suspension of the implementation of the award for twelve months so that the crisis should not affect his Federal election or the Federation itself in its crucial first year. Lyttelton, however, would not comply. He acknowledged that a year's suspension was an attractive idea but would only consider it if both sides asked for the maintenance of the *status quo* for that period. He claimed that the reason for his action was to avoid embarrassing Huggins because Welensky, rejecting any delay, had threatened to leave the Interim Cabinet to fight the territorial constitutional battle. Lyttelton was surprised that his award had proved so unacceptable as neither side had objected when he had proposed to arbitrate.[13]

To the Northern Rhodesians, Lyttelton said that he could not travel immediately, and to arrive in the midst of the Federal general election campaign would be most inappropriate. Imperiously he stated that the constitutional change would be implemented and, in any visit, he would only discuss the problems of the future.[14]

Huggins replied that there was no point in Lyttelton's visit unless, consequently, the constitutional award was withdrawn. However, he would not have been surprised when Lyttelton virtually ignored him. Indeed, Lyttelton was only prepared to comment on the timing of his visit, and told Rennie that he would hold constitutional discussions with all concerned in early 1954. Meanwhile, the constitutional award would be effected. Thereafter, if there were unanimous agreement on further change which he could accept he would allow it to be implemented immediately.[15]

The Northern Rhodesian Government was inordinately slow in transmitting this message to Welensky, and it took him almost a week to reply, but then he was fighting an election. On 22 October he demanded the suspension of the award until Lyttelton arrived because it had been rejected by both delegations.[16]

Nkumbula had intruded into this argument and into the electoral contest. On 16 October he called the new Confederate Party "vermin", and warned that there would be serious trouble if such reactionaries gained control of 6 000 000 Africans in the Federation. He proposed the withdrawal of farm labour and to maintain the campaign against the colour bar. He promised to secure a straight-forward democratic franchise based on an income of £50 p.a., a means test of £100 and the applicant's literacy in his own language. Then on 23 October he threatened that "we must not be blamed if we do things that look savage to the civilised world. We do not want to get rid of the Whites, but we are not going to allow them here as bosses".[17]

When Lyttelton again refused to suspend the award, Welensky informed him that the offer to consider the extension of the franchise had bothered the Northern Rhodesians more than the award itself because they could not see why any voter should escape the responsibilities borne by the British subject.

[13] Welensky Papers, 20/4, f. 311, Colonial Secretary to Governor-General, 2 October 1953.
[14] *Ibid.*, f. 308, Colonial Secretary to Governor-General, 3 October 1953.
[15] *Ibid.*, f. 310, Governor-General to Colonial Secretary, 3 October 1953.
[16] *Ibid.*, 7/10, f. 277, Chief Secretary, Northern Rhodesian Government, to Welensky, 14 October 1953; f. 278, Welensky to Chief Secretary, 22 October 1953.
[17] *The Rhodesia Herald*, 26 October 1953.

The spectacle of a Conservative Colonial Secretary tampering with the franchise had already caused Welensky unnecessary political difficulties in the electoral campaign. However, Lyttelton merely reiterated the reassurance that he would not allow any constitutional alteration unless it was desired by all parties. In addition, he proclaimed that he had not committed himself in any way to the enfranchisement of the British Protected Persons and would come to Northern Rhodesia with an open mind.[18]

He did not satisfy the elected Members who, in protest, promptly resigned from the Executive Council and from the committees of the Legislative Council. They intended to reserve the public announcement of their action until they had debated the unacceptability of the award in the Legislative Council which Rennie would open on 7 November. Rennie, however, did not co-operate and, in his opening speech, noted their resignations. This forced Welensky to explain that they had resigned because their request that the constitutional award be suspended, pending further negotiations, had not been granted. He said that a contributing factor to their action had been their alarm at Lyttelton's indication that he might widen the franchise in favour of the African. This affair, Welensky announced, had forced Beckett to stay in territorial politics. Despite the African rejection of the award, Moffat and Nightingale immediately declared their support for the Government.[19]

Among those taken by surprise by these events was Huggins who that day had telegraphed Welensky asking him not to act until they met in Salisbury on 10 November for a Cabinet meeting. However, the die was cast and Welensky could only reply that Rennie had forced his hand. Although *The Rhodesia Herald* called on Lyttelton to reconsider and allow the Federation time to consolidate itself, Lyttelton, on 9 November, in the Commons, merely regretted this drastic move while justifying his award. He had gathered that the elected Members would prefer that an African replace a European representative of African interests. However, he had considered that, not only was it fair to match the European gain of two seats with two African seats, but also that it accorded with the spirit of partnership on which the Federation was founded.[20]

It was a rare occasion for Lyttelton when he was the incumbent at the Colonial Office to enjoy the total support of the British Press which described the elected Members as truculent, unwise and responsible for the Federation's poor start. General amazement was expressed at the European's expectations of greater control in Northern Rhodesia. It was thought that the Federal Party was trying to impress its waverers. These Press comments seemed so pertinent to Lord Swinton that he sent them to Huggins.[21]

The whole issue was re-examined in detail on 11 November in the Legislative Council when Welensky maintained that, as the African Members had

[18] Welensky Papers, WE 7, P/C/160/52, Welensky to C. J. M. Alport, 2 November 1953; 7/10, f. 286, Chief Secretary, Northern Rhodesian Government, to Welensky, 4 November 1953.

[19] NR *Debates* (Lusaka), Col. 1 f., 7 November 1953; Welensky Papers, 7/10, f. 292, Welensky's Announcement, 7 November 1953; *The Rhodesia Herald*, 9 November 1953.

[20] Welensky Papers, 7/10, f. 293, Huggins to Welensky, (undated); f. 295, Welensky to Huggins, (undated); *The Rhodesia Herald*, 9 & 10 November 1953.

[21] Welensky Papers, 20/4, f. 304, Lord Swinton to Lord Llewellin, 9 November 1953.

rejected the award, Lyttelton could have stayed his hand, particularly as he was only being asked to visit and not to commit himself. He hoped Lyttelton would reconsider and claimed that the elected Members, who had always been reasonable and who had always advanced Africans in all fields, had been forced to act because Northern Rhodesia could not be subjected to reckless experiment. Experience elsewhere in the Empire taught that vigilance had to be constant. The elected Members had insisted on Lyttelton visiting because London had proved to be an unsuitable venue for negotiations. If Lyttelton refused, when the flying time was only 19 hours, the election would be dominated by the theme of total opposition to the British Government, which the territory could ill-afford. Welensky credited Lyttelton with the scrapping of the three pre-conditions to constitutional change set by Griffiths. These were: ratification of any changes by the African Representative Council; no adjustment within the life of the current Legislative Council despite Creech Jones's 30 month trial period; and that Welensky should hold a portfolio. However, Lyttelton had sprung the surprise of the suggestion of enfranchising British Protected Persons. Welensky rejected this because he maintained that every voter had to share the disadvantages of the British subject which were being liable to income tax and conscription. He acknowledged that Lyttelton had not committed himself on this, but experience had shown that the mere airing of such a proposal would lead the Africans to expect its implementation.

Beckett, having resigned from the Executive Council, felt he could express his resentment of the superior official attitude within it. He would refuse to have the two new Africans selected by the African Representative Council because it had committed itself to black domination. He also wanted the Colonial administration's power curbed because it looked constantly to London for guidance.

Moffat and Nightingale regretted that the elected Members had not warned them of their action because they might have been able to dissuade them from making this "appalling error of judgement". They wondered if the same would happen when the Commonwealth Secretary exercised the Federal reserved powers against the wishes of the Federal Party. If a protest was necessary, it should have been made in London. It was pointless to make fruitless gestures, and the Legislative Council was owed an explanation. After all, Moffat and Nightingale argued, the award was justified by the imbalance of the racial representation, and Lyttelton had not committed himself on the franchise. The elected Members should have realised that if Lyttelton surrendered to their demands, their opponents would have an equal right to insist on like treatment for theirs. The Africans were certainly willing to bear the responsibilities of the franchise and their delegates had acted responsibly in changing their attitude when they realised that the award was well received. Moffat and Nightingale concluded that Lyttelton had been forced to make the award when he realised that the gap between the delegations was unbridgeable, because the current constitution was so heavily criticised in Britain.

Yamba and Sokota claimed that they had not rejected the award but had merely waited to hear the verdict of their people. They reminded Welensky that Africans who had rejected federation had been called "disloyal". They claimed that the lack of preliminary discussion had been responsible for the surprise of their demand on the franchise. However, it was crucial to open the franchise to get rid of racialism, and there was a precedent because British Protected Persons had been enfranchised in West Africa in 1922. They wondered if Welensky was withdrawing the hand of friendship and consigning the African to perpetual second-class citizenship.

Welensky replied that the essential attitude of the Colonial Office, so dangerous to Northern Rhodesia, had been ignored by his critics when Griffiths could well be the next Colonial Secretary. Everyone worried about African feelings, but surely the European was entitled to reassurance. He had, in fact, tried to keep the negotiations going, but the attitude of the senior Colonial civil servant present had made even insistence on the maintenance of the *status quo* futile. It had to be remembered that the African had a position of privilege in Northern Rhodesia. He reiterated that Lyttelton had not committed himself on the franchise, but the need for vigilance was paramount. Welensky apologised if he had misrepresented Yamba and Sokota, but he could recall their bitter rejection of the award in the Press. He recalled their refusal in 1951 to negotiate, which had rendered sterile the negotiations then even though they were the most inexperienced of the Members. He denied the charge of accusing African opponents of federation of being disloyal. However, he wondered if Yamba and Sokota were really aiming at black domination. He asked if Africans would give up their exclusive rights to land to become first-class citizens. He praised Moffat's fine performance as Lyttelton's advocate, but warned that Moffat could not criticise the elected Members with impunity when he had failed to give the Africans a lead.

Finally, Welensky asked Moffat what he had meant when he had suggested that Britain should re-examine the Federation. Moffat replied that he had thought that this motion, which was unconstitutional in his view, might be used as a precedent for similar action in the Federal Assembly. Unsworth, as Attorney-General, ruled that, because this motion did not imply rejection, it was acceptable. The Council accepted the constitutional award by 13 votes to seven.[22]

Although Welensky had intended to prevent experimentation with the franchise, and not to indulge in "vote catching", the suspicions of his local and British critics that this was his intention seemed to have been borne out when there was an immediate upturn in the fortunes of the Federal Party. Welensky acknowledged, in his correspondence, that he could secure unanimous support in Northern Rhodesia if he totally obstructed the Government, but he felt that would be irresponsible. W. S. Parker, Welensky's private secretary, thought Welensky had been cunning to implant the idea that annexation was a method to enfranchise the African, because in removing protected status in a manner to which neither the Africans nor the United Nations could object, it demolished the major obstacle to the achievement of the desired dominion.[23]

[22] NR *Debates* (Lusaka), Col. 32 f., 11 November 1953.
[23] *The Rhodesia Herald*, 14 & 16 November 1953; Welensky Papers, 8/53, f. 1, W. S. Parker to J. H. Wallace, 16 November 1953; 24/151, f. 432, Welensky to F. S. Joelson, 13 November 1953.

The crisis was quickly solved. On 24 November Moffat instigated negotiations with the Government, and the resignations were withdrawn on 9 December, a week before the Federal general election. Simultaneously, Lyttelton proposed to advance the date of his Northern Rhodesian visit to early January. On the understanding that the award of September was unalterable, Lyttelton agreed to review the Constitution with the Legislative and the African Representative Councils, and firmly declared that he would not change the franchise in the life of the next legislature unless all parties, including the British Government, were agreed that it was necessary.[24]

Welensky had achieved what seemed to him to be a fair compromise and could relinquish the Northern Rhodesian leadership, but avowed privately that it would be "some time before I forget the way things were handled".[25]

The negotiations in 1957 on the Federal franchise would restore in part his confidence in the Conservative Government, but he had not diverted the Colonial Office from its aim of the rapid advancement of all its territories to self-government based on universal suffrage.

Welensky and his colleagues had attracted adverse overseas comment by their actions, and Britain itself was criticised in the UN Trusteeship Committee in October for the implementation of federation with scant regard for the advancement of the African. Thus it is surprising that the Interim Federal Government escaped similar adverse attention when it took measures in November to terminate a minor influx of Indian immigrants into the northern territories, the immigrants having acted in anticipation of a Federal ban. This is even more extraordinary when it is remembered that India, in the person of Mrs Lakshmi Menon, in alliance with Poland, led the attack on Britain at the UN. The Indian community in the Rhodesias had never been happily accepted, and one of the reasons for the Southern Rhodesian European resistance to federation was that it might allow Indian immigration which had been prohibited since the 1920s. The arguments in the constitutional Conferences over inter-territorial movement had been based on the Southern Rhodesian fear that the Nyasaland Asians might emigrate *en masse* to Southern Rhodesia.[26]

A multitude of other tasks confronted the Interim Cabinet as a nucleus of the future administration was built. The Secretary to the Treasury, Sir Andrew Strachan, was dispatched to London to discuss financial arrangements, including those for the Kafue project. The territorial Governments were prompted to amend their electoral laws and to delimit constituencies for the Federal general election. The Northern Rhodesian Government immediately upset the Copperbelt population by allocating them only two of the eight Federal seats but, when petitioned, the Governor-General, Lord Llewellin, properly referred the protesters to the judicial investigation which followed and which confirmed the validity of the decision.[27] The standing orders to serve the Federal Assembly when it was opened on 2 February were

[24] *The Rhodesia Herald*, 25 November 1953; Welensky Papers, 20/4, f. 305, Rennie to Llewellin, 8 December 1953.
[25] Welensky Papers, WE 7, P/C/169/52, Welensky to C. J. M. Alport, 5 December 1953.
[26] *The Rhodesia Herald*, 11 & 21 October 1953; *The Times*, 27 November 1953.
[27] *The Rhodesia Herald*, 21 September & 16 & 20 October 1953.

devised, and decisions were taken on the remuneration of Federal MPs, on the salaries of civil servants and on a host of other issues. The members of the Interim Cabinet could be forgiven, however, if they were preoccupied with the major task on hand, that of winning the Federal general election.

As has been related, an opposition to the Federal Party had coalesced in the interim between the Southern Rhodesian referendum and the inauguration of the Federation, with Dendy Young emerging as the leader of the new Confederate Party. This Party not only gained support in both Rhodesias, but also stole a march by being the first to publish its policy, as early as 10 September, when the Federal Party leadership was still preoccupied with the inaugural ceremonies, with the erection of a political structure in Northern Rhodesia, and with forming a new party to support Todd in Southern Rhodesia. Confederate policy reflected many traditional Southern Rhodesian European attitudes, but it had borrowed so heavily from the South African Nationalist Party that J. G. Strydom, the South African Minister of Lands, and soon to be Prime Minister, expressed pleasure at the way in which his Party's ideas were permeating the Rhodesias. Dendy Young even used the South African term "Bantu" when his opponents had dropped the traditional "Native" for "African" out of respect for African susceptibilities.[28]

The Confederate Party refused to accept that African affairs were not a Federal concern when they could obviously as crucially affect the Federation as the territories. The reason for this comment was that the Party believed that the permanency of white civilisation in Central Africa could be guaranteed by the creation of separate African states within the Federation. Therefore, the Confederates proposed to encourage the fullest development of the existing African areas and to provide a political outlet for Africans by means of separate voters' rolls. In saying this, the Confederates, like their successors, the Dominion and Rhodesian Front Parties, were naïvely confident that Britain could be induced to condone *apartheid.* They accepted that there should be a racial partnership to develop the Federation for the benefit of all, but they would limit it to politics and economics because it would be a partnership between races and not individuals. In the relationship it would be recognised that the European would lead for the foreseeable future and thus would be responsible for the social, economic and political progress of the African. The partnership would be operated on the maxim that each race's interests would be paramount in its area. As the current territorial policies had failed to promote the economic and political development of the African areas, and had driven the progressive African to neglect his natural role of leader by seeking to realise his aspirations among the Europeans, the Confederates said they would immediately set up African-administered development councils with local taxing powers. The Confederates were confident that experience would quickly produce political and economic maturity. The most serious political mistake had been the adoption of the common roll in Southern Rhodesia, and they would instead give the Africans in Southern Rhodesia true representation by the adoption of the Federal system of special Members. The Africans would have a separate roll, but simultaneously

[28] *Ibid.*, 11 September 1953; *Northern News*, 23 September 1953.

political institutions would develop in the embryo African states to meet the increasing demand for more African representation. The result would be that the African representation in the Federal and territorial legislatures would diminish progressively as the African gained greater autonomy in his areas. European immigration would be drastically increased to release the African employee so that he could use his skills amongst his own people.

Dendy Young was convinced that the Africans would readily accept this proposition and believed Huggins was mistaken if he thought that Africans could ever be removed from the common roll once they inevitably dominated it. The consequence would be a black state. As the Federal Party envisaged the partnership as one between individuals rather than races, it would remove all social, economic and political barriers which meant racial integration and, in its wake, a destruction of the stability of African society. Dendy Young said that the Federal Party was hoping to effect a gradual transition while ignoring the already apparent African rejection of their ideas. Dendy Young did not, however, explain how he would effect such radical changes when the Federal Constitution itself forbad alteration for ten years. This omission was corrected in mid-October, when the Confederates acknowledged that nothing could be done for a decade.[29]

The Federal Party countered by publishing its attitude to partnership. Constrained by the territorial responsibility for African policy, it would interpret the references to partnership and co-operation in the Federal Constitution as demanding a system which would enable the races to live together in harmony. It had to be recognised that the races had distinctive and complementary roles to play, and each should be rewarded according to his contribution to the partnership. The natural desire on the part of each race to develop on traditional lines would be recognised and considered in the provision of amenities and facilities while the current differences existed between the cultural levels of the mass of the people. However, the Federal Party said that there would be a gradual extension of political rights and privileges to those who conformed to civilised standards of behaviour and culture, with a corresponding diminution in special political representation.[30]

Apart from organisational activity, the Federal Party did little more than issue this statement as Huggins in Salisbury and Welensky in London were otherwise fully employed and had no intention of starting their campaign until mid-October, two months before the Federal election. Welensky was concerned about the inroads being made by the Confederates in Northern Rhodesia and in the Copperbelt in particular where their policy of *apartheid* seemed to appeal, but he did not think that the ground was irretrievably lost.[31]

The Federal Party was not entirely idle and, in late September, in Southern Rhodesia, had gained valuable recruits, including W. H. Eastwood, from a disintegration of the Southern Rhodesia Labour Party. Furthermore, Welensky had returned from Britain and had warned that, should the Confederates be returned, British governmental attitudes would harden and,

[29] *The Rhodesia Herald*, 11 September & 7 October 1953.
[30] *Ibid.*, 18 September 1953.
[31] Welensky Papers, 25/36, f. 15, Welensky to Sir Dougal Malcolm, 12 October 1953.

should the Federation fail, Northern Rhodesia would return to the control of the Colonial Office.[32]

When they began to campaign in earnest, within a week Huggins and Welensky, who often shared platforms, had won back the Copperbelt after a series of addresses to packed and often rowdy meetings. In an exhaustive campaign, the leaders of the Federal Party toured the three territories and would achieve almost total success. The popular appeal of Welensky's stand on the Northern Rhodesian Constitution, of course, won many votes, and a notable feature of the campaign was the abandonment in the Rhodesias of "non-co-operation" of the African nationalists who thereupon put forward candidates for the special seats. Included among these were Nkumbula, Kaunda and Nkomo.[33]

The Federal Party reminded the electorate that the main reason for federation was the need to integrate the economies of the three territories which was obviously incompatible with the Confederates' *apartheid*. Moreover, Welensky rejected the creation of "Gold Coasts" within the Federation as undesirable and unconstitutional. The racialist approach of the Confederates was depicted as merely enhancing the appeal of African nationalism. The Confederate allegation that the Federal Party intended to introduce racial integration was dismissed as a political bogey because federation would make little difference to daily life, particularly in Southern Rhodesia where the African could already qualify for the vote. Despite Confederate allegations, Welensky maintained that partnership was not meant to bring miscegenation in its wake. Anyway, to him, miscegenation was a matter of personal choice and little to do with governments. The presence of Africans in the Federal Parliament had been accepted at the referendum and would mean the social mixing of races at official functions, but that in no way infringed personal freedoms. A Confederate Party claim that its vigorous immigration policy constituted the main difference between the Parties was belied by Welensky who set a target of attracting 500 000 European immigrants in the first decade.

Both Huggins and Welensky proposed dominion status as the ultimate goal, but warned that the Federation should first prove viable. Huggins, late in the campaign, gave a foretaste of more immediate intentions by stating that the Federal Assembly soon would have to be enlarged so that it could contain a governing party and a government-in-waiting. He said this because, given the neutrality of the nine special Members on most subjects, currently the governing party needed to gain a minimum of 18 seats to secure a working majority, leaving the opposition with eight or less.[34]

One peculiarity of the electoral contest was a Confederate decision not to campaign on purely Federal matters because it was competing for territorial as well as Federal seats. Thus its candidates felt none of the restraint of the

[32] *The Rhodesia Herald*, 28, 29 & 30 September 1953.

[33] *Ibid.*, 22 October 1953; Welensky Papers, WE 7, P/C/109/52, Welensky to Gore-Browne, 25 October 1953; 42/37, f. 191, Welensky to R. Byrne, 26 October 1953; 27/1, Welensky to Sir Frederick Crawford, 26 October 1953; D. C. Mulford, *Zambia: The Politics of Independence, 1957–1964* (London, 1967), p. 36; *Central African Post*, 24 November 1953.

[34] *The Rhodesia Herald*, 19 & 27 October 1953.

Federal Party's decision to adhere strictly to Federal constitutional limitations. By so blending Federal and territorial issues, the Confederates only succeeded in confusing the electorate who frequently challenged speakers on their attitude to territorial matters such as African advancement in industry. Welensky, in particular, was asked continually to pronounce, as a Federal candidate, on African industrial advancement and, more specifically, on the implementation of the Dalgleish Report.[35]

Andrew Dalgleish, an eminent British trade unionist, had chaired a Commission in 1948 to discover what new posts the African miners could immediately fill, what training facilities they would require to advance to even more skilled and responsible employment, and how the wage structure could be adjusted to accommodate such change. The Commission found posts which the Africans could instantly fill and others for which they could be trained. It suggested that the Government and the mining industry could sponsor scholarships for further training and could alleviate dangerous frustration by persuading the Northern Rhodesian European Mineworkers' Union to accept alteration of its agreement of 1947 with the Chamber of Mines which reserved certain categories of employment for white miners.[36]

The European Mineworkers' Union was not responsive, and the Dalgleish Report was shelved and the Government argued, when taxed, that it was a domestic issue of the mining industry. Yet the Africans could hardly be expected to forget the issue, and by 1953 there was sufficient agitation for the mining companies to apply pressure on the white union. The Confederates were quick to remind the miners that the companies had recently supported the United Central Africa Association and, consequently, even though industrial relations would remain a territorial subject, the Federal general election threatened to become a men-versus-management struggle.[37]

In Kitwe on 21 October, Welensky was asked whether his Party accepted the Dalgleish recommendations when they had consistently been rejected by the European Mineworkers' Union. Expressing confidence in the Union's ability to defend its interests, Welensky replied that this was not a Federal affair. Personally, he said, he believed the Report was obsolete, "dead", and should be buried peacefully. There might be a case for a further commission to re-examine the problem, but it was, however, unrealistic to expect that the Northern Rhodesian and British Governments would ever condone a policy of segregation.[38]

Perhaps because the whole of Welensky's reply was not transmitted to London, *The Times*, on 4 November, demanded clarification as the issue of African advancement was very much alive. In any case, his reply did not satisfy his audiences because he was asked continuously, even in Southern Rhodesia, what the Federal Party would do with the Dalgleish Report. Welensky answered *The Times* by reiterating that African industrial ad-

[35] *Ibid.*, 22 October 1953; *The Times*, 2 November 1953; Welensky Papers, 24/1, f. 208, Welensky to A. Dalgleish, 9 November 1953.

[36] *Report of the Commission Appointed to Enquire into the Advancement of Africans in Industry* (Lusaka, 1948).

[37] Welensky Papers, 24/1, ff. 222–223, Welensky to A. Dalgleish, 28 August 1953.

[38] *The Rhodesia Herald*, 22 October 1953.

vancement was not a Federal responsibility but that he believed that the African should be educated culturally and economically, and then politically.[39]

Ronald L. Prain (later Sir Ronald), chairman of the Rhodesian Selection Trust group of companies, contributed to the controversy by a lengthy public pronouncement on 24 November on the opportunity presented to the Federation to work out a new deal for the African within the concept of the multi-racial society. He defended the record of the mining companies and proclaimed that the Federation would only succeed if it found a solution to the industrial colour bar. The African miners, he maintained, were right to demand change. He stimulated the African Mineworkers' Union to make such a demand, but by then the Federal Party had won the allegiance of the electorate, and in a high poll on 15 December won 24 of the 26 elected seats.[40]

The Federal Party secured all four of the Nyasaland seats, having had to compete with one Confederate and two Asian independent candidates. In Northern Rhodesia, only the Lusaka seat was lost — to Dr A. Scott, a veteran liberal politician. Similarly, in Southern Rhodesia, one seat was lost — the Sebakwe constituency to the Confederate, Dendy Young. Included among the defeated were Nkomo, because the electorate in Southern Rhodesia chose the Federal Party-sponsored candidates (M. Hove of Matabeleland, and J. Z. Savanhu of Mashonaland) and Nkumbula, whose candidacy was ignored when the Northern Rhodesian Governor nominated D. L. Yamba and M. Kakumbi. The Nyasaland nominees were W. M. Chirwa and C. R. Kumbikano. The Southern Rhodesian Methodist, the Reverend Percy Ibbotson, was returned as the Specially Elected European Representative for African Interests. Dr J. F. C. Haslam and the Reverend A. B. Doig were nominated by the Governors of Northern Rhodesia and Nyasaland respectively as the European Members for African Interests. The surprise of the election was the size of the majorities won by the Federal Party on the Copperbelt.

For the leading members of the Federal Party, the Federal general election brought no respite from political campaigning, particularly in the North where there were fewer politicians, because the territorial elections in Northern and Southern Rhodesia had still to be held. Nyasaland had no electoral system and was thus not involved. Those, like Barrow, who had won Federal seats were simply replaced by nomination. While the Parties competed for votes, both the Rhodesian legislatures witnessed embittered debates. In Northern Rhodesia there was the reaction to the constitutional award, and in Southern Rhodesia the debate over Article 29 (7) of the Federal Constitution on 23 September (described in the previous chapter) which resulted in Greenfield agreeing to seek formal reassurance that the British Parliament would never legislate unilaterally for the Federation.

While the Northern Rhodesian politicians were all involved in the Federal electoral campaign, the territorial Parties in Southern Rhodesia prepared themselves for the struggle ahead. In the first week of September, Huggins relinquished the office which he had held for 20 years, but the remainder of

[39] Welensky Papers, 24/1, f. 208, Welensky to A. Dalgleish, 9 November 1953; *The Times*, 10 November 1953.

[40] *The Rhodesia Herald*, 25 November & 31 December 1953.

his Cabinet, including Macintyre, Caldicott and Greenfield, all destined to be Federal ministers, stayed to serve Todd. The process of preparation was responsible for one fatality, for the Southern Rhodesia Labour Party which disintegrated after its congress had refused to allow men with Federal aspirations, like Eastwood, to retain their membership after joining the Federal Party.

The fusion of the United and Rhodesia Parties, seemingly effected by Todd and Stockil in Bulawayo on 4 September, soon threatened to follow suit, as four days later, the negotiations at branch level ran into difficulties in Bulawayo where the United Party insisted on retaining the leadership of Todd and its policy in any merger. A joint committee of the Parties continued to seek agreement but had to admit failure on 15 September. After this, Stockil corrected the impression that the Parties had merged on 4 September. Todd, Stockil maintained, had to explain his policy because the United Party in 1948 had proclaimed that it would curb the number of Africans qualifying for the voters' roll but had then decided in 1950 to maintain the common roll. Todd replied that his Party's adherence to the common roll was the obstacle to fusion. There was no mystery about this, unlike the Rhodesia Party's approach to African affairs. The Rhodesia Party, Todd acknowledged, had every right to reject his Party's policy but, by the same token, his Party was justified in retaining it.[41]

Nevertheless, the idea of fusing was sufficiently attractive to the rank and file of the Parties for it to survive. There was a clear need not only to fight off the Confederate challenge, but to ensure that there was a strong, independent government in Southern Rhodesia. The Parties agreed that, should a merger be possible, they would hold separate congresses to ratify it and meet thereafter to determine the structure of the new Party. However, by 15 October, it was clear that agreement was impossible. The difficulty was not the approach to African affairs, which had not been discussed, but the question of the leadership and the insistence of the United Party that, as the governing Party, it had to remain in existence until the new Party was an actuality.[42]

The next day, Todd hastily reassured the electorate that he had no intention of introducing universal franchise because it would place power in unfit hands and terminate all development by frightening away the investor. Five days later, he publicly read from a telegram from Stockil which terminated the negotiations because the United Party would not agree that both Parties should dissolve to hold an inaugural congress to settle a policy and choose a leader. The Rhodesia Party feared that the United Party would neither dissolve at the appointed moment, nor would it hazard its leader being set aside. Todd declared that his Party's counter-proposals had been rejected and that, consequently, though many people would be disappointed, it would seek election unchanged. He shook Stockil considerably by announcing that, as there was little point in waiting until March, the election would be held on 27 January 1954.[43]

However, in the interim, the members of both Parties in the Lomagundi

[41] *Ibid.*, 9, 16 & 18 September 1953.
[42] *Ibid.*, 1 & 16 October 1953.
[43] *Ibid.*, 17 & 22 October & 2 November 1953.

constituency had stolen a march on their leaders as, on 22 October, they announced that they were opening their own negotiations on fusion. Their action was immediately imitated in Salisbury, and the leadership of both Parties seemed threatened. For some days confusion reigned, but it was Stockil who was left out in the cold. On 30 October he announced that the Rhodesia Party was considering abstaining from the election, and the next day he indicated that he would not impede the fusion. On 5 November Todd was confirmed as the leader of the new United Rhodesia Party. This Party had attracted men like G. Ellman-Brown, R. F. Halsted, J. A. Ewing, H. Reedman and many others who would play a prominent part in the immediate political future. They were joined a week later by eight former executive members of the Southern Rhodesia Labour Party.[44]

Stockil was not attracted to the Confederate Party and stood instead as an independent candidate in the Victoria constituency. In any case, the Confederates, though they campaigned in all areas, virtually conceded defeat at the outset when at their first territorial congress in late December Dendy Young declared that they were aiming to form a government in five years' time. They hoped to provide an effective opposition but, because of their trouncing at the Federal polls, did not expect to be returned. Consequently, their policy statement said nothing about creating separate African states. Mention about the appointment of European representatives of African interests was also omitted, but the ideas of separate racial electoral rolls and of African-controlled local government in African areas were retained. The early attainment of dominion status was the ultimate objective, and a progressive note was introduced by a declaration that those Africans who remained in European areas should receive equal pay for equal work.[45]

The United Rhodesia Party waited for the Federal result and then the New Year before opening its short campaign. Todd, however, did declare in mid-November that, if he were returned to power, he would appoint a commission to examine the franchise because it did not satisfy African aspirations. There had to be stability for development and the African had to be drawn into politics. Yet Todd thought it necessary to reiterate that his goal was not universal franchise because government had to remain in responsible, civilised hands.[46]

In the campaign, W. A. Godlonton, a respected lawyer, agreed with Todd that the Southern Rhodesian franchise had not attracted the Africans and believed that the Federal and territorial franchises should be identical. The United Rhodesia Party urged that Africans be able to buy land in their townships — the current system being leasehold — to encourage the growth of a stable African middle class. Likewise, there had to be racial co-operation and advancement in industry. It was stressed that the European had a permanent place in Southern Rhodesia, and, to encourage economic expansion and to steal Confederate thunder, the need for large-scale white immigration was proclaimed, as was dominion status, as the ultimate goal.[47]

[44] *Ibid.*, 23, 24 & 31 October & 2 & 6 November 1953.
[45] *Ibid.*, 23 December 1953.
[46] *Ibid.*, 13 November 1953.
[47] *Ibid.*, 23 December 1953 & 20 January 1954.

Todd clearly had in mind a gradual conversion of the Federation into a unitary state when he said in Bulawayo on 12 January: "From the point of view of efficiency in the Colony [Southern Rhodesia], I am inclined to believe that if, during the next ten years, the Territorial Government could work itself out of the job, we would be acting in the best interests of Central Africa." By this process, he thought, not only would the disparate peoples of the Federation be welded into a permanent union, but the constitutional difficulties of the moment would be eliminated. Confirming this view, when referring to the claims being advanced to be the territorial capital by Gwelo and Bulawayo in the event of Salisbury being chosen as the Federal capital, Todd said that there was no need for haste because, if dominion status meant amalgamation, separate capitals would be superfluous. If Todd had attended the pre-Federal Conferences it is unlikely that he would have thought thus. In any case, once in power, he and his Government would display an independence of spirit which belied these sentiments.[48]

Investment moneys flowed into Southern Rhodesia, and the new confidence was certainly reflected in the election results on 27 January when the United Rhodesia Party secured 26 of the 30 seats in the Legislative Assembly. Todd immediately announced his Cabinet. He took the portfolios of Internal Affairs and Justice. P. B. Fletcher became Minister of Native Affairs, Health and Agriculture, G. Davenport the Minister of Mines, Public Works, Education and Defence, C. J. Hatty (later Sir Cyril) the Minister of Finance and Posts, and G. Ellman-Brown the Minister of Roads and Irrigation and of Trade and Industrial Development. However, some of these subjects would be relinquished shortly to the Federal Government as it assumed its power. The retention of Defence, for the moment, was important, as five days later the African coal miners came out on strike and troops were deployed.

After the Federal general election, the Northern Rhodesian politicians also gave their electorate a respite until the New Year. The only intrusion in the Christmas period was the mining companies' negotiations with the unions on African advancement. The companies sought to avoid European redundancy by proposing that African miners could take over certain posts at less than European rates of pay. By the end of December no comment was yet forthcoming from the European union, but the African trade unionists had immediately demanded equal pay for equal work and action instead of words.[49]

In the first week of January the Federal Party began to prepare its electoral campaign in Northern Rhodesia, and the Confederate decision to contest both the Federal and territorial elections gave an excuse to change tactics. Beckett, as the new leader of the unofficials, had wanted a "best man", "non-party" election to avoid a multiplicity of candidates which might divide the vote and produce an unrepresentative legislature, but the Confederates gave the Federal Party no choice but to fight. Although Huggins accepted the Australian dictum that federal and territorial politics did not mix, the Federal Party had neither the men nor the money to support a separate Northern Rhodesian territorial party. Nevertheless, it was confident of winning every

[48] *Ibid.*, 13 & 23 January 1954.
[49] *The Bulawayo Chronicle*, 24 December 1953.

seat after its crushing defeat of the Confederates in the Federal election. In fact, the Confederate Party was in such disarray that it reversed its decision to compete as a Party, and its candidates stood as independents. John Gaunt, a former Colonial officer, the territorial leader of the Confederates, justified this decision by reminding the electorate that the majority Party in the Legislative Council did not form the Government. He argued that the Northern Rhodesians had to pull together to obtain self-government in the shortest possible time. Moreover, he believed that matters such as African affairs should not be influenced by external interests. For these reasons, Gaunt claimed, his Party had welcomed the truce proposed by Beckett and that it could only conclude that the reason for the *volte-face* was Welensky's desire to continue to impose his will on Northern Rhodesian politics. This would be accomplished if the Federal Party won all twelve seats because then all elected Members would be subjected to control from Salisbury.[50]

While Gaunt manoeuvred for position, Lyttelton arrived having been censured by Griffiths in the Commons for his handling of African affairs and having been warned by the African Representative Council that it would expect any constitutional change to include the enfranchisement of the British Protected Person. Lyttelton, reminding Griffiths of his role as promoter of federation, defended his own record and declared: "Let no Hon. Member forget that we are the most progressive colonial power in the world and that we have all set our hands, whatever our party, to giving self-government within the Commonwealth to these territories." He did not explain then how the Federation could contain such independent territories and survive.[51]

On 11 January, after a flying visit to the Copperbelt, Lyttelton and his advisers, including Gorell Barnes, met Rennie and the official and elected Members. Welensky, though solely a Federal Minister, took the chair. The meeting examined the franchise, the order of seniority in the Executive Council, racial parity, the title of Members holding portfolios, the substitution of an African for a European representative of African interests, the power of the Governor, and the possible introduction of freehold title.

Although the meeting was lengthy and at times acrimonious, Lyttelton managed to resolve most of the issues before its conclusion. Land alone was not considered. The franchise, of course, was the crucial matter. The elected Members refused to enfranchise the British Protected Person because it would lead to universal suffrage and eliminate European political influence. However, Welensky pointed to the anomaly that Southern Rhodesian Africans, as British subjects by birth, could emigrate to the North and claim the vote if they otherwise qualified. Thus the first question to resolve was that of Federal citizenship. The meeting agreed that the Federal and Northern Rhodesian franchises should be aligned as closely as possible.

Lyttelton reassured the elected Members that no immediate change was contemplated. He would give them five years to devise a formula, but advised it was obviously better not to delay. He could see little sense in extending the franchise while retaining the sectional representation of the African, and

[50] *The Rhodesia Herald*, 7 January 1954; *Northern News*, *Central African Post*, 12 January 1954.
[51] House of Commons *Hansard* (London), Vol. 522, Col. 427, 16 December 1953.

suggested a system of two-member constituencies, African and European, provided it could be ensured that a minimum number of votes would be forthcoming from each race.

When examining the Executive Council, Beckett explained that the elected Members were only seeking frank collaboration between the Members, and not domination. He felt the leader of the unofficials should be second in seniority to the Chief Secretary. He provoked an acid debate on the circulation of documents which Lyttelton terminated by postponing a decision to a further meeting. Lyttelton refused to introduce parity between the officials and unofficials in the Executive Council because it would alter his constitutional award of September which he was sworn to uphold. He accepted, however, that Members could be called "ministers". He ordered Rennie to discuss with the Executive Council the question of replacing a European Member for African Interests with an African, once the African Representative Council had chosen its candidates. Finally, he postponed consideration of cabinet government for five years after Rennie declared it to be inopportune.

The talks were officially described as "very amicable", and at a civic luncheon that day Lyttelton expressed confidence in the possibility of solving every constitutional problem. However, when asked by the Press, Welensky commented somewhat bitterly that it seemed that Northern Rhodesia was becoming "the football ground of British politics". Indeed, he said, the last debate in the Commons had shown that all the colonies had become objects of Party convenience. He felt it was important when considering constitutional change to remember that it was unwise to advance people politically when they were not ready in an economic sense.[52]

The meeting reconvened on 13 January, but Lyttelton only promised to seek expert advice on land, and proposed that the members of the Executive Council form a "Front Bench", with the leader of the unofficials sitting next to the Chief Secretary.[53]

At the Press conference, Beckett and Welensky expressed satisfaction as they expected the Government to be more efficient. Lyttelton declared that the primary task of the next five years was to devise a constitution which would "take care of the danger of swamping the European and on the other hand the danger of giving the African the impression of political arthritis and giving him no hope on which he can advance to greater responsibilities". If the European vote was swamped, the investor would lose confidence, but if significant advancement was not achieved, the African would cease to co-operate. Thus consideration of the possibilities would begin immediately. The answer, he felt, lay neither in the retention of the *status quo* nor in "nice looking liberal-minded resolutions about the franchise". He excused his belated ruling on the enfranchisement of the British Protected Person. It had taken time to analyse the question, and ingenuity was needed because it was not just a question of Africans qualifying for the franchise and securing

[52] Welensky Papers, 7/10, f. 319, Minutes of a Meeting with the Colonial Secretary, Lusaka, 11 January 1954; *The Rhodesia Herald*, 12 January 1954.

[53] Welensky Papers, 7/10, f. 306, Minutes of a Meeting with the Colonial Secretary, Lusaka, 13 January 1954.

European seats. Lyttelton said it had to be realised that, by the end of the five year period in 1959, under the present system, a small number of African voters could hold the balance of power.[54]

By the time Lyttelton reported back to the Commons on 11 February, the question of the fifth African Member had fallen away through Rennie appointing two European representatives for African interests, Moffat and Harry Franklin, a recently retired Colonial officer. Taxed by Griffiths, Lyttelton explained that Moffat had refused, for family reasons, to continue to serve in the Executive Council and thus it had been necessary to appoint Franklin.[55]

Once Lyttelton had gone, the Northern Rhodesians could concentrate on their election. The Federal Party suffered an immediate setback when, on nomination day, 18 January, Beckett carelessly disqualified himself by failing to sign the second page of his nomination papers. The Federal Party branch committee in his constituency, Livingstone, had in any case decided to support its own choice of candidate, L. A. Oxenham. Welensky was understandably very annoyed.[56]

The campaign seemed to go so badly, on the Copperbelt in particular, that there were urgent pleas in early February for Welensky's assistance. These were particularly unwelcome as Welensky was just out of hospital. As it was associated in the public mind with the mining companies, because of the latter's enthusiasm for federation, the Federal Party was afflicted with the aspersions cast at the companies that they were advancing the African miners to gain cheap labour.[57]

Welensky summoned the energy for a late burst of electioneering and though he feared that his Party had lost many votes, on the day, 18 February, it won ten of the twelve seats, suffering defeat only in the Livingstone and Midlands constituencies. The Livingstone result was no surprise because the Federal Party had found a candidate in H. A. Thom, while its branch continued to support Oxenham. The seat was won by F. S. Derby, formerly of the Confederate Party and standing as an independent, but the margin of victory was so narrow that he only defeated Thom by 11 votes and Oxenham by 21. The Federal Party had not expected Gaunt to defeat their candidate, Brian Goodwin, in the Midlands constituency. The new leader of the unofficials was John Roberts, a young farmer from Broken Hill.[58] The elections over, the Federal Government could get on with its given task.

[54] *The Rhodesia Herald*, 14 January 1954.

[55] House of Commons *Hansard* (London), Vol. 523, Col. 1378, 11 February 1954.

[56] *The Rhodesia Herald*, *Livingstone Mail*, 19 & 20 February 1954; Welensky Papers, 42/37, f. 172, Welensky to R. Byrne, 23 January 1954.

[57] Welensky Papers, 42/32, f. 138, R. J. Bower to Welensky, 3 February 1954; 42/1, f. 70, Welensky to G. Abrahams, 29 January 1954.

[58] *Ibid.*, 42/32, f. 138, R. J. Bower to Welensky, 3 February 1954; *Northern News*, 22 February 1954.

CHAPTER FIFTEEN

The Reality of Government

The Assumption of Power and First Political Difficulties, March 1954 – February 1955

THE mood of the Federal Cabinet as it faced the task of cladding the Federal structure was, perhaps, best reflected in a comment by Welensky to a correspondent: "As I said to the P.M. [Huggins] only a day or so ago, we now have the O.K. to go ahead and it will be difficult to produce alibis in five years' time if we don't do something."[1] The immediate preoccupation was the passage of legislation to enable the new Government to assume its functions. There were unresolved constitutional issues, such as the Federal franchise, but consideration of these would have to wait until the Federal Government was a functioning entity. The assumption of the functions would not, in the event, be effected without controversy. There was enough on the Federal plate at the moment to satisfy any political appetite.

The opening ceremonies of the Federal Parliament in early February 1954 were somewhat eclipsed by a sudden eruption of industrial unrest in Matabeleland. On 1 February, the day preceding the election of T. I. F. Wilson (later Sir Ian) of Southern Rhodesia as Federal Speaker, the public was startled by an unheralded strike by the African coal miners at Wankie. This arose out of a demand for cash in lieu of rations of between three and five shillings a day, which was currently a growing preference among the African workers in Southern Rhodesia. When the Wankie Colliery Company did not respond, the leaders of the miners acted without any warning beyond a letter in late January stating that a strike was contemplated. This vagueness was understandable because the existing African trade unions were not recognised officially, because Africans were regarded as being as yet too unsophisticated. Furthermore, strikes were illegal in terms of the existing Masters and Servants Act. The coal supply was crucial because upon it depended the mines, the railways and the power stations in Northern and Southern

[1] Welensky Papers, 25/31, f. 38, Welensky to W. M. Macmillan, 25 February 1954.

Rhodesia. As the stocks of mined coal were sufficient only for a few days' consumption, a quick return to work was needed. Moreover, it was felt that serious labour unrest would affect the new Federal Government's ability to raise loans on the London Market.[2]

Even though one of the collieries was mechanised and European volunteers were maintaining a production of 2 400 tons a day, the Southern Rhodesian Government immediately invoked its new Peace Preservation Amendment Act which gave the police wide powers to restore order, including imposing curfews and searching without warrants. Prompt reinforcement of the small local police force re-established control within hours, but not before an ANC member, who advocated negotiations with the company, had been seriously assaulted, and threats of death had been issued to anyone contemplating returning to work.[3]

As the situation was reportedly under control and the limited production was not being hampered, the Provincial Police Commissioner, B. G. Spurling, was considerably surprised when, on 2 February, Todd and his Minister of Native Affairs, P. B. Fletcher, not only flew to Wankie, but, on arrival, ordered considerable military reinforcement. The Federal Government was not involved because it would only take over Defence in June. Four companies of European territorial soldiers, a company of the regular Rhodesian African Rifles, and two armoured cars were dispatched to Wankie. Todd and Fletcher later revealed that they had done this when they had found that, apart from the police, all able-bodied European men were down the mine while thousands of, what Fletcher described as primitive and potentially excitable Africans, milled about close to the white suburb.[4]

The strike only lasted another day, and on 4 February, the miners drifted back to work. They staged a "go slow", however, until 14 April when the company granted them an extra five shillings a day and announced the overhaul of its conciliation machinery. Six Africans received short prison sentences for inciting workers to strike. For the moment the military force stayed in Wankie with the exception of two companies of territorials who returned to Bulawayo to reinforce the police, in anticipation of trouble, after the banning of a public meeting called by the Southern Rhodesian Federation of African Trade Unions to discuss wage complaints.[5]

Any trouble had been nipped in the bud and, amid popular acclaim, Todd immediately pointed to the resoluteness of his Government. However, he promised an enquiry in accordance with simple justice. Prompted by the Press, Todd later declared that it was time to reconsider the recognition of the African trade unions and, in due course, they were recognised.[6]

Many felt that Todd had over-reacted, but there is no doubt that his action was popular with the Press and his electorate. He did not, however, entirely

[2] *The Rhodesia Herald*, 1 February 1954; Welensky Papers, FGC(54), 5th Meeting, Minute 9, Federal Cabinet, 1 February 1954.

[3] *The Rhodesia Herald*, 2 February 1954.

[4] Author's interview with Col. B. G. Spurling; *The Rhodesia Herald*, 3 February 1954; SR *Debates* (Salisbury), Vol. 35, Col. 807 f., 5 May 1954.

[5] *The Rhodesia Herald*, 5, 6 & 8 February & 2 March 1954.

[6] *Ibid.*, 5 & 6 February 1954.

escape public criticism. J. Z. Savanhu, the Federal MP, publicly denounced him, noting that, as recently as 29 January, Todd had pleaded for African advancement, but when the miners had struck to improve their emoluments, copying their British counterparts, he had ruthlessly employed starvation and intimidation. He had even banned a legitimate meeting in Bulawayo. Belying Todd's recent electoral commitment to partnership and racial co-operation, Savanhu noted, troops were promptly deployed when the established means for conciliation, the Native Labour Board, failed, exposing the reality of Todd's police state.[7]

Calling these allegations "wild", Fletcher answered Savanhu by revealing what he and Todd had found in Wankie. Nevertheless the veteran trade unionist, L. J. W. Keller, agreed that the troops had been used to intimidate the miners. The remainder of the Parliamentary Opposition, however, were only concerned about Todd's failure to recall Parliament, as required by law, to explain the mobilisation. Todd replied that he had not wished to do so and thereby interrupt the first session of the Federal Assembly, which was sharing the Southern Rhodesian facilities (while its Parliament was being built nearby). In any case, he believed, recall was unnecessary because his action was so clearly popular with the electorate and, indeed, with the Southern Rhodesian parliamentarians themselves. The Opposition responded by pointing out that he had, in fact, recalled Parliament within the prescribed period of 30 days for a mere six and a half hours to deal with other pressing matters. Todd ignored this and no one seemed to think it necessary to tax him further on his flouting of the law. The time would come, however, when even his closest colleagues would become irritated with the erratic and highly personal nature of his Government.[8]

With the Northern Rhodesian election campaign approaching its climax, the Wankie strike was not the only distraction of the hour. D. L. Yamba, currently a Federal MP, also threatened to steal some of the thunder by demanding the right to appear at the opening of the Federal Parliament in "traditional" dress. Fearing that he might appear in a toga, topped by a fantastic headdress, and thereby secure inordinate publicity, Huggins testily ruled that, as Parliament was based on a Western tradition, only Western dress was appropriate.[9]

The public was not, however, disappointed by the glittering spectacle presented by the formal opening ceremony on Wednesday, 3 February, with its accompanying guards of honour, bands, mounted escorts and artillery salutes. In the first speech from the throne, the Governor-General, Lord Llewellin, naturally dwelt on the historic nature of the gathering before outlining the achievements of the Interim Government and the immediate programme of legislation. He reminded the Members that the final location of the seat of government would have to be quickly resolved and, on a more domestic note, that they would not only have the pleasure of deciding their own remuneration, but also of selecting their title. The latter was resolved on the morrow by the Members accepting the Southern Rhodesian precedent of

[7] *Ibid.*, 6 February 1954.
[8] *Ibid.*, 8 February 1954; SR *Debates* (Salisbury), Vol. 35, Col. 807 f., 5 May 1954.
[9] Welensky Papers, 24/151, f. 426, Welensky to F. S. Joelson, 4 February 1954.

1923 and calling themselves "Members of Parliament".[10] This conveniently avoided the potential connotation of the initials of the alternative "Members of the Federal Assembly", though obviously in the debate no one was unsubtle enough to draw attention to this.

Before the new Assembly could consider its first bills, it had, of course, to appoint the committees of the House. The most significant of these was the African Affairs Board. The House elected Dr Haslam chairman, and the Reverend Ibbotson vice-chairman. The ordinary members were also drawn from the ranks of the Specially Appointed and Elected Members. These were Doig and Chirwa from Nyasaland, Yamba from Northern Rhodesia and Savanhu from Southern Rhodesia. Doig also found himself chairing the select committee studying the siting of the Federal capital.

As the immediate need of the Federal Government was finance, the programme of legislation was dominated at the outset by bills of a financial character. The Customs and Excise and Income Tax Bills were naturally among the first of these, as were bills relating to borrowing, coinage and currency. An audit had to be established and, to facilitate the take-over of the assigned territorial services, a Territorial Laws Amendment Bill was tabled.

The second readings of these bills gave the Members their first opportunities to air their political views. In so doing almost all the backbenchers, and Chirwa in particular, considerably irritated the Federal Cabinet by straying from the Federal into the territorial areas of responsibility.[11] However, as far as the African MPs were concerned, the racial practices of Southern Rhodesia, which segregated the post offices and barred them from hotels, had hardly made them feel welcome and, indeed, must have been a considerable provocation. They were even asked not to use the Members' toilets in the Legislative Building lest they offend the Members of the Southern Rhodesian Parliament.[12] The main northern African plea was that the Federal public service should not adopt the established Southern Rhodesian practices in employment and should offer equal opportunities for all. They also wanted the enfranchisement of British Protected Persons. In their defence, Doig felt it necessary to remind the House that, if it was surprised by these comments, these African MPs represented thousands of people who were as yet unreconciled to the fact of federation. This alone made the rapid advancement of the African imperative.[13]

The attitude of the two Southern Rhodesian African MPs, Savanhu and Hove, was noticeably different and, when Chirwa called for the implementation of equal partnership between the races, they joined the European MPs from all the territories in warning that this could not be realised immediately. Savanhu agreed with I. D. Smith that it was impossible to legislate for equality, while Hove urged the MPs to find their political affinities in

[10] Fed[eration of] R[hodesia] and N[yasaland], *Debates* [*of the Federal Assembly*] (Salisbury), Vol. 1, Col. 9 f., 3 February 1954; Col. 15 f., 4 February 1954.

[11] Welensky Papers, FGC(54), 8th Meeting, Minute 7, Federal Cabinet, 17 February 1954.

[12] This was a matter with which Todd should have dealt but he had only just assumed office. — JRTW.

[13] Fed R & N *Debates* (Salisbury), Vol. 1, Col. 73, 8 February 1954; Col. 111, 9 February 1954; Col. 156 f., 10 February 1954.

interests other than race. Welensky, for the Government, acknowledged the existence of discriminatory laws in the territorial sphere but asked the House to remember that the picture was not entirely one-sided because, in particular, the right of the European to acquire land in the North was severely restricted. He did not repent when the northern African MPs protested at his proposal to attract 500 000 European immigrants in the first decade, because he was confident that a selective immigration policy geared to the availability of resources would benefit everyone. As for the enfranchisement of British Protected Persons, Welensky could not understand why the European alone should be disqualified unless he acquired British citizenship.[14]

The most spectacular of the developments expected in the Federal era, and one which had held the public imagination since 1941, was the hydro-electric potential of the three territories. Therefore, few of the MPs who spoke in the first debate failed to comment on it. Indeed, the pressure exerted by Northern Rhodesians for the Kafue project matched that of the Southern Rhodesians for the formidable dam on the Zambezi in the Kariba Gorge, giving a foretaste of the ferocity of the argument which, combined with other inter-territorial frictions, would almost threaten the very existence of the Federation in this its first year.

It will be recalled that the hydro-electric issue had already divided the Federal camp in May 1953 after Welensky had tried to obtain £27 000 000 in Johannesburg for Kafue. His success in securing an initial promise of £10 000 000 from Sir Ernest Oppenheimer, raised Southern Rhodesian fears that Welensky would commit the Federal Government to a project which had not been conclusively proved to be better than their own. However, while Huggins merely warned Welensky that he might curtail the Federal Government's ability to borrow if he sought the remainder of the money on the London Market, no satisfactory site for the Kariba dam had yet been found and thus the Southern Rhodesian Government was reconciled to an early start on Kafue. Indeed, Huggins had telegraphed Rennie, in August, saying that his Government would fully support the Kafue project if Northern Rhodesia could obtain finance from sources not readily available to the future Federal Government, thus excluding the local and London money markets, the International Bank and the Commonwealth Development Finance Company. Northern Rhodesia, too, had to obtain an assurance from the British Government that the money raised for Kafue would not be regarded as part of the development finance required by the Federal Government, and would not prejudice the later construction of Kariba. Southern Rhodesia had to be reassured that drilling would be undertaken to discover if the cost of Kafue would be within the proposed £31 000 000. Huggins warned that he did not consider that Kafue alone would solve Southern Rhodesian power problems or those of the Rhodesia Railways, and he would not be prepared to sacrifice the Kariba project if Kafue was considered as an alternative. However, he agreed, Kafue could be a priority if these conditions were accepted.

On 3 September the Rhodesian Governments concluded an agreement

[14] *Ibid.*, Cols. 133–134, 9 February 1954; Col. 153, 10 February 1954; Col. 163 f., 10 February 1954.

which acknowledged the urgency of the power crisis and empowered the Northern Rhodesian Government to raise the necessary finance and to proceed with the project until the Federal Government assumed its responsibilities. The Northern Rhodesian Government would still not raise money where it might hamper the ability of the federation to borrow and would, in addition, actively support the building of the first stage of Kariba once Kafue was under way.[15]

The curious timing of the agreement, the day before the official birth of the Federation, may have been fortuitous but, if it was not, it only emphasises the determination of the Northern Rhodesian Government to commit the Federal Government to Kafue. A week's delay could have involved the Interim Government as a party rather than as an heir to the agreement. Clearly, the Northern Rhodesian Government felt that Kafue could no longer be delayed, and certainly not for six months until any Federal legislation could be implemented. Power, of course, was a Federal subject and, as there was a more than imperfect liaison between the Northern Rhodesian Government and the Interim Cabinet, confusion and, indeed, conflict, was inevitable.

As the Interim Ministers had not immediately divorced themselves from territorial affairs, Welensky was ordered to sound British financial circles during the Northern Rhodesian constitutional conference in London in September. Here again confusion arose because the announcement on Kafue had named the International Bank and the City as the likely sources of finance. Shortly afterwards, in accordance with the agreement of 3 September, Welensky, while in London, told the Press that the International Bank would be ignored in favour of the City and organisations like the Colonial Development Corporation and the British South Africa Company in order not to corner unfairly the public sources of finance. He expressed confidence that the money would be forthcoming, but revealed privately that the British had shown a preference for Kariba.[16]

When the Interim Government dispatched its Secretary to the Treasury, Sir Andrew Strachan, to London in October to assess the borrowing prospects for the whole spectrum of Federal development, he was firmly told that it would be positively harmful to continue to seek private finance in lieu of a Federal commitment to Kafue. The Federal Government, he was reminded, was responsible for all external borrowing and should not allow any territory to raise piecemeal loans. If the Federal Government settled on Kafue, it should approach the International Bank for the bulk of the money and the balance from the Colonial Development Corporation and similar organisations. This admonishment was softened by the warm anticipation in official and City circles of involvement in the development of the Federation. Huggins promptly ordered Strachan to invite the International Bank to send a mission to the Federation to examine the Kafue scheme.[17]

Such was the lack of co-operation between the Governments that the

[15] *Ibid.*, Vol. 3, Col. 3257, 1 March 1954; Welensky Papers, FGC(53), 6th Meeting, Minute 8, 10 November 1953.

[16] *The Rhodesia Herald*, 9 & 17 September 1953; Welensky Papers, 24/73, f. 535, Welensky to Gore-Browne, 18 September 1953.

[17] Welensky Papers, FGC(53), 5th Meeting, Minute 3, Federal Cabinet, 28 October 1953.

Interim Cabinet was considerably amazed in early November when the Northern Rhodesian Government announced the appointment of the Anglo American Corporation as the consulting engineers to the Kafue Hydro-Electric Authority. Equally, Rennie seems to have known nothing about the invitation to the International Bank because, when opening the Legislative Council on 7 November, he referred to the September agreement and announced that, with Whitehall's help, his Government was searching for finance. The Federal Government was even more startled when, almost immediately thereafter, the Northern Rhodesian Government proposed to turn the Kafue Hydro-Electric Authority into a statutory body empowered to raise loans, build the dam and generate and sell electricity. The Federal Government, which was considering a higher organisation to co-ordinate all hydro-electric development, and had no desire to be committed to an organisation devised by Northern Rhodesia, immediately invoked its powers and forbad the Northern Rhodesian Government either to legislate or enter into any contracts for the purchase of equipment or for the construction of the dam and its ancillary works. As the Northern Rhodesian Government had advanced £1 500 000, the Federal Government agreed that work in hand would continue, but henceforth it would be represented on the Kafue Authority and would be kept informed of all developments. The Federal Government then continued to plan its higher authority but, in mid-January, with the approach of the first legislative session, had to draft a short Enabling Bill to facilitate the immediate adoption of the Kafue project. The International Bank promptly demanded to see this Bill.[18]

Although the Federal House would be treated to a display of sweet reasonableness by the speakers in the debate on the Enabling or Hydro-Electric Bill, the atmosphere within the six-month-old Federation was somewhat soured by reports of Northern Rhodesian discontent over apparent neglect. The general complaint — to be expressed even in the Legislative Council — was that Southern Rhodesian parochialism, reinforced by ignorance of northern conditions, was dominating everything. An example was a complaint that Huggins, in not appointing a deputy prime minister, had ignored Welensky, thereby failing to acknowledge the importance of the northern contribution. Later, when income tax was levied at a higher rate than had been promised in the Federal campaign, many Northern Rhodesians felt betrayed. The selection of Salisbury in March as the Federal capital by the Federal Assembly, on the recommendation of a select committee, after intense lobbying by interests representing Lusaka and Livingstone amongst others, only served to confirm these feelings.[19]

[18] NR *Debates* (Lusaka), Col. 15, 7 November 1953; Welensky Papers, FGC(53), 6th Meeting, Minute 8, Federal Cabinet, 10 November 1953; 8th Meeting, Minute 10, 30 December 1953; FGC(54), 3rd Meeting, Minute 8, Federal Cabinet, 15 January 1954; 5th Meeting, Minute 3, 1 February 1954; 6th Meeting, Minute 10, 10 February 1954.

[19] Welensky Papers, 24/151, f. 419, Welensky to F. S. Joelson, 25 February 1954; f. 417, same to same, 11 March 1954; 28/96, f. 51, J. Hawkins to Welensky, 8 May 1954; NR *Debates* (Lusaka), Col. 163, 22 April 1954; J. R. T. Wood, "Siting the Capital of the Central African Federation", in J. A. Benyon, C. W. Cook, T. R. H. Davenport & K. S. Hunt (Editors), *Studies in Local History: Essays in Honour of Professor Winifred Maxwell* (Cape Town, 1976), p. 71 f.

Exacerbating these feelings was the attitude of the Northern Rhodesian civil servants, many of whom had never reconciled themselves to the Federation. This must not be exaggerated, but the attention of the Federal Cabinet was increasingly drawn to resistance by northern officials to Federal policy as well as to discontent within their ranks.[20] The officials whose departments were being absorbed by the Federal Government were offered secondment or recruitment into the new service, but on terms which could not match their current generous overseas leave and other compensations for having to live abroad. The Federal Government could, and often did, make up the leeway by promotion on appointment, but the feeling persisted and was aggravated by the fear that all the desirable positions were reserved for Southern Rhodesians. The initial appointments and later success of men like R. M. Taylor (later Sir Robert) and H. M. McDowell (later Sir Henry), both of whom would serve as Secretary to the Treasury, proved the fear to be somewhat baseless.

Crowning this northern discontent was the resistance to the Federal assumption of powers, and, as it was sometimes successful, it was considerably annoying to the Federal Government and its supporters. The Department of Public Works was never handed over, and only after protracted pressure was European Agriculture prised loose. Broadcasting was designated an exclusive Federal subject, but the Northern Rhodesian Government, with whom the Central African Council had entrusted the African service for all three territories, refused to relinquish it until there was an independent Federal broadcasting corporation. It successfully argued that African broadcasting could not be entrusted to the Federal Government itself because it affected the daily lives of the Africans. Small wonder that Federal circles looked forward eagerly to the arrival of the new Northern Rhodesian Governor, Sir Arthur (formerly A. E. T.) Benson, as he had played such a vital role in the promotion of federation in 1951.[21] Placed in new circumstances, with new responsibilities, Benson would only disappoint them.

Kafue, as van Eeden would warn in the debate on the Hydro-Electric Power Bill, had become identified with the aspirations of the Northern Rhodesians, and the threat posed to it by Kariba only worsened inter-Rhodesian relations. However, in early March Kafue seemed a *fait accompli* and the Northern Rhodesians could lower their guard. Undoubtedly because he was neutral as a Nyasalander, Barrow had been entrusted with the piloting of the Bill. Speaking to the converted, he dwelt on the need to ease the burden on the mining and transportation of coal in the light of the projected requirement within a decade of 50 per cent more coal than was currently mined. He

[20] Welensky Papers, 24/98, f. 108, S. Hill to Welensky, 18 March 1954; 42/21, f. 313, G. Beckett to Welensky, 6 April 1954; 24/151, ff. 411–412, Welensky to Joelson, 11 March 1954; FGC(54), 13th Meeting, Minute 9, Federal Cabinet, 24 March 1954; 40th Meeting, Minute 6, 26 October 1954.

[21] *Ibid.*, FGC(54), 18th Meeting, Minute 11, Federal Cabinet, 2 June 1954; 19th Meeting, Minute 10, 9 June 1954; 45th Meeting, Minute 5, 3 December 1954; 42/242A, f. 309, Welensky to Beckett, 28 April 1954; f. 299, Beckett to Welensky, 16 June 1954; 24/73, ff. 505–506, Welensky to Gore-Browne, 17 May 1954; 35/25, f. 587, Welensky to J. H. Wallace, 19 May 1954; 27/78, O. B. Bennett to Welensky, 2 July 1954; 27/1, f. 62, Welensky to Sir Frederick Crawford, 14 July 1954.

stressed also that, while Kafue would be the first scheme to be implemented, all the other projects were regarded as complementary. The Shiré Dam, in particular, was necessary if Nyasaland's bauxite reserves were to be exploited. The Bill, he explained, would allow the development of the hydro-electric potential of any river, but further legislation would be required for the distribution of electricity. In the debate, Southern Rhodesians joined the Northern Rhodesians in praising the Kafue decision as it seemed that time was the essence and, as the scheme was sound, simple and, unlike Kariba, near the railhead, it would not strain the Federal financial resources. In opposition, Dendy Young was joined by four Federal Party members, J. W. Swan, N. G. Barrett, L. M. Cullinan and Eastwood, who argued that only Kariba would benefit the Federation as a whole because it would provide, unlike Kafue, power in excess of the needs of the copper mines. Both sets of protagonists, in this good-tempered debate, supported the plea of the Nyasalanders that the Shiré scheme should not be forgotten.[22]

This declaration for Kafue did not save the Federal Government from continuing pressure from interested parties in both the Rhodesias. Work did not cease on either site, and the information being acquired was hardly secret. Within two weeks of the debate, the Southern Rhodesian Chamber of Mines publicly advocated Kariba to ensure that there would be power for Southern Rhodesia. The Northern Rhodesian Government, through its Financial Secretary, R. A. Nicholson, who was also chairman of the Kafue River Authority, displayed a determination to retain a significant influence in Kafue's development. Nicholson sought the immediate appointment of a general manager for Kafue to speed up the tempo of development while his Government requested representation on the new Authority. The Federal Government, however, resented these intrusions into its exclusive field and was determined to retain control lest the true interests of the Federation be subordinated to inter-territorial rivalry. Consequently, on 7 April, the Federal Cabinet decided to appoint a board responsible for both sites and which would be served by men of technical and administrative expertise only. Territorial representation *per se* would be excluded.[23]

However, though barely discernible, the tide had begun to turn in favour of Kariba. The new data was not yet crucial, but the Federal Cabinet felt that it should reveal to the International Bank its plans for the development of hydro-electric power in the next two decades, which was expected to cost £110 000 000. It was likely, anyway, that the Bank would be prompted by the heated public debate to ask for the Kariba data. In announcing this, the Federal Cabinet felt bound to indicate its preference for Kafue, but privately it avowed to keep an open mind.[24]

The Cabinet decision on territorial representation on the Hydro-Electric Power Board was immediately transmitted to the territorial Governments. Heedless of its import, the Northern Rhodesian Government thereupon proposed that Nicholson should serve as the Board's interim chairman until a

[22] Fed R & N *Debates* (Salisbury), Vol. 1, Col. 744 f., 4 March 1954.

[23] *The Rhodesia Herald*, 16 March 1954; Welensky Papers, FGC(54), 14th Meeting, Minute 10, Federal Cabinet, 7 April 1954; 15th Meeting, Minute 12, 14 April 1954.

[24] Welensky Papers, FGC(54), 15th Meeting, Minute 12, Federal Cabinet, 14 April 1954.

suitably experienced man from abroad had been found. If Nicholson were not acceptable for this, then he should at least be a member of the Board.[25]

The Northern Rhodesian Government was not the only source of irritation. On 6 May, Todd, in the Southern Rhodesian Assembly, was asked for a statement on Kariba. Without acknowledging his trespass in Federal preserves, Todd claimed that public opinion was hardening in favour of Kariba because it could produce significantly more power than Kafue. As new information was at hand indicating that Kariba could be ready a year earlier than anticipated, his Government would make representations forthwith to have it built. Nicholson and van Eeden hastened to remind Todd in the Press of the Federal decision on Kafue. Welensky, in a speech in Bulawayo, chastised Todd for his intrusion, and denied any knowledge of fresh evidence.[26] Welensky assured the public that his Government would not renege on Kafue, but almost immediately the Federal Cabinet discussed ways of softening the blow to Northern Rhodesia if Kariba were chosen. They considered doing this by appointing, as chairman of the Power Board, the other prominent member of the Kafue River Authority, J. H. Lascelles, who was also the executive vice-president of the Rhodesian Selection Trust. Furthermore, the Cabinet acknowledged that the new data on both schemes could no longer be ignored because of the necessity to provide as much power as possible by 1960. As this allowed little time for delay, the Cabinet proposed to adhere to its request for £30 000 000 for Kafue from the International Bank while re-examining the evidence and supplying the Bank with the relevant information. In any case, despite the public outcry, the Federal Government had yet to convince the International Bank that either scheme was workable or profitable, and, even by mid-May, neither scheme was ready for presentation and the sum needed was unknown.[27]

Work on the estimates was given priority, but the public debate was fraying tempers and the Cabinet decided on 19 May that it would have to declare its intentions. The possibility of a public meeting was rejected as this might not achieve its aim, and in any case Huggins and Barrow had addressed a recent Federal Party meeting on this subject. A statement by Barrow was composed, but before he could release it, Dr A. Scott, the independent Federal MP for Lusaka, issued the challenge which the Federal Government had hoped to avoid. The Northern Rhodesians, Scott proclaimed, having stoutly supported federation, now were wondering whether it should not have been postponed for five to ten years to allow their territory to develop. If Kariba were chosen, Scott threatened, the Legislative Council would protest to the British Government and, while the fate of Kafue hung in the balance, the Northern Rhodesian Government would be reluctant to pass any more departments to the Federal Government.[28]

The next day, 21 May, Barrow released his statement which reiterated that,

[25] *Ibid.*, 16th Meeting, Minute 5, Federal Cabinet, 12 May 1954.

[26] SR *Debates* (Salisbury), Vol. 35, Col. 860, 6 May 1954; *The Rhodesia Herald*, 10 May 1954; Welensky Papers, 42/32, ff. 130–131, Welensky to R. J. Bower, 12 May 1954.

[27] Welensky Papers, FGC(54), 16th Meeting, Minute 5, Federal Cabinet, 12 May 1954.

[28] *Ibid.*, 17th Meeting, Minute 1, Federal Cabinet, 19 May 1954; 24/73, ff. 505–506, Welensky to Gore-Browne, 17 May 1954; *The Rhodesia Herald*, 20 May 1954.

while the Federal attitude remained unchanged, it was advisable to acquaint the financial institutions with the total Federal electricity requirements and with what was known of Kariba. He added that a new, and perhaps better, site had been found in the Kariba Gorge which would have to be evaluated.[29]

In Lusaka a week later, Huggins took this conditioning of the public mind a stage further by not only reiterating that the International Bank would see all the evidence, but that the ultimate decision would be based on it. He was confident that this would satisfy any reasonable person. His Cabinet had, in fact, swung even further away from Kafue as, on 2 June, it decided that henceforth nothing should be done which would commit the Federal Government to either scheme.[30]

The Northern Rhodesian Government maintained its pressure by offering more money for the development of the Kafue site, and Lascelles, when replying to the Federal invitation, indicated forcibly that he expected Kafue to press forward. He rejected the ceiling of £10 000 on all contracts which the Federal Government had imposed until its choice of projects had finally been made. He wanted the Board to be entirely autonomous, and demanded that a general manager for Kafue be appointed immediately.

The Federal Government accepted the Northern Rhodesian offer of additional finance so that there should be no unnecessary delay should Kafue be chosen. It decided, nevertheless, that it should be spent on capital equipment which could be used at either site, and would not allow Lascelles to dictate his terms of reference.

Later in June, however, both Lascelles and the Federal Government relented. Lascelles accepted the chairmanship — but without remuneration — and agreed that, for the moment, there was no need for a general manager. The Federal Government, for its part, raised the contract ceiling to £50 000.[31]

When R. Roberts, head of the Southern Rhodesian Department of Engineering, spoke to the Federal Cabinet on 2 June, the Ministers had an opportunity to hear a first-hand account of the investigations at Kariba. Roberts claimed that the nine boreholes sunk at the new site had proved it was the best in the gorge. Further sampling was needed, but Roberts was confident that this site would lessen the expected engineering problems and therefore the cost and time of construction. The need for immediate expert advice was apparent, and the Federal Government cast around for suitable engineers.[32]

The Federal Government set the criterion that the ultimate report of the engineers had to be entirely acceptable to any investor. The consultants, therefore, had to be objective and thus entirely independent. This contrasted with the Northern Rhodesian Government's appointments to the Kafue River Authority on which, through the consulting engineers and Lascelles, both of the great copper mining corporations had been represented. The policy of conserving the sterling area's reserves ruled out American or Canadian engineers. As Halcrows had already been used as consultants, and it would be invidious to appoint another British firm, and as the British in any

[29] *The Rhodesia Herald*, 21 May 1954.
[30] Welensky Papers, FGC(54), 18th Meeting, Minute 17, Federal Cabinet, 2 June 1954.
[31] *Ibid.*, 20th Meeting, Minute 9, Federal Cabinet, 14 June 1954.
[32] *Ibid.*, 18th Meeting, Minute 17, Federal Cabinet, 2 June 1954.

case were less experienced than the French in this field, the advice of the French Department of Electricity was sought. The services of Messieurs Duffaut, Tisne and Misson were consequently secured.

Announcing their appointment in the Federal Assembly on 28 June, Huggins acknowledged that his Government had accepted Kafue as the first to be built, but he explained that new discoveries at both Kafue and Kariba had forced a reconsideration. It was now thought that Kafue could produce more power but at a higher cost, while Kariba might be cheaper and quicker to build than was originally estimated. The Federal Government could not ignore the emotion and confusion engendered by the merits of the rival schemes, but it had to serve the interests of the Federation, and to secure the best available advice.[33]

The Federal Assembly accepted this decision without demur, but Nicholson, when questioned in his Legislative Council, could not resist remarking that he could not be expected to comment on the appointment "of the gentlemen who were expected to answer in a foreign language" because this was an exclusively Federal matter. Little more could be done until the French consultants reported, but the Northern Rhodesians had not been placated, and the storm would again break with fury when the French verdict became known.

One result of this controversy was a renewed search by Welensky for sponsors for a national newspaper to serve the Federation and support its Government. The established newspapers were regionally based and territorially orientated, and Welensky had feared, in October 1953 (when he began his search), that these papers would foster rather than discourage inter-territorial rivalry. He would pursue this goal doggedly well into the next year, 1955, approaching men and corporations in the Federation, South Africa, the United States and even Belgium, but without avail. With such a small literate population, the potential readership was tiny and the competition from the established newspapers would be fierce. The outlay would be considerable while a profit could not be guaranteed and no one would take the gamble. As the internal dissemination of propaganda was a territorial function, and in the North was in the hands of often unsympathetic civil servants, the Federal Government was thus denied a formidable propaganda weapon. This is not to say that the existing newspapers, and especially those of the Argus group, withheld support, but they did favour the towns and territories in which they were based and to which their readership was almost totally confined.[34]

In June 1954, there were, of course, many other issues aside from Kariba-Kafue to distract public attention. The territories were peaceful and enjoying a boom consequent to the inflow of investment capital and a buoyant copper price. Salisbury, the focus of development, with the Rhodesian Selection Trust following the precedent of the Anglo American Corporation in establishing its headquarters there, had, by June 1954, passed an unprecedented £5 000 000 worth of building plans to become the fifth fastest growing city in

[33] Fed R & N *Debates*(Salisbury), Vol. 2, Col. 948 f., 28 June 1954.

[34] Welensky Papers, 25/202A, f. 321, R. Prain to Welensky, 7 July 1954; 24/67, J. Gliesner to Welensky, 28 October 1953.

Southern Africa. The Federation enjoyed a favourable trade balance of £9 750 000 a year later.

In June 1954, however, the white firemen — a European-reserved occupation — on the Rhodesia Railways ignored their union, rejected a pay increase and came out on strike. This strike forcibly illustrated an inadequacy of the Federal Constitution because, though Welensky was Minister of Transport and responsible for the railways, "labour" was a territorial subject and had to be dealt with, in this case, by the Northern and Southern Rhodesian Governments. Although Welensky played a considerable role in the public and private attempts at conciliation, and because the strike only spread to the North in its last days, it was Todd who, with customary vigour, declared a state of emergency because an essential service was at risk, and deported the strike leader, C. R. Taylor who, as a recent immigrant, had failed to declare his membership of the British Communist Party. The strike, which was essentially a struggle between the established leadership and the new recruits, was over in two weeks.[35]

If Northern Rhodesia had hardly been affected by the strike, it had experienced a short but vicious strike in April at the Roan Antelope mine where even the mine hospital was affected and the abandoned patients were too frightened to help each other. Yet, in the decade of the Federation, this was the least militant period for African nationalism and, as President Kaunda confirms, to many nationalists the Federation seemed so formidable that they doubted whether there was any point in sustaining their opposition. Indeed, Nkumbula and Kaunda are said to have suggested to H. J. Roberts, the leader of the unofficials, that their movement should arrive at some sort of accommodation with the Federal Party. If this is so, nothing came of it and many Africans turned to militant trade unionism to promote African aspirations. Others, however, kept the flag aloft: on 8 May, Matthew Kakumbi contradicted his maiden speech in the Federal Assembly with a fiery proclamation of his opposition to federation. He and Robinson Puta, the trade unionist, proposed to use the ANC "police" to foment discontent and bring about a labour shortage on the Northern Rhodesian European farms. In August, Puta threatened the whites with "Mau Mau" tactics.[36]

Despite these alarums and excursions, the main pre-occupation of the Federal Government was naturally the assumption of its responsibilities. This was largely accomplished by 1 July 1954, and, being efficiently done, what trauma there was did not attract public notice even if certain northern officials considerably irritated the territorial and Federal politicians in the process. Conversely, there were several instances where Southern Rhodesian attitudes and practices also frustrated the Federal aim. One of these affected the establishment of the Federal public service and, faced with the practi-

[35] *The Rhodesia Herald*, 28 & 31 May 1954; Welensky Papers, 24/73, ff. 493–495, Welensky to Gore-Browne, 8 June 1954; 24/1, ff. 190–191, Welensky to Dalgleish, 12 June 1954; 29/44, f. 102, Welensky to J. P. McDonagh, 14 June 1954; 27/78, f. 63, Welensky to O. B. Bennett, 14 June 1954.

[36] Welensky Papers, 24/1, ff. 199–200, Welensky to Dalgleish, 15 April 1954; ff. 183–184, same to same, 26 June 1954; 18/39, f. 10, Sitrep, Northern Rhodesia, 14 June 1954; K. Kaunda, *Zambia Shall Be Free* (London, 1962), p. 60; Author's interview with Sir Cecil Burney.

calities of securing manpower, and conscious of the need to satisfy the Southern Rhodesian Public Service Association from which most of the civil servants might be drawn, the Interim Public Service Commission informed the Interim Cabinet in December 1953, that there was no alternative but to establish separate branches for the races with differing conditions of service, pay and pensions. The Interim Cabinet, however, rejected this because the Constitution demanded that the categories of employment be graded without reference to race. This deadlock was not broken by a re-examination in March.[37] In the time-honoured Southern Rhodesian fashion, which had so successfully avoided the use of the reserved powers, Huggins sought the opinion of the Commonwealth Secretary. Lord Swinton responded with an acknowledgement of the difficulties, but endorsed the Federal Cabinet's view that the proposed course would breach the Federal Constitution. He urged an early grasping of the nettle, that the sooner the Federal Government declared that there would be no bar to Africans applying for the same jobs as Europeans, the better. However, civil servants were urgently needed, and the Federal Cabinet ordered further examination.[38]

No immediate solution was forthcoming, and later in 1954 the Interim Public Service Commission argued successfully that, because the seconded officers were anxious not to lose their promotional prospects in their own services, the establishment of a permanent civil service could be postponed until the period of secondment, five years, was over. In that time, it was expected, the implications of the multi-racial society produced by the policy of partnership would have been understood and the structure of the Federal public service could be modelled. For the time being, non-Europeans would be recruited into the Federal service on existing territorial conditions, while terms of service for the Europeans were devised which, after adjustment, proved acceptable to the territorial civil service associations.[39]

Southern Rhodesian attitudes also spoiled the aim of the Federal Government to remove all barriers to inter-territorial movement which the Federal Cabinet believed was a fundamental freedom of the Federation. However, the framers of the Federal Constitution, in recognition of the Southern Rhodesian fear of an Asian influx, had made "Inter-Territorial Movement" a concurrent subject. The Interim Government had prevented the minor inrush of Asians in November 1953, but then the internal barriers were still intact and Southern Rhodesia had been unaffected. However, in March 1954, it was hoped that, as the settled and prosperous northern Asian community was unlikely to move, the Federal Government could frame, without reviving Southern Rhodesian fears, its immigration legislation on the basis of the freedom of inter-territorial movement. This was a miscalculation as the Southern Rhodesian Government proposed, nevertheless, to control entry into its territory the moment the legislation was promulgated.[40]

[37] Welensky Papers, FGC(53), 8th Meeting, Minute 5, Federal Cabinet, 30 December 1953.
[38] *Ibid.*, FGC(54), 10th Meeting, Minute 6, Federal Cabinet, 3 March 1954; 11th Meeting, Minute 2, 10 March 1954; 12th Meeting, Minute 2, 17 March 1954; FGC, 15/11, 3/53, Note of discussions on the Federal Service with Commonwealth Relations Office, 4 March 1954.
[39] *Ibid.*, FGC(54), 40th Meeting, Minute 5, Federal Cabinet, 26 October 1954.
[40] *Ibid.*, 12th Meeting, Minute 12, Federal Cabinet, 17 March 1954.

Months of negotiations followed. The Federal Government argued that the British Government would be offended and its relationship with the Indian Government harmed, that the selective nature of the Federal legislation would effectively bar Asian immigration, that the settled Asians within the Federation were unlikely to move, and that the Southern Rhodesian action would have unhealthy political consequences in Nyasaland.

In early August 1954, when the Federal Cabinet examined the draft legislation, it found that a clause to prohibit the movement of "known African agitators" could be construed to prevent some of its African MPs from travelling to Salisbury. The Federal Ministers considered the postponing of the enactment of the legislation until excessive movement made it necessary and when any governmental action would not be criticised at home and abroad. Nonetheless, they decided to proceed, but Greenfield, the introducer, lectured the Federal Assembly on concurrent legislation and warned that the Federal Government would not hesitate to override any territorial action which it found to be offensive. He was not blunt enough to state at the outset that the selective nature of his Bill would be used to exclude Asian immigrants, but admitted as much when questioned in debate. A feature of this debate was that the European, and not the African, MPs claimed that the Asian stood in the way of African advancement.[41]

Despite Greenfield's threat, three weeks later the Southern Rhodesian Government introduced the Inter-Territorial Movement of Persons (Control) Bill and, although Keller and four United Rhodesia Party MPs protested, it was passed. The Bill did not specifically mention Asians, but it empowered the Minister not only to prevent the entry of convicted criminals, but also persons and classes of persons whom he deemed to be undesirable. This move was well received by the Southern Rhodesian electorate.[42]

A surprising consequence was an urgent request from Lusaka for a delay in the Federal enactment so that the internal barriers could be retained until Northern Rhodesia had taken powers to prevent an Asian influx. The Chief Secretary, A. T. Williams, when introducing legislation on 17 November, maintained that this was not meant to be offensive to Asians but to preserve the racial balance of the territory, and he promised a repeal the moment Southern Rhodesia lifted its control. The method chosen was to screen anyone from the other territories who wished to settle in Northern Rhodesia, but not immigrants because they would have been thoroughly examined by the Federal authorities. Many of the Legislative Council found this offensive because it interfered with long-established residents of the Federation, and J. C. Ng'andu was censured by Moffat and Franklin for suggesting that the true aim was to inhibit the movement of African political leaders.[43]

The Federal Cabinet disliked this legislation even more than the Southern Rhodesian Act and indicated to Benson that it would not welcome prosecution of Europeans who failed to present themselves for screening. The

[41] *Ibid.*, 29th Meeting, Minute 6, Federal Cabinet, 4 August 1954; Fed R & N *Debates* (Salisbury), Vol. 2, Col. 2084, 2 August 1954.

[42] SR *Debates* (Salisbury), Vol. 36, Col. 1859 f., 24 August 1954.

[43] Welensky Papers, FGC(54), 38th Meeting, Minute 4, Federal Cabinet, 11 October 1954; NR *Debates* (Lusaka), Col. 141, 17 November 1954.

Federal Government also had to ensure that the Southern Rhodesian Government would not prevent convicted criminals from lodging appeals to the Federal Supreme Court which was established in Salisbury on 1 July 1955.[44]

The Nyasaland Government obviously had no need to become embroiled in this affair, but it did frustrate the Federal attempts to encourage European immigration to the extent that the Governor, Sir Geoffrey Colby, ignored Federal and local European pressure and refused to allow the Federal Government to set up local advisory committees on immigration. Colby welcomed European immigrants, but felt that, because of African fears about the shortage of land, to encourage immigration openly would only provoke an African reaction. The Federal Cabinet accused Colby of trying to reserve the protectorates exclusively for Africans, in violation of the policy of partnership, but the Federal African MPs in the immigration debate confirmed that the Nyasaland Africans in particular wanted their territory closed to any further Europeans.[45]

Bound into these debates on immigration and other issues was the question of partnership, its philosophy, its implementation and its alternatives. Much had been said on the subject by July 1954, but only Moffat hazarded an attempt at codifying it. The Federal Cabinet itself took a conservative line and warned that the European should condition himself for change, that he should expect to concede a growing role for Africans in all fields, but equally that the African should not assume that there would be drastic change. The latter had to earn an equality of treatment and had to realise that the speed of change could not be allowed to shake the confidence of the investor.[46] Yamba ignored this warning and, through a motion calling for the immediate equality of treatment of all races in public places, forced the Federal Assembly to debate the subject directly on 20 July 1954.

Yamba demanded equality because educated and decent Africans were being denied the facilities offered to Europeans in the post offices and on the Rhodesia Railways, and argued that this was a necessary step in the realisation of partnership. His seconder, Chirwa, added a warning that discrimination, being humiliating, only bred hatred. He urged the Assembly to take this opportunity to display its liberalism to the world. Most of the African MPs agreed that the issue should not be dodged, but Savanhu was more cautious. He supported the motion while accepting that the longer the implementation of partnership was delayed, the more difficult it would be for the races to live in harmony. However, he was confident that the Southern Rhodesian Africans were not prepared for more than gradual change lest there be a white reaction and the consequent retardation of their advancement.

The European backbenchers opposed the motion and decried its immoderate language but agreed that the discriminatory pinpricks should be removed. Most of them accepted equal treatment in public places, though

[44] Welensky Papers, FGC 19, Minutes of the Inter-Government Meeting, Salisbury, 30 November 1954.

[45] *Ibid.*, FGC(54), 44th Meeting, Minute 4, Federal Cabinet, 23 November 1954; Fed R & N *Debates* (Salisbury), Vol. 3, Col. 2078 f., 2 August 1954.

[46] Welensky Papers, 25/98, f. 37, Copy of Moffat's Motion, 7 April 1954; f. 28, Welensky to H. J. Roberts, 28 June 1954.

I. D. Smith and van Eeden felt that there should be equal but separate facilities. Predictably all agreed with Savanhu that the pace of change had to be slow, that respect had to be earned and that legislation would not help in that direction. They suggested that the African MPs should have waited to see what action the Federal Government proposed. Advising the withdrawal of the motion, lest it damage race relations, they pointed out that most of the discrimination was territorial rather than Federal. Van Eeden maintained that demands for equality weakened the case for the special racial safeguards.[47]

Huggins, emphasising many of these points, did not hide his irritation. He declared that, in accepting federation, the electorate had not agreed to a social upheaval. Nevertheless, he promised to work with the territories to improve the lot of the emergent African. It could not, however, be done overnight. He saw the main task as the development of the Federal economy to provide for an expansion of facilities. Then, as the African advanced, the European would become more enlightened and equality would be realised. Any immediate action would merely result in unpleasant incidents. He noted that the provision of equal facilities in public places in Northern Rhodesia had not resulted in racial mixing but in the races avoiding contact.

Indulging in one of his tactless lapses for which he was famous, Huggins declared that: "You cannot expect the European to form up in a queue with dirty people, possibly an old umfazi [African woman] with an infant on her back, mewling and puking and making a mess of everything."[48] Furthermore, he insisted that the Africans should remember that it was the European who was prepared to co-operate and who had created the Federation. The motion was untimely, mischievous and deplorable because it could put the clock back ten years. It dealt mainly with territorial subjects and custom and, in any case, people could only be persuaded, not forced, to change their attitudes. He advised Yamba to withdraw the motion but knew him well enough to know that he would not as he had "sulked about London and would not help us draw up the Constitution".

Chirwa similarly was not spared because, in decrying the behaviour of most of the African intelligentsia, Huggins found him, in particular, guilty of "near sedition" as he had been telling Africans privately that the Federation was not yet a fact and that it was still possible to go to London and get it repealed.

Yamba did not withdraw the motion and commented that he had merely asked for equality of treatment in the public facilities provided by the Federal Government. He claimed that, unless the partners were equal, partnership would not exist, and he wondered if the Federal Government would ever be prepared to make partnership a reality. Chirwa said that he had expected a more statesmanlike approach from Huggins. He pointed out that Southern Rhodesia was the only territory with a rigid colour bar, and argued that Huggins could not expect to continue to operate two different systems within the Federation. On division, the motion was rejected overwhelmingly.

As Chirwa indicated, Nyasaland had never had much of an overt colour bar, Northern Rhodesia was abandoning its, and yet Southern Rhodesia was determined not to change. It would be years before the Southern Rhodesian

[47] Fed R & N *Debates* (Salisbury), Vol. 2, Col. 1483 f., 20 July 1954.
[48] *Ibid.*, Col. 1968, 29 July 1954.

Government, ever conscious of its electorate's reaction, would effect any real changes. On 11 June 1954 Fletcher, the Minister of Native Affairs, explaining his Government's view of granting Africans freehold title to land, in their townships, announced that the possibility of multi-racial hotels and clubs would soon be considered. However, he was immediately and publicly chastised for his temerity by a Government backbencher, H. D. Wightwick, because the United Rhodesia Party had not been warned about such a move. Ellman-Brown, the Minister of Roads, cleared the air for the moment by declaring that the Government would not tamper with racial segregation but would create "international" areas for multi-racial meetings under approved conditions.[49]

The Federal Government, however, having African MPs for whom it had to cater, could not wait for the Southern Rhodesian Government. On 2 August it declared the residences of the Governor-General, the Prime Minister, the Federal Assembly and King George VI Barracks in Salisbury to be extra-territorial areas where the African MPs might be entertained equally with their European colleagues and be served with liquor. This was nothing more than a stopgap as it was obvious that the Land Apportionment Act would have to be amended to accommodate certain needs. First among these was to allow the multi-racial university to be established in Salisbury. Herbert Chitepo, the first Southern Rhodesian African advocate, was suffering because he was prevented from obtaining suitable chambers for his practice. There was, in the spirit of the times, the need to make provision in town planning for the accommodation of inter-racial associations. Lastly, it was necessary to give certain hotels permission to receive non-European visitors and travellers.[50]

However, the necessary amendments were introduced in the Southern Rhodesian Parliament on 4 November. They met stiff resistance because they seemed to be the proverbial "foot in the door". Todd confidently declared the vote to be free and was considerably surprised by six of his Party voting against him in the second reading. In characteristic fashion, he nailed his colours to the mast and declared that, as his Government was committed to the university, he would resign if the amendments did not become law. Ten divisions followed in the committee stage, and the adjustments to the amendments were conservative to say the least. Inter-racial hotels would be available only to visitors from without the Federation. Multi-racial clubs could not have educational and sporting activities and had to confine themselves to cultural, religious and welfare interests. African students, lecturers and professors could live on the university campus but not their families. African advocates would be able to practise in European areas if the Minister, after discussion with the local bar association, was satisfied that there was no suitable alternative accommodation available.[51]

[49] *The Rhodesia Herald*, 12 & 13 June 1954.

[50] Welensky Papers, FGC(54), 28th Meeting, Minute 8, Federal Cabinet, 2 August 1954.

[51] SR *Debates* (Salisbury), Vol. 36, Col. 2235 f., 4 November 1954. Nonetheless, the amendments were not as radical as the drafter, Fletcher, had intended. He sought to include areas in every town where all races could trade, but Todd opposed him. — Author's interview with Sir Patrick Fletcher.

Oliver Lyttelton, the Colonial Secretary, had allowed four years in which to resolve the question of the next step in Northern Rhodesia's constitutional advancement, but Moffat, in seeking a definition of the race relations policy, inevitably re-opened the question almost immediately. Any discussion on partnership, or a philosophy to replace it, would raise Federal as well as territorial issues and thus the question of the unresolved Federal franchise inevitably arose. Moffat put forward on 29 July a four-part motion for consideration by his Legislative Council. However, seven months previously it had been decided that proposals would be put to Lyttelton and then a motion, representing a statement on partnership, suitably adjusted to the realities of the hour, would be introduced in the Legislative Council. Moffat had ignored this and, on 24 March, he had presented an alternative motion to the Governor for consideration. In this he accepted that the policy had to evolve to meet changes of circumstance, but felt that it had to conform to five principles. The first was that ultimately the Legislative Council would be elected, regardless of race, on a common roll. However, this would not be possible until, mainly through economic advancement, both races had lost their fear of racial domination. The second principle accepted that marked differences existed between the races and that, while they persisted, racial representation was inevitable. However, there should be a progressive movement towards equality of racial representation. The third principle was that, until equality was achieved, the protective legislation for Africans had to be retained. The fourth was that the officials had to hold the balance of power until the common roll had been introduced. Lastly, every inhabitant of Northern Rhodesia would have the right to progress according to his character, training, ability and industry without distinction of race, colour or creed.

Moffat explained that he sought to clarify the principles of African advancement and to persuade the European to adopt liberal principles and not to fear for his future. He thought that the ultimate objective had to be stated if the Africans were to accept it, even though the Europeans might read no further than the first line and reject the common roll as nothing less than African domination. The Governor replied that the motion should be discussed in the Executive Council and then with Roberts, Franklin and lastly with the remainder of the unofficial Members. If they all agreed, Moffat's motion would be substituted for the revised statement on partnership.[52]

When consulted, Roberts, as was his custom, sought Welensky's advice. Welensky did not understand what Moffat meant in the first clause because a common roll already existed and any African who qualified could claim a vote. On the second clause, Welensky wondered if Moffat wanted racial representation scrapped the moment the African voters could swamp the Europeans. Likewise, would protection for Africans be removed once they had an equality of voters or were in the majority? Since the official Members were always subject to the instructions of the Colonial Secretary and were far from neutral in matters affecting the interests of Africans, Welensky urged Roberts to resist strongly the suggestion that they should hold the balance of power. The fifth clause Welensky dismissed as nothing more than a platitude.

[52] NR *Debates* (Lusaka), Col. 616 f., 29 July 1954; Welensky Papers, 25/98, f. 37, Copy of Moffat's Motion, 7 April 1954.

Welensky told Roberts to advise Moffat to withdraw the motion because it would only damage race relations. If, predictably, Moffat argued that this had been the constant verdict for the past two and a half years, Roberts should reply that such a statement had been as inopportune then as it was now. The current reason was that the Federation had only recently come into existence and its Government wished to keep away from racial issues for a year and instead to demonstrate its liberal policy by its actions. Racial motions in the Northern Rhodesian Legislative Council would not assist. If Moffat proved stubborn, Roberts could threaten him with amendments recalling Lyttelton's statement that there would be four years in which to reconsider the Northern Rhodesian Constitution, and proposing an examination by a select committee or a committee of the whole House which could take four years.[53] Gaunt had also put down motions on a variety of subjects, including the Northern Rhodesian Constitution, and Moffat was also to be told that Roberts would equally oppose Gaunt. Roberts had some effect because, by 2 July, Moffat had changed the first clause, had amalgamated clauses two and three, and had re-worded the motion in more ambiguous language.[54]

On 29 July 1954, in the Northern Rhodesian legislature, Moffat moved:

"1. The objective of policy in Northern Rhodesia must be to remove from each race the fear that the other might dominate for its own racial benefit, and to move forward from the present system of racial representation in the territorial legislature towards a franchise with no separate representation for the races.
2. Until that objective can be fully achieved, a period of transition will remain during which special arrangements in the Legislative and Executive Councils must continue to be made, so as to ensure that no race can use either the preponderance of its numbers or its more advanced stage of development to dominate the other for its own racial benefit.
3. During this period of transition, special legislation must be in force to protect, to the extent that may be necessary, the interests of either race. Meanwhile this Council notes and agrees with the statement of the United Kingdom Secretary of State for the Colonies that it is the duty of Her Majesty's Government to ensure that on contentious issues the balance is fairly held.
4. Every lawful inhabitant of Northern Rhodesia has the right to progress according to his character, ability and industry, without distinction of race, colour or creed."[55]

Moffat proclaimed that the term "partnership" should be discarded, because it was interpreted in astonishingly different ways, and replaced by something more definite in the hope that both races would accept it as their goal. A system of government had to be found to which each race could fully contribute, or the survival of the European as a political or civilising force was

[53] Welensky Papers, 25/98, f. 27, Welensky to H. J. Roberts, 28 June 1954.
[54] *Ibid.*, f. 23, H. J. Roberts to Welensky, 2 July 1954.
[55] NR *Debates* (Lusaka), Col. 616 f., 29 July 1954.

doubtful. Otherwise the races would diverge and the longer the delay, the more difficult would be the solution. It was imperative to get rid of the racial fear, which had been growing in recent years, and a reasonable solution would be welcomed by almost all Africans. A reason for haste was that outside influences were working in Northern Rhodesia, spreading foreign ideologies, and while the territory was still at peace the opportunity should not be lost. There were only two solutions: either the races formed a united nation, or Northern Rhodesia was partitioned into separate racial areas.

Moffat felt he had to correct three misconceptions. The first was that the Westminster system of government could be transplanted without modification, because that could only be done when an African middle class existed and shared common attitudes with the European. The second was that democracy was desirable in current circumstances. It might be in the future, he argued, but had to be based on a stable society, and the currently tribal society was still recovering from its collision with European civilisation. The third was that partnership could be realised by political action alone.

Moffat rejected the adoption of the Southern Rhodesian Constitution, because in a dangerously short time a critical number of Africans would be enfranchised. His approach, he claimed, was the realistic one, but it would be necessary to replace the obsolete system of using Europeans to represent Africans. He was confident that the balancing factor of officials in the legislature would be needed for a long time. The motion as a whole could guarantee to the African that the future of a multi-racial society was assured and a genuine desire for this society, which he was sure the Africans shared, would remove the fear of domination by either race. Thus a heavy responsibility lay on the Africans to co-operate, as the only alternative was partition.

The African Members unanimously accepted the motion, but some of the Europeans worried about the practicalities of applying it. Gaunt agreed that the problem had to be identified and the time in which to solve it was short. However, he disliked the balance of power being held by officials who took their instructions from a government 5 000 miles away. Furthermore, he could not accept the concept of a multi-racial nation because the races were as likely to mix as oil and water. Thus he rejected the common roll. The Government's response was to declare its acceptance of the motion and to promise to disseminate it country-wide.

Roberts took the opportunity to proclaim his desire to see the Federation achieve dominion status. The first step was for the territories to prove that they were capable of governing themselves in order to gain the confidence of the British Government and to secure full autonomy. He felt that the acceptance of the motion would be a great stride towards engendering that confidence. The details naturally had to be worked out and one would be to achieve uniformity throughout the Federation of the standards of civilisation on which the franchises would be based so that they might be extended to all those willing to accept the responsibilities of a British subject. He was pleased that all the African Members had accepted the motion because it meant that they were dissociating themselves from the African demands elsewhere for adult suffrage.

Moffat was delighted not only by the acceptance of the motion, but by the high level of the debate on this the most explosive issue of the day. Outside the Legislative Council, Welensky — ever alive to the practicalities of politics — was privately to describe the motion as "all conscience and cold water". Nkumbula commended Moffat, and contrasted his motion with the usual "skin-deep liberalism" of the European. However, when Nkumbula's African National Congress declared that the consequence would be the lowering of the franchise, Moffat hastily replied that this would not happen until racial fears had diminished.[56]

Welensky had also to coach Roberts on the four motions being advanced by Gaunt. The first demanded the appointment of a select committee to examine the constitution, finances and activities of the ANC, and to recommend appropriate action. Welensky agreed that it was the duty of the Government to investigate any society which was proving to be harmful, but a select committee was useless because it could not see classified information and might, as it should, include an African Member who could well owe allegiance to the ANC. If Gaunt persisted with this, Roberts, Welensky thought, could propose an amendment merely calling for governmental investigation. The second motion recognised the need of the urban African to have stability through security of tenure, but Gaunt proposed that any alienation of urban land to an African should be matched by an equivalent excision from Native Trust Land for Europeans. To Welensky, this was ridiculous and pointless because "land" was reserved for the Colonial Secretary's discretion.

Gaunt's third motion proposed to compare the current population and financial resources of Northern Rhodesia with those of Southern Rhodesia in 1923, and for the granting of immediate self-government. In answer, Welensky suggested that Roberts move that the Legislative Council should take all responsible steps to obtain dominion status for the Federation as the correct way for Northern Rhodesia to obtain self-government.

Gaunt's last motion claimed that, for the harmony and stability of the Federation, the Legislative Council should declare it would firmly take such measures as were necessary to ensure that political control within the European areas would be retained by the Europeans residing there. This, to Welensky, was blatant *apartheid.* He thought that any amendment by Roberts would have to be couched in the widest terms, saying that, in the interests of racial harmony, control should remain in responsible hands.[57]

Gaunt dropped the first two motions and advanced the second two in reverse order. They were debated on 28 and 29 July, the day before and simultaneously with the Moffat debate. Gaunt was heavily defeated on both occasions. He maintained that, as there were insurmountable obstacles to the achievement of political equality and partnership, the alternative was political partition which was not *apartheid.* Africans, he felt, should be allowed to aspire to any height, but they should not do so at the European's expense. The European would not remain dominant for ever and any attempt by him to do so would invite disaster. All Gaunt sought was that each race should govern its areas.

[56] Welensky Papers, 24/73, ff. 476–478, Welensky to Gore-Browne, 25 August 1954; P. Mason, *Year of Decision* (London, 1960), p. 62.

[57] Welensky Papers, 25/98, f. 24, Welensky to H. J. Roberts, 29 June 1954.

Roberts condemned the motion unreservedly as a vote of no confidence in the Federation. He wondered if Gaunt realised that the European would be left with control of six per cent of the land. It would surely be better to declare that government should remain in responsible hands. Other Members argued that Gaunt would only disrupt the racial harmony and that it would be better to strive to make the Federation a success. Franklin thought that Gaunt implied that the Africans wanted a "West Coast" style of government immediately when, in fact, they all desired a genuine partnership, and the extremists, whatever they said in public, were no exception. Deny the African his political rights and he would fear for all his rights.

Replying, Gaunt said that Roberts might claim that six per cent of Northern Rhodesia would remain under European control, but the result of partnership would be total African domination. Partition was the only solution because the African was not prepared to wait forever for equality, but the European was not prepared to concede this for a hundred years. The motion was almost unanimously rejected.[58]

A like fate awaited the second motion on the morrow. Gaunt asked for immediate self-government because those who had made their homes in Northern Rhodesia could not permit their destiny to be decided overseas, particularly by a future Labour administration. Moreover, until Northern Rhodesia was self-governing, it could not speak with an equal voice to Southern Rhodesia. In passing, he felt that officials who would not make their homes and retire in Northern Rhodesia should not vote on questions affecting the future of the territory.

Roberts agreed on the desirability of self-government, but thought it was necessary first to digest the recent constitutional changes and, in so doing, prove capable of successfully exploiting them, thereby winning the confidence of the other Governments. Self-government for Northern Rhodesia would naturally result from the Federation obtaining full autonomy. Therefore he proposed that the correct path was to obtain self-government as an integral part of the Federation and to the degree which was possible within the Federal system. To this end Northern Rhodesia would support the aim of the Federal Government to achieve full self-government for the Federation when its peoples desired it and when the British Government would assent to it.

A. T. Williams, the Chief Secretary, pledged the Government's support for this. He believed that Northern Rhodesia needed development capital and, in order to obtain it, it had to maintain stability. The ultimate goal had already been stated by the British Government as self-government for Northern Rhodesia within the Commonwealth. This, of course, was not quite what Roberts had meant, but it is an early reminder of the intention of the Colonial Office from which it would never be diverted. Williams concluded by finding the aspersions cast by Gaunt at the officials to be unworthy.[59]

On 12 October 1954, Sir Arthur Benson declared in the African Representative Council that the Legislative Council would never have totally African membership because it was the policy of the British Government to develop Northern Rhodesia for all races. Nevertheless, neither he nor the defeat of

[58] NR *Debates* (Lusaka), Col. 586 f., 28 July 1954.
[59] *Ibid.*, Col. 668 f., 29 July 1954.

Gaunt deterred those in favour of partition whose ranks van Eeden joined in November. As van Eeden did not take advantage of the Federal Party congress in Livingstone in September to indicate his disagreement with the Party's policy, the public must have been surprised by this change of tune when he had worked so hard for federation. The Federal Party hierarchy, however, knew that in mid-October van Eeden was discontented, that he believed, in particular, that the current policy would not achieve dominion status because African enfranchisement would swamp the European vote.[60]

Van Eeden felt so strongly about this that he proposed to resign and contest a by-election in April 1955, when the voters' roll re-opened and many more people could be enrolled. He produced a variation of the time-worn partition proposal in which the central state, comprising the "Railway Belt" and Southern Rhodesia, would seek dominion status. He would retain racial discrimination but only for the non-emergent African. However, to classify, the "emergent" African would have to face a stiff test. A common roll would exist, but its standards would be so high that, while some Europeans would lose the vote, only half of one per cent of the 2 500 000 Africans within the dominion would qualify.[61]

The reason for van Eeden's restlessness, however, was not thought to be merely discontent with policy, and later he alleged that he had been offered a Cabinet post to keep him loyal to the Party. Huggins denied this vigorously. There is no doubt that van Eeden was highly ambitious, and perhaps he knew that Huggins had intended that Beckett should be the Federal Minister of Agriculture. When Beckett had to stay in the Northern Rhodesian Legislative Council after the constitutional crisis in late 1953, van Eeden, having played such a prominent role in the Federal campaign, can be excused if he saw himself as being the next in line, and must have been disappointed when Welensky was named as the only Northern Rhodesian in the initial Federal Cabinet. Certainly some people, and Welensky among them, believed that van Eeden aspired to Cabinet rank and, when he thought that Huggins was considering promoting van Eeden in March 1954, Beckett protested strongly.[62]

For whatever reason, van Eeden publicly announced his partition proposal on 10 November 1954. Welensky welcomed this because it offered Beckett the possibility of securing van Eeden's seat.[63]

Van Eeden continued to challenge the Federal Party. A week or so later in Lusaka, he reiterated his statement and argued that the policy of the Federal Party was pointless because the Africans would never be prepared to exchange Britain for the Federation as the protecting power. Indeed, the policy of drifting for seven years until the Federal Constitution could be reviewed, and then asking for something which the Africans would not accept, would

[60] *The Rhodesia Herald*, 13 October & 11 November 1954.

[61] Welensky Papers, 24/13, ff. 239–241, Welensky to Mrs L. Easton, 17 November 1954.

[62] *Northern News*, 2 September 1954; *The Rhodesia Herald*, 4 October 1954; Welensky Papers, 42/21, f. 321, Beckett to Welensky, 10 March 1954; f. 320, Welensky to Beckett, 19 March 1954; ff. 249–250, Beckett to Welensky, 7 October 1954; 5/24, f. 86, Welensky to N. Taylor, 1 December 1954.

[63] *The Rhodesia Herald*, 11 November 1954; Welensky Papers, 24/13, ff. 239–241, Welensky to Mrs L. Easton, 17 November 1954.

merely ensure the demise of the Federation. The Federal Party reacted by demanding his resignation, and it was obvious that such a rebel could not be tolerated within the ranks. However, he refused and was saved from expulsion, on 28 November, by Welensky declining to use his casting vote as chairman of the Northern Rhodesian division to effect it. The division, nevertheless, asked the central executive to examine van Eeden's scheme and to expel him if it was incompatible with the Party's policy.[64]

Welensky used this opportunity to declare publicly, *vis à vis* dominion status, that he was more concerned with stature than with status, because once the Federation had the stature, the formal grant of autonomy would not be refused. However, though he had only adhered to the tradition that a chairman alone should not upset the *status quo*, criticism of him from within the Party would make Welensky regret he had saved van Eeden. Nonetheless, the central standing committee of the Federal Party, of which Welensky was a member, met on 8 December to consider the Northern Rhodesian request. It decided that T. P. M. Cochran, the chairman, should state publicly that, because his proposal directly conflicted with Party policy, van Eeden would have to explain himself to the Parliamentary Caucus in January.[65]

Van Eeden thereupon blamed Welensky for this verdict, and Welensky, privately wishing that he had the freedom of a backbencher to say what he pleased, countered with a threat to resign at the Caucus meeting. Van Eeden must have been surprised when Yamba publicly advocated partition. However, Nkumbula unreservedly condemned it, and Yamba promptly recanted.

By the end of December Welensky concluded that van Eeden was courting expulsion because, without resigning, he was arranging a mass meeting in Lusaka at which to flout again the Party's authority. In the unsettled atmosphere of the time, with the hydro-electric issue never far out of sight, with industrial unrest threatening the copper industry, and a growing European intolerance of African unrest as a consequence, there was no doubt that van Eeden was gaining significant support. This was confirmed on 3 January 1955, when the Midlands branch of the Federal Party in Northern Rhodesia found van Eeden's proposal to be consistent with the Party's aim, and warned that at least two of its members would resign if van Eeden were expelled.[66]

Such threats did not save van Eeden when he met the full central executive on 7 January. He was liked by many of the Southern Rhodesian members, and Cochran, as chairman, gave him what Welensky considered to be the utmost latitude when accounting for his actions. These Southern Rhodesians pleaded with him to conform but, when he truculently refused, withdrew their support. Of the 50 members present, 47 voted for his expulsion and, declaring that he would not appeal to the Parliamentary Caucus, he left the meeting. Welensky thought that the recent ascent of J. G. Strydom to the premiership of South Africa had led van Eeden to seek to gain the support of

[64] *The Rhodesia Herald*, 29 November 1954.

[65] Welensky Papers, 24/73, ff. 457–459, Welensky to Gore-Browne, 3 December 1954; 31/56, f. 76, Minutes of the Central Standing Committee, Federal Party, 8 December 1954; f. 84, Statement by T. P. M. Cochran, 8 December 1954.

[66] *Ibid.*, 35/25, f. 83, Welensky to N. Taylor, 15 December 1954; 42/32, f. 108, Welensky to R. J. Bower, 21 December 1954; 42/21, f. 278, Welensky to Beckett, 29 December 1954.

the more extreme right-wing elements in Rhodesian politics. Nevertheless, Welensky believed that, in reality, van Eeden would not attract many voters to the party which he was believed to be forming.[67]

Welensky and van Eeden then duelled in the Press. Welensky declared that there was nothing new in partition, and that it was still impracticable. Economic *apartheid* was impossible and a policy of despair. He retained his confidence in the Federation. Van Eeden countered by pointing to the explosive situation on the Copperbelt and in Nyasaland (where, recently, radical demands had been made for the reform of its Constitution), and advised Welensky that his time was better spent resolving the pressing racial problem than trying foolishly to prove that he (van Eeden) had proposed *apartheid.* Partition at least was a positive alternative to the current helpless drift towards African domination. Concrete and constructive policies were needed, not empty platitudes. Van Eeden claimed that he was gaining support and indeed that day, 11 January, a member of his constituency committee openly joined him.

On 20 January, van Eeden held a meeting in Lusaka, attracting a large crowd who, Roberts comforted himself, were probably there out of curiosity. Van Eeden maintained that, because the British Government always surrendered to voluble demands, his policy could be forced through with sufficient European and African support. He had never liked the Federal Constitution but had supported federation as the only way to unite the Europeans to force the British hand. He claimed to have pressed for positive action, for example, on immigration, and believed that, while the Federal Party concurred, its Government was rendered helpless by the power retained by the Colonial Office. As a Rhodesian-born, he was not anti-African but believed in racial co-operation, and not in the vain policy of partnership which would only encourage racial strife. His partition proposal, he claimed, was the only solution because the Federation would disintegrate within five years. He dismissed Gaunt's partition as merely the creation of black and white "blobs". By contrast, his states would have distinctive frontiers. Asked about the inevitability of Africans swamping the Euorpean voters under his plan, van Eeden replied that it would not matter because, when it happened, they would be civilised. He gave, however, no indication of his immediate intentions.[68]

To blunt van Eeden's attack, Welensky asked his friend, Tom Reid, the veteran British Labour MP, to secure a debate in the Commons on partition. Then, on 23 January, in the Press, Gaunt outlined his new Dominion Party's policy of ensuring that the whites dominated their areas, while Welensky expounded on the immense practical difficulties of carving up the Federation which could only destroy the confidence of the investor. Effectively, Welensky said, this would mean that the Federal Government would have to go into liquidation or secure the authority of the investors to change. In any

[67] *Ibid.*, 43/*Malvern*, Welensky to Huggins, 31 December 1954; 42/52, f. 331,Welensky to D. Cole, 17 January 1955; 24/151, ff. 386–388, Welensky to Joelson, 19 January 1955; *The Rhodesia Herald*, 4 & 8 January 1955.

[68] Welensky Papers, 31/56, f. 73, Report of a Meeting, Lusaka, 20 January 1955; 25/242A, H. J. Roberts to Welensky, 21 January 1955; *The Rhodesia Herald*, 11 January 1955.

case, he pointed out, Article 98 prevented the alteration of the Constitution for nine years unless the British Government and the four Governments of the Federation were agreed.

While the African nationalists in the northern territories would support partition, if they felt it would realise their dreams of power, Welensky claimed that the vast majority of ordinary Africans would reject it if they really understood the tremendous disadvantages. In the event, partition would still leave a balance of 2 500 000 Africans living in the Rhodesian dominion, and they could not fail to be envious of their newly independent neighbours. Consequently, it would mean that the Europeans in the dominion would soon be facing the same problems as before. The partitioned states could not survive economically, and the British Government would never allow Northern Rhodesia to be stripped of its mineral wealth. Indeed, the Commonwealth Under-Secretary, Douglas Dodds-Parker — at T. Reid's prompting — had just confirmed that it was unthinkable. Equally, the Europeans in the remainder of Northern Rhodesia and in Nyasaland would refuse to live in a Central African "Gold Coast". The manufacturers would gravitate to the black states to exploit their cheap labour, leaving the white dominion to stagnate. Dominion status, Welensky stated, would be attained by maturity, and, if self-government was wanted, it already existed in Southern Rhodesia and in the Federation itself.[69]

Todd, never slow to state his opinion publicly, supported Welensky with a suggestion that van Eeden was attempting to tear down the Federal flag with its motto "Deserve to be great" in order to haul up the skull and crossbones. Partition to Todd was unthinkable.[70]

Van Eeden had commented on the lack of progress on the Federal franchise, but Welensky ignored him because his Government had not yet examined the problem. However, both Roberts and H. St L. Grenfell, who was also at the Lusaka meeting, advised that, before van Eeden did any real damage, this omission had to be rectified. Grenfell in particular felt that quick action was needed to regain the initiative, that the franchise proposals had to be submitted to the Federal Party congress later in the year. It was necessary, also, to settle this matter while the Conservatives were in power. The question of the nature of Federal citizenship would only complicate and delay the resolution of the franchise issue, so Grenfell argued that it should be shelved for the time being.[71]

Huggins was in London, so Welensky sought the advice of Greenfield who thereupon, on 3 February, agreed with Grenfell, as there was no doubt that there was public anxiety about the franchise, and because it was the best way to counter van Eeden. Welensky and Greenfield formed a committee on the franchise and the qualifications for Federal citizenship.[72] Neither problem

[69] Welensky Papers, 25/227, f. 19, Welensky to T. Reid, 22 January 1955; *The Rhodesia Herald*, 24 January 1955.

[70] *The Rhodesia Herald*, 26 January 1955.

[71] Welensky Papers, 28/80, f. 41, H. St L. Grenfell to Welensky, 24 January 1955; 8/111, f. 194, same to same, 31 January 1955.

[72] *Ibid.*, 8/111, f. 193, J. M. Greenfield to Welensky, 3 February 1955; 9/3, ff. 61–64, Meeting of Franchise and Citizenship Committee, 4 February 1955.

was as easily or as quickly solved as Grenfell had expected, but then even the battle with van Eeden would endure for much of 1955.

Van Eeden had also alluded to an impending racial confrontation in Northern Rhodesia, meaning, perhaps, the continuing *impasse* between the European miners and the copper companies on African advancement, as well as the strike by African copper miners which lasted 58 days in early 1955. The strike had a political connotation because, after a visit from Nkumbula and Kaunda, the African Mine Workers' Union had asked for an increase for every African miner of ten shillings and eightpence per shift which would give every miner the monetary qualification for the franchise. The miners were British Protected Persons, but then the African politicians were campaigning to abolish this hindrance.

The purpose of Nkumbula and Kaunda was thought to be to tighten the links between the union and their ANC which had been loosened when the president of the union, L. C. Katilungu, had refused to be associated directly with their fight against federation. Federal intelligence was aware that Matthew Nkoloma, the general secretary of the union, had been in contact with Zukas, the British Communist Party and the Russian delegation at the International Labour Organisation Conference in Geneva. He was not, however, thought to be a Marxist, but merely an opportunist who would exploit anything for his own ends. He had certainly been more active since his return from a recent trip to Europe and, it was thought, he and Robinson Puta, the militant nationalist, were seeking to oust Katilungu from the leadership of the union. When the copper companies refused to grant the increase, the miners walked out on 2 January 1955.[73]

The copper companies hoped that the leaders would soon lose support and were encouraged by a quick return to work of thousands of miners who, with their European counterparts, kept the production at 60 per cent of the normal. However, the companies had to wait more than two months for the strike to be settled, even though they paid off the strikers after four weeks.[74]

Although the strike was peaceful, the threat of violence was ever present, and again the mine hospitals suffered. Evidence of tension was seen in sporadic stonings after vehicle accidents, and in unconfirmed reports of secret oath-taking in the style of the Mau Mau. Nkumbula, who had declared immediately that there would be no violence, was nonetheless arrested along with Kaunda, but only because they were found in possession of a prohibited publication, *Africa and the Colonial World*. For this they served two months in prison with hard labour. The protest meetings at their arrest only increased the tension and deepened the European fears which van Eeden hoped to exploit.[75]

Ultimately, on 2 March 1955, at the suggestion of the British trade unionist and Labour MP, Ronald Williams, the miners returned to work, pending a settlement, at their former rates of pay, thus ending the longest strike in

[73] *Ibid.*, 19/28, ff. 110–111, Memorandum "The Security Angle", 19 February 1955.
[74] *Ibid.*, 25/202A, f. 275, R. L. Prain to Welensky, 7 February 1955; f. 281, same to same, 14 January 1955.
[75] *The Rhodesia Herald*, 7 January 1955; D. C. Mulford, *Zambia: The Politics of Independence, 1957–1964* (London, 1967), p. 39.

Northern Rhodesia. It had cost £2 000 000 in loss of production. In due course the companies awarded a modest increase.[76]

A consequence was that the union moved closer to the ANC, and Katilungu was ousted from his other presidency, that of the African Trade Union Congress, by the railway trade unionist, Dixon Konkola. The struggle to achieve the ten shillings and eightpence increase continued and the latter was again demanded in May, but was moderated to six shillings and eightpence in September. The companies for their part, conceded a copper bonus and a cost of living allowance.[77] More important was the *impasse* over African advancement on the copper mines. As has been seen, Prain of the Rhodesian Selection Trust, had fired the opening shot of the campaign in November 1953. The Anglo American Corporation agreed but, typically, adopted a gentler tone. Both, however, ignored Nkoloma's call for action rather than words. The African Mine Workers' Union, in any case, only complicated the argument by objecting to the creation of the Mines African Staff Association, which was to serve the Africans promoted to supervisory posts, because thereby the union would lose its best men. The other complication was a dispute over the refusal of the companies in 1953 to continue to deduct union dues because the companies felt that the finances of the union were being mishandled.

Through 1954 the companies maintained their pressure, but an attempt to use the persuasive powers of W. Lawther, the veteran member of the British Trades Union Congress, at a round-table conference between the African and European unions, failed in July when the European union rejected the proposals. A Commission of Inquiry under Sir John Forster, chairman of the British National Arbitration Tribunal, nevertheless agreed with the companies that the Africans were clearly ready for some advancement, but discounted the African union's claim that its members were ready to assume every responsibility. The European union objected to the retention of the African wage structure for those promoted, but the Commission argued that, if these Africans were to receive European rates of pay, all wages in the Federation and its economy would be seriously affected.[78]

The European union refused to compromise and, because it appeared to be unreasonable, Beckett appealed to Welensky to ignore the strictures of the Federal Constitution and intervene. On 4 November, the Anglo American Corporation announced that it accepted African advancement in principle but would not enforce it at the expense of the European workers. On the morrow, however, ignoring the advice of Welensky, the Rhodesian Selection Trust threw down the gauntlet. It gave six months' notice of the withdrawal of the agreement with the European miners but would consider in the meantime any further proposals.[79]

[76] Welensky Papers, 19/33, f. 14, FISB Review, 14 February 1955.

[77] Mulford, *Zambia*, *op. cit.*, p. 43.

[78] Welensky Papers, 24/1, ff. 199–200, Welensky to A. Dalgleish, 15 April 1954; FGC 19, Northern Rhodesian Memorandum on Defence, 2 November 1954; *The Rhodesia Herald*, 19 October 1954.

[79] Welensky Papers, 42/21, f. 288, Beckett to Welensky, 31 October 1954; f. 285, Welensky to Beckett, 9 November 1954; 25/202A, f. 304, Welensky to R. L. Prain, 8 November 1954; f. 300, R. L. Prain to Welensky, 18 November 1954; *The Rhodesia Herald*, 8 November 1954.

The miners appealed to Welensky, as a trade unionist of old, and he visited them on 1 December — on the pretext of inspecting the postal organisation on the Copperbelt, which came within his portfolio. The result was that they indicated to the Rhodesian Selection Trust that they would negotiate if its notice of termination was withdrawn. To demonstrate their willingness, they ended an overtime ban at Mufulira on 4 December.[80]

Prain was not in a conciliatory mood when approached by Welensky, but nevertheless announced on 6 December that the Trust was prepared to discuss equal pay for equal work with certain provisos,[81] and a week later declared that the notice of termination would be suspended for three months.

The European union sought advice from the South African Mineworkers' Union and, whatever was forthcoming, two ballots of the members of the union in February supported a limited advancement. It seemed that an agreement was possible. The Rhodesian Selection Trust proposed an interim arrangement with the pay set at the European rate. If the post had to be filled simultaneously by two Africans, then the pay and the benefits would be sub-divided accordingly.[82]

The European union leadership, however, was not yet ready to accept this, and their South African adviser, D. E. Ellis, provoked indignation when on 1 April he announced that a liaison committee of the Northern Rhodesian and South African unions would determine the rate of African advancement. He was publicly rebuked by Welensky, but claimed that he had been gravely misrepresented because he had merely said that his union would only assist when a full scale invasion of European posts was threatened.[83]

The affair dragged on. In May, the union indicated that it would concede 13 categories of employment if there would be no further African advancement without its consent. This ploy was successful because on 31 July an agreement was signed with the Anglo American Corporation which opened 24 categories of employment to Africans but allowed the European union to control any further advancement. Settlement was reached with the Rhodesian Selection Trust on 10 September on like terms, but the agreement would only endure for three years, and in that time a complete survey of skills and their employment would be undertaken. On 27 September the two agreements were combined so that the 24 categories of employment would remain open to the Africans, but the veto on their advancement by the European union would only last until the survey was completed. It seemed that the struggle was over, but in November the Europeans refused to teach the required skills to the Africans selected for promotion. Nevertheless, African advancement proceeded.[84]

80 Welensky Papers, 35/24, f. 86, Welensky to N. Taylor, 1 December 1954; 25/202A, f. 298, Welensky to Prain, 2 December 1954; 42/60, Welensky to D. Taylor, 8 December 1954; 24/1, ff.173–175, Welensky to A. Dalgleish, 8 December 1954.

81 *The Rhodesia Herald*, 6 December 1954.

82 *Ibid.*, 6 February 1955; Welensky Papers, 42/1, f. 64, G. Abrahams to Welensky, 16 January 1955; f. 63, Welensky to G. Abrahams, 21 January 1955; 42/72, f. 234, Welensky to D. Taylor, 28 January 1955; 29/9, f. 72, Welensky to V. T. Joyce, 8 February 1955.

83 *The Rhodesia Herald*, 3 May 1955.

84 *Ibid.*, 1 August 1955.

Van Eeden had also commented on Nyasaland which still lacked a territorial electoral system. Lyttelton, in the Commons on 24 May 1954, had said that in the coming months he would consult with the Governor and would announce definite proposals at the end of the year. He surprised the Federal public considerably, however, by adding that he had agreed in January to increase the African representation in the Legislative Council. This, without doubt, inspired the demand from 50 prominent Nyasaland Africans on 29 August 1954 for a visit from the new Colonial Secretary, Alan Lennox-Boyd, to hear their demand that the Legislative Council should contain ten Africans, ten non-Africans, all elected on a selective franchise, and ten officials, and that this pattern should be reflected in the Executive Council.[85]

Lyttelton had ignored the convention of consulting the Federal Government on all constitutional matters, but Lennox-Boyd did not. He sent Colby to Salisbury on 11 January 1955 with details of the intended changes. Presenting the changes, Colby warned that the Nyasaland African had awakened and would not rest until he was given political equality. The proposal was that the Legislative Council should seat twelve officials and twelve unofficials of whom six would be elected Europeans, five would be Africans and one a European nominated to represent African interests. The six Europeans would be elected on a franchise which would be modelled on that already used in the Federal election.

The Asians who qualified would be enfranchised and would vote for these men, but, if they preferred it, they would have one nominated seat and the European seats would be reduced to five. The current system of the African Provincial Councils electing candidates for the Governor's selection would be retained. The Governor would choose two to represent the Southern Province, two for the Central Province and one for the Northern Province. As currently there were five Europeans, one nominated Asian, a European representing African interests, and three Africans, Colby argued that, if the Asians were prepared to be enfranchised, the Europeans would gain a seat and, with the European representative of African interests, would effectively have seven seats while the Africans had five. If the Asians refused, there would be six Europeans in the House.

Cloak it how he liked, Colby could not convince the Federal Cabinet that this was anything less than parity of racial representation, with six non-Africans facing six Africans. As the stated Federal objective was to get rid of racial representation *per se*, parity was unwelcome and embarrassing. In any case the increase of two African seats seemed premature as the African had only entered the Legislative Council in 1949. When Colby replied that Lyttelton had committed the British Government to this, the Federal Cabinet merely asked him to convey its rejection to Lennox-Boyd. The two new African Members would only be conceded if the seat of the European representing African interests was abolished as obsolete. Likewise, the Federal Cabinet would allow the Asians no alternative but enfranchisement even though Colby maintained that their low literacy rate would disenfranchise most of them. It would accept six non-African Members elected

[85] House of Commons *Hansard* (London), Vol. 528, Col. 24, 24 May 1954; *The Rhodesia Herald*, 20 August 1954.

on the non-African common roll and five Africans nominated by the Governor.[86]

Colby informed Lennox-Boyd of this, adding that the Federal Government feared that the proposals might stimulate interest in van Eeden's partition plan. Yet Colby continued to argue that true parity was vital for Nyasaland because it would answer the aspirations of the Africans and bring peace. He agreed to the removal of the nominated Asian Member because Asians were not similarly represented in any other territory, and was prepared to sacrifice the nominated European because the Africans regarded him as a European first and their representative second.[87]

The Northern Rhodesian reaction was that Colby was merely proposing to deliver ammunition to van Eeden because, whatever Colby said, there would be a sizeable Asian intrusion into politics, capturing some, if not all, of the non-African seats. These proposals were doubly unwelcome at that moment because the Northern Rhodesian Executive Council was contemplating an upward adjustment of the franchise to compensate for the declining value of the pound, and Colby was aligning his franchise with their existing one. The Northern Rhodesian African would resent the donation of five seats to his Nyasaland counterpart when recently he had only been given four. Thus, on 28 January 1955, Benson telegraphed Colby asking him to delay any announcement by two weeks to allow the African unrest, occasioned by the Copperbelt strike, to subside.[88]

Benson had obviously seen the message from London (which the Federal Government received on the morrow, 29 January) that Colby would announce at a conference on 2 February that, although the composition of the Executive Council of Nyasaland would be unchanged, the Legislative Council would comprise twelve officials, five Africans and six non-Africans. The non-Africans would be elected on a franchise based on the Nyasaland Federal electoral regulations. Perhaps Benson succeeded because the Nyasaland Conference was postponed for a week. Roberts used the respite to persuade Benson to suggest to Colby that the income and property qualifications of the franchise should be raised from £250 p.a. to £500 p.a. In addition, the form for the application for the franchise should be worded so as to test the educational qualification. Similar advice was given to the Federal Government concerning its franchise regulations.[89]

The Northern Rhodesian Government also sought to be directly involved in the formulation of the Federal franchise and citizenship proposals, but was rebuffed by Welensky and Greenfield. Welensky, however, agreed that the income qualification should be set at £500 p.a., and thought that Southern Rhodesia had made a mistake, when revaluing its income qualification two years previously, in not tying it to the value of the pound. This would have meant that it would be worth £500 by February 1954. He was anxious, also, to ensure that the property qualification should not be abused so that three

[86] Welensky Papers, FGC(55), 2nd Meeting, Minute 12, Federal Cabinet, 11 January 1955.
[87] *Ibid.*, 20/9, f. 418, Nyasaland Governor to Colonial Secretary, 13 January 1955.
[88] *Ibid.*, 25/242A, f. 294, H. J. Roberts to Welensky, 28 January 1955.
[89] *Ibid.*, 7/14, f. 345, UK High Commissioner to Welensky, 29 January 1955; 25/242A, f. 293, H. J. Roberts to Welensky, 1 February 1955.

persons living, for example, in a servant's quarters, would not qualify because the value of the building divided by three was not sufficient for the vote.[90]

On 9 February, Lennox-Boyd in the Commons, and Colby at the Nyasaland Conference, revealed the changes and explained the removal of the nominated Asian and European seats. Colby added that Africans would not be enfranchised because they were not British subjects. The income level had not been changed.

The Europeans and the Asians cautiously accepted the proposals, but the Africans rejected them. This rejection seemed to J. Graylin, the Federal MP for Livingstone, to present an opportunity for the Federal Cabinet to press the Colonial Office to re-cast the proposals. However, the Cabinet only ordered Barrow to sound the opinion of the Nyasaland Europeans on the nationality qualification. Graylin's purpose was to advance his constituents' fears that the proposals presented an unwelcome opportunity for Asians to enter politics *en bloc* and to combine with the Africans to introduce rabid racialism. He feared that the Northern Rhodesian Africans would be inspired to agitate for similar changes which would induce the Europeans to agree with van Eeden that Nyasaland, as the black state, had no place in the Federation. Welensky replied that the Africans had rejected the proposals, and pointed out that the African strength was only being increased by one. He did not think it was likely that any Asians would be elected because only 50 had been enrolled for the Federal election.[91]

Lennox-Boyd also faced questioning by his Parliament as it wished to know why the demands of the Africans could not be met. He answered that the proposals were a reasonable step forward when only five years had passed since the Africans had gained any direct representation. He thought that there were great dangers in forcing the pace of political development.[92] There, for the moment, the matter rested.

[90] *Ibid.*, 9/3, ff. 61–64, Meeting of Franchise and Citizenship Committee, 4 February 1955.
[91] *Ibid.*, 28/78, f. 138, J. Graylin to Welensky, 11 February 1955; f. 136, same to same, 15 February 1955; f. 137, Welensky to Graylin, 14 February 1955; FGC(55), 6th Meeting, Minute 6, Federal Cabinet, 15 February 1955; *The Nyasaland Times*, 10 February 1955.
[92] House of Commons *Hansard* (London), Vol. 537, Col. 1274, 23 February 1955.

CHAPTER SIXTEEN

Early Strains

The Federal Franchise, Nyasaland's Constitution and Kariba, February 1955–February 1956

IN February 1955, Huggins attended the Commonwealth Prime Ministers' Conference in Britain and used the opportunity to explore further the British feelings towards the possible commitment of the Federation to heavy capital expenditure on the Kariba scheme. The choice of hydro-electric schemes, with van Eeden and other antagonists complicating the issue, would dominate politics for many of the remaining 20 months of the premiership of Huggins. Although this subject would affect seriously the relationship between the Federal and Northern Rhodesian Governments, other matters such as the assumption of the remaining Federal powers, the attitude of individual members, and comments on issues like dominion status had begun to create suspicion in the minds of the northern officials.

In late 1954 Huggins had indicated to Welensky that he would shortly resign to give his successor time to consolidate himself in power well before the life of the current Federal Legislative Assembly was over.[1] However, Huggins would never dance to the tune of anyone else, and would not tender his resignation when Todd called for it later in 1955 and again in early 1956. Huggins postponed his retirement for a year and thereby denied Welensky the opportunity to take the reins when the copper price was high, the Federal purse full, and the debacle of Suez and its drastic consequences still a year away.

The consulting engineers, who, on the advice of the International Bank, were reinforced by André Coyne, the celebrated French hydro-electric expert, took five months over their examination of both the Kariba and Kafue projects. While the engineers made their investigations, the Federal Ministers ignored the increasing suspicions of the Northern Rhodesians, and said nothing in public apart from an avowal by Huggins, at the Federal Party

[1] Welensky Papers, 24/151, ff. 398–399, Welensky to F. S. Joelson, 18 November 1954; 42/32, f. 108, Welensky to R. J. Bower, 21 December 1954.

congress in September 1954, that the production of adequate power for the Rhodesias was the only criterion. Everything was not, however, left to the consultants, and the Federal Cabinet established a small committee of civil servants to examine the merits of the scheme and asked the Federal Treasury to do likewise. The resultant reports were considered by the Cabinet in mid-December.[2]

The consultants found both schemes to be sound engineering propositions but had no doubt that Kariba would generate more than double the power produced by Kafue at almost half the price. They said that the Kafue scheme might rival Kariba if an additional dam were built 200 miles upstream in the Meshi Teshi Gorge, but that it would take years to acquire the necessary hydrological data. Furthermore, the data on the Kafue Gorge itself was not sufficiently complete to estimate anything more than a predictable minimum flow. Both schemes would ultimately have twin power houses. Kariba's would be immediately below the dam wall, while Kafue's would be a considerable distance away to exploit the fall of the gorge, which meant that there would be long tunnels with the inherent, if unlikely, danger of rockfalls. The first stage at Kariba, including eight generating units and transmission equipment, would cost £53 400 000. The overall cost, with an additional eight units, would be £85 800 000. By contrast, the first stage of Kafue would cost £36 500 000 and the second £55 000 000.

The majority recommendation of the working committee of the Federal Government was Kariba. The single dissenting member argued that, if the demand for power grew at the current rate, the existing thermal installations, combined with the first two stages of Kafue, could cope until 1967 when either the Meshi Teshi Dam or Kariba would have been built. He accepted the Meshi Teshi proposal and argued that the choice of Kafue would ensure no wastage of the existing capital investment in thermal units, colliery equipment and rolling stock.

The majority chose Kariba because it would meet the total power requirement. Coal would be saved and the transport system would be freed to carry other commodities. More important, Kariba would produce cheaper power than thermal generation or Kafue. They were confident of finding the necessary capital, and the speed of construction was not yet crucial as the power shortage was only expected in 1959 or 1960, and even then it could be met by the Southern Rhodesian grid until Kariba was ready. The abundance of cheap power would generate demand so there was nothing to fear. Kafue could only produce half the power of Kariba, and there was little point in speculating about the unknown qualities of the Meshi Teshi Dam. To build Kafue first, and then Kariba, would cost £115 000 000, whereas Kariba alone could produce sufficient power until 1970 and would cost £80 000 000. Furthermore, the Kafue tunnels could be blocked.

The Federal Treasury, however, preferred Kafue because it would be difficult to find more than £38 000 000. If Kariba were chosen, it would load the Federation in the next eight years with an additional national debt of £60 000 000, making it difficult to raise money for other purposes. Moreover,

[2] *Ibid.*, 15/65, f. 100, Minutes of the Congress of the Federal Party, 3 & 4 September 1954; FGC(54), 47th Meeting, Restricted Annexure, Federal Cabinet, 15 December 1954.

being so dependent on copper and tobacco, the Federal capacity to bear such a load of debt could easily be affected by matters beyond its control. If the Government had to provide such large sums the resultant heavy taxation might inhibit industrial expansion on which the demand for electricity depended. The only alternative to heavy taxation was to limit funds drastically for health, education and other programmes. The Treasury agreed with the minority report that the existing thermal equipment, which was by no means worn out and represented a considerable investment, should not be discarded. In addition, there was no fear of Kafue producing power in excess of the demand.

On 15 December, the Federal Cabinet noted that both schemes were considered technically sound, and agreed that the deciding factor was the level of demand. They dismissed any pessimism as they were confident that the Federation was about to experience a period of expansion, and decided that so little was known about Meshi Teshi that it could not be considered. Supplies for Kariba, they felt, would not burden the transport system as they would be routed via Sinoia, whereas the materials for Kafue would have to compete with coal and other supplies for the Copperbelt. The crucial consideration was that the two stages of Kafue could not meet the power demands of 1964, and the building of Kariba would have to begin in 1957. Yet, as the power shortage was only expected in the 1960s, there was still time for careful consideration.

The first step was to have the estimates of both schemes examined by the international firm of accountants, Cooper Brothers. The second was for Huggins to sample opinion in London and, if necessary, in Washington, after attending the Prime Ministers' Conference. The third was for the International Bank to begin its examination of the broad economic prospects. The public would be informed that the decision still awaited the completion of investigations. However, the likelihood of the choice of Kariba was indicated by the Cabinet's decision that further considerable expenditure on Kafue could not be justified.

Before making the announcement, Huggins sent Benson the reports of the engineers and apprised him of Federal Cabinet thinking. Benson replied with a strong plea for reconsideration because the Federal working committee had lacked experts. He was sure that all the facts had not been presented and urged Huggins and Barrow to meet the Kafue consultants. In addition, Benson proposed to provide a copy of the Northern and Southern Rhodesian agreement to build Kafue which Benson was sure Huggins was misrepresenting.[3]

Huggins announced the postponement of the decision on 2 January 1955. However, Welensky, who was despairing of Northern Rhodesian parochialism, had already been forced to state on 29 December that no decision had been made. He was responding to the *Central African Post* which had claimed that Barrow was neglecting the interests of the copper industry. Welensky seemed still to favour Kafue because he told Prain on 4 January that, in the prosperous days ahead, it could generate the capital needed for Kariba. Prain

[3] *Ibid.*, 8/82, f. 1, Sir Godfrey Huggins to Sir Arthur Benson, 22 December 1954; f. 7, Benson to Huggins, 31 December 1954.

was a staunch believer in Kafue, and Welensky may have been trying to dampen his suspicions. Nevertheless, the argument for Kariba was gathering strength. On the next day Coyne wrote to Huggins, acknowledging that the decision depended on financial considerations, but advised that the choice of Kariba would never be regretted. He found nothing to be gained from waiting, that the productive capacity of the Kafue River was unknown, but that obviously it would never rival that of Kariba.[4]

Coyne's report was published on 13 January, and in it he advised that, while the first stage of Kafue should be built immediately, the Federal Government should concentrate on Kariba. The immediate reaction was pressure from Northern Rhodesia for the publication of the recent Anglo American Kanthack report on Kafue and the possibilities of the Meshi Teshi Dam. Freer Payne, the mayor of Lusaka, even invited Huggins and Welensky to inaugurate a Kafue River Development Association. Prain advised Welensky that he expected that the availability of finance would dictate the building of Kafue. Welensky was clearly torn by conflicting emotions. As a Northern Rhodesian, he was naturally attracted by Kafue. However, he recognised the desirability of Kariba, but worried about the consequences of over-loading the Federation with debt to the extent that a fall in copper prices could ruin it. Copper prices reached a record £315 per ton in late January. In fact, in early February, Welensky believed that the question of finance would ensure that Kafue was the first priority. Yet, in London and Washington, Huggins found none of the financiers to be at all interested in Kafue. The International Bank indicated that it would not quibble about the greater amount of money required for Kariba. The British Chancellor of the Exchequer, R. A. Butler (later Lord Butler), favoured Kariba. Furthermore, Coyne visited London and again urged Huggins to build Kariba.[5]

With Northern Rhodesian rife with rumours that Welensky would not oppose Huggins, the Federal Cabinet met on 25 February to settle the matter in order to exploit the coming dry season. Huggins reported that the Colonial Development Corporation had offered £15 000 000, the Commonwealth Development Finance Company £3 000 000, and the International Bank had promised to bridge the gap if its mission approved of the scheme and the Federal Government contributed £8 000 000. The Federal Government was assured that its normal borrowing would not be affected.[6]

The Cabinet thereupon decided to build Kariba subject to a final appraisal by Coyne and approval by the International Bank. It was expected that if Coyne could make certain adjustments to his design, Kariba's first stage, with six generating units, could be in operation by 1959. The Cabinet believed it

[4] *Ibid.*, 42/52, f. 345, Welensky to D. Cole, 29 December 1954; 25/202A, f. 288, Welensky to R. L. Prain, 4 January 1955; *The Rhodesia Herald*, 3 January 1955.

[5] *The Rhodesia Herald*, 14 January 1955; Welensky Papers, 25/174, f. 15, F. Payne to Welensky, 17 January 1955; 28/80, f. 41, H. St L. Grenfell to Welensky, 24 January 1955; 25/202A, f. 281, R. L. Prain to Welensky, 14 January 1955; f. 286, Welensky to Prain, 19 January 1955; f. 279, same to same, 25 January 1955; 42/52, f. 331, Welensky to D. Cole, 17 January 1955; f. 318, same to same, 18 January 1955; FGC(55), Special Meeting, Federal Cabinet, 25 February 1955.

[6] Welensky Papers, 42/21, f. 268, G. Beckett to Welensky, 23 February 1955; FGC(55), Special Meeting, Federal Cabinet, 25 February 1955.

had made the best choice, and Welensky, in particular, ignored calls from Northern Rhodesians to cross the floor. Even if he had preferred Kafue to the end, which he did not, he certainly knew that his resignation would have disastrously split the Federal Party and the Assembly itself into territorial factions.

It was decided that Huggins would announce the choice on 1 March, but in the few remaining days of February the rumours flew and the pro-Kafue lobby busied itself with last ditch attempts to reverse the decision. Allegations abounded that, despite the cast-iron case for Kafue, the Federal Cabinet had succumbed to Southern Rhodesian pressure and, indeed, was subservient to the Southern Rhodesian Parliament. Barrow was blamed for the suppression of the Anglo American Kanthack report and for ignoring the advice of the Federal Hydro-Electric Power Board. The result, it was thought, could well be a revulsion in Northern Rhodesia against the Federal Party and a consequent formation of a purely Northern Rhodesian party.[7]

Spurning such threats and the resignation of Lascelles as chairman of the Power Board, Huggins duly announced the decision on 1 March, remarking that not only had the controversy made the final choice more difficult, but that one could be forgiven if one had forgotten that Kariba and Kafue were both Federal schemes. He assured the Federal Assembly that, only after the fullest consideration of the facts, his Cabinet had reversed its decision on Kafue despite the political embarrassment. It had to act in the interests of the Federation and have a scheme capable of expanding to meet further increases in demand. The two stages of Kafue could not meet this criterion after a decade, whereas Kariba could. The advantage of Kariba was that further generating units could be added at reasonable cost and, furthermore, the cost per unit of power could be expected to decrease. The extension of the railway line north of Sinoia for 90 miles would be a start to the building of the Kafue-Sinoia link which would bring the Copperbelt 500 miles closer to the sea. A decision had to be taken because the International Bank refused to act as arbitrator and thereby be drawn into any political controversy.[8]

Immediately Freer Payne called a protest meeting in Lusaka, Gaunt proposed to ask the Northern Rhodesian Legislative Council to adjourn for 24 hours as a mark of its disapproval, and W. F. Rendall, a Federal Party Member of the Legislative Council, threatened to resign. Welensky, however, publicly warned that he would not resign, and a few days later had even more to say on the subject. In addition, G. W. R. L'Ange, who had hitherto been thought to be organising the resistance to Kariba, on 3 March, pressed the Federal Assembly to urge the Government to prosecute its decision vigorously. The other MPs who spoke that day, except for van Eeden, favoured Kariba, but L'Ange, V. T. Joyce and Dendy Young criticised the Government's handling of the issue and felt that the Northern Rhodesian public was owed an explanation. Van Eeden called for a reconsideration because of the harm being done to Northern and Southern Rhodesian relations by what appeared to be a breach of faith. Rightly or wrongly, he claimed, the

[7] *Ibid.*, 8/82, f. 151, ? to R. C. Bucquet, 27 February 1955; f. 152, Confidential Memorandum, Kariba v Kafue, ? February 1955.

[8] Fed R & N *Debates* (Salisbury), Vol. 3, Col. 3256 f., 1 March 1955.

Northern Rhodesians had regarded the building of Kafue as a condition of federation and that a firm promise had been broken. He had read the reports and could not understand why Kariba was preferable. It seemed illogical to him that the Federal Government could accept Kafue without the Meshi Teshi Dam in March 1954, but should now argue that it was unacceptable without it.[9]

The debate was renewed on 7 March, but, in the interim, pressure continued to be exerted on all the Northern Rhodesian Federal MPs to cross the floor. The Northern Rhodesian ANC fastened upon this opportunity to cable Lennox-Boyd to re-open discussions on federation because even the Europeans were finding fault with it. Welensky responded to the critics by promising that both he and Huggins would speak in the debate, and asked the Northern Rhodesians to reserve their judgment until then.[10]

Dr A. Scott opened the renewed debate claiming that the Northern Rhodesians had been deliberately kept in the dark, that they could have built Kafue out of their copper surpluses, and that there seemed to be discernible pressure on the Federal Government to develop Southern Rhodesia at Northern Rhodesian expense. He believed the Northern Rhodesians would have rejected federation had they known the fate of Kafue. It was extraordinary that the French experts had not met the Kafue consultants, and it seemed that they had been coerced into recommending Kariba. Huggins, interjecting, called this a most libellous statement. Scott vowed to put all the facts before Coyne and the International Bank.

J. S. Moffat (who had replaced Dr Haslam as the Specially Appointed European Member for African Interests in Northern Rhodesia) made his support conditional on being satisfied that the breach of the Northern and Southern Rhodesian agreement was legal. F. S. Owen supporting the decision urged the immediate reassurance of the Northern Rhodesians. Graylin, however, claimed that only the diehards in Lusaka were upset. Yamba decried the protest, but thought that Northern Rhodesia should be compensated for the money it had spent on Kafue. Chirwa sympathised with the Northern Rhodesians because they had undoubtedly been let down, but Savanhu wondered at the fuss as both schemes were exclusively Federal responsibilites.

Barrow declared his impartiality in serving the interests of the Federation. Welensky said he had done likewise, even though he had initially favoured Kafue. He agreed that the public should be fully informed, but believed certain people were exploiting the situation. Talk of secession, cries for MPs to resign, for him to become a national hero by leading the resistance, were misguided to say the least, because the result would be a loss of confidence by the investors and, perhaps, even the destruction of the Federation itself. He accepted Northern Rhodesian disappointment, but was confident that Scott had been wrong in alleging that Lusaka would stagnate as it would share in the general development of the Federation. Having ardently promoted Kafue

[9] *The Rhodesia Herald*, 2 March 1955; Welensky Papers, 42/60, f. 223, Welensky to D. Taylor, 3 March 1955; 24/73, ff. 438–439, Welensky to Gore-Browne, 3 March 1955; Fed R & N *Debates* (Salisbury), Vol. 3, Col. 3407, 3 March 1955.

[10] *The Rhodesia Herald*, 4 & 7 March 1955; Welensky Papers, 25/174, f. 11, F. Payne to Welensky, 6 March 1955.

and attended all the meetings in 1953 prior to the Northern and Southern Rhodesian agreement, he knew Northern Rhodesia had proceeded with Kafue only on the understanding that the Federal Government would eventually take it over. Furthermore, the British Government had made it clear at the outset that any finance would have to be raised by the Federal Government. Kafue had certainly not been a pre-condition for federation as there had been no referendum in Northern Rhodesia. The question of a dam in the Meshi Teshi Gorge had only been raised when Kariba had become a rival to Kafue, but the lack of evidence had counted it out.

To Huggins, the Northern and Southern Rhodesian agreement was irrelevant because the International Bank and the British Government had indicated their preference for Kariba, and the Bank, by refusing to make its assessment in advance of a Federal decision, had forced his Government's hand. He believed that any statement of policy could be revoked if fresh evidence emerged, because no government would adhere to a policy which had subsequently been proved potentially ruinous. He denied that he had sprung any surprises and was confident that only a few merchants in Lusaka would have been really disappointed. Kafue remained a good scheme and would be needed. He drew overwhelming support in the division.[11]

Huggins then broadcast on the issue, and Welensky visited Lusaka. Welensky again refused to resign and found Lusaka quite hysterical.[12]

The Northern Rhodesian Legislative Council rejected, without a division, Gaunt's motion for a protest adjournment, but on 16 March unanimously accepted a motion which noted and shared the disappointment caused by the Federal decision which broke the September 1953 agreement. The Council demanded that its Government ensure that Northern Rhodesian power requirements, especially between 1959 and 1961, were met.

The main theme of the debate was criticism of the lack of consultation by the Federal Government with the Northern Rhodesian Government. This had contravened Article 42(2) of the Federal Constitution which prescribed that there should be consultation between the Governments on all major issues. The Members made plain their disappointment but, noting the tentative nature of the Federal decision, were determined that all the facts should be laid before Coyne and the International Bank, and that the Federal Government would meet any further expenditure on thermal units to supply the Copperbelt. Roberts supported the motion after the Chief Secretary revealed that he himself had first learnt of the Federal decision from the special edition of the local newspaper. The African Members found in the events proof for African distrust of the Federation. Sokota demanded the provision of a clause to allow secession. Franklin said there was great cause to worry over the future of Northern Rhodesia if solemn agreements could be broken after pressure from the Southern Rhodesian lobby. However, he also deprecated the wild talk of secession and the lament over what Lusaka might lose.[13]

[11] Fed R & N *Debates* (Salisbury), Vol. 3, Col. 3463 f., 7 March 1955.

[12] *The Rhodesia Herald*, 14 March 1955; Welensky Papers, 24/151, ff. 378–379, Welensky to F. S. Joelson, 14 March 1955.

[13] NR *Debates* (Lusaka), Col. 123, 15 March 1955.

Simultaneously, in the Federal Assembly, van Eeden blamed Huggins and Welensky for miserably bungling the Kariba-Kafue issue. Launching a general attack, he claimed that the immigration policy was so restrictive that the target of 500 000 European immigrants would not be realised even though it had been depicted in the Federal campaign as crucial for the continuance of European influence. No immigration department had been created, nor had land or housing schemes. Nothing had been done, despite a promise by Huggins, to alter the allocation of land in Nyasaland for the races. Van Eeden criticised the failure to finalise the Federal franchise, which was the other great safeguard, because it could keep government in civilised hands.

Van Eeden thought that, by assuming more and more power, the Federal Government could weaken the influence of the Colonial Office and bring the stature of the Federation closer to dominion status. However, it had still to assume all the powers allocated to it. Like his fellow Northern Rhodesians, he decried the Federal failure to consult the other Governments on matters of mutual interest. The supreme omission was the failure to evolve a uniform policy *vis-à-vis* racial issues in all the territories. The Federal Government was involved in racial matters simply because its legislation affected everyone and, as the senior Government, it was obliged to lead.

Van Eeden noticed the lack of ideas on attainment of dominion status although this was one of the main aims of the Federal Party. It was difficult, he agreed, but the only way was to decide on a scheme, secure the electorate's acceptance, and present it to the British Government as the choice of the people. The Nyasaland constitutional changes, van Eeden felt, could radically affect the whole Federation by ensuring that only non-European Members were returned at the next general election. Despite campaigning for the reduction of the influence of the Colonial Office, Welensky had simply condoned this change. Van Eeden was confident that his plan for partition would be accepted within five years.

Scott found he could support van Eeden, and deplored the Federal failure to establish better race relations. Instead, he claimed, the Federal Government constantly alarmed and distressed the African. This made dominion status unattainable because of the likelihood of African rejection. It also had continually upset the Northern Rhodesians.

I. D. Smith was contemptuous of van Eeden because he had so recently been the "Lord High White-washer" of the Federal Party, but Dendy Young claimed that the Federal Government, by failing to define partnership, was drifting towards racial conflict. It was imperative that the territories enjoy similar constitutional development, but again the Government had failed. The recent Nyasaland constitutional changes were the most glaring example. Young demanded the enfranchisement of British Protected Persons, and called for a reduction in the influence of the Colonial Office and for a warning to the electorate that, without an extremely liberal constitution, dominion status was unattainable.

Kakumbi thought that it was too soon to criticise the Federal Government, but Doig, Kumbikano and Chirwa found much to alarm the Africans, particularly as van Eeden was so recently in the inner circles of the Federal Party. They thought that van Eeden wanted to disrupt the Federation, and warned that any impetus towards dominion status would convince the Africans that federation was only an interim measure. They pressed the Government to take the chance it had hitherto missed to demonstrate the sincerity of partnership by providing opportunities and training for Africans. This would lessen the African fears of European immigration. Hove and Savanhu supported the training suggestion, but felt that generally everything was going well, and that Africans accepted that all the goals could not be attained overnight.

Macintyre, as Minister of Finance, expounded on the excellent condition of the economy and left the main defence of the Government to Welensky who judged van Eeden's speech as the most mischievous ever because it ignored the economic factor which was the key to progress. Welensky said that in this field much had already been accomplished and that an expanding economy was needed to bolster the immigration drive which he still supported, but not as a safeguard, because he did not fear the Africans. He noted that van Eeden had omitted to mention that, for the first time, the Nyasaland Europeans there were being enfranchised and he had chosen to forget that the Nyasaland Government would remain in control of the official majority. In answer to the criticism on the assumption of powers, Welensky listed the departments which had been transferred into Federal hands. He acknowledged that no agreement had yet been reached with the Northern Rhodesian Government on broadcasting, but claimed that success depended on co-operation and not on the "big stick". Van Eeden was being a defeatist on dominion status because through economic expansion the stature would be achieved and that was more important than the status. The policy of partnership, Welensky believed, was being implemented and, as the Constitution could not be changed for nine years, it was absurd to condemn the Federation yet. It was wrong and damaging to stir up political dissension on constitutional grounds. The need was to concentrate on achieving prosperity.

Van Eeden dismissed the arguments of the Government as cant and hypocrisy. He felt he had certainly not been answered. He reminded the House that the failure on consultation on Kafue had even alienated the Northern Rhodesian Federal Party. He had intended to work within the Constitution when seeking to change it and had not introduced racialism into the debate. He had omitted the economic aspects because the budget debate offered the opportunity for that. The current balance of payments was praiseworthy, but was only the result of a high copper price and a good tobacco season. However, the immigration target would not be met, and dominion status would not be realised as the Government would never induce the population to agree. He expected that the Government could not answer him and would depend on personal attacks and abuse. However, he withdrew the motion because only Young and Scott supported it.[14]

The Press, public and private controversy over the Kariba-Kafue issue continued unabated and forced Barrow, on 17 March, to reiterate that the production of hydro-electricity was an exclusive Federal responsibility. He confessed that the Northern Rhodesian Government had not been kept fully informed, but then neither had the other territorial Governments. A question

[14] Fed R & N *Debates* (Salisbury), Vol. 3, Col. 3857 f., 15 March 1955.

from Scott, Barrow revealed, had precipitated the debate and had left the Federal Government no time to inform the Governments of its decision.[15]

Three days later Beckett warned Welensky that Benson was deeply hurt. Thereupon, Huggins (who had chosen the title of Lord Malvern of Rhodesia and Bexley for the viscountcy which he had recently been awarded) wrote to Benson on 22 March and promised to inform all the Governments once Coyne had reported. If, as was likely, Kariba were chosen, he proposed to seek Benson's help in moving the inhabitants of the area to be flooded. Malvern, typically, could only maintain a placatory tone for a few sentences because he was considerably annoyed by the attacks on him by the officials in the Northern Rhodesian debates. Calling them civil servants of the "hybrid variety", he called their behaviour unethical and remarked that they clearly did not understand what an agreement was or why the *aide memoire* was ever signed. The Press had announced that day that Malvern had cancelled a meeting in Lusaka because the mission of the International Bank was arriving and he had undertaken that it would not be embroiled in a political controversy. However, Malvern told Benson that the real reason was that he was avoiding the possibility of being rude to one of these civil servants. The joint decision on Kafue, Malvern noted, was being referred to as an agreement when it was a statement of policy based on the information available at the time. In any case, on 23 July 1954, the Federal Government had assumed the legal and executive power with regard to hydro-electricity, and thereafter neither of the Rhodesias could continue unilaterally to implement the policy of 1953. The Federal Government, after all, Malvern reminded Benson, represented the people of the Federation and did not govern with the permission of the territorial Governments.[16]

Malvern had also forbidden Welensky to attend the protest meeting in Lusaka. Freer Payne, its organiser, however, met Malvern in Salisbury and afterwards told the Press that, while Malvern had been forthcoming, they had not agreed. Payne remained convinced that the underlying motive was political expediency. He had also discovered just how much the Federal and territorial Governments differed in their interpretation of what was an agreement. Roberts promptly and publicly denied that they did, but the Press simultaneously carried a statement by R. A. Nicholson, the Financial Secretary that there was no doubt that the Northern Rhodesian Government could have raised the money for Kafue unaided. Payne threatened to resign from the Federal Party but then recanted and, on 31 March, Coyne announced that, having examined the rival sites, there was no doubt of the superiority of Kariba. Benson, however, remained in a prickly mood, and on 6 April refused to "rubber stamp", as a member of the Railway Higher Authority, a decision on the extension of the railway north from Sinoia without fuller information.[17]

Malvern, who had been hinting about retiring, told Welensky that he

[15] *The Rhodesia Herald*, 18 March 1955.

[16] Welensky Papers, 42/21, f. 262, G. Beckett to Welensky, 20 March 1955; 8/82, f. 219, Lord Malvern to Benson, 22 March 1955.

[17] *The Rhodesia Herald*, 22 & 26 March & 1 April 1955; Welensky Papers, 42/60, f. 214, Welensky to D. Taylor, 23 March 1955; 25/174, f. 5, F. Payne to Welensky, 28 March 1955; 42/26, ff. 72–73, Benson to Welensky, 6 April 1955.

would wait for the hydro-electric fracas to die down before doing so at the end of the year. Another by-product of the row was that the Federal Party felt betrayed by its Members of the Northern Rhodesian Legislative Council.[18]

In April Dr Kanark of the International Bank arrived, and the Federal Government named the distinguished civil engineer, Duncan Law Anderson, as the new chairman of the Federal Hydro-Electric Power Board. Sir Alexander Gibb and Partners were appointed to serve as consulting engineers with Coyne. A working party was set up to examine Nyasaland's Shiré scheme which was threatening to cost £78 000 000.

In May the first tenders were offered, but Benson remained determined at least to set the record straight in his terms. On 27 June he wrote to Welensky recalling the events and defending his officials, and Nicholson in particular. Benson stated that he, like others, remained upset, not at the decision, but at the manner in which it was taken.[19]

Aside from Kariba, the public attention had been caught by van Eeden when, on 13 April, he announced that he would soon resign his seat to fight a by-election. The Nyasaland Government did not assist the Federal Party either by coincidentally raising again the reform of the Nyasaland Constitution. The summoning of the two northern Governors to London to discuss the Nyasaland Constitution, evoked a warning from Malvern that the Federal Government would expect to be consulted, not only because of the constitutional convention, but because changes in Nyasaland would affect the Federal position. Malvern wished Lord Home, the recent successor to Swinton, as Commonwealth Secretary, to be clear about his Government's objection to parity of racial representation in Nyasaland. Malvern conceded that parity and partnership were closely related, but felt that the premise for parity was an equality of knowledge and a sense of responsibility, and not one race being more numerous than the other. He warned that his Government intended to introduce the Federal electoral law in 1956 and, in framing it, would have to take into account the Nyasaland changes, as well as the decline in the value of money. It was regrettable, he said, that this matter was coming to a head just before a British general election, even though he was confident that the Conservatives would be returned.[20] His prediction was correct because, on 27 May, Sir Anthony Eden (later Lord Avon) led the Conservatives to a 61-seat victory.

The immediate British response to Malvern was a reassurance on consultation and, accordingly, he was shown the statement which Lennox-Boyd would deliver in the Commons on 15 June. This emphasised the necessity to satisfy ultimately all the inhabitants of Nyasaland. There was a strong argument against change at that moment, but it was known that the Africans felt that reform was overdue and were expecting it. For this reason Colby had held his February conference, but his proposals had drawn criticism from all sides. In particular, the Africans had sought representation in the Executive

[18] Welensky Papers, 42/60, f. 210, Welensky to D. Taylor, 13 April 1955; 25/242A, f. 270, Welensky to H. J. Roberts, 15 April 1955.

[19] *Ibid.*, 42/26, ff. 68–71, Benson to Welensky, 27 June 1955.

[20] *The Rhodesia Herald*, 14 April 1955; Welensky Papers, 20/18, f. 386, Malvern to Lord Home, 18 April 1955.

Council and parity of unofficial representation in the legislature. Lennox-Boyd would not concede the former, but felt that racial parity was feasible because the official Members would hold the balance of power. Yet, "parity" had become an emotional word and its introduction could obstruct all progress. For this reason he intended to implement the February proposals. (The Legislative Council would comprise twelve official Members, six non-African elected unofficial Members and five African unofficial Members appointed by the Governor after being elected by the African Protectorate Council.) Because the new franchise had yet to be devised with the concurrence of the Federal Government, Lennox-Boyd said, the one used in the Federal election in 1953 to elect the Nyasaland Federal MPs would be retained to elect the six non-African elected Members in Nyasaland's first general election.[21]

The Nyasaland Association (European) responded to the announcement by decrying the maintenance of a racial approach to politics. For the Africans, Chirwa, the Federal MP, cabled Lennox-Boyd reiterating their demands and protesting at the obvious influence of the Federal Government which would mean African subordination. The Asian spokesman, however, thought that henceforth stronger bonds between his people and the Europeans would have to be forged.[22] The Federal Government said nothing but it disliked the proposal to restrict the vote to citizens of the United Kingdom and Colonies rather than to British subjects because this would exclude Europeans who were of South African origin and were reluctant to give up their South African citizenship. Later, in August, it resisted pressure from the Nyasaland Government to introduce this voting restriction into the Federal arena.[23]

Colby defended the Nyasaland proposals to Welensky because he felt that, with the Africans outnumbering the Europeans by 600 : 1, it was obvious that Nyasaland was a black state. It was therefore vital to retain the official majority because it was the greatest safeguard for the European. He predicted an intensification of African nationalism and that African leaders of real calibre would emerge. To avoid providing a fertile field for agitation, Africans had to be given reasonable opportunities. It was irrelevant, Colby said, to argue that the African was not ready for change when, through rebellion, he could make the position intolerable for the European.[24]

On 11 July in the Legislative Council, Colby stated that the changes were not the last word on the Constitution and further reform would follow in due course. In particular, the racial approach to politics would be abandoned to ensure the evolution of a healthy body politic. The current changes answered the African argument that Britain was not meeting their aspirations. He was confident that the Africans recognised the need for European leadership for the present, as well as for training in the art of governing. Political maturity, he declared, would not be gained through noisy meetings at which irre-

[21] Welensky Papers, 20/18, f. 385, A. H. Reed to H. N. Parry, 19 April 1955; House of Commons *Hansard* (London), Vol. 542, Col. 12, 15 June 1955.

[22] *The Rhodesia Herald*, 17 June 1955.

[23] Welensky Papers, FGC(55), 32nd Meeting, Minute 10, Federal Cabinet, 6 July 1955; 34th Meeting, Minute 7, 3 August 1955.

[24] *Ibid.*, 42/51, f. 3, Sir Geoffrey Colby to Welensky, 24 June 1955; f. 22, same to same, 27 June 1955.

sponsible resolutions were passed. He would introduce the necessary legislation in August, and hoped that an election would be held in March 1956. The subsequent Bill, which was debated in early September 1955, provided, among other matters, for an income or property qualification of £240 p.a., and was well received in the Legislative Council.[25]

When van Eeden announced his decision to resign his seat, the Press judged his timing as perfect. Indeed, Beckett, who was nominated by the Federal Party to stand against van Eeden in the by-election, acknowledged that victory would be very difficult. F. S. Derby raised the hopes of the Federal Party by standing as the Confederate Party candidate for the seat. Van Eeden, however, was an astute tactician and worked hard at enrolling new voters, while Beckett enrolled none. Van Eeden exploited Kafue and other local grievances, at a moment when the Federal Party in Northern Rhodesia was in considerable disarray, and published his plan for partition.[26]

Inevitably racial questions featured prominently in van Eeden's campaign, and again others inadvertently came to his aid. In early August Moffat gave notice of a motion for an investigation into the basic principles of a united multi-racial nation and into the parliamentary and electoral system best calculated to serve it in the transitional period. The Federal Cabinet decided to reject it because the existing Constitution provided adequately for the transitional period, and in any event an electoral law was being devised. Simultaneously, in the Northern Rhodesian Legislative Council, Derby asked for a select committee on the Moffat resolutions of the previous year so that they should be implemented or rescinded. Derby found them to be "a platitudinous policy of temporary expediency".[27]

On 16 August Moffat spoke to his motion in the Federal Assembly and faced inevitable defeat. He hoped, however, that the House would still examine it on its merits. He intended merely to persuade the Government to examine the basic principles of its policy. The principles were clear, but it was hard to get them accepted. He thought that the parliamentary system was difficult to apply and that, while the fear of racial domination persisted, there had to be some impartial authority outside Parliament to maintain a balance between the conflicting racial claims. He did not explain to which authority he referred and perhaps was forgetting momentarily that the Federation was largely self-governing. The Federation, he acknowledged, was pledged to build a multi-racial state and thus he wanted to ascertain its fundamental requirements. Once the full implications were understood, it would be possible to achieve a unity of purpose and action throughout the Federation. However, while any racial division existed, the Westminster model would be impossible to apply. It should, therefore, be modified to suit local conditions and should be designed to allay white fears whilst simultaneously providing

[25] Ny *Debates* (Zomba), p. 2, 11 July 1955; p. 5 f., 5 September 1955.

[26] *The Rhodesia Herald*, 14 April & 13 June 1955; Welensky Papers, 42/21, f. 255, Beckett to Welensky, 14 May 1955; f. 251, same to same, 1 May 1955; 28/78, f. 129, Welensky to J. Graylin, 30 April 1955; 24/73, ff. 395–397, Welensky to Gore-Browne, 10 October 1955; 24/13, ff. 212–213, Welensky to Mrs L. Easton, 10 October 1955.

[27] Welensky Papers, 15/70, f. 56, J. S. Moffat to Welensky, 10 July 1955; FGC(55), 35th Meeting, Minute 7, Federal Cabinet, 10 August 1955.

for African political advancement. As separation was impracticable, the only real option was multi-racialism, and the motion was necessary because the political leaders seemed to hesitate lest the electorate shrink from partnership. The motion, Moffat said, represented a first step towards securing a binding commitment by all the Governments to the realisation of multi-racialism.

After Doig, the seconder, and Scott had spoken in like vein, Welensky replied, not questioning Moffat's sincerity, but commenting on his contradictory behaviour. Moffat had, in the recent budget debate, not only voted against the Government, but had urged the Federal Party to follow his example, leaving Welensky to wonder if he really wanted the Government to fall. Welensky felt that it was extremely difficult and impracticable to lay down hard and fast rules for human relationships. His Government had, nevertheless, done much in its limited fields to advance the African in its short life. Amongst others, opportunities for promotion for Africans in the postal organisation had been created, a settlement had been reached on the Copperbelt, and an agricultural college for Africans was being planned. It was difficult to understand Moffat's purpose, for the motion would only cast doubt on the integrity of the Federal Government and damage it in the eyes of the world. The Federation's problems were certainly not insuperable. As the Federal Assembly was constantly used to air racial matters, and stress was always laid on the discrimination suffered by Africans and never on that in their favour, it was necessary, Welensky felt, to remind the House that the Europeans had accepted Federation and not a social revolution. They believed, by contrast, in evolution. The Federal Government had done much and would do more, and the motion certainly did not assist.

Moffat replied that he would be content if only Welensky would say that his resolutions were acceptable. Moffat said he could not understand why the Government rejected the motion because it did nothing more than catalogue what he wanted. It was lost by nine votes to 20.[28]

Van Eeden had been continuing his campaign with the assistance of Dendy Young, after a pact between them on 21 July. Dendy Young depicted Malvern as a Little Englander *vis-à-vis* the Afrikaner, and pleaded that the Federal Assembly needed van Eeden. The tactics of van Eeden were clearly effective, and the Federal Party never really raised its hopes of defeating him. Malvern and Welensky attacked partition and racial separation, but to little avail. Kafue and other grievances told, and on 6 September van Eeden was returned to the Federal Parliament as an independent by 560 votes to Beckett's 305 and Derby's 30.[29] Although van Eeden was later to become the chief strategist of the Federal Opposition, such was his nature that within a few years he returned to the Federal Party and worked hard for it.

The Federal Party licked its wounds, while its opponents sought to exploit the situation by coalescing. A United Dominion Party was formed in Northern Rhodesia, but van Eeden and other leading lights had never been able to find common ground and did not succeed this time. By 1956 there were as many as ten parties. Welensky told his correspondents that van Eeden had

[28] Fed R & N *Debates* (Salisbury), Vol. 5, Col. 1685 f., 16 August 1955.

[29] Welensky Papers, 35/26, f. 63, Welensky to B. Weinbren, 21 July 1955; *Northern News*, 2 & 15 September 1955; *The Rhodesia Herald*, 30 September 1955.

taught the Federal Party a lesson in organisation, but had in fact gained a majority which was largely comprised of the 200 new voters whom he had enrolled.[30] However, Welensky, like Beckett, had no illusions about the sagging morale of the Federal Party and the unpopularity of his Government. Welensky acknowledged this when speaking in Umtali on 28 October, but claimed it was inevitable because the Government had put the interests of the Federation first and had spurned easily-won popularity. Accordingly, it had recently terminated the trade agreement with South Africa to end the reliance on imports and to encourage local production. The tax measures had not been well received, and Welensky had risked his personal popularity over Kariba, and would do so again in like circumstances. Yet he pointed out that the gross national product had increased by £30 000 000 in a year to £304 700 000. As the copper mines alone had a life expectancy of 50 years, he declared great confidence in the future.[31]

The political circles were more than somewhat startled when Todd chose to comment on Welensky's speech, doing so in Umtali on 4 November. Malvern was out of the country, *en route* to London to discuss, amongst other issues, the Federal franchise and, as Todd criticised him by inference, Todd's timing was deemed to be questionable. Todd declared he was speaking out because he believed that the Federal Government faced a crisis. He had recently asked, and had been told, that the Federal Government could not raise money for the development of the greatest asset of the Federation, the African himself. It was easier to secure money for African housing than education. The Federal Government was also faced with the challenge of van Eeden and his ideas on partition, but Todd expected the Federation to become more resistant to such attempts to overthrow the Constitution. A crisis such as this, Todd alleged, inevitably affected the territorial Governments, because in many ways they were subservient to the Federal Government. Consequently many, including himself, had been disappointed by the failure of Welensky to acknowledge his Government's failures. The liberal forces of the Federation were divided in their loyalties, not by their beliefs, but by the lack of efficiency and cohesion displayed by the Federal Government. This weakness, Todd maintained, was promoting nationalism among the Africans and Europeans and, as a result, racial emotion.

Todd claimed that it was generally known that Malvern would resign soon. As clearly Welensky was taking over many of Malvern's functions, Todd urged Welensky to bring in the best available men and women from within and without the Federal Assembly to strengthen the Cabinet. The crisis was only compounded, in Todd's eyes, by current talk of the formation of a party with identical aims to the Federal Party but more dynamic and energetic.[32]

Todd immediately wrote to Welensky to reassure him of his goodwill and to express the hope that, as it was necessary, Welensky would take over very soon. Todd later explained to Welensky that he had not given him any warning of his speech to avoid embarrassing him. He thereupon confused Welensky by claiming that the idea had come to him early in the morning and

[30] Welensky Papers, 24/73, ff. 395–397, Welensky to Gore-Browne, 10 October 1955.
[31] *The Rhodesia Herald*, 29 October 1955.
[32] *Ibid.*, 5 November 1955.

that there had only been time to type the speech before delivering it in the afternoon. Todd insisted that Malvern should retire at the end of 1955 rather than in mid-1956.[33]

Welensky replied that his position as Deputy Prime Minister made it difficult to do anything Todd had suggested. I. D. Smith, when telling Welensky later of the anger of the people of the Southern Rhodesian Midlands at Todd's effrontery, thought that Todd was seeking to become Malvern's successor. However, Todd had assured Welensky that he had no desire to enter the Federal field. Welensky concluded that Todd had been provoked by a refusal by the Federal Treasury to provide money for his pet schemes. He was left wondering about Todd's outburst, asking himself why, if the Federation was so prosperous, Todd should think it was so badly governed.[34]

Welensky refused to comment initially because it was Malvern's prerogative, but, when the Press persisted, he relented and admonished Todd for his impertinence. Welensky accepted the concern in territorial circles, but said it was equally important that the Federal Government should maintain broader objectives and ensure that no single territory gained a peculiar advantage. He regretted that Todd should think that the Federal Government was dividing the liberal forces. He agreed that only the best men should serve, but it remained Malvern's duty to select the Cabinet. Hinting at Malvern's retirement, Welensky assured the public that Malvern was keeping him fully informed. He felt that, if Todd found that money was unavailable for a specific purpose, he should remember that the investor provided funds for the development of the Federation as a whole.[35]

The same issue of *The Sunday Mail* carried a statement from Malvern that he would not be standing again and would be retiring soon. David Cole, a local journalist, whose letter appeared in the same paper, and Dendy Young, whose opinion was sought, could only conclude that Todd was pressing for a general election when Malvern retired so that he and at least two of his Cabinet could secure Federal seats. They thought that Todd wished to replace Macintyre with Whitehead whose eyesight had improved and had recently indicated that he would like to return to politics.

Welensky revealed the next day, 7 November, that he had unequivocably rebuffed an approach by the new political grouping, whose existence Todd had revealed, because he was satisfied with the Federal Party. He said nothing about this new body, but it was thought to represent industrial interests in Southern and Northern Rhodesia. They received some support from *The Bulawayo Chronicle* because it seemed that the Federal and United Rhodesia Parties had grounded on that most dangerous shoal, complacency. Change, the *Chronicle* agreed, was desirable but Todd should consider his own Cabinet first in that light.[36]

[33] Welensky Papers, 31/46, f. 74, R. S. G. Todd to Welensky, 5 November 1955; 25/315, f. 19, Welensky to I. D. Smith, 11 November 1955.
[34] *Ibid.*, 24/151, ff. 363–364, Welensky to Joelson, 15 November 1955; 25/315, f. 20, I. D. Smith to Welensky, 9 November 1955; f. 19, Welensky to I. D. Smith, 11 November 1955.
[35] *Ibid.*, 24/151, ff. 363–364, Welensky to Joelson, 15 November 1955; *The Sunday Mail*, 6 November 1955.
[36] *The Bulawayo Chronicle*, 7 November 1955.

Van Eeden, too, could not resist rushing into the controversy, calling Todd the "Arch-Priest" of racial integration and claiming that only political expediency had driven Welensky to embrace partnership. Van Eeden advised Welensky to look at the strange bed-fellows that he had thus cultivated because they, including Todd, had outdone his interpretation of partnership and might eclipse him.[37]

A new political group briefly surfaced, but denied that it was the one to which Todd had referred. However, like Todd, its quarrel was not with the principles of the Federal Party, but with its organisation and some of its appointments. There was as much need, it said, to get rid of the die-hards as there had been in South Africa when the United Party had split to spawn the Progressives.[38] This announcement, at least, spurred Beckett to urge the overhauling of the machinery of the Federal Party. A wider effect of the whole affair was that Todd's outburst was feared to have frightened the investors because a £10 000 000 Federal loan for general development failed on the London Market shortly afterwards. The British Press certainly enjoyed a shiver of trepidation for the time when Malvern's experienced hand would no longer be at the helm.

Todd answered these criticisms on 10 November, claiming that the uproar confirmed that people were disturbed by the lack-lustre of the Federal Government. He denied any ambition to enter Federal politics as he was fully occupied by his current role. He agreed with Welensky that there was nothing so wrong with the Federal Party and Government that it could not be rectified, but urged that it be done immediately. Explaining his outburst, he warned that the liberal vote could be split, and a third party opposed to partnership could secure power. His purpose had only been to spur the Federal Government to reform itself so that people could again support the Federal Party.[39]

He did not satisfy *The Sunday Mail* that his statement in Umtali had been anything but ill-timed. It was, *The Sunday Mail* said, on 13 November, particularly unfortunate that Malvern was out of the country and that the speech had been made on the eve of the floating of a £10 000 000 loan. It was disgraceful that the territorial tail should try to wag the Federal dog. Malvern would have to give his successor time to prepare for the next general election and it was certainly not the moment to form another Federal Party because that was precisely what the opposition wanted. Van Eeden had said that he wanted Todd to succeed Malvern because clearly Welensky was the only man capable of taking over from Malvern. This, the newspaper concluded, had been the reason for the campaign of whispering and denigration.

The Press expected comment from Malvern because more was being read into his reply than he had actually said. The London weekly, *South Africa*, predicted that Malvern would resign for he was not the sort to stay when considered superfluous. However, busy with other issues, Malvern ignored the challenges, but it is now known that he refused to go at Todd's or anyone else's bidding and postponed his retirement to the end of 1956. Welensky

[37] *The Rhodesia Herald*, 7 November 1955.
[38] *Ibid.*, 10 November 1955.
[39] *Ibid.*, 11 November 1955.

agreed with Malvern's silence because the Federation could only be harmed by the threat of his retirement. When Malvern had wanted to comment on his retirement at the Federal Party congress in Blantyre in August 1955, Welensky had dissuaded him because he had no desire to suffer the fate of N. C. Havenga of South Africa as the heir-apparent in the last days of the premiership of Dr Malan. Malvern proposed that when he was ready to retire, he would merely submit his resignation to the Governor-General and recommend Welensky as his successor. Welensky agreed to this.[40]

While Todd was attacking him, Malvern had revealed to the British Government the progress which had been made towards devising formulae for the Federal franchise and citizenship. He explained that, given five years in which to accomplish this, the Federal Government had concentrated on the more immediate and massive task of the assumption of power.[41]

As has been seen, however, the carping of van Eeden, in particular, had prompted Welensky in February 1955 (when Malvern was in Britain) to set up a committee under Greenfield to devise a franchise for the Federation. This committee confined itself to the election of the constitutionally-prescribed 26 ordinary MPs and paid no heed to the election or selection of the nine special MPs representing African interests. The reason for this was that the Constitution was frozen for a minimum of seven years and a maximum of nine. Thus it was impossible as yet to wrest the nine special seats from territorial control. Likewise, the enlargement of the Federal Assembly to allow the two-party system to operate effectively could not be considered. Another inhibition was that, in terms of the Constitution, any Federal franchise proposals applying to Nyasaland had to be accepted by its Legislative Council. The Federal citizenship issue was complicated by the existence of British Protected Persons when citizenship generally in the Commonwealth carried with it the status of British subject, and Federal citizenship had to equate with that already obtaining in Southern Rhodesia.[42]

Greenfield's franchise committee and the Ministry of Home Affairs toyed with the idea of citizenship embracing both the British subject and the British Protected Person, but it was known that the African Affairs Board would reject any suggestion that there be first and second class citizens. By the time Malvern met the Secretaries of State in November doubts had arisen whether Federal citizenship was an essential prerequisite for exercising the vote, and its replacement by an oath of allegiance was considered.[43]

The premise had been that there should be a qualified common roll, but there was a suggestion in June — to which everyone would return — that there should be dual rolls to enfranchise a wider portion of the population, while power was retained by the more educated. It was felt that Federal citizenship could be made a qualification for the upper roll. To avoid the swamping of the European electorate, the franchise committee set the income

[40] *South Africa*, 14 November 1955; Author's interview with Sir Roy Welensky; L. H. Gann and M. Gelfand, *Huggins of Rhodesia* (London, 1964), p. 254; Welensky Papers, 27/50, f. 31, Welensky to S. Brooke-Norris, 25 November 1955.

[41] Welensky Papers, FGC(55), Note of a Meeting, 15 November 1955.

[42] *Ibid.*, 9/3, ff. 61–64, Minutes of the Franchise and Citizenship Committee, 4 February 1955.

[43] *Ibid.*

qualification and its equivalent in property at £1 000 p.a. for the upper roll, and £500 for the lower roll. However, the Federal Cabinet and the franchise committee soon reverted to a common roll based on an income of £500 p.a. and the ability not only to understand English but to complete the registration form without assistance.[44]

The northern Governors contributed their ideas. Benson proposed that Federal citizenship should accommodate the desire of British Protected Persons to retain their status. All British subjects would qualify for a first class citizenship while the second class would have local significance only and would be a qualification for the vote. Consequently, British Protected Persons would declare their loyalty to the Queen, the Federation and their territory, but would retain their status.

The franchise committee, however, believed that a two-tier citizenship would only confuse the issue and would be rejected internationally. The British Protected Person might object to becoming a Federal citizen of any kind, or at least to being a second class one. It would be wrong, the committee concluded, to enfranchise a person and enable him to play an active part in politics while he could still apply to Britain for protection and redress.

To avoid African domination, Benson advised against copying older political forms from countries with homogeneous societies. The emphasis should be on quality rather than quantity. The qualification for the vote should not be based merely on financial and educational standards, because these would favour "flashy demagogues", and would exclude many hard-working loyal citizens. Thus there should be a greater variety of qualifications, to each of which should be allocated a "point", and the accumulation of four points would secure the vote. A candidate would require ten points. The aspiring voter would have to be at least 25 years old with a sound knowledge of spoken and written English and have local Federal citizenship. In addition, the voter would possess prescribed educational qualifications or income or property. Alternatively, length of service in a responsible position in the public and private sectors would be recognised. Benson suggested that civil servants below a certain rank who could score ten points would qualify as candidates. (This last proposal was in keeping with the approach of the Colonial Office to the involvement of African civil servants in politics and was something which the Federal Government abhorred.)

Benson thought that special representation would have to endure while racialism prevailed, but that it would be progressively eliminated. It could be replaced, in time, by a system under which a candidate would have to secure the votes of both races.

The Federal franchise committee preferred quality to quantity, and disagreed that the threat of African domination ruled out the adoption of traditional constitutional forms. Partnership ultimately would produce African domination, but not before the Africans had proved they could exercise political judgment. Indeed, the committee had found it was impossible to improve on the traditional formulae suitably modified for local conditions. It judged Benson's scheme to be sound only in principle because, when lauding

[44] *Ibid.*, 9/2, ff. 93–100, Note by the Investigating Committee, ? June 1955; FGC(55), 28th Meeting, Minute 3, Federal Cabinet, 7 June 1955.

length of service, he ignored the self-employed and assumed that anyone who changed employment often was less resourceful than the one who did not. The points system could be weighted to favour one race. The committee had explored such possibilities but had agreed that income, property and education were the best indicators of maturity. Benson's ideas of candidates needing to attract a proportion of votes from both races were considered to perpetuate racial distinctions. The committee felt that a common roll would only be successful if it eliminated such distinctions.

Colby argued that, while thousands of Africans in Nyasaland could fill in the registration form unaided, only 100 possessed the prescribed £500 p.a. income. This did not perturb him because within a decade the Africans retiring from South Africa with their accumulated savings, and the new prosperity of the African farmers, would mean that the African voters could predominate. What troubled him was the introduction of the common roll because very soon every Nyasaland Federal seat would be captured by Africans. The Africans would then demand a territorial common roll which was most undesirable and would be resisted by the European Members of the Legislative Council.

The franchise committee felt that Colby exaggerated, and called for more information. Meanwhile it set the minimum voting age limit at 21, and the income qualification, and its property-owning equivalent, at £300 p.a. The educational standard would be the Cambridge Overseas Certificate or something similar. If the aspiring voter lacked the educational requirement but could fill in the form unaided, his income would have to be £500 p.a. The latter would be reviewed every five years by the Federal Supreme Court and equated with the purchasing value of the pound.[45]

The Governors and the franchise committee were naturally not alone in pondering the constitutional problems. After pressure from a number of quarters, Welensky asked R. M. Taylor, the Secretary to the Federal Treasury, to examine a recent idea of Todd to merge the Southern Rhodesian and Federal Governments. Taylor agreed that, because the Constitution allowed the territories to delegate any of their powers, the merger was possible, but thought that, thereupon, the northern territories would demand the right to secede. The Africans would exploit such a suggestion and, in any case, the Southern Rhodesians would not gain any more Federal seats.[46]

Gaunt was seeking an equality in the territorial allocation of Federal seats to avoid the perpetuation of territorial rivalries. The United Dominion Party talked of gaining dominion status and demoting the territorial legislatures to provincial councils. Van Eeden constantly berated the Federal Government for its failure to produce any franchise proposals, and only Nkumbula, in a cable to the Colonial Secretary, on 6 March 1955, had made detailed suggestions. In the interests of racial harmony, he wanted the enfranchise-

[45] *Ibid.*, 9/2, ff. 44–46, Colby to Malvern, 28 September 1955; f. 16, E. I. G. Unsworth to H. N. Parry, 30 November 1955; ff. 14–15 & 26–29, Memoranda by Benson, (undated); ff. 20–21, Comments by the Official Committee, (undated); f. 12, the Northern Rhodesian Government's Observations on the Draft Proposals, (undated); ff. 22–24 & 37–40, Minutes of the Franchise and Citizenship Committee, 5 December 1955.

[46] *Ibid.*, 7/2, f. 347, R. M. Taylor to Welensky, 17 June 1955.

ment of all British Protected Persons who earned £50 p.a. or possessed £100 worth of fixed property. There should be provision for secession, and Northern Rhodesia should be given a 30-seat legislature, a prime minister and a cabinet of ten. Alternatively, he suggested a bi-cameral house elected by the races on separate rolls.[47]

Malvern discussed all this with Home and Lennox-Boyd in London on 15 November. Malvern told them that, as he assumed that citizenship would be the basic qualification for the vote, his committee had first tried to define it. However, the complexities were such that he had concluded it might be better to concentrate on the other qualifications, such as the £500 p.a. income level or the variety of equivalent qualifications proposed by Benson, and regard every resident as a potential voter. Malvern felt that the merit of Benson's suggestion was that it drew into the system a stable element of society which lacked the income qualification. Colby, however, had feared the swamping of the tiny European electorate in Nyasaland and therefore Malvern thought that it might be necessary to have a different system there.

Lennox-Boyd disagreed because Colby had said that the £500 p.a. income qualification would only enfranchise 100 Africans, and it would be a long time before the European position would be endangered. Heedless, Malvern claimed that everywhere in the Federation the reservation of the European seats might be ultimately necessary and, at least, there should be a means of adjusting the income qualification with the falling value of money. The British Ministers agreed, but warned that care would have to be taken lest such action be construed as an effort to keep the African off the roll.

Malvern stressed it was essential to introduce the franchise and citizenship laws in 1956, the third year of the Federation, and he would send someone to London to complete the negotiations as soon as possible. Citizenship, he warned, had to equate with that in Southern Rhodesia, but it would be difficult to achieve this without depriving British Protected Persons of their prized status.

Home found no insuperable difficulty because citizenship was not essential for the franchise. He promised to discuss the problem with the Home Office. Malvern hoped that Home would also establish if the Federal franchise committee's proposal, that the British Protected Person should have the right to acquire Federal citizenship (carrying the status of a British subject), was acceptable to Britain and the Commonwealth. Home agreed to do this.[48]

Malvern reported to his Cabinet on 15 December, but before then the franchise committee had more information on the voters in Nyasaland. There 80 Africans and 20 Asians would qualify for the vote with an income of £300 p.a. and the Cambridge Overseas Certificate, and 150 Africans and 100 Asians at the £500 p.a. and simple literacy level. The committee was assured that the African would gain the vote more quickly on the first basis, but even at £500 p.a. would steadily acquire it and soon eclipse the European electorate. However, the committee thought that this would take 15 to 25 years, and by then the removal of special representation for Africans would have counter-balanced the ordinary seats captured by the Africans. The committee

[47] *The Rhodesia Herald*, 7 March 1955.
[48] Welensky Papers, FGC(55), Note of a Meeting, London, 15 November 1955.

had also been attempting to frame a citizenship bill but had found it impossible without departing radically from Commonwealth practice. The committee and the Governor-General, Lord Llewellin, agreed that there should be a single class of citizenship with the status of a British subject. There should be the simplest process for registration and without a fee. An oath of allegiance was specified, but the committee rejected Todd's advice that it should be as demanding as possible of the person taking the oath because the committee believed that the British and northern Governments would baulk at strong declarations of loyalty to the Federation. The introduction of an oath might also rally support for African nationalism at a moment when it appeared to be flagging. The committee suggested that the Federal Government should consider laying its draft bill before the British Government, and ask it to terminate naturalisation in the northern territories. The bill should also be circulated amongst the Parliamentary Caucus of the Federal Party.[49]

The Federal Cabinet was somewhat taken aback to discover that Malvern had agreed that citizenship should not be a franchise qualification. He explained that the British had found the citizenship formula to be unacceptable because the idea that two-thirds of the population would not automatically qualify as citizens would be rejected in Britain and the Commonwealth, and make it difficult to amend, as was necessary, the British Nationality Act. The majority of British Protected Persons were believed to be loath to change their status and the British Government could not justify "rail-roading" them into making the change by otherwise withholding the vote. The British Ministers would not change the law of nationality but would entertain any proposals within that stricture. They would happily accept high qualifications for the franchise. Malvern reported that they promised to provide more detailed comment but, in the meantime, wished the Federal Government would refrain from discussing the issues with the territorial Governments or the Parliamentary Caucus.[50]

The Federal Cabinet and its franchise committee wondered at the British determination to extend the franchise to British Protected Persons when it was not required by the Federal Constitution and, more significantly, by the northern territorial Constitutions. Indeed, the Nyasaland Constitution had recently been amended and there had been no suggestion of this. In January the Federal Cabinet discovered that even Coutt's Report on Kenya had not suggested it. The change seemed hardly necessary when African affairs were territorial, and when there were special Federal representatives of African interests. Malvern was asked by his Cabinet to inform the British Ministers that such a change was unacceptable because it would be politically embarrassing.

Other anomalies were found. For example, British Protected Persons from Nyasaland living in Southern Rhodesia would vote for the ordinary MPs, but

[49] *Ibid.*, 9/2, ff. 22–24, Minutes of Franchise and Citizenship Committee, 5 December 1955; f. 31, Federal Citizenship Law: Report by the Chairman, 5 December 1955; 8/111, ff. 173–174, Lord Llewellin to Welensky, 15 December 1955.

[50] *Ibid.*, FGC(55), 193/55, Memorandum by Lord Malvern, 10 December 1955; 51st Meeting, Minute 4, Federal Cabinet, 15 December 1955.

not the three special representatives of that territory. There would be little point in acquiring citizenship if that status did not qualify the holder for the vote. The obvious alternative was to reserve the vote for British subjects. The Cabinet noted that the British Government had favoured the common roll and the progressive elimination of special representation, and it was possible that the extension of the vote to the British Protected Person could be used as a lever to achieve this.[51]

The franchise committee thought that there was an indisputable claim for the recognition of Federal citizenship by Britain and the Commonwealth, particularly as the proposed method of registration was simple and was without the current fee of £5 and the language test. The committee looked forward to the time when all the inhabitants, irrespective of race, controlled the Government, as only then would the appeal of nationalism be weakened. The alternative was *apartheid* on the British Colonial or South African patterns. The Federal Government, the committee maintained, should be credited with making a gesture of faith by not asking for the removal of both special representation and the African Affairs Board, and for still proposing a non-racial common roll. It would merely enroll those civilised citizens who would swear allegiance to the Queen and the Federation. By contrast, the British Government seemed unconcerned about the racialism inherent in special representation. It was obviously desirable to engender loyalty to the Federation, and this and citizenship, the committee thought, had to be the basic qualifications for the franchise. The preamble of the Constitution, after all, prescribed that the granting of dominion status was dependent on the expressed wish of the majority of the inhabitants, and a good indication of this was a voluntary drift towards citizenship.[52]

At the end of January Home expressed regret to Malvern that the latter had not induced his Cabinet to separate citizenship from the franchise because the British Government would face serious political difficulties if the franchise, by being reserved for British subjects, were closed to two-thirds of the population. Home proposed to discuss the matter further with his colleagues and asked Malvern to continue to refrain from public debate.[53]

The Federal Cabinet, however, had already reviewed the matter in mid-January when the Northern Rhodesian Government asked to be included in the discussion. The Federal franchise committee was ordered to examine ways of inducing the British Government to allow citizenship to be a qualification for the franchise. The committee was also to review the use of a points system and the elimination of special representation to allow the development of purely party politics.[54]

The committee produced a memorandum on 25 January and, a month later, after further reflection, Greenfield reported to the Cabinet on the

[51] *Ibid.*, FGC(55), 51st Meeting, Minute 4, Federal Cabinet, 15 December 1955; 8/111, ff. 170–172, Memorandum, Citizenship and Franchise Legislation, 20 December 1955; f. 169, Memorandum by Greenfield, 1 January 1956; FGC(56), 3rd Meeting, Minute 6, Federal Cabinet, 17 January 1956.

[52] *Ibid.*, 9/2, ff. 6–10, Memorandum by the Franchise Committee, 25 January 1956.

[53] *Ibid.*, 8/111, f. 166, UK High Commissioner to Malvern, 30 January 1956.

[54] *Ibid.*, FGC(56), 3rd Meeting, Minute 6, Federal Cabinet, 17 January 1956.

committee's progress to date. The problem of the British Protected Persons and the British subject status of the Federal citizen, without which the Southern Rhodesian Government would not repeal its citizenship law, was still unresolved. The conferment of British subject status on all would, of course, be tantamount to the annexation of the northern territories. The Commonwealth Relations Office had examined the draft bill and, while not objecting to any of its principles, still opposed citizenship as a qualification for the vote. A further inhibition was that, if Federal citizens were to be British subjects, Britain and the Dominions would need to amend their laws.

Greenfield noted that Article 10 of the Federal Constitution gave the power to arrange for the election of the 26 ordinary MPs, but that a constitutional amendment was needed to realise the objective of eliminating special representation progressively. This, however, remained most desirable as was its corollary, the gradual involvement of the poorer and less well-educated inhabitants in the electoral system. Thus he recommended that the northern Governments be pressed to elect directly, rather than nominate, the special representatives and to serve the cause of multi-racialism by including non-Africans in the electoral process. The existence, however, of the nine special representatives meant that the resolution of the question of the participation in the common roll could be postponed.

The committee, Greenfield said, had considered multiple voting but had found its variations to be limitless. The voter could well be given two or 100 votes. Any figure would be arbitrary, and the selection would result in privileged classes. Multiple voting could only be accepted on a basis of each voter having two votes. It would appeal to those who valued intelligence above all, but was fraught with difficulties. The committee had considered giving voters who earned £250 p.a. one vote, and those who earned £300 p.a. two. The first, however, would soon outweigh the second, and in any case the problems of delimitation would be almost insuperable. The committee therefore discarded this idea.

It had also considered very seriously the dual roll system with the "A" roll electing the 26 ordinary MPs, and the "B" roll the nine special representatives. The "A" roll qualifications would be an income of £500 p.a. and literacy in English, that of the "B" roll would be £100 p.a. and simple literacy. It found no great virtue in this suggestion.

The committee concluded that the best solution was a single roll based on an income of £500 p.a. and simple literacy. The Federal Parliament would decide if the income level should be tied to the value of the pound. If educational qualifications had to be recognised, then the committee suggested that the Cambridge Overseas Certificate should be accepted as the minimum, and that the income requirement of the voter who possessed it should be reduced to £300 p.a. The committee finally recommended that the Federal Government should decide its approach to the fundamental issues before involving the territorial Governments.

The Federal Cabinet decided that it was opportune to bring the territorial Governments into the discussions. (It was subsequently agreed with the territorial Governments to form an inter-government committee to devise the Federal franchise.) The Federal Cabinet would also advocate its franchise committee's recommendations but without irrevocable commitment. Considerable merit was found in the dual roll because it would tend to exclude the representation of the extremists, and would encourage the growth of party politics. The dual roll would introduce a system of multiple voting without the usual difficulties, and would retain control in civilised hands. This would also considerably widen the franchise without endangering standards.[55]

Aside from the deliberations within the Cabinet, Welensky had publicly expressed the hope in mid-February that the Federal Assembly might be enlarged to 60 seats, and that there would be no delay in attaining full self-government within the Commonwealth. He was undoubtedly encouraged to say this by a message from Lord Llewellin, then in England, who had seen Lord Salisbury and had gathered that the Federal constitutional review might be held earlier than the minimum of seven years because the Gold Coast would obtain its independence within two years, and the Federation was likely to be similarly treated. The most attractive aspect of this news was that negotiations for this advance would be with the current British Government.[56]

Meanwhile, there were other preoccupations. African nationalism, though apparently quiescent, was being carefully watched and the Governments were preparing themselves for possible conflict with it. Links between the local African nationalists and the Communist-penetrated South African ANC and the Communist-dominated South African Indian Congress were detected, as were contacts with Kenya, Tanganyika and the Gold Coast, with individuals like Fenner Brockway and the Reverend Michael Scott and with organisations like the Fabians, the Labour Party and the British trade unions. An increase in the dissemination of propaganda in the rural areas of Northern Rhodesia, together with the formation of youth leagues, threats to subvert the police, and the likelihood that the African trade union leaders would use their organisations for political ends, alarmed the Federal Government. Consequently, it urged the Northern Rhodesian Government to improve the security of the rural areas, which was now being left entirely in the hands of an under-staffed district administration. (It had been decided to close what few rural police stations there were in a rationalisation of the policy under which the district commissioners had always been responsible for policing the rural areas.) It is interesting to note that the infiltration of the upper echelons of commerce and industry by Afrikaner nationalism was also under surveillance.[57]

Welensky met Benson on 23 November 1955, for discussions on this and a variety of subjects, including the thorny issues of the Public Works Department, the transfer of European agriculture, the hostility of certain Northern Rhodesian officials and of the *Central African Post*. Benson promised to investigate most of these but would not introduce police into the rural areas as

[55] *Ibid.*, FGC(56), 8th Meeting, Minute 3, Federal Cabinet, 22 February 1956.

[56] *Ibid.*, 24/198, ff. 67–68, Llewellin to Welensky, 1 February 1956; *The Rhodesia Herald*, 13 February 1956.

[57] Welensky Papers, 19/33, f. 1, FISB Review October–November, 16 December 1955; f. 17, FISB Review, 13 February 1956; FGC(56), 8th Meeting, Minute 2, Federal Cabinet, 22 February 1956.

he lacked the manpower to do so effectively. He also did not want to upset the current system which employed the tribal Chiefs, particularly because he was convinced that there was no rural threat. He welcomed, however, any "plain-clothes" help which the Federal Government could supply.[58]

As African unrest had begun in rural areas in Kenya and elsewhere, the Federal Government remained wary, and the correctness of its attitude seemed confirmed in early December 1955 when Federal officials saw a copy of an oath administered by the action groups of the Northern Rhodesian ANC to their recruits. It read: "I promise Almighty God that, because the proposed Federal plan is a wicked plan, I shall continue to fight against it. I shall be ready to perform any service that this National Government shall require of me until the liberation of my people from White dominion shall come to an end." Yet the recently-declared aims of the ANC were hardly sinister. It proposed to fight for the broadening of the franchise to permit its full participation in government, but on the basis of ability rather than colour. The ANC would oppose the colour bar and seek the promotion of Africans to high office in the public and armed services. It promised to shield Africans from police brutality, secure an improvement in the lot of the Chiefs, and advance the African in commerce and industry. It would resist any proposal to standardise the policies regarding African affairs in the three territories, and any other moves towards unitary government.[59]

Nevertheless, the fears of trade union militancy were confirmed on 15 December 1955 when the African Mineworkers' Union declared itself to be highly dissatisfied with the educational requirements for the new range of mining jobs opened to Africans, and with the continuing racial disparity in pay.[60] The reports from Nyasaland likewise were of low-keyed activity by its African Congress. There had been a move to expel the Nyasaland African Federal MPs, and talk of passive resistance as a means to extricate Nyasaland from the Federation.

The Southern Rhodesian African Association had criticised Savanhu and Hove, declaring that they only sat in the Federal Assembly for personal gain. The Movement for Colonial Freedom in Britain was interesting itself in the case of Dixon Konkola who had recently been elected to the presidency of the Railway African Workers' Union but had been refused permission by the Southern Rhodesian Government to reside in its territory even though the headquarters of the union were in Bulawayo.[61]

The sins of the Federal Government were paraded before the British public on 5 January 1956 by W. M. Chirwa. He addressed meetings and Church congregations in Scotland, and as he left Britain he issued a public statement with the assistance of the Africa Bureau to correct the impression that all was well in the Federation. He claimed that the imposition of the Federation and the subsequent actions of its Government had only increased the resistance to it. He attacked that Government for allowing Southern

[58] *Ibid.*, 42/26, f. 54, Minutes of Discussions between Welensky and Benson, 23 November 1955.
[59] *Ibid.*, 33/33, f. 1, Northern Rhodesian ANC Organisation, 5 December 1955; 19/33, f. 1, FISB Review October–November, 16 December 1955.
[60] *The Rhodesia Herald*, 16 December 1955.
[61] Welensky Papers, 19/33, f. 1, FISB Review October–November, 16 December 1955.

Rhodesia to maintain its colour bar and for failing to end discrimination on the railways and in the post offices, and to give equal opportunities in the Federal civil service. Moffat's motion on the investigation into the multi-racial society, Chirwa recalled, had been dismissed. He did not fail to broadcast the worst of Malvern's parliamentary quips — the queuing behind the dirty umfazi — as an illustration of the prejudice he had to face. He depicted the daily trials of the African MPs in having to travel six miles for a meal, having to carry a pass to exempt them from carrying passes, having to use separate buses, which were not allowed to travel to the centre of Salisbury, and having to use separate entrances at the post office. The university, Chirwa asserted, would be multi-racial and yet it was planned that the African students would live and eat separately from the Europeans. Moreover, the Southern Rhodesian Government, he noted, in terms of the amendment to the Land Apportionment Act, could prevent any African student it chose from residing on the campus.

There had been African advancement on the Copperbelt but, Chirwa claimed, this was solely because of Prain. However, the Federal Government had simultaneously refused to open its civil service. There were no Africans on the immigration board, yet Africans were deeply troubled about white immigration, except where skills were needed. The Federal Government had to realise that the northern Africans would not give up their status as British Protected Persons, and could not understand why it should not be a qualification for the vote when it was in Nigeria. The Nyasaland Africans, too, were disappointed in the Nyasaland constitutional changes. Their exclusion from the franchise endangered race relations because it made them second-class citizens. In this they saw the Federal hand. Nyasaland, Chirwa maintained, was as much a black state as Uganda and should be allowed to develop along similar lines to achieve democratic self-government within the Commonwealth. The Africans wished to live in peace with the other races, he stated, but not to be dominated by them.[62]

Welensky apprised his British correspondents that Chirwa was discredited in nationalist eyes by continuing to sit in the Federal House, and Chirwa himself immediately adopted a more restrained attitude on his return. However, Nkumbula and Kaunda then re-entered the lists with virulent criticisms of all Europeans, demanding African self-government and warning of trouble if their aims were not realised shortly. Nkumbula wanted twelve Africans in the Northern Rhodesian Legislative Council in 1958, and parity in the Federal Assembly until it was dissolved. He threatened resolute opposition to any attempts to achieve dominion status.[63]

The Federal Government took this warning seriously enough to plan the composition and training of the army to deal with the widespread unrest which could be expected in 1960 when, it was anticipated, the Federal Constitution would be reviewed. It knew that it would have to rely on local resources as the British would never have any troops to spare. It considered

62 *The Rhodesia Herald*, 6 January 1956; Welensky Papers, 42/50, f. 31, Biographical Note by the Africa Bureau, 4 January 1956; f. 32, Press Statement by Chirwa, 5 January 1956.

63 Welensky Papers, 19/33, f. 17, FISB Review December–January, 13 February 1956; 24/151, ff. 357–358, Welensky to F. S. Joelson, 5 January 1956.

paratroops and planned a seven battalion force to maintain internal security.[64]

The Federal Party, which by February 1956 was planning its campaign to win the Sebakwe seat in Southern Rhodesia — which Dendy Young had recently vacated to become a Southern Rhodesian judge, remained troubled. At the Southern Rhodesian divisional executive meeting in January the Federal Government and Party were criticised for their poor efforts in the field of public relations, and for their failure to encourage industry and agriculture.[65]

The rumpus over the demands for the retirement of Malvern had died away, but in February 1956 Todd and Malvern clashed in public over a proposed inter-governmental ministerial economic council for which Todd had been pressing since October 1955. Todd was critical of the lack of co-ordination between the Governments, but Malvern felt that Todd was proposing nothing less than a return to the Central African Council which could mean the scrapping of the Federation. Malvern acknowledged that the co-ordination could be improved, but did not believe that it would be by a group of ministers sitting together waiting for divine inspiration. He was confident that the territorial Governments were equally guilty in the matter of consultation, but the difference was that his Government did not attack them in public.[66]

The Federal Party may have enjoyed Malvern's perkiness, but he remained so disliked and distrusted in Northern Rhodesia that Beckett urged that he should resign. The Northern Rhodesian feelings were exacerbated when the Federal Cabinet, in January, refused to base the new Vampire fighter squadrons at Livingstone because of its unsuitable climate. The airport there had been eclipsed, as far as international travel was concerned, by its new rival at Kentucky — outside Salisbury — and a new use for it was being sought. Graylin, the Livingstone Federal MP, fought hard for a reconsideration of the decision, but ignored pressure to resign. The Northern and Southern Rhodesian relationship within the Party, however, was most severely tested in the storm which blew up when the new estimated costs of Kariba were revealed in February. Roberts believed that it could well destroy the Federal Party in Northern Rhodesia.[67]

The revision of the estimates had been sufficiently startling for Welensky to write to Malvern in London on 12 November and allege that Barrow had given him a considerable shock by stating that the first stage of Kariba would cost £78 000 000 instead of £53 400 000. The cost of the completed scheme, when the north bank power house had been built, would be £111 780 000 instead of £85 800 000. Van Eeden was quick to gather that something was

[64] *Ibid.*, FGC(56), 8th Meeting, Minute 2, Federal Cabinet, 22 February 1956.

[65] *Ibid.*, 15/64, f. 15, Meeting of the Divisional Executive, Federal Party, Salisbury, 26 January 1956.

[66] *The Rhodesia Herald*, 9 & 11 February 1956; Welensky Papers, FGC(1), 17/55, Memorandum, 22 December 1955.

[67] Welensky Papers, FGC(56), 3rd Meeting, Minute 6, Federal Cabinet, 17 January 1956; 28/78, f. 95, J. Graylin to Welensky, 31 January 1956; f. 96, Graylin to Malvern, 31 January 1956; f. 94, Graylin to Welensky, 1 February 1956; 42/21, ff. 223–225, Beckett to Welensky, 10 January 1956.

afoot and, by alleging serious miscalculation, prompted Barrow into promising a public statement.[68]

In fact, it was Malvern who issued a brief statement in January. However, he only provoked L'Ange, the Federal Party MP for Nkana-Chingola, to compose a parliamentary motion demanding justification for Kariba. The Cabinet prepared a reply and suggested to L'Ange — who complied — that he should ask for the approximate cost, the reason for the increase, the economics of the scheme, and a report on the financial discussions. The Cabinet took care to supply Benson with an advance copy of its reply.[69]

In January the Federal Government received offers from the copper companies of £20 000 000 in loans and a gift of £10 000 000. However, in advance of the still awaited verdict of the International Bank, the Government proposed to tighten the Federal belt, to curb both immigration (setting a limit of 2 000 a year) and overseas investment. It would also control internal credit to limit inflation.[70]

The Cabinet would not have recognised the significance of the announcement on 19 February — almost on the eve of the Kariba debate — of the birth of what was to be its most formidable rival, the Dominion Party. Though, for the moment, this excluded van Eeden, it brought together S. E. Aitken-Cade, L. J. W. Keller, R. O. Stockil, R. Williamson, J. Gaunt, C. A. Aitken and a Marandellas farmer called Winston Field.

On 21 February in the Federal Assembly L'Ange spoke to his motion, castigating the Government for its secrecy and poor public relations throughout the whole affair. He had thought that the competitive price both of the construction and the product had been the reason for the choice of Kariba. He could not accept that a rise from £55 000 000 to £78 000 000 was to be expected. It seemed that the first price had been a pure fabrication to secure the choice of Kariba. He said that the least he had expected was for Malvern to recall Parliament instead of merely issuing a terse statement.

Barrow replied that the original price had never been more than an estimate. Since then further examination had revealed that a greater flow of water could be expected because the evaporation rate would be less than predicted. As a result the annual output would be 7 650 000 000 kilowatt hours compared with the original estimate of 6 500 000 000. An arch dam would replace the arch gravity dam and the two power stations would be built underground. The complexity of the calculations were such that they were only completed in December 1955, and the combined operating cost had only been known the week before. The current figures were still only estimates, as the final ones depended on loan negotiations and the placing of contracts. However, great care had been taken to be as accurate as possible. The Government had hesitated over the matter of making a bald statement on the costs before a detailed analysis was ready because it did not want to mislead the public. The leak of the cost, Barrow said, had created the situation which the Government had hoped to avoid.

[68] *Ibid.*, 43/*Malvern*, Welensky to Malvern, 12 November 1955; FGC(55), 49th Meeting, Minute 4, Federal Cabinet, 6 December 1955; *Northern News*, 30 November 1955.
[69] Welensky Papers, FGC(56), 5th Meeting, Minute 8, Federal Cabinet, 31 January 1956.
[70] *Ibid.*, 6th Meeting, Minutes 2 & 3, Federal Cabinet, 7 February 1956.

Barrow did not satisfy van Eeden, V. T. Joyce, Scott or Moffat who all dwelt on the bitterness of their fellow Northern Rhodesians, the failure of Malvern to recall Parliament, and the viability of the scheme. Van Eeden, condemning the timidity of L'Ange's motion, demanded an end to Kariba.

Macintyre thereupon detailed the sources of the money and claimed that Kariba, despite its cost, would produce cheaper power than would any other means. Welensky said that Kariba had to be continued lest there be a catastrophic loss of confidence in the Federation at home and, more important, abroad. Anyway, to propose to reject it before the International Bank had reported was particularly asinine. He recalled that Malvern had warned that the estimates would have to be revised.

Malvern maintained that power was the fundamental of all development. If Kariba were cancelled, an alternative would have to be found. The increase in the cost was due to the redesigning of the dam but also covered the Kariba village to house the construction workers and the transmission lines to distribute the power. The House, Malvern felt, ought to realise that the International Bank would also be influenced by political stability.

Nevertheless, Yamba, Kakumbi and Chirwa joined the established chorus clamouring for at least the suspension of the scheme. Doig, too, wanted to be reassured that other development would not be adversely affected. Scott expected the Federal Government to "bulldoze" the scheme through at any price, while L'Ange, when closing the debate on 15 March, remained convinced that the original estimation had been a hoax. Van Eeden could only raise five others to support his amendment, and it was lost. L'Ange's motion was accepted.[71]

The Kariba issue would further excite its opponents and partisans, but it was the issues of the franchise, the enlargement of the Federal Assembly, and the status of the Federation which would wreak greater damage to the relationship between the Federal and Northern Rhodesian Governments and engender resistance from the British Government.

[71] Fed R & N *Debates* (Salisbury), Vol. 5, Col. 1930, 21 February 1956.

CHAPTER SEVENTEEN

Malvern's Last Act

The First Bid for Federal Independence and the Franchise Tug of War, March–October 1956

SIMULTANEOUSLY with the closing stages of the Kariba debate, Malvern wrote to Lord Home, giving the latest verdict of his Government on the franchise issue. However, perhaps encouraged by Lord Salisbury's message to Lord Llewellin on the likelihood that the constitutional review could be earlier because of the rapid constitutional advances elsewhere in Africa, Malvern now asked for the Federation to be made independent within the Commonwealth.[1] This request, combined with recent statements on the desirability of dominion status and the apparent eagerness of the Federal Government to secure all power possible, aroused the gravest suspicions in the minds of the northern officials. It seemed to them that the dreaded spectre of amalgamation again stalked abroad.

On 12 March Malvern publicly stated that his Government would frame a franchise which would give the Africans an increasing share in government to keep pace with their efforts at advancing themselves. Nevertheless, he allayed fears of racial domination by saying that they would never acquire more than an equal share of the partnership.[2] Then he informed Home that the current Federal Constitution could not realise his aim of keeping government in civilised hands while at the same time eliminating racial representation and encouraging party, rather than racial, divisions. The territorial franchises, being too exclusive, would deny the African the vote for a long time. There was special representation, but the African could not be expected to remain content with that when voting systems were being introduced all over Africa. The solution was to introduce a wholly elective system in the form of a dual roll. The upper roll would elect the ordinary MPs, and the lower roll the special representatives. This would require a constitutional amendment but,

[1] Welensky Papers, 20/1, ff. 290–293, Lord Malvern to Lord Home, 12 March 1956; 24/198, ff. 67–68, Lord Llewellin to Welensky, 1 February 1956.
[2] *The Rhodesia Herald*, 13 March 1956.

in any case, one was necessary to enlarge the Federal Assembly to allow the two-party system to operate properly, and thereby eliminate racialism. There was also a need to reduce the current over-large constituencies. By this means, Malvern maintained, all aspirations would be met, but government would remain in civilised hands. The next Federal general election was due in 1958 and thus reform should be effected in 1956.

In addition Malvern warned that, if the Federation was not elevated in status to match the impending independence of the Gold Coast, Nigeria and Malaya, grave political consequences would ensue and stability could well be lost. He was aware of the British difficulties over this and thus did not propose to eliminate the safeguards, but would merely incorporate them in a treaty with Britain. This would allow the Federation to claim to be independent. Any other constitutional amendments would be effected in the established way. He would not interfere with the allocation of powers between the Governments, because it would be considered at the review in 1960. Malvern proposed to discuss this with Home during the Prime Ministers' Conference in June in London. Perhaps wishing to leave this contentious issue for Malvern, Welensky, who was *en route* to the United States of America, met Home and Lennox-Boyd in London, but only discussed the dual roll. Welensky warned that there would be great difficulty in getting the Federal Party and Government to allow the enfranchisement of British Protected Persons without a change in their status. The British Ministers replied that they could nevertheless not condone the withholding of the vote from them.

However, Home had found a compromise. This was that any British Protected Person who took the prescribed oath of loyalty should be given the vote and all the rights and obligations, but not the status, of a Federal citizen. The oath of loyalty, after all, Home argued, was something on which the Federal Ministers had laid considerable stress. Welensky found merit in this and proposed that it should be evaluated by the inter-government committee which had been formed to devise the Federal franchise. Lennox-Boyd immediately cabled the northern Governors to have this done.

Home warned that the dual roll proposal contradicted certain matters which, at the inception of the Federation, had seemed very important. It was possible, he thought, to effect amendments to the Constitution before the review but they would have to be acceptable to the British Parliament. He agreed that, if the electorate as a whole chose the African special representatives, moderates would be returned, but this would only be criticised in Britain. Furthermore, the European could not participate in the election of the African special representatives when British Protected Persons were denied the vote. Any "B" roll could not be dominated by Europeans, and special representation had to be retained until the African membership of the "B" roll was sufficient to return six African MPs in open elections. Theoretically, Home felt, the three European special representatives of African interests should be replaced by Africans but that would make the membership of the African Affairs Board entirely African and harm its efficiency.[3]

[3] Welensky Papers, 23/6, ff. 8–10, Home to Malvern, 23 March 1956.

Home informed Malvern of all this, but before Malvern could reply, the Dominion Party published its franchise proposals on the day — 27 March — before it narrowly won the Sebakwe by-election. It also chose a dual roll. There would be a common roll and an African roll to elect the six African special representatives. The three European special representatives would be elected by the two rolls voting together. For the African aspiring to the common roll, there would be more stringent standards than for the European. He would need ten testimonials from registered voters and a statement from a native commissioner or magistrate declaring that he had been living a civilised life for a number of years, had been educated to understand liberal democracy and was of good repute. In addition he might have to appear before a court of five referees who could vote by secret ballot on his acceptability. Two adverse votes would be sufficient for rejection.[4]

When Malvern replied, he commented that, if Home feared the swamping of the "B" roll by Europeans, the seats could be reserved for Africans for a decade. The African Affairs Board, Malvern thought, was useless and would be better served by nine Africans, or 18 if the size of the House was doubled. This would allow men like Moffat to hold a portfolio rather than be wasted in a task which was not appreciated by either race.

Malvern preferred to press his case for limited independence for the Federation. He expected the British to make difficulties over the clause in the Constitution's preamble which allowed dominion status only when the majority of the inhabitants desired it. However, he claimed, this had only been inserted to assure the Southern Rhodesians that such promotion was possible. It did not prescribe a plebiscite. Indeed, it was undesirable because the Constitution had rendered it impossible to gain the loyalty of the northern Africans. The Federal Government had been divorced from the Africans who were governed by people who owed their loyalty to the British Government. Consequently the African looked to Britain and not to the Federation. Furthermore, the African political organisations would certainly ensure that any expression of African opinion would be hostile to the Federal Government.

Malvern also predicted that the British Government would say that all major constitutional changes were reserved for the review. The Constitution, he explained, had been designed in response to the northern Government's fear that too much power would be given to the Federal Government, and the "freezing" of the legislative lists had been a product of this. The intention, nevertheless, was not to block any constitutional advance. Malvern felt that undue emphasis was being laid on the wording of the Constitution and this was an effect of the British ministerial and civil service changes in office since the Federal Constitutional Conferences.[5]

A month would pass before Malvern again pressed his case. Although in that time there were worrying reports from the Federal security services, at least Malvern could announce that the International Bank had approved the Kariba loan. However, the Nyasaland elections in late March, forced him to make a statement on secession. The appointment by the Governor, after

[4] *The Rhodesia Herald*, 28 March 1956.
[5] Welensky Papers, 23/6, ff. 11–12, Malvern to Home, 5 April 1956.

selection by the African Protectorate Council, of D. N. Kwenje, M. W. K. Chiume, H. B. Chipembere, D. W. Chijozi and J. R. N. Chinyama brought militant African nationalism into the Nyasaland Legislative Council. Secession, the Federal officials expected, would become their prime demand and events would prove them right. The Nyasaland African Congress lost no time in not only proclaiming its triumph but in stating that it had always been understood that federation had been accepted on a trial basis and that it could be terminated if it proved unacceptable. There was no appreciable effect when Malvern immediately proclaimed that, to the contrary, the Federation was indissoluble. As there was no constitutional provision for a termination, he explained, this could only be effected by force or, with the unanimous agreement of all the contracting parties, by a British Act of Parliament. It had been made perfectly clear at the outset that there would be no trial period and that the territories had committed themselves irrevocably. The purpose of the review, Malvern stated, was not to ask the partners if they wished to stay in the Federation, but to iron out the imperfections of the Constitution as it had been framed somewhat hastily. Nonetheless, the Constitution could, and was being made to, work.

The Congress might have gained a sizeable foothold in the Nyasaland Legislative Council but, like Nkumbula and Kaunda, J. F. Sangala, the president of the Congress, and one of his aides, T. D. T. Banda, were found guilty of possessing seditious literature.

The Northern Rhodesian ANC had not been presented with the opportunity of an election, but was determined to secure recognition as the only true representative of African opinion. The ANC was encouraged by Commander T. Fox-Pitt, then of the Movement for Colonial Freedom, who not only advised the ANC to seek a change in the Northern Rhodesian Constitution that year, but also publicly condemned the refusal of the Northern Rhodesian Government to recognise the ANC as the mouthpiece of the Africans. The Federal authorities discovered that the Northern Rhodesian nationalists were also being advised by the Fabian Colonial Bureau, the Africa Bureau, the Anti-Slavery Society and the Commonwealth office of the Labour Party.

The ANC embarked on a campaign of boycotts in Lusaka, designed to demonstrate its power, and threatened to extend it to Livingstone. The Federal Government noted that Kaunda was increasingly taking the lead. The question of African advancement continued to provoke controversy and, indeed, there was a strike over it by white miners at Mufulira.

Southern Rhodesian African nationalism remained far more politically dormant. European politicians, notably H. H. C. Holderness of the United Rhodesia Party, believed the reason was because the African could achieve political satisfaction through the common roll there. The branches of the northern Congresses in Southern Rhodesia might have been attracting more public attention, but significant steps were being taken at an organisational level by local activists. Young nationalists, like James Chikerema, Edson Sithole and George Nyandoro, with the assistance of the Nyasalander, Dundusa Chisiza, formed the African National Youth League to inject vigour into Southern Rhodesian African politics. They did so, it was reported, with some resistance from Advocate Herbert Chitepo, Stanlake Samkange and the Southern Rhodesian African National Congress.[6]

The Federal franchise was not the only one to be examined as in February the Southern Rhodesian Government had announced that its franchise would be reviewed by a judicial commission. On 19 April Sir Robert Tredgold, the Chief Justice of the Federation, and Sir Charles Cumings, the former Chief Justice of the Sudan, were appointed to the Commission.[7]

The inter-government committee on the franchise met in April and submitted its first and very inconclusive report to the Federal Cabinet on 5 May. The committee explained how its Northern Rhodesian members had resisted change in the method of returning the nine special representatives, but their Federal counterparts thought that the northern Governments should adopt the Southern Rhodesian method as a *quid pro quo* for the British Protected Persons being enfranchised on the common roll. Alternatively the African Representative or Provincial Councils might sit with the Legislative Council as an electoral college. There was some support for the Northern Rhodesian variant of the dual roll but none for their insistence that the European special representatives should be nominated. Indeed as the Southern Rhodesian special representative was already elected, it was seen as retrogressive. None of the committee could decide whether the special representatives were still needed.[8]

On 10 May Malvern wrote to Home again on the independence issue, enclosing drafts of a proposed Anglo-Federal treaty and a bill which would give the Federation independence in the same manner as Ceylon. The Federal Constitution would have to be amended and the safeguards written unchanged into the treaty. The only casualty would be the African Affairs Board which, because it had never drawn attention to any "differentiating" measures, Malvern considered superfluous. He would replace it by an undertaking in the treaty not to differentiate between the races, or by a body within Parliament with specific functions. He mainly disliked the African Affairs Board because it had impeded contact between the Federal Cabinet and the African MPs. He pointed out that the safeguards otherwise had been inserted *in toto* into the draft treaty. Everything depended on the good faith of the Federal Government, but that was assured. Malvern was confident of convincing the Federal electorate that, by this means, complete independence had been secured. Yet the position of the northern territories would not be affected. He concluded by saying that any controversy over the northern protected status could be settled later.

The bill provided that no British Act passed thereafter would affect the laws of the Federation unless the Federal Government expressly requested or consented to it. The British Government would bear no responsibility for the Federation. The Colonial Laws Validity Act of 1865 would cease to apply to Federal legislation, and the latter would no longer be void if it was repugnant to British law. British Acts would not repeal Federal laws. The treaty would prevent the Royal Assent being given to any Federal bill which proposed to

[6] *Ibid.*, 19/28, ff. 74–79, FISB Report, 22 March 1956; 19/33, f. 18, Security Review, 18 April 1956; *The Rhodesia Herald*, 14 & 23 April 1956.
[7] *The Rhodesia Herald*, 20 April 1956.
[8] Welensky Papers, FGC(56), 16th Meeting, Minute 2, Federal Cabinet, 2 May 1956.

amend Articles 9 to 13, 33, 40 (2), 44 or 47 of the Federal Constitution until the British Government had been consulted. The same restriction would apply to bills which differentiated between the races. If the British Government objected to any Federal legislation which appeared to conflict with the treaty, the Federal Government would have to obtain its agreement. The Federation would have to observe the conventions of the Commonwealth with regard to foreign affairs and accordingly would be bound by the principles of the Imperial Conferences from 1923 to 1926. The Federal Government would also undertake to convene a review conference between 1960 and 1962.[9]

While the British Government digested Malvern's message, A. D. Evans, as chairman of the inter-government committee, suggested that the Federal Government should inform the committee that a bill would soon be introduced to confer local citizenship on those British Protected Persons who swore an oath to undertake the duties of a Federal citizen. This was Home's compromise and, in any case, the only disagreement over citizenship within the committee was the oath and its form.

The franchise issue, Evans warned, was not as far advanced and could not be enacted until early 1957. The committee, nevertheless, had rejected a Southern Rhodesian suggestion to wait for the Tredgold Commission's recommendations because they would not be ready in time and might be inappropriate. Evans thought that the Federal Government should seek as much agreement as possible and then decide on the franchise, and inform the territories accordingly. He opposed the retention of racial representation because the consequences would be drastic.

The committee had examined the alteration of the methods of appointing the special representatives. It was possible but not likely that the northern Governments might, of their own accord, effect an improvement. Thus the committee had also suggested that the special representatives might become the "B" roll MPs in a wholly elective system. They could be elected by the "A" and "B" rolls voting together, or by the "B" roll and a percentage of the "A" roll.

Seeking further guidelines, Evans said the committee needed to know whether the European special representatives would be elected or nominated, and whether the British Protected Person would qualify for the vote without first securing citizenship or taking an oath of allegiance. The majority of the committee preferred that the British Protected Person should not be burdened with any more than anyone else and that any oath should apply to all. It was a way to secure their loyalty, but it could merely increase apathy towards voters' registration. Finally, the committee wanted to know whether the Federal Assembly would be enlarged and if there would be a second chamber because that could resolve many difficulties over the African Affairs Board.[10]

At the meeting of the committee on 16 May, all the territorial representatives rejected most forcibly the obligation of British Protected Persons to

[9] *Ibid.*, 23/6, ff. 13–14, Malvern to Home, 10 May 1956; 7/2, f. 314, same to same, 10 May 1956; f. 317, Draft of the Rhodesia and Nyasaland Independence Act, 1956.
[10] *Ibid.*, FGC, 87/56, Memorandum by A. D. Evans, 11 May 1956.

swear any oath in order to be enfranchised. The Southern Rhodesians thought that it was illogical to distinguish between British Protected Persons and British subjects born in the Federation, while the northerners argued that oaths were alien to African customs and could be counter-productive. At worst a boycott might be provoked, and it was pointless to press for something which might be resented. In response the Federal representatives proposed, therefore, that citizenship be conferred on all "belongers" who lacked British subject status. The committee agreed that the British Government needed to be reminded of the unique position of the Federation in this regard, but the Federal representatives insisted that the oath for British Protected Persons be retained. The committee decided that British Protected Persons should become British subjects by registration rather than naturalisation, and that any oath would merely declare allegiance.

The committee considered electing the special representatives through electoral colleges which would include the European and African common roll voters in addition to the Members of the Legislative, African Representative, Protectorate, Provincial and Town Councils. The northern representatives disliked the involvement of so many Europeans and, in any case, believed that the Africans hated electoral colleges. The committee agreed that the problem should be studied further.

While the committee as a whole accepted the franchise qualifications, its Northern Rhodesian members wanted the points system reconsidered so that people should not be disqualified by only educational and income criteria. They were apprehensive about the increase in the size of the Assembly because they believed the number of Southern Rhodesian seats should not equal those of the northern territories. They insisted that special representation should be maintained until there were enough Africans on the "A" roll to protect their interests. The committee agreed that a second chamber was not a practical proposition at the moment.[11]

The Federal Cabinet accepted that there was merit in giving citizenship to all "belongers", but that Home's compromise was equally attractive because it could be argued that, as the British Protected Person would have local citizenship, the Europeans should have a say in the election of the northern special representatives.[12]

Benson did not leave matters entirely to his representatives, and informed the Federal Government of his plans for the reform of the Northern Rhodesian Constitution, which included a dual roll, but with cross-voting between the rolls on a fractional basis. Thus, in the election of an "A" roll candidate, a fraction of the "B" roll votes cast would count and *vice versa* for the "B" roll candidate.[13]

As Benson was writing to the Federal Department of Home Affairs, he naturally did not reveal his concern about Federal intentions. There is no reason to doubt the seriousness with which Welensky, for one, viewed the political prospects if the Gold Coast, as had just been announced, would

[11] *Ibid.*, 9/3, ff. 11–18, Second Interim Report of the Inter-Government Committee on Citizenship and Franchise, 16 & 17 May 1956.
[12] *Ibid.*, FGC(56), 19th Meeting, Minute 11, Federal Cabinet, 22 May 1956.
[13] *Ibid.*, 9/6, f. 60, Benson to F. L. Finnie, 18 May 1956.

receive its independence when any steps towards that were denied to the Federation.[14] However, there is no hint in Federal Cabinet records of ambitions quite as Benson saw them. He would appear to Federal eyes to be overly and mistakenly suspicious, and certainly the facts so far revealed do not seem to support the case which he would make in a lengthy warning to Lennox-Boyd on 6 June of what he diagnosed Malvern's true intentions to be.

This dispatch would have a traumatic effect on the relationship between Benson and the Federal Government. Benson wrote unguardedly because he could not know that someone in the Colonial Office would pass his secret dispatch to Lord Home who would in turn transmit it to Malvern and later to Welensky. Benson was naturally outraged when he discovered six months later what had happened. He was even more appalled when he found that several copies had been made and that even Lord Llewellin had received one.

When Benson wrote on 6 June, Malvern was in London but, as he would only discuss the Constitution with Home and Lennox-Boyd on 15 June, Benson was in time to undermine Malvern. Benson recalled the persistent British refusal to permit amalgamation and alleged that, although Malvern had accepted the Central African Council in 1945, he had remained determined to amalgamate. Therefore, Malvern had set out to reveal its inadequacy and to hamstring it, through the Southern Rhodesian possession of coal and virtual control of the railways, to prove the need for a political union. While doing this, Malvern had not bothered to disguise his desire for amalgamation. Eventually pressure from within the Rhodesias and the financial straits of Southern Rhodesia, after heavy spending on what Benson called extravagant capital projects, forced Malvern to consider federation. Nevertheless, Benson claimed that Malvern had told him on the eve of the Officials' Conference in 1951 that nothing could be produced which would satisfy Southern Rhodesians because they would not allow their freedom of action to be curbed in any way.

When the Federation came into being, Benson asserted, it was the territorial Governments which set to work with a will to make it succeed. Malvern and the Federal Government, by contrast, were determined to see it fail. Evidence of this was a public description of the Federal Constitution by Malvern as "shocking", and in an official dispatch as "impossible". The reason was that Malvern saw the Federation as a springboard to amalgamation, and confirmation of this was to be found, said Benson, in a comment by P. F. Brereton of the Nyasaland Federal Party that, "off the record", the Federal Government was intending to federalise everything possible to facilitate amalgamation.

Benson believed that, while the Southern Rhodesian electorate had always been willing to absorb the North, the Northern Rhodesians favoured federation but would have hesitated to amalgamate. The northern motive was to thwart the desire of the Colonial Office to hand over power eventually to the Africans, and, exploiting this, the Federal Party had swept to power in the Federal and territorial elections.

Benson alleged that the subsequent actions of the Federal Government had

[14] *Ibid.*, 24/198, ff. 63–65, Welensky to Llewellin, 1 June 1956.

confirmed Brereton's statement and, ignoring the strictures of the lack of staff and money, it had set out to take over as much as possible. By mid-1954, it had confronted the territorial Governments with a flood of bills seeking to assume their powers. These arrived two, three or at most six days before they were to be introduced in the Federal Assembly, leaving no time for the preparation of views. Protests drew apologies but no action.

As Benson was referring to subjects which had been placed on the Federal exclusive list, it is difficult to see why he thought that there was anything to say about their handover. The Federal Cabinet was certainly surprised at Benson's protests, and its view was that perhaps his Government was reluctant to see part of its structure dismantled. He demanded an explanation from Malvern and was somewhat curtly told that opinion was not being sought and that the bills were being sent merely to have their drafting checked.

Benson claimed in his dispatch that, by the end of August 1954, it was apparent that the territorial and Federal interpretations of the concurrent list were very different. The Northern Rhodesian Government, he said, had certainly not expected the Federal Government to assume most of the concurrent subjects. In the course of this second bid for power, Welensky had suggested the creation of a statutory corporation to build and maintain all roads in the Federation. However, Benson said he had opposed it, not because he suspected any ulterior motive yet, but because centralisation would not improve the roads. The Federal Government had then boldly tried to take over the Public Works Department which had a building capacity of £6 000 000 and was a major contributor to the development of Northern Rhodesia. The Northern Rhodesian Government had responded by suggesting that a working party should study the implications. This was appointed, but the Northern Rhodesian representatives were considerably taken aback when all it discussed was a handover. Thereafter, extreme pressure was exerted by the Federal Government until finally, in March 1956, Benson related, he had written to Malvern to tell him that his Government would not submit.

As a result of the Federal influence on the Northern Rhodesian Federal Party, however, Benson told how the Northern Rhodesian Government had been unable to prevent the federalisation of European agriculture, although he had refused to part with animal health on the argument that the bugs that bit the tribal animals were the same that attacked those of the European.

Recently, Benson alleged, the Federal Government had embarked on a more subtle campaign, using inter-governmental committees headed by Federal chairmen, to influence territorial policy by proclaiming, for example, the necessity for a standardised labour policy. This, if accepted, would have an obvious effect on Northern Rhodesian efforts to advance the African.

Benson claimed that Greenfield had tried to diminish the influence of English Law — the code in the northern territories — by trying to pack the Federal bench with Roman-Dutch judges. However, Benson and Colby had thwarted him through the influence of their Chief Justices on Sir Robert Tredgold, the Federal Chief Justice.

Greenfield recalls that, in choosing judges, both Sir Robert Tredgold and H. J. Clayden (later Sir John), a judge whom Greenfield had recruited from

South Africa, had possessed the qualifications to work in Roman-Dutch as well as English Law. For a third judge, Greenfield had sought the assistance of Lord Kilmuir, the Lord Chancellor. Greenfield wanted an English barrister, but Kilmuir pressed him to accept a Scottish advocate who was equally qualified in Scottish and English Law. The Scot was quite acceptable to Tredgold, but he thought that the two northern Chief Justices should be consulted first. They opposed this appointment. In the event, shortly afterwards the Scot, for other reasons, withdrew his candidacy. Greenfield thereupon chose a Northern Rhodesian judge, Sir Arthur Lewey.

Benson, concluding his dispatch, quoted a recent speech of Welensky in which he claimed that two-thirds of the affairs of Northern Rhodesia were the responsibility of the Federal Government and that, in consequence, the British Government would soon realise that the Federal Constitution had to be amended before the review. This, to Benson, exactly matched the tactics which Malvern had been applying for the last 20 years. Benson had discovered that Malvern was seeking to transfer the safeguards to a treaty, and warned that the Federal Government intended to be independent before the Gold Coast. The British Government could not allow this to happen, but it was still necessary to warn Lennox-Boyd that Malvern's determination to achieve amalgamation remained unshaken, that he was paying only lip-service to federation, and that he would treat the "solemn" preamble as no more than a "scrap of paper".[15]

The furore over Benson's dispatch was months away, but the most immediate effect was felt in the coming negotiations when Malvern would discover that the Colonial Office was convinced that he was intent on amalgamation.

While Benson was thus warning Lennox-Boyd, Greenfield reported to Welensky that Todd had told him that two-tier citizenship would merely perpetuate the idea that any privileges were reserved for the Europeans. Todd's Government also opposed a dual roll and remained convinced of the need for high franchise qualifications. It felt that a lower roll voter would soon consider that he should be able to vote for anyone.

More surprisingly, as he had been chairman of the franchise committee, Greenfield agreed with the Southern Rhodesian verdict. He felt it was time to debate these issues in the Caucus to still the criticism of the paucity of information and to end the lack of unanimity within the Federal Party. Todd had also told Greenfield that their Parties would have to become more closely associated, particularly if a territorial by-election at Gwelo was to be won.[16] Nothing was done about this and, for whatever reason, the new Dominion Party won the seat.

Welensky passed Greenfield's report to Malvern, while informing him that the ANC-inspired boycott of shops had been renewed on the Copperbelt, and that the general tension in Northern Rhodesia made him all the more concerned about the current closing of rural police stations. Ten days later, on 18

[15] R. S. Hall, *Zambia* (London, 1965), p. 164; D. C. Mulford, *Zambia: The Politics of Independence, 1957–1964* (London, 1967), p. 51; Author's interview with Sir Arthur Benson; Photo-copy of Benson's Dispatch to Lennox-Boyd, 6 June 1956, in the possession of Sir Roy Welensky; J. M. Greenfield, *Testimony of a Rhodesian Federal* (Bulawayo, 1978), p. 141.
[16] Welensky Papers, 9/6, f. 64, Greenfield to Welensky, 7 June 1956.

June, he wrote that the situation was such that he had been forced to dissuade the Northern Rhodesian Federal Party from demanding the proscription of the ANC.[17]

Tempers, indeed, were raw. On 10 May the collapse of a trench in Kitwe had buried alive two Africans and had resulted in a small crowd demanding a reciprocal burial of two Europeans. On the same day in Nkana a European engine driver was threatened with death when two Africans fell off his train. The boycott of shops was proving effective and the Federal officials feared that the ANC might try to instigate industrial action as Nkumbula was reported to have told his executive that the current aim was to extricate Northern Rhodesia from the Federation by the disruption of the economy. It was also to force the Indian and European traders out of business and out of the country and to demonstrate that he, Nkumbula, was still a force to be reckoned with, even though the Colonial Secretary had refused to meet him recently in London. Nkumbula quoted a statement by Dr Kwame Nkrumah of the Gold Coast that self-government would never be achieved by non-violent means.[18] The ANC also instigated a boycott of European fish traders on Lake Mweru and had in fact driven several of them away. Thus it was not surprising that the Europeans should have demanded strong action and should have criticised the Northern Rhodesian Government's reluctance to act, for its prosecution of the small fry while Nkumbula and Kaunda remained free to do as they pleased. The arrival from England of Doris Lessing, the celebrated Rhodesian novelist, and a Paul Hogarth, was interpreted by the Federal authorities as a sign that the Communists were taking an interest in Federal affairs because these two visited local Communists as well as prominent African nationalists.[19]

Malvern had gone to Britain believing that the Constitution's preamble had been phrased in such a way that the British Government would concede independence if the Federal electorate indicated a preference for it. If this seems impossibly naïve, at least this is what he told Welensky. Welensky, for his part, wanted a package deal, rather than a piecemeal settlement, to settle the issues of the franchise and citizenship as well as granting independence. His prime concern was that the Federation should not be considered inferior to the Gold Coast.[20]

Thinking thus, Malvern began his negotiations when dining on 14 June with Lord Home, Alan Lennox-Boyd, Lord Salisbury, Alan Noble, the Parliamentary Under-Secretary of State for Commonwealth Relations, and Lord Llewellin. The British Ministers could see no insuperable difficulties with regard to the franchise and citizenship, and felt that the advance towards independence of the Gold Coast and the Sudan altered the position *vis-à-vis* the status of the Federation. Nevertheless, they felt it would be difficult to advance the date of the review.

[17] *Ibid.*, 43/*Malvern*, Welensky to Malvern, 8 June 1956; same to same, 18 June 1956.

[18] *Ibid.*, 19/28, f. 91, B. M. de Quehen to Welensky, 14 May 1956.

[19] *Ibid.*, f. 79, Sitrep, 11 May 1956; f. 91, FISB visit to Northern Rhodesia, 14 May 1956, *New Statesman and Nation*, 9 June 1956.

[20] Welensky Papers, 24/198, ff. 63–65, Welensky to Llewellin, 1 June 1956; ff. 54–58, Llewellin to Welensky, 14 June 1956; ff. 51–53, Welensky to Llewellin, 20 June 1956.

Malvern and Llewellin countered by predicting that by 1960 the Labour Party might be in power and that the actions of Aneurin Bevan and James Griffiths might prompt the Federation to declare its independence unilaterally. Malvern and Llewellin claimed that this need not happen because there was still time to grant the Federation some constitutional advance before the Gold Coast independence was ratified in 1957. However, Llewellin doubted whether the Federation could be independent if two-thirds of its territory were controlled by the Colonial Office. The British Ministers agreed. Yet, Llewellin warned, every political party in the Federation had the achievement of dominion status as its major goal and if some constitutional advance was not granted very soon, the Federal Government might find itself unable to govern. As if to prove the first point, three days later, Welensky publicly declared that dominion status would be achieved very soon.

At the dinner, Malvern and Llewellin wore Lennox-Boyd down until he agreed that possibly the Federal review could be held sooner because of the new situation created by the Gold Coast. Any revision of the Constitution, of course, would need to have the support of the Federal and territorial legislatures. Llewellin asked what role the northern officials would play in this process, but was somewhat mystified when Lennox-Boyd replied that they would be ordered neither to support nor to oppose any changes. When he heard of this, Welensky was infuriated and blamed such attitudes for many of his problems. Although Llewellin found the undertaking in the preamble ridiculous, all the British Ministers expressed a determination not to renege on it. Nonetheless, he and Malvern concluded that a plebiscite might be acceptable. Thus Llewellin advised the Federal Government to legislate on citizenship as soon as possible but to postpone finalising the franchise because there was little point in enfranchising people who might oppose further steps to independence.[21]

If Malvern thought that he had made some progress, he was in for a rude shock as, on the morrow, he was told by Home and Lennox-Boyd that the earliest the review could be held was 1960 and that change was impossible before then. Furthermore, they could not understand how Malvern thought that the Federation could be independent while the Colonial Office continued to administer two of its territories. Certainly, it could not aspire to full membership of the Commonwealth.

Malvern replied that he was not seeking to change the distribution of powers before 1960 but that the Federation could not slip behind the Gold Coast in status because the Federal electorate might consequently return in 1958 a government which could not maintain stability. He was only asking for complete control of external affairs so that the Federation could be termed self-governing. As every Party had proclaimed the aim of achieving dominion status, the Europeans could not be persuaded that no immediate steps could be taken towards that goal. Southern Rhodesia after all had been promised that its prospects of becoming a dominion would not be dimmed by federation, but now the British Government said that this was impossible unless the northern territories changed their status. Yet, Malvern noted, the status

[21] *Ibid.*, ff. 54–58, Llewellin to Welensky, 14 June 1956; *The Rhodesia Herald*, 18 June 1956.

of the Canadian and Australian colonies had not prevented their federations from becoming dominions.

Having been slightly misleading, Malvern should not have been surprised when Home and Lennox-Boyd could not understand how Southern Rhodesia could become a dominion and yet remain in the Federation. Lennox-Boyd acknowledged that the only obstacle to advancing the review was that African opinion was unlikely to be won over, and the preamble demanded that any change in status had to be acceptable to the majority, and the majority was African. In the Gold Coast there was no doubt of the support of the majority. Home advised Malvern to win African support by devising liberal formulae for franchise and citizenship. However, Malvern felt that such support would not be won until the Federal Government was given some contact with the African.[22]

Benson's dispatch had had a telling effect because Malvern reported from London to Welensky that the Colonial Office believed that they were intent on amalgamation. Malvern expected that the status of the territories would be ultimately reduced and that they would get lieutenant-governors, but he avowed that he had renounced amalgamation when he had accepted federation. He had realised that Southern Rhodesia would never become a dominion until South Africa absorbed Swaziland and Basutoland. Federation had offered another way to achieve full sovereignty. He felt it was necessary to kill the canard of his desire for amalgamation which Secretaries of State repeatedly threw at him.

After this meeting Malvern's principal private secretary, W. F. Nicholas, wrote to Greenfield that, while the British Government was likely to be prepared to amend the Constitution in an exceptional way, it had found insuperable difficulties in giving reciprocal Commonwealth citizenship, bearing the status of a British subject, to Federal citizens, some of whom would be British Protected Persons. Greenfield, however, disagreed that a departure from the general Commonwealth pattern was impossible. He favoured two-tier citizenship with the upper qualification having British subject status. As recognition by the Commonwealth was essential, Greenfield suggested to Welensky that Malvern should use the opportunity of the Prime Ministers' Conference to secure it.[23]

In a memorandum to Malvern, Home and Lennox-Boyd reiterated their difficulties with the preamble and stated that Malvern's proposals could only be considered in 1960. However, they were prepared to ask the Commonwealth Prime Ministers in 1957 if the Federal Prime Minister could attend their Conference by right instead of by invitation as was the current practice. They would also discuss with Malvern increasing Federal responsibilities with regard to exchanging high commissioners with the Commonwealth, joining more international organisations, receiving more information on foreign affairs, and allowing the Federal High Commissioner in London to attend all meetings between the Commonwealth Secretary and the Common-

[22] Welensky Papers, 23/6, ff. 37–42, Minutes of a Meeting, Commonwealth Relations Office, 15 June 1956.

[23] *Ibid.*, 43/*Malvern*, Malvern to Welensky, 18 June 1956; 8/111, ff. 160–161, Greenfield to Welensky, 18 June 1956.

wealth High Commissioners. They might also allow the Federal Assembly to legislate extra-territorially in certain circumstances. If events took a different course, the position would be reviewed.[24]

Still in London, Malvern replied in familiar vein on June 21 claiming that he had understood, when accepting federation, that it could be independent even when the Colonial Office retained a degree of control in the North. He warned that the Federal Party might force the issue by passing a constitutional amendment bill to remove the reservations. If the British Government disallowed the bill, the Federal Government would resign. He denied that he sought amalgamation or the advancement of the review. It seemed wrong, however, to have made the Constitution flexible and then to bar all amendment because of a provision for a review. He would not accept that everything depended on the whim of the majority, because his Government had to keep power in civilised hands, and for a long time these would be in the minority.

Malvern had been urged to win African support, but he reminded Home and Lennox-Boyd that the European was equally important and seemed to be swinging to the right because it appeared that too much was being done for the African. The performance of the Africans in Parliament had confirmed that their election had been premature. He expected the swing to the right to intensify with the granting of independence to the Gold Coast. It would force him to raise immediately the issue of constitutional advancement. Indeed, he claimed to have been forced to reveal his intentions publicly to avert a full-scale independence campaign being mounted.

Malvern maintained that 1960 was too late for the review because by then the Federal Government and a Labour Government could be in open conflict. He dismissed, too, a British suggestion that he should consult the territories, because their powers would be unaffected. His electorate would only feel betrayed if he were invited to attend the Commonwealth Prime Ministers' Conference by right when they believed that, after 20 years of participating in the Conference, he possessed that right. The other concessions were hardly acceptable because the Federal Government did not want to exchange high commissioners, its supply of information on foreign affairs was adequate, and he could not think of a single subject on which his Government would want to legislate extra-territorially.

As these interim proposals would not appeal to his electorate, Malvern preferred to reject them, leaving himself free to force the issue with a constitutional amendment bill. He urged the British Government to reconsider granting independence to the Federation despite the continuing presence of the Colonial administration. It should acknowledge that he was not seeking a review, or amalgamation, or any change in the status of the British Protected Person or a reduction of safeguards. At the review, Malvern did not want any examination of individual constitutions, Federal or otherwise. Finally, he urged the British Government to promote the Federation simultaneously with the Gold Coast because the Rhodesians would not accept a lesser status.[25]

[24] *Ibid.*, 23/6, f. 16, Memorandum: Provisional sequence of Events and Action to be taken relative to constitutional changes in the Federation of Rhodesia and Nyasaland, 18 June 1956.
[25] *Ibid.*, ff. 17-20, Malvern to Home, 21 June 1956.

Malvern, Home and Lennox-Boyd reviewed all this on the next day, 22 June. Malvern revealed that Professor Wheare, the Oxford expert on federations, had advised him at the outset that independence was possible despite the continuing presence of the Colonial Service, and this had persuaded him to embrace federation. Home had not known of this advice but nevertheless felt that the Federation could not be truly independent in these circumstances. Evidence of African support had to be produced.

When Malvern said that he could not influence African opinion, Lennox-Boyd pointed out that Malvern could reduce discrimination on the railways and in the post offices. He provoked Malvern to warn about white reaction. However, Malvern repeated that he had no designs on territorial powers. All he sought was for the Federation to be independent in its own field and be recognised as such in the Commonwealth. The latest British proposals, he felt, were certainly no solution.

Home argued that Malvern was only asking for a semblance of independence while risking severe African reaction and a political storm in Britain. He warned that, even if the British Government ignored the opposition and accepted Malvern's proposals, the new Commonwealth would reject them. Lennox-Boyd agreed that, as it was too early to seek full membership of the Commonwealth, it was pointless to risk a rebuff. Home suggested asking Wheare to clear up the matter of his advice to Malvern on independence. Home thought that the time to re-open these discussions was when the Gold Coast became independent.

Lennox-Boyd warned that the consequence of Malvern forcing independence could be a break-up of the Federation, but Malvern replied that economic necessity would prevent that.[26]

In a letter, Welensky provided Malvern that day with confirmation that no Party still aimed at amalgamation. He warned, however, that the independence issue was very much alive. He said he had tried in vain to keep the Federal Party off this subject and soon the Federal Government would be unable to ignore it. Malvern could certainly expect to be questioned on his return on the prospects of independence and it would be an issue in the general election. The Federal Government, Welensky maintained, could not accept a piecemeal settlement of the franchise and citizenship without any advance towards independence.[27]

He had not yet learnt that Todd had just attacked the Federal Party and Malvern by implication, again doing so when Malvern was abroad. Addressing the congress of his United Rhodesia Party at Gwelo, Todd urged the Federal Party to re-vitalise itself and increase immigration, curb the influence of the Colonial Office, speed up constitutional development and, in managing the economy, ignore the cost of Kariba. If all this were not done, then the URP would be forced to enter Federal politics in opposition. He would bitterly regret this, Todd said, because his objective was to produce a progressive, happy society. However, far from encouraging development, the Federal Government was hampering it. If it would do otherwise, the Parties would unite and Todd promised to throw his weight behind Welensky when he

[26] *Ibid.*, ff. 50–59, Minutes of a Meeting, Commonwealth Relations Office, 22 June 1956.
[27] *Ibid.*, 43/*Malvern*, Welensky to Malvern, 22 June 1956.

succeeded Malvern. Todd also attacked the three territorial African Congresses and the Colonial Office, describing the former as seditious because they were abusing the Constitution and working for the destruction of the Federation, while the Colonial Office stood by idly.[28]

Welensky immediately told the Press that he was not rejecting a fusion of the Parties but that he did not think Todd had assisted it. Welensky drew considerable support, even from R. A. Nicholson of the Northern Rhodesian Government, whom many thought led the opposition to federation among the northern officials. Todd quickly answered by criticising Welensky for replying so promptly instead of waiting for the Federal Party congress in September. Welensky, like others, concluded that Todd was bidding to succeed Malvern.[29]

In London on 25 June, Professor Wheare confirmed to Home, Lennox-Boyd and Malvern that he had not been misquoted. The key was the term "Federal Government". The Constitution's preamble specified that the Federation would go forward to full membership of the Commonwealth when the inhabitants so wished. This did not mean, Wheare said, that the Federal Government could not be regarded as self-governing in its own right and become a member of the Commonwealth. It was a constitutional possibility despite potential political difficulties. He had thought that the limitations on the Federal Government could have been removed at the review. He agreed that there were similarities between the Federation and Australia where the states had limited the authority of the Federal Government by leaving some power in British hands. The Colonial Laws Validity Act had applied to the states and not the Federal Government and it could be said that it was the Australian Federal Government which became the member of the Commonwealth. The maintenance of the power of disallowance for limited purposes was a side-door to admit the responsibilities of the Colonial Secretary.

To Home this was a large front door because the powers of the Colonial Secretary were considerable. Unless they were diminished, he could not see how the Federal Government could be considered independent even if it was a separate entity. Malvern had said that he was not seeking a review but, Home argued, what he did want would clearly prejudice it. There would be African and British opposition, and the abolition, for example, of the African Affairs Board would clearly dishonour parliamentary pledges. Wheare agreed that the realities should be faced and maintained that he had never thought that any changes should be made before 1960. Malvern replied that 1960 was too late. He found that Articles 97 and 98 allowed amendment of the Constitution before the review, but Wheare disagreed. In any case, Wheare argued, the prescribed concurrence of the African population would not be obtained.

Sir Gilbert Laithwaite, the Permanent Under-Secretary of State for Commonwealth Relations, thereupon proposed a variation of the Newfoundland formula under which the British Government would retain ultimate responsibility for African interests, but the Federation would be called a dominion even though it would not be recognised as such internationally. The danger in

[28] *The Rhodesia Herald*, 23 June 1956.

[29] *Ibid.*, 24 June 1956; Welensky Papers, 25/130, f. 3, R. A. Nicholson to Welensky, 25 June 1956; 28/104, f. 33, Dr M. Hirsch to Welensky, 25 June 1956.

this, he said, was that the entrenchment of the territorial powers would render the review in 1960 unnecessary.

Malvern warned that, before the Federal Party would accept anything, it had to be plain that an advance towards independence would be teamed with the settlement of the franchise and citizenship questions. Wheare and he then rambled on about ante-dating the review and answering Malvern's critics. Wheare thought that the Newfoundland formula might be the answer. He felt that the Africans might be placated if the Colonial Laws Validity Act applied to both the Federal and territorial Governments and suggested that the reservations should be kept in the Constitution as well as being mentioned in the proposed treaty. The treaty should be confirmed by an act of the Federal Parliament to give it local prestige. Malvern replied that the European would be singularly unimpressed.

Lennox-Boyd declared that he would decide what the reaction of the officials would be when the northern Legislative Councils were consulted about any proposals. He would, of course, require justification for supporting them, and advised that everything should be simplified so that the African could understand. Malvern explained that he had not yet consulted the territories because he wished first to know the reaction of Home and Lennox-Boyd. Finally he asked for his denial on amalgamation to be recorded.[30]

After the meeting that day, Malvern wrote to Home about dominion status, claiming they had agreed that, even though dominion status no longer really existed, a country still had first to be granted independence and then seek membership of the Commonwealth. His aim was to achieve the first. Thereafter, if the Commonwealth accepted the Federation as a full member despite the continuing British responsibility for the protectorates, the British Parliament could be merely informed of the promotion.[31]

Two days later, on 27 June, Welensky wrote to Lennox-Boyd warning that the Federal Party could lose the general election if some form of dominion status was not forthcoming. To Malvern, Welensky pointed out the irony that, while the Federation was not thought fit to be independent, the Gold Coast, currently in a state of turmoil, was. Welensky declared that, when he was Prime Minister, he would never attend a conference as anything less than Nkrumah's equal.[32]

Then Malvern informed Home, on 2 July, that he accepted Lyttelton's explanation (of 24 June 1953) of the preamble. Malvern explained why he had been so anxious for Wheare to endorse what he (Malvern) had told the Southern Rhodesians. This was because in 1953 he had assumed that the northern territories would remain protectorates for a long time and thus it appeared that only the Southern Rhodesians had something to lose. He still, however, would not accept the African veto in the preamble.[33]

On 6 July Malvern told Welensky in a letter that the British had ruled that the Federal Prime Minister would continue to attend the Commonwealth

[30] Welensky Papers, 23/6, ff. 70–78, Minutes of a Meeting, Commonwealth Relations Office, 25 June 1956.
[31] *Ibid.*, f. 21, Malvern to Home, 25 June 1956.
[32] *Ibid.*, 27/62, f. 79, Welensky to Lennox-Boyd, 27 June 1956.
[33] *Ibid.*, 11/20, f. 1, Malvern to Home, 2 July 1956.

Prime Ministers' Conference, but only by invitation. Three days later, Malvern met Home, Lennox-Boyd and Benson to demand the enlargement of the Assembly because he wanted a wider choice from which to draw his Cabinet and the select committees. Furthermore, he maintained, the Federal constituencies were so large that people turned to their territorial and not Federal representatives for assistance. Malvern wanted to double the number of seats in the Assembly while not upsetting the territorial ratio. He would double the number of African representatives but would not increase the number of Europeans performing that function. Therefore, there would be three Europeans and 15 Africans in this category.

Lennox-Boyd did not expect the northern Governments to object, provided that African representation was doubled one way or the other. Benson agreed, but thought that the African would more readily accept the enlargement if the franchise were satisfactorily resolved. Home promised to consider the question of enlargement with sympathy and then asked about the franchise and citizenship. Malvern replied that the inter-government committee had not yet completed its examination but was likely to recommend a dual roll. It was hoped to introduce Africans gradually into the parliamentary system and thus they would preponderate on the B roll thereby removing any need to reserve seats. The reserved seats would be retained until the African dominated the lower roll and elected only Africans.

Lennox-Boyd reminded Malvern that the British Government considered it was highly important that the British Protected Persons should be enrolled without endangering their status. Malvern replied that this had been considered carefully, and he favoured two-tier citizenship. This final meeting closed with the British Ministers promising to furnish Malvern with a written reply to all the questions he had raised.[34]

Lord Llewellin reported to Welensky that the British Government refused to contemplate any major alteration to the Federal Constitution before 1960. Moreover, it considered itself bound by Lyttelton's interpretation of the preamble. The British Ministers still could not see how the Federation could be independent while two of its Governors took orders from London. Llewellin agreed with them but promised to make them understand that no one in the Federation, apart from the Colonial officials, would feel bound by the promises made by Lyttelton. He would also tell them that, when they talked of the importance of African opinion, they were sacrificing to an unascertainable factor their right to act.[35]

Nicholas, Malvern's principal private secretary, revealed to the Federal Cabinet that the British officials had indicated to him that they had intended that their Government should resist all suggestions of amendment. They had advised their Ministers that all the Governments were bound to maintain the *status quo* until 1960, and that legally it was impossible to advance the Federation while the British Government controlled the northern territories. It was clear to him that Home and Lennox-Boyd had happily accepted this advice because they feared upsetting the Commons.

[34] *Ibid.*, 43/*Malvern*, Malvern to Welensky, 6 July 1956; 23/6, ff. 80–84, Minutes of a Meeting, Commonwealth Relations Office, 9 July 1956.

[35] *Ibid.*, 24/198, ff. 44–46, Llewellin to Welensky, 10 July 1956.

Nicholas felt that, if little had been gained, at least the attitude of the British Government had been discovered. He found that as none of the current British officials had been at the Federal Conferences, they knew nothing of the understandings reached there. Home and Lennox-Boyd appeared to be governed not by what they thought was right but by what they thought they could get away with in Parliament. They had seriously advised that all that was needed to win the African over was to establish a liberal franchise, remove the colour bar from the railways, and accept Africans into the civil service on equal terms. This would allow the British Government to divest itself of the protectorates in 1960. Nicholas thought that Benson seemed to agree.

Home and Lennox-Boyd would not give way even when Wheare confirmed the correctness of Malvern's assertion. Nicholas blamed their attitude on the British legal adviser, Sir Ralph Hone, who disagreed with Wheare. This was crucial because it was unlikely that the Africans would have withdrawn their objections to the Federation by 1960. It seemed that the northern Governments had greater influence on the British Cabinet than the Federal Government. It certainly appeared, reported Nicholas, that they had vetoed Malvern's proposals which were rejected out of hand probably because the northern Governors had said that they would adversely affect African opinion. The Colonial Office firmly believed that the Federal Government was intent on amalgamation and it interpreted all Federal actions accordingly. It was known that Benson believed this because evidence to this effect had been placed before Malvern by British officials. Malvern had denied the charge in writing. As Nicholas had attended all the Federal Conferences, he believed that all the understandings reached there were being ignored and thought that the British could be fairly accused of a breach of faith.[36]

Malvern arrived home on 13 July and, promising a full explanation to Parliament, said that he could not accept that dominion status could not be considered before 1960. Welensky immediately told Joelson that, if nothing were done to improve the standing of the Federation, the Federal Party would be defeated in 1958 because the electorate would not agree that the Sudanese and West Africans were better fitted for self-government. Welensky said he had never known a more "gutless" British Government. The Labour Party would succeed it but, as serious trouble was possible on the Copperbelt, he believed that any chance of enhancing Federal status would then be unlikely. The whole African situation was changing rapidly and it was ridiculous to forbid any adjustment until 1960 when the Constitution had been designed to allow amendment by agreement. After all, when the Federal review was planned in 1953, no one knew that the Gold Coast would be independent by 1957. He said that he and Malvern had succeeded so far in placating the Europeans but would not be able to continue to do so unless they became masters in their own house.[37]

To Lord Llewellin, Welensky was franker about the consequences of the Labour Party being returned. All chance of promotion would be lost. He

[36] *Ibid.*, 7/2, ff. 298–302, W. F. Nicholas to H. N. Parry, 11 July 1956.

[37] *Ibid.*, 24/151, ff. 347–349, Welensky to Joelson, 16 July 1956; *The Rhodesia Herald*, 14 July 1956.

confessed that he, too, had found it difficult to accept Malvern's conception of independence and, indeed, had tried to dissuade him from advancing it. Welensky could not accept the British view of the preamble because he believed that it had been worded to allow the wishes of the inhabitants to be expressed through the legislatures. Concluding, he noted that Malvern had done little about franchise and citizenship.[38]

Greenfield was alarmed when Malvern told the Cabinet that the three European representatives of African interests should be replaced by Africans so that there would be 18 African MPs in the new House. Greenfield felt that the franchise issue should be settled before the House was enlarged. He said he still opposed the dual roll and thought that it was time to make Todd and the United Rhodesia Party understand that the British Government and not the Dominion Party was the common enemy against which they had to unite.[39]

Malvern gave his promised explanation to the Federal Assembly on 2 August, recalling that Wheare's assurance on Federal independence in its own sphere had persuaded him to accept federation. As his Government had been, for practical purposes, independent, he would not have raised the matter had other countries not been recently advanced to independence more quickly than expected. They would be full members of the Commonwealth while the Federation was ignored, even though he, as its Prime Minister, and before as Southern Rhodesia's premier, had attended the Commonwealth Prime Ministers' Conference for the last 20 years.

Malvern had concluded that the Federal electorate would not allow this and, he feared, it would then concentrate on constitutional matters to the detriment of the main task of economic development. At the outset there had been a series of written and unwritten pledges made to the territories and to the Africans. Two of these were that amalgamation would not be effected and that the protected status of the northern African would be preserved. He had not questioned these. The autonomy and powers of the territories were inviolate because they had been frozen for ten years. He had concentrated on independence for the Federation within its own sphere. Constitutional amendment was therefore necessary and, in the process, he had proposed that the safeguards should be transferred to a treaty to be signed with Britain. The practical effect would have been little, he confessed, but the Federal Government would have been independent. It was not a bid for more power, but for international status. The Federal Government would have gained full control over external relations, but in the interests of economy would have continued to use the services of the British diplomatic corps.

His proposals, Malvern maintained, were entirely reasonable in the light of developments elsewhere, and any British Government wishing to observe the undertakings should not have found them difficult to accept. However, the political climate in which they were presented made it certain that they would be rejected. Malvern had been in London for the Prime Ministers' Conference and he felt that he would not have otherwise attracted notice. However, a leak to the Press led to immediate claims that he was seeking

[38] Welensky Papers, 24/198, f. 42, Welensky to Llewellin, 16 July 1956.
[39] *Ibid.*, 7/2, f. 296, Greenfield to Welensky, 19 July 1956.

British relinquishment of control of the territories. He acknowledged that he had chosen his moment badly, for, in any case, the Federal Government had not yet published the conditions of service for African Federal civil servants, and there was no franchise or citizenship bill. All these would have demonstrated the attitude of the Federal Government to the Constitution.

He reported that both Secretaries of State had disagreed that the Federal Government could be legally independent while the northern territories were under the control of the Colonial Office. This was totally contrary to the advice given during the Federal Conferences but, if he had achieved nothing else, he believed he had cleared this point finally.

The second British argument was that Malvern was proposing in effect a constitutional review before 1960. He denied this because the safeguards would be transferred to the treaty unaltered. The British Government had offered a few minor improvements but they did not enhance the Federation's status. In the end, it had agreed to submit new proposals which Malvern expected to fall far short of his own.

Malvern attributed the obstructive attitude of the British Government to the efforts of the Colonial Office to represent every Federal proposal as an attempt to gain amalgamation surreptitiously. Yet when he had accepted federation, he had dropped his advocacy of amalgamation permanently. The Federal Government could force a confrontation by presenting a bill to amend the Constitution provided that, in terms of Article 97, the legislative lists were unaffected. The support of two thirds of the House was required and thereafter the sanction of the territories. Everything would depend on the instructions given to the northern officials and presumably they would be to oppose the bill. If that happened, there would be a debate in the British Parliament, and rejection was certain. The Federal Government would then fight a general election on the issue. Such drastic action would risk stability, Malvern concluded, but would create an opportunity to reveal Federal views.

In the debate, the Federal Government was roundly condemned for its presumption or its timidity, according to the beliefs of its critics. Van Eeden insisted that there should be a dominion comprising Southern Rhodesia and the northern "Railway Strip". Moffat, Williamson, Doig and Scott maintained that changes were only possible after ten years, and then only with the consent of the people. Savanhu said that the Southern Rhodesian Africans would oppose any immediate changes because they wished to see first how partnership would be implemented. The northern African MPs lacked his restraint and, indeed, spoke violently enough for the impeachment of Chirwa, in particular, to be considered. They strongly opposed the exchange of British for Federal protection.

Malvern blamed the deplorable racial tone of the speeches on the use of the words "dominion status" which was misleading because, in fact, he had not tried to secure it. To prove this, he described again what he had tried to achieve and claimed that he would not have violated the Constitution. If the Africans were suspicious of Federal intentions, he reminded them that his Government was denied contact with them while others could freely influence them. The Northern Rhodesian Government had, at the outset, prevented the Federal Government from acquiring the potent means represented by the broadcasting system. The Federal Government had full control of its defence forces, one of the prerequisites of independence, and Malvern hoped that it would not have to resort to using them as had the North American colonists when dealing with a "stupid" British Government. He had tried to improve the international status of the Federation but had failed. However, he said, his failure should be forgotten as the Federation could not currently afford a confrontation. The main task was to develop the Federal economy and to advance its people. Then, when strong enough, the Federation could do as it pleased.[40]

Waiting for the British reply, the Federal Government continued to examine the citizenship and franchise questions, and soon came under pressure from the Southern Rhodesian Parliament to accept a new form of intergovernmental participation in the formulation of policy. Greenfield advised the Federal Government to concentrate on elevating Northern Rhodesia to self-government, to eliminate the Colonial administration, and then to bid for dominion status.[41] In the public arena, perhaps inevitably, Malvern and Welensky were accused of failing to lead in the matter of independence. They were attacked, too, both within and without the Federation, when British firms failed to win the main civil engineering contract at Kariba and it went to the lowest bidder, an Italian firm called Impresit.[42]

The main preoccupation, however, was the continuing unrest in Northern Rhodesia where a series of short strikes had begun on a variety of pretexts. There was strife between the African Mineworkers' Union and the Mines African Staff Association. The wrangle over African advancement continued, and there was a new objection to the wearing of protective leggings. The Federal Government, keeping its ear to the ground, noticed that the Southern Rhodesian nationalists, who were being scorned for their docility, were watching, and indeed would later comment on, what violence was achieving in Cyprus.[43] The apparent powerlessness of the Northern Rhodesian Government in the face of a campaign by the ANC to force it to recognise its sole right to speak for the African population, considerably annoyed the Northern Rhodesian Europeans, including Welensky. That Government's silence on security matters led to threats of resignation from Roberts and the other Federal Party Members of the Executive Council.[44]

The Southern Rhodesian Government at least took some action, and on 20 July expelled J. C. W. Malifa, president of the Mashonaland branch of the Nyasaland African Congress, D. K. Chisiza, a member of that branch, and A. P. Banda, general secretary of the Northern Rhodesian ANC in Southern Rhodesia. Todd explained that he could not stand idly by while disloyal

[40] Fed R & N *Debates* (Salisbury), Vol. 6, Col. 915 f., 2 August 1956; Welensky Papers, 19/32, f. 45, Welensky to Malvern, 16 August 1956.
[41] Welensky Papers, 7/2, f. 284, Greenfield to Welensky, (undated).
[42] *Ibid.*, 24/151, ff. 342–344, Welensky to Joelson, 8 August 1956; ff. 345–346, Joelson to Welensky, 20 July 1956; 24/198, ff. 47–48, Welensky to Llewellin, 28 June 1956.
[43] *Ibid.*, 39/18, f. 8, FISB Report, 27 June 1956.
[44] *Ibid.*, f. 7, FISB Report, 5 July 1956; 19/32, f. 5, Sitrep, Northern Rhodesia, 6 July 1956; 24/151, ff. 347–349, Welensky to Joelson, 16 July 1956; ff. 345–346, Joelson to Welensky, 20 July 1956; 28/115, f. 78, C. Hyam to Welensky, 31 July 1956.

elements tried to sabotage the Federation. He expressed concern about the security situation in Northern Rhodesia and revealed that he had offered police reinforcements. He had no wish to interfere, but had heard talk of driving the European out of Nyasaland, in particular, even though its Constitution provided that the territory was the rightful home of all people domiciled there.[45]

H. E. Davies, the Southern Rhodesian Federal European Representative for African Interests, urged the African leaders to accept the reality of the Federation and not to allow their personal bitterness to sway their judgment. However, the Railway African Workers' Union next threatened militant action if a variety of skilled jobs were not opened to Africans, and the Federal authorities found, by 21 July, that the Northern Rhodesian position was deteriorating so rapidly that a situation similar to the Mau Mau uprising was becoming a distinct possibility. They diagnosed this just when the provincial administration appeared to them to be forcing the pace of Africanisation at an almost frightening rate and just when the Northern Rhodesian Police were withdrawing from the rural areas to leave all control to the district commissioners and their messengers. Consequently the African attitude towards the local Europeans deteriorated.[46]

The rumour was that Benson aimed to destroy the Federation. This he resented because, in his view, he never wavered in his support for his conception of the Federation. The Northern Rhodesian Europeans looked to Salisbury for rescue and urged, in particular, the Federal Government not to wait until 1960 before revising its Constitution.[47]

The strikes spread to the Central African Road Services' Union after the dismissal of a driver in Lusaka, and on 26 July the African Mine Workers' Union planned a further series of short strikes in August, postponing the arbitration of their demand for an increase of six shillings and eight pence per shift. This campaign of strikes was implemented and led the mine managers to demand a state of emergency. They did so just as Nkumbula pledged the ANC to work for the improvement of race relations. However, it is likely that he was responding to a motion in the Legislative Council calling for an investigation into the aims and objects of his organisation. In any case, Nkumbula was reported to have simultaneously told his executive that the British Government would not relinquish anything until blood was shed and that therefore the ANC had to be prepared to shed it.[48]

The Nyasaland nationalists were just as militant but still deeply divided and consequently less active. The Federal Government for its part could only stand by and watch the situation in Northern Rhodesia since the Federal Constitution forbad any involvement. It did, however, reveal the terms and conditions of service in its public service, and most important of these was

[45] *Ibid.*, 19/28, f. 64, de Quehen to W. F. Nicholas, 20 July 1956; *The Rhodesian Herald*, 21 July 1956.

[46] *The Rhodesia Herald*, 24 July 1956; Welensky Papers, 19/28, f. 63, FISB Report, 24 July 1956; 5/27, f. 2, W. D. Gale to W. F. Nicholas, 21 July 1956.

[47] *Ibid.*, 19/28, f. 66, FISB Report, 18 July 1956; Author's interview with Sir Arthur Benson.

[48] Welensky Papers, 19/32, f. 27, FISB Report, 26 July 1956; f. 72, FISB Report, 6 August 1956; 19/33, f. 9, Security Review, 20 August 1956; 19/32, f. 47, FISB Report, 27 August 1956.

that race alone would not bar promotion. It was intended, for example, that African medical practitioners should serve in Branch 1, the highest of the employment categories. Welensky also announced that day, 23 August, that the railways would allow reasonably-dressed Africans to use its dining cars.[49]

Home wrote to Malvern on 16 August but only on the subject of citizenship. He acknowledged the merits of the two-tiered system but warned that it did not accord with the decision in 1947 to make all Commonwealth citizens British subjects, and that it could set a dangerous precedent for the disqualifying of classes of citizens within the Commonwealth. It could undermine the whole Commonwealth system by encouraging discrimination in other countries. It was also possible that the British Protected Persons might think that they were being discriminated against on the grounds of race alone.[50]

A week later Home took Malvern to task for his speeches in the Federal Assembly, insisting that his Government wanted only to see the Federation advance to full self-government and membership of the Commonwealth. The question was one of pace. Then Home recalled that Wheare had only said that theoretically the Federation could become self-governing in its own sphere and that in 1953 it was thought that it could do so in 1963 once some of the reservations had been removed at the constitutional review. Wheare had also stated that the sanction of the Africans was needed for any major alterations to the Constitution. Home remembered, too, that Malvern had maintained that, as long as Britain remained responsible for the northern territories, any change in her relationship with the Federal Government could not run counter to the preamble and Lyttelton's pledge in Parliament. However, the British Government's view was that the proposed Federal independence act would be regarded in Britain as implying dominion status or tantamount to it. This would invoke the pledge in the preamble and, consequently, demand the sanction of the majority of the inhabitants when the British Government could find no evidence of African support for the bid by Malvern for independence. This was of real concern, Home said, because the British Government could not make changes unless they were favoured by the African population.

Home suggested a joint British and Federal effort to win the support of the northern Africans, and promised that, if Malvern could suggest ways of doing this, he and Lennox-Boyd would consider what they could do to help. He was pleased that Malvern had stressed in the Federal Parliament the need to demonstrate how Federal policies would benefit the African because it could make it easier to effect changes during the review.[51]

Malvern replied that Home's comments on Wheare had only clouded the issue because all Wheare had been asked was whether it was possible to take certain action. Wheare had confirmed that it was, and any subsequent hedging on his part on timing was irrelevant. In 1953 no one had foreseen the need for early action. Malvern claimed that in 1952 he had realised that the need to

[49] Fed R & N *Debates* (Salisbury), Vol. 7, Col. 1827, 23 August 1956; *The Rhodesia Herald*, 23 August 1956.
[50] Welensky Papers, 8/111, f. 143, Home to Malvern, 16 August 1956.
[51] *Ibid.*, 23/6, ff. 27–28, Home to Malvern, 23 August 1956.

consult African opinion would bar the relinquishment of British control in the North for a long time. Thus he had sought to confirm that the Federation could become independent in its own sphere, and Lyttelton and his advisers, including Wheare, had agreed that it could, without invoking the preamble. In any case, Lyttelton had known that the pledge only related to amalgamation and had since confirmed this. Malvern explained that he had not asked Home for dominion status because it implied the removal of British control of the northern territories. Thus he was surprised that Home should be influenced by the wrong construction that the Labour Party might put on his request. Home was now prescribing African approval as a prerequisite to any advance in the constitutional field which, Malvern stated, had certainly never been contemplated at the Federal Conferences. It meant that, short of African self-government, no advance would be achieved.

Malvern described as "ironical" Home's suggestion of joint action to win over the African because he was merely displaying his ignorance of the Constitution which barred the Federal Government from virtually all contact with the rural African. The situation was that the stage had been captured by the small body of nationalists and he could cite examples of the traditional authorities, the Chiefs, publicly quailing before nationalist demagogues. There were enlightened Africans who supported the Federation but, Malvern said, it was dangerous for them to do so publicly. He knew that lack of control had been a feature of British Colonial Policy since the Second World War, but nevertheless, he asked when the British Government intended to curb nationalist activities, as the Northern Rhodesian situation was deteriorating rapidly. Although strikes were being used as political weapons, it seemed to Malvern that the British Government did not appear to realise what effect they would have on the Federal and, ultimately, the British economy.[52]

In Northern Rhodesia a campaign of civil disobedience in the form of the destruction of identity and marriage certificates had been added to that of boycotts and short strikes. Though Nkumbula intervened and even suspended the ANC official who had initiated it, feelings continued to run high. 8 000 European women petitioned the Government over the trend of events. The Federal Party threatened to crush Nkumbula's organisation if it did not cease its current activities. The Party also continued to press the Northern Rhodesian Government to act, and when the latter did it had some effect. In Livingstone the boycott ended after a local ANC leader was convicted for inciting violence. However, the arrest and acquittal on the Copperbelt of four ANC members, including a provincial president and a provincial secretary, for conspiracy against the business of the European traders, only enhanced the reputation of the ANC amongst the African population. The acquittal came after Nkumbula, appearing as a witness, claimed sole responsibility for the boycott. The ANC depicted this as a milestone in the struggle and then also claimed credit for the closure of the rural police stations.[53]

There was alarm in Southern Rhodesia when Africans working in the jute industry came out on strike, but it was soon discovered that their motivation

[52] *Ibid.*, ff. 34–35, Malvern to Home, 5 September 1956.

[53] *Ibid.*, 19/32, f. 78, FISB Report, 13 August 1956; 24/151, ff. 338–340, Welensky to Joelson, 28 August 1956; 19/33, f. 9, FISB Report, 20 August 1956; Mulford, *Zambia*, *op. cit.*, p. 46.

was not political. In Nyasaland the five African Members of the Legislative Council, all Congressmen, were enjoying considerable notoriety and copies of their speeches in *Hansard* were widely read. The Congress itself, however, remained divided and apathetic. The convention of the Capricorn Africa Society at Salima in June had seemed to impress the Southern Rhodesian Africans with the genuineness of its multi-racial approach in the Capricorn Contract which it had ratified and which had contained its ideas on race, the franchise, education and immigration. The *African Weekly*, however, had commented on, and the Federal Government feared, the likelihood of disenchantment when these high-minded ideals were not realised. By late August the Society was under attack by the Nyasaland African Members of the Legislative Council.[54]

On 29 August the Commonwealth Relations Office offered Malvern only an extension of Federal responsibilities in the field of external affairs, and direct access to the Queen. Britain would be formally responsible for the external relations of the Federation, but would allow foreign governments to deal directly with the Federal Government. There could be a limited exchange of representatives, and the British Government would support any application by the Federation to join a wider range of international organisations. The Federation was currently a member of the World Health Organisation, the World Meteorological Association and the General Agreement on Trades and Tariffs. The Federal High Commissioner in London would be invited to all meetings between the Commonwealth Secretary and the Commonwealth High Commissioners. (Currently the Federal High Commissioner was only invited when economics and defence were under discussion.) Finally, access to the Queen would be through the Governor-General rather than the Secretary of State.[55]

Malvern, when he replied one month later, only welcomed the invitation to the Federal High Commissioner. Otherwise, as the Federal Government was already dealing directly with other Commonwealth countries, he declared that something more concrete would have to be offered to satisfy the Federal public's aspirations. He regretted that he had been forced to debate the constitutional issue in the Federal Assembly because it had stirred up those who wished to join South Africa.[56]

Malvern was probably using his standard ploy with the British in raising the bogey of Afrikaner expansionism because there does not seem to have been any significant pressure from that quarter. What pressure there was came from the Southern Rhodesians whose Assembly had unanimously agreed on 9 August to send a delegation chosen by Todd and Stockil to meet the Federal Government to discuss inter-governmental co-operation and the attainment of dominion status. The United Rhodesia Party also formally approached the Federal Party on the subject of fusion.[57]

[54] Welensky Papers, 19/32, f. 73, FISB Report, 14 August 1956; 19/33, f. 9, FISB Report, 20 August 1956.

[55] *Ibid.*, 23/6, f. 30, Memorandum from the Commonwealth Relations Office, 29 August 1956.

[56] *Ibid.*, f. 36, Malvern to Home, 3 October 1956.

[57] *Ibid.*, 7/2, f. 290, M. J. Lamb to Welensky, 10 August 1956; 42/32, f. 48, Welensky to R. J. Bower, 14 August 1956.

A week later, Todd pressed Malvern to meet his delegation and to arrange a conference on co-operation. To ensure progress, Todd believed that the other Governments had to be excluded at first. He wanted greater co-operation in security, labour, immigration, industrial and economic development, the franchise and the civil services. There was adequate collaboration at official level but Todd hoped to improve the relationship between the Cabinets to derive the maximum benefit from the Federation. He thought that it would be unfortunate if each Government had to keep within its own sphere and not comment in the interests of the Federation as a whole. He was quick to reassure Malvern that he was not suggesting the re-establishment of the Central African Council because he realised that the Government responsible had to make the final decisions. Nevertheless, he wanted the views of the partners made known before the decision was taken.[58]

Malvern replied that all the Governments would have to attend the initial meeting, but Todd disagreed. The Federal Cabinet supported Malvern and, moreover, thought it would be improper to discuss certain subjects in front of Stockil. Not wanting to appear to rebuff Todd, the Cabinet decided that Malvern should discuss the problem with him.[59] The result was that Todd, on 5 September, could announce that Malvern would soon call a heads of Governments meeting.

The inter-government committee had been at work all the while and its Federal members reported to their Cabinet on 20 August, telling of the northern rejection of oaths of allegiance. The Cabinet decided not to press the matter until the British Government had revealed its views. The committee also needed to discover whether there would be a wholly elective system or whether the special representatives would be retained. Likewise they wished to know whether the Assembly would be enlarged and if there would be a single or dual roll. The committee had examined means of gradually eliminating the special representation but the Cabinet was sure that the British Government would demand that it wait for the review. The Cabinet, however, believed that as a *quid pro quo* for the enrolment of the British Protected Person, an elective system should be introduced for the selection of the special representatives and that this could involve the European voter.

The enlargment of the House, the Cabinet decided, would still be negotiated with the British Government, but it agreed with the committee that the number of seats could be safely doubled if the additional MPs were elected through the common roll. Evans explained that his committee's latest idea was to enlarge the membership to 78 and to divide it equally between the Africans and the non-Africans to give parity of racial representation. The territorial ratio of seats would be 42 for Southern Rhodesia (21 African and 21 non-African), 24 for Northern Rhodesia and twelve for Nyasaland. This, the committee believed, would keep government in civilised hands, eliminate racial politics, preserve the common roll, create a basis for partnership, while abandoning special representation. Because public opinion would not accept it, the Cabinet rejected this suggestion but thought that it was possible to work towards parity without any public declaration of intent.

[58] *Ibid.*, 9/10, f. 3, Todd to Malvern, 17 August 1956.
[59] *Ibid.*, FGC(56), 33rd Meeting, Minute 9, Federal Cabinet, 22 August 1956.

Examining the choice of dual or single rolls, the Cabinet accepted that, while there were strong arguments for a dual roll, the Africans on the lower roll would constantly demand greater representation because of their numerical superiority. Furthermore, as it was unlikely that the African would dominate the lower roll at the outset, it was thought that the British Government would reject it. In Southern Rhodesia, the European would dominate the lower roll for some years, but in Nyasaland there would be so few European voters that the African would quickly secure both rolls. It might be more acceptable to retain special representation for the masses who could not qualify, and to raise the lower roll qualification from an income of £100 p.a. to one of £220 or £250 p.a. The Cabinet proposed to ask the British Government for its opinion, but recognised the need for an early settlement.[60]

At the end of August the Federal Minister of Home Affairs, F. S. Owen, also reviewed the franchise. The existing arrangements, he thought, could be used for the general election and the franchise reserved for the review. The dual or single roll could be adopted to elect an enlarged House with parity of racial representation. Both of these would require constitutional amendment and electoral acts but the maintenance of the *status quo* would be severely criticised because the electorate expected change. Failure to increase African representation would also not conform to the Federal Party's policy. The African special representatives in the Assembly had provoked the Europeans and, Owen warned, the Government would be accused of not trying to get rid of extremism. The existing income qualification was also generally thought to be too low. Finally the northern territories were considering enrolling British Protected Persons and, if the Federal Government did not follow suit, it would be difficult to use the territorial rolls as had been done at the last election.

Owen thought that many of these difficulties could be overcome by simply legislating for the election of the 26 ordinary MPs, using higher qualifications as recommended by the inter-government committee. However, there would be no provision for the enlargement of the Federal Assembly, and any increase in ordinary seats would have to be matched by a proportionate increase in the special representation which, he said, would be incompatible with Federal Party policy.

The dual roll, Owen proposed, would not only keep government in civilised hands, but would eliminate special representation and encourage party rather than racial divisions. It would have a moderating effect, for the upper roll voter would qualify for both rolls. The upper roll would elect three-quarters of the MPs and vote with the lower roll voters to elect the remainder. The race of MPs would only be specified for the first six years to ensure that Africans were returned while the European dominated the lower roll. Accordingly, there would be six African MPs and three European reresentatives of African interests. Thus the African Affairs Board would survive.

The upper roll qualifications of an income of £500 p.a. and simple literacy would ensure European domination for the foreseeable future, except in

[60] *Ibid.*, 8/111, ff. 146–147, Minutes of a Special Meeting, Federal Cabinet, 20 August 1956.

Nyasaland. The Africans would predominate there on the lower roll at the outset, and the same was theoretically true in Northern Rhodesia. However, the influence of the upper roll voters was expected to make it difficult generally for extremists to secure any seats. The abandonment of special representation, before the African had secured significant political influence through enrolment, would be criticised, Owen said, and the dual roll would not safeguard the Europeans' position in the long term, although a generous 25 per cent leeway in delimitation might. Furthermore, the African voters might soon demand greater representation. It might also be difficult for the parties to attract the lower roll voters and, if the House were enlarged, there would be an unreasonable increase in African seats. However, he noted, this was the scheme favoured by the Northern Rhodesian Government which could be an indication of what the British Government would choose.

Owen also considered parity of representation in an enlarged Assembly. The gradual replacement of the special representatives by Africans elected by the single roll fitted the Federal Party's aim of increasing African participation and might convince the African of the sincerity of the policy of partnership. Thereby, the party political system could be established before the African nationalists dominated the voters' roll. A relatively high franchise would ensure that the African did not achieve parity of representation before he was ready.

A potential danger, Owen found, was that the African Congress might secure an undue influence in Nyasaland, but the single roll would inhibit that. A single vote was more likely to appeal to Africans than plural voting. Nonetheless, the Europeans might become alarmed at the increasing number of African voters and the Africans might demand more than parity. Furthermore, a high qualification might disenfranchise a number of Europeans and the small number of Africans qualifying might prompt the British Government to insist that special representation be retained. The party system would not develop if there were only a small number of African voters. Yet low qualifications could result in Africans exercising their vote before they properly understood the party system, and parity might be achieved too soon. The racial allocation of seats might encourage racialism but that, Owen thought, was an inherent danger in any common roll system.

Lastly, Owen examined the British Protected Person and the franchise. The inter-government committee had recommended that when registering, the British Protected Person should not have to change his status or swear any oath. The reason was that the difference between his status and that of the Southern Rhodesian African was academic. An oath would not secure loyalty and, being misunderstood, would be regarded as an instrument of discrimination. Thus the Federal Government should adopt a formula which would confer citizenship on all "belongers", but would recognise the distinction between British subjects and British Protected Persons.

Owen noted that, despite its protests, the British Government had not finally rejected this formula. The other choice was to persist with the citizenship bill as drafted and insist that both British subjects and British Protected Persons take the oath of loyalty. The British Protected Persons would secure only local citizenship but could qualify for the vote. However, Owen concluded, the inter-government committee preferred to reserve citizenship for British subjects and allow the British Protected Persons to qualify for the vote through a specific provision.[61]

The Federal Cabinet examined Owen's memorandum on 4 September but found that there were four rather than three options because provision could simply be made for the election of the 26 ordinary MPs, thus avoiding a constitutional amendment. The election of the special representatives could be deferred for the review.

The Federal Cabinet noted that the Federal Party insisted on a single form of citizenship which would be one of the qualifications for the vote. The British Government, on the other hand, would not agree to the status of a British subject alone being a qualification for the vote. Nevertheless it still had not rejected the two-tiered citizenship despite the difficulties which it had pointed out. As the sanction of the Commonwealth would have to be obtained and would take time, the Federal Cabinet felt that it might be necessary to conclude the franchise negotiations first, using the status of a British subject as a basic qualification. The Cabinet favoured the dual roll but thought that the lower roll qualification should be an income of £200 p.a. rather than one of £100 p.a.[62]

A week later Welensky and Greenfield presented the Cabinet with a memorandum advocating the dual roll. This was curious because hitherto Greenfield had opposed the dual roll and some weeks later Welensky remarked that Greenfield's continuing rejection of it was somewhat of a problem. They based their qualifications on incomes of £500 p.a. with simple literacy, or £300 p.a. and the Cambridge Overseas Certificate for the upper roll, and £200 p.a. plus simple literacy for the lower. They rejected property as a qualification, but would include citizenship if the two-tiered proposal was accepted. If it was not, nationality should be substituted and only British subjects would qualify for the upper roll.

Welensky and Greenfield proposed that elected MPs would replace the African special representatives in 1958 and the European special Members in 1963 when the African Affairs Board, they suggested, should cease to exist. If the British baulked, the African Affairs Board would be retained until 1968, but no longer. Should the British refuse to enlarge the House, the dual roll would be applied to the election of the 26 ordinary MPs, and special representation would be reviewed in 1960.

Welensky and Greenfield agreed with Owen that the dual roll system would keep power in civilised hands, while broadening the franchise. They accepted that it would not safeguard the European's position indefinitely, but felt that this could be accomplished by some honest gerrymandering in delimitation. If the dual roll was rejected, then the common roll should be based on their upper roll qualification. They wanted the citizenship bill published with an explanation that it was not yet in its final form. They knew

[61] *Ibid.*, 23/23, f. 79, Memorandum by F. S. Owen, 30 August 1956. Owen, the Federal MP for Ndola, had been brought into the Cabinet in mid-1955 as the second Northern Rhodesian. Greenfield had advised that he be made a Parliamentary Secretary, but Malvern made Owen a Minister. — JRTW.

[62] *Ibid.*, FGC(56), 35th Meeting, Minute 4, Federal Cabinet, 4 September 1956.

that the electoral bill could not be ready for some time but, as much of the administrative work could be done in advance, they expected the general election to be held on due date.

The Cabinet considered postponing the review to allow a ten year trial of the dual roll in order to discover if the party system could develop. It noted that the Northern Rhodesian Government favoured an income of £100 p.a. for the lower roll. However, the Cabinet proposed £200 p.a. to allow leeway for a compromise. It agreed that property, except where it affected income, should be discarded. Citizenship, the Cabinet also recognised, hinged on the franchise, but the publication of the citizenship bill might block some of the options. The two-tiered system was thought to be fraught with difficulties, particularly when a Southern Rhodesian African could qualify for the upper roll while his northern cousin could not. The Cabinet agreed that, when the House was enlarged, four lower roll seats for each territory would be reserved for Africans. The European representatives of African interests would continue to be elected and nominated. The idea of parity of racial representation was rejected by the Cabinet simply because the electorate would do likewise. The Cabinet thought that the current veto of the Nyasaland Government over the Federal franchise ought to be rescinded. Finally, it decided to discuss the memorandum with the Party Caucus and at a heads of Governments meeting, and to establish if the 25 per cent tolerance on delimitation would be practicable in the northern territories.[63]

While his Cabinet made these deliberations, Malvern was drawing his premiership to a close. On 13 September he addressed the congress of the Federal Party for the last time. He reviewed economic development, finding the pace to be almost dangerously fast, and African agitation, which he said was destructive. He urged that the African be brought into the democratic system and that change be made in advance of any pressure. He rejected fusion with the United Rhodesia Party because it would raise suspicion in the northern territories and identify the Federal Party with the African policy of the Southern Rhodesian Government when the Constitution forbad the Federal Government to have any such involvement. He attacked the Colonial Office with some virulence because he believed it to be guided by men whose qualifications and experience were negligible, and whose policies varied from misguided idealism to outright expediency. Success was the only yardstick of a policy and the British one was a failure by any standard. Malvern said nothing about his retirement as Prime Minister but did not offer himself for re-election as president of the Party. In a moment of emotion, he stood down and Welensky was unanimously elected in his stead.[64]

Eleven days later, on 24 September, Malvern finally told Welensky that he would end his premiership on 31 October. The formal announcement was made at the end of September. Little more was done about the franchise in the remaining weeks, and attention focussed on a state of emergency in the copper-rich Western Province of Northern Rhodesia. The Acting Governor, A. T. Williams, had chosen an opportune moment to declare it on 11

[63] *Ibid.*, 36th Meeting, Minute 2, Federal Cabinet, 11 September 1956; 24/198, ff. 18–20, Welensky to Llewellin, 13 October 1956.

[64] *Ibid.*, 15/83, f. 15, Malvern's Address to the Federal Party Congress, 13 September 1956.

September, when the world was entirely preoccupied with the Anglo-French declaration that force would be used to keep the Suez Canal open. He was forced to act when a confrontation with the miners, over the wearing of protective leggings and a "clocking in" system, prevented production. There were also threats of sabotage of mine plant and machinery. Welensky despaired because it seemed that, in a fashion typical of the Colonial Office, the Northern Rhodesian Government would never act until drastic measures were needed.[65]

With a feverish atmosphere developing around the mines, with crowds constantly needing to be dispersed, the Northern Rhodesian Government drew police reinforcements from Nyasaland. In the early hours of 12 September, 32 African leaders were arrested, including M. D. Nkoloma, general secretary of the African Mine Workers' Union, and its vice-president, J. R. Nanistengo. The president of the Union, Lawrence Katilungu, had opposed the strike and, in any case, was in Bulawayo attending an arbitration meeting. He returned some days later to plead for a return to work and was soon accused of being the mouthpiece of the Government.[66]

Simultaneously, Nkumbula and W. M. Chirwa were touring the Southern Province strongly appealing for money and support for the despatch of a delegation to London to counteract Malvern's bid for independence. They pressed the need to follow the examples of the West Africans and the Indians in their struggle for independence and to spill blood if necessary. Chirwa left Northern Rhodesia for Nyasaland on 19 September, having reportedly raised some £700.[67]

The declaration of the emergency provoked Dixon Konkola, president of the Railways African Workers' Union, who was in Britain undertaking a course of study, to proclaim publicly that it was a bid to crush the unions. There were similar protests from the British Labour Party, and in mid-October the Northern Rhodesian ANC demanded an end to the state of emergency. The ANC also declared that Northern Rhodesia should be given the right to secede at the review and that there should be immediate parity of racial representation in the Executive and Legislative Councils. British Protected Persons should also be enfranchised. The ANC was holding its annual conference, and Nkumbula, in a bitter speech, used it to explain his recent conciliatory gesture. He warned the Northern Rhodesian Government that it could expect nothing but racial strife if it did not concede to the ANC's demands. Nkumbula added that if Europeans did not support him, he would work for an exclusively African government.[68]

[65] *Ibid.*, 43/*Malvern*, Malvern to Welensky, 24 September 1956; 19/32, f. 55, 56 & 59, FISB Reports, 4, 6 & 10 September 1956; 24/151, ff. 335–336, Welensky to Joelson, 19 September 1956.

[66] Mulford, *Zambia*, *op. cit.*, p. 46; *The Rhodesia Herald*, 13 September 1956; Welensky Papers, 24/1, ff. 142–143, Welensky to Dalgleish, 13 September 1956; 19/32, f. 53, FISB Report, 17 September 1956.

[67] Welensky Papers, 19/32, f. 59, FISB Report, 10 September 1956; 42/50, f. 18, FISB Report, 26 October 1956.

[68] *Ibid.*, 42/24, f. 91, ICFTU Information Bulletin, p. 149, 15 October 1956; 19/33, f. 8, Security Review, 11 October 1956; 19/32, f. 67, FISB Report, 19 October 1956; Mulford, *Zambia*, *op. cit.*, p. 47.

Only Nyasaland was spared overt unrest as, within a week of the Northern Rhodesian action, Southern Rhodesia had its first taste of civil commotion in the form of spontaneous violence on the night of 17 September after a bus boycott in Salisbury. The main target of the rioters was a hostel for women in the African township of Harare. Considerable damage was done and some of the inmates were raped. The boycott was in protest against an increase in fares, and the Federal Government was, albeit privately, critical of the failure of the Southern Rhodesian Government to respond to earlier revelations that the African workers in Salisbury were being expected to spend more than a third of their income on transport. The Federal Government was even more critical when the Southern Rhodesian Government declared a state of emergency after African railway employees came out on strike on 23 September following a rejection by their union of an arbitration award. The strike, which equally affected Northern Rhodesia, lasted only three days because the railways' management then issued an ultimatum and, when it was ignored, dismissed all the strikers and re-engaged them at lower rates of pay.[69]

The Federal Cabinet thought that the strike could have been handled without a state of emergency being declared. Welensky ascribed the reaction of the Southern Rhodesian Government to its inexperience and to Todd's flair for the dramatic. It seemed clear to Welensky, as the strikes in Northern Rhodesia had cost £5 000 000 in lost production at a time when the income from copper was declining because the price had fallen from £400 per ton to under £200, that the Federal Government could not be expected to manage the economy unless it controlled labour and industrial relations.[70]

The Federal Government was even more concerned to discover that the Northern Rhodesian Government, in invoking the Emergency Powers Order in Council of 1939, could suspend and even amend Federal legislation unilaterally. For example, Williams, the acting Governor, had amended the prison regulations but only after consulting the acting director of the Federal prison service. The Federal Attorney-General confirmed that Williams had acted within his powers. The Order in Council had been made in accordance with the British Settlements Act of 1887 and the Foreign Jurisdiction Act of 1890 with the effect that it could suspend any other Order in Council including the Federal. Consequently a territorial Governor could suspend the Federal Constitution as well as interfere with the operation of Federal laws. This was particularly disturbing to the Federal Government because of the potential political capital it presented to the opposition parties.[71]

Greenfield had to admit that he had been unaware of the Emergency Powers Order in Council because it had only been published for the first time in the Northern Rhodesian Government Gazette on 11 September 1956. He recommended that the Federal Government should demand of Home, who

[69] *The Rhodesia Herald*, 18 September 1956; Welensky Papers, 25/344, f. 15, Welensky to J. E. Stephenson, 19 September 1956; 24/73, ff. 339–340, Welensky to Gore-Browne, 20 September 1956; 42/60, f. 150, Welensky to D. Taylor, 1 October 1956.

[70] Welensky Papers, 42/60, f. 150, Welensky to D. Taylor, 1 October 1956; 29/44, f. 89, Welensky to J. P. McDonagh, 13 October 1956.

[71] *Ibid.*, FGC(56), 38th Meeting, Minute 4, 25 September 1956; 39th Meeting, Minute 3, 2 October 1956; 7/2, f. 260, Memorandum by the Federal Attorney-General, 11 October 1956.

was due to visit in November, an amendment to prevent the northern Governors from interfering with Federal laws, even in an emergency, without the consent of the Governor-General.[72]

The necessity for declarations of states of emergency was discussed at the heads of Governments meeting in Salisbury on 8 October. It was generally agreed that there should be limited powers which could be used whenever disturbances threatened, but further study was deemed necessary.

The meeting also reviewed inter-territorial movement, labour and African policies. Nyasaland asked for advance notice of deportations, referring to the recent Southern Rhodesian action against its nationalists, and the Southern Rhodesian Government agreed to furnish it. The latter, in its turn, complained that nationalist action in Nyasaland was preventing the recruitment of labour for Kariba. Finally Nyasaland promised to do more to combat African nationalist propaganda.

The Federal Government sought the reaction of the territories to the enlargement of the Federal Assembly because their sanction of a constitutional amendment would be needed. The Southern Rhodesians welcomed this as a stabilising factor. The Northern Rhodesians agreed that a larger Cabinet was needed but doubted if they had sufficient political talent to spare in their territory to serve an enlarged Assembly. They feared African resistance to this because it would seem to strengthen the European position. If the numbers of seats were doubled, the Northern Rhodesian Government insisted that the overall Southern Rhodesian majority of one elected seat should be unaffected. The Nyasalanders argued that as any enlargement had to be attractive to the northern Africans it might be wise simultaneously to appoint one or more Africans as parliamentary secretaries.

The meeting concentrated mainly on the economic policy to be applied during the construction of Kariba. The Federal Government explained that inflation was increasing, that the commercial banks had been asked to restrict credit, that immigration was being curbed and that development of secondary industry was being viewed cautiously. The International Bank did not insist on this, but the Federal Government had undertaken to keep the economy on an even keel. Beyond established projects, only railway development would be allowed. The Federal Government had promised to spend on development any windfall from a high price of copper, consequently it was investing £20 000 000 for this purpose. Revenue was to be used to sustain growth, and the Federal Government had been asked to ensure territorial collaboration in the management of the economy.

The Nyasaland representatives expressed concern about their territory's development because it depended so heavily on federal assistance. The Southern Rhodesians were anxious that the establishment of important secondary industries should not be hampered. The Federal Government responded by promising to assess the economic situation every six months.[73]

Dominion status was not discussed by the heads of Governments meeting but the subject was kept before the public eye by Winston Field, who was gaining prominence in the Dominion Party. Twice in October, Field called

[72] *Ibid.*, 7/2, f. 256, Greenfield to Welensky, 12 October 1956.
[73] *Ibid.*, 9/11, f. 2, Heads of Government Meeting, Salisbury, 8 October 1956.

for an all-party approach to the British Government because he felt it was imperative, before too much ground was lost, to show determination to ensure that the Federation would be responsible for its own future. The fate of the Federation, he said, should not be left in the hands of a temporary incumbent of Whitehall who worried only about being returned at the next election.[74]

The gathering strength of this appeal and of the Dominion Party itself, despite its lack of a leader, caused Welensky concern about the electoral prospects of the Federal Party in 1958 if he did not succeed in enhancing the status of the Federation. Thus Greenfield's continuing rejection of the dual roll did nothing to reassure him. He was also considerably irritated in the last days of October by having a copy of Benson's dispatch of 6 June laid before him and thus being able to read it for the first time. He could not have been mollified by a report, after a visit to London, from B. M. de Quehen, the head of Federal Intelligence. De Quehen described the new unfriendly and "Fabian" attitude of the British officials and concluded that adverse reports from the Northern Rhodesian Government were responsible, as well as an increasingly socialist influence which resulted from the lessening of the tension with Russia. (De Quehen wrote this the day before the outbreak of the Hungarian revolt.) He thought, also, that India's anti-colonial attitude was having an effect. Certainly the Indian representatives in Salisbury were sending home despatches which were critical of the Federal Government while favouring the African Congresses. De Quehen knew that Doris Lessing believed there was a considerable Indian influence on Whitehall. He also felt that the British officials were preparing for the replacement of Lennox-Boyd by Aneurin Bevan at the next election. The attitude of the Labour Party, as it was currently talking of a universal franchise for the Federation, especially worried Welensky.[75]

The rumour within the United Rhodesia Party was that Malvern, despite his announcement, would not retire at the end of October because of instability at home and abroad. Todd was particularly agitated because, he told Welensky, a postponement of Malvern's retirement would prevent fusion of the Federal and United Rhodesia Parties. Todd claimed that fusion was so urgent that he could not contemplate delaying the merger much beyond the end of October. (Greenfield was surprised by Todd's sudden anxiety on fusion because he had always found him privately to be lukewarm on the subject.)[76] Todd's agitation was misplaced because Malvern was as good as his word and quietly left his office for the last time on 31 October 1956, his departure more than somewhat over-shadowed by the reports of an imminent Anglo-French landing at Suez.

It was truly the end of an era, for he had served as Prime Minister, first of Southern Rhodesia and then of the Federation, since 11 September 1933, and

[74] *The Rhodesia Herald*, 12 & 24 October 1956.

[75] Welensky Papers, 29/44, f. 89, Welensky to J. P. McDonagh, 13 October 1956; 24/157, ff. 224–225, Welensky to J. Johnson, 22 October 1956; 24/198, ff. 13–14, Llewellin to Welensky, 24 October 1956; 19/28, f. 30, de Quehen to Welensky, 23 October 1956.

[76] *Ibid.*, 31/46, f. 61, Todd to Welensky, 18 October 1956; Author's interview with the Hon. J. M. Greenfield.

this feat had not been surpassed in British and Commonwealth history even by Sir Robert Walpole. Malvern so dominated politics that, even in 1946–7 when his United Party formed a minority government through an election pact with the Southern Rhodesia Labour Party, no one rivalled him within his own ranks or on the Opposition benches. Welensky, then in his forties, had been waiting in the wings as the unquestionable successor, but never as a rival.

As Malvern dominated his Cabinets, so Welensky — though less of an autocrat — dominated his. However, while none who served Welensky doubted his ability, his grasp of issues and his determination to succeed, there are some who regret, albeit with hindsight, that the Federal Cabinet was left with no one who had as long experience or as sure a touch when dealing with the British as Malvern. They forget, of course, that Malvern had failed in his recent and unrealistic bid for independence which was a product of his tendency to seek advice from his civil servants rather than from his Cabinet and his ministerial legal adviser in particular. He took little interest in the day to day running of his Ministers' portfolios except at times of difficulty. Likewise, a master of *laissez-faire*, he ignored his Party except at election times. Welensky by contrast was keenly interested in both the Party's and his Ministers' activities and constantly sought advice. Malvern had failed to secure independence when dealing with Eden, Home and Lennox-Boyd, while Welensky would have to face Macmillan, Sandys and Macleod and the realities of the post-Suez view of the Empire. Malvern, over seventy and no longer the vigorous man he had once been, was unlikely to have fared any better than Welensky in the new era.

CHAPTER EIGHTEEN

Accord with Britain

The Enlargement of the Assembly, and the Anglo-Federal Convention, November 1956–April 1957

WELENSKY took the reins as the world waited in trepidation to see if there would be a "Big Power" confrontation over Suez. He immediately despatched a message of support to the British Prime Minister, Sir Anthony Eden.[1] Furthermore, no end was yet in sight to the Northern Rhodesian emergency, and he was continually made aware of the activities of the African nationalists in the other territories. The copper price had fallen, and the outlay on Kariba was forcing stringent economies. Undoubtedly Welensky would have been happier to take office twelve months earlier, as Malvern had intended, when the copper price was over £400 per ton and the trauma of Suez was a year away. Fate would deliver Welensky two blows almost immediately. On 22 January 1957, Lady Welensky suffered a coronary thrombosis from which she never recovered completely, and, two days later, a heart attack killed Lord Llewellin. Llewellin had been ill for some time but was still able to supply the Federal Prime Minister with invaluable advice on the British politicians whom he knew so well. He would be greatly missed. If the blows rained thick and fast, Welensky, with the aid of Greenfield in particular, would reach an accord with the British Government with relative ease on the outstanding constitutional issues. Many people would look back on this period and see it as the zenith of the Anglo-Federal relationship.

The congratulations on his attainment of the Federal premiership flowed in as well as letters commending Welensky for his public support of Eden. The blocking of the Suez Canal cut the African east coast sea route to Europe but, more importantly, interrupted the flow of oil to the West and affected the Federation sufficiently for the Government to consider seriously rationing fuel. Another effect was the postponement of Home's visit.

Lennox-Boyd was among those praising Welensky for his support of Eden,

[1] Sir Roy Welensky, *Welensky's 4 000 Days* (London, 1964), p. 68.

adding that his Government would seek an honourable way to fulfil the aspirations of the Federal Government which, he noted, were for power not status. It was most important, he said, first to restore the atmosphere of trust so that the Federation could continue to develop with full British support. The key was to win sufficient backing for a franchise which would remove the racial factor from Federal politics and ensure the participation of those who could meet certain standards.[2]

In fact, the Federal Government was wasting no time because the Cabinet met the day Lennox-Boyd wrote, 13 November, to hear Greenfield suggest that it was time to advance concrete proposals to double the size of the Federal Assembly, to formualte legislation to remove the election of the special representatives from the territorial Governments, and to eliminate the African Affairs Board in ten years' time. The first step would be to draft a bill proposing a house of 52 elected seats and 18 for representatives of African interests. The latter would comprise four African and two Europeans from each territory. In a decade these Europeans would be replaced by Africans. The alternative, he suggested, was to draw a bill without mentioning the election of the special representatives and lay it before a conference of the territorial Governments called to settle the qualifications for the dual roll, and then decide on further action. Greenfield, not wanting to be out of step, had accepted the dual roll. He insisted that the upper roll be reserved for British subjects, and warned that it would be necessary to repeal the Southern Rhodesian Citizenship Act if the formula for Federal citizenship was to be accepted.

The Cabinet, however, thought that any proposal to abolish the African Affairs Board might endanger the whole package, but it acknowledged that the proposal provided something on which to effect a compromise. It agreed to a final attempt to persuade the British Government to accept Federal citizenship as a qualification for the franchise. If, as was likely, the British refused, some of the Cabinet wanted citizenship held in abeyance, but others did not because second-generation Northern Rhodesian Europeans were unhappy at being British Protected Persons. There was also a need to assume responsibility for naturalisation.

The Cabinet decided to re-draft the citizenship bill to incorporate minor changes suggested by the territorial Governments, and place it before its Caucus with the explanation that, if the British Government refused to accept Federal citizenship as a qualification for the upper roll, the Federal Government would insist that the roll be reserved for British subjects. Thereafter, the bill would be released publicly.[3]

A Federal ministerial committee on the franchise was formed, under the chairmanship of Greenfield, but before it could achieve anything, the Federal Chief Justice, Sir Robert Tredgold, warned Welensky that the current pressure for constitutional advancement could lead the Federation into an impasse from which it could only emerge with discredit. He deplored, in particular, the growing tendency, even amongst Cabinet Ministers, to talk of resorting to unconstitutional methods. He warned that he and many hundreds of others

[2] Welensky Papers, 27/62, f. 76, A. Lennox-Boyd to Welensky, 13 November 1956.

[3] *Ibid.*, FGC(56), 45th Meeting, Minute 7, Federal Cabinet, 13 November 1956.

would offer total resistance to anything unconstitutional — with the support of the law, the responsible Europeans, all the Africans, the British Government and the world. Such talk was bringing the Federation and its leaders into disrepute.

Tredgold, having examined the proposals for advancement failed to find any advantage in them. He felt they would merely waste money and manpower which could ill be spared. The public had to understand that only prestige was at stake. It seemed madness to quarrel over prestige and alienate many whose co-operation was desperately needed. It would only harden and swell African opposition to the Federation. Tredgold declared that the whole future depended on cultivating the right relationships, and it would be grimly ironic if the European should be fiercely demanding, and the African fiercely resisting, changes which would not substantially benefit the European or particularly hurt the African.[4]

Before Welensky replied to Tredgold, Greenfield predicted publicly in Ndola, on 29 November, a long and bitter struggle to nationhood in which the Federation would be ultimately successful. Many people, he noted, were impatient with the reluctance of the British Government to accord the Federation its rightful place when it had as proud a record in both world wars as any of the dominions. He was being asked, he said, why the Gold Coast, the Sudan and Nigeria were being advanced when the Federation was not. The Federation, of course, he asserted, could achieve instant promotion if it adopted universal adult suffrage but this would be madness because, at best, the result would be a form of Liberian anarchy. There was moreover much to be done before the Federation could claim full nationhood. The northern territories had to become fully self-governing, and before then the Federal and territorial franchises had to be settled. He expected that the electorate wanted to secure the position of the civilised members of society because, while the Africans had adequate safeguards, the Europeans had none.[5]

In Sinoia a day later, Welensky demanded enhanced status for the Federation within the Commonwealth without delay. Then he assured Tredgold that he would never use unconstitutional methods. Welensky agreed that the recent proposals had no practical advantages, and claimed that he had tried to play down the question of an enhanced status. However, surprised at the amount of support it had, he had sought to control the movement to steer it towards more reasonable goals. Tredgold would notice, Welensky said, that he had never referred to dominion status in public, although on occasions he had spoken about independence. He had concentrated on a "Higher Status" because it was unreasonable to expect the Federation not to change when constitutionally it could do so. He claimed that, as he had found Malvern's idea of independence to be pointless, he had not helped him to achieve it. Indeed, he had only heard the details of Malvern's proposals through a leak from London. Nonetheless, Welensky said, the British rebuff was resented locally and made his position, as the new Prime Minister, rather awkward. He would act constitutionally when the time was ripe. However, he found it difficult to accept that the Federation, as heir to the long record of self-

[4] *Ibid.*, 7/2, f. 253, Tredgold to Welensky, 22 November 1956.
[5] *The Rhodesia Herald*, 30 November 1956.

government in Southern Rhodesia, should be forced to play second fiddle to the Gold Coast, whose Prime Minister had been in gaol five years previously.[6]

In reply to Lennox-Boyd, Welensky claimed that, even though his opponents would set the pace on the subject of the status of the Federation, the Federal Party would win the next election if the British Government assisted it. The result would be assured if the Federation was soon given some advancement in status or was publicly assured that it would happen shortly. Because he could not see why the Federation should receive any less than the Gold Coast, Welensky informed Lennox-Boyd that he was prepared to hold a general election to provide an indication of public opinion on advancement. It was distressing that his High Commissioner in London should be treated as inferior to his Commonwealth colleagues. Lennox-Boyd had urged him to remove the racial factor from politics, but with "this abortion of a Constitution that we have" Welensky wondered if he ever could. The special representatives were not forced to consider European opinion with the result that, in his time as Deputy Prime Minister and as Prime Minister, only once had an African MP sought an appointment with him. The other key factor was that the Federal Government was specifically excluded from contact with the African population.

Welensky emphasised to Lennox-Boyd that he strongly resented the allegations which Benson had made on 6 June, and suggested his dismissal because their relationship was thereby destroyed.[7] Benson did not yet know into whose hands his dispatch had fallen, but he would appear to Welensky, at a heads of Governments' meeting in December, to be nothing but obstructive.[8] This judgment was harsh because Benson, as will be seen, was party to a compromise on the enlargement of the Federal Assembly. Perhaps it was the mood of the moment, because the Federal Government was experiencing difficulties with all its territorial partners. The decision to convene the meeting was taken in late November and Welensky had immediately sent Todd a copy of the agenda. He was considerably annoyed when Todd thereupon publicly proclaimed his rejection of the dual roll. This was a deliberate intrusion into Federal affairs because Todd had handed Welensky a copy of his statement on rejection before he made it. Welensky not only rebuked Todd publicly but asked Greenfield, as a friend of Todd, to inform him that goodwill and the desire to work together did not mean that one partner should go his own way and expect everyone else to follow. Todd replied in a speech that he remained determined at least to see that the common roll should continue to apply in Southern Rhodesia.[9]

On 7 December, C. W. F. Footman, Chief Secretary of Nyasaland, then proposed that, to secure African goodwill, the Federal Government should not take over any more concurrent subjects until the constitutional review, when the territorial Governments would be able to ask for the reversion of

[6] Welensky Papers, 7/2, f. 251, Welensky to Tredgold, 4 December 1956.
[7] *Ibid.*, 27/62, f. 75, Welensky to Lennox-Boyd, 6 December 1956.
[8] *Ibid.*, 9/5, ff. 32–34, Welensky to N. Barrett, 28 December 1956; 24/73, ff. 320–322, Welensky to Gore-Browne, 29 December 1956; 24/151, ff. 325–326, Welensky to F. S. Joelson, 3 January 1956.
[9] *Ibid.*, 24/151, f. 330, Welensky to Joelson, 27 November 1956; *The Rhodesia Herald*, 7 December 1956.

some of them. The Federal view was that the Nyasaland Government must have misunderstood the position because the contracting parties to the Federation would have rejected the idea that concurrent subjects had to be delegated first by the territories to the Federal Government before it could legislate on them. The Federal officials found this proposal objectionable because the Africans would feel that their resistance had won them a partial victory.[10] Benson commented that they could not decide on the enlargement of the Federal Assembly until the potential number of voters was known through the settlement of the franchise issue. If, however, there could be no delay, he favoured the number of European special representatives remaining constant while that of their African colleagues was doubled. He would increase the elected seats by 50 per cent so that the number of elected Members of the northern Legislative Councils and of Federal elected MPs would be equal. This would mean that the Federal constituencies would cover the same areas as the territorial.

Benson's suggestions were critically examined by the Federal Cabinet and Greenfield pointed out that the current size of the Federal House had been fixed before the number of voters had been assessed. The 50 per cent increase in elected seats, furthermore, would align the constituencies only in the northern territories because Southern Rhodesia had 30 not 14 territorial seats.[11]

When the heads of Governments met in Salisbury on 13 December Benson annoyed the Federal Government by appearing totally obstructive at first despite its eagerness to settle the contentious points. He irritated Lord Llewellin, in particular, by prefacing his comments with the remark that his views would not be those of his Government because some of his Executive Council belonged to and accepted the ideas of the Federal Party. Llewellin remarked to Welensky that this was untrue as the Governor and the official Members controlled policy and could over-rule the unofficial Members of the Executive Council.

First on the agenda of the meeting was the Federal proposal for the enlargement of its Assembly. Sir Robert Armitage, the new Governor of Nyasaland, said that he would not oppose the doubling of the number of seats but preferred a 50 per cent increase because it would align the constituencies of the Nyasaland Federal MPs with those of the elected Members of the Legislative Council. The Southern Rhodesians, Todd and Stumbles, agreed without reservation, but Benson advanced his plan to increase the Federal House to 54 seats to give Southern Rhodesia 21 elected seats, Northern Rhodesia twelve and Nyasaland six. The number of specially elected and nominated Africans would be doubled to twelve, but the number of Europeans representing African interests would be unchanged. Greenfield replied that the Federal electorate would not accept a doubling of the numbers of special African representatives because it would perpetuate racialism.

The meeting agreed that the European special representatives were needed

[10] Welensky Papers, 9/10, f. 4, C. W. F. Footman to Welensky, 7 December 1956; 9/11, f. 5, W. F. Nicholas to H. N. Parry, 10 December 1956.

[11] *Ibid.*, 9/11, f. 7, Greenfield's comments on Benson's letter, 11 December 1956; FGC(56), 49th Meeting, Minute 6, Federal Cabinet, 11 December 1956.

as they were required for the African Affairs Board. The Federal Government argued that a doubling of numbers would yield a better choice of members for the Board. The Federal, Southern Rhodesian and Nyasaland delegates thereafter accepted the Federal proposal for enlargement, but Benson dissented and considerably annoyed Welensky who knew that the British Government would agree to it.

The three territorial Governments argued that Federal citizenship need not be a qualification for the vote, but the Federal Government pointed out that the Commonwealth practice prescribed that the voter had to be a citizen with the status of a British subject, and even the recent amendment to the Nyasaland Constitution had provided that. Furthermore, the Federal electorate would insist on all voters being citizens and would probably only relent if special representation were ended. After all, the Constitution prescribed adequate safeguards for the African but none for the European. A citizenship law was a mark of self-government and it would be an anomaly that Southern Rhodesia should have one, when the Federation could not. There was also the need to supply a nationality for those who had been born in the northern territories of British parentage.

Next discussed was the dual roll. The Southern Rhodesians worried that the lower roll voters might expect to vote in territorial elections in Southern Rhodesia where the single roll was likely to be retained. However, they proposed to wait for the recommendations of the Tredgold Commission on their franchise before expressing any firm opinion. They suggested that the Commission should examine the Federal franchise as well, but the Federal representatives would not risk the embarrassment of a rejection by the Federal electorate of a suggestion made by a commission appointed by the Southern Rhodesian Government.

Benson supported the dual roll if British Protected Persons were admitted to the upper roll. He argued that, if they were excluded, racial politics would be perpetuated because there would be virtually no Africans on the upper roll and the Europeans might not bother to register on the lower. In any case, if they registered, the Europeans would dominate the lower roll for some time and the Africans would be driven into the arms of the extremists.

As Armitage agreed that British Protected Persons had to be accepted onto the upper roll if the Africans were to be won round, the meeting decided that it should form a sub-committee, chaired by Greenfield, to seek a compromise to allow both British Protected Persons and British subjects to vote on a single roll to elect all or most of the Federal MPs.

The sub-committee (Greenfield, Stumbles, Benson and Armitage) was told its purpose was to keep power in civilised hands, to win and retain African support and to bring the African into the party political system to eliminate racial politics. The Federal Government thought that, if the election of the special representatives were drastically modified, the electorate might allow British Protected Persons onto the common roll. The northern Governments, by contrast, insisted that the Africans could not be denied the rights they had gained to elect the special representatives and that the spirit of the Constitution had to be preserved.

The sub-committee produced a scheme to increase the number of the elected Federal MPs and yet preserve the existing rights of the Africans, while enfranchising the British Protected Persons. This would draw the African into party politics. It proposed a house of 59 seats. Therefore, the ordinary seats would be increased by 66 per cent, the African seats doubled, and only the number of European special representatives would remain unchanged. The 44 ordinary MPs would be elected on a roll of high qualification. The voters could be either British subjects or British Protected Persons. Southern Rhodesia would have 24 of these seats, Northern Rhodesia 14, and Nyasaland six. There would be four seats reserved for Africans for each territory. The established methods would be retained to fill the existing reserved seats, two for each territory, but the new MPs would be returned by elections on the common roll. Special representation would be eliminated progressively. Thus when an African captured an unreserved seat, a reserved seat would be removed and the number of unreserved seats increased by one. Alternatively, when the African voters represented a certain proportion of the total, special representation would disappear. The sub-committee commented that it was essential to settle the franchise qualifications quickly so that the territorial Governments could publicly support the Federal Government's proposals for amending the constitution. It advised the Federal Government to point out to the electorate that, under the new Federal electoral act, 53 out of 59 MPs would be elected instead of the current 29 out of 35. The Federal Government could also explain that the increase in seats for Nyasaland was only 50 per cent because its electorate was so small.

This proposal was accepted at the second plenary session, on 14 December, as a basis for negotiation. Benson wanted the opinion of the African Affairs Board, but Welensky thought that they should not depart from the normal procedure of only referring legislation to it in due course. Benson again demanded the alignment of constituencies but was ignored. The meeting agreed to withhold any public statement until the franchise had been settled and that this should await Tredgold's report. Until then, the Governments would prepare for an inter-governmental conference on the franchise which Greenfield would chair. The Federal Government then raised the question of the territorial power to suspend Federal laws in a state of emergency. It claimed that the same end could be achieved administratively, but the northern Governments were unconvinced. The meeting ordered the law officers of the four Governments to examine the problem.[12]

A communiqué was drafted indicating that the Assembly would be enlarged but that the franchise was not yet settled. It was published in *The Rhodesia Herald* the next day, 15 December, along with a comment ascribing any difficulty over the franchise to Todd's expressed dislike for the dual roll. However, two days later this newspaper entitled its leading article "The Shadow of Whitehall" and it was almost as if the writer had seen the minutes of the meeting. He commented that one would assume that, because of his earlier public statements, Todd had been responsible for the rejection of the dual roll, but that an analysis of the communiqué indicated that the culprits

[12] *Ibid.*, 9/11, f. 22, Heads of Governments Meeting, Salisbury, 13 & 14 December 1956; 23/23, ff. 58–60, Report of the Sub-Committee of the Heads of Governments Meeting, 14 December 1956; 8/111, f. 33, Llewellin to Welensky, 18 December 1956.

were the northern Governors. As Todd was waiting for the verdict of the Tredgold Commission, the writer continued, he would have wanted to reserve his position. The action of the northern Governors showed the extent to which the Colonial Office could influence the most crucial Federal issue of who would have the vote and control the Federation. This power was conferred by Article 98 which prescribed, in the first decade, territorial sanction of any constitutional amendment, whereas in the northern territories the Governors were all-powerful whatever Benson might say. How, *The Rhodesia Herald* asked, did Benson square his claims to have a Federal Party Government in Northern Rhodesia with his rejection of the dual roll? The result, it said, was that the Federation was forced to have a single roll of high standard if government was to remain in civilised hands. Consequently, the Federation might be saddled with an undesirable and even dangerous system of representation. It seemed unlikely, the newspaper concluded, that the franchise issue would be resolved before the general election in 1958.

Benson promptly drafted the letter to the editor which he wished Welensky, as chairman of the meeting, to sign. In this letter Benson claimed that the dual roll had not been rejected by himself and Armitage. He had simply not been prepared to obtain a unanimous decision from his Executive Council on a matter which lay outside its exclusive jurisdiction. He had not wished to embarrass the Federal Party Members of the Executive Council, through a conflict of loyalties, by invoking the principle of collective responsibility. So he had decided to express the personal views of the members of the Executive Council, and accordingly had brought with him Roberts and the Attorney-General of Northern Rhodesia, B. A. Doyle. The Executive Council had exhaustively examined the proposals, but had arrived at no collective decision. Nevertheless, all members of the Northern Rhodesian Government had accepted unanimously the dual roll in principle even though they wanted its proposed form modified. Armitage had agreed, and in fact it had been the Southern Rhodesians who had rejected the dual roll.[13]

Welensky refused to sign because he believed that a newspaper was entitled to express an opinion and to ask questions. He told Benson that it would be most unwise to comment on an editorial and, in any case, the proceedings of the meeting were confidential. Furthermore, he thought that the public might be misled because Roberts had only attended on the second day. In addition the northern Governors had indeed rejected the dual roll by objecting to the exclusion of British Protected Persons from the upper roll.[14]

Benson accepted that prime ministers did not write to newspapers, but insisted that the inaccuracy had to be corrected, and reserved his right to do so. Welensky replied that he had never suggested restricting Benson's freedom of action. He commented, somewhat wearily, to the Secretary of the Federal Cabinet, H. N. Parry, that it seemed that Benson still did not understand the difference between news and comment.[15]

Benson's relationship with Welensky reached its nadir in early January

[13] *Ibid.*, 42/26, f. 36, Benson to Welensky, 27 December 1956.
[14] *Ibid.*, f. 34, Welensky to Benson, 31 December 1956.
[15] *Ibid.*, f. 32, Benson to Welensky, 18 January 1957; Welensky to Parry (note on Benson's letter); f. 30, Welensky to Benson, 25 January 1957.

when Lennox-Boyd arrived in Northern Rhodesia and told him that Welensky had received a copy of Benson's dispatch of 6 June, and was considerably hurt by it. Lennox-Boyd ignored Welensky's doubts about continuing to work with Benson and merely ordered the latter to explain himself to Welensky. Lennox-Boyd also paid no heed to Benson's demands that whoever copied and distributed the dispatch should be prosecuted under the Official Secrets Act. Benson would meet Welensky after Lennox-Boyd had returned to London.[16]

Lennox-Boyd, spending a week in Northern Rhodesia before travelling to Salisbury, used his time there to express support for the Federation. He told an audience in Ndola on 1 January 1957 that the reality of the Federation had been accepted in responsible circles and that the only remaining controversy was whether to break the links with the Colonial Office, which might be premature. He promised to tell the British public how good he had found race relations and how liberal the thinking was.[17] At other meetings he praised the achievements of the Europeans and assured the Africans that Britain would not forsake them. However, he earned criticism from the Dominion Party and the London *Economist* through his refusal to meet representatives of political parties, including Nkumbula. The *Economist* felt that Lennox-Boyd was losing the opportunity to show that he was more sensitive to African opinion and to the inevitable changes than were local whites. He responded by meeting Nkumbula, but only as a private individual.

Welensky hardly gave Lennox-Boyd time to protest his support for the Federation when on 3 January he said publicly that there would be serious trouble if the Africans continued to ignore the territorial and Federal Governments when seeking guidance. He warned the British Government that many African leaders rejected partnership because it prevented them from achieving a purely African-dominated government. The British had to understand that, if this goal were ever realised, another part of Africa would be lost to progress. It was necessary to recognise that, by contrast, those who supported the Federation intended to maintain British standards. Indeed, the Federation might become the last British bastion in Africa. Steps had to be taken to make the British way of life secure yet Britain would grant full self-government to the Gold Coast and deny it to the Federation. The British refused self-government, it seemed to Welensky, because the hands which ensured the maintenance of standards were not only white but of their kith and kin.[18] There was no response from Lennox-Boyd or the African nationalists, but James Johnson of the British Labour Party immediately reminded Welensky that the Constitution for ten years precluded a parallel advance to that of the Gold Coast. Johnson was anxious that Welensky should know that Nkumbula did believe in partnership despite the imposition of the Federation against African wishes. The same was true, he said, of the African leaders in Nyasaland even though they were more bitter.[19]

[16] *Ibid.*, 42/26, f. 29, Benson to Welensky, 31 January 1957; Author's interview with Sir Arthur Benson.

[17] *The Rhodesia Herald*, 2 January 1957.

[18] *Ibid.*, 4 January 1957.

[19] Welensky Papers, 24/157, ff. 216–217, J. Johnson to Welensky, 5 January 1957.

Welensky reinforced his warning by writing that day to Lennox-Boyd to spell out his fears. He declared that the immediate problem was to improve the structure of government and to bring the African into politics, because the European had not yet been weaned from segregation, nor had the African resistance dissipated as the benefits of the Federation increased. It was essential, he said, that the African should gradually take a larger part in the political and economic life with the full acceptance of the European. Yet as African opposition increased, European opinion hardened. The African masses might not have definite views but they were highly suggestible and were open to intimidation and could be manipulated to the advantage of the African leaders. While the situation was not yet alarming, the trends were, and the Federal Government, excluded from contact with the African, could do nothing. Major reform of the complicated relationship of the five Governments was most necessary as it was to a large extent responsible for the current situation. The progress of the whole populace was being adversely affected. The northern Africans were increasingly unco-operative and showed no desire to be brought into the political system. They rejected liberal solutions for fear of being seduced into accepting the Federation. With appreciable effect, Welensky claimed, the Congresses were endeavouring to wield power in the economic as well as the political field, aiming to achieve African-dominated self-government.

Welensky warned that current trends might affect investment and inhibit any Federal or territorial constitutional advancement. He said that the Europeans increasingly feared that the British Government would support the Africans to the Europeans' detriment because the arguments used against Malvern's bid for enhanced status would be just as valid in ten years' time. Consequently the Federation would continue unreformed. Thus, if there were no constitutional change, Welensky asserted, the Europeans would become more apprehensive. The situtation was exacerbated by the Africans becoming aware of the suspicious attitude of the Colonial officials towards the Federal Government when the latter's only contact with the Africans was through those officials. He alleged that relations with the Nyasaland Government were fine, but that the Federal and Northern Rhodesian Governments had diverged to the point that the removal of a few officials would have little effect.

Welensky maintained that Home's proposal for joint action to win over the African had been very wide of the mark, showing fundamental ignorance of the African attitude. Welensky exonerated his Government, citing the recently revealed structure of the Federal civil service, the establishment of the multi-racial university, and the opening of the facilities on the railways to all races. The Federal Government had gone further than the Colonial Office because it had accepted, in principle, that Africans could be commissioned in its army. It intended to open employment on the railways to all races, but was faced by a powerfully-entrenched European union, and industrial relations was a territorial subject. Furthermore, the economy would be endangered by a major industrial upheaval. He said the Federal Government was prepared to grant citizenship to all inhabitants but the British Government had objected because the British Protected Persons did not want to become British subjects thereby. Consequently, the Federal Government would be able to confer citizenship on only one third of the population. Welensky was confident that his Government could not be faulted on its provision of finance for African services, and the franchise would be settled as soon as a formula acceptable to the territories had been found.

Even so, Welensky said, all these changes in a liberal direction had not affected African attitudes. The fault, he believed, lay with the system which gave the impression that the British and Federal Governments pursued opposing policies and that there was still a choice between the multi-racial Federation and ultimate African supremacy. The African nationalists wished to return to full Colonial rule as a first step to African self-government, and as they expected to secure this goal after the next British election, they were not interested in political evolution within the Federal system. They also exploited the aspects of racialism and the apparently diametrically-opposed Federal and territorial policies in an effort to convince the African population that the Federation was a bar to their aspirations. They were convinced that the Colonial service was bent on implementing black rule, and the attitude of some of the officials seemed to confirm this.

Welensky continued, explaining that many of these officials had spent their lives implementing a policy different from the Federal Government's and some resented the change. Others believed that the Federal Government was intent on amalgamation. The Federal Government was left in an awkward position because two-thirds of its population was suspicious of its policies and felt a greater loyalty to Britain. It did not help for the whole population to believe that the British Government was also suspicious of Federal intentions. In many ways he felt that the proposed freedom of action of the Federal Government in its own sphere had not been realised. Protracted negotiations with the territorial Governments were often necessary on many Federal matters, which gave the British Government an indirect say in Federal affairs at a moment when British and territorial governmental attitudes had hardened against the Federation through no fault of its own.

Welensky declared that all that was needed was for Britain to make it abundantly clear to the African that secession was impossible, that the Federation would not disintegrate at the review and that, therefore, their future lay in the Federation. The British Government could show its confidence in the Federal Government by a declaration of common aims. It could declare that the territories would advance within the framework of the Federation and of the Commonwealth.[20]

Welensky wrote in like vein to Home that day, saying that, to assist in the wooing of the African, he was considering forming a small ministry, under his control, to keep race relations under constant review. For this to be successful, he said, he would obviously need the assistance of the British and territorial Governments.[21]

These letters were discussed when Lennox-Boyd met Welensky and the Federal Cabinet on 8 January. They must have had some effect because Lennox-Boyd replied to Welensky's words of welcome by stressing his sup-

[20] *Ibid.*, 20/1, ff. 284–289, Welensky to Lennox-Boyd, 3 January 1957.
[21] *Ibid.*, 7/2, f. 198, Welensky to Lord Home, 3 January 1957.

port for the Federation. Evidence of this, he proclaimed, would be found in his declarations in Northern Rhodesia of the total British commitment to the Federation. He had emphasised that secession was impossible.

The meeting deferred this discussion, and considered citizenship. Greenfield announced that a Federal citizenship bill would be introduced in February and that it would force Britain and the Commonwealth to amend their legislation if the Federal citizen were to be a British subject. He warned that his Government would expect Federal citizenship to be a qualification for the franchise. If this were rejected by the British Government, the Federal Government would demand that the voter be a British subject, but this would merely perpetuate the current system.

Lennox-Boyd replied regretting the abandonment of the dual roll. However, Welensky reassured him that it could be introduced if the problem of the British Protected Person were resolved. Lennox-Boyd promised to reconsider two-tier citizenship.

They discussed next the enlargement of the Federal Assembly and Gorell Barnes, the Assistant Under-Secretary of State for the Colonies, emphasised that it would be most undesirable to extend the system of special representation for Africans because it would entrench racial representation. The meeting accepted that this was a point on which both the British and Federal Governments could agree.

When territorial constitutional advancement was considered, Lennox-Boyd said that he was expecting proposals for self-government for the northern territories, which would almost certainly include the enfranchisement of the British Protected Person, albeit on otherwise high qualifications to ensure civilised standards. He acknowledged the need for the Governments to stress the similarity of their aims and their support for the policy of partnership. Above all, the African had to be encouraged to look to the Federal Government for his salvation. Lennox-Boyd thought that this effort could be assisted by the Federal Government producing an imaginative franchise. Welensky and Caldicott responded by saying that for that reason they had advocated the dual roll and two-tier citizenship.

Lennox-Boyd advised the Federal Cabinet against any proposal to abolish the African Affairs Board because the antagonistic British and African reaction would give the Board an importance it did not deserve. He promised that, when the status of the Federation was enhanced, its Government would be given greater control of external affairs. He attributed the territorial power, to override Federal legislation in an emergency, to an unintentional oversight, and offered to make a ministerial pronouncement on Article 29(7) — which gave Britain the power to negate any Federal law — to avert any further controversy on it.

Discussing at last Welensky's letters to Home and himself, Lennox-Boyd acknowledged that the Federal Government was not bent on amalgamation but he had, unfortunately, already found the European unions in Northern Rhodesia, for example, more eager to talk about it than their own affairs. If their views were made public, they would give the Africans good reasons to believe that this was the European intention.

Welensky answered that he had already told Lennox-Boyd that none of the political parties had made amalgamation their aim, and that the best way to scotch the fear was to make a success of the Federation. Lennox-Boyd thought, therefore, that Welensky should not only say this in public but should declare that a unitary government was not a prerequisite for dominion status.

The final matter raised by Lennox-Boyd was the African dislike for the Federal importation of Greeks and Italians as semi-skilled labour on the railways. Welensky replied that this illustrated the constitutional anomaly of the territories controlling the supply of labour, while the Federal Government was responsible for the railways. The Federal Government could not deal directly with the Rhodesia Railways Workers' Union which was very conscious of its powerful position. The railways needed semi-skilled labour and, until the union could be forced to accept Africans, immigrants such as Greeks, Italians and others were needed.[22]

The same day, 8 January, Lennox-Boyd addressed a public meeting in Salisbury and claimed that colonial rule would not endure a day longer than necessary, and that he was trying, in the meantime, to lift colonial affairs out of the British political arena. However, he could do no more for the moment, because he was forced to return to London the next day by the resignation of Eden. Yet as good as his word, he let no opportunity slip, and as he left he declared his belief in partnership.[23] He arrived home as Harold Macmillan kissed hands as Prime Minister, a fateful day for the Federation.

Retained by Macmillan at the Colonial Office, Lennox-Boyd returned to the Federation on 14 January. He went straight to Nyasaland where he continued his outspoken support of the Federation and immediately clashed with W. M. Chirwa and the African Members of the Legislative Council.[24]

Some members of the Federal Party thought that Lennox-Boyd had uttered nothing more than platitudes, but, to the contrary, Federal intelligence believed that he had shocked the Africans by his uncompromising attitude. The African nationalists in Nyasaland announced that they were not going to accept the Federation (despite its reality) under any circumstances and would achieve secession. However, Lennox-Boyd stressed the permanence of the Federation and reassured the Nyasalanders in general that its existence would not inhibit the constitutional development of the territories. He found that they did not seem to understand that it would be easier for Nyasaland to advance within a strong Federation.[25]

Lennox-Boyd then returned to Northern Rhodesia — to Broken Hill — where, on 20 January, he again asserted that the Federation was permanent and that it was idle to suppose that a successive Labour Government would destroy it. The Northern Rhodesian ANC ignored this and asked him publicly to allow the territory to secede at the review, to enfranchise British Protected Persons immediately, and to provide equal racial representation on

[22] *Ibid.*, 20/1, ff. 76–80, Ministerial Discussions with the Colonial Secretary, 8 January 1957.
[23] *The Rhodesia Herald*, 9 & 10 January 1957.
[24] *Ibid.*, 16 January 1957.
[25] Welensky Papers, 42/21, f. 199, G. Beckett to Welensky, 11 January 1957; 9/5, ff. 24–27, H. J. Roberts to Welensky, (undated); 27/62, f. 65, Welensky to Lennox-Boyd, 30 January 1957; *The Sunday Mail*, 20 January 1957.

the Executive and Legislative Councils. Nkumbula suggested that a non-racial dual roll should be adopted, using the current qualifications for the upper roll. He assured the Europeans that they need not fear being swamped because the lower roll seats would be strictly limited and would be progressively eliminated as significant numbers of Africans qualified for the upper roll.[26]

Lennox-Boyd answered the demand for secession in a radio broadcast on the African service on 23 January by repeating that everyone had accepted the permanence of the Federation and would work to make a success of it. He reminded listeners that the basis of European fears was that they would be overwhelmed by the weight of African numbers and denied their rightful place. As all development depended on the Europeans, it would be wise to reassure them. If this were done, African fears would also fall away.[27]

Lennox-Boyd fired another shot from Johannesburg on his way home by saying that there were too many irresponsible Africans in the Federation who believed that the white man had no right to be there. To the contrary there were Europeans who had been there for three generations who had more right of occupation than some of the Africans who had come in from nearby territories. Neither race, he thought, should claim superiority by virtue of numbers or intellect. He laid the responsibility for the African opposition at the door of the previous Labour Government because it had done nothing more than allow matters to drift.[28]

In the Commons on 6 February he repeated that British control of the northern territories would not last a day longer than it was needed, and he expressed the hope that the Africans would look to the territorial and Federal Governments with the same confidence with which they did to Westminster.[29]

Welensky warmly praised Lennox-Boyd because he believed that he had done some good. Welensky was, however, reeling under the double blows of the heart attacks suffered by his wife and Lord Llewellin. Lady Welensky clung to life, but Llewellin, who had been ill for a year, did not rally. Before Llewellin died at 4 a.m. on 24 January, Welensky acknowledged that he was losing a friend and a counsellor of immense value. In the coming months it was to prove impossible to find a man willing to serve who had as great a wealth of political experience as Llewellin. The search was all the more difficult because Welensky refused to have a soldier as Governor-General.[30]

It not only took a considerable time to find a replacement, but Welensky found himself for a few hours without an Acting Governor-General and was forced to act illegally and sign documents of state which needed immediate action. The Chief Justice was required by the Constitution to act for the Governor-General in his absence or on his death, but, when Welensky telephoned him at 6 a.m. on 24 January, Sir Robert Tredgold refused to comply until he had finished his work as chairman of the Southern Rhodesian

[26] *The Rhodesia Herald*, 21 & 22 January 1957.
[27] *Ibid.*, 23 January 1957.
[28] *Ibid.*, 25 January 1957.
[29] *Ibid.*, 6 February 1957.
[30] Welensky Papers, 25/202A, f. 209, Welensky to Sir Ronald Prain, 9 January 1957; f. 202, same to same, 22 January 1957; 24/151, ff. 320–321, Welensky to Joelson, 23 January 1957.

Franchise Commission. He persisted in this attitude when he met Welensky and Greenfield later in the morning and even proposed to resign as Chief Justice when Welensky insisted that he should take office. Welensky had to ask Home by telephone to persuade Tredgold to act even for a short period. Tredgold submitted and took office for a week or two. He managed, however, to clash again with Welensky later in the year. Welensky's office saw a lengthy telegram from Tredgold to Home criticising the negotiations on the Federal franchise, and Welensky immediately informed Tredgold that an Acting Governor-General could do nothing more than appoint the chairman of the African Affairs Board. He certainly could not interfere in Federal negotiations. Tredgold refused to accept this, and Welensky, by means of the telephone, again invoked the aid of Home to call Tredgold to order.

Tredgold was replaced as Acting Governor-General, at Welensky's suggestion, by Sir William Murphy, a former Governor of the Bahamas, who was farming in Southern Rhodesia and who was about to act as its Governor while the incumbent, Sir Peveril William-Powlett, took leave. Murphy filled both posts until June.[31]

A legacy of the visit of Lennox-Boyd was Welensky's confrontation with Benson. On 31 January Benson informed Welensky that Lennox-Boyd, when leaving, had told him that Welensky had received a copy of his dispatch of 6 June. As this had deeply hurt Welensky because he had hitherto regarded Benson as a friend, Lennox-Boyd had warned Benson that the outlook for further co-operation was indeed bleak. Benson asked and was told that Welensky had known the contents of the dispatch for three months. This angered Benson considerably because it meant that he had not been allowed immediately to explain himself to Welensky.[32]

Intimating that he would probably resign, Benson sought an interview with Welensky. He did not tell Welensky that he had demanded without success that Lennox-Boyd take action under the Official Secrets Act against the copier of the dispatch. Neither did he reveal that he had offered to resign but had been told to stay until he had effected the pending Northern Rhodesian constitutional change. Benson stayed and effected the change in 1958, but when in 1959 he was offered a further term of office, he declined it.[33]

On 4 February Welensky wrote to Benson agreeing to the interview and took the opportunity to correct Lennox-Boyd because it had been Malvern who had received the copy of the dispatch. Malvern naturally had shown it to him. Nevertheless, Welensky had been bitter because he felt that he had failed as a judge of character. In 1954, he recalled, Lyttelton had asked him whether he would prefer to have Sir Frederick Crawford or Benson to succeed Rennie in Northern Rhodesia and he had replied that he would be satisfied with either.[34] In fact, Welensky's correspondence of 1954 confirms his welcome of Benson even though Crawford was a personal friend.

[31] *Ibid.*, 24/151, f. 197, Welensky to Prain, 31 January 1957; Author's interview with Sir Roy Welensky; Home to Welensky, 25 January 1957 (a telegram in the possession of Sir Roy Welensky); J. M. Greenfield, *Testimony of a Rhodesian Federal* (Bulawayo, 1978), p. 153.

[32] *Ibid.*, 42/26, f. 29, Benson to Welensky, 31 January 1957.

[33] Author's interview with Sir Arthur Benson.

[34] Welensky Papers, 42/26, f. 27, Welensky to Benson, 4 February 1957.

Welensky and Benson met in Salisbury two weeks later, and the latter recalls that he found Welensky unwilling to discuss the details of the dispatch but eventually agreed to a line by line examination. Benson maintains that during this interview Welensky conceded the veracity of the allegations, but Welensky reported to the contrary to Lennox-Boyd. In his view the interview had been quite fruitless because Benson had tried but failed to justify his allegations. Welensky told Joelson that he had finally asked Benson how he could continue to maintain that a man of the calibre of Malvern would not appreciate that the British Government would never sanction amalgamation because it would bring the protectorates under local control and set the precedent for South Africa to demand incorporation of the High Commission Territories.[35]

None of these difficulties had interrupted the examination of the franchise and citizenship. On 15 January the Federal Cabinet discussed the meeting of the heads of Governments and the discussions with Lennox-Boyd and Gorell Barnes. It accepted a house of 59 seats and noted the point made by Gorell Barnes that racial representation would be perpetuated if the elective principle was not adopted. It regretted the abandonment of the dual roll but acknowledged that Southern Rhodesia was likely to oppose it. Finally it decided that the proposed inter-government committee should meet as soon as possible.[36]

Consequently, Greenfield chaired a meeting of this committee on 30 January. He began by saying that he presumed that the British Protected Person would be admitted to the single roll but, because the electorate would object, he thought that the committee should devise qualifications to accommodate the northern fears that the current high income levels would exclude most Africans. It was thought that virtually no Africans in Northern Rhodesia would qualify at the £500 p.a. income level and, because the £300 p.a. qualification was associated with the possession of the Cambridge Overseas Certificate, only 550 would be eligible for the vote in 1959 and 6 500 in 1974.

As the northern representatives happily accepted the high qualifications, Greenfield proposed a third income level of £200 p.a. which would be coupled with an adequate knowledge of English and service for a specific period in one of a series of designated responsible occupations. He had drawn, of course, on the earlier ideas of Benson.

The meeting accepted this as an interim measure and devised, therefore, a method of eliminating it by progressively raising the income level as the number of voters increased until it equalled that of the lower of the two permanent qualifications. The meeting re-introduced the concept of the possession of property as an alternative to an income of a certain standard, and re-adjusted the existing proposed income levels by adding £100 p.a. to both. The first then became the possession of an income of £600 p.a., or property worth £1 500, and two years of secondary schooling (this was an innovation) and an adequate knowledge of English. The second level was an

[35] Author's interview with Sir Arthur Benson; Welensky Papers, 27/62, f. 63, Welensky to Lennox-Boyd, 19 February 1957; 24/151, ff. 301–302, Welensky to Joelson, 19 February 1957.
[36] Welensky Papers, FGC(57), 2nd Meeting, Minute 6, Federal Cabinet, 16 January 1957.

income of £400 p.a., or property worth £1 500, and the possession of the Cambridge Overseas Certificate and an adequate knowledge of English. The third income level of £200 p.a. would have an alternative of the possession of property worth £500. The period of service in the responsible occupation would be ten years.

An immediate difficulty was that the Nyasaland delegates felt that the occupations prescribed for one territory would not suit another. For example, the ranks of the Nyasaland teachers and civil servants contained many shady characters. Moreover, a third level of qualification would mean that the Nyasaland European voters would be outnumbered from the outset. Thus the Nyasalanders wanted to retain their current veto over Federal electoral law so that they could design a system for Nyasaland's peculiar needs. The meeting decided, however, merely to designate different sets of occupations for each territory. It accepted a minimum age of 21 and the enfranchisement of women who qualified. The position of polygamous wives was unresolved.

Greenfield closed the meeting of the inter-government committee by warning that his Government would enlarge the Federal Assembly to 59 seats, including 15 for special representation of Africans, if the franchise were not settled soon. The enlargement did not need the sanction of the territories in terms of Article 98 because the ratio of ordinary and special seats would not be disturbed, but he hoped that the territories would support it. Only the Nyasalanders replied, and they agreed to support it.[37]

While Greenfield thus sought to settle matters with the territories, Welensky decided to take the initiative on the resolution of the broader constitutional issues. He knew that there could be no major constitutional amendments before the Federal review but thought he had found a number of adjustments which could be made and thus improve the position radically. The simplest way to win local popularity, and therefore the 1958 general election, was to become an open antagonist of the British Government, but he believed that he would thereby achieve only a Pyrrhic victory. He informed Joelson and Don Taylor, of the *New Commonwealth*, of his intentions and declared publicly that he would make a stand on the issue of white survival.[38]

However, before he could dispatch his proposals to London, Home informed him that there was no possibility of securing any amendments to the British Nationality Act if citizenship were not divorced from the franchise. Home wanted Welensky to assist him by making a declaration to this effect and to make it clear that he would not ask the British Protected Person to give up his status. Home and Lennox-Boyd had also decided that a two-tier citizenship was unacceptable because the decision in 1947 turned all Commonwealth citizens into British subjects. Home also declared that he and Lennox-Boyd genuinely sympathised with Federal desires for an improvement in status but were glad that Welensky understood that British parliamentary difficulties would prevent any anticipation of the review before 1960. However, wishing to satisfy some of the Federal aspirations, Home said that it

[37] *Ibid.*, 8/111, f. 85, Minutes of the Inter-Government Committee on the Federal Franchise, 30 January 1957.

[38] *Ibid.*, 24/151, ff. 306–307, Welensky to Joelson, 5 February 1957; 42/60, f. 109, Welensky to D. Taylor, 5 February 1957.

might be possible to effect some changes in the constitutional field without having to resort to British legislation.[39]

Home had cabled just as Welensky was dispatching his proposals to London and, as Welensky was also thinking of ways of improving the situation without resorting to legislation, it is possible that he had already outlined his ideas to Lennox-Boyd. Welensky claimed in his dispatch that his ideas had not yet been revealed to his colleagues and would not be until Home had replied. If necessary, he would travel to London to press his case. He said that the fundamental difficulty was the British method of exercising its responsibilities. To remedy this Welensky thought that the British Government should publicly declare that its administration of the northern territories was an integral part of the Federal system and was divorced from that of the rest of the Empire. It was also necessary to convince British Protected Persons that they were not foreigners living in the Federation and owing loyalty only to Britain, the protecting power. This could be accomplished by extending the franchise to them. However, the electorate would first have to be persuaded to accept this by Britain making a determined effort to make the Federation work and offering, at least, some prospect of an improvement in its status.

Welensky emphasised that he was not asking for independence, or for constitutional amendments other than to enlarge the Federal Assembly, or for any alterations to the status of British Protected Persons, the protectorates or the safeguards. He sought only to improve the system, to engender loyalty to the Federation and induce a feeling of security among all races. He announced that he had a number of suggestions which would improve the administration of Federal affairs. The first was the establishment of a Central African department in Whitehall to deal with both Federal and territorial matters. This would be seen as a declaration of faith in the Federation. It would recognise the unique position of the Federation in the Commonwealth and end the anomaly of the Commonwealth Relations Office being responsible for the Federation and Southern Rhodesia only, while the Colonial Office dealt with Northern Rhodesia and Nyasaland. Welensky felt that this would give the lie to the current belief that Britain was pursuing two conflicting policies and evaluating these in the light of events in her other colonies. Loyalty to the Federation would be encouraged as would the acceptance of the policy of partnership. The establishment of such a department would create a cadre of advisers with the breadth of knowledge of Federal affairs which was vital if the British Government was ever to understand Federal problems. To further their education, there could be an exchange of officers between the department and the Federal and territorial services. Evidence would thus be supplied of the effort being made by the five Governments to establish a prosperous multi-racial society. It would scotch the fear of the majority of the electorate that Britain, through the lack of a desire to co-operate, was retarding the progress of the Federation.

Welensky's second suggestion was that the civil services in the northern territories should be locally based like those of the Federation and Southern

[39] *Ibid.*, 8/111, ff. 94–95, Home to Welensky, 15 February 1957.

Rhodesia. This he felt was as urgently needed as the Central African department. The Federation would only gain if all civil servants knew that their entire careers would be spent serving it. The independence of the services would not be prejudiced, and there would be equal opportunites for Africans. He proposed inter-service promotion because he disliked the current practice of offering opportunities in the world-wide Colonial service, for he believed that it induced a feeling in the northern Africans that the current arrangement was temporary and that ultimately they would govern themselves. He knew that the protagonists of the system would argue that they could thereby secure better recruits, but the Federal and Southern Rhodesian services were locally based and were not any less efficient, and the Northern Rhodesian service was already recruiting locally at a junior level.

The third improvement would be to delegate, in terms of the Constitution, greater powers to the Federation in the field of external affairs. This was necessary, Welensky said, if only because Southern Rhodesia had possessed greater control of its external relations prior to federation. It would assist the Federation in dealing with its Belgian and Portuguese neighbours. The Federation should be responsible for all its external dealings except for those which affected the British responsibilities in the protectorates, which could not be delegated. It would not mean that Britain would be consulted any less than at present.

Welensky proposed that any necessary legislation should be as non-controversial as possible and aimed only at improving the Federal system. It would not lessen the safeguards or affect the status of the protectorates. It should be accompanied by declarations affirming the continuance of the federal form of government to allay the suspicions of the Africans on amalgamation and reassure the insecure that secession was impossible. There was need of a new British act, specifically connected with the Federation, to replace those which gave Britain jurisdiction over the two protectorates and their inhabitants. This was necessary as the Foreign Jurisdiction Act was chiefly involved and gave legal foundation to Northern Rhodesia and Nyasaland being regarded as foreign territories. This was being exploited by African nationalist propaganda. The status of either the protectorates or British Protected Persons would be unaffected because their rights were already entrenched. It was also necessary to provide that, after an appointed day, no act of the British Parliament should extend to the Federation as part of its law unless there was Federal consent for its enactment. This, he said, would undo the notorious Article 29(7).

Welensky maintained that it had never been intended, when the Federal Constitution was enacted, that a British order in council should enable a territory to supersede or suspend any Federal law. Unfortunately the Emergency Powers Order in Council of 1939 had been overlooked, and the Northern Rhodesian Government had used it to suspend certain Federal prison regulations. Although the suspension itself was innocuous, the Federal Government felt that in principle it was wrong that its legislation could be thus suspended. Any public disclosure of this anomalous situation, he stated, was likely to embarrass his Government.

Welensky felt that there was also need to adjust the Colonial Laws Validity

Act with regard to the Federal Government, and that it should be stated that no Federal law would be inoperative simply because it was repugnant to the laws of England. He wanted the power to legislate extra-territorially and believed that Federal citizens, once the Federal citizenship act was passed, would be recognised as British subjects. Finally, he asked the British Government to declare that it would convene the review at the earliest possible date, meaning 1960, and that the review would consider the date and the conditions for the complete independence of the Federation. The British Government should also confirm that the review could not consider secession. Finally he repeated his concern to win over the African and asked for British and territorial co-operation if he set up his proposed small ministry to review race relations continually.[40]

Welensky remarked to Lennox-Boyd that he was going so far to meet the British difficulties that he was risking his premiership. Home did not reply in detail, merely suggesting an immediate discussion between their officials as a preliminary to a visit by him in mid-May. It was imperative to avoid a hostile public reaction. Welensky disagreed because he thought that it was necessary for them to devise the compromise before their respective officials could supply the details. Furthermore, he had to meet Home soon because, to be effective by the next election, any bill to amend the Constitution had to be introduced before mid-June. He proposed, therefore, to visit London within a few weeks.[41]

While Welensky awaited the British reaction, Greenfield steered the Citizenship Bill through the Federal Parliament. Introducing it on 28 February, he explained the reasons for its form and how British Protected Persons could not be enfranchised without the annexation of the northern territories. Consequently the Federal Government proposed that anyone born in Southern Rhodesia, and those born of British parents in the northern territories, should automatically be Federal citizens. British Protected Persons could become Federal citizens by registering, swearing allegiance and undertaking to fulfil the duties of a citizen. Britain would have to legislate to accord the Federal citizen the status of a British subject. The Southern Rhodesian Act would be superseded.

The Bill had an easy passage through the Federal Assembly mostly because Doig withdrew his objection to the oath after reading a number of oaths currently used in the Commonwealth. What opposition there was was entirely predictable. Chirwa threatened to walk out because he could not see why British Protected Persons should change their status to become Federal citizens. Van Eeden thought that, as the process of securing British nationality would be much easier, there could be a marked increase in the number of northern Africans acquiring the vote.

Although Greenfield advised Chirwa to study the difference between Crown colonies and protectorates, Chirwa continued to oppose the Bill through all its readings. He proclaimed that the Africans objected strongly to the Bill because it should not be brought in before the review. Yamba sup-

[40] *Ibid.*, 20/1, ff. 267–275, Welensky to Home, 15 February 1957.
[41] *Ibid.*, 27/62, f. 63, Welensky to Lennox-Boyd, 19 February 1957; 20/1, f. 265, Home to Welensky, 2 March 1957; f. 264, Welensky to the Acting Commonwealth Secretary, 8 March 1957.

ported him and claimed that it seemed that, in clearly supporting this Bill, Britain was giving up her protective role. Accordingly the northern African would have to look elsewhere for a protector, or protect themselves. Greenfield replied that plainly the African MPs had misunderstood the Bill because it had no "diabolical" intentions.[42]

The franchise issue had not been resolved, but the debate on citizenship prompted van Eeden to ask for a report on progress. On 5 March he claimed that an explanation by the Government was long overdue and he could not believe that, after four years, broad intentions had not been settled. He hoped that the solution offered would not be as feeble as the formula for citizenship.[43]

Greenfield replied by outlining the negotiations, stating that the Government intended ultimately that the House would comprise only elected MPs. Then Chirwa declaimed on a supposed denial of the vote to Africans and the consequences. The other northern African MPs dwelt on the subject of "civilisation" and rejected it as a criterion for the vote. They provoked Welensky to remind them it was a criterion of their territorial Governments and the British Government. He also denounced Chirwa as "an unmitigated twister of the truth" because, while he sat in the Assembly and took part in the process of governing, he claimed that the Europeans would not share the government with Africans.

On 11 March, L. M. N. Hodson pressed the Government to deal urgently with the amendment of the Constitution to enlarge the Assembly. However, Williamson and van Eeden decried the irresponsibility of this at a time of financial stringency. Chirwa thought that the Federal Government should have concentrated on securing economic benefits for Africans. If the Federal Government had consulted the Africans it would have discovered that they regarded an enlarged House as simply a threat to their future. It was time that the European appreciated the dangers of ignoring the Africans. I. D. Smith, an advocate of the enlargement, noted that Chirwa always opposed anything that would benefit the Federation. Van Eeden closed the debate with the comment that the reason for enlargement was to accommodate the excessive numbers of aspiring politicians which the fusion of the Federal and United Rhodesia Parties would produce. Nonetheless, the motion was overwhelmingly accepted.[44]

Hodson had steered the Federal Assembly away from the franchise but it was the most topical political issue because on 14 March the *Report of the Commission on the Southern Rhodesian Franchise* was published.[45] Its findings, however, did not surprise the Federal Government because a week previously Tredgold had briefed the inter-government committee on them.[46] He had told how his Commission had sought the opinions of individuals, associations and study groups and had discovered a consensus on the retention of the common roll, but with a variety of alternative qualifications for the voters.

[42] Fed R & N *Debates* (Salisbury), Vol. 7, Col. 2619 f., 28 February 1957.
[43] *Ibid.*, Vol. 7, Col. 2800, 5 March 1957.
[44] *Ibid.*, Col. 3037, 11 March 1957.
[45] *Report of the Franchise Commission* (Salisbury, 1957).
[46] Welensky Papers, 8/111, f. 81, Meeting of the Inter-Government Committee on the Franchise, 7 March 1957.

The Commission had found that the African population could be divided into a minority of extremists and a majority anxious to co-operate with the Europeans. Nevertheless, both groups deeply mistrusted the Europeans, and the Commission had concluded that, to correct this, a greater number of responsible Africans had to be enfranchised.

The franchise qualifications had to be lowered, but the influence of the better qualified voters, the Commission maintained, should not be swamped. This could be ensured by providing three higher categories of voters, and one whose voters had low qualifications but whose votes could never count for more than half the votes cast in any one constituency. These categories would be permanent and delimitation would be crucial because it would be clearly better to establish constituencies in which the numbers of the lowest category of voters were less than half those of the higher categories rather than devalue their votes at an election.

The Commission proposed that the voters should qualify for the first category by having an income of £720 p.a., or possess immovable property worth £1 500, and an adequate knowledge of English. The second category required an income of £480 p.a., or property worth £1 000, and one year of secondary schooling. The third had an income level of £300 p.a., or property of £500, and a school certificate acquired after four years of secondary schooling. The fourth required only an income of £180 p.a. and an adequate knowledge of English.

Tredgold believed that only 10 000 Africans would qualify at the lowest level, and of those only half would register because currently only a fraction of those who possessed the existing qualifications, an income of £240 p.a., had bothered to register. There were, in fact, only 600 African voters. Nevertheless, he felt that sufficient Africans would qualify initially to ensure that the scheme would become increasingly popular. He rejected the inter-government committee's idea that the lowest category should be temporary and that the voters qualifying for it should have spent a specified time in responsible employment. He disliked it because he believed that the Africans would see it only as a method of limiting their enrolment. In any case, such regulations might inhibit people from changing employment to better themselves.

Tredgold emphasised that he had retained a single roll, but the inter-government committee (and, indeed, Welensky and others[47]) saw his proposals as much akin to a dual roll as there would be effectively two permanent classes of voters through the devaluation provision which could affect the lowest category. The committee contrasted this with its intention to eliminate its proposed lower class of voters as the Africans increasingly acquired the means to qualify on equal terms with the other members of the community. It would be difficult also, the committee felt, to explain to the Africans why their vote could be devalued and indeed, it was invidious to reduce the value of anyone's vote in an arbitrary manner. Racial voting might be encouraged, and it was possible that candidates could be returned after polling fewer votes than their rivals. In Nyasaland the special votes would have to be devalued

[47] *Ibid.*, 24/73, ff. 293–295, Welensky to Gore-Browne, 22 March 1957.

immediately because the delimitation could not produce constituencies in which the lowest category of voters did not dominate. The committee found that there were other problems, and if the economy did not prosper the voters would not be able to progress to the higher levels.

After Tredgold left the meeting, the inter-government committee re-examined its own proposals. The Northern Rhodesians found the income levels too high, while the Nyasalanders claimed that the £200 p.a. level was too low because their European voters would be immediately outnumbered. The Nyasalanders wanted it to be £300 p.a. with a time limit for its elimination. The Northern Rhodesians favoured the Tredgold formula, but the Nyasalanders disagreed unless the limit for fractional voting to be applied was lowered to a third of the votes cast. However, both northern delegations agreed to re-examine the Tredgold formula.

The Federal delegates warned that their Government would soon have to draft the constitutional amendment bill and wanted to eliminate special representation. The meeting, however, agreed that this could only be done when the Africans began to capture the ordinary seats and that the first to go should be the special European seats. Thereafter ordinary European MPs could serve on the African Affairs Board if required.

A meeting of the heads of Governments was convened for the end of March and, in preparation for this, the Federal Government reconsidered the outstanding issues. While this was being done, Home, through Lord Salisbury, was trying to avert Welensky's proposed visit to London. Salisbury, who was acting for Home who was in New Zealand, acknowledged the need for haste but feared that the arrival of Welensky would give rise to furious speculation in Britain and Africa. Such a furore would only hamper the British Government's ability to assist Welensky. Salisbury advised Welensky to agree to the preliminary discussions between their officials and to the already-announced visit by Home in May. Home was, moreover, prepared to arrive at the beginning instead of the end of May.[48]

Welensky, replying the same day, 13 March, found May to be too late. Clearly, he said, the British Government did not appreciate how little time there was to amend the Constitution, delimit the constituencies, and compile voters' rolls before March or April 1958, when the general election had to be held. The alternative, which was unthinkable, was not to enlarge the Assembly and to legislate only for the 26 elected seats. If he should not go to London, then he demanded that Home should visit the Federation in early April *en route* from New Zealand. There would be undesirable speculation but, Welensky said, it did not worry him overmuch. Officials were welcome, but Home was needed because decisions had to be taken.[49]

Welensky waited three days and then, through Lennox-Boyd, pressed Home again. Welensky reminded Home that he had attempted to minimise the British difficulties and that he was trying to avoid the question of dominion status becoming an issue in the Federal general election by presenting the electorate with a *fait accompli* which shelved the independence

[48] *Ibid.*, FGC(57), 9th Meeting, Minute 9, Federal Cabinet, 13 March 1957; 20/1, f. 262, Salisbury to Welensky , 13 March 1957.
[49] *Ibid.*, ff. 260–261, Welensky to Salisbury, 13 March 1957.

issue until the review. If agreement could be reached shortly on other issues, said Welensky, holding out the proverbial carrot, he might well be able to enfranchise the British Protected Person on the same terms as everyone else. He repeated that he was trying to avoid having to shout louder than the Dominion Party for independence because he appreciated the difficulties in which he would place the British Government.

While Welensky struggled thus with the reluctant British, he received praise from Tredgold and support from Todd. Tredgold adjudged Welensky's proposals to be a masterly method of dealing with the problems of constitutional advancement because it would satisfy the legitimate aspirations of the people of the Federation whilst avoiding any charge of flouting the undertakings of 1953.[50] Todd, for his part, wrote to Salisbury praising everything which Welensky had proposed except for the creation of a Central African department which the Southern Rhodesian Cabinet disliked because it would imply a demotion for their territory. Their electorate would insist that instead the Commonwealth Relations Office should take charge of the northern territories. There was, after all, nothing extraordinary in this because the Commonwealth Relations Office already cared for the protectorates of Bechuanaland, Swaziland and Basutoland. Todd also gave notice that, as the Southern Rhodesians would accept the Tredgold proposals to broaden the basis of the franchise, he would soon demand the removal of the reserved powers from the Southern Rhodesian Constitution. He would do so because his Parliament would be fully representative of all sections of the community and safeguards would be unnecessary.[51]

Salisbury revealed to Welensky on 21 March that Home would not break his journey from New Zealand to visit the Federation because he would be out of touch with the latest developments. Furthermore, Home considered that a flying visit would be a poor substitute for the tour of the whole Federation which he intended to make in May. Instead he invited Welensky to visit London in April, and asked him to withhold his hand from the Press. Welensky agreed with alacrity and proposed to arrive in London on 12 April with a small party which would include Greenfield and the Federal Attorney-General, V. L. Robinson (later Sir Victor). Welensky wanted to settle first the principles and then set the officials to work on the details.[52]

The meeting of the heads of Governments was in the offing, and both Todd and Benson sought Welensky's ear. Todd was anxious to explain his rejection of the Central African department. He had also always believed that there was a great need for inter-governmental co-ordination and claimed that there was a special relationship between the Federal and Southern Rhodesian Governments because they were both responsible to the Commonwealth Relations Office and were of equivalent status. He felt that they had to make a united approach to the British Government on what he saw as the three immediate issues. These were the creation of the Central African department, the merging of the office of the Governor of Southern Rhodesia with that of

[50] *Ibid.*, 7/2, f. 225, Tredgold to Welensky, 19 March 1957.
[51] *Ibid.*, 20/1, ff. 258–259, Todd to Salisbury, 19 March 1957.
[52] *Ibid.*, f. 257, Salisbury to Welensky, 21 March 1957; f. 256, Welensky to Salisbury, 22 March 1957.

the Governor-General, and the problem of constitutional advancement. His Cabinet had rejected the first categorically, the second it had accepted in principle, and the third it had not yet considered in detail but felt that it would be more appropriate if Southern Rhodesia were promoted before the Federation. To reconcile these views, Todd proposed an immediate formal meeting of themselves and their Cabinets. If no agreement was forthcoming, the Southern Rhodesian Government would seek representation at the Anglo-Federal negotiations in April or would request a later opportunity to put its views across.[53]

Welensky rebuffed Todd gently, agreeing to meet him but not his Cabinet. He claimed to favour inter-government co-operation but reminded Todd that there were subjects which were exclusive responsibilities of the individual Governments. When dealing with these, it would be useful to consult the others, Welensky said, but in doing so the Federal Government could not favour one Government by seeking its opinion alone. In any case, he felt that, if he had to secure territorial sanction for everything he wished to raise in London, he would never get there.

Welensky recalled that he had recently shown Todd his dispatch on the Central African department so that he could see it in perspective. The ideal was obviously to transfer the northern territories to the Commonwealth Relations Office but it had always been resisted by the Secretaries of State, before and after federation, because they believed that it would be unacceptable to the Commons. Furthermore, there was no doubt that it would be unfavourably received by the northern Africans. To Welensky, the greatest advantage of the proposed department was that, unlike the Colonial Office, it would not be committed to an eventual surrender of the northern territories to African domination.

As for the merging of the Federal and Southern Rhodesian governorships, Welensky believed that it might undermine the federal principle. He thought, anyway, that there would be vigorous protests from Northern Rhodesia and Nyasaland and that the impartiality of the Governor-General would be severely strained if the Dominion Party was in power in one assembly and the Federal Party in the other.[54]

Benson, perhaps still bruised from their last encounter, sought Welensky's attention because he was anxious that there should be no misunderstandings when the heads of Governments met. Accordingly, Benson carefully sketched the limitations of the Northern Rhodesian Government. It could not, for example, agree to the amendment of the Federal Constitution without the consent of the Colonial Secretary. Therefore at the forthcoming meeting, he could not agree or disagree with the proposed formulae for the Federal franchise and the enlargement of the Federal Assembly. He would be prepared to recommend wholeheartedly the enlargement if Article 13(2) were amended. If it were not, he would be faced, as a territorial Governor, with the impossible task of having to construe the new voters' roll, when used to elect the new special African representatives, as being "... a body representative of Africans". All the franchise proposals confronted him with similar difficulties

[53] *Ibid.*, ff. 253–255, Todd to Welensky, 26 March 1957.
[54] *Ibid.*, ff. 250–252, Welensky to Todd, 27 March 1957.

because they all favoured European interests. In the opinion of himself and his Executive Council, the best course would be to modify the Tredgold proposals to suit Federal and territorial needs. He enclosed a Northern Rhodesian Government memorandum showing how the Tredgold system could be adopted in Northern Rhodesia and promised to support an elective system for the new Federal African representatives if the Federal Government accepted this as a formula for its franchise.[55]

The memorandum emphasised the need to curb the influence of the ANC which had demanded that it should be recognised as the only body representing African opinion. The ANC had failed to win any seats on the urban, rural, Provincial or African Representative Councils, but its influence was such that it controlled many of the members of these bodies. Indeed, the memorandum claimed, the majority of the members of the African Representative Council, all the African Members of the Legislative Council and the Federal MPs would profess to support the ANC. The Government had resisted the ANC demands and had insisted that it should work within the system. The granting of some executive powers to the African Councils and an extension of the franchise sufficient to convince the African that to vote would definitely give him a voice in the making of policies, would stifle the ANC because the majority of Africans was well-disposed towards the Europeans. However, special representatives should be discarded because the ANC could always label them as stooges.

The intention, the memorandum continued, was that power should be retained in civilised hands, but Africans had to be able to gain seats and no fewer than the four they currently held in the Legislative Council. Such a result could be achieved by the use of a common roll and careful delimitation. The rural constituencies could ensure the return of desirable African MPs because the influence of the ANC therein was minimal and the European votes would have a moderating effect. The unreformed Tredgold scheme was unsuitable because its ordinary qualifications would exclude most Africans from voting in the next Northern Rhodesian general election in 1959, and its special votes could never count for more than half the total of the votes cast which meant that, if a European stood for any constituency and was opposed only by an African, he would be elected. Moreover, the concentration of Europeans on the Copperbelt ruled out the application of the variety of delimitation proposed by Tredgold. The memorandum recalled that subsequent discussions with Tredgold had led him to recommend that, instead of never counting for more than half the votes cast in a constituency, the special votes should be reduced in influence to a third of the total votes.

The criterion was to eliminate the influence of the ANC because otherwise the future of the Federation was in jeopardy. This could not be achieved by tighter control and police activity. The African had to be brought into the electoral systems and a variation of the Tredgold proposal could accomplish that in the Federal and territorial fields. The variation was to adjust progressively the upper value of the special votes. Accordingly, when the number

[55] *Ibid.*, 23/23, ff. 29–30, Benson to Welensky, 26 March 1957; ff. 38–40, Northern Rhodesian Government Memorandum — Application of the Tredgold Proposals to Northern Rhodesia, 28 March 1957.

of special votes cast was less than three times the number of ordinary votes, then they would not count for more than a quarter of the total number of votes polled. When they amounted to more than three but less than four times the total number of votes, they would not count for more than a fifth of the latter. The fraction would be reduced to a sixth when the number of special votes exceeded that of the ordinary votes by four or more times. Concluding, the memorandum stated that this arrangement would last for ten years when it would be abolished and the special voters then registered would become ordinary voters.

In its examination of the memorandum, the Federal Government noted that the deliberate "rigging" of the rural constituencies would ensure the return of a limited number of African MPs while it eliminated specified racial representation. These Africans would be elected where the ANC would have minimal influence and the European vote would have a healthy effect. Furthermore, after ten years the fractional voting system would be eliminated and there would be a return to a franchise of high quality. It would be difficult, however, to justify the "blatant chicanery" of the delimitation and the result would inevitably be an African demand for more seats and even equal representation. As this device was so obvious it was not worth adopting. In any case, Federal law required the use of a judicial commission for delimitation and it could not be instructed to produce constituencies for the return of members of a specified race when racial representation *per se* no longer applied. The fractional voting system could not work without such manipulation and, the Federal Government maintained, it was iniquitous anyway that the value of the vote should vary with the number of votes cast. It also disliked the elimination of the system after ten years because the special voters, on becoming ordinary voters, would outnumber the Europeans in several districts, and totally in Nyasaland. Furthermore, there was no justification for making them ordinary voters when they did not qualify. It was surely better to use normal methods of delimitation and reserve a number of seats for Africans which could be slowly removed.[56]

For its own part, the Federal Cabinet devoted two of its meetings in late March to an examination of the alternatives regarding the franchise so as not to attend the meeting of the heads of Governments empty handed. On 19 March, after an exhaustive study of the variations, Greenfield re-introduced the dual roll for consideration because, he said, as citizenship would no longer be a qualification for the franchise, Southern Rhodesia might not continue to oppose it. He argued that, after all, Tredgold had virtually proposed a dual roll there. However, the point was immediately raised that, as time was short and because there was little to choose between the proposals, it was surely better to adopt the proposal most likely to be accepted by the territories. The Cabinet agreed and ordered first the discovery of the Southern Rhodesian attitude to the Tredgold proposals and thereafter a substantial agreement with the Southern Rhodesians before the meeting of the heads of Governments.

The Cabinet met again before this was achieved to consider a memorandum

[56] *Ibid.*, ff. 62–68, Federal Government Comment on Tredgold Proposals, 28 March 1957.

by Greenfield on the three possible variations of the franchise. These were a modification of the Tredgold system, the proposal of the inter-government committee, and the Federal dual roll. The Cabinet concluded that the best compromise would be to marry the Tredgold qualifications with the dual roll because of the difficulties presented in Nyasaland by the tiny European electorate. Under the dual roll system, the European would still be greatly outnumbered within ten years, but it was better than the other ideas which would achieve that result immediately.

The Cabinet decided to ask the heads of Governments to examine the dual roll. There might be difficulties over the preponderance of European voters on both rolls, and there could be a demand for the reservation of seats for candidates specifically elected by the lower roll. However, the Cabinet expected Welensky to have to concede, in April, the admittance of British Protected Persons to the upper roll. He could then argue that his political difficulties would be such that a strong European influence on the lower roll would have to be accepted as a *quid pro quo* for the promotion of the British Protected Person. The Cabinet also predicted that the Northern Rhodesian Government would insist that lower roll qualifications should be set at a level at which the African voter would predominate. The territorial Governments might want one of the other proposals, but Welensky promised to press hard for their acceptance of the dual roll, and to that end these Governments would be given notice of his intentions.[57]

Welensky then saw Todd and persuaded him to agree to the Federal Government adapting the Tredgold qualifications to the dual roll.

The Federal Government outlined its ideas in a memorandum to be laid before the heads of Governments, stressing the need for haste. It discussed therein the three alternative schemes and, in advocating the third, expanded on it. The upper roll voters would elect all 59 MPs, while the lower roll would vote for the 15 African representatives. The upper roll voter would have three votes, one for the election of an ordinary MP, one for a European representative of African interests, and the last for an African MP. The lower roll voter would have two votes, one for the election of the European representative of African interests and the other for an African MP. Only if there were an objection from the northern Africans would the current systems of electing the special representatives be retained, and then only for the existing seats. Any additional African MPs would still be elected by the upper and lower rolls voting together. The Tredgold qualifications had been adapted to the dual roll, and the three upper roll income levels had been set at £720, £480 or £300 p.a. The alternative property qualifications and the educational standards were as described by Tredgold. The special qualification selected for the lower roll was an income of £180 p.a. and an adequate knowledge of English. The special seats would be gradually eliminated as the Africans captured ordinary seats. Wives of monogamous marriages and the first wives of polygamous marriages would be accepted as voters on the qualifications of their husbands.[58]

[57] *Ibid.*, FGC(57), 10th Meeting, Minute 3, Federal Cabinet, 19 March 1957; 11th Meeting, Minute 2, 25 March 1957.

[58] *Ibid.*, 23/23, ff. 75–78, Federal Government's Electoral Proposals, 30 March 1957.

On 30 March, after an inconclusive discussion on the taxing powers of the Federal Government, but after agreeing to accept the recommendation of the recent Fiscal Commission to reduce the Federal share of income tax by two per cent, the heads of Governments turned to the constitutional problems. Speaking with Greenfield on the Federal proposals, Welensky reserved the questions of British Protected Persons and the franchise, as well as other matters relating to citizenship, for his negotiations in London. He had thought that such a statement would provoke Benson, but it did not.

Greenfield said that the scheme of the inter-government committee was too difficult to justify. The Tredgold system of devaluation was as awkward, and trouble could be expected whenever it was applied. The dual roll, by contrast, used the same qualifications, but not the devaluation of votes. The lower roll voters, Greenfield said, would only be involved in the election of 15 MPs, and the objection that these voters would resent their special status applied equally to the unreformed Tredgold proposal. Welensky reminded the meeting of the peculiarities of the federal system and urged the acceptance of the dual roll as a means of accommodating them.

The meeting approved of the ultimate goal of returning to the common roll through the gradual elimination of the lower seats, but Todd rejected the dual roll because it consolidated racialism. The Tredgold system, he said, avoided that because the ordinary and special voters voted together for all the MPs and he was confident that adjustments could be made for Nyasaland. Stumbles and Benson thought that the phasing out arrangement suggested by the inter-government committee was being discarded too hastily. Armitage disagreed and warned that all the proposals contained difficult and disagreeable features which were almost impossible to justify. The best of the schemes was, in his view, the dual roll because, though it enfranchised few Africans on its upper roll, it would produce an African majority on its lower roll. The goal was to elect moderate Africans, and the non-Africans on the lower roll could assist in attaining it. Armitage, however, still wanted to continue to select the European and African special representatives and would allow only the additional African MPs to be elected by the lower roll. He also sought to have the lower roll qualification set at £100 p.a.

Benson rejected the dual roll because the upper roll would influence the election of the lower roll candidates. He disliked the Tredgold scheme because it would produce no African MPs, but he had adapted it to produce African representation without the specific reservation of seats. The meeting, however, criticised his proposed gerrymandering of constituencies to return African MPs. They thought that perhaps the solution was to provide for three different electoral systems.

Welensky regretted this suggestion because he was hoping that the territorial Governments would agree to common qualifications. He warned that, if there were no agreement, the Federal Government might merely legislate for the election of the existing 26 MPs because then neither a constitutional amendment nor the territorial sanction thereof would be needed. In this eventuality, the Federal Government would choose a franchise with high qualifications, one of which would be Federal citizenship. The subject of enlargement, he said firmly, would not be pursued because the Federal

Government and its electorate were not prepared to have any more African representatives chosen on the current basis.[59]

The meeting made no further progress, and Welensky prepared to go to London. He ignored a demand from Gaunt that, if the Federal negotiations failed, the Federation should first declare its loyalty to the Queen and then its own independence. However, Welensky was provoked by the British Labour MP, James Johnson, who had been invited to Northern Rhodesia by Nkumbula, and who told a meeting of Africans in Ndola that he sympathised with their plight of finding themselves "fighting alone". Publicly and privately denouncing such phraseology as offensive, Welensky wondered whom the Africans were fighting and reminded Johnson that, if he was referring to the Europeans, they, as taxpayers, paid for the education of the Africans.[60]

The British Labour Party in late March had intruded into the Federal constitutional argument by publishing James Griffiths's *Plural Society* as its plan for the Federation. This demanded, as the essential foundation of a democratic society, adult suffrage. Secondly it insisted that Britain retain ultimate control of all her plural societies until full democracy was implemented. Any transfer of power would depend on the existence of constitutional instruments outlawing all forms of racial discrimination.

Welensky paid no heed to this and, indeed, on 5 April claimed that he would soon secure a guarantee, written into the Constitution, that independence would be granted in 1960.[61]

Before Welensky reached London, a blow was dealt to the Federal Government as Lord Salisbury resigned because Macmillan decided to release Archbishop Makarios from exile in the Seychelles. Salisbury told Welensky that he had been unable to accept collective responsibility for a policy with which he profoundly disagreed.[62] The Federation had lost its staunchest ally in the British Government. No one ever really replaced him.

A more immediate danger was an effort by Todd to undermine Welensky's proposals. In a letter to Home on 10 April, Todd emphatically denied the rumour that his Government intended to veto the amendment of the Federal Constitution to enlarge the Federal Assembly, but he confessed that it disagreed with the Federal franchise proposals and viewed them with apprehension. Todd hoped that Welensky could be dissuaded from adopting the dual roll because it represented a retreat from the Southern Rhodesian non-racial outlook and aims. Todd believed in the single roll and that the Tredgold scheme was correct for Southern Rhodesia and therefore for that part of the Federal electorate which came from that territory.

Todd enclosed a memorandum which vigorously underlined the recommendations of the Tredgold Commission Report and asked why, after 34 years of responsible government in Southern Rhodesia, standards should be sacrificed to accommodate those of the least developed state in the Federation. Above all, Southern Rhodesians objected to the introduction into their political life

[59] *Ibid.*, 9/11, f. 24, Heads of Governments Meeting, Salisbury, 30 March 1957.
[60] *Northern News*, 28 March 1957; *The Rhodesia Herald*, 31 March 1957; Welensky Papers, 24/157, ff. 182–183, Welensky to J. Johnson, 1 May 1957.
[61] *The Rhodesia Herald*, 6 April 1957.
[62] Welensky Papers, 43/*Lord Salisbury*, Salisbury to Welensky, 8 April 1957.

of a system under which a specified group of people voted for special representatives. If a lower roll was unavoidable then at least its voters should vote also for the ordinary candidates. If the Tredgold recommendations could not be adopted uniformly throughout the Federation, they could be varied to suit the needs of the individual territories and would do much to eliminate racial politics.[63]

In London, on 12 April, Welensky and Greenfield met Home, Lennox-Boyd and C. J. M. Alport, the current Parliamentary Under-Secretary of State for Commonwealth Relations. Home immediately asked if the British Protected Person would qualify for the vote without sacrificing status. He also wanted to know if the alternative property qualifications would enfranchise a reasonable number of Africans because his Government had to be satisfied on a number of such points before he could reach an accommodation with Welensky. He wondered what form an agreement between the British and Federal Governments should take, and suggested that they should settle for a joint communiqué. Welensky accepted this suggestion and claimed that, despite his failure to secure the support of the territorial Governments, he was confident he could obtain public approval for any formula upon which he and Home agreed. They then examined, in the course of five cordial meetings, the issues at stake and drew up the communiqué which they published on 27 April.[64]

The British and Federal Governments prefaced the communiqué with a reaffirmation of their opposition to amalgamation or secession. They announced that they had agreed that the Federal review would be held in 1960 in terms of Article 99, and that its purpose would be to examine the Constitution in the light of experience gained since the inception of the Federation, and to agree on constitutional advances which might be made. The review would consider a programme for the attainment of a status which would enable the Federation to become eligible for full Commonwealth membership. The Federal Government was later to refer frequently to this statement when it was at odds with the British Government over the controversial recommendations of the Monckton Commission which included secession.[65]

The communiqué related that Welensky, Greenfield, Home and Lennox-Boyd had examined the progress made and had agreed that the hopes of the founders of the Federation had been justified and that a sound basis had been laid for the further development of partnership. The first product of their discussions was an acceptance by the British Government of Welensky's request for the granting of the fullest possible responsibility for external affairs, bearing in mind that the Federation was not yet a separate international entity. The Federal Prime Minister would be allowed to advise the Queen direct on certain formal and ceremonial matters. Submissions relating to the territorial Governments, however, would continue to be made by the

[63] *Ibid.*, 23/23, f. 3, Todd to Home, 10 April 1957.

[64] *Ibid.*, 20/1, ff. 227–230, Minutes of a Meeting, Commonwealth Relations Office, 12 April 1957.

[65] *Ibid.*, f. 217, Minutes of a Meeting, Commonwealth Relations Office, 15 April 1957; ff. 212–213, Minutes of a Meeting, Commonwealth Secretary's Room, House of Lords, 16 April 1957; ff. 210–211, Minutes of a Meeting, Commonwealth Secretary's Room, House of Lords, 17 April 1957; ff. 196–198, Minutes of a Meeting, Commonwealth Relations Office, 18 April 1957.

Secretaries of State. The British Government promised to consider the creation of a Central African department when it reviewed the responsibilities of its Ministers with regard to the constantly evolving Commonwealth. It agreed to legislate to allow the Federation to make laws with extra-territorial effect.

The communiqué also told how Welensky had drawn attention to the controversy over the purpose and effect of Article 29(7) and the matter of the British Parliament legislating for the Federation. The British Ministers had replied that their Government recognised the existence of a convention which applied to the current stage of the constitutional evolution of the Federation whereby, in practice, the British Government did not initiate any legislation to amend or repeal any Federal Act or to deal with any matter within the competence of the Federal legislature, except at the request of the Federal Government. This assertion would be referred to, with much bitterness, in 1962 when the British Government chose to ignore it and to act unilaterally in granting Nyasaland the right to secede.

The British Ministers agreed that locally-based civil services would eventually be established. As a first step they promised to consider the possibility of interchanging officers.

Finally, it was announced that the British Government had accepted in principle the enlargement of the Federal Assembly. No similar declaration was made on the Federal franchise because Welensky had said that formal proposals were dependent on further negotiations in Salisbury. However, he had assured the British Ministers that a bill would be introduced under which the British Protected Person, who was otherwise qualified, could register for the vote without having to change his status. The franchise qualifications would ensure that a reasonable number of such persons could qualify.[66]

The communiqué said nothing about the extension of the taxing powers of the Federal Government so that it might collect fees for some of the services it provided, but Home had promised that any bill to amend the Constitution thus would receive sympathetic consideration from his Government. The demand for the amendment to the Foreign Jurisdiction Act was dropped after Alport had claimed that the only result would be confusion and misunderstanding in the Commons. It was also agreed that, rather than mention the power of the northern Governors to suspend Federal legislation in emergencies, it should be curbed by an administrative instruction.

The suggestion for the creation of a Central African department was rejected by Lennox-Boyd because Malaya, Nigeria and the West Indies might make similar demands. Welensky replied that his main reason for asking for this department was that, as long as the Colonial Secretary was responsible for other parts of the Empire, where different policies were applied, the northern Africans would be unsettled. He had made the same point when discussing the need for locally-based civil services, but the meeting framed the published statement so as not to shock the existing Colonial civil servants. Home promised that this goal would be realised when the Federation became independent.

[66] *Ibid.*, f. 246, Joint Declaration on the Review of the Constitution, 27 April 1957.

The original draft of the Joint Declaration, which served as the preface to the communiqué, was also toned down. It had stated that the British and Federal Governments were "not prepared to consider any proposal either for amalgamation . . . or for secession". However, Lennox-Boyd, obviously accepting the advice of the Colonial Office, argued that it was necessary to persuade the Africans to participate in the review and that it would be a mistake, therefore, to give the impression that discussion on any subject might be ruled out.

Welensky and Greenfield would rue the day on which they agreed to this. Of course the communiqué was a device to achieve many of the Federal aims without having to resort to British legislation which Home feared might jeopardise the success of the review. There would be times when the Europeans of the Federation would curse Home's timidity, while the African nationalists welcomed it as something they could exploit.

Welensky nonetheless was in an aggressive mood and used the moment to reply to the Labour Party at a Press conference. He stated forcibly that the dogma of one man, one vote would not apply in the Federation in the foreseeable future and that any pretence that it could was mischievous and dangerous. Nevertheless, the cordiality of the parting between Welensky and the British Ministers was reflected in the Press reports which lauded Welensky as probably the first engine driver to have spent a night at Windsor, and credited him with the sagacity of an elder statesman. Macmillan had taken the trouble to entertain Welensky and Greenfield to lunch at Number Ten Downing Street and had impressed them with his confident air.[67] All was affability at the lunch table, but almost exactly six years later, Welensky would refuse a like invitation lest he choke on the food of the man whom he regarded as a traitor.

Welensky returned to Salisbury and presented the draft of the communiqué to his Cabinet two days before it was published. He told the Cabinet that the most important achievement was the convention that the British Parliament would only legislate for the Federation at the request of the Federal Government. Almost as significant, he said, was the promise that eventually the civil services would all be locally based. To gain these concessions, he had been forced to offer to compromise on the enfranchisement of British Protected Persons. However, he felt that this had been inevitable and even the Southern Rhodesian Government had concurred.[68]

The next and difficult task was to settle the franchise and pilot it and the enlargement of the Assembly through the Federal Parliament and past the African Affairs Board. A Federal general election had to be fought and thereafter other difficulties faced, but a significant step seemed to have been taken towards independence. Nonetheless, the stumbling block of the Colonial Office's desire for black advancement remained, and events were, in due course, to render the Federal review farcical and the ultimate consequence would be the break-up of the Federation amidst much acrimony.

[67] *The Rhodesia Herald*, 18 April 1957; Greenfield, *Testimony*, *op. cit.*, p. 154; Welensky Papers, 42/52, f. 38, D. Cole to W. S. Parker, 20 April 1957.

[68] Welensky Papers, FGC(57), 14th Meeting, Minute 4, Federal Cabinet, 25 April 1957.

CHAPTER NINETEEN

Growing Discord

Argument over the Constitutional Amendment and Electoral Bills, April 1957 – January 1958

THE Accord of 1957, as Welensky has admitted, was coolly received in the Federation[1] and he and his Government still faced the difficult task of framing and implementing the Federal franchise and the enlargement of the Federal Assembly. This would only be completed in February 1958. In the process the Federal Government would face defections from its supporters, a new militancy among the African nationalists, and collisions with Todd, Moffat and the African Affairs Board. The copper price continued to plunge, reaching new record low levels every month until November when it stood at £174 a ton, well over £200 lower than it had been in mid-1956. The situation was not helped by Todd experiencing difficulties of his own or by the exploitation of the situation by James Callaghan, a young, unknown and new Shadow Colonial Secretary. Not only did Callaghan, a member of a visiting Commonwealth Parliamentary Association delegation, abuse the rules and thus the hospitality of the Federal branch of the Association, but he committed the Labour Party to the infamous — in the eyes of the local Europeans — dogma of NIBMAR, "No Independence Before Majority Rule".

Another positive result of Welensky's visit to London was the choice, finally, of a successor to Lord Llewellin. On 24 April the new Governor-General was named as Simon Ramsay, M C, LL D, the sixteenth Earl of Dalhousie, who had been a Conservative backbencher for the first five years after the Second World War. It is interesting to note that among other men suggested were Lord Salisbury; Lord Monckton, soon to head the Commission on the Review of the Federal Constitution; Sir Robert Tredgold; Marshal of the Royal Air Force, Sir Arthur "Bomber" Harris (later Lord Harris) who began his military career in the First Rhodesia Regiment in 1914; and Lieutenant-General Sir Archibald Nye, the distinguished soldier who

[1] Sir Roy Welensky, *Welensky's 4 000 Days* (London, 1964), p. 77.

had been Governor of Madras and British High Commissioner in India and Canada. Welensky, it will be remembered, was opposed to having a soldier.[2] Dalhousie took office on 8 October 1957, and would prove a popular Governor-General.

On his return, Welensky set Greenfield to work immediately on the franchise and other constitutional issues. They would not, however, be easily solved. Welensky's first action was to answer criticism from Gaunt on his agreement with Home, spelling out publicly the political facts of life. The Dominion Party had attacked the proposal to enlarge the Assembly, but Welensky maintained that it was needed to develop the democratic two-party system. It was equally important, he said, to deviate from the racial representation of the North and, consequently, his Federal Government would not allow an extension of the system of nomination. It would keep power in civilised hands but could no longer deny the British Protected Person the vote because of his status alone. Welensky claimed that, although Gaunt might argue that the Convention on British legislation for the Federation was meaningless, the Federal population would appreciate its significance, particularly if the British Labour Party came to power.[3]

In his Legislative Assembly, Todd paralleled Welensky's arguments because the Tredgold Report was being debated and, in lauding it, he maintained that progressive measures were necessary if Southern Rhodesia was not to be overwhelmed by African nationalism and communism. He then introduced legislation to allow the establishment of multi-racial trade unions.[4]

Welensky reported to Home that their agreement had been well received in the Caucus but that two members had objected to his compromise on British Protected Persons and that one of the members would resign. Home replied explaining how the Federal control of external relations had been improved. The Federation, he said, could open direct relations with any Commonwealth country, exchange high commissioners and enter into any agreement with it. It could negotiate with foreign countries, subject to British responsibilities under international law. The British Government would allow the Federation to establish missions in capitals on the pattern already implemented in Washington (where Whitehead had been dispatched in 1956) and in Lisbon. It could appoint diplomatic agents, consular or trade representatives and accept like representation in return. The Federation would be able to join any international organisation to which it was entitled, and henceforth the British Government would keep the Federal High Commissioner in London fully briefed on foreign affairs. In return, the latter would inform the British Government of any Federal negotiations.[5]

James Johnson warned Welensky on 5 May that he was writing two articles

[2] Welensky Papers, 24/151, ff. 320–321, Welensky to F. S. Joelson, 23 January 1957; 25/202A, f. 195, Sir Ronald Prain to Welensky, 31 January 1957; f. 191, Welensky to Prain, 21 February 1957; f. 189, Prain to Welensky, 1 April 1957.

[3] *Ibid.*, 24/57, f. 104, Press Statement by Welensky, 30 April 1957.

[4] SR *Debates* (Salisbury), Vol. 39, Col. 1251, 30 April 1957.

[5] Welensky Papers, 28/17, Welensky to Home, 30 April 1957; 20/1, ff. 239–241, Home to Welensky, 30 April 1957.

for *The Rhodesia Herald* on Northern Rhodesia and Nyasaland. He explained that he had tried to encourage co-operation between the Northern Rhodesian ANC and the British Government, but had found the Northern Rhodesian Government suspicious of the new African politicians and the educated Africans. In Nyasaland he had attempted to persuade the nationalists not to talk of joining Tanganyika. He warned that he would criticise Welensky for paying heed only to Gaunt and van Eeden instead of acting like a prime minister of a quasi-dominion, and doubted whether Welensky would win the allegiance of the Africans before the Federal review.[6]

In *The Rhodesia Herald* on 7 and 8 May, Johnson maintained that the acid test of the Federation would be if, by 1960, the 6 000 000 Africans believed that they had benefitted from it. There had been a poor start but the Africans were not to blame because their suspicions had been aroused by injudicious statements by the Europeans and the short-sightedness of the Governments. After all, the Africans could eat in the railway dining cars but, unlike their Congolese cousins, they could not stoke the engines in the Rhodesias because the Federal Government feared for the votes of the European railwaymen. Furthermore, continued Johnson, when British MPs like himself spoke out for Africans, they were attacked by none less than the Federal Prime Minister. Welensky, Johnson felt, had to learn statesmanship and should study the example of Sir Robert Menzies of Australia.

Johnson wrote that he was unimpressed by the artificiality of the social mixing of the races. He criticised the administration of the northern territories and, while acknowledging faults on both sides, he minimised those of the Africans. The chief mistake of the Governments, he claimed, was to ignore the young politicians and continue to rely on the traditional authorities. He did not say that these politicians were self-appointed but warned that reactionary government would drive the African nationalists underground. Johnson was particularly shocked by the failure of the district officers to shake hands with the young politicians.

The most important of his discoveries, he said, was the suspicions of the Africans regarding the franchise. In a mood of profound mistrust, they had looked for the defect of the liberal Tredgold proposals and had found that the special votes would be devalued when they reached half of the votes cast. Their attitude would not change until they were confident that they could return Africans to the legislatures.

Johnson believed that racial parity was the way to secure legislatures which were loyal to the electorate as a whole. This would be achieved through double-member constituencies in which, by cross-voting, moderates of both races would be returned. Once political stability had been achieved, there could be a gradual return to the common roll with universal adult suffrage as the ultimate aim.

In Johnson's view the Federal Government's tactless insistence on dominion status, which he said Welensky had wisely suspended until 1960, had done great harm and it would be difficult to convince the African that the northern Europeans would not seek closer ties with the Southern Rhodesians

[6] *Ibid.*, 24/157, ff. 176–177, J. Johnson to Welensky, 5 May 1957.

at the review. That opinion, however, Johnson claimed, might be reversed if Welensky would suggest that the territories be given greater autonomy in 1960. Above all, before then the Africans had to be given a real stake in the Federation and be accepted socially, be educated and advanced in all fields of employment. Such measures would foster the growth of the vital middle class. However, Johnson, no stranger to the northern territories, concluded his articles by admitting that the quality of life for the northern African had already improved.

Johnson also attacked Welensky in the Commons and then explained privately to him that he was only anxious for the success of the policy of partnership in the short period before the review. He warned Welensky that the support of the moderate elements of the Labour Party would not be won by public comments about their "half-baked" ideas. Welensky had to remember that, just as white Rhodesians were conditioned against Labour MPs, so the British public was conditioned against "white settlers". Johnson acknowledged that he had been surprised by the good race relations. He had wondered at the moderate feelings of the Africans when their leaders on the Copperbelt had been deported in defiance of the concept of civil liberty. Finally, he declared his support for the Federation.[7]

Johnson provoked again both a private and public reply from Welensky who denied his preoccupation with van Eeden and Gaunt and thought that Johnson had been fooled by the African nationalists. In *The Rhodesia Herald* Welensky claimed that the African nationalists only dwelt on political advancement and never acknowledged the positive advantages which federation had brought. Johnson, Welensky wrote, had not given the reason for Welensky's attack on him which was for using the word "fighting". Johnson had also favoured the replacement of the provincial administration by the ANC even though an ANC leader in Ndola had declared on 4 January 1957 that "I hate Federation and I hate anyone who supports it", and this was not an isolated outburst.

Welensky noted that Johnson had wanted to extend the system of special representation and yet, simultaneously, advocated the common roll. The special representation would only serve to perpetuate the racialism which Johnson abhorred. He failed to appreciate the difficulty of breaking down social barriers, and it was particularly galling that he ignored the achievements of the white man in Africa. The most irritating part about the championing of every African cause by the Labour Party was that it taught the African to look to London for solutions. This, Welensky warned, could rebound on the Labour Party if it ever returned to power because it would then have to deal with the realities of life. The truth, he said, was that the majority of the Africans were primitive, immature and prone to extremism.[8]

While Welensky had been tussling with Johnson, the Federal Cabinet had been viewing the first fruit of Greenfield's labours, a draft of the constitutional amendment bill to enlarge the House to 59 seats. There would be 44 ordinary MPs, eight elected Africans (including the two existing Southern Rhodesian seats), four specially elected Africans from the northern territories

[7] *Ibid.*, ff. 141–142, Johnson to Welensky, 11 May 1957.
[8] *Ibid.*, ff. 174–175, Welensky to Johnson, 11 May 1957; *The Rhodesia Herald*, 16 May 1957.

and three specially elected and appointed Europeans. The racially-designated seats would, as planned, be eliminated as ordinary seats were captured by Africans. The first category to go would be the eight elected African seats, followed by the four northern special seats and, lastly, those of the three special Europeans. The latter would be retained to the end as they were needed to serve on the African Affairs Board.

The House would be enlarged at the next general election and, to provide for the possibility that the franchise had not been resolved by then, Article 11 would be amended to empower the Governor-General to adapt the existing electoral law by means of regulations. There would also be minor amendments to give the Supreme Court jurisdiction in electoral matters, and to allow the elected Africans to become members of the African Affairs Board.

Greenfield furnished the territorial Governments with an explanation of the bill as well as copies of it, doing this because, in terms of Article 98, their legislatures had to sanction the bill and there was no time to be lost. Moffat and Doig also received copies in the hope that there would be no resistance from the African Affairs Board.

Home was informed of Federal intentions, and Greenfield canvassed Todd and the northern Governors. Todd alone accepted the bill without qualification. Home and the northern Governors objected to the use of the existing electoral law, because then the British Protected Person could not vote unless he became a British subject.

The Federal Cabinet, however, felt that it could not provide by regulation what its Parliament refused to do by legislation. It would run the risk of the Assembly rescinding the regulations by a simple majority. Thus, the Cabinet argued that it might be better to place the onus squarely on the Federal Parliament to enact an electoral law to elect the reconstituted Assembly. If this proved impossible, the MPs might pass a temporary bill to elect the next Parliament.

Benson had complicated the issue by insisting that the Tredgold franchise qualifications, and not the existing ones, should be used if the regulations were implemented. Greenfield opposed the deletion of the clause providing for the regulations because he believed that it was an evasion of the issue and, in any case, they might be needed to deal with Nyasaland's electoral peculiarities.

Despite Greenfield's objection, however, some of the Cabinet underlined their reluctance to include the provision for the regulations by expressing their fear of the political capital which the Dominion Party might make of it. They also worried about the extent to which the details of the Federal franchise would have to be revealed to the territorial legislatures to persuade them to sanction the bill. If great detail were required, it might be advisable to persuade the territorial Governments to postpone their debates until after the impending Federal by-election in Mrewa, caused by the death of N. G. Barrett. The Cabinet, nevertheless, decided to publish the bill as it stood on 21 May with an explanatory statement by Welensky.[9]

The Mrewa by-election was in full swing by the time the bill was

[9] *Ibid.*, FGC(57), 15th Meeting, Minute 4, Federal Cabinet, 1 May 1957; 17th Meeting, Minute 2, 14 May 1957; 18th Meeting, Minute 2, 16 May 1957; 19th Meeting, Minute 1, 20 May 1957.

published, and the Federal Party was faring badly despite a recent reorganisation and the appointment of a full-time secretary, A. T. Adams, a South African of considerable political experience and ability. Mrewa was a rural and traditionally conservative area and, in the event, Winston Field of the Dominion Party won the seat.

Aside from being involved in the Mrewa campaign, Welensky was continuing his correspondence with James Johnson, telling him that Nkumbula and Chirwa would endeavour to prevent voters from registering despite the concession made to British Protected Persons. He also attacked the Labour Party for their ignorant meddling in Federal affairs.[10]

The Federation had never enjoyed a good Press in Britain and the Federal officials had concluded by May that it was part of a deliberate campaign which would intensify before 1960 and would be more effective than anything the African nationalists might do. The inspiration was believed to be Jennifer Rosalynde Ainslie, a South African member of the Communist Party, who was studying at London University and wrote for the *New Statesman and Nation.* It was concluded that a vigorous counter-propaganda campaign was required and later Welensky would recruit a committee in London, under the chairmanship of G. H. Baxter, similar to that of the United Central Africa Association.[11]

In mid-May Todd informed the Federal Government that he favoured abandoning Tredgold's fractional voting for a system under which the special voters would be enrolled until they represented 25 per cent of the total electorate. The special category and the devaluation of votes would then be scrapped. Todd asked the Federal Government to adopt this although the terminal percentage might have to be lowered to accommodate the different ratios of European and African voters in the northern territories. The Federal Cabinet, examining this request, asked Greenfield to secure greater details.[12]

On 28 May Greenfield reported that, in addition to what Todd had said, the Southern Rhodesian Government intended that Federal citizenship should be a franchise qualification and that it was contemplating introducing a single transferable vote. This adjustment to the Tredgold scheme narrowed the choice to this version of the single roll and the Federal dual roll proposal. Todd had found an ally because Greenfield declared that he favoured the first. Greenfield had, of course, favoured the single roll from the beginning. He argued that the dual roll violated the principle of equal rights for civilised men in introducing the concept of superior and inferior voters. He believed that this could breed more resentment than to withhold the vote altogether. It would not bring the African into the party system, and could encourage the formation of purely African parties pledged to end the inequality of voters. Furthermore, the Europeans and Asians who qualified only for the lower roll would have no choice but to vote for Africans. When the lower roll was eliminated the voters qualified on it might swamp the upper roll, and yet to disenfranchise them, he warned, was to invite serious political trouble.

However, Greenfield's version of the single roll was different from Todd's

[10] *Ibid.*, 24/157, ff. 135–137, Welensky to Johnson, 22 May 1957.
[11] *Ibid.*, 8/6, f. 24, B. M. de Quehen to Welensky, 25 May 1957.
[12] *Ibid.*, FGC(57), 19th Meeting, Minute 1, Federal Cabinet, 20 May 1957.

because he proposed the elimination of the special category of voters after a prescribed time and not when they equalled a percentage of the total electorate. He said that a time limit could be justified as giving the British Protected Person a reasonable opportunity to enroll at a low qualification. Greenfield was confident that there would not be a flood of applicants for the vote because the African had always been indifferent about registering.

The Federal Cabinet disliked the single roll because the British Government was unlikely to accept that there would be an adequate opportunity for the enrolment of a reasonable number of Africans. Moreover, there was the danger of a deliberate attempt to take advantage of the situation by the registering of an excessive number of voters, which was most undesirable, particularly in Nyasaland. The dual roll's advantage was that it permanently limited the influence of the lower qualified voters to returning a quarter of the House. The ultimate difficulty of disposing of the lower roll was thought by the Cabinet to have been exaggerated because the special seats would progressively disappear as the Africans captured the ordinary ones. When the transformation was complete, it said, the justification for the lower roll would have gone and it would be perfectly reasonable to abolish it and to disenfranchise its voters.

The Cabinet disliked the special voter having a say in the election of the ordinary MP because that could lead candidates into making wild promises to secure votes. Yet it also did not favour the lower roll voters only electing the special MPs because this would entrench racial representation. Nevertheless, it was felt that the dual roll was necessary to fulfil the promise made in London that a reasonable number of Africans would be enfranchised. The Cabinet deferred any decision, however, until after the meeting of heads of Governments on 3 June.[13]

Greenfield laid before the latter a memorandum describing the three schemes and duly indicated the Federal preference for the dual roll because it answered the British demand for a reasonable number of African voters. Citizenship was no longer a major problem and Welensky, during the meeting, stressed that his Government was prepared to enfranchise the British Protected Person.

The meeting agreed that voters who were not British Protected Persons would have to be British subjects rather than Federal citizens. The matter of the oath was not settled because Benson and Armitage believed that it would not engender African loyalty and might deter the moderate African from registering as he might feel it implied his acceptance of the Federation. If such obduracy and timidity on the part of the northern Governors irritated the Federal representatives, they did not show it. Welensky merely promised to consider an oath which demanded only loyalty to the Queen.

The meeting accepted the qualifications suggested by Tredgold, agreeing that wives should be registered on their husbands' qualifications except for the educational standard which they would have to meet themselves. These conditions would also apply to the first wife of a polygamous marriage. Existing voters would be placed on the upper roll.

[13] *Ibid.*, 21st Meeting, Minute 6, Federal Cabinet, 28 May 1957.

Benson sought a change in the method of selecting the special representatives from Northern Rhodesia because the African Representative Council, which was entrusted with this, had fallen under the domination of extremist influences. He thought that if the influence of the upper roll on the election of the lower roll candidates was reduced, he could, in terms of the Constitution, designate the lower roll as a " . . . body representative of Africans", and use it to elect the two special representatives as well as the two new elected African MPs. The Federal Government agreed to examine this suggestion.[14]

On the morrow, 4 June, the Federal Cabinet disagreed that Benson's suggestion would fit the definition of "a body representative of Africans". The Cabinet agreed that the status of a British subject, or British Protected Person combined with one year of residence, should be a franchise qualification. An oath reduced to a declaration of allegiance to the Crown, was accepted because it could also be construed as implying loyalty to the Federation. The first wife of a polygamous marriage would be allowed to qualify on her husband's means. A board, comprising a judge and two educationalists, would be established to define equivalent educational qualifications. Another board would review the income levels in the light of fluctuations in the value of money. The voters, to prove their literacy, would have to fill in their registration forms in front of an official, but those already registered on the Federal and territorial rolls would be automatically transferred to the new ones.

The last matter to be considered by the Cabinet was whether the details of the proposed franchise could be released as requested by the Nyasaland Government, whose Legislative Council was about to debate the Federal Constitutional Amendment Bill. The Nyasaland Government's difficulties were recognised, but it was felt that the endorsement of the franchise by the Caucus of the Federal Party had to be obtained first, and, before that could happen, Welensky had to discuss the oath and other matters with the British Government. Welensky left the Cabinet meeting to travel to London to attend his first Commonwealth Prime Ministers' Conference from where he cabled to say that any discussions with the Caucus had to be delayed until he returned. The Federal Cabinet did, however, in his absence finally decide to accept the dual roll.[15]

Welensky's visit to London was publicly attacked by Nkumbula and Kaunda. They were distressed by the lack of British public resistance to him travelling to London to win concessions for the Europeans in advance of the review and without first consulting the Africans. The British public, they claimed, had let their Government surrender the right of its Parliament to legislate on the affairs of the Federation, illustrating the weakness of the safeguards.

Preoccupied with the Conference, it was three weeks before Welensky could discuss the Federal issues with Home and Lennox-Boyd. However, Federal affairs were reviewed in the Conference and Lennox-Boyd stated that, as Southern Rhodesia had been on the point of attaining dominion

[14] *Ibid.*, FGC 19, GC(57), Heads of Governments Meeting, Salisbury, 2 June 1957.

[15] *Ibid.*, FGC(57), 22nd Meeting, Minute 6, Federal Cabinet, 4 June 1957; 23rd Meeting, Minute 3, 18 June 1957; *The Rhodesia Herald*, 5 June 1957.

status when the Federation was established, the review in 1960 would consider a programme for the attainment of that status by the Federation. Welensky confirmed that his Government would apply for full Commonwealth membership once the Federation had achieved full independence after 1960. He justified such aspirations by claiming that his policies compared favourably with those being applied in other parts of Africa. At least as important, he pointed out, the Federation was already economically independent. In 1956, £156 000 000 had been invested in the Federation, and of that £100 000 000 came from internal sources. Such economic strength would make political independence a reality.[16]

On 25 June Welensky reported to Lord Home and Lord Perth, the Minister of State for Colonial Affairs, and Alport that the Joint Declaration had been coolly received in the Federation but that he was not unduly worried. The Federal Party had lost the recent Mrewa by-election but then, he said, the Party had contained people who had never been entirely happy with the Federation and he had been expecting them to gravitate to the Dominion Party. The advantage which he had gained was that dominion status had been shelved, as a political issue, until 1960. He explained how he had adapted the income levels recommended by Tredgold to his own franchise proposals but warned that these were still to be ratified by his Caucus. Furthermore, although he was prepared to set the lower roll qualification at an income of £180 p.a., he had indicated publicly that it would be approximately £200 p.a. He had done this, he said, because Todd had asked for a delay in any final commitment as he was in difficulties (with his Cabinet, though Welensky did not say so) and might have to raise the £180 p.a. qualification. Welensky, however, preferred the latter.

Home agreed it was preferable, but expressed surprise at the recent announcement that the voter would have to take an oath when registering. As nothing had been said about this in April, Home feared that it would deter British Protected Persons from registering. Welensky replied that the unpopularity with his Party of the compromise on the British Protected Person had forced the Federal Government to introduce the oath. However, it was a simple declaration of allegiance to the Crown and he envisaged no difficulties. Sir Gilbert Rennie, currently the Federal High Commissioner in London, supported this as he had always found the British Protected Person eager to express loyalty to the Queen.[17]

Although Home accepted the oath, if it were kept simple and if it were presented to him for approval, Lennox-Boyd was not yet satisfied and said as much when he and Home met Welensky on 1 July. Lennox-Boyd advanced the standard Colonial Office's objection that, since the infamous Mau Mau oathings, oath-taking had fallen into disrepute and that the habit should not be encouraged. The oath would be misrepresented by agitators and British Protected Persons would refuse it. Welensky claimed his Government had never concealed its intention to have an oath in the registration process, and he repeated that it was a political necessity as a *quid pro quo* for the en-

[16] Welensky, *4 000 Days*, *op. cit.*, p. 79.
[17] Welensky Papers, 20/1, ff. 199–201, Minutes of a Meeting, Commonwealth Relations Office, 25 June 1957.

franchisement of British Protected Persons. He still believed that there would be no difficulty because the African was ever ready to declare his allegiance to the Crown. At his suggestion, the British Ministers agreed to draft the oath.

Next on the agenda was the unresolved question of the emergency powers of the northern Governors. The head of the legal department of the Commonwealth Relations Office, Major-General Sir Ralph Hone, reported to the meeting that he had visited the northern territories and had found the Governors sympathetic to the Federal point of view and willing to co-operate. The problem was that the Governors needed to act swiftly in emergencies, and that the Federal Government controlled such vital matters as the distribution of essential commodities, communications and power. Hone believed it was imperative that the Governors should be capable of immediate action in these fields.

Welensky disagreed as the granting of this power was tantamount to the abolition of the Federation. He insisted that the Federal Government should immediately recall its Parliament to confirm the Governor's assumption of power. Lennox-Boyd, however, was anxious that the action should not be stultified by the courts, and wondered if the device of the Governor-General acting on the advice of his Ministers could not be used. Hone preferred to use Article 41(1) of the Federal Constitution which allowed the Governor-General to delegate certain of the Federal powers to the territorial Governors. After examination, Welensky agreed that Hone should draw up proposals on this basis.

They discussed the Constitutional Amendment Bill and Welensky revealed that Moffat had stated formally that the African Affairs Board had examined it and had found nothing to criticise. Chirwa had not been present, so it was thought, correctly, more might be heard from the Board.

Finally Welensky asked for the speedy amendment of the British Nationality Act to accommodate Federal citizenship. Home promised to give this high priority in the next parliamentary session.[18]

As their negotiations closed, Nkumbula arrived in London and addressed the Movement for Colonial Freedom, revealing that he would ask for the secession of Northern Rhodesia, an African majority in the Legislative Council, and one man, one vote. He would not consider any association with Southern Rhodesia before his territory was independent, and denounced the dual roll as a deliberate attempt by Welensky to suppress the African.[19]

While Welensky was in London, the territories approved the Constitutional Amendment Bill but not without an uproar in the Nyasaland Legislative Council where the five African Members objected because the Bill anticipated the review in 1960 and was thus a breach of faith. After arguing that the Chiefs and other Africans had not been consulted and, after demanding secession, H. B. Chipembere led the African Members from the Chamber. In their absence, the motion was put and approved. In the aftermath, the African Congress ordered W. M. Chirwa and C. R. Kumbikano to resign their Federal seats and, when they did not comply, expelled them.[20]

[18] *Ibid.*, ff. 187–191, Minutes of a Meeting, Commonwealth Relations Office, 1 July 1957.

[19] *The Rhodesia Herald*, 2 July 1957.

[20] Ny *Debates* (Zomba), p. 14 f., 18 June 1957; *The Rhodesia Herald*, 10 July 1957.

Thereafter Greenfield introduced the Bill in the Federal Assembly, on 26 June, presenting the standard defence that it would allow the development of the two-party system, reduce the over-large constituencies, and make delimitation easier. He claimed it would ease the settlement of the franchise and would bring the African into politics. The Dominion Party did not reply, but sought an adjournment.[21]

If Welensky's negotiations and Greenfield's introduction of the Constitutional Amendment Bill were without trauma, Todd was experiencing difficulties with his Party and Cabinet for the second time that year. The first difficulty had been over an attempt by an African, Patrick Matimba, then abroad, to return to Southern Rhodesia with his Dutch wife. Matimba was married to her, but his attempt to return drew attention to the Immorality Act of 1916 which forbad sexual relations between black men and white women outside marriage. Although the Mrewa by-election was pending, and Matimba was proposing to live within that constituency, and though it was responsible for immigration, the Federal Government shunned any involvement in the issue. Todd might have wanted to do likewise, but his Party feared that the Dominion Party would exploit the affair and supported a resolution to make the Act "fair" by forbidding such relations between white men and black women.

Todd voted against the resolution in the Southern Rhodesian Parliament on 3 May, but his Cabinet supported it and it was passed by 17 votes to eight. The Cabinet had believed that Todd intended to vote with them, and felt betrayed. No legislation followed and, as Lord Blake has noted, the law was made truly "fair" in 1958 by the repeal of the Act itself by Whitehead without any fuss and with the support of the very men who had voted to extend it in 1957.[22]

Todd's second problem was a consequence of his desire to liberalise the Southern Rhodesian franchise. Under pressure from his Cabinet, he had raised the special voting qualification from £180 p.a. to £240 p.a. but had added an alternative qualification of ten years of schooling and two years of continuous employment. This elicited such opposition from his Cabinet that Todd threatened to resign. He chose to do this publicly at the annual general meeting of the Inter-Racial Association on 15 June. As this Association was regarded with suspicion by the more conservative elements, this was provocation indeed and Todd was to pay for it. He declared that, as a custodian of Rhodes's dictum of equal rights for civilised men regardless of colour, he could do nothing less than enfranchise approximately 6 000 Africans who had received ten years' education and worked in such responsible positions as teachers, agricultural demonstrators and medical orderlies. If he could not effect this, he stated that he would be forced to resign.[23]

He thoroughly confused the public (who, after all, had not yet seen the franchise proposals) and provoked Donald Macintyre, the Federal Minister of Finance, to write to Welensky criticising Todd's dramatic methods of

[21] Fed R & N *Debates* (Salisbury), Vol. 8, Col. 20, 26 June 1957.
[22] R. Blake, *A History of Rhodesia* (London, 1977), pp. 301–302; Welensky Papers, FGC(57), 2nd Meeting, Minute 10, Federal Cabinet, 15 January 1957.
[23] Blake, *Rhodesia*, *op. cit.*, p. 303; *The Rhodesia Herald*, 16 June 1957.

putting over proposals which, in themselves, were not very revolutionary. The merger between the Federal and United Rhodesia Parties had been under negotiation for some months, but Macintyre was convinced that the public reaction to Todd was such that it would be fatal for the Federal Party if the merger occurred before the Federal general election. Saying that it was imperative to return Welensky to power, Macintyre advised that, in any case, the merger should be postponed while the United Rhodesia Party was so internally rent.[24]

The day that Macintyre wrote, 17 June, Todd thought it necessary to reassure the public that he intended to keep power only in civilised hands. *The Rhodesia Herald* concluded, however, that, from his protestations, his Party was so deeply divided over the franchise that a split within it was possible. The *African News* praised Todd's stand but warned that, if he resigned, the chance for an integrated society would be lost. This was confirmed by two leading Southern Rhodesian Africans, J. P. V. Moyo and C. L. Mzingeli, who stated that if Todd went the African "liberalists" would become racialists and militant nationalism would thrive, and to counter it Southern Rhodesia would adopt the *apartheid* policies of South Africa.

S. E. Aitken-Cade, chairman of the Dominion Party, commented acidly that day on such methods of leadership, but nevertheless these methods seemed to succeed because, on 19 June, the Caucus of the United Rhodesia Party accepted the Southern Rhodesian franchise proposals. Todd revealed these publicly on 23 June. The outstanding features were, of course, the adjustment of the special qualification and the introduction of a preferential vote. Candidates had to qualify as ordinary voters, and the income levels of £720, £480, £300 and £240 p.a. would be adjusted with any fluctuation of the value of money.[25]

The Federal Party seemed to endorse these proposals because, on 27 June, it announced that it would soon merge with the United Rhodesia Party to become the United Federal Party. The Federal Party's fortunes had improved. It had suffered considerable internal dissent over the compromise on the British Protected Person, but it would win, on 1 July, the South-Western constituency in a Northern Rhodesian territorial by-election. However, despite the external appearances of unity, the Press continued to speculate that the merger could well be postponed because of disagreements over the franchises.[26]

The uncertainty about the merger was confirmed when Todd pressed Welensky to promote the fusion on his return from London. Todd also urged Welensky to adopt the Southern Rhodesian franchise formula, claiming that it was supported by both their Parties. Todd told Welensky that he was confident that Federal MPs, in opposing his franchise formula, were not reflecting the true feelings of the people. In support of this assertion he produced comments from both United Rhodesia and Federal Party branches. Three URP African branches in Salisbury (Mabvuku, Harare, and Highfield) were among those which rejected fusion unless the Federal Government

[24] Welensky Papers, 29/47, f. 38, D. Macintyre to Welensky, 17 June 1957.

[25] *Ibid.*, 8/111, ff. 1–4, Statement by the Southern Rhodesian Prime Minister, 23 June 1957.

[26] *Ibid.*, 15/7, f. 19, Federal Party Statement, 27 June 1957; *The Rhodesia Herald*, 2 July 1957.

adopted the single roll. These branches and the Northern Rhodesian Federal Party similarly insisted that Federal citizenship should also be a qualification.[27]

Welensky, however, preferred first to discuss with his Cabinet a draft of the Federal electoral bill which was ready on his return. On 11 July, his Cabinet ratified its acceptance of the dual roll and the other aspects of the bill. The only major change was that the voter had to be a Federal citizen if he was not a British Protected Person. This meant that periods of residence for the voters did not have to be prescribed. The Cabinet did not adjust the monetary qualifications, and Greenfield was asked to secure as much agreement as possible on these proposals with the Southern Rhodesian Government.[28]

Before Greenfield could initiate any negotiations, Todd sought a meeting with Welensky to settle their differences on the franchise. He revealed that Greenfield had already asked him to state publicly that the Federal franchise was none of his Government's business and that he had replied that, if he did so, he would be subjected to exacting questions from his entire electorate. In any case, Todd said, he was unable to sidestep the issue because he felt so strongly about it.[29]

There may have been a leak to the Press, for on the morrow, 13 July, the *Rand Daily Mail* speculated that a clash between Todd and Welensky was imminent because, though the northern Governors seemed to have accepted the dual roll, Todd continued to reject it. In addition, the newspaper noted, this was the third time that Todd had strongly criticised the Federal Government when the Federal Prime Minister had been out of the country. The question was again asked if Todd aspired to the Federal premiership, but he denied it.

On 16 July Welensky reported to his Cabinet that Todd had proposed to him that the Federal Government should not disturb the current machinery for electing the Southern Rhodesian Federal MPs so as to give time for further consideration of the Federal franchise after the Federal general election. Welensky and Greenfield had insisted, however, that as the Federal Party might not secure the necessary two-thirds majority in the next Parliament, the matter had to be settled promptly.[30]

There was no discussion on other disagreements with Todd, but Welensky told Joelson that they were at odds because he preferred to enfranchise the middle-aged African businessman while Todd favoured the partially-educated teachers at the mission stations whom experience had shown constituted the most seditious element in the populace.[31]

The Federal Cabinet agreed that Todd should be told that the matter of the franchise could not be postponed. It also decided to persuade its Caucus to consider the enfranchisement of ordained ministers of religion who could not satisfy the means tests. The Caucus had already rejected this but there had been pressure from the Anglican Church and it seemed to the Cabinet a

[27] Welensky Papers, 8/111, f. 18, Todd to Welensky, 4 July 1957.
[28] *Ibid.*, FGC(57), 25th Meeting, Minute 2, Federal Cabinet, 11 July 1957.
[29] *Ibid.*, 8/111, f. 33, Todd to Welensky, 12 July 1957.
[30] *Ibid.*, FGC(57), 26th Meeting, Minute 1, Federal Cabinet, 16 July 1957.
[31] *Ibid.*, 24/151, ff. 273–274, Welensky to Joelson, 18 July 1957.

welcome opportunity to give the vote to some of the best Africans. With these matters settled, it was decided that, after the Caucus had sanctioned the proposals, which it promptly did, Greenfield should make a statement on the franchise in the debate on the Constitutional Amendment Bill, which had been renewed the previous day.

In fact Greenfield's statement in the Federal Assembly on 18 July, after a successful division on the second reading, was to sour the subsequent debates on the Constitutional Amendment Bill.[32] In the second reading the Dominion Party MPs had made the points which Greenfield had anticipated when he introduced the Bill. Winston Field, making his maiden speech, had claimed that the existing House was adequate, that the cost of the enlargement was underestimated, and that too much had been done to please the British Government rather than the Federal electorate. The Bill provided that the special seats could only be eliminated after five years and he feared that Africans might capture a significant number of ordinary seats before then. He thought that the enlargement should be postponed for a decision by the electorate in the general election.

Van Eeden reiterated that the enlargement appeared designed to accommodate the new political aspirants who would emerge from the fusion of the United Rhodesia and Federal Parties. Field thought that the House should have first been shown the franchise proposals, and Scott agreed. Field warned that the African had to be brought into the electoral system lest there be serious trouble.[33]

The northern Africans agreed. Kakumbi thought that the cost of enlargement could not be justified and that the Africans would still be underrepresented. Chirwa objected to this anticipation of the review and the failure to consult Africans. He believed that the Constitution would be breached if the proposed six new African representatives were elected on a roll dominated by Europeans. He warned that the northern Africans could not be expected to be "tamed" like their Southern Rhodesian cousins.

However, Savanhu joined his fellow Southern Rhodesians, I. D. Smith and L. M. Cullinan, in supporting the Bill because he believed that it improved representation. Doig supported the Dominion Party on the current Assembly's adequacy because a stalemate in it was impossible as the nine representatives of the Africans held the balance of power. He thought that Nyasaland would be inadequately represented and cautioned that either the Africans dominated the election of all their representatives or there would be trouble.

Moffat, however, accepted the enlargement but, like Doig, disliked the special category for the four existing northern African seats. (The two existing Southern Rhodesian African seats, being elective, had been listed with the new elected African seats.) He warned that the northern Africans regarded the two Southern Rhodesian African MPs as "stooges" because they were elected on the common roll. As the northern Africans were at last showing signs of adopting partnership — or so Moffat believed — he urged the importance of all their representatives being elected by a body representa-

[32] Fed R & N *Debates* (Salisbury), Vol. 8, Col. 260, 18 July 1957.
[33] *Ibid.*, Col. 130 f., 15 July 1957.

tive of them as prescribed by Article 13. If this were done, not only would he support the Bill, but he was confident that thereby "moderate" Africans would be returned. If, however, the Southern Rhodesian model was adopted, only extremists would be elected.[34]

Greenfield, in reply, doubted if any Africans would capture the ordinary seats prematurely because the goal of electing Africans purely on their individual merits would take time to achieve. No mandate was needed because this change had been in his Party's manifesto at the last election. He denied any overbearing British influence as his Government had formulated the enlargement and then had sought the approval of the British and territorial Governments. The critics, Greenfield felt, should remember that hitherto the northern African had been excluded from the vote unless he became a British subject, with the result that only a handful had registered. However, his Government would enfranchise the British Protected Person and there should be increasing numbers of African voters. He denied that the Constitution would be infringed as his law officers had examined the Bill and had found it tailored to suit its precepts.

Answering Moffat, Greenfield stated that only the territorial Governor was empowered to assess whether the method of electing the four new Northern Rhodesian Africans would result in the election of men who were representative of African opinion. The Federal Government would have preferred not to have two methods for electing the northern Africans but was committed to gradual change and to the guarantee that the current system would not be altered before the review. He deplored the suggestion by Moffat that the new system would elect extremists. Article 98 provided for constitutional amendments if the territorial legislatures agreed and thus Chirwa was wrong in claiming that the Constitution would be breached. Finally, Greenfield maintained that, because the lower roll qualification would enfranchise a significant number of Africans, the division of seats was equitable. The Assembly accepted the second reading by 23 votes to nine.[35]

Before conducting this defence, Greenfield had, of course, revealed the Federal franchise proposals. He had described only the election of 53 of the 59 MPs because the methods of selecting the two specially appointed Europeans and the four specially elected African representatives from the northern territories were unchanged. The 53 seats consisted of 44 of unspecified race, six for the new elected Africans, the two existing elected seats for Southern Rhodesian Africans and the one for their European colleague. Greenfield had described the electoral system as one of two common rolls, calling the upper "the General Roll" and the lower "the Special Roll". The general voters would vote for all categories of representatives, while the special would only elect their MPs. All voters would have to be 21 years of age or more and be Federal citizens or British Protected Persons. They would have to swear an oath of allegiance to the Queen and fill in the registration form unaided. The qualifications remained the same but property was described as the ownership, or the long-term leasing, of land. The qualifications were waived for ordained clerics. Greenfield had closed by noting that

[34] *Ibid.*, Col. 224 f., 17 July 1957.
[35] *Ibid.*, Col. 264 f., 18 July 1957.

any Federal electoral act could not apply to Nyasaland in terms of the Constitution until the Nyasaland Legislative Council passed resolutions to that effect.

In the committee stage on 22 July, the Dominion Party decided to leave the burden of opposition to the representatives of the Africans and Scott, who bore it eagerly. Yamba alleged there was an attempt to divide and rule, accusing the Government of wanting to keep racialism, and Welensky of avoiding meetings with Africans. Scott thought the aim was to control the selection of African MPs. Chirwa agreed, and claimed that the Federal Government was whittling away the safeguards. The outcome, he said, could only be bloodshed.

Moffat was so concerned that he wanted a select committee to examine the Constitutional Amendment Bill and its possible effects. Doig supported him, but Greenfield disagreed because the Bill had been published for some time and had been discussed and accepted by the territories. Any major alteration, he said, would only result in extensive delay. Chirwa immediately pointed out that the northern Governments had ignored the unanimous opposition of the Africans in their legislatures. He found that the refusal to appoint a select committee demonstrated how little the Government cared for the African. The refusal, he warned, would merely intensify the northern opposition.

Welensky replied that he had never been asked to address an African meeting but had spoken to multi-racial gatherings, which he preferred. In fact, one of his Ministers had asked Chirwa to arrange meetings with Africans, but Chirwa had not replied. Furthermore, it was a constant complaint of the Africans on the Copperbelt that their African Federal MPs never bothered to address them. These MPs, he claimed, had the deplorable record of only making racial contributions to the debates in the House.

Welensky recalled that, in the debate on his "Resolutions", Moffat had urged the improvement of the system of representation. Thus the fuss which Moffat was making was surprising when the Federal proposals were very reasonable. The scorn of the African MPs, however, Welensky said, was expected because they did not want a democratic system. It was remarkable to him that his critics had failed to comment on the lowering of the franchise qualifications or on the concession on British Protected Persons.

Welensky did not still the protest. Chirwa retorted that democracy did not exist when the majority was excluded from voting. He denounced the dual roll because it denied the African a full voice in the election of his representatives, in violation of the Constitution. Welensky had merely proved that he was the champion of the European and nothing would dissuade Chirwa from believing that universal suffrage was the best solution.

Doig claimed to have offered his services as an intermediary between the Cabinet and the African population, but had been ignored. He thought that the current system of electing the special representatives should be retained because it gave the Africans an adequate voice. The elimination of racial representation was desirable, but he would be more impressed with the sincerity of the Government if it implemented partnership.

Welensky had said that he would never introduce universal suffrage, but Yamba maintained that nevertheless it was inevitable and was the northern

Africans' goal. The debate closed with reassurances from Greenfield that there would be no gerrymandering with delimitation because a Federal judge would head the commission, and that the Europeans would only dominate the electoral system at the outset.[36]

Field joined the continued attack by Moffat, Chirwa *et al* in the third reading on 29 July, claiming that the Bill should have been discussed first with all interested parties. Chirwa berated the British Government for failing to consult the African Affairs Board (which it was not bound to do) thereby shaking African confidence. Moffat doubted whether the Bill had any support outside the Federal Party. Doig felt the Government should have suspended the debate for further negotiations.

H. E. Davies, the specially elected European Member for Southern Rhodesia, however, supported the Government and lectured Chirwa on the powers and duties of the African Affairs Board. Davies believed that the mass of Africans anyway was not interested in politics.[37]

Moffat was granted a day's adjournment which Chirwa used to debate a motion — which Scott called unfortunate — on discrimination within Federal departments. Moffat used the adjournment to press Welensky to allow the Africans a major influence in the election of their MPs. He promised that, if the method of electing the four new northern African MPs was changed to the existing system, he and his colleagues would support the Bill. If this was impossible, he suggested that the Government should announce that it had not yet decided upon the method of the election of the four new MPs but would ensure that a substantial number of their electors were black. Moffat was prepared to extend this to all African MPs. If the Federal Caucus opposed this last compromise, he proposed that African MPs should be elected only by Africans, while their three European colleagues were elected by all races.[38]

Moffat, as chairman of the African Affairs Board, also signed a report that day, 30 July, which declared the Bill a measure which differentiated between the races. It will be recalled that the Board — albeit in the absence of Chirwa — had already examined the Bill and had found it to be acceptable and fair.

Greenfield dealt with the Board's new objection when the debate resumed on 31 July, and judged it to be inaccurate and without foundation. The Federal Government, he maintained, was being neither dishonest nor dishonourable in seeking to have the new African MPs elected on the same basis as the existing Southern Rhodesians because it believed in the party system and opposed racial groupings. He argued that there was nothing that was prejudicial in the Bill and, indeed, that it should be remembered that the Constitution offered protection for Africans alone. The Board was indulging in special pleading and advanced no counter-argument. It had linked the Federal franchise proposals with the Bill and had chosen to attack certain aspects of them and had ignored others. It had stated, for example, that the Africans were denied participation in the election of the ordinary MPs. This was untrue, he said, as the African had always been able to vote in Southern

[36] *Ibid.*, Col. 350 f., 22 July 1957.
[37] *Ibid.*, Col. 496 f., 29 July 1957.
[38] Welensky Papers, 8/111, f. 7, Moffat to Welensky, 30 July 1957.

Rhodesia and, more recently, in the northern territories. Greenfield revealed that his Government was prepared to reduce the special qualification from £180 p.a. to £150 p.a. with simple literacy, or £120 p.a. and two years' secondary schooling, but it would not withdraw or suspend the Bill.

Before a vote was taken, Savanhu, who had promised Welensky on the previous day that he would support the Bill but would thereafter resign because he believed he did not have the support of his constituents, lauded this concession. He confessed that he had been subjected to pressure from a group of Africans from Salisbury to oppose the Bill but he would not comply because he saw nothing wrong in it.[39]

At the division Savanhu and Hove were amongst the 25 who voted for the Government. The opposing group of nine comprised Moffat and the other northern African representatives, Scott, and the three Dominion Party MPs, Field, Williamson and van Eeden. The Royal Assent did not automatically follow because the British Government had to consider the protest of the African Affairs Board and it had to be debated by the Parliament at Westminster. This did not happen until November, and by then James Callaghan (the young Labour MP and future Prime Minister) had visited the Federation and tempers were raw.

The next day, 1 August, Welensky publicly praised Savanhu's action in voting for legislation in which he believed and then resigning over difficulties with his constituents. Such political acumen, he said, seemed to bode well for the Federation. Welensky, however, confided to Joelson that he believed Savanhu had been threatened with violence by the militant African National Youth League.[40] If he had been, Savanhu shrugged off the threat and stood again for the Federal Party and won back his seat in the subsequent by-election.

Welensky described Moffat's behaviour, to Joelson, as shocking. He related how the African Affairs Board had examined and approved the Bill before the debate. It had asked the Federal Government for a statement on its intentions on the franchise, but when that had been supplied, the Board had immediately rejected the enlargement because it disliked the franchise. Welensky's bitterness was also directed against the Press which had given Greenfield's reply to the Board's report minimal publicity and yet, for days, had quoted everything said by the Board itself.

The unveiling of the franchise proposals brought protests from within the Federal and United Rhodesia Parties, and some resignations. In certain circles Welensky found himself depicted as an illiberal reactionary.[41]

The Federal debate was followed by the immediate introduction in the Southern Rhodesian House of a Bill to amend that territory's electoral law. As has been seen, this adapted the Tredgold recommendations and added compulsory preferential votes when more than two candidates stood for a

[39] Fed R & N *Debates* (Salisbury), Vol. 8, Col. 655, 31 July 1957.

[40] *The Rhodesia Herald*, 2 August 1957; Welensky Papers, 24/151, ff. 268–269, Welensky to Joelson, 1 August 1957.

[41] Welensky Papers, 25/123, f. 25, Welensky to E. Musgrove, 5 August 1957; 24/33A, ff. 7–9, Dr C. Fisher to Welensky, 5 August 1957; 8/112, f. 197, A. Pedder to the Editor, *Federal Outlook*, 22 July 1957.

constituency. The special voters would disappear the moment their numbers equalled a fifth of the ordinary electorate.

In introducing the Bill, Stumbles, the Minister of Justice, strove hard to dispel the impression that it was being forced through, maintaining that it was the product of frank discussion and critical analysis. The emerging African middle class, he said, had to be catered for in such a way that the Europeans would not be swamped. The Southern Rhodesian Opposition, however, were not to be deceived and fastened on Todd's recent threat to resign.

Todd countered by saying that he had only stated that he could not continue in office if an important section of the populace was excluded, and that he had not intended to threaten anyone. The resistance was not serious, and the Bill passed easily through its initial stages.[42] There was, however, some agitation both within and without the House over a proposal to disqualify people who married polygamously. An amendment removed it.

Concurrent with this debate, Yamba's motion on discrimination followed its predictable course to defeat in the Federal Assembly.[43] Undeterred, Moffat immediately proposed the appointment of a select committee to devise a suitable Federal franchise for the next general election only, because of the revision in 1960. This was, he claimed, the only way to avoid the emotion which had bedevilled the recent debate. A democratic basis had to be found or soon the European, in particular, would find himself in dangerous circumstances. The committee, he said, had to be served by the best brains available to ensure that by 1960 the Federation's fundamental problems were understood.

Moffat stated that, for a single election, the franchise proposals would be adequate if the majority of the MPs were elected on a roll dominated by the Europeans, that the special representatives were chosen by a substantial African majority, and that the new African MPs would not suffer a loss of authority through their method of election. The racial bigots of both races, he claimed, would be eliminated by the participation of all races.

Greenfield, however, was unconvinced and dismissed the proposed select committee as the stock answer of the Opposition and minority groups to the problems of the day. He advised Moffat and Doig, the seconder, that they would accomplish more if they worked through the party system. He remarked that Davies, their Southern Rhodesian colleague, had after all joined the Federal Party. Greenfield believed that select committees were always weighted in favour of the government of the day and that, moreover, it was unreasonable to expect its members to give up their partisan interests. The franchise issue was too controversial to be successfully examined by a select committee. There had never been much time to spare for a delimitation before the election, and the African Affairs Board, by reserving the Constitutional Amendment Bill, had made it even shorter. There certainly was no time, he felt, for a select committee to re-examine the four franchises.

After Yamba, Chirwa and Williamson had dwelt on the unwillingness of the Government to consult anyone, Moffat withdrew his motion, but not

[42] SR *Debates* (Salisbury), Vol. 40, Col. 537, 1 August 1957.
[43] Fed R & N *Debates* (Salisbury), Vol. 8, Col. 597, 30 July 1957.

before he had claimed that he knew of no other public figure with a greater capacity for saying "No" than Greenfield, with the exception of Molotov.[44]

Moffat and his colleagues were not alone in maintaining pressure on the Federal Government for, on 5 August, the Action Group of Bulawayo wrote to Todd suggesting the alignment of the Federal and Southern Rhodesian franchises. As minor points of difference abounded, the Group was confident that the members of the Federal and United Rhodesia Parties would accept a compromise for the sake of uniformity. The major divergences, it claimed, were only the dual roll as opposed to the single roll, and the mechanism for the elimination of special representation. The Group urged Todd to delay the committee stage of his Bill to attempt alignment.[45]

A copy of this suggestion was forwarded to the Federal Cabinet which discussed it within two days because Todd had indicated that he would delay his committee stage. The Cabinet agreed that an alignment was desirable because it could prevent confusion amongst the voters. It, however, believed that the Southern Rhodesian Government would neither allow the British Protected Person *per se* to qualify nor accept the declaration of allegiance. There would be difficulties over the registration procedures and the property qualification which, in the Federal definition, included leasehold because of the peculiarities of the protectorates. The Federal proposals required a Cambridge School Certificate, while the Southern Rhodesians asked only for some years to be spent at school. The Federal Cabinet thought, however, the Southern Rhodesian educational qualifications could be accepted, provided an income qualification was introduced in the case of the special voters who had ten years in school and two years of continuous employment. This would equal the lowest of the prescribed Federal levels which had been reduced to £150 p.a. with simple literacy, or £120 p.a. and two years of secondary schooling.

After further deliberation, the Federal Cabinet rejected an idea that the Caucuses of the Federal and United Rhodesia Parties should conduct the negotiations, and ordered Greenfield to meet Todd and Stumbles. The Federal Caucus was informed of the effort being made, and the consideration of a draft of the Federal electoral bill was deferred for Greenfield's negotiations. It was thought that, if Greenfield was successful, a similar effort on alignment could be made with the northern territories.[46]

A product of Greenfield's negotiations was that Todd advanced an amendment in the committee stage of his Electoral Bill to ensure that the special voter would have to earn £120 p.a. if he would qualify on the basis of ten years of schooling. A number of other alignments was accepted by the Federal Cabinet on 20 August, but before then the African representatives had continued their attack.[47] On 13 August Yamba asked the House to agree that dominion status should not be granted to the Federation until the

[44] *Ibid.*, Col. 936 f., 6 August 1957.

[45] Welensky Papers, 8/112, f. 165, Memorandum by the Action Group, August 1957; Action Group to Todd, 5 August 1957.

[46] *Ibid.*, FGC(57), 28th Meeting, Minute 6, Federal Cabinet, 7 August 1957.

[47] *Ibid.*, 42/52, f. 26, W. S. Parker to D. Cole, 23 August 1957; FGC(57), 30th Meeting, Minute 2, Federal Cabinet, 20 August 1957.

majority of the inhabitants asked for it, confidently claiming that even the whites were content with the current status. Field, however, criticising the preamble of the Constitution, believed that it was impossible to discover the opinion of the majority, particularly when most Africans knew nothing of the issues. He suggested that the only way to consult African opinion was through the traditional tribal authorities.

Welensky warned that his Government would reject the motion and hoped Yamba would withdraw it because in April 1957 he and the British Government had agreed that in 1960 a programme to achieve a higher status would be considered. However, the representatives of the Africans ignored him. Moffat agreed that it would be impossible to gauge African feelings, but was confident that they would oppose any attempt to obtain a higher status while they felt a need for British protection. Kakumbi confirmed that the Africans would not co-operate until segregation had been abolished and partnership had been fully implemented.

Scott scorned the efforts of the Government to gain African co-operation but believed that once it could demonstrate to Britain and the Africans that it could take over the protective role, there would be no difficulty with the preamble. He agreed with Welensky that universal suffrage should not be introduced, perhaps, for hundreds of years. Nevertheless, he felt that the Government could do a great deal by making timely and generous concessions. Doig suggested that Welensky's statement, that nothing would happen until 1960, should be publicised because the Africans were being told that the concession on British Protected Persons was balanced by a hidden British commitment to the advancement of the Federation. Finally, Yamba claimed that to date there had been nothing to convince the Africans that the Federation had benefitted them in any way. Until that happened, he said, there would be no agreement on dominion status. He could not understand how Welensky could reject the motion if he had accepted the preamble. However, the motion was rejected overwhelmingly.[48]

The Southern Rhodesian Assembly and the committee stage of its Electoral Bill next claimed attention. The Government introduced the amendment to the qualifications of the special voters, which has already been mentioned, and Keller accused it, in return, of rushing the Bill through against the wishes of well over half the electorate. The third reading was completed on 21 August, and the Bill passed into law.[49]

The Federal Cabinet decided to print its Electoral Bill, but its implementation had to await the British verdict on the African Affairs Board's protest. There were distractions, however, in the meantime and one was the arrival of a delegation from the British branch of the Commonwealth Parliamentary Association.

The idea of inviting a delegation from the Association had been suggested to Welensky in 1956 by his biographer, Don Taylor, when they were mulling over the problem of informing the British political parties on the true state of affairs in the Federation.[50] The idea was implemented, and in early

[48] Fed R & N *Debates* (Salisbury), Vol. 8, Col. 1254 f., 13 August 1957.

[49] SR *Debates* (Salisbury), Vol. 40, Col. 1070, 21 August 1957.

[50] Welensky Papers, 42/60, f. 147, Welensky to D. Taylor, 17 October 1956.

September 1957 the delegation arrived led jointly by Richard Wood of the Conservative Party and James Callaghan, the Shadow Colonial Secretary. The Federal members of the Association had entertained previous delegations and understood that the visiting members would refrain from public comment until they reported back to their branch. Then they would publish their findings if the branch thought fit. This delegation at the outset declared it would abide by this rule.

It was axiomatic to such visits that the members did not use the opportunities provided for personal gain. Thus the locals were startled to find that Callaghan was retained by *Reynold's News* to write on what he found and was posting articles which appeared under such sensationalist titles as "Trouble Brewing: The Land of King Copper". In Southern Rhodesia Callaghan was shown, with some sense of pride, the fruits of a new African housing programme and, apparently impressed, he assured the Minister responsible, Geoffrey Ellman-Brown, that he would not fail to publicise this. He did not, and preferred to write about the Copperbelt as the "storm-centre of the Federation" and of the political, industrial and social strife which he found. Later, in 1960, when serving on the Monckton Commission, Ellman-Brown taxed Callaghan on his failure to fulfil his promise and received the reply that it had not been politic to comply.[51]

Callaghan provoked local comment when, at the end of the three week tour, he declared at a Press conference in Salisbury that dominion status could only be granted to the Federation with the support of the people of Northern Rhodesia and Nyasaland. He believed that this would be impossible in 1960 because the Federation had not yet really found its feet and needed a period of constitutional stability. He warned that he and his colleagues would not press the British Government to abrogate a pledge which had been freely entered into just because the northern Colonial administration was disliked. In any case, representative government had first to be introduced in the northern territories. There was no substantial African support for the Federation, he said, and if by 1960 the people of the Federation were unable to devise a solution acceptable to most Africans, the British Government would have to supply its own.

Callaghan reassured the Rhodesians that his Party would not introduce universal suffrage immediately, but he warned that it agreed with the African desire for bold moves in that direction. The Labour Party, he said, thought that a pre-condition for universal suffrage was the acquisition of a rudimentary knowledge of politics. Callaghan was impressed by the economic development, but was depressed by the lack of social contact between the races. He claimed that references to dominion status, particularly by Welensky, were antagonising and unsettling the Africans, and were forcing their leaders to attempt to protect their people when it was granted. Finally, Callaghan declared that a future Labour Government would demand African majorities in the northern territorial legislatures as prerequisites to independence.[52] Thus Callaghan was the first to commit his Party to the NIBMAR precondition (No Independence Before Majority Rule) which was later to be

[51] *Reynold's News*, 22 September 1957; Author's interview with the Hon. G. Ellman-Brown.
[52] *The Rhodesia Herald*, 26 September 1957.

such a stumbling block in the granting of independence to Southern Rhodesia in the aftermath of the Federation's demise.

The rest of the delegation commented that they had heard more about dominion status at this final Press Conference than they had on tour, and the next day, thanking Welensky for his hospitality, Callaghan claimed that he had been forced to answer impertinent questions. He regretted that attention had focussed on dominion status because his delegation had thus been denied the opportunity to give a balanced account of what they had discovered. He had affectionate memories of the Federation and had wished to avoid appearing to slap down the European in order to cultivate the African. He explained that although the Press had not asked him the right questions, he had criticised, in the *Central African Examiner,* the dangerous course which African nationalist factions were following, and had told the African leaders what he thought of their activities. He denied a charge laid by *The Rhodesia Herald* that he had loaded the dice against the European because the Labour Party intended to be fair to all and to meet the established obligations.[53]

Callaghan referred to a highly critical editorial in *The Rhodesia Herald,* entitled "Slap in the Face", which recalled that his Party had willingly accepted independence for India, Pakistan, the Sudan and Ghana even though their governments had been less stable than that of the Federation. The newspaper noted that Callaghan had maintained that the whites sought not only to govern themselves but the millions of blacks currently protected by the British Crown. Thus he ignored the ample evidence of the good intentions of the whites while aware that without European co-operation, capital and skill, the African had little prospect of advancement. To slap the face of the white, when moderates of all races were trying to co-operate, the newspaper warned, would only result in the hardening of attitudes. The *Northern News* similarly took up the cudgels in an article entitled "Labour View is Forever Amber", and in the *Umtali Post* a reader called for a unilateral declaration of independence before 1960.[54]

The Federal Government, however, ignored the bait and, in any case, was preparing for a lengthy visit from Lord Home. Home was greeted on arrival by a memorandum from the Dominion Party which claimed that the intention of the constitutional preamble was that the Colonial officials should assess the desires of the people and that there should therefore be active Federal and territorial co-operation in informing the populace. It proposed a Federal office of race relations[55] which Welensky had been contemplating but was not raised in the review of current issues which he, Greenfield and Caldicott conducted with Home on 1 October.

They discussed first the fate of the Constitutional Amendment and Electoral Bills. Greenfield was anxious to have the Royal Assent for the first as soon as possible so that preparations for the general election could begin. The draft order in council, he felt, should be tabled when the British Parliament resumed its sitting at the end of the month.

[53] Welensky Papers, 42/39, f. 50, L. J. Callaghan to Welensky, 26 September 1957.
[54] *The Rhodesia Herald,* 26 September 1957; *Northern News,* 27 September 1957; *Umtali Post,* 30 September 1957.
[55] *The Rhodesia Herald,* 2 October 1957.

Home, however, revealed that delay was the least of the problems. He was not confident of the full support of his Party for the Constitutional Amendment Bill and argued that, because of the objections of the African Affairs Board, it was necessary to consider the Electoral Bill simultaneously. Furthermore, the Commonwealth Parliamentary Association delegation was critical of the liberality of the proposals and its report, expected in November, might attract the support of some Conservatives, making it difficult to obtain a majority. The delegation erroneously compared the Federal solution with Southern Rhodesia's and, ignoring the lack of special MPs in the latter, criticised the provision that the special voters would not influence the election of the ordinary MPs. Home felt that the Federal Government should respond by reducing either the literacy qualifications or the special roll income level from £150 to £120 p.a.

The Federal Ministers were unyielding because they valued the literacy qualifications and believed that they could not lower the income qualifications without facing defeat in Parliament or losing the confidence of their electorate. They felt that the concession on the British Protected Person had been ignored and were concerned that the Commonwealth Parliamentary Association delegation should have passed judgment on the franchise without consultation on it. Home promised to discuss this subject again before he left.

Home announced that his Government would amend the British Nationality Act early in the next session, and would urgently consider a Federal request to be the sole authority for the issue of passports. The meeting then discussed a memorandum by the Commonwealth Relations Office on the unresolved problem of the suspension of Federal laws under the emergency powers of the northern Governors. This suggested that, until the Federal review, there should be draft regulations or instructions to be kept by the Governors for issue in an emergency. When these were needed, the Federal Cabinet would advise the Governor-General to delegate powers, in terms of Article 41(1), to the Governor to be exercised at his discretion. If possible, the Governor would then consult the Federal Government before taking action and, if there was time, the adjustments to the law would be effected normally through the Federal Assembly. The Governors would not issue any regulations which expressly stated that any Federal enactment was amended, modified or suspended unless it was unavoidable. Accordingly, the emergency regulations would be drafted to make them seem supplementary to Federal law.

Home said that he could go no further to meet the Federal demands, but the Federal Ministers were not satisfied because the regulations could only be reversed by legislation. Welensky thought that, as the northern officials were lax about security, the Federal Government could be gravely embarrassed if the implications of this proposal became known. Greenfield pointed out that, in any case, the Governor-General was not empowered to suspend the operation of Federal law and so could not delegate that power to the northern Governors.

The meeting agreed to re-examine the subject and turned to the subject of the locally-based civil servants on which Welensky reported that, apart from a limited inter-change, little progress had been made. He wanted to propose the immediate recruitment of local professional and administrative officers at the imminent meeting of the heads of Governments. He then asked about the establishment of the proposed Central African department in Whitehall and Home replied evasively that he was considering it in the broader context of the Commonwealth and the dependent territories. He had encountered many difficulties, he said, but would persist.[56]

On 1 October it was merely announced that Home was in the Federation on the first leg of a fact-finding tour and his thunder was stolen in the Press that day by Wightwick and Callaghan. Wightwick, a dissident member of the United Rhodesia Party, demanded that it should be clearly indicated to the British Government that Southern Rhodesia would secede if there was any likelihood in the foreseeable future of the equality of racial representation or if there was the slightest chance of the European losing control. Southern Rhodesia would stand on its own feet, he said, but if it could not, it would join South Africa. The reason for Wightwick's demand was Callaghan's pronouncement on dominion status and a comment to Wightwick by one of the Parliamentary Association delegation that, to be acceptable, any constitutional solution had to provide for ultimate control by the black majority. Furthermore, when asked by Wightwick, Callaghan had said that the Labour Party would not prevent the break-up of the Federation if it was the consequence of his pronouncement. The delegation had made it clear that, if the Labour Party came to power, there would immediately be racial parity in the northern legislatures and, thus, to Wightwick, there was no longer any call for kid gloves.[57]

An article in the *Central African Examiner* by Callaghan also appeared that day. In this he acknowledged that it was easier for the highly qualified European to be philosophical about African advancement than the European artisan who saw his livelihood threatened. Yet if racial harmony was ever to be established, the technical training of the African had to be improved and European immigration restricted. Political stability would depend on the African National Congresses being free to act and to exert their influence through the political system. He did not explain that the Congresses had virtually refused to participate, but warned that exclusion would force them to work outside the system. He rued the waste of the political talents of Nkumbula and the Southern Rhodesian nationalists, James Chikerema and George Nyandoro, who had all condemned the political violence in the North. This violence, Callaghan attributed not to Nkumbula but to the young nationalists flexing their muscles. The youth had to be educated in partnership and it troubled Callaghan that senior European schoolboys had no contact with their African counterparts. The European parents, if they opposed such contact, would have to be converted, but Callaghan did not expect any resistance because he had found everywhere a surprisingly humanitarian attitude. The people were clearly willing to go further than their representatives, and suffered from a lack of leadership.

Both Wightwick and Callaghan (who was promoted the next day, 2 October, to the national executive of the Labour Party) drew fire from the

[56] Welensky Papers, 20/1, ff. 176–180, Minutes of a Meeting with Lord Home, 1 October 1957.
[57] *The Rhodesia Herald* & *The Bulawayo Chronicle*, 1 October 1957.

local editors. Wightwick, a comparatively new immigrant, was asked if he yet understood that the Southern Rhodesian and Federal Governments controlled their own destinies despite the Labour Party's commitment to universal franchise. Wightwick was advised to leave the United Rhodesia and Federal Parties because he only embarrassed them.

In Callaghan's case, the editors acknowledged that bold leadership would reveal a surprising degree of liberal opinion, but he was belaboured for committing his Party to refusing any constitutional advance for the Federation until Africans dominated the northern legislatures. He was firmly told that white skills would be needed if the African were to advance at all. It could be expected that there would be work for all, and redundancy would only become a threat if the economy was artificially impeded by measures such as the reduction of immigration.[58]

Roberts claimed that it had never been intended that a Commonwealth Parliamentary Association delegation should constitute a Grand Jury judging the Constitution or status of the Federation before the British Government could. Callaghan, in particular, had over-stepped the mark, Roberts said, and he believed that the ignorant would interpret Callaghan's comment as a decision.[59]

Welensky wrote to Callaghan regretting his statement on dominion status because it had certainly appeared to slap down the European. In public Welensky declared that much of the current restlessness could be blamed on Labour's failure to acknowledge that the Federation was permanent, rather than on his or anyone else's comments on dominion status. He was not forcing any pace, he said, and had accepted the review in 1960. Welensky reminded Callaghan that elsewhere Britain was granting independence at a rate which seemed to the Rhodesians to be over-hasty.[60]

The counter-attacks on Callaghan continued: there were demands that such visits should be curbed and questions on how many people Callaghan had met in order to speak with such authority.[61] Callaghan, at the Labour Party Conference on 5 October, replied with a fierce attack on the racial practices in the Federation and, in particular, the lack of technical training for Africans, who were even denied the opportunity to become apprentices. However, a shortage of time at the Conference saved the Federation from a severe drubbing because a resolution condemning the permanent under-representation of Africans was not debated.

Callaghan followed up by writing in *Reynold's News,* on 6 October, on racial segregation in Salisbury (which he described as "the two-faced city") and on how unfit the Federation was to become a dominion. He repeated that the Europeans were asking to govern millions of Africans who wished to remain under British protection. He wrote that the cries since his visit for Boston Tea Parties and for joining South Africa only produced a counterpart to this "ugly racialism" in the African ranks. The outlook to Callaghan was

[58] *Ibid.*, 2 October 1957.
[59] *Central African Post*, 2 October 1957.
[60] Welensky Papers, 42/39, f. 48, Welensky to Callaghan, 2 October 1957; *Rand Daily Mail*, 2 October 1957.
[61] *The Rhodesia Herald*, 3 October 1957; *Midlands Observer*, 4 October 1957.

stormy even though the economic prospects were bright. The solution lay with the Europeans who had political and economic power and who could solve the racial problem by making the African feel he was a citizen with political rights and duties. If this were done, Callaghan said, the Africans would reciprocate and the Federation would become one of the greatest members of the Commonwealth.

Welensky ignored letters in the Federal Press defending Callaghan, and on 10 October described provocative remarks by visiting British parliamentarians, after a "Cook's Tour" of three weeks, as most reprehensible. It was most regrettable, he said, that the delegation should have commented publicly on the Federation's future status when it was known that it would be reviewed in 1960. The purpose of the visits was to enlighten the other parts of the Commonwealth but, if the precedent set was followed, the Association would destroy itself. Welensky reminded the public that none of the delegation had any executive authority and that they had not shown any great understanding of the issues involved.

The local Press lauded this statement as a "timely" and well-deserved rebuke. It lectured Callaghan on the inflammatory and unconstructive nature of his remarks which should have properly been made in the Commons.[62]

Welensky ignored Callaghan's precondition and, on 11 October, boldly proclaimed that the Federal Party had begun to plan for independence in 1960 when dominion status would be sought. He added that the undesirability of racial integration had been amply demonstrated by the recent events at Little Rock in the United States of America. Home, that day, was in Blantyre and argued that, as the Federation was "here to stay", it would thus be sensible to concentrate on making it work. He reviewed the unprecedented development since federation and claimed that partnership and co-operation between the races would grow. He was, without doubt, responding to demands from all the Nyasaland African Federal and territorial representatives for secession in 1960.[63]

Home had repeated to Greenfield how uncertain he was of Conservative support for the Constitutional Amendment Bill. Thus he insisted that the Federal Government should satisfy Moffat as it would be unfortunate if it appeared as if concessions had been wrung out of the Federal Government by the British Government. Therefore, it would be better to appear magnanimous and, perhaps, allow the special voters a say in the election of the 44 ordinary MPs. Alternatively, the influence of the general voter in the election of the special MPs could be limited.

Although Greenfield said that there was not the slightest possibility of Welensky agreeing to either of these ideas, Home persisted, suggesting that, in any one constituency, the votes of the general voters should never exceed in value those of the special voters. This need only apply in the next general election and the whole subject could be revised in 1960. Greenfield would not accept this either because the Southern Rhodesian voters had already elected their special MPs. Furthermore, as the Federal franchise levels would be

[62] *Western Daily Press* (Bristol), 11 October 1957; *The Bulawayo Chronicle*, 11 October 1957; *The Sunday Mail*, 13 October 1957.

[63] *The Rhodesia Herald*, 12 October 1957.

lower than Southern Rhodesia's, there could be no more concessions. Greenfield warned that, if the Royal Assent was given to the Constitutional Amendment Bill without a commitment on the Electoral Bill, the position of his Government would be untenable because the general election could not be held on the existing territorial franchises without drastic alteration. At the very least, he said, the British Government would have to commit itself to accepting the regulations which might then be made in terms of the Constitutional Amendment Bill which might be very similar to the provisions of the Electoral Bill.[64]

Before meeting the Federal Cabinet again on 15 October, Home publicly expressed his confidence that, with patience and understanding, the support of the African could be won. He doubted the claims that the majority of Africans opposed the Federation because he thought many of them had no idea of its purposes and achievements. He issued a clear directive to the northern provincial administrations to explain the benefits of the Federation, which was something Roberts and Beckett in Northern Rhodesia had urged him to do. Home was also confident that the review would serve to convince the African finally that the purpose was not to exploit him but to bring him gradually the full benefits of partnership. The African leaders might demand the immediate application of universal suffrage, but to Home this was impracticable because he believed that political growth had to be gradual.[65]

Before Home joined their meeting, the Federal Cabinet reconsidered his request to lower the voting qualifications to ensure a preponderance of African voters in Northern Rhodesia. Home wanted the £150 p.a. income level reduced by £10 because British calculations indicated that otherwise there would be slightly more European than African voters in Northern Rhodesia. Nyasaland did not trouble him because the African voters were expected to outnumber the Europeans by two to one. Greenfield believed, however, that there were likely to be fewer voters than the British predicted and that all such estimates had to be treated with reserve. The Cabinet concluded that it could make no more concessions and thus the reduction of the income qualification could not be considered. Like Greenfield, it was determined that there should be a British commitment to the Electoral Bill before it could accept a British assurance of support for the Constitutional Amendment Bill. It was responding to Home's persistent suggestion that there would have to be an alternative provision of electoral regulations if the Electoral Bill was rejected.

Thus prepared, the Cabinet met Home who asked immediately for a small concession to satisfy the Commons. He did so because he believed that it was imperative to prevent the hardening of opinions before 1960 to ensure a successful review. In particular, he said, the British political parties, needing to be convinced that a reasonable attempt had been made to meet African aspirations, would be satisfied if there were more African than European voters in the northern territories.

However, the Federal Cabinet refused to compromise because it had been difficult enough to get the Federal Party to accept the reduction from £180 to

[64] Welensky Papers, FGC 19/4, f. 26, Greenfield to Welensky, 10 October 1957.
[65] *The Rhodesia Herald*, 15 October 1957.

£150 p.a. The Federal Ministers argued that, moreover, the rising African wages in Northern Rhodesia, together with the enfranchisement of wives on their husbands' qualifications, would soon place the European voter in the minority. The Cabinet also did not want to give the impression that the franchise could be constantly changed. Thus Home could do nothing more than promise to discuss the support of the Electoral Bill with his Government, and he asked for a memorandum which would emphasise the moderate features of the franchise proposals.

Home then reported that he had instructed the district administration to proclaim the advantages of the Federation and he suggested that the Federal Government should supply the Northern Rhodesian Government with information on the economic advantages of the Federation which were not quite as apparent as they were in Nyasaland. He suggested that the Federal Ministers should also cultivate the northern officials. The Nyasaland Government had willingly agreed to disseminate information on the Federation, but the Northern Rhodesian Government had not, and he thought that there was an unnecessary amount of friction between the Federal and Northern Rhodesian Governments.

Home agreed to re-examine the suspension of Federal laws under the northern emergency powers after Greenfield had rejected the latest British proposals on them. Greenfield argued that, because Southern Rhodesia could not suspend Federal legislation, there was no reason why Northern Rhodesia and Nyasaland should be thus empowered. The Federal Government, he said, was prepared to confer the necessary emergency powers and indemnities if the need arose. Then the meeting discussed fruitlessly the proposed extension of the taxing powers of the Federal Government for which Nyasaland was seeking postponement until 1960.[66]

Finally, before departing for London, Home declared publicly that the review in 1960 would reassure all races that nothing would be done to prejudice their interests. There could be absolute confidence, he avowed, in the intention of the British Government to uphold and sustain the Federation.[67] These brave words would soon have a hollow ring.

Welensky reported acidly to Lord Malvern that Home had been influenced by the attitude of the Commonwealth Parliamentary Association that the Federation should not be made independent unless there was a marked improvement in the political rights of the Africans. Thus there was little difference, he argued, between the approaches of the Conservative and Labour Parties, in which the Europeans counted for little. Home had seen Tredgold, Moffat, Benson and Todd, and Welensky, knowing what would be forthcoming, had refused to make any further modifications.[68]

Welensky also apprised Joelson of the recent events and the influence on them of the Commonwealth Parliamentary Association. He was, however, equally concerned that, despite grave personal misgivings, he had recommended to his Party that it should fuse with the United Rhodesia Party.[69]

[66] Welensky Papers, FGC(57), 36th Meeting, Minute 1, Federal Cabinet, 15 October 1957.
[67] *The Rhodesia Herald*, 16 October 1957.
[68] Welensky Papers, 43/*Malvern*, Welensky to Malvern, 22 October 1957.
[69] *Ibid.*, 24/151, ff. 243–244, Welensky to Joelson, 23 October 1957.

The Federal Party accepted his recommendation at a congress in Ndola on 22 November, and within two months Welensky would see his doubts confirmed when the Southern Rhodesian Cabinet tried to oust Todd.

A product of Home's visit was that, on 31 October, the British Government indicated it would ignore the African Affairs Board's report and recommend the granting of the Royal Assent to the Constitutional Amendment Bill. Callaghan in the Commons immediately decried this as a mistake because the Africans had been keenly awaiting the outcome of the first ever objection of the Board. He expected the political stability of the Federation to be seriously affected and demanded a full debate. He was vindicated at least by a bitter reaction to the news amongst African nationalist circles for which Welensky blamed Moffat.[70]

Callaghan maintained the pressure and, as promised, he, Griffiths and Creech Jones tabled a motion on 13 November to prevent the Royal Assent to the Constitutional Amendment Bill. That day he also addressed the Africa Bureau on Federal affairs claiming that many Europeans were quite unacceptably blaming the failures of the Federation on the Labour Party. He predicted that the review in 1960 would be very difficult if the Europeans had not, before then, won the African round.

When heckled, Callaghan related how he had tired of Europeans attempting to brainwash him when, in fact, their only contact with Africans was with their cooks. Indeed, he had found the gulf between the races was so wide that neither knew what the other was saying or doing. Welensky had attacked him for his comments but, Callaghan said, they were the truthful product of conversations with hundreds of people. He stated that people either thought that the pace of advancement was too fast or that there was little time left for change. He proposed to inform the British public of the true state of affairs through a series of meetings, but resisted pressure from the Reverend Michael Scott and the Bureau for a commitment to the break-up of the Federation when the Labour Party was returned. Nevertheless, it seemed to the Rhodesian Press that Callaghan had implied that the Europeans were on trial and that the Federation would be dissolved if they did not meet the expectations of the Labour Party. To the Press this appeared contrary to the solemn undertaking of the Labour Party in 1953 to make the Federation work, and seemed only to encourage extremism and reaction.

Callaghan also said that, if his delegation had used different language in its report, it would have been called statesmanlike.[71] Welensky replied instantly that, as no report had been received, it could not be described as statesmanlike or otherwise. He nevertheless doubted whether the views of Callaghan would meet this criterion because it implied an open mind, and Welensky knew that, long before the visit, Callaghan had stated that the Federation would not last and had displayed that prejudice wherever he went. Welensky was unmoved by Callaghan's references to him but wanted the public to understand that Callaghan, while a guest of the local Commonwealth Parliamentary Association, was publishing articles which were highly derogatory to

[70] House of Commons *Hansard* (London), Vol. 577, Col. 187, 6 November 1957; Welensky Papers, 43/*Malvern*, Welensky to Malvern, 7 November 1957.

[71] *The Rhodesia Herald* & *The Bulawayo Chronicle*, 14 November 1957.

the Federation. This was, Welensky maintained, simply an abuse of hospitality, just as the writing of articles before the publication of the considered report of the delegation was highly objectionable.[72]

Callaghan, asked by the Press to reply, repeated that he had tried to tell the truth but would not indulge in personal recriminations with Welensky. He had not said anything derogatory and was sorry that Welensky had disapproved. Welensky, when asked in turn, urged the Labour Party to correct the impression that it was anti-European and would protect only African interests. He warned that he remained determined to proceed with the Constitutional Amendment and Federal Electoral Bills. *The Rhodesia Herald,* however, demanded that Callaghan reply to the charge of the abuse of hospitality.[73]

While the fate of this challenge was awaited, T. I. F. Wilson, the Federal Speaker and chairman of the Federal branch of the Commonwealth Parliamentary Association, informed Welensky that he had written to the chairman of the Association, Major J. G. Lockhart, suggesting the establishment of a principle that no member of a delegation should write articles while visiting. Lockhart was considering this and Wilson proposed to seek the support of the Federal and territorial branches for a demand for such a commitment from the British branch, making it clear that otherwise it would never be invited again. Wilson was personally aggrieved because he had worked hard to make a success of the tour and had been shocked to discover Callaghan writing articles when travelling at the Federal taxpayer's expense. To him it was a breach of confidence of the worst nature. He enclosed a letter to Callaghan to this effect, the posting of which he left to the discretion of Welensky.[74]

No reply was forthcoming from Callaghan, but Major Lockhart wrote to Welensky regretting the brush with Callaghan and personally accepting the blame. He said that normally the delegates were asked not to write or broadcast during their tours so that their parent branches would be the first to receive their views. This delegation, however, had toured in a recess and, as there would not have been a branch meeting for some time after their return, it had seemed unreasonable to prevent the writing of articles. Accordingly, Lockhart, when approached by Callaghan for permission to write, had concurred because there seemed to be no difference if he wrote in September or November.[75]

If Callaghan chose not to defend himself publicly, J. E. MacColl, a Labour member of the delegation, obliged. He denied that Callaghan had gone out of his way to be hostile and thought that Welensky, realising this, had shifted his attack to the articles written by Callaghan in a British newspaper which few Rhodesians would ever see. Here, MacColl conceded, Welensky was on firmer ground because there was little chance of any of his allegations being repudiated. However, the two articles had not dealt with constitutional matters, and not even Welensky, at his wildest, could call them derogatory. MacColl maintained that the local hosts had been in constant touch with their

[72] *The Times*, 15 November 1957.
[73] *The Rhodesia Herald*, 15 & 16 November 1957.
[74] Welensky Papers, 42/39, ff. 23–24, T. I. F. Wilson to Welensky, 17 November 1957.
[75] *Ibid.*, 42/39, f. 20, Major J. G. Lockhart to Welensky, 19 November 1957.

visitors and that the slightest hint that the delegation had been indiscreet would have been gratefully received. He concluded that, if the delegation was wrong in thinking that the Rhodesians would have welcomed frankness and resented platitudes, the fault was certainly not that of Callaghan.[76]

Field entered the fray, calling the comments of the delegation impertinent and saying that the Rhodesians should emphasise that they intended to run their own affairs. He described a tour by Callaghan of farms in the Marandellas area, during which Callaghan was plainly seeking to confirm his preconceived ideas and was obviously irritated by the contentment of the African employees as well as by their lack of ambition and knowledge of politics.[77]

Welensky then admitted to *Reynold's News* that neither was it an unwritten custom that visiting British parliamentarians should not contribute to newspapers, nor was it a condition laid down by the Commonwealth Parliamentary Association. Nevertheless, to him, Callaghan had ignored the code of good manners of not criticising a host when under his roof. Furthermore, Callaghan had been the guest of the local branches of the Association as an MP and not as a journalist. Welensky had read what Callaghan had written and believed that he had irresponsibly painted only part of the picture. For example, he had not revealed that the African nationalist leaders were not representative of the mass of the industrious, law-abiding African people, even though he had admitted that the current beerhall boycott had not been popular. Callaghan had also emphasised the differing racial wage levels, but had omitted to comment on the vast differences between the European and African skills, civilisation and education. He had not said that African mine labour was drawn from the rural areas and was confronted with civilisation for the first time on arrival. Callaghan had ignored the technical training provided for raw Africans at the Hodgson Technical College in Northern Rhodesia and at Domboshawa, just outside Salisbury. Overall, Callaghan had failed to paint life as it was and Welensky was confident that he could find equally unpleasant aspects of life in Britain about which to write.[78]

Welensky informed Wilson that one could not insist strongly enough on the normal courtesies from people like Callaghan. Welensky complained to Lockhart that he still had not seen the report to which Callaghan had referred. He warned Lockhart that the future of the Association was in jeopardy if the recent behaviour set a precedent because the people of the Federation certainly resented the delegation's behaviour. However, Welensky confessed that he was obviously not used to the new brand of Labour politician.[79]

Simultaneously, Callaghan moved in the Commons that the Constitutional Amendment Bill should not receive the Royal Assent. He claimed to be supported by a rare consensus of opinion on an African subject. The British Press had variously cautioned its Government and Parliament to weigh the

[76] *The Times*, 22 November 1957.
[77] *Citizen*, 22 November 1957.
[78] Welensky Papers, 42/39, f. 32, Welensky interviewed by Clyde Sanger, 22 November 1957.
[79] *Ibid.*, f. 21, Welensky to T. I. F. Wilson, 23 November 1957; f. 18, Welensky to Major J. G. Lockhart, 25 November 1957.

issue carefully. The British Council of Churches had warned of a racial reaction in Africa. The Africa Bureau, the Inter-Racial Society in Salisbury and the Capricorn Africa Society had denounced the Bill and, indeed, only the British and Federal Governments had advocated it. The tragedy, he said, was that the British Government could not amend the Bill because the Federal Constitution allowed it only the power of acceptance or rejection. His Party saw the Bill as unnecessary and he noted that it had not enjoyed the unanimous support of the Federal House. He claimed that such an amendment had not been envisaged in the Federal negotiations in 1953 and was a breach of them. He praised the African Affairs Board for a job well done and claimed that the understanding was that the British Parliament would refuse a bill against which the Board had ruled, particularly if it had scraped through the Federal Assembly by one vote. (In fact, it had received one more vote than the two-thirds it required.) To him, the justification of the Bill was "hypocrisy at its worst" and it would thus be "sheer folly" to force the Bill through. Callaghan denounced the British Government for weakening its constitutional position by the 1957 Convention and declared the latter unlawful because the Labour Party had not been consulted. He was sure the Federal aim was to secure control of African affairs simply because it disliked the Colonial Office. The Africans, knowing this, would regard the passing of the Constitutional Amendment Bill as further evidence that the British Government had deserted them. Callaghan believed that, if the Bill were forced through, then the Government was obliged to give the Africans a greater role in the government of the northern territories. Doig had written to *The Times* to protest against the Bill and Callaghan recalled his last paragraph in which he had written that the passing of the Bill would discredit the African Affairs Board in the eyes of the Africans. The Bill would undermine the confidence of the Africans in British protection, Callaghan said, and make the prospects of the review in 1960 quite dismal.

Callaghan was supported by other Labour speakers, including Dugdale who agreed that the Bill was simply a bid for power by the whites. Mrs Barbara Castle, of the Labour Party, was at pains to prove that, despite what the Government maintained, liberal opinion was not the dominant force in the Federation. She had discovered that nearly half of the recent Federal immigrants were South African born and she believed that they had gone to Southern Rhodesia because they thought that white supremacy could be permanently maintained there without violence. She claimed to have found further evidence of the illiberal nature of the Federal Government in its staffing of its immigration board in London by former South African policemen.

Alport immediately pointed out that she had mistaken the British South Africa Police of Southern Rhodesia for the South African Police. It was a trivial mistake, but, because she spoke with such authority on their affairs, it stuck in the craw of the Rhodesians and was not easily forgiven or forgotten, particularly as shortly afterwards she arrived in the Federation and appeared to emulate Callaghan's earlier and successful bid to gain prominence within the Labour Party through political posturing and the writing of lurid accounts of life in the Federation.

In the debate, Mrs Castle, like Callaghan, also made play with Doig's letter and with Dugdale's assertion that the Europeans were merely seeking power. Creech Jones warned of the dangers of undermining African confidence and, believing the European to be over-represented, he asked Lennox-Boyd to recover the African's trust by giving him a greater influence in territorial politics. Griffith wanted time for full discussion with Moffat and the African Affairs Board.

Alport replied that, despite the African belief to the contrary, there was provision for the amendment of the Constitution before 1960. The Press laboured under similar misconceptions, he said, and Callaghan had not helped by speaking of the Bill being passed by one vote when it had secured 25 votes to eight (which was one vote more than the two-thirds required). The British Government certainly did not have to accept automatically any ruling of the African Affairs Board. Furthermore, he stated, as the African voters would outnumber the Europeans in Nyasaland, while in Northern Rhodesia there would almost be equality, the Europeans would not dominate the election of the new African MPs. It was not an act of discrimination towards the northern Africans to give them an opportunity to elect their Federal representatives directly. The Bill would simply give the Africans increased experience in democracy. Alport asked the House not to divide because of the harm which it would do in Africa.

Major Patrick Wall (later Sir Patrick), a member of the recent visiting Parliamentary Association delegation, dismissed Mrs Castle's speech as a complete tirade.

Finally Lennox-Boyd stressed that the Federal Government could not retard the constitutional development of the territories. He felt that the details and merits of the Bill could not be ignored because, if they were, the Africans would be misled and, worse still, there would be in effect an abdication to the African Affairs Board. The report of the Board had been carefully considered, but the British Government believed that the Bill served everyone's best interests. A delay to 1960, he said, would merely deny the vote to many Africans until then. The House divided and the objection to the Royal Assent was soundly defeated.[80]

Welensky promptly congratulated Lennox-Boyd and Home, claiming that historians would place the proposals in their proper perspective. His Government, he said, was greatly heartened by the result.

The moment, however, was one of unease. The first rumbles of the Southern Rhodesian Cabinet crisis were being heard with Todd categorically denying that he had any intention of resigning. In Northern Rhodesia the ANC campaign of violent unrest was sufficiently alarming to prompt calls for its proscription.[81] Nevertheless, Welensky set up his department to monitor race relations.

He also informed Home on 28 November that, in accordance with British advice, a working party had begun to plan for the 1960 review. He hoped for an inter-change of ideas with the British and territorial Governments and was

[80] House of Commons *Hansard* (London), Vol. 578, Col. 808 f., 25 November 1957.

[81] Welensky Papers, 20/1, f. 169, Welensky to Home, 27 November 1957; *The Rhodesia Herald*, 28 November 1957.

confident of the full support of Southern Rhodesia and Nyasaland, but not of Northern Rhodesia. To remedy this, he wanted Benson, whom he believed would retire in 1958, replaced early.[82]

Welensky did not allow the Labour Party to go unchallenged. He publicly decried Callaghan's ignorant claim as Shadow Colonial Secretary, that it was never intended that the British Government should disagree with the African Affairs Board. He could not believe that Callaghan thought that Malvern and he would have accepted what would have been, in effect, a "Star Chamber" Government. It was clear that the Labour Party had reneged on Attlee's promise to give the Federation a fair trial. Welensky, albeit privately, was also disappointed by the failure of the British Government to reply vigorously to Callaghan. However, he did not have total local support because at least one correspondent to *The Rhodesia Herald* accused him of attacking the likes of Callaghan whenever he wished to improve his standing in the Federation.[83]

Furthermore, the rejection of the African Affairs Board's report is believed to have destroyed what faith there remained amongst the northern Africans in the safeguards. Certainly, the northern Africans thought that, unless they took drastic action, the whites would achieve their goal of independence within the Commonwealth in 1960. In the aftermath Doig resigned his seat and, in February 1959, Moffat did likewise. Benson sympathised with Moffat and Doig, and considered resigning himself.[84]

With the Constitutional Amendment Bill assented to, the next step was to introduce the Federal Electoral Bill. However, before this could be done, Benson made a late bid to extend the franchise to Chiefs, headmen and pensioners with 20 years' service to add nearly 2 000 voters to the lower roll in Northern Rhodesia. He intended to introduce this into the new Northern Rhodesian Constitution, which he had begun to devise, and believed it would be well-received because it would undermine the ANC threat to boycott the registration of voters. The Federal Cabinet, however, found that he had forgotten the literacy qualification and, while the enfranchisement of these people was desirable, the illiterate or those whose only qualification was 20 years' service with one employer were unacceptable.[85]

Greenfield introduced the Electoral Bill, on 16 December, and stressed that the delimitation commission would be chaired by the Federal Chief Justice and would have a latitude of 15 per cent in drawing up the constituencies. Field wanted a tribunal to assess a person's civilisation. He rejected the lower roll as nothing more than an attempt to patronise a proud people, the Africans.

Moffat regretted that the "magnificent" Tredgold Commission Report had not received the recognition it deserved, and he decried the departure from its principle of allowing the special voters some say in the return of the ordinary MPs. The racial approach would lose the Federal Party any African support it had gained, he said, because Africans had been assured that they would be able to elect their own spokesmen. Should he, Moffat asked, tell the Africans

[82] Welensky Papers, 20/1, f. 168, Welensky to Home, 28 November 1957.
[83] *Rand Daily Mail*, 29 November 1957; *The Rhodesia Herald*, 12 December 1957.
[84] D. C. Mulford, *Zambia: The Politics of Independence, 1957–1964* (London, 1967), p. 53.
[85] Welensky Papers, FGC(57), 44th Meeting, Minute 6, Federal Cabinet, 11 December 1957.

that the Government intended that their votes should be swamped by the Europeans?

Warming to his task, Moffat declared that it would be a lasting disgrace if, through this Bill, the Government abused the power of the minority. Indeed, because they felt so strongly about this, Moffat announced that he, Doig, Chirwa and Yamba were considering an action in the Federal Supreme Court on the premise that the framing of the franchise was outside the competence of the Federal Government and within that of the territorial Governments.

Yamba found the Bill evil because, he said, it was designed to protect the interests of the Europeans. Chirwa cautioned the British Government on breaking faith with the Africans. He believed that Nyasaland would soon secede and join Tanganyika. Scott supported the dissenters and, because Welensky had forbidden his Ministers to speak, apart from himself and Greenfield, much of the defence of the Bill came from the Federal Party backbenchers. These called the speeches of the Opposition extravagant and inflammatory and thought that the African representatives feared having to stand for election. They questioned why Moffat should be considering an action so late in the day and concluded that he was merely seeking publicity abroad. Van Eeden, however, announced that the Dominion Party would vote against the Bill because it could not accept provisions such as the 15 per cent margin for delimitation.

Chirwa interrupted the debate with a motion deprecating an alleged statement by Welensky at the Federal Party congress, in November, that someone would have to nominate MPs to fill the special Nyasaland seats when the British Government relinquished its protective role. Chirwa claimed that this had spread much alarm amongst Africans who, he reminded the House, had never accepted the Federation. The Governments had sworn that they would not allow amalgamation, but the Africans remained fearful that they would.

Welensky replied that Chirwa had merely wasted public time and money by this motion when all he needed to have done was to ask him for an explanation. In fact, at Ndola, answering a question on the likely course of events, he had predicted that constitutional progress in the northern territories was a necessary prelude to self-government and had suggested that the Nyasaland officials might be replaced at some stage by nominees of the Governor-General. Then he accused Chirwa of dishonesty because he had been demanding adult suffrage and the break-up of the Federation in 1960 when he knew that neither was possible. Welensky acknowledged that insufficient had been done to put the Federal case over to the Africans, but stressed that this was being rectified. After Chirwa had made all his familiar points in reply, his motion was rejected.[86]

On 18 December, before the final day of the second reading, Moffat wrote to Welensky and pleaded that, despite the current emotion, reconciliation was possible. The key was the degree of control which the ordinary voters, who would be Europeans in practice, would have over the election of the additional northern MPs. As the Nyasaland African voters would outnumber their European counterparts, the problem narrowed to Northern Rhodesia

[86] Fed R & N *Debates* (Salisbury), Vol. 8, Col. 1751 f., 16 December 1957.

about which he felt strongly because of the assurances which all the parties had made to the Africans. He sought discussions to settle this affair which so distressed him.[87]

Moffat's letter was immediately examined by the Federal Cabinet but it could not find a way to satisfy him. He had not helped by failing to suggest one. The Cabinet, satisfied with its formula, ordered Greenfield to terminate the debate that afternoon.[88]

This Greenfield accomplished after strongly censuring the northern Africans for calling their Southern Rhodesian colleagues "stooges". He also criticised Moffat for exaggerating the position. The Bill, Greenfield maintained, was certainly not *ultra vires* of the Constitution and, in fact, the Government had kept carefully within it when devising its legislation. The Government had therefore fulfilled its obligations to the Africans, while Moffat had failed to advise them that the Constitution could be amended thus before 1960. Moffat could hardly thereafter blame the Government. Closing, Greenfield indicated that the Government would consider enfranchising the tribal leaders if they were literate. The Bill passed its second reading by 21 votes to seven.[89]

The Federal Assembly recessed for the festive season but the battle with the Labour Party continued. The Labour journal, *The Tribune,* on 18 December demanded the abolition of the current Colonial policies to save the honour of Britain. It declared that the Labour Party would not be bound by any agreement between Lennox-Boyd and the settler governments, and would repeal any undertakings which dishonoured the pledge of a paramountcy of African interests. The Federation would be dissolved because it had failed either to win the confidence of the Africans or to improve their conditions. The northern territories would revert to undiluted control by the Colonial Office, but only in preparation for an early advance to self-government. Universal suffrage would be introduced and through democracy the African would gain his freedom. Dominion status would only be granted to governments which represented the majority of their people. Before self-government, colour bars would be abolished and full rights of speech, Press and association would be restored. (*The Tribune,* however, did not explain why it thought these freedoms had been curtailed when, in fact, apart from in the emergency situation in Northern Rhodesia, they had not been.) There would be no special privileges for Europeans and Asians, the paper continued, as all races would enjoy equal rights. Almost gleefully, it concluded that its declaration could well provoke the Europeans to make a unilateral declaration of independence before the Labour Party was returned to power.

Wilson, the Federal Speaker, still could not forgive Callaghan his trespasses and wrote again to him on 20 December defending his branch of the Commonwealth Parliamentary Association on its equal treatment of its black and white members. Wilson found that the social tension, to which Callaghan had referred in his articles, was nothing more than a figment of his imagina-

87 Welensky Papers, 25/98, f. 19, Moffat to Welensky, 18 December 1957.
88 *Ibid.*, FGC(57), 45th Meeting, Minute 2, Federal Cabinet, 18 December 1957.
89 Fed R & N *Debates* (Salisbury), Vol. 8, Col. 1915 f., 18 December 1957.

tion as the social barriers were gradually breaking down. He was confident that, if only the Labour Party would express faith in the Federation, the African nationalist movement would be deflated.[90]

On 31 December Welensky expressed extreme disappointment to Home with Moffat's emotional and illogical attack upon their Governments. He had never understood why an air of great authority and respect surrounded Moffat when, apart from being the bearer of an honoured name, he had hardly earned it by his performances in the Northern Rhodesian and Federal legislatures. Greenfield, Welensky believed, had answered Moffat effectively in the last debate but not before Moffat had done great harm to race relations because he spoke with such authority. Welensky could not forgive Moffat for the way in which he had used the African Affairs Board, but believed that Moffat's popularity had radically declined. It was clear to Welensky that Moffat was a man of some ability who found his role plainly frustrating. However, it was equally clear that he could not be brought into the Government.

Welensky told Home that he understood that his clash with Callaghan had embarrassed the British Government. This was unfortunate as he had not wished to confront Callaghan, but had been forced to by the strength of local feeling. In any case, he had been provoked because Callaghan had told him in London, before ever setting foot in Africa, that the Federation was doomed. All this was distressing because a few favourable comments from the British Labour Party on the permanency of the Federation could rectify a number of matters. As a consequence of the new militancy of the Labour Party, he claimed he was under some pressure to take a strong line on the independence of the Federation. However, he would not yield and would, as promised, raise the issue only in 1960.[91]

Home took more than a month to reply and then dealt with Moffat and Callaghan lightly. To his practised eye, Moffat was simply an old Scottish radical who, on form, could be politically awkward. He believed that, in the recent debates, Moffat had found himself out of his depth and thoroughly regretted it. Callaghan, to Home, was a young, bouncy "customer" who could take the knocks and who might well become Welensky's friend. The report of the delegation from the Commonwealth Parliamentary Association had been released and in it Home noticed that Callaghan was convinced by the economic case for the Federation. Thus it was unlikely that Callaghan desired an end to the Federation. Home suggested a change of tactics, that the Federal Government should claim that by 1960 the achievements of the Federation would be so apparent that even the Labour Party would have to recognise what had to be done and what solid prospects lay ahead. A convincing, consistent and persistent publicity drive, Home felt, could create the right atmosphere for the Federal review.[92]

Home, in fact, had also fallen foul of Welensky when, on 6 January, shortly before the committee stage of the Electoral Bill, he had cabled Welensky to say that his parliamentary difficulties were forcing a British debate on the Bill

[90] Welensky Papers, 42/39, f. 13, T. I. F. Wilson to Callaghan, 20 December 1957.
[91] *Ibid.*, 25/98, f. 15, Welensky to Home, 31 December 1957.
[92] *Ibid.*, 25/98, f. 10, Home to Welensky, 4 February 1958.

before the Royal Assent could be forthcoming. Welensky immediately replied that his difficulties equalled those of Home as at best he was likely to secure only one vote more than the two-thirds required because the Dominion Party would oppose the Bill. If this Bill failed, then the Federal Government could only issue regulations to govern the impending general election. He understood that Home had approved the Bill and had agreed that the Royal Assent would be automatic if it was unaltered. To allow the debate before the Assent would alter the established procedure, and, though he knew that convention could not bind another Parliament, he believed that the failure of the British Government to approve the Electoral Bill would be tantamount to the suspension of the Federal Constitution.[93]

In the event, the Royal Assent was forthcoming. Welensky used this opportunity to announce to Home that he would waive the means qualifications for Chiefs but could not do likewise for the headmen because of the complications and variances in the tribal structures in Nyasaland and Northern Rhodesia.

The representatives of the northern Africans and the Dominion Party fought the last stages of the debates on the Electoral Bill every step of the way. After Yamba had dwelt on the resentment which had been aroused amongst the Africans, Moffat requested an adjournment for consideration of an alternative scheme. Greenfield rejected this because Moffat had had ample time to give prior warning. Because the Government should have been aware of the degree of opposition both within and without the House, Chirwa was surprised by this refusal and concluded that the Government was not prepared to listen to anyone. Moffat maintained he had acted properly by raising his alternative in Parliament and had only asked for an adjournment for its consideration. His proposal was thereupon rejected in a division.[94]

Greenfield introduced his amendment regarding the Chiefs, placing them on the general roll, and while it was easily accepted, the northern Africans objected strenuously to the demand for literacy. Supported by the Southern Rhodesian African representatives, Greenfield refused to concede.

Next, the clauses of the Bill were fought through, with the northern African representatives objecting to the means and educational qualifications for the general roll because they favoured the European. Chirwa protested that the dual roll would turn Africans into second-class citizens. To Moffat, the most important safeguard for the Africans, that of being able to control the election of their own representatives, was being abolished.

Then the northern African representatives questioned whether the Constitution could be legally amended, but Greenfield maintained it could. Chirwa thereupon raised the bogey of interferences with land rights, while Moffat and Doig harped on their promises to the Africans that the Constitution would be frozen for the first decade.

Welensky and Greenfield replied that such promises had been contrary to the intention of the Federal Conferences. Field confirmed that the Constitution could be changed but felt that, if the representation of the African was to be doubled, the method to effect it should be the established one. In the

[93] *Ibid.*, 20/1, ff. 165–166, Welensky to Home, 6 January 1958.

[94] Fed R & N *Debates* (Salisbury), Vol. 8, Col. 1952, 6 January 1958.

closing moments, Moffat pleaded that the qualifications should be lowered to ensure large African majorities, but Greenfield would not bend because he believed it would be too great a step towards universal suffrage. The Government won the division by 23 votes to ten, with van Eeden, Field, Williamson and Scott supporting the six northern African representatives.

When the third reading began on 8 January 1958, the Assembly had before it an objection from the African Affairs Board that the Bill differentiated between the races. Greenfield disagreed because the Board's argument was based on the differing standards of wealth and education enjoyed by the races. To Greenfield, any objection had to show a disability which was imposed on the African and not on the European.

Field proclaimed that his Party believed that there should be a common roll, and a purely African roll with a civilisation test for anyone who wished to graduate from the latter to the former. Doig doubted the Government's desire to make a success of the Federation. Scott wanted the debate terminated because he had given up hope of the Government seeing reason, and he drew fire from Davies who accused him of rubbing his hands in anticipation of the African refusing to enrol. It was, in fact, the declared intention of the African Congresses to discourage the African from registering for the vote.

All this skirmishing drew Malvern from the back benches into the battle. He launched into a vigorous account of how he had been forced to accept Nyasaland in early 1952 when Lyttelton had roared "All or nothing". Malvern had asked Lyttelton why, if the Africans were fit to sit in the Federal Parliament, they would need, in addition, a "white nurse" and was told that they would still need the guidance and restraint which the European representative would provide. In Malvern's view, Doig, in particular, had never provided either guidance or restraint and indeed had only tried to lead every extremist movement. Malvern believed that everything in the country had been built by blood, sweat and tears and he was determined that the "kindergarten" should not be allowed to ruin it. The Bill, in his view, would assist the Africans to advance, and he hoped that the system would produce wise and temperate African MPs. It should, he said, because it had already produced two — the Southern Rhodesians, Hove and Savanhu.

Moffat expressed pleasure to see the Malvern of old dash into the fray with all his guns blazing and then leap on his horse and dart off in every direction at once in his time-honoured fashion. Moffat, however, remained convinced that, despite everything, the Federal Government served only its white electorate. Hove, however, disagreed.[95]

Greenfield, winding up the debate on 9 January, dealt solely with Doig's objections, asking him how he could allege that the Government did not want the Federation to succeed. Doig had also claimed that the Nyasaland Members would always be Europeans and Greenfield replied that this had been the case hitherto because the Africans had not been enfranchised unless they became British subjects. However, he said, the Federal Government would give the vote to British Protected Persons, and Africans could certainly

[95] *Ibid.*, Col. 2120 f., 8 January 1958.

replace Europeans. Greenfield had nothing more to say, and when the House divided the Government more than secured its two-thirds majority. The Electoral Bill passed into law without further trial.[96]

On 15 January, the report of the delegation from the Commonwealth Parliamentary Association finally arrived. It urged the Rhodesians to indulge in more racial mixing and to remove racial distinctions to prove to the non-Europeans that partnership was a reality. It would help, it suggested, if Salisbury could be made into a race-free precinct.[97] However, this report seems to have been almost overlooked because not only was it long delayed, but it arrived amidst the uproar over the rebellion against Todd. The Todd crisis would occupy local attention for months to come and make Welensky and some of his Cabinet regret at times the fusion of the two Parties. However, the Federal Cabinet at least had achieved the enlargement of the House and the settlement of the franchise, and could thus hold its general election on time in 1958.

[96] *Ibid.*, Col. 2196 f., 9 January 1958.
[97] *The Rhodesia Herald*, 16 January 1958.

CHAPTER TWENTY

The Course to Collision

Todd's Cabinet Revolt, and Conflict on Northern Rhodesia's Constitution, January–May 1958

IN his New Year message, Welensky forecast that 1958 could be the most important year for the Federation since its inception because, for the first time, everyone — regardless of race — who qualified for the vote could elect the Government.[1] He and his Ministers had cleared the ground for the general election and, of course, were looking beyond it to the constitutional review in 1960. They were expecting a revision of the Northern Rhodesian Constitution to be followed by some adjustment in Nyasaland. However, though they had some inkling, they did not suspect that they would be drawn into a confrontation with the British Government over Northern Rhodesia. This was partly due to the desire of Welensky and his Cabinet to preserve certain concepts, such as the goal of achieving a non-racial party system. It was also a consequence of being involved, through their Party, in Northern Rhodesian politics. More immediately, the fusion with the United Rhodesia Party in September 1957, producing the United Federal Party, brought in its wake unexpected difficulties for Welensky and his Cabinet because some people falsely concluded that he was involved in the Southern Rhodesian ministerial rebellion against Todd, welcoming the opportunity to get rid of him.

Within the Federal Cabinet, Greenfield had been the main advocate of the fusion of the Federal and United Rhodesia Parties. His reasons were pragmatic because he was much involved with party affairs and saw the advantages of a merger. In Northern Rhodesia and Nyasaland, the Federal Party operated in the Federal and territorial spheres, but in Southern Rhodesia it did not, even though most of its members also belonged to the United Rhodesia Party. Greenfield believed that much time and money could be saved by ending the overlap and proposed fusion at the FP congress in 1956. It was accepted, and

[1] Welensky Papers, 6/2, f. 119, Welensky's New Year Message, 1 January 1958.

negotiations began with the URP. Todd was believed to have been unenthusiastic and, as has been related, Welensky had similar misgivings. However, Greenfield was supported by P. B. Fletcher and others within the URP. Fletcher confessed later that he had sought the merger because he hoped that it would bring fresh influences to bear on Todd. The conversion of Wightwick to fusion was a sign that such sentiments were shared. The URP accepted the idea in September 1957, and two months later the FP did likewise. Consequently, the URP decided to hold a dissolution congress in March 1958.[2]

There had, of course, been tensions within the Southern Rhodesian Cabinet for some time, particularly over the Southern Rhodesian franchise and the Immorality Act. Ellman-Brown had been dissuaded from resigning in August, and at the URP congress in September Wightwick had proposed the replacement of Todd as Prime Minister by Fletcher. Fletcher had declined, saying that the Cabinet was a happy team. Indeed, Fletcher and Ellman-Brown successfully ordered Wightwick and his cohorts to cease their agitation.[3] Nevertheless, all was not well within Todd's Cabinet and Welensky and Greenfield were told so on their return from the FP congress on 23 November. Todd was in Inyanga and Fletcher was at Kariba and, in their absence, the three remaining Ministers, Stumbles, Hatty and Ellman-Brown, met and decided that, with Todd at the helm, the URP would lose the next election. They were worried that Todd's apparent emphasis on African advancement, and not on general economic development, would alienate the electorate. Furthermore, they were concerned by reports that Todd, without consulting or even informing them, was having talks with Joshua Nkomo, the Reverend Ndabaningi Sithole and Guy Clutton-Brock, a British missionary, who were all leading figures in the recently revitalised African National Congress of Southern Rhodesia. Fletcher returned to Salisbury before Todd and, agreeing with his colleagues, warned Todd on the evening of 24 November that the Cabinet proposed to resign because they believed he would lose them the election. Fletcher apologised for the unexpected nature of this announcement.[4]

On the morrow, appointments were muddled and Todd only saw Hatty, who claimed that Fletcher had acted without permission and declared that he had never thought that the situation was beyond recall. At the weekly Cabinet meeting, on 26 November, nothing further was said about resignation.[5] Meanwhile Welensky had been at work. He did so because he feared the damage that the crisis might do to the Federation when the fate of the Federal Electoral Bill hung in the balance. He also felt indebted to Todd for his support for that Bill which had been forthcoming despite their differences of opinion over the franchise. Welensky spoke to Todd and pointed out the embarrassment which his resignation would cause to the Federation. He also feared he would be blamed if Todd stood down.

[2] J. M. Greenfield, *Testimony of a Rhodesian Federal* (Bulawayo, 1978), p. 157; R. Blake, *A History of Rhodesia* (London, 1977), p. 305.
[3] Blake, *Rhodesia*, *op. cit.*, p. 305.
[4] *Ibid.*, pp. 305–306; Author's interview with the late Sir Patrick Fletcher.
[5] Blake, *Rhodesia*, *op. cit.*, p. 306; Author's interview with the late Sir Patrick Fletcher.

The rebellious Ministers were treated to a similar lecture from Welensky and the result was that only routine Cabinet business was discussed on 26 November. Rumours were circulating and Todd had to issue his statement denying any crisis. Welensky would pay for his services as a mediator because he soon found himself blamed for interfering and keeping Todd in power when he was no longer wanted. Later he would be accused by many, including Tredgold, Todd's daughter, Judith, and the Salisbury weekly, the *Citizen*, of engineering the downfall of Todd.[6]

Todd believed that the matter was settled and, as if to placate his Cabinet on his relationship with the African National Congress, he used a St Andrew's Night dinner in Bulawayo to defend the record of his Government and issue a stern warning to those who might seek to promote civil unrest. His Government, Todd claimed, had fostered private enterprise by denationalising the steel and sugar industries and had brought a new freedom for everyone. Local government had been encouraged, the Land Husbandry Act had given opportunities to 300 000 African farmers, and urban Africans had recently been allowed to buy their homes. The pass laws had been eased, and African education had been placed on a sounder basis. A new industrial conciliation bill had been drafted which would maintain standards but allow the African to participate in industry. The principle of wage bargaining was being extended. The liberal spirit of the times had been demonstrated by the maintenance of a colour-free franchise which, nevertheless, had sufficiently high standards to ensure political stability in the future.

Then Todd switched from defence to attack and warned that his Government was preparing security legislation designed to curb the freedom of individuals and organisations. Thus the Europeans and Africans should rise in the defence of liberty and good race relations and make the introduction of such legislation unnecessary. He knew that race relations were still sound and that there was no cause for alarm. However, there were signs of erosion and his Government believed in prevention rather than cure.

Todd claimed that the formation of the Southern Rhodesia African National Congress, on 12 September, had not alarmed his Government even though, in the light of events in the North, the name "Congress" was hardly reassuring. The constitution of the ANC was reasonable but he did not know if Clutton-Brock and its other authors had intended it to be anything more than good propaganda for the Africa Bureau and other friends overseas. Nkomo was known to be well educated, capable and responsible, but the Government did not know how much influence Clutton-Brock would have or how responsible the other leaders would be.

When asked what attitude his Government would take to the formation of the ANC, Todd had replied that it would wait and see. Since September, however, George Nyandoro had appeared to supplant Nkomo and, with the other ANC members, had attacked those wishing to join the civilised and responsible community which governed Southern Rhodesia, calling them "sell-outs, Judas Iscariots and foolish people" who would be disciplined. A leading member had recently inferred that the ANC would determine what

[6] Welensky Papers, 25/202A, f. 163, Welensky to Sir Ronald Prain, 20 January 1958; J. Todd, *Rhodesia* (Bristol, 1966), p. 61.

was in the African interest and deal with those who disagreed. European country storekeepers had been threatened with unnamed consequences if they did not provide financial support. At ANC meetings in the Reserves the authority of the Chiefs had been flouted and the police humiliated.

Todd maintained that such behaviour had shocked the traditionally courteous Africans. Moreover, it was unnecessary as in Southern Rhodesia the non-racial franchise allowed pressure to be exerted through the vote. The ANC, however, was not prepared to work within the system, despite its own constitution, and was attempting not only to exert pressure by mass action but, through threats and humiliation, to prevent Africans from participating in the democratic life of the country. Todd believed that the success of the Federation would turn on the enlistment of courageous, capable Africans into the political parties. The alternatives were co-operation or unrelenting racialism. His Government would not fail to protect its people but, if ANC leaders would support racial harmony and observe the law, nothing need be done. Times of change and development were always fraught with danger and powerful emotions could be engendered. His Government recognised this and could be depended on to keep firm control.[7]

This speech was immediately supported by the *African News*, but at least one critic attacked Todd for over-reacting to enthusiastic tub-thumping.[8]

Welensky, albeit privately, was also at odds with Todd because he had urged him to remove the unnecessary and discriminatory restrictions on inter-territorial movement, which principally affected the Asians. However, Todd had refused to comply because his electorate wanted them retained and he preferred to wait until the Federal and territorial general elections were over.[9]

Todd, satisfied that all was well, departed on a month's holiday to South Africa. However, the day he left, 16 December, the Southern Rhodesian Government published regulations raising significantly the minimum wage in industry. These were not universally welcomed and not at all by Wightwick whose jute factory in Umtali was in financial straits. On 27 December Wightwick resigned from the United Federal Party declaring that he had no confidence in Todd. His branch asked him to vacate his seat, but also called on Todd to resign.[10]

Early in the New Year, the volume of rumours grew and Welensky concluded that there was a smear campaign against Todd. D. W. Lardner-Burke, later Minister of Justice in the Government of I. D. Smith, who had unsuccessfully stood for the United Rhodesia Party in 1954, left the United Federal Party and joined the Dominion Party. Welensky shed no tears over these defections but warned his British correspondents not to underestimate the Dominion Party's burgeoning strength. The *Central African Examiner* concluded that the UFP was deeply divided and that Wightwick's resignation would have wide implications because his reasons were undoubtedly shared

[7] Welensky Papers, 31/46, f. 57, Southern Rhodesian Government Press Statement – Speech by Todd, Bulawayo, 30 November 1957.

[8] *African Daily News*, 2 December 1957; *The Rhodesia Herald*, 12 December 1957.

[9] Welensky Papers, 24/151, ff. 236–238, Welensky to F. S. Joelson, 31 December 1957.

[10] Blake, *Rhodesia*, *op. cit.*, p. 307; *The Rhodesia Herald*, 24 December 1957.

by some of the Southern Rhodesian Cabinet and many others. Todd, it believed, ignoring his last speech, had gathered the reputation of being an ultra-liberal and had flouted the maxim of Rhodesian politics which was to act as liberally as possible but to speak as toughly as possible. The journal predicted that Todd had wrecked a career of great promise and might have offered the DP the chance of victory.[11]

The news of the furore reached Todd in South Africa and he telephoned his Cabinet, offering to return on 5 January. He was assured, to his relief, that it was unnecessary. Nevertheless, something had happened to convince his Cabinet that he could not continue to lead them. The nature of this final straw was not even hinted at but, as Lord Blake has made plain, it was not the supposed reason which his colleagues decided to use as a *casus belli* — the minimum wage regulations on which they claimed that neither they nor the Federal Government had been consulted. In truth, the regulations had been discussed in Cabinet and with the Federal Government.[12] It seems doubtful that Todd was ever told what precisely had so upset his Cabinet, but it must have been of sufficient magnitude for the Ministers to ignore Welensky's stricture, of only six weeks previously, that the stability of the Federation must not be threatened. After all, amongst other matters, the fate of the Federal Electoral Bill had not yet been settled.

Todd cut short his holiday and flew home on 9 January, but did so only because he had heard that some American friends were visiting Southern Rhodesia. *En route*, at Johannesburg, he was considerably surprised to be informed by reporters who were waiting for him that he would be expected to see Welensky and then resign. Todd thought that they had mistakenly uncovered the events of late November, and issued a disclaimer. He realised his error when Fletcher immediately informed him on arrival that the Cabinet would present him with their resignations on the morrow, 10 January.[13]

The next morning Todd demolished the Cabinet's case on the regulations and then had to hear again their claim that he would lose them the general election. He asked them if they were still determined to resign and they said that they were but would give him a day to reconsider matters. After the meeting, Todd consulted friends and decided not to resign. The rebels were confident that Todd would go and did not submit their resignations as promised. Indeed, they held a Cabinet meeting — without Todd — on 10 January and took decisions on routine matters. However, Todd forced their hands and then held a Press conference.

At this he sketched the recent events and said that his Ministers believed that he could not lead the UFP to victory in the general election. He denied that they were at odds over policy but claimed they wished to attract more reactionary support. He knew that he had the support of his fellow moderates and was determined that the Party which had elected him as its leader in 1953 should decide the issue. It distressed him that men whom he admired should try to supplant him. He would not meekly step aside because he felt that the

[11] Welensky Papers, 24/157, ff. 98–100, Welensky to J. Johnson, 3 January 1958; *Central African Examiner*, 3 January 1958.

[12] Blake, *Rhodesia*, *op. cit.*, p. 307.

[13] *Ibid.*, p. 308.

rebels might have erred. Moreover, if he did, policy might be subordinated to purely political considerations and, while this might appeal to a section of the electorate, it would be abhorrent to the Southern Rhodesians as a whole. There would be no support for such short-term policies. To allow the UFP a say, Todd announced that he would hold a special territorial congress in early February. He was confident that it would endorse his decision to continue as leader.[14]

A. Pedder, the Secretary of the superseded URP, thereupon circularised all UFP branches, asking them to ascertain quickly the attitude of their members and whether, in particular, they would support Todd's decision not to resign. Pedder's presumption considerably annoyed the hierarchy of the UFP.[15]

Todd, never one to neglect the Press, issued almost daily bulletins. On 12 January he claimed to have the support of the UFP Caucus in the Southern Rhodesian Parliament and would announce his new Cabinet soon. He denied that he was flouting opinion as he was assessing it carefully and as quickly as possible while attempting to provide sound government.[16] *The Rhodesia Herald*, however, doubted that he had the support of the Caucus but agreed with the *Central African Examiner* that Todd's liberalism underlay the crisis and that desperation was the motivating force.

Todd kept his promise and, on 13 January, announced a Cabinet comprising Sir George Davenport, A. E. Abrahamson, A. D. H. Lloyd and the brothers, E. D. and R. D. Palmer. Yet *The Rhodesia Herald* was right, because a day later more than half the Caucus endorsed the rebellion.[17] In reality, the alienation had already begun because a Parliamentary Secretary, H. J. Quinton, had resigned his office and three backbenchers, H. Reedman, R. M. Cleveland and M. N. Buchan had withdrawn their support.

In the Caucus, Fletcher, Hatty, Ellman-Brown and Stumbles defended their rebellion. They referred to the dispute over the Immorality Act, the franchise and the minimum wage regulations. They disliked Todd's behaviour over African advancement and, in particular, his statement on television overseas that he expected the Africans to acquire skills and judgment equal to that of the European within 20 years. Todd was criticised for his conversations with Clutton-Brock and Nkomo. He replied with a vigorous if unsuccessful defence.[18]

Todd was determined not to resign and gambled on the support of the territorial congress of the UFP which would enable him to wait to be defeated in Parliament and then fight a general election. Welensky watched in disbelief while Todd continued to try to govern with his minority.[19] Fletcher, the

[14] *Ibid.*; Welensky Papers, 16/1, f. 3, Press Statement by Todd, 11 January 1958.

[15] Welensky Papers, 16/1, f. 5, A. Pedder to UFP branch chairmen, 11 January 1958; Author's interview with Sir Roy Welensky.

[16] *Ibid.*, 9/12, f. 113, Press Statement by Todd, 12 January 1958.

[17] *The Rhodesia Herald*, 15 January 1958; Fletcher believed that the Governor, Sir Peveril William-Powlett, had acted unconstitutionally in asking Todd to form a government when he did not command a majority in Parliament. Consequently, Fletcher refused later to be knighted by the hand of William-Powlett and received his knighthood by special dispensation from the Queen. – Author's interview with the late Sir Patrick Fletcher.

[18] Blake, *Rhodesia*, *op. cit.*, p. 309.

[19] Welensky Papers, 25/123, f. 19, Welensky to Col. R. Musgrove, 16 January 1958.

acknowledged leader of the dissidents, demanded the recall of Parliament, but Todd refused it.

In the midst of this confusion, Welensky warned his correspondents not to think that this crisis had developed out of a struggle between liberalism and reaction. There were differences in emphasis, but none of the men involved had opposed any of the enlightened measures taken. Welensky believed that five such men did not resign lightly and Sir Patrick Fletcher confirmed this verdict.[20] Tredgold, however, concluded that Todd had paid the price of moving, politically, too far ahead of his electorate. In any case, by late January, Todd began to endeavour to induce the electorate to believe that the problem had been his liberalism. Welensky was unconvinced but conceded that Todd was a skilful politician.[21]

The date for the congress was set for 8 February and the lobbying began immediately, but Welensky decided to stand aloof.[22] The rebels were confident enough for Stumbles to declare to Greenfield that Fletcher would carry the day. Greenfield was not particularly pleased at the choice of Fletcher as leader, but felt that there was no challenger. Stumbles proposed to exploit the attempt by Pedder to influence the branches, and consequently Welensky, as president of the UFP, ordered the branch chairmen to do nothing more at their meetings than to elect delegates to the congress. He feared that any premature debate could only do harm. To ensure there was no misunderstanding, Welensky told the Press what he had done. The branches complied but there were complaints from the Filabusi branch that I. D. Smith, even though he was a Federal MP, was campaigning against Todd.[23]

Todd was dissatisfied with the structure of the congress because it was being held in terms of an adaptation of the Federal Party's constitution which the URP had never had the opportunity to adopt. In particular, the URP had never voted for the FP executive who would be present. Even the number of delegates from each branch had been decided by a method which was foreign to the URP. Todd was willing to accept these arrangements, however, if those who had served on the central executive of the URP could be present with full voting rights. He was further annoyed when he discovered, from the agenda, that the congress would proceed to the election of office bearers without first debating the Cabinet crisis. He wanted to describe the recent events before the rebels could put their case. Thereafter, there could be an open debate to which he would reply.[24]

All this led to Welensky to forecast on 23 January that the meeting would be difficult. Indeed, it could be unproductive because neither side was likely to accept a verdict against them and the issue could be carried forward to the renewed session of the Southern Rhodesian Legislative Assembly on 18

[20] *Ibid.*, 42/60, f. 87, Welensky to D. Taylor, 17 January 1958; 24/101, f. 15, Welensky to H. Hochschild, 17 January 1958; Author's interview with the late Sir Patrick Fletcher.

[21] Sir Robert Tredgold, *The Rhodesia that was my Life* (London, 1968), p. 226; Welensky Papers, 24/73, ff. 241–243, Welensky to Gore-Browne, 21 January 1958.

[22] Welensky Papers, 24/73, ff. 241–243, Welensky to Gore-Browne, 21 January 1958.

[23] *Ibid.*, 16/5, f. 33, Greenfield to Welensky, 15 January 1958; f. 32, Press Statement by Welensky, 17 January 1958; f. 28, Barnes to Welensky, 31 January 1958.

[24] *Ibid.*, f. 29, Todd to R. F. Halsted, 21 January 1958.

February as a matter of confidence in the Prime Minister. Welensky told his correspondents how he had tried to dampen the controversy but he was already being informed that the congress was being packed against Todd, which he resented because it had been Todd who had demanded the congress. He had suggested to Todd that he should hold a meeting of the former URP but had received the correct reply that to do so would make a mockery of the recent fusion. Welensky told Joelson that he expected Todd, if he retained the premiership, to be an awkward bedfellow henceforth.[25]

Joelson, in fact, had irritated Welensky by accepting the rejection of liberalism as the underlying cause and had said so in his *East Africa and Rhodesia*. He wrote that Todd symbolised for the Africans and the outside world a determination to get them a square deal. He said that defeat for Todd would mean that the British had placed too much faith in the promises of the Rhodesian leaders. He believed that Todd was right when he said: "My removal from office at this moment would be widely interpreted abroad to indicate a rejection of Southern Rhodesia's moderately liberal stand, or at least a step backward from it; I know also that to the great African section of our population this is how the position would appear."

Joelson claimed that the Conservatives would not have defied the Labour Opposition in founding the Federation if they had not had confidence in the liberalism of Malvern, Welensky and Todd. He erred, of course, because Todd had been nothing more than a backbencher until late 1953 when Malvern relinquished the reins in Southern Rhodesia.

Furthermore, Joelson did not expect the Conservatives to grant dominion status in 1960, or for years after that. He related how the representatives of the overseas Press were currently recording the astonishment of the locals at Todd's international reputation and at the possibility that there should be a reaction abroad to his overthrow. However, Joelson ridiculed the claim of the *Citizen* that Welensky had engineered the removal of Todd because Welensky knew that it would lose him not only African support, but the prospect of dominion status. In Joelson's view, the Southern Rhodesians would be wise to accept a reasonably rapid advancement of the Africans, which was all Todd had asked for.[26]

Faced with mounting speculation, Welensky reminded the public on 25 January that both sides had denied differences over policy. He wanted it universally understood that the policy of the UFP and the Southern Rhodesian Government was unchanged. He acknowledged that he had no involvement in the dispute but felt obliged to speak because he knew what effect the crisis would have on the political parties in Britain where so many of the issues were being weighed and would be settled in the next few years.[27]

However, the local Press believed he was intervening to try to prevent the holding of the congress on 8 February. When asked, he refused to comment on a report by the political correspondent of *The Rhodesia Herald* that he feared that the outcome of the congress would split the UFP irreparably.[28]

[25] *Ibid.*, ff. 232–233, Welensky to Joelson, 23 January 1958.
[26] *East Africa and Rhodesia*, 23 January 1958.
[27] *The Rhodesia Herald*, 25 January 1958.
[28] *Ibid.*, 27 January 1958.

His statement reminding the public that the antagonists had denied that policy had been the catalyst also had little effect because James Johnson wrote to him on 29 January regretting that the Southern Rhodesian Cabinet should have deserted Todd because he was "a dangerous radical". This, to Johnson, was an astonishing diagnosis of Todd's paternalistic attitude.[29]

As disaffection spread within the UFP, Welensky regretted that there was no alternative to the leaders embroiled in the crisis. He thought that Whitehead, currently serving as Federal representative in Washington, might have been a likely successor if he had not expressed an intention to seek a Federal seat in the next general election. Furthermore, even if Whitehead were available, Welensky had been told that a significant number of Southern Rhodesian MPs had expressed a determination not to accept a Prime Minister who was not a member of their House.[30]

The Press had been reasonably accurate because, on 31 January, Welensky revealed privately that he had attempted to reconcile the opposing factions but had failed. He continued to believe that the congress would only widen the divisions and that the crisis would have to be settled in Parliament. He dreaded this eventuality, and was considerably irritated by the failure of those involved to see what damage was being done to the UFP.[31]

While Todd and Fletcher lobbied for support — despite a so-called truce — Welensky did not suffer from a lack of advice. Dr E. M. B. West of Bulawayo wrote endorsing Joelson's opinion of the African view of the crisis. Africans had been expressing fears to him that the crisis was the product of European reaction which might not only retard their advancement but that of the country as a whole. The Africans believed, he said, that the minimum wage award was responsible for the crisis. They did not think that there was anyone who could replace Todd and maintain the rate of progress of the previous four years. West found that African opinion was hardening along these lines, that the moderate and educated Africans felt that, if their fears were correct, they would have to join the ANC. If they did that, the ANC would only become more powerful and violent. They would join it in the full knowledge that the ultimate result would be a dictatorship.[32]

Malvern suggested that Welensky should announce his intention to get the resolution, to fuse with the URP, rescinded before the congress because this could not be done thereafter without appearing to side with the defeated faction. Malvern, expecting the URP to suffer a schism, wanted to extricate the Federal Party. He foresaw that the United Federal Party would form the Federal Government and the Dominion Party the Federal Opposition. In Southern Rhodesia, however, the DP could be the territorial Government and the UFP the territorial Opposition. He felt that this would hardly be conducive to good government.[33]

Welensky might have mused about the desirability of Whitehead securing

[29] Welensky Papers, 24/157, ff. 91–92, J. Johnson to Welensky, 29 January 1958.
[30] *Ibid.*, 9/12, f. 85, Welensky to L. M. N. Hodson, 31 January 1958.
[31] *Ibid.*, 42/60, f. 82, Welensky to D. Taylor, 31 January 1958; 24/73, ff. 236–237, Welensky to Gore-Browne, 31 January 1958.
[32] *Ibid.*, 9/12, f. 56, Dr West to Welensky, 2 February 1958.
[33] *Ibid.*, f. 77, Malvern to Welensky, 2 February 1958.

the premiership, but the Vumba branch of the UFP cabled Whitehead on 5 February asking him to accept their nomination. Whitehead replied immediately that he would if he was assured of support from both sides and could re-unite the Party. He asked that Welensky be informed of this correspondence. There were other candidates: the UFP Karoi branch proposed Ellman-Brown, while Greenfield thought that Fletcher might be an adequate replacement if Todd were defeated.[34]

As the congress approached, the pressures on Welensky and the leading members in the UFP increased. The Todd faction wanted an open debate with the Press present. However, because matters such as the election of office-holders in the new Party had also to be settled, the Press was excluded. This provoked a public protest from Todd and his supporters, claiming that the Party hierarchy had exceeded its powers. Counter-complaints that the Todd faction had broken the truce and a denial from Todd, forced Welensky to spell out the position publicly on 5 February, namely that the truce meant that neither faction would lobby for support. Accordingly, the UFP executive ordered each branch to do nothing more than elect its own delegate.[35]

There was a dispute over who was to chair the congress. Todd suggested A. E. P. Robinson (later Sir Albert), then chairman of Central African Airways, but Welensky would not allow a chairman of a statutory corporation to be involved in political controversy. Others were suggested, including Welensky, but he insisted that Greenfield should preside and Todd and Fletcher agreed. Greenfield was not pleased.[36]

Todd complained again to Welensky on 7 February when he read the congress agenda and discovered that Fletcher would speak first. He protested, he said, because his accusers, despite promises to the contrary, had not apprised him of their charges against him. However, Welensky was also beset with complaints that Todd was reviving moribund branches, with the result that when the delegates met on 8 February a committee had to be appointed to vet the challenges against some of their credentials. It is interesting that most of them succeeded.[37]

The congress that day first considered and rejected a demand to admit the Press. Then Fletcher explained the rebellion rather feebly and his fellow rebels were little better. Todd was brillant, winning applause, but the tide was running against him. The Umtali constituency advanced Whitehead's candidacy and, when Greenfield closed the wearisome proceedings late in the evening, the choice was Todd, Fletcher or Whitehead. Todd won the first ballot by 129 votes to Whitehead's 122 and Fletcher's 77. As Todd did not have an overall majority, a second ballot was held without Fletcher who was

[34] *Ibid.*, f. 61, Armstrong, Secretary of the Vumba branch, to Welensky, 5 February 1958; 16/5, f. 8, Glass to E. C. F. Whitehead, Whitehead to Glass, (undated); f. 33, Greenfield to Welensky, 15 January 1958; 9/12, f. 87, K. Fox, Chairman of the Karoi branch, to Welensky, 30 January 1958.

[35] Blake, *Rhodesia*, *op. cit.*, p. 310; Welensky Papers, 16/5, f. 11, Moore to Welensky, 5 February 1958; f. 4, Press Statement by Todd, 6 February 1958; f. 19, Todd to Welensky, 3 February 1958; f. 12, Press Statement by Welensky, 5 February 1958.

[36] Welensky Papers, 16/5, f. 18, Todd to Welensky, 3 February 1958; f. 9, Welensky to Todd, 5 February 1958; f. 5, Todd to Welensky, 5 February 1958; f. 6, Welensky to Todd, 6 February 1958; Greenfield, *Testimony*, *op. cit.*, p. 159.

[37] Greenfield, *Testimony*, *op. cit.*, p. 159.

adjudged to have been eliminated. Whitehead then gained 193 votes to Todd's unchanged 129.[38]

Welensky thereupon called on both sides to assist Whitehead. Welensky praised Todd's magnanimity and called for the re-establishment of stability and unity within the Party. Todd, in turn, urged the MPs to allow Whitehead to inherit a united team. He was grateful, he said, for the opportunity to have served his country and vowed that he had no regrets or bitterness.[39]

Nothing, however, was fated to go smoothly, and the next day, 9 February, Fletcher demanded that Todd should resign immediately as caretaker in favour of Sir George Davenport. Ellman-Brown and Hatty, however, did not support Fletcher's demand.

Whitehead flew in from Washington on 12 February and issued a self-effacing statement doubting whether he would become Prime Minister because he could not presume that the UFP Southern Rhodesian Caucus would endorse his candidacy.[40]

Seeing himself primarily as a mediator, Whitehead immediately sought to reconcile the two groups. He hoped to bring Todd, Davenport and Lloyd into his Cabinet with Ellman-Brown and Hatty. He wanted the Federal Government to "buy off" Fletcher, but would not pay Stumbles the same compliment.[41]

The rift, however, was not easily healed and even though Whitehead announced on 13 February that he could see no insuperable difficulties in forming a Cabinet, a day later he declared that he had failed. He proposed to summon the parliamentary Caucus on 16 February to assist him in attempting to avoid being forced to choose his Ministers from one faction or the other.[42] On 15 February Todd complicated matters by asking his former Ministers to choose between his faction and Fletcher's. They spurned him but, that night, Whitehead at last formed a Cabinet of men from both sides, including Todd. Whitehead took over Fletcher's portfolio of Native Affairs, Davenport those of Mines and Land Surveys, Hatty the Treasury and Native Education, Todd Labour and Social Welfare, Ellman-Brown returned to Roads, Local Government and Housing, and R. J. Knight, a newcomer, accepted Justice and Internal Affairs.[43]

Whitehead, of course, required a parliamentary seat, and on 24 February J. M. MacDonald resigned his seat in Hillside, Bulawayo, for him. Welensky concluded — perhaps prematurely — that the generosity of Todd, in accepting office, had not only contributed to the stabilising of the situation, but would convince people at home and abroad that the liberal nature of the Southern Rhodesian Government had been preserved. He acknowledged that the more militant Africans — Nkomo was one — did not believe this but he thought that they would spurn anything which would not serve their ends.

[38] Blake, *Rhodesia*, *op. cit.*, p. 310.
[39] *The Rhodesia Herald*, 9 February 1958.
[40] Welensky Papers, 9/12, f. 69, H. N. Parry to Welensky, 10 February 1958; *The Rhodesia Herald*, 13 February 1958.
[41] Welensky Papers, 9/12, f. 53, Greenfield to Welensky, 13 February 1958.
[42] *The Rhodesia Herald*, 14 February 1958; Blake, *Rhodesia*, *op. cit.*, p. 310.
[43] Blake, *Rhodesia*, *op. cit.*, p. 310.

He noted that it had only been well into the crisis that the African politicians had recognised Todd as their whole-hearted champion.[44]

The Todd crisis had not been the only issue to have attracted public attention because in early January Mrs Barbara Castle, the British Labour MP and tireless anti-*apartheid* campaigner, arrived from South Africa, seemingly seeking to emulate Callaghan. She immediately warned the locals not to assume that British MPs were ignorant of their affairs because they had passed the Constitutional Amendment Bill and would have given the Federal Electoral Bill an equally stormy reception had they had the opportunity. She told how badly Welensky's comments on Callaghan had been received in Britain, where Callaghan was recognised as a moderate. *The Bulawayo Chronicle* promptly reminded her of her own ignorance in confusing the South African Police with the British South Africa Police.[45]

Unabashed, Mrs Castle continued to express her opinions, and in a series of articles ran foul of the management of Salisbury's Meikle's Hotel and the Rhodesian Guild of Journalists for exaggerating an incident at the hotel.[46] The local Press and politicians also criticised the sensationalist tone of her writing. She, in turn, would be followed a year later by John Stonehouse MP, also apparently bent on making a name. Although the Federal Cabinet was to become embroiled with Stonehouse, it avoided the fracas over Mrs Castle. The Federal Ministers were not only preoccupied with their portfolios and the Todd crisis, but with the next constitutional problem, that of the advancement of Northern Rhodesia.

For Northern Rhodesia, 1957 had been a troubled year because the ANC acquired a new drive and broadened both its organisation and its basis of support. The ANC remained divided between those who followed Nkumbula's cautious lead and those, like Kaunda, S. Kapwepwe, M. Sipalo and other emerging young leaders, who favoured a vigorous prosecution of the ANC's aim to be recognised as the sole voice of the Northern Rhodesian African. This militancy was the product of the drive for power which was invigorated by the attainment of independence by Ghana and by the fear that, if the Federation became a dominion, the chance of attaining purely African self-government would be irretrievably lost. Sipalo, a Lozi, returned from his studies in London, Prague and New Delhi in early 1957 and injected a new sense of urgency into the ANC, particularly in the Southern Province. He tried to force Nkumbula into more aggressive leadership and, for his sins, was expelled from the ANC later in the year. Kaunda was also at odds with Nkumbula, but both heartily and publicly disapproved of the violent methods widely adopted by the new, rejuvenated branches. Both men, however, were abroad for much of the year lobbying for support and studying political organisation, and those predisposed to violence had a free rein.[47]

[44] Welensky Papers, 19/12, f. 16, Welensky to Dr West, 12 March 1957; 29/60, f. 95, Welensky to R. Meier, 12 March 1958.

[45] *The Rhodesia Herald* & *The Bulawayo Chronicle*, 21 January 1958.

[46] *The African Daily News*, 24 January 1958; *The Rhodesia Herald*, 7 February 1958.

[47] Welensky Papers, 28/78, f. 74, J. Graylin to Welensky, 15 September 1957; f. 73, B. M. de Quehen to Welensky, 18 September 1957; D. C. Mulford, *Zambia: The Politics of Independence, 1957–1964* (London, 1967), p. 63 f.

The Northern Rhodesian Government, in response, produced a series of ordinances designed to lessen the need to declare emergencies. The nationalist organisations were forced to register their branches and supply the Government with information on their activities. The police were given wider powers to control public meetings, and the penal code was revised to prevent politically-inspired boycotts — the tried weapon of the ANC — and strikes. The definition of "seditious intention" was extended to include bringing any of the Governments of the Federation into hatred and contempt. The legislation threw the ANC — albeit temporarily — into considerable disarray, but its immediate effect, combined with the protests over the Constitutional Amendment and Federal Electoral Bills, would raise the emotional temperature considerably.[48]

Against such a background the consideration of the revision of the Northern Rhodesian Constitution had begun. The Federal Government had first seen the Northern Rhodesian Government's plans in late March 1957 in the form of the memorandum on the possibility of adapting the Tredgold formula. Herein were the Northern Rhodesian ideas of fractional voting and contrived rural constituencies for the election of African Members which would curb the influence of the ANC. The Federal Government had seen the advantages but rejected the "rigging" of the delimitation.

In early September 1957, Roberts reported to Welensky that he was under pressure to settle the constitutional issue because Benson intended introducing an electoral bill in March 1958. Roberts suspected that the British Government would reject the Federal Electoral Bill and that Benson feared a snap Federal general election because he and the British Government did not want the Federal Assembly re-elected on the current basis. This desire for a prompt solution seemed to Roberts to strengthen his own hand and he believed that he would be able to gain considerable concessions.[49]

Benson proposed that the Executive Council should consist of five official and five unofficial Members. In addition, there would be two assistant ministers who would be nominated or elected African Members who would sit on the Government front bench but not in the Executive Council. The Legislative Council would comprise six official, four nominated unofficial, and 18 elected Members. The 18 would represent eight constituencies which could only return Europeans, six which could return Africans, and four which could elect either Africans or Europeans.

Roberts rejected this solution because the electoral outcome would defy prediction. He advanced his Party's proposal to have a 28-member Legislative Council. In this, there would be six official Members, 14 ordinary Members elected by constituencies which were likely to return Europeans, four by urban constituencies which would elect Africans, and four African Members nominated by the rural native authorities. A common roll would be used in the elections. The Executive Council would consist of three officials and five unofficials, and there would be, in addition, two parliamentary secretaries who would be Africans and could be either elected urban or nominated rural Members. The appointment of the latter two would be discussed with the

[48] Mulford, *Zambia*, *op. cit.*, p. 66.
[49] Welensky Papers, 8/112, f. 126, H. J. Roberts to Welensky, 13 September 1958.

leader of the majority party in the Legislative Council. For the next Legislative Council only, Roberts proposed that a class of special voters should be admitted to the common roll, but they would not be given too great an influence.

Benson countered by proposing a Legislative Council of 30: six official, two nominated unofficial, 14 ordinary Members, whose constituencies would lie along the line of rail, and eight specially elected Africans representing the rural areas. Roberts immediately objected to the lack of provision for the representation of Crown Land Areas, such as Fort Jameson and Abercorn, where Europeans lived. They would object to being represented by Africans, just as the Africans on the line of rail would reject representation by Europeans. Benson proposed an Executive Council of nine: five official Members, three elected Members and one nominated Member. He proposed to adopt the Federal franchise qualifications for everyone except Chiefs and hereditary councillors. The ordinary vote would not have an influence of more than 25 per cent in the election of the African Members. The same would apply to the special vote with regard to the ordinary Member.

Roberts then suggested a variation in which two of the 14 ordinary seats would be reserved for Europeans from the Crown Land Areas and, in return, he would accept that two of the eight African seats should be reserved for Africans in the urban areas. He reduced the percentage of the influence of the special vote to 20 per cent and demanded that this should be only a percentage of the ordinary votes cast, and not of all the votes. Benson agreed to this last demand but insisted that then the percentage should be 33⅓. Roberts would not agree, and deadlock ensued. It was not broken by the involvement of Greenfield in early November 1957.[50]

Roberts also insisted on an elected majority in the Executive Council and that the leader of the majority party should be named "Chief Minister". Benson harped throughout their meetings on the African demands for parity of racial representation, while Roberts continually reminded him that his Party sought complete self-government for Northern Rhodesia. Benson also warned that the British Government would not allow any advance unless it included the appointment of an African to the Executive Council.

Benson and Roberts met again on 11 December but still could not agree because Roberts would not permit the special voter to swing an election of an ordinary Member or the ordinary voter to do likewise with regard to the special seats. He continued to ask for an unofficial majority in the Executive Council and for the leader of the majority party to be named chief minister. He would, however, accept a parity of official and unofficial representation on the Executive Council, provided that when an African Member was later promoted to it, an official would stand down. Roberts also wanted to introduce the system, already adopted by Southern Rhodesia, of a single transferable vote to ensure that neither the new Constitution Party (recently formed by Dr A. Scott, Colonel David Stirling, H. Franklin and S. H. Chileshi) nor the ANC profited from a split vote. He continued to demand

[50] *Ibid.*, 7/10, f. 333, Minutes of a Meeting of Roberts, Collins and Greenfield, November 1957; f. 341, Minutes of a Meeting of Benson, Roberts *et al*, 12 November 1957; f. 343, Roberts to Welensky, 11 November 1957.

that the special vote should only apply to the election of the next Legislative Council, that the assistant ministers should not sit in the Executive Council, and that the candidates for nomination to the Legislative Council should have the prior approval of the chief minister.

Benson was unyielding, and again spoke of the African demand for parity, of the likelihood that the Colonial Secretary would refuse either the appointment of a chief minister before the Federal review in 1960 or any European gains without a *quid pro quo* of the appointment of an African to the Executive Council. Franklin, as a representative of African interests, currently sat in the Executive Council, but both Roberts and Benson agreed that he did not count, in the eyes of the electorate, because he was white.[51]

The deadlock continued into January and provoked Beckett to suggest to Welensky that perhaps he should ask Sir Robert Armitage, the Governor of Nyasaland, to persuade Benson to be reasonable. However, Lennox-Boyd convened a meeting in March in London with Benson, Roberts and Sokota, and at this meeting arrived at a formula as a basis of discussion. Roberts demanded that the influence of one category of voter on the election of another should never be more than 20 per cent, but Lennox-Boyd and Benson insisted that it should be 33⅓ per cent. Roberts asked for an Executive Council of five elected Members, three official Members and one African Member, and for the appointment of a chief minister. In reply, Lennox-Boyd proposed that the existing number of Members in the Executive Council remain at nine. However, he wanted the unofficial European representative of African interests replaced by an African, the number of elected unofficial Members increased by one to four and the number of official Members decreased by one to four. He also agreed to prior consultation with the leader of the majority party in the Legislative Council before any unofficial was appointed to a seat in the Executive Council. However, he would not accept that this leader should be appointed chief minister.[52]

The British proposals were embodied in a Northern Rhodesian White Paper which the meeting agreed should be laid on the table of the Legislative Council on 28 March to be debated therein and by the public at large. This recalled that it had been agreed that there would be no further change in the life of the current Legislative Council unless all parties thought it necessary. Change, however, had been anticipated, the White Paper stated, and in 1957 negotiations had begun. A wide spectrum of opinion had been examined. Partition was impracticable, it declared, because Northern Rhodesia and the Federation itself were indivisible. The ANC had asked for parity of representation with the Europeans and officials. This, however, could not be contemplated as racial parity *per se* would perpetuate racialism. Furthermore, parity ran counter to the first principle, to which the Northern Rhodesian Government claimed to have always adhered, that party politics had to be encouraged on non-racial lines. The Government, the White Paper asserted, was committed to moving away from racial representation.

[51] *Ibid.*, 7/10, f. 345, Roberts to Welensky, 11 December 1957.

[52] *Ibid.*, 42/21, f. 155, Beckett to Welensky, 12 January 1958; f. 159, Beckett to Roberts, 12 January 1958; 20/4, f. 300, Roberts to Welensky, 21 March 1958; 7/10, f. 347, W. S. Parker to Welensky, 19 March 1958.

Stability also demanded, the White Paper continued, that the basic framework of government should not be subject to change every few years. To ensure that power was in responsible hands and extremists were discouraged from looking to sectional interests alone, the Government proposed to extend the franchise to those who contributed to society and would exercise the vote with judgment. Like the Tredgold Commission, the White Paper rejected immediate adult suffrage because it would lead to a more extreme form of racial representation than currently existed. Yet, it was acknowledged that ultimately the Government would have to rest on the consent of the governed. It was accepted that the Europeans were more sophisticated than the majority of the Africans and this complicated the issue because, if only they and the few blacks who had attained their standards, were enfranchised, the Africans would be grossly under-represented for a considerable time. Thus a qualitative franchise was needed even though the common roll was the ideal. Moreover, for the next decade, a temporary set of lower qualifications would be required to ensure that the races were properly represented.

In order that none of the races should fear domination, the Government proposed that there should be a Legislative Council of 31, including the Speaker. Of these, 22 would be elected. Twelve of them would be returned by constituencies based on the Crown Land and adjacent Native Trust Lands and Native Reserves along the line of rail. Six would be elected by special constituencies which would cover the rest of Northern Rhodesia. Two further elected seats would be specifically reserved for Europeans to be returned by two re-grouped constituencies representing the total area of the special constituencies. This would cater for rural Europeans. A similar arrangement was proposed for the Africans living in the urban areas, as there were two further constituencies whose seats were reserved for Africans and which embraced the whole area of the ordinary constituencies. The remaining eight seats would be divided between six official and two nominated Members. The latter two would not specifically represent African interests, as they did currently, and would only be appointed after the Governor knew the result of the election and had consulted the leader of the majority party. This allowed the Governor to find suitable holders of portfolios in the event of a freak election producing too few members capable of serving on the Executive Council.

The White Paper proposed that the Executive Council should comprise the Governor, four officials and five unofficials. Four of the latter would be ordinary elected Members. In addition, there would be two assistant ministers who would be bound by the oath of office but would not sit in the Executive Council. They would work as directed by their ministers. Two of the eleven ministers and assistant ministers would have to be Africans.

The Federal franchise was adopted except that there would be no dual roll. Chiefs would automatically be ordinary voters, and their headmen would be enrolled for the special vote, as would pensioners who had worked for 20 years. The total of the special votes cast in the twelve ordinary constituencies would not count for more than a third of the total votes cast. The ordinary vote would suffer the same fate in the special constituencies, and the same arrangements would obtain in the amalgamated constituencies for the racially-reserved seats.

The White Paper's last and most curious recommendation was that each of the candidates in the special constituencies, who only possessed the special qualifications, would have to acquire the endorsement of two-thirds of the Chiefs in the constituency. This was an extraordinary recommendation from a man like Benson who had such wide experience of rural Northern Rhodesia. In the short time, usually three weeks, between the announcement of an election and nomination day, the candidates would have to find the Chiefs of these immense constituencies — the area of 287 640 square miles of Northern Rhodesia would be divided by six. Given good roads and dry weather, it would have been a difficult enough task in the time available, but, with almost trackless bush and flooding rivers, it was impossible. Benson was, of course, seeking to eliminate the more extreme candidates by insisting on the sanction of the most conservative element in rural life, but he had forgotten the art of the practical and the possible.[53]

The discussions with Lennox-Boyd had been private and it was agreed that no announcement would be made before the White Paper was tabled on 28 March. Thus the other participants were more than somewhat startled when Sokota not only declared publicly in London on 17 March that Lennox-Boyd had promised that Africans would sit in the Executive Council, but gave some details of what Roberts had sought. This provoked Welensky to cable Home warning that he would be asked to comment and he would reply that the Federal Government had not been consulted. Welensky asked for an early report on the progress made.[54]

Roberts, by then back in Northern Rhodesia, simultaneously protested to London that this leak had placed him in an untenable position. It had hardened the attitude of the UFP Members of the Legislative Council, he said, because Sokota had revealed their proposals before Roberts could. Consequently he and his colleagues, with regret, were forced to dissociate themselves from the White Paper as it stood. His Party would not agree to the special voters having an influence as great as a third, and thought that an Executive Council of four elected Members, three officials and an African would have been a tribute to their record and their outlook. He reminded Lennox-Boyd that the Colonial Office would still hold the balance in such a Council if the Governor continued to be its president. He revealed, however, that his Party would reluctantly allow the special and ordinary voters a 25 per cent influence in each other's election, but insisted that there should be a single transferable vote to prevent the election of any candidates from minority groups.[55]

Lennox-Boyd replied the same day, 19 March, to Roberts expressing regret at Sokota's actions. He agreed that he could lower the offending percentage, but warned that he had to be able to proclaim that the African would have a reasonable influence over the election of the ordinary Members. Home cabled Welensky and declared that Sokota had unilaterally decided to

53 *Proposals for Constitutional Change in Northern Rhodesia* (Lusaka, 28 March 1958).

54 Welensky Papers, 20/4, f. 306, Welensky to Home, 19 March 1958; *The Rhodesia Herald*, 18 March 1958.

55 Welensky Papers, 7/10, f. 368, A/Governor of Northern Rhodesia to Colonial Secretary, 19 March 1958.

make his statement. He revealed to Welensky that Lennox-Boyd, Benson and Roberts had reached agreement on a draft White Paper and promised Welensky sight of it before it was published on 28 March. He avowed he would consult Welensky if changes to the contents were needed even though the British and Federal Governments were not yet formally involved.[56]

By this time, van Eeden had entered the fray, writing an open letter to Benson which asked for an explanation of the constitutional talks. He was aggrieved, he said, because he, as chairman of the Dominion Party, had been included in earlier formal talks on the Constitution, and at these he had been led to understand that there would be a "round-table" conference which would have given his Party a chance to reveal its ideas. Clearly, he protested, this undertaking had been forgotten. However, he charged that perhaps this had been deliberate once Benson had realised that the Dominion Party would insist that there should be no change in the Constitution before 1960. Van Eeden's interpretation was that the British Government would impose its ideas without regard to local feeling.[57]

Roberts apprised Welensky of the events in London and, simultaneously, on 21 March publicly revealed the UFP's ideas on the revision of the Constitution. When the draft of the White Paper reached him three days later, Roberts protested to Lennox-Boyd that it did not specifically state that the four elected unofficial Members in the Executive Council could not be those who had only become Members through the special qualifications. On 28 March, when the White Paper was tabled in the Legislative Council, Roberts declared that he and his colleagues dissociated themselves from certain sections.[58]

He was supported by the *Northern News* which found that, despite the presence of 22 elected Members in the Legislative Council, the Governor, who was responsible only to the Colonial Office, would continue to be the executive head. He would not even be hampered by the unofficial majority in the Executive Council because, in practice, the African Member would side with the officials. Just as extraordinary was the power of the Governor to nominate two additional Members to the Legislative Council and thereby reverse the verdict of an election. The influence of a third in the election of the ordinary Members was seen as entirely unreasonable when this category of voters was designed shortly to disappear. The *Northern News* wondered at the authorship of the White Paper because it certainly did not reflect the ideas of the elected Members or those of many of the officials.

The UFP, two days later, echoed these sentiments in describing its disagreement with certain fundamental points of principle such as the composition of the Executive Council and the percentage of influence. It insisted again on the appointment of a chief minister and the introduction of a single transferable vote. Roberts commented that the influence should not be higher than 20 per cent, and added that the proposal to place an African in the

[56] *Ibid.*, 7/10, f. 369, Lennox-Boyd to A/Governor, 19 March 1958; 20/4, f. 306, Home to Welensky, 21 March 1958.

[57] *The Rhodesia Herald*, 20 March 1958.

[58] Welensky Papers, 7/10, f. 351, Roberts to Welensky, 21 March 1958; *The Rhodesia Herald*, 21 March 1958; NR *Debates* (Lusaka), Col. 472, 28 March 1958; *Northern News*, 29 March 1958.

Executive Council, on the grounds of race alone, was quite unacceptable.[59] This was something to which he had not appeared to object previously.

The Coloured community protested at the lack of either safeguards or a specific place in politics for them. Van Eeden attacked the UFP for the utter hopelessness of its policy of appeasing and conciliating the officials. He believed that the best way to combat the threat to the Europeans was to present an all-party front to the Colonial Office. The Parties should adamantly refuse any changes in the Northern Rhodesian Constitution before 1960 and until the independence of the Federation had been satisfactorily resolved. Any compromise before then, he warned, would be fatal to the interests of the European. Gaunt declared that the proposals of the Northern Rhodesian Government would result in African domination within 15 years, when the territory would sink back into "its primitive rottenness". He proposed an immediate partition to create three African protectorates and a central European-dominated state.[60]

To Aby Mayanja, secretary of the Committee of African Organisations, the White Paper, together with Lennox-Boyd's support for the Federal Electoral and Constitutional Amendment Bills, was proof that the Africans could no longer trust the Colonial Office to hold the balance of power. Mayanja declared that it was therefore imperative that the Africans should be well represented in 1960 if the "settlers" were not to confirm their dominion. It could only be prevented by the Africans being able to insist that no change be made without the sanction of a plebiscite based on universal suffrage. Mayanja also protested at the recent territorial legislation which had suppressed, in his view, the civil and trade union freedoms. The Societies Ordinance, he believed, had signed the death warrants of the African political organisations because their members had either to comply with it or face up to seven years' imprisonment with hard labour.[61]

The issue of the White Paper was rivalled by the simultaneous publication of a plan by the national executive of the British Labour Party to achieve in the Federation a genuine partnership between the races and an equality of rights for every citizen. Indeed, concerned at the aggravation of racial tensions, the Labour Party urged the Federation to make an unequivocal declaration of intent on these aims. It proposed an immediate increase of African representation in the Federal Assembly. (Thus it disregarded the development of party or, at least, non-racial politics.) Yet it wanted the true meaning of partnership taught at all levels, while racial discrimination was rapidly abolished. It demanded that dominion status be withheld until all the inhabitants could exercise full and equal democratic rights. It proposed that the Africans in the northern territories should immediately be given opportunities for greater participation in government. More specifically, the Africans in Nyasaland should be given an elected majority in the Legislative Council, and the number of African ministers should equal those of other races. The Northern Rhodesian Africans would be given parity of representation with

[59] *The Rhodesia Herald*, 31 March 1958.
[60] Welensky Papers, 35/7, f. 26, G. T. Thornicroft to Chief Secretary, Northern Rhodesian Government, 28 March 1958; *The Rhodesia Herald*, 29 March 1958.
[61] *The Rhodesia Herald*, 29 March 1958.

other races, and the franchises of both territories would be broadened without delay to begin progress towards a common roll and adult suffrage.

In its conclusion, the Labour Party condemned the British and Federal Governments for overriding the protest of the African Affairs Board and thereby weakening the confidence of the Africans in the safeguards and tragically deepening their hostility to the Federation. The Labour Party considered itself to be completely bound by the terms of the Federal constitutional preamble and would, when in power, continue the system of protection and separate governments as long as the people so desired. It thought that the powers of the Federal and territorial Governments should be reviewed to ensure that the protection was effective.[62]

A debate in the Legislative Council on the White Paper was not possible until the budget session in July, but the delay did not mean that the affairs of the territories, rather than of the Federation, would not continue to attract attention. In Nyasaland, Armitage, like Benson, had begun to explore the possibilities of constitutional revision. He met with equal, if not stronger, resistance from his European elected Members. On 19 March, all six of them declared — albeit privately — that they would use all legitimate means to defeat his intention. They would not co-operate until Nyasaland was more secure and did not believe that this would be achieved until at least a year after the Federal review. They did so with regret because, they said, they had hitherto always supported the Government. They believed that change was unnecessary and, indeed, that the advances effected in 1955 had proved unwarranted because they had utterly exceeded the capabilities of the Africans. At the time the Europeans had opposed these advances, but had been ignored. There could be no question, in 1958, of appointing an African to the Executive Council until the Africans in general supported the Federation. To do otherwise was to make a mockery of that Council and would lead, they believed, to the necessity of having a council within a council because the African would prove to be incapable of trust. They based this assertion on the record of the African Members of the Legislative Council who, since their election in 1956, had done nothing but oppose every major decision of the Government, because the aim of the African Congress was black domination. This was repugnant to the Europeans and had made them determined to prevent any increase in African representation until the African Members threw their weight behind the Federation and multi-racial government.

The Nyasaland European elected Members warned that the Europeans, having watched the procrastination over issues such as the federalisation of non-African agriculture, had come to believe that the Government would do nothing more than appease the tiny vociferous element of the African population. They said that the Europeans would continue to believe this until the Government altered course and the Africans ceased their unreasoning opposition to the Federation. While the Europeans were in this frame of mind, the elected Members said that they could not contemplate constitutional change.[63] This stand evoked immediate support from Welensky.

The Nyasaland European elected Members conducted their resistance in

[62] *Ibid.*

[63] Welensky Papers, 20/18, f. 380, Six Non-African Elected Members to Armitage, 19 March 1958.

private, while the Federal public's attention was distracted in April by the events in Southern Rhodesia after Whitehead, on the 17th of that month, failed in the Hillside by-election to gain the seat which he needed if he was to continue as Prime Minister. This defeat left him with no alternative but to call a general election.

Immediately, pressure began to be exerted within the UFP for the expulsion of Todd lest it lose the election. There was no need for such drastic action because, at a Caucus meeting on 23 April, Todd, B. Baron, H. Holderness, A. D. H. Lloyd, Ralph and Eric Palmer and M. N. Buchan announced that they were resigning to resuscitate the old United Rhodesia Party. They did so, they said, because they believed that the UFP no longer represented the principles for which they stood and on which they had been elected. They claimed that the differences in application and interpretation of policy had culminated in the split in January. (If this was true, they did not explain why they had been happy to serve under Whitehead thereafter.) The URP, in their opinion, had given Southern Rhodesia a unique record of progressive administration and, to them, if disaster were to be avoided, policies had to be courageous and fly in the face of popularity. They felt that fusion had brought detrimental outside influences to bear on Southern Rhodesian policies. Compromise within the UFP, they believed, was destroying the best influences in Southern Rhodesia.[64]

Comment was sought from Welensky, who was recuperating from an abdominal operation, and he replied that a schism was always a matter for regret, but that it was better for it to be in the open. Indeed, he said, it was not entirely unwelcome to him because, just as the Dominion Party had done so for the Right, the revived URP would provide a home for those of the Left, leaving the moderate UFP to occupy the centre. He believed that the UFP would serve the public interest best, but that the electorate now had a chance to decide for itself.[65]

The next day, 24 April, Todd publicly described the schism as a victory for Fletcher and reaction, and not for Whitehead and conciliation. The UFP, Todd said, contained men whom the Dominion Party would have been happy to recruit. He believed that these men were the major influence on Whitehead and the leadership. This meant, he said, that the UFP had lost its last chance of gaining the respect and support of either the European or the African.[66]

The Constitution Party of Northern Rhodesia had immediately made overtures to Todd, and that day provoked Frank Clements, a journalist and member of the Dominion Party, to claim that Todd, Scott and their ilk believed that the survival of the white man in Central Africa depended on concessions and bribes. He declared that it was time to stop such a policy and that his Party would do so.[67]

Speaking with Clements in Lusaka, van Eeden said that the Dominion Party would also "stop the rot" in Northern Rhodesia. He called again for no constitutional change before 1960. Simultaneously, Welensky issued a state-

[64] *The Rhodesia Herald*, 24 April 1958.
[65] *Ibid.*
[66] *Ibid.*, 25 April 1958.
[67] *Ibid.*

ment that the UFP would continue to advocate evolution rather than revolution. In contrast to his earlier comment, he criticised the advent of a movement to the Left, and defended the record of the past 25 years during which the Africans had enjoyed a medical scheme which had been largely paid for by the Europeans. He proclaimed that all inhabitants of the Federation should progress together but that it would serve no purpose in granting a section of the population privileges which, through no fault of their own, they would not yet be capable of enjoying. To do otherwise would only lower standards and create opportunities for demagogues. It would be better to ensure that financial and industrial development kept pace with political advancement, if it could not keep ahead of it. This had been the basis of the Federal franchise proposals and Welensky declared that he was not prepared to compromise.[68]

Whitehead entered the lists two days later stating that the main battle would still be with the Dominion Party, which had gathered into its fold such a wide variety of reactionary souls. On these lines the campaign was fought until polling day on 6 June when the DP attracted 18 314 votes, the UFP 17 064 and the URP 4 862. However, the preferential vote told against the DP, and the UFP was the victor on the second count. The DP had feared this consequence in the last days of its campaign and had petitioned the Governor to suspend the preferential vote. The Government had refused, and Whitehead had pointed out that the DP was virtually asking for the suspension of the Constitution and the intervention of the British Government in the affairs of Southern Rhodesia.[69]

The UFP gained 17 seats and the DP 13. The URP was eliminated. Todd had paid the price of failing to keep the support of his first Cabinet and his Parliamentary Caucus. Fletcher had retired and Ellman-Brown was defeated by Ahrn Palley, of the DP. Welensky, happy that his United Federal Party had won, believed that many a voter had sighed with relief at the result because, while they had not wanted a Dominion Party Government, they had not been prepared to support Todd at any price.[70]

Five days after the election, Whitehead appointed C. J. Hatty as Minister of the Treasury and Mines. R. J. Knight retained Justice and Internal Affairs. A. E. Abrahamson became Minister of Labour, Social Welfare and Housing, and A. R. W. Stumbles, Minister of Roads, Irrigation and Lands. H. J. Quinton was made Parliamentary Secretary in the Ministry of Native Affairs, the portfolio of which Whitehead adopted. With the power struggle in Southern Rhodesia successfully resolved from their point of view, the Federal Cabinet could turn its attention to other pressing territorial matters, notably that of attempting to achieve an acceptable revision of the Northern Rhodesian Constitution.

[68] *Ibid.*
[69] *Ibid.*, 26 April, 19 & 22 May 1958.
[70] Welensky Papers, 25/202A, f. 153, Welensky to Sir Ronald Prain, 16 June 1958.

CHAPTER TWENTY-ONE

The Benson Constitution

The Futile Federal Attempt to influence Northern Rhodesian Reform, May–December 1958

WELENSKY and others had fought hard for Whitehead but his electoral victory had not been their sole preoccupation because Northern Rhodesia had always claimed their attention. Indeed, Welensky and his colleagues would find themselves increasingly drawn into the constitutional wrangle there, particularly when it threatened to intrude into the Federal election campaign. Obstinacy would be the keynote of the confrontation, but the British Government, being in the stronger position, would inevitably win. The Federal Ministers would gain the impression that nothing more than expediency — no matter how it was cloaked — underlay the British actions.

Concern for Northern Rhodesia had led Welensky to attack the British Labour Party for encouraging African nationalism to the detriment of everything else, while Greenfield became involved in the constitutional argument. Greenfield has since said that, as the British White Paper sought to encourage the election of moderates and the development of party politics, he found little objectionable therein. Nevertheless, on 28 March, the day the White Paper was tabled, he wrote a memorandum criticising it for the Federal Government's information. On 9 May it was forwarded to the Northern Rhodesian Government. In his memorandum, Greenfield accepted the ingenuity of the proposals, but thought that they were too complicated and likely only to defeat their purpose. They would be understood by few, he felt, and could be exploited to convince the potential special voters that they were being given political rights which were little more than a sham. The African position was strengthened without any advance towards self-government which the Europeans desired. The number of African Members had been doubled (from four to eight), while that of the European Members had been increased by a sixth. The Federal Government disliked the devalued vote as it offended principles and undermined confidence. If it was necessary, Greenfield said, it should only apply to the special vote in accordance with the

Federal practice of giving responsible voters complete rights and limiting those of the special voters.

Greenfield saw the requirement, for special candidates to secure the endorsement of two-thirds of the Chiefs in their constituency, as a violation of the democratic right of any person to offer himself as a candidate. He saw it also as a loophole for bribery and corruption. He depicted the appointment of an African to the Executive Council, because of race alone, as a retrograde step on the path to responsible government. The Federal belief was that Africans should seek ministerial appointments through being members of the majority party in the legislature. Greenfield thought that the moment was opportune to appoint an elected chief minister.

It was the proclaimed aim of the White Paper to encourage party politics but in reality, Greenfield noted, one race, when under pressure, would present a united front. However, he expressed relief that the White Paper was a basis for discussion and not a firm proposal by the Colonial Secretary.[1]

Lusaka took an inordinate time (six weeks) to reply to Greenfield and then naturally defended the White Paper. It agreed that the scheme was complicated, but believed that, nevertheless, it had been widely understood. It argued that there was a substantial advance towards self-government through the changes in the Executive and Legislative Councils. In any case, it noted that Greenfield had commented only on the aspirations of the Europeans, but ignored African ambitions. The proposals represented the firmest intention to build a non-racial and not just a multi-racial state and, the Northern Rhodesian Government claimed, additional seats had been warmly welcomed by the Europeans. The devaluation of the vote would only affect the voters' second vote. Moreover, the predicted numbers of ordinary and special voters were such that a devaluation of the ordinary votes would be unlikely for some years. As for the Chiefs' endorsement of the special Members, it was felt that the rural Africans would only regard a candidacy as truly representative if it were supported by a Chief. This proviso would also allow party to cut across race, and it seemed, the Northern Rhodesian Government said, that these proposals as a whole would hasten the day when a party would be returned with the full support of the majority. The attainment of this, it concluded, would only be postponed if, at this moment, a chief minister were appointed.[2]

Greenfield was unconvinced. In a note to Welensky, he said he did not believe that the full implications would be grasped by the ordinary voter. He could not follow the reasoning on self-government and concluded that, not only did the Northern Rhodesian Government misunderstand what the electorate sought, but that it intended to resist the application of any formula through which the European could gain control. It failed, he felt, to appreciate that the increase in the number of African seats, together with the devaluation of the vote, could allow the African National Congress to ignore the European

[1] J. M. Greenfield, *Testimony of a Rhodesian Federal* (Bulawayo, 1978), pp. 163–164; Welensky Papers, 7/10, f. 64, Memorandum on the Northern Rhodesian White Paper by Greenfield, 28 March 1958; 20/4, f. 293, H. N. Parry to Chief Secretary, Northern Rhodesian Government, 9 May 1958.

[2] Welensky Papers, 20/4, f. 283, A/Chief Secretary, Northern Rhodesian Government to H. N. Parry, 18 June 1958.

voter, forcing the Europeans to abandon the two-party system to defend their position. Consequently, he believed that the officials would hold the balance in a racial confrontation, and that the Africans would lose the political training which the system, adopted by the Federation, would provide.

Greenfield still rejected the devaluation of the votes. It also seemed to him that the Northern Rhodesian Government was oblivious of the danger of intimidation to which it would expose the Chiefs. He noted that it was believed that the appointment of a chief minister would be rejected by the majority of the inhabitants. If this were so, he said, then any advance would be impossible, because the majority would never endorse it. Greenfield's last objection was the appointment of an African to the Executive Council purely because of race.

Greenfield warned Welensky that Lennox-Boyd might unveil new proposals in the midst of the Federal general election campaign. So he advised Welensky to present counter-proposals or to insist that the *status quo* be maintained until after the election in order to gain time to evolve something reasonable. It worried Greenfield that so little headway was being made on the self-government issue, and he believed that, unless a chief minister were appointed, there would be no lessening of Colonial Office influence, which was the *raison d'être* for the Federal review in 1960.

Greenfield feared for the party system if the ANC captured all eight African seats and left the United Federal and Dominion Parties to share the remaining 14. If the latter Parties tied in the contest, or one gained one more seat than the other, they would be forced to form a coalition. This could be avoided by increasing the number of seats by two, to 16, or by cancelling the devaluation of the ordinary votes, to block the dominance by the ANC candidates. An alternative, he proposed, was to nominate Members to reinforce the majority party but, in practice, this would be unacceptable. The chief minister could always increase his numbers by appointing official Members to his cabinet. A decision was obviously necessary, and Greenfield suggested a meeting with Roberts, and perhaps Whitehead, to secure one.[3]

While awaiting the Northern Rhodesian Government's reply, Welensky and Greenfield had advised Roberts on tactics after he had warned, on 26 May, that the Government intended to propose, in the Legislative Council, acceptance of the White Paper. Benson would allow the UFP to advance amendments, but Roberts knew that the officials and the Africans would vote against them despite the latter's public condemnation of the White Paper. The Africans and the UFP, however, he said, would combine against the original motion. Roberts wondered if a "take note" motion might not be better because it would allow everyone to express their opinion without the Legislative Council having to divide. Thereafter, Lennox-Boyd could assess these views and make his decision. Roberts believed that Lennox-Boyd was going to face stiff resistance from the Commons because it would want a better deal for the Africans. By contrast, Roberts said, the Northern Rhodesian Europeans were looking to the UFP to gain greater concessions for them than had the White Paper.[4]

[3] *Ibid.*, f. 274, Greenfield to Welensky, 4 August 1958.
[4] *Ibid.*, 7/10, f. 376, H. J. Roberts to Welensky, 26 May 1958.

Greenfield agreed with Roberts on the "take note" motion, but thought that Welensky might prefer Benson to be defeated or Roberts to propose the deferment of the consideration of the White Paper until 1960. Welensky predicted to Roberts on 17 June that, despite their clamour against the White Paper, the Africans would vote for it rather than allow the *status quo* to continue. As the UFP faced only defeat, he thought that Roberts should avoid the debate if possible or choose the "take note" motion. The UFP's case, Welensky urged, had to be put strongly to ensure that Lennox-Boyd understood precisely what would happen if he adopted certain courses.[5]

Such deliberation by Welensky, Greenfield and Roberts, however, was fruitless because Benson would not be diverted and set 4 July for the debate on the approval of the White Paper. Nonetheless, on 2 July, Roberts informed Benson that his UFP Caucus wished to protest at the British interpretation of certain aspects of the White Paper. He referred to a dispatch to London by E. D. Hone (later Sir Evelyn), the Chief Secretary, and a reply by Gorell Barnes of the Colonial Office. Roberts recalled his desire to protest at Hone's ideas, but Benson had persuaded him to wait for Gorell Barnes's reply. The Caucus, Roberts told Benson, was alarmed at Hone's suggestion of an African assistant minister, in addition to the African minister, and thought that, as a *quid pro quo*, the other ministers should be drawn from the ranks of the ordinary elected Members. The Caucus wanted the "leader of the majority party" to be the leader of the majority of the ordinary elected Members because, otherwise, a Member elected only by the special voters could in certain circumstances become the leader. Roberts said he had tried to secure all these changes in the Executive Council before the White Paper was published. He also thought that Lennox-Boyd and Benson should know that he could see little point, if the White Paper were passed unamended, in his Party fighting the next election because it would be defeated.[6]

On 4 July, while the ANC burned copies of the White Paper, Hone duly proposed the motion, declaring a non-racial approach to politics as the aim. He acknowledged that the final decision was the prerogative of Lennox-Boyd but claimed that a unanimous acceptance by the Legislative Council would ensure that there would be no changes. It was, after all, he said, a carefully balanced scheme.

The debate took two weeks and, predictably, the African representatives, including Franklin, thought they were not offered enough and demanded parity. The UFP advocated its proposals, while Gaunt had another scheme for partition. Roberts thought it tragic that nomination had been the method of introducing African Members into the legislature because, if they had been elected, non-racial politics would have been a reality by 1958. Hone refused a free vote to the officials because he claimed they supported the White Paper. (If they did, he did not explain why he had to constrain them.) Gaunt was defeated on partition, as was Roberts when he tried to secure the adoption of his proposals. Sokota likewise failed to secure parity. The victory of the Government can only be described as hollow. Lennox-Boyd immediately

[5] *Ibid.*, f. 378, Greenfield to Welensky, 31 May 1958; f. 384, Welensky to Roberts, 17 June 1958.
[6] *Ibid.*, f. 389a, Roberts to Sir Arthur Benson, 2 July 1958; f. 389, E. D. Hone to A. Lennox-Boyd, (undated).

invited Hone, Roberts, Gaunt, Chileshi and Franklin, among others, to London as the international situation prevented him from travelling.[7]

A day later, on 18 July, the Dominion Party congress in Salisbury not only framed the broad principles of a declaration of independence for the Federation, but condemned both the White Paper and Roberts's proposals as simply a lowering of standards.[8]

In the Federal Assembly on 23 July, van Eeden urged the Federal Government to prevent the implementation of the White Paper. There had already been a debate sponsored by Yamba on the secession of Northern Rhodesia because, he claimed, the African had been variously betrayed, one example being the rejection of the protests of the African Affairs Board in late 1957. On just this issue, two weeks before this debate, Doig had resigned his seat. Van Eeden wrongly claimed that it was implicit in the Federal agreement that there would be no territorial or Federal constitutional changes before 1960, and he insisted that the Federal Government intervene. Field agreed because, he said, he could not sit idly by while it became possible for a territorial legislature to house a majority of Members who were antagonistic towards the Federation. Scott opposed such an interference in the liberty of the territories as well as its timing. Welensky explained that territorial constitutional changes were not only possible but were expected. Thus he asked van Eeden to withdraw his motion because, if it were accepted, it would place the Federal Government in a ridiculous position. Van Eeden refused to comply, but could not even raise six supporters.[9]

Four days later Roberts warned Welensky from London that, as expected, no progress had been made with Lennox-Boyd. He suggested that Welensky inform the British Government that, after the debate on van Eeden's motion, the Federal Government would be highly embarrassed if something unpalatable were imposed. Then Roberts told Lennox-Boyd that he was stunned by the approach of the Colonial Office to a constitutional problem. He had found that far too much attention was being paid to pleasing the British Opposition and that expediency, rather than planning for the long-term goal, was the motivation. The danger, he said, was that a pattern, once set, had to be followed because the African was resistant to change. Roberts was distressed that all he had worked for might be destroyed. He warned that his Party would be horrified at the lack of progress, and that he could see no point in staying in politics if there were to be no concessions to his point of view.[10]

There had been two other Federal debates with a constitutional flavour. Both were introduced on 1 July. In the first, Moffat pressed racial cooperation. He wanted to remove the fear of racial domination, and suggested the retention of special machinery in the meantime. He acknowledged the European fear of swamping, and the African resentment of the discriminatory Federal franchise. It seemed better to provide immediately for a democratic system of government based on an African majority and designed to prevent

[7] NR *Debates* (Lusaka), Col. 216 f., 4 July 1958; *The Rhodesia Herald*, 18 July 1958.

[8] *The Rhodesia Herald*, 19 July 1958.

[9] Fed R & N *Debates* (Salisbury), Vol. 9, Col. 335, 8 July 1958; Col. 611 f., 23 July 1958.

[10] Welensky Papers, 7/10, f. 395, Roberts to Welensky, 27 July 1958; f. 397, Roberts to Lennox-Boyd, 28 July 1958.

any form of racial suppression. Otherwise, he said, the African would be forced to become more radical, there would be outside interference, and the result would be disastrous. Moffat knew that he was always accused of being theoretical, so he proposed that in 1960 the rights and privileges of the Federal citizen be defined, and machinery designed to safeguard them. This, unlike the African Affairs Board, he explained, would serve all races and would not only be able to reserve legislation, but to declare it illegal. He would use a court modelled on the United States Supreme Court, served by experienced and impartial men.

Greenfield, however, rejected this as impracticable because, firstly, it would conflict with the elected legislature and, secondly, it would be difficult to man the court. He suggested an amendment stressing the need for racial co-operation to establish a strong nation imbued with British ideals of character, freedom and justice. Each lawful inhabitant had to be able to progress in his own way, and the wide gap between the races had to be closed. Power had to be retained in responsible hands. Progress, he said, would be based on the Citizenship, the Constitutional Amendment and the Electoral Acts. A sporadic debate followed over the course of the month before Moffat withdrew the motion, berating the Government for its lack of courage.[11]

The other Federal debate on 1 July was prompted by Field demanding a conference of the political parties and the African representatives on plans for the Federal review. He sought sober discussion, he said, because he had learned in Britain in 1956 that it would not be easy to attain independence. He urged a concerted effort because plans drawn by the Government alone were likely to be matters of controversy. Furthermore, if the Africans understood in advance what was planned, they might co-operate. However, he found that to date the Federal Government had done nothing but discourage the Dominion Party. He recalled that Welensky had recently rejected publicly a united front because the world would believe that the two major Parties were combining against the African. Thus Welensky had ignored the DP's intention to include Africans in the negotiations. Nevertheless, Field thought his proposed all-party conference would ensure that any plan would be supported by two-thirds of the Federal Assembly, which would force the British to take it seriously.

Welensky confirmed his rebuff of the Dominion Party for the reason given by Field. In any case, he said, the conference would be hampered by the extreme views of some of the parties. His Government was confident of obtaining independence in 1960 as it had considerable experience of such negotiations. He felt that any negotiator had to remember the British commitment to bring all its territories to independence within the Commonwealth, and in such negotiations the Government needed a free hand even though it would keep in touch with all shades of opinion in order not to work in isolation. In addition, a conference would be inopportune as 1960 was still two years away, and before then there would be a general election. The motion was lost[12] but, nevertheless, Welensky instructed H. N. Parry immediately to plan the approach to be made in 1960.

[11] Fed R & N *Debates* (Salisbury), Vol. 9, Col. 149 f., 1 July 1958.
[12] *Ibid.*, Col. 116 f., 1 July 1958.

A further Federal debate concentrated on the activities of the African Congress in Nyasaland where, in particular, it had been trying to inculcate a hatred of the Federation in schoolchildren. This was alarming the Europeans and the moderate Africans. The Federal Parliament, it was felt, could not stand idly by and watch what could be the disintegration of the Federation.[13] In fact the Congress had done more than indulge in propaganda and other activities. It had taken the step of inviting Dr Hastings Banda to return to Nyasaland to lead the struggle for power.

The Congress had become increasingly militant as W. M. Chirwa and C. R. Kumbikano had found to their cost earlier in the year when they had been expelled from it after failing to comply with an order to resign their Federal seats. This was something that H. B. Chipembere, a Member of the Legislative Council, had been wanting to do for two years but Banda had advised from abroad against it. Chipembere, M. W. K. Chiume and other young militants had increasingly become irritated with the Congress leadership but, because of their youth, they were unable to supplant it. Consequently, they had searched for a mature but still dynamic leader who would command the respect of the African population. Only Banda (then practising medicine in Kumasi in the Gold Coast) was considered suitable. Accordingly, in March 1957, during the independence celebrations in Ghana (Gold Coast), Banda was approached. He had, however, no desire to become involved in politics and an announcement that he would return proved to be premature. Chipembere and Chiume were undeterred and the pressure continued. Chipembere informed Banda that Nyasaland needed a "saviour" and that only he had the experience, the age, the qualifications and the necessary degree of esteem of his fellow Nyasalanders. It is possible that Banda would have continued to ignore the young militants had Britain, in April 1957, not reached its accord with the Federal Government which seemed, to the Nyasaland Africans, to resurrect the spectre of amalgamation. Banda was prompted to advise the African Congress to adopt a more uncompromising attitude, including the expulsion of Chirwa and Kumbikano.

To the pleas of the Congress were added those of Doig and a Nyasaland farmer, Major Peter Moxon, who wanted moderate and more mature leadership of the Congress. In early 1958 Banda had moved to London after having been suspended — albeit temporarily — from practising in Ghana, and there he gave in. Banda thereupon conducted a brief campaign in London at meetings and on radio and television on the evils of the Federation, while Chipembere prepared a welcome fit for a "political messiah".[14]

The reception was planned for 29 June at Chileka airport near Blantyre but due to a misunderstanding Banda was not on board the plane. The disbelieving crowd threatened to burn the aircraft, a Viscount, and were only pacified when Chipembere searched it. On 6 July Banda eventually arrived at Chileka to the jubilant roar of the crowd. The wildness of the reception and the anti-Federal mood considerably perturbed the authorities and the Europeans. Banda warned that he had no magical solution with him and that a struggle lay ahead.[15] The Federal officials were wary, but they could not

[13] *Ibid.*, Col. 646 f., 23 July 1958.
[14] P. Short, *Banda* (London, 1974), pp. 82–88.
[15] *Ibid.*, p. 89; Sir Roy Welensky, *Welensky's 4000 Days* (London, 1964), p. 97.

know that Banda's intrusion into politics signalled the beginning of the end of the Federation.

While public attention was riveted on the events at Chileka, Parry submitted his memorandum on the preparation for the Federal review. He identified three separate problems. The first was the constitutional structure; the second, the re-distribution of powers in the light of experience; and the third, the necessary legal and financial amendments. The purpose of the review, Parry said, was to eliminate the elements of constitutional subordination to Britain. This would avoid the political complications of a direct request for independence. The immediate step, he suggested, was to discover from the British Government the extent of the possible agreement. When doing that, it would be necessary to explain why the *status quo* was unsatisfactory and how change would benefit not only the Federation but the British interests in Africa as a whole. He warned that British Africa was moving rapidly towards self-government and that if the Federation were left behind, tension was inevitable between its Governments and Britain. Africa was assuming a growing prominence in the East-West confrontation and the Federation would have little influence if it remained little better than a colony. Moreover, he felt that it was vulnerable to subversion sponsored by the anti-colonial movements and the Soviet Union. It would never be a firm bulwark until the majority of the population no longer believed that, through Britain, they could destroy it.

If Britain were to grant the Federal request, Parry believed that a price would have to be paid. He expected Britain to worry over the efficacy of safeguards for the Africans in an independent Federation. To assist planning, he suggested that Greenfield should chair a committee of the heads of ministries tasked to discover the likely British attitudes. Methods of attaining independence and the extent of powers to be adopted required examination with the assistance of someone like Professor Wheare. The committee would have to decide at what stage the territories should be brought into the discussions. Parry believed that it would be appropriate to begin negotiations with the British Government, at official level, in the New Year.

Parry suggested methods of removing the Federal subordination to Britain. He examined the ramifications of the secession of Nyasaland, finding much in its favour as it would remove a political and financial liability. Nyasaland would, however, face impoverishment, its whites would be cruelly abandoned, and there would be an independent African state on the Rhodesian border which would unsettle the Africans in Northern Rhodesia and jeopardise stable government. Parry also found merit in partition but decided that it would be difficult and expensive to administer. He recalled Malvern's proposed treaty with Britain which would contain the safeguards on which the British Government had postponed discussion until 1960. He suggested it include defence, trade relations and economic and financial assistance. He related that, as a counter to Malvern in 1956, the British had proposed adapting the status once enjoyed by Newfoundland. Under this, the first few clauses of the Statute of Wesminster could be exploited to ensure that, amongst other matters, the Colonial Laws Validity Act would no longer apply. In this way, laws would not be inoperative because they were repugnant to the Law of England. The Federation would be able to legislate extra-territorially and the British Parliament would be unable to legislate for it without its permission. The British Government, however, would insist on retaining ultimate authority for African affairs. Parry also considered the idea of an upper chamber assuming responsibility for the safeguards, but could see no point in pursuing it because it had so many variations.[16]

Welensky passed Parry's memorandum to Greenfield who replied that Parry had missed the most important aspect of the subordination of the Federation. This, Greenfield said, was the Colonial Office's grip on the northern territories, which had to be loosened before the Federation could achieve real independence. He believed that the British Government realised that the Federal Government would expect more than Malvern had in 1956, but Greenfield acknowledged that this had not been stated formally. It was too soon to present the demand, but it could be drafted.

A major difficulty was the British pledge not to surrender power until the inhabitants agreed and Greenfield doubted that the British Government could ever be convinced that this had been achieved. Thus, he said, it would have to be shown that positive attempts had been made to win African allegiance but that these had been sabotaged by the African leaders. He suggested that the Federal Government argue that, as it was impossible to gauge the true feelings of the Africans, the British Government would have to decide what was best for all the inhabitants. He agreed that "a pound of flesh" would have to be given and that it was worth examining what could be done in the field of African advancement.

Greenfield believed, however, that it was too early to go to London and certainly too soon to brief a constitutional expert. Preparations for the Federal review could begin, he said, but one of the most difficult problems was the involvement in them of the territorial Governments. He thought it would perhaps be best if the Federal and territorial political leaders were ranged against the British politicians, the Colonial civil servants and the Governors. He felt that concerted action by the local leaders in the pre-1953 Federal Conferences would have produced a better Constitution. Instead, he recalled, they had served in the Governors' teams with the result that the British Government had used its own civil servants as spurious mouthpieces for the northern territories. For this reason, Greenfield wanted any further conferences to be confined to the poltical friends of the Federal Government.[17]

Lord Home interrupted the deliberations on 16 August when he informed Welensky that Lennox-Boyd had decided on alterations to the Northern Rhodesian White Paper. Lennox-Boyd agreed that the ordinary vote should not be subjected to devaluation. He widened the definition of "Ministers of Religion" to include sisters and lay brothers. Existing voters would automatically enrol as ordinary voters and all aspiring voters would have to swear allegiance to the Queen. The special qualifications would be gradually raised, during their ten-year life, until they equalled the ordinary qualifications, whereupon they would be eliminated. They would only be raised if, on a specific date, the number who qualified matched or exceeded the number of

[16] Welensky Papers, 7/21, f. 138, H. N. Parry to Welensky, 8 July 1958.
[17] *Ibid.*, f. 130, Greenfield to Welensky, 7 August 1958.

the ordinary voters. Special voters would be allowed to stand as candidates, but Lennox-Boyd warned that this was an experimental measure which would be withdrawn if it were abused. He settled on an Executive Council of a Governor and ten ministers, of whom four would be officials, four elected Members and two African Members. There would be no assistant ministers. The Governor would use his common sense about whom he consulted in selecting ministers. Finally, in the six special constituencies, the ordinary as well as the specially-qualified candidates would have to secure the approval of two-thirds of the Chiefs.

Lennox-Boyd believed that this was an equitable solution even though the only Federal objection allowed was the concession on the devaluation of the ordinary vote, which would be excessively criticised. The difficulty of defining the "majority party" for the purposes of consultation had been avoided, he claimed, by allowing the Governor his discretion. The introduction of a second African minister would avoid the difficulties which one on his own would experience and obviate the need for assistant ministers. Welensky had asked for the postponement of the order in council until after the Federal general election in November, but Lennox-Boyd said he had to publish the White Paper during the British parliamentary recess which would end on 23 October. This would, of course, he promised, contain all the details of the order in council.[18]

Welensky would not accept such dictation. He protested that early publication would give the advantage to his opponents who would certainly condemn the scheme. This, he warned, could force him to make considerable difficulties for the British Government.[19]

Lennox-Boyd, however, although sympathetic, replied that he had promised the Commons the publication of the White Paper in the recess and he had to comply lest the Opposition, concluding that he was merely accommodating Federal needs, dragged Welensky's name into the ensuing controversy. Furthermore, all the details would have to be published if the debate in the Commons were not to be plagued by suspicion. As he could not delay it, Lennox-Boyd wanted the earliest possible publication so that the criticism in the Federation would die down by polling day. He deeply regretted the necessity for this action and hoped that he could stave off the Commons debate until after the Federal general election.[20]

Welensky was still unconvinced and replied that he would have to declare openly his substantial objections to the proposals. The one which made them totally unacceptable, he said, was the failure to provide for any advancement towards responsible government. The elected Members had been allocated four out of the ten seats in the Executive Council and, he observed, those appointed to them need not come from the majority party. This meant that the political parties could not promise the electorate that they could carry out any policy. He denounced the inclusion of two African ministers as merely a lamentable appeasement of the Africans which cut across the concept of non-racial politics.

[18] *Ibid.*, 20/4, f. 269, Home to Welensky, 16 August 1958.
[19] *Ibid.*, f. 266, Welensky to Home, 21 August 1958.
[20] *Ibid.*, f. 264, W. I. McIndoe to Parry, 23 August 1958.

Welensky was fundamentally opposed to the appointment of two nondescript Members, and his fears for the party system were only magnified by the requirements in the special constituencies with regard to the Chiefs, which was an unwarranted interference in the free play of politics. Such proposals were intolerable and Welensky regretted that he had been unable to discuss them personally, but would ask Caldicott to interrupt his current tour of Europe if necessary.[21]

On 3 September Welensky ordered Sir Gilbert Rennie, the Federal High Commissioner in London, to maintain pressure on the British Government. Welensky said he still wanted a predominantly elected Executive Council under the presidency of a chief minister but would settle for a Council of seven, comprising three official and four elected Members appointed on the advice of the leader of the majority party. He insisted that any Africans appointed be drawn from that party and that the unofficial point of view should dominate any conflict within the Council. He expected the British Government to transfer to the Northern Rhodesian Government its jurisdiction over local subjects. He dismissed nomination and the endorsement of the Chiefs as unacceptable. Welensky asked Caldicott to assist Rennie.[22]

Six days later Caldicott and Rennie reported failure to secure any concession. Lennox-Boyd had told them that he would consider the demotion of one African minister to an assistant minister, but that as a *quid pro quo* the ordinary vote would be devalued. They discovered that Roberts had yielded on the consultation of the leader of the majority party because Africans might capture most of the seats. Instead there would be an informal agreement that the Governor would consult the leader.[23]

Later that day, Welensky ordered Rennie to see Home and urge most strongly that Lennox-Boyd visit Salisbury because he had not properly consulted the Federal Government even though the proposals could have a profound effect on the Federation. Welensky said that the impending general election forbad him from travelling because of the unfortunate inferences which would be drawn. Finally, he said that it should be made clear that if the proposals were published unamended the Federal Government would forcibly state its views in public.[24]

On the morrow, 10 September, both Caldicott and Home cabled Welensky. Caldicott said that the publication of the White Paper had been delayed a day so that he could discuss it again with the British Ministers. He had pressed the desired changes without avail and the White Paper would be published unaltered the next day.[25]

Home told Welensky that Lennox-Boyd could not travel but that he, Lennox-Boyd and Caldicott had considered everything very carefully and had even consulted the Prime Minister, Macmillan. He explained that Lennox-Boyd was committed to publication in the recess and that, in any case, the Legislative Council would expire on 19 January 1959, and that the

[21] *Ibid.*, f. 261, Welensky to Home, 26 August 1958.
[22] *Ibid.*, f. 257, Welensky to Rennie, 3 September 1958.
[23] *Ibid.*, f. 256, Telephone conversation between Welensky and Rennie, 9 September 1958.
[24] *Ibid.*, f. 255, Welensky to Rennie, 9 September 1958.
[25] *Ibid.*, f. 244, J. Caldicott to Welensky, 10 September 1958.

electoral arrangements, embodied in a Northern Rhodesian ordinance, had to be ready by 1 October 1958. Suspicion, he said, would arise if publication were delayed, and any attempt to prolong the life of the Legislative Council could produce a violent reaction which might lead to demands for greater concessions to the Africans. Benson, he warned, could not be asked to risk an insurrection. As the proposals were hardly revolutionary and would be seen by reasonable people as giving the Europeans certain definite advantages while the Africans gained a modest advance, the British Government would not delay. It hoped that the publication of this modest plan would remove the fears of the Europeans from the Federal electoral campaign. Home believed that the obligation to consult the Federal Government had been fully met and that indeed, an important adjustment had been made to the franchise in response to its demands.[26]

In a further dispatch, Home insisted that the advance to self-government had to be sufficiently gradual to ensure the protection of the interests of all members of the community. The British Government favoured the development of party, rather than racial politics, but it thought that it would be difficult to achieve when there were 2 500 000 Africans and only 70 000 Europeans in Northern Rhodesia. The Africans were expecting the appointment of African ministers so this provision was unavoidable and Lennox-Boyd insisted that there had to be two because the experiment of appointing one elsewhere — in Kenya — had failed.

To Home the nomination of two nondescript Members was not a step away from the elective process, because it would ensure that there would always be Members capable of holding portfolios when most Africans were so inexperienced. Lastly, he defended the provision for the approval of the Chiefs because it would give the Africans, who did not qualify for the vote, confidence in the candidates. Not only did the tribal system demand this, he said, but it would inhibit the agitator.[27]

The White Paper was duly published in Northern Rhodesia the next day, but was overshadowed by the news that, in attempting to persuade the Tonga people to leave the area threatened by the rising waters of Lake Kariba, the Northern Rhodesian Police had been attacked by primitively-armed tribesmen and had shot and killed eight and had injured 14. The ANC had been persuading the people that it was unnecessary to move, and Benson immediately alluded to this by blaming the unrest on the "evil men who have told lies".[28] On their side of the lake, the Southern Rhodesian Government had eschewed persuasion and had merely ordered its tribesmen to leave the affected area. In mitigation it did provide transport and assistance to establish them on higher ground. The Northern Rhodesian Government disapproved of such undemocratic ways and tried to use persuasion, including the appearance of the Governor in full fig accompanied by a military band, but it failed and the Southern Rhodesians were vindicated.[29]

[26] *Ibid.*, f. 254, Home to Welensky, (undated).
[27] *Ibid.*, f. 252, Home to Welensky, (undated).
[28] Northern Rhodesian Government *Gazette* (Lusaka), 11 September 1958; *The Rhodesia Herald*, 11 September 1958.
[29] Author's interviews with Sir Arthur Benson and Sir Roy Welensky.

The Copperbelt also provided a diversion because the European miners came out on strike over the continuing dispute regarding the manner of opening certain categories of employment to Africans.[30]

The proposals appeared in much the same form as before, with the White Paper stressing the value of the common roll but providing a temporary set of special qualifications to ensure adequate African representation in the next decade. The removal of the devaluation of the ordinary vote was emphasised.

The publication surprised Roberts and he immediately protested to Lennox-Boyd that Benson had not yet sought the opinion of the elected Members. Indeed, Benson had only just informed him that he would publish the proposals in full. Roberts claimed that, if he had been aware of this, he would have made his views known when the Federal Government was consulted. He expected a storm of protest from the elected Members.[31]

Roberts, thereupon, publicly announced that he had called an emergency meeting of his Caucus and reserved comment until then. Welensky, despite his threat of a public protest, remained silent, but Gaunt and Rodney Malcolmson, both members of the Northern Rhodesian delegation to London, protested vigorously. Gaunt called the proposals a gross betrayal of white civilisation in Northern Rhodesia cloaked in a smokescreen of cant and hypocrisy. Malcolmson claimed that the delegation had been hoaxed into believing that it was participating in a collective decision when, in fact, decisions of this nature were taken beside trout streams or in the smoking room of the Carlton Club or at "elevenses" in Hampstead or in Bloomsbury. To Malcolmson, Lennox-Boyd was guilty of cowardice, of appeasing his Opposition.

The ANC was also disappointed because it had expected more than eight African seats, but it welcomed the provision for two African ministers. The British Labour Party agreed that little had been offered to the African.[32]

Roberts's Caucus ordered him to invite Lennox-Boyd to Northern Rhodesia to receive its final representations before the Commons debate. Roberts was also to protest strongly at the entrenching of racial representation in the Executive Council because it would be irrevocable and would destroy party politics. If Lennox-Boyd could not visit, the Caucus demanded that he should postpone the adjustment of the Executive Council for twelve months. The Caucus warned that, if it were not taken seriously, it would withdraw its members from the Executive Council and might persuade all ten elected Members to resign from the Legislative Council.[33]

Roberts, informing the Press of this, said that the British proposals made the Governor an absolute ruler, which was unacceptable. He was grateful that the ordinary vote would not be devalued but decried the granting to the special votes a weight equal to a third of the total number of ordinary votes, as this would force the voters into racial blocs whenever more than two candidates stood in a constituency. Nomination to the Council was being retained and, even more disquieting to him, was reserved for the discretion of the

[30] *The Rhodesia Herald*, 13 September 1958.
[31] Welensky Papers, 7/10, f. 400a, Roberts to Lennox-Boyd, 11 September 1958.
[32] *The Rhodesia Herald*, 12 & 13 September 1958.
[33] Welensky Papers, 20/4, f. 244, Roberts to Home, 17 September 1958.

Governor alone, who could, therefore, nullify the effects of an election. The presence of nominated Members and a substantial number of officials could wreck the party system. Moreover, a future Governor could be a political appointment. As the size of the Executive Council made it ludicrously expensive and unwieldy, the motive for the increase could not have been efficiency and economy but simply expediency. Finally, Roberts deplored the disregard for his Party's demands for the appointment of a chief minister and the transfer of certain subjects from the jurisdiction of Britain.[34]

Welensky then revealed to the Press, on 18 September, that Caldicott had arrived in London to find that the decisions had been taken and that it was pointless to make representations. Welensky had not expected anything from an all-party delegation because of its divergent views, but he had found the proposals of the UFP most reasonable. He would not say what would be done to force the British hand, but conceded that he and Roberts were consulting each other closely. He believed that the proposals would make the Federal review more difficult because the enhanced powers of the Governor entrenched the Colonial Office more strongly.

Asked to comment on Lennox-Boyd's statement that the British Government could not give up its responsibilities until the Africans regarded the Federal Government with the same confidence as they did the British, Welensky replied that the current system militated against fostering loyalty by encouraging a large proportion of the population to look to London for salvation. This would not change, he said, until the Labour Party firmly indicated that it would neither break up the Federation nor allow a territory to do so unilaterally. Welensky stated that his Government would ensure that its views were widely known in Britain in the hope that reason and common sense would carry the day. What concerned him most were the immediate priorities such as the establishment of party politics. Questioned on the calibre of the current African politicians, he expressed confidence that, within a reasonable time, they would be capable of filling junior ministerial posts. Finally, he agreed that the Northern Rhodesian proposals could have an unfortunate effect and that they should have been considered more dispassionately without a Federal general election in the offing. He refused to indicate when that election would be, but on the next day he dissolved the Federal Assembly and announced that polling day would be 12 November.[35]

Welensky's next step, in fact, was to meet R. A. Butler, the British Home Secretary, who was then on a private visit to the Federation.[36] They met on 22 September and, asked to intercede, Butler agreed to put the Federal case, without commitment, to Macmillan.

Welensky supplied Butler with an *aide mémoire* in which he outlined the Federal position. This explained the advantage which the timing of the

[34] *The Rhodesia Herald*, 18 September 1958.

[35] Welensky Papers, 7/10, f. 31, Press Conference, 18 September 1958.

[36] Welensky wondered at Butler's sudden arrival but had to wait years before discovering the real reason – from Butler himself. Butler told him that he had been due to go to South Africa to deliver the "Winds of Change" speech. However, the South African Prime Minister, Strydom, died and Butler went instead to Umtali to visit his wife's cousins, the Courtaulds. Harold Macmillan delivered the speech 14 months later. – Author's interview with Sir Roy Welensky.

announcement had given to Welensky's opponents in a highly charged political atmosphere. By refusing to be drawn into the debate until Lennox-Boyd was ready, he claimed to have been pilloried for apparent meekness. If the British flatly rejected the Federal representations, he would be called inept and helpless and would be forced to take a stronger line if the proposals were not modified substantially or at least delayed until after the Federal general election.

Welensky said that, despite the critics accusing it of hypocrisy, his Government was trying to establish racial goodwill. The critics, of course, he asserted did not have to steer between the limitless demands of the African nationalists and the natural apprehensions of the Europeans. So if British intransigence forced him to take a tough line, he and his Party would be accused of veering to the Right and, as a result, race relations would suffer. This was reason enough for delay and *The Times*, James Johnson and Todd, he said, agreed with him. However, he found that there was little point in delay unless the possibility of modification existed.

During his visit, Butler had suggested the appointment of a Royal Commission to remove the matter from the political arena and to bring fresh minds to bear. He had argued that the degree of controversy would justify this, but Welensky rejected the suggestion because it would be seen as outside interference. The commission might uphold the Federal view, but Welensky doubted that even that would sway the British Government as his confidence in the reasonableness of Home and Lennox-Boyd had been shattered. Nevertheless, he would avoid a breach with the British Government, unless asked to surrender strongly held principles, and would reconsider the commission if Butler insisted. Welensky was confident that further effort could achieve a solution.

Welensky then recalled that when formulating its franchise proposals and its constitutional amendment, the Federal Government had consulted the territorial Governments continuously. However, he said, Benson had not returned the compliment and had shown the Federal Government only his completed plans. Thereafter all the Federal representations had been rejected. Nevertheless, Welensky believed the impasse could be solved by removing the provision for Africans in the Executive Council, appointed solely on grounds of race, because they could be nominated Members and need not be the choice of the leader of the majority party. If this was done, Welensky felt he could persuade the unofficials to accept an African appointee to the Executive Council if the election produced a suitable candidate. If it did not, a by-election and not nomination, would be the answer. If it seemed to give too much power to the leading party, Welensky said he would consider election by the Council of Chiefs and, to provide a sobering influence, by European elder statesmen.

Welensky was also prepared, reluctantly, to abandon the appointment of a chief minister if, in exchange, the Executive Council was reduced to the Governor, three official and four unofficial Members appointed on the advice of the leader of the majority party. He said that, above all, it was necessary to be rid of the endorsement by the Chiefs because it would allow the ANC to use pressure to exclude all UFP candidates. If the real reason was to secure black Members then, he suggested, the colour of the candidates could be specified for the first five or ten years. He thought that he had shown what could be achieved and hoped that Butler could persuade his colleagues to allow a re-examination in the calmer atmosphere which could follow the Federal general election.[37]

Butler immediately transmitted this plea to Macmillan. Welensky, of course, was not working openly and, on 25 September, Malcolmson warned him that, although the elected Members had decided not to resign *en masse* over an unacceptable final decision, his branch (Luanshya) had unanimously demanded that he should. Welensky advised Malcolmson that something was afoot and that, as a gesture of defiance, nothing more than a mass withdrawal from the Executive Council (rather than resignations from the Legislative Council) was necessary. Otherwise, he cautioned, the United Federal Party would be denied a voice in the territory's affairs for as long as three months before the Governor was forced to call an election. Shortly afterwards the Ndola branches similarly demanded resignations because they did not think that a withdrawal from the Executive Council would be a forceful enough gesture.[38]

Before the British Government replied to Butler's intercession on Welensky's behalf, the Federal electoral campaign was in full swing and Moffat had intruded by publicly declaring that it was Welensky's standard tactic to create a constitutional crisis before an election. A good hate campaign against the Colonial Office, he said, always distracted the electorate from the defects of the Government and won their votes. If this were true, then surely, Moffat argued, Welensky would have accepted the offer of the Dominion Party to work against the Northern Rhodesian constitutional proposals.

Moffat found many inconsistencies in the UFP's case. He agreed with its rejection of the African demand for parity but believed that the ambitions of Roberts were solely responsible for the demand for a chief minister because the latter's powers would have been so slender. The UFP had apparently accepted the need for an African in the Executive Council and, Moffat said, this belied Welensky's rejection of the provision for two Africans as racialism in reverse. Such a contradiction rendered this issue a minor one. The UFP in any case, he felt, had won a major victory in securing the removal of the devaluation of the European vote and thus could hardly complain at an extra African seat in the Executive Council. There was certainly no justification for the current hysteria, and Moffat believed that only Roberts stood in the way of a compromise.

Moffat also commented on a recent attack by Welensky on his leadership of the African Affairs Board. He reminded the public that the Board was empowered to draw attention to any bill which seemed to differentiate between the races. It had done so when it had assessed the Constitutional

[37] Welensky Papers, 20/4, f. 238, Welensky to R. A. Butler, 23 September 1958; 42/38, f. 158, same to same, 23 September 1958.

[38] *Ibid.*, 42/38, f. 157, Butler to Welensky, 24 September 1958; 7/10, f. 406, R. Malcolmson to Welensky, 25 September 1958; 25/229, f. 48, Welensky to R. Malcolmson, 25 September 1958; f. 52, Luanshya branch, UFP, to Welensky, (undated); f. 50, W. Rendall to Welensky, 27 September 1958.

Amendment Bill and Welensky had not criticised its reasoning but had insisted that it should remain silent when the Federal and British Governments had decided on a course of action. Thus Welensky had ignored the possibility that the Board might have a strong case as well as a moral duty to act. However, Moffat alleged, when a territorial Government and the British Government decided on a course of action, Welensky, without any constitutional right to dispute such a decision, reacted in a manner which he would deny to the African Affairs Board.[39]

Welensky replied publicly on 6 October depicting Moffat as nothing more than a faithful former Colonial officer defending the Colonial Office. He dismissed Moffat, in the light of his advocacy of the proposals and of his record, as lacking acumen, political maturity and, indeed, responsibility. Moffat, he said, chose to ignore the shortcomings and the dangers of the African Affairs Board and, in particular, its undemocratic nature. Moffat had known that the British and Federal Governments had taken legal advice on the Constitutional Amendment and Electoral Bills and had found them not to be discriminatory. Thus, Welensky maintained, Moffat had thereafter failed in his leadership. By being a nominated Member, Moffat had always exercised power without responsibility, but Welensky believed that experience would teach him the necessity of preserving the British parliamentary tradition.[40]

The timing of the announcement, for which Welensky blamed Benson, certainly affected the tempo of the Federal general election. Aware that it had, the British Government, before answering his approach through Butler, assured Welensky on 3 October that the debate in the Commons and the Northern Rhodesian order in council would be delayed until after polling day. It also indicated that, while major alterations were unlikely, adjustments might be possible to answer some of the European criticisms. Any modification, however, would be unacceptable to the British Government if it appeared to be the result of the UFP's agitation. It was hoped that an announcement that the proposals were being studied in London would dampen the controversy. If Welensky commented, then the British Government wanted him to say that his criticisms were also being studied in London.

Butler, in particular, asked Welensky to say nothing more in case he prejudiced what Butler might achieve.[41] Welensky promised to comply and to try to keep the matter out of the election. To assist him, however, he asked the British Government to announce that the implementation of the White Paper had been suspended pending further negotiations. It should also hint at a conference in the sober post-election atmosphere.[42]

While Welensky awaited the British reply, the Dominion Party continued to exploit the situation in an election which, by October, was being fought against the background of a lengthy strike by the European copper miners and of growing African unrest in all three territories.[43] Banda was establishing

[39] *Northern News*, 29 September 1958.

[40] Welensky Papers, 25/198, f. 3, Welensky to the *Northern News*, 6 October 1958.

[41] *Ibid.*, 20/4, f. 231, Welensky to Butler, 24 October 1958; f. 236, M. R. Metcalf to Welensky, 3 October 1958.

[42] *Ibid.*, f. 235, H. N. Parry to M. R. Metcalf, 6 October 1958.

[43] *Ibid.*, 7/10, f. 414, Roberts to Lennox-Boyd, (undated); *The Rhodesia Herald*, 7 October 1958.

himself in Nyasaland and inflammatory speeches were becoming the order of the day. Nkomo copied his example in Southern Rhodesia. A split in Northern Rhodesia between Nkumbula and Kaunda led to the latter adopting a more extreme attitude.

Welensky tried to remove the issue of dominion status from the election by promising to consult all the parties before any negotiations in 1960. The Dominion Party, however, merely threatened that if it were returned, and if dominion status were refused, it would unilaterally declare the Federation independent. Welensky replied that this would only lead to armed resistance from the Northern Rhodesian and Nyasaland Police. He claimed also that thereby the DP had illustrated its lack of confidence in its ability to achieve independence.[44]

Nevertheless, the idea was sufficiently attractive — or the threat sufficiently serious — for Welensky to have it assessed. His advisers found that it would seriously divide the white population while unifying the Africans. It would not only confirm but reinforce the anti-Federal sentiments of the Africans and might even morally justify an insurrection.

The Federation would be an outcast in the international community. The operation of treaties and other legal relationships would be impossible because the Federation would not exist in international law until Britain accepted the revolt. Likewise, membership of the Commonwealth would be withheld and recognition would only come from South Africa. The United Nations would cut the Federation from financial and technical assistance from international agencies. Defence arrangements would be severed and the denial of arms supplies would mean that the Federal forces would become increasingly ineffective.

The Federal Attorney-General defined a unilateral declaration of independence as a revolt or a *coup d'état* which would mean that the judiciary would have to be persuaded to join it or be replaced.

The territorial courts, which enforced Federal law, could, in terms of the Federal Constitution, declare the legal competence of the Federal Assembly to be void. These courts were bound by the Colonial Laws Validity Act which made void any law that was repugnant to the British act which extended powers to the colony in question. The Colonial Laws Validity Act also applied to the Federal Order in Council and would render void any unilateral amendments to it. The impossibility of securing the Royal Assent to any legislation passed after the declaration of independence would exonerate any judge who refused to apply it.

The Ministry of Commerce and Industry warned that all claims to Commonwealth treatment would be invalid and that the Federation would be expelled from the sterling area. Preferential earnings of £6 000 000 in Britain by the tobacco and asbestos industries would be lost and other countries would be unwilling to supply markets. The same would apply to capital investment. If the British Government wanted to aggravate the situation it would freeze sterling balances of £113 000 000 in London. This would cause great hardship because the Federation would have to rely on barter. Britain

[44] *The Rhodesia Herald*, 13 October 1958.

could also refuse to guarantee loans from the World Bank, terminate the Double Taxation Agreement and replace Federal with American tobacco.[45]

Although irritated by the constraints of the Federal Constitution, such as that demanding the consent of the majority of the inhabitants for any enhancement in its status, Welensky accepted this advice. The time would come when he would look again at the possibilities of a unilateral declaration of independence but, for the moment, he dismissed the idea as "poppycock".[46]

Home replied in late October to Welensky's representations through Butler. He explained that, to meet Welensky's demands, Lennox-Boyd would publish a supplementary dispatch to effect certain amendments. To ensure that the Executive Council commanded a majority in the Legislative Council, to apply the principle of collective responsibility and to promote the growth of party politics, the Governor would choose his ministers first from the elected Members and in so doing would consult the leader of the majority party.

Home said that this was designed to placate Roberts, as was the second provision which stated that, should there be insufficient suitable unofficial Members to serve the Executive Council, the Governor could declare that Council to be complete despite some empty seats. Thus unsuitable Africans would not be appointed. The dispatch would also declare that, if the new constitution worked well, the appointment of a chief minister would be reconsidered if it was desired by the races and parties of Northern Rhodesia. The delegation of responsibility for certain subjects to Northern Rhodesia would be considered at the Federal review.

Home said that Lennox-Boyd thought that the logical moment for publication of the supplementary dispatch was the end of October but that he was willing to delay a couple of weeks because the British debate could be postponed until the last week of November. He dismissed, however, an all-party conference because he believed that the adjusted settlement was equitable. Concluding, Lennox-Boyd and Home hastened to reassure Welensky that nothing would prejudice the Federal review.

Simultaneously, Butler wrote to Welensky saying that, while he and his colleagues sympathised with Welensky's problems at the hustings, they nevertheless felt that because of the review in 1960 they did not want to make the northern African more intractable.[47]

Although Butler suggested that the scheme was workable and was the best that could be hoped for, Welensky was disappointed because the fears of the European had not been allayed. He threatened that, if this plan was released before his election, he would be forced to confront the British and Northern Rhodesian Governments. Although anxious to avoid this, he was bitter that the advice of Benson was always taken on timing while his was ignored with the consequence that he might lose his election outright. Thus he appealed

45 Welensky Papers, 7/20, f. 61, ? to H. N. Parry, 13 October 1958; f. 59, Parry to Welensky, 21 October 1958; f. 58, Memorandum by Parry, 21 October 1958; ff.56–57, Weinberg to W. S. Parker, 14 October 1958; ff. 62–63, N. R. Bertram to W. S. Parker, 14 October 1958; f. 66, Memorandum "What the United Kingdom could do if she wanted to get tough", 14 October 1958.

46 *Ibid.*, 7/21, f. 160, Welensky to Sir Ernest Guest, 15 October 1958.

47 *Ibid.*, 20/4, f. 233, Home to Welensky, (undated); f. 232, Butler to Welensky, (undated).

for reconsideration of the all-party conference so that, for the purposes of his election, the matter could still be said to be under review.[48]

Home conceded to further negotiations but only after the election when he would gladly receive a Federal Minister. Welensky gratefully replied that he would refer to the continuance of negotiations at an election meeting in Umtali. As the all-party conference had been refused, Welensky instructed Roberts to say, when asked, that the Federal Government was being given an opportunity to make representations and that, naturally, Roberts and his colleagues had made their views known.[49]

Nevertheless, the British had not shaken Welensky's determination to change the proposals significantly. He told Roberts on 4 November that he was expecting to see the main objectionable feature — the endorsement by the Chiefs — removed before he went to London. (Welensky had decided that he would be the Federal Minister to be received by Home.)[50]

Meanwhile Welensky had been persuaded, during the election campaign, to assist in the termination of the Copperbelt strike. Pressed by van Eeden early in the strike, Welensky refused to do anything because industrial conciliation was a territorial matter. However, when the Northern Rhodesian Government also stood aloof, Welensky intervened thereby shaming Benson into action. The strike, which was amicable, was called off in favour of arbitration, a week before the election with tributes being paid to Welensky, Roberts, L'Ange and Benson.[51]

Van Eeden, however, sourly stated that Welensky had waited too long and had allowed the Federation to sustain a considerable loss of income through the strike.[52] In fact, despite the strike, the Federation was enjoying a significant recovery with a rising copper price and ready offers of loan finance. The European copper miners thus left the stage to Banda and, perhaps, his performance did much to convince the Federal voters that they could not gamble on a change of government. On 12 November, Welensky was returned with his Party winning 46 seats, two-thirds of the House, the Dominion Party eight and the independents one. Moffat's Constitution Party was eclipsed, but Moffat accepted further nomination as a representative of African interests.

Knowing that Welensky was departing immediately for London, Beckett urged him to inform the British Government that, by 1960, Northern Rhodesia and Nyasaland would expect to be rid of every aspect of the Colonial Office administration, except for the operation of the safeguards. As Beckett believed that Benson was so determined to get his own way that he would threaten resignation, he advised Welensky to spin out the negotiations until Benson retired in the New Year. Alternatively, Welensky should demand the maintenance of the *status quo*. Above all, he should be wary of

[48] *Ibid.*, f. 231, Welensky to Butler, 24 October 1958.
[49] *Ibid.*, f. 228, Home to Welensky, (undated); 7/10, f. 443, Welensky to Home, (undated); f. 417, Welensky to Roberts, 29 October 1958.
[50] *Ibid.*, f. 418, Welensky to Roberts, 4 November 1958.
[51] *Ibid.*, 31/56, ff. 50–51, van Eeden to Welensky, 26 September 1958; f. 53, Statement by Welensky, 26 September 1958; *The Rhodesia Herald*, 4 November 1958.
[52] *The Rhodesia Herald*, November 1958.

Benson's considerable influence over Lennox-Boyd. Benson had tried to persuade some of the elected Members to accept the proposals, and thus Beckett urged the Federal Government to warn that it would brook no more interference by the British Government. Beckett was confident that the British would be easier to deal with after their election in 1959, and he believed that it was crucial that nothing should be done which might prejudice the review. Therefore, Welensky should press for the transfer of all territories to the jurisdiction of the Commonwealth Relations Office, and the early establishment of the Central African civil service.[53]

Welensky arrived in London on 18 November and stated publicly that his Government would eliminate racial representation and thus would readily accept two Africans in the Northern Rhodesian Executive Council provided they were chosen on merit alone.[54]

Welensky and Greenfield met Home and Lennox-Boyd the next day for the first of eight meetings but merely indicated their dislike of the endorsement by the Chiefs and of nomination. Welensky asked if the leader of the majority party would have to be consulted on the nomination of Members both to the Legislative and the Executive Councils. Lennox-Boyd replied affirmatively.[55]

On 20 November, while Greenfield complained that there had been no advance towards responsible government in Northern Rhodesia, Lennox-Boyd protested that no one was grateful for the concession on the devaluation of the ordinary vote. Greenfield said he was not surprised because devaluation was so indefensible that even Todd had discarded it. When Greenfield depicted as retrogressive the appointment of two Africans to the Executive Council solely on the grounds of race, Lennox-Boyd replied that the ratio of 71 000 Europeans to 2 000 000 Africans made it necessary. Welensky reminded him that he did not object to Africans in that Council but to the method of their selection. Lennox-Boyd suggested the conversion of the two nominated seats for Africans into elected ones, but Welensky preferred only one because he believed that the Africans would equate the value of one elected Member with two nominated Members. However, Lennox-Boyd refused to face the adverse reaction even from the Conservative Party if Welensky's visit resulted in a reduction of African representation. Greenfield proposed the replacement of one nominated Member by an African official Member, but Lennox-Boyd insisted that the four official Members had to be the Chief Secretary, the Attorney-General, the Financial Secretary and the Secretary for Native Affairs. He proposed to sound out Benson on the substitution of the two nominated Members by two elected African Members, but thought that, if he agreed, the proposal that the Governor need not fill all the seats in the Executive Council would have to be dropped.[56]

Lennox-Boyd continued to maintain that the endorsement by the Chiefs was essential not only for translating democracy into tribal conditions but for

[53] Welensky Papers, 42/21, f. 126, G. Beckett to Welensky, 17 November 1958.
[54] *The Rhodesia Herald*, 19 November 1958.
[55] Welensky Papers, 20/4, f. 225, Minutes of a Meeting, Commonwealth Relations Office, 19 November 1958.
[56] *Ibid.*, f. 222, Minutes of a Meeting, Commonwealth Relations Office, 20 November 1958.

preserving the traditional tribal authorities. Nevertheless, he was prepared to indicate that, if it proved unworkable, it would be rescinded. Welensky knew that it would not work because the African nationalists were capable of intimidating even the most influential Chiefs. He proposed that the Chiefs sit as a body to vet the candidates. Lennox-Boyd then suggested that a candidate should be disqualified if a third of a constituency's Chiefs positively disapproved of him.[57]

The next day Lennox-Boyd was absent from the discussions. These concentrated on the chief minister. Welensky said that this appointment would be a logical consequence of the removal of the two nominated Members, but Home deferred the discussion to 1960.[58]

Three days later the meeting resumed with Lennox-Boyd participating. Greenfield dwelt on the impracticalities of the Chiefs' endorsement but Lennox-Boyd said that its removal was a major alteration which required consultation with the Northern Rhodesian all-party delegation which had recently visited him in London. The same applied to the question of nomination. Lennox-Boyd and Home claimed that nominated Members had given valuable service elsewhere, but Welensky was adamantly opposed to them. He warned that, because the Federal Government had only been consulted after decisions had been taken, the UFP in Northern Rhodesia was contemplating going into opposition rather than associate itself with the territorial Government. However, Lennox-Boyd argued that this threat only made nomination all the more necessary.[59]

Roberts was consulted and his telegrams were laid before the meeting on 26 November. In them, he protested again at the special voters having an influence worth a third of the ordinary votes which would radically affect some constituencies. However, he confirmed that he accepted the endorsement by the Chiefs, provided that they were given guidance. He would not countenance the conversion of the nominated seats into elected African seats unless the European was given a *quid pro quo*.[60]

Despite Roberts, Greenfield spelt out again the impracticalities of the Chiefs' endorsement. He disliked giving them a veto. Lennox-Boyd was sympathetic, but said that his Northern Rhodesian advisers had insisted on a bridge between the old and the new, and that the authority of the Chiefs should be maintained. He was prepared, however, to examine the difficulties. Home agreed because Roberts and the provincial administration endorsed the proposal. Home's readiness to agree does not accord, however, with Welensky's report to Gore-Browne that Home had blatantly supported the Federal case, saying that he could not understand the Colonial Office's intentions. Welensky claimed Greenfield had argued so well that the Colonial Office officials had been plainly embarrassed and Gorell Barnes unusually silent.[61]

[57] *Ibid.*, f. 219, Minutes of a Meeting, Lord Home's Room, House of Lords, 20 November 1958.

[58] *Ibid.*, f. 217, Minutes of a Meeting, Commonwealth Relations Office, 21 November 1958.

[59] *Ibid.*, f. 213, Minutes of a Meeting, Commonwealth Relations Office, 24 November 1958.

[60] *Ibid.*, 20/5, f. 110, Benson to Lennox-Boyd, 25 November 1958; f. 109, same to same, 25 November 1958.

[61] *Ibid.*, 20/4, f. 209, Minutes of a Meeting, Commonwealth Relations Office, 26 November 1958; 24/73, ff. 169–170, Welensky to Gore-Browne, 14 December 1958.

After telephoning Roberts in Lusaka, Welensky reported that Roberts had never grasped the practical difficulties of obtaining the endorsement of the Chiefs. Furthermore, Roberts had understood from Benson that there would be one African nominated Member and one European. Lennox-Boyd replied that the presumption was that the nominated Members would be Africans, but one could be a European or an Asian. After further discussion on other aspects, it was agreed that Welensky should present a memorandum to Lennox-Boyd, listing the Federal objections, before the supplementary dispatch was issued.[62]

On 27 November Lennox-Boyd opened the debate in the Commons, defending the proposals and his rejection of the African demand for parity which he said was incompatible with the fostering of non-racial politics.

Callaghan thereupon decried the proposals because they left the African inadequately represented, failed to inspire confidence, and accordingly would worsen race relations in the entire area. The Africans would not believe that the new constitution represented an advance and would certainly not understand its complicated mechanism. He disliked the devaluation of the special vote and blamed Benson for it. The constitution, he said, would be so unworkable that it would only be used once. He rejected the role of the Chiefs because to him they were nothing more than civil servants and could be used to stifle candidacies.

Callaghan questioned how non-racial politics were being fostered when the constituencies had to be deliberately delimited to return European Members in some and Africans in others, and the special vote had to be devalued in five of the ordinary constituencies because the African voters would outnumber the Europeans. He understood white fears, but said that Britain could not betray her pledges to the Africans. The real test of British policy was the resultant quality of race relations but Callaghan believed that the proposals would only increase racial tensions and endanger the long-term prospects of the Federation.

Callaghan also censured Welensky for travelling to London, having just been returned to power, to try to reduce the number of proposed African ministers to one. This gave the impression, he said, that the Federal Government was trying to retard African progress permanently.

Other Labour and Liberal MPs sought the appointment to the Executive Council of "naughty boys" like Nkumbula so that they could contribute to society rather than be ostracised. They complained that the literacy test would disqualify thousands, and stressed the growing importance of Africa in international politics, which meant that any development in Northern Rhodesia would be keenly watched. It was also imperative to reconcile the Africans as they were anxiously awaiting the review. They could not accept the degree of power given to the tiny white population. Arthur Bottomley, who would later figure prominently in Rhodesian affairs, threatened Welensky that the Labour Party would not grant dominion status at the expense of the masses.

The Conservatives pointed out that British Protected Persons were being

[62] *Ibid.*, 20/4, f. 204, Minutes of a Meeting, Lord Home's Room, House of Lords, 26 November 1958.

enfranchised and claimed that, in the Federal election, Africans had voted for European candidates, belying claims of significant racial discord. Alport maintained that it was no good pretending that a different or more extensive franchise might solve Northern Rhodesia's problem if, as a result of intimidation or indifference, the Africans were not prepared to exercise the normal responsibilities of a parliamentary democracy.

As the debate progressed, Welensky and Greenfield from the Strangers' Gallery watched the House empty until only a handful of stalwarts was left. Then, at the division, they saw with wry amusement the MPs come flooding back to record their anxiety about Northern Rhodesia. The Conservatives won the day with a comfortable majority of 296 to 238. Callaghan, however, attacked Welensky in the Press and on the BBC. Welensky told Gore-Browne how Callaghan had claimed that he (Welensky) might appear in Britain as an avuncular, kind-hearted liberal, but at home he — a teetotaller — was a tough, whisky-swilling, sjambok-wielding European who was determined to keep the black in his place.[63]

That day, 27 November, Welensky wrote his promised memorandum for Lennox-Boyd in which he protested again that his Government had only been consulted when the Northern Rhodesian proposals were virtually unalterable, and expressed the hope that this would not recur when the alterations to the Nyasaland Constitution were considered. The Federal representations, he said, had been too lightly dismissed. The proposals would stultify the development of political partnership in Northern Rhodesia and the main Federal objection was that there would be two Africans in the Executive Council even if no one who was suitable were elected. The Federal Government would happily accept Africans who were equipped to assume responsibilities, but it abhorred gestures of appeasement.

Welensky rejected nomination by the Governor as it would be resented by the electorate. The welding of officials and unofficials into the semblance of a cabinet was already difficult and the principle of collective responsibility would be impossible to apply among mutually suspicious people. If there had to be Africans in the Executive Council solely on the grounds of race, he argued, then nomination had to be dropped because it would ruin the party system. There was anxiety to promote Africans but the truth was they still needed training. Nomination would make it difficult for the political parties to attract Africans and would leave the leader of the majority party with the unenviable task of having to placate his disgruntled Africans who had won seats but had been ignored by the Governor. Furthermore, he said, the Governor could always upset the result of an election by his choice of nominated Members.

Welensky returned to the difficulties of seeking out up to 40 Chiefs in vast tracts of country in the 28 days between proclamation and nomination day. The Chiefs might be ill, drunk or merely absent from their kraals when the unfortunate candidate arrived. These were reasons enough for reconsideration, he observed, aside from the problems of bribery and intimidation. The

[63] House of Commons *Hansard* (London), Vol. 596, Col. 563 f., 27 November 1958; *Proposals for Constitutional Change in Northern Rhodesia*, Command 530 (London, September 1958); Welensky Papers, 24/73, ff. 169–170, Welensky to Gore-Browne, 14 December 1958.

proposal violated all the principles of parliamentary nomination and showed the authors to be ignorant of the party political system. The White Paper had concentrated on the encouragement of party and not racial politics, but the scheme itself would impede that development and thus Welensky urged its reconsideration most strongly.[64]

Before leaving London, Welensky told the Press that his Party was not trying to bulldoze a path to independence, but had always maintained that the Federation had an unanswerable case to be fully independent. It did not seek it for prestige, he said, but to weld the peoples of the Federation into the partnership.[65]

Benson was briefed by Lennox-Boyd and, on 2 December, he travelled to Salisbury with Roberts ostensibly to hear Welensky's version. Benson proved intractable, while Roberts accepted the Federal case, although he wanted to involve the Chiefs because he believed that the policy of building them up in the face of African nationalism had already paid handsome dividends. Benson and his Secretary of Native Affairs, G. S. Jones (later Sir Glyn), endorsed this statement.

Benson maintained that his proposals did not depart from democratic practice although to bring in large numbers of Africans it was necessary to marry Westminster practices with the traditional African representation. He made light of the difficulties because, ignoring the prescribed 28 days between proclamation and nomination day, he noticed that there would be 60 days between dissolution and the nomination day. He believed that he was encouraging the candidates of the political parties to penetrate the rural areas which to date only the ANC had done. If none of the candidates were accepted there would be a by-election. At Roberts's suggestion, Benson said, the provincial administration would provide a guideline for the Chiefs which would ensure that candidates of other tribes could be accepted.

Greenfield, unconvinced, pointed out that the Chiefs could change their minds and withdraw their consent. Welensky thought that the UFP would not gain any of the special seats. Roberts agreed and remarked that this was even more certain if the candidates did not have the approval of the Chiefs. In the end he agreed with Greenfield on the practical difficulties and promised to enlighten his Caucus.

Benson explained that nomination need not apply to one race alone and that it would ameliorate the freak election. He disagreed with Greenfield's suggestion of substituting an African for a European official in the Executive Council because there were none with suitable qualifications. He promised to consider first the African elected Members when appointing ministers but, because men had to match their responsibilities, he was glad to retain the power to nominate. He would, he promised, always consult the leader of the majority party first and then the other leaders. He provoked the Federal Ministers to express the hope that the supplementary dispatch would not refer to the consultation of the other leaders. Next Benson objected to the idea of the appointment of a chief minister as being meaningless. The meeting

[64] Welensky Papers, 20/4, f. 196, Welensky to Home, 27 November 1958; 20/5, f. 114, Memorandum by Welensky, 28 November 1958.

[65] *The Rhodesia Herald*, 28 November 1958.

closed with a Federal expression of hope that it would be consulted properly the next time a constitutional change was contemplated.[66]

Benson then wrote to Welensky and considerably annoyed Greenfield because he dismissed his harping on matters of principle as indulgence in the "theoretical". The irritated Greenfield still could not reconcile Benson's scheme with his professed anxiety to encourage party politics. After all, Greenfield argued, the special seats were vital to the UFP if it were to secure a majority and thereby influence the choice of ministers.[67]

Greenfield urged Welensky to use Benson's letter to influence the British Ministers, but Welensky did not comply. However, he did dispatch to Home the minutes of the meeting with Benson, adding that the meeting had not been satisfactory. He explained that Benson had refused to drop the "vetting" by the Chiefs and yet had not shown that it would not be an intolerable burden on the candidates. The Federal Government still vehemently opposed this, he said, as well as the nomination of Members which Benson continued to defend. Welensky acknowledged that he could not prevent the British Government from implementing the proposals but, in a last bid to influence it, he claimed to believe that it recognised the disadvantages of "vetting" and thought that, as these were recognised by others, "it would only be graceful if you could abandon this . . ."[68]

Welensky followed this dispatch with another one to Home in which he described the current degree of influence of the ANC over the Chiefs. He did not mention that Paramount Chief Mpenzeni had delighted Benson by urging his fellow Africans to work and co-operate with the Government. Welensky's efforts to sway Home were unsuccessful because he replied on 17 December that Macmillan, he and Lennox-Boyd had agreed that they could not drop "vetting" or nomination. (Macmillan reveals in his memoirs, *Pointing the Way*, that he had in fact changed his mind since meeting Welensky on 21 November, because then he had agreed to concede "vetting", if not nomination.) Home maintained that the removal of nomination had always presented them with great difficulties and that many of the mechanical difficulties of "vetting" seemed to have been solved by Benson discovering that there would be 60 days for it. Moreover, Home said, instructions from Benson to the Chiefs would guard against abuse and, if "vetting" proved impracticable, it would be dropped. (Welensky can be forgiven if, at that moment, he despaired of the British Government; and it would only continue to disappoint him from this moment on.) Home said that, accordingly, Lennox-Boyd would announce in the Commons on the morrow, 18 December, that his proposals would stand, that he had sent a supplementary dispatch to Benson which would clarify certain points, and that he had instructed Benson to publish this dispatch.[69]

[66] Welensky Papers, 20/4, f. 194, Lennox-Boyd to Benson, 28 November 1958; ff. 182–192, Minutes of a Meeting, Salisbury, 2 December 1958.
[67] *Ibid.*, 7/10, f. 462, Greenfield to Welensky, 15 December 1958.
[68] *Ibid.*, 20/4, f. 178, Welensky to Home, 8 December 1958.
[69] *Ibid.*, 7/10, f. 443, Welensky to Home, 15 December 1958; f. 462, Greenfield to Welensky, 15 December 1958; 20/4, f. 175, Home to Welensky, 17 December 1958; H. Macmillan, *Pointing the Way, 1959–61* (London, 1972), p. 134.

Making the announcement in the Commons, Lennox-Boyd also claimed that the mechanical difficulties had been rectified, that nomination had to be retained and that, when the moment was opportune, the appointment of a chief minister would be considered.[70]

Greenfield immediately contacted Roberts but found him unconcerned. They decided that at a Press conference on 19 December Roberts would say that there were aspects of the proposals which were distasteful but that the leader of the majority party would gain significantly, particularly as he had never before had a say in the selection of the nominated Members. Furthermore, that if the Governor would take the advice of the leader, the Constitution might possibly work which meant that the electorate had to return a party in strength so that it could provide suitable candidates for the Executive Council. Roberts would also say that, if that party had enough suitable candidates, it would contest all eight special seats.[71]

Benson published the supplementary dispatch and immediately announced that nomination day would be 27 February 1959, and that the general election would be held on 20 March. Roberts held his Press conference, and Welensky released details of his negotiations and told how, while courteously treated, he had faced a *fait accompli* because the British Government had manoeuvred itself into a position from which it could not retreat. He noted that the Dominion Party was already trying to exploit his alleged failure, but he hoped that time might prove his visit to London to have been worthwhile.[72]

Greenfield did his arithmetic and told Welensky that the period between dissolution (on 19 January 1959) and nomination day (on 27 February 1959) amounted to 39 days and not the 60 which Benson had promised. Moreover, Greenfield said, the task of the special candidates would be made even more difficult because this period would be the height of the rainy season. As this was such a remarkable departure from what Benson had promised, Greenfield thought that Welensky would be justified in alerting Home and Lennox-Boyd to the degree to which Benson had failed them even at the first election under the new constitution.[73]

Welensky sought the advice of H. N. Parry, who suggested that the matter should be left to simmer. Welensky agreed, and turned his attention to the problem of Nyasaland.[74]

[70] House of Commons *Hansard* (London), Vol. 597, Col. 275, 18 December 1958; Welensky Papers, 20/4, ff. 176–177, Lennox-Boyd to Benson, 18 December 1958.

[71] Welensky Papers, 7/10, f. 446, Greenfield to Welensky, 19 December 1958; f. 465, Press statement by Roberts, 19 December 1958.

[72] *Northern News*, 23 December 1958; Welensky Papers, 20/5, f. 48, Statement by Welensky on the Northern Rhodesian Constitutional Changes, 1958, (undated).

[73] Welensky Papers, 20/5, f. 41, Greenfield to Welensky, 30 December 1958.

[74] *Ibid.*, f. 40, H. N. Parry to Welensky, 2 January 1959; f. 39, Parry to Greenfield, 6 January 1959.

CHAPTER TWENTY-TWO

The Nyasaland Emergency

The Effect of African Unrest on the British Attitude to the Federation, January-March 1959

ONLY four candidates in the six special rural constituencies in Northern Rhodesia managed to secure the support of the Chiefs. Roberts protested, but his voice was almost drowned in the uproar over Nyasaland. Indeed, the Northern Rhodesian election campaign passed virtually unnoticed in the rest of the Federation even though it resulted in resounding victory for the United Federal Party. The events in Nyasaland, coupled with the continuing unrest in Northern Rhodesia and the agitation in Southern Rhodesia, would shake the resolve of the British Government, and Welensky would find himself coerced into accepting what would become the Monckton Commission. The beginning of the end was about to be spelt out because Macmillan, as he has admitted in *Pointing the Way*, had begun to doubt whether the Federation could be maintained.[1]

On 22 December 1958, A. C. W. Dixon, the leader of the UFP in the Nyasaland Legislative Council, reported to Welensky on the action taken since June on Nyasaland's constitutional change. Dixon said that a committee had been formed which had discussed the problem with others outside the Party, including the Governor. A variety of ideas had been forthcoming but everyone agreed that an official majority had to be retained in the legislature until 1965 to encourage the moderate African to enter politics. The number of African seats, Dixon claimed, would have to be increased and an African appointed to the Executive Council. It was recognised that, with the enormous racial imbalance, an increasing tempo of change in world politics and the prospect of a Labour Government in 1960, power was likely to remain in European hands for only five more years. Constitutional change was due in 1960 and could be expected again in 1965. Dixon said that, if the moderate African by then dared not challenge the African Congress, everyone knew

[1] H. Macmillan, *Pointing the Way, 1959–61* (London, 1972), p. 135.

that life would be intolerable for the Asian and European. Even if the moderate African dared, without the support of his fellow Africans, he would be ineffective and a target for intimidation and abuse.

It was only realistic to accept immediately a modest African majority in the legislature, but the UFP, Dixon maintained, could not be expected to concede more for the moment. The Party proposed, he said, a dual roll which would give them 2 125 European voters, 370 Asians and 400 Africans on the upper roll and 15 000 Africans on the lower. The upper roll would elect six Members who could be expected to be Europeans. It would join with the lower roll to elect eight African Members. Fifteen official Members would give the Government a majority of one. The Governor could nominate two Africans to the Executive Council and, perhaps, an Asian or a Coloured as their communities were unlikely to be represented. Two of the non-African elected Members would also be appointed to the Executive Council, Dixon said, but that it was not yet practical for any of the unofficials to accept a portfolio. The Council would thus consist of the Governor, five officials, two European elected Members, two African Members and a nominated Asian.

Dixon explained that the UFP in Nyasaland realised the need for a swift resolution because Banda had promised the Africans constitutional reform in June 1959 which would return an overwhelming majority of Africans to the Legislative and Executive Councils. Banda had said that Nyasaland would secede from the Federation in 1960. Consequently, Dixon felt that it was essential that Banda be discredited by Lennox-Boyd announcing a definite and irrevocable change. Furthermore, Dixon wanted Lennox-Boyd to say that no election would be held until the current Legislative Council expired in May 1960 because Banda might then lose face and might even leave the country. Alternatively, Dixon said, Banda might become more militant and the Nyasaland Government could gaol him and proscribe the Congress.[2]

The Nyasaland Association, led by a lawyer and Member of the Legislative Council, M. H. Blackwood, preferred the common roll, with the qualifications different from those obtaining elsewhere in the Federation, to elect eight non-Africans and eight Africans. These would sit with three Members nominated to represent the Chiefs, the Asians and Coloureds, and 16 officials. Eight double-member constituencies would be delimited for the election. The Executive Council would be the Governor, three officials and four unofficials nominated by the Governor.

Greenfield preferred parity of racial representation and agreed with Dixon that the upper roll should join the lower roll in electing the Africans to give the fairest chance for the development of the party system. The Governor could then consult the leader of the majority party on the appointments to the Executive Council. Unlike the Nyasalanders, Greenfield thought that Africans should receive the portfolios of African education and African agriculture, while the Europeans took those of local government, social services and commerce.[3]

The Nyasaland division of the UFP accepted parity when it conferred with the Nyasaland Association on 30 December 1958. They agreed to eight non-

[2] Welensky Papers, 7/14, f. 359, A. C. W. Dixon to Welensky, 22 December 1958.

[3] *Ibid.*, f. 352, Greenfield to Welensky, 22 December 1958.

African Members who would be virtually elected by the Europeans, and eight African Members in whose election the Africans would predominate.[4]

The UFP appointed a sub-committee which Greenfield chaired on 20 and 21 January. On the second day this sub-committee reported to a joint study group comprising members of the Nyasaland Association, the UFP and African and Asian organisations. Greenfield asked the study group to give Welensky an opportunity to comment on any proposals before they were submitted to the Governor. He then revealed that the sub-committee had agreed that the UFP should take any opportunity to become involved in governing Nyasaland so that, when responsible government was achieved, it would form the first government. The sub-committee proposed to adopt the dual roll and the Federal qualifications. The upper roll would vote with the lower to elect the African Members. The eight non-Africans and eight Africans were accepted as a reasonable representation. Nomination by the Governor was acceptable if the leader of the majority party was consulted. The sub-committee could not agree, however, on the size of the official majority. The meeting discussed these recommendations and then turned its attention to the problem of delimitation and, in so doing, rejected the idea of double-member constituencies.[5]

Greenfield briefed Welensky on the joint study group's findings. Welensky then wrote to Lennox-Boyd, stressing that it was essential that the Nyasaland Government should place itself in the strongest possible moral position. A showdown with Banda was desirable and thus, Welensky insisted, an early announcement on the Nyasaland Constitution was needed to bring matters to a head. It concerned him that the Nyasaland Government was always on the defensive and that, no matter what the Governor said, it was never believed because the African leaders were confident that the British Government would overrule him. Welensky warned that the Federation could not succeed in these circumstances. The situation had arisen, he said, because the Federal Government had been excluded from any contact with the daily affairs of the African and, equally, because the Labour Party had continually indicated that the Federation was not permanent.[6]

The proposal of the joint study group, for eight elected upper roll Members and eight elected lower roll Members and twelve nominated Members of whom a minimum of four would be *ex officio*, worried Dixon as he preferred six upper and eight lower roll Members and an official majority. The joint study group, of course, intended that all unofficial Members of the Executive Council would vote with the Government's twelve nominated Members. However, on 24 January the plan was laid before the Governor as a basis for discussion.[7]

Welensky promptly indicated that he would not commit himself yet to

[4] *Ibid.*, f. 345a, Barrow to Welensky, 31 December 1958.
[5] *Ibid.*, f. 321, Proceedings of the Joint Study Group, 21 January 1959; f. 317, Dixon to Welensky, 24 January 1959; 20/18, f. 393, Greenfield to L. A. Little, 24 January 1959.
[6] *Ibid.*, 7/14, f. 320, Welensky to Greenfield, 23 January 1959; 27/62, f. 48, Welensky to Lennox-Boyd, 23 January 1959.
[7] *Ibid.*, 7/14, f. 317, Dixon to Welensky, 24 January 1959; 20/18, f. 397, Proposals of the Joint Study Group, 24 January 1959.

definite proposals. He and Greenfield thought that the question of whether the nominated group should be all or partly unofficial was worth debating. It depended on whether Lennox-Boyd would insist on there being African ministers. If he did, they felt that he probably would wish the Governor to nominate them. It also depended on the election returning representatives of the Asians and Coloureds. Welensky and Greenfield recognised that they would have to be non-committal about the composition of the Executive Council or risk an argument similar to that over Northern Rhodesia.

The joint study group had proposed that the Parties should produce Coloured and Asian candidates, but the Federal Government rejected specific reference to race. In any case, it felt it was difficult to define Coloured and Asian. Greenfield and Welensky expected Armitage to reject parity because he would see a need for additional African seats, but not for more European ones. They advised the UFP to argue that the current Constitution, with its racial reservation, was nothing more than *apartheid*. By contrast, the UFP could claim that its proposal would cut across race and would include Asian and Coloured candidates for at least two of the eight seats.[8]

Armitage met the UFP on 6 February and reacted as Greenfield had expected. Dixon professed the non-racial aim but Armitage insisted on specifically reserving seats for Africans because Africans might ignore the election or, worse, the upper roll voters might swamp the lower and return eight non-Africans to the lower seats. He doubted that sufficient Africans would enrol. Conversely, the UFP thought that a large number would register if there was a power struggle between Banda and W. M. Chirwa. However, Armitage believed that, if Banda was not confident of winning all eight seats, he would boycott the election.

To ensure African domination on the lower roll, Armitage suggested that the lower qualifications be dropped to an income of £100 p. a. and an educational level of one year of secondary schooling. This, he said, could yield a maximum of 20 000 voters and, if only a third registered, they would still dominate the lower roll. When he asked for a justification for the increase of non-African seats from six to eight, the UFP replied that it would fill the extra two seats with a Coloured and an Asian Member. He pointed out that another party might not have the same intention and asked why Coloured and Asian representation should not be entrenched.

Dixon replied that it was difficult to define a racial group and that it was desirable to abandon the racial approach to politics. Armitage, however, insisted on racial representation. He disliked the idea of twelve official nominated Members because some of the backbench officials never spoke in the debates. He wanted to include amongst the nominated Members a woman and, perhaps, Coloureds and Asians. Dixon acknowledged that this was within Armitage's prerogative and indicated that he was naturally expecting the four elected Members of the Executive Council to accept the Government whip. Greenfield, when reading the minutes of this meeting, despaired of his Nyasaland colleagues because they seemed determined that the UFP's role was one of permanent opposition.

[8] *Ibid.*, 20/18, f. 393, Greenfield to L. A. Little, 24 January 1959.

Dixon said that if the Governor could not secure a majority that way, then he would be expected to nominate up to four more Members. This sparked a considerable argument because Dixon pointed out that Banda's Party might win all eight lower seats and accept the Government whip. Armitage went further and claimed that the extremists might capture seats on the upper roll as well and might refuse to co-operate with the Government. In that case, Armitage asked if the UFP expected the Governor to nominate Members to the Executive Council from outside the ranks of the elected Members. The Party, Dixon said, would not because it was confident that Banda would not capture all the seats. It believed that a Congress Member might support the Government on territorial matters but would defy the whip on Federal issues. Armitage replied that after such behaviour the Member would be forced to resign. The meeting concluded with Armitage saying that he would not accept the UFP's plan unless two seats, one for an Asian and one for a Coloured, were reserved.[9]

Dixon did not press the matter and thus, on 17 February, when it was learnt that, because of the upsurge of violence in Nyasaland, Lennox-Boyd had cancelled an impending visit and was sending instead his Minister of State, Lord Perth, the Federal Cabinet began to prepare its own argument. However, two days later, Dixon produced a draft of a letter to Armitage. Greenfield not only disliked the wording of this, but was worried and confused because, he had learnt, a proposal was also being submitted by the Nyasaland Association on behalf of the existing six Nyasaland European elected Members of the Legislative Council. Amongst these were, of course, members of the UFP, including Dixon.[10]

In this proposal the Executive Council would contain four official Members and two unofficial Members elected by the upper roll and two by the lower. These four unofficial Members would be compelled to accept the Government whip. In the Legislative Council of 24 Members, there would be twelve nominated Members, comprising nine or ten officials plus an Asian, a Coloured and, perhaps, an African woman. The twelve unofficial Members would comprise six elected by the upper roll and six by the lower. The number of lower roll seats would be fixed. However, when the Africans registered on the upper roll exceeded by 25 per cent the votes of the other races on it, three of the nominated seats would be removed and added to the upper roll representation. This process would be continued at 25 per cent levels (namely at 50, 75 and 100 per cent) until all the nominated seats had disappeared. The Legislative Council would then comprise 18 upper and six lower roll seats. At this stage, if a party held a majority of the seats, responsible government would be introduced. However, before then, Africans who were elevated to the Executive Council would receive training in ministerial duties.[11]

As these proposals did not correspond with those of the UFP, which had the support of its Coloured and Asian members, Welensky ordered the

[9] *Ibid.*, 7/14, f. 310, Minutes of a Meeting, Zomba, 6 February 1959.
[10] *Ibid.*, f. 307, Welensky to Greenfield, 17 February 1959; f. 305, Greenfield to Welensky, 19 February 1959.
[11] *Ibid.*, f. 313, Proposals of the Nyasaland Association, 19 February 1959.

Nyasaland division of the Party to adhere to its own proposals. He was annoyed that the apparent double-dealing was giving the impression that the Members of the Legislative Council were being influenced by the Government.[12] In the event, Perth's visit was delayed by Armitage's declaration of a state of emergency to combat the rising tide of violence and civil disobedience. L. A. Little, chairman of the Nyasaland division of the UFP, met Perth on 17 March but was told that constitutional changes could not be considered. Little welcomed this because his Party had always preferred that change be delayed until after the Federal review when the future could be more clearly perceived. Dixon and Blackwood made the same point forcibly. Perth promised to discuss this with Welensky, and on 19 March informed the Federal Cabinet that not only were constitutional negotiations impossible during the emergency, but that he would recommend their postponement until after the review.[13]

Banda and the Congress had been conducting their own negotiations on constitutional change. In June 1958, before his return to Nyasaland, Banda with Chipembere and D. K. Chisiza had met Lennox-Boyd in London to demand, unsuccessfully, an African majority in the Legislative Council, and representation in the Executive Council. The African Members would be elected on the basis of universal adult suffrage. Lennox-Boyd asked them to wait until August when Armitage would reveal his ideas on constitutional revision. Accordingly, Banda warned the Nyasalanders at Chileka airport on his return that he had not brought self-government in his luggage. He lost his temper, however, when a reporter asked him if it would not be better for the Africans to advance economically rather than politically. The frenzy into which he worked himself was almost embarrassing and this was the public face which he was to present at meetings throughout Nyasaland in the coming months. This led his enemies to dismiss him as a mere demagogue, but the hysterical displays were undeniably effective.[14] He had, after all, lived for five years in the Gold Coast and had watched Nkrumah at his rabble-rousing best.

Nevertheless, Banda began his campaign cautiously to secure African majorities in the Legislative and Executive Councils and secession from the Federation. He was not yet asking for complete independence. Welensky and others fervently hoped that Banda would only engender opposition to himself amongst the ranks of the Nyasalanders. They hoped in vain because Banda not only brushed aside established politicians like W. M. Chirwa, T. D. T. Banda and Chinyama, but rendered them politically impotent. At the annual conference of the Congress at Nkata Bay on 1 August, he was not only elected president-general, but secured the right to appoint his own office bearers. He thereupon ignored the older men and surrounded himself with men such as Chipembere, Chiume and D. K. Chisiza whom he made respectively treasurer-general, publicity secretary and secretary-general.

[12] *Ibid.*, f. 299, Welensky to L. A. Little, 25 February 1959.

[13] *Ibid.*, f. 282, Little to Welensky, 17 March 1959; 20/1, ff. 162–164, Minutes of a Meeting with Lord Perth, Federal Cabinet Room, 19 March 1959.

[14] P. Short, *Banda* (London, 1974), pp. 88–89; Welensky Papers, 42/15, f. 89, Fedinform, Zomba, to Fedinform, Salisbury, 6 July 1958; ff. 86–87, D. Cole to Welensky, 9 July 1958.

Then, believing that organisation was the most effective weapon in his arsenal, Banda reorganised the Congress and set about ridding it of its considerable debts. Copying Nkrumah's use of the "verandah boys", the young unemployed, and of women, Banda formed Youth and Women's Leagues on the well-tried totalitarian principle that they would prove to be more militant than the adult men.

Once elected, Banda toured northern Nyasaland eliciting support, decrying amongst other matters, the "stupid Federation" of the Europeans from which he was determined that Nyasaland would secede. As Philip Short has revealed, Banda received the mass adulation with mixed feelings but was grateful at least for the confirmation of the success of his leadership. The outward display of bombastic emotion might have covered his uncertainties, but, when out of the glare of publicity, he was unfailingly courteous, humble, rather shy, yet nonetheless shrewd.[15]

When Armitage failed to reveal his plans in August, Banda vented his venom on the leading Asian association, the Asian Convention, for its temerity in suggesting that Nyasaland should adopt the Tanganyikan model which provided parity of representation for Africans, Asians and Europeans. Banda warned the Asians to stay out of politics or risk trade boycotts.[16]

Armitage remained silent on the Constitution but, on 24 October, Banda granted an interview to the Secretary for African Affairs, John Ingham. He demanded that the Legislative Council should be expanded to accommodate two officials, six elected non-Africans and 32 Africans elected by universal adult suffrage. Little progress was made but they did discuss other matters such as the official discouragement of the Chiefs from participating in the affairs of the Congress, and the prosecution of people who defied the law relating to good agricultural practices. Banda preferred that people should be persuaded, rather than compelled, to practice good husbandry. Ingham stated that as the Chiefs were responsible for law and order in their areas, the Government would not countenance their participation in politics. Although Banda pointedly referred to the use of non-violence to gain his aims, he indicated that a constitutional compromise was possible.

Ingham arranged a meeting for Banda with Armitage on 30 October as well as an opportunity to address the heads of departments on the complaints which he had against them as a result of his tour. However, before either of these could be held, "The Clocktower Incident" occurred and drastically increased racial tension.[17]

On Sunday, 26 October, after Banda had played with crowd emotions at his weekly meeting, excited Africans, waiting for buses near the Clocktower in Blantyre, stoned passing cars, slightly injuring two European women, damaged shop signs and menaced Asians. A Congress official succeeded in restoring order and the Police Mobile Platoon, which was standing by, was not needed.

The incident and the lack of official reaction thereto brought a storm of protest from the local Europeans and their Press. Blackwood called for the

[15] Short, *Banda*, *op. cit.*, pp. 90–93.
[16] Welensky Papers, 42/15, ff. 79–80, FISB Report, 11 November 1958.
[17] Short, *Banda*, *op. cit.*, pp. 93–95.

banning of the Congress and warned that, if the Government would not protect its people, they had to protect themselves. Dixon was more restrained and attributed the incident to a few extremists. Banda apologised but exonerated the Congress from any blame. This and the Government's claim that the incident was so trivial that intervention was unnecessary, brought a fresh deluge of protest, and henceforth the nerves of the Europeans were on edge.[18]

Banda had a cordial meeting with Armitage on 30 October but little progress was made because clearly the excessive demands of the Congress could not be entertained. Banda, however, hinted that he might not insist on universal suffrage and declared that he was not anti-European and had been waiting to be approached by the European politicians. It was his intention, he said, that the Europeans would be unaffected by the attainment of self-government and he would recruit more for his civil service. Banda's meeting with the heads of departments, to which he brought Chiume and Chipembere, was equally unproductive because it was clear that nothing would be done about his complaints.[19]

The new temper of the moment, however, was forcefully demonstrated by the vigorous manner in which the police dispersed the crowds that had gathered outside the meetings. Eleven days later the Nyasaland Government warned that public reaction to these incidents was such that it was compelled to stamp out lawlessness and would use Federal resources if necessary. These had been offered recently by Welensky and, in September, the Federal Army had demonstrated its ability to reinforce local forces by air-lifting 500 men of the Royal Rhodesia Regiment to Nyasaland for a week's manoeuvres. Banda criticised the Government's reaction at an amiable meeting with the Deputy Chief Secretary, P. Youens, on 21 November, and denied that he was responsible for the violence after his meetings because he advocated non-violence. He thought that the police were being provocative, but Youens denied that they were and asked him to make his audiences understand that violence could not be tolerated.[20]

The victory of the UFP in the Federal general election served only to disappoint Banda, even though he contributed to that victory by ordering his followers to boycott it. He had hoped that the Dominion Party would erode Welensky's power and thus reduce his chances of securing dominion status for the Federation. The post-election activity of the UFP in Nyasaland and the obduracy of the Government, convinced Banda and his lieutenants that greater pressure, even contravention of the law, was required to effect the changes they sought.

This mood was enhanced by that prevailing at the "Freedom Conference" in Accra in early December where Banda, Nkomo and Kaunda heard Nkrumah call for a fight to end colonialism by 1960. On his way home, undoubtedly inspired, Banda was delayed in Salisbury because the Nyasaland Government did not want him to return at a weekend and spark off a riot. Banda's fury was intensified by the Federal customs choosing to spend an

[18] *Ibid.*, pp. 96–98; *Report of the Nyasaland Commission of Inquiry*, Command 814 (London, July 1959), pp. 28–29.

[19] Short, *Banda*, *op. cit.*, p. 98.

[20] *Ibid.*, p. 99; Command 814, *op. cit.*, p. 30.

hour examining the documents which he carried. In a fine temper, he spoke at a meeting on the next day, 21 December, in the Highfields African township of Salisbury. Opening with a bellow of "Kwacha, Freedom, To Hell with Federation", he denounced moderation because moderates had never achieved anything in history. Africans had to be prepared to suffer imprisonment for their beliefs. He was, he said, ready to die for them. When he left Highfields for the airport the next day, he was seen off by an excited crowd and he concluded, with some justice, that he had rocked Salisbury from its political sleep.[21]

The Southern and Northern Rhodesian Governments responded by banning Banda from their soil, and Welensky declared in his New Year's message that trouble-makers would not be tolerated. Banda retorted that this was being done because he had "spoiled their natives for them". Shortly afterwards Chipembere and M. Sipalo of Northern Rhodesia were also declared prohibited immigrants in Southern Rhodesia. The Southern Rhodesian ANC immediately organised meetings to protest against the bannings.[22]

While Banda was away in Ghana, the disobedience campaign in Nyasaland had spread. The Government responded by taking powers to control crowds and to punish the stoning of vehicles. Banda returned to aggravate the situation with speeches demanding African domination. He proposed to embrace Communism if it would serve his purpose[23] and alarmed the Rhodesians who were watching the growing Soviet interest in Africa as unrest spread across the continent. The Belgian Congo was experiencing its first riots and thus the menace seemed closer to home. Communist infiltration and subversion had been studied in some detail by Welensky and his Government, and they had discovered that Russia had reconciled herself to a period of African capitalism after colonialism and before the Communist solution could be implemented. Her tactics would be to manipulate the African nationalist movements, foment industrial unrest, construct "front" organisations and use external and, apparently, non-Communist propaganda.

Welensky had therefore prepared a scheme for the defence of Africa south of the Sahara by the Western Powers and, in September 1958, had sent an official to London to explain it. The official had returned despairing of the *laissez-faire* attitude of Whitehall. Undeterred, Welensky had raised the matter with Macmillan when they met in London in November 1958. Macmillan, however, had replied evasively and did nothing.[24] He was, of course, by then questioning the future of the British presence in Africa and was undoubtedly determined not to become involved in its defence. One can only speculate on what might have happened if Macmillan had heeded Welensky's words.

Although his public posture was uncompromising, Banda told Callaghan in early January that he would try to secure a common sense constitutional

[21] Short, *Banda*, *op. cit*., pp. 99 & 104–105; *The Rhodesia Herald*, 22 December 1958.
[22] Short, *Banda*, *op. cit*., p. 106; *The Sunday Mail*, 4 January 1959; *The Nyasaland Times*, 6 January 1959; *The Bulawayo Chronicle*, 19 January 1959; *The Rhodesia Herald*, 21 January 1959; *African Weekly*, 21 January 1959.
[23] Short, *Banda*, *op. cit*., p. 106.
[24] Sir Roy Welensky, *Welensky's 4 000 Days* (London, 1964), p. 110.

solution. Indeed, he had already met Youens on 2 January and had indicated that he was willing to negotiate on his proposals. He did so even though he made constant references to the possibility of his imprisonment. He continued to ask for an African majority in the legislature but denied that this would be a form of self-government because he expected the Governor to retain his veto. Moreover he was prepared to consider a larger official presence in the legislature and would contemplate something less than universal adult suffrage. Asked by Youens if he would reject any Government proposals, Banda replied that it would depend on their nature. Though he and Youens failed to agree on anything, Banda indicated that he would welcome discussion with Armitage and Dixon.[25]

A meeting with Armitage and Dixon was arranged for 20 January in Zomba, but before then Banda addressed a meeting of his Women's League in Limbe on 16 January, and the tone rather than the content of his speech inspired the audience to block the nearby road and stone passing cars. When he arrived for the meeting with Armitage and Dixon, he found that the police had arrested 36 of the 40 women who had gathered to greet him and who had refused to disperse. Of the arrested, only four were charged with unlawful assembly and even these were later acquitted.

At the meeting Banda insisted on an African majority in the Legislative Council although he was vague on the precise number of seats. However, he said he would accept parity in the Executive Council because, to balance his five Africans, he proposed three officials and two elected non-Africans. Although it was pointed out to him that the will of the African majority would prevail, he would not agree because the Governor would retain his veto. He was unmoved when Armitage reminded him that the veto was rarely used. After two hours of discussion the meeting ended with Armitage convinced that it was pointless attempting to negotiate because progress was impossible unless Banda had his way.[26]

Banda and Chipembere thereupon spoke at a public meeting. Banda counselled patience because the problem was still being explored. He was intent on securing an African majority in the Legislative Council because it was there that laws were made; laws such as the agricultural rules and those that allowed 50 women to be arrested for waving at him when he passed. With much emotion he pointed out that no one was arrested in London for waving at the Queen. Nevertheless, he said, it was the legislators, and not the police who applied the law, who were to blame.

Mrs Rose Chibambo of the Congress followed with a tribute to the gallant arrested. Then Chipembere launched into an emotional tirade challenging the Government and demanding that the crowd should secure the immediate release of the arrested women. The crowd of some 500 responded by rushing to the police station and stoning its protective cordon of the Mobile Platoon. The Riot Act was thereupon read, and the crowd driven off with tear-gas and a baton charge. This was the first time that the Congress executive had directly inspired a riot.[27]

[25] Short, *Banda*, *op. cit.*, p. 107; Command 814, *op. cit.*, p. 42.
[26] Command 814, *op. cit.*, p. 43.
[27] Short, *Banda*, *op. cit.*, p. 107.

Welensky had already reviewed the preparedness of his forces. On 19 January he told the officers commanding the Federal Army and the Royal Rhodesian Air Force to expect serious trouble in Nyasaland within the next three months. The Nyasaland Government, he believed, could nip the trouble in the bud but would not do so because the Governor would first have to consult the Colonial Secretary. Welensky wanted to be able to reinforce Armitage at a moment's notice and planned to alert the regular and territorial units for air-lifting to Nyasaland.[28]

Nevertheless, Welensky believed that the situation could be contained, and it amused him, because he thought that they were panicking, when on 21 January the Dominion Party demanded the break-up of the Federation. The defeat of the UFP over the Northern Rhodesian Constitution seemed to the Dominion Party to herald a new British approach which doomed the Federation in its current form. Certainly, the DP said, Western civilisation in the area would be sacrificed to the detriment of both races. The UFP had failed to produce a plan for 1960 and therefore the DP advanced its own because the Federation and its peoples could not be allowed to drift any nearer the review without guidance. The cold facts, the DP claimed, were that the British Government was bent on achieving political equality between the races in the short term and ultimately African domination. Thus, as African states were an inevitable feature of the Federation, the DP resuscitated its "Central African Alliance" which envisaged separate black and white states under a bi-cameral dominion parliament. Welensky wondered why the DP did not realise that, even if the British Government accepted the Alliance, it would still allow the black states to become independent. Thereafter, he thought, the black states would accept some form of Russian aid which would place the future of the Europeans in jeopardy.[29]

The Nyasaland African Congress also felt that a confrontation was at hand because it was clear that negotiation would yield nothing. An opportunity to discuss other plans had already been created as, in early January, D. K. Chisiza had suggested to Banda that there should be an extraordinary conference of the Congress to pass a vote of confidence in his leadership which was under attack by W. M. Chirwa and others. It would also be possible, Chisiza had said, to discuss new ways of raising money if Southern Rhodesia banned the Nyasaland Congress and thus interfered with the flow of subscriptions from members working there. Banda had agreed, and two delegates from each branch were summoned to Limbe on the weekend of 24 and 25 January. Banda, who left most of the routine decisions and work to others, decided only to attend that part of the conference which debated his leadership. It is likely, as Short has pointed out, that his absence from the rest of the proceedings was deliberate because of the subjects discussed. In any case, Banda had lost his ability to speak freely in the vernacular. It is also probable that his three young, ambitious lieutenants did not tell him everything.[30]

The agenda of the conference was discussed at two meetings of the exe-

[28] Welensky, *4 000 Days*, *op. cit.*, p. 115.
[29] *The Rhodesia Herald*, 21 January 1959; Welensky Papers, 27/98, f. 35, Welensky to T. Arnott, 23 January 1959.
[30] Short, *Banda*, *op. cit.*, p. 108.

cutive committee on 22 and 23 January and Banda attended neither. At these the question was asked as to what action would be taken if the Government's constitutional proposals were unacceptable or if Banda were arrested. The answer was non-co-operation which meant the boycott of elections, of trade with Europeans and Asians, the non-payment of taxes, and the refusal to become members of district councils. It did not encompass sabotage or physical injury.[31]

(Present at this conference was George Nyandoro of the Southern Rhodesian ANC who had come to Blantyre to meet Chipembere and M. Sipalo of Northern Rhodesia. This was necessary because the recent ban on the latter two by Southern Rhodesia had prevented a meeting of the secretaries of the Congresses of the three territories for the purpose of drawing up an agenda for a "Summit Conference" in Blantyre on 21 February to plan and co-ordinate action. Sipalo did not arrive. Consequently, after attending the conference of the Nyasaland Congress in Limbe, Nyandora and Chipembere travelled to Lusaka where they met Sipalo and Mukupo, the secretary-general of the Northern Rhodesian ANC. No "Summit" resulted, but it left the Governments in no doubt that they were facing concerted action.[32])

The conference of the Nyasaland Congress met three times: in the morning of 24 January at a hotel in Limbe, when organisational matters were discussed; in the afternoon at Ndirande, when Banda won the vote of confidence in his leadership; and, on the next day, in the bush outside Limbe. The second meeting was public, but the first and third were secret and great care was taken to ensure that no informers were present and no one was allowed to take notes. Consequently, it is not known precisely what was discussed. However, it is clear that the conference thought it necessary to appoint Y. K. Chisiza, a former inspector in the Tanganyika Police and brother of D. K. Chisiza, as bodyguard to Banda. The Congress was also instructed to draw up a "black list" of "stooges", of unco-operative Chiefs, civil servants and others who would be punished at a later date. The method of punishment was not specified but a variety of suggestions like banishment and killing was advanced. This theme of violence featured in the discussions on other matters. There was, however, no unanimity because, while some of the delegates spoke of the possibilities of assassinating the Governor and senior officers in the police, army and district administration, others advocated non-violence. It was decided at least that the pattern of protest would encompass civil disobedience and acts of sabotage which would not injure. Illegal meetings would be held and the application of unpopular laws would be resisted by all means. Violence would be condoned if there was sufficient provocation, but submission to arrest was regarded as an honourable alternative. Indeed, the leading members of the Congress considered their imprisonment to the extent of discussing the procurement of legal representation in Britain.

Rain terminated the meeting in the afternoon and undoubtedly the delegates left somewhat confused as to the precise intentions of their leaders. The delegates returned to their homes and briefed their branches on what had

[31] Command 814, *op. cit.*, p. 49.

[32] *Southern Rhodesia Review Tribunal (Preventive Detention (Temporary Provisions) Act 1959): General Report*, CSR 27-1959 (Salisbury, 6 May 1959), p. 20.

happened. Excited crowds gathered outside the meetings on the first day; cars were stoned and a baton charge by the police, after dispersal orders had been ignored, resulted in 21 arrests. The atmosphere was clearly highly charged.[33]

Chipembere and others were pleased at the result because it brought a prospect of real action. The subsequent Commission of Inquiry, chaired by Sir Patrick (later Lord) Devlin, declared that no report was made to Banda on the discussions or the decisions of the conference. It is odd, nevertheless, that the Commissioners should have believed that the lieutenants whom Banda had appointed had not told him something of the proceedings, even if they wrote nothing down. Armitage was to comment on this, and Short goes further because he is confident that oral reports were made, though he gives Banda the benefit of the doubt as to how much he heard of the talk of violence.[34] In any case, Banda was inevitably being forced to use violence to achieve his ambition.

The conclusions of the meetings were soon sufficiently widely known for the Press to predict a campaign of, at least, disobedience.[35] Information soon filtered through to the Nyasaland Special Branch on what had been discussed; and an example of what was received later was quoted in full by the Devlin Commission in an appendix as a translation of Chinyanja notes on the meeting of 25 January. It read:

"1. Chirwa, T. D. T. Banda, Matenga etc. want a way in which to destroy Dr. Banda.
2. A person to accompany the Dr. everywhere. He was found K. Chesenza. He is our watchman.
3. If our Dr. were caught what would be do [*sic*].
   A. Word will issue from the Central Body telling all
   B. people to start war after two days.
   C. Digging up roads, destroying anything belonging to Europeans.
   D. Not to pay taxes.
   E. To hit Europeans or cut throat.
4. Hold meetings without permission.
5. End European agriculture. Hit or tie up Kapitaos [foremen]. Forestry Kapitaos are not wanted.
6. The people who discredit Congress should have their names written down.
7. There will be cycles for the leaders of Congress so that they can visit Branches.
8. If a fellow member of Congress is arrested by the police we must send a telegram to Box 30, Blantyre to advise the leaders there.
9. If a person is arrested because of Congress the case must be taken to senior Europeans.
10. Those who have maize must keep it carefully. When the real fighting starts they must send it to the towns to their fellows and Congress will pay.

[33] Command 814, *op. cit.*, pp. 49–52.
[34] *Ibid.*, p. 52; Short, *Banda*, *op. cit.*, p. 110.
[35] *Rand Daily Mail*, 2 February 1959.

11. If the Governor does not agree to what we have given him do not go to work and do not pay taxes.
    A. 32 people in Leg. Coy.
    B. On the Finance Committee there must also be Africans.
12. Our African Police must not wear puttees as putties [*sic*] make the legs thin.
13. Why did the Europeans raise the tax when people could not even manage to pay 17/6.
14. When a Congress member is caught by the police you must fight without fear.
15. If one of our people is arrested phone Box 30 Blantyre quickly.
16. If non-members of Congress do their own will leave them to themselves.
17. We must visit our Chiefs.
18. In 1953 we would have received self-Government but false leaders spoiled things there in London. They put us on trial to see if it is true. Chirwa and his fellow are there."[36]

This and seven independent reports from different parts of Nyasaland led the Special Branch to conclude that the Congress had decided that Chiume, D. K. Chisiza, Chipembere and Mrs Rose Chibambo would assume the leadership on the arrest of Banda and would designate a day, called "R-Day", when violent action would be taken. In preparation for "R-Day", criminal elements, including murderers, would be recruited for their peculiar skills. They would be assisted on the day by the inmates of Zomba Prison who would be released by the staff. Telecommunications, road and rail bridges, airfields, fuel dumps and the main power station at Blantyre would be sabotaged. District and provincial commissioners would be assassinated, as would police officers and other officials. The European and Asian populations would be murdered and their bodies mutilated. In Zomba the Governor would be killed by his servants. The African police and the soldiers of the King's African Rifles would murder their officers and join the insurrection with their arms and ammunition. "Quislings", including W. M. Chirwa, would be murdered before "R-Day".[37]

All this took time to filter through and the Nyasaland Government did nothing at first because little extraordinary happened aside from Banda's weekly speeches, which were not particularly seditious. However, events soon began to fit the pattern. Illegal meetings and processions became widespread, particularly in the Northern Province where there was strong allegiance to the Congress but pitifully few policemen. Demonstrations occurred, and on 11 February two European veterinary officers were assaulted when they were about to give evidence against Africans for transgressing the agricultural rules. As a consequence, 20 Africans were arrested. Other arrests led to the stoning of the police station in Karonga on 15 February and a riot in Kota Kota two days later. These and other incidents, combined with fresh evidence

[36] Command 814, *op. cit.*, p. 146.
[37] *State of Emergency*, Command 707 (London, 23 March 1959), p. 8; Welensky, *4 000 Days*, *op. cit.*, pp. 118–119.

on Congress intentions, convinced the Commissioner of Police to advise Armitage to act.[38]

The Devlin Commission would doubt the authenticity of the "murder plot", but it would concede that by mid-February the Nyasaland Government had to act or abdicate. Welensky, by 16 February, knew something of what the Nyasaland Special Branch was uncovering, and the rising tide of violence led him to place the Federal Army on stand-by and to invite Armitage to confer. Armitage declined because he had made his own preparations and, in any case, he believed that the Congress would stay its hand until either the constitutional changes were announced or Banda was arrested. Armitage did not want to precipitate anything which might lead to the cancellation of Lord Perth's visit at the end of the month. Thus he proposed to meet Welensky on the arrival of Perth.[39]

Welensky thought it politic to keep R. A. Butler informed, and described to him that day, 16 February, the worsening situation in Nyasaland. The law was openly being flouted, but Welensky accepted that Banda was only probing to see how far he could go with Armitage. Welensky claimed that, having listened to one of Banda's speeches, he was reminded of Hitler in 1938. It was distressing, Welensky said, to see the Nyasaland Government forced onto the defensive, with the Congress undermining everything that Armitage might say by claiming that they could go over his head to the British Government or at least to the Labour Party. This action, he claimed, was ruining the Federation and was a direct consequence of the exclusion of its Government from involvement in the daily life of the African. Welensky confessed that he had not wanted Nyasaland in the Federation, but currently found himself one of the few who insisted that it should not secede lest 2 500 000 people be abandoned to Banda.

Reporting on current progress, Welensky described a recent successful, if unpleasant, debate in the Southern Rhodesian Parliament in which Whitehead, at Welensky's insistence, had amended the law with regard to liquor and Africans so that hotels in the white areas could serve them. Welensky also revealed that the security situation in Southern Rhodesia had deteriorated as the African nationalists exerted increasing pressure. He was confident, however, that Whitehead could rectify the situation.[40]

Butler replied immediately and asked Welensky to keep their correspondence confidential to allow him freedom of action. Lennox-Boyd had privately announced that he would not stand again at the next general election and Butler explained that this was due to overwork. Butler promised to speak to Lord Perth before he left.[41]

On 18 February, the Nyasaland Government revealed to the Federal Government what it had uncovered of the Congress's plans. Welensky immediately opened a Federal operations room in Salisbury to monitor events continuously. The next day there was further rioting in Karonga, and on 20

[38] Welensky Papers, 42/38, f. 129, Welensky to R. A. Butler, 16 February 1959; Short, *Banda*, *op. cit.*, p. 111; Command 814, *op. cit.*, pp. 55–56.
[39] Welensky, *4 000 Days*, *op. cit.*, p. 118.
[40] Welensky Papers, 42/38, f. 129, Welensky to Butler, 16 February 1959.
[41] *Ibid.*, 42/38, f. 127, Butler to Welensky, 20 February 1959.

February Africans armed with pangas put the Fort Hill airfield out of action, menacing the staff, stoning a police detachment and blocking the runway after the latter had left. At the same time there was a Congress-inspired incident at the great Church of Scotland Mission at Livingstonia which was not particularly serious but nevertheless frightening for those involved. A report was also received that two Africans were overheard to say in Blantyre that Sunday, 22 February, would be "R-Day". In this atmosphere, Lord Dalhousie chaired a meeting of the heads of the Governments convened principally to consider action to deal with the deteriorating security situation in all three territories.[42]

In Southern Rhodesia the growing confidence of the ANC had led to widespread unrest. The encouragement of the flouting of the law, intimidation, open and secret threats of murder and of boycotts, the ridiculing of officers of the government and of tribal authorities, the extortion of money and other support, the claims that the ANC was more powerful than the Government, had convinced Whitehead and his Cabinet, in December 1958, that they would have to act.[43]

In Northern Rhodesia, after a bitter quarrel within the national executive of the ANC in October 1958, Kaunda, who had recently been inspired by a visit to India, led a revolt against Nkumbula. Consequently Kaunda, Simon Kapwepwe and M. Sipalo formed the Zambia African National Congress in the belief that, if Northern Rhodesia were to become self-governing and secede from the Federation, the nationalist movement had to be well organised, highly disciplined and led by self-sacrificing men. Nkumbula and his ANC certainly did not fit this description. The ZANC soon began to erode Nkumbula's country-wide support. However, its decision to boycott the general election drew the Government towards Nkumbula to encourage him to work within the Constitution and not to frustrate its attempts to enfranchise Africans. This was rather fruitless because, although Nkumbula moderated his tone, the registration of voters never came up to expectation. This was partly due to apathy, but also to the militant frame of mind in which Kaunda had returned from the Accra Conference and the support he gathered thereafter. Banda did not assist Nkumbula's reputation by telling Nkrumah that he had gathered from a senior Northern Rhodesian official that Nkumbula had secretly accepted the Federation.

Later Nkumbula's reputation was further dented by apparent Government help in obtaining the signatures of the Chiefs in his constituency. Although by February there was little increase in the – by then – normal amount of unrest in Northern Rhodesia, inflammatory speeches by Kaunda and Sipalo so alarmed the Europeans that three branches of the UFP cabled Lennox-Boyd on 20 February demanding action to silence them. Kaunda had said that his ZANC would warn the Government three times before taking action on any contentious issue. If, as a result, his party was banned, it would operate underground until independence was achieved.[44]

[42] Welensky, *4 000 Days*, *op. cit.*, p. 118; Command 814, *op. cit.*, pp. 56–58; Welensky Papers, 18/38, Red Minute Book, FISB Report, 20 February 1959.
[43] R. Blake, *A History of Rhodesia* (London, 1977), p. 324.
[44] D. C. Mulford, *Zambia: The Politics of Independence, 1957–1964* (London, 1967), p. 73 f.

These events were reviewed at the heads of Governments meeting in Salisbury on 20 February, while C. W. F. Footman, the Chief Secretary of Nyasaland, warned Banda in Zomba that, unless the situation improved, the constitutional negotiations with Lord Perth might be postponed or abandoned.[45] The impending visit by Perth was announced that day.

In Salisbury, the first subject discussed was whether the Governor-General could act as the Governor of Southern Rhodesia when William-Powlett retired later in the year. This was an obvious economy, but the northern Governors opposed it. Benson remarked that his Africans already reacted suspiciously when the Federal Chief Justice, Sir Robert Tredgold, deputised for Dalhousie.

Welensky quickly drew attention to the security situation by asking Armitage what had been done to protect women and children in Nyasaland. Armitage replied by reading from a security report, but unfortunately the minutes do not recall what it contained apart from indicating that there was adequate prison accommodation. He explained that a declaration of a state of emergency was necessary because otherwise he could only restrict a person to an area. He acknowledged that, once the emergency ended, all detainees would have to be released.

Whitehead said that his Government had no powers of arrest without declaring a state of emergency, and he was worried his ANC might exploit the stripping of Southern Rhodesia of troops for Nyasaland. He believed that the Congresses were co-operating to keep the troops in Southern Rhodesia and, consequently, he thought that the two Rhodesias should detain their subversives before the security forces departed to Nyasaland. His difficulty was to find a public justification for a state of emergency.

Benson said he had no such difficulty as he intended to take action against Kaunda and Sipalo under the Penal Code. He believed that his territory was under control. Indeed, Nkumbula was being so restrained that Benson had warned his officials not to be lulled into a false sense of security. He was confident that he could avoid any trouble before and on polling day, which was 20 March.

The meeting decided that, because of the action to be taken, Welensky should chair an inter-governmental committee on which Whitehead, Benson and Armitage would sit. Action was to be taken against Sipalo and Kaunda by 23 February, and Whitehead would declare a state of emergency on 27 February. Armitage would do what he wished thereafter, and the Federal prisons in Nyasaland would be prepared for a large influx of prisoners.[46]

The next day, 21 February, Welensky announced that reinforcements from the King's African Rifles and the Depot, the Royal Rhodesia Regiment, had been sent to Nyasaland. Proclaiming this as evidence of Federal determination to assist the territorial Governments to maintain law and order, he was confident that there were adequate forces for the task.[47]

There seemed that day to be confirmation of Whitehead's belief in a

[45] Short, *Banda, op. cit.*, p. 113.
[46] Welensky Papers, 8/34, f. 1, Minutes of the Heads of Governments' Meeting, Salisbury, 20 February 1959.
[47] *Ibid.*, 18/38, Red Minute Book, Press Statement by Welensky, 21 February 1959.

Federation-wide conspiracy, because the Northern Rhodesian Government discovered that an inter-Congress meeting would be held at Fort Jameson on 25 February. Armitage immediately asked Benson to prevent the entry of the Nyasaland delegates. Benson replied that he would if Armitage insisted, but preferred not to interfere because, within two days, he would know what had happened at the meeting. Benson had been about to arrest Sipalo, but for the same reason decided to wait until after the meeting.[48]

On 22 February a meeting of the heads of the armed services and the police in Zomba decided that the situation in the Northern Province was such that two platoons of the Tanganyika Police, already at the border, should cross it and secure the Fort Hill airfield. There was also concern for Blantyre and Limbe where there had been widespread rioting. There, Chipembere had urged the mobs to go "the whole hog", depicting the European as the enemy. The Press did not print this statement because it was too inflammatory. Chipembere ended his speech by confirming that he was attempting to provoke his arrest. Y. K. Chisiza told a crowd that London was shaking and that evidence of this was that normally Lennox-Boyd would merely announce a constitutional change but, fearing bloodshed, he was sending out Lord Perth to persuade Banda to calm his people down.

Despite these speeches and the disturbances, the Nyasaland Government did not believe that "R-Day" was imminent, and did not want to declare a state of emergency until the Congress leaders had done enough to warrant their arrest. It was decided that they would be given ten days' grace to accomplish this. There was, as yet, no plan to evacuate Europeans from the outlying areas, but Armitage had hired a Beaver aircraft for that purpose.[49]

The next day heavy rioting cut the communications between Blantyre and Limbe. On the morrow, 24 February, police fired on Africans rioting in Lilongwe, killing two and wounding one. Another African was killed at Balaka attempting to free prisoners. Banda circulated publicly a letter he had written to Armitage claiming that the importation of troops from Southern Rhodesia was evidence of a European attempt to dominate. He warned that if his people were shot, beaten or imprisoned, nothing would be solved.[50]

Into this state of anxiety stepped John Stonehouse, the British Labour MP, to tell a cheering meeting of the Southern Rhodesian ANC that, if his Party won the next British general election, it would not grant independence to the Federation unless the majority of its people wanted it. He believed that it would be a "terrible" mistake to give total power to a small minority before all had been given an opportunity to express their opinion. He declared that the whole Labour movement, representing millions of British people, was vitally interested in African problems. The Labour Party insisted, he said, that everyone should enjoy the human rights and dignities for which it had fought for a hundred years. He stated that it supported the Africans in the struggle against poverty. The Africans might have applauded Stonehouse, but he was not welcomed by the Europeans at that volatile moment.[51]

[48] *Ibid.*, Message from Benson, 21 February 1959.
[49] *Ibid.*, Report by Wing-Commander Wilson, 22 February 1959.
[50] *The Rhodesia Herald*, 23 February 1959; Short, *Banda, op. cit.*, p. 114.
[51] *The Rhodesia Herald*, 23 February 1959.

Simultaneously, two battalions of territorials were mobilised and sent to training camps outside Salisbury, Bulawayo and Umtali. Armitage appealed that day, 24 February, for more reinforcements because he was unable to curb the Congress. This, he claimed, made it difficult for him to reassure militant Pressmen and the public, and created the worst possible atmosphere for Perth's discussions with the Congress.[52]

Welensky immediately asked Lennox-Boyd to postpone Perth's visit to prevent the Congress from being able to claim credit for any changes. To deal with "self-acclaimed kings" seemed to Welensky the worst possible basis for a constitutional review. He suggested that a salutory lesson would be dealt if it were forcibly stated that negotiations would be impossible until the situation returned to normal. Armitage also cabled Perth, asking for the postponement and warning him that a state of emergency was imminent.[53]

As planned, at midnight on 25 February, Whitehead announced the state of emergency, justifying it as necessary to prevent the ANC from emulating the example of its counterpart in Nyasaland. The ANC was banned and hundreds of its members were detained in a dawn sweep.

Nkomo was abroad, but Whitehead reported to a meeting with Welensky, Footman, Brigadier Long, Commander of the Federal Army, and Air Vice-Marshal Jacklin of the Royal Rhodesian Air Force that the sweep was almost totally successful. Footman then announced that Perth's visit had been postponed indefinitely, and warned that the security forces could do little more than keep Blantyre secure. He revealed that crowded meetings throughout Nyasaland were being informed of the programme of violence, including assassination, which would be implemented on Banda's arrest. The Congress appeared to be contemplating action between 7 and 9 March. Therefore, he said, time was short if trouble was to be nipped in the bud.

Welensky asked for confirmation that all control had been lost in the Northern Province, but Footman replied evasively that it was important to restore morale. He believed that it might be possible to obtain police reinforcements from Northern and Southern Rhodesia and reduce, perhaps, the force levels in the Northern Province for re-distribution in the Central and Southern Provinces. Blantyre and Limbe would require strong forces.

Welensky produced an article in the *Daily Express* in which Donald Wise stated that he had never been in a territory where the civil servants and the civilians displayed so little confidence in their Government, and Footman had to acknowledge that this was true and that the patience of the Europeans and the Asians was becoming exhausted. His Government had thought, he said, that the trouble would start in the towns, but the Congress had realised that the Government was weakest in the districts which meant that equal attention would have to be paid to the urban and rural areas when remedial action was taken. A complication was that the 1 050 prisoners in Zomba were known to be planning to break out of their none-too-secure gaol.

All this, Footman maintained, meant that action was necessary between 3

[52] Welensky Papers, 18/38, FISB Sitrep, 23 February 1959; f. 67, Armitage to Welensky, 24 February 1959; *The Rhodesia Herald*, 24 February 1959.

[53] Welensky Papers, 18/38, f. 34, Welensky to Sir Gilbert Rennie, 25 February 1959; Welensky, *4 000 Days*, *op. cit.*, p. 122.

and 7 March and already a plan was being formulated. However, he warned, the task was difficult and strong reinforcements were needed. Footman was fearful that when the army was used it always shot to kill because it assumed that, as the civil power had lost control, the sternest and quickest measures were required to restore order. As shooting to kill was unnecessary, he preferred police action with the military in support. It was the way to achieve success, he said, while reducing bitterness to a minimum. Welensky was content because, if his army was forced to take over, he had no intention of using anything but minimum force and would not give orders to shoot to kill. Clearly he was forgetting, or did not know, that while the Federal Army was trained to use minimum force in the form of controlled fire, like all armies it always shot to kill unless otherwise instructed. Footman concluded with the chilly warning that, if action was not taken within seven days, the Congress would act with the likelihood of success.

The meeting discussed the movement of troops, including dispatching an infantry company to Kariba where a thousand Nyasaland construction workers were on strike. Footman proposed that the emergency should be declared on 3 or 4 March, but stated that the timing would depend on the level of reinforcement. However, the Air Officer Commanding was confident that, weather permitting, sufficient men could be transported.

Footman confirmed that Banda would be imprisoned even though it was Chipembere, in the main, who was the author of the plans and the promoter of the agitation. Welensky was worried that the announcement of the postponement of Perth's visit would spark off even more serious trouble and he proposed to move the troops as quickly as possible. He urged the use of the army and, because they were threatening to interfere, demanded that Julius Nyerere of Tanganyika and Tom Mboya of Kenya should be declared prohibited immigrants. However, Footman said only that the delegation from the Tanganyikan African National Union, which had arrived in Karonga, would be expelled.

Welensky agreed that the Tanganyika Police should be used to reinforce Karonga and to re-occupy Fort Hill. As the meeting closed, there was a testy exchange between Footman and Chetwynd-Palmer of the Northern Rhodesian Government over a request from Footman for two platoons of the Northern Rhodesian Mobile Police. Benson was reluctant to release them because he feared the effect that the troubles in Nyasaland, the Congo and Kariba could have on the emotional atmosphere of his election. Footman said that the platoons were only required for a week, and somewhat acidly remarked that, in any case, if the situation in Nyasaland could not be controlled, the Northern Rhodesian Government would be forced to reconsider the request. Shortly afterwards Home offered a British battalion from Kenya, but Welensky thought that his forces were sufficient.[54]

The announcement, on 27 February, that Perth had cancelled his visit to avoid provoking further incidents, indicated that a declaration of a state of emergency in Nyasaland was imminent. Further proof was provided by the continual arrival of troops at Chileka airport and an increase in the reconnais-

[54] Welensky Papers, 18/38, Red Minute Book, Minutes of a Meeting, Salisbury, 25 February 1959.

sance and "showing the flag" flights by the Royal Rhodesian Air Force. The massive reinforcement of the overseas Press corps was sufficient indication in itself. Nevertheless, while *The Nyasaland Times* questioned the seeming hesitation of the Government, Armitage informed the Press on 2 March that it would probably be unnecessary to declare an emergency.[55] He, of course, was avoiding giving the Congress any hint of his real intentions. However, the European women and children had been brought into Blantyre for protection, and units of the army, the Nyasaland, Northern Rhodesian and British South African Police were quietly reinforcing the outlying districts.

Incidents continued, and on 28 February it was reported that Chipembere had been stirring up Fort Johnston while Banda was alleged to be urging the rural population around Blantyre and Limbe to send in able-bodied men armed with knives, sticks and stones to fight the "Bwanas".[56] Whatever the truth of this, on 1 March, the Johannesburg *Sunday Times* revealed in an exclusive interview that Banda expected to be the first African Prime Minister of Nyasaland. It recorded that the interview was interrupted by a tirade from Banda on letting Welensky loose with his tear-gas and aircraft - "Let him kill my people" - as it would avail him not. There would be no compromise. Banda said he would have settled before Welensky chose to terrorise his people. Now, however, Banda declared that he would not even try to prevent the coming storm. Indeed, claiming that he could not countermand orders he had not given, he emphatically exonerated himself and the Congress from any responsibility for the disorders, maintaining that they were purely spontaneous. However, Carel Birkby, the interviewer, commented that the informed blamed the Congress and that they claimed that the northern disturbances were designed to draw troops from Blantyre and Zomba. Banda rejected this and the suggestion that the show of force had disrupted the implementation of the master plan.

When Birkby asked how Nyasaland would fend without Federal aid, Banda replied that the Nyasalanders had survived before and would starve just to be free. They would strive until they were liberated, but would still welcome Europeans in their new state.

Birkby sought clarification on violence and asked if Banda would advise the South African blacks to use it to gain their freedom. Banda repeated that he had never advocated it and had only worked constitutionally. However, he would not say whether he approved of violence because he did not know what he would do under provocation. He maintained that his people had been severely provoked by the authorities. He believed he had total support and declared that, if the Federation was broken up, he would accept self-government under the Colonial Office provided that there was an evolutionary formula for independence within the Commonwealth. The interview over, he shouted to the waiting crowd that "they" could arrest him, kill and bury him "here". In response the crowd groaned with dismay and then yelled with delight when he added that, nonetheless, his ghost would haunt "them" and still destroy the Federation.

[55] Short, *Banda, op. cit.*, p. 115.

[56] Welensky Papers, 18/38, Red Minute Book, 28 February 1959; f. 34, Nyasaland Sitrep, 28 February 1959.

The Federal Government thought that the arrival of Stonehouse in Nyasaland on 3 March – on the morning of the declaration of the emergency – would not assist Armitage and took action. Stonehouse had annoyed Field and others by telling his African audience in Salisbury to "Hold your heads high, this country belongs to you". He had, like Mrs Castle, tested the colour bar in Meikles Hotel in the company of nationalists and had visited the African townships without the necessary authority. He had arrived ostensibly on private business, having advertised in the *The Times* for commissions, but had asked for, and had been granted, the facilities normally accorded to "fact-finding" parliamentarians. He did not explain that Christian Action had tasked him to survey Federal conditions. Christian Action was an organisation which was regarded by Rhodesians with some suspicion, not just because of its left-wing stance against the whites in Southern Africa, but because it had in its ranks proclaimed humanists, agnostics and communists.[57]

Stonehouse also did not disclose that, like Callaghan, he came commissioned to write for *Reynold's News*, and was accorded privileges which were not usually granted to journalists. His actions in Southern Rhodesia provoked a considerable, if unnecessary, uproar in the local Press. Thus his presence on the eve of both the Southern Rhodesian and Nyasaland emergencies was unwelcome even though he advocated non-violence.[58]

When Stonehouse reached the Copperbelt, the Federal Government decided, with the concurrence of the Colonial Office, to ask him to leave after his tour of Northern Rhodesia and not to visit Nyasaland. Governments do not, normally, disclose their motives for such action and he could not be told that an emergency was about to be declared. On the evening of 28 February, the Chief Immigration Officer handed Stonehouse, at his hotel in Kitwe, a notice from Barrow, as Minister of Home Affairs, which said that his personal safety could not be guaranteed and, as his presence in Nyasaland was likely to lead to serious breaches of the peace, he should leave without going there. If Stonehouse would not accept this, he would be declared a prohibited immigrant and would be expelled.

Stonehouse refused to co-operate and, after waking the local District and Provincial Commissioners, declared that he would not change his plans. On 2 March he telegraphed Lennox-Boyd to protest and then travelled to Lusaka to be entertained, as planned, by Benson. The latter informed him that Lennox-Boyd had replied asking him not to go to Nyasaland. Stonehouse was telephoned by Hugh Gaitskell, the leader of his Party, asking him to return for an emergency debate on Nyasaland on 4 March. However, he was also informed by a London *Daily Herald* reporter that Armitage had just said that, if Stonehouse arrived, he would be accorded the normal privileges and facilities.[59]

Stonehouse decided to ignore a public declaration by Barrow that his visit

[57] *Ibid.*, 42/60, f. 3, Welensky to D. Taylor, 20 March 1959; J. Stonehouse, *Prohibited Immigrant* (London, 1960), pp. 167–169; House of Commons *Hansard* (London), Vol. 601, Col. 526, 4 March 1959; H. Soreff and I. Greig, *The Puppeteers* (London, 1965), pp. 32–33.

[58] House of Commons *Hansard* (London), Vol. 601, Col. 526, 4 March 1959.

[59] Welensky Papers, 18/38, Red Minute Book, 28 February 1959; Stonehouse, *Prohibited Immigrant, op. cit.*, p. 192 f.

would end on the morrow. On 3 March Benson reported to Welensky that he had done his best to persuade Stonehouse to leave and had offered to fly him to Dar-es-Salaam. However, Stonehouse had been assured by Mrs Castle of the support of the Labour Front Bench and the Conservative backbenchers and had refused to leave under duress. He thereupon had attempted to take the scheduled flight to Nyasaland that day, but it had been cancelled because of the declaration of emergency. When he had refused to board the Northern Rhodesian Government aircraft waiting to take him to Dar-es-Salaam, the Federal immigration officials had been forced to arrest him. Stonehouse had appealed to the two Northern Rhodesian policemen present but was ignored because immigration was an exclusively Federal responsibility. As he was hustled out to the tarmac, he had offered token resistance until out of sight of the Press. He had been escorted to the Northern Rhodesian aircraft and was flown to Tanganyika.[60] The Federal Government publicly denounced his display for the Press, but Stonehouse replied that he had merely shown that a British parliamentarian could not be evicted from a British territory without a struggle. Welensky replied that Stonehouse revelled in notoriety but would not gain the support of his responsible colleagues.[61] To Rhodesians Stonehouse was little better than an agitator stirring troubled waters without any intention of sharing the consequences, and it is not surprising that they were to look somewhat askance at the appointment by Harold Wilson to ministerial office of Callaghan, Mrs Castle and Stonehouse.

The uproar over Stonehouse continued in the British Parliament and Press until, on 13 March, he appeared in the Commons and gave a factual account.[62] He reserved a more romantic version for his book, *Prohibited Immigrant*. Callaghan and others persistently demanded not only explanations from the Government, but sought to influence the Speaker to rule that there had been a breach of privilege because a British MP had been arrested on other than a criminal charge when visiting a British territory. The Speaker refused because immigration was exclusively Federal and Stonehouse had been visiting privately and could not claim any immunity from the law.

In the debates, the Government steadfastly confirmed the Speaker's view. Railing against it, the Labour MPs called the Federal Government "Fascists", and described Welensky as irresponsible and unworthy to be a Commonwealth Prime Minister.[63]

In the early hours of 3 March Armitage declared his emergency, and Banda and hundreds of his followers were promptly arrested. Little resistance was encountered. Banda and his principal colleagues were flown to detention in Southern Rhodesia. As the Devlin Commission has revealed, the special constables, who effected the arrests, were rather over-enthusiastic, but they were barely trained, ill-disciplined and had been living in fear of their lives for the past weeks.[64]

[60] Welensky Papers, 18/38, f. 97, Benson to Welensky, 3 March 1959; Stonehouse, *Prohibited Immigrant*, *op. cit.*, p. 197.

[61] *The Rhodesia Herald*, 4 March 1959.

[62] House of Commons *Hansard* (London), Vol. 601, Cols. 1613–1617, 13 March 1959.

[63] *Ibid.*, Col. 40 f., 2 March 1959.

[64] Command 814, *op. cit.*, pp. 93–99.

The arrests led to attempts to release prisoners and, inevitably, there were incidents. The most serious was at Nkata Bay where the M. V. *Mpasa* was in port receiving prisoners. A crowd, bent on freeing the prisoners, milled around most of the morning while the District Commissioner tried to dissuade them. Then, bearing him with them, they advanced on four rifleman and a sergeant of the Royal Rhodesia Regiment who held them at, or just outside, the dock gates for over an hour. The District Commissioner had called for reinforcements from Mzuzu, 30 miles away, and knew that a platoon of the King's African Rifles was on its way. It arrived after the Riot Act had been read three times in the vernacular and the crowd had pushed the riflemen back to a point where the road into the docks broadened out so that they could no longer contain the crowd.

At that moment, the crowd which had whipped itself up into a frenzy, bellowing for blood, stormed the four riflemen. The reply was a short burst of controlled fire at point-blank range. The riflemen fired 18 rounds while the sten-gun of the sergeant jammed after nine. The 27 rounds killed 20 and wounded 28. The moment the crowd stopped advancing, the sergeant, a man of considerable military experience, ordered a cease-fire.[65] The author, as a young rifleman, witnessed this tragic affair from a low cliff-face, 30 yards away, where he was guarding the approach to the Boma (the district administration's offices) which had housed the European women and children before they were evacuated by ship's boat.

The collection, transportation and detention of prisoners continued for the next few days and incidents became increasingly infrequent as peace returned everywhere. The Northern Rhodesian and Tanganyikan Police were withdrawn after a week and, on 24 March, the territorial battalions were stood down, and the regular units gradually returned to their normal duties.

The Federal electorate was undoubtedly pleased by the resoluteness of the action by the Nyasaland and Federal Governments, but it provoked a storm of protest from the British Opposition, the British Press and Churches, particularly the Church of Scotland. In the Commons, hints from Lennox-Boyd at a murderous conspiracy were frankly disbelieved. Fenner Brockway, for one, claimed that Welensky and Whitehead were set on a "showdown" with the African nationalists before Labour came to power.[66]

Callaghan, on 3 March, found it sinister that, less than 24 hours previously, Armitage had declared that a state of emergency was unnecessary. Armitage, of course, had merely withheld his hand from the Press, but Callaghan wondered if he had abdicated to the Federal Government. Callaghan was also amazed that Lennox-Boyd, in maintaining that action was unavoidable, was not ashamed to camouflage the truth which was that a few panic-stricken people had precipitated the trouble. This baseless remark, particularly when made in the safety of Westminster, was to anger the beleaguered European in rural Nyasaland.

Led in this manner, the Labour Party concentrated on the alleged forcing of Armitage's hand by the Federal Government. Although Lennox-Boyd declared that Armitage alone had asked for reinforcements, Mrs Castle

[65] *Ibid.*, pp. 111–120.
[66] House of Commons *Hansard* (London), Vol. 601, Col. 218, 3 March 1959.

claimed that there had been Colonial Office pressure to bow to Federal demands. The detention of Banda in Southern Rhodesia, outside British jurisdiction, was depicted as most offensive. (Banda, of course, was not being held in a Southern Rhodesian prison *per se* because the Federal Government controlled all prisons in the territories. Furthermore, being Federal, these prisons were outside British jurisdiction wherever they were located.)

Callaghan refused to accept what he called the tired, old excuses which had been produced for the Cyprus emergency, that power-drunk, mad nationalists had to be curbed. He disagreed that Armitage had been forced to change his mind so quickly. As the Federal Government was trying to hamstring any British Government before 1960, it was imperative to reform Nyasaland so that the bulk of the population would be represented at the Federal review. Lennox-Boyd reminded the Labour Party that it had first advocated federation and that Attlee had pledged its assistance in ensuring success. He revealed that plans had been discovered which had included murder and that the Nyasaland Government had been forced to call for reinforcements. He was answered by howls of derision from the Labour Party who had heard of murder plots in every colonial emergency. Lennox-Boyd continued and indicated that there was time enough to negotiate a constitutional advance when order had been restored because the life of the Legislative Council only expired in 1960. He believed, however, that there were elements who would seek to prevent the return of tranquillity.

A. Bottomley demanded a Royal Commission of Inquiry, while Callaghan suggested a Parliamentary Commission.[67] The British Government remained convinced that an emergency was justified, but would shortly institute a Royal Commission.

Banda, on 4 March, sought the permission of the superintendent of his prison in Gwelo to retain the services of the Southern Rhodesian advocate, H. Chitepo, to make strong representations against the allegations of Lennox-Boyd on the murder plot because he and the Congress were being defamed. In fact, Chiume, who had escaped arrest by being in London, had already done this. Banda must have gathered the bones of the allegations from the Press, and these were fleshed out for him on 7 March by Commander T. Fox-Pitt, Welensky's antagonist of old. Fox-Pitt indicated that the British parliamentarians, Press and people disbelieved the massacre story. Indeed, he said, they objected to the possibility of being dragged into another scandal similar to that of Cyprus. He felt that the actions of Welensky could always be explained by his desire to be his people's hero.[68]

Fox-Pitt did not satisfy Banda as, on 9 March, he asked the Hon. David Astor, editor of the *Observer*, to ensure that the British people did not believe the allegation, which he attributed to one of his enemies, because neither he nor his colleagues had considered massacring anyone, even in the last resort.[69]

That nothing more was released immediately about the murder plot drew criticism from the Federal Cabinet special propaganda committee because it

[67] *Ibid.*, Col. 217 f., 3 March 1959.
[68] Short, *Banda, op. cit.*, p. 119; Welensky Papers, 20/11, f. 270, Dr H. K. Banda to Superintendent, Gwelo Prison, 4 March 1959; 42/15, ff. 58–68, T. Fox-Pitt to Banda, 7 March 1959.
[69] Welensky Papers, 20/11, f. 251, Banda to D. Astor, 9 March 1959.

gave Chiume and the Labour Party the opportunity to cast doubts on it. Welensky heeded this and, on 10 March, said publicly that the plans for the uprising in Nyasaland were inspired by the Accra Conference and he wished to register a protest that a Commonwealth government should welcome the evolution of such plans on its soil. On 17 March he announced that something on the massacre plot would be published soon.[70]

Welensky left that to Armitage who on the next day described to Lennox-Boyd the plot, the events and the reasons for his action. This dispatch was printed on 23 March as a White Paper to answer the critics of the murder plot. Armitage firmly maintained that, being responsible for law and order, his Government was obliged to act or condone intimidation and violence. He traced the developments before and since Banda's arrival, recalling the increasingly threatening behaviour from August 1958. After Accra came the threats of destruction, open hostility to Europeans and Asians, and the breaking of the law on processions. There was the riot at Zomba and the meetings in and outside Limbe when the "R-Day" plans were discussed.

Armitage, enumerating these plans, said that he could have only ignored them at the risk of the most serious consequences. In any case, events began to corroborate them with the flouting of the law, attacks on police stations, the building of a thousand or more roadblocks and other acts of sabotage. The events in Karonga forced him to ask the other Governments for assistance. Simultaneously, he revealed to them what he had discovered and, when fully reinforced, declared his state of emergency. He believed that he had anticipated the full implementation of the Congress's plans although some of them were realised and there was further rioting, sabotage and attempts to release prisoners. Because of the last, he had asked the Federal Government to hold the more important prisoners elsewhere. He concluded by saying that no governor liked declaring states of emergency but the events spoke for themselves.[71]

While public attention was drawn to Nyasaland, the Northern Rhodesian Government was hard at work discrediting the Zambian African National Congress's boycott. It was also, as David C. Mulford has revealed, planning its banning. A report on its meeting on 2 March furnished the evidence which the Government needed for a ban under the Societies Ordinance. The report purported to reveal plans for the assault and, if necessary, the assassination of the African candidates and voters. The Northern Rhodesian Government knew, too, of the meeting with the Nyasaland Congress at Fort Jameson. Accordingly, Benson issued the Safeguard of Elections and Public Safety Regulations on 11 March and, in the early hours of the next day, Kaunda and the leading members of his ZANC were arrested and restricted to rural areas. The ZANC was banned.

When announcing this, Benson referred to the plan at Accra for joint action, but exonerated Nkumbula's ANC from involvement in it. Describing the clandestine activity of the ZANC, Benson claimed that its reign of terror was worthy of the Mafia's "Murder Incorporated". The ban, he maintained,

[70] *Ibid.*, 25/201, ff. 35 & 38, Minutes of the Federal Cabinet Special Propaganda Committee, 6 & 11 March; *The Rhodesia Herald*, 11 & 18 March 1959.
[71] Command 707, *op. cit.*, p. 1 f.

like the action in Nyasaland, would anticipate any implementation of the plan and, in fact, his general election was held without incident, with the heavy polling by the Africans contrasting with the — albeit normal — apathy of the Europeans.[72]

It is known that the Federal and territorial Governments agreed to co-operate and that Benson would act last. However, Mulford asks if this was not part of longer term strategy to render still-born the aspirations of the African nationalists in the interests of the preservation of the Federation. He believes that the main impetus might have come, not from Welensky as was suspected, but from the British Government.

Unlikely as this might seem because of the local antagonism towards the Colonial Office, Mulford possesses a letter from Benson to that office complaining of Welensky's tactlessness and indicating that Lennox-Boyd had been pressing for the declaration of an emergency rather than the mere banning of the ZANC. Benson was referring to Welensky's public assertion in Kitwe, on 10 March, of the Federal determination to obtain independence in 1960. This infuriated Benson because he believed that Africans, who would be otherwise relieved at the removal of the ZANC from the political scene, would be driven to sympathise with it. At best, he felt, the Africans would be unsettled because they were frightened of an independent Federation. Welensky had said this even though he knew precisely when Benson intended to act and would be responsible for any bloodshed. To Benson the Kitwe speech was "criminal", "sadistic and evil" because Welensky had ample opportunity to make it after the banning and before 20 March.

Mulford believes that both the Federal and the British Governments thought that African nationalism could be dissipated by a co-ordinated effort.[73] Unfortunately, however, there is no confirmation of a joint Anglo-Federal effort against African nationalism in the Welensky Papers. The earliest attempt at co-ordination recorded is the head of Governments meeting on 20 February 1959, and there is no indication of a British involvement. This does not conform with Benson's protest to the Colonial Office.

In any case, the Federal Government remained at loggerheads with the British Government over the Northern Rhodesian Constitution. On 7 March Welensky had protested to Home, at Greenfield's prompting, over the difficulties imposed on the aspirant candidates in the six rural constituencies who had to secure the sanction of two-thirds of the resident Chiefs. Consequently on nomination day two constituencies lacked candidates because of the impossibilities of the task, even though in one, Luapula, ten candidates had sought to be accepted. There had also been the rejection by the Chiefs in other constituencies of the UFP's candidates. Rain, rivers, mud, indifference and influence had fulfilled the predictions of Welensky and Greenfield.[74]

Thus Welensky asked Home for the elimination of the Chiefs' endorsement. Nkumbula, separately and publicly, described his trials in obtaining sufficient certificates from the Chiefs in his constituency. He was experien-

[72] Mulford, *Zambia*, *op. cit.*, pp. 94–96.
[73] *Ibid.*, pp. 104–105.
[74] Welensky Papers, 20/4, f. 172, Welensky to Home, 7 March 1959; 20/5, ff. 34–35, Greenfield to Welensky, 3 March 1959.

cing difficulties despite rather obvious assistance from the Government. He said that he had been forced to walk and cycle for over 600 miles. (It would be interesting to know if any British politician would have accepted such a task before he could begin to campaign to win the allegiance of the voters.) None of the candidates was helped by being allowed 40 days instead of the promised 60, and this drew a protest from Roberts on 13 March. The depth of Welensky's own feeling is illustrated by a comment by him to Gore-Browne that he had once credited the Colonial officials with a sincerity of purpose, even if it was misguided, but that currently he was convinced that they were nothing but "bloody evil".[75] This is hardly illustrative of any accord with the Colonial Office.

Lennox-Boyd replied to the protests; defending the requirement on the Chiefs and refusing to suspend it on inadequate evidence. He argued, moreover, that the rains had been abnormally heavy. He left Greenfield, at least, amazed at his obstinacy in the face of the facts.[76]

On 12 March it was announced that Lord Perth would visit the Federation on 17 March. By 16 March, however, Southern Rhodesian politics were also attracting attention. The police were called that day to the Athenaeum Hall in Salisbury to control 5 000 Africans who were attempting to get in to listen to an address by Todd. Todd was forced to hold five successive meetings and this was an illustration of the sway which he and no other European politician had gained over the Africans.[77]

Welensky consoled himself with the degree of African support which his Party was gaining in Northern Rhodesia as the tempo of the election increased. He also knew that no one in power could compete with Todd's "airy-fairy" promises which the UFP believed would bring bitter disillusionment. Welensky preferred other methods of winning support, and that month appointed J. Z. Savanhu as a Parliamentary Secretary of Home Affairs.[78]

Todd told his meetings that it was imperative to implement a genuine partnership within months rather than years. He also attacked vigorously the current programme of Southern Rhodesian security legislation which was to induce its most virulent parliamentary critic, Dr Ahrn Palley, to resign the Dominion Party whip that very day. R. J. Knight, the Southern Rhodesian Minister of Justice, had introduced the Unlawful Organisations Bill with the design of outlawing the four territorial African National Congresses on Southern Rhodesian soil. The Bill would empower the Governor to ban by proclamation any organisation which endangered public safety or sought to promote the aspirations of certain external Communist-inspired bodies. The proclamation would be laid before Parliament and would only have force during the life of that Parliament. It would not, however, be capable of being

[75] Welensky, *4 000 Days*, *op. cit.*, p. 135; Welensky Papers, 24/73, ff. 155–157, Welensky to Gore-Browne, 8 March 1959.

[76] *Ibid.*, 7/10, f. 486, Lennox-Boyd to Benson, (undated); f. 487, Greenfield to Welensky, 22 March 1959.

[77] *The Rhodesia Herald*, 12 & 17 March 1959.

[78] Welensky Papers, 31/54, f. 43, Welensky to S. Udwin, 23 March 1959; 42/60, f. 53, Welensky to D. Taylor, 20 March 1959.

challenged in the courts. The justification for this was that the MPs were to be entrusted with determining the manner in which Southern Rhodesia would be governed. The police would not require warrants to enter any place where it was suspected that meetings of unlawful organisations were being held. Any office bearer or member of an unlawful organisation would be presumed to be such until it was proved otherwise. Any one present at a meeting of a banned organisation or possessing its documents would also be automatically assumed to be a member unless he could prove he was not.[79]

This was a radical departure from hitherto accepted principles of justice, of the dogma of "innocent until proved guilty", and was repugnant to many Southern Rhodesians. It provoked considerable public reaction despite Whitehead dwelling on the events in Accra, the Nyasaland "murder plot", and the co-ordinated efforts of the African National Congress to undermine the Federation. He reminded Southern Rhodesians that hitherto the law had proved inadequate in combating subversion and he believed that drastic changes were required because of the Cold War and the pressures being brought to bear on Southern Africa. He could not allow Communist organisations to flourish. Palley agreed with the motive but not the means.

The Bill was passed but public pressure, which included representations from the Bar Association and members of the University College and the Churches, forced Knight to withdraw a Preventive Detention Bill on 24 March. Under this not only would the Governor have the power to detain, during his pleasure, persons who were likely to endanger public safety, but five MPs, and not the judiciary, would be entrusted with the periodic review of the detentions. Knight conceded that the Bill had been too hastily drafted and that, if amended, it might become unwieldy.[80] Nevertheless, the Bill was merely re-drafted and would inflict further political trauma.

Perth visited the three Nyasaland provinces, inspected the detention centres, watched the security forces at work, and spoke to a wide cross-section of the population. Leaving for Lusaka on 18 March, he said that he had found nothing but rejection of the Federation amongst even the most responsible Africans.[81] On 19 March he flew to Salisbury, lunched with Welensky, and then met the Federal Cabinet. He repeated to them that he had discovered a widespread, unreasoning fear of the Federation, but that his visit had been only exploratory and he would recommend that his Government postpone constitutional change until after the review in 1960. He announced that, because his Government was anxious to dispel doubts in Britain, Armitage's dispatch of 17 March would be published as a White Paper, and that a commission of inquiry (the Devlin Commission) into the events in Nyasaland would be appointed. Neither of these proposals would have surprised the Federal Cabinet as not only had they been discussed with Armitage, but they had been leaked to the Press.

Perth reported that in Northern Rhodesia he had noted a widespread relief at the banning of the ZANC – a surprising conclusion after a day's visit – and he was impressed at the manner in which the election was being conducted.

[79] SR *Debates* (Salisbury), Vol. 42, Col. 2460, 17 March 1959.
[80] *Ibid.*, Col. 2717, 24 March 1959.
[81] *The Rhodesia Herald*, 19 March 1959.

affirmed his Government's determination to preserve the Federation, vealed that it believed that it should join the Federal Government in ling British doubts by appointing a Royal Commission on the Federation's future.[82]

His statement on the intention to preserve the Federation rings hollow now that Macmillan has told how he concluded on 5 March: "It looks as if the Federation plan, although economically correct (since Nyasaland is not "viable") is regarded with such suspicion by "advanced" native opinion as to be politically unacceptable."[83] This lead his Cabinet to decide, on 17 March, that a Royal Commission was necessary. As in the case of the Devlin Commission, Welensky was not taken by surprise because, in a personal message on 13 March, Home had argued that this was necessary to tie the hands of the Labour Party should it be victorious in the general election that year. Home believed that the Commission would solve many of Welensky's problems, and as he expected it to be at work by September 1959, he suggested that the difficult negotiations on the terms of reference should begin immediately.[84]

Perth said that there was such anxiety about Federal affairs in Conservative and Church circles that it was necessary to allay it. It was equally important to persuade the Labour Party not to make its threatened firm commitment to the break-up of the Federation. The issue of the Federation's future had to be removed from the British election. Ignorance had to be dispelled and a Royal Commission would keep discussion within proper bounds. To encourage Federal acceptance, Perth claimed that British colonial policy was being revised and a halt was being called to the rapid advancement of colonial territories to independence. In Tanganyika, for example, a long-term programme was being proposed. These words were also to ring hollow.

Welensky replied that, while his Government wished to assist the British with their problems, it could not accept a commission of inquiry. The reasons, he said, were various. A primary one was that, as the UFP alone was devoted to the preservation of the Federation, nothing should be done which would encourage its rivals, lest closer ties between Southern Rhodesia and South Africa result. Because of its unyielding opposition to the Federation, this danger was enhanced, he claimed, by the proposed inclusion of the Labour Party in the commission. Local European opinion would resent the Federation being on trial when it had achieved so much despite the factors which gave it a poor start. The proposal meant, he said, that the review would be removed from Federal hands and entrusted to a body without direct responsibility. It would be regarded by African opinion, Welensky concluded, as a concession to violent pressure or at least interference by London on their behalf.

The Federal Ministers believed that the commission would only highlight the Federal shortcomings. They thought that British opinion was not open to conversion, and doubted that the commission would remove the Federal issue from the British election.

[82] Welensky Papers, 20/1, ff. 162–164, Minutes of a Meeting between the Federal Cabinet, Lord Perth and M. R. Metcalf, 19 March 1959.

[83] Macmillan, *Pointing the Way*, *op. cit.*, p. 135.

[84] Welensky, *4 000 Days*, *op. cit.*, pp. 137–138.

Perth, by contrast, continued to maintain that, because of the record of the Federation, only good could come out of a full-scale inquiry if the members of the commission and its terms of reference were carefully chosen. He was confident that they could agree because they shared a common objective. He revealed Welensky's alternative suggestion that the review should be advanced. The British Government had considered this carefully, he said, but had decided that it would not serve as well as the commission. Thus Perth urged the Federal Government to accept the latter.

Perth departed to speak in the debate on the Federation in the House of Lords on 24 March. Fenner Brockway had continued his attack, and used a meeting of his Movement for Colonial Freedom on 19 March to answer a challenge by Welensky to re-assert his belief in a conspiracy inspired by Welensky and Whitehead. Brockway noted there had been no violence in Southern Rhodesia, yet Whitehead had declared a state of emergency with full Federal sanction. Simultaneously, Brockway commented, Armitage had said that a similar declaration was unnecessary in Nyasaland. Brockway found an unlikely ally in the *Daily Express* in deducing that thereafter Welensky had pressed the Colonial Office to force Armitage's hand. After all, Brockway argued, Welensky had, in 1953 and 1957, spoken of Boston Tea Parties. Brockway then read from a letter from Banda which denied the intention to murder, and which told of occasions when Africans had merely disarmed Europeans and delivered their weapons to the police. Banda claimed that he, himself, had handed in one gun. Brockway pleaded with the Africans not to use force, and urged Welensky to see that his policy was of greater danger to the Europeans than to the Africans in the Federation. Thus, Brockway said, Welensky had to abandon his policy.[85]

Home and Perth were joined by Butler in urging Welensky to accept the preparatory commission for the Federal review. Welensky replied to Butler saying that he respected his expert appraisal of British public and parliamentary opinion and would weigh his request and reply later. However, Welensky was in a critical mood and told Butler that he thought the Conservatives could have answered the Labour Party more forcefully. It concerned him, he said, that Callaghan, Griffiths and Brockway had been prepared to attack him, a prime minister of a Commonwealth country, in the manner that they did. He explained that he had challenged Brockway to repeat his accusation outside Parliament, because in Rhodesia it would lead to a charge of criminal libel. He believed that, if Griffiths or Callaghan became Secretary of State, the Federation was doomed unless they changed their attitude. He knew "that the declaration of a republic here would no doubt cause some bloodshed, but I believe nothing like as serious as some people think. The only way to prevent it, of course, would be for Britain to send troops here, and that I think is extremely unlikely. All this is dreadful to contemplate but I can tell you that people here are beginning to think along these lines and that's what disturbs me."[86]

Butler replied immediately, saying that he had discussed Federal problems at length with Home, Lennox-Boyd and Perth. They recognised the immen-

[85] Welensky Papers, 42/36, f. 4, Federal Information Department Report, 20 March 1959.
[86] *Ibid.*, 42/38, f. 124, Welensky to Butler, 20 March 1959.

sity of Federal problems but believed they had persuaded Gaitskell on the need for an inquiry into the Nyasaland crisis and for long-term preparation for the review. The British Government wanted the Nyasaland commission of inquiry limited to a judge and two assessors but knew that this would only be accepted by the British Parliament if there was a place for parliamentarians on the preparatory commission. Gaitskell had indicated his Party's willingness to serve. However, because of Welensky's warning, the Government would say in the Lords the next day that it was considering, with the Federal Government, the best way to prepare for the review and that undoubtedly the British Parliament would want to be involved. This would allow the details to be worked out while the subject itself was removed from the political arena.[87]

British and Federal officials were also discussing the concept of the preparatory commission. Meeting on 20 March, the British thought the emphasis should be placed on the appointment of the members, leaving the terms of reference vague and general so as not to embarrass the Federal Government. They suggested a membership of ten. Of these, the British would appoint five members including a Northern Rhodesian and a Nyasalander. The Federal Government would appoint three members, and the Southern Rhodesian Government two. The secretariat should be provided jointly by the Federal and British Governments, but no one from the Commonwealth Relations and Colonial Offices would serve. The terms of reference should be to examine Federal and territorial progress since 1953 in the social, economic and political spheres. Then, taking into account the Federal constitutional preamble, the commission would consider and make recommendations on changes to ensure further progress.

Like Perth, the British officials felt that the issue of the review had to be shifted into a neutral arena before the British election lest a Labour Government insist – as Callaghan already had – that there should be a parliamentary commission, the outcome of which could only be embarrassing and unsatisfactory. A further advantage was that the preparatory commission could provide a means of assessing the commitment in the preamble and avoid the need for other methods of weighing public opinion which would be unacceptable to the Federal Government. The British officials, however, thought dominion status was impossible while one or more of the territories came under British jurisdiction.

The Federal officials, needless to say, disagreed with the last because, they argued, if a formula could be found to give Cyprus full Commonwealth status, one could be devised for anything. They did not favour a commission which usurped the responsibilities of the Government, but thought it might be useful if it merely reviewed the facts. They knew that such a commission would find the faults, but believed it would favour the Federation. The Governments could assist by providing factual surveys. If the commission was politically acceptable, the Federal officials decided that its appointment would have to be accompanied by a statement affirming the indestructibility of the Federation. It should also be followed immediately by the review. Happily, the British officials agreed and suggested a compromise formula on

[87] *Ibid.*, 20/13, f. 6, Butler to Welensky, 23 March 1959.

the terms of reference. This would be to review the progress made since 1953 and to consider if it had been hampered in any way by the Constitution.[88]

The officials might have agreed but, on 24 March, Welensky told Butler that he and Whitehead adamantly opposed the preparatory commission because the electorate would believe that they had abdicated from their responsibilities. The Federal Government felt that the commission would merely sit in judgment on all its efforts since 1953. If the British Government insisted that it could solve its own difficulties in no other way, then the Federal Government reserved the right to protest at the inclusion of the British Opposition. Indeed, if parliamentary representation was allowed, then all the Federal political parties would demand places. Welensky therefore asked that the Government spokesmen should only say, when pressed in the debate, that he had been asked about parliamentary representation. He wanted an opportunity to discuss the matter personally and asked if Home could visit him.[89] Home promptly agreed and flew to the Federation a week later.

The House of Lords examined Armitage's dispatch and, predictably, the Opposition disbelieved it. Armitage, of course, had been vague because he could not identify his informants for fear of endangering them. The Labour Peers found it remarkable that, if what Armitage said was true, there had been no murders or attempted murders of isolated Europeans. Banda appeared to them not at all blood-thirsty. As expected, they advocated a parliamentary inquiry, rather than an aloof judicial one, because of the urgent need to restore the shaken confidence of the Africans in the British Government. They demanded the standing-down of the Federal forces - which, like their brothers in the Commons, they labelled "Southern Rhodesian" - and the immediate return of the detainees to Nyasaland as well as their early release. They wanted a new Nyasaland constitution and a clear indication of the Government's attitude to the Federal review.

Describing the security forces as "heavy-handed", the Labour Peers wondered why it was necessary to arrest people for throwing stones at illegal meetings or to shoot them when they tried to release prisoners. Lord Silkin listed statements by Welensky and concluded that the Africans had every reason to fear the Federation and its Government. It was the Labour belief that the confidence of the African had to be won and that subject people had to be given their freedom.

Lord Malvern, who was present, was also attacked by Lord Silkin for saying on previous occasions that there were times when people had to be compelled to comply with policy and that the Federal defence forces might well find themselves in a similar predicament to their counterparts in the American Revolution. Malvern had noted that the British seemed disappointed that there had been no European casualties (there had, in fact, been some who were victims of assault) and Silkin found this remark, and one that the British would be happier if the policy of partnership was implemented with a few European deaths, to be most improper.

The Press reported the debate as reaching a state of "pandemonium" when, unrepentant, Malvern declared that a parliamentary inquiry would be

[88] *Ibid.*, f. 8, Minutes of a Meeting, Salisbury, 20 March 1959.
[89] *Ibid.*, f. 5, Welensky to Butler, 24 March 1959.

the biggest insult offered yet to the British people living in the Federation. He claimed that great damage had been done to race relations by "itinerant politicians", some of whom were paid by newspapers. In his estimation, they had done more harm than Banda. What the itinerant politician did not understand, he said, was that the African was polite and would tell you what you wanted to know. Never one to do things by halves, Malvern pronounced Africans, until they were considerably advanced, to be "all liars". However, he explained that this was a defence mechanism.

If the Lords found these remarks to be offensive, and certainly the Press did, Malvern was only reiterating a commonly-held white opinion in Central Africa. He next criticised Griffiths for frightening the Africans when he toured in September 1951. He described commissions of inquiry as the common way of wasting the taxpayer's money to tell the Government what it wanted to know. He repeated that some seemed disappointed at the lack of European casualties and warned that the future African states would deteriorate rapidly no matter how cleverly their constitutions were worded. It was thus imperative, he said, to educate the Nyasalander in government, and it was a Federal responsibility to see that this was done.

Malvern's fellow Rhodesian peers, the Duke of Montrose and Lord Robins, also spoke. Robins defended the Federal Government, while Montrose advanced the Central African Alliance Plan of his Dominion Party which, he claimed, Banda had found more realistic than anything Welensky had produced.

Lord Salisbury defended the Federal Europeans and claimed that the African National Congresses wanted to frustrate partnership. Others warned of Communist penetration and suggested that the Labour Party had a vendetta against Welensky. Lord Perth said that, leaving the "murder plot" aside, it was clear that the Government had to act. He believed that the unsubstantiated British accusations of a Federal plot had done much harm and had alienated the intensely loyal Southern Rhodesians. He thanked the Southern Rhodesian and Federal Governments for their support of Armitage and praised the troops whom he had seen behaving in an exemplary manner. He had found the detention camps administered by humane men. The situation was under control, he said, and the Federal troops were being withdrawn. He had spoken to many Africans and had discovered how widespread intimidation had been. This, and the aspirations of young men and the fear of the Federation, he claimed, were reasons for widespread Congress support.

Perth avowed that the Nyasaland Government would restore the authority of the Chiefs which had been flouted by the Congress. Simultaneously, the civil service was being Africanised as fast as possible. Perth ascribed the fear of the Federation to the orders preventing the district commissioners from advocating federation in 1951, which had led the Africans to conclude that something had to be wrong. He listed the benefits which the Federation had brought and claimed that the Africans did not understand just how much they could lose. He urged that the Federation should not become a party issue and announced the Nyasaland Commission of Inquiry to which Devlin would soon be appointed.

Lord Home, closing the debate, stressed the value of partnership, the efforts of the Europeans and their sense of fair play. He was convinced that there had been a conspiracy. The Governor had been forced to act because the pursuit of power by other than constitutional means could not be tolerated. The House had to remember, he said, that African affairs could not be judged by the sophisticated yardstick of British society. There had to be time for the partnership to be built.[90]

The long fight over what was to become the Monckton Commission had begun, but Welensky was confident enough to tell the local Press that the recent events had not damaged the chances of a reasonable Federal constitutional advance in 1960.[91] Welensky could console himself with the Northern Rhodesian election results as his UFP had won eleven of the ordinary seats and two of the special seats for Africans, giving it 13 seats. It will be recalled that two special seats had no candidates. Consequently, by-elections would follow. The Dominion Party had won one ordinary seat, the Central Africa Party two (captured by Sir John Moffat and Harry Franklin) and a special seat. Nkumbula had been returned to the single special seat captured by his ANC.

The UFP, however, lacked a majority in the 30-seat house. Analysis later showed that it had attracted the lowest share of the African vote, six per cent, when the DP had twelve per cent. A main reason was that Nkumbula had ordered the African voters to vote for anyone other than the UFP candidate. Contrary to Benson's intention, the ordinary vote had dominated the special constituencies which meant that the men for whom the Africans had voted were not elected. The boycott by Kaunda's ZANC, of course, was partly responsible but, nevertheless, the Africans felt cheated.[92]

The UFP gained because the Constitution prescribed that Benson had to accept the suggestions of Roberts for the holders of portfolios. These were Roberts himself, as Minister of Labour and Mines; E. Carlisle, Minister of Land and Natural Resources; R. Malcolmson, Minister of Local Government; W. Dunlop, Minister of Transport and Works; G. Musumbulwa, Minister of African Education. Benson exercised his constitutional right and nominated E. Mwambwa as Minister of African Agriculture.

With the territorial matters settled for the moment, Welensky could concentrate on Federal affairs, and the preparatory commission in particular.

[90] House of Lords *Hansard* (London), Vol. 215, Col. 204 f., 24 March 1959.
[91] *The Sunday News*, 29 March 1959.
[92] Mulford, *Zambia*, *op. cit.*, p. 98.

CHAPTER TWENTY-THREE

Aftermath of the Emergencies

Commissions of Inquiry, and Argument on the Preparatory Commission, April-August 1959

THE battle over the preparatory or advisory commission, to which Lord Monckton would be appointed, had already begun and would be fought throughout the remainder of 1959. The idea was, as Welensky has described it, "the favourite device" of the British[1], and ultimately, as Lord Malvern predicted and Macmillan has revealed, it told the British Government what it wanted to hear. It was in the argument over its composition and terms of reference that Macmillan out-manoeuvred Welensky to achieve this result.

Home arrived in Salisbury on 1 April and immediately met the Federal Cabinet. He claimed that the great concern amongst the Labour, Liberals and Young Conservatives over recent events in the Federation was forcing his Government to consider taking a greater role in the administration of the northern territories. This could mean curbing Federal involvement in the North. Pressure was also developing, he said, to give the Nyasalanders the option of secession and, if this was conceded, it could not be denied to the Northern Rhodesians. This would result in the disintegration of the Federation. He warned that a real danger was that the Labour Party, with its eye on the imminent British general election, might commit itself to secession. To prevent this, he declared, it was necessary to appoint a dispassionate preparatory commission.

Home felt that the membership of the commission should not be confined to Britain and promised that the Federal Government would be fully consulted. The purpose would be to prove that the Federation was not only succeeding in its aims, but that it was essential. If the commission reported thus, he said, it would have a vital effect on Britain and the Commonwealth. The intention was not to hold an inquest or to apportion blame and the terms of reference could specifically demand that the commission should consider,

[1] Sir Roy Welensky, *Welensky's 4 000 Days* (London, 1964), p. 137.

in the light of progress since 1953, the necessary steps to effect the principles enshrined in the Federal Constitution. This would satisfy moderate opinion in Britain and might win the confidence of the Africans. It would, he said, remove any suggestion of a conspiracy between the Federal and British Governments and provide an opportunity to dispel the ignorance in Britain. Certainly, a full report by the commission would be more widely publicised than anything produced by the Governments. Above all, he believed it would probably prevent the Labour Party from advocating Nyasaland's secession.

Obviously the composition of the commission would have to be acceptable to the Labour Party, Home observed, and this would mean the appointment of at least two Labour members who would probably be Privy Councillors. It would, however, offer the first chance of a bipartisan approach to Federal problems and would, therefore, be an important development which could enhance the possibility of a successful review in 1960. Home believed that the leaders of the Labour Party were anxious to end the controversy over the Federation and that it was imperative to exploit the opportunity. In any case, he said, events in the Federation were affecting the chances of the Conservatives winning the election, and it was essential to establish the commission before then. Thereafter, it was most unlikely that a Labour Government could upset it. There was the risk that the commission could make recommendations that were inconvenient. However, he felt, it was small compared with those to be run if there were no commission because then the political attack would continue until the review when the secession of Nyasaland would be the main issue. The Labour, Liberal and Conservative Parties, in any case, would want advice on the advancement of the northern territories before they considered the review's results. If there were no commission, these Parties would demand a parliamentary one for the examination of northern affairs. As this alternative commission was bound to impinge on Federal issues, Home avowed that the British Government was anxious to avoid being forced to appoint it.

However, the Federal Cabinet rejected the commission mainly because the African would conclude that all he had to do was to riot and a commission would be sent from Britain to try the merits of his case. Nevertheless, the Federal Cabinet admitted that it would have to co-operate if threatened with the appointment of the alternative parliamentary commission. Hindsight reveals that this was a fatal admission because Macmillan would choose to interpret it as graceful acceptance.

Home, nonetheless, was forced to hear the criticisms of his idea which had already been made to Perth. The Federal Ministers believed that the commission would prejudice the review and take matters which rightly belonged to the Governments out of their hands. To them, the chief danger of the moment was not the pace of advancement, but the failure to allow the African time to digest the changes.

When they suggested that Federal public opinion would reject British interference, Home objected because they were forgetting the extent of British involvement in the northern administrations. He countered the argument, that the commission would be more acceptable if the date of the review were brought forward, by saying that he had considered this and the other alternatives but had found that none would achieve the vital bipartisan involvement. He agreed with the Federal Ministers that the outcry in Britain was a product of the purely territorial affairs of Nyasaland, but claimed that it illustrated the need to educate the British public.

When Welensky queried the ability of a Labour Government to break up the Federation, Home correctly replied that a British Government could do anything by legislation even though the necessary mechanical process might present formidable difficulties. The meeting ended with a Federal promise to reconsider the proposal, but Welensky admitted years later that, at that moment, the possibility that the Conservative Government might destroy the Federation had not crossed his mind.[2]

Home spent four days in the Federation and succeeded in persuading Welensky to accept — albeit in principle — the proposal. He returned to London to give what Macmillan recorded as "rather a bad account of Welensky. He is clearly in a very excitable and nervous state (as everyone is in Africa) but he has got him to agree to a programme in general terms, for the period preceding the 'review' laid down by the Act".[3] According to Macmillan, Home and Welensky had agreed that the ground would be cleared by a committee of officials from the five Governments before the commission began work. The commissioners would comprise representatives of the Governments and an unspecified number of Privy Councillors. They would be assisted by experts in the economic and constitutional fields. Macmillan informed his diary: "If we can only get (a) the Governors of Northern Rhodesia and Nyasaland to agree, (b) the Socialist leaders to agree, we may be able to gain a little time for serious thinking. Otherwise there is a danger of a real bust-up."[4]

The British Government took time to comment further on the proposal and, before it did, the Federal Government had to defend itself in its Assembly. Field provoked the debate by reminding the House that his Party had always believed that it might be necessary to declare independence unilaterally. However, he had to confess that he had been surprised to hear Welensky suggest on the BBC the previous evening that the Federation might become a republic. This, Field said, was a far more violent suggestion than his own.

Welensky dealt first with the reasons for the recent disturbances. The Africans, he said, had not only been encouraged by outside influences to believe that the Federation was temporary, but had been distracted by the series of conferences since Bandung in 1955 which had resolved to remove colonial regimes. However, though his Government would continue to advance the Africans in all spheres, Welensky believed he should warn the African nationalists that the Europeans had no intention of either being pushed out or of being massacred. There was no reason, nevertheless, why Nyasaland should not attain full self-government within the Federation.

Welensky took the opportunity to attack the Labour Party for its smears

[2] Welensky Papers, 20/10, ff. 251–254, Minutes of a Meeting with Lord Home, Federal Cabinet Room, 1 April 1959; Author's interview with Sir Roy Welensky.

[3] H. Macmillan, *Pointing the Way, 1959–61* (London, 1972), p. 136.

[4] *Ibid.*

and for its refusal to accept the clear evidence of plans to massacre the Europeans. He warned that, should certain Labour MPs ever dominate a future government, Anglo-Federal relations would have to be seriously reviewed. These people, he remarked, had accused the Federal and territorial Governments of conspiracy when the latter had simply co-ordinated their troop reinforcement of Nyasaland. Welensky denied pressing anyone to declare states of emergency and had merely made available the full resources of his Government. Yet the Labour's *Daily Herald*, he commented, had accused him of flinging out Stonehouse like a common criminal and of using two British Governors like "office boys". It had called him "the ruffianly Premier", a "high-handed son of an Afrikaner mother" who tried to beat the Africans into subjection. Such actions, the newspaper had alleged, had cost the Federation its dominion status. Welensky disagreed that dominion status was lost because he knew that the five Governments could devise a formula to achieve independence with safeguards which would satisfy anyone.

It was only after the Dominion Party had claimed that he could think only of attacking his critics, and the African MPs had said that he had frightened their constituents, that Welensky explained his reference on the BBC to a republic. The question, he said, had only arisen when the interviewer, Christopher Chattaway, had asked what he would do if the Commonwealth refused to accept any action taken by him in circumstances where he was forced "to go it alone". If fact, he explained, he had stressed his loyalty to the Queen and had said that the declaration of a republic would only happen in the last extreme.

Gaunt suggested a Royal Commission to study the partition of Northern Rhodesia, and Greenfield answered by claiming that the clear difference between his Party and the Dominion Party was the issue of the maintenance of the Federation. He noted that the DP was not antagonistic towards the British Labour Party because it shared its aims. The same could be said of the DP and the African nationalists, he remarked, and thus "an unholy trinity" had been formed.[5]

Macmillan decided to join the negotiations, and Welensky would discover that: "My cautious acceptance in principle of Alec Home's original proposal had been converted by some magic in Harold Macmillan's mind into willing – indeed enthusiastic – alliance with him in carrying out an exercise whose dangers and difficulties made him exult."[6] This attitude was certainly reflected in Macmillan's first dispatch in which he pressed strongly for appointment of the commission as the best method of handling a delicate situation. Blithely ignoring the utter reluctance of the Federal Government, he spoke about the broad agreement which Welensky and Home had reached and the need for the bipartisan approach to the review to calm British opinion. He found encouraging signs of the possibility of Labour co-operation but would not approach Gaitskell until he knew that the plan was sound and that it had Welensky's endorsement.[7]

When he wrote again on 17 April, Macmillan reported that his Cabinet and

[5] Fed R & N *Debates* (Salisbury), Vol. 10, Col. 31, 7 April 1959.
[6] Welensky, *4 000 Days*, *op. cit.*, p. 144.
[7] Welensky Papers, 20/10, f. 250, Macmillan to Welensky, (undated).

the Northern Rhodesian Governor designate, Sir Evelyn Hone, liked best of all the alternatives the plan of Welensky and Home. Macmillan still ignored the strenuous objections of the Federal Government. Gaitskell, he said, had not yet been approached so as to prevent the Labour Party from bargaining and, perhaps, gaining the initiative. Thus he wanted to present Gaitskell with a plan which was so reasonable that he would lose face if he refused to co-operate. This plan would be based on that negotiated with Welensky and Whitehead. The first step would be for a conference of officials to prepare material for the preparatory commission by October 1959. Welensky had wanted an official conference similar to that of 1951 but it would soon be apparent that Macmillan did not. Macmillan suggested that the preparatory commission should assemble to consider a progress report by the officials and then adjourn to await the final one. Thereafter, it would use this and information gathered from other sources to advise the Governments on the further steps needed to advance towards the achievement of the aims of the Federal Constitution, including its preamble. The work of the officials was crucial, he said, because it would temper the less desirable material which the commissioners might read of their own accord.

Macmillan had considered Welensky's suggestion of the Lord Chancellor, Lord Kilmuir, as chairman of the commission and Greenfield as a member, but felt that their presence would be inhibiting. He believed that the Governments should remain free to act. Moreover, he said, he was confident that he could obtain a chairman who would enjoy the confidence of everyone. He suggested a judge or the Master of Balliol, Sir David Lindsay Keir, or someone of similar calibre. The Federation should be represented by three members, including an African, while the territories would have two members each. He was sure that two Africans of calibre would disarm all critics.

Macmillan warned that the announcement of the commission would provoke questions in his Parliament on amalgamation and dominion status, and thought it wise to anticipate these with a statement based closely on the Joint Declaration of 1957 and the Federal constitutional preamble. He said that Welensky, as an experienced parliamentarian, would be reassured by the reiteration of the rejection of secession and would accept that the best way to ensure a good reception was to be frank.

The statement proclaimed the commission to be purely advisory. The recent past was recalled, as promised, including the Declaration of 1957, which had reaffirmed the Anglo-Federal opposition to amalgamation or secession. The purpose in 1960 was to review the Constitution in the light of progress and to agree on any possible constitutional advances. A programme for the attainment of full membership of the Commonwealth would be considered. Once that was attained the northern territories would cease to be under British protection and this would bring into play the pledges made in the preamble and in Parliament in 1953. The consent of the people of Northern Rhodesia and Nyasaland would have to be obtained, but the manner in which this would be done had not yet been prescribed. Nevertheless, the statement said, it was clear that the northern legislatures were not designed to reflect the opinion being sought.

Macmillan acknowledged Welensky's difficulties on the commission and the review, but was sure that Welensky would believe that "we are your staunch friends and that we are with you in convincing the world that your Federation is a splendid conception with a great and honourable future".[8] Welensky has described this message as "soothing as cream and as sharp as a razor".[9]

Welensky consulted Whitehead and replied to Macmillan on 22 April. He accepted the Labour Party's participation, he wrote, but wanted several modifications to the terms of reference to meet local difficulties. Indeed, he noted that Macmillan had not sent the product of the recent negotiations. What he had sent, Welensky observed, was the version which Home had advanced first and which had been rejected in favour of the simpler formula that confined the commission to advising on the constitutional framework best suited to achieve the objects of the Constitution of 1953. Home had agreed that this was very different from advising on further steps which might be necessary to achieve those aims.

In further justification Welensky recalled that, finally, because of British difficulties, he had agreed to a commission which would not investigate Federal affairs, but would advise on the constitutional aspects of the review. This was very different, he insisted, from advising on further steps to secure the objects of the preamble. If the alteration was not made, the commission might recommend a widening of the franchise to ensure a majority of African voters. It might even advocate the integration of education. None of these possibilities, Welensky warned, would escape his opponents when accusing him of "selling the European down the river". The utmost the electorate would accept, and not without difficulty, was that the commission would be confined to looking at constitutional aspects and would be debarred from delving into political controversies.

Welensky also criticised Macmillan's definition of the scope of the work of the officials because he had intended, and Home appeared to agree, that there would be a conference like that of 1951. It was not enough, Welensky demanded, that the officials should supply material on which the commission could work and, therefore, it should be stated that the officials would meet as soon as possible to evolve an outline of constitutional changes and a programme for their possible implementation.

Welensky accepted Macmillan's allocation of members and agreed to search for an African member even though it would be difficult. However, he was not happy with the suggested chairmen. He said that Greenfield and Whitehead knew and respected the Master of Balliol but considered him unsuitable. As British judges had no knowledge of the Federation, Welensky, Whitehead and Greenfield preferred Lord Kilmuir. Alternatively, they wanted Lord Salisbury or the Master of University College, Oxford, Dr A. L. Goodhart, or Lord Milverton. Whitehead suggested Mr Justice Douglas Abbott of the Supreme Court of Canada, a former Canadian Minister of Finance. Welensky wanted assurance that he would be consulted on all candidates.

As for the programme, Welensky stressed that "as this is life and death to us" only top-ranking officials could be used and, as it would be difficult to

[8] *Ibid.*, ff. 245–248, Macmillan to Welensky, 17 April 1959.
[9] Welensky, *4 000 Days*, *op. cit.*, p. 144.

spare them, work could only begin in July and would not be complete before the end of the year.

Welensky's final objection was to the last paragraphs of the draft statement because he believed that progress was more likely if effort was concentrated on a formula to retain British protection, perhaps in a new form, once the Federation was independent. Otherwise the review conference would have the impossible task of demonstrating that 6 000 000 Africans were in favour of something they did not understand. Nevertheless, Welensky said he was grateful for the expressions of friendship and hoped that Macmillan would not take it amiss if he reminded him that "our whole future is at stake in the discussions in 1960". Consequently, he concluded, everything had to be weighed carefully.[10]

Simultaneously, the Dominion Party proclaimed it criminal folly to believe that the Federation could be maintained unchanged as it was obvious that the British Government would introduce reforms which would lead to the establishment of black majority governments in the northern territories. The only way to avoid the secession of Southern Rhodesia, the DP said, was to adopt the Central African Alliance. Indeed that day, 22 April, Field introduced a motion in the Federal Assembly for the appointment of a select committee to study the idea.[11]

Field failed and four days later he was partially answered by Lennox-Boyd when addressing the Conservative Commonwealth Council. Lennox-Boyd revealed that preparations for the review had begun with the highest priority being given to the assessment of African fears. Nothing of what the African had feared in 1953 had been realised, he said, and the pledges in the preamble would remain unaltered in the future. Furthermore, it was necessary that the African should appreciate the consequences of Nyasaland leaving the Federation because they could include a chain reaction which could cause the Federation to disintegrate and the Southern Rhodesians to look to South Africa for salvation.[12]

Home and Macmillan replied to Welensky on 29 April. Home avowed that they had tried hard to incorporate Welensky's ideas. However, because there would be inevitable questions on the prescribed sanction by the majority of the inhabitants of any change, the statement had to be retained that the legislatures by themselves were an inadequate gauge of opinion. Home urged agreement while there was a good chance of committing the Labour front bench to a reasonable approach. If the opportunity was lost, he said, the agitation would begin again.

Macmillan claimed to have induced his Cabinet to accept many of Welensky's ideas. However, in the terms of reference, even though the purpose would be to examine the Constitution, he wanted to retain the ability to advise on steps to achieve the objects of the preamble. He agreed that the commission should avoid controversial subjects like integration, but doubted that any truly independent commission could accept preclusion from examining the general political background. This was particularly true of the fran-

[10] Welensky Papers, 20/10, f. 242, Welensky to Macmillan, 22 April 1959.

[11] Fed R & N *Debates* (Salisbury), Vol. 10, Col. 555 f., 22 April 1959.

[12] *The Rhodesia Herald*, 27 April 1959.

chise, he noted, which was obviously an aspect of the mechanism of the Constitution.

Macmillan also disagreed on the task of the officials because he thought a conference like that of 1951 would interfere with the work of the commission and confuse the review by presenting the former with an agreed scheme on which to pronounce. The function of the officials, he said, was merely to lay lines of argument and information before the commission. Yet he believed that he was going a long way to meet Welensky if the terms of reference stated that the officials would meet as soon as possible to survey economic, political and social developments. The officials would also analyse possible constitutional changes, he explained, and would submit progress and final reports to their Governments and the commission.

Macmillan dismissed Welensky's pessimism on the timetable but was prepared to exclude mention of a terminal date for the work of the officials. He was anxious, however, not to keep the distinguished members of the commission waiting. He enclosed a revision of the last four paragraphs of the statement and repeated his belief that they were close to agreement.[13]

Welensky was not as effusive but did acknowledge, on 1 May, that the gap had narrowed. Nonetheless, attaching the greatest importance to the terms of reference, he rejected Macmillan's revision of them as not answering his fears. The Federal and the Southern Rhodesian Governments had experienced great difficulty over their franchises, Welensky said, and they certainly did not intend to reconsider them and doubted if the commission, no matter how independent it was, could judge them. The commission could prepare for the review but there could be no other changes to the terms of reference. In other words, he explained, the commission would advise the Governments on the constitutional framework best suited to achieve the objects of the Constitution. With regard to the duties of the officials, Welensky said that Macmillan had misunderstood because he had not intended that they should be able to commit their Governments. The 1951 Conference had only produced a basis for discussion and there was a mass of small legal and technical detail which the officials would clear away. It should be stated that the officials would meet as soon as possible to survey developments and suggest and analyse any constitutional changes which might be desirable and practicable. He confessed, however, that this matter was not crucial to him.

Welensky stated that the membership question was also worrying him because the Dominion Party would object to its exclusion when the Labour Party was included in double measure. Furthermore, he politely rejected the re-wording of the last four paragraphs of the draft statement because it was merely a précis of what had been written before. The constant reiteration of the pledges was having a depressing effect in the Federation, he claimed, and there was no need for a further reference to them. He still maintained it was better to say that a formula would be devised to retain British protection than to promise to undertake the impossible task of demonstrating that 6 000 000 Africans favoured something they did not understand.[14]

[13] Welensky Papers, 20/10, f. 237, M. R. Metcalf to Welensky, 30 April 1959; f. 238, Macmillan to Welensky, 29 April 1959.

[14] *Ibid.*, f. 232, Welensky to Macmillan, 1 May 1959.

Macmillan, however, had little intention of surrendering much. He remained anxious to make it clear that the commission could not be debarred from considering the franchise. In his reply, Macmillan accepted Welensky's revision on the officials, but would not radically change the draft statement because Gaitskell and certain Conservatives would question whether the legislatures were yardsticks of their populations. He still wanted to anticipate questions but, to accommodate Welensky, he proposed to say that the manner in which opinion would be ascertained had not been defined and that it was possible that it would combine several elements. The northern legislatures, he said, could not be more than one of these elements. Macmillan, perhaps, was becoming weary of Welensky's obstinacy because he reminded him that it was not a joint statement and that he had only consulted him out of friendship. He added that the statement would be followed by half an hour of questions which would be difficult to answer off the cuff. Nevertheless, Macmillan asked Welensky to feel free to comment. As the whole issue was fraught with dangers, including violent unrest in the northern territories, Macmillan said that he wanted to proceed to settling the membership.[15]

Welensky, promptly on 6 May, accepted the amended statement. However, he replied that he could not understand why Macmillan dwelt on the franchise when he had made it clear that he would not reconsider it whatever the commission said.[16]

At this point, Welensky's senior Ministers, Barrow and Greenfield, offered their advice. Barrow said that because of the attitude of the Africans, the Governments should simply decide on the best policy for the Federation and impose it firmly. Greenfield was not as terse. He recalled the rejection of an inquisition into Federal affairs and the long duel with Home and Macmillan to secure the least damaging compromise. As he was suspicious that Macmillan might yet, when making the statement, betray the Federation on the terms of reference and the duties of the commission, Greenfield advised a reiteration of the Federal opinion on the commission and on the need for care in framing the statement. He thought that it also might be politic to ask Macmillan for four Federal commissioners to accommodate the Dominion Party and thus avoid a clash with Field over the inclusion of the Labour Party.

Greenfield also disliked the latest form of the proposal, particularly Macmillan's failure to stress the permanence of the Federation. Macmillan had to prohibit any enquiry into the continuance or otherwise of the Federation. It was not enough to allude to the Declaration of 1957, which had stressed the continuance of the Federation, because since then there had been a considerable effort to re-open the issue. The advisory but not inquisitional nature of the commission had to be categorically emphasised and Greenfield would not allow it to travel around the Federation examining witnesses.[17]

Before Welensky could implement Greenfield's suggestion, Macmillan, on 9 May, thanked him for accepting the wording. Macmillan remained con-

[15] *Ibid.*, ff. 235–236, Macmillan to Welensky, 5 May 1959.

[16] *Ibid.*, FGC(1), Restricted 6/59, Annexure D, Welensky to Macmillan, 6 May 1959.

[17] *Ibid.*, 7/15, f. 6, Barrow to Welensky, 1 May 1959; 20/10, f. 221, Greenfield to Welensky, 7 May 1959.

vinced, however, that neither he nor Welensky should say anything about precluding the franchise because that would only highlight it as a matter of controversy. He said he was hoping to discuss the plan with Gaitskell and thereafter would consider immediately the next step.[18]

After receiving this, Welensky told Greenfield that he could not re-open the issue without "upsetting the applecart" as he knew that Macmillan had already spoken to Gaitskell. Anyway, Welensky felt that he could rely on the nominees of the five Governments to be wedded to the Federal ideal. He said he was prepared to exclude the Dominion Party because those who would serve on the commission would be of no particular political complexion.[19]

Welensky was wrong if he thought that the matter was out of the melting pot because Gaitskell, Griffiths and Callaghan rebuffed Macmillan on 4 May and in subsequent meetings. Macmillan concluded that they were fanning African problems to create an election issue. He did not, however, tell Welensky this when he reported to him on 13 May. Indeed, Macmillan claimed that Labour leaders seemed anxious to be helpful even though they insisted on a parliamentary commission which would only report to Westminster. Their principal objection to Macmillan's proposal was that the Africans would be so thinly represented that their views would not be heard and this would provoke an African boycott. Macmillan did not want to force the issue yet because, in "the better atmosphere", agreement might result and he had allowed the Labour Party to reconsider its attitude in the forthcoming parliamentary recess.[20]

Macmillan reported to Welensky again in early June, but before then the General Assembly of the Church of Scotland approved overwhelmingly a report by their Committee Anent Central Africa. This recalled that in 1952 the General Assembly urged consideration of the African viewpoint because the African opposition appeared vigorous, persistent and generally well informed. The safeguards had seemed adequate but developments since 1953 seemed to justify the mounting African distrust. Chief among these were the Declaration of 1957, (inhibiting British power), the Federal Electoral Act and the dangerous and retrogressive Constitutional Amendment Act. The economic argument meant nothing to the African who had not yet enjoyed any direct benefit.

Thus the Committee demanded that the review include a fearless examination of the possibility of refashioning the Federal structure to accommodate the criticisms by the Africans, particularly those from Nyasaland. The Committee insisted on adequate African representation at the review and that the granting of dominion status without the consent of the majority of the people would be premature and dangerous. As it knew personally many of the Nyasaland detainees, the Committee disbelieved the murder plot, particularly as no Europeans were killed and furthermore as there was no assurance that evidence would ever be led publicly. It was sure that Nyasaland would never return to normal until the detainees were released or were condemned in open

[18] *Ibid.*, 20/10, f. 229, Metcalf to Welensky, 9 May 1959.
[19] *Ibid.*, f. 215, Welensky to Greenfield, 13 May 1959.
[20] Macmillan, *Pointing the Way*, *op. cit.*, p. 136; Welensky Papers, 20/10, f. 213, H. G. M. Bass to H. N. Parry, 13 May 1959.

trial. It seemed that, despite the Government's statement to the contrary, the detainees were being held for political reasons.[21]

The superficiality of the comments of the Church's experts, particularly those of the Reverend George MacLeod (later Lord MacLeod), irritated the Federal Government and, while he found the Church to be more responsible than the Labour Party, Macmillan conceded that it had "some dangerous and subtle agitators".[22]

The Committee's report might have affected the attitude of the Labour Party. Certainly *The Times* of 4 June carried a reference by Gaitskell, when meeting trade union and Labour leaders, to the great wisdom of the deliberations of the Church of Scotland. He intimated that, if the Conservatives did not change their dangerous, reactionary policies in Africa, he would ask the electorate to turn them out on that score alone. This, and a meeting with Gaitskell, on the same day, confirmed to Macmillan that the Labour Party, faced with full employment and a stable economy, could not resist exploiting the African situtation.[23]

He reported to Welensky two days later that he had failed with Gaitskell and was abandoning the negotiations because he was not prepared to give Gaitskell a veto. Macmillan said that there were also dangers in delay and that he would implement his plan in the hope that, when it was revealed, the Labour Party would be forced to accede. He proposed to capitalise on Welensky's desire to have non-parliamentary commissioners and would announce that the commission would be composed of them. However, in the hope that public pressure might force the Labour Party to relent, he would indicate that he would be willing to add two Conservative, one Liberal and two Labour Privy Councillors to the British team. If the Labour Party still resisted, he felt that the commission would probably get on better without them. At least, he claimed, he would have seized and retained the initiative and could appoint people who were independent and reliable. He had a distinguished judge who was willing to accept an appointment.[24]

Welensky agreed that Macmillan should force the issue. However, he denied that he had always wanted non-parliamentary commissioners because at the outset he had proposed the appointment of Lord Kilmuir and Greenfield. He added that it had always been difficult to accept the inclusion of the Labour Party while the Dominion Party was excluded. He, in fact, preferred that, if the members of his Government and Parliament could not serve, then the whole commission should be non-parliamentary. So he hoped that Macmillan would not make the additional offer thereby avoiding the clamour from the local parties for a *quid pro quo*. If it was essential to make it, Macmillan should not press it if there was no reaction. In any case, Welensky expressed surprise at the inclusion of a Liberal.

In accordance with the agreement on mutal consultation on membership, Welensky named his representatives as R. M. Taylor, chairman of Richard

[21] Welensky Papers, 39/125, f. 1 & f. 6, Memorandum by the Committee Anent Central Africa, 22 May 1959.
[22] Macmillan, *Pointing the Way*, *op. cit.*, p. 136.
[23] *Ibid.*, p. 137.
[24] Welensky Papers, 20/10, f. 209, Macmillan to Welensky, 6 June 1959.

Costain (Africa) Ltd. and formerly the Secretary to the Federal Treasury, A. E. P. Robinson, chairman of Central African Airways, and V. L. Robinson, the former Federal Attorney-General. Whitehead would approach Geoffrey Ellman-Brown and a judge of the Southern Rhodesian High Court. Closing, Welensky demanded, as Greenfield had urged, that Macmillan should revise his statement to emphasise the permanence of the Federation, and that the commission and the review were not concerned with secession. This, he said, was vital if local and overseas confidence in the Federation's political stability were to be restored.[25]

Macmillan hesitated because he was failing to take the Federal issue out of British politics, and decided on 19 June to invite Welensky to London in early July to re-examine the problem.[26] Simultaneously, however, the Federal Government declared the Reverend T. S. Colvin of the Church of Scotland a prohibited immigrant. This provoked Aneurin Bevan to demand that Welensky be banned from entering Britain. Welensky also alarmed the Labour Party by publicly referring to the need for a Federal police force. (This would be one of the Federal demands at the review so that the Federation would not have to continue to rely on the territories to enforce its laws. This force could also be used in intelligence and riot control. It was easy to introduce because no constitutional amendment would be required.)

All Welensky said was that, if the British Government did not supply sufficient policemen, the Federal Government would have to act because Nyasaland, for example, needed policemen not soldiers. As he had issued a written statement, distortion by the Press annoyed him considerably. It was even more irritating that the Labour Party should depict his statement as a sinister move to prevent the implementation of the British pledges to the northern Africans. Furthermore, it was rumoured in London that the Labour leadership would soon be pressed by its rank and file to declare in favour of secession of the northern territories.[27]

One matter was settled before Welensky arrived in London as, on 1 July, Home informed him that he, Lennox-Boyd and Armitage had agreed to fill the vacuum created by the emergency with a new but interim constitution to serve Nyasaland until the review. Home was sure that Welensky would agree that a significant move towards the ultimate goal of an African majority in the legislature was timely. It would placate many moderates in Britain, Home said, by showing a willingness to meet African aspirations in a reasonable way. He believed that it would be well received in the Federation and that the more the Africans shared in government, the less they would desire secession. Events would soon show just how mistaken that belief was.

The changes made were that the five unofficial African nominated seats in the Legislative Council would be increased by two to seven. The number of unofficial non-African elected seats would remain at six. Consequently, there would be 13 unofficial seats — six non-African elected and seven African nominated. The number of official seats would be increased by one, from

25 *Ibid.*, f. 206, Welensky to Macmillan, 8 June 1959.

26 *Ibid.*, f. 205, Macmillan to Welensky, 19 June 1959.

27 *Ibid.*, 8/17, f. 1, Greenfield to Welensky, 24 June 1959; 11/38, f. 44, Welensky to H. St L. Grenfell, 25 June 1959; *The Rhodesia Herald*, 1 July 1959.

twelve to 13 to preserve, with the Governor's casting vote, the official majority in the Legislative Council. In a further advance, two Africans would be nominated to the Executive Council. The federalisation of non-African agriculture was due to be announced at the opening of the Legislative Council on 7 July but, as it was feared that it would provoke a severe African reaction (a verdict with which the Federal authorities disagreed), it was proposed that the announcement of the constitutional change would be substituted.

As the constitutional convention demanded consultations with the Federal Government on such changes, the Federal Government could legitimately complain at this high-handedness but Welensky, perhaps because he was preoccupied, chose to let it pass. In any case, Armitage, in April, had informed Welensky of his ideas for an interim measure and thus must have softened the blow, particularly as Welensky had thought the introduction of two Africans into the Executive Council was timely.[28]

On 5 July, the day before Welensky and Greenfield arrived in London, the Bow Group of the Conservative Party also chose to intrude into Federal affairs with the publication of a memorandum "Central Africa. The Challenge of 1960". This demanded that a "Commonwealth" commission should be appointed to prepare for the review. To assist it, the British Government would clearly define the pledges. This was necessary because the lack of clarity was responsible for many African fears. It had to be plain that no change was possible without the consultation of the people through the ballot box and through a conference attended by the native authorities, the trade unions, the chambers of commerce, political organisations and the like.

Because the Federal Constitution could be lawfully changed only by the British Parliament, the Bow Group advocated that the principal commissioners should be Privy Councillors representing the major British Parties. They should be supported by two Privy Councillors from the Commonwealth and a sociologist, an economist and a constitutional lawyer. The chairman should be considerably experienced in public affairs, because he faced a diplomatic and constitutional problem with a considerable political bite.

However much the Federal Government disliked investigations, the Bow Group insisted that it accept a frank enquiry. It was particularly important to avoid a repetition of events surrounding the Federal franchise in which agreement had been reached in secret between Governments before anyone in Britain could discuss it publicly. Forgetting, or perhaps not knowing, that the settlement of the Federal franchise had been a prerogative of the Federal Assembly, the Bow Group demanded that, in cases where the British electorate had to decide on grave constitutional issues, it was entitled to the full facts. Agreement on African matters, the Bow Group maintained, was becoming so important that a commission whose constitution satisfied Westminster was preferable to one which met only the requirements of the British and Federal Governments. The independently-minded Rhodesians found this assertion insufferably arrogant and quite unacceptable. To them the opinion of the British parliamentarians or people, living 6 000 miles away, was of little more than passing interest.

[28] Welensky Papers, 20/18, f. 356, Home to Welensky, 1 July 1959; f. 362, Armitage to Welensky, 11 April 1959; Welensky, *4 000 Days*, *op. cit.*, p. 152.

The Bow Group intended that its commission should provide the British public with a survey of opinion in the Federation. In this, language and the lack of education would not count. The working of the Federation since its inception would be examined with concentration on the electoral system, the division of powers and the police, labour and trade union policies. The operation of the electoral system would be a measure of the success of partnership. The commission would evaluate acceptable alternatives to the Federation and these would embrace a rapid evolution to adult suffrage without transitional safeguards for the Europeans.

The Bow Group found that there were three possible alternatives. The first was the replacement of the Federation by a customs union. The second was a treaty under which the Federal Government would assume the supervisory powers of the Colonial Office without affecting the division of powers. The third was to make only marginal changes. Police, for example, would remain a territorial subject. The principle of the common roll would be developed in the territories to secure a greater participation by the Africans in the control of matters which concerned them most. The Federal Government would receive greater economic powers but would be excluded from the control of the land.

The immediate task was to re-establish the belief in Britain in the possibility of a moderate solution. Britain, the Bow Group knew, could not impose a solution but could induce acceptance of one. To this end, more African support for the Federation had to be evinced before 1960 and it meant granting more responsibility to the Africans in Nyasaland and broadening the franchise in Northern Rhodesia before October 1960. The Europeans had also to be persuaded to see their problems in perspective, that they had to work towards sharing, and not seizing, power. Otherwise, the Bow Group concluded, the result would be increasing instability and unrest in which the European could not survive.[29]

Welensky and Greenfield met Home and Lennox-Boyd on 6 July and again on the morning of 7 July before meeting Macmillan in the afternoon in the garden of No. 10, Downing Street. Welensky was offered a cane chair and was about to sit down when it was noticed that the seat had rotted through. Writing to his wife, Greenfield quipped, "Evidence of the decay of the Commonwealth."[30]

The discussion continued into the evening and became quite heated. Lennox-Boyd, in particular, seemed to have been upset by the Hola Camp incident in Kenya and the possibility that Lord Devlin would be critical in his report on Nyasaland. Macmillan found Welensky sincere but very sensitive and liable to become angrily indignant.[31] Welensky thought Macmillan was "more harassed than I had ever seen him. The effect of our Central African problems on his Party's electoral prospects appeared to be giving him considerable anxiety; he therefore exerted all his powers of persuasion on me".[32]

Nevertheless, after a lunch on 8 July, attended also by R. A. Butler, agree-

[29] Welensky Papers, 11/38, f. 66, Memorandum by the Bow Group, 5 July 1959.

[30] J. M. Greenfield, *Testimony of a Rhodesian Federal* (Bulawayo, 1978), p. 174.

[31] Macmillan, *Pointing the Way*, *op. cit.*, p. 137.

[32] Welensky, *4 000 Days*, *op. cit.*, p. 146.

ment was reached. Provided the Labour Party agreed, the terms of reference would be as previously arranged, *viz*:

> "In the light of the information provided by the committee of officials and of any additional information the Commission may require to advise the five Governments in preparation for the 1960 Review on the constitutional programme and framework best suited to achieving the objects contained in the Constitution of 1953 including the Preamble."[33]

If the Labour Party still refused to co-operate, Macmillan proposed to wait for a few days and then to announce that, because of this refusal, the commission would not be appointed and, instead, an ordinary parliamentary delegation would tour the northern territories. The Federal and Southern Rhodesian Governments would be asked to invite the delegation to Salisbury. This alternative was, of course, in Rhodesian eyes worse than the first.

Welensky informed Barrow that the British Government insisted that there be five African members and, by way of compromise, the Federal delegation would be expanded to four and those from the territories to three each. The Nyasaland delegation would contain two Africans, while each of the others would have one. If Whitehead refused to nominate an African, the British delegation would include Coloured representatives from either Malaya or the West Indies. Aside from that, the British team would contain a Canadian, possibly Abbott; an Australian, probably Frank Menzies, the brother of Sir Robert; three Conservative and three Labour Privy Councillors and an independent chairman. Lord Forster, chairman of the National Arbitration Tribunal, would be asked to take the chair. To assist the commission, there would be four experts, making the total of members 26, of which 13 would be local and 13 from Britain and the Commonwealth.

Welensky immediately told *The Times* that he would allow a commission to visit the Federation before the review. If agreement on the composition of the commission was otherwise impossible, he would accept the inclusion of members from the Commonwealth who had long experience of working federal systems. The Federal commissioners would be knowledgeable local residents of good standing and independent of the Federal Government. He did not expect that, as a result of the review, the British Government would abandon its responsibilities and, if there were to be any transfer of power, it was likely to be to the territorial Governments. However, the Federal Government might find itself made a trustee. Finally, he indicated that his Government would increase its spending considerably in Nyasaland.

This statement provoked an immediate protest from the Dominion Party which refused to accept that Welensky could make such an agreement before the Federal Assembly could debate the issue. It disliked the exclusion of the Federal parliamentarians and the "high-handed British manner" which ignored the possession by the Federation and Southern Rhodesia of sovereign governments. Van Eeden thought that, by losing the initiative, Welensky had lost the battle before it had begun. He and Wightwick objected to the

[33] Welensky Papers, 20/10, f. 202, Welensky to Barrow, 8 July 1959.

financial commitment to Nyasaland before the Federal Assembly had been consulted. Yamba and F. Chembe joined in, claiming that Welensky had again ignored African feelings. They declared that, unless the Africans were fully represented, they would ignore the commission. In reply, Barrow berated the Opposition for trying to embarrass Welensky when he was in a difficult position and when there was no doubt that he had every right to negotiate.[34]

This debate was summarised by Barrow in his telegrams to Welensky on 9 July in which he also related that Whitehead had discussed the proposal with his Cabinet and would consult Welensky before replying to Home. Barrow was anxious that Welensky should persuade Macmillan to drop the disagreeable alternative of a visit from a parliamentary delegation. In fact, Welensky was to find his interview with the Labour Party "pretty shattering" because Griffiths, for example, told him that they would not accept an African commissioner as a true representative of his people unless he belonged to the Congresses.[35]

After consulting Welensky, Whitehead replied to Home, testily complaining that his Government was only being given an opportunity to record its views after the agreement. Nevertheless, he said, his Government would accept the commission on the stated terms and would accord it the facilities granted to the Devlin Commission. If the Labour Party would not cooperate, his Government would only accept a British parliamentary delegation under the auspices of the Commonwealth Parliamentary Association and without special powers of investigation. Anything else, he warned, meant surrender to the Labour Party.

Furthermore, Whitehead continued, the Southern Rhodesian Government objected to the requirement that it should appoint an African member, because it was its firm policy to use people suited to specific tasks and, in this case, there was no African who had the necessary constitutional knowledge or the political and economic experience to be of use to the commission. The Southern Rhodesian Government wished to adhere to this policy but the alternative proposal to recruit Malayans or West Indians was equally unacceptable because their countries had gained self-government 30 years after Southern Rhodesia.

Thus, with the gravest misgivings, he said, the Southern Rhodesian Government would capitulate and appoint an African in order not to invalidate the negotiations which had just been concluded. Whitehead added that, after 35 years of self-government, Southern Rhodesia expected to be brought into negotiations earlier. The presentation of a *fait accompli*, he claimed, had caused him considerable difficulties with his Cabinet.[36]

Nevertheless, Macmillan's preparatory commission had been accepted and the process of erosion which resulted in the disintegration of the Federation had begun. As Welensky puts it: "Dismayed and reluctant, we accepted the

[34] Fed R & N *Debates* (Salisbury), Vol. 10, Col. 1517 f., 9 July 1959.
[35] Welensky Papers, 11/38, f. 23 & f. 27, Barrow to Welensky, 9 July 1959; 42/21, f. 66, Welensky to G. Beckett, 20 July 1959.
[36] *Ibid.*, 20/10, f. 198, Whitehead to Welensky, 9 July 1959; f. 195, Whitehead to Home, 18 July 1959.

Commission . . . Step by step we had been edged down a road which was to get stonier and stonier the further we were driven along it."[37]

Welensky cabled his Minister of Finance, Macintyre, ordering him to make it plain in the Federal Assembly that the extra finance for Nyasaland would not prejudice future approaches to the loan markets. He also instructed Barrow to prepare a statement on the banning of the Reverend Colvin to explain that it had been done at the behest of the Nyasaland Government which had warned Colvin of the consequences of his desire to assist African nationalism and, thereby, hurt the Federation.[38]

Then, on 15 July, Welensky replied to Lennox-Boyd's toast to the Federation at the dinner of the Rhodesia and Nyasaland Club in London, saying that it had taken ten centuries to acquire parliamentary democracy and thus it was unfair to expect the Federation to do likewise in a few years. However, he said, progress was being made. He had accepted the preparatory commission but would not allow it to put him and his Government in the dock.[39]

Later, as he left London, Welensky denied that he was seeking a transfer of power to the Federation in 1960. All he wanted, he said, was a programme which laid down further steps to be taken towards complete independence. Essential to that would be the safeguarding of African rights. He thought that it was possible, and even probable, that Nyasaland would be an African state within the Federation.[40]

Welensky and Macmillan made their formal announcements on the preparatory commission in their respective Parliaments on 21 July. Welensky mentioned the officials who were already at work and outlined the terms of reference and the membership of the commission. He recalled the Joint Declaration of 1957 and its rejection of amalgamation or secession. His Government, he proclaimed, would never have been party to an inquest on the affairs of the Governments of the Federation or have associated itself with anything which called into question the continuance of the Federation itself. Indeed, he said, "As will be seen from the terms of reference I have quoted, what we have agreed to is something very different."[41] Ultimately, Macmillan and the commission would disappoint Welensky on this particular score. He would call it betrayal.

In fact, the evasion had already begun because Macmillan, in his speech that day, made no reference to the Joint Declaration and its protestations on amalgamation and secession. Moreover, when questioned Macmillan said that, if asked about the possibilities of secession coming within the purview of the commission, he would say that the commission, in practice, would be free to hear all points of view from whatever quarter and on whatever subject. His Government, he said, had simply thought that it was right to specify terms of

[37] Welensky, *4 000 Days*, *op. cit.*, p. 149.

[38] Welensky Papers, 11/38, f. 35, Welensky to D. Macintyre, 9 July 1959; f. 39, Welensky to Barrow, 8 July 1959; f. 20, same to same, 10 July 1959; f. 9, Barrow to Welensky, 11 July 1959.

[39] *The Rhodesia Herald*, 15 July 1959.

[40] *Ibid.*, 18 July 1959.

[41] Welensky, *4 000 Days*, *op. cit.*, pp. 149–150. Curiously this statement was omitted from the Federal *Hansard* although Welensky made a clear reference to it in the subsequent debate two days later. – JRTW.

reference which accorded with what it regarded as the object of the Federal constitutional review. There was need for careful preparation for the review and, he explained, the commission would complement the work which the officials had already begun. The paramount object was to create an accord on the next stages of the political evolution of the Federation. In seeking this, he said, it was right that all the races should make their views known on the future. The commission would begin work in the northern autumn and Macmillan hoped that both sides of the House would support it.

Gaitskell reserved his ammunition for the debate on the Federation scheduled for the next day, but he did reveal that his principal objection was that the commission was unlikely to gain African support because half its members were the nominees of the Governments. Another danger, he said, was that the commission would interfere with what was properly the work of the review. It was vitally important that African opinion should be properly represented at the review. He asked if the Africans had been consulted by the Governors before this decision had been taken.

Macmillan, regretting that Gaitskell had taken such a firm position, replied that, while formal consultation had not taken place, the Governors were constantly in touch with the Africans and took their feelings into account. Gaitskell asked who would appoint the African members and Macmillan replied that his Government would do so after having taken the advice of the Governors and Governments concerned. Gaitskell questioned why ordinary British MPs were rejected as unsuitable and was told that it was better to have experienced Privy Councillors because of the serious issues at stake. When he asked if the terms of reference implied that in all circumstances the Federation would continue to exist, Macmillan made his evasive reply that the commission would be free to hear all points of view.

The remainder of the questions came from J. Grimmond, the leader of the Liberal Party — who wanted representation of the non-white Commonwealth — and from Stonehouse and Dingle Foot who declaimed on the problem of obtaining African support when African organisations were proscribed and hundreds of their fellows detained.[42]

Before the debate on the morrow, 22 July, Home warned Welensky that Lennox-Boyd would refer in general terms to the changes to be made in Nyasaland, particularly the appointment of two Africans to the Executive Council and the filling of the two extra African seats in the Legislative Council by nomination. If he made any reference to the federalisation of non-African agriculture he would say that nothing would be done until 1960 when the division of powers would be totally reviewed. On the transfer of marketing, he would make a similar comment. It was difficult, Home said, to know how Lennox-Boyd would be pressed, but it was necessary to anticipate questions. Home was sure that the more he and Welensky spoke with one voice the easier life would be.[43]

In a second message Home indicated that Lennox-Boyd would publicly support the Federal Government on the development of the Shiré River at the Nkula Falls in Nyasaland. Welensky replied that he understood the

42 House of Commons *Hansard* (London), Vol. 609, Col. 1072 f., 21 July 1959.
43 Welensky Papers, 20/18, f. 351, Home to Welensky, 21 July 1959.

British difficulties and would do nothing to increase them. However, he felt that as the transfer of marketing in Nyasaland was a specific election promise, he might have to say that it was still under consideration.[44]

In fact, Lennox-Boyd only referred to the constitutional changes. The debate opened with an hour-long speech from Gaitskell which Macmillan described as "rather academic, waspish rather than rude — quite effective".[45]

Gaitskell claimed that the high hopes of the Federation had not been realised and that the economic development — which might have been achieved without federation — had not affected the peasant in Nyasaland. The basic ill, he said, was that the Federation did not rest on consent but on force. The denial of freedom of speech had increasingly alienated the African when significant constitutional reform could have won him round. Instead, his suspicions had been deepened by a series of actions which, Gaitskell maintained, included the brushing aside of the African Affairs Board and the Declaration of 1957. The cure was immediate constitutional advancement to re-establish African confidence in their eventual achievement of democratic independence. One man, one vote was, after all, he said, becoming the norm in Africa.

Gaitskell suggested that the Africans in Nyasaland be given an elected majority in the Legislative Council and parity in the Executive Council. In Northern Rhodesia, he said, there should be parity of racial representation in both Councils. To him, these steps were necessary because only governments would attend the review and, to obtain a fair hearing, the Africans had to dominate the northern Governments. An essential prerequisite of this action was the release of the detainees lest "stooges" be elected. If the Europeans wanted to stay, they had to realise that harmony would only be born of rapid advancement and their coming to terms with African nationalism. His Party would have welcomed an advisory commission composed of parliamentarians because only that would restore the faith of the Africans in British protection. The proposed commission was inadequate, he said, because half of it would be nominated by the Governments and too few of the members would be Africans, who would be useless unless they were detainees. The Labour Party would include members from the recently independent countries of the Commonwealth.

Gaitskell demanded a statement reaffirming the pledges and affirming that there would be no Federal or territorial constitutional changes until proper democratic elections had been held. There should also be no grant of dominion status as a consequence of the review. Finally, he demanded that Macmillan erase the ambiguity between his statement on the commission's consideration of secession and Welensky's emphatic exclusion of it.

Macmillan did not comply. He dwelt on the need for the review and promised that the Africans appointed as commissioners would command African confidence. He decried the calling of any African, who co-operated in the building of a multi-racial society, a "stooge". It was also unreasonable, he said, to think that a broad-based commission would lack objectivity. His Government had nearly settled the commission's membership, and the choice

[44] *Ibid.*, f. 346, Home to Welensky, 22 July 1959; f. 349, Welensky to Home, 23 July 1959.
[45] Macmillan, *Pointing the Way*, *op. cit.*, p. 138.

of Privy Councillors was seen as a mark of the importance of the work to be undertaken. If it were necessary, he would lower the "top bar" but he still had to achieve a balance between Britain, the Commonwealth and the Federation. He defended the role of the European in Central Africa as the main agent for its development and called on the House to eschew party politics in this matter. Macmillan was supported by Major Patrick Wall who found both the Labour and Conservative Parties united on wanting the Federation to become a strong multi-racial member of the Commonwealth. It was thus unfortunate that within the Labour Party there were a number of racialists — he named Stonehouse, Brockway and Mrs Castle — who gave a different impression. Their aim, he said, was the immediate establishment of an African state based on universal adult suffrage. Other Conservatives warned that Nyasaland's secession would terminate the Federation. They thought that the criticism of the commission was unfortunate because it would only destroy its credibility in African eyes.

This appeal was ignored by the Labour speakers because they believed that the commission, as currently constituted, would be unacceptable to the Africans. They reiterated that the commission would be unwieldy and would encroach on the preserves of the review *el al.* Dugdale declared that, as they were only motivated by fear, Welensky and his Party should not be entrusted with the Government. With some perception, he postulated that the commission was a political dodge to have the whole matter declared *sub judice* before the British election. Dingle Foot questioned the right of Britain to impose the Federation and claimed that the only Africans who would inspire confidence were Banda, Kaunda and their colleagues.

Gaitskell's main support came from Callaghan, and Macmillan thought that his speech drove the wavering Conservatives back into the fold. Callaghan blamed Lennox-Boyd for consistently under-estimating the strength of the opposition to the Federation and for delaying the Nyasaland reform and thereby provoking violent protest. The commission appeared to him to be yet another concession to Welensky in the retreat in the face of Federal aggrandisement. He explained that the difficulty in finding true African representatives had led him to advocate the parliamentary commission. Any African who agreed to serve would be labelled a "Quisling". He had advocated the inclusion of Commonwealth parliamentarians because he knew Welensky regarded British Members of Parliament with suspicion.

Callaghan believed the preparatory commission would fail and would only provoke further violence. He urged that the limits to be imposed on the commission should be explained because the only way the Federation could survive would be by allowing the choice of secession. Finally he warned that this affair would be seen in Africa as a test of British sincerity.

Lennox-Boyd, when winding up the debate, was in the eyes of his supporters, including Macmillan, most impressive. He refused to discuss the division of powers, he said, because it was reserved for the review. He outlined the economic development and the steady progress in the removal of racial discrimination. He defended the 1958 Northern Rhodesian Constitution and outlined the advances to be made in Nyasaland. He had no doubts on the gravity of the consequences of Federal disintegration, for Nyasaland, in particular. Lennox-Boyd avowed that independence for the Federation still depended on the consent of the three territories and he promised to consider the points which Grimmond had made. Grimmond had said that the vast majority of Africans would support the commission if it examined the Federal Constitution and not simply justified it. Therefore it should be able to recommend structural changes. Grimmond had also thought that the commission was unwieldy and wanted not only representation of the African Congresses, but equal racial representation. He and his Liberals voted at the division with the Labour Party but the Government won it comfortably.[46] It would do likewise is a similar debate in the Lords on 27 July.

On the eve of the parallel Federal debate in Salisbury, the Dominion Party lost a motion calling for a round-table conference before the review to make the Government aware of all points of view. It argued that constitutional advance was not a matter for one Party alone. Greenfield refused the motion because it would be difficult to obtain a consensus of opinion.[47]

The next day, 23 July, Welensky drew the attention of the House to his statement on the preparatory commission. He explained how a wave of ill-informed hysteria had swept Britain after the events in Nyasaland, resulting in Labour-inspired pressure for a parliamentary commission of inquiry into Nyasaland in particular and the Federation in general. Later the Labour Party had suggested the inclusion of Commonwealth parliamentarians. The British Government had concurred but he had refused to entertain such an inquest. He had accepted the alternative preparatory commission because he hoped, perhaps foolishly, that it would result in a bipartisan British approach to Federal problems. He was not so naïve, he said, as to believe in the possibility of a selfless British colonial policy which advanced only the best interests of the colonies, but agreement on this commission might yet take the Federation out of British politics.

Welensky admitted that he did not like commissions, but had accepted this one because it could do no more than advise the Governments. As the review would not consider secession or the break-up of the Federation, he could not see what role the Federal Opposition could play in the commission and, thus, he had excluded Federal parliamentary representation from it. He would, however, consult the Opposition after the commission had reported and before the review. He closed with an appeal to the Commons to cease making his task so difficult. The calling of non-Congress Africans "stooges" and "Quislings" before appointments were made was totally irresponsible and placed the appointees in an invidious position. If British MPs disliked his Government, he said, they might at least care for the interests of the people of the Federation.

Field said he was surprised that after the reception the idea had received in the Commons, Welensky was still prepared to allow the British to nominate half the commission's membership. He recalled the promises of the UFP to obtain independence in 1960 and noted that now Welensky and, indeed, even a Federal official had stated publicly that no more than a programme for the achievement of that goal was being contemplated. Whatever Welensky said, it

[46] House of Commons *Hansard* (London), Vol. 609, Col. 1283 f., 22 July 1959.
[47] Fed R & N *Debates* (Salisbury), Vol. 10, Col. 1727, 22 July 1959.

was clear to Field that the commission — being heavily weighted against the Federation — would sit in judgment on it. It would be difficult to ignore its advice particularly if the British Government wanted to implement it. By thus deciding their fate, the commission would not only detract from the sovereignty of the Federal and Southern Rhodesian Governments, but would set an unhealthy precedent for outside interference. Field noted that in this context, Lord Malvern had said recently that the idea was nothing less than an insult to the Federal and territorial Governments, and that the commissioners would either be biased or flabby. Concluding, Field demanded that the Government should formulate a plan and take the people into its confidence and not find refuge in commissions.

To Wightwick it seemed that the initiative had been lost even before Welensky had gone to London. Welensky's tone, he said, had changed from imperious demands for independence to humiliating acceptance. In forcing Welensky's hand, the British Government had cynically disregarded the Federation's self-governing status.

The African MPs, Yamba and Chembe, stressed African suspicions of the proposed membership, though they otherwise welcomed the commission. Robert Moffat, successor to his brother Sir John as the nominated Member from Northern Rhodesia, thought that the commission would offer the African his first opportunity to express his opinion on the Federation. However, Moffat feared that the commission would be allowed to take only evidence on issues raised in the officials' report.

Replying, Welensky expressed his amazement at the Dominion Party's under-estimation of the residual powers of the British Government. These were such that the Federation could not pretend to be sovereign. Macmillan in his recent speech, after all, had plainly said that, while Federal and territorial opinion would be heard, the prime responsibility for the Federation lay with the British Parliament. Thus Welensky believed that he had accomplished no mean feat by securing half the places for Federal and territorial commissioners. He avowed that he would still attempt to obtain independence in 1960.

Answering other points, Welensky explained that when he had spoken of commissioners from the Commonwealth, he had meant only men from the long-established federations of Canada and Australia. He was confident that the advice of the commission could be ignored if it was inappropriate. As for the claim that the UFP lacked a plan, he said, it was plain that the objective had always been to preserve the Federation and to work towards achieving its independence. He could not have prevented the British Government from instituting an enquiry into the affairs of the northern territories and as that would have excluded the Federal and Southern Rhodesian Governments, he claimed that he had at least ensured that a good result was likely through the careful framing of the terms of reference and the selection of the commissioners. The British Government would not control the commission just because the British-appointed members would predominate. He avowed that the commission would be independent and would resist any sort of dictation.[48]

[48] *Ibid.*, Col. 1811 f., 23 July 1959.

Nobody commented in this debate on the Report of the Nyasaland Commission, chaired by Sir Patrick Devlin, which was published on 23 July. This lengthy document traced Nyasaland's history and then examined the recent events in detail. It began by describing Nyasaland as a "police state", albeit a temporary one, where people dared not criticise the Government. It found that, at the African Congress conference in Limbe on 25 January, the central executive and the branch delegates decided on a campaign of defiance, including violence if necessary. In particular, the enforcement of the law was to be resisted. Beyond this, nothing was clearly settled, although other forms of violence were discussed including the beating and killing of Europeans.

The Devlin Commission was not clear on the extent to which this policy replaced that of non-violence in the six weeks before the emergency. The Commission found that it seemed to vary from district to district. Certainly in northern Nyasaland where enthusiasm for the Congress was strongest, by mid-February there was sabotage, rioting and destruction of property. Government authority was being openly defied and by 3 March the Governor was forced to act. He did so on his own initiative, it conceded, and not because of Federal pressure.

The Commission believed that Banda was absent from the Congress conference on 25 January and neither authorised nor even knew of its decisions. However, it said, his failure to condemn publicly the use of violence had made such decisions possible. Despite the wild talk, the Commission concluded that neither murder nor assassination had been planned. There had been no "murder plot".

The Commission decided that unjustifiable force had been used when the arrests were made. The same criticism applied to the enforcement of the law in the disaffected areas. The casualties seemed to be higher than usual in such operations and some had been unnecessary. Amongst the numerous complaints it heard, the Commission claimed that there was no evidence to sustain charges of rape and similar outrages committed by the security forces, but that there was beating, bullying and confiscation of property inflicted not only on supposed offenders, but against the population generally. Much of this was authorised by the Nyasaland Government.[49]

Lennox-Boyd received the Devlin Report on 16 July and immediately summoned Armitage to London to discuss it with himself, Macmillan and Home. Short believes that the dismissal of the murder plot and the condemnation of the methods of the Nyasaland Government literally made the Conservatives "squirm". This was not the impression which Welensky's Conservative allies gained.[50]

The product of Armitage's visit was a further White Paper in which he answered his critics and which was published simultaneously with the Devlin Report. Armitage began by gratefully accepting the acknowledgement that he had been forced to act and had done so on his initiative. He was grateful for little else and, because it would be quoted out of context, he deeply regretted that the Commission had stated: "Nyasaland is — no doubt only temporarily

[49] *Report of the Nyasaland Commission of Inquiry*, Command 814 (London, July 1959), p. 1 f.

[50] P. Short, *Banda* (London, 1974), p. 123; Welensky Papers, 25/240A, f. 253, Lord Robins to Welensky, 30 July 1959.

— a police state, where it is not safe for anyone to express approval of the policies of the Congress party, to which before 3rd March 1959, the vast majority of politically-minded Africans belonged, and where it is unwise to express any but the most restrained criticism of government policy." This he dismissed as totally erroneous because normal opposition was tolerated and, indeed, T. D. T. Banda, W. M. Chirwa and others remained virulent critics but had consistently condemned the use of violence. The Commission agreed, Armitage observed, that no such condemnation had been forthcoming from Dr Hastings Banda and his colleagues. It had justified taking evidence in private by claiming it was protecting its witnesses from punitive action by the "police state" when the real reason was to avoid Congress retaliation. Armitage also dismissed the Commission's allegation that his earlier White Paper (Command 707 which explained the emergency) was intended to cloak his actions.

He claimed that the Commission had misled by noting that the Chiefs had not incurred Government displeasure by acting against "disrespectful demonstrations" by the Congress. The truth was, he said, that the Chiefs, as presidents of the African courts, were empowered to authorise or proscribe meetings and to penalise anyone who defied their ruling. In thus maintaining authority, they would be supported by the Government.

The Commission found that the Nyasaland Government believed that most Africans did not share the aspirations of the African nationalists. However, Armitage claimed his Government had always acknowledged, for example, the strong opposition to the Federation. The Commission had blamed the enforcement of soil erosion prevention measures for some of the bitterness. Yet, he noted, in a discourse on intimidation, it had decided that Africans regarded force as an acceptable alternative to persuasion. It had sympathised with Banda's protest at the enforcement of the soil erosion measures but had ignored the dramatic drop in convictions which indicated acceptance of them.

Armitage pointed out that he had been criticised for saying that Banda intended to force the Government to accept his aims. Yet the Commission had recorded Banda saying just that. His audiences had certainly believed that self-government was imminent, but the Commission, Armitage said, had condemned him for saying that Banda intended the Government to abdicate. It refused to accept Special Branch evidence but acknowledged that lists of "stooges" to be killed had been compiled. It attacked his claim that Banda's speeches encouraged law-breaking but confirmed that they had. It said that he lied when he claimed Banda would not compromise but it recorded the occasions Banda had informed the Government that he would not accept less than an African majority in the legislature.[51]

Short reveals that there is evidence suggesting that some of the Congress executive, and not Banda, had a secret plan, involving assassination, to implement if he was killed.[52] If this is true, it spoils the Commission's emphatic rejection of the murder plot.

[51] *Nyasaland Despatch by the Governor relating to The Report of the Nyasaland Commission of Inquiry*, Command 815 (London, July 1959), p. 1 f.
[52] Short, *Banda*, *op. cit.*, p. 124 fn.

Armitage's Government rested its case on its inability to distinguish between types of murder when there was acknowledged talk of killing. The Commission agreed it could not ignore the adoption of a policy of violence. Indeed, it accepted the crude description of the proceedings of the Congress's conference on 25 January and had reproduced it in an appendix. It had agreed that the references to beating and killing had to be taken seriously because events seemed to confirm them. The Commissioners had, however, rejected "R-Day" because only two of their witnesses had referred to it. Armitage, however, suggested in his rebuttal (White Paper, Command 815) that the rest of the witnesses were merely avoiding incriminating themselves and that the Report had revealed sufficient justification for the conclusion that there was a plot, plan, design or scheme which was accepted at Limbe and taken home by the delegates. The Devlin Commission, he said, had given no reason for dismissing the Government's evidence. Yet there had been seven witnesses, not all of whom were informers in the normal sense. They were from different parts of Nyasaland and did not know of each other, but all confirmed the violence planned on 25 January. In addition to their evidence, he noted, the Commission had recorded statements on the spilling of blood and of threats to "stooges".

Armitage said that Banda had been in frequent contact with his Congress lieutenants and could not believe that nothing was said to him about the policy of violence. Certainly, he pointed out, Banda had only condemned the uselessness of moderation, and yet his appearance, reputation and performance as a witness convinced the Commissioners that he would never approve of murder or violence. Armitage, however, found it difficult to agree and flatly repudiated the suggestion that his Government had not taken the threats of murder seriously. He said that when the Police Commissioner had told him, on 18 February, of his discovery, he would have been justified in immediately declaring an emergency, but reinforcements were needed. The Commission had also used negative evidence, he claimed, to prove the absence of a plot and had pointed out that there had been no loss of European life. Armitage preferred to believe that his resolute action had prevented this.

He maintained that the intelligence gained had forced the security forces to act secretly and swiftly with the maximum available strength to prevent the expected loss of life. However, he believed that, by examining in detail each incident, the Commission had distorted the degree of force used. There were 263 arrests before 5 March and only seven injuries in their execution, and six of these the Commission had not attributed to the excessive use of force. Nonetheless, Armitage did not condone such abuses. He felt that the Commission had drawn an unfortunate parallel with the sweep in Southern Rhodesia which had been without incident. The Southern Rhodesian Government had possessed more forces, and all those to be arrested had lived in the accessible townships.

The dispersal of crowds in Nyasaland had been criticised, he said, but many crowds had done considerable damage and the security force commanders had to be wary. In the event, 96 crowds had been dispersed since October, 60 on or after 3 March, without resort to firearms despite the ease with which such gatherings could be whipped into violent mobs.

Armitage observed that the Commission had dwelt on the degree of unrest, had told how the gangs had roamed free, and yet had wondered if "Operation Sunrise" could not have been on a lesser scale and if some warning could not have been given. The latter was hardly practicable, he said, and in any case the Commission had noted with sympathy the difficulty in which he had found himself at the Press conference on 2 March. Showing further inconsistency, the Commission had questioned the shooting of the man who had waved a spear at the District Commissioner at Rumpi, but it had ignored the coroner's verdict that it had been necessary. Armitage noted that the Commission criticised the measures taken to restore order but acknowledged that control had been lost in many areas. It denounced the punitive hut burning at Mlanje but accepted that it had been the decision of a single officer using his initiative after two days of rioting and looting. The Government had immediately countermanded such action.

The Commission, he continued, had criticised the wholesale confiscation of agricultural implements but had accepted that they could have been used as weapons. It had given him credit for not condoning unnecessary force and had found that, in every case of shooting, the perpetrator had honestly believed that it was necessary. However, the Commission was satisfied that the use of illegal force in the villages had been officially authorised even though he had specifically excluded brutality when ordering firm and, if necessary, tough action to restore order. If his orders had been misinterpreted and some bullying had taken place, it was a matter for regret. In any case, the Commission had not referred to specific incidents and Armitage said he had not seen any evidence of the use of fists and rifle butts.[53]

Welensky commented publicly that he, too, could not distinguish between types of murder and that the Nyasaland Government had been impelled to act once it knew of the plan to kill if Banda were arrested. Federal officials immediately compared the published Devlin Report with the proof copy which they had received earlier. They noticed three excisions. One was an appendix which had summarised the conclusions of the Commissioners but which they had rejected as over-simplified. The second was a statement which reaffirmed the necessity to act. The third dealt with the assumption by the Commission that the punitive action taken to eradicate the influence of the Congress had been accepted as illegal but had been expressedly or impliedly authorised from the "top". The Commission had said:

> "We have referred to the conception of these operations and to the use of the words tough and punitive. We do not suppose these words were used in orders of the day, but we are satisfied that the intention behind them was clearly conveyed to the troops who had to execute them."

However, it excised from its published version:

> "If African soldiery are allowed to be tough in a village, it must be obvious to anyone that what in fact happened is likely to happen."

[53] Command 815, *op. cit.*

The Federal Government was left wondering why it was necessary to cut this out.[54]

The Devlin Report was debated in the Commons on 28 July and in the Lords on the morrow. In the Commons the Attorney-General, Sir Reginald Manningham-Buller (later Lord Dilhorne), endorsed the conclusion that the adoption of a policy of violence had precipitated the emergency. He exploited the points made by Armitage. Like Armitage and Welensky, he could not distinguish between varieties of murder but could agree on the necessity to act. The preservation of European life, he said, was no reason to doubt the planning of murder. Nyasaland should not have been labelled a "police state" just because evidence was taken in camera to protect witnesses from intimidation and to enable civil servants to speak freely. Manningham-Buller could not reconcile the Commission's acknowledgement of the undisputed leadership of Banda with its portrayal of him as a figurehead. As the branches were told of the decisions of 25 January, he observed, Banda must have been the only member of the Congress left in ignorance. As Banda had not condemned the violence, he would appear to be a party to it and the verdict of the Commission seemed to be at variance with the mass of material it had gathered. The Opposition, he said, was asking the Government to accept the Report in its entirety but the Government could not.

Callaghan claimed that the Government was picking out what suited it and ignoring conclusions based on fact. If the Government was allowed to do this, he said, the Africans would never trust another commission, and peace would not be restored in Nyasaland. Callaghan saw the underlying cause of the crisis as frustration because the Congress had no effective way of making its views known. It had been forced into violence because it feared that it would not be represented in 1960 by men of its own choice. It had resorted, he claimed, to illegal methods because the Government had refused it permission to hold meetings. In so doing, Lennox-Boyd had ineptly divided the Nyasaland Government from its people.

Callaghan believed that Lennox-Boyd had been taken aback by the Report and had tried to resign, but that Macmillan had dissuaded him for electoral reasons. Thus Nyasaland would be denied the benefit of a new hand at the helm. Callaghan refused to sanction Armitage's actions when unnecessary and, therefore, illegal force had been used. Furthermore, Armitage was detaining the man whom the Commission had exonerated. The Government, Callaghan said, had claimed that Banda would not compromise, but Banda had written to him on 9 March declaring that he would accept the Labour idea that there should be an African majority in the Legislative Council and parity in the Executive Council. He said parity to Banda meant the number of Africans equalling that of the European officials and unofficials combined. Banda promised to seek a commonsense solution, thereby dispelling the impression of being unreasonable and unyielding.

Callaghan disputed the Devlin claim that Welensky had not influenced Armitage. Likewise, he remained convinced that panic had been the motivating force and that the murder plot had been concocted by Lennox-Boyd to

[54] *The Rhodesia Herald*, 24 July 1959; Draft: *Report of the Nyasaland Commission of Inquiry* (London, 1959) – in the possession of Sir Roy Welensky; Welensky, *4 000 Days*, *op. cit.*, pp. 132–134.

justify the emergency. He charged that the crime Lennox-Boyd had committed was not that of misleading the Commons, but of risking the Europeans in the remote areas by precipitating a crisis. The belief in the plot could explain the unnecessary vigour of the police. To repair the damage, Callaghan wished the Government to release the detainees, declare secession to be possible, and initiate constitutional talks aimed at giving the Africans control of their destiny by 1960.

The other Labour speakers agreed that the plot had been hatched in London by Lennox-Boyd and Perth and that their bungling had led the Congress to resort to violence.

In reply, Lennox-Boyd made familiar points. He praised both his Government for its record in advancing dependencies to independence and his Governors by implication. He reiterated Armitage's arguments. The strength of the opposition to the Federation had not been underestimated. Constitutional opposition had not been suppressed. Welensky had not influenced Armitage and, as the Devlin Report confirmed this, it was the height of hypocrisy for Labour to accept the Report in one breath and criticise one of its main conclusions in the other.

To Lennox-Boyd, the mere appointment of a judicial inquiry belied the allegation of the existence of a "police state". Turning to the murder plot, he recounted how he had returned from Aden on 1 March to be confronted by the Special Branch reports. He had been forced to take them seriously because they emanated from separate sources and much of the programme which had been revealed had already been implemented. He had joined Armitage in praying that the killing could be prevented, but they had to wait for troop reinforcements. The Commons tended to ignore the existence of intimidation, he said, and the Report had established the definite implementation of a policy of violence. However, when action had been taken, restraint had been exercised as the record showed. Punitive action, he maintained, had not been ordered by the Nyasaland Government and when it had occurred it had been stopped.

Lennox-Boyd explained that the new constitutional changes — which Armitage implemented in mid-August — were of an interim nature only. When the situation permitted, the constitutional negotiations would be resumed. He said that Nyasaland would move towards internal self-government, dominated by Africans but so devised to ensure that every Member of the Legislative Council cared for the interests of all races.

Lennox-Boyd stood by the pledges, recognised the opposition to the Federation, but believed that the best policy was to make a success of it. He refused to accept that Banda was a dupe of his associates when he was their undisputed leader and he would not treat him any differently from any other of the detainees who would not be released while they remained dangerous.[55]

The British Government won the debate but the Devlin revelations, coupled with those on the Hola Camp in Kenya where eleven inmates had been killed by their guards, soured many parliamentarians and shocked public opinion. Indeed, Lennox-Boyd had proposed to resign, but Macmillan

[55] House of Commons *Hansard* (London), Vol. 610, Col. 317 f., 28 July 1959.

and the Cabinet had worried about the effect on their electoral prospects. The events in Nyasaland and Kenya would inspire Iain Macleod, who would soon succeed Lennox-Boyd, to adopt a radical approach. Outside the House, Banda's former patients in London petitioned for his release. Welensky, though not pleased by the Devlin Report, was happy to have been exonerated.[56]

A comment by Home in the Lords debate on the preparatory commission, that constitutional change in both northern territories was necessary, surprised the Northern Rhodesians because the Benson Constitution had been intended to endure for ten years. Home's further statement, that these territories would become progressively more representative to the point where they would have African majorities, invoked a protest from Roberts that the basis of the Northern Rhodesian Constitution was non-racial. Home apologised as he had not intended to mislead.[57]

Northern Rhodesia, in any case, attracted attention because, on 7 August, the report of an inquiry into the action against the Zambia African National Congress was released publicly. The author was N. A. C. Ridley, a barrister in the service of the Northern Rhodesian Government. He had examined the actions of the ZANC and the ANC before and after the schism and had found that the Government had taken justifiable action to prevent wrongful interference with the general election. People had been fearful of election day, but in the event it had been calm despite 50 cases of arson. Ridley accepted that individual cases could have been dealt with by the law, but he was convinced that the broader measures had been necessary.

Ridley was satisfied with the evidence he had taken. He had seen, in the main, Special Branch material and had interviewed the restrictees and others. The evidence proved to him that there had been an intention to co-ordinate activity with the Southern Rhodesian and Nyasaland Congresses, but it had been disrupted by the declarations of emergency. A reaction, in the form of sabotage, arson and attacks on Europeans, he found had been planned if any of the leaders of the four Congresses were arrested. In Northern Rhodesia, there had been inflammatory speeches and when Kaunda and his cohorts were arrested, there had been widespread arson and malicious damage to property. The effort to dissuade people from standing for the Legislative Council and from exercising their votes had continued. To this end, pamphlets had been circulated and threats had been issued from public platforms. It was true that, on 5 March, Kaunda had been induced to ask his followers not to indulge in intimidation on polling day but he had refused to ask them to refrain until then.

Ridley had no doubt that the ZANC had conspired to organise unlawful meetings, corrupt policemen, utter false statements, foster ill-feeling between the racial groups and to publish statements on the need to refuse to vote. He, nevertheless, recommended action to meet many of the African grievances,

[56] Sir Nigel Fisher, *Iain Macleod* (London, 1973), p. 143; Short, *Banda, op. cit.*, p. 119; Welensky Papers, 25/240A, f. 249, Welensky to Lord Robins, 4 August 1959.

[57] House of Lords *Hansard* (London), Vol. 218, Col. 593, 27 July 1959; Welensky Papers, 20/5, f. 20, Draft Statement by Roberts, 14 August 1959; f. 21, Welensky to Home, 13 August 1959; 20/4, f. 153, J. Amery to Benson, 14 August 1959.

including the disparity in wages in the mining industry. He also urged the countering of the ZANC's propaganda.[58]

Mulford, pursuing his thesis on the inter-governmental conspiracy inspired by the Colonial Office to defeat African nationalism, casts doubt on the validity of the evidence seen by Ridley and believes that he failed to justify the action taken. Mulford finds little proof of a resort to violence before the banning, and thinks that the subsequent actions were used by Ridley as evidence of violent intentions. Mulford's research has revealed that the Government knew that the ZANC was not well organised enough to precipitate major violence, despite its propaganda and militant outbursts.[59] Nevertheless, in spite of Mulford's assertion, it is possible that the ZANC could have made a sufficiently significant gesture to deter the voters. The banning did disrupt the organisation of the ZANC and did lead to a revival of Nkumbula's ANC. If Mulford is right, and the Governments were indeed conspiring against African nationalism, the lack of accord between Salisbury and London is a startling discordancy.

Later in August the Report of a Tribunal comprising T. H. W. Beadle, the Chief Justice of Southern Rhodesia, and two assessors, on the action taken in Southern Rhodesia in February was tabled in its Legislative Assembly. The Tribunal found the assertions of the Southern Rhodesian Government to be proved and that there had been sufficient reasons for preventive detention. It believed that the Southern Rhodesian African National Congress had conspired to excite disaffection with the object of altering the Constitution by unlawful means. Racial hatred had been encouraged and subversive propaganda had been disseminated. Processions and strikes had been intended and native commissioners, land development officers, Chiefs, policemen and African MPs had been ridiculed and their authority undermined. Boycotts had been both threatened and implemented. Congress members had spread lies resulting in some convictions for criminal defamation. People had been intimidated to join the ANC and it had tried to infiltrate and control other African organisations.

Finally, the Tribunal related that there had been attempts at co-operation in subversion with other Congresses, though plans had not advanced beyond discussion. George Nyandoro, of the Southern Rhodesian ANC, had travelled in January to Nyasaland and Northern Rhodesia for that purpose. The draft of an agenda in Nyandoro's writing had been found, the Tribunal said, which listed the establishment of bonds of unity, plans for positive action and territorial efforts for the achievement of self-government.

The Tribunal acknowledged that these ideas were not necessarily subversive, but that they indicated the intention to act. The draft agenda had been for a summit meeting on 21 February which had been frustrated by the banning of Sipalo and Chipembere. The Tribunal said that when it asked them, Banda and Nyandoro had claimed that the agenda referred to a meeting of the Pan Africa Freedom Movement of East and Central Africa in April.

[58] N. A. C. Ridley, *Northern Rhodesia: Report of an Inquiry into all the Circumstances which gave Rise to the Making of the Safeguard of Elections and Public Safety Regulations* (Lusaka, 20 July 1959), p. 1 f.

[59] D. C. Mulford, *Zambia: The Politics of Independence, 1957–1964* (London, 1967), pp. 101–102.

However, unlike the Devlin Commission, Beadle and his assessors found both Banda and Nyandoro to be thoroughly unreliable witnesses. They said that Banda, in particular, had denied any knowledge of contact with the Southern Rhodesian ANC even though he had spent time with Nyandoro on 24 January in Limbe. He had denied knowledge of the summit meeting planned for 21 February when there was no conceivable reason why Chisiza and Chipembere should have concealed it from him. Moreover, the Tribunal noted, Nyandoro had claimed that Banda had told him of the summit because he had discussed it with Nkomo in Accra.[60]

For the time being, the restriction and detention of the African nationalists continued but could not be carried on indefinitely. The more immediate problem was to resolve the membership of the preparatory commission so that its work should be completed to allow the Federal constitutional review to be held in October 1960.

[60] *Southern Rhodesia Review Tribunal (Preventive Detention (Temporary Provisions) Act 1959): General Report*, CSR 27-1959 (Salisbury, 6 May 1959).

CHAPTER TWENTY-FOUR

The Preparatory Commission

Disagreement and Final Resolution of Its Composition, August 1959–January 1960

WHILE the results of the Devlin and the other Commissions were being examined, Macmillan and Welensky had continued to discuss the membership of the preparatory commission and the dialogue would continue until the end of the year. During this argument the British general election was held, and Macmillan's victory by 100 seats made a mockery of Home's earlier claim that the Labour Party could well win, and effect the dissolution of the Federation.

In the wake of the general election Lennox-Boyd finally resigned and was replaced by Iain Macleod. Although Macleod took his time, it soon became apparent that the Press speculation at the time of his appointment, that he would demand the release of Banda before the preparatory commission visited Nyasaland, was accurate. Just as the question of the membership of the commission would be bitterly fought, so would the argument over the timing of Banda's release.

Welensky thought that, while in London, he and Macmillan had agreed that Lord Forster, chairman of the National Arbitration Tribunal who had some experience of Northern Rhodesia, would chair the preparatory commission. So he was somewhat surprised by a dispatch from Macmillan on 10 August telling him that they first had to choose a chairman. Making no reference to Forster, Macmillan said that he wanted Lord Shawcross QC, the chief British prosecutor at the Nuremberg Trials and the Labour Attorney-General in 1945-51. As he had since become a cross-bencher in politics and a capitalist in economics, Macmillan felt that the only danger was that the Labour Party would regard Shawcross as a renegade. However, he said, it would criticise any of his choices. If Shawcross refused, then Lord Reading would be preferred. As vice-chairman of the commission, Macmillan proposed Sir Donald MacGillivray, a distinguished colonial administrator and current chairman of the Council of State in Kenya. Among the members would be Professor Wheare, Mrs Elizabeth Huxley, Frank Menzies and Douglas Abbott.

Noting that there was one place left, apart from the Privy Councillors, and ignoring the previous correspondence, Macmillan proposed to impress the Africans with a Malayan or a West Indian. He was thinking of Sir Henry Lee, a former Malayan Finance Minister, who was really more English than the English. If a non-European were unacceptable, then Sir Alexander Fleck, chairman of Imperial Chemical Industries, or an economist might be suitable. Macmillan told Welensky that he was anxious to settle the membership in case he decided to call an early election. He promised to ignore boycotts or the threat of them — referring to the Labour Party and to a recent walk out of the Northern Rhodesian Legislative Council by the six African Members in protest at the provision for only five Africans out of 26 members of the preparatory commission.[1]

Welensky asked Macmillan why Lord Forster had not been mentioned, and rejected Lords Shawcross and Reading. If Forster were unavailable, he preferred Lord Reid, the distinguished Scottish lawyer. After the experience of the Devlin Commission, Welensky felt that he and Macmillan had to exclude politicians and find someone who, because everything was at stake, could be relied on to do "the right thing". He asked Macmillan not to insist on a Malayan or a West Indian as he had difficulties enough without outraging his Parliament. He did want an economist and suggested Professor D. T. Jack of the University of Durham, who had recently conducted an economic survey of Nyasaland and had chaired an inquiry into the implementation of a 40-hour week on the Copperbelt in 1950. Welensky confessed that he had not yet found a suitable African, but otherwise that his team remained V. L. Robinson, A. E. P. Robinson and R. M. Taylor.[2]

Welensky learned from other sources that Lord Forster was unwell and, on 4 September, Macmillan informed him that he did not favour Lord Reid but had found a most suitable chairman. His choice was Viscount Monckton of Brenchley whom he had thought was too busy but who, when asked, had said that the task was of such paramount importance that it was his duty to accept. Macmillan said he was aware that Welensky and Whitehead did not want a politician. (He was forgetting that they had proposed Lord Kilmuir.) Nevertheless, he recommended Monckton because not only was he a wise and trusted friend, but he was not primarily regarded in Britain as a politician and was greatly experienced in dealing with men and affairs.[3] Macmillan did not add that, in certain cirlces, Monckton was known as the "Fixer" because of his considerable achievements as a reconciler, particularly in the crisis of the abdication of Edward VIII. He also did not say, but then he might not have known, that Monckton was terminally ill with arteriosclerosis.

Believing that they would be fortunate to recruit Monckton, Macmillan wanted an immediate reply from Welensky and Whitehead. Welensky was on

[1] Welensky Papers, 20/10, f. 193, Macmillan to Welensky, 10 August 1959; f. 191, Welensky to Macmillan, 14 August 1959.

[2] *Ibid.*, f. 191, Welensky to Macmillan, 14 August 1959.

[3] *Ibid.*, 25/240A, f. 234, Welensky to Lord Robins, 26 August 1959; 20/10, f. 188, Macmillan to Welensky, 4 September 1959.

holiday in Beira, but under such pressure he agreed promptly. Whitehead did likewise[4] and the appointment was announced on Monday, 6 September.

Monckton's biographer, Lord Birkenhead, might believe that, by September 1959, the Federation was already stricken with its fatal disease, but its symptoms were certainly not yet recognisable to the Federal Government. At least one of Welensky's friends, J. Thompson, had searched the parliamentary statements of Macmillan and Lennox-Boyd but could not find confirmation of an assertion by Welensky that it was quite clear that, in 1960, a considerable step forward could be taken and that the Federation could become independent in its own field. Welensky replied to Thompson that his discussions in London indicated that this was perfectly possible and that, to the contrary, Macmillan had indeed cleared the way for it in the Commons. He claimed that Macmillan had confirmed that powers held by the British Government could be transferred to the territories.[5]

The sincerity of this view was confirmed at a meeting on 14 September between Welensky, Whitehead, Caldicott and Greenfield. The main topic was the review, and the Federal Ministers declared that they aimed to secure independence for the Federation within its own sphere as soon as possible. This would involve the abrogation of the British power to legislate for the Federation which had been waived in 1957 but not explicitly removed from the Federal Constitution. The Colonial Laws Validity Act had to be repealed in so far as it affected the Federation. The British veto had to go and with it, obviously, the African Affairs Board. The Governor-General henceforth would be chosen by the Federal Government. The ability to legislate extra-territorially had been conceded in 1957 but had to be written into the Constitution. The appeal to the Privy Council, however, would be retained and there would be compensating safeguards, for example a constitutional amendment would require the endorsement of two of the three territories. If such an amendment directly affected a territory, then its approval would be sought. A council of state or a senate to call attention to discrimination could replace the African Affairs Board. Welensky wanted the Chiefs on this council but Whitehead considered that the Chiefs were becoming obsolete. Human rights or any such formula would not be written into the Constitution because experience elsewhere had proved that it could be suspended in times of emergency and rendered useless. There was still the long desired adjustment to end the ability of the territories to suspend Federal laws.

Greenfield reminded the meeting that the constitutional preamble contained two pledges. The first was that the northern territories could continue to have separate governments under British protection for as long as their inhabitants wished. The second allowed full self-government for the Federation when the inhabitants desired it. This did not inhibit, he said, the granting of responsible government to the territories either at once or by stages. In Northern Rhodesia a constitutional change had been effected in 1958 without a referendum of the inhabitants.

[4] *Ibid.*, f. 187, W. S. Parker to Welensky, 5 September 1959, and Parker's notes thereon, 7 September 1959.

[5] Lord Birkenhead, *Walter Monckton* (London, 1969), p. 327; Welensky Papers, 24/47, ff. 2–3, J. Thompson to Welensky, 20 August 1959; f. 38, Welensky to Thompson, 25 August 1959.

The Federal Government presumed, and Whitehead confirmed, that Southern Rhodesia would soon press for the removal of the British reserved powers. Whitehead expected that these would be replaced by a requirement for the consent of two-thirds of his Parliament for specific legislation. He and Welensky agreed to discuss the matter before any final agreement because it would set a precedent for Federal advancement. It was hoped that Southern Rhodesia would be rid of all restrictions before the review to enhance Federal chances of advancement. Welensky warned, however, that he would not agree to any lowering of the Federal or Southern Rhodesian franchises. He and Whitehead agreed to consult the Dominion Party.

The Federal Government believed that, as a result of the review, the Northern Rhodesian Government should acquire the status which Southern Rhodesia had been given in 1923. Whitehead favoured this but feared that the British would then insist that the franchise be lowered to give control to the Africans.

The Federal Government thought Nyasaland was not ready for a parallel advance but could be given the current status enjoyed by Northern Rhodesia. It would mean unfortunately that there would be Colonial Office officials appointed as Ministers. Whitehead thought that the land shortage in Nyasaland would force the British Government to amalgamate the two northern territories which would mean that the Federation would comprise two states with equal representation in its legislature.

Whitehead suggested again the combining of the posts of the Southern Rhodesian Governor and the Governor-General because there were obvious economies to be made. The northern Governments had opposed this but he did not want it abandoned without good reason. The Federal Cabinet had been reconsidering the federalisation of the police and proposed to adapt the Canadian or Nigerian systems. Whitehead, however, warned that he would never agree to the lowering of standards but, after Welensky proposed to raise them, he agreed to consult his Police Commissioner.

Whitehead refused to relinquish labour, and wanted the control of the tsetse fly because it was closely associated with African agriculture. The Federal Ministers agreed that all roads should become territorial responsibilities. Whitehead wanted health to be reallocated because he believed the curative service should be territorial while the preventive remained Federal. The Federal Ministers disagreed because the system was working well. Generally, Whitehead felt that the review should not be used by the Federal Government to secure more power regardless of principle. The Federal Ministers agreed because they really sought to hand the power of the Colonial Office to the territories. It was imperative that the northern territories were properly policed. They reviewed problems relating to the Land Apportionment Act and other issues. Whitehead agreed to allow the Federal Government to establish an African agricultural college — to be called Chibero — on European land. He was having difficulties with racial problems with regard to hotels and cafes, and urged the development of the non-racial Federal capital site at Warren Hills, outside Salisbury. Welensky, however, could not see how that would assist the Southern Rhodesian country-wide racial problems. A security council was considered to co-ordinate the efforts of the army and the police. Then Greenfield raised the problem posed by the nationalist detainees because they were crowding the prisons. Nothing on either issue, however, was resolved.[6]

On 12 October they discussed again labour, the Federal capital site, industrial expansion and economics, but not the review because they intended to meet again shortly.[7] They did not, but in preparation Greenfield wrote a memorandum which is interesting for his ideas. Unlike Welensky, Greenfield felt that the review could discuss the territorial Constitutions. At least it could examine the overall picture because in 1957 it was agreed that a programme to attain Commonwealth membership would be considered, and this plainly included the elimination of Colonial Office control. Providing an outline of constitutional advances, Greenfield proposed the removal of the Southern Rhodesian "apron strings" in 1960 and those of the Federation in 1961. In 1962 Northern Rhodesia would be granted responsible government on the 1923 Southern Rhodesian pattern. Nyasaland would be advanced in 1963 to the current status of Northern Rhodesia. The Northern Rhodesian "apron strings" would be cut in 1965 and those of Nyasaland in 1970. By then the Colonial Office would have withdrawn and the Federation would be fully independent. The territorial franchises would be determined by the British and territorial Governments in consultation with the Federal Government.

Greenfield thought that the Monckton Commission could not consider the Federal Constitution in isolation from the territorial Constitutions. However, Whitehead might prove difficult because, if he failed to secure the removal of his British veto in November, he would object to the review examining the territorial Constitutions as it would involve the northerners in the settlement of his Constitution. Greenfield advised the apprisal of the territorial leaders of the UFP of Federal ideas on the review and of the programme thereafter. The idea of Northern Rhodesia advancing to cabinet government, which meant that the UFP would spread its wings, had to be firmly implanted.

It was also clear to Greenfield that the review would discuss the re-distribution of functions. He recalled that Welensky had stressed that the advance to full Commonwealth membership did not imply that the Federal Government would grab further power from the territories. However, it was necessary to federalise the police and Greenfield proposed that Roberts and Little of Nyasaland should assist in persuading Whitehead on this. Recently, he said, Whitehead had claimed that the Canadian model, and not the more suitable Nigerian one, had to be applied because it had been an election promise. The Nigerian system, unlike its Canadian counterpart, did not allow independent state forces. Greenfield knew that Whitehead's Police Commissioner, Colonel B. G. Spurling, disliked the Canadian model but might accept the Nigerian. Greenfield had heard that Whitehead had already instructed his officials to secure in London a clear-cut division of powers so that everything connected with external or economic affairs would be Federal, but everything local or social would be territorial. Greenfield understood that Whitehead would allow the Federation to keep external affairs, defence, customs, immigration, income tax and railways. Whitehead also appeared to

[6] Welensky Papers, 7/24, f. 95, Minutes of a Meeting with Whitehead, 14 September 1959.
[7] *Ibid.*, f. 77, Minutes of a Meeting with Whitehead, 12 October 1959.

want to recover health, roads, education and European agriculture at least, but he had obviously not considered the difficulty of dismantling the current structure. It was unfortunate that Whitehead had adopted a rigid attitude so early and Greenfield suggested that he should be asked to withdraw these instructions.[8]

The correspondence on the membership of the preparatory commission had not ceased with the appointment of Monckton. Macmillan had prorogued the British Parliament immediately after announcing the appointment. On 16 September he told Welensky that the need to call the general election had been the reason for the urgency to make the appointment. However, Macmillan said he could not appoint the Privy Councillors before the election but would make preliminary soundings so that a conclusion could be rapidly reached after it. He believed that Welensky was satisfied with MacGillivray, Mrs Huxley, Wheare, Menzies and Abbott. He appreciated Welensky's feelings on West Indians or Malayans and would not press him further. He would accept Professor Jack, and Welensky's team. Privy Councillors to be considered included Sir Toby Low, Sir Alan Noble, Sir Roland Robinson and Lord Crathorne. British public opinion, Macmillan averred, made it absolutely essential to secure African members of quality, and Monckton, naturally, was anxious to recruit a sensible body of commissioners.[9]

If Macmillan was content, Home was not and he questioned the choice of Abbott the next day because his attitude to Africa was unknown and he had been a minister in a Canadian government whose general attitude to "colonialism" had been unhelpful. Moreover, the appointment of a former member of the Canadian Opposition front bench might be misunderstood in Canada. Home was confident that he could find a more suitable choice.[10]

The next few weeks were dominated by the British election campaign during which Macmillan commented, with regard to the Federation, that economic and political advancement had to be simultaneous, as independence with pauperism was a sham. Lennox-Boyd claimed that the Federation had succeeded in developing a multi-racial society, if on a limited scale. The Conservative Party policy, he said, was to assist the dependencies to attain self-government within the Commonwealth, to foster economic and social advancement, and to enable them to keep pace with political development.[11]

Callaghan maintained that the Colonial Office should do more to prepare the colonies for independence. The real failure of the Conservatives, he said, was in disregarding colonial for British interests. He claimed that in Central Africa the argument used to retard self-government was the same as that which had previously held back the British people, namely that they were too ignorant and too irresponsible to vote. The result had been the recent Nyasaland explosion which had uncovered almost universal hostility and resentment. Devlin, he noted, in discovering this, had given the Tories an opportunity to make a fresh start, but their ideas were too rigid. By contrast, Callaghan maintained that the Labour Party would allow the true leaders to

[8] *Ibid.*, 16/46, f. 9, Greenfield to Welensky, 16 October 1959.
[9] *Ibid.*, 20/10, f. 185, Macmillan to Welensky, 16 September 1959.
[10] *Ibid.*, f. 184, Home to Welensky, 17 September 1959.
[11] *The Rhodesia Herald*, 24 & 30 September 1959.

speak and would make it clear to the people that they themselves could choose the form of association with other territories. His Party was not hostile to the local Europeans and would safeguard their well-being as a minority, but the Europeans had to understand that they had to be accepted as a natural element in society. Representative government was the immediate aim, but Callaghan concluded that there had also to be rapid progress towards the implementation of adult suffrage.[12]

From South Africa, where he was on leave, Welensky contributed to the debate avowing that the trouble in Nyasaland would not cause the Federal Government to deviate from its commitment to partnership. Nyasaland had been allowed to stagnate for 100 years, he said, and the recovery of the lost ground had been beyond the resources of the Federation, even though much had been done. He did not believe that universal suffrage was the answer because it would delay his objective of introducing democracy.[13]

Macmillan returned to the membership of the preparatory commission on 5 October (three days before his general election) because the northern Governors had transmitted their nominations to him. Welensky knew that Sir Evelyn Hone wished to appoint J. Woodrow Cross, W. H. McCleland and Lawrence Katilungu, but was considerably taken aback by Armitage's selection of the recently released Orton Chirwa with G. G. S. J. Hadlow and E. K. Gondwe. Welensky refused to accept Chirwa because he was one of those who had been responsible for the disturbances and, since his release, had become the leader of a new political party pledged to break up the Federation. Chirwa would be totally unacceptable to local opinion, he said, and his appointment would entirely discredit the commission. Welensky sympathised with the difficulty in finding someone who would not be labelled "stooge", but this carried appeasement too far. Chirwa, he felt, was the worst possible choice. Although Welensky did not give this impression, he was quite flabbergasted by the suggestion.[14]

The British election intruded, and in its wake Lennox-Boyd resigned. He was replaced at the Colonial Office by the ambitious, young and able Iain Macleod who was believed by the Press to have been given a free hand by Macmillan to bring British Africa to independence within five years. It was thought that current policies would be reappraised including the removal of the "police state" stigma from Nyasaland. The early release of Banda was expected. Sir Nigel Fisher acknowledges Macleod's ambition for higher office but has discovered that he did not view his appointment as a vehicle for his own political advancement but as an opportunity to do something which was right.[15] The Rhodesians, mistakenly perhaps, were not to reach such a charitable conclusion.

In fact, Macmillan told Macleod that he had reserved for him the worst job of all, and the Press was right in that Macleod believed that only the speeding up of the advancement to independence would avoid the risk of considerable

[12] *Ibid.*, 30 September 1959.
[13] *Ibid.*, 25 September 1959.
[14] Welensky Papers, 20/10, f. 175, Macmillan to Welensky, 5 October 1959; f. 173, Welensky to Macmillan, 7 October 1959; 43/*Goldberg*, Welensky to B. D. Goldberg, 13 October 1959.
[15] *The Rhodesia Herald*, 16 October 1959; Sir Nigel Fisher, *Iain Macleod* (London, 1973), p. 141.

bloodshed. Indeed, Fisher has shown that the acceleration achieved independence for Tanganyika in 1961 (instead of 1970 as planned by Lennox-Boyd in January 1959), and 1963 for Kenya (instead of 1975). Macleod was convinced that it was more dangerous to go too slow than too fast, but to the Rhodesians he was a gambler and he soon generated a venomous suspicion in them. However, such emotion was of the future and, for the moment, the return of the Conservatives was greeted with relief by everyone in the Federation, apart from the African nationalists. Welensky pointed out to James Johnson the error of the Labour Party in over-emphasising the effect of colonial issues on the British voter who, as ever, was more concerned with parochial issues.[16]

On 24 October Macmillan revealed that Armitage had withdrawn Orton Chirwa's name and had substituted R. Katengeza who had been narrowly defeated by Chiume in the Nyasaland general election in 1956. Welensky was relieved but was disappointed to hear that Professor Wheare could not accept. He told Macmillan that Hone had helped him to find a suitable African for the Federal team, referring to G. H. Habanyama who was a respected councillor of the Gwembe Native Authority and no "stooge".[17]

When Macmillan next wrote to Welensky on 29 October, he said that the ranks of the commission were rapidly being filled with the acceptance of Professor Jack and Frank Menzies and the possible agreement of Mrs Huxley and MacGillivray. However, there had been no reply from John Diefenbaker, Prime Minister of Canada, on Abbott. Also, Macmillan continued, there was a slight complication because the Opposition had tabled an amendment to the Address from the Throne which regretted that the Address contained no proposals for ending the Nyasaland emergency, for the release or trial of political prisoners, or for an early and substantial extension of the northern franchises so that the northern Governments might truly represent their people at the review. This amendment was to be debated in the Commons on Monday, 2 November and, while he did not expect difficulties, Macmillan said it would delay his approach to Gaitskell. He proposed to ignore Gaitskell until after the debate but, in the meantime, would publish the names of the appointees, with the exception of the Privy Councillors, and intimate that the Labour Party would be approached. He hoped that the commission would be of such calibre that Gaitskell could no longer refuse to participate. To Macmillan the Labour Party was crucial lest the northern African refuse to participate and thus make it extremely difficult to create the atmosphere of trust and goodwill necessary for the review.

Hence Macmillan wished to change the composition of the commission in two ways to ensure its universal approval. The first was to substitute a Malayan for a Canadian and he was sure that he could find a Malayan who would satisfy Welensky. Such a choice, Macmillan believed, would have an important effect on the Commonwealth, particularly in the long term. The second move was to drop the insistence on Privy Councillors only. This could have a dramatic effect because, after nine years out of office, the Privy

[16] Fisher, *Macleod, op. cit.*, p. 141; Welensky Papers, 24/151, ff. 182–183, Welensky to F. S. Joelson, 16 October 1959; 24/157, ff. 43–46, Welensky to J. Johnson, 29 October 1959.

[17] Welensky Papers, 20/10, f. 170, Macmillan to Welensky, 24 October 1959; f. 171, Welensky to Macmillan, 25 October 1959.

Councillors of the Labour Party were steadily declining in number and many of the survivors were incapable of undertaking the assignment. This alone, he said, gave the Opposition justification in claiming that the commission would be one-sided. If Welensky agreed, Macmillan promised to refuse to appoint Mrs Castle or Stonehouse but would accept Callaghan because he would become better disposed to the Federation if he were a commissioner. Thus Macmillan thought that the Labour team should comprise a Peer, a Privy Councillor and Callaghan. He hoped that Welensky would concur and would persuade Whitehead. Macmillan conceded that his election success gave him greater freedom to manoeuvre but that he wanted to use it to ensure that the real danger of African opposition was removed.[18]

Welensky was irritated by another request for an urgent answer at a weekend, but did not say so when he replied immediately. Believing that Macmillan was simply using the Federation as a pawn when the Labour Party, bereft of other weapons, exploited it, Welensky apologised that he might disappoint Macmillan but he could not accept his proposal. Indeed, Welensky suggested, the moment might have come to abandon the commission itself because its underlying purpose, of keeping the Federation out of British politics, had not been realised. Home, he said, had originally wanted to educate British public opinion, but the Federal Government had been extremely reluctant to accept the commission and had utterly refused to countenance an inquiry into Federal affairs. Eventually his Government had grudgingly agreed to a commission which would merely advise on the constitutional framework. It had done so because Macmillan had urgently argued that thereby the Federation would be removed as an issue from his general election and, in the long term, out of British politics completely. Nonetheless, Welensky asserted, Federal issues had been bandied about in that election, and the latest Labour move, the amendment, showed that the second goal had not been attained. As Welensky and his Government had never wanted the commission, they suggested that it should be dropped.

Hindsight suggests that perhaps Welensky should have ended his reply there because Macmillan would never fail to exploit a door left even slightly ajar and interpret it as a willing invitation to proceed. However, Welensky continued, saying that, if Macmillan felt irrevocably committed to the commission, his Government could not agree to reconsider the question of Commonwealth coloured representation. He reminded Macmillan just how vehemently he had opposed it in London and had, by way of substitution, agreed to increase the number of African commissioners. The Federal Government would also not accept other than Privy Councillors as the British commissioners. The reason, he said, was that he had greatly emphasised the belief that membership of the Privy Council equated with responsibility. There could be no lowering of standards without the most damaging public reaction. Moreover, there would be renewed pressure for Federal parliamentary representation. He would have sufficient difficulty in explaining Macmillan's latest choice, the Right Reverend R. H. W. Shepherd — presumably because he was the current Moderator of the Church of Scotland. Callaghan,

[18] *Ibid.*, f. 167, Macmillan to Welensky, 29 October 1959.

Welensky continued, had disqualified himself, even if he were to be elevated to the Privy Council, by his irresponsible statements on 22 July. In saying this, Welensky remarked that he was ignoring Callaghan's violent personal attacks on him. In any case, the Federal Government seriously doubted whether Labour participation would induce the Africans to co-operate, and the latest amendment made it even more unpalatable to the Europeans. Welensky warned that Whitehead agreed with him and would be writing to give his own reasons.[19]

Only later did Welensky berate Macmillan for his failure to stand by his pledges. He came to realise that his refusal to concur on the issue of the Privy Councillors aroused in Macmillan and his new Government personal dislike and resentment, although this was masked for some time by repeated affirmations of friendship.[20] He would have been more irritated had he known that Macmillan would accuse him alone, in *Pointing the Way*, of changing his mind. Saying nothing of what had happened, Macmillan blandly wrote: "The truth about this man, whom I liked and respected, was that under a bluff and burly exterior he concealed an impulsive and often suspicious temperament. Yet his heart was in the right place." Continuing, Macmillan claimed that Welensky suggested, out of the blue, the abandonment of the commission because agreement could not be reached on its composition.[21] This, of course, ignores the whole history of the affair and its tedious argument.

As promised by Welensky, Whitehead wrote to Home on 2 November, the day of the Commons debate. He rejected Malayans and Callaghan and insisted on the retention of the Privy Councillors. He would not accept the proposed changes anyway, he said, unless Southern Rhodesian parliamentarians were included. He agreed with Welensky that the commission should be abandoned because it could not attain the expected objectives.

Whitehead was faced with another issue because Home had asked him that day if the British Government could announce in the debate that the Southern Rhodesian detainees would be allowed to appear before the commission and submit memoranda to it. Three months earlier, on 21 July, Macmillan had already conferred this privilege on the northern detainees and now hoped, Home said, to be able to confirm that the Southern Rhodesians would share it. Home believed that acquisition of all shades of opinion in the Federation would obviously be a factor of the greatest importance in establishing the credibility of the commission. (Thus Home implied that Welensky's suggestion on 31 October of abandonment was to be ignored. However, Macmillan delayed until after the debate before saying so directly.) Whitehead replied firmly that he did not wish anything to be said on the detainees before he began his negotiations in London later in the month. He understood that Southern Rhodesian affairs were completely outside the commission's terms of reference and wished to be assured that any attempt to give evidence on them would be ruled out of order by Monckton.[22]

[19] *Ibid.*, f. 164, Welensky to Macmillan, 31 October 1959.

[20] Sir Roy Welensky, *Welensky's 4 000 Days* (London, 1964), p. 152.

[21] H. Macmillan, *Pointing the Way, 1959–61* (London, 1972), p. 139.

[22] Welensky Papers, 20/10, f. 160, Whitehead to Home, 2 November 1959; f. 161, Home to Whitehead, 2 November 1959.

In the Commons debate, Callaghan propounded his standard themes of African hatred for the Federation and the need to regain their confidence. He believed that the commission would be ineffective without that confidence, and that this would only be achieved by associating Kaunda, Nkumbula and Banda in some manner. The most important issue, he said, was to advance speedily all three territories to independence. These sentiments were echoed by his colleagues. They thought that Banda was the key figure and that sooner or later the Governments would have to come to terms with him.

Macleod replied that the tendency to violence still existed in Nyasaland and some emergency powers had to remain in force. He stated that 830 detainees had been released, leaving 459 still in prison, of whom 37 had been tried and convicted. No one, Macleod assured, would be detained longer than necessary. He would not consider change for Northern Rhodesia because its constitution was too new and needed to be given a fair trial. He envisaged steady constitutional advance but did not think that it was necessary to use the legislatures alone to represent public opinion at the review. He was confident that African commissioners could be found who would inspire confidence, and he supported the Federation because it offered the chance of creating a multi-racial society.[23] The Government won both this debate and that in the Lords on 3 November.

On 5 November Welensky wrote to Home acidly commenting on the impracticalities of the Northern Rhodesian Constitution which Home had recently defended. Simultaneously, Macmillan thanked Welensky for his prompt reply and explained that he had delayed replying for the result of the vote in Parliament. He accepted Welensky's difficulties with the Malayan commissioner and the Privy Councillors and would not press him again. Indeed, he said he would accept and abide by Welensky's judgment and their agreement of July. He was positive that it was vitally important to retain the commission. His Government had been in no difficulty with the debate and, in fact, the Opposition had been half-hearted about it. What interested him more was British public opinion which he was sure the commission would moderate. Thus encouraged, he would wait until he had recruited all the independent members before offering Gaitskell his three places. If he refused them, Macmillan said he would fill them from the cross-benches.[24]

Replying immediately, but saying nothing more about the abandonment of the commission, Welensky demanded a reduction by three places if the Labour Party refused. If Macmillan offered the seats to the cross-benches, Welensky wanted to know in advance the likely candidates. He asked for a speedy conclusion as he was facing a short session of Parliament and wished to announce the names during it. Also, he was becoming anxious about procedural matters, especially the extent to which the commission could take evidence from politicians. He had always considered that the volume of evidence should be kept to a minimum. The terms of reference provided that the bulk of the material would be collected by the civil servants but allowed the commissioners to supplement it. What worried him was that an idea was

[23] House of Commons *Hansard* (London), Vol. 612, Col. 668 f., 2 November 1959.

[24] Welensky Papers, 20/4, f. 149, Welensky to Home, 5 November 1959; 20/10, f. 159, Macmillan to Welensky, 5 November 1959.

gaining credence that all politicians would be able to submit evidence. As the Governments were to refrain from giving evidence, Welensky said that the picture which would emerge would be very lop-sided and he hoped, therefore, that Monckton would be instructed to keep the taking of evidence to a minimum in accordance with the terms of reference.[25]

The problem was not yet solved and, indeed, would only become more complicated. The Federal Government was considerably annoyed by a decision by Monckton not to have a secretary-general who was connected with either the Federation or its territories. He chose M. D. Tennant, the Under-Secretary of the British Ministry of Labour, with whom he had worked when he had held that portfolio. The assistant-secretaries were to be J. C. Morgan and D. A. Scott (later Sir David), the heads of the Central African departments of the Colonial and Commonwealth Relations Offices. Although, because of the equal numbers of local and overseas appointees, the Federal Government proposed A. D. Evans as joint secretary-general, Evans was made nothing more than the Federal liaison officer.[26]

The ranks of the commission were slowly filling, with Professor D. G. Creighton from Canada and E. K. Gondwe from Nyasaland agreeing to serve. However, on 17 November, Macmillan had to report continuing failure with Gaitskell. Yet he believed that the Labour camp was hesitating and might accept if given a few more days' grace. He hoped that Welensky still regarded Labour participation as crucial and wished to postpone the joint announcement of the membership for a week, even though by then the Federal Parliament would have risen. Welensky agreed.[27]

Macmillan, having toured much of the Commonwealth in 1958, decided at this moment to visit Africa in the New Year. His purpose was not merely to inform himself but, by focussing public attention on African problems, he hoped to lift them above British party politics. The decision to visit was announced on 18 November by Welensky who could not refrain from claiming, at the same time, to be sickened by the sight of Britain, France and Belgium, scuttling their colonies.[28]

Welensky repeated this later in the day in the Federal Assembly when van Eeden criticised the Federal propaganda effort. What worried van Eeden was that the UFP was dominated by a "leave it to Roy" faction who believed that Welensky unaided could negotiate a reasonable settlement. They forgot, van Eeden said, that the British Government would pay inordinate attention to northern African opinion. Within the Federation, he added, there was considerable and effective propaganda being aimed at the Africans by well-meaning people who opposed any further advance for the Federation. So

[25] *Ibid.*, 20/10, f. 157, Welensky to Macmillan, 6 November 1959.

[26] *Ibid.*, f. 153, W. I. McIndoe to M. J. Lamb, 13 November 1959; f. 154, Welensky to Home, 13 November 1959; f. 149, Macmillan to Welensky, 23 November 1959. Sir David Scott, berating Welensky for glossing over the British concessions to Federal demands in his *4 000 Days*, regards Evans's appointment as the liaison officer as most generous – D. Scott, *Ambassador in Black and White: Thirty Years of Changing Africa* (London, 1981), p. 54.

[27] Welensky Papers, 20/10, f. 153, W. I. McIndoe to M. J. Lamb, 13 November 1959; f. 152, H. G. M. Bass to Welensky, 17 November 1959.

[28] Macmillan, *Pointing the Way*, *op. cit.*, p. 119; *The Rhodesia Herald*, 19 November 1959.

there had to be effective counter-propaganda. This assertion met with general approval from the House.

Welensky, however, denied the existence of the faction and claimed that not only was his Party deeply concerned, but that his Government was taking the task of countering the propaganda very seriously. African opinion would have to be consulted on any changes but would not constitute a "veto" because, if the opinion were erroneously founded, it would be judged accordingly. He believed the campaign to prevent the attainment of a higher status would not succeed. Any impartial survey would fully justify the claims for advancement and for that reason he thought the preparatory commission could do nothing but good. He could not accept the thesis that an irresistible wave of African nationalism was sweeping down Africa. To him the trouble stemmed from people becoming contemptibly ashamed of their colonies. Nevertheless, he agreed that all reasonable efforts had to be made to educate the northern African.[29]

In fact, the Federal Assembly had already concerned itself with the immediate future because, on 12 November, Gaunt had sought to make the legislatures the vehicles for the opinions of their diverse peoples on the issue of the advancement of status. He wanted the union between the Rhodesias to be declared indissoluble so that any suggestion of severance could be ignored. The return of any Federal powers to the territories would likewise be resisted because it would weaken the Federation and possibly lead to its dissolution. He explained that his intention was not to attack the Government but to persuade it to accept certain irreducible minima before the preparatory commission began work and provided, as it undoubtedly would, a blueprint for the future of the Federation.

Robert Moffat claimed that the Federal constitutional preamble had been carefully explained to the Africans and that they had been led to believe that their opinion, as they were the majority of inhabitants, would be the deciding factor in change. Chembe agreed and claimed that independence for the Federation could not be considered until the majority of Africans was enfranchised. Yamba stressed the hatred of the Africans for the Federation and their suspicions of the commission. He wondered why, if Nyasaland could enjoy an African majority in its legislature, Northern Rhodesia could not. As the Federation had reduced Northern Rhodesia to poverty, or so he believed, power had to be returned to the territories. Chad Chipunza, however, thought that the Federation was on the right course.

Greenfield convinced Gaunt and most of the House that the Assembly, anticipating the discussion and the review in 1960, should affirm its determination that the Federation should be maintained intact and that a programme should be drawn up for the attainment of full Commonwealth membership. He argued that it was time for the Assembly to state forcibly that there was no question of secession being considered. He reminded the House that the commission was purely advisory and could not bind any of the five Governments. His Government did not interpret the preamble as giving the majority of the inhabitants anything more than the right to express an

[29] Fed R & N *Debates* (Salisbury), Vol. 11, Col. 3698, 18 November 1959.

opinion. It was confident that it was outside the scope of the commission to advise how the preamble would be interpreted. The House needed reminding, he said, that the Declaration of 1957 had specifically ruled out secession and he agreed that the power of the Federal Government should not be weakened. Indeed, he and his Government had publicly stated that, if power was to be transferred, it would be from the Colonial Office to the northern Governments.[30]

On the eve of Macmillan's statement in the Commons on the preparatory commission on 24 November, the volume of criticism of the Federation was swelled by the chairman of the Rhodesian Selection Trust, Sir Ronald Prain. Earlier in the year the Trust and its rival, the Anglo American Corporation, had ceased to contribute financially to political parties, somewhat to the distress of the United Federal Party. Now Prain decided to introduce political comment into his report to his shareholders and pointed out to Southern Rhodesia the incongruity of it being the leading territory in a multi-racial federation when its legislature contained only Europeans. He called for drastic alteration to the Land Apportionment and other similar Acts to restore African confidence in partnership. Nyasaland, too, shared some of his attack because he believed that economic development alone would not satisfy African aspirations. Only in Northern Rhodesia was partnership making any strides. He warned the Europeans not to ignore events in the rest of Africa and to resign themselves to greater sacrifices if progress were to be ensured. Discrimination and restrictive practices had to go.[31]

Macmillan informed Welensky on 23 November that he would deliver his statement the next afternoon. He apologised for not enclosing his full text but said that he was still waiting for Gaitskell's reply, and that it would be sent as soon as possible. He intended to describe the objects of the commission briefly and then its terms of reference fully. Thereafter he would name the commissioners and say something about the Privy Councillors. He would express his pleasure if the Labour Party agreed to co-operate. If they did not, he would grant them a further short delay but would stress that the commission had to start work and consequently he would fill the gaps if necessary. To avoid answering a multitude of questions off the cuff, he would anticipate them with a short, precisely-worded statement that he was adhering to the terms of reference. If questioned thereafter, he would recommend trust in Monckton and his experienced team. He hoped that Welensky would agree with this course and expected him to make a similar statement.[32]

The Federal Parliament had risen, and Welensky had no parallel opportunity. In any event, this dispatch only arrived hours before Macmillan spoke and the full text of the statement only reached Welensky two hours after it had been delivered. The answers to the supplementary questions took a further two days to arrive, and Welensky found himself placed at a serious disadvantage. He had no time to comment to Macmillan on the statement and could only reply that he was being denied the opportunity to study the

[30] *Ibid.*, Col. 3491 f., 12 November 1959.

[31] Welensky Papers, 25/240A, f. 246, Welensky to Lord Robins, 12 August 1959; f. 243, Robins to Welensky, 19 August 1959; *The Rhodesia Herald*, 23 November 1959.

[32] Welensky Papers, 20/10, f. 148, H. G. M. Bass to M. J. Lamb, 24 November 1959.

statement but trusted that it would conform with his demands of 6 November. He said he intended only to reiterate publicly the terms of reference and name the members.[33]

Gaitskell again spurned Macmillan and forced him to choose his alternative course. Accordingly, Macmillan proclaimed that the commission would not merely supply the best possible advice, but could provide a common approach for all concerned. He read, as promised, the terms of reference but said that, nonetheless, he regarded the commission as free, in practice, to hear all points of view from any quarter and on any subject. The commission would decide what use it would make of the evidence it acquired and the House would surely have confidence in Monckton's ability to deal with this. In cases such as this, Macmillan considered it unwise to be too rigid in interpretation, and the terms of reference would permit the commission to consider the whole field of the redistribution of powers in either direction. It would advise on the timing of any programme and on the nature of any changes in the framework.

Before anticipating any questions, Macmillan listed the members of the commission. Sir Donald MacGillivray would be vice-chairman. The independent British members would be Mrs Elspeth Huxley, Professor Jack and the Reverend Shepherd. They would be joined by Professor Creighton from Canada and Frank Menzies from Australia. The Federation would be served by G. H. Habanyama, A. E. P. Robinson, V. L. Robinson and R. M. Taylor. The Southern Rhodesians would be Mr Justice Beadle, G. Ellman-Brown and Chief Simon Sigola; the Northern Rhodesians, J. Woodrow Cross, Lawrence Katilungu and W. H. McCleland; and the Nyasalanders, the Reverend Henry Chicuse, E. K. Gondwe and G. G. S. J. Hadlow.

Macmillan thought that the main question which the Commons would ask would be whether the commission would command the confidence of the Africans, and he hoped that his careful selection of commissioners would commend itself to men of goodwill everywhere. The reason why the African political parties in particular had been excluded, he said, was that men of unprejudiced views were required. What was really important was that all shades of African opinion would be heard and recorded. This facility would undoubtedly be extended to the detainees. Macmillan assured the House that it would debate the outcome of the review and, finally, stated that he had asked Gaitskell to supply three Privy Councillors and hoped that he would comply.

Gaitskell replied that his Party preferred a purely British, and possibly a parliamentary, commission because it would be more objective. This would avoid the problem of trying to find members who were truly representative of the Federation's population. However, if the Government were determined on its plan, more than five African members were necessary because so many millions feared the outcome. Of the five chosen, he noticed that three unfortunately were dependent on the Governments for their income and were surely unwise choices from the point of view of achieving an unbiased view.

Gaitskell asked Macmillan why he was determined to limit the British parliamentary membership to Privy Councillors. For success, it was surely

[33] *Ibid.*, f. 147, Text of Macmillan's Statement, 24 November 1959; f. 133, Welensky to Macmillan, 25 November 1959; Welensky, *4 000 Days, op. cit.*, p. 156.

necessary to include members of the African political movements because if they boycotted the commission it would lose much of its value. To assist the inquiry all detainees, including Banda, should be released or tried immediately because the Africans were bound to react favourably. African support was also assured if the commission could consider forms of association other than federation. Certainly, if this were not done many would see little point in giving evidence. Gaitskell wanted reassurance on this last point.

Macmillan answered each point in turn. He defended the formula for the membership as the best in the circumstances. There was a continuing programme for the release of the detainees. Consideration of other forms of association fell under the provision for the examination of the redistribution of powers. If Gaitskell wished to continue to negotiate, Macmillan was willing.

Gaitskell confirmed his wish to continue to negotiate, but warned that the terms of reference were not wide enough. Macmillan replied that these terms were the product of an agreement and were quite adequate for the purpose.

Grimmond, however, was not convinced that anything but the continued association with the Federation could be considered. It seemed to him that Macmillan had reneged on his statement of 21 July and he asked bluntly if the commission could recommend secession for Nyasaland. Macmillan replied that the commission was appointed to examine an existing constitution. The objective was an acceptable solution and the terms of reference were designed to give full scope for advice on its achievement. If the commission felt that the terms inhibited it, it would undoubtedly say so.

Bevan explained that what worried his Party was the recommendations the commission could make. The ambiguity made it impossible for the Labour Party to join the commission. He provoked Macmillan into repeating that the commission was allowed to consider the whole field of the redistribution of power between the Federal and territorial Governments. It was to advise on any programme of change and on the character of such changes in relation to the constitutional framework. It seemed to him, therefore, that the terms were of reasonable width. He was confident that, if the problems were insoluble, the commission would say so.[34]

Macmillan immediately informed Welensky that the Labour Party was still playing politics. However, he said, he was confident that he had won the support of sensible people by keeping the offer open. The Labour Party seemed so deeply divided that he thought that, ultimately, it would refuse. He claimed not to have yielded an inch on the terms of reference but had merely explained the text, the programme and the framework. Welensky need not have the slightest doubts. The commissioners were of such calibre that they would not be swayed by transient opinion and, anyway, tempers would have time to cool before they began work. He thought that Welensky might feel that he had gone too far in saying that the commissioners could listen to evidence of all kinds, but no one, in practice, could prevent it. However, he was convinced that the commission would not allow irrelevant material to influence its judgment. Much would be gained by letting people talk, pro-

[34] House of Commons *Hansard* (London), Vol. 614, Col. 207 f., 24 November 1959.

vided the recommendations of the commission, as they would be, were strictly within the terms of reference. Macmillan thought that an African boycott was possible but unlikely if he and Welensky calmly showed confidence and strength.[35]

Before replying, Welensky discussed with his Cabinet Macmillan's statement and the Press reports of his anwers to the supplementary questions. The Press was asking whether Macmillan had allowed the commission to consider secession. It was thought that Macmillan had been deliberately evasive because he was anxious to woo the Labour Party. Nevertheless, it disturbed Welensky that the commission would be free to hear evidence on any subject and Macmillan had not even explained that such evidence had to be viewed in the light of the terms of reference. The clear implication was that the commission could consider secession. This had not been contemplated when the Federal Government had accepted the commission. Indeed, it had publicly rejected an inquest. Thus, the Federal Cabinet felt, it was unfortunate that Macmillan had been so ambiguous in his replies to the questions on secession and other forms of association. Consequently, if the Labour Party accepted the invitation, it would apparently win a victory because secession seemed to have been conceded. The Federal Government could not participate under the terms sought by the Labour Party, and Macmillan would be told this. In addition, a Federal statement would be issued declaring that the agreed terms of reference would be honoured.[36]

Welensky accordingly wrote to Macmillan that day, 25 November, telling of his frustrated efforts to secure the full text and of how he still had only a Press version of the supplementary questions. He was being asked, he said, whether Macmillan had widened the scope of the commission, but Macmillan's personal letter did little to allay his anxiety. Welensky declared that if he could show the letter to the Press, all might be well, but it was marked "Secret". Denied anything else, the public would judge solely on the Press reports. The concern was twofold. Would alternatives to federation be considered or merely the secession of one or more of the territories? Secondly, to what extent would the commission be allowed to hear or publish evidence?

Welensky felt that Macmillan needed reminding of the clear expression of opposition to secession in the Joint Declaration of 1957. This had been understood by the Federal Government to be the basis of the terms of reference when they were accepted. The intention was to examine the objects of the 1953 Constitution and to work towards the attainment of full Commonwealth membership. Secession was a complete departure from this aim. Welensky construed the terms of reference as excluding secession, and claimed that his interpretation was confirmed by the Labour and Liberal Parties asking for a widening of the terms of reference to include it. Welensky said that he was naturally disappointed at Macmillan's failure to refuse to comply. Even more worrying was that Macmillan had seemed to suggest that consideration of secession would be possible. At least that was the Press interpretation.

Consequently Welensky warned that he had to declare unequivocally that

[35] Welensky Papers, 7/21, f. 89, Macmillan to Welensky, 24 November 1959.
[36] *Ibid.*, FGC (59), 44th Meeting, Federal Cabinet, 25 November 1959.

he would not accept any extension or interpretation of the terms of reference to allow consideration of secession or alternative forms of association to federation. With Whitehead's agreement, he would make this publicly clear the next day. In fact, he said, he had already done so in his Parliament and he quoted, for Macmillan's edification, Greenfield's successful amended motion. It seemed clear that the Labour price was consideration of secession and, if Labour accepted the invitation, people in the Federation would believe that it would be allowed. Only a clear, unequivocal statement would avoid this construction and, if it were not forthcoming, the Federal Government would have to reconsider its association with the commission.

Welensky commented that, despite the strong Federal rejection of an inquisition, Macmillan seemed to be allowing it. Thus he asked Macmillan to make it abundantly clear that the Federal Government was not being placed on trial. He was also concerned that Macmillan and Macleod should propose that evidence, including that from the detainees, could be published. Unless this evidence was strictly within the scope of the terms of reference, the idea was intolerable as it would give the enemies of the Federal Government free publicity. So Welensky asked that any irrelevant evidence, and particularly that which attempted to slander his Government, should not be published. Whitehead, Welensky warned, would ask for a similar assurance.[37]

Macmillan apologised on the morrow, 26 November, for the delayed arrival of his dispatches but was typically evasive. He hoped, if everything had arrived, that Welensky had seen how he had tried to make it clear that the terms of reference could not be altered and that he was only trying to explain the meaning of the programme and the framework. He said that he and Home had discussed Welensky's protest and affirmed that there was no intention of extending the terms to include secession. They had agreed to the terms and would stand by them. In addition, every commissioner would endorse them by accepting his appointment.

Macmillan said that he and Home also thought that all evidence had to relate to the constitutional problems. He was confident that Monckton would not admit evidence which either criticised Welensky's administration or set out grievances and accusations. An inquisition would not be allowed. Macmillan promised to discuss this with Monckton who, he said, was not only utterly reliable, but was very skilful in these matters. When speaking about evidence being taken on anything, he had meant only what was relevant and he agreed that perhaps he should have said "on any relevant subject", but he had said this in July and no one had questioned him then. Furthermore, he could not see how the submission of irrelevant material could be prevented. What mattered was what the commission did with it. He was determined that there would be no opportunity for free publicity for attacks on any of the Governments and he hoped that Welensky would reaffirm in his statement that the terms of reference had not been varied. It was, after all, due to the firm stand on this point that the Opposition had not accepted the invitation. His Government had always sought an all-party approach on broad considerations and was not going to sacrifice principles to expediency. The Labour

[37] *Ibid.*, 20/10, f. 133, Welensky to Macmillan, 25 November 1959.

Party's rejection of the terms of reference would be made plain in the final exchanges.[38]

Welensky immediately expressed his gratitude for Macmillan's proposed discussion with Monckton on the question of relevant evidence. He was grateful, too, for the clarification of the matter of the terms of reference.[39] That day he issued a public statement which was based on Macmillan's reassurance. This claimed that the membership of the commission was well balanced, and he marvelled at the continuing Labour refusal to co-operate despite their expressed interest in the Federation and the future of its inhabitants. He said he was pleased that the British Government had stood firm on the terms of reference.[40]

Macmillan welcomed this statement because he believed that it would assist him in tying up the loose ends. However, in *4 000 Days,* Welensky acknowledges that he had made a serious mistake in accepting Macmillan's reassurance and that he would regret it deeply.[41]

Simultaneously, the itinerary for Macmillan's visit arrived, and Greenfield began to prepare for discussions with him. The main topic was constitutional advancement and Greenfield feared that Macmillan might try to hide behind Monckton. Nonetheless, Greenfield felt that it was necessary for Macmillan to understand the form of the ultimate Federal Constitution when independence was obtained. In a session to be kept short so as not to weary him, Macmillan would be told that the basis would be partnership which did not mean full integration but eventual equal opportunity. There might be pressure for a measure of land segregation but that would only be possible by mutual agreement. The territories would keep their individual approaches to the franchise, African representation and to the Africanisation of the Cabinets. To provide safeguards, a council of state was preferable to an upper house because of the paucity of suitable people.

Greenfield suggested advancing his programme through which, by 1970, the Federation and all territories would have fully representative self-government. The Federation and Southern Rhodesia would become fully independent in their own spheres in 1960. Simultaneously Northern Rhodesia would be elevated to the status which Southern Rhodesia had enjoyed in 1923, while Nyasaland would receive a constitution similar to the current Northern Rhodesian one. In 1965 Northern Rhodesia would become fully responsible, and Nyasaland would be promoted to Southern Rhodesia's 1923 status. In 1970 Nyasaland would have full responsible government. It might be possible by 1965 for the Federation to receive special recognition by the Commonwealth, and for full membership to follow in 1970 with the inhabitants' consent.

Greenfield thought that the Federal Government should proclaim that, apart from police, it did not covet any territorial powers. It would produce a list of matters promised in 1957 but which had still not been effected, including the creation of a Central African civil service and the power to

[38] *Ibid.*, f. 137, Macmillan to Welensky, 26 November 1959.
[39] *Ibid.*, f. 124, Welensky to Macmillan, 26 November 1959.
[40] *Ibid.*, f. 127, Statement by Welensky, 26 November 1959.
[41] *Ibid.*, f. 128, Macmillan to Welensky, 28 November 1959; Welensky, *4 000 Days*, *op. cit.*, p. 161.

legislate extra-territorially. Greenfield suggested that the meeting with Macmillan should also discuss the unco-operative attitude of the Northern Rhodesian civil servants, defence and the futures of the Caprivi Strip and Barotseland. The meeting should also review the possibility of all the Governments coming under the Commonwealth Relations Office, the policies regarding the detainees and the preparatory commission procedures.[42]

There was indeed general concern at the attitudes of the Northern Rhodesian civil servants. Federal officials were in London at a conference preparing with their northern and British counterparts for the commission, and Whitehead returned from there on 25 November bearing the news that the Northern Rhodesians were advocating a wholesale transfer of powers to the territorial Governments which would emasculate the Federal Government. Consequently, he said, the talks were in danger of breaking down. Roberts immediately sought confirmation of Whitehead's allegation and was informed by Macleod that, within the terms of reference, the intention was to analyse the relevant constitutional proposals with complete objectivity. He said that a determination to give the best possible advice as well as a spirit of friendliness and co-operation prevailed, and that no one in fact had suggested a transfer of powers to the extent that it would destroy the federal concept. A breakdown, he felt, seemed unlikely.[43]

Sir Evelyn Hone, when copying to Welensky Macleod's reply to Roberts, expressed amazement that the Northern Rhodesian officials could be thus attacked by Whitehead. However, Welensky replied with a warning that, in any event, he would oppose any transfer of power which would jeopardize the Federation. Macleod's version of the events was somewhat dented by Evans reporting to Welensky on 10 December on the considerable tension within the officials' conference. In the first week, he said, there had been a concerted effort by the territories to strip the Federal Government of its major functions. He claimed that Northern Rhodesia, in particular, sought the return of health, education and European agriculture and would allow the Federal Government to act in the economic field only at the behest of the territory concerned. The justification was that the only way to win African confidence was to limit the Federal Government's powers. The Federal officials had not yielded despite the Southern Rhodesians also demanding some of these. The Federals had claimed full self-government for the Federation in 1960 but not full Commonwealth membership. The Northern Rhodesians did not favour any such advance until the territories had achieved considerably higher constitutional levels. Again they suggested the strengthening of the territories by the return of powers. They wanted to abolish the Federal franchise and elect all MPs on the territorial franchises. In addition there should be equal territorial representation in the Federal Parliament. They seemed to Evans to be utterly ignoring the European in their calculations.[44]

[42] Welensky Papers, 25/30, f. 210, Greenfield to Welensky, 26 November 1959.
[43] *Ibid.*, 7/25, f. 50, Sir Evelyn Hone to Macleod, 25 November 1959; f. 51, Macleod to Hone, 27 November 1959.
[44] *Ibid.*, f. 49, Hone to Welensky, 1 December 1959; f. 44, Welensky to Hone, 9 December 1959; f. 26, A. D. Evans to Welensky, 10 December 1959.

The constitutional battle was still being fought as Evans wrote and he confessed that his Federal team had not appreciated just how insistent the territorial delegations and, in particular, the Northern Rhodesians would be. Indeed, Evans believed that the saving grace was that they had over-played their hand and had not endeared themselves to the British which, he claimed, could be useful when serious preparation began. This news disturbed Welensky.[45]

The straws in the wind led Federal intelligence to predict that the British Government would make even larger concessions to the Africans in 1960. The freer rein given to the Northern Rhodesian officials seemed to indicate this and was further confirmed by a remark by R. Gribble, Assistant Security Adviser to the Colonial Secretary, that the Federal Intelligence and Security Bureau should not be regarded as permanent. He said this when discussing the training of British security officers in African affairs, and confirmation was to be found in the reduction in the number of British officers seeking the training provided by the Federal Bureau.[46]

This perhaps prompted Welensky on 22 December to propose again to Macmillan the defensive measures which he had suggested in 1958 against Communist and other menaces. Because of the unsettled state of the Belgian Congo, he wished to seek Portuguese co-operation in military intelligence, communications and propaganda, as well as to strengthen economic ties with them. He no longer thought of a sub-Saharan axis but of one across Africa from Cabinda on the mouth of the Congo River to the Moçambique border with Tanganyika on the Ruvuma River. He would have preferred to include British East Africa, but knew that there would be difficulties because of British intentions there.[47]

In London the Federal officials consulted Professor Sir Ivor Jennings who found no precedent for the transfer of powers from the Federation to the territories. The only fundamental principle underlying the division of powers in other federations, he said, was that the Federal Government should be strong. He felt that it was perhaps better to have a definite list of territorial powers so that there would be no accusations of Federal encroachment. The Federal officials were curious to hear his opinion of the statement in the current officials' conference that it would be a derogation from the northern protected status if there were a transfer to the Federal Government of any function relating to those which had been the subject of the treaties with the African Chiefs. Jennings believed that, as the treaties were made with the Crown, the Queen could exercise her powers in any way she liked. This point, he noted, had not been raised when South Africa was unified despite an abundance of such treaties. The Federal officials then revealed that it was currently argued in their conference that any removal of subordination to Britain would require the consent of the inhabitants. Yet the latter had not been consulted either in 1957, when Britain had agreed to the convention not to legislate for the Federation, or in 1958, when Northern Rhodesia had been set on the road to self-government. To Jennings the key to the problem lay in

[45] *Ibid.*, 42/21, ff. 59–60, Welensky to G. Beckett, 14 December 1959.
[46] *Ibid.*, 29/51, f. 38, FISB to W. S. Parker, 22 December 1959.
[47] *Ibid.*, f. 28, Welensky to Macmillan, 22 December 1959.

the Federal constitutional preamble which had been politically, and not legally, drafted. The crucial section, he said, was only an expression of belief or it would have been drafted differently. It could not prevent the Federation from advancing even if the inhabitants were opposed.

On the question of self-government in the Federal sphere, Jennings found that there was only a technical difference between this and full membership of the Commonwealth. It was possible, he believed, to remove all subordination and still not be a full member, as in Newfoundland's case. The British powers could be limited to territorial functions. The Federal Government would then have power through the repeal of the Colonial Laws Validity Act to prevent laws being declared invalid because they were repugnant to British legislation. It would also be necessary to have the power to override orders made under the Foreign Jurisdiction Act. Jennings favoured the Federal Supreme Court for academic advice on legislation. He believed that some form of tribunal was necessary for the administration of the safeguards, and favoured an upper house or a council of state. However, the three territorial legislatures could be used for final approval of amendments to the Federal Constitution because such amendments were never entirely Federal matters. These legislatures could also be the final arbiters of discriminatory legislation. The upper house could be similarly used. That house could be selected by an electoral college if a proper racial balance were arranged in the latter. Jennings could find no fundamental formula for territorial representation in the Federal Assembly. It was a matter for political negotiation. Finally, he agreed that an alternative word to "Federation" could be found. He suggested "Confederation", for example, but felt that it perhaps would not translate any better into the vernacular.[48]

Macmillan saw Gaitskell on 1 December and bluntly told him that he could neither change the terms of reference of the preparatory commission nor his explanatory statements. Gaitskell tried to bargain, but Macmillan simply asked for the names of his three Privy Councillors. Gaitskell promised a decision once he had consulted his Parliamentary Party and shadow cabinet. As the Labour Party censured him for proposing to visit South Africa, Macmillan concluded that they were using Africa to heal their deep internal divisions.

Macmillan, in apprising Welensky of this conversation, blamed Gaitskell for a current Press story that contact had been renewed between the British Government and the Opposition with the aim of satisfying the latter. The truth was that Gaitskell was being asked to accept or reject the offer and had indicated that he would decline it.[49]

Because of the likelihood of Gaitskell's refusal, Home that day, 1 December, sent Welensky the names of suitable alternative appointees. These were Lord (Herbert) Morrison, a man of deservedly high stature and of independent mind, Lord Shawcross who had worked extensively with Monckton on constitutional matters, and, lastly, Clement Davies of the Liberal Party who knew Africa and was a responsible man and who might be persuaded to accept the appointment independently of his Party. The Conservative Privy

[48] *Ibid.*, 7/25, ff. 32–40, Consultation with Professor Sir Ivor Jennings, 29 November 1959.
[49] *Ibid.*, 20/10, f. 117, Macmillan to Welensky, 1 December 1959.

Councillors would be Lord Crathorne, Sir Lionel Heald and Hugh Molson. Welensky, however, would not accept Davies because, he said, he had never been helpful in debates and his nomination would not ease Federal difficulties. He suggested Lord Reith.[50]

As Macmillan had expected, the Labour Party declined because parliamentary membership was being confined to Privy Councillors and because it wanted the detainees released before the commission began work. It also demanded an immediate constitutional advance for Nyasaland. Macmillan saw the refusal as a blessing because the Labour Party would not be able to indulge in wrecking tactics. A week later the predicted African reaction was realised in part in London where the self-exiled Nkomo and Chiume, speaking for the banned Southern Rhodesian and Nyasaland African Congresses, and Orton Chirwa, president of the Malawi Congress Party, declared that their members would boycott the commission because there was no point in presenting evidence. They saw the commission as a smokescreen to obscure the true situation in Nyasaland where hundreds were detained. Shortly after this, the African Members of the Nyasaland Legislative Council followed suit. On 14 December Orton Chirwa returned to Nyasaland describing meetings with Macleod, and predicting that the release of the detainees and the end of the emergency were imminent. Macmillan, however, on 15 December, did not heed the threats of boycotts and declared that, despite them, the commission would shortly assemble.[51]

However, already a section of the British Press was calling for the cancellation of the commission. This surprised Welensky considerably and he told Beckett that, as he had never wanted the commission, he was not averse to it "being strangled at birth even now, but there it is. I don't believe Macmillan can go back now, he is too far committed".[52]

The membership was still not settled. Lord Morrison's health was too frail, and for the last two places Macmillan and Home considered Sir William Heyter, the late British Ambassador in Moscow and the current Warden of New College, Oxford; Philip Mason of the Institute of Race Relations; and Sir Thomas Knox and Sir Thomas Taylor, the principals respectively of St Andrews and Aberdeen Universities. Alternatively, two women sociologists with knowledge of Africa, Professor Margaret Read and Dr Audrey Richards, were considered, but Welensky wanted no more academics. He wondered if it would not be better to reduce the commission to twelve a side. If this were unacceptable, he insisted on the remaining appointees being Privy Councillors.[53]

The search continued and, while it did, the Federal Government was distracted by a problem relating to Banda. There had been a number of people trying to interview him in prison, but most had been refused. The

[50] *Ibid.*, f. 115, Home to Welensky, 1 December 1959; f. 120, Welensky to Home, 2 December 1959.

[51] *Ibid.*, 7/11, f. 285, Press Statement by the Labour Party, 4 December 1959; Macmillan, *Pointing the Way*, *op. cit.*, p. 142; *The Rhodesia Herald*, 11 December 1959; *Evening Standard*, 14 December 1959.

[52] *The Rhodesia Herald*, 16 December 1959; Welensky Papers, 42/21, ff. 59–60, Welensky to G. Beckett, 14 December 1959.

[53] Welensky Papers, 20/10, f. 110, Home to Welensky, 14 December 1959.

latest request, in November, was from Sir John Moffat and was made through the Chief Secretary of Nyasaland, C. W. F. Footman. The intention of detention, as stated by Julian Amery, the Under-Secretary of State for the Colonies, was to remove certain people from circulation, and an exception could not be made for one of them. Accordingly, Moffat was refused because, being a politician, he would set a dangerous precedent for British parliamentarians in particular.

Moffat, never one to yield, convinced the Nyasaland Government a month later that he had to discuss the political situation with Banda. The Nyasaland Government thought that Banda might reveal that he was ready to compromise, and might also show how temperamental and unsuitable he was. To achieve this, the Nyasaland Government felt that Moffat had to meet Banda alone and in secret. Greenfield, though a reluctant gaoler, was still anxious not to set the precedent for politicians. He did not believe that Banda had given any sign of modifying his views and was sure that such a meeting could not be kept secret.[54]

Footman thereupon proposed to visit Banda himself early in 1960 while Armitage took up Moffat's cause with Welensky. Armitage claimed that his Government was about to attempt to persuade the Africans to give evidence to the preparatory commission. However, he said, the detainees could hardly be expected to present their case without some assistance in preparing it. He doubted if they would want to give evidence but he felt that the Governments could not be seen to be impeding them. He noted with some satisfaction that certain of the detainees were studying economics and thought that the long-taught lesson was at last sinking in. He wanted to say publicly that if assistance were required, it would be given provided that anything produced would only be used for presentation to the commission. Care would be taken to avoid abuse of the privilege and the definition of "expert" would exclude people like Stonehouse and Mrs Castle, but would include men with knowledge of African affairs like Moffat. Armitage wanted the earliest possible reply because Macleod was taking an interest in the matter.[55]

Whitehead, when consulted, somewhat flippantly advised that the detainees would need four years more of study before they would be ready for an examination in economics. He thought they were fluent enough to give evidence without needing lawyers. In particular, he could not understand why an opposition leader from Northern Rhodesia should be used to brief Nyasaland's subversives or why only the Central Africa Party was being given this facility. He suggested that Welensky inform Macleod that they both objected to this proposal though he appealed "don't quote me as I claim never to interfere in the affairs of the two Northern Territories".[56]

Welensky concurred and on the morrow, 23 December, rejected this proposal. He opposed the campaign to persuade the Africans to give evidence

[54] *Ibid.*, 20/11, f. 178, Greenfield to C. W. F. Footman, 16 November 1959; f. 177, Footman to Greenfield, 17 November 1959; f. 175, Footman to Greenfield, 18 December 1959; f. 173, Greenfield to Footman, 19 December 1959.

[55] *Ibid.*, f. 170, Footman to Greenfield, 22 December 1959; 20/10, f. 103, Armitage to Welensky, 22 December 1959.

[56] *Ibid.*, 20/10, f. 102, Whitehead to Welensky, (undated).

because, he felt, this was properly the function of the political parties. Citing letters from Chipembere, he expressed confidence in the ability of the detainees to write without outside help. He disliked volunteering help because it could lead to the briefing of Dingle Foot, the Labour MP, or someone worse. It was impossible to prevent the material produced from being used for other purposes. Furthermore, and echoing Whitehead's observation, he could not understand why an opposition leader should be regarded as a suitable coach for subversives. The utmost he would allow was an intimation that the requests for legal advice in the preparation of evidence would be considered but did not think that it was wise even to volunteer this. Finally, he thought that the interest being shown in economics showed a desire by the detainees to prepare themselves for ministerial posts when Nyasaland became an independent republic.[57]

Greenfield informed Footman that his timing would be most inappropriate because both he and Welensky would be away and the public was bound to draw the most unfortunate conclusion from the visit of the Nyasaland Chief Secretary. He suggested that the Federal Secretary for Law, who administered the prisons, should see Banda in advance of a visit of someone from Nyasaland of lesser rank than Chief Secretary. Greenfield added that if Footman had to come, then he should disguise his purpose as an inspection of all places of detention. Footman agreed.[58]

Neither Macleod nor Moffat yielded and, on 25 December, Franklin, Moffat's fellow representative in the Northern Rhodesian legislature, publicly claimed that Moffat had secured permission from Armitage to visit Banda, but that Greenfield had refused to co-operate. As Armitage was responsible for law and order, Franklin doubted there was any risk. He contrasted this with the freedom given to Kaunda by the Federal prison authorities to receive visitors when he was a convicted prisoner.[59]

Greenfield replied through the Press confirming the veracity of Franklin's account but quoting Amery that the purpose of detention was to remove certain people from circulation. The *Evening Standard* of Salisbury remained puzzled at the high-handedness of the Federal authorities who, after all, it noted, were holding political prisoners at the request of the Nyasaland Government. It demanded an explanation but the Nyasaland Government denied that any permission had been given.[60]

Macleod waited a week. In the meantime Macmillan had more to report to Welensky on the commissioners. Macmillan claimed that he had cast around for candidates for the last two places but, finding no suitable Privy Councillors, he wanted to appoint a close friend, young vigorous Aidan Crawley, a former MP who had left the Labour Party to become a broadcaster on world affairs. Macmillan had considered Lord Reith for the last place but believed that he was too difficult to work with unless he was in command.[61]

[57] *Ibid.*, f. 101, Welensky to Armitage, 23 December 1959.
[58] *Ibid.*, 20/11, f. 168, Greenfield to Footman, 24 December 1959; f. 167, Footman to Greenfield, 28 December 1959.
[59] *The Rhodesia Herald*, 25 December 1959.
[60] *The Bulawayo Chronicle*, 25 December 1959; *Evening Standard*, 28 & 29 December 1959.
[61] Welensky Papers, 20/10, f. 100, Macmillan to Welensky, 24 December 1959.

Welensky accepted Crawley and suggested Lord Reid for the last place, but Macmillan, on 27 December, said that Reid was too ill. As possible Labour moves against the commission were imminent, Macmillan was anxious to appoint Sir Charles Arden-Clarke, the first and last Governor-General of the Gold Coast. Welensky concurred but the list was not closed because Home cabled him on 30 December saying that, as the Reverend Chicuse had withdrawn, Armitage wished to replace him with W. M. Chirwa, the former Federal MP. Armitage believed that Chirwa would attract African support and Home avowed that Chirwa understood the advantages of federation and was fair-minded even though he did not support it. This last characteristic was hardly a qualification for membership of an impartial commission and, while Welensky wasted no time in accepting the nomination, he placed on record that Chirwa could not be regarded as other than a staunch opponent of the Federation.[62]

Pressed by Macleod, Home returned to the subject of the detainees and the preparatory commission on New Year's Day 1960. He insisted that, even if none accepted the offer of assistance, it still had to be made. The danger of being accused of politicial suppression, he warned, could not be run. It was important politically that the detainees should be provided with something more than legal advice and he wanted Armitage to announce the provision of such facilities for those who requested them.[63]

In his second dispatch that day, Home revealed to Welensky that the current campaign against the commission was being conducted through letters to the Press. These claimed, he said, that anyone giving evidence could face prosecution under the Emergency Regulation 35 of the Nyasaland Emergency Regulations or Section 52 of the Southern Rhodesian Native Affairs Act. This was incorrect, but he felt he had to reassure potential witnesses by providing the necessary immunity by legislation or by pronouncements by the four Attorneys-General as had been done for the Devlin Commission. He preferred the first method even though it would not preclude the possibility of private prosecutions. In the meanwhile he wished to state that he was consulting the Governments on the subject.[64]

Welensky replied two days later that he had never thought that prosecutions could arise out of evidence given in private and within the terms of reference. The Devlin practice, he said, ensured that its members and witnesses were fully protected. Nevertheless, he warned that neither his nor the Southern Rhodesian Government could undertake not to prosecute anyone who broke the law through the publication of evidence given to the commission. They could not provide a public platform for sedition, criminal libel and perjury.

He explained that intimidation of witnesses had been the reason for the Devlin arrangements and was just as likely in this case, but nothing more was needed than the pronouncements of the Attorneys-General which gave wit-

[62] *Ibid.*, f. 98, Welensky to Macmillan, 24 December 1959; f. 97, Macmillan to Welensky, 27 December 1959; f. 96, H. G. M. Bass to W. S. Parker, 28 December 1959; f. 95, Home to Welensky, 30 December 1959; f. 93, Welensky to Home, 31 December 1959.

[63] *Ibid.*, f. 91, Home to Welensky, 1 January 1960.

[64] *Ibid.*, f. 90, Home to Welensky, 1 January 1960.

nesses the necessary leeway. Those who wished to make seditious statements in public would not be protected.[65]

Welensky consulted Whitehead, then informed Home that they still believed that there was no justification for the provision of anything more than legal advice. He added that they felt that Home's telegrams had implied that the preparatory commission had not solved the British political problem. Furthermore, they believed that the commission was only adding considerably to Welensky's problems as it was confusing and irritating local political circles. As this was of much concern and as neither of them had wanted the commission in the first place, they again suggested its cancellation. Indeed, they suggested, cancellation could enable the Governments to achieve better results than the commission ever could.[66]

Home hurriedly replied that he and Macleod had consulted Monckton who had confirmed that most evidence would be taken in private and, when there were public meetings, that he would curb the irrelevancies and unsuitable language. Home and Macleod preferred the statement from the Attorneys-General but thought that the prescription that evidence should be taken in private would provoke further and unnecessary political controversy. They trusted that Welensky would accept a declaration that there would be no criminal prosecutions arising out of written or oral evidence accepted as relevant by the commission.[67]

Intruding into this exchange was the departure of Macmillan to Africa and with it came Press predictions that he would recommend Banda's release. There was increasing pressure for it, including a visit to the Commonwealth Relations Office by Callaghan and Sir Frank Soskice, Labour's principal legal adviser. They gathered that the decision to release Banda had been taken. Home did not comment on this to Welensky or on the other pressures, including a demand by the Bow Group for Banda's release so that he could resume his political role. The Bow Group warned that no amount of rhapsodising over economic benefits would keep Nyasaland in the Federation and that the pressure-cooker of African nationalism would inevitably burst. The Group insisted that the franchise had to be broadened before the Federation's future was considered and that Banda had to be free to participate in the elections. It felt that, if the franchise were broad enough, he would be unlikely to refuse to participate. If he won the election, he would lead his Party in a non-violent way because of the Devlin revelations. He would do this even if he opposed the Federal and Nyasaland Governments.[68]

If Home did not comment on the pressures, James Johnson did while explaining the Labour Party's attitude to Welensky. Johnson claimed that Macmillan's handling of the issue in Parliament was totally responsible for the Labour refusal. Consequently, he said, the argument had concentrated on the question of whether or not Nyasaland should be allowed to secede if the commission found it essential. The logic of events was driving the British public towards such considerations. The Bow Group and a growing number

[65] *Ibid.*, f. 88, Welensky to Home, 3 January 1960.
[66] *Ibid.*, f. 87, Welensky to Home, 4 January 1960.
[67] *Ibid.*, f. 84, Home to Welensky, 5 January 1960.
[68] *Evening Standard*, 5 January 1960; *The Rhodesia Herald*, 4 January 1960.

of young Conservatives, he predicted, would support such a conclusion and force Macleod to satisfy them. Time was short but Johnson hoped that the British Government could achieve a decent settlement. He believed that Macleod would release Banda. Macleod, of course, had by then announced an accelerated constitutional programme for Tanganyika. He had added that Northern Rhodesia and Kenya could expect similar treatment and led Beckett amongst others to advise Welensky to make a strong stand.[69]

On 6 January, Home warned Welensky that Macleod and Armitage, who had met in Dar-es-Salaam in late December, had agreed to accelerate the release of the detainees because the security situation had eased. They proposed to get down quickly to a hard-core who could not be released for some time. Home said that this, the emergency, Banda and other related matters would all be raised by Macmillan when he met Welensky and that Macleod would make a speech at Leeds in a few days' time to indicate what would happen. Home promised to send Welensky a draft of the latter.[70]

In a second dispatch, Home said that he had also discussed Moffat's request with Macleod. Consequently he reminded Welensky that, while the Federal Government was acting for the Nyasaland Government in holding the detainees, their future and treatment remained the responsibility of the Nyasaland and British Governments. It was, he said, the prerogative of Armitage to grant special privileges to the detainee and his visitor. A common-sense arrangement could be published when the need for it again arose.[71]

A third dispatch dealt with the issue of the evidence. Home had reconsidered and thought that the declaration by the Attorneys-General on immunity was unfair to the witnesses because they could not know in advance just what evidence would fall within the definition. Accordingly he wished that any evidence which was given to the commission would be privileged. This, he argued, would place the Governments and the commission above suspicion. He admitted, though, that it would lay them open to irrelevant abuse by witnesses but believed that this could be ignored.[72]

Replying the same day, 6 January, Welensky informed Home that he and Whitehead rejected both dispatches on the Monckton evidence as totally unacceptable. They were not prepared to indulge irrelevant abuse and wanted the adoption of the Devlin procedure under which all evidence was given in private. They rejected public debate as unnecessary. As Welensky's misgivings, expressed on 4 January, were now entirely justified, he and Whitehead asked again for the abandonment of the commission. The text of Macleod's speech had arrived and they demanded the modification of its references to the taking of evidence. If Macleod did not comply, they warned that they would issue without hesitation a public repudiation and ensure that the law would be enforced against any witness who transgressed it.[73]

Home's reaction was to point out that, while victory at the polls had made

[69] Welensky Papers, 24/157, ff. 40–41, J. Johnson to Welensky, 5 January 1960; 42/21, f. 57, Beckett to Welensky, 5 January 1960.
[70] *Ibid.*, 20/11, f. 152, H. G. M. Bass to Welensky, 6 January 1960.
[71] *Ibid.*, f. 161, Bass to M. J. Lamb, 6 January 1960.
[72] *Ibid.*, f. 82, Bass to Lamb, 6 January 1960.
[73] *Ibid.*, 20/10, f. 79, Welensky to Home, 6 January 1960.

his Government secure, the Federation's future depended on the ability of his Cabinet to satisfy the Conservative Party and that this was more difficult because of the election of so many new young men. The commission was already winning support in Britain and he was quite certain that it would be disastrous to cancel it because it would seem to be a Labour victory over Welensky.

Home recommended the commission as the best and indeed the only way to convince people that the Federal structure was the correct one for the circumstances. Without preparation for the review and the correction of ill-informed opinion, there was, he said, a great risk that British parliamentary support would be lost. He explained that the retention of this support was the reason for the emphasis on the method of giving evidence and the facilities for the detainees. Even *The Times* that day, he added, had joined the critics on these issues. It would greatly assist if all parties, and Welensky in particular, appeared reasonable and anxious to ensure that all views were heard.

Home agreed that a few witnesses might attempt to blackguard the Federal Government, but promised that they would be curbed. Furthermore, the risk was surely negligible compared with the prize of a commendation of the Federation by the commission. Therefore he urged that the British and Federal Governments should make a plain declaration on the protection of witnesses and the assistance to be given to the detainees. He stated that unsuitable persons like Stonehouse could not be advisers and that lawyers and others solely deemed fit by the Governor would be employed. In any case, the question was likely to be academic because the detainees undoubtedly would refuse to give evidence. Nonetheless, the Governments had to be seen to be encouraging them to give evidence.[74]

In his speech at the opening of the Commonwealth Week at Leeds, Macleod acknowledged the public anxiety over the future of Nyasaland, but hoped that the preparatory commission and the review would allay it. He attached the greatest importance to the British pledges and declared that protection would not be withdrawn unless the people of the northern territories desired it. He said that the moment had arrived to deal again with the constitutional advance of Nyasaland and that he would visit there as soon as possible. Accordingly, the emergency had to be ended as soon as practicable. He was reviewing it continually and was happy to announce that Armitage felt that the release of the detainees could be accelerated. Macleod promised that the Governments would ensure that the commission received evidence from every quarter and that facilities would be provided for legal assistance in its preparation.[75]

Welensky had secured his amendment because Macleod said nothing more than that protection for witnesses was being discussed. He enlightened Beckett on this success but acknowledged that Macleod was tough and set on making a name for himself as Colonial Secretary. He added that he had heard that Macleod was determined to rid Britain of all her colonies within five years and felt that there was no smoke without fire.[76]

[74] *Ibid.*, f. 75, Home to Welensky, 7 January 1960.
[75] *Ibid.*, f. 81, Text of Macleod's Speech, 7 January 1960.
[76] *Ibid.*, 42/21, f. 53, Welensky to Beckett, 12 January 1960.

Welensky informed Lennox-Boyd that the membership had been finalised but, nevertheless, he was considering the abandonment of the commission. The membership, however, was not settled because, as Welensky learned later that day, W. M. Chirwa was hesitating about accepting and Armitage was ordered to send him to London to confer with Macleod and Monckton. Welensky acknowledged to Home that such action was the prerogative of the British Government, but he wanted to know if he would be informed of the discussion since, if Chirwa laid down conditions for his acceptance, a serious situation would develop. In any case, Welensky questioned the propriety of Chirwa seeing Monckton at all. An undesirable consequence of any leakage, he said, could be the demand by other commissioners for special privileges.[77]

Rumours of the imminent release of Banda spread after Footman visited him in Gwelo on 5 January. The Press discovered a popular belief that Macmillan, then in Accra, wanted the healthiest possible climate for his talks and thought that Banda should be released. Armitage reacted by stating that Banda would be released when public safety would not be endangered. The local Press found this sensible and reassuring. *The Sunday Mail* pointed out that, while it was fashionable in Britain to see anyone detained after racial trouble as a martyr, Banda was not one and should be held while the danger of unrest existed and until Nyasaland had permanent and effective security legislation. The newspaper noted that even under the Emergency Regulations the Nyasaland African Congress had been able to operate, and evidence of that was the burning down of the house of the Reverend A. D. Kayira who had promptly resigned from the Legislative Council in fear of his life. An improvement, however, was seen in the security situation in Northern Rhodesia because, on 9 January, Kaunda was released from restriction.[78]

Home told Welensky that he was anxious that he should understand that Monckton had expressed strictly private views which could not be quoted. He said that in any case, however great his authority, Monckton could not commit the commission to any final decision on procedure without the agreement of its members. Home sought to avoid subsequent misunderstandings.[79]

However, Welensky and Whitehead indicated to Home, on 11 January, that they had not shifted their ground on the taking of evidence and on the prosecution of those indulging in sedition. Using Home's uneasiness about Monckton's assurances, they argued that the only solution was to take evidence in private. After all, they argued, the purpose was to educate the Governments and the public, and this could hardly be done if the Press could highlight part of the evidence before the commission could evaluate it. Welensky proposed to raise this during Macmillan's visit.[80]

That day, 11 January, was an eventful day for Welensky. Armitage wrote enclosing a detailed account by Footman of his visit to Banda. He had found Banda in excellent health, glad to see him and without complaint at his

[77] *Ibid.*, 27/62, f. 31, Welensky to Lennox-Boyd, 7 January 1960; 20/10, f. 77, Bass to Lamb, 7 January 1960; f. 76, Lamb to Bass, 7 January 1960.

[78] *The Rhodesia Herald*, 8 & 9 January 1960; *The Sunday Mail*, 10 January 1960.

[79] Welensky Papers, 20/10, f. 73, Bass to Lamb, 9 January 1960.

[80] *Ibid.*, f. 71, Welensky to Home, 11 January 1960.

treatment. Banda indicated that he would happily give evidence to the commission if he were free. He did not know if the Malawi Congress Party would give evidence because he said he knew nothing about it. Then Footman explained the purpose of the Federal review and that its delegations would be chosen by the Governments but added that, as Macmillan had said, the northern legislatures were not broadly-enough based and that a cross-section of other opinion would be represented. This meant, Footman told Banda, that the United Federal, the Central Africa, the Malawi Congress and the Congress Liberation Parties would all be considered. Banda thought there was little point in including the Central Africa Party (a comment which would have hurt Moffat) and did not want the Asians represented. He had not known that all Parties would be considered and thought that the delegates should not be selected by the Governments, but be elected by the people.[81]

Reverting to a well-worn theme, Banda declared to Footman that civil servants should not be politicians and, in particular, should not sit in the legislature. He dealt next with an end-of-the-year statement by Welensky which mentioned the possibility of the Federation becoming independent in its own sphere. (He was not alone in his alarm as *The Times* had reacted with wrath because Welensky had also suggested the scrapping of the African Affairs Board.[82]) Banda appeared quite impressed when Footman read Macmillan's statement of 22 July which confirmed that protection by Britain would only be terminated and the Federation acquire full independence when all were agreed that protection was no longer needed. The independence within the Federal sphere, Footman explained to Banda, related only to Federal functions which the commission would examine when discussing the redistribution of powers and the constitutional framework to effect it. Thus it was necessary for the Africans to put forward their views and not to boycott and prejudice their case not only with the commission but in the eyes of the world. If the Africans felt that the Federation were unacceptable, they should substantiate that view. Banda answered that the reason for the boycott was the detention of all the leaders. If they were released, evidence would be freely given.

Feeling that he was getting nowhere, Footman tried another tack and sought to discuss the Nyasaland Constitution. However, Banda refused to do so while he was in detention. When Footman raised administrative subjects, Banda urged him to be bold and get the European civil servant out of politics, but he would say little else while he was in detention. The only way to peace, he said, was to release the detainees.

If he convinced Footman, the latter was thoroughly disappointed by the surly "hard-core" detainees he visited at Marandellas on the next day. Believing that they would endanger the peace, Footman recalled that Banda had never been able to control them. It was very possible, he thought, that not just the district commissioners but the people themselves would not welcome their return. He could not imagine that Banda would either.

The representative of Federal intelligence in Nyasaland also reported to

[81] *Ibid.*, 20/11, f. 125, Armitage to Welensky, 11 January 1960; f. 127, Secret Report on Discussions with Dr Banda, 6 January 1960.
[82] *Ibid.*, 31/96, f. 28, Welensky to O. Woods, 12 January 1960.

Welensky on 11 January. He said that three days previously he had attended a meeting of the Nyasaland intelligence committee to discuss the possible effect of the accelerated programme for the release of the detainees. The original plan was to have only 55 detainees left. As the meeting was not asked if the acceleration was desirable, it was clear to him that the Nyasaland Government had been ordered to effect it whatever the circumstances. It seemed to Federal eyes that Nyasaland was again heading for trouble and that little was being done to prepare for it. The new idea was to release all but a dozen detainees by the end of April when the emergency would end. Before then security regulations would be introduced to ensure the maintenance of order and to allow the hard-core to continue in detention. The committee found the cause of the unrest and the solution to be political. The situation had not changed during the emergency in the view of most Africans and the preparatory commission seemed to hold little attraction for them. It was believed that the Malawi Congress Party had established a territory-wide organisation to be presented to the leaders on their release. These leaders were expected to be more bitter and more formidable than ever. Militancy was predicted and, indeed, it was felt that the arrogant and confident mood of Orton Chirwa was already percolating through the ranks, making them ripe for exploitation. The arrival of the commission could well spark off demonstrations. Another contribution to instability was the widespread knowledge that the detention of Banda would be reviewed in March, the anniversary of the emergency. If the result were unfavourable, a violent reaction was possible. Furthermore, Orton Chirwa had returned from London declaring that there would be a reform of the Nyasaland Constitution in February.

Overall, intelligence gleaned indicated that the Africans were expecting a renewal of the struggle in March, and the confident mood of the politically-minded would be bolstered by the acceleration of the release, seemingly because of Orton Chirwa's demands. Abuse and violence against non-Africans and their property, as well as acts of revenge by the ex-detainees, were likely. Loyal and co-operative Africans would feel confused and betrayed. This would particularly affect the African civil servants, undermining the Government. The speed of the proposed release was such that it would not allow time for an assessment of its effects. As a general strike was probable, coupled with a campaign of violence, disobedience and intimidation, the Nyasaland intelligence committee was particularly disturbed by reports from Northern Rhodesia predicting widespread trouble in April which would dissipate the strength of the security forces.

Thus the committee recommended the imposition of control orders on all released detainees even if they were likely to be totally ineffective and even if they were removed with the ending of the emergency in April. Finally, it endorsed the opinion of the Acting Police Commissioner and the Federal Army Commander in Nyasaland that the new programme could spark trouble before forces could be deployed.[83]

Despite this finding, Armitage that day, 11 January, reminded Welensky that he had told him in December that, if an advantageous opportunity arose

[83] *Ibid.*, 29/51, f. 30, H. Bridgeman to W. S. Parker, 11 January 1960.

for the early release of Banda, it would be taken. Ignoring the opinion of his intelligence committee, Armitage said that, if Nyasaland continued to be so quiet, all but the "hard-core" would be released by April. By then there would be adequate security legislation to deal with all eventualities. Armitage, however, for some unexplained reason, did not include Banda within the definition of "hard-core" and revealed that his Government was considering when best to release him. A hopeful development, he felt, was that Banda had asked to see W. M. Chirwa after previously spurning him. Armitage thought that, as Chirwa's friends were more moderate, older Africans, who might be encouraged to play a political role, it might be possible to exploit this *rapprochement*.[84]

This prospect did not look so rosy on the morrow when the Malawi Congress Party claimed that W. M. Chirwa was being secretly flown to London and that he had been persuaded to fill the vacant place on the commission. Although the Nyasaland Government denied this statement, the MCP wished Chirwa to know that the boycott would be so total that not even a hen would give evidence.[85]

The final blow delivered to Welensky on 11 January was a report of a television interview with Lord Shawcross by the celebrated interviewer, John Freeman (later Lord Freeman). In the interview Shawcross said he was distressed by the critical reaction of the Labour Party to his appointment, but, having left politics, he found it impossible to refuse an invitation from the Prime Minister to perform a public duty. Furthermore, he considered himself a free agent. He noted that there had been much discussion on the terms of reference but he could not recall a commission which had felt inhibited by them. He vowed that he would not hesitate to write a minority report if he thought that it were needed.

Freeman suggested that the point at issue was whether the terms of reference would permit the preparatory commission to recommend not how the Federation might be modified but how it might be abolished. Shawcross commented that, as it had been stated publicly that the commission could hear evidence from any quarter on the entire subject of the Federation's future, he would feel free to suggest what he thought was the right conclusion. However, he said, he could not speak for the rest of the commissioners. Pursuing the point, Freeman asked if, after discovering that responsible and representative African opinion was implacably and universally opposed to the Federation, Shawcross would regard it as a matter of conscience to report against the Federation. Shawcross agreed that he would certainly feel that. He would disregard white opinion if it dissented from the African view because Britain was pledged to allow the will of the majority of the inhabitants of the Federation to decide its future. Finally, he stated that he did not pretend to know much about Africa but he had visited it once or twice.[86]

Lord Shawcross told Lord Birkenhead that he realised that, if the commission remained under attack from the Labour Party, it could not function

[84] *Ibid.*, 20/11, f. 125, Armitage to Welensky, 11 January 1960.

[85] *Evening Standard*, 12 January 1960.

[86] Welensky Papers, 20/10, f. 71, Welensky to Home, 11 January 1960; *Northern News*, 12 January 1960; *The Listener*, 28 January 1960.

because it would receive virtually no co-operation from the Africans. Thus he decided to make it clear to the Labour Party and the British public that, despite any interpretation of the terms of reference, secession could be considered. He took care first to consult Lord Monckton who agreed that there could be no rigid interpretation of the terms of reference.[87]

Welensky promptly asked Home for an urgent reply on the assurances given to Shawcross which had led him to accept his appointment. After all, Welensky said, he knew that Monckton had written to all his commissioners on 14 December asking them not to make statements to the Press without consulting their colleagues.[88] (Possibly Lord Birkenhead did not know of this instruction because he certainly does not comment on it.)

Welensky, who told Joelson "the inside story of the Monckton Commission would make you writhe", received his reply two days later. Home explained that Shawcross had not been given any assurances and that the interview had been arranged before he had accepted his appointment. Home imagined that, faced by the question, Shawcross had meant to say that, if he came to the conclusion that the task of the commission was impossible, he would report as much. Home believed that every commissioner would do the same because, after all, Macmillan had indicated in the Commons that they could. Home hastened to assure Welensky that Shawcross had no preconceived ideas about the Federation and that Macmillan could tell him more about the man when they met shortly.[89]

Welensky again consulted Whitehead who drafted a joint dispatch demanding the dismissal of Shawcross. Lord Birkenhead claims that Welensky cabled Home to this effect but he did not quite do that. He told Home that he and Whitehead had seen the full text of the broadcast and could not accept Home's explanation because Shawcross was an experienced politician and lawyer and could have parried the question. Their view, he said, was that Shawcross had displayed a bias before the commission had even met and that they considered him unsuitable because of his open declaration of willingness to ignore the terms of reference. As the news of the interview had disturbed the Federation, they had decided to issue a joint statement to the effect that they had considered Shawcross's statement and deplored his decision to publicise his views a week before the commission met and in a manner which appeared to be at variance with the terms of reference. They would say that they felt so strongly about this that they had informed the British Government that this would be the first subject which would be discussed with Macmillan on his arrival.[90] This statement duly appeared in *The Rhodesia Herald* on 14 January.

Shawcross explained his actions to Home and offered to resign but Home consulted Monckton and found that it would not be necessary. Birkenhead

[87] Lord Birkenhead, *Walter Monckton: The Life of Viscount Monckton of Brenchley* (London, 1969), p. 342.

[88] Welensky Papers, 20/10, f. 71, Welensky to Home, 11 January 1960.

[89] *Ibid.*, 25/151, f. 172, Welensky to F. S. Joelson, 12 January 1960; 20/10, f. 69, M. R. Metcalf to Welensky, 13 January 1960.

[90] *Ibid.*, 20/10, f. 66, Welensky to Home, 13 January 1960; Whitehead's Draft Reply, 13 January 1960; Birkenhead, *Walter Monckton*, *op. cit.*, p. 342; Welensky, *4 000 Days*, *op. cit.*, p. 169.

has shown that Sir Lionel Heald discussed the terms of reference with Monckton and both agreed that secession should be discussed. Indeed, Heald avowed that he would resist any pressure on him to do otherwise and if necessary would, giving his reasons, resign. Hugh Molson asked Home if secession could be considered and Home said that it could be. Molson, too, said he would not have served if it had been otherwise. Aidan Crawley averred that he only agreed to join on precisely the same conditions. Monckton told Crawley that he had never had terms of reference which he could not interpret as he thought best. Home knew by the time the commission left England that it would listen to evidence on secession but he did not believe that it was entitled to recommend it.[91]

Yet Macmillan had told Welensky in November that he had not wavered on the terms of reference and had not conceded an inch on the question of secession. Had Welensky and Whitehead known of the interpretation of the task by Monckton and his British commissioners, they undoubtedly would not have confined themselves to demands for the abandonment of the commission, but would have effected it by withdrawing their teams. It is also clear that they would not yet have been prepared to accept Crawley's pre-examination diagnosis that the situation was so desperate that the decision to discuss secession was in reality a last bid to save the Federation.

To cap Shawcross, W. M. Chirwa, *en route* to see Macleod, declared on 14 January that he believed that secession was inevitable and that Macleod agreed. Chirwa said that the Southern Rhodesians deluded themselves that, led by "strong Sir Roy", they could impose their will on Nyasaland. If secession were opposed, violence would erupt and Chirwa was confident that, by the end of the year, Banda would have led Nyasaland out of the Federation. An alternative federation of Northern Rhodesia, Nyasaland and Tanganyika seemed a possibility to him. Chirwa maintained that Macleod's promise of independence for Tanganyika, and the developments in the Congo, had given the Africans new inspiration and they had full confidence in Britain's intention to help them realise their ambition.[92]

Later, when he returned from London on 27 January during the second half of Macmillan's visit to the Federation, Chirwa publicly stated his terms for serving on the commission. These were the prior release of all detainees, including Banda, the appointment of more independent members, the broadening of the terms of reference to include consideration of any subject, including secession, and a public declaration to that effect. He said that Macleod had not been able to concede these points but had tried to arrange a meeting with Macmillan while he was in the Federation. Chirwa was confident that the release of the detainees would not disturb the current peace of Nyasaland.[93]

When, in mid-February, Chirwa accepted his appointment, he wasted no time in further shocking the Federal public in an interview on the local radio. He acknowledged that the official attitude was that the commission was to advise on the best way forward for the Federation, but he believed that the

[91] Birkenhead, *Walter Monckton*, *op. cit.*, pp. 342–343.
[92] *Evening Standard*, 14 January 1960.
[93] *The Rhodesia Herald*, 27 January 1960.

weight of evidence would lead it to report in favour of secession. In his view the commission offered an opportunity for the Africans to ensure that secession was considered at the Federal review. He was confident that his acceptance of the appointment would assist in ensuring the demise of the Federation. He knew that most Africans wanted the commission to hear their demands for secession, and Shawcross had said that it would. Chirwa said that there would at least be a report by the minority advocating secession and, perhaps, it might be by the majority.[94]

The local Press greeted Chirwa's appointment with disbelief. His commitment to the break-up of the Federation, it said, made his selection destroy Macmillan's claim that the commission would solely advise on the best way forward for the Federation.[95]

With its facade of impartiality shattered, the commission was hardly making an auspicious start. Indeed, after Macmillan's departure from the Federation — but before Chirwa's broadcast — Welensky would again ask for the suspension of the commission pending further negotiations. However, that was three weeks away and on 15 January, while preparing to receive Macmillan, Welensky wrote to Lord Perth to say that he retained his faith in the commission despite it being largely discredited by the attitude of the Labour Party and by Shawcross's outburst. He pinned his hopes on the "good men" in the commission and believed that they could make something of it.[96]

However, Welensky's current mood indicated that he did not wish to be rude to Perth. Welensky had gout and was feeling short-tempered and this was not surprising because he had just received a dispatch from the British Government indicating that it would allow its civil servants in the northern territories to give evidence to the commission in their personal capacities. In the past the British Government had permitted its African civil servants to belong openly to political parties and seemed ever eager to allow practices which it would forbid in Britain. It was always happy to accept people such as Banda and Kaunda as representing universal African opinion despite their self-appointment to the position. It is unimaginable that a self-proclaimed spokesman for, say, the Cornishmen would be told to do anything more than get himself elected to Parliament before demanding that the British Government should negotiate with him alone.

The Federal and Southern Rhodesian Governments had never deviated from their inherited British traditions and, consequently, replied that they could not depart from the cardinal principle that their civil servants had to carry out the policy of the governments of the day and thus could only express their views through the ballot box. Civil servants could hardly be

[94] Welensky Papers, 42/50, f. 6, Federal Broadcasting Corporation Interview with Chirwa, 12 February 1960. Sir David Scott - Scott, *Ambassador in Black and White*, *op. cit.*, p. 67 - in his account of this affair ignores Chirwa's statements in January 1960 and claims that the radio interview ("Mr Chirwa had been buttonholed by a reporter") was on 15 February, the eve of the first plenary session of the Commission at which Monckton appealed to the Commissioners not to make statements to the Press. - JRTW.

[95] *The Bulawayo Chronicle*, 15 February 1960.

[96] Welensky Papers, 20/1, f. 126, Home to Welensky, 9 February 1960; 25/183, f. 1, Welensky to Lord Perth, 15 January 1960.

allowed to give evidence to a body which would advise their Governments and, if the northern Governments needed to know the opinion of their civil servants, they only had to ask them. The British Government had suggested that this evidence could be given in private, but the Federal Government believed that this departure from practice could hardly be kept a secret. It hoped to hear that the British Government had abandoned this proposal.[97]

Such was the mood of belligerence as the Federal Government prepared to meet Macmillan.

[97] *Ibid.*, 20/10, f. 64, H. G. M. Bass to M. J. Lamb, 13 January 1960; f. 63, Lamb to Bass, 15 January 1960.

CHAPTER TWENTY-FIVE

The Winds of Change

Macmillan's Visit, and Discord over the Release of Banda, January–April 1960

THE Federal Government accepted that Banda could not be detained indefinitely but was anxious that he should not be released while Nyasaland was still in a state of ferment. Macleod, by contrast, believed that it was better to grasp the nettle sooner rather than later. In any case, spurred on by ambition, or perhaps, a clarity of foresight, he was anxious to accelerate the process of change in British Africa. Neither he nor Macmillan had to live with the consequences nor appeared to care about them, unlike the local European. If Macleod was anxious to deal directly with unelected, self-appointed leaders, the Federal Government was not. He believed that there was no rival to Banda and, although he was right, he allowed no other leader time to emerge in his haste to bring Nyasaland rapidly to self-government under a majority-rule constitution. Any means justified the end, and the nationalist leaders would find henceforth that it was unnecessary to seek to be elected to secure a place at the conference table. The Federal Government had conceded an African majority in the Nyasaland Legislative Council and was prepared for the emergence of an African leader through the ballot box, but Macleod could not wait for that. All this underlay the Federal Government's first clash with Macleod. He was prepared to take action which he would have abhorred in Britain but was surprised and hurt by the local European reaction to him.

A clash was perhaps inevitable between Macleod and Welensky because the latter, while acknowledging Macleod's ability, has written that they never seemed to speak the same language. "To me his mixture of cold calculation, sudden gushes of undisciplined emotion and ignorance of Africa was perplexing and discouraging."[1] The Federal Government sensed that direct negotiations with Banda could spell the beginning of the end, and was proved to be right.

[1] Sir Roy Welensky, *Welensky's 4 000 Days* (London, 1964), p. 187.

The clash over Banda was still in the future, and the preoccupation of the moment, in early January, was the preparation for Macmillan's visit. The Federal officials reproduced the timetable for independence by 1970, compiled by Greenfield, for presentation to Macmillan lest he attempt to postpone discussion until the preparatory commission's recommendations were at hand. The officials believed that he had to be convinced that the commission was only a means to an end, a tool which could give the Federation its right shape. Greenfield had planned on obtaining full membership of the Commonwealth for the Federation in 1970 but the officials now thought it could be attained as early as 1965. They advised that it should be stressed that the Federal Government was not intent on acquiring more powers. Control of the police was the sole exception. It was also important to remind Macmillan of the number of decisions taken in 1957 which had not yet been implemented.

The Federal officials also advised that the Nyasaland situation should be examined. They felt that the Federal reply on allowing the detainees political interviews should be that it was a British responsibility but the Federal Government should be consulted. The future of Bechuanaland should also be discussed and, more specifically, the problem of working a section of the railway line there which the Federal Government had recently bought. What was needed was a British declaration that, whatever the future held for Bechuanaland, the agreement on the railway would not be upset before 1979.[2]

Britain's recent and arbitrary decision to widen its tobacco imports to embrace all countries, thereby adversely affecting Federal tobacco exports, would be raised with Macmillan in an agenda of some eight items. There would be discussions on constitutional matters (including the preparatory commission and the statement by Shawcross), defence, and the lack of consultation of the Federal Government with regard to territorial affairs. An examination of the Nyasaland emergency and the future of Banda would follow. The alarming pace of events in the Belgian Congo and its possible effect on British advancement of the northern African should be aired, and details sought of the recent Anglo-American talks on Africa.[3]

Evans reported to the Federal Cabinet on the findings of the officials' conference which had prepared the ground for the preparatory commission, reiterating how the territories had sought to strip the Federation of its powers, abolish the Federal franchise and secure equal territorial representation in the Federal Assembly. The Southern Rhodesian view was that 1960 offered the last chance to adjust the distribution of power, but the northerners merely sought to stave off an enhancement of the Federal status so that their territories might become more powerful. The Federal delegation could see no reason to change the distribution of power and claimed that the intention of the Federal constitutional review was not to design a new constitution, but to adjust the existing one.

The territorial Governments had sought, Evans said, the right to implement treaties with regard to subjects which they controlled, but he believed that it had not been well received by the British. All the territories, in fact, had wanted to recover health, but the Federal delegation had argued that only

[2] Welensky Papers, 29/51, f. 21, Memorandum: Prime Minister's Office, 15 January 1960.
[3] *Ibid.*, 20/10, f. 51, Memorandum and Agenda, 15 January 1960.

a re-definition of services was necessary. On non-African education, Nyasaland had opted for the *status quo* (namely Federal control of non-African education and territorial control of African education). However, the Northern Rhodesians had argued that only the return of non-African education to territorial control would make multi-racial schools possible. The Southern Rhodesians, Evans reported, had also sought the return of non-African education but later retracted when they realised the multi-racial implications. Both northern territories had wanted to recover European agriculture while Southern Rhodesia was content with the current arrangement and the Federal officials had wanted to acquire African agriculture.

Evans told how an argument had arisen over marketing because the Northern Rhodesians had claimed that Federal administration of marketing was unsympathetic to their problems and, furthermore, had antagonised the Africans. The Northern Rhodesians had sought to re-acquire the land banks because they affected African interests. They had disputed the Federal right to acquire land in European areas for the provision of telecommunications and other services. All the territories had wanted the return of the control of prisons but the British delegates had doubted whether their Government would be pleased because it would open a new field for questions in the Commons. The Federal delegates had demanded the federalisation of the police but the territories had rejected it. Finally, the territories had sought to remove all roads from Federal control.

Evans described a major clash on the question of total Federal self-government. Eventually, he said, it was agreed that the review should provide the final settlement because deadlock had ensued after the Federal and Northern Rhodesian officials had revealed their ideas and the Southern Rhodesians had supported the former. As the review was likely to break down on this issue, and as the British legal advisers had advanced arguments which were difficult to counter, Evans suggested that Sir Ivor Jennings be retained to advise the Federal Government. Evans expressed disappointment at the British failure to give the lead as they had done in the previous conference in 1951. The Northern Rhodesians had been openly hostile at the present conference, he said, and their every suggestion was tainted with suspicion of the Federal Government which had an unfortunate effect on the British. The same rancour was not forthcoming from the Nyasalanders but they gave the impression of being unable to cope. By contrast, the Southern Rhodesians had been generally helpful to the Federal cause.

Evans concluded that, lacking a policy, the British Government was hoping that the preparatory commission would provide guidance. He gathered that the main British aim was to protect their relationship with the non-white peoples of the world. Thus, he said, the Federation was only a pawn in a larger game and policy would not be framed on the merits of the case. The advantage held by the northern Governments, he felt, was that they had all Federal communications relayed to them while the Colonial Office denied the Federal Government sight of theirs.[4]

Evans advised Welensky that the most important card in his hand was the

[4] *Ibid.*, 7/25, ff. 4–25, Report by A. D. Evans, January 1960.

Declaration of 1957. He believed that it should not be played too soon and, even if Macmillan issued a reassurance thereon, Welensky was not to make more than a casual reference to it. If Macmillan then indicated that he thought that his Government was bound by the Declaration, Welensky could demand a firm statement. If Macmillan hesitated, Welensky should make no more than a mental reservation.[5]

Welensky immediately reassured Evans that the card would not be played too early. He knew that the Federal public was alarmed by a statement by Macmillan in Lagos but he, having the full text before him, was not concerned. A greater worry, he said, was the number of Rhodesians who were talking of emigrating because the situation had become so serious.[6]

What Welensky referred to was a Press conference in Lagos on 15 January at which Macmillan was recorded as saying:

> "Before the British Government's ultimate responsibility over Nyasaland and Northern Rhodesia is removed, the people of the two territories will be given an opportunity to decide on whether the Federation is beneficial to them. This will be an expression of opinion that is genuinely that of the people."

Macmillan also said he hoped that all but a few detainees would be released shortly.[7]

This prompted a spate of sensationalist headlines in the British and Rhodesian Press which claimed that Nyasaland would be free to decide whether to stay in the Federation and that, in fact, no territory would be compelled to remain. The *News Chronicle* noted that Macmillan had chosen Lagos as the place in which to slap down Welensky's demand for full Commonwealth membership. However, the Press had missed an equally pertinent comment which Macmillan had made at a banquet in Accra when he had spoken of a "wind of change" blowing through Africa.[8]

Macmillan arrived in Salisbury on 18 January, appearing to Welensky to be both bland and unrepentant. Early the next morning he met Welensky, Whitehead and Greenfield to discuss two points of acute anxiety: the preparatory commission and the Federation's future. Welensky told him of the widespread alarm caused by Shawcross. Henceforth, he warned, extremists on both sides could be expected to use the commission to give their ideas undesirable publicity, making it difficult to devise a formula to give witnesses the required immunity. Welensky, Whitehead and their Cabinets were also concerned about the British attitude to the future of the Federation. Hitherto they had believed that the British Government favoured its continuance but had been shaken by recent developments. There had been rumours about the impending release of Banda about which they had hoped to be consulted but apparently the decision had been taken. If this were true, they warned Macmillan, an early release would simply increase the risk to Nyasaland's security.

[5] *Ibid.*, 25/30, f. 168, Evans to Welensky, 18 January 1960.
[6] *Ibid.*, f. 165, Welensky to Evans, 18 January 1960.
[7] Welensky, *4 000 Days*, *op. cit.*, p. 171.
[8] Welensky Papers, 20/1, ff. 158–159, London Press Comment, 18 January 1960.

Whitehead reminded Macmillan that Southern Rhodesia had been self-governing since 1923, and might have achieved independence if it had not joined the Federation. Recent events, he said, had encouraged the favouring of secession because independence seemed even more remote under the Federation. He believed staunchly in the Federation but, he said, it was difficult to combat this idea even though the destruction of the Federation would be disastrous, particularly for Nyasaland. However, he feared that the Southern Rhodesians would cease to support the Federation unless their minimum demands were met at the review.[9]

Macmillan has revealed that he was surprised by the "almost metaphysical argument" about the terms of reference, particualrly as he thought that it had been settled before he left London. However, he does concede that his statement in Lagos and that of Shawcross had contributed.[10]

Macmillan began his reply smoothly, saying that, if the Governments could find a common strategy, they would be better able to handle the tactical situation. His Government, he declared, believed that the Federation was to the benefit of all despite the sacrifices of the partners. He hastened to affirm that there was no change in British policy towards the Federation. However, he said that uncertainty about the Federation was affecting some sections of British public opinion, possibly because of the Church of Scotland's propaganda and probably because of a sympathy for the growth of national consciousness in Africa. The Labour Party had tried to capitalise on the situation, placing the British Government in difficulties because liberal and sentimental opinions could be easily exploited. It was necessary, therefore, to educate public opinion on the political and economic advantages of the Federation because difficult decisions had to be taken by the end of the year. He was adamant that the hostile propaganda had to be combated and claimed that already there were signs that public opinion was steadying and that the preparatory commission would have a very valuable influence by presenting the true facts as well as appraising the practical means for further progress. It was certainly not appointed to destroy the Federation, he avowed, and the terms of reference were quite clear on that point. He promised to clarify this publicly on the morrow when he spoke to the Rhodesia National Affairs Association. He would also clear the misunderstanding which had arisen over his statement in Lagos because what he had meant to say was not that there was a possibility of secession but that the component parts of the Federation had an eventual right to decide whether they should belong to an independent federation.

On the question of immunity for the commission's witnesses, Macmillan proposed that action should not be taken against those whose statements the commission decided to publish. Nevertheless, he agreed that the commission should not be used as a vehicle for libellous or seditious statements and that the perpetrators should not escape prosecution if their comments were simultaneously or subsequently published by the Press. He proposed to discuss Banda's future with Welensky after he had visited Nyasaland. The timing of

[9] Welensky, *4 000 Days*, *op. cit.*, p. 171; Welensky Papers, 20/1, ff. 148–153, Minutes of a Meeting between Macmillan, Welensky, Whitehead and Greenfield, 19 January 1960.
[10] H. Macmillan, *Pointing the Way, 1959–61* (London, 1972), p. 143.

the release was a tactical matter and the main objective was to end the emergency and resume constitutional progress in Nyasaland. Rapid constitutional revision, he urged, was required or the achievement of independence by the Federation would be delayed.

Greenfield, however, still felt that they were at cross purposes over the commission. The Federal Government, he said, had accepted the commission only if its terms of reference specifically excluded the consideration of any alternative forms of association. Thus it had been considerably embarrassed by subsequent interpretations which had appeared to widen the commission's scope. Particularly damaging had been Shawcross's statement, but so had been the British commitment on evidence to be taken from the detainees. Consequently, he claimed, the northern Africans were being encouraged to give evidence against the Federation. A direct invitation to do so had been issued by the Northern Rhodesian Government journal, *Nshila*, and through it, he alleged, the northern officials were campaigning against the Federation.

Macmillan thought it would be worse if the northern Africans boycotted the commission but, before anyone took him up on this, Whitehead raised the question of immunity because he doubted whether his Parliament would allow evidence to be given in public. The reason, he felt, was that public opinion would be inflamed if the extremists were given this opportunity to fill the Press with inflammatory statements. Immunity could only be given for evidence given in private. Macmillan replied that Monckton preferred that evidence should be heard in private but the difficulty was that the commission had not yet met to decide its procedure. Macmillan was anxious, however, to settle the problem because the local legislatures had to pass the necessary legislation and a statement had to be made in his Parliament when it reassembled on 26 January. Welensky closed the meeting with the suggestion that, because of Shawcross, he and Macmillan should issue a joint statement. Macmillan agreed to consider this.

Later in the day Macmillan met the whole Federal Cabinet and explained that his purpose was partly to complete his tour of the Commonwealth which he had begun in 1958, and partly to study the problems of the Federation. There were difficulties but he was not pessimistic. He urged support for the Federation because it was greatly advantageous to the area. Its destruction would be disastrous. He ascribed the current British pessimism to idealism and to the support of the underdog as well as to the narrow selfish views of certain people who were bent on personal gain. He believed that the positive aspects of the Federation had not been sufficiently publicised. He claimed that the commission, with its purpose of ensuring further steady progress and its inspiring membership, would do much to assist by providing accurate material and information on the fairness of the concept. The British people like to look forward and for that reason, he said, it was necessary to advance Nyasaland as quickly as possible to correct the constitutional imbalance between the territories.

Possibly for the Cabinet's benefit, Welensky reiterated that the Federal public regarded Shawcross as unsuitable. Greenfield declared that Macmillan was mistaken about the trust which the commissioners would inspire in view of the current opinion of the Federal public. Caldicott demanded that the

Lagos and Shawcross statements be publicly corrected lest doubt and uncertainty became dangerous.

Macmillan replied that he had been misquoted and would make amends on the morrow. He found the comments of Shawcross to be unfortunate but knew that Shawcross had an open mind and would make a valuable contribution. He was sure that the commission would be a source of strength and hoped that it would take most of its evidence in private. He thought that immunity could be provided for witnesses whose evidence was published. The commission, he repeated, had already contributed to a swing in British public opinion.

Macintyre expressed relief because the Federal ability to borrow would be seriously affected if doubts were not expelled. Nevertheless, Welensky drew Macmillan's attention to the statements of Lyttelton on 24 February and 24 June 1953 that secession could not be contemplated. Barrow warned that Orton Chirwa and his Malawi Congress Party were creating a situation similar to that of early 1959 and that an accelerated release of the militants was dangerous. He feared even the exile of Banda in Britain because the Africans would merely compare this with the treatment of Makarios of Cyprus and Nkrumah of Ghana. He wanted the British Government to accept responsibility for any bloodshed. Macmillan replied that he would discuss the release with Armitage and then with Welensky. He closed the meeting with an acknowledgement of the need to inspire confidence in the investor.[11]

The next day, 20 January, Macmillan addressed the Rhodesian National Affairs Association in a Salisbury cinema while his speech was relayed to an adjourning one and to a crowd gathered in Union Avenue outside. He described the purpose of his visit, warned of the growth of African nationalism and praised what he had seen of the Federation's development. He spoke of the British decision not to impede the spread of national consciousness in the Empire and of the successful granting of independence since 1945. He acknowledged the soundness of the Federal economic progress but thought that it had to be complemented by progress in the political and social fields. There was no call for pessimism because similar multi-racial problems had been overcome in Malaya and the West Indies. He was confident that the Federation would meet the challenge and find a peaceful racial *modus vivendi* but it could not be done in a day and would need mutual tolerance and self-discipline. However, before Britain transferred her powers to the Governments of the Federation, she would want to know that democracy was understood by every inhabitant. Every man would have to enjoy the full protection of the law.

In due course, Macmillan hoped to welcome the Federation to full membership of the Commonwealth but not before the people of the northern territories had consented. To clear the misconception of Lagos, he quoted directly from a tape-recording of his speech. He had said that his Government had made it abundantly clear that it would not remove protection until it was the expressed wish of the inhabitants of the northern territories to enter into

[11] Welensky Papers, 20/1, f. 154, Minutes of a Meeting with Macmillan and the Federal Cabinet, 19 January 1960.

an independent Federation. Thus protection would endure for some time while territories were advanced to self-government before the Federation became independent. He said that this had been prescribed by the preamble to the Federal Constitution. However, he pointed to the exercise encompassing the preparatory commission which was designed not to destroy the Federation but to advise it on the best way to progress. The British Government, Macmillan vowed, stood firm on the terms of reference and expected the commission to be constructive. Otherwise, he claimed that the destruction of an experiment which was only seven years old and had made considerable progress would be nothing less than act of treachery to the high ideals which had underlain the Federation. It was for the benefit of all and was not, as some of its critics claimed, an act of aggression. Forebearance, he said, was the key to success.

Macmillan pledged British aid for Federal development and declared that, if they succeeded, the people of the Federation could show the world that a new society could be built on a true and developing partnership. He received applause but, as he rightly says, the European at least soon reverted to a state of anxious suspicion.[12] Macmillan does not seem to allow that this was justified even though the Europeans knew that they were being marched unerringly and unceasingly towards their political extinction by historical inevitability aided by their kin in Whitehall.

Welensky replied with a short speech in which he said that Federal problems had to be solved by locals of all races. He reminded the audience that the British and Federal Governments had agreed on the commission's terms of reference and that his Government was determined that they should be fully honoured. As far as he was concerned, the destruction of the Federation was unthinkable.

Lord Salisbury had commented in *The Times* the day before on the fallaciousness of the Lagos statement because it had said that neither of the northern territories would be forced into the Federation when, in fact, both were already part of it. As an author of the Federation, Lord Salisbury said that he could not emphasize strongly enough that the purpose of the review was to make the Federation function more smoothly and not to destroy it. He quoted Lyttelton who, on 24 March 1953, had said: "I emphasise that this conference is not to decide whether Federation has succeeded or failed or whether it should be abolished or continued." The review, Salisbury said, was merely to make the adjustments which the first decade had proved to be necessary. Salisbury could utter these brave words, but Macmillan's Press entourage indicated to the Federal officials that they expected the Federation to be "fractured soon". Nonetheless, they wrote in their newspapers that Macmillan had reassured the Rhodesians.

After his address to the RNAA, Macmillan met the Southern Rhodesian Cabinet and then had further discussions with Welensky and Greenfield. Welensky immediately demanded that his and Whitehead's Governments should be brought into the full confidence of the British Government. He wanted a reciprocal arrangement to that existing for the northern territories

[12] *Ibid.*, 25/30, f. 16, Macmillan's Address to the RNAA, 20 January 1960; Macmillan, *Pointing the Way*, *op. cit.*, pp. 146–147.

under which they received copies of all Federal and Southern Rhodesian dispatches. He complained that he had just discovered by indirect means that the northern Governments had attended a recent conference in East Africa on security even though defence was the prerogative of the Federal Government. Greenfield added that he had just read in *The Times* of a conference on Roman-Dutch Law under the chairmanship of Lord Denning and could only conclude that three of the Governments involved with the Federation were ranged against the remaining two. Indeed, he said, the Commonwealth Relations and Colonial Offices seemed to have formed a front against the Federal and Southern Rhodesian Governments. Sir Norman Brook, Macmillan's Secretary to the Cabinet, replied that this was not the Colonial Office view and he proposed an investigation. Welensky said he had learned of Anglo-American discussions on Africa through the *Economist* and asked Macmillan for an account of them. Unabashed and without apology, Macmillan said that they were a useful development in foreign affairs.

Welensky asked if there would be any objection to the establishment of a line of defence across Africa with his close friends, the Portuguese, who were as worried as he about the events to the north. Guardedly, Macmillan replied that this was preferable to one involving South Africa. Welensky said that he was not unduly worried by the unrest and disorders in the Belgian Congo because the Federation had little commercial or other ties with it. He expected blood to be spilled but not wide repercussions.

Macmillan and Welensky agreed that the preparatory commission should take evidence in camera. Welensky proposed to ask Whitehead to influence his commissioners to demand this and Macmillan said he would do likewise with the northern Governors. Finally, Macmillan and Welensky accepted that immunity could be granted for evidence given to the commission but it would not be extended to that given to the Press.[13] Later, Whitehead accepted this formula.

Welensky replied that day to Armitage's letter of 11 January which had told him that Banda's release was being considered. He would not disguise from Armitage his deep concern for the consequences of an imminent release. Indeed he revealed that he had felt compelled to tell Macmillan that Banda should be held until the preparatory commission had reported. Welensky said that his security reports on Nyasaland were most disturbing and that he did not believe that he would be exaggerating to say that the release of Banda together with the "bully boys" would be the catalyst for disturbances. He told Armitage that he had warned Macmillan that the result would be bloodshed for which the British Government had to accept responsibility. Consequently Macmillan had promised to discuss Banda's release with Armitage.[14]

Macintyre suggested to Welensky that he should get Macmillan to commit himself to paper because his speech had been ambiguous and had seemed to give the territories three options. They could stay as they were or enter an independent federation or secede. This could not have satisfied the whites,

[13] Welensky Papers, 20/1, ff. 144–147, Minutes of a Meeting between Macmillan, Welensky, Greenfield and Sir Norman Brook, 20 January 1960.

[14] *Ibid.*, 20/11, f. 123, Welensky to Armitage, 20 January 1960.

Macintyre said, and the blacks would not co-operate until Macmillan declared secession impossible. Welensky replied to Macintyre, when Macmillan was in Northern Rhodesia, and claimed that he had "worked hard" on Macmillan with the result that he had declared that the British Government was committed to the terms of reference. Macmillan, he said, had "slapped" Shawcross down and had tried to wriggle out of the Lagos statement. However, he had refused to do more because he claimed that he had come to listen and learn and not to interfere with constitutional matters. It was clear to Welensky that he would have to use Lyttelton's statements to the full, and noted with satisfaction that *The Sunday Mail* had already quoted one of them.[15]

In Northern Rhodesia, Macmillan, by inviting Kaunda's new United National Independence Party to meet him, conferred on it the official recognition which the Northern Rhodesian Government had been withholding. Their meeting, however, was fruitless even though Macmillan lectured the Africans at large on the negative aspect of the decision to boycott the preparatory commission. Sir John Moffat did nothing to assist the Federal cause by telling Macmillan that there would be an insurrection if the Federation remained in being. The visit was nearly marred by a violent incident when someone dropped four sticks of fused dynamite down the coal shute of the boiler room of the Savoy Hotel in Ndola. Fortunately, they were discovered before they were shovelled into the boiler, but the security officials could not discover who was responsible.[16]

While Macmillan was in Northern Rhodesia, on 23 January, the British South Africa Police, unbeknown to the Federal authorities, were taping a conversation between Banda and his legal adviser, Dingle Foot QC. Two days later Welensky was given the transcript in which Foot began by saying that he knew Monckton very well and that he was "certainly taking the line that he is not going to be restricted by the terms of reference". Foot said he had also spoken to Macleod, whom he knew slightly, and had gathered that Macleod and Monckton were extremely anxious to release Banda. Other sources had confirmed this anxiety but Foot believed that Macmillan and Monckton intended to release only Banda. Thus he wanted to discuss whether Banda should give evidence to the commission and claimed that Macleod was willing to see Banda.[17] (Macleod later denied these assertions when Lord Lambton, the Conservative MP, who was endeavouring privately to assist the Federation, confronted him with the transcript on 31 July 1961. On the same day, Lord Monckton informed Lambton that he had spoken to Foot on 7 January 1960, but had said nothing to justify Foot's statement to Banda. Indeed, he had told Foot, and others who had raised the point, that he could not commit himself until he had consulted his commissioners as he had no authority to issue a ruling on the matter. He had done nothing more than make a note of the conversation with Foot. He acknowledged that he and Foot had discussed

[15] *Ibid.*, 25/30, f. 103, Macintyre to Welensky, 20 January 1960; f. 101, Welensky to Macintyre, 21 January 1960.

[16] *The Daily Telegraph*, 22 January 1960; *News Chronicle*, 22 January 1960; Welensky Papers, 25/30, f. 94, FISB Report, 22 January 1960.

[17] Welensky Papers, 29/27, f. 18, Transcript of Foot's conversations with Banda, 23 & 24 January 1960; Welensky, *4 000 Days*, *op. cit.*, p. 178; Author's interview with Colonel B. G. Spurling.

the release of Banda, but denied saying that he wanted him to be freed even though he knew that Banda would then be more likely to give evidence. He had never requested the release at any time because he was powerless so to do.[18])

The transcript related that Foot and Banda discussed petitioning the Queen and whether they should issue a writ against Lennox-Boyd, presumably for wrongful detention. Then Banda asked Foot if Macleod were a better Colonial Secretary. Foot replied that he was and that he had been appointed to make a change. Nevertheless, Foot stressed that Lennox-Boyd had many admirable qualities.

This discussion continued until D. K. Chisiza and Chipembere came into the cell and asked if Macleod would alter the Colonial policy. Foot believed that, at least, Macleod would do what Lennox-Boyd had refused to do and that was to make Kenya independent on the basis of adult suffrage. Furthermore, he said Macleod was certainly considering the shortening of the timetable for independence in the Empire. The meeting then discussed the visit of W. M. Chirwa to London and decided that it must have been Chirwa and not Macleod who had taken the initiative.

The next morning, Foot asked Banda for his opinion on exile in Britain as a condition for his release, suggesting that he could resume his practice of medicine or claim compensation for the loss of his practice in Nyasaland. However, Banda wanted to know who, in his absence, would negotiate on the new constitution. Foot replied that the Government intended a virtual dictatorship and would not consult Banda even though it should. He thought that Banda could accept exile because it had not done Makarios any harm and could not be permanent. Banda's acceptance of exile, Foot said, should be on the condition that he had freedom of speech.

Foot intended to meet Macmillan the next day in Nyasaland and wanted a letter from Banda demanding the lifting of the emergency, the immunity of the commission's witnesses and that their evidence should be freely given and in public. Banda agreed, and Foot claimed that the letter would put Macmillan completely "on the spot", compelling him to answer Banda. The letter would also ensure that Macmillan found time to see Foot. Foot was confident that a decision was about to be taken because Macleod had said as much and was definitely anxious to end the emergency. Foot thought that it might be a good idea to publish the letter.

Chisiza and Chipembere were called in again and a long letter was composed which included a demand to allow the commissioners to advocate secession. On the advice of Foot, the letter was changed to a memorandum so that it might be published and not break prison regulations, presumably because letters were subject to scrutiny. Foot took care to take with him the rough drafts and proposed to show the memorandum not only to Macmillan, but to Macleod and Monckton, marking it "private" in each case. He asked if he could also pass it to certain people in London, including David Astor (of the *Observer*) and the Africa Bureau, but Banda wanted only Astor to see it.

The next day Macmillan was given a boisterous welcome in Nyasaland. He

[18] Welensky Papers, 29/27, f. 24, Conversation between Macleod and Lambton at White's Club, 7.15 p.m., 31 July 1961; f. 26, Monckton to Lambton, 31 July 1961.

hurt Armitage with his cold indifference, and Macleod was to do likewise when he visited Nyasaland two months later.[19] The reason was probably because Armitage was still attempting to adhere to his instructions on appointment in 1956 to make the Federation work, and appeared to be an ally of the Federal Government. The uproar over the emergency and the Devlin Report had not endeared him to Macmillan or Macleod.

Macmillan saw the usual cross-section of local politicians and found time for Dingle Foot who told him of Banda's conditions for co-operation. The Malawi Congress Party organised a demonstration outside Ryall's Hotel when Macmillan arrived to attend a multi-racial civic luncheon on 26 January. He was greeted by booing, whistling and the waving of placards which had hitherto been hidden under the demonstrators' shirts because the emergency was still in force. Scuffles developed as the police tore up the placards and as the crowd tried to break throught the cordon of linked arms. The commotion lasted half an hour until the police arrested 30 of the demonstrators and a sudden rainstorm deluged the crowd. It was a trivial incident in which the local Press noticed the restraint of the police in the face of provocation. Welensky was informed that, while the police had handled the crowd firmly, he could expect exaggerated Press reports.[20]

The prediction was proved correct for two days later the British Press carried lurid versions of what had happened. The *Daily Herald* called the incident shameful, brutal, unnecessary and provoked by senior policemen. The *Daily Mirror* agreed and demanded that there should be an immediate end to this "police state". *The Daily Telegraph*, more moderate in tone, nevertheless agreed that the police had provoked the riot by tearing down the placards. The *Daily Mail* claimed that a European policeman had struck and kneed Africans. It said that women had been punched by senior policemen who had encouraged their juniors to stamp on bare feet. Both the *Daily Mail* and the *Daily Express* were confident that a good-humoured London bobby could have controlled the crowd single-handed and dispersed it without incident.

The Press was encouraged by an exchange in the Commons after Dugdale had demanded a statement on the riot and Macleod promised an official report. Dugdale drew attention to the stupid and truculent actions taken by certain police officers. The crowd were, after all, he alleged, only demonstrating against the imprisonment of Banda and the apparent determination of the Governor to include Nyasaland in the Federation (a curious remark when it had been included seven years earlier). To Dugdale, this incident only confirmed the correctness of the Labour decision not to serve on the commission unless it discussed secession. Macleod regretted what had happened but felt judgment had to await a full report. Grimmond agreed but found it disquieting that the reports had appeared in normally sympathetic newspapers. He wanted confirmation that the police were controlled by the Nyasaland, and not the Federal, Government and demanded an impartial inquiry. Macleod agreed to consider it.[21]

[19] Author's interview with Sir Robert Armitage.
[20] Macmillan, *Pointing the Way*, *op. cit.*, p. 149; *The Rhodesia Herald*, 27 January 1960.
[21] House of Commons *Hansard* (London), Vol. 616, Col. 169 f., 27 January 1960.

Mr Justice Southworth of the Nyasaland High Court subsequently conducted the inquiry with almost pedantic thoroughness and found the overseas Press corps guilty of gross exaggeration. He noted that the amount of skin lost by the public and the police was approximately a square inch and that the amount of blood spilled would not have filled a mustard spoon. Despite the reports, he found that batons had not been used and heavy boots had not stamped on bare feet. Knees had not been raised and policemen had used force only to extricate themselves. He had brought the reporters involved back to Blantyre to testify and regretted the expense of exposing their distortion. Southworth might have enjoyed himself but this incident, along with many others, accounts for the local suspicion of the British Press which has endured. This can be dismissed as pathological, but the Rhodesians and Nyasalanders sympathised with the policeman who commented, on seeing the reports, that he and the Press must have been present at different incidents. Lips curled at the confessions of the newsmen that they had coloured their reports later, that they knew little of local conditions and that they had based their reaction on experience elsewhere.[22]

On the afternoon of the incident, Macmillan, saddened by the general sense of failure in Nyasaland, returned to Salisbury and dined that evening with Welensky, Whitehead and Lord Malvern. Macmillan has recorded that there followed a useful talk, but claims that he had no opportunity for detailed discussion with Welensky on what he had discovered or even, having seen Armitage, on the question of Banda's release. He left Salisbury the next day without at least even imparting his feeling that the Federation could only survive if it were supported by men such as Banda.[23]

Welensky, of course, had listened to Foot's conversation with Banda and was indeed most anxious to hear what Macmillan and Armitage had decided. He recalls that Macmillan had evaded the subject at the dinner table and afterwards had retired immediately to bed. At the airport the next day, he was just as elusive and avoided discussing Banda in a conversation which lasted half an hour. Later, from South Africa where he had gone to deliver his "Winds of Change" speech, he promised to consult his Cabinet on Banda and reply to Welensky through Home.[24]

Welensky immediately wrote to Home and described Macmillan's visit as very successful and his reception, apart from the incident at Ryall's Hotel, as very good. Nevertheless, he complained that he had been left in the dark about Banda's release, the Nyasaland Constitution and a proposed visit by Macleod. Moreover, the Federal Government was still not receiving copies of the correspondence between the Nyasaland Government and Macleod. Nothing, Welensky said, was known officially of Macleod's talks with Orton and W. M. Chirwa though they had received considerable publicity and Federal intelligence had picked up what had been said in private. Orton Chirwa had returned saying that Banda would be released and, Welensky reported, that Dingle Foot had not only confirmed this but had said that Macleod was

[22] *The Southworth Commission Report, 1960* (Zomba, 2 May 1960).

[23] Macmillan, *Pointing the Way*, *op. cit.*, p. 149; Welensky Papers, 20/11, f. 111, M. J. Lamb to M. R. Metcalf, 29 January 1960.

[24] Welensky, *4 000 Days*, *op. cit.*, p. 179.

anxious to effect it. Welensky said that Macmillan had denied that any decisions had been taken but had felt it would be advantageous to release Banda when possible.

Welensky acknowledged that Nyasaland's constitutional change was inevitable but wanted it postponed because he believed that the Federal review would produce something quite dramatic for Nyasaland. He reminded Home that the events in Nyasaland had already been used as an excuse to postpone for the review the agreed federalisation of European agriculture in Nyasaland. Somewhat testily, he recalled how plainly he had expressed his contempt for the "gutless" British attitude towards Nyasaland. Yet, he said, he had done his best to persuade the Nyasaland Europeans to accept the British line and they still blamed him for doing this.

He was so irritated by the lack of information that he protested that he had only heard of Macleod's visit through the Press. It had been rumoured that Macleod and Armitage had quarrelled over Banda and that Armitage had threatened to resign. Yet Welensky had been told little but noted that thereafter Footman had been sent to see Banda to discover if he was prepared to negotiate. He was not critical of this action but felt he should have been told of the intention. These complaints, he said, were laid before Macmillan who was told of the embarrassment which the Federal Government was suffering as it appeared that the British Government did not trust it. As the Federal Government was responsible for defence, it was reasonable for it to expect to be kept fully informed.[25]

The next day, 29 January, the *Citizen* of Salisbury claimed that Banda's release would coincide with Macmillan's departure from South Africa. The delay, it said, was only to avoid antagonising the Afrikaner nationalists before Macmillan could discuss with them the terms under which South Africa could stay in the Commonwealth once she became a republic. Banda, the *Citizen* claimed, had been offered exile in Britain but had refused it and would be released unconditionally.

Aside from such speculation, there were other developments before Home replied. The Northern Rhodesian Legislative Council on 28 January rejected a suggestion by Sir John Moffat that its delegation to the review should demand an association other than federation because the latter had been opposed from its inception by the majority of inhabitants. Moffat believed that the Africans looked to Britain for salvation simply because they mistrusted the Federation. This lack of trust was making solutions difficult and, he felt, was compounded by Southern Rhodesia being developed to the detriment of Northern Rhodesia. The situation was confused by the growing realisation that the Federal link could not preserve European political power. He asserted that the Federation was responsible for the frustration of the African Congresses and the resultant growth of racial animosity. All that was left was the choice of the Federation disintegrating peacefully or being broken up by force. Thus, he concluded, there was a need for something to replace the Federation, and his motion was the only way to reassure the population. Franklin and the Opposition African Members supported the motion but the

[25] Welensky Papers, 28/17, f. 58, Welensky to Home, 28 January 1960.

United Federal Party preferred to debate it after Monckton had reported. The Government believed that Moffat wished to prejudice the review.[26] Three days later, at the Central Africa Party congress, Moffat warned again of a violent disintegration of the Federation and called once more for an alternative association to be devised at the review.

Whitehead also chose to speak publicly about the review on 29 January warning that he would refuse to sign any resultant document if Southern Rhodesia's conditions had not been met. If he did so, he promised to seek the opinion of the electorate in a referendum or a general election on the whole question of Southern Rhodesia's continued membership of the Federation. There were three Southern Rhodesian conditions. The first was the removal of the constitutional reservations and he believed that, but for the Federation, Southern Rhodesia would have been a dominion in 1955. A condition of entry into the Federation had been that Southern Rhodesia would not sacrifice its advancement but, if this were to happen, he felt that his electorate was entitled to comment.

The second condition was that control would remain in civilised hands because it was on this basis that the Southern Rhodesian electorate had accepted federation. This condition also underlay the Federal franchise. However, Whitehead recalled that the British Government had insisted that African affairs remain territorial. Thus, he felt that, if control in the Federal sphere were lost to the African majority, the comical situation could arise in which European education would be the prerogative of an African-dominated Federal Assembly, while African education fell under the almost completely European territorial Parliament. The third condition was that there should be no African nationalist governments in the northern territories as it was essential that the Federation should remain a buffer between militant black and white nationalism in Africa. It had to be wedded to the middle way represented by partnership. Finally, Whitehead demanded a definite result from the review because otherwise economic uncertainty and racial unrest would continue. He was anxious not to break up the Federation. Indeed, he said, he would fight for it but only up to a certain point.[27]

William Harper, the leader of the Southern Rhodesian division of the Dominion Party, who expected the Federation to terminate at the review, rejected these conditions as impracticable. The United Federal Party was alarmed at Whitehead's departure from its stated policy of excluding secession. It believed that political frustration drove Whitehead to make his statement without apparently first informing Welensky. Industrialists in Southern Rhodesia, however, believed that the colony could survive if it seceded.

By contrast, the Northern Rhodesians generally deplored the statement because they felt that the Southern Rhodesians could only afford to talk about "going it alone" after receiving a seven-year-long injection of Northern Rhodesian finance. Many decried such a prejudgment of the review and the preparatory commission but some agreed that Whitehead was right to indicate

[26] NR *Debates* (Lusaka), Col. 765 f., 27 January 1960.

[27] *The Rhodesia Herald*, 30 January 1960; Welensky Papers, 42/75, f. 146, Record of Whitehead's Press Conference, 30 January 1960.

his minimum requirements. Nonetheless, the UFP in Northern Rhodesia gathered that its public morale had been shaken by Whitehead.[28]

Welensky endorsed the statement because he knew that Whitehead had heard that there would be a determined effort to lower the qualifications for the Federal franchise. Welensky supported the Southern Rhodesian bid for independence because, if it succeeded, the Federation, as senior partner, could be given no less.[29]

Answering questions in the Commons, Butler would not allow reconsideration of the preparatory commission's terms of reference even though they did not satisfy everyone. In any case, he stated that Macmillan's visit had done much good and had made it easier for the commission to operate.[30]

Welensky, however, had reason to doubt the adherence to the terms of reference and wrote accordingly to Macmillan on 1 February. Despite the agreement with Macmillan, Welensky said that Monckton would interpret the terms as widely as he thought fit. This made a number of minority reports most likely. He also believed that Monckton and Macleod favoured the early release of Banda and his fellow detainees. Orton Chirwa had told close associates that Banda would be released to travel to consult Macleod and then to America. Banda would not return until the commission had reported, but would then become Nyasaland's first prime minister. Welensky was sure that, if Banda and his lieutenants gave evidence, it would be highly coloured, tendentious and favour only secession. He knew that Banda believed that Kaunda's Party could be persuaded to follow the same course. The latter and the Malawi Congress Party were known to be considering a closer association with Tanganyika, but Nyerere did not welcome it.

Welensky then revealed that he knew of a secret bid by Dingle Foot to induce Banda to give evidence. However, he said, Banda had adhered to his statement to Footman that he would not give evidence unless he and the other detainees were released and the emergency lifted. Welensky alleged that Foot had simply followed the standard Labour Party line of doing all he could to break up the Federation and, of course, he was legal adviser to Christian Action and the Africa Bureau, both of which opposed the Federation. The Communist Party did likewise and Welensky was convinced that its indirect and unobtrusive influence on left-wing organisations and newspapers was greater than was realised. His purpose, he said, in exposing Foot's activities was to warn that he might try to prejudice Monckton against the moderate, reasonable and often inarticulate opinion of all races.[31]

On the eve of Macmillan's "Winds of Change" speech in Cape Town, Home replied to Welensky's dispatch of 28 January giving him "an equally harsh shock" to that which Macmillan would give his Southern African audience. Macmillan had conferred with Home and Macleod and had informed them of the concern of Welensky and the two northern Governors at

[28] *The Rhodesia Herald*, 1 & 2 February 1960; Welensky Papers, 27/17, f. 28, J. A. Clarke to Greenfield, 30 January 1960; 27/40, f. 84, C. D. Burney to Welensky, 5 February 1960; *The Sunday Mail*, 31 January 1960.
[29] Welensky Papers, 24/2, ff. 127–128, Welensky to Mrs C. Davies, 5 February 1960.
[30] House of Commons *Hansard* (London), Vol. 616, Col. 371, 28 January 1960.
[31] Welensky Papers, 7/11, f. 190, Welensky to Macmillan, 1 February 1960.

the security risk which would be run if Banda were released while the preparatory commission was still in the Federation. However, Macmillan, Home and Macleod did not think that Banda could be held until the commission had completed its work because, aside from political pressures, the Federation was in jeopardy unless the political impasse in Nyasaland was quickly broken. Furthermore, Home insisted, an essential ingredient of the success of the review was that the Africans should be able to see clearly that they could advance in the territorial sphere. Thus the question of the Nyasaland Constitution had to be re-opened and Armitage agreed that this could not be done without releasing Banda. The British proposed that Macleod should meet Banda immediately after his release and persuade him to co-operate. Home said that exile for Banda in Britain had been considered but rejected as it would make little impression on him because it was not legally or practically feasible and would not reduce the risk of disturbances in Nyasaland during the visit of the commission. In any event, Home maintained, Banda would have to be released soon and, although there was the attendant security risk, it could be reduced considerably by cutting to a minimum the time between the release and the meeting with Macleod. Extra forces could be brought in and the other detainees held until the repercussions of Banda's release had been assessed.

Consequently Home and Macleod proposed that, in mid-February, Armitage would announce Macleod's arrival on 27 February in Salisbury and that two days later he would reach Zomba. Banda would be released just before or just after Macleod's arrival. In the meantime, Welensky and Sir Evelyn Hone would be consulted about the discreet reinforcement of Nyasaland. If Banda agreed to further discussions, a Nyasaland constitutional conference would be held in London after the commission's visit. This would help to restrain Banda and his followers and perhaps persuade them to give evidence to the commission. Home hoped that Welensky would agree that this was the wisest course and declared that the British Government would accept responsibility for all the risks incurred.[32]

On receipt of this dispatch, Welensky summoned M. R. Metcalf, the British High Commissioner in Salisbury, to a meeting with himself, Barrow and Whitehead to express his grave concern at the taking of this decision without the further consultation promised by Macmillan. At the meeting, Welensky said that Home had not mentioned the Nyasaland preventive detention act which the British Government had promised would replace the Emergency Regulations. Moreover, the proposed release of Banda just as the preparatory commission arrived would seriously prejudice its chance of resolving the Federal problems. Indeed, Welensky observed, separate constitutional discussion between Macleod and Banda would make a "nonsense" of the commission's work. Whitehead told the meeting that the release would create security and political problems for Southern Rhodesia. In fact, he maintained, a worse moment could not have been chosen, and his Government might fall. A general election would follow, fought solely on the issue of secession. Barrow decried the timing of Banda's release because it could affect

[32] *Ibid.*, 20/1, ff. 132–134, Home to Welensky, 2 February 1960; Welensky, *4 000 Days*, *op. cit.*, p. 179.

the reaping and processing of Nyasaland's export crops. Welensky wondered if he should regret his restrained reasonable behaviour and insisted that henceforth he should be told the exact intentions of the British Government so that he could plan accordingly. He asked Metcalf to request Home to visit the Federation as soon as possible. Otherwise, he warned, he and Whitehead would go to London immediately.[33]

In Cape Town, Macmillan obviously knew nothing of Home's dispatch to Welensky because, on 5 February, when sending good wishes and expressing his desire to keep in touch, he informed Welensky that he had been in contact with his colleagues and that they would soon reveal their plans to Welensky. He knew the next day what had happened because, instead of Home visiting the Federation, he invited Welensky to meet him in London on 17 February and promised that, until then, nothing would be said or done.[34]

Macmillan was at sea, returning home, when Home wrote on 9 February expressing anxiety because Metcalf had reported that Welensky might ask for the initial meeting of the preparatory commission to be deferred until after he had completed his talks with Macmillan in London. Home begged Welensky not to do so because, if the discussions in London uncovered difficulties which were so fundamental that they defied solution, the future of the commission and other issues would have to be reconsidered. The commission's postponement would have such serious consequences that it should be avoided. As the future relationship between the British and Federal Governments was involved, Home felt that Macmillan and Welensky should first review these grave issues before any hint of a serious disagreement was given. He hastened to reassure Welensky that the British Government wished to see the Federation grow in strength and prosperity, and pressed Welensky to believe in British sincerity. He asked Welensky to be available for discussions the moment Macmillan returned to London and to do nothing until then.[35]

Welensky's criticisms also prompted Macleod to write expressing his determination to keep Nyasaland in the Federation. He did not want to discuss Banda in this letter, he said, but looked forward to doing so when he met Welensky. He knew that Welensky was distressed at the lack of consultation. He agreed that it was imperfect, but recalled that he had furnished the Governments of the Federation with copies of his only speech on Federal affairs — at Leeds — before its delivery. Since then, however, the quick flow of events in Parliament had prevented like consultation but he earnestly hoped that their meeting would remedy it.[36] Saying this, he ignored the Federal request for copies of all correspondence between himself and the northern Governors.

Roberts also expressed dismay to the British Government at the risk being run by releasing Banda because he believed that it would be acclaimed in Northern Rhodesia as a victory for the extremists. It would give impetus, he said, to the declared campaign of boycotts and disobedience during the visit

[33] Welensky Papers, 20/1, ff. 129–130, H. N. Parry to M. R. Metcalf, 3 February 1960.
[34] *Ibid.*, f. 128, Macmillan to Welensky, 5 February 1960; f. 127, Metcalf to Parker, 6 February 1960.
[35] *Ibid.*, f. 126, Home to Welensky, 9 February 1960.
[36] *Ibid.*, 25/27, f. 92, Macleod to Welensky, 9 February 1960.

of the commission. He warned that he would be unable to silence the protest within his Party. Sir Evelyn Hone transmitted this message on 10 February telling Macleod that rumours of an imminent release were rife.[37] A report from Ndola claimed that Macleod was pressing Armitage but that he, Hone and Welensky still had considerable misgivings about the release.[38]

Macmillan was clearly still reluctant to face Welensky because, on 11 February, Home informed Welensky that Macmillan was sending him to Salisbury. By that day, even Blackwood, as a leader of the UFP, saw fit to warn publicly of the inevitable dangers of an immediate release because Banda could not control his supporters. He recalled that trouble had been nipped in the bud in 1959 but felt that the Government had been so criticised for its action that it would be reluctant to react swiftly again. He thought that Banda should either be detained permanently or exiled because he had no rival to challenge him. Blackwood could see no point in releasing Banda if Nyasaland had to call for outside reinforcement. However, he knew that Macleod was pressing for the release and that it would be effected before the preparatory commission arrived.[39]

The next day Welensky was asked by Home merely to announce his visit because no decision on Banda's release had yet been reached by the British Cabinet. Welensky concurred but warned that it should not be assumed that he had revised his view on the grave consequences of the release.[40]

Home might have persuaded Welensky to remain silent, but the public speculation continued. Banda was expected to be returned to Nyasaland for his release on Sunday, 14 February, and a crowd of a thousand Africans waited to greet him all day in a drizzle at the Clock Tower in Blantyre only to be disappointed. The Colonial Office refused to comment on speculation by the British Press that its plan to release Banda before the commission arrived had been foiled by Banda refusing to be released. *The Sunday Mail* thought that the delay had been caused by a major constitutional crisis in which Armitage was likely to resign and a breach would open between the British and Federal Governments. It believed that the British Government had decided that it would be prudent to wait a little longer. The newspaper blamed Macleod for the expectation of the release that day because it had been mentioned so often in reports from London, and by the itinerant African policitians, that Macleod must have leaked it. The resulting tension, it said, was sufficient for the Rhodesian African Rifles to be sent to Blantyre. With some accuracy, *The Sunday Mail* predicted that the authorities would not release Banda before the commission reached Nyasaland on 21 March because, if he was footloose before then, the results would be incalculable. However, whatever the British action might be, the newspaper believed the Federal Government would avert a tragedy.[41]

[37] *Ibid.*, 25/242A, f. 54, Hone to Macleod, 10 February 1960.
[38] *Evening Standard*, 9 February 1960.
[39] Welensky Papers, 20/1, f. 123, Home to Welensky, 11 February 1960; *Evening Standard*, 11 February 1960.
[40] Welensky Papers, 20/1, f. 121, Home to Welensky, 12 February 1960; f. 122, Welensky to Home, 12 February 1960.
[41] *The Sunday Mail*, 14 February 1960; *The Rhodesia Herald*, 15 February 1960.

The next day, 15 February, Federal public attention was distracted from Nyasaland to the Victoria Falls where the preparatory Advisory (Monckton) Commission assembled for its first meeting. One of the commissioners, Lord Crathorne, found that the Commission, under the "brilliant" chairmanship of Monckton, soon welded into a team even if they never quite achieved unanimity. Geoffrey Ellman-Brown, however, recalls his service on the Commission as the unhappiest period of his life and he, after all, had been through the Todd crisis and would experience the trauma of UDI in 1965 and the unfolding tragedy of Rhodesia at war. In addition, A. D. Evans would report regularly on the discord in the Commission.[42]

Evans told Welensky on 16 February that the Commission was deciding whether evidence should be taken in public or in private and that he knew that the Federal commissioners and two of the British were adamant on the latter. Appalled at Chirwa's appointment, the Federal and Southern Rhodesian commissioners had asked Monckton to ensure that the Commission could not recommend secession. Monckton had assured them that he had no doubts about the limits imposed by the terms of reference but was anxious to avoid discussing them at the first plenary session. Evans had met Mrs Elspeth Huxley and Menzies and found them to be sympathetic to the Federal cause.[43]

The next day Evans informed Welensky that Monckton seemed worried by difficulties with some of the British commissioners over the lines of investigation and the making of a precise statement at this early stage. Monckton had invited A. E. P. Robinson to dine, so Evans drew Robinson's attention to Macmillan's statement that the purpose was not to destroy the Federation but to advise it how best to go forward. Robinson thus reminded Monckton of this and he agreed that it was a sound basis for their work. Consequently the Federal and Southern Rhodesian commissioners decided that they and Welensky would be satisfied if Monckton would declare this even though there would be no limit on the evidence to be received. At Evans's urging, these commissioners included the Northern Rhodesian and Nyasaland commissioners in their deliberations and there was an immediate agreement on the need for a clear statement on the terms of reference.

The group felt some sympathy for Monckton, Evans said, because of the diverse opinions of his commissioners. Chirwa, in particular, was proving troublesome because just before the first meeting he had promised in his radio interview to advocate secession. In the meeting, however, he had endorsed the decision to eschew contact with the Press, but Evans, knowing Chirwa's sentiments on secession, worried if he would. However, he reported that the Commission decided to be guided by Macmillan's statement although it could not anticipate its conclusions.[44]

Welensky promptly sent Macmillan a transcript of Chirwa's radio interview and asked if he still approved of him as a commissioner. He warned that if Macmillan did not rebuke Chirwa, he would. Evans showed Monckton the

[42] Lord Birkenhead, *Walter Monckton: The Life of Viscount Monckton of Brenchley* (London, 1969), p. 344; Author's interview with the Hon. G. Ellman-Brown.
[43] Welensky Papers, 20/7, f. 268, A. D. Evans to Welensky, 16 February 1960.
[44] *Ibid.*, f. 261, Evans to Welensky, 17 February 1960.

transcript and a consequent leading article in the *Evening Standard.* These distressed Monckton who declared that he would demand an explanation from Chirwa who had already vowed on three separate occasions that he would not err again. Evans doubted Monckton's strength as chairman. The commissioners had started taking evidence in Northern Rhodesia and Evans's next complaint was that it was apparent that the African witnesses had received official help with their evidence.[45]

Welensky replied to Macleod that day welcoming his statement supporting the Federation. He claimed that even his advisers were pressing him to let Nyasaland go but, although he and Malvern had been forced to include it, he would not concur because it would be catastrophic for all its inhabitants. He recognised the growth of nationalism and the dislike of the world for paternalistic governments. He favoured constitutional changes in Nyasaland to make it clear that the African had a part to play in government. Nevertheless, he said, it had to be plain that no concessions were being made to extremism. The changes had to be effected before Banda was released because, if Banda were allowed to negotiate with Macleod on the Constitution, there would be no alternative to a government dominated by him. Welensky reminded Macleod that the confidence of thc whites had to be retained because they would supply the capital, the administration and the integrity for a considerable time. It was necessary, he concluded, to prove to the world that people of different races could live together.[46] This appeal, however, would mean nothing to Macleod because he had set himself a different course and had chosen Banda to lead Nyasaland.

As Home's visit was in the offing, Greenfield supplied Welensky with a list of subjects to be raised. This included complaints about the Monckton Commission. The Federal Government, he said, had been most embarrassed by Macmillan's remarks about the terms of reference and by his retention of Shawcross and Chirwa. Compounding these were statements by Monckton which were quite at variance with those of Welensky. This left the Federal Government only with the private assurances of Macmillan and Monckton, and in these Greenfield had no faith. It had become apparent to him that evidence on secession would be taken when Shawcross and Chirwa had indicated their preferences for it. More serious, Greenfield said, was the encouragement of people to give evidence on the need for secession because consequently some of the commissioners, and perhaps most of them, would argue that the volume of this was such that the terms of reference would have to be ignored if the Commission were to serve a useful purpose. It particularly disturbed Greenfield that the ideas of Macmillan and Macleod had superseded Welensky's statement that there was to be no inquisition and that the terms of reference would be adhered to strictly. He knew that Welensky accepted Macmillan's statement as compatible with the terms of reference but he felt compelled to point out that Macmillan had in fact indicated that the terms had been extended. Even though Macmillan had confessed that he should have used different words, his appointment of Chirwa and his failure

[45] *Ibid.*, 42/50, f. 5, W. S. Parker to M. R. Metcalf, 18 February 1960; 20/7, f. 255, Evans to Welensky, 18 February 1960.
[46] *Ibid.*, 25/27, f. 83, Welensky to Macleod, 17 February 1960.

to rebuke Shawcross confirmed Greenfield's opinion. The Federal Government had after all, he said, been consulted on all the appointments except for that of Chirwa. As the Commission had begun work there was little which could be done about Shawcross and Chirwa, but Greenfield wanted Home to know that the Federal Government now had little faith in the British Government's word. Greenfield was quite prepared to say this.

Greenfield was also anxious about the Federal franchise because Macmillan had refused to exclude it from the terms of reference, and because Whitehead had warned that Home was considering lowering it. Confirmation of this, Greenfield said, was to be found in the actions of the Northern Rhodesian officials, including their fraternisation with Kaunda. Thus he believed that the Federal Government was entitled to ask Home if this was what he wanted and, if so, why neither he nor Macmillan had said anything about it. Home had to understand that the Federal Government would not give way on this issue.

Greenfield called attention to a statement by Home that there should be immediate discussions on the Nyasaland Constitution. Clearly, Greenfield claimed, Home felt that he did not have time to consult the Federal Government and had therefore betrayed the undertakings of Lennox-Boyd and had ignored the convention that such matters would be *sub judice* until the Commission reported. Monckton had stated that he would take evidence on any subject and obviously an examination of the Nyasaland Constitution was part of his task. As the British Government wanted the best of both worlds, Greenfield declared that the Federal Government had to make a firm stand.

He argued that there was no point in discussing the Nyasaland Constitution with Banda as secession was his declared aim. He could be deported under Article 25 of the British Central Africa Order in Council of 1902 to any British territory which was willing to have him. He could not be detained indefinitely but, alternatively, if his principal lieutenants continued in detention and Orton Chirwa was denied access to him, Greenfield felt that he could be released under a restriction order combined with a prohibition on addressing public meetings. Nyasaland would have to provide the necessary legislation. If the British Government did release Banda, Greenfield insisted that it should declare that secession could not be considered. However, bearing in mind the Shawcross and W. M. Chirwa incidents, he believed that this was unlikely and that the Federal Government would have to resist strongly any suggestion of release.

Lastly Greenfield advised that the veto of the Northern Rhodesian Chiefs should be raised again; that there should be a protest at the activities of the northern officials and another at the extent to which both Chirwas enjoyed the confidence of the British Government. Reassurance should also be sought that the review would not be postponed until 1961.[47]

Compiling his notes for the forthcoming discussions with Home, Welensky wrote that he agreed that Africans had to be granted a greater participation in government, but only on the basis of merit which would make it clear that there would be no concession to extremism. To achieve this, he felt, Banda

[47] *Ibid.*, 28/17, f. 28, Greenfield to Welensky, 19 February 1960.

could not be released before any change was made. It would be better to detain Banda until the Commission reported because then his opinions would be viewed in the light of its recommendations. Welensky thought that the early release of Banda would disastrously affect the Commission's deliberations and give support to those who regarded the Commission as a means to effect the dissolution of the Federation.

Welensky totally rejected the British claim that the release would induce co-operation in Nyasaland, just as the appointment of W. M. Chirwa must have only encouraged those in favour of secession. The Europeans would interpret the release, and the subsequent negotiations between Banda and Macleod, as appeasement. Welensky believed that the reports of the recent Kenyan conference, at which majority rule had been conceded, Macmillan's recent ambiguous statements, threats of a new, tough Colonial policy and reports of conciliatory interviews with the Chirwas, would convince the Europeans that the British Government was abandoning them and their kin in Kenya. Public morale was low and the release of Banda would only lower it. Furthermore, the Africans would conclude that there was everything to be gained from extremism. Because Banda would consider nothing other than secession, Welensky decided that he had to be exiled to Britain if his release were unavoidable.

He recalled that six months previously, when introducing Nyasaland's interim Constitution, Armitage had declared that the next change would be dependent on the outcome of the Federal review. Therefore, Welensky noted, the contemplation of change as well as the release of Banda could only be regarded as panic measures to appease the African nationalist because of pressure from the Labour Party. As it was impossible to deny similar constitutional revision to the other territories, confusion would only increase, while confidence declined. Thus it was possible that Home might be induced to consider a compromise which Welensky had suggested and which would include reassurance for Northern Rhodesia. (Unfortunately, the details of that compromise are unknown.)

Welensky intended to protest at the lack of consultation and would insist that the only conclusion was that the Chirwas were more in Macleod's confidence than the Federal Government. He noted that nothing was yet known in Salisbury of the northern Governors' opinion on the release, and yet the Commonwealth Relations Office had kept them informed on the Federal attitude. He would express disappointment at Monckton's ambiguous interpretation of the terms of reference. Ignoring Macmillan's categorical pronouncements to the contrary, Monckton had been reported as saying that, if there were overwhelming evidence on the need for secession, the Commission would view it in the light of the statements of Macmillan and Welensky and thereafter would decide what to do. Welensky would protest at the failure to rebuke W. M. Chirwa.

The Northern Rhodesian official attitude was troubling Welensky. A reliable source had revealed to him that the Northern Rhodesian Minister of Finance intended to ignore the agreement that the Governments would not give evidence, and that he would submit a memorandum on what it cost Northern Rhodesia to belong to the Federation while devaluing the financial gains from it. Welensky had also been told that the Northern Rhodesian Attorney-General had recently asked a Federal official in Lusaka what he would do once "we have succeeded in unscrambling the Federation". Another report told that Africans had been encouraged by northern officials to appear before the Commission and give evidence against the Federation. This had already been defended by the Acting Chief Secretary, thus Welensky, convinced that there were senior officials bent on damaging the Federation, perhaps because of personal grudges, wanted them removed.

Welensky found the British Government guilty of failing to support the Nyasaland Government. For example, it could have expressed confidence in the Nyasaland Police after the incident at Ryall's Hotel and have prevented a loss of morale amongst all ranks. His last point was that nothing in Macmillan's recent statement would inspire any confidence in the investor.[48]

As Home prepared to depart for the Federation on 19 February, Macmillan sent Welensky a message of hope, revealing that long discussions on the Federation were being held, but he gave no details. He hoped that a settlement was possible and urged that everyone have faith even though he knew that Welensky's was as strong and undiminished as his own[49] (an assurance to which hindsight has given a ring of insincerity).

Macleod also hastened to reassure Roberts who had protested that the decision to give Kenya independence based on adult suffrage would affect all the British territories. Macleod acknowledged that it would and that all those Governments would have to adjust their policies but it did not mean that their territories would be advanced at an unsuitable pace. After all, he recalled, he had recently said in the Commons that it was too soon to tear up the Northern Rhodesian Constitution, and the Kenyan decision had not caused him to change his mind.[50]

However, ten days later, Michael Blundell from Kenya warned Welensky of the British intention to rid themselves of Kenya before tackling the Federal problem. Blundell said he found Macleod aggressive, tough, ruthless, difficult and very ambitious. He was clever and was very close to Macmillan. He was not likeable and was not straightforward. Having caught him lying, Blundell disliked him. He warned that Macleod had no sympathy for the Federation and would take the least sign of flexibility as a new opportunity to erode the Federal standpoint.[51]

On 20 February Welensky welcomed Home to a meeting of the Federal Cabinet, asked everyone to be frank and gave his Ministers the floor. Barrow immediately claimed that there was a great fear in the Federation that Banda's release was imminent. If this were true, he said, a grave security risk would be run, against the advice of the four local Governments. If Banda were released while the Monckton Commission was still in Nyasaland, Barrow was adamant that no moderate African would dare give evidence. These Africans and the Chiefs were fearful and had been much disturbed by the reports of the Chirwas. He expected Banda to demand secession and

[48] *Ibid.*, f. 27, Notes by Welensky, 19 February 1960.
[49] *Ibid.*, 20/1, f. 120, Macmillan to Welensky, 19 February 1960.
[50] *Ibid.*, 25/242A, f. 43, Macleod to Roberts, 19 February 1960.
[51] *Ibid.*, 42/29, f. 17, M. Blundell to Welensky, 29 February 1960.

independence, and would be faced by only a handful of European policemen supported by an unreliable African force. Thus, if he were released, Banda had to be exiled to Britain despite the obvious disadvantages. Otherwise, the release would be an act of criminal folly. It would indicate that European interests in the northern territories were being sacrificed. It would result in an increased demand in Southern Rhodesia for secession, and the northern African would conclude that Britain had weakened in its resolve to resist violence. This would drive the moderate African underground and produce a situation worse than that in 1959. The Federal Government would be left to bear the brunt and, Barrow concluded, anyone who believed that Banda could be persuaded to give up his demands for secession had no appreciation of his character and little understanding of the African mentality.

John Graylin claimed that there would be wide repercussions in Northern Rhodesia because the African nationalists would be encouraged by this example of what violence could achieve. He pleaded for a firm policy against extremism because the lack of one had allowed Banda to gain his current influence. He warned that there was a strong anti-British feeling in the Federation. B. D. Goldberg confirmed that this was so in Southern Rhodesia. Caldicott told of a recent and most disturbing conversation with Armitage and his Acting Police Commissioner from which he gathered that army reinforcements would be needed in Nyasaland. Thus Caldicott warned that, if a call-up of territorials were necessary, there would be a most violent reaction amongst the parents and relatives of the young men who would be placed in a considerable amount of danger because of a most ill-considered act by the British Government. Barrow, who had protested at the lack of consultation, sought details of the new Nyasaland Constitution and reminded Home of Lennox-Boyd's reassurance to the European Members of the Executive Council that there would be no further constitutional revision before the Federal review.

Promising to be frank, Home first wanted to dispel the idea that his Government was chiefly concerned about the opinion of the Labour Party or the British electorate. Nevertheless, he said, the British Parliament remained a factor because only it and the Southern Rhodesian Government could, as signatories, break up the Federation. His Government aimed to preserve the Federation but, to achieve it, he stressed that the co-operation of the northern territories had to be secured and the Nyasaland political impasse had to be broken. Only political advancement would do this, and the British Government was convinced that progress was impossible unless talks were held with Banda as a free man. This, he said, did not apply to D. K. Chisiza and Chipembere. As it was impossible to detain Banda indefinitely, Home argued that the best alternative was a controlled plan under which Banda would be released soon to talk to Macleod and leading Nyasaland Africans on constitutional advancement. If progress were made a conference would be held in London in mid-year. However, its results would not be implemented until after the review. Banda might not co-operate but would then alienate his support overseas.

Home acknowledged that there might be unrest, but this was just as likely if Banda were not released. Without committing Macleod, Home thought

THE CRISIS YEARS 1959-1962

25 Catalyst for the destruction of the Federation: Dr Hastings Banda, Nyasaland's first African physician and its first Prime Minister. He is seen here with Winston Field, the Southern Rhodesian Prime Minister, in 1964 after the break-up of the Federation. Its demise was the result of Britain's decision to satisfy the aspirations of Banda and his followers. *(Picture: National Archives of Zimbabwe.)*

26 A force to be reckoned with: Northern Rhodesia's Kenneth Kaunda (in dark suit, seen here restricted to Salisbury Airport in May 1963) forced the pace of constitutional change. When Britain granted Banda, and then Kaunda, the right for their territories to secede, the Federation could no longer endure. (*Picture:* The Herald *and National Archives of Zimbabwe.*)

27 The also-ran: Harry Nkumbula, breathed life into Northern Rhodesian African nationalism but was surpassed in militancy and organisation by Kaunda. (*Picture: C. Leys and C. Pratt,* A New Deal in Central Africa *(London, 1960) and National Archives of Zimbabwe.*)

28 The betrayed: Sir Mwanawina Lewanika, Paramount Chief of Barotseland (seen here visiting Southern Rhodesia's Governor-Designate, Sir Humphrey Gibbs, and Lady Gibbs in November 1959). Lewanika's wishes were to be ignored by successive British Secretaries of State as they strove to satisfy the African nationalists. A late bid for independence for Barotseland was to be supported by the Federal Cabinet in 1963. *(Picture: R. D. K. Hadden, Federal Information Dept.)*

THE CRISIS YEARS 1959-1962

29 A resolute supporter: Sir Robert Armitage (right), Governor of Nyasaland, is greeted at Salisbury Airport by Sir Peveril William-Powlett, Governor of Southern Rhodesia, in May 1959. Armitage's firm support for the Federation was incompatible with the aims of Harold Macmillan and his new Colonial Secretary, Iain Macleod. (*Picture:* The Herald *and National Archives of Zimbabwe.*)

30 A sign of partnership: The first African given Federal ministerial rank, J. Z. Savanhu, takes his oaths of office before the Governor-General, Lord Dalhousie, at Government House, Salisbury, on 1 April 1959. He was appointed Parliamentary Secretary to the Ministry of Home Affairs. (*Picture: R. D. K. Hadden, Federal Information Dept., in the possession of Mrs Joan Bridge.*)

31 The executor of change: Harold Macmillan, the British Prime Minister, is welcomed to the University College of Rhodesia and Nyasaland, Salisbury, on 19 January 1960, by the chairman of its Council, Lord Malvern. Macmillan visited the Federation *en route* to deliver his "Winds of Change" speech in Cape Town. His decision to seek membership of the European Common Market accelerated the process of de-colonisation and brought the demise of the Federation in its wake. (*Picture: National Archives of Zimbabwe.*)

32 The new broom: Iain Macleod (left), the new Colonial Secretary, is met by Welensky on arrival in Salisbury on 24 March 1960. Macleod's haste for change provoked such a reaction in the Federation that Macmillan removed him from office. (*Picture:* The Herald.)

THE CRISIS YEARS 1959-1962

33 The fatal recommendation: The verdict of the Monckton Commission was that the territories should be given a qualified option to secede. Welensky rejected it but it was a mortal blow to the Federation.

Front row (left to right): A. Crawley, Prof D. C. Creighton, W. M. Chirwa, Sir Donald MacGillivray, Viscount Monckton of Brenchley, Sir Charles Arden-Clarke, Mrs Elspeth Huxley, Frank Menzies, A. E. P. Robinson.

Second row (left to right): G. Ellman-Brown, Rev R. H. W. Shepherd, Lord Crathorne, H. Molson, Mr Justice Beadle, G. G. S. J. Hadlow, Sir Lionel Heald.

Third row (left to right): E. K. Gondwe, W. H. McCleland, J. Woodrow Cross, Prof D. T. Jack, Sir Victor Robinson, Lawrence Katilungu, R. M. Taylor.

Absent: Lord Shawcross, Chief Simon Sigola, G. H. Habanyama. (*Picture: Federal Information Dept., in the possession of Sir Albert Robinson.*)

34 A fateful step: Joshua Nkomo (right) and the Reverend Ndabaningi Sithole walk out of the Southern Rhodesian constitutional talks on 15 May 1961 in Salisbury. History could have taken a different course had Nkomo stayed.

35 Political trauma: The flight of white refugees from the newly independent Belgian Congo (now Zaire) had a profound effect on both black and white political opinion in the Federation. A plane-load of refugees is seen here disembarking at Salisbury in July 1960. (*Pictures:* The Herald *and National Archives of Zimbabwe.*)

THE CRISIS YEARS 1959-1962

36 Constitutional accord: On 1 June 1961, Sir Edgar Whitehead, Prime Minister of Southern Rhodesia, and Duncan Sandys, the Commonwealth Secretary, announce in Salisbury that they have reached complete agreement on a new constitution for Southern Rhodesia. This was endorsed with enthusiasm by the largely white electorate at the subsequent referendum, but the liberal mood soon dissipated. (*Picture: Federal Information Dept.*)

37 Promoters of change: Both Sir Evelyn Hone, Governor of Northern Rhodesia (left), and Sir Glyn Jones, Governor of Nyasaland (right), were to steer their territories through to majority rule and in the process angered the Federal Cabinet. Lord Alport (centre), although at heart a Federal supporter, also earned Federal dislike by the way he discharged his duties as British High Commissioner. (*Picture:* The Herald.)

38 A target for assault: George Mennen Williams, US Secretary of State for African Affairs (right), was to be punched on the nose in Lusaka on 28 August 1961, five days after this photograph with Welensky was taken. Williams's comments on Africa had angered local whites.

39 Macleod's replacement: A wary Welensky greets the new Colonial Secretary, Reginald Maudling (left), in Salisbury on 29 November 1961. Maudling's solution for Northern Rhodesia negated almost all Welensky had wrung from Macleod. (*Picture: Mrs Joan Bridge.*)

40 False optimism: Sir Edgar Whitehead announces on 30 January 1962 his intention to repeal the Land Apportionment Act. He seriously misjudged the enlightenment of his electorate and would pay for his temerity at the polls at the end of the year. (*Picture: Federal Information Dept., in the possession of Mrs Joan Bridge.*)

41 The lull before the storm: At the Commonwealth Relations Office on 2 March 1962 are (left to right) Whitehead, Sandys, Welensky, Maudling and Greenfield. By then, Maudling had made his changes which would bring Kaunda to power, and Sandys had told Banda that Nyasaland could secede. A week later Macmillan placed the winding-up of the Federation in R. A. Butler's hands. (*Picture: Sport & General Press Agency Ltd.*)

that Nyasaland would not be advanced as far as Northern Rhodesia as the official control of the Executive and Legislative Councils was necessary. However, the franchise might have to be lowered below that of Southern Rhodesia because of differing levels of incomes. He concluded by giving the assurance that there would be no Northern Rhodesian constitutional changes until the end of the life of the Legislative Council in 1964. (This commitment would be angrily recalled a year later when Macleod proposed amendments.) Finally, Home believed that the Monckton Report would be far less effective without evidence from Banda.

The Federal Ministers replied that the African moderates would not give evidence because W. M. Chirwa's presence on the Commission was a sufficient deterrent. Greenfield agreed with Barrow that the security risk was not the only danger because it would be clear that there was a plain choice between Banda and the interests of the European. It would also be assumed that he would be the first African prime minister because no other African would dare negotiate once he was at large. Barrow wanted the constitutional change effected before the release because there was great advantage in forcing Banda onto the defensive for once.

Home did not think that an imposed solution was the answer and said that the Federal review would be in jeopardy if Banda remained in detention. He remarked that there was a considerable advantage in involving Banda in the constitutional negotiations because if he rejected reasonable proposals he would lose much sympathy. Constitutional advancement would also enable the British Government to retain the support of its Party for the Federation which was endangered by the increasing African hostility. Home denied Banda had been chosen as the first African prime minister and confirmed that the emergency would only be lifted when there was legislation to prevent another outbreak of violence. He thought that there were good grounds for the continued detention of Banda's lieutenants. Finally, he asked what Barrow thought of the risk of keeping Banda in prison. Barrow replied that it had only become likely through Macleod's hints of an early release. The Federal Ministers *en masse* declared that only firm handling, which would not include an inclination to treat with Banda, would resolve the political difficulties of Nyasaland which could affect the rest of the Federation. To them any action which smacked of appeasement held grave consequences. Greenfield told Home that Sir John Moffat had asked again to see Banda and he thought that it could be granted if Moffat promised to report fully to the British and Federal Governments. Home, however, wanted time for reflection because he feared that Moffat and Banda might agree on a form of constitutional advance before Macleod could reveal his ideas. This could be extremely embarrassing.

Caldicott drew attention to rumours that the British Government wished to lower the Federal franchise at the review and warned that the electorate would resist. He also sought further reassurance that the Federal Constitution would not be revised. Home placated him on both issues. Goldberg raised the attitude of the northern officials, and Home, expressing concern, promised to discuss remedial action with Macleod.[52]

[52] *Ibid.*, 20/11, f. 79, Minutes of a Meeting of the Federal Cabinet with Home, 20 February 1960.

The meeting adjourned to the next day and in the interim Home and Welensky exchanged messages. Welensky told Home that he had received information that Banda had accepted an offer of £200 from Jeremy Thorpe, the Liberal MP, on behalf of Associated Rediffusion Television of London for the exclusive right to interview him on his release. Home revealed a timetable for the release of Banda and that he was seeking ways of avoiding giving the impression of appeasing extremism. Macleod would leave London on 28 February and would spend three days in Salisbury, two in Lusaka and seven in Nyasaland. Banda would be released on 8 March, two days after Macleod had arrived in Nyasaland. There could be an adjustment by a day or two but no longer lest the release and the departure of Macleod clash with the arrival of the Monckton Commission in Nyasaland on 21 March. Home proposed that, in the next few days, it would be announced that Macleod would visit to find a basis to re-open the constitutional negotiations. Nothing would be said about Banda's release. If Macleod could induce Banda to agree, a constitutional conference would be held in May or June but the implementation of its conclusions would await the review. The Nyasaland constitutional changes were not contingent on the outcome of the Monckton Commission or the review but there would be time to re-examine them before they were implemented. Home did not divulge that, at that moment (as Macmillan has revealed), he was warring with Macleod because, in fact, he sympathised with the Federal view that Banda should be detained until the Monckton Commission had completed its visit.[53]

When the meeting resumed the next day, 21 February, Greenfield expressed concern at the interpretation by the Monckton Commission of its terms of reference. He reviewed events, so familiar to Home, recalling his Government's reluctant agreement to restrictive terms of reference to advise on the constitutional framework and a programme for constitutional advancement. Greenfield regretted that Macmillan had thereafter unfortunately given the impression that the terms could be extended. Macmillan had privately reassured the Federal Government, but had not been unequivocal in public. Greenfield believed that the manner in which Africans were being persuaded to give evidence, and the emphasis being placed by Monckton and others on the taking of evidence from Banda and the detainees, would only deepen the suspicion that secession could be entertained. The Federal Government, he said, was particularly distressed over the Shawcross and Chirwa affairs. The invitation to London had endowed W. M. Chirwa with an unwarranted importance and he had not been rebuked for even more reprehensible statements than Shawcross. Greenfield added that Monckton, by his statements on possible action if overwhelming evidence on secession were received, had also disturbed the Federal Government and the public mind.

Home replied that the Federal Government knew that the terms of reference had been carefully framed but that it would be difficult to muzzle people. Nevertheless, he said, the firm statement on the terms had brought the Labour refusal. The evidence taken could be quite different from what might be contained in the report. Home blamed the Press for being mis-

[53] *Ibid.*, 28/17, f. 47, Welensky to Home, 20 February 1960; ff. 50–51, Home to Welensky, 20 February 1960; Macmillan, *Pointing the Way*, *op. cit.*, p. 165.

leading on what Monckton had said. He knew that, if there were an overwhelming demand for secession, the Commission would have to decide whether it could adhere to its terms of reference or conclude that it could not report. Home had spoken more than once to Shawcross and had found him to be lacking preconceived ideas. Furthermore, he had been told that Chirwa had been rebuked.

Greenfield, however, maintained that evidence on secession was inadmissable because the terms of reference related to the Federal constitutional preamble which envisaged nothing but the continuation and advancement of the Federation. He hoped that Monckton clearly understood these limits. Home assured him that Monckton did. Welensky expressed appreciation for the difficulties confronting Monckton but warned that his Government would repudiate any report which transgressed the terms of reference. He agreed that the Commission could say that it could not fulfil its function within the terms of reference.

Home promised to convey the Federal anxieties to Macmillan, but Greenfield had more to say. He felt that the Commission could consider the stages of progress, and the territorial Constitutions in general, but could not examine detail like the territorial franchises. Home agreed, but Greenfield then asked him why the British Government was considering separate negotiations which would include Banda, why there would be a double inquiry. Home, however, could see no harm in an independent investigation and believed that Whitehead would expect to be similarly treated. Indeed, Home asserted that it would assist the Commission if it knew what constitutional possibilities existed.

Greenfield feared that the Commission's conclusions might conflict with those of the British Government, but Home was confident that the modest revision which the British Government had in mind would not prejudice the Commission's deliberations. Greenfield was still not satisfied because he could not see any advantage in taking evidence from Banda when he would only demand secession. Home maintained that the cross-examination of Banda would be valuable, but Greenfield reminded him that Lennox-Boyd had assured Nyasalanders that there would be no constitutional change before the Federal review. Home, while agreeing to remind Macleod of this, warned that the assurance had been given in very different circumstances. The Federal Ministers responded by arguing that, therefore, non-African agriculture in Nyasaland could be transferred to the Federal Government, but Home preferred that this be dealt with at the review.

Barrow had a report from Nyasaland that many Africans had decided not to give evidence to the Commission because of Chirwa's appointment, and he believed that this was an indication of the effect of the release of Banda. Home said that he had heard that a great number of Africans would give evidence in Northern Rhodesia, but the Federal Ministers remained convinced that the greater risk would be run by releasing Banda. They considered the British ideas academic because Banda was bound to demand the release of his fellow detainees.

This drove Home back to his standard argument that Banda would simply appear to be unreasonable. He repeated that he fully appreciated the risk but that, after lengthy consideration, his Government had decided it was necessary because of the political difficulties in Nyasaland, the overall political needs of the Federation and, above all, the necessity for progress at the review. He declared that the Nyasaland emergency would not be lifted and that steps would be taken to contain the situation. Macleod would visit, without any declared intentions, to see if Banda would co-operate, and would do so before the Commission reached Nyasaland. If Banda would not co-operate, Home said, Macleod would then be able to review the situation directly with Armitage and the Federal Government.

The Federal Cabinet nonetheless remained convinced that the release would be accompanied by the greatest turbulence, no matter how willing Banda was to curb it. If that happened, Home replied, he would be willing to return Banda to prison.

However, he did not convince the Federal Ministers that such action could be publicly justified. They preferred to exile Banda to Britain, but Home felt that it would not secure the political advantage being sought. The Federal Cabinet, though, stated obstinately that it would not tolerate the renewal of violence because of its effect on British public opinion, as the fracas at Ryall's Hotel had shown that the most minor incident would be distorted. They still could see no point in releasing Banda because he would only hinder the work of the Monckton Commission.

Home, equally stubborn, maintained that deferment of the release would lose the political advantage and give the impression that Banda would be deliberately kept away from the Commission. He continued to urge that everything would be gained from associating Banda at the outset with the Nyasaland negotiations because it would keep him under control in that crucial year. The Federal Ministers, quite unmoved, declared that the security situation dictated that Banda be detained until mid-year. Home reminded them of the criticism in Britain and abroad and insisted that confidence had to be restored by constitutional progress in Nyasaland which would only be assisted by Banda's release. Welensky closed the discussion by saying he wished to consult his colleagues further. He thought the best solution was for Macleod to see Banda in prison because thereby the Governments could discover what they could expect and would not be planning in the dark. There was after all, he said, a great difference between a calculated and a blind risk.[54]

Further consultations wrought no change in the Federal attitude, and on the next day, 22 February, Welensky informed Home that his Government opposed Banda's release. If the British Government insisted, then Banda should be held until the Monckton Commission had left Nyasaland so that the moderate African should not be discouraged from giving evidence. His Government decried the poor handling of the issue and wished to protest because it was inevitable that a most serious situation would be precipitated. Macleod could see Banda in prison but the Federal Government could not agree to his release. At best it could promise to remain silent, but would probably be prevented from doing so by its Parliament.

[54] Welensky Papers, 20/11, ff. 73–78, Minutes of a Meeting of the Federal Cabinet with Home, 21 February 1960.

Home proposed the compromise of the deferment of the release until the Commission left Nyasaland but not the Federation itself. Greenfield, however, maintained that the earliest possible date for Banda's release was the completion of the Commission's work. If it were effected earlier, it had to be accompanied by an unequivocal statement that the Commission could not consider secession as clearly there had been a tacit extension of the terms of reference and there had to be a return to the agreed basis.

Barrow was even more vehement and declared that the release would be criminal folly and that the British motive was to appease British opinion. Obviously the British Government was indicating that the non-Africans in Nyasaland were expendable. He warned that, as Macleod had treated the Government of the Federation so shabbily, the European was being provoked to throw off the British yoke. He insisted that, if the British Government decided to release Banda, it should delay until the Commission had left the Federation because there were other ways of taking evidence from Banda. Otherwise, the impression would be given that only the views of Banda were important. Barrow concluded that the British Government had to be prepared to accept full responsibility for its actions.

Caldicott supported Barrow, adding that, to avoid alarming the moderate Africans, there should be no leakage of the decision to release Banda. He and his Government, he said, were already extremely bitter about the leaks for which Macleod was entirely responsible.[55] (It seems, from this remark, that the Federal Government had discovered Macleod's practice of meeting selected Pressmen to brief them on an "off-the-record" basis in order that inspired editorials and articles should erode the position of his adversaries.[56])

Home acknowledged the difficulty and seriousness of the position. The Federation was not expendable but, he said, it was his duty to explain policy. He could not imagine anything worse than a dispute over Banda's release or a public discovery that the British Government had given way on something on which it held such strong convictions. Powerful opposition to the Federation had developed in past months and he had to repeat that it was essential to secure the support of the British Parliament and the international community which demanded the release of Banda and constitutional progress in Nyasaland. In particular, overseas opinion insisted that Banda should give evidence as a free man in Nyasaland. It would not matter, he said, if Banda advocated secession because many others would do likewise and there was advantage in forcing him to justify his argument before an expert and critical audience. There was, in any case, no other African with whom constitutional discussion could be held and, if Banda could be steered towards acceptance of a modest constitutional programme, the current deadlock could be broken. The situation would only worsen if Banda were held until the northern autumn.

Home said he had considered the Federal Government's views and wondered if it might not be possible to separate the release from the programme of the Monckton Commission. For instance, if Banda were freed a month before the Monckton visit to Nyasaland, any deterioration in the security situation could be measured. If it were serious, his Government would be

[55] *Ibid.*, ff. 67–72, Minutes of a Meeting of the Federal Cabinet with Home, 22 February 1960.
[56] Author's interview with the late F. S. Joelson.

prepared to remove Banda from the scene. Home said that this was a compromise which he was confident his Government would accept.

The Federal Ministers, however, disliked it because of the effect on African moderates. Welensky still maintained Banda could be held for another five weeks while Macleod explored the possibilities. He continued to believe that the release on or before the arrival of the Monckton Commission in Nyasaland would merely provide a focus for unrest. If there were trouble he vowed that his Government would act responsibly and protect European life and property.

Home interjected that it would seem that Banda was being kept from the Commission, but Welensky was unrepentant because he continued to believe that evidence could then be taken from Banda without setting him at large in Nyasaland. Having gone as far as he could to meet the British Government, Welensky warned that he would have to consider seriously if he could continue to negotiate.

Caldicott agreed because he could see no danger in delay. The atmosphere in Nyasaland, he said, was friendly and, unlike a year ago, the Federal troops were being warmly received, but he warned that it could change overnight. Barrow wondered why the Commission could not go to Nyasaland immediately and Banda be released thereafter. Home proposed to report the impasse to London before meeting the Federal Cabinet again. Welensky closed with another warning that, if there were any early release, his Government would feel compelled to take the initiative in the ensuing public dispute.

In his communications with London (as Macmillan has revealed) Home, in fact, advocated that Banda should be held until the Monckton Commission had departed from Nyasaland and, if Sir Nigel Fisher is correct, Macmillan agreed. Macmillan indicates that he did not. Macleod, however, for the reason given by Home to Welensky, was so adamant that there had to be an early release that he was prepared to resign. For days Macleod and Home were deadlocked but the Press gathered no hint of the battle and did not complicate the affair. On 24 February, Macmillan hit upon a compromise which Macleod grasped eagerly. This was that Banda should be released three days before the departure of the Monckton Commission from Nyasaland instead of three days after it. This would allow Banda to give evidence in his country as a free man.[57]

Home accepted this but it is not clear when he told Welensky because in their final meeting they only discussed other issues, including the Federal review. Welensky asked when it would be held and Home said that it should be December, but that January was more likely because Monckton had said that he would not report before October, and time was needed to consider the Commission's findings. Welensky and Home agreed that the Governments would choose the delegates to the review. Welensky proposed to include a member of his Opposition in his delegation. Home wanted the Nyasaland and Southern Rhodesian constitutional revisions completed before the review agenda was drawn up. He repeated that the Northern Rhodesian Constitution would remain untouched. He avoided questions on the future of Bechuana-

[57] Macmillan, *Pointing the Way*, *op. cit.*, p. 165; Sir Nigel Fisher, *Iain Macleod* (London, 1973), p. 157.

land because he said he had enough problems without provoking South Africa. Welensky told him that the Federation was contemplating opening an office in Nigeria and, finally, that Tredgold should be a candidate for the next Governor-General. Home agreed to consider both ideas.[58]

Before leaving, Home explained to the Press on 26 February that he had been discussing the future with the Federal and Southern Rhodesian Governments because he did not believe in surveying matters from London alone. He said that his discussions had been fruitful and encouraging (a brave statement when they had been the most difficult he had ever had with the Federal Government). He had reviewed the Southern Rhodesian Constitution with Whitehead who had accepted an invitation to visit London in April. Likewise he had examined the Nyasaland Constitution with the purpose of implementing an orderly, timely and just advance. He vowed that in each case he had borne in mind that each territory for which Britain was responsible had to be treated on its merits. He made it quite clear that Britain was not abdicating from her responsibilities and that she would see justice done to all the races. Timely progress was necessary, but it had to be orderly and just. He acknowledged the current uncertainty but claimed that the Federation had such good prospects that they deserved recognition. Finally, he reaffirmed the 1957 Declaration and its opposition to both amalgamation and secession. He did not add that he had been extremely reluctant to reaffirm this but had given in to pressure from the Federal Cabinet.[59]

The local Press concluded that Home had cleared the air, and Welensky publicly declared that he interpreted Home's remarks as rendering futile any further talk of secession. He said he believed that the British Government was determined to provide for orderly progress and for the stability of the Federation and its territories. The Dominion Party, however, thought otherwise and promptly called for secession. Whitehead replied that he would put the safety and integrity of Southern Rhodesia first, but would not abandon 80 000 northern whites without a fight.[60]

Privately, Welensky gave a variety of impressions of Home's visit. R. M. Taylor, his former Secretary of Transport and currently of the Monckton Commission, wrote to say, as did Evans, that it had been a mistake to incorporate the word "Federal" in the name of the United Federal Party because the Federation was blamed by the African for actions taken at the territorial level. Agreeing, but arguing that the change of name would not be easy, Welensky informed Taylor that, after a week with Home, he wanted to book accommodation in the Ingutsheni Mental Hospital. Another correspondent was informed that reasonable assurances had been given on the Federation and its territories but that there had been a considerable disagreement over the release of Banda.[61]

[58] Welensky Papers, 28/17, f. 44, Welensky to Greenfield, 26 February 1960.
[59] *Ibid.*, 28/17, f. 46, Home's Press Conference, 26 February 1960; J. M. Greenfield to the Author, 8 January 1981.
[60] *The Sunday Mail*, 28 February 1960; *The Rhodesia Herald*, 2 March 1960; SR *Debates* (Salisbury), Vol. 44, Col. 3048, 1 March 1960.
[61] Welensky Papers, 7/11, f. 227, R. M. Taylor to Welensky, 23 February 1960; f. 226, Welensky to Taylor, 27 February 1960; 27/50, f. 9, Welensky to S. Brooke-Norris, 26 February 1960.

Welensky told Joelson that Home had discovered facts of which he was unaware, in particular, that Macleod had disclosed his plans to the Chirwas, that the latter two had announced that the detainees would be released in greater numbers, that the constitutional negotiations would be re-opened and that Banda would be freed in February. The Chirwas had even been able to date these events. Welensky explained that Whitehead's threat to withdraw Southern Rhodesia from the Federation had been a result of his resentment of the British attitude. No one had pulled any punches with Home and Welensky said that his own resentment had mounted when he discovered that Foot had seen Macleod and then had divulged everything to Banda. Welensky confessed that he was uncertain of his standing with Macmillan but that he had accepted his personal assurances and believed that they would be honoured, even though his colleagues thought differently.[62]

Lord Robins was informed by Welensky that Home had been told that many British-born responsible people were talking about "cutting the painter". Welensky said that he understood this mood even though he did not share it because he knew that ultimately decisions would not be made in London but in Salisbury. He had always tried, he said, to co-operate and not embarrass his British friends but had made it clear to Home and Macmillan that there were limits beyond which he would not be pushed. There had been a considerable row over Banda's release but, on the positive side, he had been assured of constitutional revisions which would bring the much desired stability.

The position, he believed, would improve after the year's end. The Nyasaland talks would soon re-open and the British proposals, being reasonable, would have his blessing. He had backed Whitehead on the independence issue and was confident that Southern Rhodesia would gain it. There would be safeguards, but the Southern Rhodesians were safe from being dragged down in a welter of African nationalism. Home, Welensky concluded, was a decent man and it seemed that the British Government was going to help the Federation through the difficult period ahead.[63]

Welensky must have been told of Macmillan's compromise with Macleod on Banda's release and must have accepted it as a *fait accompli* because Home reported to him that he had spoken to Macleod who said he was looking forward to his tour. (Without any record in the Welensky Papers, one can only surmise that the British unilateral decision on Banda's release would have been greeted with acrid distaste by Welensky and his Cabinet after their bitter and assiduous struggle to influence the British against an early release.)

Home said he had informed Macleod of Welensky's strong feelings on the issues at stake. He urged Welensky to convince Macleod on the virtues of the Federation, to make him understand the essential liberalism that underlay Whitehead's policies. Macleod, Home said, had to be made to realise that Southern Rhodesia was the nucleus of a nation dedicated to ultimate racial co-operation. Home was confident that, as Macleod was very interested, he would soon grasp the realities.[64] (Nevertheless, Home was revealing a remark-

[62] *Ibid.*, 24/151, ff. 168–169, Welensky to Joelson, 3 March 1960.
[63] *Ibid.*, 25/240A, f. 213, Welensky to Lord Robins, 1 March 1960.
[64] *Ibid.*, 28/17, f. 36, Home to Welensky, 29 February 1960.

able lack of confidence in Macleod, and one must wonder why he did not undertake the task of converting him, instead of delegating it to Welensky.)

Macleod wrote thanking Welensky for his assistance in a difficult situation. The Monckton Commission was enjoying success, he noted, to the extent that the boycott had been ineffective. Indeed, Hone, who had feared for the security situation in Northern Rhodesia, was prepared to release police reinforcements for Nyasaland. Macleod felt that it was necessary to make an announcement on Nyasaland on 2 or 3 March. He proposed, however, to say nothing about Banda, beyond indicating that his release was Armitage's responsibility. Nevertheless, it seemed to him that speculation on the release was unavoidable as the arrival of the Monckton Commission approached. Referring briefly to W. M. Chirwa, whose "ebullience" Home had said had caused anxiety, Macleod revealed that Chirwa had at first made his acceptance of the Monckton Commission appointment dependent on Banda's release. However, when Macleod would not allow it, he had given way.[65]

On 2 March Welensky announced in Salisbury that Macleod would soon visit the Federation. Simultaneously, the news was received in the Federation that on the previous day Macmillan had declared in the Commons that, while Banda's release was a matter for Armitage, ultimately it was the responsibility of Macleod who need not accept the advice of Armitage and could remove the latter, though that would be a grave step to take.[66] This was an extraordinary statement to make when the fiction at least was that a colonial governor accepted his appointment from the Monarch and was beholden unto her alone and could accept or reject the advice of the Colonial Office. In any case, it was more than Macleod had promised would be said.

Macmillan's statement provoked Blackwood and Dixon to ask Welensky to inform Macmillan that they felt that this was a disgraceful comment on a Governor's discretion. In particular, they believed that Armitage should not be saddled with a decision taken in Britain. Furthermore, they said, this decision would be totally rejected by the UFP and the moderate Africans and Asians in Nyasaland, and the British Government would be responsible for any bloodshed. They felt that Welensky would have to say this publicly because, if it were suspected that he had consented to such a decision, his Party would lose all credibility in Nyasaland.

Blackwood and Dixon wanted to know of any agreement with Macleod on the Nyasaland Constitution before they met him. They were determined, in any event, not to negotiate until a month after Banda's release or until he had established his *bona fides* and his respect for law and order. Even then they would hold off until Macleod had shown his hand as they were tired of always having to reveal their ideas while the Colonial Office kept its proposals secret. They believed that the Colonial Office had made its decision and thus they had to force it to explain its intentions at the outset. Even so, they warned Welensky, they would not co-operate until Banda, or any other African leader, had been compelled to accept the British proposals on the Nyasaland Constitution as a basis for discussion. They aimed to gain for the UFP the

[65] *Ibid.*, 25/27, f. 60, Macleod to Welensky, 29 February 1960.
[66] *Ibid.*, f. 55, Press Statement by Welensky, 2 March 1960; House of Commons *Hansard* (London), Vol. 618, Col. 1030, 1 March 1960.

negotiating position of strength which had hitherto always been denied to similar parties in other colonies.[67] They would never realise this goal.

Consequently Welensky immediately asked Home to warn Macleod that he would experience difficulties in the Federation because there was a growing demand for the protection of the rights of the European. He said that Macleod's Kenya solution, in particular, had caused concern because it appeared to renege on Macmillan's commitment in Cape Town on advancement on merit. There was a demand for a united front, but Welensky said he would resist it because he could not fuse with the Dominion Party, which was devoted to the break-up of the Federation. Nevertheless, Macleod had to understand that any progress was dependent on his ability to inspire confidence in the Europeans. It would help greatly if Macleod could reiterate that the Northern Rhodesian Constitution would survive the life of the current Legislative Council. Welensky expressed his sympathy with the view of a local editor that stability was impossible when there was a constitutional change every twelve months. He was weary of the political battle, he said, and would see out 1960 and then decide his future in the light of the outcome of the Federal review.[68]

His appeal had some effect because a week later Macmillan publicly declared that, while it was proper that the African should be given an increasing share in the life of the territories, nothing should be done to destroy the rights and privileges of the Europeans. Later, in Northern Rhodesia, Macleod obliged with a statement on the permanency of the territory's Constitution.[69]

Callaghan immediately proclaimed that the British Government had to break faith either with the Africans, whom it was pledged to advance, or with the Europeans, who believed that the Federation was created to stem that advancement. He insisted that henceforth secession had to be considered by the Monckton Commission because, as Southern Rhodesia had been allowed to state its minimum conditions, so should the northern territories. Home and Welensky also drew fire by separately, on 15 March, describing Nyasaland as a neglected "Imperial slum" which was not ready in any sense for independence.[70]

Blackwood and Dixon were waiting for a reponse from Greenfield on constitutional proposals for Nyasaland which they had drafted for submission to the Monckton Commission. They had envisaged a Legislative Council of 26, comprising twelve mostly-official Members plus six unofficial upper roll elected Members and eight unofficial Members elected by the upper and lower rolls combined. The electoral qualifications would match those of the Federal franchise. The nominated ranks in the Legislative Council would not

[67] *Ibid.*, 7/14, f. 258, M. H. Blackwood to Welensky, 4 March 1960.

[68] *Ibid.*, 28/17, f. 35, Welensky to Home, 7 March 1960; 7/14, f. 257, Welensky to Blackwood, 7 March 1960.

[69] *The Rhodesia Herald*, 16 March 1960; Welensky Papers, 20/1, f. 118, Macleod to Welensky, 5 April 1960.

[70] *The Rhodesia Herald*, 15 & 16 March 1960; House of Commons *Hansard* (London), Vol. 619, Col.1137 f., 15 March 1960; Welensky Papers, 28/17, ff. 30–32, SAPA Reuter Report, 15 March 1960.

merely contain officials, but could have seats for representatives of Asians, Coloureds and, perhaps, African women. The number of lower roll seats would be fixed. However, when the Africans registered on the upper roll equalled 25 per cent of the total registration on that roll, three of the nominated seats would be removed and added to the upper roll representation. This process would be continued at 25 per cent levels (namely at 50, 75 and 100 per cent) until all the nominated seats had disappeared. The membership of the Executive Council would be adjusted in sympathy with this process but Blackwood and Dixon had not worked out the details. Official control of government was to be maintained, and thus the Executive Council would seat eight Members. Initially four of these would be official nominated Members plus two unofficial elected upper roll Members and two unofficial Members elected by the upper and lower rolls combined. On appointment to the Executive Council, all the unofficial elected Members would accept the Government whip.[71]

Acknowledging their ingeniousness, Greenfield nevertheless rejected their ideas because he felt that, as long as British officials controlled Nyasaland, the Federation could not become independent. He knew that, because of the sparseness of the European population, officials had to be in control but, he said, they should belong to an internal and not an external civil service. Greenfield also felt that the lower roll should fade out in harmony with the Federal Constitution. He did not believe that accepting the Government whip was conducive to harmony and it seemed clear to him that Blackwood and Dixon were ever reluctant to accept portfolios. The most alarming aspect of the proposals to Greenfield was that they envisaged total African domination.[72]

Preparations were being made for Macleod's visit and for the release of Banda. Blackwood warned Welensky that the release would destroy a substantial pro-Federal movement in the Southern Province which was supported by the Chiefs and headmen. He and his colleagues had tried to persuade the Nyasaland Government to negotiate openly with Chinyama, Kwenje and other African Members of the Legislative Council. Blackwood had taken issue over the continual boosting of the image of Banda to the detriment of all other African politicians. He was sure that the Colonial service was responsible for most of the mystique which Banda had acquired and he thought that Welensky could attack Macleod on this.[73]

A sample of the Nyasaland Government's views on current issues was circulated on 18 March by Footman's successor as Chief Secretary, G. S. Jones, to all his heads of department and to the regional heads of the Federal departments. He stated that Britain intended to bring all dependent peoples to a stage where they were competent to manage their own affairs in conditions which would ensure a fair standard of living and a stable form of government under which individuals of all races would feel free and secure. He said that the population ratios, of course, made it inevitable that the

[71] Welensky Papers, 7/14, f. 273, Blackwood's and Dixon's Constitutional Proposals, 23 February 1960.

[72] *Ibid.*, 7/14, f. 266, Greenfield to Welensky, 8 March 1960.

[73] *Ibid.*, 27/69, f. 191, Blackwood to Welensky, 12 March 1960.

African would exert the predominant influence on any variety of responsible government. The current or any other Government could not endure indefinitely without the consent of the majority of the governed.

Thus to seek to gain this consent was not, Jones said, an act of appeasement, but one of common sense. African nationalism was rampant and had to be diverted into constructive channels lest it submerge everything including the minority races on whom the welfare of Nyasaland and its inhabitants depended. This nationalism, he observed, made the African politicians so frustrating to deal with because they would not view issues objectively.

Nevertheless, the hope that more moderate and constructive leaders would emerge after Banda was detained had not been realised. In any case, Jones said, if the Devlin Report were to be believed, Banda was a victim of his principal lieutenants who had used him as a front. As no one had challenged his leadership, Banda was the key to the situation, even though he had only lived in Nyasaland for nine months in the past 30 years. The Government accepted that he had not yet proved himself, but it knew that the demand — both internally and externally — to allow him to do so would not diminish. It was quite clear that he had to be brought into the negotiations if any progress were to be made. Banda's release, Jones explained, would be determined by several factors, including the threat to security, but the longer it was delayed the greater would be the tension. Thus he would be released in the near future and without warning. However, the hard core of the detainees would not be freed and public security legislation would be enacted before the state of emergency was ended.

Jones maintained it was vital to confront Banda with a definite plan for orderly constitutional development. The process, he argued, had to be evolutionary for stability because responsible government could not be introduced overnight. Yet the plan had to attract Banda to ensure that he would make it work. The framework was currently being devised with the assistance of Macleod and it would include protection for the rights of the minorities. Jones hoped that Banda could be lured towards the more stable and mature Africans, and away from the Malawi Congress Party and its Youth League. Thus Jones warned that a potential security situation had to be faced but, despite it, the Government would resist all pressure from Banda to release the hard core. As the future was fraught with danger, the Government looked for support from its senior officials.[74]

When they saw this letter, Greenfield and Welensky would describe it as shocking. They were particularly annoyed that it should have had such a wide circulation despite Home's agreement on the secrecy of the issue of Banda's release. Moreover, Jones seemed to be re-stating the superseded doctrine of paramountcy of African interests. Greenfield wondered how many countries had the consent of the governed. Nevertheless, he observed to Welensky that Jones had admitted how vital the European was for the welfare of Nyasaland even though the African nationalists refused to recognise it. The appeal for help from the officials reminded Greenfield of the French Government in

[74] *Ibid.*, 42/15, f. 21, G. S. Jones to Provincial Commissioners, etc., 18 March 1960; f. 20, P. W. Youens to Dr P. R. Stevens, Director of Medical Services, 22 March 1960; f. 19, Youens to H. N. Parry, 22 March 1960.

1940. He noted that Jones had also made it clear that Banda had been chosen as the key to the situation and, indeed, as the future prime minister. As this letter only came into their hands during Macleod's visit, Greenfield told Welensky that it confirmed that Macleod was not being candid with them because he had just assured them that Banda was only one of the leaders to be consulted.[75]

Part of the preparation for Macleod's visit included consultation with Banda, and to this end Macleod wished to employ as an intermediary the American Quaker, George Loft, as well as G. S. Jones. Home had met Loft but what Macleod perhaps did not know was that the Federal Government had discovered that he had already been using Loft as his agent in discussions with Banda on what he would say on his release as well as the mechanics of it. Loft was employed by the American Friends Service Committee and had spent two years in the Federation during which time he had become intimately acquainted with the African nationalists. He had regularly visited the detainees as a religious adviser, and had attended the African nationalist conferences outside the Federation as an observer. He was on the committee of Christian Action and was connected with the Southern Rhodesian Detainees Legal Aid and Welfare Fund and the Fellowship of Reconciliation Group in Salisbury. He was in contact with the Africa Bureau, and kept Chiume informed of Banda's health and other matters. The Federal Government saw him as a source of potential embarrassment but could not claim that he had indulged in any subversive activity. Nonetheless, the Federal Government stalled on the admission of Loft to the prison until it was almost too late, but had to admit Jones.[76]

Jones saw Banda in Gwelo Prison on 10 and 11 March and explained that his purpose was to make his acquaintance. He said he had seen the other detainees in Nyasaland and was carrying on where Footman had left off. Banda was cheerful and without complaint. When they exchanged their life stories, Banda admitted not only his debt to Britain and America for his education, but that his home was really in London. However, he was dedicated to Nyasaland and would die there. He denied any complicity in the "R-Day" murder plot and hoped that the races could live amicably in Nyasaland. He promised to foster white immigration once self-government had been achieved. He recognised the importance of the white civil servant and would not persecute the Europeans who opposed him if they held their views honestly. Field's ideas on partition intrigued Banda but he was more interested in Gore-Browne's proposal of joining North-Eastern Northern Rhodesia to Nyasaland because it would re-unite four tribes.

Banda said he was not embittered because Nkrumah, de Valera, Ghandi and Nehru had suffered imprisonment before him. It was his intention to lead Nyasaland to self-government or to return to gaol to die. He was willing to give evidence to the Monckton Commission but only when he and his

[75] *Ibid.*, 42/15, ff. 15–16, Greenfield to Welensky, 2 April 1960.

[76] *Ibid.*, 25/27, f. 61, Macleod to Welensky, 3 March 1960; f. 63, G. Loft to Macleod, 26 February 1960; 20/11, f. 115, M. J. Lamb to H. G. M. Bass, 25 January 1960; 25/27, f. 59, FISB Report, 1 January 1960; 20/11, f. 44, Armitage to Welensky, 15 March 1960; f. 42, D. D. O'Donovan to H. N. Parry, 21 March 1960.

fellow detainees had been released. However, he thought there were circumstances when he would consider being released alone, but Jones did not respond by revealing any details of his release.

Banda expected to be involved immediately in constitutional negotiations and then to attend a round-table conference in London. (Thus it is clear that he was being kept informed of British intentions.) He said he did not oppose federation *per se* provided Nyasaland was self-governing, but he rejected the current Federation because Welensky and his Party had attempted amalgamation. Indeed, he favoured a federation of Northern Rhodesia, Nyasaland and Tanganyika. He wanted an immediate overwhelming African majority in the Legislative Council but was prepared to realise his goal of universal suffrage gradually. He acknowledged the need for tranquillity, and promised to control the Malawi Youth League but expected the police to refrain from provoking his followers. He claimed leadership of the Malawi Congress Party, even though it had been formed in his absence, because Orton Chirwa was his friend, confidant and legal adviser. He acknowledged that he lacked enough educated Africans to administer his new state, but had sufficient for a Parliament and felt Britain could train his youth. He proposed to retain the native authorities and the Chiefs, but would reduce their role to that of the squirearchy in Britain.

The Press confronted Jones as he emerged from the gaol and would not be fobbed off with a statement that he was merely on his rounds as the new Chief Secretary. *The Rhodesia Herald* suggested that Jones had tried to persuade Banda to accept his release. It believed that Banda was withdrawn and, from choice, was spending much time alone in his cell. Nonetheless, the newspaper concluded that Banda had refused to be released without the other detainees.

Jones denounced this report as unfortunate and deliberate although he felt it would not affect Banda because he was far too intelligent and shrewd. Assessing Banda, Jones said that he had shown an ability to lead and that detention might have persuaded him to use patience and diplomacy. He believed that Banda might become so engrossed in the negotiations that he would prevent violence. However, Jones thought that he would revert to agitation if he met stiff opposition to his views, and that only time would tell.[77]

There was one other visitor from the Nyasaland Government because, later in March, its Salisbury representative, G. N. Burden, decided to see Banda. Burden asked Banda about the renewal of violence in Nyasaland, including the burning of the house of E. K. Gondwe of the Monckton Commission, the intimidation of the families of certain Africans, and the political indoctrination of children. Banda condemned violence but claimed that, in 1958, the Government had intimidated certain Chiefs into supporting the Federation. He disliked the indoctrination of children but denied that it was happening, claiming that the children acquired their attitudes from their parents. In addition, they were only reacting to the pro-Federal propaganda in the schools.[78]

Welensky, who still privately expressed confidence in the future of the

[77] *Ibid.*, 42/15, f. 25, Report of Discussions with Banda, 10 & 11 March 1960.
[78] *Ibid.*, ff. 45–46, D. D. O'Donovan to Welensky, 24 March 1960.

Federation, prepared his case for representation to Macleod. Constitutional advancement in Nyasaland was acceptable but it had to be a recognition of merit and not a concession to extremism. Any changes were not to be effected before the Federal review and, if there were to be change, the Federal Government wanted the question of the federalisation of non-African agriculture to be re-examined. He knew that the British Government hoped Banda would be open to reason and would negotiate and prevent violence, but the Federal Government expected him only to demand secession. Like all extremists, he would eschew compromise and reason except as a deliberate bluff to gain a point. He would refuse to do anything until his lieutenants were released, but Welensky proposed to remind Macleod that Home had promised that the British Government would be steadfast in its refusal to free the hard core. Home, Welensky noted, had also declared that the British Government would not hesitate to re-detain Banda if he were associated with violence or if his presence led to violence. Above all, Welensky wanted Macleod to understand that the Federal Government dissociated itself from the decision to release Banda and would accept no responsibility for it.

In his preparation notes, Welensky wrote that he would insist on the expansion of the Nyasaland Police and would warn that, in the event of trouble, public opinion would expect vigorous Federal action. The emergency would have to endure until a preventive detention act was enacted. Reassurance would be sought on Home's statement that the Northern Rhodesian Constitution would survive the life of the Legislative Council and Macleod would be asked to remind his Government that the Monckton terms of reference would not be extended. Welensky intended to demand that not only should corrective instructions be issued to the Northern Rhodesian officials, but that he should receive copies of them and subsequent reports on their implementation. He would also insist that the attitude of certain senior officials warranted their replacement. He would complain about the lack of consultation of his Government and, finally, would seek the views of Macleod on a recent American offer of US $20 000 000 for education in the northern territories.[79]

These demands were undoubtedly made to Macleod when he arrived in Salisbury on 24 March, but no record has been seen of the meetings held with him in the next two days. However, Welensky has recorded that Macleod was cool and withdrawn and that they achieved no rapport. Macleod declared that he had no fixed ideas on the northern territories beyond knowing that, for the sake of the Federation, there had to be constitutional progress. He intended merely to explore. He repeated this to the Press but added, when asked about the release of Banda, that he could not discuss the cases of individual detainees.[80]

On 27 March, Macleod endured a violent demonstration on his arrival in Lusaka. His car was struck with sticks, and fists were shaken in the windows. It took the police ten minutes to clear a way and restore order. When he reached Government House, he was confronted with a two-hour long demon-

[79] *Ibid.*, 25/27, f. 44, Notes for Talks with Macleod, 21 March 1960; 25/240A, f. 202, Welensky to Lord Robins, 21 March 1960.
[80] Welensky, *4 000 Days*, *op. cit.*, p. 187; *The Rhodesia Herald*, 25 March 1960.

stration outside. Not surprisingly, when he met Kaunda on the following day, he told him how unimpressed he was. This had the desired effect because there were no further demonstrations. Another consequence was that Kaunda announced the next day that Macleod had invited him to London for further discussions.[81]

At a civic luncheon Macleod declared that the British Government would uphold the Federal constitutional preamble and would not forgo its responsibilities until asked by all the inhabitants. He said he had no plans to amend the Northern Rhodesian Constitution but could not predict the outcome of the Federal review. However, he surprised the Federal Government because, wishing to placate African fears, he stated that the delegations to the review would be composed of more than just members of the Governments and the legislatures.[82] Thus, Macleod made an opening for Banda and other African nationalists by departing radically from the agreement with Home and Macmillan that the review would be confined to delegations chosen by the Governments.

C. D. Burney provided Welensky with the only record of discussions with Macleod in Lusaka. Macleod told him and Roberts that there were no definite plans for the Nyasaland Constitution, but that it seemed to him that many people laboured under the misapprehension that the British Government only gave way to threats of force and that the African nationalists believed that they would gain their ends by demonstrations. This was nonsensical, Macleod said, because such tactics had only brought delays in Kenya, Nyasaland and Cyprus. He knew how greatly intimidation had hampered the UFP's efforts to enlist the support of the moderate Africans. It was clear that, as long as the African nationalists claimed that they would take power in October 1960, the moderate African would be reluctant to risk joining the UFP. Thus Macleod said he would publicly deny that this would happen.

In response to a question from Roberts, Macleod confirmed that there were no plans for Northern Rhodesian constitutional change although the review might alter the situation. However, he considered the Constitution too complicated to survive for long. Roberts then demanded that any changes should be announced in Lusaka and not in London. Macleod noted this but warned that he could not give the impression of accepting the UFP's opinion because he had to appear at all times to be impartial.

Burney maintained that there would never be any stability as long as the British Government could unilaterally issue an order in council or impose a new constitution. However, Macleod would not promise more than to consult the Northern Rhodesian and Federal Governments before any action was taken, and to adhere to the spirit of the preamble. Burney asked how far the Northern Rhodesian Government could move towards self-government within the bounds of the current Constitution and franchise, and was told that the franchise was too narrow for anything to be done. This was the standard

[81] *The Rhodesia Herald*, 28 March 1960; Welensky Papers, 20/1, f. 118, Macleod to Welensky, 5 April 1960.

[82] D. C. Mulford, *Zambia: The Politics of Independence, 1957–1964* (London, 1967), p. 150; Welensky Papers, 20/1, f. 118, Macleod to Welensky, 5 April 1960.

British reply, but Burney had trapped Macleod because he then asked why the Federal Government was a responsible government when its franchise was equally as narrow. Macleod evaded the question, and Burney concluded that he would require tough handling. It seemed that what chiefly worried Macleod was the security situation which might arise if Northern Rhodesia were promoted to the status which Southern Rhodesia had gained in 1923.[83]

Welensky felt impelled to correct an impression given by Kaunda, and did so in the Federal Assembly on 29 March. His reason was that African MPs had protested that only nationalist extremists were ever invited to meet the Secretaries of State. The truth, he said, was that Macleod had simply invited Kaunda to call when in London. Welensky quickly passed on to describe a visit from an unofficial Katangese delegation which had suggested that he should befriend Katanga when the Congo became independent in mid-year. There had been speculation that Katanga might join the Federation, but, while he was prepared to be friendly to any neighbour, Welenksy told the House he felt that any move towards a closer association would have to come from the people themselves.

The idea of gaining another black province did not appeal to the Dominion Party, but its spokesman, Wightwick, believed that the degree of the Imperial withdrawal was such that it was time for a "showdown" with the British Government. He insisted that the Federal delegation to the review had to tell the British Government unequivocally that it wanted independence because there would be no security under British rule. Independence, he said, might have to be taken if the British Government refused to concede it. The Federal Government, he averred, was in a powerful position and, as the Federation could only survive if political power remained in white hands, it could counter the threat of the creation of black majorities in the northern territories with sanctions because it controlled not only the railways, the postal service and the defence forces, but the purse. Britain could retaliate but not without hurting her taxpayer. If Britain was determined to withdraw from Africa, Wightwick demanded that serious consideration be given to the Central African Alliance.[84]

If Wightwick was attempting to shake Macleod's resolve, he did not succeed because, as planned, on 1 April at 9.25 a.m., Banda was delivered at Government House, Zomba, by the Federal authorities, having been released from Gwelo Prison before dawn.

[83] Welensky Papers, 27/40, f. 75, C. D. Burney to Welensky, 30 March 1960.
[84] Fed R & N *Debates* (Salisbury), Vol. 12, Col. 36, 29 March 1960.

CHAPTER TWENTY-SIX

The Seeds of Destruction

Macleod's Reform of the Nyasaland Constitution, and the Monckton Inquiry, April–August 1960

THE release of Banda, as part of Macleod's programme to bring him into the political system, regardless of the cost to Nyasaland or the Federation, would place in power the catalyst for the destruction of the Federation. Welensky would resist this process fiercely, but Macleod would out-manoeuvre him. Macmillan did not assist by transferring Lord Home, the Federation's only real friend in his Government, to the Foreign Office and by replacing him with Duncan Sandys (later Lord Duncan-Sandys) who knew little of the issues at stake. The result was that the Federation found itself bereft of an advocate in the Commonwealth Relations Office, while the Colonial Office remorselessly pursued its goal of introducing majority rule into its dependencies. With Macleod at the helm, that process of change had already become dramatically faster.

At Government House, Zomba, on the morning of 1 April 1960, Macleod and Banda reviewed the situation for an hour and a half. Then Orton Chirwa arrived and took Banda to his home. The news of the release spread like the proverbial wildfire, but the Pressmen and others were struck by the friendliness of the crowds which gathered to hear Banda appeal for calm because success was at hand. Later, Banda, Orton Chirwa and Armitage broadcast appeals for tranquillity. Macleod told the Press that his current conversations with Banda were the start of negotiations which might be continued in London at a later date. Otherwise he proposed to concentrate on short-term problems such as ending the emergency and to leave the long-term ones to Monckton. He was confident that Banda wanted a relaxation of tension and a start to the constitutional negotiations. The only condition of the release was that Banda should appeal for calm.[1]

Armitage declared that there was no change in the pattern of release which

[1] Welensky Papers, 7/26, f. 316, A. D. Evans to Welensky, 2 April 1960; P. Short, *Banda* (London, 1974), p. 131; *The Bulawayo Chronicle*, 2 April 1960.

was based on the premise that, when a detainee no longer represented a menace to law and order, he could be released. He thought the last to be freed would be the Chisiza brothers and Chipembere.

Dixon told the Press that a problem of safeguarding the freedom of movement and of speech had been created because law and order would still have to be maintained. Welensky and Field refused to comment, but the Central Africa Party regretted that the release had been so long delayed. Harper, of the Dominion Party, claimed with some prescience that "the Federal Dream is shattered" and wanted to throw out the United Federal Party before its policies affected the situation in Southern Rhodesia. Wightwick believed that the release was evidence that neither Armitage nor Welensky could stand up against Macleod. The British Labour Party unreservedly welcomed the news, but *The Bulawayo Chronicle* felt that Macleod was gambling on being able to influence Banda. Worse than that, it felt he was counting on Banda's ability to control his followers which he had not yet been able to do. The die was cast, the newspaper believed, and there would be cold comfort for the Federation if Macleod's gamble on Banda failed. The *Northern News* thought that the release would be cautiously welcomed because it inferred that Armitage was satisfied with the security situation.[2]

As the discussion in Zomba continued, *The Bulawayo Chronicle*, mulling over the affair, concluded that, if Macleod believed that he could influence Banda, he must have decided that Nyasaland should at least become semi-detached from the Federation under a majority-rule government because Banda would never accept a position of subservience to Welensky. Thus, the newspaper predicted, Macleod might have stolen a march on the Federal Government and have raised the possibility of a looser and, perhaps, purely economic association of the territories.

As if to confirm these fears, Banda emerged from one session with Macleod to tell the waiting crowd to refrain from disorder to enable Macleod to do for Nyasaland what he had done for Kenya. It was noticed that Macleod and Armitage were cheered whenever they appeared in public and it was concluded that this had been ordered.[3]

Welensky found Macleod able but obstinate and likely to learn the hard way. Their meetings, he told his correspondents, had been cordial and he had tried to be reasonable with Macleod. He had rejected the release but Macleod had replied that he could not survive politically if the Federal Government dictated the policy on Banda. Welensky had been forced to concede that Banda was a British prisoner and that his release was their prerogative. He had wished to avoid antagonising African and British opinion, but had warned Macleod that he might be forced to state in public that he had opposed Banda's release. Nonetheless, he had been comforted by Macleod's reassurances on the northern constitutions and wondered at Banda's reaction when the British Government finally told him that secession was impossible.[4]

Banda continued to appeal for calm even though he appeared anything but

[2] *The Bulawayo Chronicle*, 2 April 1960; *Northern News*, 2 & 4 April 1960.

[3] *The Bulawayo Chronicle*, 4 April 1960; Welensky Papers, 7/26, f. 309, A. D. Evans to Welensky, 4 April 1960.

[4] Welensky Papers, 25/240A, f. 197, Welensky to Lord Robins, 4 April 1960.

calm himself. At Limbe on 4 April, gesticulating excitedly, he urged the crowd to leave all trouble-making to him. He promised to do this in Zomba and London but would eschew the use of stones and spears and rely on his brain and his tongue. Macleod, he proclaimed, was a good Christian and wished to help him. Macleod had, after all, displayed great courage in defying Welensky who had wanted to detain him until 1961. Macleod had suggested a conference in London and Banda revealed that he would attend. He said he would go immediately to Britain and the United States. However, he frustrated the Press by refusing any interviews because, of course, he had the exclusive contract with Jeremy Thorpe.

Orton Chirwa announced that Banda would succeed him as leader of the Malawi Congress Party, that there would be an election in October, and that independence would be granted before the end of the year. Blackwood countered by pointing out that Macleod was still exploring the possibilities of a conference in mid-year, and that a final decision on the future was, therefore, most unlikely before the Federal review.

The same day, 4 April, criticism of Macleod by van Eeden brought applause from both sides of the Federal Assembly. Van Eeden claimed that it was widely believed that no action would be taken while the Monckton Commission deliberated. Thus the Federal Assembly had been profoundly disturbed to hear of Macleod's visit and even more so when his purpose had become clear. Van Eeden claimed that Macleod was currently negotiating with a man who had been incarcerated as a dangerous agitator, but who was now deemed the proper representative of his people. Thus Banda was either unfit for the given role, or had been wrongly imprisoned. Such double-dealing only served to bring Macleod and the Colonial administration into disrepute. The Federal Assembly should not tolerate such interference. Van Eeden did not blame the Federal Government and only asked it to convey the House's opinion to the British Government. Greenfield, in reply, refused to comment on matters which were the prerogative of the Colonial Secretary.

Welensky was ill and did not comment, but *The Rhodesia Herald* demanded that he should because the "ambitious" Colonial Secretary appeared intent on a greater "sell-out" than he had achieved in Kenya. Banda, it said, was still intent on breaking up the Federation and Macleod seemed to be his willing partner. It was hoped that at least Macleod would expand on his refusal to revise the Northern Rhodesian Constitution.[5]

The next day, while the Federal Assembly resumed its criticism of him and his apparent abdication to Banda and Kaunda, Macleod reported to Welensky on his tour. He described his warning to Kaunda on the demonstrations and its salutory effect. He claimed that he had repeatedly said that there would be no revision of the Northern Rhodesian Constitution before the review, thereby showing that he rejected the demands of the African nationalist Parties for radical change before October 1960. However, the repetition by every African whom he met of the fear that they would not be adequately represented at the review had led him to say publicly that representation would not be solely confined to the legislatures and the Governments. Banda's release had been

[5] *Evening Standard*, 4 April 1960; *The Rhodesia Herald*, 5 April 1960; Fed R & N *Debates* (Salisbury), Vol. 12, Col. 286 f., 4 April 1960.

uneventful, he said, and he seemed anxious to keep the peace. Macleod did not expect to influence Banda at this early stage and had settled for a constitutional conference in London, even though there would be widely differing views to reconcile. The best time for the conference was mid-July. He proposed to announce this at the end of his visit and after consulting Welensky in Salisbury.[6]

Welensky did not reply and there is no record in his papers of any further discussions with Macleod on his return to Salisbury. However, Welensky told Beckett that he would demand an explanation of a statement by Banda that Macleod had told him that he had wished to release him in February but that people in Salisbury and Zomba had objected and he had been detained for a further two months. This was the truth, but Welensky wanted to know if Macleod had told Banda. Macleod had assured him that there would be no exceptional changes in Nyasaland but Welensky could not see how Banda could accept that. Nonetheless, if Macleod did what he said he would, the outlook was reasonable but Welensky had grave doubts about British integrity and wondered if such promises would be honoured.[7]

The barrage of criticism of Macleod from the Federal Assembly led Gaunt to press the Federal Government to declare that it would not subscribe to any change which would diminish the rights of the Europeans who had colonised Northern Rhodesia. Questioning the right of the Federal Government to be consulted on all changes, and because it was clear that the Northern Rhodesian Constitution would soon be changed without the consent of its electorate, Gaunt sought a constitutional amendment so that any territorial constitutional revision would have to win the consent of the Federal House.

Greenfield replied that, as the Monckton Commission was considering all the Constitutions, the whole matter would be examined at the review when the Federal Government would exert its maximum influence to secure the territorial changes it desired. Chief of these was the transfer of the powers of the Colonial Office to the northern Governments. Any change to franchises would be opposed in case the basis of the Federal franchise was undermined. Likewise, any revision which would impede the attainment of responsible government would be resisted. He felt that Gaunt was too defeatist in assuming that Banda would be the first prime minister of Nyasaland. The Federal Government, Greenfield said, could not support the motion because it had responsibilities for the interests of all races. It was accordingly amended to a defence of civilised standards and of the rights of all sections of the community, and was accepted.[8]

Evans, in Nyasaland with the Monckton Commission, watched the actions of Banda and concluded ruefully that the Nyasaland Government had abdicated. For example, Evans told Welensky, the ban on meetings, still in force while the emergency endured, was rescinded to avoid any incident before Banda left for Britain on 6 April. Typical of the moment was the sight of two African police constables joining in the applause for Banda's praise of Macleod and his call for the ignoring of "stooges" and the United Federal Party.

[6] Welensky Papers, 20/1, f. 118, Macleod to Welensky, 5 April 1960.
[7] *Ibid.*, 42/21, f. 48, Welensky to Beckett, 6 April 1960.
[8] Fed R & N *Debates* (Salisbury), Vol. 12, Col. 353 f., 6 April 1960.

Senior officials were believed to have "thrown in the sponge" when meeting Macleod and, certainly, they had given the Monckton Commission the impression that all was lost. Their attitude had prompted Menzies to tell Evans that Welensky should be given a free hand to restore authority and control.[9]

Despite Banda's and Kaunda's favourable reception of Macleod, the northern African Congresses had persisted with their boycott of the Monckton Commission. However, the Commission had been enjoying some success because none of the boycotts had been total. From Northern Rhodesia, Evans had continued to report to Welensky that the Commission was constantly faced with complaints about territorial matters for which the Africans mistakenly blamed the Federal Government. An increase in the price of postage, Evans said, was often the sole real complaint against the Federal Government. The presentation of evidence was mostly very poor and in many cases when it was good, it clearly had been rehearsed. There were occasions when the presentation was quite sophisticated, but the presenter had been unable to answer questions on it. There had, however, been the rare African who was prepared to reveal details of the current spate of nationalist intimidation, and what they found soon began to influence the commissioners in favour of Federation. Examples of the lack of co-operation with the Federal Government, such as the African school on the Copperbelt which taught nothing about the Federation, irritated the commissioners and confirmed their impression that the Federation had not recovered from the Colonial administration's failure to recommend it to the Africans.

In mid-March, Evans reported, the evidence presented was particularly poor and W. M. Chirwa sought to have it ignored but was told that the Commission would record what it had found. A day of particular gloom for Evans was 16 March when Sir John Moffat informed the Commission that the Federation could only be maintained by force. However, the day had brightened when Beadle and Taylor had tied up Harry Franklin by challenging him on his evidence. This seemed to recruit Sir Charles Arden-Clarke and Lord Crathorne to the ranks of the Federal enthusiasts which included Dr Shepherd, Menzies and Mrs Huxley. Consequently Evans urged Welensky to ensure that men of the highest calibre gave evidence when the Commission reached Salisbury.[10]

In Nyasaland, Evans said, the boycott seemed to be effective until witnesses in the Southern Province began to appear despite demonstrations by the Malawi Congress and Congress Liberation Parties. At Fort Manning the Commission was confronted by the sight of severed telephone lines and of Asians being intimidated by the Malawi Youth League wielding axes and assegais. In the Central Province the Chiefs, to a man, declared their opposition to the Malawi Congress Party and asked why it was not banned. They were amazed at the weakness of the Government. Evans thought that there was a solid core of support for the Federation but that the Nyasaland Government was fast losing control and did not support those who defied the MCP. Chief Sigola of the Southern Rhodesian group of commissioners was

[9] Welensky Papers, 7/26, f. 256, A. D. Evans to Welensky, 6 April 1960.
[10] *Ibid.*, 20/17, ff. 156, 137, 123, 113, 75 & 71, A. D. Evans to Welensky, 11, 14, 15, 16, 18 & 19 March 1960.

astounded when the Nyasaland Chiefs feared to return home after giving evidence. Dr Shepherd had been shocked and furious when, as Moderator of the Church of Scotland, he had been refused entry to the Livingstonia Mission. He gave no notice to the mission at Ewandeni and was warmly welcomed. However, the next day the walls of the mission were plastered with posters threatening death to the Reverend Gondwe who lived in the area. Shortly afterwards his house was burned down and Evans concluded that all control had been lost in the Northern Province. When in Mlanje, in the Southern Province, witnesses had been threatened with death, Hugh Molson had asked Evans for Welensky's likely reaction to a recommendation of secession. Evans replied that Welensky would not hesitate to describe publicly the precise conditions on which he had accepted the Commission. The boycott had meant, however, that little evidence against the Federation was forthcoming.

The best evidence was from the officials but they gave an overriding impression that they had lost control and this affected the Commission to the extent that, on 6 April, Evans described the members as dejected, disheartened and gloomy. They cheered up in Southern Rhodesia, he said, where peace reigned and police escorts were unnecessary.[11]

The day before Macleod left the Federation, Banda arrived at London Airport where reporters pursued him relentlessly, shouting questions which he ignored because he had reserved his first statement for Jeremy Thorpe's ITV programme, *This Week*. Brian Connell introduced Banda on the programme with the comment that he was from Nyasaland which was a British protectorate "which does not want to become part of the Central African Federation". Small wonder Rhodesians questioned the reality when they read the transcript. Thorpe asked first how Banda had fared in prison and was told that he was very well treated and had spent the time teaching his lieutenants British history from Alfred of Wessex onwards. He had found Nyasaland, on his return, in excellent fettle and more militant than ever. The opposition to the Federation was greater and he had earned greater loyalty. His intention was to ask for immediate self-government and secession from the Federation. Macleod was a great and good man who understood the problems and was helpful. Banda could not say if the Monckton Commission would serve any purpose because its terms of reference were limited, but he would not give evidence until all his men were free. Thorpe wondered, referring to the recent shootings at Sharpeville in South Africa, if events there would affect Nyasaland. Banda replied that they would strengthen his case because there was no difference between South African and Southern Rhodesian policies. He believed that Nyasaland did not want to be federated with Southern Rhodesia. He had various objections to the Federation, the chief being that it had been formed by the Europeans to prevent Nyasaland from becoming an African state. The Africans had opposed it because they did not want to share the fate of the Southern Rhodesian Africans. He saw no prospect of a future economic link with Southern Rhodesia, but a federation was possible with Northern Rhodesia and Tanganyika.

[11] *Ibid.*, f. 1, Evans to Welensky, 30 March 1960; 7/26, ff. 401, 396, 316, 286–289, 202, 191 & 184, same to same, 30 & 31 March, 2, 6, 11, 12 & 13 April 1960.

Banda hastened to reassure the Europeans or anyone else living in Nyasaland that there would be no violence and none of the repressive measures which were currently being taken in Ghana. He proposed to negotiate solely with Macleod, who was a "good Christian gentleman", and would ignore Welensky. Pressed, he would say no more about Welensky than that he was a bully. He looked forward to a federation with East Africa and Northern Rhodesia which would ultimately bring in the Congo, the Portuguese colonies and Basutoland. When he stated that it was the British Government's duty "to give us self-government. Now! Now! Now!", Thorpe asked if Nyasaland was economically viable and was told that it had been in 1953. Thorpe noted that Banda called himself the extremist of the extremists and Banda replied that he had been called that and was not afraid of it even though, in reality, he did not believe in violence. He would return to Nyasaland and expected that Macleod had already announced, or would shortly announce, the date of the Nyasaland constitutional conference. He closed by thanking the British people for their support when he and his colleagues were arrested and some of them were killed.[12]

Freed from his obligation to Thorpe, Banda faced a televised Press conference and was more specific about the constitutional conference, surprising everyone by announcing that it would be in June. However, he vehemently declared that he would not negotiate until the detainees were released. His hysterical tone had a detrimental effect on his viewing audience at this and subsequent interviews, and his reversion to extravagant condemnation of Britain's Colonial policies led Sir Nigel Fisher to advise him to leave the wild talking and constant denigration of the British Government to Welensky. Banda concurred, and for 18 months refused to give either Press or television interviews. This corrected the British impression that he was a fanatic, and Fisher believes that, if people did not think he was a moderate, at least they found him less tiresome than Welensky.[13]

Macleod was still in the Federation and was keeping his counsel though the Press believed that he had been embarrassed by Banda's premature statement on the Nyasaland constitutional conference. Armitage informed the Federal Government that Macleod had not revealed any constitutional proposals and had only offered Banda a round-table conference in July. Armitage reaffirmed that nothing would be implemented before the Federal review and declared that he and Macleod had steered clear of any discussion on the Federation's future. Moreover, no matter what happened in London, the Governor-in-Council would remain in effective control of Nyasaland. He warned that detention had only made Banda more extreme in his demands. Banda wanted a 60-member Legislative Council with an African majority and an enlarged Executive Council.

The Federal regional liaison officer in Nyasaland, T. R. Wade, noted that Banda had demanded secession in London and concluded that the British Government could only either capitulate or use force to restore firm government and to keep Nyasaland in the Federation. Wade, however, predicted

[12] *Ibid.*, 20/11, f. 20, Banda's ITV interview, 7 April 1960.

[13] *Ibid.*, 42/15, f. 9, Banda's televised Press Conference, 7 April 1960; Sir Nigel Fisher, *Iain Macleod* (London, 1973), p. 161.

that the latter course was politically unacceptable to the British Government.[14]

Dixon, reporting to Welensky on his meetings with Macleod, confessed that he was confused. If Macleod was honest, he said, then the minorities in Nyasaland had nothing to fear. If he was just another professional politician pursuing appeasement, then the future was obscure. However, the degree of chicanery would only become apparent at the mid-year conference but, until Macleod flew his true colours, Dixon was prepared to believe that he was honestly seeking to advance the African and the Federation. Indeed, Dixon said, Macleod had informed the Executive Council that it was unthinkable that Nyasaland should be anything but an integral part of the Federation. Like Armitage, Dixon reported that Macleod had no constitutional proposals. He had told Dixon that he was a great believer in the Federation and intended to secure African acceptance of it. Therefore Macleod said he would seek to provide for African participation in the Government of Nyasaland, but felt there was no prospect of African self-government for many years. The hard core would remain in detention and the emergency would obtain until there was security legislation.

Continuing his report to Welensky, Dixon said that both he and Blackwood had explained to Macleod that their Party and the moderate Africans accepted the inevitability of African self-government but believed that the Nyasaland Africans were not yet ready for it. Macleod agreed and asked how the UFP would provide training for responsibility, warning that, if there were no provision for self-government, the Africans would reject it. Blackwood and Dixon thereupon produced their proposals for a gradual increase in the number of African seats. They thought that a constitution should last at least ten years to provide stability and that it was necessary to end Colonial Office rule. Macleod agreed it was necessary to keep control in the right hands and claimed to have been forced to release Banda to prevent the Monckton Report from being considered one-sided. It also had to be recognised that Banda was the only leader with significant following, even if it were recruited by intimidation. Dixon replied that it was nevertheless impossible to negotiate with Banda while he was committed to a policy which had forced the Government to imprison 1 500 people and, if he did not advocate secession and independence, he would be disowned. Asked what he would do if Banda and the Malawi Congress Party refused to consider his constitutional proposals, Macleod replied that he would impose them.

At their last meeting, Dixon asked what Macleod thought of Banda. Macleod replied that, from reading his speeches, he appeared "a vain little man" and meeting him had only confirmed that impression. Moreover, he had discovered just how ignorant Banda was about economics and the problems of governing a country. Macleod confirmed that agreement was improbable unless Banda materially altered his line. There would also be a security risk when it dawned that the aims of the Malawi Congress Party would not be realised. Macleod's most important statement to Dixon was that his "ante" would fall far short of Banda's highest bid.

[14] Welensky Papers, 7/14, f. 250, Meeting between Armitage and T. R. Wade, Zomba, 7 April 1960.

Dixon warned Macleod that no European would deal with Banda in his current mood, and Macleod replied that his first task was to drip cold water down Banda's neck in preparation for the cold douche. Dixon urged the continued detention of the hard core even though the most dangerous of all, Chiume, was still at large, in London. Macleod said that Banda had declared that he would not negotiate until they were released, but Dixon gathered that they would not be before the Nyasaland constitutional conference. Nevertheless, Dixon told Welensky, he wondered if Macleod would be strong enough to resist the pressure and, even so, the problem of Chiume remained because Banda would not exclude him from his delegation despite the detention order which was still to be served on him whenever he returned to Nyasaland. Finally, Dixon had discovered that Macleod was thinking that the conference should be attended by four delegates from the MCP, four from the UFP, two Asians, Armitage and his Secretary for African Affairs, J. Ingham.[15]

Macleod dined with Welensky in Salisbury on 7 April and on the morrow, before leaving for Mauritius, announced to the Press that there would be a mid-year constitutional conference. He declared that neither had he discussed secession nor would the conference. He acknowledged, however, that there was little prospect of success unless certain attitudes changed. His greatest anxiety was that Nyasaland should return to normality and advance constitutionally in common with Britain's policy for all her dependencies. He was heartened, he said, by the current calm in Nyasaland and, if it continued, he thought the release of the detainees could be accelerated. He denied that he had clashed with Armitage over the release of Banda as it was a matter of practical politics that Banda should be allowed to go to the conference as a free man. There seemed to be enough common ground for the conference, but Macleod hoped that people would not adjust their attitudes before then. He had not brought with him any constitutional proposals, but thought that he had reached a stage where some could be considered. After the conference, he believed that Banda and one or two others might be invited to the review. He described his contact with Welensky as enjoyable but, when questioned, answered sharply that the advancement of Nyasaland was the responsibility of the British Government. He had no plans for Northern Rhodesia and simply wanted Nyasaland to make up lost time. However, Macleod acknowledged that there remained the possibility that the Monckton Report might recommend changes in both northern territories.[16]

The Rhodesia Herald demanded comment from Welensky without success. However, Blackwood obliged saying that the conference was unlikely to be held that year because there was little prospect of the detainees being released. Even if the Africans were given a majority in the Legislative Council, he was confident that they would not secure control of the Executive Council before 1970 because they had so much to learn about economics and administration. The newspaper felt that Macleod had left with enhanced prestige, particularly because he had forced Banda out on a limb by firmly stating that the conference would not consider seccession. Macleod was clearly, it said, an

[15] *Ibid.*, 7/14, f. 222, A. C. W. Dixon to Welensky, 14 April 1960.
[16] *Evening Standard*, 8 April 1960.

exponent of divide and rule.[17] Tom Stacey of the *Daily Express*, by contrast, thought that the visit had radically changed Macleod's ideas and must have made him despair of a solution.[18]

Whitehead urged the Federal public not to think that Banda would have his own way because if he did Nyasaland would starve. He was confident that Banda's hysterical gesticulations on television would alienate much of his British support. Todd said that the lines of conflict between the races were more sharply drawn and he wondered, publicly, about the future of his Central Africa Party. Chad Chipunza of the UFP felt that clearly Banda had become a major political figure with whom one would have to deal. I. D. Smith called for a united front of responsible opinion and drew support from van Eeden.[19]

Macleod wrote to Welensky from Mauritius promising to keep in touch. He was confident that, despite the pitfalls, he and Welensky could "bring it off", and the degree of trouble in South Africa and the Congo meant that they dared not fail. Welensky did not reply, but informed Lord Salisbury that Macleod had left a wiser man. Welensky found Banda's constant emphasis on surrender loathesome because he had never believed that the Africans should be denied a role in government, but simply that they should earn it on merit. To him what was happening in the Congo, where the Belgians were preparing a hasty withdrawal, was not progress, and he had warned Macleod that he would prevent a similar occurrence in the Federation. Welensky asked Salisbury, as principal architect of the Federation, to give evidence to the Monckton Commission when it reached London.[20]

Greenfield, on 12 April, thought it pertinent to remind the Federal Assembly of recent British ministerial statements. Home, for example, he said, had recalled that the Declaration of 1957 had stated that the review would not consider other forms of association. Macleod had added that secession would not be considered at the Nyasaland conference. The Monckton Commission would not deliberate on secession even though Macmillan had not precisely excluded it. Macleod had also said that there would be no immediate revision of the Northern Rhodesian Constitution unless it was recommended by the review. Greenfield revealed that the UFP, however, did not intend that territorial constitutional development should stall, and would see that responsible government was introduced, while maintaining standards of responsibility. It was too soon to revise the franchise and the UFP would resist any such move, but Greenfield felt there was no need to worry because Macleod had confirmed that his Government had no desire to revise it. Despite the unique set of circumstances in Nyasaland, the UFP was determined that its future lay in the Federation. Finally Greenfield reminded the House that Welensky had never promised that dominion status would be attained in 1960 as the Federal Government recognised that territorial constitutional deve-

[17] *The Rhodesia Herald*, 9 April 1960.

[18] *Daily Express*, 11 April 1960.

[19] *The Sunday Mail*, 10 April 1960; *The Rhodesia Herald*, 11 April 1960; Fed R & N *Debates* (Salisbury), Vol. 12, Col. 565 f., 11 April 1960.

[20] Welensky Papers, 25/27, f. 28, Macleod to Welensky, 12 April 1960; 43/*Lord Salisbury*, Welensky to Salisbury, 12 April 1960.

lopment should precede the final stage of the attainment of independence. However, he said, this did not preclude any advance in the Federal sphere, and the Government would vigorously seek this because events were moving so swiftly in Africa.[21]

The Opposition immediately demanded again that control should be in responsible hands and, in the course of the debate, van Eeden urged that a great effort be made to win over the British people.[22] (In fact, the Federal Government had already retained the London publicity firm, Voice and Vision, which had assisted Macmillan in his landslide electoral victory in 1959 — with the wooing of the British electorate with the slogan, "You've never had it so good".)

Banda, meanwhile, had been campaigning in Britain for support. He proposed to address the General Assembly of the Church of Scotland, sought money for a university at Livingstonia and threatened to break up the Federation or return to gaol. He wanted a constitution which reflected the numerical strength of the Africans and, if that were treason, he was willing to accept the consequences. He would not discuss secession at the Nyasaland conference but would pursue it thereafter. His precondition for any negotiations remained the release of the detainees. He described his arrest as a means to exclude him from the Federal review so that the "so-called" African moderates would not experience any difficulties.[23]

On 13 April Banda and Kaunda arrived in New York to attend the "Africa Freedom Day" of the American Committee on Africa. They also spoke on television and at a luncheon of the National Press Club. Banda again gesticulated wildly as he thundered against the Federation. A Federal official present thought that he should be given maximum public exposure because he invited ridicule. However, when he and Kaunda addressed the American-African Institute, the Federal officials conceded that his performance was masterly.[24]

Although Banda continued to appeal for calm in Nyasaland, Welensky remained concerned and informed Macleod of incidents of intimidation, including threatening actions by African policemen as well as assaults on them. He believed that the morale of the Nyasaland Police was generally low. He sought the replacement of the Nyasaland Attorney-General because he had given defeatist evidence to the Monckton Commission. Later, Welensky asked Macleod for extra policemen for Nyasaland because he thought that there would be trouble in July when Banda discovered that he could not have his way on secession. He did not want to use the Federal Army and suggested that, if police recruits were not forthcoming, then men should be seconded. Macleod replied that the Attorney-General was retiring but said nothing about extra police. He lauded the virtues of G. S. Jones, the Chief Secretary (whom he would soon promote to Governor), and thought that it might

[21] Fed R & N *Debates* (Salisbury), Vol. 12, Col. 619 f., 12 April 1960.

[22] *Ibid.*, Col. 671 f., 13 April 1960.

[23] *The Scotsman*, 12 April 1960; *The Bulawayo Chronicle*, 13 April 1960.

[24] Welensky Papers, 20/11, f. 12, R. B. N. Wetmore to Secretary, External Affairs, 14 April 1960; f. 8, Banda's Speech to the American-African Institute, (undated); ff. 184–186, D. G. Madgett to Secretary, External Affairs, 22 April 1960.

comfort Welensky to know that Banda had done his cause great harm by disappointing the Press and the Labour Party.[25]

For some reason Blackwood and Dixon had abandoned their plan to submit their constitutional proposals to the Monckton Commission and had forfeited UFP confidence. Consequently, Greenfield was worried that these two would attend the constitutional conference, representing the UFP, without any firm plans for Nyasaland's future. To Greenfield it was also unfortunate that Macleod would hold the initiative because, while he had promised to consult the Federal Government, he would do so by correspondence, effectively preventing any timely counter-action. Thus it was essential, before Macleod became wedded to a set of constitutional proposals, to attempt to persuade him to accept something palatable to the Federal Government. Thus Greenfield suggested that if the Blackwood and Dixon constitutional proposals, which were quite reasonable, were revived and endorsed by Welensky and Barrow, the British Government might accept them. That Government had also to be persuaded to consider the Federation's future as a whole as only Banda would profit from the current Anglo-Federal conflict. Greenfield found there was a triangle of interests because the UFP wanted Nyasaland in the Federation, but without Colonial Office control, while Banda agreed with the latter aim, but wanted secession, and the British Government wished to keep Nyasaland in the Federation under the Colonial administration until it had effected an African take-over, regardless of African capabilities.

Greenfield believed that the best which could be hoped for was that in July Banda would be told that his plans were inadmissible. It was likely that Macleod would retain control through the Colonial officials and, at worst, impose a "partial Kenyan sell-out". The Nyasaland conference was supposed to be exploratory and was not to prejudge the Monckton findings, but it could lead to dangerous pronouncements. The rebuff of Banda could produce tension which might delay or seriously prejudice the review. Therefore an understanding with the British Government on security matters was desirable, but one which also embraced constitutional issues would be preferable.

Before abandoning their proposals before the Monckton Commission, it appears that Blackwood and Dixon had adjusted them by divorcing the Executive Council from the Legislative Council, and it was in this, Greenfield told Welensky, that the embryo of a solution lay. He recalled that Welensky had already, albeit reluctantly, accepted these proposals. Consequently, he believed that Welensky should place them before Macmillan and Macleod when he visited London for the Commonwealth Prime Ministers' Conference in May. In addition, Greenfield wanted Welensky to raise in London the question of the removal of Colonial Office control of the northern territories because it would block Federal advancement and, in any event, its policies had failed in Africa. However, he acknowledged that it could not be removed overnight, but he felt that its removal could be planned. It was also imperative to speak to Macleod before July and not just to correspond with him.[26]

[25] *Ibid.*, 25/27, f. 29, Welensky to Macleod, 13 April 1960; f. 24, same to same, 21 April 1960; f. 51, Macleod to Welensky, 21 April 1960.
[26] *Ibid.*, 7/14, f. 230, Greenfield to Welensky, 21 April 1960.

Perhaps because Welensky was unenthusiastic, Greenfield again pressed him on 27 April to consider this plan, adding that, to sell it, a device could be proposed which could involve the local populace meeting around the village tree. Greenfield thought it might help if Sir Conrad Corfield, the distinguished former official in the Indian civil service who had inspired this plan, saw Macleod. However, he said, there were difficulties because Blackwood and Dixon had already discarded the "tree meetings" and had indiscreetly told Macleod that they did not care how low the franchise standard was set. The other territories would insist on the maintenance of the Federal standard but Greenfield feared Macleod might take advantage of this indiscretion. Blackwood and Dixon had produced two further versions of their scheme but both were undesirable because they envisaged the retention of the official majority and a quick surrender to the black majority which Corfield did not. As Macleod would impose a solution, because agreement was unlikely, Greenfield believed that there was no harm in trying to influence him.[27]

Welensky departed for London from where he advised Whitehead that Butler thought that, by the end of the year, Southern Rhodesia would get its independence if the issue were not overplayed. The Conservative Party simultaneously produced a blueprint for the Federation which the UFP instantly rejected because it proposed self-government for Nyasaland based on adult suffrage. However, it did suggest an amalgamation of the Colonial and Commonwealth Relations Offices which was welcomed in the Federation. The Dominion Party criticised the writing of such a document without first-hand knowledge, while the Central Africa Party thought that Southern Rhodesia would have to be promoted ahead of Nyasaland.[28]

Home had sent Whitehead a draft of a statement on Southern Rhodesia which warned that the withdrawal or reduction of the reserved powers would depend on there being alternative safeguards covering discrimination, land and constitutional amendments. Whitehead and his colleagues accepted this statement with reluctance but wanted to be able to announce that their constitutional negotiations would be completed before the Federal review.[29]

The morale of the Federal Cabinet was somewhat shaken when information came to hand that Whitehead had concluded that the Federation could not survive and that the Southern Rhodesian division of the UFP had to plan accordingly. He could see no point in retaining Nyasaland, and expected an imminent and severe internal crisis. Just as disturbing was the news that Beadle had suggested to the Monckton Commission a Central African alliance of six or seven governments and had gained the support of Ellman-Brown and, more important, Whitehead. Greenfield transmitted these revelations to Welensky in London.[30]

On the evening of 8 May Welensky was summoned from his bed by Macmillan to be told of an incident on the Copperbelt involving a Mrs Lilian Burton, her three children and a pet dog. A mob stoned her car to a stop and

[27] *Ibid.*, f. 218, Greenfield to Welensky, 27 April 1960.
[28] *Ibid.*, 42/75, f. 138, Welensky to Whitehead, 3 May 1960; *The Rhodesia Herald*, 4 May 1960.
[29] Welensky Papers, 42/75, f. 137, Whitehead to Home, 5 May 1960.
[30] *Ibid.*, 28/79, f. 38, Greenfield to Welensky, 7 May 1960; 20/16, f. 366, A. D. Evans to Welensky, 4 May 1960.

then set it on fire. Mrs Burton extricated herself and her children but could not save the dog. As she did this she was savagely assaulted. She died a week later. In order to convict her murderers, the Northern Rhodesian Government had to ask the Federal Government for an aeroplane to fly African witnesses to safety. Years later in independent Zambia, streets were named after her executed assailants. Macmillan, Macleod and Welensky composed a statement and then, deeply shocked, Welensky declined a conciliatory share in a bottle of champagne offered by Macmillan.[31]

This savagery brought a storm of protest from the European population. Roberts was convinced that it stemmed from the current lionising of Kaunda by Macleod and Sir Ronald Prain. The local Press had reported that Macleod would receive Kaunda officially and Roberts was determined to prevent it. He also blamed Macleod for procrastination over issuing a firm statement on the British Government's attitude to the demands of the United National Independence Party and the expectations of immediate constitutional change. Sir Evelyn Hone warned Macleod that Roberts, Malcolmson and Dunlop were considering resigning from the Executive Council unless this statement was forthcoming. The Federal Government responded to the violence by placing army units on stand-by, while the Northern Rhodesian Government called up its police reserve. On 10 May the Northern Rhodesian Government announced measures to restore order, including the banning of UNIP in the Western Province.[32]

Not surprisingly, northern internal security was the main topic when Welensky met Macmillan, Home and Macleod on 9 May. Indeed, defence was the chief topic at most of Welensky's meetings with the British Government and led to an adjustment to the Federal commitment to the Middle East. At the suggestion of the British Chief of General Staff, Lord Mountbatten, the Federal contribution was changed from an infantry brigade to a squadron of the Special Air Service Regiment. Welensky proposed that the European strength of the Nyasaland Police should be doubled but Macleod said Armitage had asked for only 40 experienced men. Macmillan thought that they should wait to see the effect of this reinforcement. If a military presence was required, he wanted to use British troops so that the Federal economy should not be disrupted by a call-up. Welensky, however, preferred the Federal Army.

Referring to Northern Rhodesia, Macleod said that Hone wanted to announce that, while there would be no constitutional changes in 1960, Africans would be able to express their ideas at the Federal review. Welensky concurred but thought Hone should stress that no changes would be made until after the review. In addition, it should be made clear that the choice of African representatives at the review was the prerogative of the Governments. The British Ministers agreed and Macleod and Home undertook to compose Hone's statement and to consult Welensky before it was released. Macleod agreed to consider the construction of an irrigation and power project at the

[31] *Ibid.*, 25/23, f. 1, Welensky to Col. N. L. D. Mclean, 30 May 1960; Author's interview with Sir Roy Welensky.

[32] Welensky Papers, 7/45, f. 72, Roberts to Welensky, 9 May 1960; 25/242A, ff. 29–30, Hone to Macleod, 9 May 1960; *The Rhodesia Herald*, 11 May 1960.

Nkula Falls on the Shiré River in Nyasaland. Home promised to consult the Foreign Secretary, Selwyn Lloyd, on Federal defence co-operation with Portugal.[33]

Discussion between the directors of Federal intelligence and the British MI6 appeared to reveal a British determination to preserve the Federation. Further encouragement was an indication from Lord Monckton that he disliked Beadle's ideas and did not intend to recommend radical change either in the Federal franchise or in the distribution of seats in the Federal Assembly. He wanted to placate African opinion, but not appease it. Greenfield gathered that the Commission might recommend the return of some services to the territories and might urge Southern Rhodesia to amend the Land Apportionment Act and other discriminatory legislation. Monckton thought that the Africans should be given better opportunities to secure seats in the Southern Rhodesian Assembly. He wanted some discussion, albeit *sub rosa*, with the Federal Government in London in June. All this encouraged Greenfield, but later he would be bitterly disappointed by Monckton.[34]

Another source of Federal satisfaction was Macleod's firmness on 17 May in insisting on seeing Kaunda in London without his entourage and telling him that a constitutional revision could not be considered. He said that he was gravely disturbed by a report from Hone that, despite his statement to Kaunda's Party in Lusaka, it had been widely claiming that there would be a major change in 1960. Such misrepresentation, he warned, would have serious, even dangerous, consequences. Indeed, in the Commons on 10 May, he had already ascribed the current violence in Northern Rhodesia to the agitation of the extremists, and he repeated the warning he had given Kaunda in Lusaka that violence would retard political progress as the British Government was not amenable to this kind of pressure. Nevertheless, he praised Kaunda's statement in New York which had unreservedly condemned the use of violence. Macleod said he would make it understood in Northern Rhodesia that his Government would not alter a constitution which was so new. In any event, he added, they had to wait for the Monckton Report which meant that change was impossible in 1960. Macleod assured Kaunda that Africans would be adequately represented at the Federal review. It was too early to choose delegations or even to define their composition, but he declared that they would be widely based and not solely drawn from the legislatures. There had been pressure in the Commons for the renunciation of violence, and consequently Macleod warned he would support any action by Hone.

Kaunda explained that the violence stemmed from the belief of the ordinary Africans that it had achieved independence in the Congo and a revision of the Nyasaland Constitution. Macleod replied that, nonetheless, the only result would be a delay of at least 18 months. He drew attention to the faster progress being made in Tanganyika, Sierra Leone and Nigeria, where violence

[33] Welensky Papers, 20/1, ff. 114–117, Minutes of a Meeting between Welensky, Macmillan, Home and Macleod, 9 May 1960; ff. 111–113, Minutes of a Meeting between Welensky, Watkinson, Alport and Lord Mountbatten, 10 May 1960.

[34] *Ibid.*, 7/39, f. 1, FISB discussions with the Director-General, Security Service and Head of MI6, 16 May 1960; 7/11, f. 117, Greenfield to Welensky, 12 May 1960.

had not been employed. Kaunda claimed to have difficulty in getting his Party to appreciate this, but promised not to deviate from his personal commitment to non-violence. He agreed to explain that there was no prospect of immediate political advancement even though, in so doing, he might be committing political suicide. He asked at least that there should be some discussion on Northern Rhodesia's future at the review to compensate for the risk he was taking. He also wanted a relaxation of the rules governing meetings because they offered such useful opportunities to release public tension. Macleod replied that he would consider this once peace had been restored and he agreed, at Kaunda's request, to investigate prison conditions.[35]

After telling Welensky that he had found Kaunda attentive and constructive, Macleod affirmed publicly on 21 May that constitutional alterations for Northern Rhodesia would not be considered until after the review. Kaunda condemned the violence and proposed to hold meetings to speak against disorder. Roberts doubted this, and was vindicated a week later by UNIP clamouring for change by October.[36]

Macleod's declaration on Northern Rhodesia led Dixon immediately to demand a similar denial of Banda's repeated promises of secession and independence in 1960 so that the Africans would not be disappointed by the result of the conference in July. Macleod ignored Dixon and simply informed Armitage that the conference would be held on 24 July and would be attended by four delegates from the MCP, four from the UFP, one from the Congress Liberation Party, two African Members of the Legislative Council, two Asians and one Coloured.[37]

On 20 May, the day before Macleod made his statement on Northern Rhodesia, the Committee Anent Central Africa of the Church of Scotland intruded into Federal affairs by recommending the re-casting of the Federation on looser lines and the granting of an option to the territories to secede after a fixed period. If this were impossible, it claimed, then the painful step of reverting to former identities might be necessary. However, the acceptance of its report was deferred after a vigorous counter-attack in the Church's General Assembly led by Dr Shepherd.[38]

With such opinions being aired, Welensky thought Evans should know his views on the break-up of the Federation. Evans was in London by then, 26 May, because the Monckton Commission had concluded its tour. Writing from Salisbury, to where he had returned on 23 May, Welensky told Evans that, if Nyasaland were allowed to secede because of certain intransigent African leaders, the Federation would be destroyed as secession could not then be denied to either of the Rhodesias which were at least economically viable. It would be a major tragedy because the Zambezi River would become

[35] *Ibid.*, 20/5, f. 2, Interview between Macleod and Kaunda, 17 May 1960; 20/1, ff. 103–104, Note of a Meeting with Macleod, London, 20 May 1960.
[36] *Ibid.*, 20/1, ff. 103–104, Note of a Meeting with Macleod, London, 20 May 1960; *The Times*, 21 May 1960; *The Rhodesia Herald*, 24 May 1960.
[37] Welensky Papers, 7/14, f. 245, Dixon to Armitage, 24 May 1960; f. 239, Macleod to Armitage, 25 May 1960.
[38] *The Rhodesia Herald*, 20 May 1960.

a barrier, a Maginot Line, between black and white. Nyasaland's secession would seal the fates of Southern Rhodesia and Bechuanaland. Welensky believed that Southern Rhodesia could survive alone, but with much reduced standards. The northern territories would be hostile to it and would deny it markets by developing their own industries. The Rhodesia Railways would lose its copper revenue because Northern Rhodesia would send its minerals out through Angola. It would then only be a matter of time before Southern Rhodesia joined South Africa.[39]

Evans replied with the cheering news that the Commission had already worsted two Cambridge dons and had "pasted" the Scottish Council on African Questions which had submitted a memorandum that contained, in his view, not only misrepresentations, but special pleading. Evans concluded that, as most of the memoranda from Scotland resembled each other, there was collusion. The Commission had been particularly disturbed by an attack from within the Church of Scotland on Shepherd and on the African commissioners whom it called paid Government officials.[40]

If Evans's revelations were cheering, somewhat depressing evidence came to hand in Salisbury that the old ally of the Federation, the copper mining company, thc Rhodesian Selection Trust, had finally turned against it because its American leadership concluded that the Federation could not survive the disaffection of its African population. The American directors diagnosed the fatal weakness as being the failure of any prominent politician, official or European businessman, with the sole exception of their Sir Ronald Prain, to attempt to make contact with the Africans. As in Kenya, the short-sightedness of the European leadership had driven the Africans to revolution and, inevitably, to violence. The intransigence of the Malawi Congress Party, however, caused RST to withdraw an offer of £90 000 to develop a coffee industry in Nyasaland.[41]

On 30 May, before leaving for the West Indies, Macleod wrote to Welensky to explain that his paper on Nyasaland had not yet appeared because the collection of ideas and comments by the Nyasaland Government would only be complete in mid-June. However, he still promised Welensky an opportunity to comment. The real problem was Northern Rhodesia and not Nyasaland, and Macleod was not optimistic about the Congo which, with a month to go before independence, was daily becoming more unstable. He knew that the Federation offered the best future for the three territories but felt its chances of survival had to be improved. He believed that Monckton and the Federal review would find a clear way forward, but to assist this he wanted to grant Kaunda's request for a statement that a Northern Rhodesian constitutional conference could be held after the review.

Recommending this, Macleod conceded that Kaunda was difficult and unreliable, but preferred him to the rest of his colleagues. Macleod expected Roberts to oppose this idea and believed that Roberts was too responsive to

[39] Welensky Papers, 20/16, f. 352, Welensky to Evans, 26 May 1960.
[40] *Ibid.*, f. 310, Evans to Welensky, 27 May 1960.
[41] *Ibid.*, 25/151, ff. 12–13, F. T. Ostrander to D. Cole, 27 May 1960; f. 1, H. Hochschild to Ostrander, 31 May 1960; ff. 3–9, Ostrander to Cole, 9 June 1960; f. 8, FISB Memorandum, July 1960.

pressure from his electorate to be a source of strength. Indeed, the greatest single danger to the Federation was the "Canute-like" attitude of Blackwood and Roberts to the inevitability of change. One could still move at one's own pace, Macleod claimed, but "move we must". The first step was to obtain Hone's views on the advisability of a Northern Rhodesian constitutional conference. The situation in Northern Rhodesia appeared to have been well handled, and the tension seemed to be dissipating which would not have happened if Roberts's advice had been taken. If a state of emergency had been declared, Macleod predicted, great difficulties would have been encountered and the reputation of the Federation would have suffered greatly.[42] Thus, with no great finesse, he was trying to drive a wedge between Welensky and the Northern Rhodesian division of his Party. It was also clear that, like the Rhodesian Selection Trust, he had chosen Kaunda as the heir-apparent.

To ensure the success of the forthcoming Nyasaland conference, Macleod proposed to Welensky to use a third party to influence Banda. Two men seemed best able to do this. They were Oliver Woods of *The Times* and Sir Jock Campbell of the Campbell, Booker Carter Group which had interests in Nyasaland. (The idea of employing Campbell would not have pleased the local Europeans. One Nyasalander described him — rightly or wrongly — as the "evil genius" behind the recent events in that territory.[43] Campbell not only recruited his staff from the ranks of the Fabian Society and the Labour Party, but he was a sponsor of Christian Action, a supporter of the Africa Bureau, and, later, became a vice-chairman of the Southern African Freedom Group and would have been regarded with the gravest suspicion by local Europeans.) Macleod would not use Dingle Foot because he found him untrustworthy and inefficient.

Macleod maintained that the only way to prevent Nyasaland's secession was to grant an immediate generous constitutional advance. However, perhaps to reassure Welensky, he declared that the Chisiza brothers and Chipembere would continue to be detained even after the emergency had been lifted just before the conference. He wanted to retain firm official control of the Executive Council and knew that this, at least, would be accepted by Blackwood and Dixon. He proposed, therefore, to have an Executive Council composed of the Governor, four officials and five unofficials of whom three would be Africans and two would be Europeans. This would at least give the appearance of an unofficial majority. He would have an African majority in the Legislative Council by giving the Africans between 18 and twelve seats while the Europeans kept their current six even though they were not really entitled to them. As the Governor had to get his legislation through, he would retain the power of nomination. In addition, Members appointed to the Executive Council would accept the Government whip. Macleod proposed to adopt the Federal franchise for the non-African seats but said he would have difficulties with the African seats because both wings of the Conservative Party would support the African clamour for universal suffrage. Macleod would not grant this but felt he would have to lower the limit to an income of £75 p.a. with or without literacy.

[42] *Ibid.*, 20/1, ff. 98–102, Macleod to Welensky, 30 May 1960.
[43] *Ibid.*, 7/14, f. 246, J. Foot to Welensky, 30 May 1960.

Welensky did not reply immediately even though he continued to worry about Nyasaland, reminding Home on 4 June that he had been misunderstood in London as he wanted policemen, not the British Army, because the result of using troops was always so drastic. In fact, Greenfield was examining Macleod's proposals. He noticed there was no mention of granting portfolios to unofficials and that Macleod seemed determined to retain racial separation and separate voters' rolls. It was also clear that Dixon and Blackwood were reconciled to having 18 African Members of the Legislative Council and a lowered franchise.

Greenfield would accept these 18 but wanted some of them to be elected by the general roll. He thought that Macleod should be persuaded to accept a device to enable the UFP to win some African seats. There could be six double-member constituencies returning Europeans and Africans on the basis of the Federal general roll. The six constituencies would then combine to elect an Asian. Each voter would be given three votes. This could result in the UFP dominating 13 constituencies until the number of Africans on the general roll increased. Special roll voters would only have one vote and Nyasaland would be divided into six constituencies, each returning two members. By this device the UFP might win some of these seats. These six constituencies would combine twice to elect a European and an Asian and this method would give the special voter three votes but, in reality, their effect would be halved. The Legislative Council would therefore contain 26 unofficial and four official Members. The leader of the majority party would be entitled to nominate two Africans and one European to the Executive Council, leaving his rival the opportunity to nominate one African and one European. Alternatively, the composition of the Executive Council could relate directly to the ratio of the seats gained in the Legislative Council.

Greenfield found Macleod's reference to Canute most disquieting as it seemed to confirm that Macleod would appease African nationalism. Macleod clearly wished to discover Welensky's reaction to a Northern Rhodesian constitutional conference designed to pacify Kaunda. He was placing the Federal Cabinet in a dilemma because its Party aimed at securing self-government for the territory and Macleod would co-operate provided Kaunda, and not Roberts, became prime minister. To uncover his true intentions, Greenfield believed that Macleod should be given a non-committal reply.[44]

Welensky was in no hurry to reply and before he did, Macleod announced the composition of the delegations to the conference. While the UFP was content to have four places, the MCP was not. Banda called the allocation "insulting". Evidence of intimidation in both northern territories accumulated and provoked Welensky to warn publicly on 10 June that he would oppose any political advancement of Africans until their leaders showed themselves capable of controlling the intimidation and the use of the stone and the petrol bomb as political weapons. He conceded that progress might not be fast enough, even though some thought it was too fast, but, if the thuggery did not stop, he would use all his influence to block any movement towards responsible government. Simultaneously, Roberts announced a plan

[44] *Ibid.*, f. 235, Welensky to Home, 4 June 1960; f. 210, Greenfield to Welensky, 6 June 1960.

to combat the terrorism by curbing the movement of itinerant work-seekers, by expanding development projects to accommodate the genuinely unemployed, and by providing street lighting and police foot patrols in the African townships.

Harper contributed to the confusion with a demand for a looser federation and, in the background, were the ominous reports from the Congo including an attempt to establish an independent government in Katanga.[45]

Depressing reports from Evans in London of tensions within the ranks of the Monckton Commission cannot have improved the mood of the Federal leaders. However, Evans did say that most of the material submitted was of a constructive nature. Sir Ronald Prain had called for equal territorial representation in the Federal Assembly and a lowering of the Federal franchise. The Conservative Commonwealth Council was most enthusiastic for the Federation, which attitude contrasted with hostile written evidence from Northern Rhodesia. Colin Leys, the author of the book, *A New Deal in Central Africa*,[46] appeared before the Commission and not only had his inaccuracies pointed out to him, but when he refused to make any recommendations was asked why he had sought an interview. His fellow author, Philip Mason, was treated more kindly because he appeared less of a polemicist. It was disturbing that mutual suspicions between the commissioners seemed to be growing and, outside their ranks, Shepherd had been subjected to vilification from within his Church. Unbowed, he remained proud of his achievement in securing the enlargement of the Committee Anent Central Africa which would weaken the influence of its chairman, the Reverend George MacLeod.[47]

On 15 June Evans described the agitation of Woodrow Cross over a memorandum which Molson had submitted to his Monckton Commission subcommittee. Woodrow Cross did not have a copy of the memorandum, but listed its contents from memory for Evans. Molson had asked that the Federation should not be maintained by force and that, to meet the aspirations of the African nationalists, there should be territorial constitutional changes which would ultimately lead to self-government. Accordingly all functions affecting the lives of the people had to be territorial and those currently in Federal hands had to be immediately surrendered. The Federal Government would keep control of economic matters and anything which related to foreign affairs. To effect the promises in the Federal constitutional preamble, positive steps had to be taken to implement partnership. Woodrow Cross worried about the implications of the words "to meet African Nationalist aspirations". Evans advised him to oppose the proposal as he did not believe the Federation had to be maintained by force. Evans was disappointed but not surprised by this suggestion, and took comfort in its early emergence. Greenfield, however, can only have been disturbed when this report was capped by one from his son, Ewen, then working for the Bulawayo municipality, warning of widespread African dissatisfaction with government poli-

[45] *The Bulawayo Chronicle*, 3 June 1960; *Northern News*, 14 June 1960; *The Rhodesia Herald*, 10 & 15 June 1960.
[46] C. Leys and C. Pratt, *A New Deal in Central Africa* (London, 1960).
[47] Welensky Papers, 20/16, ff. 277, 263, 258 & 242, Evans to Welensky, 7, 9, 10 & 14 June 1960.

cies which the National Democratic Party (which had succeeded the banned African National Congress) intended to exploit.[48]

Before he replied to Macleod, Welensky informed Home that Greenfield would be in London in July and wished to see Macleod. Home agreed but rejected Welensky's second request which was to convene the Federal review before the Monckton Commission reported.[49]

Welensky wrote to Macleod, on 17 June, opposing an announcement of constitutional discussions for Northern Rhodesia in 1961 because it would appear to be a concession to UNIP and its campaign of violence. To bolster this argument, he referred Macleod to a recent statement by the Northern Rhodesian Government on the criminal activities of that Party. In the first five months of 1960, 85 office bearers had been convicted of 117 criminal offences, including attempted murder, riot, assault on the police, damage to property and the advocation of violence. Thus he and many others viewed most cynically the protestations of Kaunda on "non-violence". Indeed, Welensky said, Kaunda's statement on the impossibility of constitutional advancement had been simply blackmail and made a concession at this moment appear the worst kind of appeasement. Moreover the current constitution was barely a year old and it had been said in the Northern Rhodesian Legislative Council that the word "constitution" lost its meaning when it was constantly changed. However, he did expect some progress towards responsible government, but only with the preservation of standards, including the franchise. He felt strongly enough to warn that he would vigorously oppose any action which made a mockery of the current Constitution and which appeared to be an abandonment of principles, just because of African nationalist pressure. He hoped that Macleod would adhere to his statement of not giving in to violence, and commended the Governor, Hone, for his Address from the Throne which noted UNIP's attempts to embarrass the Government and warned against the expectations of immediate constitutional change. Thus it seemed to Welensky that enough had been said on the subject of change.

Welensky warned Macleod that everything done in Nyasaland would affect the rest of the Federation and, in particular, the weakening of the influence of the European would affect race relations in Northern Rhodesia. The problem was to grant a reasonable advance without abandoning principles. Thus he agreed with the substance of Macleod's constitutional proposals for Nyasaland because they met African aspirations to a reasonable extent, whilst retaining power in responsible hands. He accepted that the number of African seats should be increased, but to twelve and not 18, because otherwise Nyasaland would have a larger legislature than Southern Rhodesia, which would be absurd. He did not enthuse about the retention of official control of the Executive Council because all sections of the community disliked it, but he knew that it was necessary at present. He urged the avoidance of outright racial representation, but acknowledged the difficulties. The lowering of the franchise qualification to £75 p.a., he told Macleod, was unacceptable because

[48] *Ibid.*, f. 231, Evans to Welensky, 15 June 1960; 28/79, f. 36, E. Greenfield to J. M. Greenfield, 16 June 1960.
[49] *Ibid.*, 20/18, f. 314, Home to Welensky, 17 June 1960.

it was lower than any other franchise in the Federation and would not only provide fuel for criticism of Southern and Northern Rhodesia, but would cast doubts on the whole basis of the qualitative franchise which protected civilised standards in the Federation.[50]

Welensky reserved for Joelson his opinion that the Colonial Office should be abolished the moment Nigeria gained independence. He also told Joelson that Armitage was being treated badly by being left out on a limb while the Colonial Office searched for his replacement and had to scrape the bottom of the barrel.[51]

Welensky immediately asked the Colonial Office for the paper containing the Nyasaland constitutional proposals, but had to wait ten days for it, and by then further dismal news was at hand. The Northern Rhodesian Central Race Relations Committee on 20 June publicly despaired of the Federation and advocated its replacement by an adaptation of the East African High Commission. The UFP was incensed by this contradiction of its policy by a committee which was served by ten members, four of whom were civil servants. In Britain, the Federal and territorial Monckton commissioners were becoming so impatient with the slow rate of progress that Beadle angrily interrupted a session of the Commission to suggest that he might have to buy a house in London. However, it seemed that the commissioners would recommend the continuation of the Federation, which was an achievement in itself. Welensky nevertheless asked Evans to warn him immediately anything appeared to go wrong so that he could take it up with Macmillan.[52]

The Federal Cabinet was encouraged by an agreement by the Southern Rhodesian division of the UFP to examine the *raison d'être* for the Land Appointment Act and to reduce the pass laws to the carrying of an identification certificate. This agreement was welcome to the Federal Cabinet but only if the outside world did not think that Whitehead was frightened. The British Press greeted with relief the final acceptance by Banda of the arrangements for the Nyasaland conference, but events in the Congo continued to alarm. In fact, on 24 June, Welensky declared publicly that the West was losing the battle for Africa. He condemned the action of the Imperial powers in handing over crippled economies which would be targets for the Communists who would deny the resources of Africa to the West. He saw the new freedom as freedom to starve.[53]

Macleod's proposals arrived on 27 June with a warning that great harm would be done if it became known that they had been shown to the Federal Government. (This was said despite the constitutional right of that Government to be consulted.) Macleod claimed that the proposals were only a basis for negotiation and that a number were only opening bids. An example was

[50] *Ibid.*, 20/1, ff. 94–97, Welensky to Macleod, 17 June 1960.

[51] *Ibid.*, 24/151, ff. 151–152, Welensky to F. S. Joelson, 17 June 1960.

[52] *Ibid.*, 20/18, f. 315, K. H. Towsey to Barrett, 17 June 1960; f. 309, M. R. Metcalf to Welensky, 27 June 1960; 7/11, f. 79, W. S. Parker to H. J. Roberts, 16 June 1960; 20/16, f. 236, Evans to Welensky, 20 June 1960; f. 229, Welensky to Evans, 25 June 1960; *The Rhodesia Herald*, 20 June 1960.

[53] Welensky Papers, 25/240A, f. 159, Welensky to Lord Robins, 21 June 1960; *The Daily Telegraph*, 22 June 1960; *The Rhodesia Herald*, 24 June 1960.

the franchise level of an income of £120 p.a. which would only produce an electorate of some 10 000–15 000 Africans, which was clearly indefensible and might have to be dropped to £75 p.a. with an alternative qualification of the attainment of the age of 40. In the Executive Council it might be possible to allow an unofficial majority, but the opening bid was parity at five officials to five unofficials.

Macleod explained that he had used the ideas he had gathered during his visit and was well aware that, because of the divergence of opinions, the conference would only succeed if there were a will to co-operate. He proposed an African majority in the Legislative Council but would provide a substantial role for the non-Africans. Africans would be elected on a broad-based franchise, but the executive power of the Governor would be unimpaired as the Executive Council would remain advisory to him. The unofficial Members of the Executive Council would nonetheless be involved in the day-to-day administration. These, he said, were well-tried principles which had guided other Commonwealth countries. The five unofficial seats in the Executive Council would be divided between the Africans and the Europeans in the ratio of three to two and, when filling them, the Governor would be guided by the state of the parties in the Legislative Council. The Governor would control the latter through his power of nomination, aided by the five unofficial Members of the Executive Council accepting the Government whip. The Legislative Council would comprise a Speaker and six Members elected on the general roll and twelve elected by the special roll. All electors would have to be 21 years old and be British subjects or British Protected Persons. The special qualifications were literacy and an income of £120 p.a. or the possession of property worth £500. The general roll required an income of £720 p.a. or property worth £1 500; or primary education and an income of £480 p.a. or property worth £1 000; or four years of secondary education and an income of £300 p.a. or property worth £500.[54]

The Federal Government immediately estimated that an income level of £75 p.a. without a literacy qualification would enfranchise 15 000 Nyasaland Africans. With literacy, the figure would be 8 400. However, because Greenfield was going to London in early July, the Federal Government only commented to Dixon and Blackwood who protested in reply that the Nyasaland Government was anxious only to avoid upsetting the African. Consequently, they said, control had been lost and the Government was being treated with contempt daily. Their concern was shared by the Federal Assembly which agreed that all possible measures had to be taken by the territorial Governments to fight intimidation. Evidence was produced on the risks run by those who had the temerity to oppose the African nationalists privately or publicly. An African who had been photographed speaking to the Queen Mother during her recent visit had been so badly assaulted that he had nearly lost an arm. Blackwood and Dixon had thought of resigning, but had felt that they would not thereby force the Nyasaland Government to act.[55]

[54] Welensky Papers, 20/18, f. 309, M. R. Metcalf to Welensky, 27 June 1960; 20/1, ff. 91–93, Memorandum by Macleod, 27 June 1960.

[55] *Ibid.*, 20/18, f. 301, K. H. Towsey to Greenfield, 30 June 1960; 7/14, f. 190, Dixon to Barrow, 4 July 1960; Fed R & N *Debates* (Salisbury), Vol. 12, Col. 843 f., 29 June 1960.

Dixon's lack of immediate criticism of Macleod's proposals worried Welensky because they were only the opening moves and no one knew what Macleod intended to do. Welensky believed that it would be fatal to abandon the literacy qualification because then universal suffrage might follow. If Nyasaland adopted this, Northern Rhodesia and the whole Federation would be affected. Dixon, however, pleased Welensky by persuading three Chiefs to join his delegation. Furthermore, on 9 July Welensky transmitted an urgent message to Macleod from Dixon that the proposals seemed unacceptable to Banda and the result could be the failure of the conference and widespread violence. Dixon had the support of Barrow in expressing disquiet at the loss of control by the Government. It was particularly galling to find the Malawi Congress Party policing wide areas. Dixon urged the speedy reinforcement of the police because the Europeans were disgusted at the Government's failure to provide security. He acknowledged that racial tension had been reduced, but that the price was too high.[56]

Although he was a Northern Rhodesian, Roberts felt that he should comment on Macleod's Nyasaland proposals in detail. He confessed to Hone that it was difficult to be specific without knowing the method of delimitation, the political patterns or the potential voting population. He believed that Macleod was attempting to hold the position in Nyasaland until it became clearer. It might be a reasonable policy, but in Northern Rhodesia's case he would want the objectives and principles defined. One essential was to force the parties to nominate candidates of all races which the Nyasaland proposals did not do thereby merely giving a fillip to racialism. He believed that in Nyasaland the cry, during the election of the twelve special roll Members, would be to oust the whites. This would engender a reaction amongst the latter to exclude Africans from the six general roll seats. Such a struggle would affect Northern Rhodesia.

Seeing the number of special roll seats in Nyasaland as excessive, Roberts proposed their reduction by two to ten while the general roll seats be increased by two to eight. This was necessary because no European would secure a special roll seat, while there was every likelihood of an African capturing a general roll seat. He disliked the lack of provision for party government, the Governor's sweeping powers, and doubted that the Executive Council could contain the UFP and the MCP because their views were so divergent.

It disturbed him that mere literacy was demanded when Northern Rhodesia prescribed a minimum of two years of secondary schooling. He believed that, if standards were not maintained, the qualitative vote would lose its meaning and there would be no incentive to reach the standard. He declared that, because there was no provision for the fading away of the special roll, the Northern Rhodesian system would be undermined. Finally, he found that there was no machinery for amendment which meant that, when it was needed, a new constitution would be required.[57]

Greenfield's discussion with Macleod in London yielded only clarification.

[56] Welensky Papers, 7/14, f. 188, Welensky to Barrow, 7 July 1960; 20/18, f. 292, Welensky to Sir Gilbert Rennie, 9 July 1960.

[57] *Ibid.*, 7/14, f. 170, Roberts to Hone, 8 July 1960.

Macleod indicated that six seats for the Europeans was over-generous and that the Northern Rhodesian Constitution had to be revised because it was "quite fantastic". Nevertheless, he pleased Greenfield by giving him a written promise that anything gained by Nyasaland would not automatically apply to Northern Rhodesia. Greenfield was seeking to negotiate on the Federal review because the British Government evinced a reluctance to convene it before February 1961, which would give many more opportunities to the trouble-makers. Furthermore the Federal Government wanted to exclude the latter from the review.

When they met on 7 July, Home rejected as impossible the holding of the review before mid-January 1961, but Greenfield warned that his Government would insist on the promise of 1957 being fulfilled lest the investor and the public entertain doubts. He maintained that delay would only benefit African nationalism. Another argument against delay was Whitehead's declared intention to hold a general election between March and June 1961. The Federal Government preferred the first three weeks of December 1960 for the review, followed by an adjournment for Christmas, after which the sub-committees could set to work. The final plenary session would be held in January. Home seemed surprised that so much work was intended, but acknowledged that a start could be made in December, though there would have to be time for parliamentary debates on the Monckton Report.

Greenfield raised next the composition of the delegations, warning that his Government believed that they should be drawn only from the legislatures. Nevertheless, it would include in its delegation two Africans from the UFP and two members of the DP, including Field. The fundamental principle was that the delegations had to be confined to those who agreed that the Federation should continue.

Home, however, continued to maintain that each Government was free to decide the composition of its delegation. His Government would include representatives of the principal African Parties in the northern delegations and give them as much freedom as Field to express their views. Greenfield replied that then the purpose of the review, using Lyttelton's definition, had to be clearly explained. He asked if the territorial Constitutions would be considered and was told that they would be, but only superficially. He disagreed because these Constitutions could radically affect the Federal claim to be self-governing and would have to be related to the overall objective. Home agreed that the primary aim was to make the Federation independent in its own sphere and thereafter to devise a programme for all constitutional development. Greenfield explained that his Government was anxious to secure Federal independence as soon as possible because it would not win the loyalty of the northern Africans until it was clearly permanent. He and Home considered the implementation of the findings of the review and, as Home did not want to introduce a complicated bill in the British Parliament, decided that the Federal Parliament would make the necessary amendments. Home agreed to consider a council of state because Greenfield thought that it was the appropriate method of providing permanent constitutional safeguards. Greenfield reported to Welensky that Home had insisted that representatives of Kaunda's UNIP and Banda's MCP should attend the review. It appeared that Home thought that responsible government would not be granted for ten years.[58]

Evans was still reporting daily and, on 27 June, had believed that the Monckton Commission had unanimously agreed on the detrimental effects of the break-up of the Federation. He accorded this great significance because it would exclude consideration of any alternative forms of association. The Commission had also identified the forces working against the Federation and suggested how to combat them. The commissioners had decided that functions should not be divided on a racial basis and, consequently, that agriculture and education should be entirely territorial responsibilities. Marketing could remain Federal, but not production. A. E. P. Robinson dissented and would only apply these measures to subsistence agriculture because production affected the economic functions of the Federation. He believed that the Federal Government should, in time, become responsible for all agriculture. Education was, to the commissioners, clearly a territorial function, but they thought that the Federal Government should be the arbiter of standards and provide a uniform teaching service and educational grants. Inevitably there would be multi-racial schools. Health was also accepted as a territorial function. Evans found that the commissioners had discarded the idea of equal territorial representation in the Federal Assembly, but some were considering an idea of equal racial representation. The franchises and a council of state were being examined.[59]

These revelations prompted Welensky to warn A. E. P. Robinson that the commissioners should not support ideas which would be politically indefensible in the Federation. A proposal to integrate education, for example, would lose an election in Southern Rhodesia. Thus he again asked to be alerted to any such dangers so that he could take them up with Macmillan and Macleod.

Evans and Robinson next reported that the Commission wanted to change the name of the Federation because of African opinion. Welensky had no objection but replied that: "If you call a rose a violet it will smell just as sweet." Evans also reported that some commissioners were still being difficult. Aidan Crawley was trying to promote universal suffrage which even the African commissioners rejected as impracticable. Hadlow of Nyasaland believed that nothing could save the Federation, and, with other divergent opinions being aired, Evans was doubtful about the result of a forthcoming plenary session. However, Monckton indicated that he would champion the Federal cause and appeared to be supported by MacGillivray, Arden-Clarke and Crathorne. Beadle believed that the British commissioners would be instructed to ensure that the Federation continued and that they were casting round for a form in which it could.[60]

The result of these revelations was that Greenfield had carried to London instructions from Welensky for Evans. Welensky reiterated that the mainte-

[58] *Ibid.*, 7/21, ff. 116 & 58, Greenfield to Welensky, 24 June & 8 July 1960; 20/1, ff. 71–77, Minutes of a Meeting between Home, Greenfield, Evans and Rennie, 7 July 1960.
[59] *Ibid.*, 20/16, f. 226, Evans to Welensky, 27 June 1960.
[60] *Ibid.*, 7/11, f. 47, A. E. P. Robinson to Welensky, (undated); 20/16, f. 200, Evans to Welensky, 29 June 1960; 7/11, f. 45, Welensky to Robinson, 6 July 1960; 20/16, f. 189, Evans to Welensky, 2 July 1960.

nance of the racial separation of education was of prime importance because, if it reverted to the territories, the question of discrimination would arise and with it fears of integration. Cost, in any case, ruled out the provision for the same standard of education for all races. The result would be a lowering of the standards of non-African education and this would be something which Southern Rhodesia would not accept and the Federation would be destroyed. However, post-certificate classes could be multi-racial and one Government, perhaps, could provide technical education. Health was not as crucial nor was agriculture, but Welensky noted that the African farming unions were advocating federalisation. He warned that he would resist strongly any tampering with the composition of the Federal Assembly because it had been adjusted in 1957 with the consent of the five Governments. Furthermore, the British Government had privately recognised that the Federal Government should mainly be concerned with European affairs. (Thus, though he did not say it, an overbearing African influence was not warranted.) He was adamant about the permanency of the franchise and hoped that the Commission understood that he would not change it. The Commission had to grasp that any proposals had to be acceptable to the Federal electorate. Otherwise he and Whitehead would denounce the Monckton Report. To Robinson, he said that it would be madness to divide the Federal Assembly equally on a racial basis, and revealed that he had no faith in either Macmillan or Monckton.[61]

Welensky was distracted from these problems by events in the Congo. The *Force Publique*, the 23 000-man Congolese army, had mutinied in early July and incidents of murder, assault and rape, as well as the abuse and arrest of their European officers, had become widespread. On 7 July, Patrice Lumumba, the new and first Prime Minister, dismissed Lieutenant-General Emile Janssens as Commander and promoted all privates to corporal. Units of the Belgian Army tried to restore order but their Government, like those of Britain and the United States, would not exercise its right to intervene, and their citizens fled the Congo. The action of the Belgian units was only welcomed in the rich copper-mining province of Katanga whose President, Moise Tshombe, asked them to disarm the mutineers and thus ensured peace. Tshombe also asked for reinforcements from the Federal Army. On 11 July, less than two weeks after the Congo had become independent, he proclaimed the secession of Katanga. This declaration was ratified six days later by the Legislative Assembly of Katanga. It is pertinent to note that the Katangese, with the exception of one tribe, the Balubas, had always considered themselves to be apart from the rest of the Congo. The Balubas, however, were not motivated by a love for the pro-Marxist Lumumba but by a fear of the Lundas of whom Tshombe was one. Tshombe's action was not surprising because he had from the outset sought a measure of independence for Katanga by advocating the creation of a federation rather than the unitary state which the Belgians had proposed and the rest of the Congo had accepted.

The news of Tshombe's request for Federal reinforcements came from the Press on 10 July. Knowing that the request had been routed through the British Mission in Elizabethville, the capital of Katanga, Welensky tele-

[61] *Ibid.*, 20/16, f. 220, Welensky to Evans, 5 July 1960; 7/11, f. 45, Welensky to Robinson, 6 July 1960.

phoned the consul there to be told that the latter was not anxious to pass on any messages from Tshombe because the British Government did not want to encourage Katanga's secession. He suggested that Welensky ignore the request. Although temporarily stunned by this high-handedness, Welensky refused publicly to intervene without a request from the Congolese Central Government. The British and Northern Rhodesian Governments issued similar statements.[62]

The next morning, however, Welensky was confronted with the news that the British Government had stated that Federal troops could not be used in the Congo. He protested to the British High Commissioner and to London but was told that a statement would be issued that afternoon. Welensky's tone, however, prompted Home to telephone him at 1.20 p.m. providing Welensky the opportunity to warn that, unless given a satisfactory explanation, he would issue a statement on the position as interpreted by his Government. He was promptly shown by the High Commissioner the full text of the British reply to Tshombe and thereupon declared publicly that the Federal Government would use its forces in the interests of the Federation. He added that Britain was not in any way concerned with the manner in which the Federal Government deployed its troops.

Welensky did not wait for the British reaction before reviewing the situation with his Cabinet on 12 July. By then the position in Katanga was apparently improving with a reconstituted *Force Publique* gradually restoring order, and with the Union Minière, the copper-mining company, deciding to support Tshombe. However, it was not known if Tshombe's declaration of independence was recognised either by the Congolese or Belgian Governments. Clearly trouble was imminent because the neighbouring province of Kasai was against Tshombe and the tribal clashes within Katanga were expected to continue. A worrying aspect was the reported satisfaction of the Northern Rhodesian Africans at the plight of the white Belgian refugees who were streaming through their country. Welensky revealed that, on humanitarian grounds, he had offered Tshombe food supplies.

The Federal defence chiefs were called in to review the military situation. There was no air threat because the Congo possessed no air force, but the Federal air strike capability was affected by a shortage of bombs and rockets. A battalion of territorials had been stationed at Kitwe, while the regular African battalions manned the border with Katanga. As Nyasaland could erupt if Banda returned frustrated from London, it was thought that another battalion of territorials and an African battalion should be dispatched there as well. However, it was likely that the Nyasaland Government would resent this action because of the possible effect on its forthcoming constitutional conference and the Federal Cabinet decided that a Minister should accompany the defence chiefs on a visit to Nyasaland for discussions with Armitage. A battalion of territorials was alerted for a move to Nyasaland, and British Ferret armoured cars were purchased to improve the army's reconnaissance capability. Lastly, because of Katanga's importance as a barrier against Communist encroachment, the Cabinet intended that the British Government

[62] *Ibid.*, FGC(60), 27th Meeting, Federal Cabinet, 12 July 1960; *The Daily Telegraph*, 12 July 1960.

would be pressed to support the efforts for recognition of Katangese independence.[63]

When Home wrote to Welensky on 14 July, he said that he and Macmillan had tried, when answering questions recently, to avoid the constitutional ramifications of the possible dispatch of Federal troops to the Congo by insisting that it would only be done after consultation between the British and Federal Governments. However, he warned, Welensky's subsequent statement would force him to say, when asked, that the external movement of troops would require British sanction in terms of international law. He hoped that henceforth Welensky would avoid differing with him because they were united in their aims. Welensky concurred, but protested at the BBC release of the British decision on Federal troops, and at the British failure to consult him on a subject which directly affected Federal interests. This, he told Home, he found arrogantly inept because, in fact, he had informed Tshombe that he could not assist. He hoped that the Foreign Office understood that the events across the border would have profound political repercussions in the Federation, that the Federation had a greater degree of sovereignty than a colonial dependency and that its Government was quite capable of judging certain matters for itself, including their international implications. He promised to try not to embarrass the British Government when asked by the Federal Assembly if he had protested to the Foreign Office.[64]

The Ghanaian High Commissioner in London had claimed that the Federation was interfering in the Congo, so Welensky protested immediately to Nkrumah that this was incorrect. He reminded him that the deployment of Federal troops was a matter for the Federal and British Governments, and not for Ghana. He added that those concerned for the welfare of the Congo should not exploit the situation for their own propaganda purposes.[65]

That day, 14 July, at the request of Lumumba, the United Nations' Security Council called on Belgium to withdraw her forces from the Congo and proposed their replacement by troops from Ghana, Guinea, Mali and Tunisia. Four days later these forces began to arrive, but before they did, Macmillan felt that the relationship with Welensky had ebbed so low that he had to intervene. He wrote acknowledging that the Nyasaland conference and the Congo were worrying both their Governments and that certain elements would use them to attempt to divide Welensky and himself. This had to be prevented. He blandly continued that he was sure that the Federal and British Governments were right to withhold their troops while there was hope of maintaining Congolese unity. The situation would be different if the Congolese Government collapsed or Tshombe managed to maintain his independence for some time. Either of these eventualities would force some *ad hoc* recognition. However, until then, neither Government should let itself be accused of breaking up the Congo because without Katanga it would be impoverished and ripe for Communist exploitation. The first task was to

[63] *Ibid.*, FGC(60), 27th Meeting, Federal Cabinet, 12 July 1960.

[64] *Ibid.*, 20/12, f. 227, Home to Welensky, 14 July 1960; House of Lords *Hansard* (London), Vol. 225, Col. 23, 11 July 1960; House of Commons *Hansard* (London), Vol. 626, Col. 983, 11 July 1960; 20/12, f. 226, Welensky to Home, 14 July 1960.

[65] *Ibid.*, 20/12, f. 225, Welensky to Dr Kwame Nkrumah, 14 July 1960.

restore order and Macmillan believed that the UN was best able to do this. Thus, he said, his Government would inform the UN Secretary-General that it would co-operate if he could devise a practical plan.

Macmillan told Welensky that he knew that Banda would dislike Macleod's constitutional proposals and hoped that he could be persuaded to accept a middle course. If Banda would not agree, then there would have to be prompt action to prevent widespread disorder. As simultaneously troops would be required on Northern Rhodesia's border with the Congo and in Nyasaland, Macmillan offered again British military assistance, hastily adding that he recognised the Federal responsibility for defence. He argued that the Federal Army would be overstretched, and that, politically, it was in their interests to be seen to be working together. The deployment of European territorials might only increase the political difficulties and possibly jeopardise the Federal review, and joint action could more easily be defended internationally. He proposed immediate Anglo-Federal planning on expected troop requirements and reinforcement by four British Army units. Important issues were at stake, he warned, the most crucial being the Federation's future.[66] It is, perhaps, unkind to suggest that Macmillan's constant harping on British military involvement arose out of more than a concern for the Federation. A sizeable force would have given Whitehall the means to influence policy in the Federation which the current Federal control of the armed forces denied to it.

Two days later the British Government informed Welensky that it had just refused a request from Tshombe for recognition because the Congo might still emerge united and reasonably friendly towards the West. At least it might be neutral. If this were possible, it would be better if Katanga remained in the Congo to prevent it from becoming impoverished and turning to Communism. If unity were possible, nothing should impede the UN's task. Yet, if the Congo were to dissolve into chaos, the chance to save Katanga should not be lost. However, clearly it would not survive without the armed support of the Governments which might recognise it, and this could involve white soldiery defending Katanga against states who were working for African unity with the approval of the UN and the assistance of the Communist bloc.[67]

Nonetheless, Welensky pointed out to Home that Tshombe had managed, with local and Belgian forces, to restore order. The result was the return of the whites and the restoration of normal copper production. The internal peace of Katanga, he said, sharply contrasted with the continuing chaos elsewhere in the Congo. Moreover, Tshombe appeared to be gaining support from the provinces of Kivu and Kasai and from Ruanda-Urundi. He had even won over his parliamentary Opposition, including the Balubas. This last achievement was important, Welensky asserted, because Northern Rhodesia and Katanga shared some tribes. Furthermore, Tshombe's Government was freely elected. The vital question to Welensky was what action the UN would take if Lumumba insisted that Katanga should return to the fold. Would they take military action against a stable, productive Katanga just because they

[66] *Ibid.*, f. 219, Macmillan to Welensky, 15 July 1960.
[67] *Ibid.*, f. 218, M. R. Metcalf to Welensky, 17 July 1960.

were asked to by the African states and the Russians? Tshombe, in contrast to Lumumba, at least favoured the West and, if Lumumba gained control of Katanga, the Russian influence could have a serious effect on the Copperbelt and its strategic minerals. Welensky believed that the safety of Southern Africa therefore required the *de facto* recognition of Katanga by as many countries as possible. This would strengthen Tshombe's position and make action unlikely by the UN at Lumumba's request. The ultimate compromise would be a federation of the Congo, including Katanga, and the *de facto* recognition of Tshombe would not preclude this.[68]

Home, however, told Welensky that he was satisfied with the composition of the UN force and was confident that General Alexander of Ghana would quickly bring the situation under control. Indulging in this wishful thinking, he argued that the Russians were trying to profit from keeping the Congo unsettled and that the sensible approach was to deal with Tshombe but not to recognise Katanga. Home's aim was to have order restored by the UN and to heal the rift because he believed that Katanga would call the tune after the re-unification, because it produced two-thirds of the Congo's revenue. If Lumumba were replaced by a new leader in the next few weeks, unity could well be quickly restored.

For Welensky's enlightenment, Home enclosed the instructions for Sir Pierson Dixon, the British Ambassador to the United Nations, which demanded that all aid to the Congo should be channelled through the UN. There would be no intervention in Katanga as long as law and order was maintained. It was particularly important to prevent the Central Congolese Army from entering Katanga. Any settlement to be effected would preserve Katanga's rights as a province and guarantee the interests of the West there. Dixon would inform the UN Secretary-General that Britain would not recognise Katanga's secession because it would create more problems than it would solve. The best arrangement would be for the Congolese Central Government to grant sufficient provincial autonomy to Katanga to maintain order, protect the whites and make the Katangan wealth available to the rest of the Congo. The British Government approved the choice of a man who was not connected with the military and administrative effort to represent the Secretary-General in Elizabethville. It was glad to see that the UN forces would not be concerned with the internal politics and that their deployment would be delayed until more immediate problems, such as the restoration of law and order, had been solved. Finally, Dixon was told that Home believed that the Federal Government agreed with these views.[69]

Welensky promptly explained his actions in the Federal Assembly, while praising the local efforts in assisting the thousands of refugees. He said that, contrary to the accusations that the Federal Government was interfering in the internal affairs of the Congo, it had not done so. He admitted, though, that it had been a difficult decision to deny Tshombe military assistance because he was determined to maintain order. Such assistance, however, was unconstitutional, but the ill-considered statement by the British Foreign Office had no bearing on the Federal relationship with the Congo as it was a

[68] *Ibid.*, f. 217, Metcalf to the Commonwealth Relations Office, 17 July 1960.
[69] *Ibid.*, f. 214, Home to Welensky, 18 July 1960.

domestic matter for arrangement between the British and Federal Governments. Nonetheless, Welensky said he would only supply Katanga with food.[70]

Faced with Katanga and the prospect of enduring internal unrest in the Federation, the Federal Cabinet decided to recruit sufficient forces to assist the civil power without resorting to external reinforcement. A regular European battalion (later named the Rhodesian Light Infantry) would be formed. The external commitment would be met by a locally-raised squadron of the Special Air Service and a reconnaissance squadron (the Selous Scouts) would drive the new Ferrets. All units, including the battalions of territorials, would be re-armed with FN rifles and machine guns.[71]

Barrow reported that he had accompanied the defence chiefs to Nyasaland and had discovered that Armitage was opposed to any reinforcement by the Federal Army in case it affected the negotiations with Banda. It was evident that he would risk a flare-up rather than upset Banda. In any case, he had indicated that he would prefer reinforcement by British troops who would be answerable to him rather than to the Federal Government. Provoked, Welensky immediately informed Macmillan of the probable unfortunate political repercussions of the deployment of British troops. He expressed dismay that British policy should have made a clash inevitable in Nyasaland.[72]

He informed Home that his Government accepted the main British argument and was pleased with the firm line which had been taken on non-interference in the Congo. However, he discounted the prospects of a settlement in the Congo unless Lumumba were replaced by someone very different. All would be lost once Lumumba effectively controlled the whole area with inevitable Russian help. Welensky accepted the approach of the UN and promised to resist the strong pressures to recognise Katanga. Yet he hoped that eventually Britain would consider recognition because it was the best method of preserving their mutual interests as well as those of Tshombe. He hoped the British would provide Tshombe with good advice and moral backing. For example, Tshombe should be discouraged from courting a rebuff from the UN over independence. If he had time, Tshombe might gain from procrastination.[73]

Welensky also apprised R. A. Butler of the latest events, including Armitage's refusal to allow the Federal Army to show the flag. This distressed him because he believed that only those of criminal intent found policemen provocative.[74]

Welensky's concern about the internal tensions in the Federation was fully vindicated when, on 20 July, African nationalist mobs went on the rampage in Salisbury's African townships. A day of intimidation and stoning necessitated the mobilisation of a battalion of territorials. The violence quickly spread to Gwelo and Bulawayo and took a week to bring under control, with the first deaths in Southern Rhodesia (eleven in Bulawayo) resulting from police

[70] Fed R & N *Debates* (Salisbury), Vol. 12, Col. 1345, 18 July 1960.
[71] Welensky Papers, FGC(60), 28th Meeting, Minute 1, Federal Cabinet, 18 July 1960.
[72] *Ibid.*, (Restricted) Minute, Federal Cabinet, 18 July 1960.
[73] *Ibid.*, 20/12, f. 212, Welensky to Home, 19 July 1960.
[74] *Ibid.*, 42/38, f. 122, Welensky to R. A. Butler, 20 July 1960.

action, since the uprisings in 1896. Statements by the leadership of the National Democratic Party and by Todd, calling for British military intervention to end the "oppressive" minority rule, provoked cries of "treason", and demands for deportation, from the white electorate.[75] The NDP had been formed by Michael Mawema, in the absence of the self-exiled Nkomo, on 1 January 1960 to replace the Southern Rhodesian ANC which Whitehead had banned in February 1959.

Todd travelled to London to meet Nkomo where, at a Press conference, they displayed a letter they had written to Home. This claimed that they had urged the British Government for years to widen the franchise to ensure the political security of Central Africa. No one had listened, the letter said, and instead the UFP had preferred playing politics with the reactionary Dominion Party, ignoring the 8 000 000 people who lacked the vote. The pretext of law and order was used to silence any protests. The maintenance of policies by force was directly responsible for the unrest. Thus it was imperative that the British Government should immediately establish a new and democratic regime in Central Africa to avoid a disintegration which would bring suffering to all. If the British Government would not intervene, it should say so in order that the protestors would know that they would have to rely on their own strength and resources to gain their freedom. This would inevitably bring intervention by the United Nations, but not before there had been much unnecessary suffering. Nkomo and Todd hoped that the British Government, which had brought freedom to so many millions, would not flinch from upsetting the current regime.[76]

When questioned by the Press Nkomo blamed the current crisis on Whitehead because he answered requests for involvement in government with bullets. He had information on Whitehead's intention to use South African troops to quell the disturbances. This gambling with the lives of all races had to stop and the British Government had to take action immediately. Todd claimed that the explosion had been inevitable, but that the whites had learned nothing from the Congo and had not given way. The situation was so serious that only British intervention could rectify it. Asked how the European would react if the British Government suspended the Constitution and sent in troops, Todd replied that he did not think that Welensky would order his forces to fire on them but, if there were no prompt British action, there were years of trouble in store.[77]

Two days later, on 28 July, Todd resigned from his Central Africa Party over his call for outside intervention. Gaunt demanded the abrogation of Todd's citizenship, but Welensky ignored him. In London, Evans was most alarmed at the eagerness of the British Press and others to accept totally the allegations of Todd and Nkomo. However, the British Government kept Todd at arm's length. He secured an interview for himself with Home, but half an hour before it he did not ask Home but simply informed him that he

[75] *Ibid.*, FGC(60), 29th Meeting, Minute 2, Federal Cabinet, 21 July 1960; 8/31, f. 4, Southern Rhodesian Sitreps, 21 July 1960; *The Rhodesia Herald*, 21, 22 & 25 July 1960.

[76] Welensky Papers, 31/46, f. 49, Todd, Nkomo, P. Mushonga and E. Dumbutshena to Home, 26 July 1960.

[77] *Ibid.*, f. 45, Todd's and Nkomo's Press Conference, 26 July 1960.

would be accompanied by three Africans. Home promptly cancelled the interview, making his annoyance plain.[78]

The Monckton Commission had continued to be rent by internal dissension. It was disturbed by the truculence of W. M. Chirwa and other Africans and their eagerness to exploit the Southern Rhodesian riots. Such was the trend of the Commission's deliberations that Evans sought the advice of Professor Jennings who denied the possibility of secession. If this was of cheer, the news that Duncan Sandys would succeed Lord Home as Commonwealth Secretary, was not.[79] Sandys was unknown to the Rhodesians and Home was the Minister who was most familiar with their problems and, perhaps, the most sympathetic towards them.

A luncheon with Lord Monckton in London greatly encouraged Greenfield. He warned Monckton that the impact of the events in the Congo was such that Whitehead wanted the Commission to return to see the effect. Though this would be widely welcomed, Greenfield considered it unnecessary. However, he said, there had been an inevitable reaction against liberalism, and some whites saw in the events confirmation that Africans were thinly-veiled savages unsuited to government. The Rhodesians had heard stories of atrocities from the thousands of Belgians billeted in their homes. The Africans, by contrast, had been excited by the sight of Europeans fleeing and it would be difficult to persuade them that violence did not pay. The riots in Southern Rhodesia illustrated the point while supplying ammunition to the Federation's British critics. These events had made Greenfield and Welensky more convinced that the Federation had to succeed lest partnership be trampled under by the African nationalists. The Federal Government was all the more determined to ensure that the review would be held that year. Greenfield believed that it was being said in London that a territory should have the right to secede when it gained its independence. For Monckton's benefit, he recalled Lord Swinton's vehement rejection of this in January 1953. It was obvious to Greenfield that, if such a provision were inserted in the Federal Constitution, all financial and administrative arrangements would be unsettled and a victory over partnership would be conceded to the African nationalists. The Federal Government could not accept this. Even more crucial was the franchise because, while it was non-racial, it would keep control in civilised hands. As the Africans raised their standards, so control would pass to them. Thus the Federal Government, he said, would reject radical alteration. The Constitutional Amendment Act of 1957 had been approved by the five Governments and provided for the fading out of the colour labels. Therefore the idea of equal racial representation was unthinkable.

Greenfield also made it clear that non-African education would not be surrended by his Government. It would strenuously oppose the transfer of agriculture, and would have to be convinced that something more than a

[78] *The Rhodesia Herald*, 28 July 1960; Fed R & N *Debates* (Salisbury), Vol. 13, Col. 2067, 1 August 1960; Welensky Papers, 20/16, f. 89, Evans to Welensky, 28 July 1960.

[79] Welensky Papers, 20/16, f. 148, Evans to Sir Ivor Jennings, 19 July 1960; f. 99, Memorandum by Jennings, 23 July 1960; f. 87, Evans to Jennings, 28 July 1960; 20/1, f. 69, Home to Welensky, 26 July 1960.

measure of decentralisation of the health service was needed. The only function it wished to acquire was that of the police because experience had taught that it needed to control them in emergencies. Finally, Greenfield reminded Monckton that the main purpose of the review was to achieve independence for the Federation in its own sphere as it was the best way to secure the future and win the loyalty of the African population.[80]

Monckton replied that he sympathised with the Federal Government and would see that it was not betrayed. Encouraged, Greenfield supplied him with a record of their meeting but was disappointed when Monckton made no comment on it.[81]

The Federal Government was not involved in the Nyasaland constitutional conference but, on 20 July, Welensky informed Macleod that he objected to the suggestion that the income qualification should be lowered, and abandoned when a voter reached the age of 40 because there would be a demand for this to apply to Northern Rhodesia. It appeared to him that Macleod misunderstood the importance of the franchise qualifications to the Federal Government. This illustrated the need to improve co-operation and consultation between the Governments because, without doubt, Macleod would not suggest such an irrevocable step if he understood the depth of feeling in the Federation.

Welensky claimed to have done his utmost to avoid embarrassing the British Government over the Nyasaland Constitution only to discover that Macleod was determined to place him in difficulty at a time when the Congo had appreciably added to his problems.[82]

The criticism of the lack of co-operation bit so deeply that, within an hour of the opening in London of the Nyasaland Constitutional Conference on 25 July, Macleod wrote his first report to Welensky. With the exception of one violent speech, he said he had not found the first session at all exciting. He would not intervene until the initial debate was over because he knew that by then the delegates would still be poles apart. He thanked Welensky for his views on the franchise and agreed that it might be better to maintain its high standards, even though they were inapplicable to Nyasaland, and to compensate by enfranchising people such as Chiefs and headmen. Everything depended on Banda and to date he had behaved well and appeared genuinely to desire a settlement. However, Macleod admitted that Banda was unpredictable and that anything could happen. Finally, Macleod dismissed the idea of separating the executive and the legislature as quite inappropriate.[83]

Evans and the Press reported that the "violent" speech had come from the erstwhile nationalist, J. R. N. Chinyama, who directly accused Banda of using intimidation and said that if he denied it he would only emphasise the insincerity of the African leadership. The response from Banda's delegation was cries of "nonsense". Banda declared that he had faith in the ability of Macleod to produce a solution acceptable to the people of Nyasaland. Macleod won applause for an opening sentence in Chinyanja. He stated that he

[80] *Ibid.*, 20/10, f. 19, Greenfield to Monckton, 25 July 1960.
[81] J. M. Greenfield, *Testimony of a Rhodesian Federal* (Bulawayo, 1978), p. 176.
[82] Welensky Papers, 20/1, f. 86, Welensky to Macleod, 20 July 1960.
[83] *Ibid.*, 7/14, f. 163, Macleod to Welensky, 25 July 1960.

sought orderly democratic evolution while providing stable government which would allow Britain to protect the people for as long as they desired. A. C. W. Dixon proclaimed that, despite malicious statements to the contrary, his UFP sought only the advancement of all.[84]

After this first session, Banda sought an accommodation with the Africans of the UFP, Chinyama, Kwenje and Matthews Phiri, but was repulsed. If this was surprising, it was no less so than his mild speech to a meeting of the Movement for Colonial Freedom before the Conference. It appeared to Evans that Banda was indicating that he would take what Macleod offered rather than be depicted as unreasoning and uncompromising. This, Evans observed, could be disconcerting for the UFP. At the same meeting, Enoch Dumbutshena from Southern Rhodesia, and Mainza Chona from Northern Rhodesia, provided a violent contrast to Banda, speaking wildly to a totally sympathetic audience who seemed prepared to subscribe to statements such as being ready to say "*voetsak*" to all Europeans. From the platform, Stonehouse belittled the stories of atrocities in the Congo because he had seen a picture of a white child in the arms of a black policeman, omitting to say that the picture was taken of Belgian refugees in the neighbouring French Congo.[85]

Macleod's prediction about the Nyasaland Conference was soon confirmed because the United Federal and Malawi Congress Parties proved irreconcilable. He introduced his proposals, keeping the £120 p.a. income level, but seeking to enfranchise Chiefs and headmen. On hearing of this on 31 July, Welensky lost no time in expressing his gratitude to Macleod for this understanding of Federal problems. He was quite prepared, he said, to accept the enfranchisement of Chiefs and headmen, provided they met the monetary qualifications. He assumed that, if a settlement were possible, Macleod would leave the framing of the details to the officials. Welensky asked to see the final scheme before it was published.[86]

Welensky's implied lack of trust, by the latter demand, touched Macleod on the raw. He replied recalling Federal objections to the lowering of the franchise and the complaints about the lack of consultation which hurt because he had always endeavoured to keep Welensky informed and had deferred to him whenever possible. He had provided a preview of his proposals, and Greenfield's amendments had been used wherever appropriate. He had given up the simplest method, that of enfranchising everyone, regardless of qualifications, when they reached the age of 40. Instead, he had enfranchised a small group by specifying certain categories of person to avoid having a ridiculously small special roll electorate of 8 500. He had done all this to help Welensky. He closed with a firm commitment to the Federation, and promised to report daily on the Conference.[87]

Welensky did not spare Macleod's ruffled feelings by immediately calling Macleod's attention to the mention of several categories when previously only literate Chiefs and headmen had been considered. He reserved for Joelson

[84] *Ibid.*, 20/16, f. 109, Evans to Welensky, 27 July 1960; *The Rhodesia Herald*, 27 July 1960.
[85] Welensky Papers, 20/16, ff. 111 & 109, Evans to Welensky, 25 & 27 July 1960.
[86] *Ibid.*, 20/18, f. 282, Welensky to Macleod, 31 July 1960.
[87] *Ibid.*, 20/1, f. 65, Macleod to Welensky, 1 August 1960.

only, however, the comment that Macleod might report daily but always after a decision had been taken, thereby denying him any influence.[88]

Although the Press thought otherwise, by 2 August Dixon believed the Conference would break down. He reported to Welensky that Macleod had proposed a legislature of eight general roll and 20 special roll seats with the special roll qualifications set at an income of £120 p.a. and the ability to fill in the form in English, or ten years of tax paying and the ability to write in the vernacular. Chiefs and headmen would be given the vote by virtue of their position. These qualifications could produce an electorate of 100 000. Banda had reduced his demand for seats from 46 to 30, of which six would be elected by the general roll and 24 by the special roll. However, although he did not say so, it was clear that he sought universal suffrage, which was unacceptable to Macleod.[89] Reporting that day to Welensky, Macleod told how he had enunciated the principles of his proposals and how, by some miracle, they had not been leaked to the Press. The first reaction of the Malawi Congress Party, he said, was to walk out and "return to gaol", but Banda had persuaded them at least to examine the proposals. Thus the MCP had learnt that they would not get self-government, universal suffrage, or anything else approaching their aims. That they were still prepared to talk was an achievement in itself. However, it was clear that the enfranchisement of the Chiefs and headmen was insufficient, and thus the inclusion of other categories was being considered to produce the desired electorate. Macleod believed that Dixon and Blackwood would accept the enfranchisement of the over-forties, but he would not introduce it because of Welensky's strong objections. As for the numbers of the elected Members, he was proposing between twelve and 18 special roll Members but he did not think that the number was crucial while the power to nominate obtained. He did not intend to impose a solution while a chance of agreement remained. He was, nonetheless, expecting the Conference to collapse any minute.[90]

A day later he could report a unanimous agreement that the general roll Members would be elected on the existing basis and that the special roll qualifications would be, in part, an income of £120 p.a. and literacy in English. Discussion currently centred on how it could be proved that taxes had been paid for ten years. The MCP had suggested that three years was enough and good humouredly accepted the imputation that they sought to disguise universal suffrage. The Conference had agreed to the inclusion of sensible categories such as pensioners, in addition to the Chiefs and headmen. The MCP had raised the enfranchisement of women and Macleod had referred it to a sub-committee of officials. The Africans had thought that there were not enough special roll Members and Macleod had suggested 20 matched by two more general roll Members. The UFP had not only concurred, but had suggested the use of double-Member constituencies which Macleod thought was possible.[91]

[88] *Ibid.*, 20/18, f. 266, H. N. Parry to M. R. Metcalf, 2 August 1960; 24/151, ff. 139–142, Welensky to Joelson, 9 August 1960.

[89] *Ibid.*, 20/18, f. 265, Dixon to Welensky, 2 August 1960.

[90] *Ibid.*, f. 269, Macleod to Welensky, 2 August 1960.

[91] *Ibid.*, f. 262, Macleod to Welensky, 3 August 1960.

On 4 August Macleod revealed to Welensky that the MCP had asked for nine African ministers, but he had clung to his Executive Council of five officials, three unofficials nominated from the ranks of the special roll Members and two from the general roll. Blackwood had suggested an additional appointment of two or three parliamentary secretaries who would not belong to the Executive Council. Macleod felt agreement was close.[92]

This was correct because, a day later, a basis for agreement had been found which included a declaration that the delegates would make the Constitution work and would give it a fair trial. Macleod was confident that a great advantage had been gained by the MCP acceptance of an arrangement which differed so greatly from its aims.[93]

Evans wrote to Welensky describing how deeply the Monckton Commission had been impressed by the reasonable attitude of the UFP delegates at the Nyasaland Conference. Lord Blake has assumed that the delegates from the UFP would not have signed if Welensky had objected to the new Constitution. Welensky, of course, was in Salisbury and, through Macleod's daily reports, was one day behind events at the Conference. Not being in London, he could not be urgently consulted. Greenfield, who makes this observation, also reveals that, in fact, "Welensky and his Ministers were horrified" at what had been accepted, and Blackwood would later maintain that he and Dixon had been led into a trap.[94]

Nevertheless, Welensky thereupon apologised to Macleod for the inference on the lack of consultation and praised his efforts to keep him informed. However, he expected Kaunda to demand the same concessions and asked Macleod to stand firm against the revision of the Northern Rhodesian Constitution. This was particularly important, he said, because the presence of 10 000–13 000 Belgian refugees was affecting the mood of the Federal electorate. The latter was undoubtedly unsettled by the MCP declaring that the result of the Nyasaland Conference was that the Federation was a dead letter and by Banda confirming that his aim was to break it up. These statements, however, might have been interpreted as a reaction to the Congress Liberation Party claiming the Conference as a defeat for Banda.[95]

Welensky had said in a debate on partnership that the advancement of Africans in all fields would be accelerated to enable them to take an increasing part in government. However, Greenfield felt that he should welcome the Nyasaland agreement because it acknowledged the numerical superiority of the Africans by giving them better representation while granting the non-Africans greater responsibilities. It would involve the African and European unofficials in the daily administration, and it should be noted that all Parties had pledged themselves to the success of the Constitution and its existence

[92] *Ibid.*, f. 260, Macleod to Welensky, 4 August 1960.

[93] *Ibid.*, 7/14, f. 128, Agreement on the Working Basis for the Next Stage of Constitutional Advancement — published as *Report of the Nyasaland Conference*, Command 1132 (London, July & August 1960); 20/18, f. 248, Macleod to Welensky, 5 August 1960.

[94] *Ibid.*, 7/14, f. 125, Evans to Welensky, 5 August 1960; Greenfield, *Testimony*, *op. cit.*, pp. 184–185, citing R. Blake, *A History of Rhodesia* (London, 1977), p. 331.

[95] Welensky Papers, 20/1, ff. 63–64, Welensky to Macleod, 5 August 1960; 20/18, f. 129, Telex from Rhodesia House, London, 5 August 1960.

for a substantial period. As much of the agreement related to the aims of the UFP, Greenfield thought that attention should be called to this. He believed that it might have been possible simply to give the endorsement of the UFP, but Banda thereafter had spoken not only of breaking up the Federation, but of joining East Africa. The great pity, Greenfield said, was that Macleod had not emphasised that the basis of the Constitution was the continuation of the Federation. Dixon had referred to self-government, but had been misinterpreted by the Press as meaning that, when self-government had been achieved, Nyasaland would have the option of leaving the Federation. As this was inaccurate, Greenfield drafted a statement for Welensky which praised the agreement and the declarations of the delegates, but emphasised that it was implicit that Nyasaland was being dealt with as part of the Federation. Welensky would also comment on Banda's subsequent disturbing statements. Banda had called the agreement the beginning of the end of the Federation and thus had discredited his declaration of intent to make a success of the new Constitution, even though he might have only been indulging in face-saving. Banda needed reminding that statements like Nyasaland would never be in a federation with Southern Rhodesia were meaningless when it was in fact a part of the Federation, and the Constitution which he had just accepted was based on that fact. Furthermore, he had to remember that the future prosperity of Nyasaland was dependent on continued association with the Federation.[96]

While Greenfield drafted this statement, Welensky congratulated Macleod on his skilful handling of the Conference. They would have to wait to see how Banda interpreted his undertakings and Welensky thought that he had made an inauspicious start. As if to confirm this, Banda contradicted Macleod. Leaving Britain on 9 August, he declared — wrongly — that Macleod had been misreported in the Press the previous day and that there would be elections in Nyasaland in November, which meant that they would be held before the Federal review. He repeated this on arrival in Nyasaland after having excitedly bellowed, "Kwacha! To Hell with Federation!" He dismissed the administrative difficulties of an election by saying that the civil servants would just have to work harder. Dixon had to understand that, if he thought that independence would be delayed for ten years, he was living in a fool's paradise. Banda labelled Chinyama and Chijozi "stooges" and the UFP as "stupid fools", and asked his audience at Chileka airport to believe that Macleod and the Tory Party had recognised a new era.

Before Banda finished speaking, the crowd of some 10 000 started to drift away. The MCP delegation was considerably affronted by having to submit to customs formalities which delayed them for three-quarters of an hour while they paid duty on watches and clothes. This led Leonard Ingallis of the *New York Times* to proclaim that Banda's party should never have been thus humiliated. The Federal officials and the local Europeans were equally irritated to find their movements at the airport curtailed by the MCP "Malawi Police".[97]

[96] *Ibid.*, 7/14, f. 118, Greenfield to Welensky, 8 August 1960.

[97] *Ibid.*, 20/18, f. 247, Welensky to Macleod, 8 August 1960; *Evening Standard*, 9 August 1960; Welensky Papers, 20/18, ff. 233 & 200, Confidential News Reports, 10 & 11 August 1960.

The Federal Government was none too pleased to hear that, simultaneously with Banda's speech at Chileka Airport, Whitehead, when announcing to the Southern Rhodesian Assembly that he intended to enlarge it and to ensure that some Africans were elected, stated that he did not care if Nyasaland seceded. Evans, however, at least found the Monckton Commission agreeably surprised by Whitehead's constitutional intentions.[98]

Welensky had learnt never to allow anything to slip by when dealing with Macleod and thus informed him of a local rumour that he would appoint Banda immediately to the Nyasaland Executive Council. Welensky asked if this were true because Banda's current behaviour was not very encouraging. Indeed, he seemed bent on wrecking Macleod's compromise settlement.[99]

When Macleod wrote on 15 August, he answered Welensky's earlier question on Northern Rhodesia. He appreciated the fears of repercussions from the Nyasaland settlement, but reminded Welensky that he had stated at the Conference that the proposals suited the special circumstances of Nyasaland. He could therefore argue that they were inappropriate for Northern Rhodesia. Nevertheless, he said, there was clearly a need for a Northern Rhodesian constitutional conference in 1961.[100] (Thus, in less than six months, Macleod had moved from a position where he had declared that there would be no overturning of the Northern Rhodesian Constitution of 1958, because it was too new, to advocating its replacement.)

He answered Welensky's second question on 17 August and denied that he had any immediate plans to bring Banda into the Executive Council. However, he was clearly contemplating such a move because he declared that, despite Welensky's critical attitude towards Banda's current behaviour, it would make him face the economic and political realities. It would be even better if one of his aides were brought in as well. Such an experiment had worked well in Kenya, and it was clear that Banda's early involvement with government was most desirable. Macleod did not minimise the difficulties because, for example, Banda might demand the resignation of all the existing Members of the Executive Council. Macleod could not agree to that. Banda might refuse to serve while his men were detained and it might be advantageous, if tension diminished, to effect their early release. Furthermore, Macleod maintained, as the MCP would attend the Federal review, there were obviously great advantages in Banda being there in an official capacity.[101] (Macleod again was obviously trying to condition Welensky for change.)

Macleod had more to answer because, on 15 August, Welensky had warned him that Gaunt was about to protest in the Federal Assembly against the implementation of the new Nyasaland Constitution because it would lead to the early demise of the Federation. Welensky had said that Greenfield would reply that the provisional agreement of the Conference on 4 August was based on the two fundamentals that the delegations declared that they would

[98] SR *Debates* (Salisbury), Vol. 45, Col. 1217, 10 August 1960; Welensky Papers, 24/151, ff. 134–135, Welensky to F. S. Joelson, 22 August 1960; 20/16, f. 30, Evans to Welensky, 12 August 1960.

[99] Welensky Papers, 20/18, f. 210, Welensky to Macleod, 11 August 1960.

[100] *Ibid.*, 20/1, ff. 61–62, Macleod to Welensky, 15 August 1960.

[101] *Ibid.*, ff. 48–49, Macleod to Welensky, 17 August 1960.

support it and that Nyasaland would not secede. Greenfield wanted to refer to Macleod's oral agreement with the Federal Government that there would be no implementation of the new Constitution before the Federal review. As Macleod might be embarrassed, Welensky had wanted to know what line Greenfield should take. In any case, Welensky said, this was needed because hitherto Macleod had remained silent in the face of Banda's demonstrations of bad faith. Greenfield was thus proposing to say that not only had strong representations been made to Macleod on this subject, but, if Banda did not change his tune, the UFP would reconsider its position in relation to the agreement.

Welensky had also felt impelled to draw Macleod's attention to the campaign of intimidation against all opponents of the MCP. The law had been contravened, and the Federal Government was studying the situation with a view to making representations to the Governor for the institution of criminal proceedings. In the light of this behaviour, Welensky stated, the inclusion of Banda in the Government was clearly intolerable.[102]

Macleod nonetheless replied that, as a staunch supporter of the Federation, he was determined to involve the African politicians, and Banda especially, in the Government of Nyasaland to make them aware of the necessity for the Federation. Banda, he believed, was volatile by nature and had to be given time to settle down. Moreover, it was to be expected that Banda, having failed to achieve his aims, would cast around for an issue which would cloak this failure and maintain his position. It was the duty of the Governor to deal with Banda. Jones, the Governor designate, had advised that Banda's involvement in the Executive Council would blunt his attacks even though it would not silence him. Macleod felt that he and Welensky should be guided by Jones. He did not want Greenfield to emphasise that the agreement had depended on Nyasaland staying in the Federation because that was acknowledged. He supported the Federation and had told the MCP that he disagreed with their views, but had never stipulated that the acceptance of the Federation was a prerequisite for the adoption of the new Constitution. Macleod's fear was that, through Greenfield's action, he might be accused of bad faith by the MCP and be forced to repudiate the Federal Government. The declaration of intent by all parties had been crucial to the agreement and thus he would prefer that Greenfield should say that the purpose of the Conference had been merely to advise the Colonial Secretary on the next stage of constitutional development, and that the relationship with the Federation had lain outside the terms of reference. Greenfield could then dwell on the declaration of intent and claim that, if everyone abided by it, there would be prospects of peace and progress in Nyasaland. Greenfield could note that the Governor would keep control while the African politicians proved themselves, and that any further transfer of power would depend on the British Government being satisfied that the necessary experience had been gained. Macleod warned that a public statement, to the effect that the UFP was reconsidering its attitude, would only damage the Federal cause. It would be most inopportune, he said, because the agitation in Britain was subsiding.[103]

102 *Ibid.*, 20/18, f. 184, Welensky to Macleod, 15 August 1960.
103 *Ibid.*, f. 179, Macleod to Welensky, 17 August 1960.

Welensky replied that Gaunt's motion had been dropped for lack of a seconder, but only after the UFP had brought pressure on Robert Moffat. Welensky said he had sought Macleod's opinion because he wished to co-operate with him. Indeed, he had just restrained Dixon from making a public protest over a physical assault on Phiri and Kwenje of the UFP by members of the MCP. He wished to correct also Macleod's impression that he and Greenfield had believed that the Nyasaland agreement was dependent on that territory remaining in the Federation. It was clearly implied that Nyasaland would remain in the Federation. Welensky protested that Banda had not deviated from his course of repudiating his declaration of good faith, and that his speeches and actions were directly responsible for the assaults on Phiri and Kwenje.

Welensky was concerned about the latitude which was being given to the "Malawi Police". The Malawi Youth League was drilling in Kota Kota, wearing insignia inscribed "Malawi Civil Police" and "Malawi Government Police". Welensky proposed to protest to Jones on this, and would refuse a Northern Rhodesian constitutional conference his support if it meant a lowering of the franchise or an acceleration of African advancement to the detriment of the other races. There had been Press leaks on the Monckton Commission's findings and Welensky warned that, if they were accurate, he would act as he saw fit.[104]

Welensky secured a reaction because Jones, on 25 August, wrote to say that he would make a public statement with which Macleod wished to be associated. He would note that a far-reaching step forward had been taken in the ordered constitutional development of the territory. The agreement at the Nyasaland Conference had been reached between people of widely differing views and was a tribute to their wisdom and statesmanship. He would promise the prompt implementation of the Constitution, but would warn that it would take some eight months, including a period for the registration of voters. The Federal review would precede the implementation, but Jones would recall Macleod's promise that African opinion would be adequately represented at it. Jones hoped that the people of Nyasaland would persuade their leaders to continue to display patience and goodwill in this period of preparation. (This was a peculiar view of leadership and an odd request for a Governor.) Jones would remind the people that the basis of the Constitution was the freedom of the individual. This was necessary because the contrary had been unhappily demonstrated by shameful occurrences in which the irresponsible had tried to victimise their political opponents. This he would condemn unequivocally and would promise a vigorous reaction. He would hope that all politicians and responsible people would condemn anything which endangered the achievements of the Conference. His Government proposed to ensure that the new Constitution was implemented in an atmosphere of peace and goodwill, and would call on the people to demonstrate that they were fit to bear the new responsibilities which the new Constitution would confer on them.[105]

Other matters, such as the leak of the Monckton Report to the Press, were

[104] *Ibid.*, f. 159, Welensky to Macleod, 22 August 1960.
[105] *Ibid.*, f. 119, G. S. Jones to Welensky, 25 August 1960.

demanding Welensky's attention and he might not have recognised that Banda was right in saying that the death-knell of the Federation had been sounded by Macleod, however distantly and faintly.[106] The new Constitution would bring Banda to power, despite the retention by the Governor of the executive power, and the British Government would allow him to take Nyasaland out of the Federation and set the precedent which destroyed it.

[106] *Ibid.*, 20/1, f. 44, Barrow to Duncan Sandys, 25 August 1960; 20/18, f. 233, Confidential News Report, 10 August 1960.

CHAPTER TWENTY-SEVEN

The Monckton Report

The Federal and British Reaction to It, and the Review Conference, July–December 1960

THE purpose of the Monckton Commission was to prepare the ground for the Federal review. However, its recommendation to give the territories qualified options to secede was precisely what the Federal Government had sought to avoid.

This transgression of its terms of reference destroyed the Report's acceptability to the Federal Government. Welensky did say that he would consider the other recommendations, but had to force the British Government to hold the review and, when it did, its choice of delegates rendered remote the likelihood of any progress being made in terms of Article 99. This prospect was dimmed even further by the British Government failing to control the review conference, allowing each delegate to have his say without ever interjecting or expressing an opinion or attempting to steer the speaker towards constructive argument. Macmillan, Macleod and Sandys (Home's successor as Commonwealth Secretary) would stand aloof from the proceedings, allowing them to become farcical.

In late July 1960, as the Monckton Commission began to analyse its evidence, Welensky asked Sandys to set the date for the review because delay would be detrimental to the Federation. It was important that the promise of 1957 to hold the review in 1960 was upheld, and he believed this could be done if it were convened in London in early December and then adjourned to the Federation after Christmas. He wanted to be able to announce this, to dispel the current uncertainty, before the Federal Assembly rose in mid-August.

Sandys, however, wanted to visit the Federation in mid-September before committing himself to anything, and asked Welensky to delay making any statement. Welensky was rather unwilling to comply because he claimed he would face considerable political difficulties if the date were not fixed immediately. He proposed, therefore, to announce that he hoped that the five

Governments would soon agree to convene the review conference in early December.[1]

This exchange was interrupted by a report by Walter Terry in the *Daily Mail* on 15 August which most disturbingly resembled the rough drafts being prepared by the Monckton Commission of its findings. Terry said that the Monckton Report would shock Welensky as it demanded major alterations to the Federation's political structure to meet African aspirations by sharply reducing white power. The economic structure, which the Commission regarded as crucial, however, would be left intact. To bolster African confidence, the British protective power would be retained until the Africans wished its removal. Terry had discovered that Macmillan would have the full Report by the end of August and had already seen a draft. It would be published in mid-October and Terry predicted an explosive reaction. Nevertheless, he said, it was unanimous and was a triumph for Macmillan, although it ignored the effect of the Congo on the Federation's affairs, which would enable Welensky to argue convincingly for caution with regard to Africanisation. However, Terry expected Welensky to realise eventually that the Report offered a basis for negotiation.

Simultaneously, Whitehead discovered that the Report would suggest equal racial representation in the Federal Assembly. Further Press speculation on a trial period of five years for the Federation prompted Barrow, as Acting Prime Minister while Welensky holidayed in Cape Town, to protest to Sandys. Sandys deplored the rumours and suggested that, to stem them, the Report be published earlier than planned.[2] Terry's forecast was so accurate that Evans hurried back from Scotland to London to ask Monckton if there had been a leak. Monckton merely replied that a commissioner must have spoken unguardedly to the Press. He expected the speculation to increase. His explanation convinced the Federal Government there was some substance in the rumours, and it immediately informed him of its concern.[3]

Evans made his final report to Welensky on 27 August. On the previous day, he said, he had met Monckton for the last time and was baffled because he was not giving a lead and had fallen in with the majority of the commissioners without reservation. He had ceased to hold plenary sessions and was writing chapters and submitting them to his sub-committees for comment. Evans acknowledged Monckton's difficulties but did not forgive his failure to lead. Sir David Scott, defending Monckton, claims that he was so acutely aware of the breadth of the differences within his Commission that he deliberately refrained from giving too firm a lead.[4] Scott makes no mention of the leaks.

[1] Welensky Papers, 20/1, ff. 66–67, Welensky to Duncan Sandys, 28 July 1960; f. 59, M. R. Metcalf to Welensky, 11 August 1960; f. 58, Welensky to C. J. M. Alport, 13 August 1960.

[2] Welensky Papers, 7/11, f. 28, J. A. Clark to Welensky, 16 August 1960; *Evening Standard*, 15 August 1960; Welensky Papers, 20/1, f. 44, Barrow to Sandys, 25 August 1960; f. 42, M. R. Metcalf to Barrow, 31 August 1960.

[3] Welensky Papers, 20/10, f. 12, Barrett to Parry, 16 August 1960; f. 11, same to same, 17 August 1960; f. 10, Parry to Barrett, 18 August 1960.

[4] *Ibid.*, 20/16, f. 7, Evans to Welensky, 27 August 1960; D. Scott, *Ambassador in Black and White: Thirty Years of Changing Africa* (London, 1981), p. 76.

Evans had discovered that the Report would be signed on 2 September but, because it would be edited thereafter, that Sandys would not bring copies with him to Salisbury which he was planning to visit in mid-September. Evans had also asked again about the leaks, but Monckton had weakly claimed that, though he had read "the Riot Act", he could do little more because none of the commissioners would admit their guilt. He had only his suspicions and could not act. Evans had heard that W. M. Chirwa was using Stonehouse and Fox-Pitt to write his minority report. Habanyama had been lost to the enemies of Federation, but Katilungu and Gondwe would sign the main Report. Evans had interviewed the European commissioners from the Federation and was particularly annoyed with Sir Victor Robinson because he would only say that the Report was not "too bad" and, indeed, was better than he had expected. Beadle puzzled Evans because he was writing several minority reports, and his intentions remained mysterious. Beadle supported the reversion of functions to the territories and equal racial representation, but opposed any lowering of franchise qualifications. He said that, although two recommendations would infuriate Welensky, they would give him room to manoeuvre. He was seeking to lure the British commissioners into the middle of the road to assist Welensky when he came to negotiate. To him, the British opinion was crucial and it was imperative to attempt to modify it. Ellman-Brown and Woodrow Cross were also writing a minority report advocating equal racial representation. Such activity pleased Evans because he believed that the more minority reports there were, the better the Federal cause would be served. He lauded A. E. P. Robinson and Taylor as the real Federal champions even though he disagreed with their decision to sign the Report. They had fought off many of the more revolutionary ideas. Evans expected Welensky to condemn most vehemently much of the Report, including its language. Evans had discovered that secession was recommended but hedged by qualifications which A. E. P. Robinson and Taylor had secured. He wanted a refusal of secession but believed that this might have induced an opposite reaction from the British commissioners. Instead Taylor and Robinson had succeeded in watering it down to the point where it would have little effect. They were pleased with their achievements and would report fully. However, Evans expected Welensky to disapprove of that particular chapter. They had opposed the transfer of agriculture and health, but would allow the reversion of education despite Evans's strenuous disagreement.

Before Robinson and Taylor could report, Macmillan told Welensky that he expected to publish the Report in the third week of October as he was most anxious to prevent further leakage prejudicing the review. He also announced that Jones was to succeed Armitage and would lead the Nyasaland delegation at the review. Macmillan added that he had seen roneoed copies of the Report. Welensky asked for one as soon as possible, and agreed that there should be the earliest publication because the leaks were already making it difficult for him not to comment, particularly as it was clear that a loosening of the Federation and a five year trial period had been recommended. He noted that Barrow had already warned Sandys of the serious view he would take of such recommendations. As if seeking to confirm Welensky's fears, the

African Daily News proclaimed on 5 September that whatever the Report said, the Federation was doomed and that Welensky would possibly be its last Prime Minister.[5]

On 6 September Robinson and Taylor composed their detailed chapter-by-chapter explanation and criticism of the Report.[6] *The Report of the Advisory Commission on the Review of the Constitution of Rhodesia and Nyasaland* (Command 1148) comprised 19 chapters and a minority report by Chirwa and Habanyama. The Report was signed by 23 out of the 25 commissioners, but only eight did so without reservation. Chapter One contained the introduction, the terms of reference and other matters. Chapter Two gave the history of the Federation, while Chapter Three contained an account of the views which the Commission had gathered. It had found a considerable degree of political bullying in the northern territories but, nonetheless, believed that the dislike of the Federation there was not only widespread, sincere and of long standing, but almost pathological. This was associated with a hatred of Southern Rhodesia. The hope that these attitudes would be softened by the economic advances had not been realised and the genuine fear was that British protection would be replaced by white domination from Salisbury. The oft-proclaimed desire of the Federal leadership to enhance the status of the Federation had only deepened this fear, while events elsewhere in Africa were also having a powerful effect and made it appear that the white community blocked African aspirations. Federation had not been commended to the northern Africans but nonetheless they would have been hostile. Equally important was the failure to take significant steps towards demonstrating the reality of partnership. Racial discrimination was still particularly galling in Southern Rhodesia and specially affected the emerging middle class. Aside from the indignities they suffered, the Africans believed that the Federal Government provided better educational and agricultural services, and thus thought that the benefits of the Federation were for Europeans only. Furthermore, after 1957 the Africans no longer trusted the British Government to overrule the Federal Government. The reconstituted African Affairs Board was regarded as an insufficient and unreliable safeguard. The siting of the Federal capital in Southern Rhodesia and the influx of white immigrants only increased African fears. "Federation" had become a hated word and should be changed.

However, most of these findings did not apply to Southern Rhodesia where many Africans supported the Federation for a number of reasons. One was to strengthen their numerical position *vis-à-vis* the European by association with the large northern African communities. They were more aware of the economic benefits of the Federation and, in any case, the Federal Government seemed more liberal than their own. Some feared that the Federation's disintegration would lead to Southern Rhodesia joining South Africa and the consequent implementation of *apartheid*. Nevertheless, the Southern Rhodesian Africans criticised the implementation of partnership and wanted a greater political role. Although there was also support from the Europeans,

[5] Welensky Papers, 20/10, f. 7, W. S. Parker to Welensky, 31 August 1960; f. 4, Welensky to Macmillan, 3 September 1960.

[6] *Ibid.*, 18/41, ff. 1–16, A. E. P. Robinson and R. M. Taylor to Welensky, 6 September 1960.

Asians and Coloureds for the Federation, the Commission concluded that such was the hostility of the northern Africans that the Federation could not endure unreformed.

In Chapter Four, the Commission recognised the advantages and achievements of the Federation. It had a healthy, expanding economy, utilising the common market of the three territories, their enhanced credit-worthiness and complementary economies. The Federation had attracted £804 000 000 in capital investment, and the national income had risen from £303 000 000 to £440 000 000 in 1959. Exports had increased dramatically, Kariba had been built, industries had been nurtured and imports cut. Expenditure on the social services had been doubled and, should they revert to the territories, they would cost more and function less efficiently. If the Federation were dismembered, markets would contract and employment opportunities diminish. The credit-worthiness, which was probably the greatest achievement, would disappear and the three territories would have to seek aid on their own for their ill-balanced economies which had much less to offer by way of securities. Britain would incur heavy liabilities for the current Federal loans and would have a moral obligation to prevent economic collapse. The demise of the Federation would prejudice the attainment of racial partnership and the failure of the great experiment in race relations would profoundly affect the rest of Africa. It would be an admission that there was no hope for any multi-racial community in Africa because the differences of race and colour were irreconcilable. The Commission rejected that verdict and would prefer merely to recast the Federation in a form which was more acceptable to its inhabitants. A. E. P. Robinson and R. M. Taylor thought that this conclusion would provide the lever to induce the British Government to exercise its authority in the North, and to decide how quickly to make concessions.

Chapter Five contained the general conclusions on a solution but dwelt first on how ill-suited the territories had been for a federation. One had been virtually self-governing, while the others were subordinate to Britain. Southern Rhodesia had been firmly under the control of the local whites, while the northern territories had started towards African self-government in accordance with Colonial Office policy. African rejection of closer association had been noticed by the Bledisloe Commission but, nevertheless, the Federation was founded on the hope that African opinion would change. Quite the reverse, African opposition had reached such an intensity that only drastic and fundamental structural changes to the Federation and Southern Rhodesia would dispel it. It was pointless, therefore, to continue on the current course because ultimately the Federation would have to rest on general acceptance or be maintained by force. Prompt and far-reaching reforms were required if the current advantages were to be maintained.

The Commission had examined and rejected alternative forms of association. These were the Central African Alliance, a loose consultative association and a copy of the East African High Commission. The first would be rejected by the Africans, and the second and third would lack sufficient central control. With the exception of Katilungu and Gondwe, the commissioners recommended that the Federation should continue but with a major reduction in Federal functions and a number of radical changes affecting the composition of the Federal Assembly, the franchise, the machinery of co-operation and the protection of minorities. The territories would resume responsibility for all matters relating to the daily lives of the people, but the Federal Government would continue to manage the economy, external affairs and defence. Partnership would be truly implemented through the legislature and the franchise, while deep-seated racial fears would be answered by safeguards.

The Commission acknowledged that its terms of reference confined it to constitutional matters, but felt it had to advise that everything could not be achieved by constitutional changes alone. It was most important to demonstrate that the Federation was not an obstacle to African constitutional progress by immediately implementing political advancement in the northern territories. Action was also needed on racial discrimination, on the promotion of economic development, on the re-siting of the Federal capital, and the re-naming of the Federation. No form of federation would survive without popular support, and thus the Commission recommended that, under certain conditions, the territories should be given the opportunity to secede. It is interesting that neither A. E. P. Robinson nor Taylor dissented from this conclusion.

The detailed recommendations were made in the remaining chapters. The composition of the Federal Assembly and its revised franchise were described in Chapter Six. The size of the Assembly, the Report said, should not be reduced, but Africans should secure a higher proportion of seats therein. The franchise should ensure representation of the broad opinion of both races. It should remain qualitative but without devalued or weighted votes and should include Africans of experience and judgment who lacked the income and educational qualifications.

The commissioners could not agree on the distribution of seats and offered several courses. The first was to divide the Assembly into three equal parts: the first would accommodate Europeans elected on a communal roll; the second, Africans elected on a communal roll; and the third, representatives of both races elected on a common roll. Both communal rolls would have low qualifications. To a small number of commissioners, the great preponderance of Africans prescribed an African majority in Parliament, but most commissioners thought that support could best be won for the Federation by providing equal racial representation. Others preferred a gradual attainment of the latter. The majority of commissioners demanded the immediate adoption of a common roll or at least a proclamation that it was the ultimate objective. They would rely on delimitation to secure the representation of each race. They chose a House of 60 MPs and a Speaker, with 30 African seats (ten for each territory) and 17 European seats for Southern Rhodesia, ten for Northern Rhodesia and three for Nyasaland. The majority wanted a committee to study the franchise, but the minority thought that it should be settled at the Federal review. Points to be borne in mind when considering the franchise were the waiving of the literacy test, for those who qualified in other ways, and the question of varying the qualifications to meet territorial circumstances to ensure that voters on the territorial rolls were not disqualified. Finally, the question of separate representation for Asians and Coloureds had to be considered.

Woodrow Cross and Ellman-Brown, however, did not like parity or the lowering of the franchise qualifications or the radical alteration of the territorial representation. Parity was particularly objectionable because thereby racialism would be introduced into the highest legislative body, contradicting the Commission's desire to see partnership introduced effectively. Instead, they wanted to broaden the current franchise to recognise age, position and experience. They would increase Northern Rhodesia's representation by three at the expense of Nyasaland and would provide a seat for Asians. In addition, they would increase the lower roll seats from eight to 17. Mrs Huxley, Professor Jack, McCleland, A. E. P. Robinson and Taylor also rejected parity and advocated a combination of communal and common roll representation. Robinson and Taylor told Welensky of their long battle to preserve the Federal Assembly in its current form. They had been defeated but had succeeded in securing a recommendation for a similar-sized House. They advised the Federal Government to draw attention to the diversity of suggestions as an illustration of the complexity of the subject, and to claim that there was need for further study before the review.

Chapter Seven advised the British Government to declare immediately that further constitutional advance towards self-government in Northern Rhodesia would be made and that a conference would be convened as soon as possible. The bulk of the commissioners recommended an African majority in the Northern Rhodesian legislature and an unofficial majority in the Executive Council. Some thought that it was too soon to have an African majority, while Gondwe and Katilungu wanted one in the Executive Council. If the franchise could not be lowered, then the Commission suggested that there could be special seats for tribal authorities. It urged that the authority of the Chiefs should be maintained and that intimidation had to be stamped out. The special position of the Barotse needed separate consideration.

Chapter Eight dealt with the allocation of functions. The Commission believed that everything relating to the day-to-day life of the people had to be a territorial responsibility. There should be no division on a racial basis. External relations and the regulation of the economy were clearly Federal subjects, but all the commissioners agreed that non-African education, roads and prisons should revert to the territories. The majority of them also wanted to transfer health and non-African agriculture. The Commission recommended that education should be supervised by a council comprising the three territorial Ministers of Education and the Federal Minister for Higher Education. A. E. P. Robinson told Welensky that a Mr Woodhead, the education authority of the Colonial Office, had recommended the continual improvement of European education to keep pace with Britain. Robinson thought that this could be useful ammunitition should the African nationalists demand that European education be held at the current standard or be debased to provide equal racial facilities.

The Commission decided in Chapter Nine that the Federal Government should keep its broad taxing powers and fiscal arrangements. In Chapter Ten it proposed the improvement of the machinery of co-operation by the institution of regular inter-governmental meetings and of an advisory economic development council and, perhaps, a tariff advisory committee. In Chapter

Eleven, the Commission repeated its recommendation that all forms of racial discrimination should be abolished, and in a minority report, Crawley, Molson, Gondwe and Katilungu decried the recent decision to reinforce the Federal Army with purely European units and, in addition, the formation on the Copperbelt of a European Home Guard.

Chapter Twelve dealt with the constitutional safeguards which would comprise a declaration of rights and a constitutional council. The twelve members of the Federal constitutional council would be members of similar territorial councils and would be appointed by the Governor-General and the four Chief Justices. The northern territorial constitutional councils would in each case comprise a chairman and at least six members appointed by the Governor in consultation with the Chief Justice and the Secretary of State. Southern Rhodesia would devise its own form but in a manner which would ensure its independence. The commissioners, however, could not agree as to what form racial representation should take on these councils or if they should be non-racial in character. They recommended that the councils should not veto legislation but should be able to delay it and report on it to the legislatures if it seemed to be discriminatory. The councils would not affect emergency legislation but the latter would have to be renewed every two months. Legislation would be reserved for the Monarch's pleasure as long as the two northern territories remained protectorates. The bills of rights and constitutional councils would be entrenched in the relevant Constitutions and could only be amended by two-thirds majorities and special referenda. They would be retained as special features of the Constitutions when the territories became self-governing.

Chapter Thirteen recommended that the name of the Federation should be changed and that, while for the moment, Salisbury should remain the administrative capital, the Federal Assembly should meet in each of the territories in turn. Later the Federal Government should weigh the political disadvantages of Salisbury against its administrative and financial advantages. Chapter Fourteen recommended the long desired locally-recruited civil service for the Federation and the three territories. Chapter Fifteen called for British financial assistance for the northern territories.

Chapter Sixteen examined the question of secession and found, like Professor Jennings, that the current Constitution conferred no express or implied right to secede.[7] The attainment of responsible government did not impart such a right and only a British Act of Parliament would do so. However, the Commission believed that the principle of secession was not incompatible with the theory of federation and recommended that the Federal review should discuss secession. It thought that a declaration of intent by the British Government to permit secession (if it were requested after a certain time or when a certain stage was reached — such as the attainment of self-government) would be most beneficial and could ensure that the reformed Federation was given a fair trial. Indeed, the Commission urged the British Government to make such a declaration. Any territory which seceded would be responsible for its share of the Federal public debt and it was most

[7] *Ibid.*, 20/16, f. 99, Memorandum by Sir Ivor Jennings, 23 July 1960.

desirable that it should thereafter enter a customs union. Most of the commissioners thought that it was unnecessary to prescribe the precise method of ascertaining the wishes of the inhabitants on secession, but some disagreed. The Commission proposed that the declaration of intent by the British Government should be included in the amended Federal constitutional preamble.

Chapter Seventeen dealt with the elements of subordination and recommended that the current practice for choosing a Governor-General should be continued until the Federation was fully independent. The right of appeal to the Privy Council should be entrenched and could obtain after the Federation achieved full independence. The Commission urged that effect should be given to the agreement of 1957 to allow the Federation to legislate with external effect. There should be no change in the powers relating to foreign affairs, but the Governor-General would no longer reserve legislation if the proposed safeguards were adopted with the exception, in the interim, of the constitutional amendment. The right of the British Parliament to legislate for the Federation, and the application of the Colonial Laws Validity Act, 1865, would have to be retained to provide for the future constitutional development of the Federation.

The programme for constitutional advancement was contained in Chapter Eighteen on which the Commission recommended that there should be no delay. A new constitution for Northern Rhodesia and a readjustment of the Southern Rhodesian Constitution should be effected before the Federal review. The Federation, in the view of the Commission, could only attain full independence when all the territories were fully self-governing. It would do so after a fixed period for the consideration of secession, if the British Government adopted that recommendation, or the Federal Government might be allowed to demand independence the moment that one of its territories opted to secede.

Fourteen different reservations by the commissioners littered the Report and, finally, appended to it was the minority report of Habanyama and Chirwa. They agreed with many of the recommendations but could not accept the continued existence of the Federation because it was not based on consent. They felt that the Report failed to deal effectively with the all-important question of constitutional advancement in the territories, and declared that it was intolerable that there should be a further period of the imposition of the unacceptable Federation. They were willing to test this through a referendum of all the inhabitants on the subject of secession but without the recommended delay. They criticised the current system, attitudes and practices in the Federation and, in particular, in Southern Rhodesia. They welcomed the current talk of providing seats for Africans in the Southern Rhodesian House but knew that the Europeans would prevent the Africans from dominating the electoral roll. The transfer of control of the defence forces to the Federal Government they depicted as a betrayal. To them the economic development had resulted only in the European and Southern Rhodesia getting the lion's share. The lack of co-operation between the Governments had also led to uneven development. Chirwa and Habanyama decried the failure of the Monckton Report to deal with Southern

Rhodesian constitutional advancement or to recommend an ultimate goal for the constitutional progress of the territories. What was needed was a British declaration that it aimed to implement a full democratic system based on universal suffrage. If Southern Rhodesia made a like declaration, the political atmosphere would be transformed.

Chirwa and Habanyama believed that political advancement had to be accelerated. As the Northern Rhodesian Africans had been most annoyed that Nyasaland alone had received a new Constitution, a Northern Rhodesian conference had to be convened before the review. Nothing less than an African majority would satisfy the Africans, and a chief minister should be drawn from amongst their ranks. A qualified franchise was acceptable but only for a limited time. Two-thirds of the Southern Rhodesian House should be Africans. The councils of state of Chirwa and Habanyama would have powers to act. They sought the immediate return of agriculture, health and education — including higher education — to the territories. They would add immigration because Stonehouse wished to visit the Federation again. The Federal Government would keep its economic powers, but the Federal Assembly would be reformed to reflect the population ratio. The franchise would be adjusted to achieve this aim. The European would retain a valuable role but not domination.

It would be some days before either the letter from Robinson and Taylor or the Monckton Report would arrive in Salisbury and could be studied by the Federal Government. The Federal Cabinet, with the exception of Welensky who was on holiday, however, was especially busy with the ramifications of the crisis in the Congo and a stream of refugees, while warily watching the UN forces occupy that country.

Preparations were in hand for the visit from Sandys, and Southern Rhodesia was attracting a great deal of attention with Whitehead predicting a considerable liberalisation of the Constitution, and Todd proclaiming that events in the Congo, together with urban unrest in Southern Rhodesia, spelt the end to white rule. The National Democratic Party declared that, no matter what reforms Whitehead achieved, the Africans would not register as voters.

The Monckton Commission had welcomed the change in attitude in Southern Rhodesian governing circles and, without doubt, would have approved of the recommendations of a select committee of the Southern Rhodesian Assembly for the abolition of discrimination with regard to land.[8] This, if implemented, would have been a timely, enlightened move, 19 years before it was actually accomplished. There can be no doubt that the white fears of a massive African intrusion into their areas would not have been realised because only an insignificant number of Africans could have afforded to buy either farms or urban properties in the white areas. The removal of such discrimination would have denied the African nationalists ammunititon which they were later to use with devastating effect. However, the recommendation of the select committee could hardly have come at a worse moment

[8] *Ibid.*, 25/273, f. 15, Notes for Discussion with Sandys, 7 September 1960; *The Rhodesia Herald*, 20 & 27 August 1960; *Second Report of the Select Committee on the Resettlement of Natives*, LASC (1960) (Salisbury, 1960); SR *Debates* (Salisbury), Vol. 45, Col. 1548 f., 18 August 1960.

with the European alarmed by the Congo and Africa generally. When adopted by the Southern Rhodesian division of the UFP, the recommendation gave the Rhodesian Front (soon to be formed from the nucleus of the Dominion Party) one of the main planks of its successful electoral platform. Depicting the Land Apportionment Act as the *Magna Carta* of the European, the Rhodesian Front proposed to defend it while securing independence for Southern Rhodesia to preserve the *status quo*. Thus the UFP would give the DP the rallying point which hitherto it had lacked. Enlightened though the proposal might have been, it was, in terms of the sentiments of the electorate, before its time. Whitehead would prove incapable of conquering the fears of the embattled whites who were beginning to react to the aggressive displays by the African nationalists by retreating into the laager. The virtual collapse of the Central Africa Party was symptomatic of this retreat.

Welensky grew angry at the defeatism which abounded even before the findings of the Monckton Commission were publicly known.[9] Nevertheless, in the New Year, Whitehead managed to promulgate legislation which gave the African the right to own land in certain designated areas.

The mood of the moment was reviewed by Federal intelligence in preparation for the negotiations with Sandys. It believed that the African nationalist movements had not yet won over more than 20 per cent of the Africans. Communism had made few inroads, but many of the left-wing organisations which supported African nationalism had been penetrated. Russia was beaming propaganda broadcasts at the Federation, and Africans were being attracted to conferences and universities behind the Iron Curtain. Thus Federal intelligence believed, the threat from Communism would intensify. The Pan-African organisations, it said, had the potential to threaten the Federation but, as yet, they lacked strong leadership. Likewise, within the Federation, there was no unity between the movements and only a degree of contact. They were financed by the All-Africa Peoples' Convention, the Afro-Asian Peoples' Solidarity Conference, Ghana, Christian Action and sources in the United States, notably the American Committee on Africa.

Federal intelligence found that, despite the disappointment over the terms of the Nyasaland constitutional agreement tension had eased in that territory when it was realised that a considerable advance had been achieved. However, the European remained concerned at Banda's verbal attacks on his opponents and the physical assaults by his young thugs on those not belonging to the Malawi Congress Party. Banda was reportedly concerned about these assaults but did not condemn them publicly. The conviction of certain members of the MCP had been greeted with warm relief, illustrating their unpopularity. The officials drafting the legislation to effect the Nyasaland constitutional agreement were consulting Banda regularly and gathered he would demand an early election. His MCP was looking forward to its next major event which was its first annual conference, on 21 September, to which Nyerere of Tanganyika, Lumumba, Tom Mboya of Kenya, Kaunda and Mawema (president of Southern Rhodesia's National Democratic Party) had been invited. At that moment it could be expected to demonstrate its strength and

[9] Welensky Papers, 43/*Salisbury*, Welensky to Lord Salisbury, 18 August 1960.

its prestige. The air of uncertainty was afflicting Nyasaland to the extent that the Asian businessmen were exporting their capital, and the Federal Army was keeping a wary eye on its askari.

Turning to Northern Rhodesia, Federal intelligence said that tension had abated there after the United National Independence Party had modified its claim for independence by October. Kaunda, who had avoided a threatened schism, had managed to persuade UNIP that his negotiations with Sir Evelyn Hone and Macleod should not be imperilled. Nonetheless, Federal intelligence said, UNIP planned a vigorous non-violent campaign if the negotiations failed. Disturbances could be expected if the Monckton Report indicated that only violence would end the Federation, or if it reinforced the position of the moderates. A recent Race Relations Ordinance had opened hotels and public places to all races and had been greeted with some ugly incidents and a death could spoil everything. The UNIP leadership appeared uneasy, with Kaunda, Sipalo and Sokota eyeing each other with suspicion.

By contrast, Federal intelligence found that racial tension in Southern Rhodesia had increased after the arrest of some members of the National Democratic Party. This Party, it said, had become without doubt the mouthpiece for African opinion, as the moderate Africans, although concerned at the violence, had accepted that it was the only organisation which would make any headway. The disarray of the Central Africa Party, unemployment, and the mounting cost of living, as well as the feeling that 1960 was "Africa's Year", had contributed. The Southern Rhodesian Government was unveiling a programme of reform, but the NDP was quick to attribute this to its agitation. The proscription of the NDP was pointless because another organisation would simply replace it. The multi-racial political Parties would continue to attract members but most Africans thought that a purely African Party was necessary if their demands were to be sufficiently pressed. A multiracial "National Indaba" was being planned but could only improve the situation if its recommendations were officially adopted. It would do considerable harm if they were not. Federal intelligence concluded that the Monckton Commission could have a similar effect.

Federal intelligence also reviewed the Congo and warned that, if Lumumba secured control of the whole area, the danger to the Federation from saboteurs trained behind the Iron Curtain would increase immeasurably. The reason for this belief was that the Russians and the Czechs would be behind any victory by Lumumba. The task of retaining the Federation within the Western sphere of influence would be much more difficult. Any weakening of the economies through secession would only play into the hands of the subversive, and there was little hope that the seceded territories would be able to resist the seduction of the Communist world.[10]

Federal officials suggested to Welensky that Sandys should be reminded that Greenfield had demanded the review in December and that the Declaration of 1957 had, in fact, specified October. Sandys, they said, should be made to understand the urgency created by the current political uncertainty which was affecting capital investment, business, immigration and creating

[10] *Ibid.*, 25/273, f. 13, FISB Security Appreciation, 8 September 1960.

unemployment, and which would be aggravated by any controversial recommendation by Monckton. There would still be adequate time before December for studying the Monckton Report and defining positions. The immediate task would be to digest the Monckton Report which could be done before Sandys completed his visit. Then the Governments would have to decide what they wished to discuss before the Federal review. They could do this at heads of Government level without special arrangement. If necessary the British Government could send out another Minister for informal negotiations. However, nothing should delay the review. The question of who would attend the review had also to be settled. It was known that the northern delegations would be large and would not be drawn entirely from the legislatures. However, the Federal officials advised that, apart from genuine experts like Professor Jennings, observers should not be admitted despite the precedent of the Nyasaland Conference.

The officials advised Welensky to emphasise the Federal distress at the Monckton leaks and to remind Sandys that anything exceeding the terms of reference would be repudiated. He should be warned that, if the leaks became embarrassing, Welensky would break his silence. The Federal Government wanted the Report published by 10 October because its Parliament would sit a week later.

Welensky would declare, the officials suggested, that he was concerned about the comments of Banda and would insist on public reassurance on secession, on the delay of the implementation of the new Constitution until after the review, and on the impossibility of the premature appointment of Banda to the Executive Council. Sandys would also have to ensure that Macleod would resist demands for a Northern Rhodesian constitutional conference in 1961. Finally, Welensky should dwell on the dangers of the Congo, of Russian intervention there, and the submergence of Tshombe.[11]

The Congo, in fact, was a subject with which Barrow had to deal in the absence of Welensky. He had written to Macmillan after receiving a message from Tshombe that, while the West observed the UN Resolution, Russia was sending aid and military and civil advisers to Lumumba. Tshombe believed that Katanga could not hold out against such odds for very long and was seeking aircraft, weapons and markets from the Federation. Barrow had promised only to examine the question of trade. He found a real danger in the neutral attitude of the NATO powers and, like Tshombe, he urged the West to meet its moral and political obligations to ensure that Katanga did not become another Hungary.[12]

However, Macmillan simply replied that, if NATO appeared to take sides, it could be accused of intervening for its own advantage, which could have an adverse effect in the UN. It might antagonise the African states and frustrate the aim of keeping the great powers out of Africa. Any Western support for Katanga would not only destroy African confidence in the UN, but would alienate influential men like Nkrumah. Macmillan believed that the UN should restore order in the whole of the Congo to prevent it being lost to Communism. He was glad that Barrow had refused to supply arms because, if

[11] *Ibid.*, f. 15, Notes for Discussion with Sandys, 7 September 1960.
[12] *Ibid.*, 20/12, f. 207, Barrow to Macmillan, 31 August 1960.

he had done so, he would have placed the British and Federal Governments in an unjustifiable position.[13]

Welensky returned from holiday to greet Sandys on 12 September and, while there is no record in the Welensky Papers of their first discussion, he has said that he tried to reach an understanding on problems which were not of his own making. However, he found Sandys as inscrutable as Macleod. He appeared dogged, tenacious and ruthless, and they made little progress.[14]

Welensky agreed to furnish Sandys with written proposals, and prefaced these with a declaration that a joint approach to the review seemed impossible because he was utterly opposed to secession and to the lowering of the franchise. Rejecting the Monckton revision of the Federal Assembly, he considered that the Commission had transgressed its terms of reference. He proposed further discussions when Sandys returned from the North, where he had gone.[15]

More information can be gleaned from Welensky's report to Joelson. He said that they had spent two and a half hours together and he had liked Sandys's clear mind, despite his tough and brusque manner. Sandys had wondered if the Federation could be saved but had read the Monckton Report and could be forgiven for being influenced by its ideas. Welensky had been bitterly disappointed to find that the leaks on the Report had been accurate, and described it as one of the worst documents he had ever seen. Its whole purpose was to weaken the Federation for no other reason than political expediency "to satisfy the ravings of the lunatic fringe in the United Kingdom and the African extremists here". He had boiled with rage while reading it and had been tempted to tell Macmillan of his outright rejection. He had held his tongue because of the opportunity to discuss it with Sandys. He justified his feeling of outrage by revealing that he had an assurance in writing from Macmillan that secession would not be considered. It had also been confirmed by the best legal opinion that secession was *ultra vires* of the Federal Constitution even after the Federation attained independence. It appeared that the British Government preferred that the Federation should die a lingering death. The Report would destroy any prospect of borrowing. Welensky was surprised that the Federal commissioners had signed the Report, but understood their dilemma. The position had been aggravated by Whitehead's threat of secession and his appointment of two Monckton commissioners who were out-and-out secessionists.[16]

Welensky warned Major Patrick Wall that, if the Report were adopted at the review, he would resign and fight an election on it with Whitehead's support.[17]

In this belligerent mood, Welensky wrote to Macleod on 16 September to remind him that he had already rejected as intolerable the appointment of Banda and a colleague to the Executive Council of Nyasaland. Banda's conduct, he said, had made a mockery of his pledges in London. He had persistently avowed to "smash" the Federation and denounced his opponents

[13] *Ibid.*, f. 205, Macmillan to Barrow, 10 September 1960.
[14] Sir Roy Welensky, *Welensky's 4 000 Days* (London, 1964), p. 270.
[15] Welensky Papers, 20/1, f. 39, Welensky to Sandys, 13 September 1960.
[16] *Ibid.*, 24/151, ff. 128–129, Welensky to F. S. Joelson, 13 September 1960.
[17] *Ibid.*, 43/*Wall*, Welensky to Major P. Wall, 14 September 1960.

in a manner calculated to inspire physical assaults on them. He had also publicly misrepresented the Nyasaland constitutional agreement. Welensky conceded that, after the election, Banda would be appointed to the Executive Council, but saw no reason to promote him beforehand. Once in the Executive Council, Banda could not be denied sight of secret and confidential information which, Welensky warned, would be used against him and the UFP at a crucial moment. Welensky did not share the belief that the acceptance of office would make Banda responsible, although he might act thus to gain his ends. He made no mention to Macleod, though he did later to Sandys, of a request from Banda for the release of the detainees which the Federal Cabinet had dismissed as unjustified.

Welensky rejected Macleod's suggestion that a Northern Rhodesian constitutional conference be held in 1961 or, perhaps, before the review. He did so, he said, because on 19 March 1960 Macleod had declared that he was not considering any revision, though he could not anticipate the outcome of the review. He could only conclude that Macleod contemplated radical change which would seriously unsettle the Federation. Macleod had spoken about Northern Rhodesia going forward at "our" pace and in "our" time, but the African nationalists would immediately demand concessions matching those in Nyasaland and for greater African membership of the Executive Council. Welensky added that his fears, that the Monckton Report would be disastrous, were confirmed. Its mere publication would destroy the Federation and, almost without exception, its recommendations would strengthen the hands of the extremists. Its philosphy of appeasement would rule out advancement on merit. "The secession proposals," Welensky said, "are the final straw and I consider them to be a complete breach of the understandings upon which I agreed to the appointment of the Commission." He believed that, if the situation were not most carefully handled, the end of civilised and responsible government in Central Africa was at hand. He knew that this might not seem to be "such a disaster in Whitehall. But those of us who have made our homes and lives here have no alternative but to resist to the bitter end".[18]

Macleod's suggestions were not all that concerned the Federal Cabinet about the northern territories because the chairman of the African Affairs Board, the Reverend J. L. Pretorius, had suggested the holding of the Nyasaland elections before the review. He argued that Banda had realised that his followers would not allow him to accept an appointment to the Executive Council without being elected. Pretorius believed, like Macleod, that this would make Banda amenable to a compromise on secession at the review.[19] It is curious that a man of Pretorius's experience should have believed this because Banda never gave a hint of being anything but uncompromising.

Welensky mentioned nothing of this when he informed Sandys of the Federal Government's views on the Nyasaland detainees. He recalled that it had reluctantly agreed to Banda's release because the "whitewashing" by the Devlin Commission had made it impossible to detain him any longer. However, it had been reassured that further releases would be viewed very differently because Chipembere and the two Chisizas had been clearly impli-

[18] *Ibid.*, 20/18, f. 106, Welensky to Macleod, 16 September 1960.
[19] *Ibid.*, 25/205, f. 41, J. L. Pretorius to G. S. Jones, 8 September 1960.

cated in the plans for violence. Home and Macleod, Welensky said, had promised to resist any pressure until after the review but, within six months, had recanted even though, with the campaign of intimidation in full swing, the moment was most inopportune. Intimidation was curbing political freedom, and the release would simply ensure that the Nyasaland general election was unrepresentative. However, Welensky conceded that this was a matter solely for Jones, and promised not to criticise publicly any decision taken.[20] It was perhaps a mistake for him to say this because Jones did not hesitate in surrendering to Banda and releasing the detainees on 28 September.

Although no record has yet been seen of the second and final round of the discussions, it is known that the date and venue of the Federal review was fixed at 5 December in London. There is also a list of Welensky's tentative suggestions which were submitted to Sandys. They were tentative, but they displayed a determination to reject secession. Welensky acknowledged that the non-Government delegates at the review could raise the question, but he expected all Governments to condemn it. Racial parity in the Federal Assembly, or elections on communal rolls, were equally unacceptable. The number of seats reserved for African Members could be increased but only if the principle of "fading out" was maintained. Amendment of the Electoral Act, to lessen the influence of the upper roll on the election of these Africans, was similarly unacceptable. Its commitment to the maintenance of standards, forbad the Federal Government from accepting any lowering of the upper roll qualifications, although it might allow a broadening to include responsible people. As it believed in partnership and not in entrenching power in the hands of either race, it was equally opposed to African majorities in the Northern Rhodesian Legislative and Executive Councils.

The Federal Government, Welensky continued, agreed that higher and technical education could become concurrent but would not relinquish non-African education. It was not, however, averse to the establishment of multiracial private schools. It would consider some decentralisation of the health service into territorial or local government hands, but would not do likewise with non-African agriculture. It would, however, consider making both varieties of agriculture concurrent. It would retain its control of the defence forces and its right to establish a federal police force. It would willingly hand back the administration of roads, old age pensions, the care of minors, and town planning, but would have some reservations about the prison service.

As a safeguard, the Federal Government would accept a bill of rights provided that it did not interfere with the maintenance of standards in non-African education even though African education had to lag behind for some time. A council of state was an appropriate protection provided its membership was not dependent on concurrent service with a territorial council. Consideration should be given to reference from the council to the Federal Supreme Court.

To compensate for concessions on matters such as the composition of the Federal Assembly, the Federal Government would expect the British powers of reservation to be removed as well as the Colonial Laws Validity Act. Also

[20] *Ibid.*, 20/1, f. 34, Welensky to Sandys, 20 September 1960.

there would have to be statutory recognition of the 1957 Declaration *vis-à-vis* the power of the British Parliament to legislate for the Federation. Finally, the Federal Government wanted to be able to enact extra-territorial legislation and to be consulted about the appointment of the Governor-General.[21]

Perhaps because he had made little headway with Sandys, Welensky warned Macmillan that, if the Monckton Report were published unaltered, the consequences would be disastrous. The Commission, he said, had exceeded its terms of reference and its recommendations on secession were totally unacceptable. He was confident that Macmillan would reject secession if he recalled that, in 1952-3, Lord Swinton had dismissed a secession clause as a "sentence of death", and Lyttelton had pledged that the review would not consider it. This had been reaffirmed in 1957 and, when the terms of reference had been discussed, Macmillan had agreed that there should neither be an inquest nor the consideration of secession. Thereafter, Welensky told Macmillan, he had committed himself irrevocably against secession, and the Labour Party and the African nationalists had boycotted the Commission because it could not be considered. If the Commission had disagreed, it should have said so, because its witnesses could have expressed their views on the effects of secession. Consequently, Welensky said, it appeared that he had misled the public, and this forced him to reject the recommendations on secession. He asked Macmillan to do likewise. He assumed that the Report could not be amended, but warned of the gravest consequences if they did not issue a joint statement when it was published. The appeasement of African nationalism made the Report so unsatisfactory that Welensky warned that he was tempted to use the pretext of the transgressions of the terms of reference to repudiate it entirely. He was being urged to do this, but, to save the review, he would consider changes in the composition of the Federal Assembly and a re-distribution of functions, provided there was a *quid pro quo*. He would not accept parity or the debasing of the franchise. The late publication of the Report had compelled him to defer his parliamentary session to 25 October, but the first debate would force him to declare his rejection of secession. He hoped, therefore, that Macmillan would not embarrass him by adhering to the custom of welcoming the Report by saying that it contained useful and constructive suggestions.[22]

Welensky informed Lord Salisbury that the Monckton Report was "shocking". Its proposal that the territories might secede when they reached a certain degree of self-government, he said, had undone everything achieved in 1953 and had reduced the Federation to a status less than that of Southern Rhodesia. Because he had received from Macmillan a written reassurance, he had believed secession would not be considered, and the major political Parties had expressed no opinion on it to the Commission. Sandys had confessed that the British Cabinet had been taken by surprise at the interpretation of the terms of reference. Welensky found himself in the position of having misled the Federal public, albeit in good faith, through trusting the British Government. He had told Sandys that, because he had been so gullible, he was not fit to lead the Federation at the review, and must resign.

[21] *Ibid.*, 7/27, f. 136, Tentative Suggestions submitted to Sandys, 21 September 1960.
[22] *Ibid.*, 29/50, f. 8, Welensky to Macmillan, 21 September 1960.

What annoyed him particularly was that Monckton had not hinted that he would ignore the terms of reference. Sandys had repeatedly reminded Welensky that the Report contained no more than recommendations, but he had retorted: "You don't realise you are dealing with Africans not Europeans, and Africans will take the recommendations as a sort of British Government view of the minimum they ought to receive."[23]

Sandys extended his visit, thereby giving the impression of a crisis. The Press believed that Welensky might ignore the Report and that the situation was, therefore, explosive. Nothing is known of further negotiations, but after Sandys's departure, Welensky commented privately that not only was Sandys ignorant of Federal affairs, but that rumours that Britain had made a change of policy on Africa, which had prompted Lennox-Boyd to resign, seemed confirmed. Lennox-Boyd, however, has since denied that he resigned for anything other than personal reasons. Welensky told Greenfield that, while he would not compromise on secession, he would not comment on the other recommendations until the review. He would concentrate on the argument that not only had the Commission exceeded its powers, but it had not given the major political Parties the opportunity to comment on secession.[24]

On his return to London, Sandys had another bombshell to drop and did so perhaps because he misunderstood the mood of the Federal Government. He revealed to Welensky that he and Macleod had discussed with Macmillan advancing the announcement on the Northern Rhodesian constitutional conference which was hitherto to coincide with the publication of the Monckton Report. The reason he gave was that there was a clear threat of trouble in early October in Northern Rhodesia. Furthermore, the Labour Party had asked to see Macleod about Northern Rhodesia. As it would be most unfortunate if it appeared that concessions had been wrung out of them by disorder and political pressure, the British Ministers proposed to issue the statement in two days' time, on 28 September, but promised Welensky a draft before it was released.[25] This was a typical example of Macleod's technique of hurrying the Federal Government from one crisis to another to give it little time to resist or even think.

The draft arrived on the morrow and said that Macleod had authorised informal discussions with the political Parties in preparation for a formal conference at the earliest possible date. Welensky replied immediately, saying the warning of the announcement alone had given rise to embarrassing local speculation. He insisted, successfully, that the statement be amended to say

[23] *Ibid.*, 43/*Salisbury*, Welensky to Lord Salisbury, 21 September 1960. Sir David Scott (Scott, *Ambassador in Black and White*, *op. cit.*, pp. 80–81) mulling over Welensky's reaction to the Monckton Report, concludes that it was the product of advice from Lord Salisbury *et al.* This letter to Lord Salisbury makes it clear that this was not so. The issue of the terms of reference is crucial to understanding the Federal reaction because any recommendation of secession meant the end of the Federation. Welensky might say after the event that he was poorly advised, but his reaction on reading the Report was to reject it and this was a product of Macmillan's evasion over the terms of reference. Lord Salisbury had not yet read the Report when Welensky wrote to him. — JRTW.

[24] *The Rhodesia Herald*, 23 September 1960; Welensky Papers, 42/50, f. 21, Welensky to D. Taylor, 26 September 1960; Author's interview with Lord Boyd of Merton; Welensky Papers, 7/26, f. 68, Welensky to Greenfield, 26 September 1960.

[25] Welensky Papers, 20/4, f. 145, Sandys to Welensky, 26 September 1960.

that Macleod had consulted Hone and Roberts and that they had agreed that the conference should be held concurrently with the review. After the statement was released, Roberts revealed that he had proposed this to Welensky because Northern Rhodesia would not settle down until the conference had been held.[26] Nevertheless, Macleod had stolen a march.

Macmillan felt he ought to placate Welensky and, replying to his dispatch of 21 September, described how he and Sandys had discussed the Federal problems at length. Being greatly concerned about the Federation, they thought that it had gained immensely from the wholehearted recommendation of the Monckton Commission that it should continue. He suggested that the Commission should be formally thanked in a public statement which indicated that its recommendations were being studied. He acknowledged, however, that the secession recommendation was something which he and Welensky would have to solve, but he believed that neither Government should say anything before the publication of the Report.[27]

Sandys also wrote and, characteristically blunt, stated that neither he nor Macmillan thought that the terms of reference had been exceeded even though the secession recommendation would be an embarrassment when confronting the Labour Party. He thanked Welensky for his frankness and claimed to understand Welensky's point of view. He enclosed a draft of a statement on the Monckton Report. This reminded the public that the Commission had been appointed to advise on measures for the continuation of the Federation and the furtherance of its aims. The Governments had arrived at a clear understanding and had publicly said that the commissioners would exceed their terms of reference if they recommended the dissolution of Federation or the secession of any of its territories. This had not happened because the Commission had only suggested that the territories be given a qualified option to withdraw from the Federation in certain circumstances at a future date. This recommendation had not been foreseen by the British and Federal Governments when they had drawn up the terms of reference, but they noted that the Commission had stressed the advantages of the Federation and had suggested secession as a means of making it more acceptable to its population. The Governments, moreover, agreed that a solution was imperative because the current situation was damaging the economic prospects of the Federation.[28] Welensky immediately asked for an amendment recording that Macmillan had given him a written assurance that secession would not be considered. This had justified his statements in the Federal Assembly. He wanted the Governments to reaffirm that neither secession nor looser forms of association would be considered at the review.[29]

Then he drafted a statement for issue if the British Government failed to

[26] *Ibid.*, 20/4, f. 144, Text of Macleod's proposed announcement, 27 September 1960; f. 143, H. N. Parry to M. R. Metcalf, 27 September 1960; f. 142, Press Communiqué No. 140, Northern Rhodesian Government Information Department, 28 September 1960; *The Rhodesia Herald*, 29 September 1960.

[27] Welensky Papers, 20/1, f. 26, Macmillan to Welensky, 27 September 1960.

[28] *Ibid.*, f. 24, Sandys to Welensky, 27 September 1960; f. 22, Draft Statement on the Monckton Report, 27 September 1960.

[29] *Ibid.*, f. 19, Welensky to Sandys, 28 September 1960.

agree with him. In it, he recalled his statement of 21 July 1959 rejecting an inquest or any consideration of the Federation's continuance. On 23 July 1959, he had declared that the Commission would not examine secession or dissolution and he had received a clear reassurance from Macmillan on 28 November 1959 on this. Accordingly, the Federal Government had refused to place either subject on the agenda of the review. In support of his assertions, he quoted Lyttelton who had said in 1952:

> "Who is going to take service with a Federation under a perpetual sentence of death?"

Lyttelton had also said in 1953:

> "The review will not decide whether Federation should be abolished or discontinued . . . it is a conference to make such alterations in the detailed workings of the Constitution as experience of its working has shown to be necessary during this decade, the first decade of its life."

Welensky quoted Swinton on not providing advice on divorce in the marriage service. He would reject secession, Welensky averred, not just because his honour was at stake, but because a fundamental principle was involved. The recommendation was a gross discourtesy to himself and Macmillan after their clear indication that secession would not be considered. Therefore he was forced to hold the British Government to Macmillan's undertaking to stand by the terms of reference. He believed that the Commission should have invited the Governments to give evidence on secession and, certainly, its witnesses had thought that secession was not under consideration. His Party had fought the last election, in 1958, on maintaining the integrity of the Federation, and he would not deviate from it.[30]

Sandys thereupon decided that a joint statement might be inappropriate lest it seem that the British and Federal Governments were anticipating the outcome of the review. However, he wanted to attempt another draft. He conceded that anything which contributed to further uncertainty would be detrimental to the Federal economy, but felt that discussion on secession at the review could not be prevented. Thus, if the question were asked if secession could be considered, the British Government would have to reply in the affirmative.[31]

Welensky replied the same day, 1 October, preferring separate statements because the British Government would not support him on secession. Nevertheless, he thought it would be wiser not to display any differences, adding that any mention of permitting discussion on secession would create the impression that the British Government was reconsidering its support for the Federation. He asked, therefore, for a reaffirmation that the Federation served the best interests of all the inhabitants and that the British Government would approach the review in the spirit of 1957.[32]

[30] *Ibid.*, ff. 8–11, Draft Statement by Welensky, 28 September 1960.
[31] *Ibid.*, f. 13, Sandys to Welensky, 1 October 1960.
[32] *Ibid.*, f. 7, Welensky to Sandys, 1 October 1960.

Welensky provoked Macmillan to remind him that the Report was not a legal judgment which had to be accepted or rejected. Its value lay in the consideration by intelligent, well-disposed people of the various problems which had to be solved at the review. He would not include the reaffirmation which Welensky sought and suggested that he and Welensky should merely say that the Report was just a contribution — albeit an important one — to the preparation for the review.[33]

Lord Salisbury wrote to Welensky expressing his shock at the flouting of the terms of reference. Ashamed of the current leadership of his Party, he wondered if the British Government would accept the Report in its entirety as Welensky expected. He advised him not to resign because no one thought him either gullible or unfit to govern. On the contrary, Welensky would be seen as an honest man who had been betrayed by those whom he had every reason to trust. Resignation would only detrimentally affect his authority. Salisbury considered that Welensky was right to wait for the British reaction but thought that he should publish Macmillan's reassurances whatever happened.[34]

Welensky replied that Macmillan and Sandys had not said that they would accept the Report without reservation and had conceded that, if there were a period in which secession would be allowed, it would only do incalculable harm. What angered Welensky was that no one in the Colonial or Commonwealth Relations Offices could remember anything about the events of 1952 and 1953. Welensky told Salisbury that, when he stressed this point, Sandys had replied: "Oh, times have changed since then." It embittered Welensky that any promise made to a white man was regarded as irrelevant. He recounted the recent exchange on the Report and promised to consider Salisbury's advice on resignation. If, as Sandys had said, any subject could be examined at the review, he would be forced to make a stand. He had lost all faith in the British Government, despite its protestations of friendship, and would prefer that it should declare that it would break up the Federation, if that were its intention. It was probable that the Union Jack would fly nowhere in Southern Africa within a decade. Indeed, a visiting Conservative parliamentarian had sat in his office and warned that his Government would "sell the white man down the river" if it suited it. It appeared, Welensky concluded, that the Federation was an embarrassment.[35]

Greenfield recalled that Dingle Foot had informed Banda that the terms of reference would be ignored. When tackled by Welensky, Monckton had hotly denied this assertion and had offered to show Welensky his notes on his interview with Foot. Greenfield wondered if it would be unkind to remind the British Government and Monckton that Foot's prediction had come true.[36]

Welensky's mood cannot have been lightened by Kaunda, on the same day, 5 October, proclaiming a victory for his Party by forcing the British Government to hold a Northern Rhodesian constitutional conference concurrent

[33] *Ibid.*, f. 5, Metcalf to Welensky, 3 October 1960.
[34] *Ibid.*, 43/*Salisbury*, Lord Salisbury to Welensky, 27 September 1960.
[35] *Ibid.*, Welensky to Salisbury, 4 October 1960.
[36] *Ibid.*, 7/22, f. 56, Greenfield to Welensky, 5 October 1960.

with the review. He demanded adult suffrage, 44 African seats in a house of 58, and an Executive Council of three officials and nine unofficials chosen on the advice of the leader of the majority party.[37]

On 7 October, Welensky informed Macmillan of his disappointment that they would not present a united front. He still thought it would be fatal to British interests in the Federation to allow discussion on secession at the review. This would only encourage African nationalism while shaking white confidence. It could render the demise of the Federation certain. It was already suffering alarmingly from an economic standpoint. He agreed that the Report was not a binding judgment but that did not lessen the harm its publication would do. If the Governments did nothing, the repercussions would go further than imagined.[38]

As he wrote, a dispatch arrived from Sandys threatening that, if Welensky issued his statement, the British Government would have to reply in an equally spirited fashion, giving the impression of an "unholy row". As this would detrimentally affect the review, he appended a revised statement which he believed went some way to meet Welensky. Although the British Government still maintained that the Commission's recommendation was within its competence, Sandys said that to help Welensky his Government would repudiate it. It would also declare that Welensky had been justified in assuring his public that secession would not be considered. Reference would be made to Macmillan's statements on this subject. It would be acknowledged that it was technically improper for the Commission to have recommended a qualified option to secede even though it had also urged that ways and means should be found for the Federation to continue by securing its widest possible acceptance. These and other relevant matters would be discussed at the review. Sandys revealed that the Monckton Report would be issued on 11 October with the customary expression of gratitude from the British Government. If he would not accept the joint statement, Sandys expected Welensky to comment only on the secession recommendation and asked him to delay for a few hours to avoid the morning Press highlighting the issue.[39]

Welensky, unmoved, continued to threaten to release his statement. Expressing regret at this, because the British Government had been prepared to justify Welensky's interpretation, Sandys withdrew the offer of a joint statement. He reiterated that the terms of reference had not been breached and refused to state publicly that secession would not be discussed at the review because no permanent solution would be found without African support. This was not appeasement, Sandys said, but realism, because support could only be engendered by not inhibiting discussion. A refusal by Welensky to discuss secession publicly would reveal an open breach between them and might render it impossible to convene a representative review conference. This would definitely jeopardise the Federation's future. Sandys acknowledged that his reply was contrary to what Welensky had asked of Macmillan on 7 October, in respect of maintaining confidence in the Federation. Never-

[37] *Northern News*, 6 October 1960.
[38] Welensky Papers, 20/1, ff. 2–3, Welensky to Macmillan, 7 October 1960.
[39] *Ibid.*, 20/2, ff. 174–176, Sandys to Welensky, 7 October 1960; f. 177, Draft Statement by Sandys, 7 October 1960.

theless, he recommended that Welensky speak only on the terms of reference so that the British Government could support him. There should be no reference to the review. He asked to see Welensky's statement as soon as possible.[40]

Welensky turned to Home, informing him that, because of his long association with the Federation and because it appeared that the Federation was a pawn in international politics, he wished him to appreciate his current stand. He would have no choice but to fight against the odds if he were to be told, in effect, that expediency cancelled out British promises made to him. He recalled their agreement on the Commission and subsequent assurances that men of integrity would agree that secession could not be considered. His public statements had led responsible people not to give evidence on secession and consequently he felt that he had failed them. However, he had been persuaded not to resign because neither was it the moment for personal feelings, nor was it timely to submit the Federation to the turmoil of an election. Equally he could not indulge in "double talk" because it was clear the British Government would no longer support the Federation openly. He said this because Sandys had refused to end the British statement with an avowal of support for the Federation and a promise to conduct the review in the spirit of the 1957 Declaration. It seemed clear to him that the British Government did not understand the local consequences of the publication of the Monckton Report. He had hoped for a British repudiation of secession to discourage the African nationalists and to restore African confidence. Denied that, he had to act alone. He had been proved gullible by Dingle Foot who had been right when he told Banda that the terms of reference would be ignored. Home had sent him Foot's denial but the statement so closely resembled that of Monckton's great friend, Shawcross, that collusion was apparent. Clearly Monckton and his close colleagues were determined to recommend secession and had brought the British and Federal Governments to the parting of the ways. Henceforth, both Governments would have to do what they thought best. He expected to see the Federation suffer a similar fate to that of Kenya but warned it would not submit tamely.[41]

Claiming to be depressed by the accusation of a breach of faith, Home replied immediately that he had read the recent correspondence and could find no evidence of betrayal. After all, the British Government was prepared to endorse Welensky's interpretation of the terms of reference. He said he had been surprised by the Commission's recommendation, but could find nothing in the proposed British statement which indicated a lack of support for the Federation. Indeed, he reaffirmed his Government's belief in the Federation. He would not contradict Sandys on the review because he had always believed that open discussion was essential.[42]

Years later, Home told Lord Birkenhead that there had been a technical breach of the assurances given to Welensky and, to that extent, Welensky had a grievance. However, Home was sure that Welensky must have realised that there would be some reference to secession by the Commission because it was

[40] *Ibid.*, ff. 171–173, Sandys to Welensky, 9 October 1960.
[41] *Ibid.*, ff. 169–170, Welensky to Home, 10 October 1960.
[42] *Ibid.*, f. 156, Home to Welensky, 11 October 1960.

well known that it had taken evidence on it. Home thought that the Commission would have been wiser to record that they had heard overwhelming evidence on secession and to have left it at that. Once Welensky rejected the Report, Home believed that the Federation was doomed.[43]

At 4.15 p.m. on 11 October, the Monckton Report was released in London with an accompanying statement by the British Government that the terms of reference had not been intended to cover contemplation of either dissolution or secession. It had, in fact, refused to extend the terms to cover these aspects because they were not in keeping with the Federal review and thus, it said, Welensky had been justified in assuming that neither dissolution nor secession would be recommended. However, the Commission, while stressing the advantages of the Federation, had merely proposed that each territory should be given a qualified option to secede. Sandys had obviously had his way because the statement concluded that, whatever view was taken of this, it was clear that the Federal review had to be free to discuss this and any other relevant matter.[44]

Simultaneously, at a Press conference in Salisbury, Welensky described the recommendation on secession as "completely unacceptable". Otherwise the Report, he said, was a mixture of good and bad, of logic and expediency. It was almost unanimous on the continuation of the Federation and, if it had only left matters there, it would have been regarded as well-intentioned, if impractical at times. However, by recommending secession it had rendered sterile its conclusion that the Federation was beneficial to all. It would have immediate and long-lasting ill effects and had breached the terms of reference and the clear understanding he had been given on its scope. To make his point, Welensky quoted his own statements and the Declaration of 1957 which had ruled out consideration of amalgamation and secession. He noted that the Labour Party had refused to serve because secession could not be considered. The other recommendations could be negotiated, but secession would have to be rejected out of hand because it dishonoured undertakings given to the Federal Government, and would destroy the Federation. Asked what he thought of the recommendation that racial parity should be introduced into the Federal Assembly, Welensky replied that such an introduction of racialism would be a retrograde step. At 8.15 p.m. he spoke on the radio, rejecting the defeatism inherent in the secession recommendation but promising to consider the others. He would adhere to a liberal policy despite his critics at Westminster and elsewhere.[45]

Sir John Moffat claimed that the Commission had realised that the choice lay between a weaker association or no Federation at all. Whitehead criticised the number of reservations, but William Harper rejected any criticism of the Report and, in particular, the secession recommendation because it merely confirmed what the Dominion Party had been saying for years. The divisions within the Dominion Party, however, were amply illustrated by Winston

[43] Lord Birkenhead, *Walter Monckton: The Life of Viscount Monckton of Brenchley* (London, 1969), p. 358.

[44] Welensky Papers, 20/2, f. 158, Statement by the British Government, 11 October 1960.

[45] *Ibid.*, 7/22, f. 125, Welensky's Press Conference, Federal Assembly, 11 October 1960; 20/2, ff. 162–166, Welensky's Broadcast, 11 October 1960.

Field decrying the Report because it would contribute so little to a just and realistic settlement. He acknowledged that the Commission had only offered advice and that many of its recommendations would never be implemented. He particularly disliked the recommendation on agriculture because it was contrary to all the evidence which had been submitted. More objectionable was the proposal to introduce racialism into Federal politics. The adoption of the Report, he warned, would force him to lead a secessionist movement in Southern Rhodesia while there was still time. He would do this regardless of the economic consequences and despite his efforts to keep the territories together because domination of Southern Rhodesia by the two northern territories was intolerable.[46]

Kaunda and Banda were quick to reject the Report. Aleke Banda, general secretary of the Malawi Congress Party, avowed that the Report would not discourage his Party on secession. He did not believe that any adjustments to the Federation would make it acceptable. The Associated Chambers of Commerce of Rhodesia and Nyasaland and the Association of Rhodesian and Nyasaland Industries confirmed that the Report would harm the economy, and the Rhodesian National Farmers' Union attacked it for its inconsistency. A newspaper poll, conducted in Salisbury, revealed total support for Welensky's attitude.[47]

At the Conservative Party Conference on 11 October, Macleod recalled that Macmillan had said in the Federation that the purpose of the Commission was not to destroy the Federation but to find how it could prosper. Thus he welcomed the emphasis on the value of the Federation. This made it, he said, possible to discuss secession. Nevertheless, it was clear that, at the review, grave and momentous decisions would have to be taken.[48]

When the Commons debated the Report, Callaghan predictably claimed that the Commission had echoed what his Party had been saying for years. It had confirmed the African opposition to the Federation and that the latter could not continue unaltered. He was opposed to the Balkanisation of Africa but agreed that the only way to preserve the Federation was to give the territories the right to withdraw. He accepted that the abolition of racial discrimination in Southern Rhodesia, the introduction of immediate racial parity in the Federal Assembly, followed shortly by an African majority, together with a redistribution of functions, would attract African support and save the Federation.[49]

Welensky had more to say — in two interviews for British television. In the first he declared that the British Government would have no right to raise the subject of secession and drew support from Lord Salisbury who publicly denounced the recommendation as *ultra vires*. Salisbury wondered why Macmillan had not insisted on its excision. In the second interview, Welensky, answering a question on the nature of the assurances, would only say that they were binding on the British Government. He could not disclose them

[46] *The Rhodesia Herald*, 12 October 1960; Welensky Papers, 7/22, f. 49, Statement by Field, 13 October 1960.
[47] *The Rhodesia Herald*, 12 October 1960.
[48] *Ibid.*
[49] House of Commons *Hansard* (London), Vol. 629, Col. 370 f., 3 November 1960.

because of the confidentiality of inter-government correspondence. He acknowledged that, because of the lack of a written constitution, the British Parliament could legislate on anything. It could vote to turn Canada and South Africa into Crown Colonies. It could also "pass an Act turning me into a sixteen-year-old girl but it would not have much practical effect".[50]

Welensky told his private correspondents that he had discovered an interesting point, that only late in the day, when all the evidence had been gathered, had the majority of the commissioners realised that the territories did not have an inherent right to secede upon attaining self-government. He had gathered that, in their haste to scramble out of Africa, the British regarded the Europeans as expendable. Southern Rhodesia was experiencing its worst outbreak of violence but, having lent Whitehead troops and having persuaded him not to take drastic action, Welensky was pleased to see peace returning after a considerable number of arrests. In turn, Welensky wrote that he was grateful for Whitehead's support with regard to the Monckton Report, even though his comments in January 1960 on secession had done considerable damage. The violence in Southern Rhodesia, however, led to the postponement of a visit from C. J. M. Alport, the Under-Secretary of State. This worried Whitehead and he protested to the British Government because he wished to complete his constitutional revision before the Federal review in December.[51]

The debate in the Federal Assembly on the Report gave Welensky a further opportunity to air his views. He reminded everyone that the Commission's recommendations were not binding and declared that his purpose was to gather the opinions of Parliament. His quarrel with the Commission was that it had given "the benediction with one hand and the death stab with the other". His disagreement with the British Government was that it disregarded its earlier assurances of faith in the Federation and preferred to make hair-splitting points on interpretation. The Commission had argued that the Federation could be dissolved when an eminent Commonwealth authority — Professor Jennings — had confirmed that the Act of 1953 regarded the Federation as indestructible and that secession was only possible through a British Act of Parliament which, according to constitutional convention, had to be sanctioned by the Federal Government. Welensky agreed that the Federation could not be maintained by force but that the purpose of the review was to discover what adjustments were needed to ensure that it gained willing acceptance. In passing, he noted that, despite provisions for secession, no one suggested that Canada, Nigeria or the United States were maintained by force.

Welensky said he could not accept the argument that the recommendation for secession was designed to hold the Federation together and he hoped that the reaction of the African nationalists to the Report had convinced the commissioners of their mistake. They had highlighted the achievements of the Federation but had failed to compare them with those of other countries

[50] *The Rhodesia Herald*, 15 October 1960; *The Daily Telegraph*, 20 October 1960; Welensky Papers, 25/240A, f. 137, Welensky to Lord Robins, 21 October 1960.

[51] Welensky Papers, 25/240A, f. 137, Welensky to Lord Robins, 21 October 1960; 20/9A/A, f. 62, Whitehead to Metcalf, 20 October 1960.

south of the Sahara. They had dwelt on the frustration of aspirations but not on the means to avoid it. He agreed with them that intimidation had to be eradicated but he wondered how, having acknowledged the latter, the commissioners could claim to have accurately measured African opinion. If the African nationalists truly represented African opinion, they would not have to resort to intimidation. The Commission, in its judgment on the franchise, had laid itself open to a charge of superficiality and had contradicted itself in suggesting parity while insisting that there should be no racial divisions in the legislatures. Welensky intended to ignore the recommendations on the franchise because it had only been introduced two years previously, and with British consent. He declared positively that his Government would not be influenced by expediency when considering any transfer of functions, and would avoid upsetting the civil service. He reaffirmed his faith in the Federation and avowed that his Government would be guided only by reason, logic and the principles of good government. It would not accept any appeasement.

Field noted that, despite everything, the inquest had been held. He took credit for alerting Welensky after making an early discovery that secession would be discussed. He described the Report as "bad" and promised support for Welensky. He suggested that the Report should be simply ignored.

The debate ran its predictable course with the northern Africans rejecting the Federation and the Europeans, in the main, the Report. Robert Moffat declared that the opinion of such eminent men could not be ignored. He criticised the Report for not recognising the implacable African opposition but believed that, if the African nationalists and the Governments sought a solution, it would be much like that suggested. He acknowledged the intimidation but did not attribute the expressions of opposition to it. He believed that, until the African was given a reasonable share of government, the violence would continue. He preferred the minority report but considered the Report itself praiseworthy.[52]

While the Federal debate continued, informal discussions began on the Northern Rhodesian Constitution. Kaunda declared that the Federation was dying and demanded a legislature of 61 Members, of whom 44 would be Africans. In Southern Rhodesia, Whitehead, of course, was anxious to complete his constitutional revision. Welensky, as has been seen, agreed but found Whitehead's other proposal to introduce draconian security legislation a potential source of embarrassment and advised that nothing should be done until the constitutional negotiations were complete. Whitehead, however, was in no mood to agree as he had been forced to flee from a hostile meeting in Harare and his Ministers had been confronted by angry Europeans who threatened to arm themselves and take the law into their hands. As a result, the notorious Southern Rhodesian Law and Order (Maintenance) Bill was unveiled on 1 November.[53]

Departures from accepted practices, such as the suggestion of preventive

[52] Fed R & N *Debates* (Salisbury), Vol. 14, Col. 3142 f., 25 October 1960.

[53] Welensky Papers, 7/12, f. 341, Note on Informal Discussions at Government House, Lusaka, 21 October 1960; *Central African Post*, 28 October 1960; Welensky Papers, 20/9A, f. 59, Whitehead to Metcalf, 31 October 1960; 24/1, ff. 5–6, Welensky to A. Dalgleish, 27 October 1960.

detention beyond the reach of the courts, would provoke a storm in Southern Rhodesian and a reaction from the British Government. However, before that happened, Welensky was embroiled in yet another clash with the British Government, provoked by a dispatch from London at the end of October, confirming that the northern territorial delegations at the Federal review would reflect the main shades of opinion. To make matters worse, the British Government indicated that it might include in its own delegation members of the Labour Party. Welensky reacted with "amazement". He conceded that all shades of opinion should be represented but could find no precedent for the inclusion of the Labour Party. He wondered facetiously why the Liberal Party should be ignored but, becoming serious, rejected the suggestion firmly because of the anti-Federal attitude of the Labour Party and its advocacy of secession. He trusted that the idea would be dropped because it would be so harmful. He could not understand why the review conference was described as "advisory" because he had understood that it would take decisions like its predecessors in 1952-3.[54]

The Southern Rhodesian Government agreed with Welensky and found confirmation in Article 99 of the Federal Constitution. Thus, it said, because decisions were to be taken, Southern Rhodesia would prefer to appoint only parliamentarians to its delegation rather than representatives of broad shades of opinion. However, as there were no Africans in Parliament, four Africans would be invited, one being Advocate Herbert Chitepo of the National Democratic Party. The Southern Rhodesian Government hoped that the difference in the basis of choosing delegates would not inhibit the taking of decisions because the current state of uncertainty was damaging both economic affairs and race relations. It was most surprised by the proposal to invite the Labour Party and also wondered if the Liberals would be asked.[55]

The relationship with the British Government was only worsened, on 1 November, by a message from Macmillan announcing that he had telegraphed a copy of his recent speech in the Commons. He hoped that Welensky would agree that he had fairly described the circumstances surrounding the Monckton Commission. The telegram revealed that, after describing the origins of both the Federal review and the Commission, Macmillan had immediately drawn attention to the almost unanimous verdict that the Federation should continue. His Government had refused to allow the Commission to consider dissolution but, on 21 July and 24 November 1959, he had conceded freedom to hear any evidence and to decide what use to make of it. He had sent Welensky the same message and had not been surprised that Welensky had concluded that secession could not be discussed and that the Commission had thus exceeded its terms of reference. Macmillan disagreed with this as the Commission's recommendation had been in the context of how the Federation should continue. Clearly, the Commission felt that, without its recommendation on secession, its other proposals were useless. The correctness of this

[54] Welensky Papers, 20/2, f. 154, Views of the British Government on the Composition of the Delegations to the Federal Review Conference, October 1960; f. 152, M. J. Lamb to H. G. M. Bass, 1 November 1960.

[55] *Ibid.*, ff. 44–46, Views of the Southern Rhodesian Government on the Composition of the Delegations to the Federal Review Conference, 1 November 1960.

would be judged at the review. Macmillan had denied that he had prior knowledge of the secession recommendation as neither he nor Monckton had thought it proper for them to discuss the Report between themselves. He had found two remarkable facts. The first was that none of the commissioners had ever questioned whether secession was outside the Commission's terms of reference. Secondly, most of the recommendations were hedged with reservations but the one on secession had enjoyed virtual unanimity. It had been suggested — by Lord Salisbury — that Macmillan should have returned the Report because it was *ultra vires*, but to do that would have been unrealistic and discourteous to the distinguished people who had given up months of their time. It would have been different if a commissioner had queried the validity of the Report. Gaitskell had asked if he would consider a request for secession but Macmillan, as the Report had recommended, had reserved it for the review. He agreed with the Commission but did not want to prejudice the review. His main concern was to clear the misunderstanding on the terms of reference and to emphasise the spirit in which the Report had been written. It was necessary for all to approach the review with patience, understanding and faith.[56]

In reply, Welensky unfailingly pointed out that the telegram had arrived after the statement had been delivered. He did not comment on the discourtesy of this action, but criticised Macmillan's account. Macmillan had acknowledged in his covering letter that he had made a mistake in delivery in the Commons but felt that it was inconsequential. Welensky disagreed because Macmillan had said, referring to his assurances, that he had used "the same words" rather than "the same sense". As this had an important difference in meaning, Welensky insisted on a public correction because Macmillan had certainly not written the same words in his message as he had used in Parliament. Welensky warned that he felt so strongly about this that, in the Federal debate on the Report, he would reject Macmillan's account and offer to publish the exchange of messages to allow people to judge which version was correct. He would also challenge Macmillan's assertion that none of the commissioners had asked whether secession lay outside the terms of reference because he knew that at least two of them had done so at the outset.[57]

Rubbing salt into the wound on this particular issue, Welensky did not wait for Macmillan to reply and issued a Press statement claiming that the commissioners had changed their minds on secession after their legal advisers had informed them that evidence on it was admissible. His own legal advice on this verdict was that it was erroneous. He regretted that Macmillan should have been misinformed.[58]

On 3 November Macmillan drew Welensky's attention to the correction which he had just made in the Commons. He was willing to agree to Welensky publishing their dispatches, if it were necessary, on condition that he deleted the reference to the Labour Party in his dispatch of 24 November 1959. If Welensky published the material, he would publicly say that he and

[56] *Ibid.*, 20/2, f. 151, Macmillan to Welensky, 1 November 1960; ff. 149–150, Macmillan's Statement in the Commons, 1 November 1960.
[57] *Ibid.*, f. 147, Welensky to Macmillan, 1 November 1960.
[58] *Ibid.*, 7/22, f. 32, Welensky's Press Statement, 2 November 1960.

Welensky had agreed that this was all that was relevant to the point at issue. However, in all friendship, he felt impelled to say that it was, perhaps, unwise to be the first to breach the tradition of the confidential exchange between Commonwealth Prime Ministers. Alternatively, he thought that Welensky should say in the debate that he had received explicit assurances from Macmillan in November 1959 which justified his belief that the Commission would not deal with secession and that, accordingly, it had exceeded its terms of reference. He could also say that Macmillan had protested about this matter on receipt of the Report and had taken appropriate action.[59]

Macmillan has said that he looked forward to being challenged by Welensky because he did not think that his reputation would suffer by the publication as he had not altered the terms of reference. Furthermore, he had not been responsible for the manner in which the Commission conducted itself or for its interpretation of the terms of reference. The only action which he could have taken was to suppress the Report, which was unthinkable. He claims, therefore, to have been disappointed when Welensky withdrew the challenge so as not to be the first to break a Commonwealth tradition. Macmillan recorded in his diary: "I am glad, because I think it would be a very bad precedent. But Lord Salisbury has revived the charge of 'bad faith' in a letter to *The Times* (if not directly at least by innuendo) which is rather a bore, as I cannot now answer it by publishing the text."[60]

Welensky did not withdraw his threat without regret and he reminded Macmillan that he felt betrayed because on 24 November 1959 Macmillan had written to assure him that: "We agreed the terms of reference and we will stand by them." He acknowledged that the Report could not have been suppressed but that he had at least expected Macmillan to agree that the Governments could not discuss secession at the review. He revealed that Professor Jennings had ruled the Commission's view of secession to be constitutionally unsound and that secession was impossible. This proved, Welensky said, that secession had not been in the terms of reference.[61]

If Macmillan was grateful for Welensky's withdrawal, he did not say so, but in reply regretted the deterioration in their personal relationship. However, he professed to understand how heavy were the responsibilities of the Federal and Southern Rhodesian Governments.[62]

Welensky naturally commented on this exchange when he wound up the Federal debate on 10 November. He defended his reliance on Macmillan's promises and said that he would not have accepted the Commission if he had known it would recommend secession. However, he would resist pressure to publish Macmillan's assurances because it would break a custom observed by Governments. Likewise, he would not resign because the consequent general election would concentrate solely on the Anglo-Federal relationship and give the Monckton Report undue importance. If he had been gullible, his electorate would deal with him at the next election. He would not comment on the detail of the Report because his Government was still studying it. He knew

[59] *Ibid.*, 20/2, ff. 141–142, Metcalf to W. S. Parker, 3 November 1960.
[60] H. Macmillan, *At the End of the Day* (London, 1973), p. 300.
[61] Welensky Papers, 20/2, f. 137, Welensky to Macmillan, 3 November 1960.
[62] *Ibid.*, f. 134, Macmillan to Welensky, 8 November 1960.

that the Federation could not be maintained by force but he would preserve law and order. He would make a determined effort to find a solution for the Federation but would not assist its violent break-up. He would also reject any lowering of standards and anything which did not foster racial harmony. The urgent need was to increase the productivity and living standards of the lower income groups, because on them depended political progress, and to remove unnecessary discrimination. Finally, he intended to press for improvement in status for both northern territories to provide balance in the Federation and to move towards the goal of independence.[63]

Macmillan had referred to the heavy burden which Southern Rhodesia was carrying but not to its latest controversy. This was to be used by Sandys to cancel Alport's visit which was to have settled the revision of the Southern Rhodesian Constitution before the Federal review on 5 December. The controversy seemingly arose out of Whitehead's determination to proceed with his Law and Order (Maintenance) and Emergency Powers Bills. The recent outbreak of violence had been suppressed but the National Democratic Party had reshuffled its leadership on 31 October and had replaced, as president, Michael Mawema with Joshua Nkomo to give it a new look of militancy. The next day, Reginald Knight, the Minister of Justice, had unveiled the Bills — neither of which, incidentally, Welensky liked.[64]

The nature of the Bills, in refusing access to the courts, was controversial enough without the Federal Chief Justice, Sir Robert Tredgold, choosing to resign over them. He proclaimed to the Press, and wrote in his autobiography, that it appeared to him that Knight had sat down with the Declaration of Human Rights and had erased it clause by clause.[65] His resignation did much to damage Whitehead's standing in the eyes of many, including the British, but it was, in fact, something which Tredgold had been contemplating for some time and the Bills simply provided the catalyst. Indeed, Whitehead had recently asked Welensky if he knew that his Federal Chief Justice had been "dabbling in politics" with a group in Bulawayo. Welensky had heard something to that effect but promised to ask Tredgold for confirmation. He summoned Tredgold who unhesitatingly acknowledged that the allegation was true.

He shocked Welensky even more by saying that Whitehead had failed and that he, Tredgold, should replace him. Welensky lectured him on the duties of a Chief Justice, but Tredgold was unrepentant, and further surprised him by asking him to persuade Whitehead to stand down. Tredgold clearly did not see any difficulty in securing a seat and in persuading the Southern Rhodesian division of the UFP to accept him as their leader.

Welensky relayed Tredgold's astonishing request to Whitehead who, not surprisingly, rejected it. However, Tredgold was not entirely discouraged and informed Welensky that he would, nonetheless, resign to enter politics. Welensky asked him to reconsider, but 24 hours later received his written

[63] Fed R & N *Debates* (Salisbury), Vol. 14, Col. 4082 f., 10 November 1960.
[64] Welensky Papers, 20/9A, f. 56, Sandys to Whitehead, 3 November 1960; 24/1, ff. 5–6, Welensky to A. Dalgleish, 27 October 1960.
[65] *The Rhodesia Herald*, 2 November 1960; Sir Robert Tredgold, *The Rhodesia that was my Life* (London, 1968), p. 229.

resignation and read in the Press that he had done so in protest at the repressive legislation. Tredgold, declaring the Bills to be outrageous, called them an unwarranted invasion by the executive into the preserves of the courts. He acknowledged that order had to be maintained by firm and, in some cases, stern measures, but there should be no panic action which would equally harm the innocent and leave a legacy of bitterness which would endure for generations. He proposed a national political front of all the Parties to clear the way for a national government. This would be based on three principles: the maintenance of firm government, without the sacrifice of basic human rights; the whole-hearted co-operation of the races; and the continuation of the Federation. He thought that Whitehead had lost the co-operation of the entire African population when Southern Rhodesia represented the key to the success of the Federation and the Federation was the key to progess in Africa. If Southern Rhodesia did not reform itself, the repercussions would be far reaching.[66]

It seems that Tredgold had taken his political friends in Bulawayo by surprise and, in the event, as Welensky warned Tredgold that it would, the movement fizzled out. Rejecting Tredgold's protest, Whitehead declared he would proceed with his Bills. The United Federal and Dominion Parties promptly spurned Tredgold, leaving only the rump of the Central Africa Party to support him.[67]

Sandys's reaction was to tell Whitehead that Alport could not visit. Whitehead turned to Welensky for help and the latter immediately wrote to Sandys claiming that the unveiling of the legislation had improved public morale, both African and European. He recalled how Tredgold had refused to act as Governor-General when Llewellin died and had even threatened to resign lest his work for the Franchise Commission for Southern Rhodesia should be interrupted. Shortly afterwards, Welensky said, Todd had claimed that, if the Southern Rhodesian Franchise Bill was rejected, both he and Tredgold would resign. A few months later, when acting as Governor-General, Tredgold had written to Home expressing his views on the Federal Electoral Bill, and, because he had not been entitled to do this, he had drawn a further protest from Welensky. Home thereupon had informed Tredgold that he was not entitled to interfere. Recently, in June 1960, Welensky continued, the Federal Government had become aware of efforts to persuade Tredgold to return to the political arena and had subsequently been embarrassed by the spectacle of its Chief Justice dabbling in politics. Bearing this in mind, Welensky said he was sure that Sandys would not want to give the impression of interfering in Southern Rhodesian politics and would realise that the cancellation of Alport's visit would be most unfortunate. He recalled that he and Home had come to a clear understanding that the Southern Rhodesian constitutional revision would be effected before the review and that this understanding had largely influenced the decision to release Banda and to hold the Nyasaland Conference. Thus Welensky declared that he fully sup-

[66] J. M. Greenfield, *Testimony of a Rhodesian Federal* (Bulawayo, 1978), p. 142; Author's interview with Sir Roy Welensky; Welensky Papers, 27/14, f. 22, Welensky to T. P. Cochran, 22 November 1960; *Evening Standard*, 2 November 1960.

[67] *The Rhodesia Herald*, 3 November 1960; Author's interview with Sir Roy Welensky.

ported Whitehead on the timing of the revision and was gravely concerned by the British decision.[68]

Whitehead then also wrote to Sandys that he not only regretted the cancellation but insisted that Southern Rhodesia's constitutional reservations should be removed before the Federal review. He reiterated a request for a conference on 21 November and complained about the number of times he had tried to arrange it. He was most dissatisfied, he said, with the reasons for the postponement because Tredgold's resignation was an internal matter which would not affect any negotiations.[69]

Claiming that the Tredgold affair had been poorly received by the British Press and Parliament, Sandys thanked Welensky for the interesting explanation but would not give way on Whitehead's conference. Instead, he suggested that it should be held concurrently with the Federal review. Whitehead responded by demanding, and receiving, an invitation to informal discussions in London a week before the review. If progress were made, he said, he would consent to a concurrent conference. However, he chided Sandys for commenting on the internal politics of Southern Rhodesia without knowing the latest state of affairs. Whitehead and Welensky thereupon agreed that the convening of the review could be formally announced.[70]

This was done on 13 November, and Banda immediately welcomed it although he declared the Federation was dead and all he wanted was secession. His reason, he said, was out of courtesy to Macleod. In Northern Rhodesia that day Hone lifted the ban on the United National Independence Party imposed in May.[71]

Despite the announcement Welensky painted a gloomy picture for Lord Salisbury and Major Wall because Whitehead was contemplating resignation over the British Government's failure to revise Southern Rhodesia's Constitution before the Federal review. There was a growing anti-British feeling in the Federation, Welensky wrote. In the Congo Lumumba seemed to be consolidating his position. Smallpox had entered the Federation from the Congo and, in Nyasaland, Banda was believed to have taken the care to have himself vaccinated but would not assist the Federal teams which were trying to vaccinate the whole population. However, in Southern Rhodesia the presence of troops had been welcomed by the moderate Africans who had wanted to see their areas policed and patrolled. By contrast, in Nyasaland effective administration had disappeared and the MCP was running its own police. Britain appeared to have decided on disengagement in Africa and the Federation had to pay the price. It was the beginning of the end for the British Commonwealth.[72]

Welensky informed Joelson that he had been pressed by Conservative

[68] Welensky Papers, 20/2, ff. 138–139, Welensky to Sandys, 3 November 1960.

[69] *Ibid.*, 20/9A, f. 53, Whitehead to Sandys, 5 November 1960.

[70] *Ibid.*, 20/2, f. 135, Sandys to Welensky, 8 November 1960; 20/9A, f. 46, Whitehead to Sandys, 11 November 1960; f. 51, Welensky to Sandys, 10 November 1960; f. 49, Sandys to Welensky, 10 November 1960.

[71] *The Rhodesia Herald*, 14 November 1960; *Northern News*, 14 November 1960.

[72] Welensky Papers, 43/*Salisbury*, Welensky to Lord Salisbury, 10 November 1960; 43/*Wall*, Welensky to Major P. Wall, 14 November 1960.

backbenchers to stop harassing their Government but would not comply. It appeared that no one, apart from Lord Salisbury, was prepared to stand up to the Party's leadership. Welensky revealed that Whitehead had also embarrassed his British friends, but his security Bill had been necessary and it was, after all, only a Bill and was still capable of amendment. In any case, Welensky said, there was no doubt that Nkomo and his Party were bent on subversion. Turning to the Federal review, he said that he, like Sandys, expected little from it, but wanted it held because it was prescribed by the Constitution. He knew, however, that no British help would be forthcoming. He was trying to stiffen Roberts to prevent Macleod out-manoeuvring him. Hone was intent on parity of racial representation in the Northern Rhodesian Legislative Council but Welensky said he would not agree. An African majority, he felt, was even more abhorrent because it would destroy the Federation. It was the fear of Macleod's intentions for Northern Rhodesia which underlay his anxiety to have Whitehead's position strengthened before the Federal review.[73]

As Welensky wrote, the report of the National Convention or Indaba was released. The Indaba had been suggested by, amongst others, Sir Charles Cumings, a former Chief Justice of the Sudan and a born Southern Rhodesian. It had met in early November under the chairmanship of the former Governor of Southern Rhodesia, Sir John Kennedy. The report called for Southern Rhodesia to reform itself and to eliminate unfair racial discrimination. It urged the early introduction of a substantial number of African MPs through a broadening of the qualitive franchise and the retention of the multi-racial common roll. It rejected parity or universal suffrage despite the warning of its African delegates that nothing short of this would satisfy African aspirations and restore political confidence and stability.[74]

Macmillan invited the leaders of delegations to spend a weekend at Chequers during the Federal review. He asked Welensky to read the lesson at church on the Sunday but Welensky refused, jokingly telling Gore-Browne that he had done so because, as a Jew, he feared that all the Christians present would be excommunicated. He confided that he and Macmillan did not speak the same language, as the latter was "an exponent of the art of using phraseology loaded with different meanings". He was assured by Lord Salisbury that the correspondence with Macmillan bore out that assumption. However, if that confirmation imparted a feeling of well-being, Welensky had to listen to threats from the NDP, to boycott any Southern Rhodesian constitutional discussions, and to witness a triumphant return by Nkomo from two years of exile.[75]

On 25 November, Welensky left for London saying that he would fight for the continuation of the Federation and would not be party to its lingering demise. Banda, who arrived in London brandishing a wooden spear to show that he was on the warpath, was received by a somewhat hostile Press conference which asked him to send a message to his people to cease resisting

[73] *Ibid.*, 24/151, ff. 105–107, Welensky to F. S. Joelson, 16 November 1960.
[74] *The Rhodesia Herald*, 18 November 1960.
[75] Welensky Papers, 24/74, ff. 229–230, Welensky to Gore-Browne, 21 November 1960; 43/*Salisbury*, Lord Salisbury to Welensky, 21 November 1960; *African Daily News*, 18 November 1960.

vaccination. He refused to comply, he said, because there was no epidemic, only exaggeration by the pro-Welensky Press and, furthermore, he had come to London as a politician and not as a physician. The Federal authorities, nonetheless, noted that they were facing twice the resistance to vaccination compared with 1959 despite the unrest of that year.[76]

Welensky, Whitehead and Sandys discussed Southern Rhodesia on 28 November and, in particular, a British request to increase the size of the Southern Rhodesian delegation to the Federal review to include the NDP, the Central Africa Party and others. Whitehead said his Cabinet, however, would only accede to this if there were a firm British commitment on the Southern Rhodesian constitutional revision. Welensky was anxious to avoid an African boycott of the review and hoped that Sandys would give Whitehead the commitment he sought so that he could justify to his Cabinet the enlargement of the Southern Rhodesian delegation. Sandys, however, rightly thought that the composition of the delegation at the review had little to do with the revision of the Southern Rhodesian Constitution and could not be the subject of a deal. Thus he would promise nothing, but he did think that agreement on the revision was possible if, as safeguards, there were a council of state, a statement on discrimination written into the Constitution and a right of appeal on it to the courts and, ultimately, to the Privy Council.

Whitehead was prepared to welcome these ideas but wanted the removal of the British power of disallowance and the right of Westminster to legislate on subjects which were within the competence of the Southern Rhodesian Government. This presented Sandys with a considerable difficulty because he doubted if his Parliament would acquiesce until Southern Rhodesia was completely independent. It might, however, agree that it could only legislate at the request of the Southern Rhodesian Government. However, by then Whitehead had reconsidered Sandys's suggestions and rejected appeals on political matters to the courts. He knew that the Federal Constitution had a provision for the review of legislation but noted that was by the African Affairs Board which was a political body. He certainly would not accept any proposal that there should be retrospective reviews.

Sandys thought that the retrospective effect could be limited, but thought that his Parliament would reject any protection against discrimination which was less effective than that of the Federal Constitution. In respect of the review, he warned that Whitehead would find himself in difficulties if, by refusing to broaden his delegation to include the main African Parties, he appeared to cause the review's abandonment. The effect would be that the British Government would not be able to give Whitehead the commitment he sought. The meeting agreed that Whitehead would confer with Welensky and consult Sandys again.[77]

Consequently, on the next day, Whitehead and Sandys somewhat startled the Rhodesian Press by announcing that a constitutional conference would be held concurrently with the review and that ten more Southern Rhodesians

[76] *Evening Standard*, 21 November 1960; *The Rhodesia Herald*, 25 November 1960; Welensky Papers, 27/90, f. 81, Memorandum: Dr Banda and Smallpox, 27 November 1960.

[77] Welensky Papers, 11/44, f. 222, Minutes of a Meeting between Sandys, Welensky and Whitehead, London, 28 November 1960.

would attend the review including Coloureds, Asians, and representatives of the NDP and Central Africa Party. Perhaps to dampen any alarm, Whitehead added a comment that it would be at least 15 years before the Africans dominated the Southern Rhodesian Parliament. This might have seemed like a life-time to the British public, but to the Dominion Party and to certain members of the UFP, 1. D. Smith being one, it was unacceptable even then.[78]

Sandys informed Welensky and Whitehead the next day that he had seen Nkomo at the latter's request and had found him reasonable, diffident and pleased to be invited to the review and the Southern Rhodesian conference. Nkomo, however, had wanted to bring ten delegates. Sandys had replied that this would be seen publicly as unreasonable, but Nkomo had promptly asked if he could then bring eight advisers. Sandys said he thought that Nkomo was anxious to have about him the leading members of his Party if he had to make any decisions and had replied that a request for more than one or two advisers would appear equally unreasonable. Nkomo had then wondered if he could attend when a large number of his colleagues had been detained without trial under the new legislation. Sandys had refused to comment on this but, promising to tell Whitehead of it, had warned Nkomo that it would be a grave mistake to make attendance dependent on the release of thc detainees. Nkomo, Sandys said, had seemed to agree.[79]

On 2 December Whitehead told Sandys that he had informed Nkomo that he would only grant him two places but had just heard that Nkomo had declared to the Press that he would not attend unless he was given ten. Whitehead would allow Nkomo one adviser who had to be Southern Rhodesian and not British. Whitehead was annoyed that Sandys should have said anything on the subject of detention with Nkomo because it was purely the concern of the Southern Rhodesian Government. It was a habit of the British Ministers, he asserted, to dabble in matters which did not concern them with extremists who cared little for the fate of most Africans. This practice, he said, made life awkward for him. Sandys, apologising, asked Whitehead to read his note again because he had told Nkomo that detention was entirely a matter for the Southern Rhodesian Premier.[80]

Banda did not leave the limelight to Nkomo and conducted a Press interview from his bed forcefully stating that he would demand secession and would not negotiate on the continuation of the Federation. He dismissed the Southern Rhodesian Europeans as pigheaded and said that "a bunch of fourth-class artisans rule Southern Rhodesia". On 4 December he, Kaunda and Nkomo said that they would attend the review but reserved the right to walk out if it were used to delay the Northern and Southern Rhodesian constitutional talks.[81]

On 5 December, the first day of the Federal Review Conference, the ominous news from Nyasaland was that a small crowd of Africans had stoned the police after Chiume and Chipembere had addressed them. Later the

[78] *The Rhodesia Herald*, 30 November 1960.
[79] Welensky Papers, 30/7, f. 32, Sandys to Welensky and Whitehead, 1 December 1960.
[80] *Ibid.*, f. 33, Whitehead to Sandys, 2 December 1960; f. 31, Sandys to Whitehead, 2 December 1960.
[81] *The Sunday Mail*, 4 December 1960; *The Rhodesia Herald*, 5 December 1960.

house of Katsonga, president of the Christian Democratic Party, was set alight. The news from the Congo was that the Congolese General Mobuto, a former sergeant-major and later a journalist, had arrested Lumumba.[82]

Macmillan and Welensky had dined together on 26 November and Macmillan recalls: "Fortunately, Welensky, although often somewhat impetuous, had a generous mind . . . He was most friendly, although rather pessimistic. He in effect withdrew all his accusations (or imputations) of bad faith against me, although he still feels very bitter against Lord Monckton . . . The stage was now set for the opening of the Conference on the future of Federation."[83] Welensky remembers Macmillan's eyes filling with tears as he claimed that he had been betrayed by Monckton. Also, his view of the relationship between the Governments differs from that of Macmillan. "As the British Government saw it," Welensky says, "I had most tactlessly compelled them to honour at least one of their obligations — their 1957 pledge to hold this Conference —and they were determined to make me pay for my Colonial stubbornness by turning it into a withering indictment of the Federation and all its works, and of myself."[84]

After coffee at 10 a.m. at Lancaster House, the 89 delegates and officials trooped into the Conference Room to be briefly addressed by Macmillan. He urged them to be patient, courageous and charitable. He confessed he had no solution to offer but believed that the delegates could find "a happy outcome" which would lead to peace and stability.[85] They turned to procedural matters and surprised Macmillan by their lack of antagonism. Banda asked if discussion on secession would be allowed and was assured by Macmillan that it would be. The only by-product from this session was a cable from Harry Nkumbula to the *Central African Post* in Lusaka claiming that Kaunda had surrendered to Banda his right to speak for the Africans.[86]

Sandys took the chair on 6 December and Welensky opened the debate by recalling Lyttelton's declaration, on 24 June 1953, that the Review would not decide to abolish or continue the Federation. He noted that the British and Federal Governments had confirmed this in 1957 when speaking of a programme to attain full Commonwealth membership. To him the impressive records of the Federal and territorial Governments indicated that there was little fundamentally wrong with the Federation, though certain improvements were necessary. He believed that the first task of the Conference was to draw up a programme under which the Federation could attain full independence in its own sphere. Such a step was fully justified when, elsewhere in Africa, territories with far less experience were being made independent. It was necessary to remove the British reservations to counter the belief of a large section of the population that the British Government did not trust the Federal Government and that it, and not the latter, remained the effective authority.

[82] Welensky Papers, 8/21, f. 30, Fedinfo. to Welensky, 5 December 1960.
[83] Macmillan, *At the End of the Day*, *op. cit.*, p. 301.
[84] Author's interview with Sir Roy Welensky; Welensky, *4 000 Days*, *op. cit.*, p. 285.
[85] Welensky Papers, 35/7, f. 1, Minutes of First Meeting of the Review Conference, 5 December 1960.
[86] *Central African Post*, 7 December 1960.

Welensky dwelt on the Federal achievements of enfranchising British Protected Persons, creating a non-racial university, a non-racial civil service, abolishing racial discrimination in the Federal services, advancing Africans in industry and other fields, and curbing inflation. He dismissed the fears of the Africans which the Monckton Commission had discovered to be groundless, even if British protection were removed, because the Federal constitutional preamble forbade the introduction of Southern Rhodesian practices in the North. Safeguards were necessary and he would happily accept the councils of state suggested by Monckton. He called on the British Government to fulfil its promise on extra-territorial legislation, and to give statutory effect to the convention which prevented the British Parliament from legislating for the Federation without the express wish of the Federal Government. His Government did not oppose the advancement of the territories provided it was on a non-racial basis and took account of experience and responsibility. He did not agree with the Monckton view that radical alteration was required to ensure Federal survival. He likewise rejected its appeasement of African nationalism. He found its proposals for the Federal Assembly to be contrary to the practices of partnership. Nevertheless, he said, he was keeping an open mind and would consider any scheme which would benefit the Federal people and further Federal objectives.

Chief Mwase of Nyasaland then called for secession because the Federation had been imposed and because Africans feared the loss of their land and freedom. Sir John Moffat of Northern Rhodesia noted that, contrary to expectation, the African opposition to the Federation had intensified with time, and warned that any attempt to ignore this would end in disaster. He decried the lack of genuine attempts to establish the society envisaged in the preamble. The Federation, in its current form, was doomed and the only question was whether it would end by agreement or disagreement. He called the Monckton Report "a truly magnificent achievement" and favoured its idea of a massive reform but knew that neither the Federal nor the Southern Rhodesian Governments would concur. Responsible African opinion to his knowledge did not condemn the Federal system but merely the attempt to preserve white control. He believed that the only possible form was an economic association which might make closer links desirable in the future. The Europeans had to accept the inevitability of majority rule or the future would be grim. He hoped for an agreement which would make non-racialism a reality in the territories.

Field claimed that, despite its misgivings, his Dominion Party had tried to make the Federation work. He declared that the Southern Rhodesian delegation had no intention of destroying the Federation but would not pay any price to preserve it. He questioned the attitude of the British Government because, while it claimed that the Federation was the only way to racial harmony, it did nothing to ensure its success and had not even put across the Federal concept in the northern territories. It had altered the northern constitutions, without regard to Federal wishes, while doing little to develop the northern territories. Indeed, as the British Government withdrew from Africa, he believed that it saw difficulties in maintaining the Federation and favoured its disintegration. Therefore Britain would have to assume full responsibility for the financial and other consequences of its policy. He claimed that there was a Press campaign, which might be inspired, to force Southern Rhodesia to secede.

As the uncertainty was damaging the economy, Field suggested that it should be ended by the adoption of the Central African Alliance plan. He would not be a party to any lowering of standards or territorial changes without consultation with the Federal Government. He would oppose both interference in Southern Rhodesian domestic affairs and the introduction of racial parity in the Federal House. He claimed that Southern Rhodesia would have been a dominion but for the Federation. Southern Rhodesia's sanction and that of the British Government was required for any change and he would not condone the creation of any artificial association simply to permit the British to unload their responsibilities in Africa.

Finally Chief Mapanga, on behalf of all Northern Rhodesian Chiefs, demanded secession, and the Asian representative, Patel, decried the lack of representation for the Asian and Coloured communities or of mention of them in the preamble.[87]

On the third day, 7 December, Kaunda called frequently for dissolution to avoid immediate and serious racial conflict. He complained about discrimination and the high level of the franchise. He called Welensky's attitude to discrimination "unchristian" and criticised the curbs on inter-territorial movement and the lack of freedom of association and expression which proved that the Federation had become a police state. Africans would reject the continuation of the Federation as its economic achievements had failed to better their lot and had drained Northern Rhodesia. Their opposition, he warned, would ruin the economy. He knew that, as the African preferred his political freedom to belated social reform, the African would not embrace Communism. Kaunda promised that, once independent, Northern Rhodesia would protect the minorities and, indeed, would relieve the white of his bondage of fear.

Harper stressed the necessity of maintaining white control until the African was ready to play his part. He criticised Malvern for deceiving the Southern Rhodesians at the outset and claimed that the Federation had diluted Southern Rhodesia's financial efficiency. He rejected integration and thought that the abolition of discrimination would create problems. He suggested a loose economic association of independent states.

Banda, like Kaunda, made frequent reference to the need for secession and claimed to have suggested an economic association in the early 'fifties. He did not reject federations freely entered into and reassured the Europeans that they had nothing to fear from an African state.

Matthews Phiri of the UFP wanted the Federation re-modeled to make it more acceptable to the inhabitants, but Nkumbula thereafter demanded its demolition. After a long criticism of Federal performance, he, like Kaunda, warned of bloodshed if the Federation were allowed to continue.[88]

Nkomo spoke on 8 December and dwelt on the non-representative character

[87] Welensky Papers, 35/7, f. 7, Minutes of Second Meeting of the Review Conference, 6 December 1960.

[88] *Ibid.*, f. 8, Minutes of Third Meeting of the Review Conference, 7 December 1960.

of the Southern Rhodesian Parliament and dismissed the Monckton assertion that the Southern Rhodesian Africans did not reject the Federation, as they feared that its economic strength would intensify their oppression. He believed the Federal immigration policy had prevented African advancement, and he criticised the British Government's silence on the detentions. The only cure was the granting of universal suffrage and Britain, as the custodian, had to make a stand on human rights. He looked forward to a federation of the liberated states of Southern Africa.

Blackwood demanded clarification of the Federation's fate because he was sure that many Africans would accept it if it were permanent. Chief Chikwanda said that African nationalism was too strong to be suppressed, and G. T. Thornicroft, the Coloured representative, decried the lack of care for the fate of minorities.[89]

After this, the fourth session, the delegates from the Malawi Congress Party met the Press to answer a challenge on intimidation from six British Conservative and Labour MPs who had recently toured the Federation. They insisted that their Party had not been alone in committing atrocities and that their members had also suffered. They stressed that Banda had advocated peace and that the people had responded. The British MPs, they claimed, had been misled by Welensky, who was frightened of Banda's intention to destroy the Federation, and was resorting to propaganda.[90]

Whitehead opened the fifth session to the constant heckling of Banda and Orton Chirwa. He declared that the Federation was needed to care for the expanding populations and believed that those who were advocating its dissolution were subordinating the true interests of the people to their own political ambitions. His Government would not exclude Africans from politics, but would not lower standards to appease nationalists. He urged the Conference to agree on the continuation of the Federation in the interests of economics and race relations.[91]

Before Whitehead finished, Banda, Chirwa and Paramount Chiefs Mwase and Katumbi walked out. Outside the Conference, Banda said that he had walked out because he hated hypocrisy, and Whitehead and Welensky were hypocrites.[92]

The session continued in their absence and van Eeden and Savanhu defended the Federal record while Sipalo and Chief Lundu demanded the break-up of the Federation. At the conclusion — it being Friday — Sandys, Macleod, Welensky, Whitehead, Field, Harper, Nkomo, Banda and Kaunda departed for Chequers and, in doing so, sparked off much Press speculation. During this bizarre weekend, they talked together only once when, on the Saturday after dinner, Sandys urged that, as the various points of view had been well-aired, they should proceed to the second stage. He warned that his Government would not consider the Federal dissolution until it was con-

[89] *Ibid.*, f. 11, Minutes of Fourth Meeting of the Review Conference, 8 December 1960.

[90] *Ibid.*, 27/90, f. 70, Banda's Press Conference, 8 December 1960; *The Rhodesia Herald*, 8 December 1960; Welensky Papers, 27/90, f. 75, ? to ?, 9 December 1960.

[91] Welensky Papers, 35/7, f. 13, Minutes of Fifth Meeting of the Review Conference, 9 December 1960.

[92] *The Rhodesia Herald*, 10 December 1960.

vinced that it was impossible to make the Federation more acceptable. He gathered that those in favour of the Federation were willing to countenance change. He diagnosed the hatred of the Federation as its identification with white supremacy and its imposition. No one, he said, appeared hostile to the concept itself.

Banda, as usual, was in no mood to compromise and demanded immediate secession and berated the British Government for betraying the Africans in 1953. He acknowledged British military power to re-impose the Federation, but warned that it would be a costly and useless act. He agreed with Sandys that he would happily accept a federal association, but only one in which all governments were fully representative. He favoured a greater federation of East and Central Africa, but warned that his people would insist that the current Federation would have to be dissolved first.

Nkomo agreed that federation could not be discussed until all the governments were representative, when they would undoubtedly advocate it. He appeared to shake Sandys considerably by saying that he thought the current allocation of powers between the Federal and territorial Governments was correct.

Blatantly leading him, Sandys suggested that perhaps Nkomo had meant to say that the composition of the Federal Assembly and the structure of its franchise should be changed first.

Welensky reminded the meeting that it sought to discover who wanted the Federation. Kaunda claimed that political oppression had increased during the Federation and consequently people would only consider dissolution. He suggested that common services could be administered by a commission until the three territories had advanced to the point where they could meet as equals and could discuss what political structure they wanted. This led Welensky and Whitehead to describe the difficulties suffered by the Central African Council because it had lacked an effective political superstructure. Kaunda, however, believed that the difficulties had stemmed from the very different natures of the three Governments involved. He did not convince Welensky that his proposed commission would do any better.

Summing up, Sandys claimed that everyone appeared to agree that the Federation was desirable for economic and administrative reasons, and that some wanted a revision of the current structure while others wanted to start afresh despite the severe dislocation. Therefore, he said, the outcome of the review depended on progress in the Northern and Southern Rhodesian constitutional revisions.[93]

The next morning the delegates attended the Church service at which it was thought to be symbolic that Banda should read the first lesson and Sandys the second. It was an occasion which Welensky did not enjoy. Macmillan joined them for dinner that evening and thought that the weekend had achieved some accord, but Welensky thought the gap was as unbridgeable as ever. Thus Macmillan, and not Welensky, was taken aback on the morrow when the sixth session was dramatically terminated by a walk-out by Kaunda, Sipalo, Banda, Chirwa, Chisiza, Nkomo and the Reverend Sithole. Kaunda

[93] Welensky, *4 000 Days*, *op. cit.*, p. 286; Welensky Papers, 20/2, ff. 130–132, Minutes of a Meeting at Chequers, 10 December 1960; 43/*Malvern*, Welensky to Malvern, 14 December 1960.

told the Press that, as they had put their case, they could see no further point in remaining.[94]

Macmillan, who blamed the harsh glare of publicity for the Africans' behaviour, hastily conferred with Sandys and Macleod and announced that the Southern and Northern Rhodesian constitutional conferences would be postponed until the situation was clearer. Sandys and Macleod then worked to repair the situation, while Macmillan lunched with the Nyasaland delegation the next day and lectured them. The Review continued without those who had walked out. Whitehead, in Macmillan's view, then complicated the issue by dismissing Nkomo from his delegation, automatically barring him from the Southern Rhodesian conference which he particularly wished to attend.[95]

Macmillan reviewed matters on 15 December with Sandys, Macleod, Welensky and Whitehead, recording that he found the latter in a very bad mood. Indeed, he claims that Welensky stayed behind to explain frankly his difficulties with Whitehead. In the event, Nkomo apologised to Whitehead, saying that he had not meant to be discourteous to Whitehead as the Prime Minister. Indeed he wished to work with Whitehead and was anxious to attend the Southern Rhodesian conference though he reserved his right to refuse an invitation to the Review when it reconvened in the Federation. Kaunda, who had led the walk-out, had by then led the delegates back into the Review Conference.[96]

While the Review continued, Welensky prepared and submitted his concluding speech to Macmillan and his Ministers. Macmillan persuaded him to delete attacks on the African leaders and found the speech to be hard-hitting but reasonably fair. Macleod praised Welensky by saying that he could not believe that he could be both tough and reasonable but that he had succeeded.[97]

Welensky delivered this speech on 17 December, beginning by describing as extraordinary the silence of the British Ministers and the northern officials throughout the Conference. As Macmillan had ruled at the outset that nothing would be irrelevant, Welensky said that the Conference had been forced to listen to many irrelevant and unhelpful comments. Much time had been wasted when the purpose of the Conference, in accordance with Article 99, was not to decide whether the Federation should continue but to review its Constitution. Instead, the delegates had dwelt on whether the Federation should have been formed. The most interesting aspect of the tirades was that it was not the Federation and its Parliament which had been the chief target of criticism, but the administration of the northern territories for which the British Government was responsible. It was a matter of congratulation that

[94] Macmillan, *At the End of the Day*, *op. cit.*, p. 302; Welensky Papers, 35/7, f. 17, Minutes of Sixth Meeting of the Review Conference, 12 December 1960; *The Rhodesia Herald*, 13 December 1960.

[95] Macmillan, *At the End of the Day*, *op. cit.*, p. 303; Welensky Papers, 35/7, f. 20, Minutes of Seventh Meeting of the Review Conference, 13 December 1960.

[96] Macmillan, *At the End of the Day*, *op. cit.*, p. 304; Welensky Papers, 15/22, f. 14, Nkomo to Whitehead, 19 December 1960.

[97] Welensky Papers, 11/45, f. 169, Macmillan to Welensky, 16 December 1960; f. 171, Macleod to Welensky, 17 December 1960.

the delegates had succeeded so well in "kicking the United Kingdom in the backside while simultaneously patting it on the head" by urging the continuation of protection, yet criticising the oppressive laws of the territories.

At the outset, Welensky recalled, he had challenged the Conference to point out frankly any instances in which the Federal Government had departed from the undertakings given in the preamble. He had produced evidence to prove that the Federal Government was not bent on white domination. Nevertheless, the white contribution could not be ignored and to him the slogan "Africa for the Africans" was tragically irresponsible. He had demonstrated that the use of brutality belied the claim of the African leaders to have total support. It seemed that these leaders saw in the dissolution of the Federation their easiest path to power. Indeed, O. Chirwa had spoken of seizing the whole continent.

Welensky pleaded for effective counter-measures against intimidation and warned that his Government would meet force with force. He believed that the ambition of the African leaders would produce only a drastic reduction in the already low standard of living. The truth hurt because when Whitehead had made this very point earlier, Banda had constantly heckled him and then had walked out. Welensky could find no case for the dissolution of the Federation nor any serious criticism of the performance of his Government in its use of its constitutional powers which contradicted the criticism of the division of powers. He was confident that any fears could be met by providing safeguards which were more effective than a bill of rights. Sandys would sum up the debate, but Welensky hoped that the British Government would not cast itself in the role of judge because the Federal Government was not on trial. Neither could the British Government expect to remain a benevolent neutral as it was one of the five contracting parties to the Review. Therefore it had to indicate where it stood and whom it backed. He expected the British Government to answer unequivocally two questions: would it back or break up the Federation; and, would it support the promoters of partnership or the African nationalists who sought to destroy it? If there were no answers forthcoming, there was little point in reconvening the Review.

Sandys ignored the challenge and, in his concluding speech, set out to analyse the views expressed during the Conference. The problem, he said, appeared to be one of political power and the differences, not ones of principle, but merely of pace and timing. Once timing was accepted as the key, an acceptable solution should be possible if goodwill could be engendered. He firmly condemned violence and intimidation as methods to secure political ends, but reserved any statement of policy because it was necessary first to examine the views which had been expressed and to consult the relevant Governments. It would be unwise to present the Conference at this stage with any cut and dried opinions. British policy was based on its obligations to all races and could only be discharged if the races co-operated to develop a true partnership. The Federation had promoted economic and social progress and it would be a serious matter indeed if anything were done which retarded economic advancement. Of particular importance was the growth of African confidence in the Federation and this could only be ensured by greater African participation in its government.

Sandys said that the reconvened Conference would have to decide on the composition of the Federal Assembly, on the franchise, the division of powers and the safeguards. The immediate task was to proceed with the Northern and Southern Rhodesian revisions (the Southern Rhodesian Conference was a day old and the Northern Rhodesian was about to begin) and then to decide when to reconvene the Review. He considered that the contacts made in the current session could assist in securing a mutual understanding. Macmillan thought that this speech was admirable, but to Welensky, Sandys appeared evasive and anxious only to thrust the onus for developing partnership onto the Federal Government.

Closing the Conference, Macmillan endorsed Sandys's remarks and stressed the need to take account of African aspirations while acknowledging the rights and contributions of the other races. Britain had responsibilities to all the races, he said, but could not discharge them unless everyone co-operated to build a non-racial society. He believed that, once partnership was accepted, everything else would fall into place. A vigorous economy was needed to meet all the aspirations of the races, and a satisfactory settlement depended on full racial co-operation.[98]

Macmillan had offered no solution to Federal problems and would never find one, short of dissolving the Federation. If this were a solution, his aim of peaceful stability was to prove thereafter an elusive goal. The Conference, which had become nothing more than an exercise in futility, adjourned with Macmillan congratulating himself on avoiding a breakdown. It would never be resumed.

Macmillan invited Welensky to lunch and later confided to his diary: "We had a good talk. He is a very attractive man but like so many heavy, fat, solid-looking characters, strangely mercurial. He cannot refrain from continual attacks on H.M.G. — although we are, in fact, his only friends."[99] Welensky has not recorded the view from the other side of the lunch table but can be forgiven if he pondered on the quality of the friendship being offered when British pledges were broken to appease self-elected — although popularly supported, to a degree — demagogues. Were treacherous friends indeed better than none at all? Welensky, however, would have had little time to spare for such reflections, because he faced immediately a battle royal with Macleod over Nyasaland and Northern Rhodesia.

[98] *Ibid.*, 35/7, f. 32, Minutes of Eleventh Meeting of the Review Conference, 17 December 1960.
[99] Macmillan, *At the End of the Day*, *op. cit.*, pp. 304–307.

CHAPTER TWENTY-EIGHT

Confrontation with Macleod

The Deadlock over the Northern Rhodesian Constitution, December 1960–February 1961

THE Federal and Southern Rhodesian delegates returned home and indulged in face-saving, saying that the Federal Review Conference had cleared the air.[1] At a Press conference, Welensky said that he hoped to have the Review completed by May 1961, and was confident that it would be satisfactory because the British Government had seen the need to persist with partnership. He told Lord Salisbury that, when he last saw Macmillan, he had hammered home the point that a satisfactory solution in Northern Rhodesia was most necessary and that the criterion was the enrolment of the responsible element of the community regardless of race. If that were adhered to, colour did not matter. To him the obstacle was Macleod who was "the most sinister influence in the British Cabinet today". Nevertheless, he thought that the situation had improved.[2] He did not believe this for long because he was compelled to confront Macleod within days, and by February 1961 both sides were contemplating using force.

Nyasaland was the cause of the immediate clash with Macleod. It was not entirely unexpected because Welensky knew that Dixon had rejected the report of the Nyasaland constitutional working party because it had departed from the agreement reached in July at the Nyasaland Constitutional Conference in London. The working party had recommended that, in addition to British subjects and British Protected Persons, certain others should be enfranchised by virtue of their paying tax and of their length of residence. These were in fact Africans who had infiltrated from Moçambique. Secondly, receipts relating to 1960 were deemed sufficient proof of ten years of tax-paying, one of the qualifications for the vote. Married women of ten years' standing should also qualify. However, the existing voters would not be automatically transferred onto the new upper roll and might find themselves

[1] *The Rhodesia Herald*, 20 & 22 December 1960.
[2] Welensky Papers, 43/*Salisbury*, Welensky to Lord Salisbury, 22 December 1960.

placed on the lower roll. Moreover, Dixon suspected that Macleod would not give the new Constitution the "fair trial" which he had promised. However, Greenfield could not see how Macleod could be forced to admit this. Nonetheless, Dixon, using a draft letter prepared by Greenfield, made that attempt.[3]

In early December 1960, J. Foot, a Nyasaland Federal MP, warned Barrow that he had discovered that the Nyasaland Government had no intention of allowing the Parties to discuss the details of the Constitution which had been formulated by the official working party. The Government's reason, he said, was that the United Federal Party might demand delay for discussion of the details, and this delay, the Government felt, would be regarded as a provocation to the Malawi Congress Party. Such provocation, Foot knew, was unthinkable to the Government. Foot also believed that the MCP was planning violence and, as if to confirm this, Chipembere (who had stayed behind while Banda attended the Review Conference in London), called publicly for the living body of Blackwood which he would tear to pieces. This earned him a three-year gaol sentence.[4]

Blackwood, who had managed to see Macleod in London during the Review, had accepted the need for elections as soon as they could be properly arranged. He pleased Macleod who, writing on 19 December, revealed to him that he had been resisting considerable pressure for early elections because he wished to ensure that the electoral regulations were properly drafted. These were ready, Macleod said, but there was no time to debate them in the Legislative Council as delimitation and other matters had to be effected before the New Year. In any case, he would not allow the Legislative Council to revise decisions of a conference which was more representative than it was. Furthermore, he asserted, the responsibility for the final decision was his. However, Macleod said he would happily concede some of the points which Blackwood had made. For example, existing voters could be transferred onto the upper roll even if they did not qualify under the new arrangements. Postal voting would be allowed. Nonetheless, Macleod rejected the objection to the inclusion of African immigrants from Moçambique, the demand for the proper searching of the tax rolls and the restriction of polling to a single day. He gave administrative reasons for the last two, and for the first claimed that some 20 000 voters would be lost if the Moçambique Africans were excluded.

Macleod sent Blackwood and Greenfield copies of the constitutional regulations and asked them to note that a reasonable standard of literacy was required. He defended his action of implementing the Constitution by regulation by pointing out that, after the regulations were published, 27 weeks would pass until an election could be held. This would mean that a whole year would have passed after the conclusion of the Nyasaland Conference. Thus, he maintained he could not be accused of rushing matters through or of cutting corners. Finally, he pleaded that success would depend on the generous co-operation of the Members of the Legislative Council.[5]

[3] *Ibid.*, 7/14, f. 115, A. C. W. Dixon to Macleod, 12 November 1960; f. 104, Greenfield to Welensky, 18 November 1960; 27/69, f. 134, Dixon to Macleod, 29 November 1960.

[4] *Ibid.*, 20/18, f. 92, J. Foot to Barrow, 9 December 1960; P. Short, *Banda* (London, 1974), p. 142.

[5] Welensky Papers, 20/18, f. 100, Macleod to M. H. Blackwood, 19 December 1960.

Greenfield had accompanied Blackwood on his visit to Macleod in London and thus was privy to their discussion on Nyasaland's Constitution. Also having seen Macleod's letter to Blackwood, Greenfield informed Macleod that he did not want existing voters to have to re-register. He disliked the suggestion on the Portuguese nationals and expected Welensky to object to it because it was wrong in principle and would set an unhealthy precedent for Northern Rhodesia and its Congolese residents. He warned that polling on more than one day could invite the pressurising of the voter but he acknowledged that this could be avoided by delaying the announcement of early results.

Most distressing to him was the decision to enact the electoral laws by regulation instead of by ordinance through the Legislative Council. This, he said, was a display of contempt for the Legislative Council and was something which, if he were a Member, he would resent greatly. The Members had a wealth of experience, and to bypass them was a most extraordinary action. If Macleod would not be diverted from his course, Greenfield hoped that he, Blackwood and Dixon would at least see the final version of the regulations.[6]

Greenfield advised Welensky on 23 December to question Macleod on the Portuguese nationals. Welensky accordingly warned Macleod that the Federal-Portuguese relationship should not be strained, but was ignored. On 30 December Blackwood wrote to Greenfield that the final version of the regulations had hardly been changed. He was not disposed to give in on the Portuguese Africans, the failure to require the search of the tax records or the insistence of re-registration. The last would disenfranchise anyone who was away on leave.[7]

Blackwood proposed to be guided by Welensky and Greenfield on any action to be taken, but before they could act, Macleod regretfully but brusquely explained that no further changes could be allowed because the agreement of August demanded the earliest implementation, and even so an election would only be possible by June 1961. He understood the views expressed but would not permit the Legislative Council to decide on a matter to which it had not been a party. The regulations had been framed on the recommendations of the official working party, which was an extension of the Conference, and ultimately any decision was vested with him. He had asked Jones to associate the Legislative Council more closely with the regulations but could do no more. Governor's regulations, he said, were not usually shown to other than legal advisers so the perusal by Blackwood had in itself been an extraordinary privilege.

As for the detail, Macleod believed it was practically impossible to identify the Africans from Moçambique, and the Foreign and Commonwealth Relations Offices would not allow discussions with the Portuguese Government. An automatic transfer of voters was not desirable, and responsible people would take the trouble to re-register. Anyway, Macleod noted, Blackwood had admitted that the register was out of date. Pressure on voters could be avoided by withholding early results. The regulations were not perfect, but

[6] *Ibid.*, f. 96, Greenfield to Macleod, 23 December 1960.
[7] *Ibid.*, f. 95, Greenfield to Welensky, 23 December 1960; 20/2, f. 129, Welensky to Macleod, 26 December 1960; 20/18, f. 50, Blackwood to Greenfield, 30 December 1960.

delay was not warranted. He had accorded to Greenfield and Blackwood alone the privilege of this discussion and did not want any public reference to it.[8]

When the constitutional regulations were published on 3 January 1961, Dixon publicly outlined the departures from the agreement and claimed that Nyasaland had been "sold down the river". Welensky immediately protested to Macleod that not only had his representations been ignored, but that he had been given no time to consider the regulations. He thought that Macleod had appreciated how strongly he objected to the enfranchisement of the Moçambique Africans.

He disliked the undue haste and pointed out that two days of public holiday had intervened between his receipt of Macleod's dispatch and the publication, leaving him embarrassingly powerless. The regulations were now law and the Portuguese nationals could be enfranchised in Nyasaland despite any unfortunate repercussions. Henceforth, the Federal Government would be accused of discrimination when it refused to enfranchise these Africans as Federal voters. Thus once again, Welensky said, his Government was being placed in an awkward position not of its own making. It seemed strange that the working party's report had not been published so that objections could have been made. The promulgation of the regulations had, of course, made their revision very difficult, he said.[9]

The exchanges between Welensky and Macleod would be even more bitter over Northern Rhodesia. After the opening sessions in London, both the Rhodesian Constitutional Conferences had adjourned on 20 December, with expressions of satisfaction, to be reconvened shortly in their respective territories. Roberts, however, warned Beckett that Macleod would expect parity of racial representation in the Northern Rhodesian Legislative Council as well as three or four Chiefs sitting on the cross-benches. A few officials would hold the balance of power. This was obviously a move towards African majority rule, Roberts believed, and would only be acceptable to Southern Rhodesia (as one of the Federal partners) if it were given the right to secede. Beckett concluded that Welensky, Whitehead and Roberts should plan a common strategy. He thought that Welensky should warn Macmillan that Southern Rhodesia would secede if such constitutional advancement were pushed too far. To Beckett, the only encouragement was that the Africans had over-played their hand at the Northern Rhodesian Conference and must have created a poor impression. Furthermore, Roberts had been forced to criticise the official delegates for not rebutting attacks on their administration. They had given the distinct impression of being cowed by the presence of Macleod.[10]

Roberts returned home in an aggressive mood, declaring that he and his fellow Members of the Legislative Council would resign and fight by-elections if Macleod advanced proposals which conflicted with the UFP's views on advancement on merit. However, he did not particularly worry Macleod. Welensky agreed with Roberts and warned Macmillan that both

[8] *Ibid.*, 20/18, f. 44, Macleod to Welensky, 31 December 1960.
[9] *Ibid.*, f. 38, Welensky to Macleod, 4 January 1961.
[10] *Ibid.*, 42/21, f. 37, G. Beckett to Welensky, 20 December 1961.

parity and the concept of someone holding the balance of power was unacceptable. Africans had to win their seats through the qualitative franchise.[11]

At that moment, 3 January 1961, Welensky was also annoyed with Whitehead who, without warning, had announced that he would submit any constitutional change in Southern Rhodesia to a referendum. To Welensky this was an unnecessary gamble because if the referendum was lost, a general election would be inevitable and Whitehead's chances of winning would be in doubt. It would have been better simply, he felt, to hold a general election. Welensky was not entirely despondent because Macmillan had affirmed the continuation of the Federation and this had lifted the public spirit. It appeared to Welensky that events in the Congo had influenced the British Government's attitude to the Federation. However, this hope was short-lived because, three days later, Joelson informed him that one of Macleod's colleagues was proclaiming widely that the Federation was finished and that any attempt at rescue would be unrealistic. Joelson was convinced that these were Macleod's thoughts because this statement so obviously served his purpose. Furthermore, Macleod took Welensky by surprise when he indicated to him that he would shortly announce that the Northern Rhodesian Conference would be reconvened in London at the end of January. As everyone had understood that the Conference would be held in Northern Rhodesia, Welensky promptly asked that it should be, in order not to aggravate the bitter mood engendered in Federal and territorial political circles by the manner in which the Nyasaland constitutional changes had been rushed through by regulation.[12]

Macleod replied equally promptly regretting that Welensky believed there had been undue haste over the Nyasaland regulations when he had carefully alerted him, as well as Blackwood and Dixon, to the date of their publication and had considered their objections. Practical considerations, he said, forbad further delay just as they had prevented the exclusion of the Moçambique Africans from the franchise. There had been nothing sinister in his refusal to publish the report of the working party because it had been shown to all the delegates of the Nyasaland Conference and they had been allowed time to comment. They had commented, and the report would be published soon. He understood Welensky's disappointment that every one of his points could not be met, but this was true of many other by-products of the Conference, and he could only make a fair and reasonable decision within the limits of the agreement and the practicalities.[13]

This dispatch arrived just as Roberts publicly warned that a solution for Northern Rhodesia based on Nyasaland's would be unworkable, and Welensky told the Press that, if there were any evidence of double-dealing, he would be forced to break off negotiations and advocate a policy of non-cooperation. He did not believe, he said, that a final solution for the Federation

[11] *The Rhodesia Herald*, 30 December 1960; Welensky Papers, 42/21, f. 35, Welensky to G. Beckett, 3 January 1961.

[12] Welensky Papers, 42/21, f. 35, Welensky to Beckett, 3 January 1961; 43/*Lisson*, Welensky to J. Lisson, 4 January 1961; 24/151, f. 98, F. S. Joelson to Welensky, 6 January 1961; 20/4, f. 140, M. R. Metcalf to Welensky, 6 January 1961; f. 139, Welensky to Macleod, 7 January 1961.

[13] *Ibid.*, 20/18, f. 27, Macleod to Welensky, 7 January 1961.

was possible until a pattern of territorial constitutional development emerged. He called on Macleod to reveal the true position to belie the current propaganda. Macleod largely ignored him, merely promising to assess the mood of the delegates when they arrived to see if a further meeting in Northern Rhodesia was needed.[14]

Perhaps because Macleod and Welensky were becoming so estranged, Macmillan decided to intervene and wrote to Welensky giving his ideas on Northern Rhodesia. He recalled that he and Welensky had agreed that much depended on the successful outcome of the Conference, that if a reasonable agreement was reached, however painfully, the prospects of the Federation would be greatly improved. He had to acknowledge, nevertheless, that the gap between the aspirations of the African nationalists and what was reasonable appeared wide. His ideas were the product of his discussions with Macleod, Alport and Home, as Sandys was away. They thought that the Legislative Council should comprise six official Members, two or three nominated unofficial Members, one of whom would be an Asian, some Chiefs, who would not have the right to vote, and 30 elected Members. Macmillan remembered that he and Welensky had spoken of parity being achieved through adjustment of the franchise on a non-racial basis. This, however, seemed impossible, he said, because the Africans would obstinately demand a large majority. A token African majority of, say, 16 seats to 14 European seats could be granted because, in reality, the European elected Members, when combined with the official Members, would still outnumber the Africans. A similar arrangement in the Executive Council would retain power in responsible hands. This concession of a small majority would displease the Europeans, but the Africans might moderate their demands and thus ensure the success of the Conference and avoid the need to impose a settlement. To secure European acceptance, Macmillan needed the persuasive powers of Welensky and his colleagues. Thus he asked for Welensky's advice on the proposals and the handling of the Conference because an agreed settlement would place Northern Rhodesia on an even keel for some time to come.

Macmillan enclosed proposals which described the Legislative Council; the Executive Council of four official Members and three African and three European unofficial Members; and the appointment, at the Governor's discretion, of three parliamentary secretaries, of whom two would be Africans. The aim was to secure an African electorate of 100 000 while maintaining standards of responsibility and utilising experience. The details of the franchise would be reserved for negotiation in the Conference. If they accorded with the ultimate Federal settlement, there would be a bill of rights and a council of state. Finally, the proposals showed that Macleod was greatly pressed to include Barotseland in the scheme but, in accordance with Barotse wishes, would deal separately with the Paramount Chief.[15]

Before Welensky could reply to Macmillan, Macleod revealed some of his intentions to the *Financial Times* after it had said that it was just as disastrous

[14] *The Rhodesia Herald*, 7 January 1961; Welensky Papers, 20/4, f. 136, Macleod to Welensky, 8 January 1961.
[15] Welensky Papers, 20/4, f. 132, Macmillan to Welensky, 9 January 1961.

to advance too fast politically as it was to go too slow because there had already been a marked economic decline in most of the territories affected. Macleod disagreed because, he said, rapid advancement had averted the need for emergencies in which businesses would have foundered. Confidence depended on stability, and rapid advancement would achieve that. As the African leaders, he believed, wanted to retain European expertise, the rights of the Europeans would only be endangered by acts of folly by one race or the other. However, there were many people of both races who were determined to prevent such acts. Asked how long British control would last and if he intended to be the last Colonial Secretary, Macleod replied that the policy enunciated by Creech Jones in 1948 still obtained and would guide all territories to self-government within the Commonwealth while ensuring for all a fair standard of living and freedom from oppression. British control, Macleod said, would last for as long as it took to achieve those aims. He did not think that he would be the last in his office, though it might at some stage be merged with that of Commonwealth Relations.[16]

Welensky confided in Joelson his fear for Northern Rhodesia while apprising him on other matters. He feared for its future because Macleod was incapable of hiding his intentions from him. He wished that Roberts was of tougher fibre, and revealed that there was considerable criticism of the latter's leadership. If the Conference were held in London he would be unable to coach him as he was currently doing. As for Macleod, he had read his latest pronouncements and had restrained himself with difficulty. He could not promise to continue to do so, particularly as the Northern Rhodesians were aware that a storm was imminent. The European Mineworkers' Union, in fact, had just urged him to declare the independence of the Federation and take the consequences. He wondered if events in the Congo meant nothing to Macleod. People in Africa, he said were being led prematurely to independence, and already they were starving.[17]

Condemning Macleod as "the most calamitous Colonial Secretary in History", and warning him that his ambition to be Prime Minister was fading, the *Daily Express* concurred with this judgment. The Rhodesian Press warned that the alarm in Northern Rhodesia was such that there was public pressure for the Federal Government to be represented at the Conference, to curb Macleod, and there was talk of forming a national front.[18]

Welensky replied to Macmillan on 14 January and, never willing to accept Macmillan's embroideries of the truth, denied that he had accepted parity of racial representation when they last met. Indeed, he said, not only had he rejected it, but had argued that the surest way to destroy the Federation was to devolve power onto an African majority prematurely. He noted that Macmillan had made no mention of the ultimate objective of making all elected Members responsible to all the races. To the contrary, he charged, the next advance for the Africans would merely be at the expense of the Europeans. Macleod, he said, had clearly abandoned partnership and it was thus necessary to remind him that, in 1958, Lennox-Boyd had rejected separate

[16] *Financial Times*, 10 January 1961.
[17] Welensky Papers, 24/151, ff. 96–97, Welensky to Joelson, 11 January 1961.
[18] *Daily Express*, 13 January 1961; *The Rhodesia Herald*, 12 January 1961.

representation for the races in favour of the development of non-racial politics. Macmillan's proposal of racial representation, Welensky continued, equalled, in its despair, that of the Dominion Party to partition Northern Rhodesia. The Federal Review had clearly shown that the choice lay between African nationalism and partnership, and he challenged Macmillan to choose the latter rather than assist those who were trying to divide the Federation into black nationalist states. The adoption of either parity or an African majority was an indication that a "Kenya" was about to be perpetrated and, he warned that he would fight it with everything at his disposal. He could see no reason to defer to African nationalists just because they were applying pressure, when it was only two years since the last constitutional change, and less than a year since Macleod had said publicly that it was too soon to overturn it. The pace, Welensky said, was presumably being forced by the impetus given by the changes in Nyasaland. If the Federation were to survive, he could not accept changes which would transfer power to the African nationalists. He could not allow the number of European unofficial Ministers to be reduced, and would not be cajoled by the outnumbering of African Members by the combination of Europeans and officials because many of the latter opposed the Federation and would support the Africans over crucial issues. Anyway, he said, the Europeans in the Legislative Council could be expected to belong to political parties while the Africans coalesced on a nationalist basis, and the only hope for responsible government would lie in the powers retained by the Governor.

Welensky, therefore, asked Macmillan to reveal his true intentions. If, as it appeared, the purpose was for Britain to disengage, then these proposals were a betrayal of the European in Northern Rhodesia which would destroy the Federation. It was imperative to foster the Federation and partnership, and he believed a promising start had been made. The Conference had been called, he said, and adjustments would have to be made, but these need not affect any principles. The Legislative Council could be enlarged and African representation increased but not to the point of parity. An important amendment would be to remove the endorsement of two-thirds of the Chiefs in the rural constituencies. As the Press had predicted, Welensky was sufficiently disturbed by the British proposals to ask Macmillan for observer status for his Government, and for Federal MPs to be allowed to join the delegations from the territorial divisions of their Parties. This was necessary, he said, because consultation by the British Government had been so inadequate. He reminded Macmillan that, although Macleod had consulted the Federal Government over Nyasaland, he had ignored its representations. He had rushed through the regulations, contemptuously bypassing the Legislative Council. In doing so, Welensky said, Macleod had far exceeded the agreement and had made him determined not to allow it to happen to Northern Rhodesia. Europeans were aware of what was being proposed and feelings were running high enough for very little to spark off serious trouble. Although he might greet this with disbelief, Welensky told Macmillan that he could not emphasise enough the dangers of the situation.[19]

[19] Welensky Papers, 20/4, f. 127, Welensky to Macmillan, 14 January 1961.

A day later Roberts informed Hone that Macleod's proposals were grossly insulting to the elected Members who had played such a significant role in the Government. He said he did not dare put these proposals before his Party because it would withdraw from the Conference. He was embarrassed because he had understood that there would be no major changes and had publicly said so without any refutation by Macleod.[20]

Dixon, too, decided to exert pressure on Macleod for the automatic transfer of existing voters onto the Nyasaland upper roll. Blackwood, however, understood that this would be allowed and wanted Welensky to continue to harp on the enfranchisement of the Moçambique Africans, using it to demand a *quid pro quo* for Northern Rhodesia. Blackwood, at least, was still optimistic that everything was not yet lost if a satisfactory Northern Rhodesian solution could be procured.[21]

Welensky next told Macmillan of his economic problems. The building industry was static, he reported, but general economic output had increased significantly in 1960, and the gross domestic product should rise by six percent. The adverse balance on the current international account had improved but the worrying aspect was the recent drying up of the capital inflow which was the result of a loss of confidence in Africa and in the Federation in particular. An early settlement, he said, was the only answer to the danger posed by widespread unemployment.[22]

In another letter to Macmillan, Welensky described the danger to the Federation from events in the Congo. An invasion from the north, he said, was threatening Katanga's stability, while the United Nations inhibited Tshombe. He asked Macmillan to condemn, at the UN, all those who supported the Lumumbist forces. He urged support for the moderate African countries and for an improvement in the quality and quantity of the UN forces to prevent certain African countries from using their detachments for political ends. There had to be UN commanders whom Tshombe and Joseph Kasavubu, the President of the Congo, could trust, and a firm political initiative which would recognise separatist aims. He was particularly concerned by reports from Cairo that the Afro-Asian Solidarity Council had appealed openly for arms and troops for the pro-Lumumbist regime in Stanleyville.[23]

Replying on 23 January, Macmillan regretted that Welensky rejected his ideas on Northern Rhodesia. His purpose, he said, was to try to maintain the Federation based on an effective racial partnership. However, the situation had altered radically since 1958 and unavoidable prerequisites to the maintenance of the Federation were a substantial increase in the African membership of the Northern Rhodesian legislature and the alteration of the franchise to allow the greater representation of African opinion. Otherwise there was no hope of keeping Northern Rhodesia in the Federation. Therefore he was trying to devise ways of broadening the franchise to produce an electorate of

[20] *Ibid.*, FGC(1), 1a/61, H. J. Roberts to Hone, 17 January 1961 (draft).
[21] *Ibid.*, 20/18, f. 15, Blackwood to Welensky, 16 January 1961; f. 12, Blackwood to Macleod, 19 January 1961; f. 9, Blackwood to Welensky, 19 January 1961.
[22] *Ibid.*, 20/2, ff. 127–128, Welensky to Macmillan, 21 January 1961.
[23] *Ibid.*, 20/12, f. 191, Welensky to Macmillan, 23 January 1961.

reasonable size which measured up to standards of responsibility and experience. He would preserve the elements in the Constitution which promoted the development of non-racial politics, and was concentrating on having two electoral rolls under which every voter would register on the lower roll, but only those who qualified would be placed on the upper. Hone and he were particularly anxious to abandon the system of evaluating every voter on the lower roll because Monckton had commented on it. The new franchise would produce a balance between the African and European controlled seats whilst firmly maintaining the non-racial approach.

Macmillan said he was convinced that non-racial politics would be stimulated by what he was advancing. What was needed were constituencies which could be expected to return Africans, and others which would elect Europeans through the efforts of the political parties. Agreeing with Lennox-Boyd's opposition to parity through racial reservation, Macmillan said it would be achieved through a non-racial electoral system. Whatever method was chosen, he declared, there was still the comfort of knowing that the European and official Members would out-number the Africans, with in reserve, of course, the Governor's power of nomination. It had to be remembered also that the Executive Council could only advise the Governor. Macmillan rejected the suggestion that the official element was anything but loyal to British policy.

He believed that the likelihood of an African walk-out at the Conference impelled him to offer at least parity. Any hope of an agreed solution lay between parity and the token majority of two seats. As Welensky would have to convince the Europeans, Macmillan asked him to give the proposals his urgent attention. Almost as a sop, Macmillan accepted that the approval of two-third of the Chiefs would be dropped, and that Federal MPs could join the territorial Party delegations, provided that their inclusion did not increase the size of the latter. He would not, however, grant the Federal Government observer status because it was unprecedented and might cause difficulties. Hoping Welensky would not press this matter, Macmillan turned to the issue of consultation and found Macleod not guilty because of the pace of events. Where the British Government had responsibilities it was inevitable, Macmillan argued, that decisions would not always accord with Welensky's views. However, the British Government did wish to work with him in reconciling the competing interests of the Federation's peoples.[24]

Welensky's reply was blunt. Macmillan's proposals, he said, offered no basis on which the UFP could negotiate. He considered himself a fair judge of the realities as he was a Rhodesian with everything at stake. The situation had changed since 1958 but that surely did not mean that the British Government would not adhere to sound principles. The pace of events was certainly no justification for the appeasement of the forces of evil. At Cape Town, after all, Macmillan had propounded the thesis that merit and not race had to be the determining factor, yet now his proposals were based on what he chose to call "the realities of the situation". On the issue of consultation, Welensky acknowledged that Macleod had shown his speech to Roberts and himself, but had ignored their resultant comments.

[24] *Ibid.*, 20/4, f. 123, Macmillan to Welensky, 23 January 1961.

Welensky told Macmillan that the proposals were totally unacceptable if only because the UFP could not accept that people who advocated and practised violence, and used every vile means of intimidation, could measure up to any standards of responsibility. Macmillan's proposals, he said, would certainly not foster non-racial politics, and all the seats would be captured by extremists of both races. The crucial question of how long the Governor would retain power had not been answered. As Kaunda and Sir John Moffat believed that there would be a short transitional period before majority rule, Welensky warned Macmillan not to be surprised if he was distrusted. However, Welensky said, it was possible that Kaunda and Moffat knew more about British intentions than he did. Certainly, the record of the last Conference showed Moffat supported the British official approach. Welensky wondered if Macmillan knew that Kaunda was already offering blandishments to expatriate civil servants. He added the warning: "Whom the python wishes to devour he first covers with saliva." The offer to keep in close touch, he said, hardly encouraged him when it appeared that Macleod was free to take decisions which far exceeded agreements reached at conferences. It was clear, Welensky claimed, that the impending Conference was doomed to disaster if the current line was adhered to and thus, unless there were a change, the UFP would refuse to attend. As Macmillan had clearly not understood the gravity of the situation, Welensky asked for the Conference's postponement for further discussions between them.[25]

Macmillan had heard that his latest dispatch had been discussed by the UFP in Northern Rhodesia and immediately chastised Welensky for thus abusing his private correspondence. He hoped, he said, that there would be no repetition. He was in fact giving some ground because, although he refused to postpone the Conference, he revealed that he had ordered Macleod to delay tabling the proposals for a few days. However, Macmillan said there was little time for negotiation, because the delegates would expect the proposals in the first week of the Conference, but there was room for manoeuvre between the expectations of the African nationalists, the Northern Rhodesian Europeans and the British public. He felt that there was no need to remind Welensky of the serious implications if the Conference broke down.[26]

Sandys was due in Salisbury to attend the Southern Rhodesian Conference and Macmillan wished him to take over the Northern Rhodesian discussions with Welensky. However, Sandys was delayed, and thus Welensky continued this correspondence with Macmillan. He denied that Macmillan's dispatch had been discussed because all he had told his Northern Rhodesian division of the UFP was that the British proposals were unacceptable and that Federal MPs could be included in the delegations. Field had been given exactly the same message. Welensky said he was indeed aware of the serious implications of a breakdown and had only been trying to draw Macmillan's attention to them. The solution, he said, was postponement and further Anglo-Federal negotiations. Nonetheless, he had been impelled to advise the UFP delegation not to attend the Conference and felt bound to say that Macmillan appeared

[25] *Ibid.*, f. 120, Welensky to Macmillan, 26 January 1961; *Northern News*, 25 January 1961.
[26] *Ibid.*, f. 119, Macmillan to Welensky, 26 January 1961.

bent on destroying the Federation. This, Welensky averred, he was determined to prevent.[27]

The next day, 28 January, Welensky declined to comment when the Press asked if he was responsible for the decision of the United Federal and Dominion Parties to delay attending the Conference, thus forcing Macleod in turn to delay submitting his proposals and to spin it out until they relented. When his opinion was sought, Kaunda said that he could not see why Macmillan should be bullied by Welensky's satellites or why there should be Federal representation at the Conference. He was confident of achieving his Party's aims.[28]

Welensky refused to be provoked into replying, but, if he remained silent in public, he made sure that Lords Salisbury and Winterton understood Macleod's clear intentions. He did so, he told them, because it was crucial to thwart Macleod or lose the Federation, because Southern Rhodesia would secede the moment the African nationalists gained power in the North. Thus Welensky said he wanted Macleod attacked from every quarter.[29] A month later Lord Salisbury would do so most effectively.

Welensky also dispatched Greenfield, at Macmillan's suggestion, to London to join Roberts in discussions with Macmillan and Macleod. He planned to recall the Federal Assembly immediately if these discussions went wrong. Macmillan, perhaps to soften Welensky, asked him to join the British attempt to influence moderate African opinion to intervene in the Congo and assist the UN effort there.[30]

On the morning of 2 February, the third day of the Northern Rhodesian Conference, Greenfield and Roberts telephoned Welensky to describe a "Mad Hatter's Dinner" with Macleod at which he had put forward new proposals which he thought would satisfy them. These envisaged a dual roll system with 100 000 Africans on the lower roll. The upper roll would elect 14 nondescript (of any race) Members, ten of whom could be expected to be white and the remainder black because of delimitation. The lower roll would likewise elect 14 Members, two of whom would be white similarly because of delimitation. Through this, he expected the UFP to capture the majority of the seats. The Executive Council would comprise four official, four African and four European Ministers.

Macleod proposed to tell the Conference, after stringing it along, that, because its delegations remained irreconcilable, he would impose a solution. He hoped the UFP would pretend to resist to belie any suggestion of collusion with him. He argued that something had to be laid before the Conference lest the delegates threaten an insurrection.

Greenfield informed Welensky that he had replied that the scheme would be entirely unacceptable, and that, in any case, the Federal Government would want its implications examined by its officials. Macleod had responded

[27] *Ibid.*, f. 118, Macmillan to Welensky, 27 January 1961; f. 117, Welensky to Macmillan, 27 January 1961.

[28] *The Rhodesia Herald*, 28 January 1961.

[29] Welensky Papers, 43/*Salisbury*, Welensky to Lord Salisbury, 27 January 1961; 42/79, f. 7, Welensky to Lord Winterton, 31 January 1961.

[30] *Ibid.*, 20/12, ff. 186–189, Macmillan to Welensky, 31 January 1961.

by seeming to sulk. Yet he surprised Greenfield, before the dinner ended, by suggesting that Macmillan should invite Welensky to London.

Agreeing with his rejection of Macleod's proposals over dinner, Welensky told Greenfield that he would not come to London unless the demand for an African majority in the standing British proposals was dropped. He said that opinion in the Federation was hardening and that Whitehead would also reject such proposals. Furthermore, because of a statement by Kaunda (demanding independence under black majority rule), the European Mineworkers' Union was threatening to withdraw its £8 000 000 worth of investments from Northern Rhodesia to South Africa or Britain. Thus Welensky ordered Greenfield to take a firm line with Macmillan when he dined with him that evening. Welensky thought that only Sandys understood the gravity of the situation. However, Greenfield and Roberts replied that Macleod had appeared quite desperate. (Macleod, of course, by then had strung his conference out for three days in the hope of settling with Welensky.) On hearing this, Welensky ordered Greenfield to be blunt: to say that, if he came to London, he would not exceed the brief he had given Greenfield. Finally, he agreed to a British request that Greenfield might stay in London to examine any new proposals and said he would send Evans over to help.[31]

Welensky telephoned Greenfield the next day to hear what Macmillan had said at dinner. Greenfield replied that he had been given "the full treatment", that Macmillan was all charm and had done nothing more than hint. He had invited Greenfield to Chequers for the weekend to discuss the philosophical aspects of the question and Home would join them on the Sunday. It appeared that Macmillan wanted to discuss a formula to end the Federation. However, he had made it plain that Welensky should not come to London until the Commonwealth Prime Ministers' Conference in March. He also appeared to want all decisions to be deferred until then. Greenfield told Welensky that he had warned Macmillan of the dangers of dragging on indecisively but, in truth, saw virtue in deferment, to be spared the "half-baked" ideas of Macleod. Welensky agreed that Greenfield should stay with Roberts in London for as long as the Conference endured.[32]

Greenfield would be quizzed extensively over the weekend but he has never quite understood why he was invited because Macmillan played the role of philosopher and never examined their particular problem. However, Macmillan recorded for posterity in his diary that the problem seemed simple. The Europeans, he wrote, really did not want any African advancement but could accept one short of parity. The Africans sought universal suffrage but would accept parity or a small majority. He weighed the odds. If he favoured the European point of view, he would destroy African confidence in the British Government and provoke serious unrest in Northern Rhodesia and perhaps in the Federation as a whole. The result would be that some of his Ministers would resign, dividing his Government and Party. If he supported the Africans, he would demolish the faith of the whites and provoke Welensky to declare the independence of the Federation and effect a *coup*

[31] *Ibid.*, 20/4, f. 111, Telephone conversation between Welensky, Greenfield and Roberts, 2 February 1961; f. 107, Greenfield to Welensky, 2 February 1961.

[32] *Ibid.*, f. 109, Telephone conversation between Welensky and Greenfield, 3 February 1961.

d'état in Northern Rhodesia. If the Northern Rhodesian Governor defended himself, there would be a civil war over which British Ministers would resign, dividing his Government and Party. At this point, Macmillan could not see the path to safety.[33]

Macmillan thought that the relationship with the Federal Government might be improved by a change of British High Commissioner in Salisbury and persuaded C. J. M. Alport to replace M. R. Metcalf. Macmillan recommended Alport because his knowledge of Federal affairs might contribute to saving the Federation. The appointment was announced on 3 February and was generally welcomed, though Blackwood inferred that Metcalf had been removed because he was too keen a supporter of the Federation. Blackwood, however, was in as belligerent a mood as Welensky and was contemplating publicly provoking the British Government by arguing that it must be planning the granting of full independence to the Federation by the end of the year because it had not opposed a United Nations' resolution which had called for an end to all colonies by that date.[34]

Speculation was mounting that Welensky would fly to London to deal with the UFP boycott of the Northern Rhodesian Conference because it was deadlocked and would have to be adjourned. However, the news was not entirely grim. Under the guidance of Sandys, the Southern Rhodesian Conference had been making headway, and on 5 February it was announced that all delegations, except for the Dominion Party's, had agreed to sweeping changes. The purpose was to bring in 10 000 additional African voters through a dual roll system. There would be 50 upper roll and 15 lower roll seats and a cross-voting system whereby the upper roll would have a 25 per cent influence on the election of the lower roll Member in each constituency, while the lower roll voters would have a similar effect on the election of the upper roll Member. The British reserved powers would be removed on the establishment of a council of state which would administer a declaration of rights. The British Government would also agree to a convention whereby its Parliament would not legislate for Southern Rhodesia except at the request of the latter's Government. A White Paper describing the changes was issued two days later and Whitehead broadcast an appeal for national unity because, he said, he had achieved an end to British involvement in the internal affairs of Southern Rhodesia. Harper, however, stated that the removal of some British powers did not mean that Southern Rhodesia would be independent.[35]

Welensky could safely leave all this to Whitehead and concentrate on Northern Rhodesia. He ordered Greenfield on 5 February to present Macleod with the Federal ideas. Telling Macmillan of this, Welensky claimed that the situation was so grave that disaster was imminent if they did not agree over Northern Rhodesia. Public anxiety was reaching such a pitch, he said, that

[33] J. M. Greenfield, *Testimony of a Rhodesian Federal* (Bulawayo, 1978), p. 198; H. Macmillan, *At the End of the Day* (London, 1973), pp. 309–310.

[34] *The Rhodesia Herald*, 3 February 1961; Lord Alport, *The Sudden Assignment* (London, 1965), p. 4; Welensky Papers, 27/69, f. 172, Blackwood to Welensky, 3 February 1961.

[35] *The Rhodesia Herald*, 4 & 5 February 1961; *Report of Southern Rhodesia Constitutional Conference in Salisbury*, Command 1291 (London, 1961); Welensky Papers, 7/4, f. 101, Whitehead's Broadcast, 8 February 1961.

there was an almost pathological antagonism towards the idea of a black majority. In any case, the remarkable achievement of Sandys in Southern Rhodesia made agreement all the more imperative as it should not be hazarded by Northern Rhodesia. It might be an idea to consider adapting certain of Sandys's ideas for Northern Rhodesia.[36]

Welensky and Greenfield conferred again by telephone on 6 February and Welensky stressed that they could not abandon the encouragement of non-racial politics. There could not be representation on the basis of race alone. Welensky told Greenfield he had discussed the problem with Sandys and had informed him that he was fending off Macleod's wild ideas. Sandys, at least, he said, was anxious to preserve the non-racial approach which he had achieved in Southern Rhodesia. Greenfield told Welensky he had met Alport and had suggested the addition of six African seats, but under the control of the upper roll. Welensky replied that the issue was clearly so complicated that it could not be resolved hastily and he wondered if the Conference could be delayed. Greenfield said he had suggested this to Macmillan but that he had been evasive and was clearly hoping that something would arise out of discussions with Sandys on his return.

Two days later, when Welensky rang, Greenfield had little to impart except that the Southern Rhodesian settlement had been well received in London. He nevertheless expected trouble in convincing the Southern Rhodesian electorate and thought that he and Welensky would have to assist Whitehead. Welensky believed that Whitehead was getting cold feet, but that the agreement was remarkable because it had avoided representation by race and had gained independence for Southern Rhodesia within the Federal framework. He said he was going to support Whitehead publicly in Bulawayo and would attend a special UFP congress.

On events in London, Greenfield reported that Macleod would spin out the Northern Rhodesian Conference for a few more days. Greenfield said that he and Alport had tried to see Sandys that day, but he had been in a special Cabinet meeting. Welensky asked to be alerted to the slightest hint that Macleod would table anything unacceptable so that he could summon the Federal Cabinet and take action which he did not wish to describe on the telephone. He and Greenfield agreed that they could argue next with the British that the Southern Rhodesian settlement had not yet been ratified and could still be imperilled. Sandys had asked to be warned if this was a possibility and they agreed that Greenfield should tell him that it was. Welensky knew, of course, that there was no love lost between Sandys and Macleod.

Welensky informed Greenfield that he had just made as much mischief as possible in an interview with the *Daily Mail.* He had maintained to the newspaper that he sought merit and not race as the criterion of public life and noted that Macmillan agreed even if Macleod did not. The views of Macleod, Welensky had said in the interview, were revealed in the contrast between the Northern and Southern Rhodesian proposals because the first, unlike the second, laid the emphasis on race. The changes in Southern Rhodesia would

[36] Welensky Papers, 20/4, f. 106, Welensky to Sir Gilbert Rennie, 6 February 1961.

strengthen the Federation while those proposed for Northern Rhodesia could destroy it. He believed that Britain was too quick to heed demands for power based on violence and not on ability and responsibility. The granting of an African majority on the premise of racial representation alone would, in all likelihood, lead to a demand for secession by Southern Rhodesia. Asked if he expected trouble from the Europeans in Northern Rhodesia, Welensky had said that he did not because they were responsible people, but feelings were running high and men of achievement and courage would not lightly throw away everything for which they had worked. Everything depended on the British Government, but it was a savage indictment of that Government that the *Daily Mail* should need to ask such a question. Finally, asked whether there was a clash between himself and Macleod, he replied that he was conducting negotiations at the level of Prime Minister and if Macmillan differed from Macleod it was not his concern.[37]

Welensky had praised the progress made in Southern Rhodesia but, in reality, Whitehead was already confronted by a complication in the form of a subsequent refusal by Nkomo and the National Democratic Party to accept the White Paper because it did not provide for universal suffrage, which was their aim, even though its outlawing of racial discrimination and other features were most laudable. The NDP had, in fact, endorsed the White Paper but had been criticised for doing so by its London representative, Leopold Takawira. Nkomo flew to London to discipline him but returned to revise his thinking.[38] There is speculation that it took more than persuasion by Takawira to effect this change and it is hinted that local white liberals played some role. The African countries and other suppliers of funds might also have had an influence. Rhodesians would rue the day that Nkomo changed his mind.

Whitehead, however, immediately informed Sandys that he would not be deterred by the opposition of the NDP and the Dominion Party. Sandys, in any case, had other matters on his mind because he had been drawn into the Northern Rhodesian negotiations. Indeed, Greenfield had met him on 8 February to be told that he had thought up a "fantastic" scheme which he pressed to the exclusion of all other ideas. Greenfield found that in negotiating with Sandys "one moves at the pace of an ox". Sandys expanded on his idea on 10 February by which time Kaunda and his Party had declared that they would stay away from the Northern Rhodesian Conference until Macleod tabled his proposals. That day's session was cancelled and the British Cabinet held an emergency meeting. Kaunda warned the Press of the danger of an uprising which "by contrast would make Mau Mau a child's picnic".[39]

Greenfield reported to Welensky that Sandys proposed a legislature of 15 Members sitting in nondescript seats elected by the upper roll voters living along the "line of rail", 15 rural lower roll and 15 national Members. This is

[37] *Ibid.*, ff. 102 & 100, Telephone conversations between Welensky and Greenfield, 6 & 8 February 1961; *Daily Mail*, 10 February 1961.

[38] *The Rhodesia Herald*, 9 February 1961; R. Blake, *A History of Rhodesia* (London, 1977), p. 334.

[39] Welensky Papers, 20/9A, f. 42, Whitehead to Sandys, 9 February 1961; 20/4, f. 99, Greenfield to Welensky, 9 February 1961; f. 98, same to same, 10 February 1961; Greenfield, *Testimony, op. cit.*, p. 199; *The Rhodesia Herald*, 10 February 1961.

what Greenfield describes as "the All White XV", "the All Blacks XV" and "the Greys XV". Sandys intended that the national Members be elected by both rolls voting together in a manner which would mean that the influence of the upper roll would just predominate. Greenfield had opposed the idea and no progress had been made. Sandys had tried to mollify him by saying that the British Government would not lay any proposals before the Conference without prior Federal sanction. However, Greenfield informed Welensky that Macleod was hinting that the reverse was true.[40]

Sandys and Macleod were believed to be at odds and, even if they were not, Roberts described to Welensky over the telephone how he had met Macleod and had found him in such an abject state of nerves that he was almost incoherent. If he had not seen it, Roberts said he would never have thought that a British Minister could get into such a state. Macleod had warned that he would not be blackmailed by anyone. He would take his decision and submit his proposals to the Conference on 12 February. Roberts thought that this threat should be taken seriously because Macleod had just received "an awful drubbing" when meeting the Conservative Commonwealth Committee. Indeed, he had been sufficiently provoked to greet Roberts with a shouted accusation of "taking a swipe" at him in addressing a meeting of Conservative MPs. When Macleod said that he would make his decision whatever happened, Roberts started to walk out saying that, if that were the case, their ways would part forthwith. Macleod called him back and attempted to placate him. However, Roberts warned Welensky, he remained convinced that the threat was real. He claimed that the British Ministers were faring rather badly as Lord Perth, in the recent debate in the Lords, facing criticism from both sides, had been forced to concede that the Nyasaland Legislative Council should have been allowed to consider its electoral regulations. In the Commons, Macleod had only partially answered the same question and Roberts told Welensky that Blackwood and Dixon should resign from the Nyasaland Executive Council as the moment was ripe for exploitation and they had little to lose. Welensky agreed to transmit this suggestion and apprised Roberts that Voice and Vision, the Federal public relations consultants, were about to give every British MP a copy of a protest by Dixon at the manner in which the electoral legislation had been brought into force. Roberts endorsed this idea and noted that sections of the British Press were exploiting Kaunda's "Mau Mau" threat.[41]

Macmillan decided that day — 10 February — that it was time to calm the troubled waters and wrote to Welensky acknowledging the Federation was being damaged by the uncertainty. He proposed to raise the matter of reconvening the Federal Review the moment that significant progress was made in the territorial Conferences. Agreement seemed likely in Southern Rhodesia and he hoped that the same would soon be true in Northern Rhodesia.[42]

[40] Greenfield, *Testimony*, *op. cit.*, p. 199; Welensky Papers, 20/4, f. 98, Greenfield to Welensky, 10 February 1961.

[41] *Daily Mail*, 10 February 1961; Welensky Papers, 20/18, Telephone conversation between Welensky and Roberts, 10 February 1961.

[42] Welensky Papers, 20/2, f. 125, Macmillan to Welensky, 10 February 1961.

However, despite a motion from 65 Tories demanding a slowing of the hand-over of power in Africa, Macmillan showed quite a different face the next day when he wrote to Welensky stating that the Northern Rhodesian Conference could not be prolonged any longer and that decisions were imperative. He said the delegations were so far apart that a solution would have to be imposed. Not giving an inch, though acknowledging Greenfield's help, Macmillan announced that the Africans would have a slight majority. He knew that this presented Welensky with difficulties, especially when Whitehead had to win his referendum, and thus he argued that perhaps Sandys had found the answer because the double-Member constituencies would force candidates to appeal to both races, thereby promoting the non-racial ideal which he and Welensky favoured. The African nationalists would reject the idea, he said, and the Governments would have to face a period of strife. The Northern Rhodesian problem had to be settled quickly so that the Review could be reconvened and he wanted Welensky's ideas as swiftly as possible. Macmillan appended the gist of two schemes. The first, based on Sandys's idea, proposed that the legislature should contain six official, two nominated and 45 elected Members divided in the ratio 15:15:15. The upper roll would choose the first 15, the lower the second, and both together would elect the third. The advantages were that the scheme was simple, it favoured multi-racial politics and could not be labelled as providing either parity or a majority for either side. The alternative was a house of six official Members, two nominated unofficial Members, 16 Members elected by the upper roll, 18 Members elected by the lower roll, and 12 national Members elected by both rolls. Amongst the last would be three seats reserved for Africans, five for non-Africans and the rest would be nondescript. The upper roll franchise would be unaltered, but the lower would be adjusted to achieve an electorate of 70 000 and not the 100 000 which had been proposed. The size of the Executive Council would be settled after the Review had decided on the re-distribution of functions, but the leader of the majority party would be consulted on all appointments and portfolios. There would be an advisory house of Chiefs and, finally, a decision would be taken as to whether the scheme would affect Barotseland.[43]

On receipt of these schemes, Welensky telephoned Greenfield to say that he liked neither. The British Government thought that the UFP would win twelve of the nondescript seats, but Welensky thought that it was more likely that Moffat's Liberal Party would capture at least five. Greenfield, however, said that he had already rejected both schemes because they contained too many imponderables. They were probably unworkable and would depend heavily on delimitation. Sandys had expected his reaction, Greenfield said. Welensky told him that he had suggested that the existing Constitution should be adjusted by more reserved seats for Africans, but that the idea had been rejected by Macleod when he proposed an enlargement of the upper roll influence on the lower roll elections. Welensky said he had also asked for the postponement of any decision to allow examination of the two alternatives being offered. He would be meeting his Cabinet and Whitehead, and hoped

[43] *The Rhodesia Herald*, 11 February 1961; Welensky Papers, 20/4, f. 90, Macmillan to Welensky, 11 February 1961.

to furnish Sandys with counter-proposals. He warned Greenfield that, if Macleod took his decision at the time he threatened to do so, the Federal Government would have to act and the die would be cast. In a letter written after this conversation, Greenfield warned Welensky that Sandys was determined to proceed with his 15:15:15 scheme.[44]

On the next day, 12 February, after the Federal Cabinet meeting, Welensky informed Sandys that both schemes were unacceptable. The British, Welensky said, were quite wrong in believing that the upper roll would be entirely European because advancement in employment would make increasing numbers of Africans eligible. The effect of this would be to ensure an African majority, if the upper and lower rolls were to influence equally the election of the national Members. There were already 3 000 non-Europeans on the upper roll, and by 1965 there would be 8 000. In addition, the Asians had already aligned themselves with the African nationalists. Welensky thought that delimitation would present insuperable difficulties and revealed that his Cabinet disliked the abandonment of cross-voting. The schemes were equally unacceptable to the Southern Rhodesian Government, he said, and it threatened secession if either were implemented. Indeed, he added, Whitehead was about to tell him (Sandys) that their agreement on Southern Rhodesia would be broken if the schemes were accepted.[45]

As the tabling of the proposals in the Northern Rhodesian Conference was imminent, the Federal Government had hurriedly drawn up two alternative schemes and Welensky informed Sandys of them in a second dispatch on the same day. The first had 25 upper and 15 lower roll Members and eleven official Members. Each roll would exercise an influence of 20 per cent on the election of the other's Members. The second would have 18 upper and 16 lower roll Members and ten special Members who could be relied on to support moderate policies. The franchise would be broadened for the lower roll and there would be a 20 per cent cross-voting influence. The ten special Members would include officials holding portfolios and men drawn from commerce, mining and other walks of life. In both schemes the Executive Council would be chosen on the advice of the leader of the majority party. Both schemes would have bills of rights, constitutional councils and entrenched clauses which could only be amended by special referenda.[46]

At the meeting of the Federal Cabinet, Welensky had declared that the position was so serious that "open conflict" with the British Government was highly likely. Agreeing, his Ministers accepted that the imposition of unpalatable proposals should be resisted by every possible means despite any consequences. Both Whitehead and Field had indicated that they would support any resistance, and it was suggested in the Cabinet that the Federal Army should be mobilised as a token of determination. However, it was agreed that it would be sufficient to call out the Northern Rhodesian territorial battalions which would be entirely justifiable in the light of the tension resulting from Kaunda's "Mau Mau" statement. It was decided that this

[44] Welensky Papers, 20/4, f. 95, Telephone conversation between Welensky and Greenfield, 11 February 1961; f. 23, Greenfield to Welensky, 11 February 1961.

[45] *Ibid.*, f. 86, Welensky to Sandys, 12 February 1961.

[46] *Ibid.*, f. 88, Welensky to Sandys, 12 February 1961.

would be done immediately and all the Northern Rhodesian Acting-Governor would be told was that it was a necessary precaution. Accordingly, Welensky informed Sandys of the action to be taken.[47]

Then Welensky telephoned Sandys in the evening to read out the Federal electoral schemes for Northern Rhodesia. However, Sandys rejected them because both had upper roll majorities. He lauded the virtues of his 15:15:15 scheme, but Welensky maintained that the upper roll majority was the bulwark of European interests. Sandys was quick to remark that this contradicted Welensky's assertion that responsibility and not colour had to be the criterion. Then they argued about the merits of cross-voting and cross-benches. Welensky repeatedly demanded an examination of the two Federal schemes, but Sandys ignored him and continued to press the advantage of his. Welensky could not understand how Sandys could claim that the national seats would not be captured by extremists when nobody yet knew what the constituencies would be. Sandys promised that, if Welensky accepted equal numbers of upper and lower roll Members, he would consider any reasonable method of electing the national Members, except one which would produce a European majority. He also ruled out electoral colleges as a retrogressive step. At that moment the line was cut.[48]

Greenfield also furnished Sandys with his objections to his scheme. The foremost of these was the abandonment of basic principles on which the current Constitution was founded. There was a need for more Africans in the legislature, but he felt that their representation should not be increased disproportionately. It was also important to retain control in the responsible hands of the upper roll. To divide Northern Rhodesia three times for delimitation would create immense difficulties and impossibly large constituencies. Greenfield claimed that the British eagerness to overthrow the existing Constitution was only aggravating the situation in Northern Rhodesia. The Constitution was only two years old and, he asked, what hope would there be of the new one lasting any longer? He told Sandys that he appeared to have no qualms in placing Africans in power when there were no senior African civil servants and not a single black lawyer, chartered accountant, dentist or architect. There were only two or three African doctors, a number of clergymen and a substantial number of school teachers, but few with degrees. Greenfield, however, proposed to supply ideas of his own.[49]

The seriousness of the situation was forcibly illustrated by a message which Greenfield sent to Welensky warning that prominent members of the Southern Rhodesian division of the UFP were planning to demand the secession of Southern Rhodesia if the Northern Rhodesian Conference produced something they disliked. Greenfield wondered why the UFP should waste its money on the Southern Rhodesian division and its referendum when its leaders were prepared to double-cross the Party.[50]

On the morrow, 13 February, the mobilisation of the Northern Rhodesian

[47] *Ibid.*, FGC(61), Special Meeting, Federal Cabinet, 12 February 1961; 20/4, f. 86, Welensky to Sandys, 12 February 1961.

[48] *Ibid.*, 20/4, f. 77, Telephone conversation between Welensky and Sandys, 12 February 1961.

[49] *Ibid.*, f. 71, Greenfield to Sandys, 12 February 1961.

[50] *Ibid.*, 7/6, f. 8, Greenfield to Welensky, 12 February 1961.

battalions was announced and *The Times* depicted it as unwarranted because Kaunda, a moderate, had only warned of the dangers ahead. Welensky's first action of the day was to inform Sandys by telephone that his Cabinet and Whitehead had again rejected the British 15:15:15 scheme. He said that he and Whitehead thought it might be best if they went to London but they did not expect to be welcomed as Macleod was about to table this scheme. However, Sandys surprised Welensky by welcoming the proposed visit. Sandys held out little hope, however, for the acceptance at the Conference of the British scheme, because it did not provide parity, and asked again for Federal ideas which would not produce a European majority. Welensky replied that Whitehead rejected parity even between the rolls, but Sandys warned that there was little point in resuscitating old ideas because they would not be considered. These included upper roll majorities or anything which could be labelled a European majority. Sandys thought that, if the only result of Welensky's visit to London was deadlock, the situation would be immeasurably worse. Sandys still preferred the British scheme and felt that assurances could be furnished on future political evolution but that, as the course of events could not be guaranteed, it was desirable to avoid accusations of bad faith.

Welensky wished to avoid any misunderstanding and asked Sandys to be frank if he did not want him to come to London. If he did not, Welensky warned that "the balloon would go up". Sandys had to understand that Whitehead's support was necessary, and that it could only be secured by providing a majority of two or more upper roll seats. It was pointless to suggest to Whitehead that the British Government would receive him only on condition that he did not advance any ideas. However, Sandys was equally obstinate and continued to press the unacceptability of the label of "European majority". He revealed that Macleod had at first greeted the 15:15:15 scheme with hostility and it was a major step forward that he should have accepted it. Welensky nevertheless spurned any preconditions to discussion and Sandys rang off after rejecting the two extra upper roll seats. However, he agreed to speak to Macmillan and telephone back in an hour.[51]

Welensky's luggage was ready and two aircraft seats had been reserved for himself and Whitehead when Sandys telephoned at 11 a.m. to say that Macmillan and he thought that the situation would be dangerously aggravated if they arrived. He feared that any outcome would be ascribed to their pressure and any consequent action would be adversely affected by Welensky's dramatisation. It would be better to adjourn the Conference and reconvene it in Lusaka. Welensky replied that he would prefer not to go to London, and Sandys then claimed that, because the Conference had to be given something, he had suggested to Macleod that he should briefly outline the 15:15:15 scheme in a statement to it. Welensky maintained that the British Government was accordingly proposing parity, but Sandys disagreed because it only applied to two-thirds of the seats and, moreover, the word "parity" would not be used.[52]

[51] *Ibid.*, 20/4, f. 75, Telephone conversation between Welensky and Sandys, 10 a.m., 13 February 1961.

[52] *Ibid.*, f. 68, Telephone conversation between Welensky and Sandys, 11 a.m., 13 February 1961.

At 6 p.m. Welensky rang Sandys to say that his senior Cabinet colleagues and Whitehead had accepted the proposed statement but only as a basis for negotiation. A reasonable number of the national roll seats had to be controlled by the upper roll to keep power in responsible hands. Sandys disagreed because this implied an upper roll majority and would wreck everything. Welensky had feared this reaction but claimed that not only were his Ministers adamant on this, but that their suggestion was reasonable. He knew that if the 15:15:15 scheme were presented unaltered, Kaunda would immediately detect the concession of parity and make much of it. Sandys, however, expected Kaunda to dismiss the scheme as an utterly unacceptable betrayal. Indeed, he revealed, Kaunda had just written to Macmillan demanding again African majorities in the Legislative and Executive Councils. Welensky was not surprised because, in his opinion, Kaunda had been encouraged to make such demands.

Welensky explained that he could not persuade Whitehead to go any further. He thought, though, if a holding formula for further negotiations could be discovered to satisfy all parties, he might be able to bring Whitehead round. Sandys said that he was not seeking any public statements from Welensky. He just wanted to know where he stood. Macleod would keep his proposals secret but there was the danger of leaks. If Welensky felt impelled to say something, he could indicate that he had accepted the 15:15:15 formula as a basis for negotiation. Welensky replied that he had considered this, but Whitehead had insisted that, if there were leakage, he could only say that negotiations would be based on domination by the upper roll. Sandys then recapitulated: the Conference would be told of the 15:15:15 scheme in general terms and would be adjourned for discussion between the parties and the Governor in Lusaka. Welensky would then arrive for the Commonwealth Prime Ministers' Conference in two weeks' time and negotiations would be resumed.[53]

They spoke again at 6.45 p.m. and Welensky reported that Whitehead had, with the utmost reluctance, agreed to the proposed course, provided that there was no public statement outside the Conference. Sandys agreed and wanted Welensky also to remain silent so as not to affect adversely either the Northern Rhodesian Conference or the Southern Rhodesian referendum. Welensky terminated the call by saying that he was sick of being in the middle, of being "the ham in the sandwich".[54]

Sandys summed up the day's exchanges in a telegram that night and asked Welensky to call him early in the morning if necessary. Welensky duly telephoned because Sandys had omitted to mention in the telegram that he and Whitehead had agreed without commitment. He also demanded that Macleod should be deliberately vague on the national roll Members because something other than their election should be considered. Sandys hoped Welensky would not persist with this because electoral colleges could not be considered.

Welensky, however, would not allow any doors to be closed because such formidable difficulties had to be resolved. Sandys doubted that Macleod

[53] *Ibid.*, f. 65, Telephone conversation between Welensky and Sandys, 6 p.m., 13 February 1961.

[54] *Ibid.*, f. 64, Telephone conversation between Welensky and Sandys, 6.45 p.m., 13 February 1961.

would accept such late changes to his statement, but said he would try to secure his co-operation.[55]

On the previous evening Welensky and Whitehead had addressed a packed political meeting and Welensky had drawn applause by declaring he would hold the British Government to Lennox-Boyd's promises in 1958 on the exclusion of racial representation and that it had to proclaim its support either for African nationalism or partnership and moderation. He had warned the African nationalists that, if they continued to seek domination, they would force the white man to look after his own interests.[56]

Apparently Sandys had not been told of this speech but a rumour reached him that Welensky had mobilised two territorial battalions in Southern Rhodesia and he was sufficiently alarmed to telephone Welensky at 12.45 p.m. for confirmation. Denying the rumour, Welensky suggested that the Press had misinterpreted the call-up of 15 signallers from Southern Rhodesia to serve with the Northern Rhodesian battalions. He wondered if Sandys thought he was preparing a *coup d'état,* but Sandys merely asked to be informed if Welensky thought it necessary to call up further battalions.

When Welensky promised to comply, Sandys questioned the second rumour that the Federal Assembly had been recalled for the morrow. Welensky denied it and, as he was going fishing for the day at Kariba, hoped that all crises could be postponed until his return. Sandys, for his part, trusted that there would be no leakage of their private conversations to avoid accusations of private assurances. Welensky avowed that he would say nothing. Then he told Sandys of the meeting on the previous evening. It had attracted the largest audience ever, he said, and he and Whitehead were so well received that he was hopeful of success in the referendum.[57]

Welensky and Sandys confirmed their conversations by cable. Welensky hoped that they had removed the possibility of disagreement over Northern Rhodesia. He reiterated his lack of commitment and his demand for discussion on the national roll Members. He wanted a copy of Macleod's statement to the Conference immediately. Sandys, in his cable, repeated his anxiety about the secrecy of the negotiations because of the possible effect on the Conference. He had to confess that Welensky's demands for changes had only been known half an hour before Macleod's delivery of his statement of which the delegates had already received copies. Nonetheless, Sandys assured Welensky, when speaking, Macleod had met his point, saying that the British Government would consider methods of achieving the same aim. Sandys said he had telegraphed Macleod's speech and would send the record of the Conference when it was ready. Finally, he confirmed officially that Welensky had furnished his ideas as to how he wanted the amendments to the Northern Rhodesian Constitution effected.[58]

[55] *Ibid.*, f. 56, Sandys to Welensky, 14 February 1961; f. 60, Telephone conversation between Welensky and Sandys, 9.45 a.m., 14 February 1961.

[56] *The Rhodesia Herald*, 14 February 1961.

[57] Welensky Papers, 20/4, f. 55, Telephone conversation between Welensky and Sandys, 14 February 1961.

[58] *Ibid.*, f. 59, Welensky to Sandys, 14 February 1961; f. 62, Sandys to Welensky, 14 February 1961; ff. 53–54, Macleod's Statement to the Northern Rhodesian Conference, 14 February 1961.

Welensky told his Cabinet of these exchanges and of his acceptance without commitment of the British 15:15:15 scheme, emphasising that the method of electing national roll Members had not yet been devised. He was confident, he said, that the strong Federal stand had improved his Government's position and would strengthen its hand at the Review. He would press for the reconvening of the Review in May.[59]

If, in fact, Welensky was satisfied with his efforts, he would be shocked out of his complacency when he read the telegraphed statement as well as a report of what Macleod had said in delivering it to the Conference. Both varied significantly from what Sandys had led him to believe the statement would contain. Macleod had unveiled the 15:15:15 scheme and had then committed himself to allowing the upper and lower rolls equal influence in the election of the national roll Members. Thus he had trodden underfoot Sandys's agreement with Welensky. Macleod had gone further and had said that the franchise would be adjusted to bring a greater number of Africans onto both the upper and lower rolls. Nevertheless, he had refused to elaborate on the adjustment and had drawn abuse from the African delegates who believed that he was selling them into Welensky's hands. He had closed his statement by indicating that the next step would be consultation by the Governor with all Parties before making final recommendations to the British Government.[60]

The perusal of this statement provoked instant accusations of betrayal from Welensky and Whitehead. Welensky protested to Macmillan that Macleod had exceeded his understanding with Sandys and, consequently, the Federal Government could not accept the statement as a basis for further negotiation. The particularly offensive embellishment, he said, was the commitment to adjust the upper roll franchise, including its income and educational qualifications. He had insisted also that the question of the election of the national roll Members remain open and had attached the greatest importance to it, but Macleod had ignored him. Macleod had also been evasive on the constitutional council and the bill of rights.

Welensky told Macmillan that he could not understand why Sandys had only received his message half an hour before the Conference, as it had been sent on an emergency basis hours earlier. In the event, he said, Macleod had ignored him and had "slammed the door" by saying that the votes for the national roll seats would be shared equally between the upper and lower rolls and that any method chosen had to achieve this result. The effect was that not only would there be parity of representation for the upper and lower roll voters, but parity of influence between the rolls in the election of the national roll Members. If this were not enough, Macleod had then spoken of bringing more Africans onto the upper roll. This was a complete "sell-out" to African nationalism and would put paid to Whitehead's chances of winning the referendum. Welensky said that it gave him no other choice but to reserve his position.[61]

Whitehead protested equally strongly to Sandys that, if the proposals were

[59] *Ibid.*, FGC(61), 6th Meeting, Federal Cabinet, 14 February 1961.
[60] *The Rhodesia Herald*, 16 February 1961.
[61] Welensky Papers, 20/4, f. 51, Welensky to Macmillan, 15 February 1961; f. 52, Whitehead to Sandys, 15 February 1961.

implemented, Southern Rhodesia would be forced to secede. He warned that he would support any action which Welensky might take to prevent their implementation. He and Welensky, nonetheless, could take some comfort from a demand by 91 Conservatives for caution with regard to British action in Africa. Macmillan averred promptly to Welensky that he was examining the protests and that there was still time to negotiate because the Conference would last a few days longer than expected, and a public statement was only required by Monday, 20 February. This gave ample opportunity, he said, to correct what seemed to be poor drafting.[62]

Welensky and Whitehead immediately held a joint session of their Cabinets early on the morning of 16 February. The Cabinets accepted that Macleod had exceeded the understanding with Sandys and that thereby the African nationalists would gain a majority in the Northern Rhodesian legislature which would force Whitehead to lead a secessionist movement. A grave situation confronted them and remedial measures were required. Welensky agreed with Macmillan that there was still time, but he felt that a firm stand was imperative. Nevertheless, he did not want to make empty gestures or to throw down a gauntlet which the British Government would be forced to pick up. As the security situation was explosive and the Federal economy was grinding to a standstill, he urged that nothing should be done which would exacerbate the affair unless it was unavoidable.

Whitehead was more hot-headed as he believed that only firm action by the Federal Government would impress the British. He was convinced that the British Government was so intent on implementing its policy that it would use force if necessary. Time was of the essence and it would be dangerous not to mobilise the four effective territorial battalions because only they would deter the British from contemplating the use of force. The public would welcome such a clear lead. He promised that his Government would support any effort, but he warned that, if Northern Rhodesia was beyond saving, he would have to put Southern Rhodesian interests first.

The meeting felt that measures should be taken to defend the main airfields even though little could be done if the British were determined to land troops. A resolution could be tabled in the Federal Assembly demanding independence but the taking of it would be unconstitutional and would have to be backed by force. Sufficient notice had to be given to reservists, and the problem was one of tactics, of how to prevent the British Government riding roughshod over their views. Strongarm tactics had to be countered by like methods. It was most important not to lose the initiative, and there was little time because the Macleod statement would be leaked and, once it was, alteration would be impossible. Henceforth no reliance could be placed on British ministerial promises.

Welensky remained cautious and wanted time to allow Macleod to make amends. As long as this was possible, he wanted no irrevocable action taken or last ditch stand made because the consequences of confrontation would be immense and far-reaching. He proposed that he and Whitehead should warn the British High Commissioner of the gravity of the circumstances, that,

[62] *Ibid.*, f. 50, Macmillan to Welensky, 16 February 1961.

unless Macmillan made amends, he would have to recall the Federal Assembly and explain the situation. The meeting concurred and suspended all action until Macmillan replied.[63]

Accordingly, Metcalf was informed at 10.55 a.m. by Welensky and Whitehead of their objections to Macleod's statement. They rejected the commitment on the equal influence of the rolls in the election of the national roll Members because it "sold the pass". If adjustments were not made before the statement was leaked, the Federal and Southern Rhodesian Assemblies would have to be recalled. Above all, Metcalf had to convey the message that, if nothing were done, the Federal experiment would be considered to be terminated and Southern Rhodesia would secede.[64]

Within hours Macmillan replied claiming that, before Metcalf's message had arrived, he had decided to revise the entire section dealing with the franchise, leaving mention only of changes in the lower qualifications. The European grip on the upper roll seats would be retained through the qualifications and by delimitation. No final decision would be taken until Welensky's views were known. The intention was to add no more than 2 000 voters to the upper roll, but this would not be discussed in the Conference. Macmillan would send the revised version as soon as it was ready. With regard to the national roll Members, Macmillan said he had understood that Welensky had agreed to the equal influence but without commitment and would, with reluctance, allow the Conference to examine it. Macmillan could not understand why it was thought that the African nationalists would capture all these seats when the weight of the upper roll would be equal to that of the lower. In any case, there was the additional safeguard inserted by Macleod that, to be successful, a candidate would have to gain a fixed percentage of votes from both rolls. Furthermore, Macleod was prepared to consider other methods to achieve the same result. Therefore, Macmillan could not accept that there had been any departure from the agreement with Sandys. As further evidence of this, he enclosed what Macleod had said about the constitutional council and the declaration of rights.[65]

Before replying, Welensky telephoned Greenfield, finding him mystified by a sudden request to spend "a happy weekend" with Sandys working on Macleod's statement after it had been presented to the Conference and then withdrawn. Greenfield could not understand how, if it became necessary, Macleod would be able to explain that he (Greenfield) had assisted in its revision. Greenfield had tried to discover if the Conference would consider a revised statement but could get nothing out of Alport who had "wriggled and writhed". The British Government was telling him nothing. Welensky informed him that he understood from Macmillan that as the Conference was being prorogued that day, it would not examine the revised statement which would be issued as a White Paper in three days' time, on Monday, 20 February. He wanted Greenfield to work on the White Paper and eradicate

[63] *Ibid.*, ff. 44–45, Minutes of a Meeting of the Federal and Southern Rhodesian Cabinets, 16 February 1961.
[64] *Ibid.*, ff. 41–42, Minutes of a Meeting between Welensky, Whitehead and M. R. Metcalf, 16 February 1961.
[65] *Ibid.*, f. 46, Macmillan to Welensky, 16 February 1961.

the equal influence of the rolls *vis-à-vis* the election of the national roll Members so that it would be possible to reconvene the Federal Review and save the Southern Rhodesian referendum.

Greenfield confessed to have been surprised when Sandys had said that Welensky had accepted the electoral arrangements as a basis for negotiation. Welensky, somewhat fiercely, replied that he had done so without commitment and on the understanding that the method of selecting the national roll Members would not be defined. Greenfield maintained that Sandys had used this as a "beach-head" for an advance. Accordingly, Welensky ordered Greenfield to make it clear to Sandys that it would be hopeless to insist that the national roll seats be divided equally between the upper and lower rolls. Greenfield suggested that Welensky should explain to Macmillan that the new Nyasaland upper roll had been based on the existing Northern Rhodesian one, and that this arrangement would be undone by Macleod. In addition, the retention of the power to nominate would demote Northern Rhodesia to Nyasaland's position before the recent revision, when in 1958 Northern Rhodesia had been constitutionally far advanced compared with Nyasaland.[66]

That day, 17 February, the expected leak occurred for which Welensky blamed Macleod. Consequently, the Press revealed the 15:15:15 proposal and wondered if Welensky's seemingly sudden return from the fishing trip to Kariba heralded a constitutional crisis.[67] This crisis, of course, was in fact weeks old and not nearly over.

Replying to Macmillan, Welensky recalled his agreement with Sandys and its aim to keep control in responsible hands. He acknowledged that he had accepted, without commitment, parity between the upper and lower roll seats and believed that there would be a system of weighting for the election of the national roll Members to favour responsible elements. He had urged that doors should not be closed on the ways in which this could be achieved. Macmillan, he said, had referred to the message from Sandys on 14 February but had ignored the subsequent telephonic and telegraphic exchanges. In these Welensky had insisted that all Macleod should say was that he favoured a method of election of the national roll Members, which would receive a substantial measure of support from both rolls, and he would welcome any suggestions on achieving this. Yet Macleod, Welensky noted, had committed himself to the equal influence and had said: "The votes from each of the two rolls would be equalised by averaging the percentage of the votes cast on each roll which is secured by each candidate." This would certainly give control to the more immature. Intimidation was already having its effect and, in addition, the Asians had thrown in their lot with the African nationalists. By 1965 there would be 10 000 African upper roll voters and many would vote on racialist lines. If the African nationalists failed to gain a majority at the first election, they would at the second. African moderate opinion would be swamped and it was utterly unreasonable that it should be done through the election of the national roll Members.

Welensky hoped the matter could be rectified and the question of method

[66] *Ibid.*, f. 20, Telephone conversation between Welensky and Greenfield, 11.20 a.m., 17 February 1961.

[67] *The Rhodesia Herald*, 17 February 1961.

be left open. The White Paper should make no reference to the equalising of votes and say only that both rolls would have an influence. The requirement of a minimum qualifying percentage for each successful national roll candidate would disqualify most aspirants, as anyone proposed by one party was most unlikely to gain its rival's support. Such a device introduced the power of boycott and would make a mockery of the election because the party attracting the least support from both rolls was likely to capture the seats. The idea of bringing in 2 000 upper roll voters was equally unpalatable to those who believed that this roll should contain the responsible elements. This was a cardinal principle which could not be altered, and certainly nothing similar had been suggested for the Southern Rhodesian upper roll. Welensky said he knew that the Press had been given some details on the lower roll, and he demanded to see them. Another objectionable feature was Macleod's failure to limit the power of nomination. Welensky wished to ensure that the pass was not sold as, if his ideas were rejected, he and Whitehead would face a grave situation. Consequently, Welensky warned, Whitehead was writing in a similar vein to Sandys. Welensky thereafter promptly briefed Major Wall.[68]

A crisis seemed imminent when all nine London Sunday papers headlined the deadlock of the Northern Rhodesian Conference. There were stories of the Strategic Reserve of the British Army being alerted, and a flurry of meetings at Admiralty House "to save the situation". *The Sunday Times* and the *Sunday Observer* greeted with disdain the apparent behind-the-scenes haggling with Welensky.

Against this background the exchanges began that day, Sunday, 19 February. Firstly Macmillan explained to Welensky that the factual account of the Conference, which would be published on the morrow in the White Paper, had to contain Macleod's statement exactly as he had delivered it to the Conference. Thereafter Macleod would inform the Commons of the next step, and the draft of this explanatory statement was *en route* to Salisbury. Macleod could not be vague at this stage, but would leave a number of important matters for negotiation by Hone in Lusaka. Macmillan promised Welensky that he would be consulted throughout. Macleod had indicated that the upper roll changes would be minor, and Macmillan thought that his Government had gone far to meet Welensky "even though it involved destroying any hope there was of obtaining African agreement at the Conference". Macmillan welcomed any comments from Welensky, and declared that both he and Sandys would be standing by to answer them. He looked forward to discussing the whole issue with Welensky in London in March at the Commonwealth Prime Ministers' Conference.[69]

In his draft explanatory statement to the Commons, Macleod said that the lack of agreement forced him to impose a solution. This he described without omitting the minimum percentage to be secured by successful national roll candidates or the averaging of the votes cast on each roll. Indeed, he argued that these devices should substantially increase the number of African seats, while preserving the non-racial approach. The modification of the lower roll

[68] Welensky Papers, 20/4, ff. 17–19, Welensky to Macmillan, 17 February 1961; 43/*Wall*, Welensky to Major P. Wall, 18 February 1961.
[69] *Ibid.*, 20/4, f. 14, Macmillan to Welensky, 19 February 1961.

would secure an electorate of 70 000. The upper roll would be broadened slightly by lowering the income and educational qualifications. At least two African and two European unofficial Members would be appointed to the Executive Council on the advice of the leader of the majority party. A bill of rights and other machinery would protect the individual, and the changes would be discussed with the Paramount Chief of Barotseland. The sop for Welensky was contained in Paragraph 13 which said that many matters naturally remained to be settled, including delimitation, the return of the national roll Members and adjustments to the franchise.[70]

Macleod's draft explanatory statement had barely arrived in Salisbury when Sandys telephoned at midday seeking Welensky's opinion and was bluntly told that it had been quickly discussed with Whitehead and was unacceptable. Sandys replied, equally bluntly, that his Government, having met Welensky on practically every point, could go no further. The only matter which had not been altered to suit Welensky was the parity issue. Welensky disagreed vehemently because the statement went back on almost everything on which they had agreed. For example, the upper roll qualifications would still be adjusted. He warned that the matter would be reviewed that afternoon jointly by the Federal and Southern Rhodesian Cabinets.

Then Welensky asked if the Press was correct in reporting the imminent dispatch of British troops to Northern Rhodesia. Sandys replied that the War Office had denied this publicly. What he wanted was Welensky's objections to the statement. Welensky obliged saying they centred on the weakening of the upper roll influence. Sandys, however, warned that anything favouring that roll was unacceptable to "world opinion". Welensky prophesied that the scheme would only ensure the return of Moffat and his Liberal Party, but Sandys maintained that it would suit the kind of multi-racial party which Welensky had always claimed to lead. However, Welensky remained convinced that power would pass to the least responsible element.

Greenfield was in the room with Sandys, and Sandys offered to leave while they talked, but Welensky replied that the matter was too serious for such niceties. Welensky thereupon told Sandys that Whitehead had to meet his UFP territorial congress on 22 February, and that it would reject the proposals as they stood which would mean the end of the Federation. Sandys wondered at the effect of Nkomo's repudiation of the Southern Rhodesian agreement, but Welensky said that Whitehead intended to ignore it and make the changes. It was the Northern Rhodesian proposals, Welensky explained, that left Whitehead at a loss for something to say.

Sandys said he had Macmillan's permission to reveal to him that there had been a Cabinet crisis the previous day and that he believed it was imperative to avoid the serious situation which would arise if the Northern Rhodesian Africans rioted on discovering that their ambitions had been frustrated by pressure from Welensky. Unmoved, Welensky replied that Macleod's usual technique was merely being exposed and that he liked everyone to dance to his tune. This was exactly why the UFP had boycotted the Conference. Welensky said his own position was becoming impossible.

[70] *Ibid.*, f. 15, Text of Draft Statement to be delivered by Macleod on Monday, 20, or Tuesday, 21 February 1961, (undated).

Sandys demanded again Welensky's specific objections, asking if he would accept the minimum percentage. Welensky rejected it as totally unacceptable. Sandys next asked about the equal influence of the rolls *vis-à-vis* the election of the national roll Members, suggesting that Welensky should ignore the racial aspects. Welensky replied he would not because African and Asian voters were being intimidated. Sandys claimed that Macleod had left the matter of this election open, but Welensky found that, to the contrary, there were specific commitments which meant that either candidates with minor support would be elected, or there would be deadlock. Sandys hoped that the matter could be reconsidered, but Welensky doubted that it would be. Macleod, he said, had also omitted a constitutional council though he had mentioned the declaration of rights. Welensky thought that Macleod had realised that land rights could thereby be raised and the privileges of the Africans questioned.

Sandys stated that at least his Government had met its obligations on the upper roll. Welensky disagreed because the qualifications would be lower than those of Nyasaland. He confessed that he lacked the skill to give words multiple meaning and had construed Macmillan's original proposals as stating that the upper roll would only be affected by the addition of one or two minor categories. Sandys thought that the proposed addition of some 2 000 voters could be classified as minor, but Welensky saw the point of difference as being the retention of power in responsible hands. Sandys asked Welensky again for the "background" to his objections and warned him that he would have to bear responsibility for the consequences of the Africans realising that he had thwarted Macleod. Welensky agreed, but thought that he could not be asked to accept anything which would sound the Federation's death-knell. He wished Sandys to understand that he knew he had been deliberately manoeuvred into this position.

Sandys yielded the telephone to Greenfield and Welensky quickly described the state of affairs since Nkomo's repudiation of the Southern Rhodesian constitutional proposals. One likelihood was that the resolution accepting them would be rejected by the UFP territorial congress unless the Northern Rhodesian proposals were changed. He said he had advised Whitehead to withhold the resolution, since it was hopeless, and to consider only Southern Rhodesia's interests. Their Cabinets would meet jointly that afternoon and a stand had to be made because it was "now or never". Macleod had won, as Welensky knew he would, but, nevertheless the Federation's demise was unthinkable. Greenfield agreed that the conditions for the election of the national roll Members and the changes to the upper roll were completely unacceptable.[71]

At 4.15 p.m. Welensky informed the Cabinets that he had rejected Macleod's draft explanatory statement. Then he telephoned Greenfield who was working with Sandys on the White Paper. Greenfield reported that mention in it of changes to the upper roll qualifications had been removed and that a reference to the constitutional council had been inserted. In addition, the commitments on the election of the national roll Members had been erased,

[71] *Ibid.*, f. 9, Telephone conversation between Sandys, Greenfield and Welensky, 12.55 p.m., 19 February 1961.

and thus room for manoeuvre had been gained. The tactic henceforth should therefore be to play for time. However, Greenfield was not sure that Sandys knew Macleod's intentions and thought that Welensky should accept the White Paper as a basis for negotiation, laying particular emphasis on the aspects relating to the upper roll. Sandys, he said, had given him some details of the clash within the British Cabinet and he believed that Macleod would be dismissed. Greenfield and Welensky, nonetheless, felt that this would only happen in the aftermath. Greenfield said that Sandys was in a conciliatory mood and he had shown the changes to Macmillan who had accepted them, but was not sure that he could convince Macleod. Greenfield, with Sandys's permission, would elicit the support of Lord Kilmuir.

Welensky immediately informed the joint Cabinet meeting of what Sandys was prepared to delete from the White Paper and they then discussed the prospects for amendment to it in the light of the commitments already made by Macleod to the Conference. Any success depended on Sandys's ability to carry Macmillan and his Cabinet against Macleod. It was important to exploit the split in the British Cabinet, but not to make Sandys's task impossible. Nonetheless, it was the duty of the British Government to solve the problems created by Macleod.

Whitehead explained the difficulties of persuading his congress to accept the Southern Rhodesian proposals after Nkomo had repudiated them. The meeting accordingly agreed that Welensky should insist that the responsible element should dominate the election of the national roll Members and that the moderates should not be swamped by the lower roll. Thus it would be necessary to have a qualification of literacy in English as well as a minimum age of 30. The word "lowering" should not be used with regard to the upper roll, though some "broadening" was possible, provided Northern Rhodesia stayed aligned with the electoral systems in the rest of the Federation. Welensky would emphasise the importance of the constitutional council as the watchdog for the bill of rights. Mention would also be made of the absence of provision for amendment of the Constitution. It was agreed that Welensky would write thus to Macmillan, while Whitehead would tell Sandys that he would ignore Nkomo's repudiation.[72]

Welensky immediately wrote to Macmillan recognising, nevertheless, that any amendment to the White Paper to accommodate his views would be noticeable as departures from what Macleod had said at the Conference. Consequently, Welensky thought the British Government would have to claim that the changes reflected its current thinking.[73]

Macmillan answered Welensky after a meeting of the British Cabinet the next day, 20 February. However, before the dispatch arrived, Greenfield telephoned at 10 p.m. that day to say that he had just seen Macmillan and Sandys and had found them in a great muddle. They had made minor alterations to Macleod's explanatory statement which he would table in Parliament with the White Paper, but it was difficult to discover which would

[72] *Ibid.*, FGC(1), 7/16, Record of a Meeting of the Federal and Southern Rhodesian Cabinets, 19 February 1961; 20/4, f. 8, Telephone conversation between Welensky and Greenfield, 4.30 p.m., 19 February 1961.

[73] *Ibid.*, 20/4, f. 12, Welensky to Macmillan, 19 February 1961.

be the governing document. Macmillan and Sandys would not allow the upper roll to control the election of the national roll Members but had left some room to manoeuvre, with the result that Greenfield wanted all action suspended so that he could return to Salisbury as he found it difficult to work by telephone. Welensky, however, disagreed because Macleod's explanatory statement would be made public in the Commons debate on the morrow and would have a "shattering effect". Because of this, he said he would mobilise the remaining territorial battalions and recall the Federal Parliament. He suggested that Greenfield should tell Sandys of this action and warn him not to underrate the gravity of the situation. Welensky proposed to act only after he had read the published explanatory statement. Although Whitehead had argued strongly against any warning, Welensky thought it would be unwise not to give some notice. Believing that there was still room to manoeuvre, Greenfield agreed. Indeed, Welensky felt it might be as well to delay crossing the Rubicon until the White Paper had been examined. Greenfield revealed that he had asked Sandys to visit the Federation and that Sandys was considering it. Welensky welcomed this as he wanted to prevent commitments to the changes in the upper roll and to the equality of influence of both rolls on the election of the national roll Members. He ordered Greenfield to warn Sandys that, if his objections were ignored, he would act as he saw fit. Perhaps to reduce the temperature of the moment, Welensky then informed the public that he had been reassured by the British Government that it was not sending troops to Northern Rhodesia. He claimed he had sufficient forces to assist the territorial Governments to maintain order.[74]

At 8 a.m. on the next day, 21 February, Welensky laid Macmillan's answer before the Federal Cabinet. Macmillan had declared that it was impossible to erase all that had been said on the election of the national roll Members but that the question of the method had been left open. On the lower roll, 45 000 out of the 70 000 voters would be literate and the remainder would be headmen and the like. The reference to the downward adjustment of the upper roll had been removed and Macleod's explanatory statement would simply dwell on the possibility of changes to bring in 2 500 voters. There would be a reference to the constitutional council but none to constitutional amendment because, while Northern Rhodesia remained a protectorate, Britain could not divest herself of her responsibilities.

The Federal Cabinet found that these concessions amounted to nothing. Welensky believed that they would secure an African majority in the Legislative Council from which would emanate a spate of anti-Federal resolutions that would inevitably make the Federation unworkable. In Southern Rhodesia the position would become intolerable because pressure would be generated for far greater political advancement than was currently contemplated. He thought that he should tell Metcalf that he would recall Parliament and take certain military precautions which were amply justified. However, the recall, he said, could not be immediate because the Speaker wanted to give a week's notice. Wightwick had proposed a motion which called for a declaration of independence, but Welensky preferred to keep the motion in reserve and

[74] *Ibid.*, f. 6, Telephone conversation between Welensky and Greenfield, 10 p.m., 20 February 1961; *The Rhodesia Herald*, 21 February 1961.

instead table a "take-note" motion to test the feeling of the House. It would, of course, be necessary, he warned, to go to the country on the independence issue.

The Cabinet worried about preventing the outflow of capital and about holding the position while the country was being appealed to with regard to the independence issue. It might be preferable to adopt the independence motion and ask the electorate to endorse it. Welensky spoke of the wholly aggressive attitude of Whitehead who was demanding strenuous action to resist the imposition of the Northern Rhodesian proposals as a condition for his support for the preservation of the Federal structure. The Cabinet agreed that the situation was serious enough to warrant the adjournment of the current UFP congress. It decided to mobilise that evening four battalions of territorials and to ask Whitehead for his police reserve. Parliament would be recalled and action would be taken to prevent the flight of capital.[75]

At 10.20 a.m. Welensky told Metcalf it was clear that Macmillan would ignore Federal and Southern Rhodesian advice and allow Macleod's explanatory statement to be tabled. Welensky warned that the statement was totally unacceptable but promised to stay his hand until he had seen it. Thereafter he would announce his reasons for rejecting it, recall Parliament and mobilise troops to maintain order. He would hold the British Government responsible for whatever happened. He believed that his Government had been entirely reasonable in asking for time for further examination of the election of the national roll Members and that there should be no lowering of the upper roll qualification just to bring in 2 500 extra voters. Macmillan had refused to listen and consequently the majority of the seats would be captured by the African nationalist Parties, which would mean the end of the Federation. The British Government had not been left in any doubt as to Welensky's attitude as, since January 1960, he had warned that Southern Rhodesia would secede if African nationalists were allowed to dominate the two northern territories. The Northern Rhodesian proposals and what had happened in Nyasaland left Southern Rhodesia little other choice. By ignoring all advice, the British Government had cast the die and there was little chance of persuading the Southern Rhodesian division of the UFP to accept the constitutional proposals before it.

Roberts, who was present, pointed out that the policy of 1958 had been reversed and he and his two UFP colleagues had no choice but to resign from the Executive Council. Metcalf considered it his duty to state that his Government had taken considerable pains to meet the views of the Parties. He thought that, given goodwill, the Northern Rhodesian scheme could work and that the contemplated actions were extremely serious. Nevertheless, as decisions had been taken, he would inform his Government at once.[76]

Once Metcalf had gone, Welensky informed Greenfield by telephone of the morning's events and asked him to return to Salisbury as quickly as possible. Greenfield said that he had taxed Macmillan on the failure to consult the Federal Government on the franchise and that "the shot had gone home". He

[75] *Ibid.*, FGC(61), Special Meeting, 8 a.m., Federal Cabinet, 21 February 1961; 20/4, f. 5, Macmillan to Welensky, 20 February 1961.

[76] *Ibid.*, 20/4, ff. 3–4, Minutes of a Meeting between Welensky and Metcalf, 21 February 1961.

had commented to Macmillan on the Nyasaland upper roll being based on the current Northern Rhodesian one and that the cross-voting system was being eradicated in Northern Rhodesia just as it was being introduced in Southern Rhodesia, and was sure that these comments had hurt. He suggested that he should delay his return to watch Macleod deliver his statement in the Commons. Welensky agreed. He then asked Greenfield to brief Lord Salisbury.[77]

Welensky wrote to Joelson and others to ensure that they understood what was happening. Macleod duly delivered his statement with only the minor amendments effected by Macmillan and Sandys at the same time that he tabled the White Paper: *Northern Rhodesia: Proposals for Constitutional Change,* Command 1295. Welensky thereupon issued his public rejection of the proposals and described how he had striven to induce the British Government to abandon the system of racial representation and to keep government in responsible hands. By contrast, he said, the scheme proposed would promote bitter racial politics and entrench racial representation. The most objectionable feature would be the passing of control from responsible hands through the lower roll not only having 15 seats, but having an equal influence in the election of thc national roll Members. In addition, the African membership of the upper roll would steadily increase as wages improved. Thus power would pass to the African nationalists. It was a cardinal principle that government had to remain in responsible hands, and on this the Federal Government would make its stand. However, he thought that the African nationalists, when seeking election as national roll Members, would fail to secure the prescribed minimum percentage of the upper roll votes. Equally, moderate candidates would not secure the minimum percentage of the lower roll. Thus the result would be a mockery and he intended to resist it with everything at his command. Delimitation presented serious difficulties, and it was clear that the whole exercise had been unduly rushed. He had tried to persuade the British Government to delay a decision, and had taken the strongest exception to Macleod's technique of holding a conference without adequate preparation and then attempting to force a solution on all concerned without giving them time to consider the consequences. The British Government had seen fit to publish the proposals and had to accept responsibility for whatever happened. It left him with no alternative but to recall Parliament and mobilise a number of territorials.[78]

A situation of some embarrassment then developed because the Federal Army mobilised but Whitehead, failing to live up to his earlier bellicosity, did not call out his thousands of police reservists. He told a surprised Welensky that he did not think it was necessary and that his Police Commissioner, Colonel Spurling, had resisted the mobilisation as unwarranted because it

[77] *Ibid.*, f. 2, Telephone conversation between Welensky and Greenfield, 11.15 a.m., 21 February 1961.

[78] *Ibid.*, 24/151, ff. 85–86, Welensky to F. S. Joelson, 21 February 1961; *Northern Rhodesia: Proposals for Constitutional Change*, Command 1295 (London, February 1961); *Northern Rhodesia: Statement by the Secretary of State for the Colonies on the Proposals for Constitutional Change*, Command 1301 (London, February 1961); Welensky Papers, 7/12, f. 284, Welensky's Press Statement, 21 February 1961.

would disrupt his mens' lives when Southern Rhodesia was peaceful. Whitehead had not told Spurling the purpose of the exercise.[79]

Welensky would have been even more annoyed had he known that four days later Macmillan would record in his diary that he had received "a good telegram from Whitehead — who remains calm, rather enjoying Welensky whom he clearly regards as a bull in a china shop". Whitehead could afford to do so because his congress had not, as feared, rejected the Southern Rhodesian constitutional proposals. Yet, on 22 February, he joined the Federal Government, Field, van Eeden and the African nationalists in echoing Roberts's rejection of the proposals for Northern Rhodesia as "diabolical". Roberts, Dunlop, Malcolmson, Carlisle and Musumbulwa thereafter resigned from the Executive Council and were replaced by Sir John Moffat, Franklin and others. Greenfield, in London, declared that, in a continent already torn by strife and chaos, these proposals only added a new threat of disaster and disintegration.[80]

The Federal Attorney-General commented on a declaration of independence and adjudged it to require a *coup d'état* which would make those involved rebels guilty of treason and sedition. The Government, he said, would cease to have a legal existence, and it was probable that the territorial Governments, their judiciary and police would ignore the Acts of the Federal Government and refuse even to enforce laws validly enacted before the *coup*. As the new government would not be a successor to the existing Government, the civil servants would no longer be employed, though they might be re-engaged. In addition, their pensions would be in doubt because it would be impossible for the Government to raise loans.[81]

The Federal Cabinet nevertheless continued to examine the ramifications of any action. (This was paralleled in London where, as Macmillan now admits, preparations were begun to combat an open rebellion with force.) The Federal Cabinet decided to impose exchange control to curb the flight of capital, and re-examined the problem of protecting airfields. Alerted by sources within the Royal Air Force, the Federal defence chiefs warned of an abnormal build-up of British military and air strength in East Africa. They feared and wished to prevent a landing in the Federation, but had to concede that any decision would be based on politics. The Federal Ministers took note of these fears but thought it unlikely that the British Government was contemplating a pre-emptive act of aggression. It was more likely that it was preparing a counter to a possible *coup* by the Federal Government. In any case, they said, such British forces might not be unwelcome in the vicinity in the event of a major upheaval in the Congo where its Prime Minister, Lumumba, had just been murdered. Defence was a Federal function and, in normal circumstances, the British could not land troops in the Federation without permission. However, the possibility had to be faced that the British Government might act to defend its rights in the northern territories.[82]

[79] Author's interviews with Sir Roy Welensky and Col. B. G. Spurling.

[80] Macmillan, *At the End of the Day*, *op. cit.*, p. 311; *The Rhodesia Herald*, 22 February 1961.

[81] Welensky Papers, 20/2, f. 122, Federal Attorney-General to H. N. Parry, 22 February 1961.

[82] *Ibid.*, FGC(61), 7th Meeting, Federal Cabinet, 22 February 1961; Macmillan, *At the End of the Day*, *op. cit.*, p. 311.

In the event, Welensky ordered a photo-reconnaissance of Nairobi airport. In the course of that mission, a Canberra bomber of the Royal Rhodesian Air Force landed at Nairobi to the evident embarrassment of the Royal Air Force officers whose transport aircraft were assembled there. Two days later, by some means, the RRAF intercepted a secret telegram which denied the reports that Britain was preparing to take unilateral military action in Northern Rhodesia. All that was happening, it said, was that a mobility exercise, which had been planned for some time, was being held in Libya and Little Aden. However, because the British Government believed that the Africans might foment trouble in Northern Rhodesia over the constitutional proposals, the telegram did acknowledge that a force of transport aircraft was being built up at Nairobi for quick response to a call from the Federal Government if trouble spread to Nyasaland and Southern Rhodesia.[83]

(After the event, the British Secretary of State for the Air, Julian Amery, told Welensky that in fact Macleod had ordered the implementation of one of the contingency plans designed to prevent a *coup d'état*. The result was a warning to Amery from the senior ranks of the RAF that the move could not be kept secret because of the pro-Federal sympathies within their force. Amery, who had not known until that moment of Macleod's action, immediately went to Macmillan and demanded that the action be stopped. Macmillan complied.[84])

Macleod defended his explanatory statement in the Commons that evening, 22 February, declaring that, while he was bound to consult the Federal Government, the final decision on the Northern Rhodesian Constitution was his responsibility. He criticised the UFP for boycotting the Conference while it condemned the African leaders for their walk-outs at the Federal Review. He hoped that the UFP would re-consider and co-operate with the Governor so that his recommendations would reflect the opinion of the entire population of Northern Rhodesia.

Macleod was supported by the Conservatives but was roundly condemned by the Labour Party for producing racial proposals. Callaghan noted that Macmillan and Macleod had managed to discourage and offend every one of the major Parties. They had failed to gain any significant support for the proposals because they were believed to favour African majority, but had failed to offer this. Macleod, he said, seemed to be backing his horses in all possible ways.

To Callaghan, Macmillan's behaviour was even more curious, but he acknowledged that Macmillan suffered from the disadvantage of not being trusted by the Europeans in the Federation because of his assurances on secession and the Monckton Commission. Welensky was clearly determined not to be hoodwinked twice. Callaghan was sure there would be no solution until the Africans and Europeans heard the British Government speak with one voice. Part of the problem, he said, was that the Conservatives were split on Colonial issues and, in particular, over the relationship between black and white. The result was that Macleod was not only insulted publicly by Welen-

[83] Sir Roy Welensky, *Welensky's 4 000 Days* (London, 1964), p. 296; Welensky Papers, 7/45, f. 90, H. Hawkins to W. S. Parker, 24 February 1961.

[84] Author's interview with Sir Roy Welensky.

sky in the midst of the most delicate negotiations, but was stabbed in the back by 96 Conservative back-benchers.

Callaghan criticised the minimum percentage of votes which a national roll candidate would have to secure from both rolls because it would offset the tremendous numerical advantage enjoyed by the Africans in most constituencies. It would be more honest to reserve seats for the different races than to pretend the scheme was non-racial. Macleod interjected that his system had fewer disadvantages than reservation, but Callaghan could not see the electorate accepting for long that the national roll candidate who received the most votes was not elected. He welcomed the increase in African voters but found that it was not enough considering the vast African population. His advice was to hold any further negotiations in London because tempers were too raw in Northern Rhodesia. It seemed unlikely to him, however, that "this sketch" could be turned into a constitution.

Callaghan felt impelled to call attention to the Federal Government's "malevolent" influence and referred to a letter in *The Times* in which Sir Arthur Benson had maintained that its actions, omissions and repeated declarations of intent had only served to make the Federal Government hated and feared by the northern Africans. They rejected the Northern Rhodesian Constitution, Benson had written, because they were not given the casting vote on secession. They blamed the British Government for their mounting despair and for not standing up to Welensky. Accordingly, they were attracted to African nationalism.

Callaghan wondered at the Federal mobilisation because its army could only be used to maintain order at the request of the territorial authorities. As the Governors had not been consulted on it, he said, the suspicions of a *coup* were not surprising. He asked Macleod for reassurance that Federal troops would not act until requested to do so by the British Government. Callaghan said he would not vote against the Government, but only because he did not want to give comfort to the Federal Government. Indeed, he declared, the Commons had to warn Welensky that it was united on the question of resisting any assumption by Welensky of British responsibilities.[85]

Joelson would likewise warn Welensky that the British Press would give vent to a great outburst of hostility if he declared independence. He advised Welensky to put all the facts before the Federal public and leave the next step to Britain. A declaration of independence would, in his opinion, unite the British Cabinet and merely embarrass the friends of the Federation. Wall also pressed Welensky to avoid the final breach.[86]

Welensky remained belligerent and publicly dismissed the debate in the Commons as predictable. He promised to account for his actions in the Federal debate on 27 February. He credited Callaghan with shrewdness in not calling for a division of the House, not just because he did not wish to side with Welensky, but because his policy was being implemented by a Tory Minister.[87]

[85] House of Commons *Hansard* (London), Vol. 635, Col. 513 f., 22 February 1961.
[86] Welensky Papers, 24/151, ff. 78–80, Joelson to Welensky, 23 February 1961; 43/*Wall*, Major P. Wall to Welensky, 27 February 1961.
[87] *The Rhodesia Herald*, 24 February 1961.

Welensky was also advised by Whitehead who, having been the advocate of confrontation, now maintained that the pen was mightier than the sword. He suggested that Welensky should reveal everything to the Federal Assembly which would discredit Macmillan and encourage the British Opposition to demand a Royal Commission of Inquiry. He believed that the documentary evidence would bring down Macmillan's Government and the negotiations could start afresh. Greenfield, however, preferred to conserve that ammunition because he believed that the threat of its disclosure would suffice. Whitehead disagreed because such forewarning might induce the British Government to contrive a cunning defence based on its documentary evidence. Greenfield had to concede this possibility.[88] Welensky would give his verdict on this idea a week later.

On 27 February, Welensky asked the Federal Assembly to view with the gravest concern the Northern Rhodesian proposals and the failure of the British Government to give the Federal Government a proper opportunity to discuss them before the publication of the White Paper. He called on the House to demand the publication of an account of the recent events and to resist the transfer of power into unfit hands. He explained that, until the events of 21 February, he had ignored demands for the recall of Parliament because he did not want to endanger his negotiations. However, Northern Rhodesia could not be considered in isolation and Macleod had forced his hand.

Welensky rued the departure of Lennox-Boyd from the Colonial Office because he had always brought integrity to bear. Since then, Welensky claimed, although mutual trust was fundamental to their relationship, the Governments had not spoken the same language. For 18 months, he had constantly been forced to remind the British Government of its undertakings and its subsequent contradictions. He cited the Monckton Commission pledges and found it extraordinary that, in Nyasaland, an official committee could be allowed to overrule a constitutional conference. There was pressure for change, but he thought it was exaggerated by outside influences. He would not withhold power from Africans but he would defend the principles on which the Federation was founded and which had been enshrined in the 1958 Northern Rhodesian Constitution.

Welensky recalled how Macleod had ignored the moderate Africans at the Federal Review. Despite his success in being elected to the Legislative Council, thereby confirming his popular support, even Nkumbula had not enjoyed the special treatment accorded to Kaunda. The current level of intimidation in the northern territories was a measure, to Welensky, of the irresponsibility of the people on whom power was shortly to devolve.

Describing the negotiations, Welensky revealed that in the past three weeks no less than four different schemes had been submitted and the one which was accepted was equally new. He had been given only a weekend for the exacting investigation to which any constitutional proposal had to be subjected, which was hardly "adequate consultation". Furthermore, the implications were impossible to assess when the British Government could not say

[88] Welensky Papers, 7/12, f. 232, Greenfield to Welensky, 25 February 1961.

how it would bring a further 2 000 Africans onto the upper roll. This figure seemed to have been fixed arbitrarily and someone still had to discover how to achieve it. It was hardly reasonable to be asked to allow the lower roll an equal influence on the election of the national roll Members when the new qualifications of that roll had not been revealed. Delimitation was a fundamental issue but nothing had been said about it. Therefore it was not surprising that the Federal Government had found the proposals unreasonable and unacceptable. Yet, Welensky said, he had tried to keep the door open and there had been a moment when it had seemed that agreement was possible because Macleod agreed not to specify methods to elect the national roll Members but to consider a number of such methods. However, Macleod had then described the method of election without reserve and had proclaimed that any variation of the method had to achieve the same result.

Despite this setback, Welensky claimed to have kept the matter open. He had offered to go to London, but had been rebuffed. He had failed to discover Macleod's reason for haste, but had remained determined to preserve standards and would not accept any proposals which did not allow the moderate African to participate fully in the Government and the Legislative Council. Whitehead had rejected the scheme totally, he said, because it would force him to confront a strong, and perhaps irresistible, movement for secession which would destroy the Federation.

Welensky believed that the result would be the return of a powerful bloc of African nationalists on whom the moderating influence of the upper roll would count for nought. He stated that this body, as Kaunda had already said, would work for the swiftest overthrow of any checks and balances in the way of its ambition. The nature of the lower roll election would force the upper roll electors to abandon party politics to defend their racial interests with the disadvantage of having a few thousand Africans on their roll. The 15 national roll Members would not have a moderating influence because of the manner of their election and the effect the lower roll would have upon it. The uncertainty of this, Welensky maintained, turned the whole scheme into an unacceptable gamble. Of course, he said, no one yet knew how the national roll Members would be elected, but there seemed to be little place for moderate Africans. The scheme was not as simple as it might appear to British MPs who were nurtured in a different tradition. He said that a further aspect of the farce was that, as recently as 3 January 1961, the Nyasaland upper roll had been aligned with that of Northern Rhodesia, yet, before the Nyasaland elections had even been held, Macleod proposed the broadening of the Northern Rhodesian upper roll. Likewise, cross-voting was being eliminated in Northern Rhodesia when it was being introduced in Southern Rhodesia.

The need for stability was paramount, but Welensky found that "we are changing constitutions as fast as some people change their shirts". This, after all, he said, was the third constitutional adjustment in Northern Rhodesia in seven years. He did not oppose an improvement in African representation and had himself proposed changes which would have improved it spectacularly. Much had still to be done in the Federation, but he wondered what progress was possible if standards were continually lowered. He offered the

House a free vote on whether there should be orderly progress or if the risk of events similar to those in the Congo should be run.

Field congratulated Welensky on the finest speech he had ever made. The Federal Government had been gullible, he said, but it was still deplorable that the British Government had so consistently broken faith with it. He suggested that, as it wished to withdraw from Africa, the British Government might be inciting one of the territories to secede, thereby destroying the Federation. Whatever the intention, there was no excuse for the rudeness of Macleod and Sandys and it was their Government's duty to disclose its plans so that the Federal Government could make its own. To Field, the Southern Rhodesian proposals were equally unacceptable and he was amazed that Whitehead could have accepted them when they were so similar to those to which he objected in Northern Rhodesia. He endorsed Welensky's stand but thought that he should have done so a long time ago. He wondered why the British Government had not refused to contemplate change when Northern Rhodesia remained in turmoil. He pledged his support to Welensky but queried his reluctance to say anything about what he intended to do next.[89]

While Wall warned Welensky that the Conservatives were closing ranks behind Macleod, Macmillan confided to his diary his relief that Welensky's motion was not as violent as he had feared. Welensky, however, had not quite withdrawn from the brink, as in a resumé for Lord Salisbury he warned: "The decisions I have got to take really depend on whether or not I lead a revolt." He said he knew that people were expecting the revolt and, even if a solution were found, their bitterness would only deepen, and simply because Macleod was in a hurry.[90]

However, the Press believed that Welensky had lowered the temperature and that the prospect of the revolt had receded. As was his custom, he apprised Joelson of the events, saying he was renewing the negotiations. However, he warned that if he did not obtain a reasonable solution, he might lead a secessionist movement in Southern Rhodesia in the hope of keeping the UFP in power, because the prospect of a government headed by Harper was so abhorrent. Before contemplating that, he said he would make one more attempt to settle and then would resign and put the facts squarely before the electorate, offering it a choice of "going it alone" or knuckling down to the British plans. Either choice would end the Federation. He claimed that Macleod's plans were already affecting both the Federal economy and public confidence, and that the strain had left him physically exhausted.[91]

In the continuing debate in the Federal Assembly, Robert Moffat berated the UFP for not attending the Northern Rhodesian Conference. He pronounced the proposals workable particularly as final adjustments were still possible. He appealed to Members not to behave in a manner which would preclude further negotiations because the situation would be far worse if the

[89] Fed R & N *Debates* (Salisbury), Vol. 14, Col. 4175 f., 27 February 1961.

[90] Welensky Papers, 43/*Wall*, Major P. Wall to Welensky, 27 February 1961; Macmillan, *At the End of the Day*, *op. cit.*, p. 311; Welensky Papers, 43/*Salisbury*, Welensky to Lord Salisbury, 27 February 1961.

[91] *The Rhodesia Herald*, 28 February 1961; Welensky Papers, 24/151, ff. 75–77, Welensky to Joelson, 28 February 1961.

plan were scrapped. The crucial factor was stability, and the uncertainty had to be ended. He believed that most people did not care if there were an African or European majority in the Legislative Council as they did not think the former would be irresponsible. In his opinion the British Government, far from ignoring the Federal Government, had taken great pains to consult it. The Federal Government should remember that the ultimate responsibility lay with the British Government, and Macleod was not bound to do more than listen to its opinion. Moffat found that Welensky, by mobilising troops and summoning Parliament, had provoked the population of Northern Rhodesia and confirmed their fears. He declared that African rule in Northern Rhodesia was inevitable and, if the Southern Rhodesians disliked it, they should say so in order that the Federation might be peacefully dismantled.

Gaunt warned Welensky that Northern Rhodesia was at the end of its tether and that there could not be extended negotiations. Williamson chided Welensky for giving no hope for the future and for not indicating courses of action. The Federation, in his view, was bound to fail. Pretorius cautioned against losing British friendship (a point which Macmillan would shortly make to Welensky). Lord Graham (the Duke of Montrose) and Clifford Dupont (later the first President of Rhodesia) were disappointed at the anti-climax created by Welensky. Hove and Lewanika congratulated Welensky on his stand, but Chembe supported the British Government. Greenfield conducted a re-examination of the proposals and found they blatantly promoted racialism.[92]

On 2 March Welensky summed up in the House reiterating that control had to remain in responsible hands. He resented being depicted as an opponent of African advancement and believed that, as the British Government had no real responsibility for the Federation, it did not care how it was managed. Its only concern was that the Federation should not embarrass it in the eyes of the world. It was also fashionable to yield to every pressure which was cloaked in slogans such as "self-determination", "nationalism", or "anti-imperialism". However, the British Government offered only blandishments, not real advances, but in so doing, undermined the standards on which real advancement was based. The simple truth, he said, was that the Federal Government, by standing by its principles, was serving the interests of the African population.

Van Eeden had criticised Whitehead, but Welensky thought that there had been no alternative but to declare that Southern Rhodesia could not stay in the Federation if control were to be handed to the northern extremists. He lauded Whitehead for his constant support of the Federal Government. He reiterated the need for stability and noted that, while every White Paper had agreed on this need, their effect had been to the contrary. He would not support the idea that the British had been forced to impose a solution because, if this were indeed the case, it was the result of Macleod's tiresome tactic of holding conferences which were attended by people of totally opposing views and thereby rendering serious negotiations impossible. The inevitable consequence was that the British Government would advance pro-

[92] Fed R & N *Debates* (Salisbury), Vol. 14, Col. 4217 f., 28 February 1961.

posals to satisfy those who threatened violence. Hone had claimed that the proposals would promote non-racialism, but Welensky was not convinced and quoted statements by Lennox-Boyd in 1958 rejecting election on racial grounds and parity of racial representation. Welensky acknowledged that he was accused of being weak, but he had not precluded further negotiations. His intention was to resume the negotiations when he went to London shortly for the Commonwealth Prime Ministers' Conference. If he failed, he would inform the House and then resign to seek a fresh mandate. He hoped his Government would not be forced into drastic measures to resist proposals which threatened the Federation's existence. His current mobilisation, he explained, had been to guard against internal disorder. The Federation had no choice but to defend itself because his warnings to Britain and America, on the possible repetition of the events in the Congo, had been ignored. The House divided and only I. H. Samuwiro, Robert Moffat, Yamba, Chembe and J. G. S. Chingattie rejected the motion.[93]

One of Welensky's final actions before renewing the negotiations with Macmillan was to reject Whitehead's earlier advice to induce the Labour Party to force the appointment of a Royal Commission to condemn Macmillan's policies with regard to the Federation. He preferred to continue "step by step". If the British Government would not give way, he would issue a White Paper which would disclose the entire story and let the British Government attempt to discredit him. Copies would be placed in Labour hands if Whitehead had such faith in them. Welensky had no such trust but knew that the Labour Party would try to exploit anything. He felt that Greenfield, to whom he was writing, had "sensed that I have a feeling that I have fired enough bullets that have been prepared by Edgar [Whitehead]".[94] Such was his mood as he faced another round of — ultimately fruitless — negotiations with Macmillan.

[93] *Ibid.*, Col. 4398 f., 2 March 1961.
[94] Welensky Papers, 7/12, f. 231, Welensky to Greenfield, 1 March 1961.

CHAPTER TWENTY-NINE

The Second Confrontation

The Illusory Settlement of Northern Rhodesia's Constitution, March–June 1961

THE Northern Rhodesian question had been kept open, but only to a limited extent and, in the event, the Federal Government would discover that the British adherence to the terms of the White Paper was almost total. Given this rigidity, the issues would prove as difficult as ever to solve. Macleod was determined to achieve his goal, and months of negotiations culminated in an almost exact repetition of the events of late February, except for the movement of troops. A settlement was finally reached, but the matter did not end there.

Welensky's first action on arrival in London for the Commonwealth Prime Ministers' Conference was to review the recent events with Sandys on 4 March and with Macmillan on the next evening. He reported to Whitehead that they had asked him to formulate a new basis for discussion because Macmillan was considerably anxious about the fate of the Southern Rhodesian referendum.[1] Welensky recalls that he and Macmillan dined alone at Admiralty House and Macmillan proved that he was "one of the most accomplished actors in public life". His performance was "truly magnificent". His eyes moist and his voice vibrating with emotion, he expressed great sympathy and understanding for Welensky and the Rhodesians. The tears rolled as he asked Welensky, with regard to Northern Rhodesia, if it were possible that he, who had seen the horror of two world wars, would have tolerated an armed clash between Britishers who had fought as allies on so many battlefields. Welensky interrupted him to reveal what his Canberra had found at Nairobi airport. Macmillan sighed and acknowledged that everyone made mistakes. Nevertheless, he said he had never intended to use the troops being assembled there except to assist Welensky. Then he asked for Welensky's proposals and insisted they reach agreement before he returned to Salisbury.[2]

[1] Welensky Papers, 20/9A, f. 41, Welensky to Whitehead, 6 March 1961.
[2] Sir Roy Welensky, *Welensky's 4 000 Days* (London, 1964), p. 304.

Macmillan recalls that Welensky was "pleasant enough" and that he agreed to furnish alternative proposals. The next day, Sandys noted that Welensky had agreed to do this, and expressed to him his confidence in a Northern Rhodesian settlement because the White Paper had left so much room for manoeuvre. Sandys urged haste because Hone had postponed his consultations in Lusaka until the proposals were known. Sandys was also anxious about the fate of the Southern Rhodesian referendum. Welensky, by contrast, doubted that there was much room for manoeuvre and warned that, as he was attending the Prime Ministers' Conference, his time was limited and it would be difficult to produce anything quickly.[3]

That day, the Lords debated the recent events, giving Lord Salisbury his opportunity for a vitriolic attack on Macleod. He ascribed the current acute tension between the British and Federal Governments to a crisis of confidence. He said that mistrust had clouded the issue when, only a few months previously, the white Rhodesians had been so intensely loyal to Britain. For this Macleod was responsible. He was intellectually brilliant, brave and resolute, but had adopted a wrong approach to the white community and, in so doing, had been "too clever by half". This denunciation hurt Macleod and is accepted as having given him the greatest set-back of his political career. Salisbury, however, did not spare Macmillan or Monckton for their part in creating the deplorable suspicion. Lord Perth defended the Government, while Lord Hailsham decried Salisbury's most violent personal attack on Macleod. Whatever damage Salisbury did, one of the 96 Tories who had demanded earlier in the Commons a revision of British African policy, William Aitken, now warned Welensky that they would not vote against the Government because the White Paper offered so much room for manoeuvre.[4]

Greenfield had tried to influence the Lords debate by briefing the Duke of Montrose who had flown from Salisbury to participate in it. Montrose duly revealed the details of recent British ministerial behaviour and Greenfield, watching, detected unease amongst the peers. However, Montrose then ruined the effect with a rambling account of Rhodesian loyalty to the Crown. Greenfield next sought to put his Government's case to the British public through the medium of *The Times*. Dismissing Press accusations that Lord Salisbury had expressed the views of the Federal whites and that they were all blind to the need for change, he maintained that the white leaders had demonstrated in the Nyasaland agreement and in the liberal changes in Southern Rhodesia that they were aware of the realities. The urgent necessity was to persuade the Southern Rhodesian electorate, before the referendum, that the British Government was not bent on seeing the black "racialists" gain power in Northern Rhodesia because, he said, their ideas were the antithesis of partnership.[5]

On 14 March Welensky presented his proposals, but some days would pass before they were considered because both he and Macmillan were preoc-

[3] H. Macmillan, *At the End of the Day* (London, 1973), p. 312; Welensky Papers, 7/12, f. 219, Sandys to Welensky, 7 March 1961; f. 218, Welensky to Sandys, 7 March 1961.

[4] House of Lords *Hansard* (London), Vol. 229, Col. 306 f., 7 March 1961; Welensky Papers, 7/12, f. 215, W. Aitken to Welensky, 10 March 1961.

[5] J. M. Greenfield, *Testimony of a Rhodesian Federal* (Bulawayo, 1978), pp. 202–203.

cupied with the crisis which would lead to the virtual expulsion of South Africa from the Commonwealth. Eventually Macmillan invited Welensky and Greenfield to lunch with himself and Sandys on Saturday, 18 March. Before Greenfield went to the lunch, one of the pro-Federal Tories, a junior Minister, advised him to have a notary public present when he talked to Macmillan. Thus Greenfield arrived in sombre mood but the lunch was pleasant enough, although Macmillan rebuked Welensky for something which he had said to the Conservative backbenchers. The real discussions began after the meal, with Welensky leaving much of the argument to Greenfield. Their effort was in vain because Macmillan and Sandys would not allow the upper roll to predominate. Macmillan asked to see Welensky alone, and Greenfield returned to his hotel. Macmillan claims that he "practically persuaded" Welensky to allow the negotiations to resume in Lusaka even though his sole and unacceptable aim appeared to be to secure a built-in majority for the UFP. Macmillan insisted that, in any election, there had to be an element of uncertainty. This seemed to shock Welensky.

Macmillan also strove hard to persuade Welensky that the British Government was the Federation's only friend. He pointed out that the Federation was opposed by the British Labour and Liberal Parties, by "all" the Africans, and Moffat and the other Liberals. He knew Whitehead would abandon it to save Southern Rhodesia. Thus he asked why Welensky insulted and quarrelled with him and his Government and incited the Conservatives to revolt when he knew that if it fell it would not be replaced by Lords Salisbury and Lambton. It would simply mean that his only friends would be out of power.[6] In the event, this alleged friendship would count for nothing.

Welensky remembered this conversation as being most unpleasant, but he and Macmillan did reach an agreement. Yet, when Greenfield and A. D. Evans later examined the agreement, they found that Welensky had misunderstood the position and that there were still large areas of disagreement. However, Welensky only conceded this after he had telephoned Sandys for confirmation. Consequently, he wrote to Macmillan the next day, 19 March, confessing that he had thought they had settled all the major issues but that discussion with Greenfield had revealed that there was still a considerable measure of disagreement. Sandys had confirmed this to be correct. Hence, Welensky wrote, agreement before he returned to Salisbury seemed impossible. Three main issues were clear, he said. The first was that the Federal Government could not accept any downward adjustment of the upper roll income and educational qualifications. It could allow, though, a broadening of the roll by certain categories and these could be settled in Lusaka. Secondly, the upper roll had to predominate, but on the basis of responsibility, not race. He had done his best to make the British understand that any departure from this principle would wreck Whitehead's referendum campaign and the chances of the Federation surviving. He said that it was, after all, indisputable that it would be fatal to place power in the hands of the immature who were so susceptible to intimidation and chicanery. The third issue flowed from the

[6] Welensky Papers, 7/12, f. 217, Macmillan to Welensky, 14 March 1961; 20/7, ff. 210–212, Welensky to Macmillan, 19 March 1961; Greenfield, *Testimony*, *op. cit.*, pp. 200–201; Macmillan, *At the End of the Day*, *op. cit.*, p. 312.

second because it was therefore impossible to contemplate the equalising of the influence of the two rolls on the election of the national roll Members. It seemed odd, Welensky observed, that he should be making the same points he had made to Sandys before the White Paper was published. He protested that, in an effort to meet Macmillan half-way, he had gone further, over the lunch, than he had intended to reach a settlement and would not be thanked by his Party.

However, Welensky continued, unless there was an equal British desire for a solution, one was impossible and the result would be tragic. He was hoping to avoid the latter but was not encouraged by Sandys as all concessions were expected to come from him. He hoped that Macmillan would see him again.[7]

Macmillan responded by meeting Welensky alone at the Commons on 20 March. They reached agreement again and a Press communiqué was issued which stated that the British Government would consider proposals within the spirit and framework of the White Paper and the ministerial statements. These proposals were to be put to Hone by the Northern Rhodesian political Parties and then would be forwarded by him to London. Due attention would be paid to the views of the Federal Government. In the meeting, Macmillan issued an emotional appeal to Welensky not to jeopardise their relationship at a moment when the Conservative Party was deeply shocked by the withdrawal of South Africa from the Commonwealth.

Greenfield disliked the agreement and felt that Welensky should have stayed in London to secure a final solution. However, Welensky had an important engagement in Northern Rhodesia and chose to go. He told the Press on his arrival home that he had made reasonable progress and, as a result, the UFP would participate in the Northern Rhodesian negotiations. The Press, however, expected the northern Africans to reject the proposals.[8]

Welensky informed his Cabinet that he and Macmillan had agreed to consider the appointment of a chief minister and that the established system of cross-voting would be maintained. The Governor's powers would not be increased, nor would the number of nominated Members. The legislature would be empowered to run the country, and the Governor would only intervene if it failed. The upper roll qualifications would only be expanded to include some additional categories of responsible people. The national roll seats would be retained, but other methods of filling them, including an electoral college, would be considered. The Northern Rhodesian Conference would not be reconvened, but each party, including the Federal Government, would negotiate with the Governor. Welensky hoped that the issue would be settled before the Southern Rhodesian referendum in June. He and Macmillan had discussed the Federation's future and Macmillan had said that he was considering making it independent it its own field. The general aim was to settle the future of the Federation by August or September of that year.[9] This, of course, would never be realised.

[7] The Hon. J. M. Greenfield to the Author, 8 January 1981; Welensky Papers, 20/7, ff. 210–212, Welensky to Macmillan, 19 March 1961.

[8] The Hon. J. M. Greenfield to the Author, 8 January 1981; *The Rhodesia Herald*, 21 March 1961; *African Mail*, 21 March 1961.

[9] Welensky Papers, FGC(61), Special Meeting, Federal Cabinet, 22 March 1961.

Thereafter Welensky reported to Lord Salisbury and others that he had achieved enough for negotiations to be re-opened. On 27 March, Hone began his discussions with the major Parties.[10]

While Welensky had tussled with the British Government, the Southern Rhodesian constitutional issue had been attracting almost as much attention as Northern Rhodesia. The Southern Rhodesian division of the Dominion Party had decided in February to reject the proposals and had drawn significant support from within the UFP.

A list of defectors grew, headed by I. D. Smith, who argued that he was not opposed to the presence of Africans in the Southern Rhodesian Parliament, but merely to the proposed method of placing them there. These defections came at a moment when the Federal MP for Ndola, W. F. Rendall, and J. G. S. Chingattie of Nyasaland chose for differing reasons to resign from the UFP. They were followed by L. M. N. Hodson who resigned because he thought that the Federal division of the UFP should stay out of the Southern Rhodesian quarrel.

The tide was not entirely favouring the DP because, on 6 March, van Eeden threatened to have its Northern Rhodesian division back Whitehead because Harper, the leader of the DP's Southern Rhodesian division, refused to support Welensky's efforts on Northern Rhodesia. In the event, van Eeden left the DP and later joined the UFP. The National Democratic Party, having repudiated the proposals, also began to campaign against them, using intimidation and threats to withhold the payment of taxes. The political temperature in Southern Rhodesia was high enough for Welensky and Whitehead to have a torrid time at a meeting in Bulawayo in early April. Welensky later warned Alport that success at the referendum seemed unlikely unless there was a reasonable settlement in Northern Rhodesia which retained power in responsible hands.[11] The news of continuing strife in the Congo, and of frenzied crowds greeting the announcement that Tanganyika would be made independent, hardly contributed to the peace of mind of the European in Southern Rhodesia or to the likelihood of success in the referendum.

Hone was faring almost as badly in Lusaka with the Parties not only confirming their rejection of the proposals in the White Paper, but also resisting his efforts to re-open the negotiations. On 11 April the United National Independence Party declared that the proposals would only upset race relations and destroy the economic structure. It believed the best way to serve everyone's interests was to grant an African majority in the legislature and reconvene the Northern Rhodesian Constitutional Conference. It maintained Britain had no reason to withhold African majority representation when she had granted it to her other territories. The next day the UFP opened its negotiations with Hone and pressed for upper roll predominance, the appointment of a chief minister and other matters. However, Roberts and

[10] *Ibid.*, 43/*Salisbury*, Welensky to Lord Salisbury, 24 March 1961; 43/*Wall*, Welensky to Wall, 27 March 1961.

[11] *The Rhodesia Herald*, 16 February & 6, 20 & 25 March 1961; Welensky Papers, 25/315, f. 5, I. D. Smith to Welensky, 25 March 1961; 25/229, f. 10, W. Rendall to Welensky, 26 March 1961; 24/106, ff. 15–17, L. M. N. Hodson to Welensky, 11 April 1961; 42/38, f. 119, Welensky to R. A. Butler, 10 April 1961.

Burney reported to Welensky that Hone appeared to have been instructed to keep as close as possible to the White Paper and that, unless he was told by Whitehall to accept the predominance of the upper roll, there was little point in continuing the discussions. Yet they felt there might be some prospect of a working arrangement if Nkumbula was wooed. At the same moment that Hone rebuffed Roberts, Macleod did likewise to a Barotse delegation which called on him in London seeking independence from Northern Rhodesia.[12]

While awaiting the outcome of the talks in Lusaka, Welensky preoccupied himself with the Southern Rhodesian referendum campaign, the bitterest in his experience. He informed Sandys that it was essential to settle the Northern Rhodesian question a month before the referendum if success were to be assured, as already the DP was making capital out of the fears that it might mean African majority rule in the North. However, when he replied, Sandys dwelt only on the fears of the Barotse of being absorbed by an African nationalist-dominated Northern Rhodesia. The Barotse had made a considerable effort to free themselves, he said, but Macleod had resisted. It was in a second dispatch, on 21 April, that Sandys regretted that Whitehead seemed to make everything difficult for himself. Turning to the need for an early settlement in Northern Rhodesia, Sandys declared that his Government would accept any variant of the current proposals, short of upper roll dominance. He hoped that Welensky would state his preferences so that the matter could be settled quickly. He was not concerned about the question of time because many of the Southern Rhodesian details had not yet been finally decided.[13]

If Welensky was having a worrying time politically, the revelation of a record export total of £206 000 000 and a favourable trade balance of £55 000 000 was encouraging. Nevertheless, on 26 April he complained to Lord Robins that an imposition of a tax on alien workers by Whitehead was causing embarrassment, and threatening the success of the referendum. He wrote as he awaited the verdict of the Southern Rhodesian Caucus on his request to make the taxation changes more palatable because they had so aroused the white farmers.

By that day, Welensky told Robins, Macleod had indicated that the Northern Rhodesian Constitution could be settled before the referendum, but Welensky was fearful of a quick solution. Whitehead had sent his final Southern Rhodesian constitutional proposals to Sandys with a request for the referendum to be in July. From the Federal point of view, Welensky said, any delay only made the situation more serious. Certainly, after the Southern Rhodesian budget in July, Whitehead's position would be more difficult. Welensky explained that he had known that the British Government had intended to "play it cool" with regard to the Constitutions of both Rhodesias, without understanding what would happen. The result was that the NDP had exploited the uncertainty, and thus the Southern Rhodesian security situation was deteriorating rapidly. The NDP was declaring that it would soon be the

[12] *The Rhodesia Herald*, 11 April 1961; Welensky Papers, 20/7, f. 203, Minutes of a Meeting with Hone, 11 April 1961.

[13] Welensky Papers, 25/272, f. 38, Welensky to Sandys, 19 April 1961; 20/9, f. 25, Sandys to Welensky, 21 April 1961; 20/7, f. 198, Sandys to Welensky, 21 April 1961.

Government and was urging the people to disobey the soil conservation laws. Whitehead had limited means to combat this and had admitted to him that there were areas where the native commissioners could not go without a police escort. Whitehead, he said, faced the dilemma of knowing that strong action would be poorly received in Britain, but he dared not let the situation get out of hand. Whitehead also had budgetary troubles arising out of improvements in African housing and in African teacher and police salaries. He was further bothered by a lack of personal popularity. Record tobacco and maize crops were being gathered, but fresh capital was not coming in and unemployment was rising. Yet, Welensky said, it was impossible to persuade the British Government that it was fiddling while the Federation burned.[14]

Welensky wrote twice to Sandys on 28 April. In the first dispatch, he rejected an assertion by Macleod that the Northern Rhodesian proposals did not affect the Litunga of Barotseland. In the second, he complained that he did not understand what Sandys had meant by referring to the preponderance of the upper roll. He pointed out that the White Paper had a "built-in bias" towards the African extremists because the upper roll contained increasing numbers of African and Asian voters who already favoured the extremists and were, in any case, easy targets for intimidation. The Federal Government had always maintained that power had to remain in responsible hands and Sandys had never questioned this assertion. It could only be secured by the upper roll predominance. If Sandys would not concede this, Welensky warned, no progress would have been made since January.[15]

Lord Salisbury wrote to say that he was delighted that Welensky was standing firm because there was nothing to be gained from appearing too pliant. If he did, he would be "edged from point to point". Salisbury warned that the British Government might be thinking that, once the Southern Rhodesian referendum was out of the way, it could take a firmer line on Northern Rhodesia. This would be a dangerous gamble, he said, and could lead to the break-up of the Federation which the British declared they wished to avoid.[16]

Macmillan, Home, Macleod and Sandys decided to attempt to influence the new Federal High Commissioner in London, A. E. P. Robinson, and invited him to discussions at Admiralty House on the evening of 4 May. Macmillan and Macleod were still in Parliament when Robinson arrived and he had to deal with Sandys and Home first. Sandys, while proclaiming his Government's desire to do everything to help the Federal Government over Northern Rhodesia, warned that any changes had to be within the framework of the White Paper because Macleod was committed to it. None of the variations could guarantee an automatic majority for the UFP on the upper roll. When he arrived, Macleod confirmed this view, adding that he felt frustrated because he did not know what would help the Federal Government. Robinson, confessing he lacked a brief, believed the problem was to prevent Kaunda or any other extremist gaining a majority in the next election.

[14] *Ibid.*, 25/240A, ff. 101–102, Welensky to Lord Robins, 26 April 1961.
[15] *Ibid.*, 20/9, f. 23, Welensky to Sandys, 28 April 1961; 20/7, ff. 177–182, Welensky to A. E. P. Robinson, 10 May 1961.
[16] *Ibid.*, 43/*Salisbury*, Lord Salisbury to Welensky, 4 May 1961.

If Kaunda formed a government, Robinson said, Whitehead would lose the referendum and there would be a complete breakdown of Anglo-Federal relations. However, Robinson thought that his Government would accept a formula through which an African majority was avoided in the immediate future, but was not ruled out for consideration at a later stage. Such a majority could be achieved through increasing numbers qualifying for the franchise and not simply by constitutional changes which were designed to please the extremists.

Macmillan arrived at that point and welcomed Robinson, hoping that informal communication would avoid the misunderstandings which arose out of cabling. He avowed he would support the Federation, although it might be necessary to effect some changes in the Federal and territorial Constitutions. He asked that Welensky, for whom he expressed warm affection, be informed that he did not want Northern Rhodesia to fall into irresponsible hands. The British Government was committed to the White Paper, but was prepared to consider some changes. Suggestions for these had been prepared by Sandys and Macleod, he said. For example, the nomenclature could be varied: "urban" could replace "upper", and "rural" could be substituted for "lower". Cross-voting could be introduced and the qualifying percentages varied. The ratio of the division of seats could be changed slightly to get away from the 15:15:15. Finally, some of the national roll seats could be racially reserved to ensure the reduction of extremist influences. He said that there was an *aide mémoire* which Macleod would hand to Robinson on the evening of Sunday, 7 May. Macmillan suggested that Robinson fly to Salisbury to explain it to Welensky to avoid any misunderstanding. Robinson said he would consult Welensky about this once he had the *aide mémoire*.

Robinson explained that Welensky wanted a final settlement by mid-May so that the Southern Rhodesian referendum could be held in July and the Federal Review reconvened in August. Sandys noticed that Whitehead had shifted the date of the referendum from May to June and now to July. Macmillan asked — as Lord Salisbury had predicted — if the referendum could not be held before the northern settlement, but Robinson replied that the only result would be that the Southern Rhodesian electorate would suspect that the British Government intended to bring in an African nationalist government immediately after they had voted. He said that there was no more certain way of conceding the referendum to Harper. Macmillan accepted that Welensky was the best judge of tactics, but wondered if everything could be accomplished at the pace demanded. Macleod thought that a Northern Rhodesian settlement was only possible by the end of May which would allow time to hold the referendum in July. Macmillan added that the Review could be reconvened in August or September.

Robinson underlined his Government's anxiety to complete the Review to end the uncertainty. The situation, he said, was not a parallel to Kenya, which the British Government had supported financially when there had been serious capital outflow due to political uncertainty. The Federation was an independent economy with its own central, commercial and merchant banks, discount houses and money market. However, when dealing with an economic and financial crisis caused by political uncertainty, it possessed only the orthodox weapon of exchange control to curb the outflow of funds. Therefore British financial aid would be needed and he asked about the fate of a British Treasury loan of £10 000 000, which was currently being sought.

Macleod said that progress was being made on this, but that there were still difficulties. Reverting to Northern Rhodesia he said that his Government was taking a considerable risk in proposing any variation of the White Paper. While prepared to consider anything, he did not want to minimise the dangers which he and Sandys would run, as any variation would be attacked by the African nationalists and their supporters in the Commonwealth, by the Labour and Liberal Parties, and by the left-wing Press. Robinson promised that Welensky and Whitehead would assist in the presentation of any change and that they would not hail it as a political triumph but as the product of adequate consultation and of a determination to keep the Government out of extremist hands.

Macmillan wanted the record corrected because he had never agreed to the appointment of a chief minister. However, Robinson replied that Welensky believed that he had. Unrepentant, Macmillan suggested that Welensky would be wise not to embody it in the proposals, that he should let the election take place and then ask for that appointment, which Macleod would grant. His reason, he said, was that the UFP might not be returned and Northern Rhodesia then might be better off without a chief minister. Macleod agreed with this verdict and reminded Robinson that, because Northern Rhodesia's civil servants took their orders from the British Government, which was committed to the Federation, they were the bulwark of the Federation and would ensure that control remained in responsible hands. Robinson pointed out the obvious: that the bulwark depended on the Tories, and not the Socialists, being in power in Britain. Therefore, he said, this was not a very reliable safeguard and already the Federal Government had seen those civil servants supporting the nationalists. He acknowledged that the same officials had supported the Federation of late, and Macmillan ascribed that to the change of Governor. Robinson thought that Moffat and his Liberal Party would be the casualties of any election, but Macleod was confident that they would win five or six seats because they had been prepared to serve in the Executive Council.

After Sandys left the meeting, Macmillan treated Robinson to a long monologue. He wanted the Federal public to understand that he was doing everything possible to ensure the Federation's continuation and he wished that Welensky would place his trust in him instead of agitating Lords Salisbury and Lambton and seeking to divide the Conservative Party, which could do no good. He knew that sometimes Welensky was provoked to feel animosity towards his Government, but this was only because he was carrying an intolerable burden. Macmillan claimed to be luckier because he had men like Sandys and Macleod to assist him. He felt that Welensky would be greatly helped if Whitehead gave him the support he owed him. The British and Federal public should appreciate, as he did, just how liberal Welensky was. The British Government, Macmillan declared, believe in advancing slowly and in a piecemeal fashion, and the result was that, in a continent of turmoil, British Africa was faring best. Kenya, for example, was "over the hump" and would have a multi-racial government. He did not believe that the Africans would automatically fall for the Communist line and, in any event, Cuba had shown that South America was the next target. Nonetheless, he felt that Communism was conquering the world and that events in the Congo were very worrying. Tshombe, he said, had gone to confer with the Central Government at Coquilhatville and there was concern for his safety. (Well there might be, because Tshombe was arrested and detained there.)

Robinson replied that the security of the Federation depended on establishing a strong and stable government in Katanga. Accordingly, he said, Welensky had asked Home for strong pressure on the United Nations, but still awaited a reply. Welensky was annoyed at how little information was passed to him relating to the Congo. Macmillan promised that henceforth Welensky would be kept fully informed. Macmillan said that the Portuguese Empire was doomed and that it was thus even more essential that the Federation was supported by his Government. This support would increase as more and more Africans became associated with the Government of the Federation. On Northern Rhodesia, he promised that, once an agreement had been reached, there would be no delay in a working party producing the details.

The mention of working parties prompted Robinson to point out that the Federal animosity towards Macleod was a direct product of his "Lancaster House technique". For example, Robinson explained, the Federal public had noted that the details of the Nyasaland Constitution had differed from the agreement at the Conference. Macleod warmly denied any attempt to mislead. The effect of the enfranchisement of the Moçambique Africans, he said, had been noted by the Conference and the UFP could have opposed it then, but did not. Unabashed, Robinson maintained that a major principle had been at stake and prompted Macmillan to promise that this would not happen again. Macleod agreed. Macmillan then said that he did not want the Review attended by 200 people. It was also essential that the Governments agreed beforehand on what was to be done.

In conclusion, Macmillan and his Ministers agreed to speak freely to Robinson as Welensky's representative and promised that everything would be done to support the Federation. Macleod reminded them that he had just done so in a major speech, and Robinson was sufficiently convinced to report to Welensky that he believed that Sandys and Macleod had decided to try to help, even at the risk of unrest in Northern Rhodesia. He only hoped that his optimism was justified and that he would not be disappointed as Welensky had been in the past.[17]

Macleod duly delivered the *aide mémoire* on Northern Rhodesia which said he still would not allow upper roll control of elections because he could not justify it in Parliament. All changes had to be in the spirit of the White Paper and had to produce broadly the same result. He had re-examined cross-voting and the devaluation of votes. The Constitution, he felt, could be more akin to that of 1958 if three or four rural seats were reserved for Europeans and *vice versa* for Africans in the urban areas. However, he said, Hone had rejected

[17] *Ibid.*, 20/7, ff. 191–197, Robinson to Welensky, 6 May 1961.

this as a manifest departure from the White Paper which would be strongly opposed by the Parties. He would ignore Hone if necessary if this idea were part of a scheme which was otherwise acceptable. The 15:15:15 scheme stood the best chance of being accepted in Lusaka but he would consider reducing the national roll seats to 14 and increasing the upper and lower roll seats to 16 each. There could be a form of racial reservation but it would be opposed in Lusaka. There could be four European, four African and four nondescript seats and this could be achieved by dividing Northern Rhodesia into four constituencies and allowing them to return one European, one African and one nondescript candidate. He felt Welensky would understand that the upper and lower rolls would have to have an equal influence in any system. Furthermore, the prescribed minimum percentage of votes (which the national roll candidate would have to secure from each of the upper and lower rolls) could be set at about ten per cent, but it had to be possible for the candidate to achieve it to avoid frustrated elections. Any suggestions from Welensky would be welcomed. There could, for example, be minor alterations to the upper roll, but it was essential that the Parties should agree and a decision could not be taken until the consultations with Hone were complete. The question of the chief minister should be left open because it could be introduced administratively. If Welensky were to comment, he had to remember that time was short. Macleod enclosed an illustration of how the 16:16:14 scheme could work.[18]

Writing to Welensky on 8 May, Robinson explained that Macleod would reduce the qualifying percentage to four or five per cent. Robinson did not think that there was much point in arguing over the appointment of a chief minister. Macleod, he said, was anxious to publish the new White Paper on 28 May at the latest and had made much of the difficulties which Hone had encountered with the suggestion of cross-voting and with the devaluation of votes. Hone had also asked Macleod that, if Robinson should fly to Salisbury, he should make a pretext of other business. Robinson was surprised by Hone being so firmly wedded to the existing White Paper. Macleod, by contrast, was willing to consider variations but was anxious to carry Hone with him. Macleod was currently examining a scheme by Roberts and might adopt it, Robinson said, because it had a device to avoid frustrated elections. Macleod wanted to know if Welensky wished to pursue this line, while Macmillan had asked for Welensky's reaction within 48 hours.[19]

Welensky did not reply immediately but informed Lord Salisbury that the Northern Rhodesian proposals were an affront to his intelligence and were totally unacceptable. He said he would tell Macmillan precisely what would happen if Macleod stayed on his current course. As a final step, he would resign to fight a general election and publicly expose everything which had brought about the current impasse. He no longer believed the British protestations about keeping the Federation in being, he told Salisbury, and was satisfied that they had decided to join the Common Market and would not be worried unduly if it meant the end of the Commonwealth. He said nothing of this to Joelson, but told him of a rumour that two British Ministers whom he

[18] *Ibid.*, ff. 189–190, Macleod's *Aide Mémoire*, 7 May 1961.
[19] *Ibid.*, f. 186, Robinson to Welensky, 8 May 1961.

did not name — Macleod and Perth — had been involved in raising funds for the African nationalists in Kenya. He said that pressure was being exerted to ensure that the story did not break, and he had warned one "individual" that if it were suppressed in Britain, he would see to it that it appeared in the Federation.[20]

On 9 May Robinson both cabled and wrote to Welensky because, he said, Macleod had written to him to say that Hone had rejected the cross-voting in stronger terms. The Colonial Office was urgently examining Roberts's scheme. (Welensky thereupon commented to Greenfield that the British desire to back-pedal might turn to the Federation's advantage for a change.) Robinson revealed that there had been a new development because Alport, from Salisbury, had complained at being left out when he heard that Macmillan, Sandys and Macleod had been talking to Welensky through Robinson and not through him. Macleod was anxious to reassure Alport, but Robinson was confident that Welensky would not mind how many actors there were on the stage provided there was an acceptable result. Thus Robinson proposed to keep in close contact with the British Ministers and had seen Sandys and had convinced him that it might be wise to reserve seats for Barotseland.[21]

Telling his security adviser, de Quehen, that there was every indication of "a first-class blow-up" over Northern Rhodesia, as the proposals were unacceptable and as it had been leaked to the British Press that he was preparing for a confrontation, Welensky waited the full 48 hours given him before replying. While he waited, Beckett urged him to fight for what they thought was right if the British Government forced a "show-down". If that happened, Beckett said, there should be no attempt to keep the Federation intact. Instead, the "line of rail" should be amalgamated with Southern Rhodesia.[22]

On 10 May Welensky telegraphed Robinson to tell Macmillan that his proposals were quite unacceptable as he must have realised when he formulated them. Macmillan, he said, had not ruled out the preponderance of the upper roll when they had met on 18 March, and the next day he had confirmed to Macmillan that this was essential. On that basis the negotiations had continued and the UFP had decided to participate in them. This explained why, Welensky said, he had been considerably upset when Sandys had written on 21 April and had ruled out the upper roll domination. Welensky recounted that he had replied, pointing to the built-in bias for the extremists, and had warned that, if the upper roll were not allowed to dominate, matters would be back to where they were in January. If Macmillan was still obdurate on this point, Welensky warned, they were at the parting of the ways.

He told Robinson that, in all the schemes advanced by Macmillan, there was a determination to ensure that the majority of the seats in the legislature went to racialists bent on the Federation's destruction. Welensky felt this was

[20] *Ibid.*, 43/*Salisbury*, Welensky to Lord Salisbury, 8 May 1961; 24/151, ff. 71–72, Welensky to Joelson, 8 May 1961.

[21] *Ibid.*, 20/7, f. 185, Robinson to Welensky, 9 May 1961; f. 184, Macleod to Robinson, 8 May 1961; f. 183, Robinson to Welensky, 9 May 1961; f. 185, Welensky to Greenfield, 11 May 1961.

[22] *Ibid.*, 7/12, f. 181A, Welensky to B. M. de Quehen, 9 May 1961; 42/21, ff. 27–31, Beckett to Welensky, 9 May 1961.

difficult to reconcile with British protestations on the continuation of the Federation. He had repeatedly stressed that the referendum would be lost if Macmillan did not meet him on this issue. He likened the comment in the *aide mémoire*, that alternatives would be considered provided they produced the same result, to the colour which Henry Ford had offered to his customers.

Welensky said that the statement, expressing hope that all misunderstandings had fallen away, meant little to him. Any illusions which he had gained in London of a fair compromise had rapidly dissipated despite Macmillan's frequent protestations. The concession on cross-voting was valueless because the eyes had been picked out of it. It still seemed incredible that, when it had worked reasonably well, it should be eradicated in Northern Rhodesia at the moment it was being introduced in Southern Rhodesia. The persistence with the equal influence of the rolls was a complete gamble. The substitution of the words "rural" and "urban" would remove a difficulty of delimitation, but this was only a minor improvement as long as Macmillan insisted on equal numbers in the two categories. The racial reservation of seats was unacceptable because the aim was to produce a non-racial approach. If the upper roll controlled the election of Europeans, and the lower that of Africans, steps were being taken towards *apartheid*. It was thus essential that the upper roll dominate the election of both races to ensure a working political partnership. If the lower roll were given this control, the sort of European elected would co-operate with the African nationalists in destroying the Federation and in achieving a hand-over to African racialists. The variation of the 15:15:15 ratio to 16:16:14 would make no practical difference. He told Robinson that the suggestion of four triple-Member constituencies was "utterly fantastic" because the voter would have five votes to cast for five different candidates when most voters were voting for the first time and faced difficulties enough. Each constituency would cover an area as large as England and Scotland combined. Macmillan had to reflect on the problems which would overlap each other in multi-Member constituencies.

Welensky said he had always opposed minimum percentages and was amazed that he should be asked if he wished to vary them. The European could gain nothing from them because intimidation would always ensure that the white candidate never secured the African percentage. In London, he stated, Macmillan had avowed that he would not adjust the income and educational qualifications of the upper roll, but now he appeared to be weakening. Welensky declared that he could not agree that any amendment would be a substantial improvement. Indeed, in some ways the scheme had become more dangerous.

He attached great importance to the appointment of the chief minister and recalled that Macmillan had not objected to it in March. The subsequent refusal of this appointment only indicated that the British Government thought the less responsible elements would win the election. Again he was being told that the need for speed was imperative, when his Government had always reacted expeditiously. Thus time was again being used as a weapon. Finally, he thought that there was little point in Macleod considering new methods of electing the national roll Members unless the upper roll issue was settled in a manner acceptable to the Federal Government. What he really wanted to know, he told Robinson, was whether any scheme, as outlined in the *aide mémoire*, were to be imposed.[23]

A day later Welensky informed Robinson that Alport was urging consideration of a suggestion from Roberts to have a middle roll. The voters who would qualify would comprise those qualifying for the upper roll and the upper part of the lower roll. Their influence would be balanced numerically and Alport claimed that the advantages were that there would be no devalued votes. It was simple, within the spirit of the White Paper, and promised control by the moderates. However, Welensky said he had pointed out to Alport that the middle roll idea would be upset by an increase in enrolment, which brought them back to the need for preponderance by the upper roll. As Alport did not deny this, Welensky said he concluded that the British were trying to secure his acquiescence to the gradual diminution of the influence of the responsible voter. Consequently, he had forcefully replied to Alport that he was tired of British manoeuvres and that they were back to where they had been in March. However, Alport was most concerned lest he dismiss the idea before the British had finished studying it. Nonetheless, Welensky told Robinson, he had plainly warned Alport that, if no solution were found, there would be a fundamental change in Federal attitudes. He realised that Hone was making difficulties, but that was not his problem. He was not prepared to make any more of the running and noted that the whole affair was complicated by the desire of the British Ministers to lower standards despite their high-sounding phrases and complicated suggestions. For example, he knew that their reluctance over the chief minister was based on their belief that extremists would be returned. He was completely frustrated, he said, by their technique and was determined that they should give way on the influence of the responsible voter and on the maintenance of the standard of his qualifications.[24]

These exchanges were punctuated by British messages on the Congo seeking Federal co-operation to restrain the Katangese because Tshombe had been arrested and detained at Coquilhatville when meeting the Congolese Central Government. The British wanted the Katangese to wait for the UN mediation to succeed.

There was also a report to Welensky from Lord Lambton on a conversation with Macleod. Lambton said he had asked if, to prolong the Northern Rhodesian negotiations, Macleod would consider postponing the referendum and the imposition by Sandys of the new Southern Rhodesian Constitution. Lambton, answering his own question, had thought Welensky and Whitehead were unlikely to agree because they were losing men at both extremes of their Party.

Lambton, of course, was displaying a lamentable knowledge of the degree of independence enjoyed by Southern Rhodesia, and Macleod did likewise by saying that he thought Welensky and Whitehead would welcome an imposition because they were good men who were close to his way of thinking. He had revealed to Lambton that Welensky had moved so far towards him that he would accept racial parity in the Northern Rhodesian legislature because

[23] *Ibid.*, 20/7, ff. 177–182, Welensky to Robinson, 10 May 1961.
[24] *Ibid.*, f. 174, Welensky to Robinson, 11 May 1961.

he knew that the official element would always provide a comfortable white majority.

Lambton said he had replied that, to the contrary, Macleod had moved towards Welensky in abandoning his desire for a black majority. However, Macleod had denied that he had ever suggested more than parity. He had thought that the referendum should be held before the Lusaka negotiations ended. Lambton had disagreed because of the mistrust of Macleod by Welensky and Whitehead, who would see this as a bid by Macleod to fiddle the Northern Rhodesian Constitution once the pistol had been removed from his head. Macleod had agreed that they would, but had insisted that time was of the essence.

Lambton said that, somewhat rudely, he had claimed that nothing would be settled while Macleod remained Colonial Secretary. He did not record how Macleod received this impertinence, but simply that Macleod had expressed great concern about the whole situation in Africa and determination to do his best. He had doubted if anyone else could deal with the blacks or the left wing of the Conservative Party and could not imagine what reason he could give for resigning. Unkindly, Lambton had replied that the loss of confidence of Welensky and Whitehead was enough to satisfy honour. Appearing close to tears, Lambton reported, Macleod had refused to contemplate such a course and described his resentment at Lord Salisbury's attack. If he were to have a future in politics, Macleod had said that he would have to see the matter through. He had become even more upset when Lambton had again insisted on his resignation and maintained that he had set the right course. He had embarrassed Lambton with his obvious emotion and loss of confidence.[25]

In reply to Lambton, Welensky commented that for Macleod and Sandys to talk of imposition was unbelievably naïve. Such action, he said, was legally impossible even if Whitehead connived at it and even then its suggestion would do enormous harm. He wished Lambton to know that he had not accepted parity and that the tendency in Britain to think that he was bluffing was quite erroneous.[26]

Whitehead was preparing a final version of the Southern Rhodesian Constitution and summoned all delegates who had attended the last Conference. On 15 May, after a short address from Whitehead, the NDP delegates walked out because Whitehead had been "high-handed" in only giving them two days' notice. They also protested at the current ban on meetings in the rural areas and at Whitehead's intention to discuss the issue of African land, as land was land and was neither European nor African. It appeared to them that they would not be taken into Whitehead's confidence and that the stage had been reached when the Africans would not tolerate decisions being taken on their behalf. Alport tried to dissuade Nkomo from leaving, but was sharply told that his duty was to support the Africans in their fight against the oppressive "Settler Government". The conference ended the next day and it asked the British Government to accept what had been agreed. What annoyed Welensky was that certain local Europeans were encouraging Nkomo. He was

[25] *Ibid.*, 29/27, f. 30, Report of a conversation between Lord Lambton and Macleod, (undated).
[26] *Ibid.*, 29/27, f. 35, Welensky to Lord Lambton, 19 May 1961.

also irritated that the British Exchequer should find it difficult to find £10 000 000 for the Federation when India had just received £40 000 000 and Kenya £14 000 000.[27]

On 19 May a further *aide mémoire* on Northern Rhodesia arrived and D. A. Scott of the British High Commission and Evans met to discuss it. It described the middle roll proposal for which the qualifications would be an income of £215 p.a. or property worth £250. Literacy in the vernacular would apply to the lower roll voters who qualified by virtue of their position in society. This would produce an electorate of 55 000 of which 30 000 would be from the lower roll, thus fulfilling the equalising commitment. The twelve middle roll Members would be returned by the four three-Member constituencies covering the whole of the territory. The commitment to the equalising principle led Evans to tell Scott that there was nothing to commend the idea to his Government.

Evans drew Welensky's attention to the income level of £215 p.a. and said he had pointed out to Scott that the British Government, while equalising the rolls, had forgotten the existence of 5 000 Asian and African voters on the upper roll. This meant that the middle roll would comprise 23 000 Europeans and 32 000 non-Europeans. The manipulation of the lower roll, he said, was only possible at the first election because the income level would be fixed then and would prevent future equalisation because the number qualifying through it would have increased progressively. By 1970 the non-European element of the upper roll could be expected to be 49 000. Scott had eventually understood the argument, but wanted to check the figures with Northern Rhodesia. Although he believed Alport was anxious to help, Evans felt it imperative first to discover where control would lie before manufacturing schemes.[28]

Evans had a proposal of his own which involved rural and urban constituencies, cross-voting, and some reservation of seats. He believed that this fell within the framework of the White Paper but would keep power in responsible hands. Parity was also a possibility because he aimed at producing a house of 23 Europeans and 23 Africans. Double-Member constituencies would defeat racial politics, he said. Life would be difficult for the African extremist as he would not attract European votes whereas the moderate African would.[29]

Greenfield found merit in Evans's proposal but thought that some details would have to be changed. If there were to be a confrontation, he asked Welensky to remember that there had to be a budgetary session before going to the country. He hoped that threats of resignation would induce the British Government to be more conciliatory, but said there was little sign that they would. The ball had clearly been removed from Hone's court, and thus it was time to tell Alport that Welensky wished to participate in the referendum campaign but could not until a reasonable Northern Rhodesian settlement was achieved. This had to be effected by mid-June at the very latest. Alport would be told that the latest proposal was unacceptable and that there would

[27] *The Rhodesia Herald*, 16 May 1961; Lord Alport, *The Sudden Assignment* (London, 1965), p. 52; Welensky Papers, 24/151, ff. 63–64, Welensky to Joelson, 17 May 1961.
[28] Welensky Papers, 7/12, f. 168, Evans to Welensky, 19 May 1961.
[29] *Ibid.*, 7/12, f. 175, Evans's proposal, (undated).

be a "show-down" if the upper roll influence was not conceded. If, by the end of May, agreement on this was not forthcoming, the Federal Assembly would be recalled. A Federal White Paper would describe the negotiations and, after a short budgetary session, Parliament would be dissolved. Greenfield wanted Welensky to consider establishing a Federal police force. This action, while perfectly possible in terms of the Constitution, would indicate that the Federal Government was deadly serious. It might be necessary to alert the supporters of the Federation in Britain to ask questions. The British Government might stall on the referendum date by way of an answer.[30]

Greenfield thought that Evans should discontinue his negotiations with Scott. Evans, however, advised that a dignified, responsible attitude had to be preserved for as long as possible in case it was necessary to publish what had been done. Nevertheless, the initiative should not be lost nor should the position be irretrievably weakened. Welensky should not be forced into the role of an aggressor and should always be able to show that he had done everything to avoid a serious and desperate course. It was always best to prepare for the worst when undertaking difficult negotiations as nothing was so unsettling as knowing that there was no alternative plan of action. Welensky would have to work within the Constitution and only act unconstitutionally when there was nothing else to do. The legal, proper and responsible course of action was to seek a fresh mandate from the electorate. This would give Welensky confidence and convince the British of the seriousness of his intentions. The threat of it might be sufficient because a Federal general election would cut across the referendum, the consequences of which the British surely understood. A Federal defeat over Northern Rhodesia would have an equally disastrous effect on the referendum, and Evans wondered if the British could persist on that course in that eventuality.

He proposed that the Federal Government resist, legally or illegally, the imposition of any of the variety of the current British proposals. He suggested that the governing of Northern Rhodesia be made impossible. The first step towards this would be taken when Welensky felt that negotiations with the British had reached breaking point. He would then threaten to resign and seek a fresh mandate from his electorate, and, if ignored by the British, would do so and publicly reveal the account of British machinations which underlay his decision. If at the resultant general election Welensky were returned with a sufficient majority, he would call up all his forces, in particular those in Northern Rhodesia. Making certain that Northern Rhodesian civil servants were included in the call-up, he would grant no exemptions. The purpose was to embarrass the Northern Rhodesian Government because it would be bereft of civil servants to register voters under the British-imposed constitution. Any Northern Rhodesian official who refused call-up would be tried by special Federal courts or by courts martial, if the northern judges refused to co-operate. Consideration would be given to their deportation if they were not Federal citizens. Entry of people from Britain, including parliamentarians and military personnel, would be prevented by force if necessary. Such action would be regrettable, but at least would be legitimate. Every other possible

[30] *Ibid.*, 20/7, f. 166, Greenfield to Welensky, 25 May 1961.

action would be taken to prevent the registration of voters and the holding of elections. All postal and telecommunications services, including those serving the Governor, would be withdrawn. Communications with Britain would not be severed, but would be made as difficult as possible, and the news reports would be censored to keep the British guessing as to what was being done. Federal control of transport would be used to regulate the supply and distribution of petrol and other commodities to the Northern Rhodesian Government to cause it as much discomfort and embarrassment as possible. However, supplies and services to the private sector would be maintained as far as possible. Northern Rhodesian officials would be prevented from travelling by train or air, and their shortage of petrol should restrict their movement by road.

If all legal steps failed, Evans warned, troops would have to be used to halt the registration of voters. Thereafter, a *coup d'état* might be necessary as the British Government would be bound to try to intervene forcibly. This would test the loyalty of the Federal Army, particularly its commander. If he would not co-operate, he would be replaced.

Evans acknowledged that these suggestions were frightening, but said that if no action were taken, the cause would be lost. It was imperative to plan and to hope that it was never necessary to act, but the British Government should have no illusions about the action taken. This would face it with the need for preventive action which might lose it the support of its electorate. The Federal Government should exploit the potentialities of this, Evans concluded, as it was a powerful weapon.[31]

Welensky did not match Evans's bellicosity but he did describe the situation to Lord Salisbury as "a proper mess" because the British Government was finding that it was increasingly difficult to honour his agreement with Macmillan on 20 March to work within the spirit and framework of Macleod's White Paper. Consequently, the latest proposals were, if anything, worse than the White Paper itself.[32]

On 25 May Welensky apprised his Cabinet of the latest developments and that he was making a stand on the principle of control by the responsible pro-Federal element. He was insisting, he said, on a place for both moderates and extremists. The British Government would disagree and the prospect of reconciliation was remote. It had seemed that Roberts's suggestion might make it possible for the responsible electorate to dominate for a reasonable period. The British Government, however, had suggested an income qualification of £215 p.a. which would ensure that this did not happen. He had conveyed his findings to Alport that morning who had urged that nothing drastic should be done as a reasonable settlement was still possible, perhaps through retaining the dominance of the upper roll, but simultaneously broadening it with a few additional categories. This suggestion, Welensky said, was being examined and final discussions would be held with Sandys who was coming out at the weekend ostensibly to finalise the Southern Rhodesian Constitution.[33]

[31] *Ibid.*, f. 168, Evans to Welensky, 23 May 1961.
[32] *Ibid.*, 43/*Salisbury*, Welensky to Lord Salisbury, 23 May 1961.
[33] *Ibid.*, FGC(61), 18th Meeting, Restricted Annexure, Federal Cabinet, 25 May 1961.

Alport had gone away dispirited, Welensky told Roberts. It was also clear that Hone had rejected all he had agreed with Macmillan on 20 March. A solution was almost impossible. British and Federal officials were still talking but, Welensky informed Lord Salisbury, there would be a "terrible row". He had ordered the destruction of the Federal Cabinet papers in preparation for a general election and would do everything to retain control in responsible hands.[34]

Before Sandys arrived, Alport chose to explain to the Federal public that British policies were not matters of personalities and could not be ascribed directly to Sandys, Macleod or anyone else. (Such a claim must have rung hollow in Welensky's ears because the current crisis, as Alport knew well, was a product of Macleod's determination to have his way.) Alport acknowledged that British policy contained a measure of opportunism but that it was the ingredient which had given Britain the flexibility that had enabled her to survive so many disasters. People, he felt, misunderstood the British approach because they knew nothing of the social revolution which had made Britain a happier country than it had been some centuries before. As he was aware of this, he said, he was not alarmed by the appearance of new forces and the possibilities of change in Africa. For more than a century, Britain had been bringing self-government to her dependencies and, on the whole, the policy had been successful, although it had not always been possible to control the timing of the transfer of power. If Britain consistently put her interests first, it was because she wished to harbour her strength for the benefit of her friends. She based her concept of the Commonwealth on the recognition of the strength of nationalism. In advancing the dependencies, he said, she always tried to strike a balance between the interests of the majorities and the minorities. The problem was to meet their legitimate desires but not to jeopardise political progress. Alport concluded by saying that he had always favoured the Federation because it had the manpower and the resources to stand firmly on its feet in the modern world.[35]

Meeting Welensky and Greenfield in Salisbury on the evening of 28 May, Sandys asked why the middle roll proposal for Northern Rhodesia had been rejected when it was simply a variation of Roberts's suggestion. Welensky explained that the preservation of the equalising factor had rendered it unacceptable. It had taken no account of the number of non-Europeans on the upper roll. The whole system would cease to function after the first election because, as standards of living improved steadily, the number qualifying for the lower roll would increase, but the standard was fixed and the equalising factor would be lost. Sandys understood the objection and agreed that the ultimate result was contrary to British intentions.[36]

Welensky informed his Cabinet that Sandys had said that his Government was anxious for an agreement and that he had come to negotiate a scheme which fitted the framework of the White Paper and was acceptable to everyone. Welensky said he had made it clear that the majority in the Legislative

[34] *Ibid.*, 24/242A, f. 16, Welensky to H. J. Roberts, 25 May 1961; 43/*Salisbury*, Welensky to Lord Salisbury, 23 May 1961.

[35] *Ibid.*, 27/108, f. 8, Lord Alport's speech to the RNAA, 26 May 1961.

[36] *Ibid.*, 7/12, f. 143, Evans to Welensky (Notes on the talks with Sandys), 28 May 1961.

Council had to be responsible and favour the continuation of the Federation. The middle roll scheme was unacceptable because the Federal Government wanted an income qualification of between £400 and £500 p.a., while the British Government chose £215 p.a. The better hope was Sandys's 15:15:15 scheme with the voting equation changed to 2:1 in favour of the upper roll when both rolls voted for the national roll Members. However, inevitably, to offset the effect of this, the British Government wanted to increase the new African voters on the upper roll from 2 000 to 8 000. Welensky said he wished the upper roll to be dominated by Europeans for at least two elections to ensure stability, but 8 000 new voters could give the national roll seats to extremists. He related that he had told Sandys that no more than 1 000 new voters was justifiable, and that he and the Northern Rhodesian Government had disagreed on the assessment of the European voters because the Federal Government believed that there were 23 000 and the Northern Rhodesian Government 25 000.[37]

Before they met again on the morrow, Welensky could not resist sending Sandys a note asking if he knew who was financing the African nationalists in the Federation. Some money, Welensky said, came from local businesses and some from Cairo, but a large amount could not be accounted for. This gave him the opportunity to reveal that he knew that Macleod and Perth had been involved with fund-raising for the Kenyan African nationalists. If this were not true, he suggested that the rumour had to be killed.[38]

When Sandys met Welensky and his Ministers, Evans produced two papers and for the first time the British appreciated that the addition of African voters would have a considerable effect on the elections. The papers showed that four to seven seats could be captured by Africans on the upper and middle rolls.[39]

After that, Greenfield, Evans and Burney, of Northern Rhodesia, re-examined the British middle roll proposals. Burney doubted if there were 20 000 European voters and argued that an additional 8 000 African voters would swing control into the hands of the non-European electorate. However, it was noted that Sandys had seemed to agree that the figure might be reduced to 6 000 but no further. The Federal Government, on the other hand, would go no higher than 5 000, and obviously the idea would be very difficult to sell in Northern Rhodesia. They recalled that Sandys had felt that additional categories could be accepted for the middle roll on a "pump-priming" and "once and for all" basis, which held several attractions. It avoided the addition of large numbers of otherwise unqualified Africans to the upper roll, and excluded vast numbers of lower roll voters from the middle roll elections. If the upper segment of the lower roll could be frozen, then, as time wore on, the middle roll would be dominated by the upper roll as more and more voters qualified for it. The freezing of the upper segment of the lower roll was attractive also because it meant the Federal delimitation could apply as there could be 14 upper roll and 14 lower roll seats and 7 double-Member constituencies in which teams of one European and one

[37] *Ibid.*, 20/7, f. 164, Welensky's report to the Federal Cabinet, 29 May 1961.
[38] *Ibid.*, 27/27, f. 20, Welensky to Sandys, 29 May 1961.
[39] *Ibid.*, 7/12, f. 143, Minutes of a Meeting with Sandys, 29 May 1961.

African could offer themselves for election. This would adhere to the partnership concept and create a hazard for the African nationalist Parties because they might find it difficult to put up European candidates.[40]

Despite this recommendation from Greenfield, Evans and Burney, both Welensky and Hone, who arrived for the meeting with Sandys on 30 May, rejected the middle roll proposal. The reason was that Welensky would not accept an increase of more than 3 000 upper roll voters, while Hone demanded 8 000 because he believed that the African nationalists would not accept less. No progress was made, but they agreed to meet again on the next day.[41]

At this meeting, Welensky suggested that upper roll votes should dominate the election of the national roll Members on a ratio of 2:1 over the lower roll votes. In addition only a fixed number of categories of lower roll voters would be eligible to vote for the national roll candidates. Hone and Sandys rejected these ideas. A proposal for the adjustment of the ratio to 60:40 was examined, but it was believed it would not gain public acceptance. With deadlock threatening, Sandys and Welensky retired for private discussions, and Alport, strolling in the gardens of Welensky's official residence, was shocked to discover from one who accompanied him just how deep the antagonism towards the British Government was in Federal ministerial ranks.[42] The hatred and distrust which Alport uncovered was only to grow as the years progressed towards Rhodesia's UDI and beyond.

After the defects of the middle roll had been pointed out to Sandys, he agreed to drop it, and the 60:40 ratio was resuscitated and given to Hone to re-examine during the luncheon recess. Before doing so, Hone asked for 1 000 Africans to be added to the upper roll, but the Federal representatives would not allow more than 500. Welensky, Greenfield and Evans then retired.

When the meeting re-assembled, there was considerable argument on delimitation. Hone said that he would decide on which areas were suitable for double-Member constituencies, but the Federals insisted on a judicial delimitation commission. Welensky agreed to the addition of some categories of voters, but rejected the minimum percentage of votes from both rolls which the national roll candidate had to secure because, when set at ten per cent, the European would have to secure 700 lower roll votes while his African rival would only have to secure 200 upper roll votes. Welensky knew that an equalising formula could be introduced but denounced it as vexatious and unnecessary. He reminded the meeting that the African nationalists had rejected the minimum percentage and that it had only been welcomed by the Northern Rhodesian Liberal Party.

Afterwards, Welensky informed Alport that he would accept the modification of the national roll constituencies to make six of them double-Member, each returning an African and a European. In the remaining three single-Member constituencies, the candidates would have to gain 100 votes from each roll. He then met Sandys again who suggested seven double-Member constituencies only, each returning an African and a European. Welensky

[40] *Ibid.*, f. 147, Evans to Welensky, 30 May 1961.
[41] *Ibid.*, f. 143, Minutes of a Meeting with Sandys, 30 May 1961.
[42] *Ibid.*, f. 141, Minutes of a Meeting with Sandys, 31 May 1961; Alport, *The Sudden Assignment*, *op. cit.*, p. 56.

would accept this but suggested that the ratio of seats should be 14:14:14 and Sandys agreed because it would assist delimitation. Sandys also thought that the minimum percentage could be replaced by a specified number of signatures on a nomination paper. They argued over the number and finally settled on 50. They agreed that there should be a delimitation commission.

Sandys left the meeting to consult Hone, and returned to say that there could be no cross-voting. He said that between 2 000 and 2 500 Africans would be added to the upper roll through the addition of categories, and that the 60:40 ratio of dominance by the upper roll in the national roll Members' election could be allowed, provided that it was based on the number of votes cast and not on the number of voters enrolled.

Sandys departed for London and Welensky informed Robinson that an agreement in principle was likely if Hone could persuade the other Parties in Northern Rhodesia to agree. Macleod, however, recoiled at the proposals and, consequently, Sandys explained to Welensky on 3 June that, as it was a radical alteration to the White Paper, only the 60:40 ratio would be publicly revealed by Hone because it was less offensive to the other Parties than the dropping of the minimum percentages and the other proposals. Sandys believed that Welensky would be content with this because the gap between them had been narrowed. He did not say anything of his battle with Macleod. This battle would continue into the next day, leading Macmillan to conclude that even a scheme devised by the Archangel Gabriel would be rejected. He feared that resignations from Macleod or Sandys were imminent.[43]

Welensky discussed the state of the negotiations with his Cabinet, and on 6 June wrote most forcibly to Sandys. Of their agreement, he noted, only the 60:40 ratio had survived which meant that the minimum percentage would be retained. This idea of the percentage, he recalled, was Sandys's to make the scheme more palatable to the UFP. Yet the latter had rejected it, and it was strange that it was retained even though the African nationalists would also dislike it. Welensky said he could not see what great principles were involved when, without the percentage, the national roll candidate would still have to strive hard to obtain the support of both the upper and lower rolls. The Federal idea of double-Member constituencies made this even more certain because, when the Parties had to put up black and white candidates, they would have to ensure that they appealed to both races. Sandys, he said, had exaggerated the need for this appeal but, as the proposals stood, an African national roll candidate could secure the minimum percentage from the African upper roll voters without attracting a single European vote, which was discrimination in reverse. For that reason, the minimum percentage was unacceptable. He recalled that Sandys had said it was necessary for Hone to get the agreement of the other Parties, but Welensky hoped that thereby they were not gaining a veto. It certainly seemed that they might be, he said, because Sandys spoke of finding a new course if they rejected the 60:40 ratio of upper roll influence. Sandys had referred to a paper by Greenfield which had contained the other amendments, and Welensky reminded him that this had been written at his (Sandys's) dictation. If seven double-Member consti-

[43] Welensky Papers, 20/7, f. 163, Welensky to Robinson, 2 June 1961; f. 162, Sandys to Welensky, 3 June 1961; Macmillan, *At the End of the Day*, *op. cit.*, p. 314.

tuencies were unacceptable, Welensky said he was willing to reduce them to six, and add three single-Member constituencies. However, he would not allow the minimum percentage to be applied to them. He would accept a prescribed number of signatures from another race on the nomination paper.

Welensky expressed amazement that, after all their discussions, Sandys could persist with such an impractical device as the minimum percentage. He assumed Hone would reveal to the Parties the scheme which contained five double-Member and five single-Member constituencies, all being fettered with the minimum percentage. If he did, Welensky warned that he would protest most strongly. Furthermore, he had understood that the discussions at this stage would not involve the other Parties, and to include them was contrary to the spirit of the negotiations. He closed protesting again at the minimum percentage and hoping for a quick resolution because Whitehead was pressing him to assist him in the referendum campaign. However, Welensky said, he would not until he had achieved a reasonable settlement for Northern Rhodesia.[44]

The Press was growing restless at the continuing silence from both the British and Federal camps, and speculation mounted that an agreement had been reached. Welensky cannot have assisted by declaring at a dinner that the British policy in Africa was running away with itself and that it was time to halt the "sell-out" and bring back responsibility to Colonial affairs. He said that there could be no prolongation of the constitutional negotiations over the Federation without there being damage to the economy. He acknowledged that Britain had suffered from pressure for change from both the West and the East, but that the result was a succession of tragic failures to ensure the colonial people progressed towards competency and integrity in their independence.[45]

Roberts also spoke out, accusing the Colonial Office of exploiting the silence of his Party on the current talks in Lusaka. He referred to a claim in the British Press by a Colonial Office official that the Europeans had accepted an African majority in the Legislative Council. Such tactics, Roberts said, were clearly designed to get Macleod's White Paper proposals through as quickly as possible.[46]

Welensky and Roberts might issue such challenges over Northern Rhodesia, but public attention at that moment was captured by Sandys announcing in the Commons, on 8 June, that the Southern Rhodesian Constitution had been finalised. The African, he said, would gain a significant and growing presence in the Legislative Assembly. Safeguards, comprising a declaration of rights, a constitutional council and an unqualified right of appeal to the Privy Council, justified the removal of the British reserved powers. Five days later, he laid before the House two White Papers which described the changes that, as has been seen, contained the principle of cross-voting, through which only 25 per cent of the "B" roll votes would count towards the election of "A" roll Members and, likewise, 25 per cent of the "A" roll votes would affect the

[44] Welensky Papers, FGC(61), 20th Meeting, Restricted Annexure, Federal Cabinet, 5 June 1961; 20/7, f. 161, Welensky to Robinson, 6 June 1961.
[45] *Central African Post*, 7 June 1961; *The Rhodesia Herald*, 8 June 1961.
[46] *The Rhodesia Herald*, 9 June 1961.

election of "B" roll Members. The Native Reserves and Special Native Areas would be renamed Tribal Trust Lands and be cared for by a board of trustees. The Legislative Assembly would require a two-thirds majority to amend the Constitution, but could not without British sanction alter the Declaration of Rights, the Constitutional Council, the right of appeal to the Privy Council, the security of civil service pensions or the provisions regarding the amendment of the Constitution itself. Alternatively, the Southern Rhodesian Government could hold four separate referenda of the races on such amendments. Thus Sandys had set the stage for the referendum.[47]

A *Face to Face* interview conducted by John Freeman on British television gave a further impression of Macleod. In this he predicted that popular democracy would take over in Southern Rhodesia, but at a different rate from that in the North because of the larger white population. He admitted his distress at the opposition to his policies within his own Party. He shared Lord Salisbury's anxieties but, unlike him, he thought it was dangerous to advance slowly, though he conceded that events were moving too swiftly in Africa. He saw himself as a traditional Tory in the mould of Disraeli and Lord Randolph Churchill, which meant a "Left" approach to home affairs and a robust foreign policy. He had given his heart to the Colonial Office, he said, and did not want to move.[48]

That day, 15 June, the Northern Rhodesian Liberal Party withdrew its candidate from a by-election in Chingola in protest at British pressure to modify Macleod's White Paper. Matters, in fact, were coming to a head with Macleod. Barrow protested furiously to Sir Glyn Jones at the role being played by Nyasaland officials in local politics and, in particular, the presence of a provincial commissioner on Banda's political platform. In a letter to Sandys, Welensky again rejected both the unmodified Northern Rhodesian White Paper and the middle roll proposal as totally unsatisfactory. He indicated that, with reluctance, he would accept the 60:40 ratio of upper roll influence on the election of the national roll Members if the minimum percentage were eradicated. He continued to urge the adoption of seven double-Member constituencies but, if the British Government were obdurate, he would accept five double- and four single-Member constituencies, provided there was a judicial delimitation commission. Hone still wanted the minimum percentage applied even to the single-Member constituencies but Welensky reminded Sandys that this idea was favoured by the Liberal Party alone. Welensky said he would only allow the percentage to be applied to four single-Member constituencies, and wanted it to be no higher than five per cent. He recalled the British Government's frequent assertion that the level of the percentage would be set in consultation with him. He thought that the percentage should only apply to the upper roll and that, for the lower roll, the national roll candidate should be required to secure an equivalent number of votes. Thus, for example, if there were 2 000 upper and 6 000 lower roll voters, and the national roll candidate had to attract five per cent of the upper roll votes (in effect 100 votes), he would therefore have to attract 100 lower

[47] House of Commons *Hansard* (London), Vol. 641, Col. 1392 f., 8 June 1961; *Southern Rhodesia Constitution*, Command 1399–1400 (London, June 1961).

[48] Welensky Papers, 25/27, f. 7, Telex report of the Freeman interview, 15 June 1961.

roll votes. Welensky reiterated that the matter should be settled because the Southern Rhodesian referendum campaign was now being fought in earnest. He asked for the British decision early in the coming week and warned that, if it were adverse, he would fly to London.[49]

Local Press speculation concluded that the Northern Rhodesian White Paper was being radically altered to suit Welensky which represented a swing from the Macleod policy of: "Give the masses the vote, the sooner the better, and hope for the best."[50] This provoked Kaunda to release the text of a cable which he had sent to Macleod to warn that the Africans would never accept the Welensky-Sandys plan. He pleaded that because "untold racial strife and bitterness hang over our otherwise peaceful country", Macleod should use his powers "to do the right thing now. Failing this our reasonable attitude will turn to fanaticism demanding complete independence now".[51] Simultaneously, it was reported that Hone would resign if the latest proposals, which were believed to favour the UFP, were implemented.[52]

On 18 June, Kaunda informed the largest political gathering (15 000) yet seen in Northern Rhodesia that he would increase the tempo of the anti-Federal campaign to clip Welensky's "dirty wings", but that he would do it non-violently. He did not, however, entirely catch Federal public attention because, in Southern Rhodesia, the NDP special congress announced that it would conduct its own referendum on the basis of one man, one vote.[53]

That day, Alport was informed by Welensky "in his most intimidating manner" that he had heard that the British Government would accept the formula of equal influence between the rolls in electing the national roll Members, which would mean the end of the Federation. Alport, who incidently was an advocate of the 60:40 ratio, asked for the source of this news because he had heard nothing. Welensky replied that it was unimpeachable and that, therefore, he would go to London the following week, even though he would risk hastening the demise of the Federation. Alport believed that his task was both that of British representative and counsellor to the Federal Government and sought to divert Welensky from falling prey to those Conservatives who wished to use him in their fight against Macmillan. He rightly knew that the intrusion of Welensky into British politics would not only be resented, but that, when put to the test, the Conservatives would close ranks to preserve their balance of power. Thus only the Federation and Welensky stood to lose.[54]

Having thought, on Saturday, 17 June, that nothing would happen over the weekend, Robinson was suddenly summoned by Sandys who was about to depart for Chequers where the British Cabinet was discussing entrance into the European Common Market. Sandys told Robinson that he, Macmillan and Macleod had just met Hone who had reported the rejection of the 60:40

[49] *Ibid.*, 8/66, f. 23, Barrow to Sir Glyn Jones, 15 June 1961; 20/7, f. 153, Welensky to Robinson, 16 June 1961.
[50] *The Rhodesia Herald*, 16 June 1961.
[51] *Northern News*, 17 June 1961.
[52] *The Bulawayo Chronicle*, 17 June 1961.
[53] *The Rhodesia Herald*, 19 June 1961; *African Daily News*, 19 June 1961.
[54] Alport, *The Sudden Assignment*, *op. cit.*, pp. 60–61.

ratio of upper roll influence. Sandys reminded Robinson that the British Government had agreed to support this ratio only if it received popular endorsement. It was therefore obliged to return to the equal influence of the rolls, but would attempt to meet Welensky in other ways. One was to base the minimum percentage on race and not the rolls. Thus the national roll candidate would have to secure 12½ per cent of the votes cast by each race, or 200 votes from each of the two major races (African and European) in his constituency, whichever was the lower. In the double-Member constituencies, the equivalent figure would be 400 votes from each race, which meant in practice that the candidate would have to get 12½ per cent of the European vote and only four per cent of the African vote, because there would be so many more African voters. The votes could be obtained on either roll or from both combined. The delimitation commission would be established, and Welensky would be consulted about its terms of reference. The upper roll would be broadened only by the introduction of new categories. Sandys said no decision had been taken on the distribution of national roll seats or on the racial reservation of them. Welensky's suggestion of five double-Member and four single-Member unreserved constituencies was being considered, but Sandys wondered if Welensky would not prefer seven double-Member unreserved constituencies because the minimum percentage would be based on race.

Sandys asked for Welensky's reply by 11.30 p.m. that day. Evans, who had telephoned from Salisbury, told Robinson that this request was ridiculous, and thus the time was extended to 5.30 p.m. on Sunday, 18 June. Hone claimed that he could avoid producing racial rolls by leaving it to the polling officer to determine race by appearance. Robinson ridiculed this because a few deceptive appearances could vitally sway the issue. Evans expected Welensky to reject the equality of influence of the rolls in the election of the national roll Members, and suggested that Robinson should remind Sandys of Welensky's insistence on upper roll domination.[55]

The final decision was expected at the British Cabinet meeting on Tuesday, 20 June, and Welensky, the veteran of so many British-inspired weekend Federal Cabinet meetings, was told that the British Cabinet would meet later that day (Saturday, 17 June). He informed Lord Robins that the news "only produced a horse laugh on my part because I don't believe the British Cabinet would meet on a Saturday unless the end of the world was in sight".[56]

In fact, on Monday morning, 19 June, the Ministers concerned with the Federation, and a few others with knowledge of it, such as Lords Kilmuir and Home, were summoned by Macmillan because Alport had reported that Welensky was again threatening to come to London to gather support for his last stand. Undaunted, they decided to endorse the decision on the equality of influence of the two rolls. Macmillan's account of what happened is a little confused because he records Sandys flying to Salisbury when he did not.[57]

The Federal Cabinet met that day, 19 June, at 2.15 p.m. to hear Evans

[55] Welensky Papers, 20/7, f. 151, Evans to Welensky, 19 June 1961.
[56] *Ibid.*, 25/240A, f. 96, Welensky to Lord Robins, 19 June 1961.
[57] Macmillan, *At the End of the Day*, *op. cit.*, p. 315.

describe his conversations with Robinson. On the previous evening, he said, he had told Robinson that the equality of influence of the rolls was completely unacceptable and that, consequently, Welensky would leave for London on Thursday, 22 June, to protest at the rejection of the 60:40 ratio of upper roll influence. Later, Evans recounted, Robinson had telephoned that no decision had been taken and that the British Cabinet would meet at 3 p.m. on 19 June. Robinson had said that Sandys had informed him that, while the 60:40 ratio could not be considered, the introduction of a middle roll could. Robinson had agreed to recommend it provided there was a means of keeping control in responsible hands. Sandys had also warned that any announcement of Welensky's imminent arrival would only precipitate decisions.

Welensky described to the Federal Cabinet Alport's efforts over the weekend to dissuade him from going to London, arguing that the only result might be the demise of the Federation. Alport had urged delay because the British Government had indicated that it might consider a fresh scheme (presumably meaning the middle roll). However, Welensky had insisted that he had to make a stand. He told the Cabinet that he was not rejecting further suggestions, but knew from experience that there was little likelihood of significant change. His officials had calculated that the equal influence of the rolls would give the nationalists a majority at the next election, while the 60:40 ratio would have only given the moderates a reasonable chance. There was no prospect of the Federation's survival when two of three territorial Governments opposed it. He said he had told Alport that the British decision would, at the very least, prejudice the success of the Southern Rhodesian referendum, and that he would go to London to dissuade Macmillan. He had also informed Alport that if he failed, he would tell Macmillan that he would resign and hold a general election, and that he was considering forming a national government.

The Federal Cabinet noted that nothing had ever been received in writing on the middle roll and that there was no indication that the principle of equal influence would not be applied to it. Indeed, the income level of £215 p.a. would ensure that the lower roll would soon predominate. Yet the Cabinet acknowledged that the current suggestion of basing the percentages of votes, which the national roll candidates had to secure, on race might produce a better result than the 60:40 ratio of the upper roll influence. The Cabinet agreed on a firm stand and that Welensky should go to London the following evening (Tuesday, 20 June). A deadline of midday on Tuesday, was set for the consideration of any new British proposals. The opinion of the Litunga of Barotseland would be sought and Robinson would be told that the middle roll proposals were not understood, but would be considered once they were. The announcement of Welensky's departure would be delayed until 1.00 p.m. on 20 June.[58]

Alport was informed at 11.30 a.m. that day (Monday, 19 June) that a favourable decision by the British Cabinet would persuade Welensky not to go to London. Any message had to arrive early enough to be studied before his aircraft left the following evening.[59]

[58] Welensky Papers, FGC(61), Special Meeting, Federal Cabinet, 19 June 1961.
[59] *Ibid.*, 20/7, f. 150, Evans to Welensky, 20 June 1961.

Welensky received a message the next day from Lord Salisbury who understood that he could retreat no further without surrendering, which would be fatal to his own position and to the referendum. Thus Salisbury advised him to stand fast and leave the next move to the British. He thought the middle roll might offer Macleod a less obvious "climb-down" and, if this were possible, Welensky should delay his departure.

Evans telephoned Robinson in London for news, and was told that it was generally believed that the British decision was made and that it was pointless to negotiate further because Kaunda had been given the power of veto. Evans indicated that, while Welensky remained open to suggestion, in reality he was at the end of his tether. Anything further would have to be in writing before Welensky would consider it. The decision to fly to London that evening would be announced at 1 p.m. and Welensky would go because he was convinced of the need for decisive action.

Robinson reported to Evans that Sandys had telephoned him the previous day (Monday, 19 June) to say that a final decision had not been taken and that further negotiations were possible. Sandys had said he could reveal that there would be seven double-Member constituencies, four of which would be racially reserved. The minimum percentage would be set at 12½ per cent or its equivalent at 400 votes, and not 200, which should secure the national roll seats for the moderates. Robinson asked Evans for Welensky's reaction although he had told Sandys that the principle of the equal influence of the rolls was unacceptable.

Robinson then said that he had been asked to request Welensky to delay his flight to await the British proposal, which could not arrive until late that afternoon (Tuesday, 20 June) and then would be even longer delayed because it would have to be decoded.[60]

At 10.00 a.m. that day (Tuesday) the Federal Cabinet examined the concessions, which Sandys had transmitted through Robinson, and then discussed Welensky's visit. It concluded that, if decisions had been taken, there was nothing to lose by a delay of 24 hours and that it might be worth waiting to see the British proposal. However, little concession was expected and the conclusion was that, as there might be considerable advantage in Welensky starting for London before any doors were closed, he should fly that evening as planned.

Before the Federal Cabinet met again that afternoon, Alport revealed to Welensky that the proposal was being transmitted. He wished Welensky to recognise the strenuous efforts being made to meet his requirements, even if the 60:40 proposal had been rejected. He said that Sandys had telephoned to say that, while any Federal ideas on the middle roll would be considered, his Government had not examined it closely because the Federal Government seemed to have rejected it.[61]

The Federal Cabinet, when it met at 3.45 p.m., thought that this could be another delaying tactic as there were serious practical difficulties involved. It agreed that the qualifying standards had been set too low but that nothing should be abandoned which might produce a settlement, and that last-minute

[60] *Ibid.*, f. 145, Evans to Welensky, 20 June 1961.

[61] *Ibid.*, f. 147, Alport to Welensky, 20 June 1961.

negotiations should be sought. The Cabinet, recalling Macleod's acknowledgement to the Litunga of Barotseland that his acceptance of any constitutional proposals was necessary, confirmed that the latter should be urgently consulted.[62]

The British proposal arrived within the hour. In it Macmillan conceded the minimum percentage of 12½ per cent and the equivalent of 400 votes, whichever was the lower. For practical reasons of delimitation, he said, there would be seven double-Member constituencies, with four of them racially reserved. The upper roll qualifications were inviolate, though the roll would be broadened through the addition of new categories. He confirmed that there would be a delimitation commission and that Welensky would be consulted on its terms of reference. Regretting the abandonment of the 60:40 ratio of upper roll influence, Macmillan claimed to understand Welensky's views, but reminded him that the British Government had difficulties of its own, particularly as it was responsible for law and order in Northern Rhodesia. He hoped that the new proposals would be accepted as a sincere effort to achieve a settlement which would satisfy Welensky and yet stay within the framework of the White Paper. The middle roll had not been considered seriously because of Federal reluctance and the consequent failure of Hone to air it in Lusaka. However, Macmillan said, if Welensky wished it examined, he had only to inform Alport.[63]

The dispatch was welcomed by the Federal Cabinet at its third and last meeting of the day at 4.45 p.m. because the new minimum percentage and its equivalent would create difficulties for the African nationalists. It agreed that the middle roll should not be discarded and thought that it could be based on race. As it was better to negotiate in London, Greenfield and Evans were to fly there that evening, and Welensky, Roberts and Burney would follow a day later.

Welensky was not optimistic and he alerted Joelson, John Connell, the journalist and biographer, and Wall to the victory of Macleod over Sandys on the 60:40 ratio. He told them that he would go to London to prevent a breakdown in the negotiations. He said he would see Macmillan on Thursday, 22 June and return to Salisbury on Sunday, 25 June to dissolve Parliament to discover the will of the electorate. He would resist the imposition of the Northern Rhodesian changes and revealed that he had toyed with a unilateral declaration of independence but thought there were better methods of achieving his objective. His Cabinet had agreed that he could go no further down the slippery path.[64]

The British Government had heard that Kaunda and Sir John Moffat would be flying to London that evening (Tuesday, 20 June), and was relieved that Welensky would not arrive with them. Moffat's declared purpose was to warn Macmillan of the violent consequences of yielding to UFP pressure. Roberts responded by criticising Moffat for speaking wildly when he was a Minister in the Northern Rhodesian Government. Indeed, he maintained,

[62] *Ibid.*, FGC(61), 22nd Meeting, Federal Cabinet, 20 June 1961.
[63] *Ibid.*, 20/7, f. 148, Macmillan to Welensky, 20 June 1961.
[64] *Ibid.*, 24/151, f. 57, Welensky to Joelson, 20 June 1961; 43/*Connell*, Welensky to J. Connell, 20 June 1961; 43/*Wall*, Welensky to Wall, 20 June 1961.

what Moffat said amounted to intimidation because he knew that the question of constitutional change had been left open and that the proposals could be altered in terms of the White Paper. In any case, Roberts was confident that the Northern Rhodesian Government could deal with any consequences. The *Daily Express* denounced the British Government for taking notice of Kaunda as he dealt in fear. It quoted Kaunda as saying that he was sure that the British Government would take a firm stand against Welensky and would make the right decision, if only for fear of what might happen in Northern Rhodesia.[65]

On Wednesday, 21 June, Welensky informed Macmillan that, contrary to the British belief, the Federal Government was not discarding the middle roll and would be willing to reconsider it. He was eventually told by Alport that Sandys would comment the next day. Welensky agreed not to fly to London until he received the dispatch.[66]

In the meantime, Greenfield and Evans had arrived in London that day and proposed to Sandys that the Coloured and Asian votes should be excluded from the equivalent influence formula because thereby the result could be achieved which the 60:40 ratio would have produced. The Asians and Coloureds would be compensated with a national roll seat, bringing the total of those seats back to 15, thus restoring the 15:15:15 formula. Welensky ordered them to secure a promise that, whatever happened, there would be no further constitutional changes for five years to gain valuable breathing space. Robinson advised Welensky that Roberts should not come to London because, as leader of the Northern Rhodesian UFP elected Members, Roberts would have to deal directly with Macleod, thereby creating three-cornered negotiations which would be difficult to co-ordinate. As Burney was not on Roberts's level, and thus would not have to deal with Macleod, Robinson suggested that he be sent over immediately so that at least Greenfield would have a Northern Rhodesian at hand. Robinson also suggested that Welensky delay his own departure to the point that he came only to contend with major issues.[67]

Nothing was released to the public, much to the dissatisfaction of the Northern Rhodesian Europeans who threatened to demonstrate, thereby throwing the outcome of the Chingola by-election into doubt.

Welensky briefed his Cabinet and Whitehead on the morning of Thursday, 22 June. He revealed that he had informed Macmillan that he would consider the middle roll, provided the equation set the Europeans on one side and the non-Europeans on the other, and that the Constitution would be reviewed after five years. In his view all this accorded with the White Paper and would remove many of the difficulties which were inherent in the latest proposals. He had been told late on the previous evening that Macmillan was out of London and would return that morning. As Macmillan could therefore not consider his reply, Sandys and Alport had urged him to delay his departure. Greenfield, Robinson and Evans had agreed because they believed the middle

[65] *The Rhodesia Herald*, 21 & 22 June 1961; *Daily Express*, 21 June 1961.
[66] Welensky Papers, 20/7, f. 133, Telephone conversation between Welensky and Alport, 21 June 1961; f. 135, Telephone conversation between Evans and Welensky, 21 June 1961.
[67] *Ibid*., f. 139, Telephone conversation between Welensky and Robinson, 21 June 1961.

roll would thereby be more favourably received. If the British proposals were to stand, Welensky said, Greenfield wanted the separate seat for the Asians and Coloureds. In addition, Greenfield proposed a prerequisite of 25 per cent of the upper roll votes to be obtained by any successful national roll candidate. The latter would still have to obtain the minimum percentage (12½ per cent) from each of the two major races (African and European) in his constituency. The 25 per cent requirement, Welensky explained, was designed to eliminate Moffat's Liberal Party and would be called "the Moffat hurdle".

Whitehead felt that the stark racial nature of the British proposals augured ill for the future. To him 12½ per cent was too high a hurdle for the European candidate and he disliked the provision for a review in five years because it would induce instability. The uncertainty, he said, would have a detrimental effect on his referendum, particularly as no one could say that there would not be an African-dominated government at the first election.

Welensky was not as gloomy because, he replied, there was a chance, if Greenfield were successful, of a responsible government being returned. The British had made a number of important concessions, one being that there would be no lowering of the upper roll qualifications, and that pro-Federal candidates should be able to capture at least eight of the national roll seats. If this did not happen, the Federation would end, the territorial economies would be ruined, and racial tension would increase immeasurably.

The Cabinet agreed that a moderate party and the Federation itself could not exist without African support. Thus it was imperative that the moderates should be able to capture the national roll seats to give the Government a working majority. It was happy that there should be a review after five years because no one could forecast the course of events. However, it did not expect an agreement as the British Government had manoeuvred itself into the position of having to impose the solution. It advised that the best argument to advance in the referendum campaign was that the Northern Rhodesian Government was remaining in responsible hands, and that, as Southern Rhodesia was getting a great measure of independence, it would be better able to deal with any future developments. As Britain would be unable to interfere in Southern Rhodesian internal affairs, this was a most powerful argument. Welensky cautioned the Cabinet against complacency because the British reaction to the latest proposals was unknown and he might still have to fly to London the next evening (Friday, 23 June).[68]

After the meeting, Evans telephoned Welensky from London to say that the British Cabinet was in session. He wished to know the verdict on the separate Asian seat and it became clear that he and Greenfield intended to exclude the Asians from voting for the other national roll Members. This, he believed, was the best idea to date, and Welensky agreed it should be advanced as a basis for discussion. Evans thought there could be other changes because Sandys had suggested the reduction of the 400 equivalent votes by 50 and the minimum percentage to 10 per cent. This pleased Welensky.

Evans reported that the consensus of opinion in Britain was that Macleod

[68] *Ibid.*, FGC(61), Special Meeting, Federal Cabinet, 22 June 1961.

was "going to pull a fast one" over Welensky because his resistance to the British proposals appeared to be a bluff. To counter this, Evans said, Greenfield would hold an "off-the-record" session with the Press that evening and was considering a full Press conference. Macleod was cock-a-hoop and was talking of a defeat for Welensky. It was necessary to deflate Macleod. Greenfield would stress the building of a multi-racial community and would discount any threat to Northern Rhodesia's internal security. Evans said he had informed Sandys that morning that it was extraordinary that Hone should maintain there was a current security situation, yet had never alerted Welensky to it. It was then decided that Welensky's departure depended on what the British Cabinet produced. Finally, Welensky revealed to Evans that he had annoyed the Northern Rhodesian officials by being in contact with the Litunga.[69]

Later the same day, Evans reported that the British seemed certain to accept the elimination of the Asian and Coloured vote from the calculation of the minimum percentage, and the reduction of the latter to ten per cent and its equivalent to 350 votes. More time had been asked for consideration of the 25 per cent additional qualification — "the Moffat hurdle". The British had not rejected it, but had claimed that the Commons debate on Southern Rhodesia that day had demanded Sandys's attention. An answer was expected on the morrow, Friday, 23 June at 10.00 a.m., and consequently the Federal team in London advised Welensky not to fly that night because he should not come to discuss matters of pure detail. Welensky was interested to hear that the British had accepted two of the modifications (which were based purely on race), but had not as yet accepted "the Moffat hurdle" (the 25 per cent of upper roll votes which the national roll candidate would have to secure). He felt that, if he did not travel immediately, there was little point in going until Monday, 26 June. Evans's main concern was that Welensky should read any statement by Macleod before it was released and said that Sandys had thought this possible.

Greenfield came on the line to review the reasons for Welensky travelling. The first was to push for a final settlement, but that was not apparent yet. The second was if the negotiations broke down, which they had not. However, if Welensky boarded the aircraft, it would be assumed that a break-down had occurred. Monday was a more appropriate day because by then the climax would have been reached. Welensky said that the Press had discovered that he was booked on the aircraft that evening (Thursday) and Greenfield advised him to say he was going the next day (Friday). Welensky felt that it was an impossible situation, and that he could not keep on playing that game night after night.[70]

Little of the following day's events are recorded, but Welensky did write to his supporters, claiming that the British Government had deliberately leaked the 60:40 proposal so that Moffat and the African nationalists would protest and it could then claim that the ratio was unacceptable. He asked his supporters to grin and bear it because within 24 hours the crisis would be resolved one way or the other. W. S. Parker, his principal private secretary, in

[69] *Ibid.*, 20/7, f. 125, Telephone conversation between Welensky and Evans, 22 June 1961.
[70] *Ibid.*, f. 129, Telephone conversation between Welensky, Greenfield and Evans, 22 June 1961.

fact, had information that UNIP would accept less than parity to gain access to the Legislative Council, provided that the UFP did not secure a majority. Parker had heard that there was pressure for a meeting between Welensky and Kaunda. [71]

Evans was told by Sandys at 4.30 p.m. that day (Friday, 23 June), during a short adjournment of the Cabinet, that some concession would be made to the Africans. Evans rejected an idea to replace English with the vernacular as the literacy qualification for the lower roll because it would have added another 25 000 - 30 000 voters and would have a devastating effect on the election of the national roll Members. Sandys had argued that this was necessary because of the current security threat. Unconvinced, Evans said that Welensky would accept nothing more than the addition of 500 voters to the upper roll by selecting special categories. Three-quarters of an hour later, Evans was informed that the British Government accepted the addition of the 500 voters to the upper roll but, in exchange for the exclusion of the Asians and Coloureds from the national roll elections and the inclusion of the 25 per cent "Moffat hurdle", it wanted yet another 500 voters added to the upper roll. At that point Evans telephoned Welensky to advise him to leave for London.[72]

Welensky recalls that not only was he fighting for fundamental principles, but that the hour by hour messages from Greenfield convinced him that he should go to London. Consequently, on the evening of Friday, 23 June, he went out to the airport and his luggage was already loaded into the aircraft when Alport, who had not been told of his departure, and had rushed from the bath to intercept him, informed him that Sandys wished to speak to him on the telephone. Sandys asked him not to come because if he did everything would be thrown back into "the melting pot". Welensky asked if this was a threat, and Sandys confirmed that it was. Sandys pleaded that he should be allowed to reach an agreement with Greenfield. If he failed, he promised that Macmillan would see Welensky. Sandys was confident of a reasonable settlement.[73]

As Alport had rung Sandys, Welensky thanked him for interceding and departed for home with his wife muttering typically to Alport that she had nothing in the house for "the old man's dinner". Alport was nonetheless affronted that no one had told him that Welensky was going to London. He went off to a dinner at the local army mess, but, half way through it, had to reassure Sandys who had seen a Press service tape which said that Welensky had flown.[74]

Although the next day was Saturday, everyone was busy. One of the first events arose out of Sandys maintaining, and Welensky denying, that there would be a serious security situation if the proposals which would suit the Federal Government were implemented. As Sandys was adamant that the advice of the senior Northern Rhodesian officials could not be ignored,

[71] *Ibid.*, 27/41, f. 21, Welensky to J. C. Burke, 23 June 1961; 7/12, f. 101, Welensky to G. W. R. L'Ange, 23 June 1961; 27/84, f. 14, W. S. Parker to Welensky, 23 June 1961.
[72] *Ibid.*, 20/7, f. 118, Telephoned message from Evans, 24 June 1961.
[73] Welensky, *4 000 Days*, *op. cit.*, p. 307; Alport, *The Sudden Assignment*, *op. cit.*, pp. 63–65; Macmillan, *At the End of the Day*, *op. cit.*, p. 316.
[74] Alport, *The Sudden Assignment*, *op. cit.*, p. 65.

Welensky took the obvious course and asked the area commander of the Federal Army in Lusaka to see the Acting Governor to demand to know why, if a serious security situation existed, he had not been informed. He received a categorical denial that there was any such situation, and this proved to Welensky the lengths to which Hone would go to have his own way.[75]

At 10 a.m. Greenfield sent a telephoned message to say that he believed Welensky had seen a copy of the statement which Macleod was going to make, and that he had received his at 11 p.m. the previous evening. He explained that he had been virtually excluded from the previous day's negotiations and only with the greatest difficulty had seen Sandys for ten minutes. Consequently, Evans had been forced to use his own initiative and had suggested the additional 500 voters on the upper roll. Greenfield had learned from Sandys that Welensky had accepted this. If this were true, then there were only three outstanding issues. The first was the 25 per cent "Moffat hurdle". The second was the manner in which the minimum percentage had been fixed so that the number of African votes required was always greater than the number of European votes, with the result that there was discrimination in favour of the European candidate. The third was a late bid by the British Government to reduce from two years to one the period in which the upper roll voter's income qualification had to be earned.

Greenfield thought that they had to resist the *quid pro quo* of the second additional 500 voters for "the Moffat hurdle". If pressed, the Federal Government should concede the period of the income qualification. He wanted "the Moffat hurdle" to apply to both rolls to force the candidate to attract 25 per cent of the votes of either, and not just of the upper. Macleod, he warned, had described the delimitation commission in his statement as independent and not as judicial. Nor did Macleod mention what principles would apply. As Macmillan had conceded that the terms of reference would be drawn up in consultation with Welensky, the latter should ask if this arrangement had been superseded. Greenfield said he had pressed for the new constitution to be permanent, but was told that it might last one or two general elections. Thus he felt that it was necessary to secure some sort of commitment on this.

Criticising Macleod's text, Greenfield pointed to a Press prediction of complete victory for Macleod and said that his statement was designed to confirm this, while giving the credit to Hone. Close examination would show that Macleod had not departed from the original 15:15:15 formula and, indeed, had gained 500 African voters. There was no reference to the negotiations with the Federal Government. If this were to be so, Greenfield said, then the Federal Government would have to issue a simultaneous statement without any warning, lest the British Government foil it. The British would protest, but too late. If the Federal Government did nothing, Welensky would appear to have been totally defeated, leaving Macleod to enjoy his victory.

Greenfield noted that Macleod's statement was vague about the Asians and Coloureds and the election of the national roll Members. Nor did it say that

[75] Welensky Papers, 43/*Wall*, Welensky to Wall, 3 July 1961.

the Asians on the lower roll would vote for the Asian national roll Member. There was no reference to the number of nominated Members, which Greenfield thought was necessary, and he wanted a last-minute bid to reduce the number of official Members. Furthermore, Macleod had to be prevented from effecting alterations by regulation, as he had in Nyasaland. Finally, Greenfield said he was anxious to leave London because he was acutely embarrassed at being completely by-passed by Sandys. Yet, he knew that his presence might prevent detrimental changes and, if he stayed, he could maintain contact with the Federation's supporters.[76]

Evans also reported to Welensky on his activities, saying they would negotiate on "the Moffat hurdle" that morning.[77] Welensky then told his Cabinet that Sandys had alleged that his arrival in London would have prejudiced negotiations which were "within 500 votes of agreement". He had agreed not to go after he had been promised that he would see Macleod's statement before it was delivered and that, if necessary, he could see Macmillan. The Cabinet read the statement and, like Greenfield, noted that there were several omissions. Alport was summoned and agreed to raise certain matters with his Government that evening. In addition he would transmit the Federal Government's displeasure over the demand for its views at short notice and without knowledge of the new White Paper which was being drafted on the recommendations of Hone. However, the Cabinet did not share Greenfield's distaste at the lack of acknowledgement of the Federal negotiations because it preferred to issue its own statement declaring that the solution was being imposed and that, despite some improvement, it was only the best of a bad bargain.

The Cabinet pointed out to Alport that the 25 per cent "Moffat hurdle" was merely designed to ensure good government and did not favour any racial group. Thus the addition of a second 500 African voters to the upper roll as a *quid pro quo* for it, was unacceptable. In any case, the likely membership of both the upper and lower rolls was now so equal that the additional voters would destroy the balance. If necessary, "the Moffat hurdle" itself should be abandoned. The Cabinet was at a loss to know why the British should wish to bargain over it because it was reasonable and completely impartial. The reduction of the income period, from two years to one, had been associated with the 60:40 ratio of upper roll influence and should have fallen away with that ratio. The Cabinet wondered why the reduction of the income period had been revived without a *quid pro quo*. It was not a material point, but could be used to bargain for "the Moffat hurdle". With regard to the minimum percentage, the Cabinet wanted an equivalent, if it were less than 400 votes, to apply lest it favour the African nationalists. The judicial nature of the delimitation commission had to be stated and its terms of reference drawn up in consultation with Welensky. All rolls should now have 14 seats to assist delimitation, and, to give some permanency, no constitutional alteration should be possible except at the request of the majority of the elected Members. There should be no immediate alterations to the new White Paper by means of regulations. The power to nominate Members (to safeguard the

[76] *Ibid.*, 27/14, f. 121, Telephone message from Greenfield, 24 June 1961.
[77] *Ibid.*, 20/7, f. 118, Telephone message from Evans, 24 June 1961.

interests of minority groups) should fall away because there would be an elected Asian seat. The number of official Members should be reduced to the three or four which would be required for the Executive Council. Finally, Sandys would be held to his promise to allow Welensky to see Macmillan if necessary. Although Alport agreed to convey all this, the Cabinet decided that Welensky would write to Sandys to make doubly sure. Greenfield and Evans would stay in London until Macleod had delivered his statement in the Commons.[78]

Macmillan recalls that, on 25 June, on the advice of his physician, he was resting at home when the telephone rang and thus his "treatment was brutally interfered with". He was told that Welensky was pressing for more concessions but he refused to yield as they had already granted him two of his four demands, and it was vital to stop the argument.[79]

Welensky could not know this, but Evans telephoned him early on Sunday, 25 June, to say that on the previous day there had been much activity and "gnashing of teeth", and that matters had appeared to deteriorate until Welensky's message had arrived, when everything had brightened. Indeed, Evans reported, the basis of a final settlement had been produced after a working dinner arranged by Sandys and attended by Robinson. Agreement had been reached and the results were also being telephoned to Macmillan. As a result, Macleod had to accept or reject the agreement by lunchtime and had complied after some disagreement with Sandys. The 15:15:15 formula had been retained. The 15 national roll Members would comprise an Asian, elected by the Asians and Coloured voters using Northern Rhodesia as a single constituency, and 14 Members of either major race (African and European) who would be elected by the upper and lower roll voters in seven double-Member constituencies. The minimum percentage which each national roll candidate had to secure from the European and African voters in his constituency remained at 12½ per cent or its equivalent of 400 votes from each of the two races. There was some doubt about the acceptability of "the Moffat hurdle" but, Evans said, Robinson would still make a last minute bid to have it written in because Sandys had indicated that it might still be included if it were reduced from 25 to 20 per cent. Robinson would also press for the 14:14:14 formula, the discarding of the Governor's power to nominate, the reduction of the number of official Members from four to three, and the amendment of the Constitution to be effected by the Legislative Council and not by a British order in council. Evans explained that, in terms of the agreement with Sandys, the Coloured voters could opt out of voting for the Asian national roll Member and could choose to be regarded as Europeans for electoral purposes. This did not particularly please Welensky. The votes of those Coloured and Asian voters, Evans continued, who voted for the Asian national roll Member, would not count in the election of the other 14 national roll Members. Only 500 Africans were to be added to the upper roll. This, said Evans, was the product of a fight which lasted until two that morning. Furthermore, the period in which the income qualification had to be earned

[78] *Ibid.*, FGC(61), Special Meeting, Federal Cabinet, 24 June 1961; 20/7, f. 116, Welensky to Sandys, 24 June 1961.

[79] Macmillan, *At the End of the Day*, *op. cit.*, p. 316.

was reduced from two years to one. Finally, there would be a judicial delimitation commission.

Welensky agreed that, once "the Moffat hurdle" *et al* had been pressed for the last time, the Federal delegation in London would be empowered to accept the final British decision after perusing Macleod's amended statement. Macmillan had pleaded that this should be "the very end" as he could take no more quarrelling, and Greenfield and Evans advised that he should be given this assurance. Evans said that Macmillan knew how bitter the affair had made Welensky, and had appealed that he should be content with this settlement. Macmillan accepted that Welensky had to say something in public but asked him to remember that Governments had to act responsibly, and to leave the bitterness and personal vindictiveness to Kaunda. There should be no Federal statement before Macleod's announcement. (This plea by Macmillan for an end to the affair would be acidly recalled in the coming September when the British Government re-opened it.)

Robinson came on the line to say that the Sunday Press, due to Voice and Vision's efforts, was favourable to Welensky and had dismissed any victory for Macleod. Lawrence Katilungu had arrived, representing the Northern Rhodesian ANC, and Robinson said he had organised a Press conference for him at which he alleged that, amongst other matters, Moffat would leave his Liberal Party for Kaunda's UNIP, and that the latter was not representative of Northern Rhodesian Africans.[80]

Macmillan recalls writing in his diary that he still hoped for the best. He thought if Welensky acquiesced "and does not crow or lament", if he made no foolish threats, if the Southern Rhodesians saw the settlement as fair and sensible and voted for the new Southern Rhodesian Constitution, if confidence returned, bringing with it investment in the Federation, if the Commons and the Press were temperate, then "all these terrible weeks of strain" would have been worthwhile. He knew that events had left his Ministers on edge. "Macleod, with many faults," he wrote, "has been persistent, imaginative, and ingenious. Sandys has been most loyal to me and absolutely tireless." Macmillan closed his account with the proud boast that, in making concessions to Welensky, they had not sacrificed anything of principle.[81]

The last-minute representations on "the Moffat hurdle" at least had some effect because, when Macleod delivered his statement on the new White Paper and tabled the latter in the Commons on 26 June, he set the minimum percentage at 12½ per cent and its equivalent at 400 votes, but he added that a national roll candidate would also be expected to secure at least 20 per cent of the votes cast on either the upper or the lower roll. Callaghan called the White Paper a "dog's breakfast". At least, though, Macmillan could record that the Conservative Party was calm and united.[82]

Welensky met his Cabinet and offered to resign because there had been a

[80] Welensky Papers, 20/7, f. 110, Telephone conversation between Welensky, Robinson and Evans, 25 June 1961.

[81] Macmillan, *At the End of the Day*, *op. cit.*, p. 316.

[82] House of Commons *Hansard* (London), Vol. 643, Col. 33, 26 June 1961; *Northern Rhodesia: Proposals for Constitutional Change*, Command 1423 (London, June 1961); Macmillan, *At the End of the Day*, *op. cit.*, p. 316.

misunderstanding over the basis of the election of the national roll Members which related to the race of voters. He, unlike Greenfield, had understood that it would be thus based. The Cabinet, however, dismissed the matter as one of detail. In the Federal Assembly, Welensky confirmed to Field that, regrettable though it might be, the British Government could meddle in Northern Rhodesia. He promised a statement on Northern Rhodesia later in the afternoon and looked forward to the Federal Review's resumption.[83]

In the afternoon, he acknowledged that the protracted negotiations had produced an imposed settlement which would please no one, but which was somewhat better than the original White Paper. It could produce a workable constitution, but would need the good sense and moderation of all. It was not a "sell-out" to either race, and forced the political Parties to appeal to both. It was not a good constitution because it was inspired by doubtful principles, overshadowed by political expediency, and bedevilled by haste. He described the scheme in detail, outlined the objections of his Government, and told how difficult it had been to manoeuvre because of rigid British adherence to the original White Paper. However, the scheme would at least inspire confidence in the continuation of the Federation, and he looked forward to the successful outcome of the Federal Review. Privately, Welensky wondered how Macleod could continue in office after all the concessions which had been wrung from him.[84]

With the Conservative Press hailing the settlement as a victory for Welensky and moderation, Welensky and Macmillan exchanged messages of congratulation.[85] If it were a victory of sorts, it would be short-lived. However, Welensky could immediately direct his energy towards helping Whitehead with his referendum campaign. The referendum would be convincingly won, but, of course, the Northern Rhodesian question was still far from settled.

[83] Welensky Papers, FGC(61), Special Meeting, Federal Cabinet, 26 June 1961; Fed R & N *Debates* (Salisbury), Vol. 15, Col. 25 f., 26 June 1961.

[84] Fed R & N *Debates* (Salisbury), Vol. 15, Col. 34 f., 26 June 1961; Welensky Papers, 25/240A, f. 91, Welensky to Lord Robins, 26 June 1961.

[85] Welensky Papers, 20/7, f. 106, Welensky to Macmillan, 27 June 1961; f. 108, Macmillan to Welensky, 26 June 1961.

CHAPTER THIRTY

The Dismissal of Macleod

The Re-opening of the Northern Rhodesian Constitutional Issue, June–October 1961

ANY euphoria over the Northern Rhodesian settlement and the forthcoming referendum victory in Southern Rhodesia was quickly dispelled by events in Katanga and by growing unrest in two provinces of Northern Rhodesia. Nonetheless, only the suspicious by nature would have predicted that the British Government would succumb to pressure from Kaunda and Sir John Moffat to re-open the Northern Rhodesian negotiations. The resulting antagonism, together with the failure to resolve the issue, would be partly responsible for Macmillan's replacement of Macleod with Reginald Maudling in October.

Amidst the clamour which greeted the apparent settlement (the *Daily Express*, for example, attributed the victory to Welensky[1]), the Federal Prime Minister expressed his pleasure at succeeding in limiting the extremist influence. He intended to re-join the battle for the referendum immediately, but there was one more pressing matter. The Nyasaland general election was in the offing and the Malawi Congress Party arranged a series of broadcasts over the Tanganyikan Radio. The Federal Broadcasting Corporation protested, but its Tanganyikan counterpart replied that it was a governmental matter over which it had no control. Welensky asked the Commonwealth Relations Office to forward his displeasure at such outside interference, but it was reluctant to become involved and risk offending Julius Nyerere. When forced to protest, it did so feebly and without effect. In the event, however, the broadcasts were rather ineffective.[2]

Although the United National Independence and Dominion Parties and

[1] *Daily Express*, 27 June 1961.

[2] Welensky Papers, 24/2, f. 88, Welensky to Mrs C. Davies, 27 June 1961; 20/8, f. 65, Welensky to Lord Alport, 27 June 1961; f. 64, Alport to Welensky, 30 June 1961; f. 63, Welensky to Robinson, 7 & 13 July 1961; 24/151, ff. 38–40, Welensky to F. S. Joelson, 31 July 1961; 20/8, f. 57, W. F. Nicholas to H. N. Parry, 5 August 1961.

others condemned the Northern Rhodesian settlement, Welensky was congratulated by a wide cross-section of his supporters and acquaintances. Lord Salisbury thought the settlement was as good as he would get. Wall was pleased with the terms secured and that Welensky, after frightening the Party whips, had not been forced to divide the Conservative Party. Welensky replied that he had to prick Wall's "happy balloon" as he was most unhappy at the outcome because it left a number of matters still to be settled. However, he said he would still attempt to make the new Constitution work.[3]

While the choruses of congratulations and denunciation continued, Welensky broadcast on 30 June on the proposed Southern Rhodesian constitution and warned of the wide effects of any refusal to accept change. In view of the new British policy, he said, it was vital that Southern Rhodesia should obtain as great a measure of independence as possible. It was imperative also that there should be direct African representation in Parliament. The proposed constitution would provide this without lowering standards, and he insisted that the Africans had to have a forum in which to air their views. He believed that the proposed constitution would end the current uncertainty and would revive the economy.[4]

He argued in the same vein in Bulawayo the next day, and it was along these lines that Whitehead and he fought the campaign. It would — with a streak of anti-semitism — be one of the toughest and dirtiest campaigns in his experience. He was rewarded, however, by attracting some of his biggest audiences. In the process he annoyed Macleod who complained to Burney that Welensky could never refrain from attacking the British Government.[5]

While Welensky campaigned, he was distracted to a degree by the Nyasaland general election and a crisis in Kuwait to which he responded by reinforcing the RAF in the Middle East with transport, fighter and bomber aircraft. Always a loyalist, even in his darkest moments, he did this with alacrity even though he knew that his forces might be needed to reinforce Southern Rhodesia if Nkomo's threats of unrest bore fruit. Kaunda was being equally aggressive, returning on 5 July fuming about a customs search, and breathing fire about Macleod's betrayal. More important, however, to Welensky was the welcome news of a resounding win by his Party in the Chingola by-election. Almost as pleasing was Lawrence Katilungu's retention of the south west constituency for the African National Congress in another by-election caused by Nkumbula's imprisonment for a driving offence.[6]

Although he was concentrating on Southern Rhodesia, Welensky resolved to harry Macleod at every turn, with the able assistance of Robinson. They protested to Macleod about his receiving Kaunda in London on 3 July without reference to them. They enlisted the aid of Voice and Vision and

[3] *Ibid.*, 43/*Salisbury*, Lord Salisbury to Welensky, 27 June 1961; 43/*Wall*, Major P. Wall to Welensky, 27 June 1961; Welensky to Wall, 3 July 1961.

[4] *Ibid.*, 7/5, f. 152, Welensky's Broadcast, 30 June 1961.

[5] *Ibid.*, f. 110, Welensky's Speech in Bulawayo, 1 July 1961; 43/*Scott*, Welensky to J. Scott, 19 July 1961; 7/9, f. 160, Welensky to Lord Boyd, 29 July 1961; f. 148, Welensky to E. I. Salzman, 31 July 1961; 27/40, f. 34, C. D. Burney to Welensky, 7 July 1961.

[6] *Ibid.*, 24/151, f. 54, Welensky to Joelson, 3 July 1961; 43/*Connell*, Welensky to J. Connell, 7 July 1961; *The Rhodesia Herald*, 5 & 8 July 1961.

supplied it with evidence of Macleod's duplicity and scheming since 1959 over the Constitutions for the northern territories.[7]

By 18 July Whitehead decided to warn the National Democratic Party, which was planning its own "mock referendum" and a national strike, that his Government would not tolerate any illegal attempt to disrupt the constitutional process. He promised to protect the loyal African against intimidation and to crush any attempt to defy the law. In reply, the NDP, while maintaining that it would use legal means to prevent the imposition of the proposed constitution, uttered threats of mass violence, and dismissed moderate Africans as mere puppets. Consequently, on 19 July, troops were moved into the African townships while all police reserves were placed on stand-by.[8]

With few incidents, the NDP attempted to hold its referendum on Sunday, 23 July. However, poor organisation produced something which smacked of a farce. Two whites voted twice and at least one African boasted to the Press that he had done so eleven times. It soured the atmosphere, Africans stayed away from work, and the next day arrests were made for intimidation at the Ford motor assembly plant in Salisbury. There was a sabotage attempt on the main water pipe from Hunyani to Salisbury. When a stone-throwing crowd became threatening in Salisbury, the police opened fire, killing two and wounding four. Windows were smashed in similar incidents in Bulawayo, but by 25 July normality began to return and the Africans streamed back to work. Whitehead expressed confidence that no harm had been done to his cause because he was sure that these events were abhorrent to the bulk of the African population. He won the approval of two-thirds of the electorate for his constitution two days later.[9]

Credited with a major contribution to Whitehead's victory, Welensky was able to depart on a speaking tour of Nyasaland. In his wake, in Southern Rhodesia, there was a significant development because the United Group which, under the chairmanship of a wealthy farmer, D. C. Lilford, had fought Whitehead, decided to enter the political field at both Federal and territorial levels to contest the next election. This would become the Rhodesian Front, led by Winston Field, and then by I. D. Smith.[10]

In Nyasaland Welensky discovered that his Party could achieve dominance of the upper roll, but he did not expect it to gain more than a single lower seat. He found Nyasaland, with intimidation rife, to be "explosive" and said as much to the Press. This drew an instant, if private, protest from the Governor, Sir Glyn Jones, who acknowledged that there was much intimidation which was mostly insidious, impalpable and therefore difficult to track down. The police were dealing with anything that was visible or violent with considerable success. Jones therefore believed that intimidation was not

[7] Welensky Papers, 20/2, f. 119, Welensky to A. E. P. Robinson, 13 July 1961; f. 120, "The Colonial Secretary's negotiations with African extremists", (undated).

[8] *Ibid.*, 7/5, f. 86, Whitehead's Statement, 18 July 1961; *Evening Standard*, 19 July 1961; *African Daily News*, 20 July 1961.

[9] *The Rhodesia Herald*, 24, 25 & 28 July 1961; *The Sunday Mail*, 30 July 1961; Welensky Papers, 8/33, f. 47, Sitrep, 24 July 1961; f. 53, Sitrep, 25 July 1961; 7/5, f. 33, Whitehead's Press Conference, 25 July 1961.

[10] Welensky Papers, 43/*Wall*, Wall to Welensky, 28 July 1961; *The Rhodesia Herald*, 3 August 1961.

cowing the population. He hastened to add that he wished to preserve the Federation by the consent of the people and thought that it could be obtained.[11]

In his statement to the Press on violence in Nyasaland, Welensky promised to protest to the British Government and proposed to set up a distress fund for the victims. Blackwood suggested postponing the election, but *The Nyasaland Times*, normally his supporter, thought that this would be dangerously provocative. Philip Short hints that the campaign of intimidation might have been an illusion created by the UFP in a last minute attempt to stave off defeat. There is nothing in the Welensky Papers to suggest that this was true and, indeed, the leadership of the UFP had been resigned to defeat for some time. It is true, however, that one of their candidates, Gideon Makambo, and six supporters were later convicted of conspiracy for setting fire to their own homes in Kota Kota and perjuring themselves to secure the wrongful imprisonment of others.[12]

Welensky replied to Jones that the word "explosive" was the product of poor reporting, but that his fears on the level of intimidation had been confirmed in Nyasaland. His Party's supporters had provided him with irrefutable proof that not only was their success jeopardised by intimidation, but that it even affected their candidatures. He was convinced that intimidation was having a profound effect and that it was wrong to pretend that the election result would not be prejudiced by this "unpleasant weapon".[13]

Concurrently, parts of Northern Rhodesia were of equal concern as, after Kaunda's return, the incidence of arson, sabotage and other acts of violence began to increase markedly until, on 10 August, the Northern Rhodesian Government was forced to ban UNIP in the Northern Province and to curb the activities of its Youth League in the Western Province. The Federal Army provided two battalions of African regulars to assist in the restoration of order.[14]

This inspired Welensky to write that day, 10 August, to Sandys on intimidation in all three territories. The situation was grave, he said, and he wished Sandys to induce the respective authorities to increase their efforts to eradicate it. He reported that in Nyasaland he had found the candidates fighting intimidation and not the election. Those from his Party faced abuse, threats of violence, the manhandling of women and children, and damage to property. Outside the registry offices, the MCP officials had set up tables and warned everyone that the registering officers would demand to see their MCP cards. Jones was trying hard, but his efforts were insufficient. The territory was calm but only because of intimidation.[15] As if to confirm this, *The Times*, when reporting on Nyasaland, declared that the election was one of the quietest ever conducted in Africa. However, it dismissed the intimidation as insignificant and merely part of normal African political activity, but it did

[11] *The Rhodesia Herald*, 5 August 1961; Welensky Papers, 20/8, f. 55, Sir Glyn Jones to Welensky, 5 August 1961.
[12] P. Short, *Banda* (London, 1974), p. 152.
[13] Welensky Papers, 20/8, f. 54, Welensky to Jones, 8 August 1961.
[14] *The Rhodesia Herald*, 9 & 10 August 1961.
[15] Welensky Papers, 20/8, f. 52, Welensky to Sandys, 10 August 1961.

not shake Welensky's belief in what he had seen, and he made sure that selected people, other than Sandys, knew what was happening.[16]

Welensky then pressed Hone to do more about security in Northern Rhodesia, meeting him with Caldicott and Greenfield. He found him nervous and at a loss to know quite what the Federal Government wanted of him. Welensky felt some sympathy for Hone because he knew that there would be no British support for firm action. Nevertheless, Hone did promise to deal firmly with the Northern Province.

The meeting had an unexpected result because Hone revealed that he was under pressure from Kaunda, Sir John Moffat and certain elements in Britain to reconsider the Constitution and, in particular, the Asian representation, the 20 per cent "Moffat hurdle", and the 12½ minimum percentage. He took the opportunity, quite cleverly, Welensky thought, to suggest that it would be worthwhile considering minor adjustments if these would satisfy Kaunda. He noted that the constitutional instruments had not yet been drawn up and implied that some alterations were still possible. Welensky tried to be non-committal but could not resist saying that, if there would be any reconsideration, he wanted "the whole blasted thing" thrown into the "melting pot" and the 1958 Constitution re-established. Hone said no more, but Welensky did not need hindsight to understand that Hone had planted a seed. Warned by this, Welensky seriously viewed Kaunda's latest action in departing for London to appeal to the British public and the Commonwealth to avert what he said was going to be a "very sad" affair. Kaunda claimed, rightly, that the constitutional proposals were too complicated and thus should be abandoned. He called on the British Government to listen or face the implementation of the third phase of his "Master Plan", the details of which he withheld, saying only that they were non-violent.[17]

In Nyasaland, late on 15 August — polling day — it was clear that the MCP would dominate the Legislative Council. An extraordinarily high poll was achieved with the lower roll recording 95,1 per cent, and the upper 85 per cent. The MCP gained 99 per cent of the lower roll votes, but the UFP managed to secure five out of the eight upper roll seats, even though 42 per cent of the votes had been cast for it and 43 per cent for others.

In his biography of Banda, Short makes much of the lack of intimidation and of the efforts of the MCP to avoid incidents. Blackwood, writing on 17 August, gave a very different impression. His lower roll candidates, he said, had given up the unequal struggle before election day and he had been told by one returning officer that it was frightening to see the solid, silent phalanx of voters who were completely organised and marshalled without a word. This left Blackwood wondering how such intimidation could be countered. In the upper roll elections, he believed that he had lost two of the seats because the civil servants had either voted against his candidates or had abstained. He ascribed this to a memorandum circulated by the Civil Servants' Association, the effect of which he had only managed to counter in the Southern Province. The author, S. Hoyle, the chairman of the Association, had drawn attention

[16] *The Times*, 12 August 1961; Welensky Papers, 43/*Connell*, Welensky to J. Connell, 14 August 1961.

[17] Welensky Papers, 7/12, f. 50, Welensky to Barrow, 15 August 1961; *The Times*, 14 August 1961.

to a rumour that the Federal Government was responsible for a delay in the introduction of new conditions of service for Colonial civil servants and for these conditions being set at a lower level than those offered to their counterparts in East Africa.[18]

Telling Wall, Lord Salisbury and others that a campaign had begun to force the reconsideration of the Northern Rhodesian Constitution — Margery Perham had urged it on the previous day in *The Times* — Welensky ascribed the result in Nyasaland to three years of intimidation and virtually no government. It had radically affected even the official circles in Southern Rhodesia, he said, and had undone the referendum campaign there. (The accuracy of this statement would be proved at the polls in Southern Rhodesia a little over a year later.) He was equally alarmed by the failure of the Northern Rhodesian Government to use the troops he had provided because the death toll had reached ten, and every man who had been arrested was a UNIP official. He concluded that Macleod intended to let the trouble smoulder so that, at the right moment, he could demand an inquiry and proceed as he had in Nyasaland.[19]

However, when an emergency had to be declared in the Luapula Province, it was Kaunda, and not Macleod, who demanded that the British Government appoint a commission of inquiry. He declared from London that the Africans could not be blamed for turning violent because it was pointless to talk to the British Government. They felt betrayed, he said, because they had been convinced that the British Government shared their democratic aspirations but, when Welensky roared his disapproval, they had seen it change sides. His reiterated intention was to appeal to the people of Britain and the Commonwealth.[20]

Having failed to evoke a response, on 27 August Kaunda repeated this demand, threatened an increase in violence, and revealed that he had written to President Kennedy of the United States of America, Nehru, Prime Minister of India, and Nkrumah of Ghana blaming the security forces and government policy for the violence. He exonerated himself and his Party. Indeed, he claimed that he was not allowed to visit certain areas, and drew a retort from the Northern Rhodesian Government that it had only banned his Party from those areas and not individuals in their private capacity. The Government also denied that the UNIP headquarters near Fort Roseberry had been burnt down by the security forces.[21]

Moffat was also in London and, as Welensky predicted, supported Kaunda, adding that the trouble would end in a week if there were constitutional changes. He would not ascribe the violence to one man, but to the frustration of a people. He ignored, of course, the evidence that almost all those arrested belonged to UNIP.

[18] Short, *Banda, op. cit.*, pp. 150–153; Welensky Papers, 27/69, f. 146, Blackwood to Welensky, 17 August 1961.

[19] *The Times*, 17 August 1961; Welensky Papers, 43/*Wall*, Welensky to Wall, 18 August 1961; 43/*Salisbury*, Welensky to Salisbury, 18 August 1961; 42/60, f. 12, Welensky to D. Taylor, 23 August 1961.

[20] *Tribune*, 24 August 1961.

[21] *The Sunday Mail*, 27 August 1961.

Kaunda kept up the pressure, issuing a statement on 28 August which alleged that torture and violence had been used by the Northern Rhodesian Government. Therefore he called for the resignation of the Chief Secretary, Martin Wray, and for a general election based on adult suffrage.[22]

Northern Rhodesia would be discussed by Sandys and Robinson the next day, but foremost in the minds of Welensky and Robinson was the fate of the adjourned Federal Review. Thus Robinson began by emphasising to Sandys Welensky's desire to reconvene it after the British negotiations on the Common Market in September. The reason, Robinson said, was the need to end the uncertainty about the future of the Federation. The reconvening of the Review was a matter for the British and Federal Governments alone, but Sandys maintained that the condition for this was that the territorial elections should have first produced new Governments. He reiterated that his Government unreservedly supported the Federation. The adjournment of the Review, he said, was intended to facilitate the negotiations between the Governments, and prior consultations with the Federal Government were welcome provided that no impression was given of a "behind-the-scenes" deal with Welensky and Whitehead. He warned, however, that independence in the Federal sphere was impossible until governments, which were representative, sanctioned it. (He was, therefore, conceding a veto to the territories.)

Sandys insisted that the British attitude to the Northern Rhodesian settlement was unchanged, but agreed that events in the territory would inevitably force a reconsideration. He stoutly denied that his Government would be influenced by outside pressures, but believed that Welensky had underestimated the situation and that Hone's fears had been justified. Sandys did not convince Robinson who believed that the situation had been exaggerated and that the majority of the population remained law-abiding. The trouble, after all, he said, was confined to two provinces. He asserted that Hone had also been wrong in his assessment of the influence of Moffat's Liberal Party.

Next Sandys and Robinson reviewed the situation in Katanga where the United Nations had just used force to remove the European officers serving with the *gendarmerie*. This action was based on a UN Security Council resolution of 21 February 1961 which had demanded the expulsion of all mercenaries. On 24 August, President Kasavubu of the Congo had ordered the deportation of all non-Congolese serving with the Katangese forces and had asked the UN to effect it. The UN role was to use force only to separate warring Congolese and not to implement the dictates of the Congolese Central Government. Sandys acknowledged that the UN action was illegal but, displaying lamentable weakness, said that, unless the United States could be induced to support it, protest was useless.

Robinson criticised the lack of British support for the regime in Katanga, reminding Sandys that chaos in the Congo could affect the Federation. However, Sandys continued to emphasise the difficulties of taking effective action at the UN. In any case, he believed that there was no UN desire to destroy Tshombe's regime in Katanga. He said that Tshombe was only being encouraged to join the rest of the Congo by removing his foreign advisers.

[22] *The Bulawayo Chronicle*, 28 August 1961.

Robinson wondered why the other regime in Stanleyville, Orientale Province, which was threatening secession, was not similarly treated instead of being allowed to acquire Communist arms and material. Sandys doubted that this was true, but Robinson was adamant that it was and concluded that the British did not want to offend other African countries by supporting Katanga.[23]

Robinson reported to Welensky on 30 August that he would seek advice from the Federation's friends on the postponement of the Review until 1962. He warned that the British public was being bombarded by pro-African nationalist propaganda. He advised that a counter-blast was required which Voice and Vision, Rhodesia House and the pro-Federal Press could not supply, although they were doing their best.[24] The propaganda effort was not assisted that day, however, by Welensky having to apologise publicly to the US Government for a punch on the nose which had greeted George Mennen-Williams, the Secretary of State for African Affairs, on arrival in Lusaka on 28 August. A local European was arrested and achieved some notoriety for the deed because Mennen-Williams had been adversely outspoken on Federal affairs. If the punch warmed some local hearts, which had long been irritated by self-opinionated, itinerant politicians who made up their minds before they arrived, it did nothing for the Federal image abroad.[25]

In the continuing anti-Federal campaign, a letter from Kaunda appeared that day in *The Times* claiming that the Africans had been assured by successive British Ministers that the Federal Government would not interfere with the political development of the two northern territories. In a world torn by violence, Northern Rhodesia had been an island of comparative peace until Welensky had interfered and had used the long period of negotiations to demonstrate that he would not allow smooth changes in the territory. He had indulged in boycotts and had called out the army. Assisted in these actions by Voice and Vision and the "Lord Salisbury school of thought", he had succeeded in causing the British Government to capitulate. By contrast, Kaunda claimed to have only called for a campaign of non-violence and had faced real difficulties through Government intimidation of UNIP. A European member of UNIP, he said, had been warned that he would never be employed by the Government and had been banned from travelling to certain areas. The security forces had been equally provocative.

Kaunda pointed out that the fate of the Europeans was in his Party's hands, yet none had been killed. He blamed events in the Northern Province on the Government, and claimed that African efforts, firmly to found their new nation on "love and respect for humanity", were being undermined and that the future was daily becoming grimmer. He noted that a correspondent in *The Times* had accused his Party of only ever making inflammatory speeches. He replied that it spent much of its meagre funds on scholarships. It also had in its ranks 280 Europeans — including Sir Stewart Gore-Browne. He maintained that many people would prefer a UNIP Government to a UFP one. He wanted the Northern Rhodesian problems settled calmly, and assured

[23] Welensky Papers, 20/2, ff. 109–112, Report of a meeting with Sandys, 29 August 1961.
[24] *Ibid.*, f. 108, Robinson to Welensky, 30 August 1961.
[25] *The Rhodesia Herald*, 30 August 1961.

his audience that leading Africans sought neither racialism nor the European's expulsion. The Monckton Commission, he said, had noticed intimidation by his Party, but he was glad that it had been wise enough to discover the cause and the remedy and had recommended African majorities in the northern legislatures. Since the Commission had reported, Nyasaland had gained its African majority, and why, he asked, should Northern Rhodesia not do likewise?

To the *Daily Mail* Kaunda denied that he could not control his Party and that extremists were taking over in some areas. He claimed it was, nevertheless, very difficult to control a Party in as vast an area as Northern Rhodesia except by personal visits and, of course, he had been banned from travelling to the troubled areas. He was desperately trying to avoid bloodshed, but the security forces were making it increasingly difficult. The recipe for peace was to give the Africans a fair chance through constitutional change. Thus he was making a last appeal to the British Government to help him restore the situation. However, he wondered how long the British could expect him to be reasonable.[26]

Still in London, Moffat claimed publicly that the situation would inevitably deteriorate. The difficulty facing African leaders, he said, was that they were expected to call off the troublemakers before any negotiations. Obviously they could not do this until there had been negotiations. Then Moffat, when seeing Lord Perth, threatened to resign from the Northern Rhodesian Executive Council unless Asians were allowed to vote for all the national roll Members. The minimum percentage of votes required by the successful national roll candidate also had to be reduced to five. Reporting this, *The Times* claimed that the Colonial Office greatly valued Moffat because of his calming influence on an inflammatory situation.[27]

Kaunda's constant call for an inquiry provoked Macmillan to declare that there was no justification for it. He greatly regretted that, despite the sincere advice of the Colonial Secretary and others, a large number of the members of UNIP should have resorted to violence to gain their ends. He refuted Kaunda's statement that the constitutional settlement of June had been framed deliberately to provide a built-in majority of Federal supporters to entrench white supremacy. The failure of any of the parties to agree had forced the British Government to impose a settlement which adhered to the principles laid down by Macleod in December. These would increase substantially African representation based on a practical balance between the races at or near parity, whilst encouraging non-racial politics. Whatever the disappointment at the imposed solution, there was no excuse for the lawlessness of the recent weeks, and it was the duty of the Northern Rhodesian authorities to restore peace. If there were any allegations of improper behaviour by the police, he said, they should be reported to allow investigation. He promised an inquest for every death.[28]

[26] *Daily Mail*, 30 August 1961; Welensky Papers, 7/12, f. 35, Kaunda's letter to *The Times*, 30 August 1961.
[27] *Evening Standard*, 31 August 1961; *Northern News*, 1 September 1961; *The Times*, 31 August 1961.
[28] *Northern News*, 31 August 1961.

Kaunda was undeterred. On 1 September, in Belgrade, he informed the Conference of Non-Aligned Nations that the situation in Northern Rhodesia was a threat to peace in Africa, and alleged that concentration camps had been established. Indeed, he concluded that "a well-planned operation of genocide is being conducted against three million innocent and unarmed Africans". Before going to Belgrade he had seen George Brown (later Lord George-Brown) of the Labour Party and Lord Perth, and consequently Brown had suggested that Macleod should visit Northern Rhodesia to devise fresh amendments which would be fair to both sides. The alternative, he had said, was a collision with African nationalism. Contradicting Kaunda, the Chief Secretary of Northern Rhodesia, Martin Wray, revealed that there had been 1 400 arrests since the outbreak of trouble. Of these 650 had led to convictions, of which 550 involved UNIP members.[29]

As Kaunda had flown to Belgrade, claiming to be more hopeful, the Press concluded that the White Paper was not the last word on the constitutional revision. It also noticed that violence had not abated in the affected provinces where schools and cattle kraals were being burnt. *The Sunday Mail* credited Kaunda with giving a skilful impression of an innocent abroad. It said that he disclaimed responsibility for the current reprehensible violence yet demanded constitutional revision as the price of peace. The newspaper suggested that Moffat should resign from the Executive Council.[30]

While not blind to the purpose of Moffat and Kaunda, Welensky was concentrating on the Congo. Irish and Indian UN troops had seized installations in Elizabethville in an effort to rid Tshombe of his European officers, and Robinson was distressed by the British determination to stand aloof. Welensky was equally anxious to secure an intervention, and was annoyed to discover from Mennen-Williams that the United States believed that the UN should assist the Congolese Government if it decided to subjugate Katanga by force, even though it possessed a popularly-elected president. Welensky found it most offensive when his consul-general in Elizabethville reported on 31 August that the UN civilian representative in Katanga, the Irishman Dr Conor Cruise O'Brien, had told him that all Tshombe could do was to crawl to the new Congolese Prime Minister, Cyrille Adoula, to make his peace.[31]

Welensky admitted to Lord Salisbury that he might be prejudiced, but Tshombe had an appeal to him because he had maintained law and order whilst keeping the Communist-orientated regimes of the late Patrice Lumumba and Antoine Gizenga (of Orientale Province, who threatened secession from the Congo) away from the Federal border. He was using his influence to persuade Tshombe not to provoke the UN because they would seize any opportunity to subdue him. Tshombe had continued to indicate that he was willing to negotiate with President Kasavubu but that each time he telephoned him he was switched through to the UN officials, apparently to prevent him from speaking to Kasavubu. Tshombe was fearful of placing himself in UN hands, and Welensky sympathised with him. The British Government had assured Welensky that Dag Hammarskjold, the Secretary-

[29] *African Daily News*, 1 September 1961; *The Bulawayo Chronicle*, 1 September 1961.
[30] *The Sunday Mail*, 3 September 1961.
[31] Welensky Papers, 20/12, f. 133, Welensky to Robinson, 26 August 1961.

General, was a good lawyer and would not infringe the law. Yet action was being taken at Adoula's request, and Welensky wondered when the UN had become the Congo's lackey. He regretted if his actions distressed the British Government, but nevertheless was determined to prevent further chaos. The indifference of the United States convinced him it wished to see all that he stood for destroyed. In fact, he had told Mennen-Williams that he would resist the UN's intentions with all possible means. He asked how the Americans, while watching the Berlin Wall being built, could reconcile the actions of the UN in the Congo with their abhorrence of Communist expansion.[32]

The extent of the British reluctance to become involved in the Congo was revealed by their annoyance on 31 August when Welensky declared in the Federal Assembly that he had assurances from the British Government that it would not agree to any attempt to take Katanga by force. Sandys immediately questioned this statement and Welensky replied quoting, as proof, letters from Home of 25 April and 10 May 1961, and one from Macmillan of 12 May.[33]

The next day, 1 September, Robinson described the British outrage at Welensky's temerity to refer publicly to confidential correspondence, breaking established Commonwealth practice. Sandys threatened not to comment further on Katanga unless Welensky reassured him that the offence would not be repeated.

Unrepentant, Welensky expressed his amazement at the British reaction because he understood that it was improper to disclose the actual terms of undertakings in personal and secret messages, but not their existence. If Sandys were correct, such undertakings were worthless and any further exchanges were pointless. In any case, on 10 May Home had merely said that his Government had repeatedly urged the UN Security Council to interpret the resolution as not including the use of force, except to prevent clashes between the Congolese.

Welensky said he had not referred to the representations which had been made to the United States or to Hammarskjold. He wondered how much reliance could be placed on a British undertaking and would reserve his position and act as he saw fit.

Welensky was bitter because his reliance on the undertakings had encouraged him to mislead Tshombe into believing that he should settle with the Congolese Central Government. Once more, he had been proved gullible but vowed that he would not be caught again. He thought that anyone was naïve who believed that the UN action was not part of a deliberate plan to discredit the Katangese Government to facilitate a UN take-over. O'Brien had just accused Tshombe's deputy, Godefroid Munongo, of forming a group to kill UN officials. The absurdity of this was proven by the charge being based on the evidence of a convicted Belgian criminal, André Cremer. Ignoring the dubious character of Cremer, O'Brien had asked Tshombe to dismiss Munongo and, when he refused, broke off UN relations with Tshombe, hinting that he might implement Adoula's wishes to subjugate

[32] *Ibid.*, 43/*Salisbury*, Welensky to Lord Salisbury, 31 August 1961.
[33] *Ibid.*, 20/12, f. 130, Welensky to Robinson, 31 August 1961.

Katanga. Welensky warned Sandys that only resolute British action would correct the situation.[34]

Before he wrote thus, Welensky and his senior Ministers had met Bernard Braine (later Sir Bernard), the Joint Parliamentary Under-Secretary of State for Commonwealth Relations, and Alport. Braine had come to discuss the Federal Review, but naturally the Congo was discussed first. Welensky expressed fears that the illegal and ill-advised actions of the UN might produce riots and chaos and present the Federal Government with not only a refugee problem, but another arising out of the ethnic links between the tribes of Katanga and Northern Rhodesia. He criticised the British Government's failure to honour its undertakings to him because he had been trying to persuade Tshombe to negotiate with Adoula, all the while believing that Britain would not be a party to Katanga's subjugation.

Alport maintained that nothing had changed, that Britain recognised Katanga's importance to the Federation, but that she was unable to control the UN unilaterally. Hammarskjold had been told of the British and Federal views, but little more could be done without American support. Welensky, however, knew that there had been nothing more than an exchange of views with Hammarskjold who had proclaimed the UN action to be fully justified. In Welensky's view there had been insufficient British pressure and a strong stand had to be taken if British assurances would mean anything. Britain, after all, was an important contributor to the UN exchequer. It seemed pertinent to mention a rumour that Hammarskjold's brother was heading a new Congo Development Corporation which was being formed in the United States. He asked Alport to discover if this were true.

Braine defended his Government, claiming that it did its best to promote the Federation's interests. Alport promised to transmit the Federal Government's concern and its desire that nothing further should be done to weaken and discredit the Katangese Government. Alport, needless to say, was convinced the UN sought only to reunite the Congo and was taking similar action against the Gizengist secessionist faction.

They discussed the Federal Review, and Braine said that Sandys wished to know the reason for the pressure for its resumption because he understood that all parties had agreed that it would not be reconvened until the new territorial Governments were in power. Welensky said he was amazed at this because he had always pressed for the earliest possible settlement of the Federation's future and had informed Sandys and Macmillan that he expected the resumption towards the end of the year. A speedy resumption was necessary because of the rapid changes which would follow the British entry into the Common Market and the consequent general election. In any case, there was not a great deal to settle. It boiled down to the allocation of functions, the composition of the Federal Assembly and the franchise. Greenfield found a reference in March 1961 to the commitment to reconvene the Review in that year, but Alport claimed that the British Government wanted Nyasaland to settle down first. Braine agreed to transmit Welensky's views and reaffirmed British support for the Federation.

[34] *Ibid.*, f. 129, Robinson to Welensky, 1 September 1961; f. 126, Welensky to Robinson, 1 September 1961.

Greenfield complained about Tanganyika harbouring and supporting African nationalists who were the Federation's enemies. He asked why that territory, together with Kenya and Bechuanaland, should be hurried to independence while the Federation was not. Welensky wondered how long the British would tolerate Ghana's anti-Federal activities. Braine replied that the problems of the East African territories were less complicated than those of the Federation. He acknowledged the dangers of Ghana's policies but ascribed them to its jealousy of Nigeria. Alport claimed that Ghana's funds for sponsoring opposition were depleted and advised waiting for opposition from the Monrovian states to bring Ghana to its senses.[35] These remarks indicated that the British Government would not protect the Federation.

It was Banda, and not the Congo or Northern Rhodesia, who attracted attention on 4 September by holding a Press conference after the Nyasaland ministerial appointments had been announced. He was particularly pleased that the UFP had decided to refuse its Executive Council seat because he did not want a coalition. Magnanimous in victory and ignoring the prerogative of the Governor, he claimed that he had been prepared to offer the seat, but would not have allocated it a portfolio.[36]

It was Jones, of course, who had offered Blackwood, as a leader of the UFP, a seat without portfolio, suggesting alternatively that L. A. Little could be Minister of Works. He reserved parliamentary secretarial posts for the lower roll but promised that his official Members would support the Federation until its fate was decided at the Review. After that, Blackwood assumed that one should expect the worst. Jones had been evasive when Blackwood asked to whom the other upper roll seat would go. However, Blackwood presumed rightly that it was intended for Colin Cameron, a lawyer who had stood as an independent backed by the Malawi Congress Party. Blackwood disliked this appointment and preferred not to be associated with Cameron. As the UFP had a majority of the upper roll seats in the Legislative Council, Blackwood believed it should have two seats. Jones, however, disagreed because of the overall distribution of representation in the Legislative Council. Nonetheless, Blackwood could not understand why an independent should be appointed.

Jones, though, seemed actively to encourage Blackwood to refuse his offer by emphasising the role which the Opposition ought to play. When Jones said: "I consider my offer of one seat is the maximum I can possibly give you within the spirit and letter of the Lancaster House Agreement", it sounded to Blackwood as if Macleod was speaking.

Blackwood was in a quandary because five Europeans in the Opposition could do nothing but be destructive. As he did not relish sitting alone in the Executive Council, he sought Welensky's advice. Welensky and Barrow told him to refuse the offer and, on 2 September, he complied. The Executive Council comprised: from the upper roll, Mikeka Mkandawira as Minister without Portfolio, and Cameron as Minister of Works and Transport; from the lower roll, Banda as Minister of Natural Resources and Local Government, Chiume as Minister of Education, and Augustine Bwanausi as Minister

[35] *Ibid.*, f. 122, Minutes of a Meeting with Braine, 1 September 1961.
[36] *The Bulawayo Chronicle*, 4 September 1961.

of Labour. Orton Chirwa and Dunduza Chisiza became parliamentary secretaries.[37]

Banda proclaimed that his next aim was the dissolution of the Federation. However, perhaps more worrying to the Federal Government was the news from London that Macleod had told Kaunda that he would reconsider the method of electing the national roll Members if the local security situation would allow it. Thus Macleod was reported as having asked Kaunda to restrain his Party.[38]

The veracity of this report would be confirmed on 9 September, and it would not have surprised Welensky because, when consoling an angry Blackwood on 4 September, he said that it was plain that Macleod was relentlessly achieving his aim (of implementing African majority rule in the territories) and that the Federation's only hope was a British Cabinet reshuffle. He found the British conscience very elastic on constitutional matters and advised Blackwood to concentrate on vigorous opposition. On 6 September a meeting of the northern Governors in Lusaka excited Blackwood's suspicions and he warned Barrow that plans were afoot for the amendment of the Northern Rhodesian proposals and for the weakening of the Federation by the concentrated efforts of Hone and Jones. He said that they would apply Macleod's instructions to appease Kaunda and Banda and create a situation from which the whites could not escape in a political sense. He warned the Federal Government to beware of a further *fait accompli.* Jones had given Blackwood the impression that he was bitter and dangerous and that he disliked the Federation, the Federal Cabinet and Southern Rhodesia. Blackwood informed Welensky that he feared Jones would make a deal with Banda to keep the Federal issue in the background until the Review, and then get rid of it. Blackwood therefore proposed to bring the Federation into every discussion and believed that Jones was the ideal sniper's target because he reacted so violently.[39]

However, as the UN had largely failed to remove Tshombe's European officers, the potentialities of that situation demanded Welensky's attention. On 6 September, after a Federal Cabinet meeting, he warned Macmillan that Katanga would make a stand and that the outcome would be that either the UN would have to admit defeat, which was unlikely, or it would have to take stronger action. O'Brien was visiting the UN military base at Kamina, and Welensky expected the UN forces to begin an offensive the moment O'Brien returned to Elizabethville. The exact intention was unknown, but it was likely to be an attempt to disarm the Katangese *gendarmerie* and to arrest the remaining Belgian officers and administrators. Welensky thought that the quality of the local UN judgment was most dubious as O'Brien appeared bitterly anti-British and anti-colonial, while his deputy, the Frenchman M. Michel Tombelaine, was a Marxist. O'Brien was thought to interpret his instructions as the elimination of Katanga's independence and would use any

[37] *Ibid.*; Welensky Papers, 7/14, f. 42, Blackwood to Welensky, 24 August 1961; f. 41, Welensky to Blackwood, 28 August 1961; 27/69, f. 141, same to same, 4 September 1961.

[38] *The Bulawayo Chronicle*, 4 September 1961; *Northern News*, 4 September 1961.

[39] Welensky Papers, 27/69, f. 141, Welensky to Blackwood, 4 September 1961; f. 140b, Blackwood to Barrow, 6 September 1961; f. 140, Blackwood to Welensky, 7 September 1961.

means to achieve it. For example, he had falsely reported to the Press that Tshombe had suffered a heart attack. Either the UN headquarters in New York was being misinformed by O'Brien, or it was misleading the British Government. There would be a deliberate attempt to bring anarchy to Katanga when it had enjoyed a year of efficient administration under an elected African Government. Macmillan had to realise that matters had reached a stage where Britain could no longer avoid an open and categorical repudiation of the UN actions. For his part, common prudence compelled Welensky to consider deploying his forces to protect the Northern Rhodesian border.[40]

Macmillan replied that his Government was in the closest possible contact with Hammarskjold. Yet he had to admit that he had been given no warning of the latest action. It appeared, therefore, that O'Brien had misinterpreted the instructions from New York. His statements and actions increasingly worried the British Government, and the information available tallied with Welensky's assessment. Welensky's concern was appreciated, but Macmillan disagreed that a repudiation by the British Government would be opportune. Nonetheless, it was doing its utmost to convince Hammarskjold that all prospect of Katangese co-operation in an overall settlement might be destroyed. The British Ambassador to the UN, Sir Patrick Dean, would approach Hammarskjold again about O'Brien not conforming with the intentions as they were known in New York. The British Government was committed to the UN Security Council Resolution of 21 February, and as a new Congolese Central Government had been formed under Adoula, of whom even Russia approved, the threat of a secession by Gizenga in Stanleyville had receded. In fact, Gizenga, a sworn enemy of Tshombe, had been made one of two vice-presidents of the Congo.

Macmillan, therefore, did not want the Congo to lose the wealth of Katanga and had always felt that the longer Tshombe delayed in coming to terms with the Congolese Central Government, the less likely was a reasonable settlement. If Tshombe did not co-operate, Adoula would have less chance of keeping the Gizengists in check. Without the Katangese balance to the Stanleyville regime, civil war was likely. Tshombe had to understand that, by repeatedly rebuffing the Leopoldville Government, he was alienating moderate opinion in the West. Britain, through her understanding of Tshombe's difficulties, was also suffering through doubts being cast on her desire to see the emergence of a peaceful and united Congo. Macmillan assured Welensky that he could rely on him to do his best to persuade the UN to be cautious and he hoped, sincerely, that Welensky would not deploy his troops, lest such action be misinterpreted.[41]

Welensky nonetheless deployed his troops, but could only wait for O'Brien to act. In anticipation of the Review being reconvened, Greenfield prepared the Federal requirements for constitutional change. Furthermore, two motions in the Federal Assembly on 6 September forced the Federal Government to speak on the Review. Hodson called for a Royal Commission on the

[40] *Ibid.*, 20/12, f. 120, Welensky to Macmillan, 6 September 1961; H. Macmillan, *Pointing the Way, 1959–61* (London, 1972), p. 442.
[41] Welensky Papers, 20/12, f. 118, Macmillan to Welensky, 8 September 1961.

Federal franchise to make it more acceptable to the whole population. Greenfield rejected this because it would delay the Review and, in any case, a Royal Commission was unnecessary as there was an abundance of treatises on the subject to assist the Government. Robert Moffat wanted to replace the Federal franchise with the territorial ones, but Greenfield insisted on uniformity and warned that no one knew what the territorial Governments intended to do with their franchises.[42]

The Review, of course, was not really the issue of the moment. More straws were in the wind because Wall, who had hitherto urged Welensky to hasten the Federation's independence, warned that he and many of his parliamentary colleagues would not support a bid for it until after the Northern Rhodesian general election. Wall and friends were struck by the pressure being exerted on the British Government by Kaunda and Sir John Moffat, and by the maximum publicity which was being given to their assertion that a few minor concessions would prevent widespread disturbances in Northern Rhodesia. As Macleod believed the same, Wall thought that any pressure for the Review would not win support.[43]

However, on the day before Wall wrote, 7 September, Moffat, leaving London, said with some disappointment that Macleod had given neither promises nor indication of changes to the constitutional proposals. Within 24 hours, however, the picture altered because political and government circles in Lusaka believed that Banda would consider keeping Nyasaland in the Federation if the changes demanded by Kaunda and Moffat were effected. He was using his new office to attempt to secure an African majority in Northern Rhodesia. Nyerere's hand was also seen in this because there was much activity amongst UNIP officials living in Dar-es-Salaam. Kaunda was reported as telling Macleod that unless there was a change there would be "trouble with a capital T". He was ready to implement the third stage — whatever that might be — of his "master plan".[44]

Given the susceptibilities of the British Government, Welensky would not have been surprised by a warning from it through Alport on 7 September that it had been considering the reactions in Northern Rhodesia since the announcement in June and wished to know his views on the position. It averred that no political discussions would be held until order was re-established, but the problem was whether, when peace returned, there should be a further effort to secure acquiescence for the new Constitution. If it were announced that further adjustment was impossible, lawlessness could erupt. The British Government thought that the security forces could probably cope, but the political consequences would be far-reaching, and Moffat had informed Macleod that, if UNIP boycotted the election, his Liberal Party would follow suit. In such an event, it believed it would not be feasible to introduce the new Constitution and it would obviously be impossible to continue to operate the existing one. Therefore, the Governor would have to rule directly. The

[42] *Ibid.*, 20/2, ff. 95–105, Greenfield's Draft Proposals, 8 September 1961; Fed R & N *Debates* (Salisbury), Vol. 16, Col. 2150, 6 September 1961.

[43] Welensky Papers, 43/*Wall*, Wall to Welensky, 8 September 1961.

[44] *The Rhodesia Herald*, 8 & 9 September 1961; *Evening Standard*, 8 September 1961; *The Times*, 9 September 1961.

result would be an indefinite postponement of the Review because it was recognised that it could not achieve finality until the three territories had new and more representative Governments. Thus it would be worthwhile, once order was restored, to make the effort to settle, and the British Government was considering an announcement to this effect. The Governor would reopen his discussions with the Parties but would not commit himself to anything unless agreement seemed likely. The British Government thought this was the best course for the Federation because deadlock and violence would deny it African support. The matter was urgent, but any decision would await Welensky's comment. The British Government wished to make a statement on Tuesday, 12 September.[45]

Lord Alport has since revealed that he delivered this message without conviction because he was opposed to any capitulation to violence. Yet he says he was aware of the forces at work in London and was not surprised when he was ordered to deliver the message. At that moment he was attending a periodic conference of the northern Governors in Lusaka and recalls that the change of heart led to an embittered conversation there. He was particularly disappointed because he understood the local situation and knew that, if the Federation were to survive, there had to be firmness. As by September order had been largely restored, he advised his Government to announce that it would ignore the demonstrations and implement the new Constitution as announced in June. He continued to give such advice after delivering the message, informing Whitehall that the consequence of capitulation would be the dissolution of the Federation, the granting of premature independence to the three territories, and the elimination of Britain as a major influence in Africa south of the Sahara. The High Commission Territories would be isolated and could fall prey to South Africa. African and European nationalism would be polarised in Southern Africa and Britain would be incapable of steering policies in a liberal direction. Moreover, the strategic and economic advantages of British political control of Central Africa would be lost.

Alport would discover after the British capitulation to Kaunda and Moffat was publicly known that it only encouraged the Southern Rhodesian African nationalists to continue to reject the territory's new Constitution. Nkomo and Robert Mugabe, Zimbabwe's future Prime Minister, made it clear to him at the time that they now understood that direct action was the most effective method of obtaining power. Alport declares that again any prospect of success was being destroyed by a decision taken in isolation to ease a local situation, regardless of the consequences. He believes that, in fact, this was the *coup de grâce* to the Federation.[46]

However, Alport gave Welensky no hint of his personal feelings when delivering the British message on Northern Rhodesia on 7 September. Indeed, as the British representative, he would be irritated by Welensky's resultant comment about British gutlessness. He confirmed the message in writing on Saturday, 9 September, and yet again Welensky and his Cabinet were presented with the prospect of a ruined weekend while their British counterparts

[45] Welensky Papers, 20/7, f. 103, Alport to Welensky, 1961.

[46] Alport, *The Sudden Assignment* (London, 1965), pp. 88–90.

departed for their country homes. However, Welensky refused to be hurried. He wanted time to consider the issue fully and replied, threateningly, that he would probably deliver the Federal verdict in London himself. As there was no visit from him in the offing, this must have surprised the British Government considerably.[47]

The Federal Cabinet, Whitehead and Roberts met on Monday, 11 September, with the morning's Press carrying a claim by Kaunda in London that Macleod had informed him that the election of the national roll Members would be re-examined if the violence ended. Welensky explained that Alport had given him the gist of a British message on 7 September about re-opening the Northern Rhodesian constitutional discussions but that he had insisted on seeing it in writing and had only received the dispatch at midday on Saturday, 9 September. He had protested strongly at the lack of time for consideration and had refused to summon his Cabinet over the weekend to avoid unwelcome public speculation. He had indicated that he had been considerably annoyed that the Press should have known that a statement would be issued on 12 September before he had been informed of it. He had also asked Alport to discover if the British Government would issue the statement on time no matter what the Federal Government said. If this were so, then he wished to inform his Parliament. He had told Alport that he was prepared to go to London and had provisionally booked four seats on the aircraft on 16 September.

The Cabinet noted that nothing was known of the changes contemplated. It would not accept voting by Asians and Coloureds in the election of the national roll Members, but thought that it might be advantageous to reduce the minimum percentage to five with a *pro rata* reduction in the equivalent from 400 to 160 votes. Yet it believed it was undesirable even to consider this because the capitulation to violence would not go unnoticed in Southern Rhodesia.

Roberts questioned if the lawlessness would spread, as the British suggested, and declared that any apparent victory by Kaunda would considerably weaken the UFP while strengthening the influence of UNIP. Moderate Europeans and Africans would feel betrayed, and the UFP would fare poorly in any subsequent election.

Whitehead, recalling his assurances during the referendum campaign, agreed that the UFP's credibility would be severely damaged. As the capitulation to violence would have repercussions in Southern Rhodesia, he wanted the British suggestion categorically rejected. Concurring, the Cabinet proposed to reply that any renewal of discussions would simply be an abject submission and encouragement to violence. It would remind the British Government that it had committed itself in Parliament to impose the Constitution and that the terms of the latter had undoubtedly affected the Southern Rhodesian referendum. It would strongly challenge the assertion that the Federal Review had been adjourned to await the revision of the territorial Constitutions. To underline its rejection, the Cabinet thought that Greenfield should go to London to be followed by Welensky, if necessary.

[47] Welensky Papers, 20/7, f. 97, Welensky to Alport, 11 September 1961.

Finally, it decided in a spirit of resentment, to withhold its answer to Alport until the next morning to give Macleod little time to consider it if he was determined to make his statement.[48]

Accordingly, Welensky composed a lengthy reply to Macmillan alleging that, due to Press speculation, he had not been surprised by the British suggestion but, nonetheless, was totally opposed to the negotiations being re-opened. He had, after all, on 26 June, the day that Macleod had tabled the new White Paper, promised that the UFP would attempt to make the Northern Rhodesian solution work although many of its features were unpalatable. The Dominion Party and the African National Congress had adopted the same attitude, but since then, literally by blackmail, UNIP had been attempting to ensure that it was returned to power. It had been assisted by the Liberal Party which, in lending its support, had been prepared to condone violence, doing so while condemning the UFP for forcing changes in the White Paper of February.

Kaunda, Welensky noted, pretended to abhor violence while threatening the Governments with a three-stage master plan which was allegedly non-violent but which would culminate in his arrest and incarceration. His encouragement of lawlessness had resulted in hundreds of serious and violent crimes, many of them perpetrated by his Party. Welensky drew Macmillan's attention to his statement that day in the Federal Assembly on the subject and wondered if Macmillan knew that the outbreak of violence had been confined to only two provinces. Kaunda had departed to appear in London and elsewhere as a modern Ghandi. At Belgrade he had accused the British of genocide in the Northern Province.

Welensky hoped Macleod would attempt to deny any accusations of a surrender to blackmail by stating that nothing would happen while lawlessness existed. Nevertheless, Macleod was obviously submitting to political blackmail although he had said so often that violence would not pay. Clearly, any weakness at that moment would encourage further blackmail and provide an example for Southern Rhodesian extremists to force change. Moreover, the revival of the Northern Rhodesian negotiations would be seen as a betrayal by the Southern Rhodesian electorate which had been told that the Northern Rhodesian solution of June had been final. He and Whitehead had replied to questions on Northern Rhodesia in the campaign in good faith only to be grossly betrayed. The revival of negotiations would adversely affect the Federal economy, and the deference which had already been paid to Kaunda, followed by a concession to his demands, would confirm the Federal public's suspicion that he was chosen to receive the reins of power.

Welensky pointed out that the possible intensification of the unrest was being advanced as an argument to re-open the discussions when Hone had informed him that he was using minimum force and that his forces had never really been extended. Kaunda's Party appeared a spent force and, if violence were renewed, it could be contained. The threat that UNIP might boycott the general election meant little to Welensky because its strong rival, the ANC, certainly would not, and the Liberal Party was of little political account.

[48] *Ibid.*, FGC(61), Special Meeting, Federal Cabinet, 11 September 1961.

Those who participated could certainly form the Government. There was no necessity for direct rule by the Governor.

Welensky challenged the assertion that, because it was recognised that no agreed solution would be forthcoming until the three territories could be represented by Governments elected under new and more liberal constitutions, the Federal Review had been adjourned. Macleod might believe this, Welensky said, but no hint of it was given to him and Whitehead in December 1960. The minutes of the Review Conference merely showed that it was adjourning to allow the talks on the Rhodesian Constitutions to continue. There was no suggestion of waiting for the implementation of any constitutions which might result. The final communiqué had said that the Review would be reconvened in the New Year, and on 18 March 1961 Macmillan had agreed with him to discuss reconvening it in September long before the Northern and Southern Rhodesian Constitutions could come into force.

Welensky rejected again the re-opening of the Northern Rhodesian negotiations, adding that the UFP in that territory agreed with him. If he was ignored, he expected to have the same facilities to state his case as had recently been accorded to Kaunda and Moffat. To do this he would send a senior Minister or come himself.[49]

The Press believed that there would be changes favourable to Kaunda. The *African Daily News*, however, expected that, in a test of wills, Macmillan would prefer Welensky to Kaunda. This did not matter because, the newspaper predicted, the Federation had but two years to live.[50]

Alport was holidaying in Southern Rhodesia's Eastern Districts, but a report on 12 September from his deputy to Sandys, that Welensky might disclose confidential correspondence, prompted Sandys to summon Robinson at 5.30 p.m. that day to warn that, if this were true, the British Government would henceforth only correspond on the basis that everything could be published. Robinson knew nothing about this and could only conclude that his Government must have been provoked. Sandys then revealed that Welensky's reply had just been received and he was about to discuss it with Macmillan.

The report continued to worry the British Government because at 7 p.m. on the same evening Sandys telephoned Robinson demanding an assurance that there would be no such publication except with British sanction. Sandys promised that, if Robinson provided this, Macmillan would see him at Admiralty House at 10.30 p.m. and would discuss the Northern Rhodesian issue. If he did not, then Macmillan would still see him and hear him out on the issue but would not comment. Robinson unsuccessfully tried to telephone Welensky but, although he could not supply the assurance, Macmillan kept the appointment and treated him to a lengthy monologue. Robinson replied that the proposed British statement (which he must have seen and which, as it transpired, was not released until 13 September) would conflict with Macmillan's assurance in May that power would not be given to irresponsible extremists. Moreover, in June Macmillan had accepted the scheme as entirely satisfactory. Thus it was clear that any proposal to allow change would be

[49] *Ibid.*, 20/7, f. 97, Welensky to Alport, 11 September 1961.
[50] *African Daily News*, 12 September 1961.

merely a capitulation to violence and would only encourage more demands with every prospect of success. The Southern Rhodesian electorate would be betrayed and, as Tshombe had been supporting Nkumbula's ANC, a victory for UNIP would seriously affect Tshombe.

Macmillan felt, however, that there was clearly a misunderstanding about the procedures for effecting constitutional changes in the colonies. He claimed that, in parliamentary terms, the discussions in February had been the second reading, those in June, the committee stage and now, in September, the report stage had been reached when, though the principles were fixed, adjustments could be made. Once these had been considered, his Government would draw up the final order in council. He assured Robinson that there would be no changes to the framework and that Kaunda and Moffat had been told nothing more than that their representations could not be considered until the threat to the internal security of the territory ceased to exist.

Robinson spurned such a feeble argument. He replied that the two aspects which, according to the proposed British statement, could be considered, namely the Asian seat and the minimum percentage, were hardly matters for a report stage and were conveniently and precisely what Kaunda and Moffat wanted changed.

Appearing somewhat disconcerted, Macmillan promised to reconsider the text of the statement. Nevertheless, Robinson gathered that it would be issued after Macmillan had consulted his Cabinet. It appeared that Macmillan had been persuaded that the changes were necessary if law and order were to be maintained. It was perhaps significant that he thought Kaunda would reject the British statement and implement his master plan which would force the British to detain him. Robinson warned Macmillan that, if the statement were issued, Welensky would fly to London. Macmillan regretted this because Lord Lansdowne, the Joint Parliamentary Under-Secretary of State at the Foreign Office, was about to travel to the Congo and was hoping to go on to see Welensky. However, Robinson doubted if this would change Welensky's mind.[51]

The next day, 13 September, the Press reported an intrusion by the Labour Party into the argument. Callaghan had informed Macleod that the situation was alarming and that the one-sided proposals had been genuinely and bitterly rejected and were directly responsible for the wave of violence. Thus the Labour Party called for new proposals.[52]

This demand, however, was overshadowed by the news that in Elizabethville O'Brien had sent the Gurkhas of the UN, supported by Irish armoured cars, to seize the post office and other installations. The battle for the post office raged for more than two hours and the last man, while surrendering, was flung from its roof to his death. O'Brien proclaimed that the Katangese secession had ended, but did so prematurely because the fighting did not abate with the capture of the installations. The UN garrison at Jadotville was besieged by the Katangese *gendarmerie* and by tribesmen. A UN column going to its aid was halted by an attack by one of two Katangese Fouga Magister jet trainers. The other strafed Elizabethville airport, O'Brien's

[51] Welensky Papers, 20/7, f. 93, Robinson to Welensky, 13 September 1961.
[52] *The Rhodesia Herald*, 13 September 1961.

headquarters, and the UN military base at Kamina. The Jadotville garrison would soon surrender to the Katangese.[53]

The Federal Cabinet, meeting that day, naturally assessed the situation before reconsidering the Northern Rhodesian issue. Welensky had been told that Sir Patrick Dean would tell Hammarskjold of increasing British concern at the actions of his forces in the Congo. Dean would dismiss the allegations that Britain favoured the Katangese secession but would maintain that the action in Elizabethville could only worsen the situation. The British Government wished to know under what authority O'Brien acted. If he had received orders from Hammarskjold, then Dean would ask for justification. If O'Brien had exceeded his instructions, then it was clear that the British Government was not being properly informed and, because it had no ambassador in the Congo, it was sending a Minister from the Foreign Office to examine the situation. Welensky understood that the UN had replied evasively and this had only deepened the suspicions about Hammarskjold's intentions. The Federal Cabinet examined the reports available and noted that Tshombe and his Ministers had escaped arrest. It agreed that reinforcements should be sent to the Congo border. Hone would not be consulted on their deployment because it was not an internal matter and, it was decided, Welensky would explain the situation to the Federal Assembly. (He did so later in the day, condemning the action and describing it as an application of the law of the jungle, a cynical abuse of power.)[54]

Northern Rhodesia was the second item on the Federal Cabinet's agenda. The Cabinet reviewed Robinson's messages and Welensky's conversation with Alport, and the possibility of Welensky going to London. It felt that the British Ministers might wish to oppose a visit from Greenfield but that they could hardly refuse to see Welensky's emissary after the official recognition they had accorded Kaunda and Moffat. It decided to await the draft of the proposed British statement before finally deciding on what to do. Accordingly Welensky did nothing more than ask the British Government to allow him to state his case before any statement abrogated the existing agreement. He would send a Minister to London immediately if necessary.

Replying the same day, Macmillan acknowledged that the proposed statement might be misinterpreted as a surrender to violence. Yet his Government believed that constitutional advance was impossible until order was restored and it did not think it was a sign of weakness to say as much. Moreover, he said, as Alport would have explained, the issue at stake was not the immediate restoration of law and order, but the long-term consequence of political boycott by the largest and best-known political Party. It would encourage a campaign of widespread civil disobedience which would lead to violence, mass arrests and the need for concentration camps as had happened in Kenya. Race relations would be embittered and all hopes of attracting African support for the Federation would be lost. Pressure from the Afro-Asians at the UN and in the Commonwealth, and perhaps from the United States,

[53] S. Hempstone, *Katanga Report* (London, 1962), p. 133; Sir Roy Welensky, *Welensky's 4 000 Days* (London, 1964), p. 231.

[54] Welensky Papers, FGC(61), Annexure to the 32nd Meeting, Federal Cabinet, 13 September 1961; Fed R & N *Debates* (Salisbury), Vol. 16, Col. 2507, 13 September 1961.

would effect the release of those who had been arrested, but not before they had become martyrs. This was clearly a price which should not be paid.

Macmillan could understand that the Federal view would be different, but, he reminded Welensky, the ultimate decision was his responsibility. There was no question of re-opening the negotiations, but it would be wise to follow the usual practices in the hope of securing a more general agreement, or at least of improving the situation. The risk of failure, with all the disadvantages which Welensky had described, had to be run. He promised Welensky the statement that evening.

Finally Macmillan denied that there had been any negotiations with Kaunda and Moffat or any promises made to them. Accordingly, he felt there was no reason for a visit by a Federal Minister and assured Welensky that he would be consulted before any decision was made. He hoped that Welensky would understand the British reasons for acting, even if he disagreed with them. He regretted that this had arisen during the crisis in Katanga which must be worrying Welensky intensely.[55]

The British statement, released at 5.30 p.m. GMT, declared that the reactions to the June proposals had been considered and that it was clear that, while the major features were acceptable, there was still significant criticism. As usual, it said, the British Government had been prepared to consider any reasonable representations but could not ignore the recent serious outbreak of lawlessness in certain parts of Northern Rhodesia. This, it warned, could delay the constitutional advancement which everyone was anxious to secure. The first task was to restore law and order but, when that had been done, representations could be made on the points of disagreement. After these had been considered, the process of converting the proposals into law would be completed and preparations could begin for a general election.[56]

The Rhodesian Press published the statement on 14 September and Welensky read it out in the Federal Assembly. As he had threatened, he recounted the history of the affair and emphasised such points as the promises on which the referendum campaign had been fought. He had thought in June, he said, that a final settlement had been reached and it was clear that the Northern Rhodesian Government had concurred because it had issued a booklet to explain it. UNIP alone had rejected it and had been responsible for the recent violence. It was, therefore, deplorable that the British Government should retreat in the face of violence. However, he had not been surprised by this announcement because the British Press had forecast it accurately.

Field and the majority of the Parliament shared his feelings and thus inevitably a considerable uproar of disbelief greeted a claim by Robert Moffat that the security forces were burning kraals, grain bins and the like.[57]

The only message from the British Government that day was that Lansdowne would still visit the Congo and the Federation despite the continuing hostilities in Katanga.

Wall wrote to Welensky urging an effective counter-attack in the form of Welensky's arrival in London. Replying, Welensky regretted that for the

[55] Welensky Papers, 20/7, f. 89, Macmillan to Welensky, 13 September 1961.
[56] *Ibid.*, f. 91, The Text of the British Statement, 13 September 1961.
[57] Fed R & N *Debates* (Salisbury), Vol. 16, Col. 2629 f., 14 September 1961.

second time in 18 months he had been forced to admit in Parliament that he had misled the Federal public. In a radio interview that evening, he also hinted at a possible break with Britain. He acknowledged the ultimate responsibility of the British Government for any decision, but said that, once it had been exercised, his Government would decide its course. If, in the meanwhile, an agreement could be reached with the territorial Government, it would be difficult for the British Government not to accept it. He thought that it could be a step towards declaring independence.[58]

Lord Salisbury wrote expressing amazement at the British surrender to violence. He had not expected this even from Macleod and wondered if the truth was that the latter would not have welcomed any excuse to give way. Welensky replied describing his anger at the British statement which had been issued only after a considerable campaign by the British Press on behalf of Kaunda. It was infuriating, he said, that the British Government should have the power to turn this matter "on and off". He grieved that he had misled the Southern Rhodesians and that the "sell-out" had made his position impossible. He believed that the sooner he "cut the painter" the better the situation would be. He found the change in the British attitude since 1953 quite incredible.[59]

Joelson and others were told a similar story, with Welensky adding that Hone had taken his time and had used the absolute minimum of force in contrast to the events in Southern Rhodesia where Whitehead had been decisive, and with Federal assistance, had quickly restored order. Hone had obviously not wanted a quick result because he had not used one of the Federal battalions, which had been allocated to him. Welensky believed that Macleod was seeking to use the tactics he had employed in Nyasaland so that "his heaven-sent chosen instrument", Kaunda, could easily assume the office of chief minister when "the prophet", Macleod, decided it was opportune. Thus, to Welensky, it seemed hopeless to continue to negotiate with the British Government.[60]

For the moment, however, Northern Rhodesia was driven from everyone's minds by the Congo. It dominated Welensky's correspondence on 17 September and he told Lord Salisbury that he had just agreed to allow Tshombe to meet Hammarskjold at Ndola on the morrow.

The actions of the UN Command in the Congo had brought Hammarskjold to Leopoldville where he reprimanded O'Brien for them. By that day, having gambled on overcoming a handful of mercenaries, the UN forces were hard pressed. The Irish garrison at Jadotville had surrendered and O'Brien's headquarters were under attack. Furthermore, there was a growing distaste abroad for the action which had been taken when, in terms of the Security Council's resolutions, the UN was only allowed to use force in the last resort to prevent civil war.

[58] Welensky Papers, 43/*Wall*, Wall to Welensky, 14 September 1961; 20/12, f. 114, Robinson to Welensky, 14 September 1961; 43/*Wall*, Welensky to Wall, 15 September 1961; *The Rhodesia Herald*, 16 September 1961.

[59] Welensky Papers, 43/*Salisbury*, Lord Salisbury to Welensky, 16 September 1961; Welensky to Salisbury, 17 September 1961.

[60] *Ibid.*, 24/151, ff. 29–31, Welensky to Joelson, 17 September 1961.

On the previous day, from his hide-out in Elizabethville, Tshombe had declared a state of "total war" and then had proposed a cease-fire. He suggested that he and O'Brien should meet on neutral ground, but O'Brien would only attend a meeting in Katanga. Hammarskjold intervened and secured a meeting in Northern Rhodesia. He insisted that a cease-fire should precede the meeting, but Tshombe replied by imposing conditions on it. Undeterred, Hammarskjold decided to fly from Leopoldville to Ndola in the DC6 of the UN Commander, General Sean McKeown. His aims were, in addition to the cease-fire, to secure a reaffirmation of the agreement to dismiss all European military and political advisers and to obtain Tshombe's co-operation in the re-opening of discussions with the Congolese Central Government. O'Brien tried to divert Hammarskjold to Kamina so that he might travel with him to Ndola, but was ignored and was left only too aware that Hammarskjold thought that he had let him down.[61]

Presumably to foil the Katangese Air Force, a deception plan was followed in which Hammarskjold appeared to board Lord Lansdowne's aircraft in Leopoldville but, in reality, it flew ahead of him with its navigational lights on, following the normal flight path. (This action was later to be ignored by the UN Commission of Inquiry, but not by the Federal Commission.) Then, with Hammarskjold aboard, SE-BDY *Albertina* flew east in a wide half circle (presumably to avoid Katanga) without filing a flight plan, without lights and maintaining radio silence.

After five hours, SE-BDY reported to the Salisbury flight information centre that it was heading south over Lake Tanganyika at 17 000 feet, but gave no hint as to who was on board. It began to descend, with Salisbury's permission, at 9.08 p.m. There followed three more terse conversations with Salisbury which included a refusal to disclose its destination after Ndola. At 9.35 p.m. SE-BDY informed Ndola airport tower that it was abeam of it and that it would land at 10.20 p.m. Ndola tower replied with weather information and the QNH pressure setting for the altimeter. A minute later Ndola tower gave clearance for a descent to 6 000 feet. At 9.42 p.m. Ndola tower asked if SE-BDY would stay the night or go to Salisbury, and received the reply "negative" to both questions and was told that these would be answered on the ground. An intermittent conversation continued until 10 p.m. when a large piston-engined aircraft was seen from the ground heading west. Ten minutes later SE-BDY reported: "Your lights in sight, overhead Ndola, descending, confirm QNH."

Ndola tower replied: "Roger, QNH 1021 millibars — report reaching 6 000 feet."

SE-BDY answered: "Roger, 1021."

That was the last ever heard from SE-BDY. It flew across the airfield and into the darkness to the west. At approximately 10.13 p.m., with one wing-tip slightly down, indicating the completion of a turn, in line for the runway, with wheels down and locked and flaps down, SE-BDY struck the trees growing on a hundred-foot high ridge seven miles from Ndola airport, and caught fire. All except for a security guard, Sergeant Julian, were killed.

[61] C. C. O'Brien, *To Katanga and Back* (London, 1962), p. 285.

Hammarskjold was flung out of the wreckage with his neck broken. Julian pulled the safety tab on a window and managed to run out beyond the fire, but was burnt in the process and died after a few days from kidney failure. He uttered few coherent words before he died.

Several people, both black and white, some distance away from the airfield heard an explosion, but the tower saw nothing and, while continuing to call SE-BDY, concluded that it had flown back to the Congo. Both Tshombe and Lansdowne were at Ndola but, because Hammarskjold had not wanted him to be present during the talks, Lansdowne took off in his aircraft for Salisbury. At 11.15 p.m. the air traffic controller at Ndola telephoned the police to discover if there had been any reports of an accident but was told that there were none. Fifteen minutes later "Overdue Action" commenced, and Salisbury and Leopoldville were asked if they had any news. They had none. At 00.15 on 18 September, a European policeman, van Wyk, telephoned Ndola police station to report having seen a flash in the sky, but a ground search revealed nothing. At that moment Ndola airport tower closed down for the night.[62]

Alport, who had arranged the meeting, waited until 1.17 a.m. and then crossed the tarmac to two United States Air Force Dakotas, which possessed powerful radios, and asked the crews if they knew where Hammarskjold had gone. They knew nothing and he retired to his Royal Rhodesian Air Force Canadair to sleep.[63] In the early hours of 18 September, ground and air searches began while surrounding territories were asked for any information. At 1 p.m. three Africans found the aircraft wreckage and shortly afterwards the police arrived.

SE-BDY was mechanically sound, its altimetres were correctly set and it had not been shot down or sabotaged. It was a clear night and it will probably never be known what caused the pilot to err. He must have thought that he still had a thousand feet to descend. Much has been written on the subject and the normal board of inquiry was followed by two Commissions appointed by the Federal Government and the UN respectively.[64] They exonerated the Federal Government and discovered nothing tangible except that Per Hallonquist, the pilot, had flown more hours than he should have that month and that, having never landed at Ndola before, he might have used the landing instruction for Ndol*o* in the Congo, as opposed to Ndol*a*. Even though this was thought unlikely, the *Jeppeson Manual* found in the aircraft lacked a page for Ndol*a*, and the *United States Air Force Approach Chart Manual* was found open at Ndol*o*.

Whatever happened, the enemies of Welensky and the Federation grasped the opportunity to make scurrilous comments. Allegations of murder were and are still bandied about. Investigating rumours that SE-BDY had been shot down from the air by Federal or Katangese aircraft, both Commissions found that the Royal Rhodesian Air Force was not flying that night and

[62] Welensky Papers, W/S/C/2, Chronological Story of Crash SE-BDY, 17 September 1961; Report of the Commission on the accident involving aircraft SE-BDY (Salisbury, 1962).
[63] Lord Alport, *The Sudden Assignment*, *op. cit.*, p. 120.
[64] (Unpublished) *Commission to Investigate Conditions and Circumstances resulting in the Death of the Secretary-General and Members of his Party* (New York, 1961).

neither was the Katangese Air Force. In any case, the surviving Katangese Fouga was on the ground at Kolwesi, 230 nautical miles from Ndola and its effective range was only 135 miles. Moreover, it was not equipped for night flying, let alone night fighting.[65]

On his return to Salisbury, Alport found Welensky haggard from lack of sleep and shaken by the news.[66] Tshombe stayed in Ndola to meet Mahmoud Khiari, the chief of UN civil operations in the Congo, and on 20 September they concluded a preliminary cease-fire. Colonel Maurice Barber, the Federal Director of Civil Aviation, set up an immediate inquiry as required by law and in the aftermath, the Federal Government appointed its Judicial Commission under the Federal Chief Justice, Sir John Clayden, and served by Sir George Lloyd-Jacob, an English judge, and Group-Captain Newton of the International Civil Aviation Organisation in Montreal. The UN doubted the integrity of these men and set up its own commission.

Welensky met Lansdowne early in the morning of 18 September and both still wondered where Hammarskjold had gone. Welensky took the opportunity to demonstrate that the allegations that he was interfering in the Congo were quite untrue. He had not, he said, persuaded Tshombe to secede. Lansdowne responded by describing his conversation with Hammarskjold and, in particular, Hammarskjold's denial that O'Brien had acted on the instructions of the Congolese Central Government. Hammarskjold had claimed that the action had been a logical outcome of the increasing tension in Katanga and the bid to remove the European officers of the *gendarmerie*. However, Welensky had been informed by his vice-consul in Elizabethville that O'Brien had said that his main task was to destroy the Tshombe Government.[67]

The Ghanaian, Swedish and Indian Press denounced the crash as murder, while Nkomo found it hard to believe that it was a normal accident because of the attitude of the British Government and Welensky's contempt for other nations and his defiance of the UN. It appeared to Nkomo that the crash was "an imperialistic tactic designed to eliminate one who had ceased to be their instrument".[68]

The Northern Rhodesian issue was, of course, more pressing. Arriving home on 19 September, Kaunda said that peace could only be restored by the removal of Federal forces. He thought that Roberts and Welensky were most unreasonable to protest at Macleod's statement. He appealed for a spirit of

[65] *The Herald* (formerly *The Rhodesia Herald*) reported on 20 & 22 May 1980 that a recent Swedish television programme had discussed seriously the possibility that a twin-engined De Havilland Dove, equipped for photo-mapping and flown by white mercenaries, had bombed SE-BDY with a cannister of TNT. If it did, it seems remarkable that such a slow aircraft, not equipped for night interception, could have landed a bomb on an aircraft which was flying without lights, against the darkness of the uninhabited bush, at a relatively high speed. Mr Dixon Buleni, a charcoal burner, living in the area told the United Nations' Commission that he had seen a smaller aircraft attack SE-BDY, but later admitted that he had been paid £50 by Kaunda's Party to say so. Nonetheless, subsequent to the above Swedish television programme, the author established in a confidential interview that Federal intelligence agents had found and destroyed a De Havilland Dove on a Katangese airstrip. It was loaded with handgrenades but was not airworthy. — JRTW.

[66] Alport, *The Sudden Assignment*, *op. cit.*, p. 121.

[67] Welensky Papers, 20/12, ff. 107–110, Minutes of a Meeting with Lord Lansdowne, 18 September 1961.

[68] *Northern News*, 22 September 1961; *African Daily News*, 19 September 1961.

reconciliation between the races similar to that which had been displayed in June.[69] The Northern Rhodesian division of the UFP called an emergency congress, but Robinson and Joelson from London warned against over-reaction which Macmillan might call intimidation. Nevertheless, on the Copperbelt there were demands for Northern and Southern Rhodesians to unite and declare themselves independent.[70]

At the emergency congress, Roberts described the negotiations, emphasising the statements on the finality of the settlement in June. He believed that UNIP had just reached the nadir of its popularity when Macleod, through his statement, "lifted it out of the mire". Roberts expressed his intention to support Welensky, including his call for the resumption of the Federal Review. Roberts could find little point in continuing to attempt to negotiate with men such as Macleod who "went back on their promises". Greenfield was present — substituting for Welensky — and told of his bitterness and how he was detested by Macmillan, Macleod and Sandys. Indeed, Sir Roy Welensky recalls Sandys, during one round of negotiations, asking for an adjournment for a private discussion with him. When everyone else had left the room, he asked Welensky to remove Greenfield from the meeting because he could no longer endure his baleful glare.[71]

The resolution before the congress utterly condemned the British retreat in the face of violence and claimed that the British Government had forfeited the confidence and respect of all races. Faced with wild resolutions and knowing that only strong words would satisfy the angry meeting, Greenfield warned that it would be extremely difficult to bring the British Government to heel by constitutional means. He acknowledged that there were constitutional cards still to be played, but that they were not strong ones. Unconstitutional action was probable, he said, and when the time was ripe he would support it. The congress concurred and, accordingly, adopted a resolution to resist by all possible means the introduction of changes which the Federal and territorial leaders of the Party considered adverse to Northern Rhodesian and Federal interests. This, Greenfield believed, would leave Welensky's hands free. The congress also set up an action committee of four members to plan resistance to any changes. Greenfield advised Welensky to mount a campaign which would culminate in a visit by Welensky to London in November.[72]

Reacting sharply to these fulminations, Kaunda proclaimed that the "day of the white man" was over and that the UFP was a spent force. He said that the UFP's "stupid" propaganda and, in particular, its "political blasphemy" against the Malawi Congress Party had clouded the Nyasaland issue, but that Nyasaland had eventually emerged a happy country. He wondered if Northern Rhodesia would do the same, and was awaiting British reaction to the UFP's threats.[73]

[69] *Northern News*, 20 September 1961.
[70] Welensky Papers, 16/11, f. 8, Robinson to Welensky, 21 September 1961; 24/151, ff. 25–27, Joelson to Welensky, 22 September 1961.
[71] *Ibid.*, 16/11, f. 12, UFP NR Emergency Meeting, 24 September 1961; Author's interview with Sir Roy Welensky.
[72] Welensky Papers, 24/151, f. 24, Greenfield to Welensky, 26 September 1961.
[73] *African Daily News*, 26 September 1961.

The Katangan crisis had prevented Welensky from attending the Northern Rhodesian UFP congress. He had invited Tshombe to meet him secretly at New Sarum air base outside Salisbury and had persuaded him not to lose the initiative created through forcing a preliminary cease-fire. Consequently Tshombe declared publicly that he desired to solve the problems of the Congo and end the 15 months of strife through negotiation. He would not, however, do so under duress, and appealed to Adoula to meet him on neutral ground. Macmillan welcomed this, but already the UN was reinforcing its troops in Katanga and the struggle would soon be resumed. Banda assisted the struggle by condemning Tshombe as a traitor because he used white mercenaries.[74]

In early October, the British reaction, to Welensky's public protests at Macleod's statement of 13 September on Northern Rhodesia, was still awaited. However, Hone informed Welensky that he had received a petition from the Barotse Government pleading that its territory should be made the fourth state of the Federation. Hone found that this deviated from the understanding which Macleod had reached with the Barotse in London earlier in the year.

Hone added that his information indicated that the separation of Barotseland from Northern Rhodesia would be unpopular with the Barotse people, and that the unrepresentative and outmoded Government of the Litunga was already meeting with formidable opposition. If the populace discovered that the Litunga was seeking the separation from Northern Rhodesia, the discontent might be serious enough for the Litunga to be confronted by rampant African nationalism and political conflict.[75]

In fact, the Federal Government had been developing its informal relationship with the Barotse Government. Greenfield, who knew nothing about Hone's letter to Welensky, called on the Litunga at Mongu in the course of a tour of prisons. The Litunga and his court asked for improvements in the health service and then raised the political situation. It was soon clear that the Litunga was most concerned at the increasing activity of UNIP in his territory and at the inadequacy of the police forces stationed there. Greenfield explained the constitutional proposals and that they would produce a majority for UNIP. He believed that Macleod would make Kaunda the prime minister. He related how the Federal Government had made representations, but that they had been ignored. The Barotse Government, he said, had to realise that it was in a stronger position, *vis-à-vis* the changes to the Northern Rhodesian Constitution, than the Federal Government because the Litunga had to endorse anything which would affect his territory. Macleod had claimed that the changes would not affect Barotseland, but Greenfield had no doubt that they would. He hoped the Barotse would assist his Government in resisting British efforts to favour UNIP, and offered to draft a letter to Hone. He promised to supply a constitutional adviser. Greenfield was disappointed by the lethargy displayed by the Litunga and in the ensuing months would

[74] Welensky Papers, 20/12, ff. 97–99, Minutes of a Meeting with Tshombe, 26 September 1961; f. 96, Tshombe's Press Statement, 27 September 1961; 27/90, f. 10, Banda's Press Conference, 2 October 1961.

[75] *Ibid.*, 20/9, f. 21, Hone to Welensky, 2 October 1961.

attempt unsuccessfully to galvanise him into action.[76] In the event, Barotseland would be submerged in the new Zambia.

Welensky praised Greenfield's efforts in Mongu and declared that the opening had to be exploited. On 11 October he replied to Hone to correct the record because he understood that it had been with difficulty that Macleod had persuaded the Barotse not to press their claim for separation. The renewal of activity by the African nationalists, Welensky said, explained why the Litunga should again make this demand. He added that the Barotse fears were not allayed by Macleod's decision to re-open the June settlement. He did not believe that the Barotse Government was tottering and thought that it had to be offered something. He revealed that Greenfield had visited Mongu and had discussed the threat from UNIP. Welensky did not advocate the separation of Barotseland from Northern Rhodesia but thought that a federal relationship between the two was perfectly possible.[77]

Welensky said nothing about a dramatic change in the overall situation. On the previous day, Macmillan, tiring of the constant tension over Northern Rhodesia and the bickering between Sandys and Macleod, had dismissed Macleod from the Colonial Office. He had replaced him with Reginald Maudling, the 44-year-old President of the Board of Trade. Macmillan had masked his action and saved Macleod from ignominy by giving him the prestigious posts of Leader of the House of Commons, Chancellor of the Duchy of Lancaster, and chairman of the Conservative Party.

It must be significant that, in warning Welensky of the change, Macmillan asked him to be generous when commenting on Macleod. Welensky complied but felt that Macleod's hatred for him was almost pathological. However, Macleod did not display it in his most courteous last message to Welensky in which he reaffirmed British support for the Federation and predicted that Welensky would like Maudling. As Sir Nigel Fisher acknowledges, Macleod had alienated the right wing and thereby forfeited his chance of ever leading the Conservative Party. However, in an interview on television in 1970, he was asked, if he could choose again, whether he would have done what he did in Africa or whether he would have aimed to become Prime Minister. He replied that he could not have chosen any other course than the one which he had followed if he had wanted to stay in politics. He thought that the lot of the politician was to accept the consequences of what he believed to be right. He had put his ambition aside in so doing. Kaunda's prediction that he might be welcomed into the Commonwealth, as the first Prime Minister of Zambia, by Macleod as British Prime Minister, would never be realised.[78] The Federal electorate sighed with relief at the departure of Macleod, but would soon find that Maudling was cast in the same mould.

[76] *Ibid.*, 20/6, f. 248, Greenfield to Welensky, 6 October 1961.

[77] *Ibid.*, 20/9, f. 19, Welensky to Hone, 11 October 1961.

[78] *Ibid.*, 24/151, ff. 17–19, Welensky to Joelson, 13 October 1961; 20/2, f. 78, Macleod to Welensky, 10 October 1961; Sir Nigel Fisher, *Iain Macleod* (London, 1973), p. 198; *Voice of UNIP*, 16 October 1961.

CHAPTER THIRTY-ONE

Maudling's Settlement

The Resolution of the Northern Rhodesian Constitution, October 1961–March 1962

REGINALD Maudling was unknown to the Federal Government but, Macmillan has said, as a successor to Macleod he would prove, if anything, to be further to the Left.[1] It took Maudling four and a half months of bitter negotiations to settle the Northern Rhodesian Constitution and, when he did, he pleased no one.

In this period, however, public attention was not entirely riveted on Northern Rhodesia because a second outbreak of warfare in Katanga offered much distraction and hardened the resolution of the Federation's Europeans to prevent a similar occurrence in their territory. This, of course, only added to Welensky's burden.

Macleod's dismissal as Colonial Secretary came at a moment when organisations like the Northern Rhodesian European Mineworkers' Union, as well as individuals, tired of the inertness of the United Federal Party and demanded action. One response from the UFP was the launching of the Build-a-Nation campaign in mid-October to win support for non-racial politics by attempting to persuade those Africans who qualified for the vote to claim it.[2]

While Maudling found his feet and allowed Hone to receive further representations on the Northern Rhodesian Constitution, the Federal relationship with the British Government was dominated by a dialogue between Home and Welensky on the Congo. By mid-October, both expressed disappointment at the lack of progress being made by Adoula and Tshombe in their negotiations following the preliminary cease-fire. What worried Welensky was the influx of UN reinforcements which, despite the cease-fire, no attempt was made to hide. He concluded that O'Brien was bent on subjugating Katanga by any means, and believed that until he was removed there would be no settlement. (In fact, O'Brien was removed shortly thereafter.) It dis-

[1] H.Macmillan, *At the End of the Day* (London, 1973), p. 318.
[2] *The Rhodesia Herald*, 11 & 12 October 1961; *Northern News*, 11 October 1961.

tressed Welensky that the United States, by supplying massive aid to the UN forces, seemed to support O'Brien in his vendetta.[3]

Welensky was particularly annoyed by allegations that the Federation was supplying arms to Katanga and allowing the recruitment of mercenaries. Although these were unjustified, he was prepared to strengthen the border control at Kipushi where a grass airstrip extended from the Congo into Northern Rhodesia and which had given rise to the suspicion of unusual traffic there. His Government's power to prevent the passage of mercenaries through Federal territory into Katanga was limited, but he assured Home that, in an effort to co-operate, he would stretch the law. He asked Alport to supply the names of suspected mercenaries but reserved his Government's right to act. "Ridiculous charges" were being laid against the Federal vice-consul in Elizabethville and Welensky, resenting them, asked Home to ensure that the vice-consul was not expelled. He also supplied Home with evidence of atrocities committed by the UN forces.[4]

Another matter of concern was the intention of the Southern Rhodesian division of the UFP to repeal the sacrosanct Land Apportionment Act, widely regarded as the corner-stone of European political dominance. It decided at its territorial congress to effect this after the next general election and ignored its more liberal elements who wanted an immediate repeal of the Act. Whitehead believed that this was an expression of white public opinion, but Welensky, although wanting the repeal, had a better grasp of the realities and knew it was not. Indeed, he had to intervene behind the scenes at the congress to prevent the passing of a resolution which would have been a complete breach of the undertakings given to the electorate during the referendum. Unlike Whitehead, he could see the storm clouds gathering over the UFP in Southern Rhodesia and knew that the suggested repeal of the Act had supplied the Dominion Party with a "ready-made programme". This was true because the defence of the Land Apportionment Act would be one of the main aims of the soon-to-be-formed Rhodesian Front Party. He approved at least of Whitehead's decision, having made the commitment, to allow the electorate to express its opinion at the polls. There was, Welensky said, a year until the election and events might assist the UFP in convincing the electorate. However, quite the reverse would happen. Todd, speaking in Cleveland, Ohio, was more accurate in his predictions because he claimed that great changes in the next three years would topple the bastion (of white supremacy) which Welensky had tried to erect.[5]

Todd was also right in predicting that Southern Rhodesia would hold out the longest against African nationalism. However, at that moment, there was much concern about sporadic violence which was occurring between the rival groups of African nationalists and which was being perpetrated by them against the African population in general. In mid-October a member of the National Council of Chiefs died in a petrol bomb attack. Another prominent

[3] Welensky Papers, 20/12, f. 87, Lord Home to Welensky, 10 October 1961; f. 83, Welensky to Home, 12 October 1961.

[4] *Ibid.*, f. 83 & f. 84, Welensky to Home, 12 October 1961.

[5] *Evening Standard*, 6 October 1961; Welensky Papers, 24/151, ff. 17–19, Welensky to Joelson, 13 October 1961; *African Daily News*, 17 October 1961.

African had his store set alight and his house stoned, but he was sufficiently undeterred to declare that Nkomo was far from his objective of taking over the country. Nonetheless, the UFP, experiencing considerable difficulties in the Build-a-Nation campaign, because of the unsettled nature of the African areas, soon discovered that the National Democratic Party had more influence there than the Southern Rhodesian Government. The UFP officials discovered NDP plans, never to be implemented, for a massive demonstration to be launched on 17 November at the risk of considerable casualties. After three days, Nkomo intended to demand intervention by the UN to preserve law and order and to prevent "further bloodshed by the settlers." The aim was virtual civil war, a trial of strength with the Government.[6]

Katanga continued to be a concern. A final cease-fire had been signed between the UN and Tshombe on 13 October but had never been implemented. Within five days Welensky found it necessary to warn Home that the situation was deteriorating. The UN had refused to evacuate strong points and O'Brien had rejected mixed control of Elizabethville airport. The result was that Tshombe refused to exchange prisoners with the UN and demanded O'Brien's removal. Welensky, who agreed with these sentiments, asked Home to effect the latter. Home did not comply, but the situation seemed to improve to the extent that, on 28 October, he could reply expressing pleasure at the exchange of prisoners. He understood Welensky's exasperation at the apparent duplicity of O'Brien, but was confident that there were two sides to the story and that it would be unwise to demand his removal. Home preferred that Tshombe be pressed to be more reasonable because he was demanding that the Congolese Central Government recognise Katanga as a separate entity in reply to a conciliatory note from Adoula. The result, Home said, could be a UN Security Council resolution to assist the Congolese Central Government in conquering Katanga.[7]

The Federal Government was still embroiled in the aftermath of the Hammarskjold crash and was being criticised and slandered by Nehru and other Afro-Asian leaders. However, Northern Rhodesia remained a major preoccupation because it was apparent that Hone would soon pronounce that, as the unrest had ended, he could re-open the constitutional negotiations.

While he waited for Hone to act, Roberts revealed his plans to Welensky. As there was no indication of what could be discussed, he said he would write to Hone for clarification. Roberts assumed that the two issues, on which Hone would take evidence from the Parties, would be the Asian national roll seat, and the minimum percentage of votes which each national roll candidate had to secure from each of the two major races in his constituency, namely from the upper (European) roll and the lower (African) roll. As Sir John Moffat had told him that he would support the Asian seat, Roberts thought the negotiations might centre on the percentage. He recalled that hitherto the UFP had argued that either the June settlement stood or the whole matter should be thrown open. Now, he suggested reconsideration because at least

[6] *The Rhodesia Herald*, 25 October 1961; Welensky Papers, 15/22, f. 56, J. A. Clark to Welensky, 31 October 1961.

[7] Welensky Papers, 20/12, f. 77, Welensky to A. E. P. Robinson, 18 October 1961; f. 76, Home to Welensky, 28 October 1961.

the concept of the national roll Members preserved the non-racial aspect. He revealed that pressure was being exerted on Hone to reduce the percentage from 12½ per cent to five per cent, but proposed to demand an increase to 15 per cent.[8]

Roberts said nothing in public, unlike Kaunda who, on 19 October, was in New Dehli attending a conference on Portuguese colonialism and boasted that the British Government would either have to accede to his demands or to build more prisons. Appreciating the fears of the Europeans, he believed that he could allay them if he allowed the Governor to hold the portfolios of defence and foreign affairs. He used this opportunity to claim that not only was the Federal Government co-operating in securing mercenaries for the Congo, but that he had strong views on the crash of SE-BDY on which he would not elaborate. He criticised the British Government for failing to control Federal activities in the fields of foreign affairs and defence. The result, he said, had been pacts between the Federation, South Africa and Portugal.[9]

No change in the British attitude to Northern Rhodesia could have been expected because, in the Commons on 19 October, Maudling emphasised that the Government, and not individuals, formulated policy. Thus, he said that a "Macleod Policy" did not exist and that he was waiting for the violence to cease before reconsidering the Constitution. He also ordered Hone to tell Welensky that he was surprised that the Barotse should ask for their territory to become the fourth state of the Federation. The Litunga had to be told that it would be unwise to pursue the idea. Accordingly, Hone sent an officer on this errand, instructing him also to persuade the Barotse to accept the proposed new Northern Rhodesian Constitution.[10]

More disturbing news for Welensky came from Joelson who had been informed by Maudling in confidence that there should be immediate action on Northern Rhodesia and that UNIP should be rewarded for calling off its campaign of violence. Joelson said he had disagreed and, when Maudling asked what else he could do, advised him to make a friend of Welensky. Joelson had warned him that Welensky would not easily give up either the Asian seat or the minimum percentage of 12½ per cent. Maudling had asked what concession could be made to Kaunda, and Joelson had replied that he was not worthy of any.[11]

Joelson failed to convert Maudling and, on 2 November, Hone declared that, as law and order had been restored, he was lifting the bans on UNIP and its Youth League. Representations could be made on the Constitution but he warned that there would be no further constitutional review. Roberts described this statement publicly as most extraordinary after the hundreds of convictions for crimes of violence of UNIP members. UNIP retorted that it would have the legislature examine the behaviour of the security forces.[12]

[8] *Ibid.*, 20/6, f. 239, H. J. Roberts to Welensky, 16 October 1961.
[9] Northern News, 19 October 1961.
[10] *The Rhodesia Herald*, 20 October 1961; Welensky Papers, 20/9, f. 17, Sir Evelyn Hone to Welensky, 20 October 1961.
[11] Welensky Papers, 24/151, ff. 14–15, Joelson to Welensky, 24 October 1961.
[12] *The Rhodesia Herald*, 2 November 1961.

Nevertheless, after consulting Greenfield, to whom Welensky delegated the task of advising the territorial leaders, Roberts immediately made his representations to Hone, while warning that his Party objected strongly to this re-opening of the negotiations in deference to violence, particularly as it had agreed to assist in making the June settlement work even though it disapproved of it. This time, he demanded, there should be no leaks to the Press and no alterations to the franchise. He also wished to see the other submissions. He anticipated that the Liberal Party and UNIP would ask for Asian participation in the election of all 15 national roll Members, but said that this was totally unacceptable even if the Asian votes would not count in the calculation of the minimum percentage.

Roberts opposed the rumoured elimination of the numerical equivalent of the minimum percentage whereby each national roll candidate had to secure 400 votes from each of the two races (African and European) in a double-Member constituency. Roberts also opposed the rumoured reduction of the minimum percentage to five per cent because, he said, intimidation would make it difficult to attract African votes. He reminded Hone that the courts had just convicted more than 2 000 UNIP members for intimidation. The numerical equivalent of 400 votes would not in any case be easy to obtain in constituencies as vast as those proposed, even though it might represent four or five per cent of the African electorate. It would be no more difficult for the African national roll candidate to secure 12½ per cent of the European votes than it would be for the European candidate to secure 12½ per cent of the African votes. Furthermore, the European candidate would also experience difficulty in securing his 12½ per cent of the European votes because he would be competing with other European candidates from other Parties for a roll which was much smaller than the lower roll. An answer was to reserve racially all seven of the double-Member constituencies which would simplify delimitation. This was all Roberts said he would propose and he warned that the UFP was utterly opposed to anything else.[13]

Greenfield informed Welensky of Roberts's action and of Godwin Lewanika's recent visit to Barotseland during which he had discovered that Hone's emissary had chided the Barotse for departing from their agreement with Macleod but that in reply they had simply decried the concession being made to UNIP by the re-opening of the constitutional issue. As Macleod had promised always to consult the Barotse Government on constitutional matters but had failed to do so, Hone's representative could only retire in confusion, vowing to return. Because the Barotse had stood their ground, Greenfield felt that close contact should be maintained with them.

Turning to the Federal Review, Greenfield wanted to correct a Press report that Sandys had told Welensky to "play it cool". Moreover, as Welensky would shortly address the Institute of Directors in London, Greenfield wanted him to use the opportunity to ask Sandys when he would visit Salisbury because he had said that it was pointless resuming the Review until he had come out to settle with the Federal and other Governments the course to be pursued.[14]

[13] Welensky Papers, 20/6, f. 226, UFP NR to Hone, 3 November 1961.

[14] *Ibid.*, f. 222, Greenfield to Welensky, 3 November 1961.

Before he left for London, Welensky offered to meet any of the territorial African leaders but was mostly ignored because, as the African Press explained, he had called them agitators and power-hungry demagogues, and had never accepted them as leaders of their communities. Kaunda did reply but said that he would only discuss the dismemberment of the Federation. The National Democratic Party was equally scornful. Greenfield disliked this offer because the Press had concluded that Welensky was proposing a round-table conference, ignoring Roberts's resistance to the re-opening of the Northern Rhodesian negotiations. Indeed, Hone had promptly suggested a similar conference of all Northern Rhodesian political Parties except for the Dominion Party. Roberts had spurned the offer and Hone had replied that, as Welensky had proposed a round-table conference, Roberts was the one out of step. Unabashed and being thoroughly awkward, Roberts merely queried why the Dominion Party had been excluded when it was quite as representative as the Liberal Party.[15] Hone's reply is not recorded.

Roberts then informed Greenfield on that day, 7 November, that he would publicly announce that he had agreed to submit a written representation on the election of the national roll Members. He proposed to add that Hone had suggested a round-table conference of all except for the Dominion Party, and that, although he thought it pointless, and would not attend, he would welcome direct negotiation with the two African nationalist Parties. He told Greenfield that he would say this because he was under considerable pressure to take the initiative, and he thought that it was a mistake not to advance alternatives. His idea of meeting the African nationalists, he said, was to squeeze Moffat out.[16]

On 8 November, in London's Albert Hall, Welensky drew the attention of the Institute of Directors to the wider issues of the Commonwealth, calling for a re-dedication to its old principles and, above all, allegiance and loyalty to it. He attacked the metropolitan powers for avoiding their responsibilities to their colonies and for giving way to the pressure of African nationalism and the fear of the "colonial stigma". They were surrendering to extremism and violence in the name of liberty in the hope that power would bring responsibility. In the process, excuses were made for behaviour and actions which would never be tolerated in Britain and Europe. A double standard had thus emerged. He warned of Communist penetration which was already supplying the Pan-African Movement with money and guidance. He believed that the survival of the Commonwealth depended on a new awareness of the grave errors of the last decade and of the disaster which now threatened. The Commonwealth, more than ever before, faced problems of colour and the danger of disruptive nationalism. It did so when its ties had been eroded to a few slender threads. He predicted that it would disappear soon, for ever, if there were no common allegiance to the ideals of the West.[17]

There was thunderous applause from the audience of 2 500, but Macmillan,

[15] *African Daily News*, 6 November 1961; *The Rhodesia Herald*, 7 November 1961; Welensky Papers, 20/6, f. 218, Greenfield to Welensky, 7 November 1961.

[16] Welensky Papers, 20/6, f. 219, Telephone conversation between Roberts and Greenfield, 7 November 1961.

[17] *The Rhodesia Herald*, 9 November 1961.

who spoke next and who was surprised to receive the same measure of applause, thought that Welensky had indulged himself in "a sort of parody of a parody of what Rudyard Kipling was supposed to believe". Nonetheless, one supporter paid thousands to have Welensky's speech reproduced in full in the *Daily Express*.[18]

A day later, Northern Rhodesia recaptured public attention because the Press reported that Hone's round-table conference, despite the absence of Roberts, had broken down. The five-man team from UNIP thereafter demanded that the constitutional negotiations should begin entirely afresh. Roberts repeated his earlier invitation to the African nationalists, but UNIP declined until, it said, all the Parties had accepted an African majority in the Legislative and Executive Councils. The next day, 10 November, the rival ANC suffered a crippling blow when its current leader, Lawrence Katilungu, was killed in a car crash on the Congo pedicle road.[19]

Nevertheless, Hone succeeded in persuading Kaunda and Roberts to meet under his chairmanship. So important did Maudling rate these talks that, lest they be prejudiced, he asked on 18 November that the announcement of his visit to the Federation at the end of the month should be delayed. The visit was announced on 21 November because the Press had wind of it, but by then Roberts and Kaunda were no closer to reconciliation and Hone terminated the talks by asking them for their written representations.[20]

Welensky had used the opportunity of being in London to hold discussions on a variety of subjects and reported on them to his Cabinet on 22 November. Firstly, he said, he had persuaded Sandys to hold the Federal Review in Salisbury. He had promised to seek common ground with other political leaders, while Sandys agreed to visit in the New Year. The Cabinet asked what concessions were expected but Welensky said he had not discussed them. Of more immediate concern was Northern Rhodesia and Welensky revealed that Sandys and Maudling wanted to retain the Asian seat and eliminate the numerical alternative. As compensation, they would increase to five the number of racially-reserved double-Member constituencies. Welensky had found this inadequate and had replied that, as the June settlement had been said to be final, his Government would reject further concessions. He intended only to present the case against alteration. The Federal Cabinet agree that, if the question were to be re-opened, a considerable *quid pro quo* was expected. The Ministers had just received Maudling's itinerary and were irritated to notice that there was no provision to meet them. They demanded rectification because negotiation by correspondence was so unsatisfactory.

Nyasaland was considered next because Banda had refused to allow the development of the hydro-electric potential of the Nkula Falls if Federal finance were used. Welensky proposed to try to dissuade him after Maudling's visit. He said that the appointment of Banda as chief minister of Nyasaland had also been raised in London. Welensky had replied that, as Banda had been a minister for less than three months, his capabilities were not yet

[18] Macmillan, *At the End of the Day*, *op. cit.*, p. 318; *City Press*, 17 November 1961.
[19] *The Rhodesia Herald*, 10 November 1961.
[20] Welensky Papers, 20/7, f. 86, Barrow to Welensky, 15 November 1961; 20/2, f. 74, Maudling to Welensky, 18 November 1961; *The Rhodesia Herald*, 21 November 1961.

known. He had not faced a session of the Legislative Council. Accordingly, the Federal Government would not endorse his promotion. The Federal Government was also irritated by the Nyasaland Education Department's behaviour since Chiume had taken charge. Moreover, the Nyasaland Government had tried to attach its representative, also Chiume, at the Commonwealth Education Conference to the British delegation and not to the Federal. Consequently, the Federal Government threatened to withdraw from the Conference if the Nyasaland Government had its way.

Finally, Welensky reported on his discussions on Katanga at the Foreign Office. He said he had been able to persuade the British Government to move towards his approach and away from that of the United States. He had since been urged by the Foreign Office to press Tshombe to meet Adoula in Leopoldville. The Federal Cabinet agreed that he should comply but only if the Great Powers guaranteed Tshombe's safety. Consequently, Welensky informed Alport of this condition and asked that the United States be pressed to influence Adoula to be reasonable. Welensky argued that a coerced and defeated Katanga would be of little use in the inevitable fight with the other secessionist province, Gizenga's Orientale.[21]

The news from Nyasaland immediately confirmed Federal suspicions of Banda's irresponsibility because he declared that no one would be prosecuted for ignoring the agricultural rules, although he was a member of the Government which was enforcing them.[22] It was clear that no one censored Banda because later, on 27 December, he told the Press: "I am not aware of anything about this stupid Federation and we were not party to it." Referring to the Nkula Falls hydro-electric project and its funding, he said: "I would rather see the whole of Nyasaland starve to death than accept charity from Welensky."[23]

On 28 November, Welensky described to Lord Salisbury how the African nationalists were preparing demonstrations for Maudling's arrival. The Lozi of Barotseland were denied any such opportunity because Maudling would meet the Litunga in Lusaka where there were very few of them. Violence was expected, and Welensky rued that "we sit like paralysed old women doing nothing". This was not quite accurate because the next day the Southern Rhodesian Government banned open-air meetings by the NDP until it could control its followers. Later, on the last day of Maudling's visit, 9 December, the NDP was finally banned altogether because of the continuing unrest it inspired.[24]

Waiting for Maudling to arrive in the Federation, Welensky also wrote to Sandys relating how, with extreme reluctance, Roberts had agreed to make his Party's representations on the Constitution when Hone had asked for them. Welensky's view of the changes was that they were designed to make the task of the anti-Federal Parties easier and that of the UFP more difficult.

[21] Welensky Papers, FGC(61), 45th Meeting, Restricted Annexure, Federal Cabinet, 22 November 1961; 20/12, f. 72, Welensky to Lord Alport, 22 November 1961.
[22] *Ibid.*, 27/90, f. 10, Speech by Banda, 24 November 1961.
[23] *Ibid.*, Banda's Press Conference, 27 November 1961.
[24] *Ibid.*, 43/*Salisbury*, Welensky to Lord Salisbury, 28 November 1961; *The Rhodesia Herald*, 29 November 1961; 8/33, f. 21, Sitrep, 9 December 1961.

He recalled that, at their recent meeting, Sandys, without commitment, had claimed that the British Government would retain the Asian seat but would eliminate the numerical equivalent and reduce the minimum percentage. The number of reserved constituencies would be increased to five. Thus, Welensky said, it was obvious that the British Government had forgotten the "package deal" in which the Asian seat had been bargained for 500 extra upper roll voters. Having considered the proposals, Welensky said he was finding it increasingly difficult to assist the British Government in its alleged desire to solve Kaunda's difficulties. The problem was Kaunda's demand for a built-in African nationalist majority. This implied the end to the Federation and the Federal Government therefore could not assist.

Sandys, he recalled, had made another suggestion which he found remarkable: that their exchanges to date on Northern Rhodesia should be regarded as the formal consultation which the Federal Constitution required. Welensky hoped that he had made it clear to him that he could not accept this interpretation and that he expected to be properly consulted at the appropriate time. Before then, Hone had to collect the Parties' written representations and advise the British Government thereon. Growing angrier as he wrote, Welensky acknowledged that perhaps the British Government had already made up its mind. However, if it had, then the Northern Rhodesian discussions were being turned into a hollow sham. He hoped that Maudling would meet him after his visit to Northern Rhodesia and said he had asked Alport to arrange this. Welensky closed by reiterating that the seriousness of the situation should not be under-estimated if the new Northern Rhodesian Constitution made it certain that the anti-Federal Parties would control the Northern Rhodesian Legislative Council.[25]

On arrival in Salisbury, Maudling denied that Britain intended to rid herself of her responsibilities in Africa as quickly as possible. On the contrary, he said, she was determined to ensure that her African territories attained self-government and independence at the right moment and not in the quickest possible time. His purpose was to listen and learn. He avowed that he had no preconceived notions and intended to take a fresh look at the problem.[26]

He went first to Nyasaland and, amongst others, met Blackwood, Little and Phiri of the UFP. Unimpressed, Blackwood reported to Welensky that Maudling was little different from Macleod and that expediency would govern him. They had discussed the attitudes of the Colonial Office, the Governor, and the Nyasaland and Federal Governments. They had examined the resistance to the Nkula Falls scheme, to a visit from the Governor-General, to school textbooks which mentioned the Federation, and to the proposed widening of the Blantyre-Zomba road by the Federal Government. Maudling, Blackwood said, would give no firm assurances and indicated that he would do nothing which would cause trouble.

Jones, who was present, likewise gave the impression to Blackwood that he would not cross Banda unless his hand was forced. Jones had denied that the textbooks had been withdrawn but Blackwood said he had evidence to the

[25] Welensky Papers, 20/7, f. 53, Welensky to Sandys, 29 November 1961.

[26] *The Rhodesia Herald*, 30 November 1961.

contrary and that he found his argument specious and unsatisfactory. Neither Jones nor Maudling would give an assurance that the Nkula Falls scheme would be implemented but Jones did suggest that, if everyone treated Banda pleasantly, it might yet be built. He knew nothing about the Zomba road, but Blackwood told him that he had been briefed by the engineers about the resistance.

Blackwood informed Welensky that, when discussing the constitutional issue, he had produced certain documents, in particular, a written assurance from Macleod, dated 3 August 1960, that, if the Malawi Congress Party agreed to the Report of the Lancaster House Conference, it would drop its demand for immediate majority rule, for a chief minister and for an African majority in the Executive Council. Macleod had depicted this as a great achievement by the UFP and had hoped that it would endorse the Report. Blackwood said that his reading from this letter had clearly disturbed Maudling and Jones, and that their consternation had only increased when he produced a memorandum from Macleod which stated that the appointment of a chief minister, being a constitutional change, required the sanction of a further plenary conference and discussion on a bill of rights, a constitutional council and other appropriate safeguards which had not been raised at the Lancaster House Conference.

The officials present, Blackwood said, had denied that the appointment of a chief minister required any of these, though it would be necessary to eliminate the post of Chief Secretary. Blackwood, Little and Phiri had been unconvinced and, Blackwood related, continued to claim that such an appointment would be a breach of the Lancaster House Agreement. They had produced further evidence proving that a chief minister could not be appointed until there had been a constitutional review.

Maudling, however, would give no assurances, and Blackwood concluded to Welensky that they should expect "the normal British swindle" in which, if expedient, any undertaking would be repudiated. He told Welensky that he had thought of threatening to publish the letters from Macleod but had reconsidered because he knew that Maudling had been ignorant of them. It was clear, he said, that Maudling and Jones had imagined that they could promote Banda when it suited them and had therefore received an unpleasant surprise.

Blackwood said he had maintained that Macleod's letter had persuaded the UFP to accept the Report of the Conference because it was anxious to secure a period of stability in which no changes would be made. Accordingly, he had argued that Macleod had agreed to a full constitutional conference before any alterations could be effected. Maudling, he reported, had tried to discount this claim because the Agreement had provided for the removal of two officials from the Executive Council. Blackwood told Welensky he suspected that, as soon as Chipembere completed his prison term, the two official seats would be replaced by two unofficial ones. He said he had asked Maudling for an assurance that there would be no constitutional amendments without prior consultation and a full constitutional conference. When Maudling refused this, Blackwood had repeated that the Agreement would therefore be breached. Thus, Blackwood warned Welensky that all British Ministers were tarred with the same brush and that any negotiation had to be conducted in the expectation of a swindle.[27]

Welensky arrived at a similar conclusion, telling Lord Malvern on 5 December that the British knew what was really happening in Africa, but that their senior civil servants had quite cynically "written us off". Greenfield revealed to Welensky that Roberts would suggest that the lower roll should elect 14 nondescript, three European and four African Members. This would really mean, he said, that 18 African and three European Members would be returned. Using a similar process, the upper roll would elect 17 European and four African Members. Welensky disliked this because the small majority which the Africans would gain represented an outright victory for Moffat. Furthermore, the UFP would be unable to gain any of the lower roll seats while it had no certainty of winning all the upper roll seats. Roberts had proposed allocating two seats to the Asians and Coloureds, but Greenfield disapproved. He felt it would be better to accept a reduction to 7½ per cent in the minimum percentage of votes, which the national roll Member had to secure from both races, and also to reduce its numerical alternative to 200 votes.

However, he agreed that it was advisable to have alternative plans in case the British Government tried to impose something unacceptable. This was all the more imperative, he said, by a declaration by Maudling that secession would be considered at the Federal Review which also made the Federal threat not to reconvene the Review more pertinent.[28]

Not surprisingly, Evans found himself composing yet another lengthy memorandum on Northern Rhodesia noting that the purpose of Maudling's visit was to secure concessions, but that he had not gained any from the UFP in Northern Rhodesia because it had hitherto taken an uncompromising stand and could not appear to weaken.

However, as it was recognised that some concessions were inevitable, it was agreed that they would be made during the negotiations between the British and Federal Governments. Evans urged that Maudling should be made to understand that these negotiations would not constitute the formal consultation demanded by law, nor would a telegram which required an answer within hours or over a weekend.

Evans identified four controversial issues. These were: the Asian seat; the 20 per cent "Moffat hurdle" which the national roll Member had to obtain from either the upper or the lower roll; the miniumum percentage; and the number of racially-reserved constituencies. The Asian seat had eventually been "bought" for 500 extra African upper roll voters and Maudling should be reminded that this had nearly brought Welensky to London. If this seat were eliminated, then the upper roll had to be reduced by 500 voters. There did not appear to be any objection to "the Moffat hurdle" but, if there were, the British Government had to remember that it had been a *quid pro quo* for the reduction of the period in which the income qualification had to be earned. In any case, the "hurdle" had been reduced from 25 to 20 per cent.

[27] Welensky Papers, 27/69, f. 131, M. H. Blackwood to Welensky, 2 December 1961.
[28] *Ibid.*, 43/*Malvern*, Welensky to Lord Malvern, 5 December 1961; 20/6, f. 191, Greenfield to Welensky, 6 December 1961.

As these concessions had affected the size of the lower roll, and therefore the minimum percentage, any move to tamper with the "hurdle" should be resisted.

Evans concluded that the numerical equivalent could not be removed lest the minimum percentage favour the African nationalists. Thus Maudling should be told of Macmillan's demand in June for an end to the negotiations. Evans welcomed the proposed extra racially-reserved double-Member constituencies but argued that if all the national roll constituencies were thus reserved, the minimum percentage was unnecessary.[29]

Maudling hinted at his ideas on Northern Rhodesia to the Press in Lusaka on 9 December. He found little prospect of complete agreement and warned that it should not be assumed that there would be any alteration to the June settlement. He did not intend either to alter the franchise or to hold a further conference. He knew that the issue had to be quickly resolved but considered this impossible before Christmas as he had to consult his Cabinet. What had surprised him, he said, was the width of the divergence of opinion.[30]

Roberts and others met Maudling but failed to persuade him that the re-opening of the issue represented a breach of faith. Nor was he concerned that he might be capitulating to violence because he found an analogy to an industrial strike in which there would be no negotiations while the strike endured. The UFP dismissed this as erroneous because the violence had been confined to the Northern Province and had been virtually dealt with by the security forces before Macleod decided to capitulate. Maudling wondered why the views of the Federal Government had to be taken into account. He also felt that the UFP's references to UNIP amounted to intimidation. He was reluctant to discuss the past and maintained that his brief began with Macleod's statement on 13 September. He was surprised that the Asian seat was seen as a concession to the Asians and had to be reminded that this was something for which the Asians had always pressed until recently when they had clearly been intimidated into rejecting it. Maudling thought that the initiative should have come from the Asians but agreed that his officials should check the record about their demands.

Roberts warned Maudling off from tampering with the minimum percentage because it would be so much easier for the African nationalists to attract the necessary European votes. Another result would be that the lower roll vote would become more valuable than the upper. If the principle of equalisation were to be upheld, then Roberts maintained the task of the UFP candidate should be no greater than that of the UNIP. He said that the factor of intimidation had also to be considered. Maudling acknowledged that he knew nothing about it but promised to investigate. He asked Roberts at what level the minimum percentage should be set and was told that anything less than eight per cent was meaningless. Maudling's second question was whether the UFP would make concessions to other Parties, but Roberts replied that it was simply being asked to dig its own grave. Roberts thought that, as the British Government had chosen to re-open the constitutional issue, it was

[29] *Ibid.*, 20/6, f. 187, Evans's Memorandum on the Northern Rhodesian Constitution, 8 December 1961.

[30] *The Rhodesia Herald*, 10 December 1961.

obliged to find the solution. Maudling confessed to being still confused and to changing his mind at every meeting.[31]

Roberts had little effect on Maudling because, when he met Welensky on 9 December, Maudling, as expected, asked for the removal of the numerical equivalent because the minimum percentage was high enough to ensure that the national roll candidates had to appeal to voters of both races. He also wanted to abolish the Asian seat, the racially-reserved constituencies, and "the Moffat hurdle", arguing that anyone who secured the minimum percentage would clear the "hurdle". He was confident that he was simplifying the scheme while ensuring that candidates appealed to both races. He believed that, in practice, the majority was so small that none of the Parties would secure it, which would mean that the Governor and his officials would continue to dominate. He agreed to commit his thoughts to paper and declared that he would wait for the Federal reply before doing anything.

Maudling's paper was considered by the Federal Cabinet on Monday, 11 December, when it quickly discovered that all its concessions in June would survive, but that all those which it had extracted from the British Government would be eliminated. Moreover, it noted that Maudling was proposing changes only a month after Sandys had acknowledged that the settlement was a "package deal". The Cabinet asked Welensky to tell Maudling bluntly that his proposals were unacceptable.[32]

Welensky complied immediately, confessing his shock to Maudling. He imagined, he said, that Maudling had not understood some of the fundamental issues. He recalled that he had already made the point to him that the June settlement had been accepted as final. Yet, he noted, Maudling was asking the Federal Government to give up every concession it had gained. If this were so, his solution was worse than Macleod's in February, over which Anglo-Federal negotiations had nearly collapsed. The Federal approach, he stated, was almost entirely different from Maudling's because it sought to preserve the Federation and secure its independence.

Welensky believed that his Government was entitled to Britain's support in this as she was the author of the Federation and had repeatedly affirmed her faith in it. By contrast, he said, Maudling was simply proposing a body-blow to the Federation. His proposals would make the task of the Federal supporters impossible, while making that of its enemies easy. Under the June settlement, at least the supporters might gain a slight majority, but Maudling would prefer at best a stalemate, contemplating it with what he euphemistically termed realism. However, Welensky commented, experience had taught him that, if the national roll seats were not filled, the constitutional issue would be re-opened and further concessions to extremism would be made. It seemed wrong to implement a scheme which could not be fully realised.

Welensky maintained that the elimination of the numerical equivalent would remove the single aspect of the scheme which made it tolerable to his Government. He calculated that the removal of the equivalent and the reduc-

[31] Welensky Papers, 20/6, f. 173, Minutes of a Meeting between Maudling and Roberts, 11 December 1961.

[32] *Ibid.*, 20/6, f. 186, "A Possible Solution" by Maudling, 9 December 1961; FGC(61), 49th Meeting, Restricted Annexure, Federal Cabinet, 4 December 1961.

tion of the minimum percentage to ten per cent would improve the chances of Kaunda's Party by 20 per cent at the cost of the pro-Federal Parties. The latter would be badly affected because the policy of granting long leave to civil servants meant that polls of more than 65 per cent were unlikely. It would also be almost impossible for these Parties to attract the immature voter, he said. Nyasaland had experienced a regimented 95 per cent poll, 99 per cent of which was anti-Federal. The elimination of the numerical alternative, therefore, would deny the pro-Federal Parties a single national roll seat. For that reason he could not accept this proposal.

Equally unacceptable to Welensky was the proposal that not only would the Asians lose their seat, but their votes would not count in the minimum percentage because they had to be totally excluded from the election of the national roll Members and not just from the calculation. In any case, he said, Maudling had not suggested removing the *quid pro quo* of 500 African upper roll voters. Maudling had done likewise with regard to the *quid pro quo* of "the Moffat hurdle" when arguing that the latter was unnecessary. If it was unnecessary, he argued, there should be no objection to retaining it, and it would be manifestly unfair if the seat went to the candidate who barely scraped together the minimum percentage from both rolls, when his rival had just failed to secure the percentage from one roll but had the overwhelming support of the other.

The proposal to remove the double-Member constituencies, Welensky warned, also ignored yet another hard-fought battle. The concept of partnership demanded that parties should have teams of candidates and, in the current circumstances, this could only be forced on them by racial reservation. An even stronger objection was that the moderate African would lose any chance of representation, which would mean that all hope could be banished of maintaining reasonable standards through the development of multi-racial parties. The elimination of these constituencies, he claimed, would play into the hands of UNIP.

Welensky told Maudling that he disliked being destructively critical, but felt no obligation to assist when the British Government had unilaterally decided to reconsider its June decision. His only suggestion was to pare the national roll constituencies to four racially-reserved ones and to retain the Asian seat. This would deal with the alleged unfairness of the numerical alternative because each candidate would be competing equally with others of his own race, and the reduction to nine seats would produce the narrow majority favoured by Maudling. It would make delimitation easier. Welensky closed hoping that he had convinced Maudling not to upset the settlement.[33]

After his return to Britain, Maudling expressed to Robinson on 14 December his disappointment at Welensky's remarks. He asked if there was anything to add to Welensky's comments, and Robinson replied that it seemed that Maudling had neither understood the length of the negotiations which preceded the settlement in June nor the concessions which had been made. Moreover, he had ignored the firm agreement which had been produced by Macmillan's intervention. Maudling, however, disputed the word

[33] *Ibid.*, 20/6, f. 176, Welensky to Maudling, 11 December 1961.

"agreement" because, he said, the British Government had the constitutional right and duty to decide Northern Rhodesia's future. Not disputing this, Robinson explained that his Government had the right to be consulted and that consultation had a positive meaning and was not just the submission of information. Maudling agreed that consultation was an active exchange of views, but that it did not derogate from British constitutional duty. Robinson explained that, because of the unilateral re-opening of the issue after the settlement, his Government would not advance any further proposals. Maudling accepted this verdict.

As his Government would nevertheless restate its case, despite this breach of a formal agreement, Robinson thought that Maudling should allow him to recount the history of the negotiations and the reasons for Welensky's objections. Maudling agreed and, as he did not think that action was possible before the New Year, he proposed to circulate copies of his exchanges with Welensky amongst his ministerial colleagues. Robinson began to explain the need for the minimum percentage, but Maudling refused to discuss the details. Nevertheless, Robinson pointed out that Maudling's ideas would only achieve a victory for Kaunda's Party which, amongst other matters, would undermine the British support for the pro-Western regime of Tshombe. Maudling agreed this was undesirable but felt he could not design a constitution which would ensure the UFP's return to power. Robinson concluded that Maudling still aimed to produce a stalemate at the polls so that the Governor could continue to rule.[34]

Welensky praised Robinson for his stand and agreed to the circulation of his exchanges with Maudling. He thought that Maudling's pronouncement on British duties and responsibilities made "a nice theory". However, Maudling should not forget that the Federation was vitally affected by his actions and, while the British Government had the right to impose its will, it did so at the risk of destroying any friendship which existed between itself and the Federal Government. The release of the Federal Government from its obligations was cold comfort, he said, but at least it allowed him to insist on the consultations being renewed with all the vigour of the negotiations between February and June.

Welensky told Robinson that he wished Sandys and Maudling to understand that he would insist on being properly consulted, and in London. He hoped that no decision would be taken during the British parliamentry recess. He noted that Maudling had not mentioned a timetable but that it was becoming imperative to know his intentions because the Federal Government had its own parliamentary commitments. It appeared, he thought, that the British Government would ditch the numerical alternative and reduce the minimum percentage to five. He did not believe that Maudling would want a stalemate at the polls because it would not assist Kaunda's cause. As a solution could not be implemented within a year, Welensky felt that the Federal Government had to continue to resist. He was also aware that, to minimise opposition, it was being rumoured in London that he was reconciled to inevitable change. As this was untrue, he wanted Robinson to make it

[34] *Ibid.*, 20/7, f. 76, Memorandum on a discussion between Maudling and Robinson, 14 December 1961.

clear to the British Government that he would not tolerate a betrayal over Northern Rhodesia. Amongst others, Robinson had to brief Lord Salisbury fully. Welensky told Robinson to inform them that he would reject the changes proposed and would take drastic action if necessary. He would call a general election and expose the whole affair.[35]

In the Commons on 20 December, Maudling declared that he would not settle Northern Rhodesia hastily, but said he would act early in the New Year. Robinson then met Sandys but gathered little from him. The Conservative MP, F. M. Bennett (later Sir Frederick), however, was more successful with Maudling because he discovered that he did not feel bound by previous negotiations or responsible for the re-opening of the issue. Displaying a degree of obstinacy, Maudling declared to Bennett that any negotiations would have to be based on the changes which he had proposed. However, he would consider any practical solution proposed by the Federal Government. Bennett advised the Federal Government to take advantage of this. He also claimed that Maudling wanted to avoid being accused of double-dealing by either the African nationalists or the Federal Government. Bennett thought that, nevertheless, the Federal Government should declare that the June agreement was binding and threaten to disclose all the facts. Lord Salisbury offered the same advice when he heard Maudling's ideas on the constitutional changes.[36]

In December, events in the Congo caused greater concern than Northern Rhodesia and, in addition, Southern Rhodesia had briefly stolen the limelight on 9 December by banning the NDP because of the continuing unrest it inspired.[37] The problem in Katanga was the product of months of increasing pressure on Tshombe. After the final cease-fire had been signed in October, the Congolese Central Government had resolved to invade Katanga, which meant that the negotiations for a settlement between Adoula and Tshombe could not progress. Furthermore, even before the cease-fire, O'Brien had been steadily reinforcing the UN forces and had acquired air support in the form of F86s from Ethiopia, SAAB fighters from Sweden, and a number of Canberras from India.

Under pressure, on 1 October, Tshombe dismissed from his service a number of mercenaries but refused, four days later, to allow the Cease-Fire Commission to visit his strongholds at Kipushi, Kolwezi and Jadotville. On 20 October a Congolese force invaded northern Katanga from Kasai. The resultant riposte by the Katangese Air Force was not only labelled a "flagrant" breach of the cease-fire, but provoked the UN to provide six SAABs to cover the Congolese invaders. A week later, Katangese forces inflicted a heavy defeat on the Congolese, and were again pilloried for a breach of the cease-fire. The same day, 5 November, Tshombe once more offered to negotiate with Adoula. The Congolese invaders suffered a series of defeats and, by looting, raping and murdering, alienated the local population. The Katangese did not achieve success in Kivu where not only did they suffer

[35] *Ibid.*, f. 71, Welensky to Robinson, 19 December 1961.

[36] *The Rhodesia Herald*, 21 December 1961; Welensky Papers, 20/7, Robinson to Welensky, 23 December 1961; 43/*Salisbury*, Lord Salisbury to Welensky, 27 December 1961.

[37] *The Rhodesia Herald*, 10 December 1961.

defeats from the Gizengist army, but also from the tribesmen. The UN similarly suffered a defeat in a sense when 13 Italian airmen serving with them were murdered at Kindu by drunken Congolese soldiers after having been mistaken for mercenaries.

Nonetheless, the UN was only concerned with the Katangese cease-fire violations because Tshombe was also re-supplying and reinforcing his troops. On 13 November the Congolese Central Government asked the UN Security Council for direct assistance in the maintenance of law and order in Katanga. It also wanted all mercenaries handed over to it for punishment, and a clearer mandate for the UN forces. The draft resolution before the Security Council, sponsored by Ceylon, Liberia and the United Arab Republic, authorised the Acting Secretary-General, U Thant, to take resolute action, using force if necessary, to remove all mercenaries from Katanga. It also decried the secessionist activities of the Katangese Government and its resistance to the UN. The United States made an attempt to have the Gizengist secession covered by this Resolution and wanted further negotiations between the Congolese Central and Katangese Governments, but its efforts were brought to nought by a Soviet veto. The Resolution was passed on 24 November by all members of the Security Council, excluding Britain and the United States, who abstained. Thus U Thant could act as he saw fit to end Katanga's secession.

Tshombe reacted to the Resolution by warning his people that there would be war. U Thant sought further reinforcements, while tension was increased by an incident on 28 November in Elizabethville when Brian Urquhart, a UN special adviser, and his assistant, George Ivan Smith, later Secretary-General of the Commonwealth, were kidnapped and brutally assaulted by the Katangese *gendarmerie.* They were released after Tshombe intervened. Yet Tshombe was still prepared to negotiate and, despite the fighting in northern Katanga, flew to Brazzaville in the hope that Adoula would meet him there. The UN Command then ordered Tshombe to co-operate or face the consequences.

Sporadic incidents on 2 December led to a marked increase in tension. Tshombe had been using Welensky as an intermediary, and Adoula, at that moment, protested to Welensky over his interference in Congolese affairs. He drew a reply from Welensky that the UN involvement in the Congo implied a right by all countries to express views on the manner in which it conducted itself. Certainly, he said, the common border and the resulting security problems gave the Federation a better right to say something than India and Ghana. He hoped that Adoula would allow him to appoint a representative to Leopoldville to avoid further misunderstandings. He reminded Adoula that he had never worked against the Congolese Central Government and had only spoken out against the use of force and outside interference. He pinned his hopes on a peaceful settlement and said he was heartened by Tshombe's recent acceptance of outside mediation.[38]

There was no relaxation of tension, and on 4 December Tshombe warned that, if there were a fresh armed intervention, U Thant would bear the heavy responsibility for the consequences. The next day, while Welensky was

[38] Welensky Papers, 20/12, f. 68, Welensky to C. Adoula, 2 December 1961.

anxiously watching the developments, Home wrote to explain why Britain had not used her veto in the Security Council, something of which Lord Salisbury was bitterly critical. It had not been used, Home said, so as to retain a chance of influencing events. In any case, he did not think that the Resolution had warranted the belligerent outburst from Tshombe, because U Thant intended to use conciliation and General McKeown had recently publicly stated that force would only be used in the last resort, in self-defence or to remove the mercenaries. The Resolution, Home noted, did not direct force to be used for ending Katanga's secession. He acknowledged that the recent incidents made co-operation between the UN and the Katangese more difficult, but he knew that the UN Secretariat understood it would be hopeless to embark on a military campaign against Katanga because the Swedes, Irish and Indians did not want to fight. He said he was pressing the United States for a meeting between Adoula and Tshombe on a warship to reassure Tshombe about his personal security. He thought Tshombe only did his cause harm by continuing to harbour mercenaries (estimated to be a 100 at that time) and believed that, if they were removed, much tension would be relieved. Home continued to pin his hopes on negotiations between Adoula and Tshombe and said he knew that Welensky could be counted on to help.[39]

As Home wrote, however, Urquhart claimed that the Katangese forces were infiltrating the bush around Elizabethville airport and called it the final act of bad faith. Minutes later, the Gurkhas attacked the main Katangese roadblock on the airport road, leaving 38 *gendarmes* dead. Deputising for Tshombe, who was in Paris, Godefroid Munongo responded with a call to arms. The UN quickly established control of the air and began bombing Katangese communications. It destroyed four aircraft on the ground at Kolwezi. USAF Globemasters flew in troops, armoured cars and artillery, and fighting spread throughout the city with the Katangese securing a vital underpass through the agency of a white mercenary unit led by a former chef at Meikles Hotel, Salisbury.

The fighting was still continuing on 7 December, with the UN deliberately mortaring the hospital in Elizabethville, when Robinson telephoned Welensky to report on a meeting with Home late the previous evening. Home had asked what could be done. He thought that the UN could hardly be asked to halt the flow of reinforcements when it believed itself threatened. Robinson said he had suggested a visit by U Thant to Katanga to arrange a cease-fire and Home had promised to consider this. Welensky told Robinson that the situation was still confused and that the UN Command was still prepared to tell blatant lies such as that the Katangese Government had fled. He was convinced that the UN intended to destroy Katanga but he thought that, while it might secure the urban areas, it would face a full-scale bush war. He said that Home should be told what the aim of the UN was and asked Robinson to request him to intervene personally at the UN in New York.[40]

Welensky wrote that day to Home expressing his distaste for the current events and criticising the United States for failing to press Adoula to meet

[39] *Ibid.*, 20/12, f. 66, Home to Welensky, 5 December 1961; 43/*Salisbury*, Lord Salisbury to Welensky, 4 December 1961.

[40] *Ibid.*, f. 63, Telephone conversation between Welensky and Robinson, 7 December 1961.

Tshombe. Clearly, he said, the Congolese Central Government had interpreted the Security Council Resolution as aid to subdue Katanga. He was annoyed by the lack of American understanding of the position and its false assumption that unity in the Congo meant stability and that fragmentation would bring chaos. It had to be realised that Katanga would fight.

The United States had asked for the closure of the Kipushi airstrip (which straddled the Northern Rhodesian-Congo border), but Welensky regarded this request as "impertinent" and unnecessary because the Federal authorities controlled air movement there, and there had been very little. In addition, there had been no movement by road out of the Congo since 21 November. He welcomed U Thant's statements about the UN taking purely defensive action, but warned that the UN were launching particularly aggressive air attacks. Contrary to Home's belief, it was clear that the Indian troops were most willing to fight, and Welensky could not accept Home's assertion that it was best to work behind the scenes. He was not prepared to sit back to wait for Armageddon even if it meant offending members of the UN.[41]

Welensky maintained the pressure, and the next day again demanded Home's personal intervention at the UN. Home replied that he shared Welensky's anxieties and agreed to remind the UN Secretariat of the need for reconciliation. However, he did not believe that the UN forces could be expected not to defend themselves or their lines of communication. It would be fruitless and unwise, therefore, to suggest a cease-fire until the UN had achieved the stated objective of securing the safety of their troops and lines of communication. It would be a different matter, he said, if the scope of operations was widened beyond that. He was prepared to accept the assurance he had received from the UN that the nature of the operation was purely defensive and had nothing to do with the latest Resolution. When the situation was clearer, he believed that every effort would be made to renew negotiations between the Congolese Central and Katangese Governments.[42]

A British announcement that day, 8 December, that it would supply two dozen 1 000 lb bombs to the UN galvanised Welensky into action. He did not know that U Thant requested the bombs for attacks on roads, bridges and fuel dumps, but saw the request as a bid to commit Britain to the UN cause, and he was determined to prevent it. He alerted the Press, particularly the *Daily Express,* and Lord Salisbury and other British parliamentarians, and composed a statement for release at midnight on 10 December. In this he declared that the British decision had shocked most thinking people and would not be supported by the British public once it knew the facts. He revealed that the British Government had prescribed that the bombs could only be used for defensive purposes, but how, he wondered, could anyone rely on the UN Command with its history of deliberate distortion? He could not accept that Canberras armed with 1 000 lb bombs were defensive weapons, when obviously they would be used to subdue Katanga. He said that he could not influence events directly, but that he had refused to allow the passage of the bombs through the Federation because they would be used

[41] *Ibid.*, f. 60, Welensky to Robinson, 7 December 1961.

[42] *Ibid.*, f. 57, Robinson to Welensky, 8 December 1961; f. 56, Alport to Welensky, 8 December 1961.

against an almost defenceless people who were fighting for their homeland against at least one of the Great Powers.

The threat of the publication of this statement brought a plea from Macmillan for it to be withheld but, tired of what he called "the gutless attitude of the British Government", Welensky rejected it. He warned Alport that if the UN, which had already destroyed most of the Katangese Air Force, attacked the Kipushi airstrip, he would consider himself free to take reprisals. However, as the US Government was still agitated about that airstrip and the UN was "agog" with stories of attacks from there, he suggested it should be inspected by the United States consul-general. Saying this, he reminded Alport that Kipushi, in good weather, could take a DC3 but, in the rain, only light aircraft.[43] Welensky's supporters secured debates in the Commons and the Lords while the UN air attacks continued, setting a fuel dump alight and hitting the Le Marinel Hospital, fortunately without causing any casualties.

Welensky informed Home of his alarm and distress at the indiscriminate killings and the ferocity of the UN attacks. He was even more convinced that the aim was to destroy Katanga and, for this reason, he said he had just issued his statement on the 1 000 lb bombs. He knew that the Katangese Air Force was reduced to a few light planes and felt it was necessary for Home to recall that Hammarskjold had assured Lord Lansdowne that the jet aircraft he was seeking would only be used to neutralise the single Katangese Fouga jet trainer. Yet those aircraft, Welensky noted, were being used for cannon and rocket attacks against targets on the ground. In addition, the UN had mortared hospitals, fired on civilian convoys and had destroyed houses in which civilians were sheltering. He repeated that he believed the UN had been preparing for some time for this "show-down" and was astonished that anyone could think this was a defensive operation. He said it was strange that the US Ambassador to the UN, Adlai Stevenson, could issue a statement blaming Tshombe for the crisis, when the US Government had done nothing to promote a meeting between Tshombe and Adoula. Consequently, Welensky urged Home to demand the reinstatement of the cease-fire, an impartial investigation, and severance of diplomatic relations with the United States if necessary.[44]

Welensky's statement on the bombs embarrassed the British Government and achieved his aim because, on 12 December, the UN announced that the bombs were no longer required. The British Government could be thankful that he said nothing about the 20mm cannon shells which he knew it was supplying. The UN also declared that its purpose was not to force a political solution by destroying the military strength of the Katangese leadership. The UN's goal, it said, remained only to secure the freedom of movement of its forces, to restore law and order, and to ensure there were no further attacks on its personnel.[45] However, as the UN issued this statement, the hospital at

[43] Macmillan, commenting on the crisis, calls it "internal" and makes no mention of Welensky's role even though he certainly knew of it — Macmillan, *At the End of the Day*, *op. cit.*, p. 449; Author's interview with Sir Roy Welensky; Welensky Papers, 43/*Salisbury*, Welensky to Salisbury, 10 December 1961; Sir Roy Welensky, *Welensky's 4 000 Days* (London, 1964), pp. 247–248.

[44] Welensky Papers, 20/12, f. 52, Welensky to Robinson, 11 December 1961.

[45] Welensky, *4 000 Days*, *op. cit.*, p. 248.

Shinkolobwe was strafed by Indian Canberras killing four and wounding 50 inmates, despite a huge red cross painted on its roof and its isolation of some 1 500 yards from other buildings. Railway installations, trains and electric generators were also hit. It was difficult to see just how these acts safeguarded the UN lines of communication. Furthermore, as the forces of the UN Commander, General K. A. S. Raja, began to encircle Elizabethville, mortar bombs began to fall on a variety of civilian targets. The next day, a battalion of Ethiopians was flown in and the fighting reached a new pitch in ferocity. One of the casualties was a Red Cross official whose ambulance was hit by a bazooka shell and whose body was later discovered nearby in a shallow grave.

After an appeal from Tshombe, the British and American Governments began to press for a cease-fire. In a dispatch to Home, Welensky welcomed this and urged Britiain's use of the veto or at least a withdrawal of support for the UN operations. He warned that the fighting had welded the Katangese into a nation and that they would fight indefinitely. Northern Rhodesia could not escape the consequences, he said, and Britain would be continually embarrassed by accusations that she was assisting the Katangese guerillas.[46]

Home replied that a meeting between Tshombe and Adoula had been arranged, in Kitona, and that all hope of a peaceful outcome was pinned thereon. He expected that Welensky might have to use his influence to ensure that Tshombe went to Kitona. Welensky complied, informing Tshombe that he could thereby achieve peace. However, Welensky also applied pressure on the US Government by writing to Mennen-Williams advising him that the only way to peace was through negotiation and not through the subjugation of Katanga. The best outcome, he believed, would be a federation. The United States, he said, had to ensure that Adoula met Tshombe at Kitona.[47]

When Mennen-Williams replied, on 19 December, a cease-fire was less than a day old. The Katangese Government had escaped the encircling grasp of the UN and had moved to Kipushi. Simultaneously, train-loads of white women and children had been evacuated to Northern Rhodesia. Despite a final assault, the UN failed to secure the whole of Elizabethville before the cease-fire came into effect. On the previous day, however, U Thant had declared that his troops would not stop short of their objectives, prompting Tshombe to inform President Kennedy that he was prepared to negotiate through the US Ambassador, Edmund Gullion. Late on 18 December, Tshombe and his Finance Minister, J. B. Kibwe, drove to Kitwe where they met Gullion and Alport. On the next day, Tshombe and Gullion flew to Kitona, while the West was somewhat taken aback by India's sudden invasion of Goa. Mennen-Williams, in his dispatch, expressed delight at Welensky's acceptance of the need for a united Congo, something which, in fact, Welensky had always favoured. He appreciated Welensky's persuasion of Tshombe and hoped the latter would remain a provincial leader. He noted that the UN had gained a military advantage in Elizabethville but had failed to solve the problem of the mercenaries.[48]

[46] Welensky Papers, 20/12, f. 51, Welensky to Home, 13 December 1961.
[47] *Ibid.*, f. 50, Home to Welensky, 14 December 1961; f. 44, Welensky to Tshombe, 15 December 1961; f. 47, Welensky to Mennen-Williams, 15 December 1961.
[48] *Ibid.*, f. 45, Mennen-Williams to Welensky, 19 December 1961.

While Tshombe travelled to Kitona, Welensky was interviewed by the BBC and was angered by the offensive tone of the interviewer who implied that he was smuggling arms into Katanga. This led to a confrontation with Alport over the general British attitude, and a promise to question the BBC. Welensky was even more annoyed to receive a dispatch from Sandys which implied similar allegations. Sandys hoped for success at Kitona but warned that the UN regarded the cease-fire as a temporary affair to last only as long as the negotiations endured. He was concerned about the mounting suspicion that aid was reaching Katanga through the Federation. He believed that the answer was to invite the UN to post observers on the border and at airports so that there would no longer be reliance on rumours. He argued that it was better to anticipate a request from the UN, because it was difficult to refuse one, and that anticipation would gain not only the initiative but also an important propaganda advantage. He hoped that Welensky would lose no time in issuing the invitation.[49]

Alport describes Welensky as being "shrill with indignation and self-righteousness" as he submitted his reply to Sandys through him. In this Welensky informed Sandys that he thought he had lost his capacity to be surprised by the British Government, but had been proved wrong as the last dispatch contained one of the most objectionable suggestions ever made to him. He could not believe that the British Government could seriously expect him to agree to the UN checking on his Government's actions. He would investigate any complaint, but would not allow the stationing of observers. He noted that none of the charges laid had survived critical examination, and reiterated his statement of 16 December that the Federation had done all it reasonably could to prevent military assistance reaching the Congo. He was sure that nothing had evaded Federal control. He did not think it would be difficult to refuse a UN request and believed that, in fact, it would be more difficult to persuade the Federal public that observers were necessary because it knew so much about the cynical brutality of the UN and its disregard for the truth. The public, he said, would regard this as capitulation to the forces of "rank unreason" and an admission of culpability, which indeed it would be. There was, after all, no reason why the UN should not station observers on the Katangese side of the border. Welensky declared that he was rapidly losing patience because he had adhered strictly to the rules and yet stood accused while the UN had openly broken the terms of the previous cease-fire by bringing in reinforcements, guns, armoured cars and ammunition. Thus he refused to make the conciliatory gesture which Sandys expected and warned that, if the UN made any more unsubstantiated charges against his Government, he would withdraw the facilities they had been enjoying.[50]

The settlement talks in Kitona produced, after much pressure, an eight-point outline of a possible agreement which would end the Katangese secession. The original provisional Constitution of the Congo, the *Loi Fondamentale,* was to be accepted by Katanga and thus the Congo would remain

[49] *Ibid.*, 24/151, ff. 1–2, Welensky to Joelson, 20 December 1961; 20/12, f. 41, Sandys to Welensky, 20 December 1961.

[50] Lord Alport, *The Sudden Assignment* (London, 1965), p. 160; Welensky Papers, 20/12, f. 40, Welensky to Sandys, 21 December 1961.

undivided. Kasavubu would be recognised as President as would the authority of the Central Government over all parts of the Congo. Katanga would participate in a commission to prepare a new constitution for the Congo and Katangese senators and deputies would sit in the new national legislature. UN resolutions would be respected and their execution facilitated.

Gullion publicly proclaimed this as an agreement, but Tshombe, on his return to Ndola, informed the Federal Government that he had not agreed to anything but, to gain time, had proposed to put the plan to the Katanga Assembly which was bound to reject it. He had been given an ultimatum on the eight points and was bitter and depressed and blamed Gullion for the lack of an agreement. In support of this assertion, he related how, whenever agreement seemed likely, Adoula left the room to consult Gullion and the UN representatives who were sitting next door. Adoula always returned with reasons why progress could not be made. Gullion had prevented any display of flexibility and Tshombe had gathered that only his capitulation was sought. Indeed, Gullion had told him that, if he did not accede, Katanga would be completely destroyed. Welensky thereafter told Sandys and Home that the attitude of the US State Department was so distorted that he had not been surprised by the result. As the United States had failed to settle the affair, he trusted that proposals for an end to it would be forthcoming from Britain.[51]

Macmillan and Kennedy were holding a "summit meeting" at Bermuda and Home cabled Welensky from there that all were agreed that the only hope for peace was the Kitona "Agreement". If Tshombe were dissatisfied with some of the articles then negotiations had to continue. Home conceded that Tshombe might have been subjected to pressure in Kitona but felt that, as Tshombe and Adoula were alone for many hours, no one really knew what had happened. However, Home accepted that it was incredible that Tshombe should have agreed to such a document unless he had been offered a *quid pro quo* in the constitutional review. Home said he had instructed the British Ambassador to the Congo to ensure that the contact between Tshombe and Adoula was maintained as he feared that an incident could sever it. President Kennedy had promised Macmillan that he would ensure that Adoula reached an enduring agreement. The British were most encouraged by Kennedy's anxiety to keep the negotiations alive and to prevent a recurrence of the fighting.[52]

The British Government was still concerned about the UN suspicions of the Federation, and on Christmas Day, Alport asked Welensky to reconsider the stationing of UN observers on Federal soil. Welensky again refused and warned that public feeling was such that the observers would be in personal danger. Alport was undeterred, and on Boxing Day advanced a number of suggestions to deal with the allegations of Federal military aid to Katanga. He has since claimed that he did this on his own initiative and had not consulted London before so doing, but Welensky, in *Welensky's 4 000 Days,* and the relevant documents show distinctly the hand of London in the matter.[53]

[51] Welensky Papers, 20/12, f. 36, Welensky to Robinson, 21 December 1961.
[52] *Ibid.*, f. 34, Home to Welensky, 23 December 1961.
[53] Alport, *The Sudden Assignment*, *op. cit.*, p. 161; Welensky, *4 000 Days*, *op. cit.*, p. 252.

Be that as it may, Alport told Welensky that, because of certain international developments, such as the Bermudan summit and the Indian invasion of Goa, the British Government had reassessed its policy towards the Congo. Britain and the United States, he said, were more aware of the dangers of the current UN policy and had realised that it was being dictated by a number of Afro-Asian countries for their own ends. The new Anglo-American policy was to end the hostilities and secure agreement between the Katangese and Congolese Governments. He had thus been instructed to urge the Federal Government to show that it was doing everything reasonable to prevent military supplies and mercenaries reaching Katanga. The British Government would not insist on the UN observers but it would expect a tightening of border control.

Alport suggested, therefore, that the Northern Rhodesian Government should supplement the Federal effort. He knew that Hone was keen to assist and this would draw off the propaganda effort against the Federation and would be a valuable demonstration of Federal sincerity. In particular, the Northern Rhodesian Police could reinforce the effort at Kipushi on the pretext that the airstrip was on Crown Land. In addition, a UN representative could be invited to the Federation to discuss the control of supplies to Katanga. By way of persuasion, Alport argued that, as Welensky had been so successful in inducing a change in the Anglo-American attitude, he should thus further demonstrate the responsible nature of his policies.[54]

Although encouraged by the new attitude, Welensky only promised that his Cabinet would consider Alport's suggestions that afternoon. Alport then asked for pressure on Tshombe to keep the negotiations going because a Katangese delegation was leaving for Leopoldville that day and the Katanga Assembly would be meeting in the New Year to consider the Kitona "Agreement".

The Federal Cabinet rejected Alport's suggestions because there was no evidence that it had been anything but neutral. Indeed, it could not understand the defensive attitude of the British Government and thought that the time had come to take the offensive and demand of the British and Americans an impartial inquiry into the conduct of the operations of the UN forces. This was the way, the Cabinet felt, to counter effectively the campaign of distortion and untruths being directed against the Federation. By contrast, it said, the tightening of controls affecting passengers in transit could only be irksome to *bona fide* visitors to the Federation, when the problem was not of sufficient magnitude to endanger the tourist industry and discourage immigration. The British Government had asked for four Britons, whose names appeared on a list of mercenaries supplied by U Thant, to be declared prohibited immigrants to the Federation, but the Cabinet found the evidence against them so scanty that it refused to comply.[55]

Thereafter Welensky publicly expressed confidence in the ability of the Federal officials to safeguard the Federation's neutrality, and decried the lack of evidence to substantiate the UN charges. Then, at a meeting with him, Welensky told Alport that his suggestions were rejected because the existing

[54] Welensky Papers, 20/12, f. 31, Alport to Welensky, 27 December 1961.
[55] *Ibid.*, FGC(61), Special Meeting, Minute 1, Federal Cabinet, 27 December 1961.

controls were adequate and because the lack of evidence regarding the passage of military supplies over the border gave no reason for change. Indeed, he said, the suggestions were merely a slur on Federal efficiency.

However, Alport doggedly maintained that it was necessary to demonstrate Federal neutrality. Barrow, who was present, disagreed because each Government's responsibilities were clear and Federal control of customs and immigration did not require strengthening. Alport hastily corrected any impression that the responsibilities and position of the Federal Government would be undermined. He thought, perhaps, that Hone had not done enough to stop the passage of illegal supplies through Northern Rhodesia and that discussions would clarify the position. He suggested that Welensky and Barrow inspect the adequacy of the border control and thereby gain a propaganda advantage. The British Government, on its part, Alport said, would continue to exert pressure on the United States and the UN to secure the negotiated settlement. However, if it were to succeed, the Federal Government had to be absolutely correct in its dealings with Katanga.

Capitulating somewhat, Welensky agreed that he and Barrow should visit Lusaka to discuss co-operation and then inspect the border control. However, he refused to invite a UN representative to Salisbury. Alport recalls his pleasure at gaining these concessions and attributed them to the intense pressure he had been exerting on Welensky. If this was so, Welensky made no comment on it to his confidants, like Lord Salisbury.[56]

Welensky, Barrow and a party of officials duly travelled to Lusaka. Welensky outlined the accusations to Hone, expressing particular anger at an allegation by the US Air Attaché that Ndola had been used as a base for bombing the UN in Katanga. He mentioned also a telegram to U Thant from UNIP claiming Federal complicity in the alleged arms traffic and alleging that a convoy of 40 armed Land-Rovers had left Northern Rhodesia at Kipushi. When asked for an explanation by Welensky, the Federal Controller of Customs replied that there were 13 Land-Rovers, ordered in the normal way by a Katangese firm, together with 17 three-ton trucks, laden with food. They had been searched at the border, and if they had contained arms then, the Controller said, "they must have been broken into very small parts". Hone acknowledged that he had only heard rumours of arms smuggling, but he did wish to improve border control. He reported that Mainza Chona of UNIP claimed to have seen the Land-Rovers at Solwezi and that the Northern Rhodesian Police, though present at all other border posts, were not stationed there.

Welensky agreed that the police should be stationed at Solwezi and should patrol the border and inspect all vehicles to prevent the passage of arms. Hone wanted to close the Kipushi airstrip but Welensky did not want to impair normal commercial relations with the Congo. He felt that the use of the roads would end once the rail service was resumed, but he did not object to Hone's suggestion that details of all cargo destined for the Congo should be published, though he thought it would make little difference. Hone asked

[56] *Ibid.*, 20/12, f. 29, Minutes of a Meeting with Alport, 28 December 1961; Alport, *The Sudden Assignment*, *op. cit.*, p. 161; Welensky Papers, 43/*Salisbury*, Welensky to Salisbury, 28 December 1961.

about the tightening of control of airline passengers in transit, but Barrow would not allow this because the International Civil Aviation Convention stated that visas could not be demanded of such passengers. Welensky added that he had requested the British Government to ask the metropolitan powers to prevent their citizens from going to Katanga.[57]

Welensky then publicly dismissed the allegations about the Land-Rovers and the passage of military supplies in general. In doing so, he drew attention to a report of a request by U Thant for howitzers, tanks and more troops. Welensky also called for an impartial inquiry into alleged UN atrocities in the Congo. In a letter to Sir Patrick Dean, British Ambassador to the UN, U Thant promptly denied that he had asked for anything more than additional troops. He expressed anger at Welensky's demand for an inquiry. To deal once and for all with the rumours of the passage of military supplies through the Federation, U Thant asked for UN observers to be stationed immediately at selected Federal airports and roads in accordance with Paragraph Five of the recent Security Council Resolution. He said he would make a similar request to Portugal in respect of Angola.[58]

This demand was conveyed to Welensky by Alport on New Year's Day, 1962, with the advice that it might be necessary to accede to it. As the British Government was already aware of Federal feelings on this subject, Alport urged that at least a UN official should be invited to Salisbury to discuss the matter. Welensky agreed but would not allow the stationing of observers. He intended to invite U Thant himself to Salisbury to question him on the questionable actions of UN forces because he had evidence from the British diplomats in the Congo as well as from surgeons and others working in Elizabethville.[59]

Welensky issued the invitation but the Press soon gathered that U Thant was annoyed that it had come directly from Welensky and not from the British Government. Furthermore, it was believed that the British Government was embarrassed by Welensky's invitation, and U Thant was not expected to accept it.[60]

Welensky commented publicly on 7 January 1962 revealing that he had rejected the stationing of UN observers in the Federation. However, as he had nothing to hide, he proposed an inspection by the Red Cross because of its established impartiality and integrity. He invited U Thant again to visit Salisbury to deal with any misunderstanding and to discuss "the shocking reports of atrocities perpetrated by the UN forces". U Thant again rebuffed him, through the British Government, but then relented somewhat and agreed to send a UN official in his stead.

Still anxious, Alport explained to Welensky on 18 January that the British Government wanted to avoid any publicity to ensure the success of the visit

[57] Welensky Papers, 20/12, f. 21, Minutes of a Meeting with Hone, Lusaka, 29 December 1961.

[58] *The Times*, 29 December 1961; Welensky Papers, 20/12, f. 20, U Thant to Sir Patrick Dean, December 1961.

[59] Welensky Papers, 20/12, f. 19, Alport to Welensky, 1 January 1962; 43/*Salisbury*, Welensky to Salisbury, 3 January 1962; 20/12, f. 12, D. Dunnett to British Ambassador, Leopoldville, 4 January 1962; *The Rhodesia Herald*, 5 January 1962.

[60] *The Rhodesia Herald*, 6 January 1962.

of the UN official. It also insisted that at any meeting the Federal dossier on the alleged UN atrocities should be handed to the UN official by Alport. This, Alport said, would enable Welensky to tell the UN official that the correct constitutional procedure had been followed. He would also be able to demand that there be no repetition of such acts and that the UN commanders should exercise discipline.

Welensky insisted on knowing the name of U Thant's representative before he would agree to anything. He feared that nothing would be done after the dossier had been read. Thus he was prepared to publish it. He demanded that the British Government ensure that action would be taken as he was horrified that the atrocities had been perpetrated without any outcry. Alport replied that U Thant's attention had been drawn by Home to the atrocities and, in particular, to those of the Ethiopian contingent. Alport urged the avoidance of broad allegations which might force the UN to protect its servants. U Thant, after all, he said, was under pressure from all sides and was currently faced with threats of the withdrawal of troops. Alport did not know if his Government would supply the assurance sought by Welensky but thought that it should play a role. Welensky asked for time to think. They then discussed the question of the observers but Alport thought it was no longer urgent.[61]

Simultaneously, Robinson met Lord Home who questioned him on the mercenaries and asked again that Welensky influence Tshombe to get rid of them. He believed that, if Tshombe concentrated on settling with Adoula, he would not need them and that thus his influence on the affairs of the Congo would increase. Home also examined the Federal dossier on the alleged UN atrocities and noted that it contained no first-hand evidence. Robinson, nevertheless, warned that Welensky did not want them glossed over. Home agreed that the British Government's own evidence of UN atrocities would be handed over to the UN official by Alport in Salisbury together with the Federal dossier. Alport would also inform the UN official that, as the border control was perfectly satisfactory, observers were unnecessary. If he disagreed, Alport would suggest that observers be stationed on the Katangese side and that the UN and the Federation co-operate in border control. However, Home did not want to support the Federation openly over the observers in case he fomented trouble.[62]

Replying through Robinson, Welensky told Home that he had just seen Tshombe in Salisbury, at the latter's request, and had learned that a Katangese delegation had been sent to Leopoldville as evidence of the sincerity of the desire to continue settlement negotiations with Adoula. However, Tshombe had maintained that the UN and the United States were still impeding the negotiations. He had invited a noted jurist to assist him and for that reason there had been a delay in the consideration of the Kitona "Agreement" by the Katanga Assembly. Another difficulty was the continual change in the UN personnel. Tshombe's main concern, Welensky said, was to regenerate his shattered economy and he had protested at the UN refusal to cease occupying the installations of Union Minière, the giant copper mining

[61] Welensky Papers, 20/2, ff. 65–71, Minutes of a Meeting with Alport, 18 January 1962.
[62] *Ibid.*, 20/12, f. 4, Robinson to Welensky, 18 January 1962.

company in Katanga. The economy had to be restored to end the problems of unemployment and of supporting the refugees who currently lived in camps under UN protection.

Digressing from Tshombe, Welensky told Robinson that evidence on the atrocities was still emerging and he hoped that Britain would not condone the double-standard under which colonial administrations were always pilloried and UN actions ignored. He said he had not discussed the mercenary problem with Tshombe, beyond saying that it embarrassed the Federal Government, as he did not believe that further pressure would have the desired effect. Tshombe's main purpose was to procure sorely needed food.[63]

Welensky informed Lord Salisbury that he would supply Tshombe with food and fuel worth £50 000. He added that Tshombe was not short of weapons and was planning his next military campaign. Tshombe had asked if Katanga could join the Federation if it could break away from the Congo, but Welensky said he had replied that it was not the moment to discuss it as the first objective was survival.[64]

On 22 January, Welensky enlightened the Federal Assembly on the Congo. He claimed there was no immediate prospect of a settlement and, in describing the Congo's history since independence, defended Tshombe against the slanders of the Afro-Asian bloc which, he said, would deride any regime that acquired stability from the employment of non-indigenous skill. He also explained why he had rejected the UN observers.[65]

Alport believes that Welensky's health gave way in mid-January because of the pressure he was exerting on him over Katanga. Welensky was ill and required a brief rest, but Katanga was not his only worry. The British Cabinet was not yet ready to consider the Northern Rhodesian problem, but in Southern Rhodesia the formation of the Zimbabwe African People's Union by Nkomo after the banning of the NDP had brought a renewal of intimidation and violence as the new Party confronted both the Southern Rhodesian Government and the recalcitrant African.[66]

ZAPU's particular concern was to prevent the registration of voters which had begun that month after the new Constitution had been formally introduced in December. To counter this effort, the United Federal Party, through its Build-a-Nation campaign, hoped to encourage the African to register as a voter.

During this campaign, Whitehead began to raise certain white hackles, including those of *The Sunday Mail*, by talking of totally removing racial discrimination and, in particular, that affecting the ownership of land. Welensky supported Whitehead at a Press conference on 30 January at which the scrapping of the Land Apportionment Act was proposed and discussed. Consequently, Austin Ferraz, the editor of *The Sunday Mail*, wrote to Welensky saying that it saddened him to see him support this. He said that his editorial had brought a flood of letters opposing the repeal, indicating just how politically inopportune this proposal was despite its recommendation by

[63] *Ibid.*, f. 2, Welensky to Robinson, 19 January 1962.
[64] *Ibid.*, 43/*Salisbury*, Welensky to Salisbury, 20 January 1962.
[65] Fed R & N *Debates* (Salisbury), Vol. 16, Col. 2173, 22 January 1962.
[66] Alport, *The Sudden Assignment*, *op. cit.*, pp. 161–162; *The Rhodesia Herald*, 9 January 1962.

a select committee of the Southern Rhodesian Parliament and by a UFP study group.[67] The myopia of the European electorate, fostered by the soon-to-be-formed Rhodesian Front, would win the day and would not change until confronted by the realities as portrayed by the American Secretary of State, Henry Kissinger, in 1976.

Nyasaland, with Banda beginning to trumpet for secession, was also causing concern. In mid-January, Alport visited the territory to assess the situation through a series of meetings with a cross-section of the population. The Settlers and Residents Association asked him what the European's position would be if the British Government tried to force secession on Nyasaland. Alport replied that the Federation was not a British creation but one which was forced on them by Huggins and Welensky. He wondered what benefits the Federation had really brought and was told that they were formidable.[68]

Blackwood saw Alport and asked if a British policy existed. Alport said that there might not be one beyond a general determination to maintain the Federation because it had achieved so much. The principal difficulty, he remarked, was to obtain an endorsement of the Federation by Banda and his African electorate. From that remark, Blackwood deduced that Alport attached little importance to Northern Rhodesia in current circumstances because there could not be a new Government there for a year. Alport agreed that Banda appeared to be the key to the situation and had to be persuaded to support the Federation but had had no idea how this could be done. Blackwood insisted that an obdurate British stand would change Banda's attitude. He suggested it should say that it was confident that the population did not understand the effects of secession. It should be made clear that, until Banda could demonstrate that the Nyasalanders knew how the Federation affected them and that he could solve the problems of secession, there could be no consideration of the Federation's dissolution. Moreover, Blackwood said, until Banda had shown his capabilities in public office, there could be no further political advancement. He should be firmly told that he would get no further until he had either accepted the Federation or had shown that he fully grasped the implications of the alternative and that he and his electorate possessed the answers for them.

Blackwood decried the Governor's proposal to grant Banda's Malawi Congress Party a further seat in the Executive Council as simply the pointless discarding of a bargaining counter. It should at least be used to secure the Nkula Falls scheme. Alport agreed it was necessary to persuade Banda to accept the scheme and again was told that all that was needed was governmental firmness. Blackwood suggested that Alport, when seeing Banda that afternoon, should tell him that Jones would be instructed to assist the Federal Government in the construction. (In fact, after meeting Alport, Banda was to announce that the barrage, the first part of the scheme, would be built.)

[67] *The Sunday Mail*, 28 January 1962; Welensky Papers, 42/75, f. 56, Joint Press Conference, 30 January 1962; 16/43, f. 13, A. Ferraz to Welensky, 31 January 1962; 42/75, f. 54, Statement by B. W. Ewing, chairman of the Rural Committee on the Removal of the Land Apportionment Act, 30 January 1962; f. 52, Report of the Sub-Committee on the Urban Areas, 30 January 1962.

[68] Welensky Papers, 15/16, f. 11, Report on Alport's Meeting with the Settlers and Residents Association, 11 January 1962.

Alport asked Blackwood his opinion on the appointment of a chief minister and Blackwood produced Macleod's letter on this and threatened to distribute copies. Blackwood was not being entirely unconstructive because he suggested a way to give Banda his secession and yet maintain the Federation, proposing that the territories should all secede and then re-form in another federation. Alport wondered how Nyasaland would be restrained until this could happen, but Blackwood was confident that the Federal Army could cope with anything Banda, with his limited resources, could muster. Alport raised the likelihood of pressure from the UN and the United States, but Blackwood thought it could be ignored provided the British Government kept its nerve.[69]

Alport also visited Northern Rhodesia and later briefed Welensky on his tour of the two territories. He said that the northern Governors were particularly anxious to revive the inter-governmental discussions on the Federal Review and on an impending fiscal review. Sandys had wanted him to attend these, but now, Alport announced, Sandys intended to visit the Federation shortly. Alport felt it would be wiser to hold a heads of Governments meeting before Sandys arrived, but Welensky replied that he had already discouraged Whitehead from making such a request lest Jones be embarrassed as Ministers would also be invited and Banda would certainly refuse. Moreover, Welensky said he was heavily committed in February and that the fiscal review had been postponed because the chairman, Sir Jeremy Raisman, thought it would be inopportune. Welensky could see no advantage in a heads of Governments meeting but promised to consider it. Alport then related how Banda had rejected the production of electricity at the Nkula Falls because it would be administered by the Federal Power Board and that, consequently, he would only allow the barrage to be built. Nonetheless, Alport was confident that he would eventually win Banda round.[70]

Simultaneously, Robinson wrote to Welensky to announce Sandys's intention to visit the Federation. He said that Sandys wanted to discuss the Federation's future fully in preparation for, or in lieu of, the Federal Review, but would neither see the African leaders nor act as the intermediary between them and the Federal Government. If Welensky wished to appear to invite him out, Sandys would be happy to concur. Robinson thought that Sandys was sincerely anxious to help.[71]

Welensky replied welcoming the visit if Sandys would bring the British proposals on Northern Rhodesia and was empowered to negotiate on them as well as on the Federation's future. He preferred that Sandys should announce his visit and agreed that he should ignore the African nationalists. He thought it was pointless for Sandys to come, though, if he did not discuss Northern Rhodesia. There was also little point in visiting if, in the meantime, the British Government had taken an adverse decision on Northern Rhodesia.[72]

Sandys accepted these conditions and Welensky immediately ordered Robinson to discover if the object was to conclude a comprehensive agreement on Northern Rhodesia. He wanted it understood that, if he failed to agree

[69] *Ibid.*, 20/8, f. 48, Report on discussions between Alport and Blackwood, 11 January 1962.
[70] *Ibid.*, f. 40, Minutes of a Meeting with Alport, 18 January 1962.
[71] *Ibid.*, 20/2, f. 63, Robinson to Welensky, 18 January 1962.
[72] *Ibid.*, f. 62, Welensky to Robinson, 20 January 1962.

with Sandys, he would go to London to appeal to Macmillan before a final decision was announced.[73]

A public comment by Lord Lambton, that deadlock within the British Government on Northern Rhodesia had led to the shelving of the proposals, was poorly received in Lusaka. UNIP immediately protested to Macmillan at the delay and threatened a strike on the Copperbelt.[74] The Press concluded that there was discord within the British Cabinet over Northern Rhodesia and was not very wide of the mark because, on 24 January, Robinson warned Welensky that Sandys was having difficulty in persuading his Cabinet to sanction his visit. Sandys appeared concerned, he said, that Maudling might not allow him to discuss Northern Rhodesia and that this would restrict his discussions to the Federation's future. Robinson reported that he had reminded him that Welensky insisted on Northern Rhodesia being the reason for the visit. Sandys thereupon asked Robinson to write to him formally requesting that he should be thus empowered and expressing Welensky's hope that any decision would be postponed until their talks were concluded. His purpose, he said, was to prevent Maudling from acting independently and he did not want mention made of Welensky's desire to see Macmillan, in the last resort, because it would only make his relationship with Maudling more difficult.[75]

Welensky accepted this because he was anxious to avoid a breach with the British Government which might prove to be permanent and render Sandys's visit pointless. However, he insisted on retaining the right to see Macmillan, but asked Robinson to convey to Sandys his warm regards.[76]

The Federal Cabinet was equally troubled by further ominous moves in Nyasaland where the Press had just discovered that the MCP would soon be given two more seats in the Executive Council to give it a majority. As Banda had not changed his attitude towards the Federation, the other Governments were expected to object. The Press did not fail to note that there had already been friction between the MCP Ministers and the Federal Government.[77] The reason for there being the two vacant seats in the Executive Council was the impending retirement of two European senior civil servants. The Nyasaland Government expected their ministerial places to be filled by D. K. Chisiza and O. Chirwa, giving Banda control of seven of the ten seats. The three remaining seats were held by the Chief Secretary, the Attorney-General and the Minister of Finance.

In the Federal Assembly on 24 January Gaunt, supported by I. D. Smith, called on the Government to reveal its plans in reaction to the MCP's policy on secession. Gaunt was confident that, because of the sway held over him by his lieutenants and the leaders of East Africa, Banda could not renounce secession even if he wanted to. Smith believed it was imperative to resolve the Federation's future immediately and that the Federal Government had to

[73] *Ibid.*, f. 61, Robinson to Welensky, 23 January 1962; f. 60, Welensky to Robinson, 23 January 1962.
[74] *The Rhodesia Herald*, 23 January 1962.
[75] Welensky Papers, 20/2, ff. 58–59, Robinson to Welensky, 24 January 1962.
[76] *Ibid.*, f. 57, Welensky to Robinson, 26 January 1962.
[77] *The Rhodesia Herald*, 24 January 1962.

face the bitter truth that power now reposed in the hands of Banda and the MCP. Greenfield replied that his Government was totally opposed to secession and reminded the House that the dissolution of the Federation required British legislation which, in terms of the 1957 Convention, had to be requested by the Federal Government. He noted that most of Banda's statements on the subject had been made before he accepted office and that, in any case, it was the actions of the Nyasaland Government which counted. He reminded the Assembly of the Federal economic achievements and pointed out that each territory could achieve self-government within its own sphere, giving great scope to the nationalist leaders. The secession of Nyasaland would have severe repercussions with regard to Northern Rhodesia and, in addition, he believed that the constant harping on the subject in the Federal Assembly was doing great harm. The motion was withdrawn after Gaunt had said that he had only tried to teach the Government the facts of life.[78]

Banda reacted to these comments by threatening Britain with a worse confrontation than that of 1959, while acknowledging that only the British Parliament could dissolve the Federation.

Implying a coalition of the UFP and the MCP, Blackwood told Jones on 27 January that he could see no reason why the two vacant Executive Council seats could not be filled by his UFP. He claimed that, otherwise, Jones's earlier argument, when he offered the UFP only one seat, would be destroyed. However, Jones merely tried to persuade him that the Parties could not possibly work together. Blackwood disagreed because, to date, there had been no major clash between the Parties either in or outside the legislature. He believed that Jones really feared that the UFP could claim the two upper roll seats on the Executive Council (which he had denied the UFP on 4 September after the election) and thus force the dismissal of the current occupants. Blackwood also asked about the fate of the Nkula Falls scheme and was mystified by Jones's reply that pressure should be exerted on Alport.[79]

Greenfield, however, was not convinced that a UFP/MCP coalition was practical, despite there being an advantage in having a finger in the pie, because of the embarrassment which the UFP would suffer in the Federal and Southern Rhodesian spheres. Even if an attempt to secure the seats were successful, he said, Jones might allocate all the portfolios to the existing five MCP Ministers. While Barrow saw merit in asking for the seats, to embarrass Jones, he agreed that a coalition was impossible and that, if it were attempted the UFP would soon have to resign because of Banda's attitude towards the Federation. On the Nkula Falls scheme, Barrow concluded that, because Jones had told him he would not overrule Banda because he could not face a constitutional crisis, it was clear that he was "passing the buck" to Alport. Barrow thought that the pressure on Jones had to be maintained. Welensky replied to Blackwood advising him not to accept any seats on the Executive Council even if they were offered because he would only find himself in an embarrassing situation. As regards the Nkula Falls scheme, Welensky said he

[78] Fed R & N *Debates* (Salisbury), Vol. 16, Col. 2888 f., 24 January 1962.

[79] *The Rhodesia Herald*, 29 January 1962; Welensky Papers, 7/14, f. 17, Blackwood to Welensky, 29 January 1962.

had heard nothing from Alport. He added that all Alport had suggested was a heads of Governments meeting which, Welensky said, he was anxious to avoid until he had heard the fate of Northern Rhodesia.[80]

Blackwood told Welensky he was dissatisfied because he felt that Nyasaland was sliding out of the Federation through neglect. He declared that the UFP had to fight to retain some of the confidence of the public. The Nyasaland Government was attempting to undermine the UFP by proclaiming that life in Nyasaland after secession would be tolerable, that secession was inevitable and that already Federal Ministers dared not visit. Blackwood said he had learned from a close friend of Jones that he had always been an opponent of the Federation and had only ever paid lip-service to it. Thus it was important that the Federal Cabinet was aware of the deceit being practised at the highest level, and that it understood that the British Government would ease Nyasaland out of the Federation. Blackwood related how, in the latest incident, Lady Jones, as head of the local Red Cross, had asked the Federal Government to remove the red cross symbol from all ambulances because it could not be used without the Governor's permission. The gloom within the UFP was such, he said, that he pleaded again for Federal ministerial visits.[81]

Welensky replied that he was fully aware of the events in Nyasaland and was currently fighting for the very life of the Federation. To that end he had just spent two days in Moçambique because Portuguese support could be so vital in the future. As for the UFP, he felt that the Nyasaland division had to understand that it was not its efforts which would decide if its territory would stay in the Federation, but his negotiations with the British. He promised to attend to the matter of the Red Cross and hoped that this bitter correspondence was at an end.[82]

Sandys's arrival was imminent and there was increasing expectation that Macmillan would give greater concessions to Kaunda. Welensky was in no easy mood because, in particular, the British habit of leaking everything to the Press, to hamstring him, had aroused his ire. The London Press was speculating that he would have to accept the proposals which Sandys would bring or cause the biggest revolt yet in the British backbench. The Press knew that there had been several British ministerial meetings and that there had never been such close attention given to any colonial issue. Tom Stacey of the *Sunday Times* understood that the African nationalists would be given a small but vital majority in the Northern Rhodesian legislature and that Kaunda, if elected, would be named chief minister. There would, however, be Europeans in the Executive Council and thus, Stacey said, UNIP would have to ally with Moffat's Liberal Party. Stacey believed that nothing more than the dropping of the minimum percentage and its numerical equivalent was being offered to the African nationalists. However, little was also being done to foster multiracialism and a severe struggle could be expected. Stacey thought Maudling hoped that the granting of an African majority in Northern Rhodesia would persuade Banda to drop secession and that, if the Southern Rhodesians saw

[80] Welensky Papers, 7/14, f. 22, Greenfield to Welensky, 1 February 1962; f. 20, Barrow to Welensky, 1 February 1962; f. 14, Welensky to Blackwood, 2 February 1962.

[81] *Ibid.*, 27/69, f. 122, Blackwood to Welensky, 2 February 1962.

[82] *Ibid.*, f. 121, Welensky to Blackwood, 7 February 1962.

the new system working successfully in the North, they would hasten to liberalise their own Constitution. The opinion of the Federal Press was that, short of using the Federal forces, there was little Welensky could do to alter the course of events. It concluded that the Federation was doomed because the aims of Welensky and the African nationalists were irreconcilable.[83]

Sandys arrived in Salisbury on 7 February with the local Press telling Welensky that he was about to be "put in his place". Sandys immediately announced that he would be going to Nyasaland and then to Barotseland. As both territories were outside his area of responsibility, this announcement considerably startled the Federal Cabinet particularly because he had said he did not want to meet or deal with any African nationalists. Thus the Cabinet was anxious to discover his intentions. Independently of the Cabinet, but as a warning, *The Sunday Mail* provided a list of broken British promises for Sandys's benefit.[84] All suspicions of Sandys's motives for visiting Nyasaland would be justified.

Nevertheless, the Federal Government's discussions with Sandys seemed to go well at first. Sandys indicated that the numerical equivalent would have to be dropped, but that the minimum percentage would be retained, which would make the UFP's task at the polls more difficult but would make Kaunda's no easier. Welensky thought that the system would not force a political coalition between the races because the African nationalist would only accept total control. Thus he would consider a reduction in the minimum percentage if the racially-reserved double-Member constituencies were increased to seven. In fact, he said, he would settle for six. He would oppose the removal of the Asian seat. Greenfield thought that the minimum percentage could be safely reduced to eight and revealed that his Party would attempt to secure a pact with the ANC which hated both UNIP and the Liberal Party. Welensky warned Sandys that there had to be a comprehensive settlement which would make the Federation independent in its own field, on the same basis enjoyed by Southern Rhodesia. He would increase the African membership of the Federal Assembly, but would not accept an African majority. However, Sandys insisted that, as Banda was the key to the Federation's survival, he needed the inducement of a secession clause, as suggested by the Monckton Commission, with the difference that it would carry with it an immediate grant of independence to the Federation. Sandys wanted each territory to have the option of secession when it acquired independence within the Federal framework. Welensky agreed that, despite the risks, something revolutionary was needed to shake the Federation free of the British Government. Thus he declared that his Government was reconciled to losing some of its powers, but would not allow the reconvened Federal Review to be held on the same basis as before.[85]

Sandys was more subdued than expected. He surprised Welensky by saying gratuitously that the British Government would never take up arms

[83] *Ibid.*, 43/*Connell*, Welensky to J. Connell, 4 February 1962; *The Rhodesia Herald*, 5 February 1962; *Sunday Times*, 4 February 1962.

[84] Welensky Papers, 25/240A, f. 48, Welensky to Lord Robins, 7 February 1962; 25/272, f. 26, Barrow to Welensky, 8 February 1962; 43/*Ferraz*, A. Ferraz to Welensky, 9 February 1962.

[85] *Ibid.*, 43/*Salisbury*, Welensky to Salisbury, 10 February 1962.

against the Federation, and that Britain had no desire to retain her Empire. This left Welensky wondering if even trade links would be preserved. Indeed, Sandys added gloomily that Britain no longer had the will to govern. A week later he would repeat this statement, with more dramatic effect.

After meeting Sandys, Welensky asked Greenfield to examine immediate secession or an amendment of the Constitution to enable Nyasaland to secede five years after the Federation had attained independence. Welensky assumed that the Federation would be given a reasonable degree of independence in the near future. Another possibility, he thought, was that Nyasaland might withdraw and thereafter rejoin a reformed federation. Welensky sought to ensure that Sandys fully understood the implications of secession but he did not want him to think that he was yielding on the question of keeping the Federation together.

Greenfield believed that what was needed was a full commission of inquiry, an official working party, and plenty of time for reflection. Nevertheless, after a day's thought, he committed his ideas to paper. He suggested that, at the outset, Sandys should be reminded that the dissolution of the Federation required a British Act of Parliament which could not be introduced without the Federal Government's consent in terms of the 1957 Convention. In pure legal theory Greenfield acknowledged that the Convention could be disregarded but that it would be difficult to implement the British Act of Parliament without local co-operation. In any case, immediate secession — which he saw as an act of supreme folly — would take at least a year because of the intricacies of the withdrawal.

Lacking the terms for secession, Greenfield found it difficult to assess the implications. It depended on whether there would, in fact, be immediate secession, which had just been granted to Jamaica, or if Britain would retain control during a period of transition to avoid chaos. Other factors were the possibilities of Nyasaland joining Tanganyika immediately, the compensation which might have to be paid to the Europeans, and the future relationship between the Rhodesias. The latter was obviously crucial because Banda probably would not rest until the Rhodesias separated. Moreover, once Banda secured secession, it would be difficult to deny it to Kaunda. However, it seemed that it might be possible to exact, as the price for letting Nyasaland go, a British promise that the ties between the Rhodesias were indissoluble, although such a promise would have to be regarded cynically.

A union between the Rhodesias was possible but Greenfield knew that it would depend on British determination and, of course, on the composition of the Northern Rhodesian legislature and the measure of power given to the African nationalists. He thought that a unitary state was the best bet, but that the British would defer to the wishes of Kaunda. The two Rhodesias could survive without Nyasaland, but the same could not be said of the northern territories if Southern Rhodesia alone seceded. Nonetheless, Southern Rhodesia on its own would be threatened by its neighbours whose poverty would be exploited by the Russians and Chinese.

Greenfield claimed that the secession of Nyasaland would damage the economy but not too drastically if there were a customs union and the retention of common services. However, there remained the public debt, the loss of Federal revenue, and compensation for the Europeans who had sunk everything they possessed into Nyasaland. Britain would have to subsidise Nyasaland but could not do so indefinitely, and the United States might have to step into the breach. Greenfield inferred from Sandys's "loss of will to govern" that Banda would not be restrained. Sandys had appeared to believe that Nyasaland's secession could only be prevented by force because power had virtually passed to the MCP. Sandys had doubted if Southern Rhodesia would allow its territorial soldiers to serve continuously in Nyasaland and had thought they might be needed at home. However, Greenfield was convinced that a show of determination by the British Government would keep the MCP in check, but knew that Sandys might be correct in saying that the will to do so had gone. Greenfield wondered if Banda would risk ruining Nyasaland through an insurrection, but thought it would be foolish to expect him to be guided by logic or common sense.

These considerations led Greenfield to ask if Nyasaland should not be allowed to secede and to "stew in her own juice". However, he said, the amputation had to be skilful if gangrene were not to endanger the whole body. If Northern and Southern Rhodesia were to survive united, the existence of the united state had to be completely guaranteed. The biggest and most obvious risk was the demand from the African nationalists in Northern Rhodesia for secession. To counter this would be the British guarantee on the insolubility of the Federation, if one could be obtained, but Federal history was already littered with the corpses of British guarantees.

Greenfield thought the best course was immediate independence and, if the Federal form of government survived, the Northern Rhodesian extremists had to be prevented from gaining a stranglehold. It would be best to bid for unitary government or, failing that, a single parliament for the Federation and Southern Rhodesia. The Northern Rhodesian legislature would then deal only with its territorial functions. If all these were impossible and the Federation and Northern and Southern Rhodesia kept their separate legislatures, then Greenfield wished police to be Federal.

As a condition for secession, Greenfield wanted the establishment of Russian and Chinese embassies in Nyasaland forbidden and a guarantee that Nyasaland would not stimulate subversion in the Rhodesias. Being responsible for Nyasaland's external relations, Britain could effect this by using the lever that the common services had to survive. He would soften the blow of secession for the European by ensuring that the Federal Government continued to run the non-African schools and hospitals.

He believed that, if a high price were exacted for immediate secession, it could strengthen the Federation. Part of this, he thought, could be independence with power remaining in responsible hands. He disliked the alternative of including a secession clause to be implemented in five years, because the other territories would demand like treatment. To be effective, there would have to be a strong bond between the Rhodesias, while Nyasaland was allowed a looser rein. Under this, the return to Nyasaland of such services as non-African education, health, marketing, roads, prisons and power would save considerable Federal expenditure. Standards in education and health could be guaranteed by the use of private agencies. Nyasaland Federal MPs could be elected on the Nyasaland franchise and, to show that the old derided "stupid" Federation had given way to a better one, the name could be changed to "Rhodesia and Malawi". Aside from the Governor's veto, Nyasaland would be completely self-governing but, Greenfield maintained, the Federation should also be independent in its own sphere and Northern Rhodesia should be made self-governing in a manner in which power would remain in responsible hands.[86]

The Federal Treasury advised that secession in five years would only depress the economy. Barrow wanted Sandys to be made to understand that the Northern Rhodesian European electorate never achieved more than a 65 per cent poll, while Evans had examined a proposal by Sandys to reduce the minimum percentage to four but found that eight per cent would produce the desired effect.[87]

Clearly, nothing could yet be said in public but, inevitably, when the Federal Assembly opened on 12 February, Field demanded a debate on secession because it was a good opportunity to give Sandys first-hand knowledge on local opinion. Welensky naturally would not allow such a debate during the negotiations. Nonetheless, he warned of the consequences and difficulties of secession and avowed that, while he would make necessary adjustments, he would fight for moderation.[88]

If he would say nothing in public, Welensky had to deal forcefully with certain Northern Rhodesian Europeans who were reviving the idea of partitioning Northern Rhodesia. He told one, D. A. Sparrow, that no African nationalist would accept half the country. However, when another, S. Turner, suggested a Northern Rhodesian federation within the Federation, Welensky proposed it to Sandys but the latter adamantly refused to contemplate dividing Northern Rhodesia.[89] Yet the search for a solution would lead Alport to suggest just such a scheme in the next few days.

Sandys had spent the weekend in Nyasaland and had, albeit secretly, cast the die by telling Banda that Nyasaland would be allowed to secede. He was believed to have dumbfounded Jones by thus discarding the main bargaining card. He was, of course, also poaching in the preserves of Maudling and the Colonial Office.

Knowledge of this crucial statement would be hidden from Welensky and others until April. Indeed, Blackwood, in an interview with Sandys, was most encouraged but later told Welensky he hoped that he had not seen "the smile on the face of the tiger". Sandys gave him the impression of searching for ways of avoiding secession, although he recognised the difficulties of selling any of them to the African nationalists. Blackwood urged him to ignore popular feeling because Banda could do anything he chose for at least another year. Banda was simply trying to appear moderate in the eyes of the world, Blackwood told Sandys, by claiming that he was unable to persuade the

[86] *Ibid.*, 20/19, f. 131, "Nyasaland and the Federation" by Greenfield, 10 February 1962.
[87] *Ibid.*, f. 213, Evans to Welensky, 12 February 1962; 20/6, f. 93, Evans to Welensky, 13 February 1962.
[88] Fed R & N *Debates* (Salisbury), Vol. 17, Col. 19 f., 12 February 1962.
[89] Welensky Papers, 20/6, f. 111, Welensky to D. A. Sparrow, 12 February 1962; f. 109, Welensky to Greenfield, 12 February 1962.

Nyasalanders to give up secession. When Blackwood said that the UFP, including Welensky, had always accepted that there would be an African Government in Nyasaland, Sandys wished Roberts was blessed with as much foresight and earned a lecture from Blackwood on the essential difference between the situations in the two territories.

They discussed alterations to the Federal Constitution and what powers should revert to Nyasaland. Sandys found the main stumbling block was Banda's rejection of the Federation because it was controlled by Europeans, but Blackwood expected the Federal franchise to answer that by producing an African prime minister. He believed that the majority of the Federal MPs from the northern territories, who would be returned at the next general election, would be Africans and that there would probably be some from Southern Rhodesia.[90]

Despite whatever Sandys had hoped to accomplish, on 14 February Banda publicly rejected even an economic association with the Rhodesias. Sandys met Welensky that morning and induced him to agree to meet Banda. It was a forlorn hope because Banda, when asked, replied that he would comply provided Welensky understood that his decision on secession was irrevocable. All he would discuss were the implications and methods of secession. Furthermore, any invitation had to come from Sandys, and the meeting had to be in the British High Commissioner's residence in Salisbury. Not surprisingly, Welensky rejected these conditions.[91]

Sandys, Alport, Welensky and Greenfield met the next afternoon. The Welensky Papers lack a record of the meeting but Welensky recalls that, when he maintained that all that was needed in Nyasaland was firmness, Sandys had blurted out: "No Roy . . . You see, we British have lost the will to govern." Greenfield had snapped back: "But we haven't." Alport confirms the substance of this account, but believes that Sandys meant that there was no will in British or Federal circles to govern by force. Welensky claims that stormy glances were exchanged, which is not surprising because, as has been seen, there was no love lost between Sandys and Greenfield.

Sandys's remark so shook Welensky that he suffered a migraine. He was told later that Alport was also sufficiently upset by it to vomit after the meeting. Alport, however, denies this, though he concedes that he was extremely angry because Sandys had thereby given his Rhodesian critics justification for the myth they were nurturing that the British were played out and spineless, while they, by contrast, faced their problems with manly determination.[92] Alport might thus fulminate and fume, but Rhodesians could be forgiven for believing the evidence before them that Britain was not prepared to stand up to anyone. The curious aspect of both accounts is that neither mentions that Sandys had already commented thus on 9 February, and one can only presume that it was the finality with which he said it that so startled his audience.

[90] *Ibid.*, 20/2, ff. 34–38, Robinson to Welensky, 4 February 1962; 27/69, f. 109, Blackwood to Welensky, 15 February 1962.

[91] *Ibid.*, 27/90, f. 10, Banda's Press Conference, 14 February 1962; 20/19, f. 171, Sandys to Welensky, 14 February 1962.

[92] Welensky, *4 000 Days*, *op. cit.*, p. 319; Alport, *The Sudden Assignment*, *op. cit.*, pp. 167–168.

Sandys did not entirely ruin the meeting because a version of the long-standing idea of partitioning Northern Rhodesia into three states was advanced and discussed. The middle or "Railway Strip", however, would not join Southern Rhodesia but would have a similar constitution. Alport claims authorship because, he says, he had thought of it when searching for ways to break the virtual deadlock between the British and Federal Governments. The idea was given to Evans to translate into practical terms.

Consequently, Evans produced on 17 February a skeleton outline together with statistical evidence. He advised his Government that, as Banda was in full cry, demanding secession "Now, Now", he should be depicted as irresponsible. By contrast, the Federal Government should give the appearance of being most concerned that he should understand the folly of his actions which could cause the starvation of millions. Care would have to be taken to show the world just what the British Government was prepared to condone. After that Banda could be presented with the option to secede, in the knowledge that he would accept it thereby proving his recklessness. In giving the option, the Federal Government should prescribe four conditions for secession. These should be that Britain had to compensate the Europeans and the Federal Government for their assets, ensure that Nyasaland met its share of the public debt, and grant the new Rhodesian Federation its independence. Evans proposed that if Banda decided not to secede, his decision should be declared final and irrevocable. Britain should share responsibility for Nyasaland seceding, and the cost of compensating the European should be emphasised. Banda was due in London in April, but Evans thought he should be summoned earlier to be given his option so that Federal dignity could be preserved and the initiative wrested from him. Kaunda could be invited to accompany him and could be shown up in the same reckless light.[93]

Evans's proposals on the partition were thoroughly examined in a meeting with Sandys on 19 February. Then, before leaving the next day, and to avoid misunderstanding, Sandys summed up in writing. He said he had negotiated without commitment but that his Government had indicated that it wanted the Northern Rhodesian numerical equivalent to the minimum percentage of votes, which the national roll Member had to secure, to be dropped, though it was undecided about the 20 per cent "Moffat hurdle". He had sought views on reducing the minimum percentage to four per cent instead of the current 12½ per cent in return for the retention of the Asian seat. Sandys noted that Welensky had in principle opposed any changes but would, under protest, accept the elimination of the numerical equivalent if the minimum percentage were set at eight per cent, and the Asian seat retained. Welensky had also wanted the racially-reserved double-Member constituencies increased from four to six. If this was unacceptable to the British Government, Welensky had reserved the right to see Macmillan. Sandys, however, made no reference to the tentative proposals on partition which he carried to London.[94]

Welensky referred to this letter on 21 February when briefing his Cabinet.

[93] Welensky Papers, 20/19, f. 192, Evans's Memorandum, 17 February 1962; f. 196, "Further Thoughts on Methods of Presentation", 17 February 1962.

[94] *Ibid.*, 20/19, f. 177, Evans to Welensky, 19 February 1962; f. 170, Sandys to Welensky, 20 February 1962.

He described Banda's refusal to meet him, and circulated copies of the tentative proposals on partition discussed with Sandys. If these were accepted, Welensky said, the British Government would announce that it had considered the views expressed at the Federal Review Conference, and the desire of the Nyasalanders to secede and of the Barotse to separate from Northern Rhodesia. It had assessed the opposition to the Federation and its economic benefits. It would acknowledge that dissolution would gravely prejudice the economic progress of all, but would concede that experience in working the Federation had shown a need for radical alteration to its structure. Accordingly, the British Government would say that Northern Rhodesia would be divided into three separate protectorates comprising Barotseland, North-Eastern Rhodesia and Central Rhodesia. The last would absorb the current Central, Southern, Western and North-Western Provinces and would have a constitution similar to that of Southern Rhodesia. Each protectorate, on attaining full internal self-government, would be able to negotiate freely with the Federal and other Governments to remain in the Federation or to secede totally or to join a loose economic association. Once three or more territories had attained full self-government, and if two or more had decided to remain in the Federation, the British Government would convene a conference to consider matters such as the franchise, territorial representation and the distribution of power. Thereafter, the British Parliament would effect any required changes, and immediate independence would be granted to the Federation and to the seceding territories. The Federation's independence would terminate the protectorate or colonial status of the remaining constituent territories.

Welensky warned his Cabinet that Sandys had made it clear that the British would not attempt to influence Banda on secession because they had lost the will to govern and they believed it was impossible to keep Nyasaland in the Federation. To do this, Sandys had said that large numbers of territorials would need to be mobilised. He had claimed that such massive deployment would damage the Federal economy, and the morale of the troops would suffer because there would be no prospect of retaining Nyasaland.

Welensky said he had been reluctant to discuss secession but Sandys had given him no option. Thus he had agreed to consider the partition of Northern Rhodesia, while insisting that, if Nyasaland seceded, the Federation would immediately become independent in it own sphere, and that Nyasaland would meet its financial and other responsibilities. Sandys, however, had refused to consider such matters of detail, but had eventually agreed to recommend to his Cabinet that a commission should study the effects of secession and the distribution of assets and liabilities. Sandys had suggested at first that the future Federation should comprise only "Central" and Southern Rhodesia and that Barotseland and North-Eastern Rhodesia should merely be associated territories. His premise was that the majority of Europeans lived in the central portion. Later Sandys had thought that this idea would be unacceptable to his Cabinet and had proposed to grant every territory the right to secede as it gained self-government. Welensky said he had resisted this, but had eventually been persuaded to endorse the proposals as a basis for discussion. Sandys had refused any financial support for Nyasaland, and appeared to view with equanimity the prospect of Nyasaland fending for itself.

The Federal Cabinet, blaming the Nyasaland situation on deliberate British policy, suggested that Welensky visit London to discover if the British Government would fulfil its pledges on the Federation. If it would not, he should try to create a rift in the Conservative Party, thereby pressurising the Government.

The Cabinet doubted the prospects of partitioning Northern Rhodesia, and expected that an unacceptable constitution would be imposed which would lead to the erosion of the Federal structure. This would force the Federal Government to consider drastic measures. In particular, unless there was a *quid pro quo*, it would refuse to sanction Nyasaland's secession. It was seriously worried by the news that the British Government would not subsidise Nyasaland, because it would force Banda to look to undesirable sources of finance, which might pose a threat to the Rhodesias.[95]

Robinson was informed that Welensky might arrive at short notice and was asked to plan meetings with Macmillan. Robinson replied that he had recently met Macmillan and he no longer appeared totally preoccupied with Europe and Russia. He reported that Macmillan was irritated with Gaitskell's constant questions on Federal affairs and had said that ultimately the people of the Federation would resolve their own difficulties. Macmillan felt there was little anyone could do if they decided to declare their own independence.[96]

The next day, 22 February, Robinson told Welensky that he would see Sandys on the morrow and that, in the meantime, Wall would warn the British Government through the 1922 Committee of the Conservative Party of a possible revolt against unacceptable Northern Rhodesian constitutional proposals from Maudling. S. E. R. Wynn of Voice and Vision counselled Welensky against any leakage of the current negotiations, but Welensky hinted that little progress was being made when he informed a UFP congress that the whims of others might force him into an early election. He also told the *Daily Express* of his burning desire to prove that a moderate state could exist in Africa. He would accept an African majority in the Northern Rhodesian legislature provided that the African nationalists did not secure control. He said his intention was that Africans should share fully in government, but that power should remain in responsible hands. Whitehall's mistake, he added, was to treat the problem as a cold mathematical formula. However, already that day *The Times* had prophetically declared that Maudling had decided that the next Northern Rhodesian election had to produce an African majority even though he knew that it would demand secession.[97]

On 23 February Sandys informed Robinson that he had only discussed the partition proposals in general terms with Macmillan, Maudling, Home and

[95] *Ibid.*, f. 120, Minutes of an Informal Meeting of the Federal Cabinet, 21 February 1962.

[96] *Ibid.*, f. 128, Evans to Robinson, 21 February 1962; 32/28, f. 11, Robinson to Welensky, 21 February 1962.

[97] *Ibid.*, 20/19, f. 125, Robinson to Welensky, 22 February 1962; 16/7, f. 11, Welensky's Address to the UFP Congress, 22 February 1962; *Daily Express*, 22 February 1962.

Kilmuir. However, they had preferred to settle the Northern Rhodesian Constitution before examining the wider Federal problem.[98]

While Welensky waited for the British decision, he was forced to advise Tshombe, who was facing fresh demands from the UN, to vacate certain bases. Tshombe had not yet succeeded in reaching an agreement with Adoula. Welensky also briefed Joelson and Lords Salisbury and Robins on Northern Rhodesia and warned that he was expecting Macmillan to perform one of "his usual tricks". In fact, Macmillan reveals that, while he was confident of settling the Northern Rhodesian question, he felt that it was only a preliminary to "the hideous trouble" which would result from the secession demands of Banda and Kaunda.

Welensky told Salisbury that Sandys had clearly indicated that Nyasaland would be given self-government in October. Sandys had examined the problem as a whole, he said, but it now appeared that Macmillan feared to tackle it and would merely introduce a new constitution for Northern Rhodesia on Thursday, 1 March. This decision was forcing him to fly to London, he explained. Describing the bitterness of the recent negotiations and "the lack of will to govern", Welensky claimed that Sandys had miscalculated because he believed that he would deal with a sick old man and was surprised to find that trouble invigorated him. It was Sandys, he said, who looked exhausted when they had finished.

Welensky added that the only British Minister whom he admired was Home. Sandys was a complete cynic because he could claim that, despite everything, he was an imperialist. Welensky had only sought some British resistance to Banda because that was all he needed to hold the Federation together. The time might have come to ignore Britain and declare independence. It would mean that he would have to arrest the Governor-General, Lord Dalhousie, and take care of a few other matters, but they did not amount to much. The biggest problem, Welensky felt, could be the attitude of the Federal High Court.

Welensky said nothing to Salisbury about the partition proposals which Sandys had carried to London, but told Lord Robins that, although they were most unpalatable, he was considering them for the sake of a final solution. Such consideration would be fruitless if Maudling decided only to settle the Northern Rhodesian constitutional issue on 1 March. Welensky said he resented the British art of piecemeal negotiations, which stripped one bare, and vowed he would not fall again for that ploy.[99]

Again considering tactics, Evans warned that success depended on swift action. He advised Welensky to fly to London before Maudling made any announcement on Northern Rhodesia's Constitution in the British Parliament as Sandys might not give sufficient warning for counter-action. He suggested a total onslaught on the British Government through interviews with the Press, and by attacks in the British Parliament by the friends of the Federation, assisted by Lords Malvern and Graham, who would travel to Britain for

[98] Welensky Papers, 20/2, f. 52, Robinson to Welensky, 23 February 1962.

[99] *Ibid.*, 20/14, f. 272, Welensky to Tshombe, 24 February 1962; 8/44, f. 1, Welensky to Joelson, February 1962; 43/*Salisbury*, Welensky to Salisbury, 25 February 1962; 25/240A, f. 45, Welensky to Lord Robins, 25 February 1962; Macmillan, *At the End of the Day*, *op. cit.*, p. 319.

that purpose. No one should be spared, and Sandys should be condemned along with Macmillan and Macleod. Evans felt that Sandys deserved this because of his callousness *vis-à-vis* the financial future of Nyasaland and because of his admission of the British lack of will to govern.

Evans recommended that the British Government be pilloried for its lack of decision, for its vacillation over Northern Rhodesia, and its frightened reaction to Kaunda's threats. The question should be asked why Kaunda was receiving so much attention when he was not even in the legislature. The British public should know the true, sad state of affairs — the callous view of its Government of the future of the Federation's people, as well as the damage being caused to the Federal economy. The British failure to keep promises had to be contrasted with Welensky's constant reasonable and helpful attitude. Maudling should be quoted as saying that his Government was seeking abortive and frustrated elections. A full account of the recent talks in Salisbury would reveal that Sandys had virtually ignored Northern Rhodesia, because the overall Federal problem seemed more important, and accordingly had taken with him proposals which might solve the wider problem, but of which nothing had since been heard. The next question was why so much time had been wasted on these proposals when the real intention was to impose an unacceptable Northern Rhodesian Constitution. It should be stated that a serious breach of faith would result if this Constitution was not shown to Welensky before it was released, and that it would be the latest on a formidable list of failures to consult the Federal Government. Welensky should warn that he could not continue to be reasonable and might impede the implementation of the Constitution and its operation. He could, like Kaunda, utter the threats which the British Government so feared. He might indicate that the Federal public was ready to cut the British connection. The British Government, Evans felt, should learn that the Europeans could be most defiant, aggressive and, if necessary, violent.[100]

When the British Cabinet held a sudden and lengthy meeting on the evening of 26 February, Robinson ascribed it to Federal pressure. The next day he telephoned W. S. Parker, Welensky's principal private secretary, to say that R. H. Turton, Wall and a number of other Tories had warned that Welensky would only weaken his position by coming to London that day, because he would appear to be trying to influence the British Cabinet before its decision, favourable or otherwise, was known. He might indeed provoke it to favour the African nationalists even more. He had to realise that the British public and most parliamentarians thought that only the Northern Rhodesian issue was at stake. Thus confusion would result and support would be lost if Welensky arrived demanding that the overall Federal problem should be settled first.

Robinson reported that Turton, the acknowledged leader of the pro-Federal backbenchers, had suggested that the Federal Government would have to be satisfied if the British Government postponed the decision on Northern Rhodesia to allow consideration of the new partition proposals. However, Turton had continued, the Federal Government would have to

[100] Welensky Papers, 20/19, f. 170, Evans's Memorandum, 26 February 1962.

welcome a decision to implement the Northern Rhodesian proposals as it might trick the Labour Party and the African nationalists into denouncing them. Then it could be argued that the proposals should be shelved. Welensky should only come to London if the Asian seat were dropped. He would then attract backbench support because the June settlement was being breached. Wall had agreed with Turton, Robinson said, but thought the British Government might yet have something to offer.[101]

Within the hour, Welensky telephoned Robinson to reject Turton's idea because it ignored the breaking of promises. Robinson, however, had news from Martin Redmayne, the Conservative chief whip, of a likely compromise: the Asian seat would be retained but the number of racially-reserved seats would not be increased. Welensky received this coldly as reason enough to fly to London. Although Sandys was to brief Robinson at 3 p.m., Welensky said he would board the aircraft because the British decision would jeopardise the Federation by installing an anti-Federal Government in Northern Rhodesia. He would make a stand on the June settlement and, unless something else happened, he would fly that evening.

Robinson then warned of the disarray of the Federal supporters over whether the wider Federal settlement should take preference. Nonetheless, he said that Turton was intending to warn Macmillan not to depart from the June agreement. However, Redmayne had argued that there had only been an oral agreement in June but had been answered by Turton producing the relevant document with which Robinson had furnished him. Robinson and Welensky concluded that Macmillan was likely to advance the same argument.[102]

Sandys informed Robinson that afternoon that he had written to Welensky telling him that the decision would be taken on the Northern Rhodesian Constitution, making the two changes which the Federal Government had been prepared to accept. However, it was impossible to grant the *quid pro quo* of increasing the racially-reserved seats, but this seemed unimportant. The changes which were to be made (and which would tip the balance in Kaunda's favour) were the elimination of the numerical alternative and the reduction of the minimum percentage to ten. Robinson, nevertheless, replied that Welensky would want the *quid pro quo.* He warned Sandys that his dispatch had to arrive in Salisbury early because Welensky was deciding whether or not to fly to London.[103] Sandys gave no reasons for the decision, but Macmillan has since revealed that he was deeply troubled by the prospect of renewed violence in Northern Rhodesia and a demand for the UN to examine political liberty in Southern Rhodesia. It appeared to him and his Cabinet that the disintegration of the Federation was certain because inevitably a Northern Rhodesian demand for secession would follow that of Nyasaland. Thus all the Cabinet agreed to risk drastic Federal action and to settle Northern Rhodesia. Maudling was the only dissenter, but was eventually persuaded and the decision was taken on 27 February.[104]

[101] *Ibid.*, f. 7, Telephone conversation between Robinson and W. S. Parker, 27 February 1962.
[102] *Ibid.*, f. 10, Telephone conversation between Welensky and Robinson, 27 February 1962.
[103] *Ibid.*, f. 28, Sandys to Robinson, 27 February 1962; f. 29, Robinson to Sandys, 27 February 1962.
[104] Macmillan, *At the End of the Day*, *op. cit.*, p. 320; R. Maudling, *Memoirs* (London, 1978), p. 99.

Despite Robinson's urging, Sandys did not hurry and Welensky, waiting impatiently in Salisbury would hear first from the Press that Maudling would make the announcement on Northern Rhodesia on the morrow. At 6.20 p.m. Welensky warned Robinson that nothing had arrived, but immediately thereafter Alport drove up to his house bearing Sandys's dispatch. As time was short, Alport read the dispatch to Welensky and then urged again that Welensky should not go to London. He argued that a strong card would simply be discarded. He believed it would be unwise to appeal to the British public and Parliament over the head of the British Government. He did not say that he suspected that Welensky was beginning to bore the British and that, once he did, his cause was lost.

Welensky thanked Alport and excused him from attending his departure at the airport. However, Alport drove to the airport and was received coldly by the Federal Ministers gathered there. He denies that the late arrival of Sandys's dispatch was designed to deter Welensky from travelling, but knew that Welensky thought this. However, he did not feel inclined to make excuses because not only was his advice being ignored but he was confident that Welensky would not embarrass the British Government and would only diminish his personal standing.[105]

Welensky read the dispatch on the aircraft. In it, Sandys related how he had informed the British Cabinet that Welensky feared that even the arrangement in June would produce a pro-secession majority and that, if secession were granted to Nyasaland, it could not be refused to Northern Rhodesia. Sandys said he had produced the partition proposals and had explained that they were the product of a search by himself and Welensky for a means to secure popular acceptance of the Federation. He had stressed that change had to be achieved on the basis of consent and that, at an appropriate moment, each territory would be offered the option of secession. He had warned the Cabinet, however, that Welensky preferred to deny any right of secession and, in particular, was fearful of losing the riches of the Copperbelt for Southern Rhodesia. He had told of Welensky's prediction that the general election in Southern Rhodesia would produce a pro-secession majority which would immediately take advantage of any right to secede and that, for this reason, Welensky wanted the Northern Rhodesian decision postponed to allow for consideration of a wider Federal scheme. The British Cabinet had been unconvinced, and had decided that the Northern Rhodesian issue had to be settled because it had been under discussion for more than a year, and because it was clear that an early settlement of the wider Federal problem was impossible. It had also been influenced by the conclusion of the Federal Review that there could be no progress until the territorial Constitutions had been settled. Thus, Sandys said, Maudling would announce the next day that the June settlement would be upheld with the two changes. The British Cabinet was prepared thereafter to tackle the wider constitutional problems of the Federation.[106]

Welensky's departure was not kept secret and the Press soon gathered that Macmillan did not welcome his arrival. When Maudling announced the

[105] Welensky, *4 000 Days*, *op. cit.*, p. 321; Alport, *The Sudden Assignment*, *op. cit.*, pp. 170–171.
[106] Welensky Papers, 20/2, ff. 49–50, Sandys to Welensky, 27 February 1962.

changes, they were so slight in the eyes of the British Press that it wondered why Welensky had come to London. Nonetheless, Macmillan did not see Welensky until Maudling had made the announcement. In his account, Welensky does not refer to the meeting in detail, but Macmillan, in his, claims that, appearing calm but subdued, he only half-heartedly complained about the delay of the dispatch. Macmillan, who did not really understand why Welensky had come over, says he then had to endure a barrage of complaints about the treatment meted out to Welensky over the years. Welensky warned that he would dissolve his Parliament and seek a mandate to save the Federation. Macmillan did not feel inclined to ask him for his reasons, or if he would use force to preserve the Federation because of his complaint that the Press continually misinterpreted his use of the word "fight".[107]

If Welensky had been subdued in Macmillan's presence, he did not hide his annoyance from Sandys when, on 1 March, he replied to his dispatch describing how he had waited all afternoon on 27 February and then had only received a rough draft from Alport. He had to learn first from the Press that Maudling would make his announcement on the next afternoon and was only allowed to see Macmillan after the deed was done.

He would not accept Sandys's account of their discussion as, for example, while he had never pretended to like the June settlement, he had never said he thought it would produce a pro-secession majority. In fact, he had believed that, if a pro-Federal party was not returned to power, there would be a stalemate. The point which he had made on Nyasaland's secession was that it would be difficult thereafter to retain Northern Rhodesia unless the Federation was made independent on Nyasaland's departure. He had never said that Nyasaland was beyond redemption and, indeed, his demand for firmness had brought the "loss of will" reply. It was only thereafter that he had reconsidered the desirability of keeping Nyasaland in the Federation. He reminded Sandys that he had asked for compensation for the Europeans who were forced to leave, for Nyasaland to meet its share of the public debt, and for a guarantee for abolition-of-office terms for all civil servants. He had never spoken of the danger of losing the Copperbelt but of Central Rhodesia, which was considerably larger. He had also made the point that an immediate decision on Northern Rhodesia would prejudice the settlement of the whole Federal problem.

It was pointless, Welensky maintained, to refer to eleventh hours when it was the British Government which had decided in September to overturn the June agreement. Such action had led him to question the value of reconvening the Federal Review. The real issue, he said, which had escaped the British Cabinet was that, as long as the Northern Rhodesian settlement was regarded as more important, a wider solution was impossible. The prospects of the latter were made less likely by an impending visit by Banda to London. As experience had taught that conferences did not serve to settle constitutions, he would write off the Federal Review. He was not prepared to accept any changes to the June settlement because it was a definite agreement with

[107] *The Rhodesia Herald*, 28 February & 1 March 1962; Macmillan, *At the End of the Day*, *op. cit.*, p. 321.

him, on the strength of which the Southern Rhodesian referendum campaign had been fought. As the agreement had been broken unilaterally, he would have to make his own dispositions to meet the new situation. He could only assume that Maudling's decision to advance the Northern Rhodesian announcement to 28 February was designed to ensure that he would not have the opportunity, which he had frequently sought, to have final discussions with Macmillan. He had not even been given the courtesy of a reply to his requests for those discussions.[108]

Welensky had failed to dissuade Maudling from taking the piecemeal decision on Northern Rhodesia, but at least he had, through his persistence, secured a moderation thereof which was something the Press misunderstood. However, he knew that, with Banda calling stridently for secession, the end was nigh unless he could induce the British Government to show greater resolution in its support for the Federation. He would have to change course and needed the support of his electorate. However, he could not know that Macmillan was contemplating yet another ministerial change in the hope of salvaging something of the Federation, or, perhaps, of dispatching it with full decorum.

[108] Welensky Papers, 20/19, f. 73, Welensky to Sandys, 1 March 1962.

CHAPTER THIRTY-TWO

The Appointment of Butler

The Responses of Macmillan and Welensky to the Future of the Federation, March–April 1962

MACMILLAN has revealed that by 28 February 1962 he had concluded that the system of using both the Commonwealth Relations Office and the Colonial Office to deal with the Federation and its territories was impossibly cumbersome. He believes also that it was being used by "all the local notables" to render negotiations difficult through accusations of broken faith and the conflict of policies. He decided to create the single ministry which the Federal Government had sought for so long. However, he gave no hint of his intention to Welensky who, as has been seen, decided that, in the circumstances created by Maudling's decision on Northern Rhodesia, he needed a fresh mandate. He would confess that he would not have done this if Macmillan had only indicated his intentions.[1]

Macmillan would keep the conversations going, despite the strained atmosphere, while he made his new dispositions, and thus said nothing about them when he, Sandys and Maudling met Welensky, Greenfield and Robinson on 1 March.

He welcomed the chance for a general discussion while Welensky was in London. Agreeing, Welensky felt that the prospects of a settlement had been made immeasurably more difficult by Maudling's announcement. Maudling later disagreed with his verdict. Macmillan raised the reconvening of the Federal Review, but Welensky evinced no enthusiasm. When Macmillan asked if Nyasaland was quiet, Welensky said that it was only superficially so and complained that his Government was not being supported by the Colonial officials. This prompted Macmillan to enquire if the Nyasalanders were using the Federal services and paying their taxes. Welensky said that they were but that he knew, however, that economic benefits meant little to Banda and the Malawi Congress Party. Agreeing, Sandys pointed to the resistance to the

[1] H. Macmillan, *At the End of the Day* (London, 1973), p. 321; Fed R & N *Debates* (Salisbury), Vol. 18, Col. 27, 26 June 1962.

Nkula Falls scheme. He advised waiting for Banda to demand secession but, in the meantime, deciding on policy. Macmillan expected Banda's mandate to force him to do something about secession.

Sandys asked if the Federal Government wanted to hold Nyasaland by force, and earned a rebuke from Macmillan. Then Welensky claimed that his Government was wooing the African, but Macmillan was more interested in Banda's intentions. Sandys predicted that Banda would bluntly ask whether secession would be allowed and that, if it were not, he and his Party would resign from the Government. It was a matter of great regret to Macmillan, Sandys and Maudling that principle should come before practicality and that secession was more important than economics. Macmillan wondered if Banda would secure foreign aid, and Welensky replied that the Russians and Americans would give him enough to make trouble, but not to become a pensioner.

Welensky only answered obliquely a question on what he wanted done, pointing out that it would take a year to implement the new Northern Rhodesian Constitution which would add another year to the last four years of waiting for the Federal settlement, during which the economy had run down. Macmillan was not so pessimistic because he felt elections could be held in the Rhodesias by October. Thereafter Nyasaland's desires could be met and the Federal issue settled, completely clearing the air. Maudling was prepared to offer Banda secession, provided that it was effected in an orderly manner.

Welensky claimed that, through intimidation, the MCP was already the *de facto* Government. He added that his UFP could have reached the same position if it had used the same tactics. It was also necessary to stress that, despite years of being several steps ahead of Nyasaland, Northern Rhodesia had not yet achieved the current constitutional position of Nyasaland. Maudling attributed that to the dominance of a single Party, but Welensky maintained that nonetheless 15 years of virtual self-government in Northern Rhodesia had been ignored.

Macmillan raised the tentative proposals for the Federation, asking whether Northern Rhodesia could be partitioned when it had been founded in such an arbitrary fashion. Welensky replied that there was some merit in the scheme because it would satisfy Banda and the Litunga, and offer Kaunda the premiership of a large territory, while everyone enjoyed the economic benefits of the Federation. Welensky said he would give every territory the right to secede except for Central Northern Rhodesia and Southern Rhodesia, lest their credit-worthiness be destroyed. Although the partition contradicted everything he stood for, he felt he could justify it because it would provide some stability. Kaunda and Banda would secede, but the Litunga would not, leaving a federation of three states.

Welensky asked for the implementation of partition as soon as possible. Maudling, however, doubted that the majority of the Barotse would want to stay in the Federation. He provoked Welensky to retort that the British had given the guarantee to the Litunga and therefore were bound to support him. There was no apparent threat to the Litunga's authority who was assisted only by elderly councillors and a handful of police. Maudling ignored him.

Macmillan asked about the situation on the Copperbelt, and Welensky replied that it was quiet, although there was a possibility of a strike. Maudling, confirming this, added gloomily that it could spread. Welensky doubted that it would without intimidation, and regretted that the British Government always yielded to such threats. Stung, Macmillan reminded Welensky that it was to him that the British Government had surrendered in March 1961 over the Macleod White Paper on Northern Rhodesia. He knew of many situations, Cyprus, for example, which could have been held if the British had copied the Germans in stringing people up in villages. The French, after deploying a million men in Algeria, had still suffered a humiliating defeat. It was naïve, he charged, to think one could exercise control by force, and declared he was unlikely ever to use British troops for that purpose.

Welensky angrily dismissed the Algerian analogy because, he said, the transfer of power to the black majority in the Federation had been accepted. All that was sought was a reasonable policy, and he was simply arguing that enclaves for moderates might be needed. What the British Government failed to appreciate was that African political advancement in the Federation had been faster than elsewhere in Africa. The African nationalist pursued immediate power while Welensky said he preferred development at a reasonable pace. He acknowledged that he embarrassed the British Government, but he had come to London because a solution was imperative as unemployment was growing. He had no wish to fight a rearguard action and knew that the Rhodesians could join the South Africans, but he did not like *apartheid.* However, it was clear that, if the Federation were dissolved, Southern Rhodesia would have to look south because she could not survive alone. The fate of the moderate African had to be considered, as widespread intimidation had already made his life intolerable. Such Africans, he averred, had suffered dreadfully when Kaunda had last indulged in murder and arson.

Macmillan inquired if Kaunda was responsible for the emergency of September, and Maudling admitted that he was. Then Macmillan asked Welensky if the strength and stability of the Federation would be affected by Nyasaland's departure. Welensky replied it would not be, but claimed that the precedent would have been set for Kaunda.

Summing up, Sandys deduced that the main problem was to keep Central Northern Rhodesia and Southern Rhodesia together. He said the immediate aim was to retain the multi-racial Parties in power to prevent secession. However, he believed it was necessary to have a contingency plan to meet the situation which would arise, if two months thereafter Banda was told that secession was impossible for the time being.[2]

On television that evening, Welensky brusquely dismissed again the parallel with Algeria. In Salisbury *The Rhodesia Herald* revealed for the first time that the Federal mobilisation of February 1961 had not been for the defence of the Federation's border with Katanga, as the public had been led to believe, but had been in response to a discovery of a British military build-up in Kenya at the height of the argument over Macleod's original proposals for Northern Rhodesia. The build-up, the newspaper said, had been to pre-empt any

[2] Welensky Papers, 20/19, f. 68, Minutes of Meeting with Macmillan and Sandys, 1 March 1962.

Federal resistance to the imposition of the proposals, but the mobilisation had rendered this impossible and in fact had caused the abandonment of the proposals themselves.[3]

Whitehead flew to London to join Welensky and Greenfield in their meeting with Sandys and Maudling on 2 March. Sandys continued to ponder on what could be said to Banda when he arrived in London, but Welensky said he found it difficult to help because his own views on the unacceptability of secession were too well known. He simply advised that Banda be informed that "there is no such thing as secession", which might induce him to remove himself and the MCP from the Executive Council and force Jones to form another Government. Alternatively, Jones could govern by decree or nominate official Members to fill the vacant places on the Council. However, Sandys wondered if this could be done peacefully. Welensky thought that it might not, but felt that he could not be asked to succumb to Banda's threats of opposition and bloodshed.

Whitehead, growing impatient, interjected that the problem of Nyasaland could not be isolated and that an overall plan for the Federation had to be presented to Banda when he arrived in London. In response, Sandys asked if it would be necessary to partition Northern Rhodesia, and Whitehead acknowledged that therein lay a germ of a permanent settlement. He feared that, if the problem were not settled soon, the UN would use the excuse of internal unrest to intervene. He believed that the solution was to make the Federation independent. Maudling wondered about the reaction of the Northern Rhodesians to partition, but was ignored by Whitehead who began pressing the scheme, calling it his "Northern Ireland" solution. He believed that the Federation's survival depended solely on large-scale investment and the retention of white skills. He warned that fourth and fifth generation white Rhodesians could not be persuaded that they lived on sufferance, that their livelihoods could be removed at will and that racialists could tell them how long they could stay. Nonetheless, he said, they would share and work with Africans in a scheme such as his because the prospects were so good. There was, however, not a moment to be lost.

Welensky agreed that Nyasaland could not be dealt with in isolation but warned that he would not make any suggestions as to how Nyasaland could be accommodated. Undeterred, Sandys maintained that it was Welensky's responsibility to solve the problem. However, Welensky would not yield because he said he was totally committed to the Federation and probably should not have considered partition in the first place. Clearly, he added, the Federal Review could not be reconvened and that the Federation's future had to be decided by the Governments.

Whitehead remained adamant that his was the only course and that a quick solution was needed if economic catastrophe were to be avoided. Sandys obstinately maintained that the "ball" was with Welensky. Equally obstinate, Welensky continued to lay the responsibility at the British door. They provoked Whitehead to admonish them for quibbling. He proposed to take the initiative and to submit a plan to them for consideration. Unabashed, Welen-

[3] *The Rhodesia Herald*, 2 March 1962.

sky replied that his duty was simply to keep the Federation intact, but Sandys continued to demand proposals from him lest the fate of the Federation itself be considered in isolation.

Whitehead reminded them that the situation was serious and could not be allowed to drift into violence. He said he was prepared to formulate proposals because the future of Southern Rhodesia was at stake. There was no time to haggle because the threat from the Afro-Asians had to be met, and there should be no surrender to racialists. He remained confident of finding a solution but warned that the immediate excision of Nyasaland could not be contemplated because it would set a precedent for demands from an African nationalist government in Northern Rhodesia. If frustrated, that government would nationalise the copper mines and endanger Federal revenue. Quiet consideration was needed but he preferred, with good reason, that the credit for anything which he produced should be given to Macmillan.

Maudling agreed that someone had to take the initiative but feared a violent reaction to the transfer of parts of Northern Rhodesia to Southern Rhodesia. He asked how Whitehead's idea differed from the Dominion Party's long-standing proposal for a Central African Alliance. Whitehead explained that the DP's Alliance did not contemplate a multi-racial parliament and that its proposed two African states in Northern Rhodesia would not be part of the Federation. Sandys questioned how Whitehead's ideas could be implemented and was told that the first step would be an agreement between the Governments. Then the boundaries would be drawn and the two outer Northern Rhodesian territories (Barotseland and North-Eastern) would be given the option of secession. The territorial representation in the Federal Assembly would be revised, but he warned that Southern Rhodesia would not tolerate the possibility that the Federal Government could be racialist in character. Central Northern Rhodesia and Southern Rhodesia, as the kernel of the Federation, could not have the option to secede because together they represented the areas of greatest investment and produced all the revenue. An African-dominated Federal Government was not feared provided it was not racialist in character. Whitehead said he would strive to prevent an uneducated African majority from securing power, but accepted it as a necessary risk. He would not, however, permit a stampede to allow the irresponsible to take control. Partition would leave Britain responsible for only a million Africans in Central Northern Rhodesia, thus considerably reducing its current responsibility. As he could see many advantages in his proposal, he sought the British reaction.

Before the British Ministers could reply Welensky indicated that he concurred but still would not propose anything of his own. The British seemed at a loss over Whitehead's proposals because Maudling only expressed anxiety about keeping them secret, while Sandys reminded Whitehead that Britain had a responsibility to make its own decisions.

Whitehead dismissed these comments as unhelpful, but understood Welensky's position. Indeed, he felt that it was quite "monstrous" to ask Welensky to produce proposals along the lines suggested by Sandys. He agreed that the British had very definite responsibilities and one of them was to find a solution. Welensky, agreeing, confessed to being intrigued that his advice was being sought when hitherto it had been ignored. Sandys suggested that Whitehead commit his thoughts to paper for consideration by the British and Federal Governments. The meeting agreed, but warned that something would have to be ready before Banda arrived. It thought that some unanimity was necessary by the end of March or the position would be intolerable, and even desperate.[4]

The next day Whitehead submitted "A New Plan for Central Africa". In this, after an economic and historical survey, he insisted on a permanent and genuinely non-racial settlement to preserve for everyone's benefit the £200 000 000 which had been invested in the Federation. The settlement had to be swiftly implemented to avoid complete disaster. He intended that the new central state (Central Northern Rhodesia and Southern Rhodesia) should adopt the 1961 Southern Rhodesian Constitution but preferred the current Nyasaland formula for North-Eastern Northern Rhodesia. Barotseland would have full autonomy and the option to secede. To accommodate Banda, Nyasaland would be offered either economic ties or secession. The two African states in Northern Rhodesia (Barotseland and North-Eastern) would achieve self-government at an early stage but, in view of the growing Afro-Asian interference, the new central state had to be independent immediately after its first general election. Whitehead hoped that, as its prosperity grew and its non-racial character became apparent, the other territories would be encouraged to take advantage of an association with the new central state. He concluded with a warning that, if nothing were done, the danger of a clash with African nationalism would continue to impair the economic prospects of the whole area.[5]

Whitehead left public comment to Welensky who explained to the Press why he had come to Britain. He denied that his journey was a last desperate attempt to induce the British Government to change course, as he had known an hour before he flew that Maudling would make his announcement the next day. He had known that he could not influence the decision, but had come to state his objections and to consider the effects of the decision. His main objection, he said, was that the changes favoured those who wanted to dismember the Federation. This was not surprising, he claimed, because the British Government had never helped materially with the building of the Federation or the fostering of partnership. The Federation, unlike other countries, had received no British money except for the University College in Salisbury and he suggested that those who alleged that advancement was too slow should provide means to accelerate it. The Federation should have at least received the moral support of the British Government, but every constitutional change it had effected had only increased Federal difficulties. He had sought the views on the Federation of Macmillan, Maudling and Sandys, but had not received an unequivocal reply. The British Government had also disregarded the interests of moderate Africans, yet they were in the majority and had made the policy of partnership possible, despite intimidation. The moderates would have no place if the extremists succeeded in their aims. The current Northern Rhodesian Constitution had ensured that multi-racial poli-

[4] Welensky Papers, 20/19, f. 62, Minutes of a Meeting with Sandys and Maudling, 2 March 1962.
[5] *Ibid.*, 7/34, ff. 23–28, Whitehead's Memorandum, 3 March 1962.

tics could thrive but, before it was two years old, the British decided on radical change, providing not only increased African representation, but making it easy for the anti-Federal African nationalist to secure power.

Welensky said he had tried to persuade the British Government to give the pro-Federal Parties a sporting chance. In June 1961, he had, with difficulty, secured a final and very definite agreement with Macmillan which left the scales precariously balanced between the pro- and anti-Federal elements. Thereupon Kaunda had led a campaign of violence in the Northern and Luapula Provinces to induce the British Government to make changes in favour of his Party. After a wave of murder, rape and robbery, the security forces re-established control. Then, to Federal dismay, the British Government decided to re-open the constitutional question, thus indicating clearly that violence paid. As he had believed that the June 1961 settlement was final, Welensky said he had therefore misled the Southern Rhodesian electorate. The only result of Maudling's decision would be frustrated elections which, apparently, the British did not mind because the Governor could then rule directly. However, the experience of the Governor ruling in Nyasaland, with the Executive Council advising him, was not encouraging because, in reality, Banda ruled. Frustrated elections would provoke fresh violence and further changes to suit the extremist. The British anxiety to bring in a UNIP government puzzled Welensky when its journal, *Voice of UNIP*, had idolised the murderers of Mrs Burton, and UNIP itself had 2 000 members convicted for their misdeeds. It was encouraging to find that the British public was tiring of continual surrenders to racial extremism. Thus he appealed to the British Government to re-examine its policies, even at that late hour, and seek a fresh solution to secure the continuance of the Federation and its early independence with territorial governments which were totally responsible.[6]

Passing through London, Nkomo also issued a statement saying that the days when Britain took decisions for colonial peoples had gone. Thus the current negotiations with Welensky and Whitehead were pointless because there was no African participation. He had just returned from New York, he said, where he had successfully appealed to the UN for an inquiry into the status of Southern Rhodesia. He knew that Welensky and Whitehead were opposed to the UN inquiry and he concluded that the current negotiations were being held in secret, without Africans, "to preserve the Union Jack".[7]

Leaving for Salisbury on 3 March, Welensky was considerably irritated by a last effort by Sandys to convince him that he was really a true friend of the Federation. Sandys did not deter Welensky from informing the Governor-General on 4 March that he intended to dissolve the Parliament. Four days later, before dissolving it, he briefed the Federal Assembly and declared that he would seek a mandate to resist the dissolution of the Federation and to negotiate an improved Federal Constitution. If necessary, he said he would use force to preserve the Federation.[8]

An immediate result of Maudling's settlement of the Northern Rhodesian

[6] *Ibid.*, 20/6, ff. 73–77, Welensky's Press Statement, 2 March 1962.

[7] *The Rhodesia Herald*, 3 March 1962.

[8] Welensky Papers, 32/28, f. 16, Welensky to A. E. P. Robinson, 4 March 1962; Fed R & N *Debates* (Salisbury), Vol. 17, Col. 824, 8 March 1962.

Constitution was a decision by Kaunda to seek election for the first time to the Legislative Council. Nevertheless, he made this conditional upon: delimitation by an independent commission; the refusal by the Governor to nominate anyone to fill seats rendered vacant by frustrated elections; the postponement of the Federal Review until Northern Rhodesia had acquired elected representation of the majority; an amnesty for all banned and imprisoned political leaders; and the holding of the general election earlier than October.[9]

The other result, of course, was Welensky's decision to dissolve Parliament which provoked Alport to secure an interview with him. As has been seen, he had believed that Welensky should not have gone to London because he would only have considerably diminished his standing in Britain and the Federation. It seemed to Alport, during the interview, that Welensky had realised his mistake. Alport had discovered from Field, in Welensky's absence, that his Dominion Party would boycott any election because he thought it would be irresponsible and ill-timed to hold one. Field's attitude, therefore, made empty Welensky's gesture in dissolving Parliament and encouraged Alport to tell Welensky that he would regret making it. However, Welensky told Alport that he had to wrest the initiative from British hands because they were allowing matters to drift.

Later, Alport discovered that Whitehead also regretted that the election was being held, but conceded that it was the right of any prime minister to call one when he thought fit. However, all the African nationalist Parties in the Federation decided to join the Dominion Party's boycott of the Federal election. Nkumbula greeted the announcement with the cry: "Hallelujah! Sir Roy has killed the Federation himself."[10]

Field had told the Press that the Federation's current form could only be maintained by force and that at least four battalions from Southern Rhodesia would be required in Nyasaland. He could not understand why Welensky needed a fresh mandate, and revealed that the DP no longer favoured a unitary government for Northern and Southern Rhodesia because of the deterioration of the northern situation. Welensky acknowledged the criticism but, nonetheless, maintained that he needed to sound his electorate. A further consideration, he said, was that there would shortly be elections in Northern and Southern Rhodesia, and probably in Britain.[11]

Nevertheless, Lords Salisbury and Boyd were puzzled. Salisbury pointed out to Robinson that Welensky had declared to the Federal Assembly that he would refuse under any circumstances to accept the Federal dissolution but, in the same breath, had indicated that he would consider proposals which would maintain the Federation in a different form. It was urgently necessary to clarify this, Salisbury said, because the British anti-Federal elements wished to exploit what they saw as his too rigid stance and the more flexible attitude of Whitehead. Salisbury felt that, if Welensky pinned his hopes on maintaining the Federation in its current form, he would deny himself room to manoeuvre. For example, he asked, what would Welensky do if, with

[9] D. C. Mulford, *Zambia: The Politics of Independence, 1957–1964* (London, 1967), p. 227.
[10] Lord Alport, *The Sudden Assignment* (London, 1965), pp. 172 & 178.
[11] *The Rhodesia Herald*, 10 March 1962; *The Sunday Mail*, 11 March 1962.

British approval, Banda demanded secession? The supporters of the Federation were particularly anxious that there should be no cleavage between Welensky and Whitehead because of their significant British following. Together they made a strong team. Salisbury advised that Welensky should proclaim that, while he would not shirk his responsibilities, he would consider anything which would serve the Federation's interests.

Lord Boyd told Robinson that he was surprised by Welensky's attitude because, when he left London, he had indicated that he would seriously consider the Whitehead plan. He wondered if Welensky feared that the British Government might accuse him of being the first to suggest the Federal break-up. Like Salisbury, Boyd urged that Welensky should seek a mandate to consider anything, including the Whitehead plan. He should also declare that any changes were dependent on a firm British undertaking that there would be no further erosion. Boyd, for his part, would seek a declaration from men like Lord Chandos to support any such solution.[12]

Before Welensky could reply to Salisbury and Boyd, Macmillan at last decided to inform him of his intention to create the Central African Office to handle the affairs of the Federation and its territories.[13] It is clear that, apart from the current cumbersome arrangement of using both thc Colonial and Commonwealth Relations Offices, he was tired of the ministerial conflicts between Sandys and Macleod, and Macleod's successor, Maudling. In any case, at official level, throughout the Federal period there seems to have been no love lost between the Commonwealth Relations and Colonial Offices.

On 9 March Macmillan persuaded R. A. Butler to accept the new portfolio in addition to his existing one of the Home Office. Butler had some knowledge of Southern Rhodesia from his relatives, the Courtaulds in Umtali, and Welensky had already drawn him into discussions on Federal problems. Although Welensky was unlikely to have known it, Butler also opposed, within the Cabinet, the appointment of the Monckton Commission. Moreover, unlike Sandys and Maudling, Butler was not entirely despondent about the Federation. He accepted the portfolio after Lord Home had expressed the hope that something of the Federation might be saved and after Macmillan had been even more persuasive, telling him that he "could make his name". (This was a belief which Butler would share with many other British Ministers who dealt with Rhodesia.) He, however, knew that his reputation was at stake but accepted out of a sense of duty as well as one of adventure.[14]

On what he recalls as 17 March, but which appears to have been two days earlier, Alport reached the same conclusion as Macmillan on a Central African department. A year previously he had suggested a single ministry and, he says, that night he pressed it again on the Commonwealth Relations Office. He was ignorant of Butler's acceptance of 9 March but, in the early hours of 16 March, telegrams for Welensky arrived telling of the creation of the new department. Macmillan, however, warned that this did not herald a change in policy. Alport conveyed the telegrams to Welensky and records his

[12] Welensky Papers, 32/28, f. 15, Robinson to Welensky, 13 March 1962.
[13] *Ibid.*, 20/2, f. 47, Macmillan to Welensky, 15 March 1962.
[14] Macmillan, *At the End of the Day*, *op. cit.*, p. 322; Lord Butler, *The Art of the Possible: The Memoirs of Lord Butler* (London, 1973), p. 211.

"profound astonishment" and his confession that, if he had known this, he would not have called an election. Welensky told Alport that he had left London convinced that Macmillan would do nothing to assist him, but it cheered him to think that at least his visit had achieved this change. Alport faulted this reasoning but, pitying Welensky, felt that he should not disabuse him.[15] Whatever Alport thought, it is clear that the discord over Northern Rhodesia and other issues had prompted Macmillan to make the change. Maudling would have no more to do with the Rhodesias, but the Rhodesians had not seen the last of Sandys.

If Welensky was as astounded and mortified as Alport suggests, his letters do not betray this. To Robinson, Welensky claimed to be shaken, not by Macmillan's move, but by Lords Salisbury and Boyd doubting his willingness to negotiate, although he had told them that he had given Sandys alternative tentative proposals. Justifying his dissolution of Parliament, Welensky claimed to have been in an impossible situation while he lacked a mandate to negotiate any changes. He proposed to tell the electorate what had happened and felt that, with a new British Minister, the negotiations could start afresh. He would inform Butler that he would negotiate on anything short of the Federation's demise. Welensky said that his reason for making this assertion was his discovery that Sandys, in trying hard to get him to advance alternative proposals, was putting him in the position that, if he agreed to Nyasaland's secession, the entire blame for the break-up of the Federation could be pinned on him and not on Sandys. He added that Sandys would not admit any British responsibility for Nyasaland's share of the public debt or for the fate of the civil servants who would be rendered redundant. However, Welensky did not want to be saddled with millions of pounds worth of expenditure simply because the British lacked "guts". He warned Robinson that he would not renew any negotiations until he was returned to Parliament. He reiterated that he had advanced the tentative partition proposals as merely a basis for discussion because they would present such great difficulties for the British Government. Yet he had agreed that Whitehead should continue his negotiations on them during the Federal electoral campaign. He expected that the idea of the rump of Northern Rhodesia being included in an indissoluble federation with Southern Rhodesia would be more acceptable than Whitehead's suggestion of the amalgamation of these two areas on the Northern Ireland pattern.[16]

Welensky was not alone in arriving at this conclusion because on the previous day, 15 March, Lord Robins had written to him in this vein. Butler, whom Robinson saw immediately, wanted to visit the Federation but agreed to wait until after the Federal general election. When he expressed his anxiety about a solution, Robinson immediately warned him that, although he was open to suggestion, Welensky would not propose anything. Thus Robinson urged Butler to take the initiative.[17]

[15] Alport, *The Sudden Assignment*, *op. cit.*, pp. 174–175; Welensky Papers, 20/2, f. 47, Macmillan to Welensky, 15 March 1962.

[16] Welensky Papers, 32/28, f. 17, Welensky to Robinson, 16 March 1962.

[17] *Ibid.*, 25/240A, f. 40, Lord Robins to Welensky, 15 March 1962; 20/2, ff. 41–42, Robinson to Welensky, 16 March 1962.

Welensky and Whitehead publicly welcomed Macmillan's decision to establish the Central African Office, while the Labour Party cried, "Resign". Gaitskell described it as one of the most extraordinary decisions in his experience. Sir John Moffat thought it "a very bad move", while the Rhodesian Press considered it sound, if it was intended to give the handling of Federal affairs an appearance of firmness. The Zimbabwe African People's Union saw it as a "subtle manoeuvre" of British collusion with "the settler" to achieve Federal independence under white domination.[18]

Welensky could not dwell on Macmillan's new move because he had to reply to Alport on Northern Rhodesia. On Saturday, 10 March, Alport had handed him the draft of the Northern Rhodesia (Electoral Provisions) Order in Council, 1962, and asked for his comments by Monday, 12 March. Yet another British request for an urgent answer over the weekend brought the inevitable refusal, and Welensky only answered by 16 March. It also annoyed him that such documents were always presented unannounced and in a piecemeal fashion. He noted that the declaration of rights had not been included. He objected not only to the departure from the normal practice of allowing the Legislative Council to decide the disqualification of voters but to the failure even to hint at this departure in the negotiations, or to indicate that the existing disqualifications would be changed. The matter was not purely academic, he said, because it was apparent that it would be possible for convicted criminals to qualify. The Federal Government opposed both the method and the intention of this change. Also objectionable was a provision allowing changes to the Order in Council by regulation, thereby by-passing the Executive and Legislative Councils. In the Federal view, any such alteration had to be effected through the legislature. The Order in Council specified the residence qualifications of voters, but the Federal Government felt it should be determined by the Legislative Council. The Federal Government opposed the re-registration of existing voters and disapproved of the delimitation proposals. It objected to Coloureds being allowed to choose, for electoral purposes, to be Asians or Europeans, as they had always been classified as Europeans on the voters' roll and no separate record had been kept of them. Welensky wondered who would determine whether or not a man was a Coloured.

After listing other smaller points, Welensky came to the intention to apply the new Constitution to Barotseland. As he knew that the Litunga and his Government opposed it, he urged that the whole matter be reconsidered. Finally, he reminded Alport that the agreement of June 1961 specified that the Federal Government would be consulted on the terms of reference of the judicial commission of delimitation and he trusted that this would happen soon.[19]

London and Lusaka took a week to reply. Alport was asked to point out to Welensky that the Order in Council was only a pilot order to allow the registration of voters to begin. Its provisions, he said, would be subsumed in a later comprehensive order in council which could not be ready for some months. However, it was necessary to complete the registration by the end of

[18] *The Rhodesia Herald*, 16 March 1962; *Evening Standard*,16 March 1962.

[19] Welensky Papers, 20/7, f. 57, Welensky to Alport, 16 March 1962.

June, and by then the Federal Government would have been consulted on the delimitation commission. The inclusion of the voters' qualifications was right in the current circumstances, Alport maintained, and, indeed, it was expected that the Federal Government would bless the decision that the legislature could not alter them. It followed that the disqualifications should be similarly treated. The use of regulations rather than an ordinance would allow the Governor to proceed with the registration, but copies of the regulations would be forwarded to the Federal Government. Welensky's point on the re-registration was rejected because accurate rolls were necessary and all that would be asked of the voter was to return a form in the post. There should not be any confusion over delimitation, and Welensky's memory was questioned because Evans had agreed that Coloureds would choose the race with which they wished to be identified for electoral purposes. A definition of "Coloured" had been worked out with Hone and no practical difficulties were expected. Some of Welensky's minor points were accepted and it was hoped that his doubts had been removed as the registration was to start in five days' time, on 28 March.[20]

Once again, Welensky would not be hurried and he replied only on 26 March. He welcomed the promise of copies of the regulations but reiterated his protest at the by-passing of the Legislative Council and its preclusion from debating the issue. He remained convinced that the underlying motive was the enfranchisement of convicted criminals and concluded that the way was being opened for the latter to become candidates. He found the prediction, that his Government would bless this act, to be ominous because it showed "you realise that the course upon which we are now set is likely to lead to irresponsible Government". If the later comprehensive order in council could not be ready for months, he saw no reason why the Legislative Council could not enact some of the legislation. In fact, he did not believe that this was a pilot order in council as it contained far-reaching changes to existing law. The matter of delimitation was of major importance and he expected ample time for study. He wondered if the British Government understood just how difficult the delimitation would be. However, he would not press the point on the re-registration and acknowledged that he had been mistaken over the Coloureds, but would remind the British Government that they would still be excluded from the national roll elections. He said he was grateful for the minor concessions.[21]

Welensky had already denied to Lord Salisbury that he had ever adhered too rigidly to the existing form of the Federation, but said he was in the embarrassing position of holding a mandate to do something which he had failed to achieve. Another reason for resigning was, having been badly double-crossed in the past two years, he wished to show the British Government that "even a worm would turn". He hoped that Salisbury had read his parliamentary speech and had noticed that the British Government had refuted none of his charges. Although he had spared no one, he said he had been largely ignored by the British Press. Resignation was the right and only course open to him. Henceforward he would make no proposals because he

[20] *Ibid.*, 20/7, f. 53, Alport to Welensky, 23 March 1962.
[21] *Ibid.*, f. 51, Welensky to Alport, 26 March 1962.

knew that the British Government would only reply that it would consider them. He would not put himself at a disadvantage as well as having to pay for British decisions. He had no desire to either liquidate the Federation or to realign its boundaries. The British Government continued to appease Banda, and thus must pay. In the electoral campaign, he would declare that as he proposed to consider anything, he needed a fresh mandate. He welcomed the creation of the Central African Office but wondered at Macmillan's motive. He said he did not know Butler well, but had dealt with him and found him decent. He proposed to open negotiations with Butler immediately after the election.[22]

Salisbury welcomed this clarification as most important because, he said, there were those who were trying to separate Welensky and Whitehead. He rued that the British Press had ignored Welensky's charges, but it was important that they were on record and could be used. He accepted Welensky's reasons for resigning, and welcomed the appointment of Butler. He thought that Butler was not a strong character, but was honest, experienced and knew something of Africa. It was also very important to Butler to make a success of this appointment. John Connell wrote to Welensky describing Butler — accurately — as the undertaker, but Welensky replied that Butler would find the corpse not quite dead.[23]

Having dealt with Northern Rhodesia, Welensky still could not begin to electioneer because, almost inevitably, the Nyasaland Government gave notice that it considered that the African Protectorate Council no longer met the requirement as the body designated as being representative of Africans in terms of Article 13(3) of the Federal Constitution for the purpose of choosing the Nyasaland special representatives of African opinion in the Federal Assembly. Instead the Nyasaland Government proposed to designate all the elected Members of its legislature as a body representative of Africans in terms of the Article. Regulations would be issued making the Clerk of the House the returning officer, and all candidates for these Federal Assembly seats would have to possess the same qualifications as the Members of the Nyasaland Legislative Council. Their proposers and seconders would be registered voters and one would have to be an elected Member of the Legislative Council. Nomination day would be 9 April, and polling day, 27 April.[24]

Welensky replied to Jones acknowledging his powers as Governor in this matter, but regretting that he had to interpret this as a demonstration of the hostility of the Nyasaland Government to the Federation. He said his reason was that, if the current Legislative Council were designated as an electoral college, it would be tantamount to Jones deliberately and publicly handing two Federal seats to the Malawi Congress Party. If, as anticipated, the MCP boycotted the forthcoming Federal election, such a move by Jones could only be interpreted as cynical acquiescence to opposition to the election. A MCP boycott would attract world attention and ridicule because Nyasaland's

[22] *Ibid.*, 43/*Salisbury*, Welensky to Salisbury, 18 March 1962.
[23] *Ibid.*, Lord Salisbury to Welensky, 28 March 1962; 43/*Connell*, Welensky to Connell, 24 March 1962.
[24] *Ibid.*, 20/8, f. 38, Secretary, Zomba, to Secretary, Home Affairs, Salisbury, 22 March 1962.

Specially Elected African Members in the Federal Assembly would be chosen only by the remaining five Members (all of them white) of the Legislative Council. Barrow had protested strongly and Welensky agreed that only the worst interpretation could be placed on Jones's intentions.[25]

Jones regretted Welensky's distress, but reminded him that he had to designate a body as representative of Africans when the Provincial Councils were defunct and only 36 Nyasaland African voters were registered on the Federal rolls. To designate these 36 voters would indeed invoke world-wide ridicule. He denied totally that he was demonstrating his Government's opposition to the Federation and denounced Barrow as unconstructive because no one could deny that the elected Members were representative of Africans, having been elected by 111 500 people, most of whom were Africans. Whatever body was designated, Jones maintained, the MCP would secure the two seats in the Federal Assembly. If the MCP boycotted the election, it would not matter how the Members were elected, as they could not be called representative. All this, he suggested, had surely occurred to Welensky when he called the Federal election. At least, Jones claimed, his method would fill the seats, unlike the more obvious and easier step of designating only the African Members of the Legislative Council as an electoral college.[26]

During this exchange, Whitehead stole the limelight by having to deal with a bid by the UN Committee of Seventeen on Colonialism to induce Britain to withdraw the 1961 Southern Rhodesian Constitution. Nkomo had given evidence to the UN in New York in favour of this bid and had invited Todd to support him. Todd accepted and, leaving Salisbury on 19 March, declared that he would criticise the British Government for capitulating to the Southern Rhodesian Government when it could still legislate for that territory. Thus it was pointless for anyone to protest in London. He saw the need for a strong and independent third party (the UN) to resolve this racial conflict. Whitehead promptly replied that no one knew better than Todd that Southern Rhodesia had been self-governing since 1923. Furthermore, he said, Todd's actions as Prime Minister did not accord with his current views. His Electoral Act had been less favourable to the Africans than the one against which he was protesting. Whitehead recalled that Todd had said that the reason for Nkomo's appeal to the UN was the Southern Rhodesian Government's refusal to negotiate further with him. In fact, Whitehead said he had never refused to see Nkomo, but had told him that once the electorate accepted the Constitution it would be implemented. It was pertinent to note also that the UN motion was sponsored by Mali, which was aligned with the Communist bloc, and seconded by Russia. Moreover, the Iron Curtain countries and the Afro-Asians had fully supported the resolution.[27]

En route to New York, Todd replied from London that he was not concerned with the niceties of whether or not Southern Rhodesia was self-governing. He was troubled by "the mess" in which Southern Rhodesia

[25] *Ibid.*, f. 36, Welensky to Sir Glyn Jones, 24 March 1962; 35/3, f. 295, Secretary, Home Affairs, to W. S. Parker, 24 March 1962.

[26] *Ibid.*, 20/8, f. 34, Jones to Welensky, 26 March 1962.

[27] *The Rhodesia Herald*, 17 March 1962; *Evening Standard*, 19 March 1962; *African Daily News*, 19 March 1962.

found itself and sought to resolve it. Moreover, whatever Whitehead said, Southern Rhodesia was not yet really self-governing.[28]

In New York, Todd called for a meeting between the Southern Rhodesian Government and a satisfactory representative of the people to devise a new constitution. He thought that the Declaration of Rights and other safeguards were worthless substitutes for British protection, and he described the 1961 Constitution as a "bad one" and nothing more than a swindle designed to keep power in white hands. He believed that, if it were not repealed, it would lead to bloodshed and a rout of the whites.[29]

Afterwards Todd described his own speech as "horrible", which encouraged the *Evening Standard* to question why he had made it at all because he was under no compulsion and had not given the 1961 Constitution a fair trial. He was simply playing into the hands of the enemies of democracy, it said, when everything he sought could be achieved under the current Constitution. The newspaper noticed that the Russian delegate was delighted by Todd. *The Rhodesia Herald* called Todd's speech a reckless, irresponsible attempt to worsen race relations and to endanger the economy of his own country. Whitehead had the last word as, on 31 March, he revealed that he had consulted the British Government and had been assured that there would be no constitutional changes, although it would receive a UN delegation.[30]

Welensky kept silent and, in any case, by late March, with Butler assuming power, he had much else to think about. On 26 March, Robinson had reported on his final meetings with Sandys and Maudling. He said that Maudling expected the main problem of the future to be Southern Rhodesia because great pressures would be exerted to hand over power to the Africans earlier than the Constitution envisaged. The problem appeared to Maudling to be as complex and as dangerous as that of Algeria. In regard to Northern Rhodesia, he thought that there was no reason why power could not be handed rapidly to the Africans because so many of the Europeans were temporary residents. The failure of the UFP to attract significant African support added grist to his mill. He advised the bringing together of all the political leaders to work out a federal arrangement which would be acceptable to all. The result could be a common services organisation rather than a federation, but nothing imposed would endure.

Sandys understood that Welensky did not want to appear to be taking the initiative in breaking up the Federation, but he suspected that Welensky had tried to manoeuvre him into the position of saying that the British Government wanted the Federation dissolved. However, Robinson refused to believe that Sandys was serious in saying this. Sandys regretted that he would no longer be responsible for Central African affairs and that the whole matter had not been brought under him at the Commonwealth Relations Office. However, he said, it had been thought that such a move would only arouse African antagonism.[31]

Robinson had also seen Wall and other friends and they had promised their

[28] *Evening Standard*, 20 March 1962.
[29] *The Rhodesia Herald*, 23 March 1962.
[30] *Evening Standard*, 23 March 1962; *The Rhodesia Herald*, 24 & 31 March 1962.
[31] Welensky Papers, 32/28, f. 20, Robinson to Welensky, 26 March 1962.

support, but were anxious that Welensky and Whitehead should continue to work together.

Unlike the others, Wall, when he wrote to Welensky, claimed that the purpose of Welensky's visit had been generally misunderstood, but that his "tough talk" had at least sounded a warning. By contrast, he said, Whitehead's standing was high because he had offered a moderate compromise, in a speech to the Commonwealth Affairs Club, and had made Welensky appear too rigid in his approach. Nevertheless, Wall thought that the British Government was unlikely to consider Whitehead's plan seriously because it would contravene the Federal constitutional preamble. He knew that Butler intended to investigate the matter thoroughly and Wall thought that a solution would have to involve the re-drawing of internal boundaries and, perhaps, links with Bechuanaland and Moçambique.[32]

Welensky had not received these dispatches on 27 March when he informed Robinson that he was anxious that Butler should visit in May so that no time should be lost. He was pleased that Robinson had given Butler a written account of the reasons for Federal distrust of British motives. He remained adamant that he would not advance any proposals but he wished Butler to understand the essential differences between the scheme he had given to Sandys and that of Whitehead. Robinson should emphasise the far-reaching nature of the Federal proposals as an indication of Welensky's flexibility and willingness to find a solution. He welcomed the prospect of dealing with one man and hoped there would be no personal prejudice and muddled thinking. If his visit to London had yielded little, at least it had achieved this.[33]

Welensky replied to Wall on 1 April reiterating his disappointment that he should be thought to be rigid when he had been most receptive to ideas in the past few years. However, he had reached the end of his tether and had forced Macmillan to act. He had warned Macmillan that he would dissolve his Parliament but had not been believed. He had been told by a leading journalist that one of his Secretaries of State had said that the intention was to allow the problems to worsen so that the Federation would inevitably dissolve. Prospects of a settlement were not improved by a strong swing to the Right in Southern Rhodesia and there was every possibility of the UFP losing the impending Southern Rhodesian general election. Whitehead knew very well that he could not win without his support because already three branch committees, Mazoe, Umvukwes and Umtali, had resigned, together with many members. The main reason for the defections was Whitehead's soft handling of the African nationalists. Almost as important was his intention to tamper with the Land Apportionment Act and a proposed minimum wage in agriculture. Welensky told Wall that he wanted Whitehall to appreciate that it was dealing with Britons who preferred to turn and face trouble. Therefore, Butler should visit the Federation as soon as possible.

Welensky was more frank with Robinson in answering his plea for solidarity with Whitehead. He said that Whitehead had been acting strangely of late and that he had reacted to the prorogation of the Federal Parliament by telling those about him that the British Government would intervene and

[32] *Ibid.*, 43/*Wall*, Major P. Wall to Welensky, 26 March 1962.

[33] *Ibid.*, 20/2, ff. 39–40, Welensky to Robinson, 27 March 1962.

dissolve the Federation before the Federal election. The result had been a widespread rumour of this, and a public attack in the Press on him (Welensky) by someone signing himself "Southern Rhodesian Division United Federal Party". Yet, he said, Whitehead had then acknowledged that he would need his support if he were to win the Southern Rhodesian election.

Turning to his own problem, Welensky thought that the Federal Government had to permit the secession of Nyasaland, but on conditions which ensured the continued association of the Rhodesias. He confessed that he had known for a long time that he would make no progress with Maudling who, though more likeable, was, if anything, more to the Left than Macleod. He asked Robinson to assure Sandys that he had not tried to manoeuvre him into any position. He simply would not allow himself to be placed in the position of being held responsible for the break-up of the Federation.[34]

In his first comment on the Federation in the Commons, Butler avowed that any solution had to have general acceptance. This prompted Sir Evelyn Hone to dismiss publicly Whitehead's partition plan.[35]

Robinson discovered more about Butler's intentions when he met him on 4 April. Butler dismissed any question of Britain abandoning its responsibilities and said that there was every intention to co-operate in the search for solutions to the current problems. Such action as was necessary to restore confidence in the Federal economy would be taken before July. He would reassure the northern civil servants that their positions would be protected and they could have full confidence in the future.

Butler's critical frankness about Macleod prompted Robinson to recall that it was Butler who had recommended Maudling to the Federal Government and that he had proved difficult, inexperienced and over-hasty in reaching decisions. Robinson also revealed to Butler that he knew that Sandys had told Banda in Zomba that Nyasaland would be allowed to secede. Butler appeared to confirm this and added that Sandys had gone to Nyasaland and Barotseland without authority and accordingly had angered the Colonial Office and had embarrassed the British Government. Butler promised to inform the Nyasalanders that there would be no early secession and that any decision thereon would have to be part of a general settlement which would be preceded by an exhaustive inquiry.

As a four-year development plan for Nyasaland was about to be reviewed, Robinson wanted to know if the constitutional issue would be settled first. Butler did not reply directly but said that Banda's demands for secession would force the British Government to take a "tougher" attitude. Robinson concluded that Butler would attempt to ensure a continuing relationship with Nyasaland, possibly in the form of a common market, because he indicated that he was examining the possibilities and practicalities of Nyasaland either joining Tanganyika or remaining in an association with the Rhodesias. Butler said that there were several important matters which he would discuss the next week, but would not elaborate. However, Butler admitted that something had to be done to prevent Banda from coming to Britain and exploiting Press interviews to gain publicity for his cause. Thus Robinson predicted that

[34] *Ibid.*, 43/*Wall*, Welensky to Wall, 1 April 1962; 32/28, f. 21, Welensky to Robinson, 1 April 1962.
[35] *The Rhodesia Herald*, 4 April 1962.

Butler would want to make an announcement on Nyasaland's future immediately after he had spoken to Welensky.

Butler warned Robinson that Hone was most annoyed that the Whitehead plan did not envisage consultation with the Northern Rhodesian Government. Butler said, however, that while the plan was still being studied, the amalgamation of Central Northern Rhodesia and Southern Rhodesia was impossible as Whitehead appeared to have forgotten that the Federal constitutional preamble specifically forbad it. Consequently Robinson gathered that Butler preferred the Federal solution.

Butler also reported that Lord Boyd had assured him of his support. In return he had promised to consult him and Lord Salisbury periodically. Butler was pleased to hear from Robinson that George Brown, the deputy leader of the Labour Party, had been invited to the Federation. Butler was irritated by the attempted intrusion into the affairs of Southern Rhodesia by the UN sub-committee. He had no intention of discussing Southern Rhodesia with it. Almost telling tales out of school about Sandys and Maudling, he claimed that Macmillan had realised that the division of responsibilities was aggravating the position and was particularly annoyed with Sandys's intrusion into the affairs of Nyasaland and Barotseland. Maudling had happily accepted the change, but Sandys had not because he had hoped to be the architect of the final Federal solution. In Butler's view, Sandys's greatest error was to give the impression to everyone in the Federation that Britain wanted to abdicate.

Butler wished Welensky to know that he was arranging his affairs so that he could devote his entire attention to the Federation. He would also assure him that he would not attempt to manoeuvre him, as co-operation was the key to any solution. There had to be no confrontations, but Welensky would have to accept that federation was not the only possible form of association. He realised that Welensky had to speak several times during his campaign but hoped that he would ignore the past and try to create a better atmosphere so that talks could begin on a cordial basis. He convinced Robinson that he would endeavour to reach an understanding with Welensky, and Robinson agreed that the great opportunities of the future should be stressed rather than the shortcomings of the British.[36]

Consequently, Welensky suspended the publication of his paper on the broken promises of the British until he had seen what negotiations with Butler produced. He was, of course, preoccupied with his electoral campaign but was becoming confident of a good result, despite the growing defection of the Southern Rhodesian members of his Party and an upsurge in violence in Northern Rhodesia as Kaunda's UNIP prepared to enter the electoral race against the ANC. The violence was sufficient to evoke threats from the Northern Rhodesian Government to ban meetings and a warning from Welensky that he would use force to defend the Federal Constitution.[37]

Welensky succeeded, at one of his meetings, in annoying his British friends

[36] Welensky Papers, 20/2, ff. 34–38, Robinson to Welensky, 4 April 1962.
[37] *Ibid.*, 29/27, f. 4, Welensky to Lord Lambton, 6 April 1962; 43/*Salisbury*, Welensky to Salisbury, 6 April 1962; 16/18, f. 106, Minutes of a meeting with the Umvukwes delegation, 2 April 1962; *Northern News*, 10 & 11 April 1962.

as well as Lord Dalhousie, the Governor-General, because he spoke of leaving the Commonwealth and had also confessed that he would not have called the election if he had known in time about Butler's appointment. Dalhousie warned him not to overplay the anti-Macmillan card because the Conservative Party was losing support, and criticism of its leader was resented in times of crisis.[38]

Welensky was enjoying an almost free run because of the electoral boycott by the Dominion Party. However, Field could not stand entirely aloof and, on 5 April, proposed a common market of the three territories. The lack of opposition was also too much for Todd. In Salisbury, on 11 April, he attacked Welensky, describing the general election as "a sputnik out of control" which could destroy the UFP. He decried Welensky's inability to see, as the new factor in politics, the will of the people. However, Todd was comforted that the British Government was not so blind. He believed that Butler would bring a new decisiveness to British policy which would mean that Welensky would be confronted at the Federal Review by the determination of the British, Northern Rhodesian and Nyasaland Governments to outlaw racial discrimination, which meant the introduction of African majority rule. Todd advised Southern Rhodesians not to run or fight but to co-operate with the African. He thought Southern Rhodesians had more reason to have faith in African leadership than the inhabitants of any other African country. Thus the right decision in any Federal negotiations, he said, was to transfer power to where it rightly belonged.[39] Few Europeans would have agreed with him.

On 9 April Butler transmitted a further and most disturbing message to Welensky through Robinson. Accepting that it was his Government's duty to make proposals, he claimed that, as the problem of Nyasaland was urgent, he wished to make an early announcement that its demands would be investigated. Because Welensky had agreed, in the partition proposals which Sandys had brought to London, that structural alteration was required, Butler assumed that he would not object to an immediate declaration on Nyasaland and its demand for secession. The alternative was to say nothing until after the Northern and Southern Rhodesian elections, but the economic damage done in the interim could be irreparable. The Labour Party was pressing for a debate on the Federation, but the Leader of the House, Macleod, would postpone it until after the Easter recess to allow ample time for consultation with Welensky. In the debate, Butler said he would recognise the legitimacy of Nyasaland's demands and suggest that a committee should investigate the desirability of a form of association between Nyasaland and the Rhodesias, as well as the maintenance of close ties between the latter. The committee would comprise a constitutional expert, an economist and certain individuals specially instructed to investigate Nyasaland's position. Work would begin after Butler's visit to the Federation. In recognising Nyasaland's claims, Butler would declare that nothing would be done until the inquiry was completed. The viability of Nyasaland either as an independent entity or as part of some form of association would be thoroughly investigated.

Robinson refused to comment until he knew who would serve on the

[38] Welensky Papers, 28/4, f. 30, Lord Dalhousie to Welensky, 12 April 1962.

[39] *Marandellas and Watershed News*, 4 April 1962; *The Rhodesia Herald*, 11 April 1962.

committee. He warned, however, that Welensky would reject anything like the Monckton Commission especially if evidence would be called from people and organisations. Butler replied that the purpose was to collate all the advice and recommendations, that had been received from every quarter, on the future of the territories so that an acceptable plan could be formulated. The alternative, which was dangerous, was to do nothing.[40]

His suspicion aroused, Welensky commented to Robinson that it appeared that Butler would tell Banda what he proposed, without prior consultation with the Federal Government. Welensky revealed that, after experiencing difficulties with the Federal Cabinet, he had sent a message to Butler asking him to visit before making any statements in Parliament. Welensky had informed his colleagues on the previous day, 12 April, of Butler's intentions, explaining that Banda would soon be in Britain demanding secession and that the British Government felt it could not ignore him. He told them that Butler was hoping to wrest the initiative from Banda through his announcement, and also believed that a factual analysis and boldness would help to restore confidence in the Rhodesias. He said Butler thought that there was nothing worse than continuing the current uncertainty until after the territorial elections, because there was a risk of irresistible separatist pressures. The British Government was not anxious to take action, but knew that the Federal Government could not take the initiative. There was no desire to have a "Monckton" commission, but a detailed and realistic examination was needed. The committee would report only to Butler but would maintain close contact with the Federal Government, and all the Governments would see its report, which would be ready by 30 September.

Welensky explained to the Federal Cabinet that this message had arrived during the weekend and, because he was away, Alport had relayed it only to Whitehead. Welensky said he had seen Alport but had insisted on consulting his Cabinet before making a definite reply. Alport knew that Butler was prepared to delay his arrival in May by a few days, but that he was determined to make his announcement in the debate in Parliament in late April.

Welensky reported that he had asked Alport to confirm that Sandys had informed Banda that secession would be allowed. Alport had replied that Banda had certainly understood it would but that Sandys had denied giving any such impression. Welensky had then asked whether Whitehead, when he was in London, had been told of the intention to appoint Butler, but Alport had doubted this and had assumed that Whitehead was using hindsight to attach undue importance to his discussions in London.

The Federal Cabinet also had before it a report from Robinson that Jones, when informing Banda that Butler would appoint a committee to study Nyasaland's demands, had assured him that the secession issue would not be prejudiced. Jones had said that the British Government was not committing itself because, while it acknowledged the strength of the opposition to the Federation in Nyasaland, it believed that the continued association of the three territories held great advantages for all their people. Thus it suggested a careful examination of the ramifications of secession. Surprisingly, Banda had

[40] Welensky Papers, 20/2, ff. 31–33, Robinson to Welensky, 9 April 1962.

welcomed the inquiry and had demanded it should begin immediately. Jones had warned him that any decisions would await the report of the committee and the consultation of the Governments.

Welensky informed his Cabinet he had replied that it had to be clear that, before he would agree to it, the inquiry would prejudice nothing. There should be no misunderstandings on its purposes or how it would be conducted. The Cabinet, however, worried that he might have given the impression of qualified approval. It suspected that the British Government wished to discover what effect Nyasaland's secession would have on Britain because it wanted to evade any consequences of the break-up of the Federation. It was certainly anxious to do that in the Federation of the West Indies which would dissolve on 18 April.

Some of the Cabinet wished to reject the proposal because it would inevitably develop into a repetition of the Monckton Commission and because, if the Federal Government accepted the inquiry, it would be accused of surrendering. Other Ministers were prepared to believe that Butler would want an investigation for his own edification. They thought that, if there were no public announcement by either the Federal or British Governments, an inquiry could do no harm and that, if it were realistically conducted, it could only discover that Nyasaland could not stand alone. An announcement, however, would be tantamount to a public acceptance of secession and certainly Banda would believe that.

Butler's motive was thought to be an effort to stave off the secession demands in the hope that the longer Banda was in office the sooner he would realise that Nyasaland had to remain in the Federation. However, some Federal Ministers suggested that even a secret inquiry was unacceptable because knowledge thereof was bound to be leaked either by the British Government or by Banda. In any case, Federal Ministers could not appear before the committee of inquiry and would have to reserve their evidence for Butler himself. It seemed that the true intention was not only to facilitate Nyasaland's withdrawal but to plan for a reversion to a form of the Central African Council.

The Cabinet recalled that Welensky had asked Maudling in December 1961 to institute a departmental inquiry into the effects of Nyasaland's secession and thought that it was a remarkable admission of ineffecency now to propose such an inquiry. It was difficult to believe that the British Government was not already in possession of all the necessary facts. Nonetheless, it had to be borne in mind that, since Maudling's visit, Banda would have known of the proposed inquiry as well as being led to believe that secession would be permitted. This would make the currently suggested inquiry very different from that of December 1961. Whitehead had also been told of the inquiry and, in reply, had suggested as an alternative that Butler should be accompanied by advisers on his visit and that they should stay behind to collect further information.

The Federal Cabinet noted that Robinson had gathered information from Butler which was not forthcoming from Alport. This included Butler's description of the Nyasaland question as "pressing and difficult" and as requiring an early declaration that Nyasaland's demands should be investigated.

The Cabinet recalled that Butler had unjustifiably assumed that Welensky believed that a revision of the Federation's structure was necessary and that he would not object to such a declaration on Nyasaland. Butler had suggested that the only other course was to postpone all consideration of the future until after the Northern and Southern Rhodesian elections. Thus he had argued that, in the imminent Commons debate, he had to say that Nyasaland's demands should be recognised but that there should be the inquiry and the postponement of the Federal Review until after the territorial elections. In effect, the Cabinet found, he had indicated that secession had been approved.

In the light of Robinson's revelations, it seemed clear to the Cabinet that it was forced to reject the proposals. As Butler had recalled Alport, Hone and Jones for consultations, he should be asked to travel to Salisbury before doing anything as the matter was too important to be decided through correspondence or third parties. It was imperative not to sour relations with Butler so soon after his appointment, but he could use a visit to the Federation to forestall that of Banda to London by arguing that he was coming out to see him. The Federal Cabinet decided that the reply to Butler had to make these points in terms which would not antagonise him.[41]

The Cabinet met again that day, 12 April, at 6.30 p.m. at Welensky's home to consider the draft of a reply to Butler. This reaffirmed a willingness to co-operate but declared that what he had proposed would only worsen economic and political uncertainties. The point was made that the announcement would make it clear that the break-up of the Federation was henceforth in issue. It was argued in the draft that Banda would claim that the appointment of advisers was public recognition of his demands. The announcement would cause widespread confusion and alarm in the midst of the Federal general election. On these grounds the counter-proposal was made that Butler should postpone action for full discussions with the Federal Government in Salisbury which would complement those he had already held with the northern Governors and Alport. It was also necessary to avoid any further misunderstanding through correspondence and the transmission of messages through third parties. Banda could be informed that his visit to London was unnecessary.

The Federal Cabinet thought that the reply should be more emphatic with regard to the anxiety felt and in its rejection of Butler's proposal. Yet Butler should not be antagonised, and it was felt that a stronger stand should be reserved for his rejection of this reply. Nevertheless, it should be made clear that the proposed announcement would imply the acceptance of the dissolution of the Federation and the public acknowledgement of Banda's victory. As the reply was to be transmitted through Alport, he had to be made to understand how strongly the Federal Government felt and how difficult it had been for it to reply in so mild a manner. Nothing would be written about the acuteness of the feeling, but Alport would be aware of it.[42]

Signed by Welensky, the reply was given to Alport on 13 April by Barrow. Alport read it and, visibly indignant, expressed his disappointment because it

[41] *Ibid.*, 32/28, f. 24, Welensky to Robinson, 13 April 1962; FGC(62), 11th Meeting, Minute 6, Federal Cabinet, 12 April 1962.
[42] *Ibid.*, FGC(62), 11th Meeting, Minute 6, Federal Cabinet, 12 April 1962.

appeared to be an outright rejection. He warned that, as the Federal Government was being unconstructive, his Government would have to make its own dispositions. Barrow quickly pointed out that, unlike the northern Governors, Welensky had yet to be given the opportunity of full discussions with Butler. He said that Welensky had indicated that he was prepared to consider anything which would achieve a lasting solution and that he was doing no more than ask for a delay for discussions with Butler. Barrow warned of the Federal belief that any announcement would be interpreted as heralding the dissolution of the Federation. It would therefore be small consolation for the public to know that other forms of association would be considered. Although the British intention might be otherwise, Banda would hail the announcement as an acceptance of his views. The Federal Government did not intend to question Butler's right to appoint advisers but believed that all the necessary information was readily available and objected to the announcement.

Alport argued that, as his Government had been informed that the Federal Government did not contemplate keeping Nyasaland in the Federation by force, it believed that the only way to achieve this was by negotiation. Thus, he said, Butler was only trying to seize the initiative before Banda took the law into his own hands. Butler was prepared to accept responsibility for finding the solution, and believed that the problem was bedevilled by Nyasaland's relationship with the Federation. Once the relationship was put into perspective, talks could begin on retaining and strengthening the economic and political association. The greatest danger lay in allowing matters to drift.

Barrow, however, asked Alport whether it was necessary to prejudice matters with a public announcement when Butler's advisers could work privately, as they normally did in assisting a Minister. Alport replied that the purpose of the announcement was to prevent isolated action by Banda because the latter had agreed to accept the inquiry without a prior commitment to secession. This could break the stalemate because, hitherto, Banda had refused to discuss anything but secession. Any delay could encourage the extremists to persuade Banda not to co-operate. For that reason, Alport said, the British Government felt strongly that the announcement should be made before Butler visited. In this way, the accusation would be avoided that Butler was being subjected to pressure from elements within the Federation.[43]

In *The Sudden Assignment*, Alport explains that he thought Butler had to make his declaration before he arrived to appear to have a fresh and impartial mind. He recalls that this would be in contrast to Butler's predecessors who only ever revealed their intentions after visiting.[44] Alport told Barrow, when concluding their meeting, that the early announcement would clearly indicate that the British Government had taken the initiative, but Barrow merely thought it would show an unwillingness to hear the Federal point of view. He

[43] *Ibid.*, 20/2, ff. 28–30, Welensky to Alport, 13 April 1962; ff. 24–27, Minutes of a Meeting between Alport and Barrow, 13 April 1962. For some reason, Welensky in his *Welensky's 4 000 Days* (London, 1964), pp. 334–335, and Alport in his *The Sudden Assignment*, *op. cit.*, p. 180, claim that Welensky and not Barrow conducted this meeting. However, the minutes give Barrow's name. — JRTW.

[44] Alport, *The Sudden Assignment*, *op. cit.*, p. 177.

said that Welensky and the Federal Cabinet had asked him to make the British understand that a serious view would be taken of any announcement made before the visit.

No reply was forthcoming from Butler for twelve days, and Welensky again felt that the ground was slipping from under his feet. He already knew that, in addressing the United Nations in New York on the previous day, Kaunda had wept when describing the current treatment of Africans and when demanding the dissolution of the Federation and a new constitution for Northern Rhodesia. His allegations raised more than one cynical eyebrow in the Federation because the Press was full of accounts of riots, assaults and even a murder as his Party strove to dominate.[45] On 14 April Nkomo was given a hero's welcome as he returned to Salisbury from New York and declared that Southern Rhodesia would be granted independence under African domination in early 1963. A few days later, he stated that he would accept nothing less than his ZAPU taking over Southern Rhodesia, maintaining that it was just a matter "of straightening up the papers" before the African was in power. He would not accept any qualification of the franchise.[46]

Banda contributed wild comments, and Field added fuel to the fire by lauding as admirable the appointment of Butler, but claiming that it would make no difference to the Federation's fate as Banda would soon obtain a date for independence and would thereupon demand secession. Field described Whitehead's plan as "pathetic and too late" and merely an outdated copy of his own. He said that he had advised Welensky not to call an election, when the Federal Assembly still had two years to run, because it would only create a crisis. He asserted that his reason for boycotting the election was to avoid emotional debates, which could provoke a security situation, and because it was unnecessary.[47]

Welensky ignored Field but publicly clashed with Adlai Stevenson, US Ambassador to the UN, after the latter had addressed a seminar in Illinois and had blamed the whites for the troubles of Africa. Welensky stated that Stevenson's attack was bitter and unreasoned, but Stevenson replied that Welensky could not have read the speech because it was temperate and factual.[48]

On 25 April, before departing for Broken Hill for his last Federal election speech, Welensky confided to Joelson that he was already finding Butler most difficult. He was irritated, too, that Alport should consider himself the local "overlord". The result was, Welensky said, that the northern Governors had not consulted him once that year. He was depressed about the UFP's prospects of winning the Southern Rhodesian general election because Whitehead was such an unattractive public figure. Welensky wondered if his own influence would be enough to ensure success. He found irony in Whitehead becoming the "blue-eyed boy" in Britain, while he was cast as the villain,

[45] Welensky, *4 000 Days*, *op. cit.*, p. 335; *The Rhodesia Herald*, 13 April 1962.

[46] *The Sunday Mail*, 15 April 1962; *African Daily News*, 18 April 1962.

[47] Welensky Papers, 29/90, f. 10, Banda's Press Conference, 16 April 1962; 28/49, f. 17, Notes on Field's Speech to the RNAA, 17 April 1962.

[48] *Ibid.*, 35/24, f. 540, Adlai Stevenson's Speech, 14 April 1962; *The Rhodesia Herald*, 18 April 1962.

because a year previously he had received representations from Britain to get rid of Whitehead. The latter was courting the British and Welensky had warned him against burning his fingers. Lord Salisbury was equally disappointed by Butler as he had spurned his advice.[49]

On 20 April, it had been announced that Butler would arrive on 11 May, and five days later Welensky was informed by Butler that discussions between them could not be held until then because of the Federal election. Moreover, he advised, the Federal Review could not be reconvened until the Northern and Southern Rhodesian elections had been held. Nonetheless, Butler said he was anxious to seize the initiative and end the current damaging uncertainty. He claimed that, as his Government was willing to receive any ideas on a solution, it had to open a channel for them. He thought that the initiative he had proposed would hold the position until his committee of inquiry had concluded its deliberations and it could offer a constructive approach to Nyasaland's future in the context of the continued association of the territories.

As Welensky had said in a recent speech that he was seeking a mandate to achieve a lasting solution, Butler found that their ideas coincided to a degree. He accepted that an announcement before the Federal election could be harmful and proposed to postpone it until 8 May. He could not delay further, he said, because the British and Federal Governments could be confronted by a demand for Nyasaland's secession in the immediate future. He was particularly anxious not to be forced to make a statement on Nyasaland alone since it would rob his initiative of much of its impact as a constructive and comprehensive approach to the whole problem.[50]

Returning from Broken Hill on 26 April, Welensky informed Alport that Butler had ignored his most important points, as he had not commented on the assertion that the announcement would be interpreted as an admission that the Federation was finished and that Banda would then be able to claim that his demands had been recognised. Welensky said that already a statement by Sir Patrick Dean to the UN, that the British Government was not committed to any solution in Central Africa, had resulted in a number of enquiries as to whether the British Government had abandoned the Federation. Welensky felt it was impossible to convey the strength of the Federal feeling on this point by correspondence and that it was vital to prevent further loss of public confidence. He could not accept that time was so pressing that the announcement could not be delayed a few days so that Butler could hear Federal views. If it were necessary to make the announcement on 8 May, Butler should visit the Federation before then. Welensky complained that he still did not know who the advisers on the committee of inquiry would be or how they would work. He could only deduce that another public inquiry was contemplated and that it would receive suggestions for a solution from any quarter. If this were true, he said, it would contradict the statement by Sandys in the Commons on 8 March that he would receive

[49] Welensky Papers, 24/152, ff. 186–189, Welensky to Joelson, 25 April 1962; 43/*Salisbury*, Robinson to Welensky, 17 April 1962.

[50] *The Rhodesia Herald*, 20 April 1962; Welensky Papers, 20/2, ff. 21–22, Alport to Welensky, 25 April 1962.

proposals, from the Governments, which were passed through the appropriate channels. Welensky again pleaded for a termination of this long-range negotiation and for the chance to put his case in person.[51]

Butler did not reply for five days, but, with the Federal election on 27 April, Welensky was fully occupied. Greenfield, on 25 April, had seen Whitehead who believed that Nyasaland would be allowed to secede but that the British would maintain the links between the Rhodesias. Greenfield, however, disagreed because Alport had indicated that looser ties were contemplated. Whitehead was unconvinced because he thought that Britain wanted a tight union, although it would only allow Northern Rhodesia to be partitioned if nothing else could be done. Alport had assured him that his plan would be considered in due course. Greenfield argued that Hone's public rejection of partition had ruled it out, but Whitehead disagreed.

Whitehead then shed some light on his public claim to have been given prior knowledge of Butler's appointment. He said that at that time he had met Macmillan at Chequers and had been told of the constant disagreements between Sandys and Maudling, caused by the differing advice which they had received from their officials. Macmillan had indicated that he was anxious to have one department, and Whitehead had assumed that he intended to amalgamate the Colonial and Commonwealth Relations Offices. Later he had received a message that he should see Butler before returning home, but had not understood why. He had gathered that Sandys had favoured partition, but that Maudling had thought the Federation was doomed. The only chink he had discovered in Maudling's armour was an anxiety that the security forces of Northern Rhodesia after secession might be unable to cope if tribal warfare spilled over from Angola and the Congo. Maudling had expected Southern Rhodesia to assist Northern Rhodesia in such circumstances, but Whitehead had predicted that the UN would have banned interference by neighbouring states, and Maudling had agreed that it would. Maudling could see the benefits of a working arrangement between the territories with regard to the railways, but was not perturbed by the prospect of their separation. This had provoked Whitehead to shock Maudling by suggesting that Southern Rhodesia could impose heavy railway rates. However, Whitehead, knowing that the Lobito line could alleviate Northern Rhodesia's position, now suggested to Greenfield that defence was the stronger card to play.

Greenfield tried to discuss the Federal solution with Whitehead but received little response beyond the comment that Macmillan had advised a study of the political associations being tried out in the Common Market. Greenfield considered that this was confirmation that the British Government was contemplating loosening the Federal ties to substitute a solution on the lines of the Central African Council. Whitehead disagreed, but gave no reason. Greenfield asked him if he wanted to participate in the discussions with Butler, but Whitehead said that he did not want to create a situation where the Federal Government would have to include Jones and Hone in the discussions. Recalling that the last heads of Governments' meeting had preceded the emergencies in all three territories in 1959, Whitehead thought that

[51] Welensky Papers, 20/2, ff. 19–20, Welensky to Alport, 26 April 1962.

a "Chequers-type" meeting might, nevertheless, secure a general agreement if attended by those who had "paraded for church" in 1960. He said that Nkomo would expect to attend, but would prefer to believe the advice of his Afro-Asian friends that the 1961 Southern Rhodesian Constitution would be abandoned before the year's end. Trouble could be expected from the Zimbabwe African People's Union, but Whitehead was determined to ensure that the 1961 Constitution would be unaffected by whatever fate the Federation suffered. He understood Welensky's reluctance to advance any proposals, but, because he disliked leaving matters in other people's hands, he thought an alternative should be prepared. This was particularly necessary, he believed, because all British dependencies would be independent within three years.

Whitehead aired his financial problems declaring that, if he did not obtain British loans, he would have to cancel African housing projects and face increasing unemployment. He disliked the current Northern Rhodesian practice, which Kaunda had attacked at the UN and Sir Patrick Dean had defended, of employing Africans at salaries which Europeans would refuse, and suggested that the attention of the trade unions should be drawn to this. He knew that Banda feared that Southern Rhodesia would repatriate 150 000 Nyasa workers and, because of this, he would consider a trade relationship. Greenfield wondered if Southern Rhodesia would be willing to lose Nyasa labour because the local Africans were unwilling to work on farms. However, Whitehead thought that only tobacco farms would be affected.[52]

Two days later, Whitehead asked Welensky to frame a suitable reply to a motion in the Southern Rhodesian Legislative Assembly on the necessity of finding a final solution to the Federal problem that year. However, Welensky was even more preoccupied with his election because it was polling day. In his last message to his electorate, he again gave his reasons for dissolving Parliament, arguing that the great changes and new pressures since 1958 required him to acquire a new mandate. Acting in good faith with regard to the Monckton Commission in 1960 and the Northern Rhodesian Constitution in 1961, he acknowledged that he had twice misled the people of the Federation. The faltering nerve of the British Government made negotiations with it crucial to the survival of the Federation and he needed a wide brief to conduct them. Tilting at Field and the Dominion Party, he expressed surprise that those who criticised his handling of affairs should have abstained and denied the voter the opportunity to vote, thereby negating the parliamentary system. He warned against the idea that Southern Rhodesia could survive alone the consequent economic difficulties and the appearance of rampant African nationalism on its borders. As there was a testing time ahead, Welensky urged that moderates had to be returned to the Federal Assembly and, when their elections were held, to the Northern and Southern Rhodesian legislatures. He closed with the plea to give him the support to enable him to negotiate from strength.[53]

Forty members of the UFP were returned unopposed, and in the remaining

[52] *Ibid.*, 42/38, f. 86, Greenfield to Welensky, 26 April 1962.

[53] *Ibid.*, 20/9A, f. 31, Whitehead to Welensky, 27 April 1962; 34/3, f. 41, Welensky's Election Message, 27 April 1962.

15 constituencies, only one independent, Williamson, secured a seat. The remaining 14 were retained by the UFP. Amongst the defeated was John Gaunt.

Welensky had obtained a mandate of sorts, but the Dominion Party, by boycotting the election, had prevented him from discovering the true opinion of his electorate. He now faced the awesome task of attempting to persuade the British Government to save the Federation at a moment when he was being described by Julius Nyerere as the "one drunken crazy man" in Central Africa who would resist Kaunda, Banda and Nkomo and bring the bloodshed they wished to avoid.[54] Confronted with this task, Welensky, far from elated, felt old and tired, at the age of 55.[55]

[54] *Tanganyikan Standard*, 28 April 1962.
[55] Welensky Papers, 42/21, f. 11, Welensky to G. Beckett, 30 April 1962.

CHAPTER THIRTY-THREE

The Fatal Admission

Butler's Statement on Secession, and Attempts to lull Federal Fears, April–August 1962

UNTIL the last minute, Welensky would attempt to persuade Butler not to make any acknowledgement on secession in the Commons, but to no avail. Butler made it and then was even more emphatic on the subject at a Press conference in Zomba during his visit to the Federation. The die was cast, but Butler, waiting to see the results of the territorial elections in Northern and Southern Rhodesia, would buy time by trying to persuade the Federal Government that his committee of inquiry into Nyasaland's demands for secession could well produce a solution to save the Federation.

In the aftermath of the Federal general election, Welensky immediately reshuffled his Cabinet, while Field, freed from Federal politics, helped to form the right-wing Rhodesian Front in March and became its interim leader. In the Federal Cabinet there were two new Ministers: J. A. Clark, Minister of Commerce and Industry, and J. P. G. Duncan, Minister of Education. There were two new parliamentary secretaries: G. M. Lewanika, External Affairs, and S. S. Sawyer, Defence, Economic Affairs and Power. W. H. Eastwood retired and Sir Donald Macintyre intended to do likewise in September when he would be replaced, as Minister of Finance, by J. M. Caldicott. Barrow became Deputy Prime Minister and Minister of Defence, Economic Affairs and Power; Greenfield, Minister of Home Affairs and Law, assisted as before by J. Foot and J. Z. Savanhu as parliamentary secretaries; Caldicott, Minister of Public Service; F. S. Owen, Minister of Posts and Transport; B. D. Goldberg, Minister of Health; J. C. Graylin, Minister of Agriculture; and G. W. R. L'Ange, Minister of Works. Welensky kept External Affairs.

The negotiations with Butler were renewed almost immediately but, before they were, Macintyre reported to Welensky about his fruitless visit to Britain and the United States in search of capital, and on two meetings with Butler. Butler had told him that he had not wished to visit during the Federal election and would give Welensky a week to settle down thereafter. In any case, Macmillan was in the United States, and Butler was acting as Prime Minister and could not get away. He had promised to say in Parliament that he would consider the position of the Federal Government fully. He would also announce the appointment of his advisory committee on Nyasaland and would await its report before reaching any conclusions. Macintyre had asked him to postpone the statement on the advisory committee until after he had visited the Federation, but he had indicated politely that he was irrevocably committed to the debate. He had also claimed that any delay would rob him of the initiative he had gained by persuading Banda to await the results of the committee's investigation. He had thought that Welensky had misunderstood his intentions and declared that he would give him time to study his statement to Parliament. He had accepted that any indication that secession would be allowed would be fatal and had also agreed not to conduct any negotiations in a piecemeal fashion. Macintyre then had explained the difficulties produced by the economic uncertainties, commenting that even the World Bank was showing signs of hesitation.

Despite Butler's protestations, Macintyre had sensed that his attitude was hardening against the Federation and that the possible reason was that he had just seen Kaunda. Nevertheless, Butler had said that it was imperative to give the voters in the Rhodesias guidance on secession and its dangers. Macintyre had discovered that Robinson believed that a firm line was necessary with Butler because he intended to allow Nyasaland to secede, but not before the end of the year when he would have the results of the elections in the Rhodesias on which to formulate his views.[1] Hindsight confirms that Robinson was right.

Further glimpses of Butler were given to Welensky by Roberts who had seen him in London on 1 May. Butler had asked him first about the unrest in Northern Rhodesia, and Roberts had replied that none of the African nationalist Parties was capable of a sustained economic or violent campaign on a territory-wide basis. He was confident the police could handle most eventualities and had said that Butler should ignore the unrest in deciding what to do. Asked for his opinion of the investigation into Nyasaland, Roberts had described it as a very unwise move. Curiously, Butler had agreed and had said he would not make a statement thereon until he saw Welensky. He had also declared that he would not consider secession, but later had indicated that some special arrangements would have to be made within the Federal structure for Nyasaland. Roberts had replied that the only result would be demands from the other territories for similar treatment. He had stressed the advantages of the Federation and had claimed that the situation would improve if the British Government openly supported it. He would allow some internal adjustments, but would preserve the Federation. In Northern Rhodesia he would give more power to the regional authorities to lessen the fear of the Federation. He would also bolster the traditional tribal authorities in the face of nationalism.

Butler had asked if Welensky had really meant what he said in his references

[1] Welensky Papers, 29/47, f. 12, D. Macintyre to Welensky, 28 April 1962.

to the use of force, and Roberts had confirmed that he would use all available means to prevent the break-up of the Federation. Roberts had asked if Britain would subsidise an independent Nyasaland, and Butler had replied that she would not, except in the short term. He had wondered if Roberts thought that Nyasaland should remain in the Federation. Roberts had said that it should, even though it was a drag on the progress of the rest. Butler was anxious not to upset Welensky. Indeed, he had thought that he needed "calming down", but Roberts had said that the only way to accomplish this was to support the Federation and control the nationalists to allow more responsible Africans time to emerge. The African nationalists were, after all, only the first flush of African politicians.[2]

The chairman of the East African Group of the Conservative Party, Elizabeth Owen, had met Butler and reported to Welensky that he had thought that the Federation should change its name and its constitution radically, though without losing too much political power. He had understood that Welensky would not accept merely a common market of the three territories. Butler's first aim was to achieve stability, but he had agreed that his Government had made Welensky's position more difficult and promised to make amends. Owen concluded that Butler's ideas were sound, but that Banda would be his stumbling block.[3]

Federal officials examined the consequences of secession, calculating that the gross domestic product of each Nyasalander was £9 10s 0d p.a. Nyasaland's high rate of growth was ascribed to Federal aid which had amounted to £35 000 000 in nine years. On secession, Nyasaland would lose the Federal subsidy of £6 000 000 p.a., which would drastically affect government services. Secession would reduce investment and wages. In a declining economy, the Federal civil servants would have to be replaced, the national debt serviced, and new markets found outside Rhodesia in the face of fierce competition. While all this was happening, the population would continue to increase.[4]

The correspondence with Butler was renewed on 1 May when Alport delivered a draft of Butler's parliamentary statement. Alport informed Welensky that the British Government maintained that its acknowledgement of the Malawi Congress Party's desire to secede would simply be a statement of political fact. British policy was contained in the final paragraph, he said, which was to examine the consequences of a withdrawal and the possibilities of alternative forms of association. Butler would stress the achievements of the Federation and the importance of a continuing association, and would welcome a method of preserving the Federation. The Labour Party would reject the motion, Alport warned, because the new Northern Rhodesian Constitution was not sufficiently progressive and because there was no acceptance of secession.

Alport suggested that there were points which Welensky ought to consider before publicly denouncing the statement. For example, he said, by regarding the section on Nyasaland in isolation, Welensky would think that it conceded

[2] *Ibid.*, 30/52, f. 28, H. J. Roberts to Welensky, 2 May 1962.
[3] *Ibid.*, 28/5, f. 9, G. Dashwood to Welensky, 1 May 1962.
[4] *Ibid.*, 42/38, f. 71, Alex ? to W. S. Parker, 1 May 1962.

secession, but Alport argued that others would not because it was part of a comprehensive speech. He did not doubt, however, that Banda would make political capital out of it. The second point was that condemnation by Welensky would reduce the effectiveness of Butler's initiative and give a valuable advantage to the Federation's critics. Thus Alport advised Welensky to wait to see Butler. He confirmed that Butler could not arrive earlier, but avowed that he would say that his committee's investigation would not become a public inquiry. It would be responsible to him only. Butler would discuss the composition of the committee and its approach when he visited the Federation.[5]

Welensky, however, could not understand why Butler had to condemn the Federation publicly two days before he visited it. The damage would be irreparable, he said, even if the statement on Nyasaland was contained in a comprehensive speech. It would render impossible a solution based on the amendment of the current Constitution. Indeed, Welensky said, Butler was obviously looking for looser forms of association. He would make the secession of Nyasaland a certainty and the continued association of the two Rhodesias doubtful. He would visit the Federation as its liquidator, and not as negotiator. Thus Welensky said he had to condemn the statement as disastrous. Facing the Federation's ruin, he asked again that Butler should visit before making the statement.[6]

Welensky told Joelson and others of this attempt to get Butler to visit or to water down his statement. Then he met Alport on 7 May and learned that Butler believed his statement would be seen in Britain and the Federation as a balanced interpretation of the situation. He thought the Federal Government was attaching undue importance to the references to Nyasaland, which he acknowledged were misleading when taken out of context. The motion, he said, was only seeking a solution to the problems of Central Africa. The Labour Party would propose an amendment to adopt the major recommendations of the Monckton Commission to permit secession and impose a constitution on Northern Rhodesia based on African majority rule. The Government would oppose this even though Jones had warned that Banda's reaction would be "excitable", especially in view of Butler's comments on Federal achievements and the necessity for preserving the Federation. Thus Butler advised Welensky to reserve his position until they met. He firmly believed that his statement was the basis for constructive discussion and that the Federal position would be weakened if Welensky repudiated it. Welensky replied that he would study the speech and would only issue a statement if forced so to do. Thereafter Welensky informed his Cabinet that he had reserved comment until he saw the full text.[7]

In the Commons that day, 8 May, Butler duly made his statement, adding that he thought the multi-racial concept should be fostered. Although at different stages of constitutional advance, he claimed that all the territories

[5] *Ibid.*, 20/2, ff. 16–18, Alport to Welensky, 1 May 1962.
[6] *Ibid.*, ff. 13–15, Welensky to Alport, 3 May 1962.
[7] *Ibid.*, 24/152, ff. 180–182, Welensky to Joelson, 5 May 1962; 20/2, ff. 11–12, Minutes of a Meeting with Alport, 7 May 1962; FGC(62), 12th Meeting, Restricted Annexure, Federal Cabinet, 8 May 1962.

were heading in the same direction. The 1961 Constitution of Southern Rhodesia might not appear to be as progressive as that of Northern Rhodesia, but was a considerable advance. For the first time, 15 Africans were being seated in the Legislative Assembly, and by sheer weight of numbers the African would gain an increasing influence. The European electorate had overwhelmingly accepted the change and in so doing had revolutionised its thinking.

Butler realised that many Africans were dissatisfied with the pace of political advance, but hoped that they would participate in the Southern Rhodesian election and take advantage of the opportunies offered. He had told the UN Committee of Seventeen, when it visited London, that his Government could not unilaterally set aside the Southern Rhodesian Constitution. Yet that Committee had ignored him, he said, and was still asking for this, but his Government would answer that it had no right to intrude.

Butler maintained that it had been very difficult to settle the Northern Rhodesian Constitution but that Britain had remained true to her objective of meeting the aspirations of the population, while providing stable government and preserving the non-racial approach to politics. He avowed that protected status would be retained for as long as required. He dismissed, as impractical, the Opposition's amendment asking for the adoption of the recommendation of the Monckton Commission for African majority rule, because the Constitution did not prescribe a majority for any race or party. Furthermore, he noted, all the Parties were contesting the elections. The clashes between the rival Parties were most disquieting, and he would support Hone fully in the maintenance of order. He was reluctant to introduce any restrictions, but peace had to be maintained and Hone had thought it right to prevent meetings which would lead to breaches thereof. Progress could and would be made under the existing Constitution, he said, and the British Government was not prepared to adjust it for the moment.

Butler reported that Nyasaland was progressing well after Banda's electoral victory and that currently seven of the ten Executive Council seats were filled by unofficial Members. Yet, he claimed, the broader problems of the Federation were reflected intensely in Nyasaland. Federation had brought great economic advantages, but the population still rejected it. It faced economic and other problems, but Butler sought an acceptable solution which would retain the very real advantages of the association of the three territories. When mentioning its failures, its critics forgot its major economic advantages. The key was political advancement which the Africans felt was too slow and the Europeans thought was too fast, but it was the British Government's task to persuade the races to co-operate for their mutual advantage. He looked forward to his visit and avowed that he would be receptive to any ideas from any quarter.

He said his Government could not accept the Opposition amendment on secession because it approached this grave problem in too general and too negative a manner. He sought a constructive approach, not one which would "just pull the bricks out and let the structure collapse".

Butler acknowledged that the Malawi Congress Party wished Nyasaland to secede but felt that first there should be a full examination of the territory's financial needs and economic viability as well as of all possible forms of association between the territories. He said there was no desire for another public inquiry, and that he would appoint advisers to himself who would give the Federal Government the fullest opportunity to present its views. He hoped to see a continuing association of the territories which was acceptable to them and based on the goodwill of the people. There was no British intention to abdicate from its responsibilities and, therefore, he was taking the initiative.

Denis Healey, for the Labour Party, nonetheless argued that the problems were not only dangerous and complex, but that they were the most important which had faced the British Government in Commonwealth affairs since the granting of India's independence. Butler's mistake, he said, was not to recognise African opinion. It was tragic that Britain, who had given freedom to so many millions in the past 15 years, should be attacked in the UN by those whom she had liberated. The British Government had brought this on itself by creating the Federation. The result, Healey claimed, was that the European minority had inhibited and distorted British Colonial policy.

Healey had no doubt that the majority of Africans were bitterly opposed to the Federation, with the result that its survival was at stake. He blamed the European for failing to dispel the fears of the African, and the steady erosion of the British Government's protective power, which had started with the rejection of the recommendation of the African Affairs Board in 1957. Consequently, the Africans hated the Federation and would be satisfied with nothing less than total independence for the three separate territories. Healey argued that, therefore, the Monckton Commission recommendations should be implemented. Instead, the British Government vacillated about the Federation's future. He noted that, since Monckton had reported, Nigeria, Tanganyika, Sierra Leone, Somalia, Uganda, Kenya and Zanzibar had all negotiated their independence, while the Federal Africans were refused the rights accorded elsewhere because of the opposition of a tiny European population. It would not be long, he averred, before the moderate African nationalists could no longer resist the pressure for bloody revolt. Thus the British Government had to move quickly because there was the probability of external intervention. He did not blame the European minority for defending its privileges, or Welensky for fighting to preserve what he believed in passionately. However, he wished that Welensky had less voice and more vision.

Healey, while claiming to understand white attitudes, reminded Parliament that it had an inescapable responsibility to the African majority. The British Government, he said, had to declare that no more rights would be surrendered to the European and that it would keep tight control on Federal foreign policy. He wanted Butler to assure Banda that the first issue the Federal Review would consider would be secession and that he could have internal self-government if he requested it. As Northern Rhodesia was the key, Healey hoped that Kaunda would be returned because he was risking his political reputation and, perhaps, his life, by accepting a constitution which was designed to leave in doubt whether the African majority could gain even parity in the Legislative Council. He urged that Kaunda had to be assured that the Federal troops would not interfere in the election. Finally, Healey said, Butler had to secure parity for African representation, based on a common roll, in the Southern Rhodesian legislature.

Butler replied that no further powers would be surrendered, but warned that intimidation had to be curbed, and that the Europeans also had to cease threatening the use of force.[8]

Before the Commons debate, Butler had told Welensky that, by couching everything in a general statement, commitments would not be noticed, but he did not disguise them from Beckett who found "disastrous" the refusal to hold the Federal Review before the territorial elections. However, Butler was not without local advice because, amongst others, Sir Keith Acutt and H. F. Oppenheimer told him before he left London for Salisbury that the solution should not be based purely on economic considerations. Acutt also warned Welensky that the British public was disinterested in the fate of the Federation, and that the Press depicted him as an "ogre" who sought only white domination. Acutt, however, added that he had discovered that the City would welcome reassuring news from Rhodesia because it was looking for fields of investment.[9]

Butler arrived in Salisbury on 11 May, but the Welensky Papers have no official record of the first two meetings. In public, Butler declared that he had no preconceived notions. He did not attempt to dissuade the Zimbabwe African People's Union from boycotting the Southern Rhodesian election. Indeed, he stated that there would be no change in the Southern Rhodesian Constitution, and reiterated his desire for a continued association between the three territories.[10]

Welensky told Beckett that he had spent much of the first meetings with Butler describing what would happen in Northern Rhodesia. He said that Butler rejected partition but hoped another idea would emerge. Welensky vowed he would do everything to win Butler over, but the truth was that he was dealing with a British Government which lacked courage. Nonetheless, Welensky informed his other correspondents that it was a pleasure to deal with Butler because he was frank, decent and willing to listen.

Welensky was urging all Northern Rhodesians, including Beckett, to ensure that all Europeans voted because the prescribed minimum percentages would be difficult to obtain, and took the opportunity to reveal just how little support he was enjoying. He said it was useless suggesting that he could rely on Whitehead because he always put Southern Rhodesian interests first. Moreover, the attitude of some of the Southern Rhodesian Ministers was most puzzling because they really believed that their territory could survive alone.

Whitehead, he said, was determined to spend every penny on African education, and currently educated proportionately more of his population than did India. Welensky could see little point in educating people in an academic sense unless they could be employed and be given opportunities of

[8] House of Commons *Hansard* (London), Vol. 659, Col. 235 f., 8 May 1962.
[9] Welensky Papers, 42/21, f. 10, G. Beckett to Welensky, 11 May 1962; 27/110, f. 16, Sir Keith Acutt to Welensky, 11 May 1962.
[10] *Ibid.*, 42/38, f. 66, Butler's Press Conference, 12 May 1962.

bettering themselves. However, he said, the most important factor was that Whitehead knew that he could not win his election without his support.[11]

Records do exist of the meetings with Butler on 14 May in Welensky's office. In the first of these, Greenfield expressed pleasure at Butler's appointment and confidence that a better understanding would result. He claimed that a difficulty had been to get a clear indication of British thinking on the future of the Federation, and thought that all doubts should be cleared because it appeared that the British considered a new form of association inevitable. He said that Butler's comments on the precise nature of the commitment to Banda would also be appreciated. A statement was also sought on the comments of certain British Ministers and officials, which ignored the existence of the properly constituted Federation, when they indicated that the consent of the territories was a prerequisite to any new association. Greenfield said he understood that the British Government would consider itself bound by a commitment on secession to Nyasaland but that it hoped to persuade Banda to remain associated with the Rhodesias after the Federation had been dissolved. The Federal Government felt strongly that it should have been consulted on this. In fact, he declared, without its consent, no such commitment was legally binding. In terms of the Convention of 1957, Sandys had had no right to act unilaterally. Greenfield acknowledged that the Lord Chancellor had recently given a different interpretation but, simultaneously, Butler, in the Commons, had placed great reliance on the identical Convention *vis-à-vis* Southern Rhodesia. The Federal Government was mystified, but was determined to be in at least as strong a position as Banda. Then, somewhat to Butler's annoyance, Greenfield showed him a copy of a letter he had written to *The Times*, commenting on the British contradictory statements on the Conventions.

Greenfield also expressed concern that certain British official circles assumed that the Federation was "on its last legs". The Federal Government was also perturbed at the manner in which its policies and practices were depicted at the UN and felt that there was a need for consultative machinery which would ensure that its case would not go by default.

To illustrate Greenfield's point, Welensky said that Kaunda had claimed at the UN that more money had been spent on rescuing animals from the rising waters of Lake Kariba than had been used for the resettling of the Africans who had lived there. Welensky protested that Kaunda had not been corrected by the British representatives at the UN. There was, Welensky said, a general and deplorable lack of spirit shown in repudiation and he hoped that the British diplomats would consult his officials more often.

Speaking first on secession, Butler said that, prior to his appointment, there had been considerable contact between Banda and the British Ministers and that their discussions went far towards recognising Banda's views on secession. Banda had intended to go to London to demand secession and only with considerable difficulty had he been dissuaded. Butler explained that the only real commitment which had been made was in the Commons on 8 May when he had recognised that Banda and his MCP, with the support of a firm

[11] *Ibid.*, 42/21, f. 6, Welensky to Beckett, 13 May 1962; 27/108, f. 26, Welensky to S. M. W. Andreasen, 13 May 1962.

mandate, were not prepared to remain in the Federation. He had gone no further, and the Labour Party had been soundly defeated in seeking the approval of secession. The Conservative Party had fully supported the examination of the consequences of Nyasaland's withdrawal, and of possible alternative associations.

Butler said he was shocked to learn how the MCP Ministers had interfered in the matters of health, and promised to speak to Banda about this. He doubted, however, whether relations between the Federal and Nyasaland Governments could return to normal without his committee of inquiry. He declared that the British and Federal Governments had the same aim because it was in both their interests that there should be an effective association between the Rhodesias. In particular, he claimed, the British Government would find it difficult to make good the consequences of secession, but yet would not contemplate using force to keep Nyasaland in the Federation against the MCP's will. The British Government believed that the wisest course was an alternative form of association.

Butler said that his legal advisers, when examining the 1957 Convention, had found that the power of the British Parliament was unrestricted in matters which did not fall within the compass of the Federal Government. However, he did not wish to discuss this as he could not foresee circumstances when both parties would resort to the strict letter of the law. He claimed he was embarrassed by the manner in which Federal domestic affairs had been discussed at the UN, and was convinced that Nkomo's current refusal to meet him stemmed from Nkomo's reception in New York. Despite the demands at the UN, the British Government had made it clear that it had not been able to intervene in Southern Rhodesia since 1923. Butler said he had no intention of altering either the Northern or the Southern Rhodesian Constitutions and that Sir Patrick Dean would make a statement to that effect. The Commons would demand that any changes had the support of the majority of the Federal population but would interpret this requirement liberally and sensibly. Butler avowed that he had no preconceived notions on the future association, but had in mind an economic one which would retain close ties, while leaving the territories independent in their own spheres. The union between Southern and Northern Rhodesia should be close while Nyasaland, as a predominantly African country, would be left on a looser rein which would still require the Federation to be generous in its subsidies.

Welensky replied that the British responsibility towards the Federation was too often overlooked. Britain, he said, had created the Federation and thereafter had not defended it against many malicious and ill-informed attacks. The Federal Government had been left to defend itself when it could not counter effectively a campaign sponsored by the Afro-Asian bloc at the UN. He could not understand why a convention, deemed to be binding in the case of Southern Rhodesia, did not apply to the Federation. However, he deferred to Butler's wishes not to discuss it.

Greenfield said he was glad to learn of the limited extent of the British commitment to Banda on secession and that therefore a vital Federal bargaining point had survived. He insisted that, in any negotiations on alternative associations, the Federation's existence had to be recognised. Furthermore, the destruction of the existing relationship between Northern and Southern Rhodesia should not be the prerequisite to discussion which sought to accommodate the MCP's aspirations. The power of the African rabble-rouser had to be realised because it was difficult, if not impossible, to determine the will of the semi-educated or illiterate Africans as their emotions were so easily swayed by the demagogue. Greenfield stressed the importance of retaining as much of the existing Federal structure as possible, and did not approve of destroying it to build an edifice on the foundation of the shaky "acceptance of the people concerned".

Barrow welcomed the enlightenment on the nature of the British commitment on secession. Butler, he said, had claimed that there was less tension in Nyasaland than in the other territories, but Barrow felt that this would only be so as long as the MCP had its way. The Europeans in Nyasaland were despondent, and the morale of the police and civil servants was low. All organised opposition to the MCP had been crushed by intimidation, and that Party was cementing its position by legislation. The Lancaster House Agreement stipulated that the Executive Council would be advisory to the Governor, but it was being allowed to act as a cabinet and Jones never seemed to refuse a request or a recommendation by Banda. An example of Jones's refusal to exercise his responsibilities was his lack of resistance to Banda over the Nkula Falls scheme although it would benefit everyone.

Barrow did not believe that Nyasaland should be treated differently in case the precedent was set for Northern Rhodesia. He knew that Nyasaland did not have a viable economy and could not have one in the foreseeable future. When Banda understood this, and that Britain would make no more concessions, he would moderate his demands. Thus, Barrow said, Butler had to look hard at the situation because, if unchecked, Nyasaland would slide towards tragedy.

Caldicott made the same point about the 1957 Convention applying to Southern Rhodesia and not to the Federation. He said he was worried that Hone would follow the example of Jones and abdicate to Kaunda, when the Barotse had been told that their position was safeguarded by the retention by the Governor of his powers. Another matter of concern was defence which would be radically affected by Nyasaland's secession.

Greenfield was gravely worried about the precedent being set for Northern Rhodesia both on secession and on the powers of the Governor, particularly as Jones had not been prepared to exercise his power to curb the MCP Ministers' anti-Federal acts, even when they were to the detriment of Nyasaland. The result, Greenfield said, was the fiction that Nyasaland was self-governing, when it was several stages from it. If the experience were repeated in Northern Rhodesia, the future would be very bleak.

Butler asked if the Federal Government would prefer a composite approach to one dealing only with Nyasaland. Welensky confirmed that it would, and Butler could see no harm in taking the current relationship as a starting position as advocated by Greenfield. No final views had been formulated on the association of the Rhodesias, but Butler believed Nyasaland's position was different, and he hoped that the Federal Government would consider returning certain functions to that territory. He promised to acquire a clearer picture of Nyasaland, and said he took a serious view already of the lack of co-operation with regard to health and the Nkula Falls scheme. He declared that, in his speech in the Commons, he had dealt with the misunderstanding created by Sandys, and vowed that he would adhere to the position which he (Butler) had taken. He realised the need to settle matters, but was not in as much of a hurry as the Southern Rhodesians. The Convention of 1957 would be re-examined and he would report on it as soon as possible.

For Butler's benefit, Macintyre produced a forecast from his Treasury on the consequences of secession. This related that, to date, the two Rhodesias had contributed to basic income tax while Nyasaland had consistently been a net recipient of the revenue that accrued from it. In the years 1954/55 and 1957/58, Northern Rhodesia's contribution to tax had greatly exceeded that of Southern Rhodesia, but in the last three years the fall in the copper price meant that Southern Rhodesia's contribution was greater than that of Northern Rhodesia. In a single year, 1960/61, Nyasaland received £5 750 000 for Federal Government services, and to date had received £34 000 000 for those services. Secession would bring a sharp contraction in income and expenditure which would affect the level of services provided in Nyasaland. There would be higher taxes, prices, reductions in employment and investment, and a continual preoccupation with the deficit on the balance of payments. It had to be remembered that the demands of a developing country were irresistible, and an example was the allowance by the Federal Government for an annual twelve per cent increase which, however, in 1961/62 had proved inadequate and had led to an appeal to the British Treasury for assistance. These predictions would be sadly inadequate if Southern Rhodesia decided to send home 140 000 Nyasalanders.

Butler welcomed these accounts and promised to study them. He understood that the MCP Ministers were expecting a sharp contraction in their finances. However, he thought it was too early for the Federal Government to declare under what circumstances it would assist Nyasaland. Macintyre rejected this assertion and replied that Federal support could not continue until the shape of the new constitution was seen.[12]

The meeting adjourned until the afternoon and Welensky took the opportunity to reveal to Acutt that Macmillan had asked Butler to improve the relationship with the Federal Government and that he had achieved this. He believed that the morning's session had shaken Butler on the consequences of secession and it seemed that the Federation, in a modified form, would survive. Nonetheless, Welensky said he knew he had so annoyed the British Government on his last visit that "the word went out" that he had to be cut down to size. As for the "ogre" image, he believed that it was being fostered by the African nationalists. He revealed that on the previous day Nyerere had openly incited the Northern Rhodesians to violence with the aim of unseating him. This had induced him to protest to Butler at the manner in which the British Government had stood back dispassionately to give the impression that the problem was Welensky's alone.[13]

[12] *Ibid.*, FGC 19/3, f. 1, Minutes of a Meeting with Butler, 14 May 1962; J. M. Greenfield, *Testimony of a Rhodesian Federal* (Bulawayo, 1978), p. 215.

[13] Welensky Papers, 27/110, f. 15, Welensky to Sir Keith Acutt, 14 May 1962.

When the meeting resumed at 4 p.m., the Federal Ministers asked what had happened to the declaration of rights promised for Nyasaland at Lancaster House. Butler said he would discover why it had not been produced, and Greenfield offered to assist in drafting it. Greenfield then complained that the Federal Government had not been consulted over the appointment of Sir Edgar Unsworth as Chief Justice of Nyasaland. As the Chief Justice was *ex officio* a judge of the Federal Supreme Court, Greenfield said, the Federal interest in the appointment had hitherto been recognised. Butler noted the objection.

Greenfield asked for an account of Butler's recent interview with Kaunda, and Welensky pointed out that Kaunda's position was not a parallel with that of Banda. Welensky hoped that the British Government was not going to recognise Kaunda as the only significant Northern Rhodesian African leader because the African National Congress had considerable support. Butler accepted this view and said he had found Kaunda subdued. They had not discussed any constitutional issues and Kaunda had merely given him an account of his negotiations at the UN and had asked for the release of political prisoners. Butler had impressed on Kaunda the need for all intimidation to cease and reminded him that Britain, and not the UN, was responsible for political advancement. Butler had denied the existence of any political prisoners because the substantial number of UNIP members in gaol had been convicted on criminal charges. Butler proposed to see all leaders in Northern Rhodesia and would not give Kaunda the impression that he expected him to win the election.

Greenfield and Welensky asked about the terms of the delimitation of Northern Rhodesia on which they were to be consulted. Butler replied that these were being drafted and that they would be consulted shortly. Greenfield queried the disqualification of candidates because, normally, a man could not stand for five years after serving even a minor gaol sentence. This idea had been discarded in Kenya and Nyasaland, and the Federal Government feared it would happen in Northern Rhodesia. Butler promised to examine this, but confessed that he would prefer that men like Kaunda and Nkumbula should not be disqualified.

The Federal Ministers returned to the subject of intimidation in Nyasaland — calling it "rank terrorism" — and claimed that free elections were impossible. The people of the territory, they said, had been so regimented that the MCP had secured 90 per cent of the votes. Fear of intimidation had caused the Federal Government to resist the setting of the minimum percentage at ten per cent. They acknowledged that intimidation, being largely based on superstition, was very difficult to suppress. In Northern Rhodesia the police had dealt wisely and firmly with the violence in September 1961, but since then their morale had slumped. A senior policeman had indicated that there was a constraint in acting against intimidation because of the impression being given that Kaunda was the chosen instrument of political advancement and should be allowed to develop his tactics freely.

Butler reiterated that he had ordered Kaunda to eschew intimidation and had committed himself to support the Northern Rhodesian efforts to maintain the law. Greenfield asked if there were any possibility of removing Moffat and Franklin as Ministers because they were avowedly anti-Federal and were leaders of a Party which commanded no support in Northern Rhodesia. Not surprisingly, Butler said that he could not dictate who should be Ministers.

The Federal Ministers asked about Butler's advisers and wanted ample time to brief them. Butler explained that he had wanted to meet them before devising the committee's terms of reference. He did not want a public inquiry or a published report, although he said he would consider a White Paper. He had invited Sir Ralph Hone, the constitutional expert, and Professor Arthur Brown, the economist, to serve and would engage an expert in government. He would employ a British civil servant and might also use Lord Inchyre who, as Sir Frederick Hoyer-Millar, had been the Permanent Head of the Foreign Office. The committee would not be independent and would seek to produce a unanimous report. It would not treat Nyasaland in isolation in examining future associations. It would report on the economic situation and on the political structure required to give the whole Federal area economic stability. Alport would be used for liaison with the Federal and territorial Governments. Butler stated that the committee would not take oral evidence and that, once its advice was forthcoming, he would consult the Federal Government before taking any action. He promised this, he said, because he realised that it was only at that point that the Federal Government could properly present its views on the purely political aspects.[14] On receipt of this promise, which was never to be honoured, the meeting terminated.

Butler met the Southern Rhodesian Cabinet and heard its complaints about its economic straits because it was forced to rely on Federal ability to borrow on the open market. Alport records that Whitehead could barely conceal his impatience with the policies and activities of the Federal Ministers.[15]

Todd was granted an interview with Butler and advanced a plan to save the Federation and still satisfy African aspirations. Afterwards he claimed that Butler had listened with interest because the plan would make it possible for Banda, Kaunda or Nkomo to become Federal Prime Minister through an immediate widening of the Federal franchise which would give the Africans control of the Federal Assembly. Todd then called on Britain to exercise her legislative power to bring in these changes because, he said, although the whites would oppose them, they faced an alternative fraught with the gravest consequences. If the idea were adopted, the problem of Southern Rhodesia would be solved within a year. Todd criticised Welensky bitterly for endangering the future of the Federation's people by clinging to power. The *African Daily News*, while agreeing with the aim of securing majority rule, thought that Todd's idea would be unacceptable to the African nationalists because of their long-expressed anti-Federal views.[16]

As Butler was going to Nyasaland, Greenfield briefed Blackwood saying that Butler had been prepared to answer questions directly. He had promised, Greenfield said, that there had been no further commitment to Banda and had proposed a full investigation before taking a decision. Butler did not

[14] *Ibid.*, FGC 19/3, f. 12, Minutes of a Meeting with Butler, 4 p.m., 14 May 1962.
[15] Lord Alport, *The Sudden Assignment* (London, 1965), p. 184.
[16] *African Daily News*, 17 May 1962.

expect any reaction from Banda on this score and, indeed, hoped that he would remain associated with the other territories in some way once he appreciated the financial perils of secession. Butler seemed aware of the impending disaster in Nyasaland and was not prepared to foot the bill, which gave the Federal Government a significant bargaining counter. He was copying Sandys, with the difference that he did not want Nyasaland thrown to the wolves and thought that the Federation should continue to buy Nyasaland's products to keep Banda sweet. Greenfield was highly impressed with Butler's quick grasp of Macintyre's figures and praised him as the most brilliant member of the British Cabinet.

For Blackwood's benefit, Greenfield told of Barrow's impressive briefing of Butler on the situation in Nyasaland, while Goldberg had explained the difficulties being experienced by the health service there. Butler had commented to Goldberg that, if the events he had described were exposed in the Commons, they would cause a sensation. Greenfield advised Blackwood to leave the economic case to Macintyre and concentrate, like Barrow, on the "Nazification" of Nyasaland and the resultant collapse of morale in the police and civil service. He believed that Butler was worth treating as a friend and with respect. There was no need to be obsequious, but Butler should be accorded more deference than Sandys *et al.* Butler seemed to respond to friendliness and thus should not be addressed like a jury which was, Greenfield confessed, his normal habit. He said that Butler was convinced that, through his speeches, he had made the best of the situation created by Sandys and Maudling. Thus Blackwood had to take care in the Legislative Council not to disturb the situation and rattle Butler by forcing him to save Banda's face. Butler had been frank about his predecessors, but it would be unwise to prompt him on the subject. Greenfield's final comment to Blackwood was that it was important that Butler should see the African UFP members.[17]

Greenfield's enthusiasm for Butler would not last long. In fact, the Federal Government's view of him soured when he gave a Press interview in Zomba and declared that the British Government acknowledged that, because of its mandate, the MCP was not prepared to allow Nyasaland to remain in the Federation. He said that, amongst a wide cross-section of the population, he had seen Banda and looked forward to further discussions with him in London. However, he disclosed that Banda had reserved his position on any future association with the Rhodesias. Butler described the nature of his proposed advisory committee's inquiry but refused to say much more than he had already said in the Commons.

After meeting Butler, Banda was more than usually jovial and claimed to the Press to be completely satisfied because: "All I want is dissolution, Nyasaland out! That is all. I have no interest in the Federal Review Conference." Butler has since revealed that Jones had warned him to invite Banda to London or run the risk of an insurrection.[18]

The Press interpreted Butler's statement in Zomba as meaning the end of the Federation. Welensky was furious with Butler, but Alport persuaded him

[17] Welensky Papers, 32/63, f. la, Greenfield to M. H. Blackwood, 15 May 1962.
[18] *Ibid.*, 42/21, ff. 14–33, Butler's Press Conference, 17 May 1962; *The Rhodesia Herald*, 18 May 1962; Lord Butler, *The Art of the Possible: The Memoirs of Lord Butler* (London, 1973), p. 213.

to hold his tongue. Nevertheless, Welensky told Robinson: "This fellow [Butler] was sweet reasonableness when he met us and yet you read what he said in Nyasaland, your hair stands on end . . . should not be shocked or surprised — ought to know by now." Complaining to Lord Robins, he claimed that he had protested, through Alport, to Butler who merely replied that he had said nothing more than he had said in the Commons.[19]

Butler was more restrained in Northern Rhodesia when consulting Kaunda and other political figures. He was confronted by a serious bid by the Barotse for separation from Northern Rhodesia, but gently refused it for economic and other reasons. In any case, he thought that it was too early for decisions and preferred to await the verdict of his proposed advisory committee.[20]

Butler reported to the Federal Cabinet on 23 May saying that he had been subjected to considerable pressure in the North. Banda had been almost pathological on secession, he said, and had seemed to have been expecting an immediate answer. He and his fellow Ministers had insisted that he should be made chief minister immediately. However, they had agreed to a postponement until Banda visited Britain in June or July. The Nyasaland Europeans had appeared so nervous of the MCP that Butler believed they would welcome a move towards self-government, provided that there would be a bill of rights. Explaining his Press conference in Zomba, Butler declared that he had only repeated what he had said in the Commons but that it had appeared to be more dramatic in Nyasaland. The position had not changed, he assured the Cabinet, and there would be a final examination before any decisions were taken. The MCP Ministers were bent on secession but he had warned Banda of its dangers and had not promised any British aid. He proposed that a special representative from Nyasaland should assist his advisory committee and, to calm Federal fears, he declared that he was under no obligation to accept any advice which was forthcoming or to publish it. He had discussed the Nkula Falls scheme twice with Banda, as well as the health issue, and hoped that he had made an impression.

Butler said he had gathered in Northern Rhodesia that, if isolated, it would still have a viable economy. However, intelligent opinion still seemed to favour association with Southern Rhodesia. He had enjoyed his conversations with the UFP, but had found the African nationalists immature. Kaunda seemed to possess none of the qualities attributed to him by the Press and others. The result of the Northern Rhodesian general election was likely to be a coalition of African nationalists, but Butler insisted it should be held before any settlement of the overall problem. He had found again the pathological, almost unreasoning, dislike of the Federation, even amongst the Chiefs, which led him to favour a change of name for it. Finally, he referred briefly to his meeting with the Barotse representatives and said he was glad that they had accepted the new Northern Rhodesian Constitution. However, he did not mention their desire to secede from Northern Rhodesia.

Butler's reiteration that he had said nothing more in Zomba than he had in

[19] Alport, *The Sudden Assignment*, *op. cit.*, p. 183; Welensky Papers, 32/28, f. 35, Welensky to Robinson, 21 May 1962; 25/240A, f. 31, Welensky to Lord Robins, 22 May 1962.

[20] Welensky Papers, 20/9, f. 10, Report of a Meeting between Butler and the Representatives of Barotseland, 21 May 1962.

the Commons did not save him from the wrath of Barrow who claimed that the Europeans had been bitterly disappointed by his comments. Barrow agreed that the Europeans would accept a greater measure of self-government for Nyasaland with safeguards, but claimed that this was simply a measure of their despondency, and that they knew that a bill of rights would be valueless after independence. Greenfield and Caldicott reminded Butler that Jones did not always have to accept the advice of his Executive Council and hoped that Butler would ensure that Jones sometimes rejected it. This was particularly important, they said, as the Barotse had been persuaded to accept the Northern Rhodesian Constitution on the understanding that the Governor retained and would exercise his powers. Butler found excuses for Jones and thought that a greater measure of self-government would have to be discussed at a full constitutional conference.

Greenfield warned that the Federal Government disliked the suggested committee of inquiry because it smacked of a foregone conclusion. In any case, he recalled, Butler had argued that the announcement of the proposed inquiry would deter Banda from travelling to London but he was still going. Greenfield said that the Press interpretation of Butler's remarks had made the Federal Government's position very difficult, forcing it to continue to maintain that its consent was necessary before the Federation could be dismembered. Greenfield had noticed that Butler appeared to favour the retention of the economic links at the expense of the political ties, while giving every consideration to the opinions of the opponents of the Federation. There was still no support for the Federal Government from the British Government but what had to be discovered was whether the latter thought there was any future for the existing Federation. Greenfield criticised Butler for repeating in Zomba that any solution had to be acceptable to Nyasaland and be based on the goodwill of the people because he believed an acceptable settlement was unlikely if it depended on the consent of the people as represented by the African nationalist leaders.

Welensky, endorsing these views, stressed the importance of retaining the current Federal structure with the necessary adaptations. If the Federation were dismantled, he said, there would be insurmountable obstacles to a future association. Butler replied that he was not considering holding a referendum to discover the true feelings of the people, but was bound by the Federal constitutional preamble which prescribed that the northern territories could not be held in an association with Southern Rhodesia against the will of the people. He warned that his Parliament would reject a solution based on force and said that he would retain a close relationship between the Rhodesias while forging a special link with Nyasaland, and would do so despite the wishes of certain politicians.

Greenfield maintained that the preamble described the attainment of full Commonwealth status and not dismemberment, as the latter had not been envisaged when the Constitution was drafted. The important fact was that the Federation existed and its Government could not be ignored. There was no Federal desire, he said, to adopt a negative or unrealistic attitude but, if it was clear that the Federation would be dismantled before there was agreement on any alternative, the Federal Government would be driven to hold what it had.

Butler said that there were three courses open to him. The first was to do nothing. The second was to allow secession, and the third was to make a sincere effort to hold at least the major portion of the Federation together, perhaps under a new name, with a fresh division of powers. The first course was impracticable; the second regrettable; and the third was the right solution, although it would attract criticism. There was a need for close Anglo-Federal co-operation. He did not know if a further Federal Review was desirable, but would consider it in the light of events.

Greenfield replied that his Government did not advocate the retention of the *status quo* at all costs, but could not stand idly by while its bargaining position was gradually eroded. He asked if the advisory committee would look only at secession, and Butler replied evasively that there should be a team of three for Nyasaland and another three to examine alternative associations, as there could be an interchange between the teams. Welensky urged him to keep the committee numbers small.

Caldicott demanded that there be a lasting solution for the Federation. He argued that it should be recognised that a Party like Kaunda's could win the election with a similar massive majority to that of Banda. Therefore, should Nyasaland secede, it was essential to ensure that Kaunda would not be able to question Northern Rhodesia's relationship with Southern Rhodesia. Welensky agreed that there was little point in anything unless it was permanent. It was also necessary to secure a degree of independence for the Federation to recover public confidence.

Butler appreciated the need for a long-term solution and wanted Federal opinion on what changes were possible. Welensky replied that he could not discuss an overall solution until the composition of the new Northern Rhodesian Government was known, because on this depended the re-adjustment of issues like education. He said he had made it clear that his Government would consider modifications, but did not want to make any proposals lest they be regarded as an opening for negotiations. He believed it would be fatal to divide the Rhodesias because the economic links would be valueless without political ties. He hoped none of the decisions to which Butler had referred would be taken unilaterally and that the Federal Government would be fully consulted.

Butler reiterated that he did not wish to base his case on legal interpretations of the powers vested in the Governments. He recognised that the Federal Government held strong views, but reminded it that his Government was entitled to have some of its own. He wished to restore confidence between the Governments but thought that Nyasaland was a problem which should be treated differently. He had wanted to preserve the links with Nyasaland and had been disappointed by the short-sighted attitude there. He could not promise that the British Treasury would compensate Nyasaland for secession. More money than it currently provided would be available, but it would not find £6 000 000 p.a.

Welensky promised that, if his Government knew that the close relationship between the Rhodesias would be preserved with Nyasaland on a looser rein, a Federal contribution to Nyasaland would be made, possibly in the form of services, but not at the current level. If such an assurance were forthcoming, the Governments could settle down to the task of devising the new association and achieving a substantial measure of agreement. He said he could not help being concerned about the Nyasaland Europeans.

The meeting discussed the reallocation of functions and thought that the Governments should co-operate on this. Such willingness much encouraged Butler. The meeting agreed to consider what could be offered to the civil servants before opening negotiations with them on matters such as the abolition of office. Barrow asked about the Nyasaland appointee to the advisory committee because he feared that Banda might secure the services of an American or Ghanaian. Butler promptly assured him that Jones would control the choice. In any case, he said, a liaison officer and not an adviser would be appointed.

Butler then reiterated that the final draft of the terms of reference of the Northern Rhodesian Delimitation Commission was being prepared and that he hoped that, after the Federal Government had seen a copy, the terms could be approved by the Privy Council in June. Greenfield asked for time to study the terms because his Government had asked about them months previously and had received no reply. He did not want a British judge as chairman because he preferred the Chief Justice of Northern Rhodesia who understood local conditions.

Greenfield referred again to the Convention of 1957 and suggested that Lord Malvern could enlighten Butler on this subject. However, Butler was confident that the Lord Chancellor was right about the position in pure law but thought that it would be a sad day if agreement had to be reached on such a basis. Greenfield acknowledged the right of the British Parliament to legislate on anything ultimately, but noted that there was disagreement on the scope of the Convention. Welensky offered to provide a paper on the subject.

Regarding Federal independence, Butler declared that it was important that the territories should enjoy under it a considerable measure of autonomy. He wondered what power could be given to the Federation to amend its own Constitution. Greenfield replied that this would depend on the final form of the territorial Constitutions and on the agreements between the territorial and British Governments. He thought it important that the Federation should achieve the greatest measure of independence possible. It was anomalous, for example, that Southern Rhodesia should already be more independent than the Federation.

Finally they discussed the Nyasaland share of the Federal public debt which Macintyre calculated to be between £9 000 000 and £10 000 000. Butler promised to study the problem and then summed up, describing the meeting as having been very useful. He welcomed Welensky's acknowledgement of a solution which aimed at retaining the strength of the Federal association with certain adaptations, including recognising the special position of Nyasaland. He was impressed by the degree of territorial interdependence and was anxious to get his inquiry under way. He emphasised his desire to co-operate with the Federal Government and hoped that everyone now understood the other's point of view.

Welensky was equally anxious to co-operate, but warned Butler that he would resist with everything at his disposal any solution which was based purely on economics and which abandoned effective political control.[21] On that note the meeting ended.

However, Welensky indicated to his confidants that he had recovered his faith in Butler. He believed that he had persuaded him that Kaunda was not suitable to lead Northern Rhodesia, that there were no easy solutions, and that there would be "a first class row" if something worthwhile were not produced. Butler, Welensky felt, should have been sobered by meeting Banda. He had appeared to indicate that he would prefer a victory by the UFP in Northern Rhodesia. Welensky recalled that Butler had endured a hostile reception from the African nationalists when he arrived at Salisbury airport, but when he left they had cheered him.

However, Nkomo had publicly accused Butler of conspiring with Whitehead against ZAPU to protect Europeans of British origin. Butler had informed a Southern Rhodesian audience that he would not brook interference by the UN in their affairs and that his Government would neither suspend nor reform the 1961 Constitution, and Nkomo interpreted this as an attempt to ignore the people's will and to bless in advance any reckless action by the "Settler Government". Such hypocrisy, Nkomo believed, would merely lose Britain the friendship of the Africans because it could not continue to give greater loyalty to the Europeans than to the masses while pretending to be leading its colonies to independence on the basis of majority rule. Nkomo warned that any banning of his organisation would make little difference to the African struggle. He explained that he had refused to meet Butler because he would not discuss only polite generalities.[22]

Banda told a rally in Zomba that he would return to prison if there were no secession. He called for Welensky's immediate resignation and revealed that he had threatened to resign if Jones allowed the Nkula Falls scheme to proceed. He attacked the University College of Rhodesia and Nyasaland in Salisbury for turning the African students into "stooges", and announced that he was withholding all Nyasaland scholarships.[23]

In the Federation and in Britain, Butler was depicted as returning home in triumph and it was noted that Welensky had made a compromise possible by agreeing publicly that there could be major changes and by hinting that he might accept a degree of autonomy for Nyasaland. It was hoped that the British Parties would allow Butler to grope his way forward to a solution.[24]

On 29 May Butler reported to Robinson that the visit had gone well. He appreciated the concern of the Federal Cabinet but said that no one could yet see a solution. However, they would seek one on the basis of the existing Federal association. The next stage was to appoint the advisory committee on Nyasaland and then tackle the broad problem. Butler said he understood why Welensky wanted more than an economic association to survive.

Robinson asked Butler about the amount of aid being provided by certain Commonwealth countries for the African nationalists. He said Ghana was assisting Nkomo and was widely believed to have threatened to cut off aid

[21] *Ibid.*, FGC 19/3, f. 17, Minutes of a Meeting with Butler, 23 May 1962.
[22] *African Daily News*, 26 May 1962.
[23] Welensky Papers, 27/90, f. 10, Banda's Public Meeting, 28 May 1962.
[24] *Yorkshire Post*, 28 May 1962; Butler, *The Art of the Possible*, *op. cit.*, p. 216.

after Nkomo had accepted the 1961 Constitution, with the result that he had recanted. Nigeria had financed Nkomo's recent trip to the UN. Robinson said he mentioned this because he feared that Butler might find that outside influences would undermine any agreement he might secure with the African nationalists. Butler ignored this and spoke with alarm of Whitehead's warning of imminent major unemployment and a financial crisis. He was glad that a man of Whitehead's steely character was in charge. He was disappointed in Kaunda, who seemed "dim", and in his delegation which had arrived half an hour late, with two members failing to appear at all. Butler said he expected a stalemate in the Northern Rhodesian election.[25]

Welensky issued a public statement giving some of the details of the talks, including the Federal fears expressed on Nyasaland. He welcomed the British inquiry as something for which his Government had long pressed.[26]

On 1 June Welensky wrote to Butler thanking him for his friendly, frank approach. Welensky revealed that his Government was most encouraged to find at last that the British Government believed in strong bonds between the territories. Nonetheless, he noted with concern the British Government's insistence that any settlement of the Federal problem should be dependent on the consent of the inhabitants and that Butler had constantly invoked the Federal constitutional preamble in this respect.

However, Welensky maintained that the preamble only required the consent of the inhabitants in two cases. The first allowed the inhabitants to keep their territorial method of government for as long as they pleased. This was to prevent amalgamation. The second demanded their consent if the Federation were about to acquire dominion status. Their consent might also be required for the termination of British control over the northern territories, but this did not present a problem because all parties were anxious for independence for their territories in the not too distant future. The only question was how they would get it.

Welensky believed that Butler had not yet given enough weight to the Federation's existence. Moreover, he needed to remember that, when the British Government had created the Federation, it had ignored the alleged lack of consent of the northern Africans. If it were suggested that the sanction of the inhabitants was needed for any new association, the Federal Government would insist that this was only part of the requirement. Welensky said he emphasised this because the consent of the Federation's four Governments was necessary for any major alteration of the current Constitution. Equally, the people of one or more of the territories could not be allowed to withdraw without the consent of the Governments, including the Federal Government. If this were understood, a compromise was possible. To give weight to this argument, Welensky quoted the comments made by Lyttelton and Swinton in 1953 which confirmed that the Federation could not be liquidated without the consent of the four Governments. Therefore, Welensky warned that his Government would insist that there should be no radical revision of the Constitution without its consent. Before giving that, the Federal Government would consider its responsibilities to its creditors, civil

[25] Welensky Papers, FGC(1), 22/62, Minutes of a Meeting with Butler, 29 May 1962.
[26] *Yorkshire Post*, 28 May 1962.

servants and public. Yet its willingness to negotiate showed a far more constructive attitude than did the northern African nationalists. As the constitutional conventions forbad unilateral British action on secession, the Federal Government did not intend to co-operate until a decision had been reached on the continuation of the Federation. A temporary solution would be unacceptable, and only independence would protect the Federation from attack at the UN.

He said that a purely economic association was not feasible and that there were other factors to be considered. For example, it would not be politically possible to surrender non-African education even though the Federal Government would shortly introduce legislation to allow the establishment of multiracial schools.[27]

Welensky also informed Butler that his Government, after a hurried examination of the draft order in council for the Northern Rhodesian Delimitation Commission, disliked it. He proposed to offer simpler terms of reference which would meet the Federal objections, while favouring all Parties. As it stood, he said, the order in council was excessively complex, would be difficult to explain, and might lead the African to conclude that the intention was sinister. There was too much uncertainty about the pattern which would be produced. The prescribed 50 per cent degree of latitude in the delimitation of each constituency would make a mockery of the concept of the national roll seats, and thus of the whole Constitution, because these seats were supposed to return only candidates who could secure the support of all races. It could put a premium on the vote in one constituency and debase it in another. The Delimitation Commission would clearly be impartial, but it was obvious that the framers of the terms of reference believed that it had to have a very great latitude and that a balanced distribution of voters was unattainable. There were great differences in the distribution of voters, but the Federal delimitation had been achieved without needing the prescribed variation of 25 per cent.

Another unnecessary complication, Welensky said, was the distinction between urban and rural constituencies. The proposal that the lower roll should be delimited by population rather than by voters was objectionable because it would lead to an uneven distribution in the ordinary and national roll constituencies, making the task of the national roll candidates very difficult. As the population was unevenly spread, this proposal could favour one Party. The national roll constituencies would inevitably be a combination of rural constituencies where the European population was sparse, and thus the principle of the candidate seeking the support of both races would be destroyed.

Welensky claimed that all objections could be overcome simply by dividing Northern Rhodesia into seven national roll constituencies on the basis of an average ratio of voters, ignoring urban and rural distinctions. The national roll constituency with the highest number of upper roll voters would then be divided into three upper roll and two lower roll constituencies. The national roll constituency with the greatest number of lower roll voters would be

[27] Welensky Papers, 20/2, ff. 2–8, Welensky to Butler, 1 June 1962.

divided into three lower roll and two upper roll constituencies. The remaining five national roll constituencies would each be divided into two upper roll and two lower roll constituencies. Four of the national roll constituencies would be designated racially-reserved double-Member constituencies. The margin of delimitation would be 15 per cent and, in exceptional cases, not more than 25 per cent. As such great differences of opinion were apparent, Welensky asked for more time to consider the matter.[28]

As Welensky had written officially to Butler, he furnished a private explanation of his attitude. The main point, he wrote, was that the bulk of the rural population lived in the Northern, Eastern and Luapula Provinces where Kaunda drew his strength. The small European population there comprised mainly missionaries and civil servants who thought differently from those who had deep roots in the territory. With only a few hundred European voters in those provinces, the ten per cent cross-voting would thus be a farce. Sandys had assured the Federal Government that it need not fear the delimitation because it would achieve a result favourable to it, but, Welensky told Butler, he was seeking fairness to all Parties.[29]

While Welensky argued thus, the Southern Rhodesian Delimitation Commission reported that it could not complete its task in time for an election in October as Whitehead intended. Consequently, Whitehead announced a postponement without naming an alternative date. His action was hailed as a victory by the African nationalists for their threat of a boycott, and they claimed they would prevent the election from ever being held. They proposed to concentrate on inducing the UN to force Britain to change the Constitution, because the UN General Assembly had decided to debate the matter after the Special Committee on Colonialism had suggested, on 12 May, that it should.[30]

When shown Welensky's dispatch of 1 June to Butler, the Northern Rhodesian Government immediately pointed out several misinterpretations. Consequently, on 7 June Welensky acknowledged to Butler that he had misunderstood an ambiguous section on the composition of the national roll constituencies which were, in fact, to be mixtures of upper and lower roll constituencies. This misunderstanding did not deter Welensky from pressing his alternative because, he said, the current registration of voters was revealing that there was no correlation between the voters and the population distribution. The registrations in the urban areas were greatly in excess of those in the rural. To date, he reported, 4 735 lower roll voters had registered in the Northern, Eastern and Luapula Provinces, in contrast to 19 019 in the towns of Chingola, Ndola, Kitwe and Lusaka. Yet, on the population basis, those provinces would be given six or seven of the 15 lower roll seats which would drastically affect the national roll seats, making the result very unpredictable.[31]

Butler replied on 12 June that he and the Northern Rhodesian Government had studied Welensky's proposals carefully, but had to reject them because they would produce peculiar results. He said he was bound by the White

[28] *Ibid.*, 20/7, f. 45, Welensky to Butler, 1 June 1962.
[29] *Ibid.*, f. 40, Welensky to Butler, 1 June 1962.
[30] *Ibid.*, 16/1b, f. 126a, Report on a Meeting with UFP Branch Chairmen, 5 June 1962.
[31] *Ibid.*, 20/7, f. 34, Welensky to Butler, 7 June 1962.

Paper of 20 February 1961 which specified that the upper roll constituencies should cover the urban areas, while the lower served the rural. He justified the use of population as the determining factor because only one African in 15 would be a voter. In any case, he claimed, the White Paper had promised that the unwieldly size of the rural constituencies would be reduced. Butler hoped the rural registration would improve, because the potential discrepancy was not very great as there should be three rural voters to every four urban ones. The urban and rural constituencies, he suggested, could be combined to achieve uniform national roll constituencies, and the 50 per cent margin was included only to secure adequate representation of the rural areas and to ensure that the boundaries of the three types of constituencies coincided. The latter was essential if the voter were to understand the system. However, Butler was prepared to reduce this percentage to 25 per cent for the urban and 33⅓ per cent for the rural constituencies. He was confident that the order in council would not favour one Party and had amended it to ensure that no part of Barotseland was included with a part of Northern Rhodesia. He hoped he had satisfied Welensky, and reiterated that he could not avoid the commitment in the White Paper of 20 February 1961, on using population as the basis for delimitation.[32]

Welensky was grateful for Butler's concessions but expressed his disappointment, when replying on 16 June, that these had not included matters of principle, such as the use of population in the delimitation formula. However, he disputed only the decision to use an "average ratio" of upper and lower roll votes to delimit the national roll constituencies. He said that the pattern emerging from the current registration encouraged his Government to claim that the ratio of urban to rural votes would be three to one, rather than four to three as Butler maintained. It believed also that 60 per cent of voters would live on the Copperbelt. Its sole concern, he asserted, was to achieve a fair and equitable system, and the "average ratio" would render this impossible. The fundamental principle was that the national roll Members should have the substantial support of both races, and it was desirable that the voters should represent all communities. The task of each national roll candidate should be the same, and thus the number of votes in each constituency should be almost equal. The number of European and African voters should also be the same. If the basis of the division used was the ratio between the numbers on the two rolls, there could be unlimited variations. For example, if the ratio were three to seven, one constituency could contain 300 upper and 700 lower roll voters, while another had 3 000 and 7 000. Ten per cent of the former would be 30 Europeans and 70 Africans, but in the latter it would be 300 Europeans and 700 Africans. Persuading 30 voters was obviously easier than persuading 300. The order in council did not insist that the ratio should be absolute in all the national roll constituencies, so further distortions were possible. Moreover, the "average ratio" included Asians, who were mostly upper roll voters, when the Constitution specified that they would be excluded from the national roll elections. It had also to be remembered that there would be 4 500 Africans on the upper roll and virtually no Europeans on the lower.

[32] *Ibid.*, f. 31, Alport to W. S. Parker, 12 June 1962.

The Federal Government had a simple formula to replace the "average ratio". This was to divide the number of Europeans on the rolls by seven and to do likewise for the Africans, using a ten per cent degree of tolerance. If there were 21 000 Europeans and 4 200 Africans on the upper roll, and 70 000 Africans on the lower, each national roll constituency would have 3 000 Europeans and 10 600 Africans. This would meet the requirements for the ten per cent hurdle and would not create difficulties for aligning the boundaries of the constituencies. It would mean that all the national roll candidates would have the same task.[33]

Butler replied that he was sure that his and the Federal aims were similar, but that his Government could not accept a formula based on race. The Northern Rhodesian Delimitation Commission could, therefore, not be instructed to delimit in that way except to exclude the Asians. The Federal idea of dividing by seven was not flexible enough, he said, and the British Government believed the Commission would have to delimit the national roll constituencies independently, and thereafter align the others as best it could. Greater flexibility should be allowed whilst avoiding the unlimited variation on which Welensky had commented. Butler said he would amend the order in council so that the total number of registered voters in any national roll constituency should not be less than a tenth of the total number of voters registered in Northern Rhodesia.[34]

On 23 June Alport was asked to convey to Butler Welensky's deep disappointment at the rejection of his proposals because they had provided a most equitable method. He was dissatisfied with the British formula but, as time was short, would accept it with essential modifications to secure public confidence. These were that the number of upper and lower roll voters in the national roll constituencies should not vary by less than ten per cent or more than 18 per cent. He remained concerned, however, that there would be no racial registration and that the voter's race would only be positively identified on arrival at the polling station.[35]

By the date of this correspondence, the Federal Government had presented Lord Home with a memorandum on UN atrocities in the Congo. The Federal Government intended that this should be submitted to the UN in New York, but was gently rebuffed by the Foreign Office which argued that it would be fruitless to press for an international inquiry because it would only limit the British ability to influence events in the Congo and could lose support for Britain's stand on Southern Rhodesia. The Foreign Office felt that the publication of the memorandum could jeopardise the current talks between Adoula and Tshombe and might involve the Federation in an inter-Party controversy in Britain. Home and Butler agreed with these sentiments and thought that delay in publication was advisable to await the outcome of the UN debate on Southern Rhodesia. The Federal Government reluctantly concurred, while Sir Patrick Dean cautioned the UN General Assembly on debating Southern Rhodesia when the Federation's whole future was under review. He was supported by the United States and Ireland, but otherwise

[33] *Ibid.*, f. 28, Welensky to Butler, 16 June 1962.
[34] *Ibid.*, f. 26, Alport to Welensky, 21 June 1962.
[35] *Ibid.*, f. 24, H. N. Parry to Alport, 23 June 1962.

was ignored because the General Assembly decided to debate the issue fully on 14 June.[36]

This debate, however, had to be postponed a day because of a lack of speakers. Welensky dismissed the UN decision publicly as a piece of chicanery which cared little for the interests of Southern Rhodesians. Whitehead commented that, as the UN lacked the power to interfere in the internal affairs of Southern Rhodesia or any other state, any resolution could not have legal force, and the African nationalists were being misled into thinking that it would.

Todd rued that the UN debate had not preceded the 1961 Southern Rhodesian Constitutional Conference because, he said, the result would have been very different. He urged Whitehead and the British Government to act immediately to change the Constitution and to convene without delay a conference of the "White" Government and the African leaders.[37]

In the event, the UN adopted the resolution which affirmed that Southern Rhodesia was a "non-self-governing territory" and which urged the Committee of Seventeen to continue its efforts to ensure that Southern Rhodesia emerged as an independent African state. It accepted a Bulgarian amendment demanding universal suffrage. Seventy-three nations voted for the resolution and only South Africa opposed it. Sir Patrick Dean walked out as the vote was taken after arguing that the Assembly was acting *ultra vires*. Before then, Butler had declared in London that he would not delegate the problem to any outside body because his task was to reconcile the obvious differences of colour and race to build a contented multi-racial community. In doing so, he would protect the rights of the minority and would build a state where merit alone would count. This was something, he said, which the UN did not understand. He would not brook intimidation and violence, and would not weary of the challenge.[38]

Support from the New Zealand delegation for the British stand drew a protest from Todd to the New Zealand Prime Minister, K. J. Holyoake (later Sir Keith). Todd said that the Africans in Southern Rhodesia were shocked by New Zealand's support for the British attitude because the Southern Rhodesian Government maintained its position by repressive laws, harsh punishments, bannings and the use of the security forces against women and children. It would be serious, he declared, if the "White" Commonwealth ranged, on the basis of blood, against the establishment of a black majority government in a country where the whites constituted only seven per cent of the population, but held the reins of power. He welcomed the UN Resolution because he aimed to see Southern Rhodesia emerge immediately as a free and independent African state in which all men were equal and the Government was based on one man, one vote, thereby bringing freedom, justice, peace and security.[39]

[36] *Ibid.*, 20/13, f. 23, Sir Roger Stevens to Robinson, 8 June 1962; f. 21, Parry to Alport, 12 June 1962; *The Rhodesia Herald*, 13 June 1962.
[37] *The Rhodesia Herald*, 15 & 16 June 1962; Welensky Papers, 42/75, f. 30, Whitehead's Press Conference, 19 June 1962; *African Daily News*, 20 June 1962.
[38] *The Sunday Mail*, 24 June 1962.
[39] *The Rhodesia Herald*, 26 June 1962; *African Daily News*, 30 June 1962.

Reviewing the Southern Rhodesian situation for his correspondents, Welensky decried the official American attitude that Russia sought only to foster African nationalism merely to create chaos. Even the support for Britain by the US Ambassador to the UN, Adlai Stevenson, was qualified because he wanted the Southern Rhodesian election postponed to allow time for Britain to reflect. Welensky wondered how anyone could have respect for the UN because it broke its own rules when they embarrassed the political inclinations of its vocal section.[40]

Welensky revealed that he thought the UFP was steadily losing ground to the Rhodesian Front. He attributed much of the blame to Whitehead but knew there was no one to replace him. He criticised Whitehead's belief that Britain would defend Southern Rhodesia. Whitehead had irritated him by taking it upon himself to announce the Federal decision to build a railway line to the Lowveld sugar estates and by seeking to appoint a Federal representative to Washington without reference to him.[41]

Welensky was called back to Federal affairs when, on 26 June, in the Federal Assembly, Williamson asked him what further mandate he felt the general election had given him. He asked this, he said, because Welensky had admitted publicly that he would not have dissolved Parliament if he had known that Butler would be appointed. Williamson felt that the delay in settling the Federation's future was retarding development. He criticised Welensky for failing to fulfil a promise to consult all political leaders.

Welensky promptly denied this last charge because he had striven to see Banda but to no avail. As far as the Dominion Party was concerned, he claimed to have found great difficulty, before dissolving Parliament, in identifying its leaders because so many of them intended to abandon Federal for Southern Rhodesian politics. He welcomed the appointment of Butler as an acknowledgement of the importance of the Federal problem and had enjoyed discussing that problem with him on his recent visit. Then Welensky revealed that Butler's advisory committee would report to Butler personally and would be assisted by the Federal Government. Asking that this should not be interpreted as a sign of weakness, Welensky emphasised that the Federation was not dead, but was a living entity which had made its mark in the international arena as well as in the Commonwealth. It was certainly stronger, he said, than it had been nine years previously. The duty of the Federal Government was to uphold the Constitution, but it conceded that it might be necessary and desirable to make adjustments to it, although not to the extent of destruction. Welensky remained abhorrent of the familiar spectacle of expediency masquerading as principle.

Noting the UN debate on Southern Rhodesia, Welensky commented that opposing the reasonable stand of the British delegation were 22 dictatorships, 23 countries which had not paid their membership fees, and two (Saudi Arabia and the Yemen) which tolerated slavery. He believed that the African nationalists thought they had found a short cut to power and accordingly looked to the UN, and not to Britain, for comfort and aid. He felt that many countries lost their critical faculties when dealing with problems in which

[40] Welensky Papers, 24/151, ff. 164–166, Welensky to Joelson, 25 June 1962.

[41] *Ibid.*, 43/*Salisbury*, Welensky to Salisbury, 21 June 1962.

race was only one facet. All too often universal franchise was seen as the solution to the Federal problems. He recalled that only three months previously, the Archbishop of York had noticed that the majority was often wrong and that "mobocracy" and not democracy was often the result. Welensky claimed that what was happening in New York, however, was not critical for Southern Rhodesia or the Federation and that it might only hurt the UN. The forthright attitude of the British Government was welcome, he said, and its refusal to implement the decision of the UN General Assembly, on the grounds that it would be powerless to do so even if it wanted to, was equally welcome. A result of the UN debate, Welensky explained, was that he had strengthened the Federal mission in Washington with two experienced men (the action which Whitehead had precipitated) and had invited the Nigerian Prime Minister and some of his parliamentarians to visit the Federation.

Welensky was appalled that a high-ranking American official, Mennen-Williams, could claim that the Communist inroads into Africa had been halted. Welensky was equally affronted by Kaunda's response to Butler's warning on 23 June that violence and intimidation would not be brooked. He related that Kaunda had threatened to paralyse Northern Rhodesia with strikes and a scorched earth policy if the British Government refused to sever the links between the Rhodesias after Nyasaland had left the Federation. Welensky reminded the House that, at the Conference of the Pan-African Freedom Movement of East and Central Africa in February, Kaunda had described the execution of Dedan Kimathi and his Mau Mau colleagues as "assassination" and had stood with the rest of the Conference in silence for a minute in their memory. He recalled that Kaunda had once threatened to make the Mau Mau seem like "a child's picnic". Welensky then went on to expound on the threat of Communism and to warn the West that appeasement never paid.[42]

The next day, 27 June, Greenfield reassured the African MPs in the Federal Assembly on the secession of Nyasaland, claiming that it was now *sub judice* and that Butler had taken care not to commit himself. He denied that any promise had been given to Banda by Maudling and Macleod as alleged. (Greenfield omitted to say that Sandys was responsible.) He praised the African MPs for their reasoned contribution to the debate and said that their request for greater representation was a matter for the Federal Review.

While Greenfield was thus engaged, Welensky was answering a telegram of protest from Kaunda about his statement in Parliament. He pointed out to Kaunda that he had confined himself to Kaunda's own words. Kaunda had claimed, in his protest, that he was prepared for a period of constructive thinking, but Welensky contrasted this attitude with his violent statements and the violent acts of his followers. Thus he asked Kaunda to condemn the Mau Mau publicly for the vile movement that it was and to similarly condemn its leaders to whom he had paid public tribute. He requested him also to renounce intimidation and violence and to prove that his Party had forsaken them. Only then could he accept Kaunda's thinking as constructive.

[42] Fed R & N *Debates* (Salisbury), Vol. 18, Col. 27 f., 26 June 1962.

As he had not asked too much of a reasonable, civilised man, Welensky said he awaited Kaunda's reply with interest. There appears to have been no reply, but on 19 July Kaunda did publicly appeal for European support for his Party and claimed that he had intervened to prevent a strike on the Copperbelt, thereby denying Welensky an excuse to send in his troops.[43]

The aggressiveness of the African nationalists in Southern Rhodesia by the end of June was causing the UFP much concern because it was having to cancel meetings as a result of intimidation and because Africans were becoming afraid to be associated openly with the Party. There was a plea for leading UFP officials and Ministers to assist by attending house meetings with Africans. The Build-a-Nation campaign, designed to induce Africans to register as voters, was continuing at considerable expense, but with little success.[44]

Banda was in London and, as a result, a delegation of Nyasaland Europeans went there in early July to see Butler to protest at an ordinance dealing with Africans on private estates because it appeared to threaten European rights. It was argued that, if Jones gave his assent to the ordinance, it would give the lie to the British argument that a bill of rights was unnecessary, while the Governor retained his executive powers.[45] As far as the talks with Banda were concerned, the British Government only gave a glimpse of them when, on 3 July, it informed the Federal Government that a communiqué would be released on the morrow. This revealed that Butler, Banda and Jones had met on four occasions and had discussed all aspects of Nyasaland's constitutional future. Consequently, Butler had promised to convene a constitutional conference in November to consider further advancement. Banda had insisted on secession at an early date, but Butler had re-affirmed his decision of 8 May that an inquiry had to precede any final conclusion. Consequently, it was agreed that Butler's committee of inquiry, which had been appointed, would start soon.[46]

When the communiqué was released *The Rhodesia Herald* noted that the Nyasaland constitutional conference would be held exactly one month after the Northern Rhodesian general election. Thus, it observed, the election could be expected to have a profound effect on the conference. If the communiqué was somewhat terse, Banda, in typical fashion, proclaimed in London that the Federation was dead and that his "main business is to get its burial certificate". He declared he would not discuss any form of political or economic association until Nyasaland was out of the Federation.[47]

Caldicott had gone to London and met Butler on 6 July in the company of Robinson. Butler had just announced his advisory committee: Sir Roger Stevens of the Foreign Office, Professor Arthur Brown, Professor of Eco-

[43] Welensky Papers, 35/3, f. 270, Welensky to K. D. Kaunda, 28 June 1962; *African Daily News*, 19 July 1962.

[44] Welensky Papers, 16/1b, f. 143, A. D. Butler to A. T. Adams, 29 June 1962; *The Rhodesia Herald*, 28 June 1962.

[45] Welensky Papers, 20/8, f. 31, Greenfield to Welensky, 2 July 1962.

[46] *Ibid.*, f. 30, Commonwealth Relations Office to Alport, 3 July 1962.

[47] *The Rhodesia Herald*, 4 July 1962; Welensky Papers, 27/90, f. 10, Banda's Statement, London, 5 July 1962.

nomics at Leeds University, D. A. Scott, the Deputy British High Commissioner in Salisbury, and Sir Ralph Hone, the constitutional expert. Proclaiming that they were highly suitable, Butler reminded Caldicott that Professor Brown had contributed to a recent symposium on Nyasaland and had stressed the benefits of closer association. Butler confirmed that he was trying to prolong the Nyasaland issue until after the Northern Rhodesian election in October. He assured the Federal representatives that he wanted to maintain the links between the Rhodesias, but reminded Caldicott of the unbridled opposition of the African leaders and confessed that he would be influenced by the results of the Northern Rhodesian election. Moreover, the problem was complicated by Whitehead wanting to retain the disparity in the relationship between the Rhodesias, while Butler was sure that the new Northern Rhodesian Government would want parity. Thus the allocation of tax revenue would be a problem, aside from the political opposition to the continued links. Butler said he had experienced difficulty with Banda and that it had proved impossible to withhold a greater degree of self-government from Nyasaland. Blackwood had concurred, he said, but had demanded a bill of rights. Banda had displayed an enduring pathological hatred of the Federation which had manifested itself throughout the talks. Only very occasionally had he shown a more reasonable attitude towards a new association. Caldicott and Robinson asked if Banda would barter secession for a new form of association, but Butler did not know if he would. He indicated that, at the forthcoming Nyasaland conference in November, two of the three official seats in the Executive Council would be eliminated, but he avowed that he had not promised Banda anything. (It was clear, however, to Robinson that Butler thought that secession had to be granted. It was also apparent that he had no ideas on any future association.) Butler said he believed that Banda might agree to the Nkula Falls scheme and regretted that the Federal Government no longer seemed interested in it.

Butler explained the difficulties which his Government was encountering in attempting to persuade de Gaulle to allow Britain to join the Common Market. He said that, although he had informed U Thant of his disapproval of the UN intervention into Southern Rhodesian affairs, Britain would pay her dues to the UN. Banda, who had ordered the Nyasaland students home from Salisbury, had told him that he would establish his own university with external financial aid. Butler was worried by the unemployment in Southern Rhodesia but hoped to secure aid from the British Treasury. He reiterated that the Northern Rhodesian election would be in October and Robinson gathered a distinct impression that he would pretend otherwise but would do nothing until its result was known because, while he favoured the union between the Rhodesias, he was not sure that it would survive the return of a new anti-Federal Northern Rhodesian Government.[48]

Perhaps Robinson's assessment of Butler's intentions was correct, because the latter, on 10 July, told the Rhodesia and Nyasaland Club at its dinner at the Savoy Hotel in London that investors in Britain and the Commonwealth should put money into the Federation because, if they did, the British

[48] Welensky Papers, 20/3, ff. 205–207, Minutes of a Meeting with Butler, 5 July 1962.

Government would underwrite them.[49] These words would soon have a hollow ring.

In Salisbury, at the suggestion of the British Government, Welensky invited Tshombe to meet him to discuss British anxiety about the prospects of a settlement with Adoula. Tshombe claimed that Adoula was not genuinely interested in settling with him and was simply jealous of Katanga's sound administration and prosperity. Welensky thought it important that Tshombe continue to seek a settlement and furnish financial aid to the Congolese Central Government and that, as the UN had lost credibility somewhat, time was on his side. Although constantly accused of involvement with the mercenaries, Welensky said he would continue to supply the UN with its needs, but not to the extent that stockpiling was possible. He promised to suspend supplies if the UN became aggressive. Then they talked about Katanga's forthcoming second anniversary independence celebrations and matters such as transport. Nothing was said to the Press about their discussions beyond a statement that they had been about trade and commerce.[50]

No hint was given about the financial aid which Tshombe was providing for Nkumbula's ANC. However, it did encourage someone within the Federal ranks to advocate, in a memorandum, "a dirty tricks squad" for the UFP because the Northern Rhodesian election would be a battle for survival. Using Tshombe, somehow it was hoped to persuade UNIP to boycott the election because the British Government feared this most. The ANC was judged to be useless and as Pan-Africanist as UNIP, so a coalition between the UFP and ANC was not feasible. It was felt that the Federal Government had to mount an anti-Pan-Africanism campaign. It could ban all external financial aid and deport key men such as the editor of the *African Mail* and James Skinner, UNIP's lawyer, and later Chief Justice of Zambia. There should be skilful propaganda and forceful demonstrations by the Royal Rhodesian Air Force and the Federal Army. The Federal Ministers should tour Northern Rhodesia, and material inducements should be surreptitiously offered to voters. Financial aid should be given to the Barotse National Party and others. The Catholic Church should be confronted over its support for the African nationalists, and external broadcasts should be jammed.[51] No record exists of any reaction to these suggestions but it is clear that later in the Northern Rhodesian election campaign considerable money was expended and "a dirty tricks squad" was at work under the leadership of a friend of B. M. de Quehen of the Federal Intelligence and Security Bureau.

If Butler was seeking to avoid confrontations, Welensky was in no mood to comply. He protested stiffly on 5 July when he discovered, from a public announcement in London, that there would be a separate adviser on the Barotseland issue. R. S. Hudson, the former Northern Rhodesian Secretary for Native Affairs, was later appointed, but Butler had first replied apologising and telling Welensky he thought he had mentioned it in Salisbury.[52]

[49] Sir Roy Welensky, *Welensky's 4 000 Days* (London, 1964), p. 345.
[50] Welensky Papers, 20/13, f. 125, Minutes of a Meeting with Tshombe, 3 July 1962; *The Rhodesia Herald*, 5 July 1962.
[51] Welensky Papers, 8/69, f. 40A, Memorandum, July 1962.
[52] *Ibid.*, 20/9, f. 9, Alport to Welensky, 14 July 1962.

The day that Butler apologised, 14 July, was the day after Macmillan's "Night of the Long Knives" when he dismissed seven of his Ministers. Four days later Macmillan rid himself of another nine in an attempt to boost Conservative fortunes. Butler survived and left the Home Office to become the First Secretary of State and the Deputy Prime Minister, as well as being responsible for Federal and Common Market negotiations.

Macmillan's action left Welensky, amongst others, wondering at its effect, but Welensky was in no mood to allow Butler time to settle back in the saddle because he and his advisers had completed their examination of the revised draft of the Northern Rhodesian constitutional order in council. Despite the prescription in the White Paper of February 1961 of a declaration of rights, there was no mention of it so Welensky asked Butler if there was to be a separate order in council to accommodate it. He reminded Butler that the Federal Government attached considerable importance to this safeguard. Welensky also wished Butler to remember that he and Greenfield had pointed out that a constitutional retreat was being effected and not an advance because, though African representation was being increased, no progress was being made towards self-government. Another example of the retreat was that, while currently the power of nomination was limited to two seats, in future it would be unlimited. Not to be unnecessarily obstructive, Welensky did not insist on a specific limitation of this power and said he would accept an assurance that not more than one or two Members would be nominated, and only to make up deficiencies in the electoral ranks with regard to "ministerial timber". He added that a further example of the retreat was the provision for four official Members of the Executive Council when the White Paper had only suggested three. The White Paper had also not specified the offices to be held by these Members, but the order in council had and could prevent suitably qualified men from being appointed. Welensky criticised the continued use of the title "Minister of Native Affairs" because it was an anachronism in an era of non-racialism.

Welensky objected to the title of "appointed Member" instead of "unofficial" with regard to the Executive Council, because it might be used to limit the number — six — of the elected Members who could be chosen. To accommodate one nominated Member, he said the Federal Government would insist on five elected Members being appointed so that no more official Members could be included. Of these five elected Members, two had to be Africans and two Europeans so that the political Parties would be forced to attract support from both races. The order in council only prescribed that, when the number of "appointed Members" was above four, two of them had to be Europeans and two Africans. Welensky also requested that the Governor be required to consult the leader of the Party with the majority of elected Members when choosing the Executive Council. He pointed out that Nyasaland was about to have its leader appointed as the chief minister.

Welensky noted that the race of the voter would be determined at the moment of voting. He preferred that the rolls should identify the voter. If this were impossible, then the determination had to be done audibly in the presence of scrutineers, and both the candidate and the voter should be able to appeal against the verdict. If this were not done, the system could be

THE BREAK-UP OF THE FEDERATION 1962-1963

42 Whitehead's last Cabinet: Two new ministers, B. V. Ewing (extreme left) and G. Ellman-Brown (second from left) are sworn in by the Chief Justice of Southern Rhodesia, Sir Hugh Beadle, on 24 September 1962. Looking on (from the left) are A. R. W. Stumbles, Whitehead, C. J. Hatty and H. J. Quinton. *(Picture: Federal Information Dept.)*

43 A new Parliamentary Secretary: C. M. Chipunza is sworn in by Lord Dalhousie (second from right) on 28 November 1962 in the presence of (from left) G. M. Lewanika, Parliamentary Secretary to the Ministry of External Affairs; J. A. Clark, Minister of Commerce and Industry; Sir Malcolm Barrow and Sir Roy Welensky. *(Picture: Federal Information Dept.)*

44 A pointless visit: R. A. Butler (right) visits the Federation on 19 January 1963 in search of a solution. He had, however, already conceded Nyasaland's right of secession. *(Picture: Federal Information Dept., in the possession of Mrs Joan Bridge.)*

45 The death-knell: Sir Roy Welensky announces the break-up of the Federation at a Press conference under the chairmanship of the Federal High Commissioner, Sir Albert Robinson (centre) at Rhodesia House, London, on 29 March 1963. Also present is J. M. Greenfield (right), Minister of Home Affairs and Law. *(Picture: Rhodesia House, in the possession of Sir Albert Robinson.)*

THE BREAK-UP OF THE FEDERATION 1962-1963

46 The farewell: Lord and Lady Dalhousie (right) depart on 7 May 1963. They shake hands with their temporary successors, Sir Humphrey and Lady Gibbs. Waiting in line (sixth from the left) is Winston Field, Prime Minister of Southern Rhodesia.

47 The holding operation: Sir Humphrey Gibbs is sworn in as Acting Governor-General on 7 May 1963 by the Federal Chief Justice, Sir John Clayden (second from left). Watching are (from left) J. C. Grayling, Welensky, Rex L'Ange, Greenfield and Caldicott. (*Pictures: Federal Information Dept.*)

48 Misplaced confidence: On 27 June 1963, the eve of the Federal Dissolution Conference at the Victoria Falls, Butler (centre) convinced Field (left), if not I. D. Smith (right), that Southern Rhodesia would soon be independent. (*Picture:* The Herald.)

THE BREAK-UP OF THE FEDERATION 1962-1963

49 Dissolution: At the Victoria Falls on 28 June 1963, the Southern Rhodesian delegation listens to Butler as he rings down the curtain on the Federation. From the left are Sir Cornelius Greenfield, I. D. Smith, Winston Field, Clifford Dupont and William Harper. *(Picture: Mrs B. A. Field and National Archives of Zimbabwe.)*

50 The last salute: Welensky responds to a salute at the moving farewell parade of the Federal Army on 9 December 1963 in Salisbury. Behind him are Brig R. R. J. Putterill (left) and Maj-Gen J. Anderson. Behind them are units of the Royal Rhodesia Regiment and "C" Squadron of the Special Air Service. (*Picture:* The Sunday Mail.)

51 The final agenda: The Federal Cabinet meets on 17 December 1963 for the last time. From the left are J. P. G. Duncan (Public Service); J. A. Clark (Commerce and Industry); J. M. Caldicott (Finance); Sir Malcolm Barrow (Deputy Prime Minister and Defence, Economic Affairs and Power); Sir Roy Welensky (Prime Minister and External Affairs); J. M. Greenfield (Home Affairs and Law); F. S. Owen (Transport); B. D. Goldberg (Education); H. N. Parry (Secretary to the Cabinet); A. J. Saich (Assistant Secretary to the Cabinet). *(Picture: Federal Information Dept.)*

THE BREAK-UP OF THE FEDERATION 1962-1963

52 The last toast: Two redoubtable protagonists, Sir Roy Welensky and Sir Athol Evans drink a toast to the Federation at the final banquet held in Salisbury on 12 December 1963. (*Picture: In the possession of Mrs Joan Bridge.*)

53 The Last Post: The Federal Flag is lowered in Salisbury for the last time on 31 December 1963. (*Picture:* The Herald *and National Archives of Zimbabwe.*)

54 Seven years on: Some of the principals in the rise and fall of the Federation of Rhodesia and Nyasaland at a social gathering in Salisbury in 1970. They are (left to right) Sir Malcolm Barrow, Sir Ernest Guest, Sir Roy Welensky, Lord Malvern, Sir Robert Tredgold and Sir Humphrey Gibbs. (*Picture:* The Herald, *in the possession of Mrs Joan Bridge.*)

abused as a polling officer might be tempted to assist a candidate to secure his ten per cent from each race. The strictest care was needed, and justice in an electoral sense had to be seen to be done. The order in council provided that the decision of the polling officer was final, which seemed to Welensky to be very dangerous.[53]

Welensky, letting nothing pass, wrote again to Butler on 17 July dwelling on a number of points of detail such as ambiguities. He also raised further matters of principle. The first was that the Governor would enact the requirements of the order in council by regulation and not by ordinance. Welensky felt that at least the regulations should be tabled in the Legislative Council so that they could be debated and that he should receive an advance copy of them so that he could comment. The second matter was the total removal of the disqualification for criminal conviction which deeply disappointed him because he said he had hoped the Federal and Southern Rhodesian model would be adopted. He deplored this retrograde step when the battle to maintain standards was constantly being fought.[54]

Butler replied on 3 August that, if he did not comment on the minor drafting points, Welensky could assume that they had been corrected. He declared that there was every intention to have a declaration of rights but he thought it was understood that further consultation was required and that this would be held once the main order in council had become law. He confirmed that the intention was not to have more than one or two nominated Members, but the wider provision had been included to allow the Governor to act in abnormal circumstances. The British Government had thought that four official Members in the Executive Council were needed, but Butler said he agreed with Welensky that there should be a provision for a reduction to three without the need for a constitutional amendment. Royal Instructions would serve this purpose. Butler sympathised with the desire to change the title of the Minister of Native Affairs, but understood that the Africans had wished to retain it. He wanted the question of the chief minister postponed until after the election (possibly because he hoped to see who won it). He said there was no intention of appointing less than six unofficial Members to the Executive Council, and that their title would be changed, though he preferred the use of "appointed" because it allowed the appointment of official and nominated Members in extraordinary circumstances. He had arranged that the Royal Instructions would compel the Governor to consult the leader of the majority party on the appointments to the Executive Council. He wanted to avoid the retrogressive step of racial registration and could neither see the difficulties nor approve of appeals being conducted at polling booths. He felt that the question was simplified by the Asians and Coloureds being separately registered and the whole conduct of the poll being carried out in the presence of the polling agents. Candidates, after all, would have the normal redress for malpractice. He was prepared to promise that, if the regulations could be drafted in time, they would be tabled for debate. Hone, he said, would provide Welensky with a copy.[55]

[53] *Ibid.*, 20/7, f. 18, Welensky to Butler, 14 July 1962.
[54] *Ibid.*, f. 14, Welensky to Butler, 17 July 1962.
[55] *Ibid.*, f. 9, Alport to Welensky, 3 August 1962.

Butler had not, however, entirely satisfied Welensky, who on 9 August further questioned the composition of the Executive Council and the identification of voters. He recalled that the White Paper had specified that the Executive Council would have nine Members of whom three would be official Members and the remaining six would always be unofficial Members. Accordingly, he disputed Butler's "entirely new" suggestion of the possibility of filling the unofficial seats by appointing additional official Members, and insisted that the original commitment be honoured because of the principle that each race had to seek the support of the other. He maintained that the appointment of nominated Members to the Executive Council destroyed this principle and could create an opportunity for the appointment of an unofficial who had been defeated in an election. Butler had improved the identification issue, but Welensky suggested that differently-coloured ballot papers should be used to make the computation of the ten per cent possible. Such a device would satisfy him as it would give the candidates and their agents a chance to see the colour and to protest if necessary. Welensky dealt with some more minor points in a separate dispatch and accepted most of the explanations which Butler had provided.[56]

Butler replied with an assurance that, in normal circumstances, the Executive Council would contain no less than six unofficial Members but thought it would be prudent to provide for an emergency by allowing the Governor to draw on talents outside the legislature. He accepted the differently-coloured ballot papers and declared that local opinion would be consulted with regard to the bill of rights but said this would not be done before the election. The title of Minister of Native Affairs would remain because it was inappropriate to use a new constitution to change it. He closed by saying that the order in council would be in force by 1 September.[57]

There were no further Federal protests and the way was clear for the crucial Northern Rhodesian election which, coupled with that of Southern Rhodesia, would hasten the end of the Federation.

[56] *Ibid.*, ff. 7 & 5, Parry to Alport, 9 & 10 August 1962.
[57] *Ibid.*, f. 2, Alport to Welensky, 18 August 1962.

CHAPTER THIRTY-FOUR

The Right to Secede

The Election of Kaunda and Field prompts the Decision on Nyasaland, July–December 1962

KAUNDA's accession to power in Northern Rhodesia, albeit in somewhat confused circumstances, and the ousting of Whitehead by the Southern Rhodesian electorate, and his replacement by Winston Field of the reactionary and isolationist Rhodesian Front, meant that the Federal Government alone wished to preserve the Federation. However, any real chance of achieving that would be destroyed by Butler unilaterally conceding to Banda, in mid-December, the right to secede.

While Welensky had negotiated with Butler on Northern Rhodesia, Whitehead, having postponed his election, had decided in mid-July 1962 that it was time to amend the Land Apportionment Act. He did this because he believed that it would be disastrous if the African did not participate in every aspect of life. He argued that industry had to be able to expand, while the Government had to reach all the Africans and bring them into the main stream of development by dropping all purely racial barriers. True to his word, he introduced a bill to amend the Act to permit Africans to acquire land in industrial and commercial areas, which had been zoned as European, and to allow the Europeans to buy and develop land in African urban areas for the first time since 1931. The amendment would complement the parallel Federal Education Amendment Bill, introduced concurrently in the Federal Assembly, to allow private schools to admit Africans, Asians and Coloureds. Whitehead was, of course, implementing the recommendations of the Plewman Report of 1958 rather than the Second Quinton Report of August 1961 which had sought the total repeal of the Land Apportionment Act and had encouraged the UFP congress of October 1961 to adopt the repeal as policy.[1]

The proposed legislation sparked a great deal of controversy and opposition which included comments from the Southern Rhodesian Chief Native Com-

[1] *The Rhodesia Herald*, 18 July 1962; SR *Debates* (Salisbury), Vol. 50, Col. 595 f., 19 July 1962.

missioner, S. E. Morris. In his annual report, Morris took the extraordinary step of criticising his Government's declared policy, rather than the Bill, claiming that the amendment of the Land Apportionment Act dishonoured the solemn agreement made by the British and Southern Rhodesian Governments with the Africans in 1931, under which their rights to acquire, hold, encumber and dispose of land were taken away for a *quid pro quo* of 8 000 000 acres designated the Purchase Area. He argued that the current proposal to transfer 4 000 000 acres from the Purchase Area to the Tribal Trust Lands would reduce the Purchase Area farms from 17 000 to 7 000 and was therefore a breach of faith. Furthermore, he said, it was specious to claim that 5 000 000 acres of European farm land was "unreserved" when the terms and conditions of purchase were different from those in the Purchase Area. The price was also greater and the quality of land was unlikely to accommodate the 10 000 African farmers envisaged for the original Purchase Area.[2]

H. J. Quinton replied to Morris, saying that his Commission had been well aware that they had proposed a return to the *status quo* before 1931 in order that anyone, regardless of race, could acquire land. Quinton had little effect because the Rhodesian Front had already declared that it would totally oppose any such reform. Later, it exploited white feelings on the subject with telling effect when the general election was eventually held in December 1962.[3]

Whitehead's postponement of the election led Nkomo to declare in late July that it would never be held. He warned that his Zimbabwe African People's Union would cease to use constitutional methods if Southern Rhodesia did not shortly become a free and independent African state. He said that the ZAPU national congress would be held within two months, when he would announce a deadline for British action on the Constitution. The British reaction would then determine the course which he would follow. Three courses were open: the first was negotiation; the second, complete economic chaos; and the third, bloody revolution. He would not negotiate with Whitehead's Government but only with the British Government because it was responsible for "the mess" in which the territory found itself. If Britain refused to act, the Africans would free themselves. He said: "If it means some of us will be six feet under by the time we are free, so be it."[4]

Whitehead dismissed this as "absolute nonsense" and warned that anyone who tried to obstruct the election would be dealt with under the law. He declared that he had ample forces for this purpose. There was no prospect of constitutional change before the election, and he reminded Nkomo that he had been a signatory to the 1961 Constitution. Nkomo immediately corrected Whitehead because, he said, he had not signed the Constitution. Whitehead hastily denied that he had said more than that Nkomo had accepted the draft agreement at the end of the Constitutional Conference in February 1961.[5]

Welensky was drawn into Southern Rhodesian politics, although the electoral campaign had not yet started, when a UFP constituency delegation from

[2] *The Rhodesia Herald*, 25 July 1962.
[3] *Ibid.*, 27 July 1962; SR *Debates* (Salisbury), Vol. 50, Col. 1030 f., 31 July 1962.
[4] *The Rhodesia Herald*, 30 July 1962.
[5] *Ibid.*, 31 July 1962.

Milton Park, Salisbury, sought an interview and queried the apparent disagreement between himself and Whitehead, arising out of his public rebuttal of Whitehead's suggestion that the Federal Government take back broadcasting from its statutory body, the Federal Broadcasting Corporation. Welensky categorically denied that there was any split between the Federal and Southern Rhodesian divisions of his Party even though he acknowledged that there were points of difference between himself and Whitehead, simply because they served different interests. He said that they had differed over the control of broadcasting as the FBC had rejected a Southern Rhodesian Government advertising slogan, "Claim Your Vote", because ZAPU would have to be allowed to counter it. Although he would not interfere, Welensky felt that the FBC should support the Government of the day. He was also annoyed by a FBC broadcast which had unduly emphasised the opinion of the Indian officers serving with the UN in the Congo that the Federation was their next target. This had forced him, he explained, to consider stationing aircraft on the Copperbelt to restore public confidence. Nevertheless, he described his disagreements with Whitehead as healthy and said he respected the difficulties in which Whitehead found himself, especially as the UN critically watched his every move while he strove to maintain law and order in the face of continued unrest. He declared that he would not hesitate to support Whitehead.[6]

He confessed to Joelson that, in fact, Whitehead had considerably embarrassed him and that, since his retort on broadcasting, they had not seen each other. It annoyed him that Butler seemed to prefer Whitehead because he toadied him in the hope of securing British financial aid. However, Welensky told Lord Salisbury that he did not think that Whitehead could satisfy the British and Southern Rhodesians simultaneously. In the event, Butler only contributed to the lowering of Whitehead's fortunes by indicating that he might accept the British Labour Party's suggestion that further consideration was needed before there could be any additional transfer of power to Southern Rhodesia. An allegation in the *Daily Mail* that Butler was seeking to create a confederation of Central Africa but had no place in it for "a Bismarck", meaning Welensky, drew from the latter a retort to Wall: "Well, why burn down the house because there is a cockroach in it? Why not kill the cockroach?"[7]

Welensky also found himself embroiled in a dispute with Blackwood. Welensky had forwarded to him a complaint from Nyasaland about the docility of the UFP in the local Legislative Council in the face of discriminatory legislation, and about its claim that it acted only on orders from Salisbury, reserving action for real controversies. Welensky told Blackwood he was surprised by the latter allegation because it had been Blackwood who had sought advice on how to handle Banda. Welensky believed that the Africans On Private Estates Bill warranted firm action and said he was

[6] Welensky Papers, 16/1b, f. 139a, Minutes of a Meeting with the UFP Milton Park Branch, 23 July 1962.

[7] *Ibid.*, 24/152, ff. 152–155, Welensky to F. S. Joelson, 27 July 1962; 43/*Salisbury*, Welensky to Lord Salisbury, 1 August 1962; 43/*Wall*, Welensky to Major P. Wall, 28 July 1962; Sir Roy Welensky, *Welensky's 4 000 Days* (London, 1964), p. 345.

disappointed that it had been allowed to go through in a day. He was dismayed because Greenfield, when giving Blackwood advice on 15 May, had stressed that, while it was important not to upset Banda unnecessarily, flagrant maladministration had to be exposed.

Welensky drew a furious response from Blackwood who said he had always understood that he had to work to Welensky's instructions on overall policy, as opposed to daily affairs. Blackwood added that he had also made it quite clear that any needling of the Nyasaland Government could cause it "to go berserk". Blackwood explained that, as Greenfield and Barrow had urged caution, the UFP in Nyasaland had decided to play a passive role in the March legislative session. He maintained that the stream of invective provoked by his speech on the Budget had shown that no criticism would be tolerated. Discussions with Jones, Banda and the MCP Ministers had revealed that they would accept amendments outside the Legislative Council but not within it. Nothing which could affect Banda's "face" would be tolerated. It had become clear that the most effective way to work was through private submission from influential bodies. It was only issues such as the future of the Federation which warranted a "show-down". Federal actions like Welensky's correspondence with Nyasalanders and unannounced visits by J. Foot, Greenfield's parliamentary secretary, not only angered him, Blackwood said, but made his position difficult. He wondered if Welensky had lost confidence in him and offered to resign. He agreed that there could be no half measures but felt that if attack were to be the *modus operandi,* Welensky had to guarantee protection for all Europeans in Nyasaland.[8]

Welensky hastened to assure Blackwood that what he had accomplished, and the position in which he found himself, was appreciated. Nevertheless, he firmly believed that at least an Opposition had to point out governmental mistakes lest it be accused by Banda of being inconsistent when it was forced to speak. He denied that he was responsible for the attitude of his Party, but acknowledged that he should have discussed Foot's visits with Blackwood.[9]

Blackwood remained adamant that the Opposition could do little more. He thought it important to persuade Banda that the Federation, or a fresh association, was a good and reasonable idea and that this was unlikely if the Opposition launched violent attacks. In fact, the Federal Cabinet had already reached a similar conclusion after considering a number of legitimate ways of embarrassing the Nyasaland Government. A Cabinet committee continued to examine the idea but no action was ever taken. When, in late August, the Federal Government adjusted tariffs, Jones protested that he had not been consulted. Welensky replied, expressing amazement at this protest when there were so many instances of the Nyasaland Government refusing to consult or co-operate with the Federal Government. Welensky described Jones's protest to Blackwood as most offensive.[10]

[8] Welensky Papers, 27/69, f. 60, Hayes to Welensky, 14 July 1962; f. 54, Welensky to Blackwood, 20 July 1962; f. 51, Blackwood to Welensky, 28 July 1962.

[9] *Ibid.*, f. 49, Welensky to Blackwood, 6 August 1962.

[10] *Ibid.*, f. 48, Blackwood to Welensky, 6 August 1962; FGC(62), 20th Meeting, Minute 8, Federal Cabinet, 18 July 1962; FGC(1), 25/62, Sir Glyn Jones to Welensky, (undated); 27/69, f. 40, Welensky to Blackwood, 27 August 1962.

In late July, the nervous reaction of the Northern Rhodesian Government to a threat from Kaunda, to boycott the election if his people continued to be arrested in the Northern Province for their excessive activities, aroused Welensky's contempt. Precisely at this moment Welensky crossed swords with Whitehead over broadcasting, but at least Roberts pleased him with his industrious approach to his electoral campaign. However, he would be further disappointed in August by the resignation of J. Z. Savanhu, the joint parliamentary secretary for Home Affairs. Savanhu became a vigorous opponent of the Federal Government. He resigned, he said, because little was being done to appoint Africans to senior posts in the civil service. Welensky denied the charge because of the great difficulty in finding suitable Africans. One had been appointed, he explained, but had immediately resigned for a more lucrative position in commerce.[11]

The forced landing in Katanga of a chartered DC3 of a private company, Rhodesian Air Services, after it was hit by fire from the Congolese Army, brought Welensky back into Congolese affairs as he attempted to secure the release of the aircraft and its crew. For the moment, he was unsuccessful. However, benefit was being derived from the relationship with Tshombe who had considerable influence with the Northern Rhodesian ANC, though he did not appear to understand how serious the position would be for himself and the Federation if Kaunda won. If Kaunda did, Welensky knew that Butler would say: "Sorry. Had you been able to hold the situation in Northern Rhodesia, it would have been a different story." Saying this to Lord Colyton on 15 August, Welensky claimed that Butler's advisory committee (whom he called the "four foolish virgins or four wise men, according to one's point of view") had made little impact to date. Indeed, it had been reported to him that one had slept peacefully through an interview.[12]

As August closed, Southern Rhodesia caught the public eye because of the implementation of two security measures designed to curb intimidation. It aroused the Churches, Tredgold and others to protest, despite the current violence. Welensky was appalled when the grieving relatives of the leading African nationalist, Dr T. S. Parirenyatwa, who had been killed in a car crash, were beaten up at his funeral because they were unpopular with the hierarchy of ZAPU. Nkomo would later allege that the Southern Rhodesian Government had conspired to assassinate him and that Parirenyatwa had been killed instead. This was dismissed by the Government as nonsense.[13]

In early September, Todd joined in, telling a meeting of the African Trade Union Congress that the Churches, the trade unions, workers and professional men should submit written demands to the Government to respect the will of the people. With such a unified effort, he believed the country would progress

[11] *Ibid.*, 24/152, ff. 152–155, Welensky to Joelson, 27 July 1962; 8/69, f. 45, H. J. Roberts to Welensky, 27 July 1962; 25/276, f. 17, Welensky to Greenfield, 15 August 1962; f. 12, Welensky to J. Z. Savanhu, 15 August 1962; f. 11, Savanhu to Welensky, 15 August 1962; *The Rhodesia Herald*, 15 August 1962.

[12] Welensky Papers, 20/13, f. 123, Lord Alport to R. A. Butler, 30 July 1962; 43/*Colyton*, Welensky to Lord Colyton, 15 August 1962.

[13] *Ibid.*, 43/*Salisbury*, Welensky to Salisbury, 16 August 1962; 43/*Millin*, Welensky to S. G. Millin, 30 August 1962; *The Rhodesia Herald*, 7 September 1962.

peacefully. If the Government refused to listen, it would run the danger of violence being used against it.[14]

Two days later, Todd's warning was verified by violence following a meeting, in Sakubva Township in Umtali, which had been called to discuss a sit-down strike by African students at the Teachers' Training College. The police reserve was mobilised, two Africans received gunshot wounds and a number of arrests were made. Intimidation led to a growing list of African resignations from the UFP. *En route* to London that day, 6 September, Nkomo called for a new constitution because the UN demanded it, and that Britain should respect the UN's wishes. He said that ZAPU would set a date for independence and direct all its efforts towards it, whatever the British said.[15]

Welensky was following Nkomo to London to attend the Commonwealth Prime Ministers' Conference from which he and the Rhodesian Press half expected him to be expelled. Just before he left Salisbury, he received the welcome news that the Northern Rhodesian delimitation could ensure a favourable result for him, and at least 13 upper roll seats seemed certain. He was also told that Kaunda had met Tshombe and had demanded that he stop aiding Nkumbula, because he was interfering in the internal affairs of Northern Rhodesia. Kaunda was certain he would win the election and had proposed that Tshombe should assess the potential of his Party. However, Tshombe had reminded him of his criticism of Katanga's secession, when he was seeking secession himself, and had pointed to interference by UNIP in Katanga. He had doubted whether UNIP would win the election and had suggested that it should join in a coalition with the ANC. Kaunda had replied that any such move would split his Party, but he proposed to speak to Tshombe again after having consulted his "political bureau". Another report claimed that Nkumbula was mistakenly confident of winning the election, though he complained about being short of money. Nevertheless, he did not want any overt Federal assistance lest his reputation be fatally damaged.[16]

Katanga and Northern Rhodesia were highlighted in a speech by Donald A. Bruce of Indiana in the US House of Representatives, on 12 September, which revealed the formation of a Swedish-American combine designed to break the monopoly of the Union Minière and to exploit Katanga's mineral resources. The combine was headed by Gustav Hammarskjold, the brother of the late UN Secretary-General. Bruce also described the Swedish Rhodesia Campaign Committee which was supported by the Swedish Liberal Party and the Social Democrats and the editors of the three main Swedish newspapers. Accordingly, Bruce said, these two major Parties were proposing to interfere in the internal affairs of a British protectorate, Northern Rhodesia. There had been a campaign of vilification of Welensky and the whites by the Swedish Press, which had led the British Paper, *The Sunday Telegraph,* to claim that a first instalment of £20 000 from the Swedish Rhodesia Campaign

[14] *The Bulawayo Chronicle*, 3 September 1962.
[15] *The Rhodesia Herald*, 6 & 7 September 1962.
[16] Welensky Papers, 20/13, f. 105, Secretary, External Affairs, to Robinson, 8 September 1962; 27/109, f. 28, A. T. Adams to Welensky, 12 September 1962; 28/96, f. 23, J. Hawkins to Welensky, 13 September 1962.

Committee for Kaunda had embarrassed Tage Erlander, the Swedish Prime Minister. However, he had replied that, as the intervention in Northern Rhodesia was a private initiative, his Government's stand of strict neutrality was unaffected. Be that as it may, Bruce reported, Bjorn Beckman, president of the Committee, had claimed that Erlander's Democratic Party had exhorted its branches to contribute to the Committee's fund.[17]

Butler had given the impression of merely awaiting the outcome of the Northern Rhodesian election before making a decision. However, while this in fact was his state of mind, he, Alport and the advisory committee were puzzling over future courses. Anxious about the maintenance of standards and the continuation of development, Alport thought that Britain should play a direct role for at least another decade. He favoured a composite approach as well as a resumption by Britain of some direct responsibilities. He wanted to include in his new initiative the acknowledgement of the right to secede of all the territories, which should mean that a completely new Federal structure was required. He wrote confidently to Butler on 18 July to explain that a new association was possible if the Nyasalanders understood that the Southern Rhodesians were also keen to secede. He proposed a timetable which envisaged the completion of the advisory committee's work in late September and their report in mid-October. He suggested that Welensky visit Britain in early September and Whitehead in late October. The Northern Rhodesian election would have been held by the end of October, and in mid-November the British Government could publish a White Paper on his proposed new association. Butler should then visit the Federation in early January and thereafter negotiate with the Federal and territorial Governments. The Southern Rhodesian election would follow in early April, and by July the amending legislation to bring in the new association could have been passed through the British Parliament. The plan could be revealed to Welensky and Whitehead during their visits to London, and the secession issue would be dealt with in the Nyasaland Conference in November as part of the settlement.[18]

In a second letter to Butler, on 6 August, Alport reiterated his proposals but warned that Nyasaland's secession could not be dealt with in isolation. He assumed, he said, that the Northern Rhodesian election would produce an anti-Federal majority and that Nyasaland would be granted a wide measure of self-government which would lead to independence. However, he thought that Southern Rhodesia would control the current wave of unrest, and that the Federal Government would be inclined to resist change, which would mean the British Government would have to push through its solution with determination. It was clear that the current Federal system could not continue because it lacked support. Thus it was necessary that, after a transitional period, each territory should be given the right to secede. In the transitional period the functions of the Federal Government would be transferred to a council of ministers drawn from the Federal and territorial Governments under the presidency of a British nominee. The Federal Assembly would elect the two Federal representatives and the territorial legislatures theirs.

[17] *Ibid.*, 29/20, f. 17, Transcript of Bruce's Speech, 12 September 1962.
[18] Lord Alport, *The Sudden Assignment* (London, 1965), p. 187.

Thus the Federation would be transformed into an association of states, each of which would have a wide measure of independence but which would delegate to the council of ministers the responsibilities for the common services. Britain would have to assist with the defence of the northern territories and in servicing the public debt. It would have to provide aid for education and compensate Federal civil servants. In the transitional period, he concluded, a permanent form of the association would emerge.[19]

Alport suspects that his proposal shocked Whitehall, but he knew that there were precedents for Britain reversing the trend of disengagement. Butler stalled Alport to allow his advisory committee to consider the idea, but disliked it from the outset because of the disruption it would cause. He replied to Alport on 23 August, revealing that his committee also wished to replace the Federal Government, but with a high commission. (It had in fact suggested this as a transitional device.) However, Macmillan and Butler agreed that nothing could be done which might be interpreted as "shooting the Federal Government dead". Whitehead had warned them of Welensky "doing a Samson", and Butler said that, while threats could not be entertained, the strong feeling of the Federal Ministers on the retention of a positive association between the Rhodesias had to be respected.

Butler acknowledged the pertinence of the advisory committee's argument that the Federal Government had to understand the realities of the Northern Rhodesian situation. Thus, he said, the committee had proposed a conference on Northern and Southern Rhodesia in early 1963. However, he had not been convinced and was not yet prepared to decide on any action beyond the Nyasaland Conference because he wished to await the outcome of the Northern Rhodesian election. Moreover, he thought that any new association had to control defence and external affairs, while Alport and the committee had proposed to split defence between the territories. He said he would consider a transitional period, and acknowledged the necessity for an early decision which would be acceptable to all. Everyone had to realise that something new was being attempted, and at least, he noted, Welensky had indicated that he would examine fresh ideas. If he did, he had to be encouraged but, if he did not, the British Government would be justified in taking an independent line. Butler said he had hitherto ignored the possibility of Northern and Southern Rhodesia demanding secession and would deal with it if it arose. He proposed to prepare Welensky, when meeting him in London, for a statement in November which would concede secession to Nyasaland. Butler said he would also "throw a fly over him" so as to seek the best way to preserve some of the current association between the Rhodesias, while warning him of Kaunda's likely reaction. However, Butler declined to go further because, he said, everything depended on the outcome of the Northern Rhodesian election.[20]

The first negotiations conducted by the party accompanying Welensky to London concerned Katanga. On 13 September, H. N. Parry, secretary to the

[19] *Ibid.*, p. 188.

[20] *Ibid.*, p. 191; Lord Butler, *The Art of the Possible: The Memoirs of Lord Butler* (London, 1973), pp. 218–220; D. Scott, *Ambassador in Black and White: Thirty Years of Changing Africa* (London, 1981), pp. 115–116.

Federal Cabinet, reviewed events there, including the abortive attempts at settlement. The Rhodesian Air Services' DC3, which had been forced down in Katanga, had still not been returned. Also, the Federal Government rightly suspected that the UN was stockpiling fuel and food for further military adventures.[21]

The real negotiations began on 14 September when Welensky, Caldicott and Robinson met Butler to review current affairs. Butler described the advantages and disadvantages of associate membership of the Common Market for which they might be tempted to apply, and then turned to the Federal constitutional problems. He said he did not wish to say much until his advisory committee had reported in October and until the Northern Rhodesian election was over. He was most concerned about Southern Rhodesia because of the pressure to which his Government was being subjected in the UN and elsewhere for the reform of its Constitution. He warned that the argument that Britain lacked the constitutional power to intervene there was being rejected by significant British and foreign groups. Being under such pressure, he feared that incidents might occur in Southern Rhodesia which might be exaggerated by the hostile Press (and further weaken the British case).

Welensky agreed that the Southern Rhodesian situation was serious. He said that, to implement the 1961 Constitution, Whitehead would have to dissolve Parliament and hold a general election. However, Welensky revealed, Whitehead had evidence that the African nationalists were planning further trouble for the near future and knew that, if he did not combat this energetically, his Party would lose the election. It was possible to obtain African candidates, but intimidation would deter the Africans from voting and thus ensure victory for extremism of both races. As a result of the pressure exerted on him, Welensky expected Whitehead to hold the election in March 1963.

Caldicott dismissed Whitehead's electoral chances in the near future because, he said, the electorate was critical of his apparent lack of will to govern. This was unjust, Caldicott explained, because Whitehead realised that any ill-timed action against ZAPU would only give Nkomo a propaganda advantage at international level. Nevertheless, Whitehead would have to act soon to contain the situation.

Butler appreciated Whitehead's problems and said he was very ready to discuss them with him when he came to London. He hoped that a British loan of £3 500 000 would ease the situation. He knew that the Southern Rhodesian Government's efforts to liberalise its laws had not been widely appreciated and he proposed to arrange a meeting with British parliamentarians so that Whitehead could describe them. The British diplomatic missions abroad had explained the circumstances, but friendly nations were reluctant to support a constitution of which the majority at the UN disapproved.

Moving on to Nyasaland, Butler said that he would probably grant it self-government at the Constitutional Conference in November and, to safeguard the minorities, a bill of rights would probably be added. He reserved absolutely the question of Nyasaland's independence, but believed that it

[21] Welensky Papers, 20/13, f. 100, Minutes of a Meeting between Federal and British Officials, Foreign Office, London, 13 September 1962.

would be difficult to delay indefinitely on the question of secession because the MCP desired it and would form the Government after November. He confirmed that Sandys was largely responsible for the British commitment on secession.

Welensky asked if the Federal Government would be consulted before a decision was taken and received the somewhat evasive reply that the British Government felt that nothing positive could be achieved in Nyasaland unless secession was conceded, but that it would "keep in touch". Welensky, however, would not deal with the Federal Constitution in an *ad hoc* manner and warned he would insist that the resolution of Nyasaland's future be part of the overall constitutional settlement. He would object strongly to any isolated acts, as it was necessary to settle the Federal problem within the next six months.

Butler understood this point of view, but did not think the problem could be resolved so quickly. He believed the proponents of the Federation had to accept that Nyasaland was virtually an African state, and thus was a special problem. He argued that, if the emotional issue of secession could be settled, the MCP might be induced to be constructive about trade links. The first step, therefore, was to grant secession to Nyasaland.

However, Welensky remained adamant that there could not be a piecemeal settlement and thought he owed the people of Rhodesia and Nyasaland an attempt to keep them together. He was not prepared to see control given to Kaunda who, despite having a degree of support, could not be called a national leader because he was strongly opposed by the Barotse and other important tribes. Caldicott warned that the Federal Government would be reluctant to invest if Nyasaland were allowed to secede.

Butler believed that his advisory committee would recommend that Nyasaland should assume a fair share of the responsibility for capital investment. He hoped that the Federal Government would be reasonable and generous towards Nyasaland as it would be in the Federal interest to prevent slum conditions developing there. He promised to consult the Federal Government once his committee reported.[22]

Later that day they met again to hear Welensky reiterate Whitehead's difficulties because he had discovered that ZAPU had promised to cause trouble in Southern Rhodesia in return for Russian assistance in drafting the recent UN resolution. Any action by Whitehead against ZAPU, Welensky said, would lose him support at the UN. Conversely, lack of action would lose him the election, especially as he had lost European support by proposing a revision of the Land Apportionment Act. He added that Whitehead had already implemented a number of liberal measures and, if he tried to allay foreign criticism by widening the Southern Rhodesian franchise, he would have no hope of re-election.[23]

Welensky also met Home that day and agreed to press Tshombe to co-operate with the reconciliation process which the UN wished to implement. Four days later, in the Commonwealth Prime Ministers' Conference, Welensky had to defend Southern Rhodesia and Tshombe from attacks by Nehru

[22] *Ibid.*, 20/3, ff. 194–204, Minutes of a Meeting with Butler, 14 September 1962.
[23] *Ibid.*, ff. 192–193, Minutes of a Meeting with Butler, 14 September 1962.

and Kawana of Tanganyika and to refute Britain's right to intervene in Southern Rhodesia.[24]

While Welensky fended off these attacks, Northern Rhodesia's delimitation was published and it encouraged the UFP to believe it would win 15 seats. In Southern Rhodesia, the Rhodesian Front issued its policy and disappointed *The Rhodesia Herald* by being vague on major issues such as the Federation's future, the 1961 Southern Rhodesian Constitution and franchise and the problem of land ownership. Yet the RF did indicate that there would be changes in the franchise if it came to power. It intended to retain the Land Apportionment Act, to increase the power of the Chiefs, and to introduce compulsory education and unemployment insurance.[25]

From Salisbury, Greenfield wrote to Welensky on 17 September to say that he had met the advisory committee but had gathered little from it as it was still hearing evidence and had found no solutions as yet. The committee had asked if Banda could be persuaded to keep silent if he did not have his own way, and Greenfield had replied that Banda had been saying for years that the Federation was dead and probably could happily say it for a few years more. Banda knew that, if he started causing trouble now, he would put all he had gained at risk. Thus Greenfield doubted that Banda would implement his threats. He thought it would be most unwise to give in to Banda as it would cause the Federation to dissolve and allow Russia a foothold in Nyasaland. Secession could only be considered if there were a definite plan to keep the Rhodesias together, but he did not think the British Government would accept his ideas. Yet, if Nyasaland were allowed to go, Kaunda could not be denied the same concession, because Northern Rhodesia had a viable economy. Greenfield reported that after the meeting with the advisory committee Evans had told him that he (Greenfield) had surprised the committee because it had expected him to be more legalistic and bitter. Greenfield added that the committee had met eleven Lozi in Lusaka and that they had wanted to secede from Northern Rhodesia and gain the Queen's protection. Greenfield thought that such protection without Federal troops would be ineffective.[26]

Meeting again on 19 September, Butler, Welensky and Caldicott agreed that Britain should join the Common Market, and then examined Northern Rhodesia. Welensky complained that his Government was not seeing the memoranda submitted by the Northern Rhodesian Government to the advisory committee. He maintained that this constituted a deliberate breach of the understanding between himself and Butler and that this had been done despite the dispatch to all the other Governments of copies of the Federal submissions.

Butler promised an investigation but reminded Welensky that the result of the Northern Rhodesian election would be as important as the advisory committee's report. Welensky then sought Butler's views on the possible

[24] *Ibid.*, 20/13, f. 103, Welensky to Barrow, 14 September 1962; 8/69, f. 88, Welensky to A. D. Evans, 18 September 1962.

[25] *Ibid.*, 8/69, f. 86, Evans to Welensky, 14 September 1962; *The Rhodesia Herald*, 14 September 1962.

[26] Welensky Papers, 28/79, f. 23, Greenfield to Welensky, 19 September 1962.

request from the UN to send an investigating team to the Federation and to Southern Rhodesia, in particular, warning that neither he nor Whitehead would permit such a visit. He offered assistance from the Federal mission in Washington to deal with the attacks in the UN General Assembly.

Butler agreed that a visit from the UN would be undesirable, but warned that his Government was having difficulty with its allies. The US Government was especially critical and it seemed impossible to convince it that Britain could not intervene constitutionally. He thought Whitehead should put forward internationally as good a case as possible for Southern Rhodesia in the near future. He wondered if Nkomo's current activities would lead Whitehead to proscribe ZAPU soon. Butler could see the necessity of this from the security angle, but felt it would only increase British difficulties at the UN. He asked if there was anything Whitehead could do to improve the situation.

Welensky said that Whitehead could not liberalise his Constitution, to answer African nationalist and international criticism, because he would have to hold another referendum. He knew Whitehead was under pressure from the Europeans and moderate Africans to act against the extremists and that, in any case, the likelihood of concessions on the franchise satisfying Nkomo and his lieutenants was remote. It would be an absurd gesture when 70 000–80 000 Africans were already being prevented from registering as voters by intimidation, which was only increasing in intensity. Caldicott agreed because the Southern Rhodesian record of recent years was good and, furthermore, Whitehead had committed himself to the repeal of the Land Apportionment Act if returned to power. Butler reiterated that he was powerless to intervene. Then they discussed the role Ghana was playing in Federal affairs and, in particular, the training it offered to African nationalists in sabotage. Returning to the Southern Rhodesian problem, Welensky said the immediate task was to re-establish respect for law and order but he felt that, despite the aggravation of high African unemployment, there was no need for undue alarm.[27]

Welensky reported on 20 September to Greenfield that Butler had not decided anything and would do nothing until the Northern Rhodesian election. He said that he and Butler had crossed swords over Nyasaland during a private meeting at Butler's house. He had gathered that, when Butler saw Banda in November, he would tell him that the British Government would accept his secession in principle. He would do this, hoping that Banda would be more reasonable after such a signal victory. Welensky had replied bluntly that he would only deal with solutions to the whole problem. He had made Butler understand that he would not accept a purely economic union but wanted an association of the Rhodesias which would delegate defence and foreign affairs to the central Government, while all other subjects were returned to the territories.[28]

The degree of violence in Southern Rhodesia was such that no one should have been surprised when, in the early hours of 20 September, Whitehead banned ZAPU and had its leading members, including whites, arrested.

[27] *Ibid.*, 20/3, ff. 187–191, Minutes of a Meeting with Butler, 19 September 1962.
[28] *Ibid.*, 11/55, f. 8, Welensky to Greenfield, 20 September 1962.

Nkomo escaped the net by being in Northern Rhodesia where he had declared, just before the banning, that he would not lift a finger to stop the violence because the Africans were so frustrated that "the lid had blown off". The *Northern News* noted that he had said this without any tone of regret.[29]

The next day Nkomo declared that ZAPU would carry on as normal, but pleaded for a British assumption of power in Southern Rhodesia. His London office proposed to make representations to the UN. UNIP supported Nkomo and called for active British intervention. U Thant recommended that the question be taken up by the UN Trusteeship Committee.[30]

The British *Daily Mirror* correspondent in Salisbury claimed that Whitehead's main concern had not been the effect of ZAPU's petrol bombs, but the threat of "gun-toting whites" taking their revenge in the African townships.[31] That the reporter was indulging in fantasy is borne out by subsequent history, as never in the darkest days after 1972 did anything remotely like that happen.

The uproar which greeted the banning was mostly external and the Press reported a general calm and even relief amongst the African population, even though the Special Air Service had to be dropped into the forest estates at Melsetter to curb a wave of arson. On 22 September, in Lusaka, Nkomo promised to return to join his colleagues in restriction although he did not recognise the Government's right to ban ZAPU. He declared that, for the moment, he would establish a temporary headquarters in Lusaka.[32]

The freedom allowed Nkomo by the Northern Rhodesian Government infuriated Whitehead who protested to Alport. The latter was astonished to receive this protest and asked why the Federal Government had done nothing. However, after having had his constitutional position explained to him by Barrow, Alport agreed to telephone Hone. As no action was taken immediately, Whitehead threatened to cut communications with Northern Rhodesia, and Barrow avowed that Welensky would protest at the incredible position which would arise if Nkomo were allowed to establish himself and operate from there. Pressure was probably brought to bear on Nkomo because, on 23 September, he moved to Tanganyika. Although he was thinking of it, he denied any intention to form a "government-in-exile".[33]

Whitehead reshuffled his Cabinet because R. J. Knight and R. M. Cleveland had resigned. He brought in G. Ellman-Brown and B. V. Ewing. Any comment on this was drowned by the torrent of criticism of Nkomo's failure to return to Southern Rhodesia from African trade unionists and nationalists because he had declared that he would always share the fate of his followers. Noting this, *The Bulawayo Chronicle* thought that Nkomo had expected the violence to topple the Government as it had done elsewhere. Not surprisingly, it had not, and the newspaper decided that anyone who had so misread the

[29] *Northern News*, 20 September 1962.
[30] Welensky Papers, 7/42, f. 4, Comments on the ZAPU Banning, 21 September 1962.
[31] *Daily Mirror*, 21 September 1962.
[32] *The Rhodesia Herald* and *African Daily News*, 22 September 1962.
[33] Welensky Papers, 8/69, f. 94, Barrow to Welensky, 22 September 1962; R. Cary and D. Mitchell, *African Nationalists in Rhodesia: Who's Who* (Bulawayo, 1977), p. 23; *Northern News*, 25 September 1962.

situation deserved political oblivion. Perhaps to the surprise of many, Nkomo declared at the end of the month that he was ready to return because he had created a committee — headed by the Reverend Ndabaningi Sithole — to run his Party's affairs from Dar-es-Salaam in his absence. True to his word, Nkomo returned and was restricted to the Kezi district near Bulawayo. From there he demanded that Whitehead should hold constitutional talks with him or face the prospect of having to keep the security forces on duty forever.[34]

The Southern Rhodesian action was roundly condemned at the annual conference of the Labour Party which urged the British Government to re-open the constitutional negotiations. Protest was planned at the UN. On 8 October Whitehead countered the criticism by saying that Nkomo could again lead an African nationalist party, provided he kept within the law. Indeed, Whitehead said he would welcome an African nationalist party which would encourage voters to register. He thought that it could easily hold the balance of power in the next Parliament and that, with ZAPU removed, his Government could positively concentrate on meeting the aspirations of the Africans. This had been impossible while ZAPU had operated. Whitehead advised the UFP branches to enrol as many Africans as possible to give them a forum to express their views as well as an opportunity to learn that there were Europeans who were anxious to work with them to remove their grievances.[35]

Whitehead, however, was still faced with a steady loss of supporters to the Rhodesian Front which continued to maintain stoutly that it would defend the Land Apportionment Act. Nkomo blamed Britain for the "present chaos" in Southern Rhodesia and called for the resignation of Sir Hugh Foot, the British Ambassador to the UN. He warned Whitehead that he would be deported when ZAPU took over. To counter ZAPU's influence in New York, an independent multi-racial group, led by a young businessman, A. D. Butler, decided to put the opposing view to the UN. However, before they could have any effect, Foot resigned, on 12 October, because he felt that he could no longer defend Southern Rhodesian policies, even though the Southern Rhodesians could detect no outward signs that he had ever agreed with them. The Conservative Press denounced Foot's action as a stab in the British Government's back, but he was unrepentant and declared that he had kept a pledge to Nkomo to resign if Britain refused to intervene in Southern Rhodesia.[36]

The Federal Government was not drawn into the defence of Southern Rhodesia, but it did find itself and Southern Rhodesia under attack in Salisbury from Savanhu for alleged racial inequalities in pay, conditions and other acts of racialism. On 12 October, Savanhu called an inter-racial conference to devise a non-racial franchise, new elections and an interim government. He denounced the Europeans as unfit to govern African countries and revealed that a request from the UFP to help it win the Northern Rhodesian

[34] *The Bulawayo Chronicle*, 25 September 1962; *The Rhodesia Herald*, 29 September 1962; *African Daily News*, 4 October 1962.

[35] Welensky Papers, 8/69, f. 188, M. J. Lamb to Welensky, 3 October 1962; *Federal Outlook*, 8 October 1962.

[36] *Central African Mail*, 9 October 1962; *The Rhodesia Herald*, 9 & 15 October 1962.

election had prompted him to resign, because he would not be party to the thwarting of the "legitimate aspirations to self-government" of the Northern Rhodesian Africans.[37]

On the previous day, 11 October, the Federal Government had been considerably irritated by a message from Alport that Butler's Central African Office had telephoned to say that it was to announce that day that the Nyasaland Constitutional Conference would be held on 12 November. Alport had conveyed the Central African Office's apologies for the lack of consultation with the Federal Government on this announcement and had explained that it had been under the impression that Jones had kept Federal officials informed. This feeble excuse had been rejected, and a formal protest had been lodged with Alport who had replied that not only was the omission unintentional but that he had tried, too late, to have the announcement postponed. The Federal Government's irritation was compounded when it received, the next day, a copy of a dispatch dated 29 September from the Central African Office to the Nyasaland Government. This had invited the Nyasaland Government to attend the Conference, and a copy should have been furnished immediately to the Federal Government. The invitation allowed the MCP six delegates, and the UFP three. Each of the two Parties were allowed one adviser. There would be a seat for an independent so that all shades of opinion were represented. All invitees had to be Members of the Legislative Council.

Despite the lack of formal consultation, the Federal Government had known indirectly of the invitation because Blackwood had been told of it and had been striving, with a degree of success, to secure better representation at the Conference for the UFP. In the event, the Federal Government received profuse apologies. By way of additional placation, Butler wrote to Welensky assuring him that the Conference would only discuss Nyasaland affairs and not the wider Federal issue.[38]

Blackwood warned Welensky that it seemed that Butler would grant Banda his secession because the Nyasaland officials had dropped all pretence of supporting the Federation. Welensky replied that Butler ought to make it clear to all at the Conference that he would only discuss Nyasaland's future and not that of the Federation. If this were done, Welensky said, unlike Butler and others, he did not think that "Banda would go up in smoke", provided that the carrot of the premiership of Nyasaland and internal responsible government was held out.[39]

Welensky maintained the pressure, writing on 22 October to Butler to warn him that he knew that the advisory committee had reported, and demanding that Butler consult him. Indeed, he thought that discussions in Salisbury would be useful before Butler presented anything to the British Cabinet, recalling that Butler had suggested this to him during his visit to London. He was particularly anxious about Professor Brown's proposed budget for Nyasaland because it was believed to be an underestimation. In addition, Welensky

[37] *The Bulawayo Chronicle*, 13 October 1962.

[38] Welensky Papers, 20/8, f. 21, K. H. Towsey to Welensky, 12 October 1962; f. 21, Butler to Jones, 12 October 1962.

[39] *Ibid.*, 32/90, f. 8, Welensky to Blackwood, 15 October 1962.

suggested that there should be the closest Anglo-Federal liaison during the Nyasaland Conference.[40]

Butler promptly summoned Alport to London on 27 October to discuss consultation with the Federal Government and hastily assured Welensky that he would proceed cautiously and only after consultation. He warned that, nevertheless, Nyasaland had to be dealt with urgently even though secession was formally excluded from the agenda of the Conference. There was also no prospect of his visiting Salisbury because of his duties as Deputy Prime Minister. He would take Federal advice but warned that consultation had to be based on purely British conclusions. In reply, Welensky disagreed because Butler had recently promised full Anglo-Federal consultations on all matters affecting the Federation's future before any conclusions were reached. As Butler had not yet heard the Federal view, and because Butler could not visit, Welensky said he reserved the right to go to London because he refused to act through intermediaries.[41]

Before Alport returned to Salisbury, the Northern Rhodesian general election was held and the Federal Cabinet anxiously awaited its result because it believed that Butler would base his plans on its outcome. As it knew that any political association between the territories was doomed if UNIP was returned overwhelmingly, the UFP had issued instructions in March that none of its speakers would oppose the ANC. Welensky met Nkumbula on 20 July and, while nothing is known of what was discussed, it is clear that the collaboration between their Parties was established. As Mulford has described in his able and detailed account of the election, the resources of the Northern Rhodesian division of the UFP were diverted, to an extent, to assist Nkumbula. However, what is curious is that, while Welensky was attending the Commonwealth Prime Ministers' Conference in September, the Federal Cabinet decided to stand aloof from this crucial campaign. It did so until, in the last week, Welensky quickly toured the major towns and undid Kaunda's wooing of the Europeans, and Kaunda "wept from frustration". This was the first election which did not involve Welensky in a major role. The die was cast but, if he had begun earlier, he might have swung a few more vital votes. He was faced, nonetheless, by a formidable UNIP organisation.[42]

In the event, Moffat's Liberal Party was eliminated. The UFP won 13 upper, the ANC three lower, and UNIP one upper and twelve lower roll seats. As predicted to the unheeding British, ten of the national roll constituencies had frustrated elections because none of the candidates secured the minimum percentage. Of the remainder, the UFP and the ANC gained two national roll seats each, while an Asian, sponsored by UNIP, won the special national roll seat. This gave the UFP 15 seats, UNIP 14 and the ANC five. The UFP had secured a majority, but its chances of forming the Government depended on the outcome of the ten national roll by-elections and on Nkumbula's continuing co-operation.

[40] *Ibid.*, 20/3, ff. 185–186, Welensky to Butler, 22 October 1962.
[41] *Ibid.*, f. 184, Alport to Welensky, 27 October 1962; ff. 182–183, Welensky to Alport, 27 October 1962.
[42] D. C. Mulford, *Zambia: The Politics of Independence, 1957–1964* (London, 1967), pp. 268 & 283; Author's interview with Mrs J. Bridge.

The Federal public was distracted from the elections in Northern Rhodesia, crucial though they were, by a renewed external effort against the Southern Rhodesian Government. Not only did the Reverend Sithole, on BBC television, and the African Students' Association in India accuse Welensky and Whitehead of brutally murdering Dr Parirenyatwa, but Ghana, Poland, the Ukraine, Brazil, Indonesia and Burma denounced, in the UN Trusteeship Committee, Southern Rhodesian policies and demanded intervention. This brought Whitehead to New York where, as a co-opted member of the British UN delegation, he spelt out the facts to the Committee while acknowledging that he did not expect to change his critics' views. He spoke of his intentions to integrate education at post-certificate level, of scrapping the Land Apportionment Act and of outlawing racial discrimination in public places. He believed that the 1961 Constitution would herald a new era for Southern Rhodesia in which it would confound its critics.[43]

Questioned afterwards at a Press conference in New York, Whitehead evaded the issue of mediation by U Thant and rejected the concept of parity because he did not want the races to oppose each other. He acknowledged that he had predicted that it would take 15 years to achieve his aim, but stressed that there were no racially-designated seats and that the lower roll had an influence on the election of the upper roll candidates. His idea, he said, was to ensure the acquisition of power through education, and already one-third of the members of the UFP policy committee were Africans. He explained the extent of British power, and the limitations placed on Southern Rhodesia by the Federation but said he was in favour of the latter's continuation. He claimed that he would lift the ban on ZAPU if it eschewed violence and intimidation. He would not allow interference in the internal affairs of Southern Rhodesia, but wanted the occasional loan from the British Government as well as its support. He found Nkomo charming, but thought him a weak leader.[44]

Writing to Welensky on 1 November, Butler claimed that, while in London, Alport had influenced a change in British policy but did not explain in which direction. However, Alport says that he failed to effect any change because he had argued fruitlessly that the overall Federal problem be resolved first and that the announcement of the decision on Nyasaland's secession be postponed until the outcome of the elections in the Rhodesias was finally known. (In the case of Northern Rhodesia, because of the by-elections, this could not be known until some time in December.) He had declared to Butler that these results were crucial to the chances of salvaging anything of the Federation and that they should not be allowed to be affected by the prior concession to Banda of the right to secede. Moreover, he had believed that the British Government would not want to appear to influence the outcome of the elections. The further result would be that the blame for the Federation's break-up would be laid at the British door. He had acknowledged that the risk in delay was that a frustrated Banda might inspire further unrest, but had

[43] Welensky Papers, 24/152, f. 148, Joelson to Welensky, 16 October 1962; 15/46, f. 150, Memorandum, 23 October 1962; *African Daily News*, 24 October 1962; *The Rhodesia Herald*, 29 October 1962.

[44] Welensky Papers, 16/1b, f. 174, Whitehead's Press Conference, 31 October 1962.

thought this unlikely. Alport says he had still been advocating the partition plan he had suggested earlier, but had known that the inherent danger was that the Federal Government, in resisting it strongly, might resort to force. Yet he had remained convinced that, with British participation, an association between the three territories was still possible.[45]

Alport was ignored and he returned to Salisbury on 2 November with orders to tell the Federal Government that the announcement on the acceptance of the principle of secession would be made in London on 12 November, the opening day of the Nyasaland Conference. Welensky received this frigidly and asked Alport to address the Federal Cabinet. Alport discounted the possibility that Welensky would take a "desperate course" and attempt to frustrate British policy by force. However, he was worried by a hint from Welensky that he might not assist Whitehead to be re-elected.[46]

Welensky informed Lord Salisbury that Alport had explained that Butler, wanting to keep the two Rhodesias together, would visit soon to discuss how it could be done. He said that Butler had given him a week in which to signify his attitude towards the announcement of secession, and yet, only three weeks previously, Blackwood had been assured that it would not be discussed. Affronted, Welensky had informed Alport bluntly that he would vigorously oppose any statement on Nyasaland which did not give a clear assurance of the continuing association of the Rhodesias because he had learned his lesson about relying on the good intentions of the British Government. He was extremely bitter at the news, but was somewhat cheered by the UFP victory in the Northern Rhodesian elections, if only because it had shocked the British. He knew that Kaunda had appealed to Nkumbula to form a coalition and that currently Ghana's Director of Information was pressing Nkumbula to co-operate. This, Welensky told Salisbury, showed the degree of outside influence being tolerated. He said he had warned Alport that, if any hint of Butler's decision on secession were to be leaked to the Press, he would consider himself free to say what he pleased, because he had learned to his cost the extent to which British opinion could be conditioned by a constant flow of leaks to the right quarters.[47]

On 5 November Welensky informed his Cabinet of his strong reaction to the British decision. He said that Alport had added that Nyasaland would have to meet its share of the public debt and of the cost of the redundancy of the civil servants. Whitehead was in London and had been asked to comment on Welensky's belief that the Southern Rhodesian election (now due in December) and the Northern Rhodesian by-elections would be adversely affected by the decision. Welensky said that Alport had claimed that Whitehead had replied that the Federal Government alone, amongst the four Governments, supported the Federation's continuation. This was a serious charge and Welensky proposed to confront Whitehead on his return. (Later he would discover that, when meeting Butler, Whitehead had committed himself extensively to Nyasaland's secession.)

[45] *Ibid.*, 20/3, f. 171, Butler to Welensky, 1 November 1962; Alport, *The Sudden Assignment*, *op. cit.*, p. 203.
[46] Alport, *The Sudden Assignment*, *op. cit.*, pp. 204–206.
[47] Welensky Papers, 43/*Salisbury*, Welensky to Salisbury, 3 November 1962.

The Federal Cabinet asked if Alport had indicated who would meet Nyasaland's deficit on current account and Welensky replied that he had not dwelt on it specifically. However, he said he had gathered that Britain was reconciled to providing financial assistance, but hoped to keep it to a minimum and that the Federal Government would maintain at least a trading arrangement.

One of the Cabinet declared that, unless the relationship between the Rhodesias was settled and announced simultaneously with the secession of Nyasaland, close ties would be impossible. The Cabinet decided to tell Alport that, although it was anxious to hear the British point of view, it would do nothing more than listen and would not make any quick decisions. The possibility was raised that Nyasaland's secession would so radically alter the Federation's structure that every Federal civil servant would be freed from his obligations and could choose whether he wanted to serve the new association.

Greenfield agreed that this was correct, but pointed out that the British Government, in pure law, could legislate to change this situation, although it would infringe the 1957 Convention. Finally, it was suggested that Britain was putting "the cart before the horse" by proposing to concede secession prior to a composite solution to Federal difficulties.

Joining the meeting, Alport explained that Butler had decided that, as secession was inevitable, the problem was one of choosing the moment to announce it to ensure the continuation of the relationship between the Rhodesias and the retention of practical links with Nyasaland. Alport had said he had gone to London to ensure that the decision was taken in the interests of the Federation as a whole and not merely in response to Banda. Butler had agreed and had decided that the best moment was just before the opening of the Nyasaland Conference. He had been influenced by the possibility that delay might improve the chances of the anti-Federal elements of preventing a continuing association between the Rhodesias. The new Southern Rhodesian Constitution had been implemented on 1 November, and its electorate might henceforth feel more immune to the effects of events in the northern territories. The Nyasaland Conference would be amenable towards the protection of the rights of the Europeans and to the retention of economic links with the Rhodesias. Alport claimed that Butler's advisory committee had done much to bring the Nyasaland Government to face the economic realities and, with the secession issue resolved, he thought Britain's position as the future supplier of financial support could be used as a lever. Butler, he said, had considered the Federal view that it was imperative to settle first the future association between the Rhodesias, but believed that this was impossible without the imposition of a settlement on Northern Rhodesia, which would only provoke resistance. Alport had also sought to ensure that there would be an accompanying statement on the immediate steps to deal with the consequences of secession, but Butler had decided to consult the Federal and territorial Governments only after the elections. Therefore, Butler would visit the Federation in mid-January 1963, and would arrange for a conference on future association. Alport closed by stating that Butler's decision was an exercise in political judgment and not weakness in the face of pressure. It was designed to achieve the best prospects for the continuing association of the two Rhodesias and the maintenance of the valuable links between them and, if possible, Nyasaland.

The Federal Ministers expressed their amazement to Alport that Butler considered the withdrawal of Nyasaland inevitable and that he should have reached definite conclusions on it. Accordingly, there seemed little point in prolonging the discussions with Alport. However, he argued that he had understood that they had accepted it would be unrealistic to consider holding Nyasaland by force. Thus it was logical to regard secession as inevitable.

The Federal Ministers emphasised that they had always stressed the importance of the overall settlement and that Butler was merely eroding their position before the composite formula had been conceived. They had the right to prior consultation and would not admit the British Government's right to decide unilaterally on Nyasaland. Alport acknowledged the sincerity and strength of these convictions and claimed that they had been carefully weighed by Butler in reaching his decision. Butler, he explained, had simply thought that his proposal would produce the climate of opinion which would favour the Federal Government's intentions.

The Federal Ministers, however, declared that the assurance that secession would not be considered at the Nyasaland Conference had been rendered worthless because "the pass will have been sold" before the Conference began. In fact, they asserted, Blackwood had been deliberately misled and the British Government had thus resorted to the most dubious tactics to induce in Banda some pliancy of mind. Alport claimed to be ignorant of this but thought that there might have been some misunderstanding. However, he said he would urge Blackwood to attend the Conference, despite the decision, to represent the minority. Alport maintained that the Federal Government had been properly consulted through the means of the current discussion.

The Federal Ministers rightly disputed this because, they said, the decision had been taken and it was not clear that their views would have any effect on Butler. Alport assured them that their views would be given due weight. They asked to see the report of the advisory committee, but Alport did not think it relevant to the issue because Butler had taken a political decision, while the committee had produced an economic appreciation of secession which had not changed the MCP's attitude.

Alport continued to be attacked for terming the decision an exercise in political judgment. The decision was called an inadequate and insubstantial reason for taking a most serious step which would lead to the destruction of the Federation. It was claimed that the announcement would do irreparable harm and would directly affect the election results in the Rhodesias. Alport doubted that it would because he was sure that purely territorial issues would dominate. He thought that sight was being lost of the long-term benefit of cutting the ground from beneath the feet of the extremists.

Welensky thanked Alport and commented that his Government disputed the right of the British Government to reach a decision on Nyasaland without consulting it. Certainly, he declared, the manner in which Butler's conclusions had been laid before it was not consultation. Alport withdrew in what he recalls as "a somewhat ruffled frame of mind — leaving behind me a buzz of angry conversation". He was correctly aware that he had exhausted the goodwill of the Federal Cabinet, with the consequence that, thenceforth, they regarded him as a legitimate target for their anger and indignation. He knew that his continued presence would be of little value. After he left, the Cabinet reviewed the implications and agreed that an urgent effort should be made to prevent the announcement.[48]

Alport had found Welensky coldly detached, but clearly he was reserving his anger for Butler when writing on 7 November to express his Government's profound shock at the British conclusions. He said he was uncertain whether the British decision was final or whether the Federal representations would have any effect on it. He warned that his Government relied strongly on the 1957 Convention in maintaining that its consent was required for such a change to the composition of the Federation. Indeed, the consent of the Southern Rhodesian Government was also required. However, he acknowledged that the British Government could legally disregard the Convention and pass an act to effect the change. Nonetheless, he recalled, Butler had said in May that he hoped agreement with the Federal Government was possible. In deciding on unilateral action, Welensky noted, Butler had also ignored the Federal desire for an overall settlement, including Nyasaland. Yet in May he had indicated that Nyasaland's future could not be considered in isolation. He had categorically assured Blackwood and himself that secession would not be discussed at the Nyasaland Conference, and that he would proceed cautiously, and only after consultation, which was the very antithesis of the message brought by Alport.

To emphasise the point, Welensky quoted from the minutes of 14 May in which Butler had declared that he would consult the Federal Government after his advisory committee had reported to him, and before any decision was taken. Butler had said he appreciated that it was only at that stage that the Federal Government could properly formulate its views on the purely political aspects of the problem. Welensky maintained he had therefore expected to see the committee's report and to be able to comment on it, especially as his Government had taken care to provide information for it. Butler had also asserted, on 14 September, that no decision could be taken until the Northern Rhodesian election results were known. As ten by-elections were pending, Welensky could only assume that Butler was hoping to have a drastic and disastrous effect on them through his announcement. Alport had described the decision as "an exercise in political judgment". Yet, Welensky said, clearly it had been arrived at after consultation only with Alport and Jones. Butler's assessment of the political situation was, to Welensky, "astounding" considering that the outcome of the electoral stalemate in Northern Rhodesia was impossible to predict. If the announcement were made on 12 November, then, contrary to Alport's view, the anti-Federal elements would rally and Northern Rhodesia could enter a bitter period of extreme racialism, with dire consequences. Southern Rhodesia, Welensky warned, would be radically affected as a Rhodesian Front victory at the polls was certain.

Welensky stated that the "unfortunate and disastrous" timing of the state-

[48] *Ibid.*, FGC(62), 35th (Special) Meeting, Federal Cabinet, 5 November 1962; 20/3, ff. 179–181, Statement by Alport to the Federal Cabinet, 5 November 1962; Alport, *The Sudden Assignment*, *op. cit.*, p. 207.

ment would do more to kill Butler's objective of a continuing association of Northern and Southern Rhodesia than anything else. He said it would prevent him from honouring an undertaking to the Federal Assembly that it would be able to debate any questions on the future of the Federation before any decisions were taken. The announcement would weaken the Federal Government's position with regard to Nyasaland's share of the public debt and on the protection of the minorities. It would alarm the Federal civil servants. It was intolerable to consider forcing them to serve other Governments, but it would be ruinously expensive to compensate them, unless the British shouldered the burden. The difficult task of recruiting civil servants would be made impossible. The African nationalists in Northern Rhodesia would be tempted to follow the example of Banda and, if they did, any negotiations on a new Rhodesian association would be pointless. The Pan-African Movement and a large number of whites would understand that the Federation had been effectively destroyed. There would be a large exodus of whites from the territories and, in fact, it had already begun. The raising of loans would become extremely difficult, and the future level of all the Government's revenues would be very uncertain. If the Federal Government could not curb thc high level of withdrawals from the building societies soon, there would be a national financial crisis. The collapse of confidence could lead to greater efforts to evade exchange control.

Welensky pointed out that he and his Ministers had spent nine years of their lives creating and preserving a new nation, but would now be betrayed by those to whom they had the right to turn for support. He acknowledged that it was within Butler's powers to take the decision, but declared he would resist it because he was determined that the secession of Nyasaland would be part of a general settlement, which included certain terms to be announced simultaneously with secession. These would include compensation and guarantees for minorities, a method of maintaining the Federal public service and the liabilities of the Governments for the public debt. This was not all, Welensky concluded, because the British Government would have to underwrite the public debt and assume responsibility for pensions and other matters.[49]

This dispatch brought Alport to the Federal Assembly that day, 7 November, where Welensky was facing a vote of no confidence, which he easily handled before speaking on the UN and Southern Rhodesia.[50] Alport informed Welensky that he had been told by Butler that he would make his announcement on Monday, 12 November, but that he believed sincerely that the period following it could be used constructively and usefully to cement the Rhodesian association. Butler felt keenly that the Federal view, that the announcement would be destructive, was wrong. He would ignore the immediate impact of the announcement and pursue the examination of the future relationship between the Rhodesias. In fact, Butler claimed, the announcement would be a prelude to a constructive settlement of the problems of the two territories.

Welensky was unimpressed and bluntly declared that, if the British Govern-

[49] Welensky Papers, 20/3, ff. 173–177, Welensky to Butler, 7 November 1962.
[50] Fed R & N *Debates* (Salisbury), Vol. 19, Col. 1836 f., 7 November 1962.

ment would not postpone the announcement, he would simultaneously issue a statement, in the Federal Assembly, which would reveal "the whole sorry train of events", while laying the total responsibility for the destruction of the Federation at the British door. Then he angrily told Alport that he had gathered from Butler that Alport had influenced the British attitude. Asking for confirmation, he asserted that, when he had agreed to accept a politician as the British High Commissioner, it had been on condition that he would not interfere with policy. Alport replied stiffly that he could not divulge the advice he had given Butler, but that, in his opinion, he had borne in mind the best interests of Britain and the Federation. His conscience, he said, was clear and, if necessary, he would defend himself in public. He was in full agreement with Butler's assertion that the announcement could be a prelude to a Rhodesian settlement.

Welensky warned that, if he were to be ignored by the British Government on this issue, he would not be hypocritical and participate in the Southern Rhodesian election when he knew that the British Government did not intend to preserve the Federation. Alport hoped that Welensky would not abstain lest he give the impression of not caring for the Federation or its inhabitants. He maintained that the British Government believed that the only just solution was to have the closest possible links between the Rhodesias and an economic association with Nyasaland. Welensky replied that, therefore, the widest possible divergence between their Governments was being revealed.[51]

Alport, in his account, omits the personal attack on him and claims that Welensky was more restrained than ever. He recalls arguing that Welensky's failure to participate in the election would deny any chance of an association between the Rhodesias and would frustrate the efforts of the past two years to direct Southern Rhodesia on a more liberal course. The Federal record is somewhat at variance with that. Alport alleges that he said this because he had the interests of the Federation at heart, and had made personal sacrifices on its behalf. He did not take seriously Welensky's threat to boycott the Southern Rhodesian election because he did not think it was meant, or that Welensky would wish to be responsible for Whitehead's defeat. Having seen Welensky's reaction to Field's boycott of the Federal election, Alport was certain that Welensky could not ignore his own good sense and fighting spirit and stand back and watch his Party being defeated.

Although he had advocated a composite approach, Alport now believed that any postponement of the announcement would be dangerous from his Government's point of view. Thus he said nothing to Welensky about his fears that Butler might still change his mind. He was sure that the intention to make the announcement was widely known in London and in Salisbury and that a postponement would be construed as weakness. Postponement would also encourage the MCP to be recalcitrant and give Welensky time to make life difficult for the British Government. Equally, it would allow Whitehead's opponents to accuse Britain and the UFP of subterfuge. Alport still did not believe that if the announcement were made before the Southern Rhodesian election it would place Whitehead in any sort of difficulty. To the contrary,

[51] Welensky Papers, 20/3, ff. 167–169, Minutes of a Meeting with Alport, 7 November 1962.

he believed that Welensky could use it to advantage in a denunciation of the British Government and offset the anti-British and racialist approach of the Rhodesian Front. Therefore, Alport urged Butler to make the announcement on 12 November.[52]

After his meeting with Alport, Welensky reported to his Cabinet and then telephoned Butler seeking a reaction to his dispatch. However, Butler said it was still being considered by the British Cabinet. As this was his first direct contact with Butler since Alport's return from London, Welensky asked for confirmation of the date of the announcement. Butler was not as unyielding as Alport and said that, though his Government wished to solve the problem of Nyasaland before that of the Rhodesias, it wanted to know the Federal opinion of its plans. Welensky offered to fly to London, but Butler was satisfied that the Federal case had been put sufficiently clearly in the dispatch. He pleaded for account to be taken of British difficulties. Welensky replied that he appreciated them, but remained troubled because the announcement could have tragic and chaotic consequences if it affected the results of the Rhodesian elections. He said he was due to attend Whitehead's UFP divisional congress at the weekend but that he would not decide whether to appear until he had heard from Butler. He avowed he would not participate in the electoral campaign if the announcement was made, because the Federation would have been destroyed and he would have no standing in Southern Rhodesian politics. It was, he said, inevitable that Northern Rhodesia would follow the same path as Nyasaland.

Butler replied that no decision had been taken on the fate of Northern Rhodesia and that the announcement was necessary for agreement at the Nyasaland Conference. Nonetheless, his Government had not yet made up its mind and Welensky's views would be considered. He urged Welensky to attend the UFP congress, and Welensky commented, threateningly, that if he did not, Whitehead would lose the election. Butler could give Welensky no date for the announcement but assured him that it would be accompanied by a statement on the desirability of the continued association of the Rhodesias. Welensky felt that this would not carry much weight, but accepted that Butler was trying to help. He did not believe he was asking for too much in requesting that the announcement be postponed until after the elections.[53]

Leaving London that night, Whitehead denied at a final Press conference that he and Welensky were at odds and indeed claimed he had Welensky's strongest possible support. He accepted that some changes were necessary but thought it would be an act of insanity to destroy the practical and acceptable association of the territories.[54]

Anxious to secure Whitehead's backing, Alport briefed the Southern Rhodesian Cabinet but failed to win its support for Butler's decision on secession and assumed that the Rhodesian lobby in Britain had brought influence to bear. In fact, it was Welensky who was the major influence and who secured Whitehead to his cause through a "showdown" with him in which he

[52] Alport, *The Sudden Assignment*, *op. cit.*, pp. 207–208.

[53] Welensky Papers, FGC(62), 36th Meeting, Minute 2, Federal Cabinet, 7 November 1962; 20/3, ff. 164–166, Telephone conversation between Welensky and Butler, 7 November 1962.

[54] *Ibid.*, 24/152, ff. 143–144, Joelson to Welensky, 7 November 1962.

threatened not to attend the divisional congress. Consequently, Whitehead telegraphed Butler on 8 November protesting at the failure to consult the Southern Rhodesian Government although it had been "a high-contracting party" to the formation of the Federation. He reminded Butler that, at their recent meeting, he had expressed fears of the effect of the secession announcement on the Northern Rhodesian by-elections and claimed that he now had reason to believe that the announcement would be construed as direct British interference in those elections. He said that the Southern Rhodesian election would also be affected if, at the outset of the campaign, the UFP's Federal and Southern Rhodesian divisions parted company. Thus he urged that the announcement be postponed until at least 15 December and that secession be considered only in the inter-Government negotiations in January 1963.[55]

Alport thought the "high-contracting" argument was pure gamesmanship, but ingenious nonetheless. Although Southern Rhodesia had been a principal party in 1953, he did not accept the argument as either politically or constitutionally sound. Believing that Whitehead would agree with him, Alport warned Butler that a climax was imminent and asked for permission to act on his own initiative when the announcement produced the inevitable explosion. Then in a second cable he submitted to Butler his opinion of Whitehead's argument. He has regretted this action because he believes that his message caused more alarm than he intended and simply added to the pressure being applied by Welensky, Whitehead, Lord Salisbury and his friends, thereby placing Butler in a difficult position.[56]

Alport waited most of 9 November for Butler's reply, and Welensky had to wait even longer because Alport had to transmit it to him. During this time, others were writing letters which proved Whitehead's contention that the imminence of the announcement was widely known in influential circles. An anonymous writer warned A. T. Adams of the UFP that Hone had told Roberts that day that there might be disturbing news about Nyasaland. Roberts was engaged in negotiating the electoral pact with Nkumbula and hoped that there might be a way still of sabotaging the announcement.[57] (It is interesting to note, in passing, that the financial support for this pact was estimated to be £100 000 p.a., which was deemed worthwhile because it would maintain the *status quo* and yet cost less than the annual upkeep of a battalion. Despite its expected benefits, Federal intelligence feared it might provoke a violent reaction from the ranks of UNIP.[58])

Welensky spent at least part of the day writing to his confidants warning that "things could not look blacker", and telling Sarah Gertrude Millin that, if he expressed his thoughts on the British Government, the paper would burn.[59] At 5 p.m. GMT, Butler summoned Robinson because he wished to relay the latter's comments to the British Cabinet later in the evening and

[55] Alport, *The Sudden Assignment*, *op. cit.*, p. 209; Welensky Papers, 20/3, f. 163, Whitehead to Butler, 8 November 1962.

[56] Alport, *The Sudden Assignment*, *op. cit.*, p. 209.

[57] Welensky Papers, 8/69, f. 150, Anonymous Note, 9 November 1962.

[58] *Ibid.*, 8/69, f. 162, FISB Memorandum, 8 November 1962.

[59] *Ibid.*, 42/21, ff. 2–3, Welensky to G. Beckett, 9 November 1962; 43/*Millin*, Welensky to S. G. Millin, 9 November 1962.

promised they would be taken very seriously. Robinson said he did not want to repeat all Welensky's arguments, but remarked that his Government believed its consent was required for secession and that this consent had to be part of an overall agreement. If the statement were made before it met, the Conference would inevitably consider secession and the prospect of sovereign independence, not just self-government, within the framework of the Federation. Blackwood, he said, had discussed the matter with him and had declared that, as he and his delegation were not competent to deal with Federal affairs, they would probably withdraw.

Robinson was confident that the Rhodesian elections would be gravely prejudiced. He drew Butler's attention to a statement by the ANC that it would delay its decision on participation in any coalition until after the by-elections. He thought that the announcement on Nyasaland could prejudice this delicate situation and, in particular, the position of the moderates. As a quarter of the seats had yet to be filled, the result could not be forecast. He praised Butler for transforming the political atmosphere and urged that he should not destroy all that had been accomplished by setting in train events which would have the most serious consequences. He hastened to add that he was not threatening Butler but was merely emphasising the gravity of the situation. The Nyasaland delegation of the UFP had informed him that it genuinely feared the announcement could have serious implications in the territory. For example, wild celebrations could result in a security situation.

Responding, Butler placed his confidence in the security forces and warned that his Government would not give up the idea of secession. It had always tried, he said, to make it clear that Nyasaland had to be treated as a special case. It saw secession as inevitable, and it was sure that Welensky and Whitehead would not want to hold Nyasaland by force. He had concluded that Nyasaland could no longer be held and certainly not until his visit in January. This was because secession had been discussed for so long and because the Nyasaland Africans were pathological about it.

Butler acknowledged the fears of the effect on the Rhodesian elections, and claimed to take the Federal representations very seriously, but could not accept the Federal prediction of the outcome. He and the British Cabinet had consulted the Lord Chancellor, the Law Advisers, Lord Home and others and were satisfied that they could legally do what they proposed. Professor Jennings and others might hold a different view, but they were a small minority. Lord Home, after all, had reconsidered the Convention of 1957 and the history of its negotiations, and had agreed that it related strictly to matters within the Federal sphere of influence. As for Nyasaland becoming self-governing, Butler could not accept that it had to be within the Federation because, even if the secession announcement were not made, the new Nyasaland Constitution would be valid, whether the territory remained within the Federation or not. The Conference, however, would confine itself to matters such as the appointment of a chief minister and the removal of two official Members from the Executive Council. The new Nyasaland Constitution would be the stock model of colonial self-government with the addition of a bill of rights.

Robinson declared that the Federal Government had not been consulted on the Convention and would not accept the British interpretation. Butler ignored him and reiterated that he had always stressed the urgency of the Nyasaland question. He believed that he had consulted the Federal Government on this subject fully during his visit, when Welensky was in London, and during the current interchange. Robinson was unmoved and declared that the announcement of 12 November would be tantamount to a British unilateral declaration of intent to destroy the Federation. The consequences, he said, would be severe and tragic, and Butler's visit in January might well be unnecessary. The Federal Government expected consultation to be a properly convened meeting to consider the overall picture for the purpose of devising a formula for the future relationship of the Rhodesias and Nyasaland. Once devised, the formula would be presented to the parties concerned.

Butler argued that the pathological attitude of the MCP made this course impossible. Until secession was conceded, he claimed, the MCP would not consider any new form of association. As the situation could no longer be held, action had to be taken. Nevertheless, the British Cabinet would consider the question of timing, and he hoped to be able to inform Robinson later of the result. Butler said he was under great pressure to act and expected to experience extreme difficulty with his Cabinet. He hoped that, if he satisfied the Federal Government on the question of timing, his relationship with it would improve so that they could work together in the future.[60]

The Federal Government won the day. Late in the evening of 9 November, a message from Butler was transmitted through Alport which began by assuring Welensky that his views had been considered carefully and that there were points on which the Governments had to agree to differ. For example, the Federal view of the 1957 Convention was unacceptable and thus the current proposals were not seen as a violation thereof. The message said that Welensky had not been told that he would see the report of the advisory committee and that Butler had made it plain that committee was attached to him personally and that its views would only be part of the consideration which would underlie the British decision. The Federal claim that the Rhodesian elections would be affected adversely had been studied, but the British Government believed that the voters should have been aware for some time that it would be impossible to hold Nyasaland in the Federation. The British Government thought that it had to be seen to be striving for an agreement on the association of the Rhodesias and that Nyasaland's secession had to be accepted as a regrettable necessity. The only alternative was for Britain to attempt to keep Nyasaland in the Federation by force, which would have immediate and serious consequences. By contrast, the economic and financial aspects of secession could be dealt with by statesmanship and careful planning. As a result of the deliberations, the message ended, and deferring to the Federal fears regarding the effect of the announcement on the elections, the British Government had decided to postpone the imminent announcement of the acceptance of Nyasaland's secession until just before the Christmas recess in mid-December.[61] Thus Welensky's pressure had at least gained him some time.

[60] *Ibid.*, 20/8, f. 6, Minutes of a Meeting with Butler, 9 November 1962.
[61] *Ibid.*, 20/3, ff. 160–162, Butler to Welensky, 9 November 1962.

Alport gave this message to Welensky early the next morning, 10 November, and it was greeted with apparent satisfaction. Deciding, after all, to help Whitehead, Welensky left immediately for the UFP congress in Bulawayo and, on arrival, excused his lateness by blaming Alport. Disappointed, Alport proposed to resign because Butler had ignored his advice. However, Butler would not accept his resignation. Welensky was not, of course, really satisfied, and privately described the recent events as "a bloody row", claiming that he had contemplated resigning and publishing everything worth revealing. He was sure the Northern Rhodesian election results had upset Butler's calculations, and revealed that he had financed Nkumbula, although he did not trust him, and had helped him to win the seats he had secured. Efforts, Welensky said, were now concentrated on securing an electoral pact with him. Welensky claimed that he had failed to prevent discussion on secession with Banda in London despite the undertakings which he and Blackwood had received. He had complained to Alport that: "We don't speak the same language", and had received the reply: "Oh, in fact it [secession] won't be discussed in the Conference, it will be discussed before".[62]

While Welensky waited until the Nyasaland Conference ended, on 23 November, before replying to Butler, Greenfield and others wasted no time in examining the situation. Greenfield thought that, to explain the British announcement on secession, Welensky would have to recall Parliament on 17 December, the date the British Parliament rose for the Christmas recess and on which it was expected that the announcement would be made. He believed it was worth making a final effort to persuade Butler not to make the announcement. At the same time plans were needed for action to be taken when Butler made the announcement, as inevitably he would. The Federal Government could inform Butler that it rejected outright the decision on secession and that it would resist attempts to implement it. Alternatively, it could tamely submit and receive Butler in January to negotiate the new association between the territories. Another course was to protest vehemently and to challenge the British right to act, simultaneously acknowledging that the Federal Government had no choice but to submit. It should warn that a precedent should not be set for Northern Rhodesia, and that it would bend its energies to keeping the two Rhodesias together, and would strongly resist any effort to unscramble the Federation without its agreement. Everything would turn on the by-elections in Northern Rhodesia on 13 December and the general election in Southern Rhodesia on 15 December, and there would be little time in which to decide what course to take. Hence there was a need for careful planning, which had to be co-ordinated closely with Whitehead lest the British be given any opportunity to exploit a division.

Greenfield did not advocate the adoption of the first course of outright rejection and a campaign to prevent any implementation, because he did not think it would be effective, particularly as the public had been "softened up" by the Press for over a year. There was also little desire amongst Rhodesians to keep Nyasaland. The second course, of tame submission, would be exploited by Kaunda and would produce most undesirable results. The only

[62] Alport, *The Sudden Assignment*, *op. cit.*, p. 210; Welensky Papers, 24/152, ff.139–142, Welensky to Joelson, 11 November 1962.

practicable one was the third course, of vehement protest and acknowledgement of the British right to act. Along with the Federal protest, he said, a White Paper could be published which would show the economic effects of secession, and there could be a declaration of determination to keep the two Rhodesias together. Everything would depend on Welensky's ability to arouse popular sentiment, and Kaunda had to be shown as being incapable of implementing his secession proclamations. Consideration had also to be given to an attempt at a final settlement with the British before 17 December on a package deal. For this purpose, work would have to begin immediately on a constitutional arrangement for the two Rhodesias.[63]

Robinson offered two courses of action. The first was to object to the announcement and to indicate what action would be taken if the objection was ignored. The second was to regard the recent exchanges as formal notification of the intention to allow secession and to demand that Butler begin formal negotiations thereon with the Federal Government, so that the implications could be fully examined. Butler had, after all, expressed the hope that the Governments could work constructively together and Robinson's chief concern was that the Federal Government should take the initiative.[64]

J. A. Clark, Federal Minister of Commerce and Industry, felt that the British Government should be forced to "buy" Nyasaland's secession. The price, he suggested, would be a firm union between the Rhodesias in the form of a federation. In this way, Nyasaland would not set the precedent for Northern Rhodesia. He believed that current public opinion saw Nyasaland's secession as inevitable and even desirable, and thus secession, coupled with a continuing Rhodesian association, would be greeted as statesmanlike. The British Government, after the long bitter struggle with the Federal Government, might welcome the opportunity to co-operate, rather than fight. He suggested a secret trip to Britain by two Federal Ministers after the Nyasaland Conference to achieve this settlement so that the announcement of 17 December could be made jointly by the British and Federal Governments.[65]

Welensky's view was that the British Government had chosen 17 December as the date for the announcement because it knew very well that it would be impossible for anyone to exert any political pressure during the Christmas recess. Thus he told Evans that it was important to revive immediately the support which the Federation had hitherto enjoyed amongst the ranks of the Conservative Party. He confessed to Lord Salisbury that he was puzzled by Butler, although it was clear that the latter was disappointed and surprised by the Northern Rhodesian general election because he had wanted Kaunda to win so that he could argue that, as two African nationalist territorial Governments rejected the Federation, it would be best to dissolve it. Moreover, he said, Whitehead had already indicated that he could not work with two such Governments. The Northern Rhodesian election had spoilt the game, but, while Welensky fumed against the chicanery of the British Government, he had to confess that he was still in a weak position because no one wanted to retain Nyasaland. He wished that Butler would make a forthright statement

[63] Welensky Papers, 32/63, f. 5, Greenfield to Welensky, 13 November 1962.
[64] *Ibid.*, 32/80, f. 19, Robinson to Welensky, 12 November 1962.
[65] *Ibid.*, 20/3, ff. 157–158, J. A. Clark to Welensky, 15 November 1962.

which would accept full responsibility for the secession of Nyasaland, while keeping the two Rhodesias together. In exchange, he would accept radical changes to the structure of the Federation. However, he did not think that Butler ever committed himself firmly to anything. He knew that, until the Southern Rhodesian election, he had to take care not to damage the UFP's prospects. Thereafter, if the terms did not suit him, he would make a full statement in Parliament and have it published in the Press. What distressed him most was Home's acceptance of Butler's version of the 1957 Convention. He found this "incredible". He felt that he had only two courses left: either to resign or to defy the British Government.[66]

Of prime interest to the public was the wooing of Nkumbula by UNIP and the UFP. Immediately after the elections, Mainza Chona, UNIP's secretary, claimed that a pact had been concluded with the ANC, but John Banda, its secretary, promptly denied it. By 7 November the ANC was still resisting, and Kaunda attempted to induce the senior Chiefs to exert their influence to secure the pact in case the "Federal oppression" continued for another five years. The UFP was equally busy and was looking for something with which Nkumbula could save face. They agreed, at least, not to compete for seats.[67]

On 14 November Nkumbula publicly rejected pacts with either Party, but Kaunda was still hopeful because the next day he dismissed a claim by Roberts to half the seats in the Executive Council and declared that UNIP and the ANC would demand to be the Government. Two days later, Kaunda and Nkumbula announced the conclusion of a pact, somewhat to the distress of Tshombe whom they hastened to reassure. The nature of the pact mystified everyone because their candidates continued to compete against each other for the vacant seats. The mystery was cleared in late November when Nkumbula and Kaunda announced from London that they had agreed to form the Government after the by-elections. This statement was made after Nyerere had provided Nkumbula with an aircraft to bring him to Dar-es-Salaam. A consequence was that Nkumbula joined the Pan-African Freedom Movement of East and Central Africa. The Federal Government detected a strenuous bid, including finance, to ensure the by-elections went the Pan-Africanist way.[68]

Nkumbula and Kaunda had gone to London hard on Banda's heels to see Butler to ask for a conference on a new constitution for Northern Rhodesia. The Nyasaland Conference had opened in London on 12 November but had confined itself to the self-government issue and was quickly over. Welensky and Joelson concluded that Butler and Banda had reached a private agreement on secession. The Conference was marked by a degree of accord which endured throughout the week of its existence. Nyasaland received a cabinet

[66] *Ibid.*, 32/90, f. 15, Welensky to Evans, 13 November 1962; 43/*Salisbury*, Welensky to Lord Salisbury, 15 November 1962.

[67] *African Daily News*, 2 November 1962; Welensky Papers, 8/69, f. 142, Price to W. S. Parker, 2 November 1962; *Central African Post*, 5 November 1962; *The Rhodesia Herald*, 8 November 1962.

[68] Welensky Papers, 35/22L, f. 15, G. W. R. L'Ange to A. T. Adams, 7 November 1962; 8/69, f. 162, Memorandum, 8 November 1962; *The Rhodesia Herald*, 15, 17 & 20 November 1962; Welensky Papers, 33/33, f. 117, "News Flash", 28 November 1962; 8/69, f. 186, Welensky to Robinson, 26 November 1962; 24/152, ff.133–136, Welensky to Joelson, 20 November 1962.

comprising a prime minister, not more than eight elected ministers and an *ex officio* minister of finance. The new Legislative Assembly would contain the existing number of elected Members for the time being, and its enlargement, as well as an extension to the franchise, would be negotiated later. A bill of rights would be introduced for the protection of minorities. It is, perhaps, pertinent to note that the subsequent Conference Report made no mention of the Federation's existence.[69]

While Welensky waited for Butler to complete the Conference, he shared election campaign platforms with Whitehead, but not his confidence. Whitehead's tactic was to declare that the African who had earned it by merit had to be treated as an equal. He proposed to abolish the Land Apportionment Act in accordance with a resolution of the UFP congress of 9 and 10 November. He would outlaw social discrimination and integrate education at the sixth form level. He also contemplated an early reform of the franchise.

The Rhodesian Front countered with promises of no forced integration, no lowering of standards, no abdication of responsible government, no repeal of the Land Apportionment Act, and no appeasement of the Afro-Asian bloc. The RF declared that it would promote freedom with responsibility. It would secure understanding and co-operation between all the people and promote self-help, as well as achieving a lasting, mutual understanding with neighbouring states. Welensky urged the electorate to ignore these blandishments and return the UFP to power or face an economic and political retreat. He warned that the RF would take Southern Rhodesia out of the Federation, despite the effect on the economy and the burden of defence.[70]

While the final plenary session of the Nyasaland Conference was in progress, Welensky replied at last to Butler, explaining that he had not wanted to exacerbate feelings during the Conference. He rejected outright the British Government's assertion of its right to break up the Federation unilaterally in defiance of the 1957 Convention, when it had recognised the binding force of an identically-worded convention relating to Southern Rhodesia. After their meetings in May and September, when Butler had emphasised the need for consultation, Welensky claimed that he had become confident that they would find a solution. This was why, he said, he had been so shocked by the unilateral British proposal which Alport had brought back. In any case, it would be extremely damaging to Federal interests if Butler proceeded as he proposed. The economy, which was already suffering from the constitutional struggles of the past few years, would be particularly affected. Already, property was virtually unsaleable, and the Europeans were emigrating in a steady stream. Accordingly, Welensky asked that no announcement be made until he and Butler had reviewed the situation, perhaps during Butler's visit in January. The least he asked was to be allowed to send a Minister to discuss the issue. If Butler were determined to persist with the announcement,

69 Welensky Papers, 24/152, ff. 133–136, Welensky to Joelson, 20 November 1962; 32/90, f. 22, Final Press Communiqué of the Nyasaland Constitutional Conference, 23 November 1962; f. 21, Report of the Nyasaland Constitutional Conference, November 1962 – published as Command 1887.

70 *Ibid.*, 42/75, f. 915, Whitehead's Speech, 21 November 1962; 8/69, f. 178, Message from Welensky, 22 November 1962.

Welensky wanted to discuss its terms without delay, and warned he would summon his Parliament and use every possible means to prevent further disintegration of the Federation, even at the risk of a direct confrontation with the British Government. He rejected Butler's view of the dangers of delaying Nyasaland's secession until the future association of the Rhodesias was settled. Indeed, he believed that the consequences would be far graver if secession was premature. Closing, he reiterated a demand which he had made earlier for a visit from officials from the British Treasury and the Bank of England to ascertain the economic implications of the British decision.[71]

Welensky thereupon revealed to Greenfield and Robinson that Alport had tried until 9.10 p.m. that evening, 23 November, to persuade him to remove certain parts of his dispatch. Alport was worried about the reference to the possibility of confrontation, but Welensky said he would not erase it because he and Butler had vowed at their last meeting never to use force against each other. While half admitting responsibility for many of the British ideas, Welensky related that Alport had tried to convince him that Macmillan, Sandys, Home and Butler supported the Federation. He had retorted that Alport could tell Butler, in particular, that he had been a bitter disappointment to him.[72]

Welensky's predicament won him the further sympathy of Joelson, Lord Salisbury and others. Writing on 28 November, Joelson wondered if the Nkumbula-Kaunda pact, just announced, would cause Butler to "trim again". Hone had declared that only a party with 23 seats would become the Government, but Joelson wondered if Hone and Butler would now change their minds. The pact was also likely to make Butler waver with regard to the retention of strong ties between the Rhodesias. Joelson advised Welensky to be utterly plain in his denunciation in the Federal Assembly so that everyone who read it would understand. Welensky had proposed to buy advertising space in every British newspaper to highlight the accusation against the British Government which would be contained in his speech, but Joelson thought this unorthodox. It would anger the British Cabinet and could lead to an accusation of interference in the internal affairs of Britain. However, Joelson felt that Welensky could reply that he was being forced to do this by the unilateral British action.[73]

Lord Salisbury told Welensky he could not understand the mentality of his former colleagues and, in particular, their argument on secession. He agreed that the Minister responsible for the subject could say that it could not be discussed at a conference, but that it could be raised afterwards. To allow it to be discussed before the Conference, and yet not in it, was intellectually dishonest. However, he said, it was now apparent that not only was Nyasaland lost to the Federation, but so was one of Welensky's main bargaining counters for an ultimate settlement. The dice were now loaded against Welensky, and Salisbury did not wonder at his bitterness. He hoped that the British Government would realise that there was a point beyond which they

[71] *Ibid.*, 20/3, ff. 151–156, Welensky to Butler, 23 November 1962.

[72] *Ibid.*, ff. 149–150, Welensky to Greenfield, 24 November 1962; 32/28, f. 40, Welensky to Robinson, 24 November 1962.

[73] *Ibid.*, 24/152, ff. 128–129, Joelson to Welensky, 28 November 1962.

could not push Welensky. Salisbury was also surprised by the argument that secession was not a Federal matter and thus did not invoke the 1957 Convention. It shook him that Home and the legal advisers could agree to this interpretation. He urged Welensky to continue to reject this argument, but to agree reluctantly, in terms of the Convention, to secession on the grounds that the inclusion of Nyasaland had never really been wanted. He warned that the strongest possible stand would be needed to prevent the use of Nyasaland's secession as the precedent for that of Northern Rhodesia.[74]

Salisbury was not alone in thinking that the pass was already sold because *The Times* on the previous day, 29 November, had reached that conclusion. It believed that, as a consequence, secession should be effected swiftly so that the Northern and Southern Rhodesian relationship could be resolved. It noted that both Kaunda and Nkumbula wanted a conference to ensure that they would gain a certain African majority and the right to secede.

There was no response from Butler for ten days, but Welensky, together with Malvern and others, was fully occupied with the Southern Rhodesian election, claiming that the RF was determined to turn the clock back. As the campaign wore on, however, the UFP's Federal division was disheartened by being unable to discover any evidence that Whitehead would win. The Congo was also a distraction, and Welensky had to deal with Tshombe and Lord Home over a UN proposal to impose sanctions on Katanga.[75]

If Butler was in no hurry to reply, at least Blackwood wrote to Welensky, on 3 December, describing a meeting between himself, Little, Butler and Jones in London. Butler had told him that he was still determined to make his announcement on 17 December, though he gave the impression that he had not finally decided what he would say, beyond stating the general principle. Blackwood and Little had rejected his right to make the announcement and had warned him that nothing would be achieved apart from a direct confrontation with Welensky. They had insisted that he would first have to institute negotiations between all the Governments concerned. Butler had replied that he wished to avoid a collision with Welensky because he was his best friend. He had emphasised his desire to strengthen the ties between the Rhodesias and to preserve economic and defence links with Nyasaland. Blackwood had said that he disliked economic ties because they would mean that Southern Rhodesia would continue to have a stranglehold on Nyasaland's economic development. Butler had confirmed that he had no intention of granting independence to Nyasaland for the time being and had said that he had told Banda not to ask for it until the end of 1963. This had displeased Banda. Butler had also agreed to consult the Nyasaland Opposition on the matter. He had hoped Banda would accept five reserved seats for Europeans when demanding the abolition of the upper roll.

Blackwood reported that, when condemning Banda's attitude to the Nkula Falls scheme and praising that of Barrow, Butler had been interrupted by Jones to denounce the Federal refusal to return the control of "power" to Nyasaland in order that Banda would be able to accept the scheme. Butler

[74] *Ibid.*, 43/*Salisbury*, Lord Salisbury to Welensky, 30 November 1962.

[75] *Ibid.*, 16/1b, f. 172, Lord Malvern's RTV Broadcast, 30 November 1962; 20/13, f. 73, Welensky to Robinson, 1 December 1962; f. 72, Home to Welensky, 3 December 1962.

had made it clear that Nyasaland would be expected to effect economies and to raise additional revenue for education and health. However, he had said that his advisory committee had predicted a growth of 2½ per cent in the gross domestic product, so the problem would not be too great. Blackwood had replied that he expected it to fall.

Blackwood related that, during the meeting, a telegram had arrived from Whitehead demanding the postponement of the announcement on secession. This had seemed to so startle Butler that Blackwood thought it timely to reiterate that Whitehead would lose his election if Welensky did not support him.[76]

On the same day as his meeting with Blackwood, 3 December, a British Opposition motion forced Butler to break his public silence on secession. However, he informed Welensky that he would avoid a premature disclosure of his intentions in the debate that day.

In the Commons, Healey called on the Government to respect the wishes of the people and to dissolve the Federation and reform the territorial Constitutions so that early independence could be achieved under representative democratic governments. The Government replied with an amendment which welcomed the constitutional changes in Nyasaland and noted the pending elections in Northern and Southern Rhodesia and endorsed the Government's efforts to promote a constructive solution to the problem of the future association of the territories.

Healey naturally commented that nothing was known of those efforts but that it was clear that Banda was not being allowed to realise the wishes of his electorate on secession. He noted the lack of progress in Northern Rhodesia where, two years after the Monckton Commission had recommended African majority rule, nothing like it had been achieved. He blamed the European for the collapse of the multi-racial ideal because the UFP had ignored the African voter, whereas UNIP had visited white homes and had addressed white meetings. The general election, he said, had shown the great degree of support that existed both for UNIP and for secession. If Butler was to be consistent, Healey claimed, then he had to apply to Northern Rhodesia the same principles which he had applied to Nyasaland. He argued that there was no need to hide the decision on secession from the Commons because, according to Welensky, Butler had already decided to concede it to Nyasaland.

Butler described Healey's motion as depressing and unconstructive. He said he was pleased with the success of the Nyasaland Conference. He explained he was negotiating with Kaunda and Nkumbula, but would first gauge the outcome of the Northern Rhodesian by-elections. He believed that the Southern Rhodesians had to find their own racial solution, but that their new constitution provided a basis for progress. However, only the people there could guarantee that progress, but then many of the Europeans were wedded to the non-racial concept. The association of the territories might have to be changed radically and, if this were so, the main aim would be to preserve the benefits of the Federation. It was clear that the consequences of a withdrawal by Nyasaland would be serious, but it had not shaken the

[76] *Ibid.*, 32/63, f. 14, Blackwood to Welensky, 3 December 1962.

resolve of the MCP Ministers. Nonetheless, he was comforted by the report of his advisory committee that the MCP Ministers had agreed to measures to right some of the economic imbalance which would occur at secession.

Butler would not say more than that his Government had the matter under constant review. It was obviously necessary, he said, to retain an association, particularly between the Rhodesias, but that the appropriate time to review this was in the New Year. He felt that the debate was premature because it was impossible to devise solutions until the territorial elections had revealed what sort of Governments would emerge. The amendment was put and accepted overwhelmingly.[77]

The next day Robinson met Butler and pointed out that parts of his speech in the debate would be interpreted in Salisbury, and certainly by Welensky, as meaning that Nyasaland could secede. Appearing confused, Butler protested that he had not meant that and asked that Welensky be told so, because he and his staff had thought that his remarks were strictly in keeping with his undertaking not to mention the matter at this stage. He grew silent, however, as Robinson read to him from *Hansard*, but did not fail to remind Robinson that Welensky had mentioned the secession of Nyasaland in a radio broadcast while campaigning in Southern Rhodesia, despite his request to Butler to remain silent on the subject until polling day. Yet he agreed that Robinson might assure Welensky that the British Government would not rely on this speech to claim that it had informed everyone of its intentions.

Robinson warned Butler that the Federal Government would not agree to the announcement being made before the Christmas recess nor would it condone the lack of consultation. Considerably annoyed, Butler claimed to have been consulting the Federal Government since his appointment in May. This provoked a tirade from Robinson who told him precisely what he thought of "his non-existent methods of consultation" and of his failure to keep him informed. He wondered if Butler sought to resolve the future with the Federal Government or merely to provoke its open hostility, which he had almost achieved. Clearly taken aback, Butler agreed to receive a Federal ministerial delegation, but said that Welensky should not come to London because he would alarm the public.

Butler said that he would state on 17 December that the parties would be consulted on the inter-territorial association, but on the understanding that Nyasaland could secede. He would cover the consequences of secession, maintain that Nyasaland would have to meet its financial obligations, and emphasise strongly the need for a future association between the territories. He had not written a final draft of the statement and promised Robinson to discuss it with the proposed Federal ministerial delegation. He was alarmed at the state of uncertainty in the Federation, but claimed to be one of its best friends. He proposed to arrive in Salisbury on 19 or 20 January but would not come earlier because he wanted to avoid any involvement in the argument over who should form the new Northern Rhodesian Government. He said he had seen Kaunda and Nkumbula and had answered their request for a new constitution by saying they should work the current one first. They had told

[77] *Ibid.*, 20/3, f. 147, Butler to Welensky, 3 December 1962; House of Commons *Hansard* (London), Vol. 668, Col. 942 f., 3 December 1962.

him they would form a coalition, and had asked for secession. He had replied that he would discuss it when the results of the by-elections were known. Kaunda had then rambled on about Tshombe, while Nkumbula looked uncomfortable. It appeared that Tshombe was trying to protect his rear in case of conflict with Adoula. Robinson then expressed the hope that Welensky would send over a ministerial delegation, and Butler agreed because he wanted Greenfield to discuss the 1957 Convention with Lord Dilhorne, the Lord Chancellor. Welensky concurred and sent Greenfield, Caldicott and Barrow to London a few days later.[78]

On 7 December Butler confirmed to Robinson that the date of the announcement was 17 December, but indicated that he would consider arguments for a postponement. Robinson obliged with two. The first was to give the Federal Ministers time to report back to Welensky in person. The second was that there was to be a debate in the Lords on 19 December, which would be unfortunate if it turned into one of triumph for secession, and could have serious repercussions.

Butler proposed to prevent that debate because he disapproved of it. He did not want Welensky to recall the Federal Parliament because statements might be made there which would make his visit in January more difficult. Robinson replied that the recall was unavoidable because Welensky had given his Parliament an undertaking on this if the question of secession arose. Butler responded by saying that then the situation was really serious and that perhaps he should reveal to Welensky something of the advisory committee's report. He said that it had recommended an economic association, but he felt it should be remembered that the committee members were intellectuals and that their suggestions should be considered in that light. The committee had now dispersed and would play no further part in the formation of plans for the Federation.[79]

The prospect of the Lords debate prompted Welensky to find time between his speaking engagements in both Rhodesian territorial electoral campaigns to seek support from Lords Salisbury, Boyd and Colyton. He did so arguing that their work as architects of the Federation was being destroyed. He revealed that he was sending Barrow, Caldicott and Greenfield to London and asked for assistance for them. He declared that, if Butler made the announcement on secession without giving him guarantees on finance, the future of the civil servants, and on a satisfactory relationship between the Rhodesias, he would confront the British Government violently, even though he knew that he would not win a lasting victory. He would do as much harm as he could. He found that there was no limit to the degree to which the British Government would pander to the extremists, citing Butler's willingness to see Kaunda and Nkumbula, and allow them to talk about new constitutions when the by-elections under the newly-introduced one were still being fought. It angered him that the British politicians could continue to talk about achieving an African majority in the Northern Rhodesian legis-

[78] Welensky Papers, 20/3, ff. 143–145, Minutes of a Meeting with Butler, 4 December 1962; 32/63, f. 11, Telephone conversation between Welensky and Robinson, 4 December 1962; f. 18a, Robinson to Welensky, 5 December 1962.

[79] *Ibid.*, 20/3, ff. 141–142, Minutes of a Meeting with Butler, 7 December 1962.

lature when one already existed. He was infuriated by the British attitude to the 1957 Convention and with Home, in particular, for endorsing it. He said he would ignore Butler's wishes and would recall the Federal Assembly on 17 December.[80]

On his own initiative, Blackwood wrote to Lord Boyd in similar vein, but Welensky warned him not to expect too much from Boyd because of the practice that former Ministers should not criticise the current administration. Blackwood also had a none too cordial discussion with Jones on the subject. He began by alleging that leaks from Britain, and possibly from the Nyasaland Government, on secession were having a disastrous effect. He said he was being approached daily by Nyasaland Asians anxious to transfer money to Southern Rhodesia, if they could not get it out of the Federation. Jones was unconcerned because he believed that it was better that those who had lost confidence in Nyasaland should leave. Blackwood replied that Nyasaland could not stand alone economically, and he could not see how people could be expected to have confidence in an economic absurdity or in a Government which was prepared to acquire estates but would not pay more than £1 per acre for them. Moreover, on these estates the owners were given six months in which to raze all buildings and to cut down all trees. Jones coolly wondered why people were still prepared to sell, and Blackwood answered that it was because of the incursion of trespassers and the Government's refusal to act against them. Jones agreed that there were numerous reports of trespassers, and Blackwood asked why he did nothing about them.

Blackwood hoped that the optimism in Zomba about Nyasaland after secession was not misplaced, and Jones angrily replied that it was necessary to have confidence in the country. He hoped there would be an economic association with the Rhodesias, and knew Southern Rhodesians who considered it possible. Blackwood understood that the Rhodesian Front contemplated a common market, but expected, provided Welensky supported it, the UFP to be returned *en masse* in Southern Rhodesia. Jones claimed that an African coalition was likely in Northern Rhodesia, but Blackwood disagreed as he was confident that the UFP would gain more seats in the by-elections. Jones was displeased to hear this, and predicted another state of emergency in Northern Rhodesia if a coalition between the ANC and the UFP was formed, or if the latter alone became the Government. (Blackwood gathered that Jones and, perhaps, Hone were greatly concerned that the UFP might prevent UNIP, together with the official Members, from gaining an absolute majority of seats. Obviously, Jones thought it was necessary to have an African nationalist Government in Northern Rhodesia.) Jones and Blackwood then argued about trivial incidents in the recent Conference and about, as Jones put it, the obstructive and insulting attitude of the Federal MPs from Nyasaland. They agreed at least that there would be utter confusion if the British Government tried to legislate without Federal collaboration.[81]

On 10 December, Barrow, Caldicott, Greenfield and Robinson met Butler

[80] *Ibid.*, 32/63, f. 10, Welensky to Lord Boyd, 5 December 1962; 43/*Colyton*, f. 43, Welensky to Lord Colyton, 5 December 1962; 43/*Salisbury*, Welensky to Lord Salisbury, 8 December 1962.

[81] *Ibid.*, 32/63, f. 15, Blackwood to Lord Boyd, 4 December 1962; f. 16, Welensky to Blackwood, 7 December 1962; 27/69, f. 40, Blackwood to Welensky, 6 December 1962.

in London. Barrow declared that Butler's message (that the decision on Nyasaland's secession had been taken) had come as a shock because the Federal Government had thought that the Nyasaland issue would be discussed in January, when Butler visited the Federation. Barrow still expected that there would be a full examination in January of any unilateral decision to give Nyasaland secession and warned that, unless it was accompanied by a firm declaration on the future of Northern and Southern Rhodesia, it would have a profound effect.

Butler replied that his Government had no desire to break up the Federation but deemed the statement was necessary because Nyasaland would not adopt a constructive attitude until secession was conceded. He found it impossible to pledge anything on the future relationship of the Rhodesias until all the Governments had been consulted. He said that in his announcement he would grant secession but would withhold action thereon until mid-1963. Currently, his purpose was to secure agreement on the announcement, even if the Federal Government reserved its position.

Barrow was in an awkward mood and declared that Butler's purpose was really to appease the MCP. He maintained that Banda knew already that he would get secession and, for that reason, was prepared to wait until mid-1963. Butler acknowledged that there was a tacit understanding with Banda, but declared that it had now to be implemented. Sarcastically, Barrow replied that undertakings given to the MCP had to be honoured, while those given to the Federal Government could be ignored. Greenfield pointed out that the granting of the right to secede would merely result in the disintegration of the Federation. He said he could understand the desire to induce Nyasaland to co-operate, but it was to him less important than holding the Rhodesias together. The result might be a success for Nyasaland and a failure for the Rhodesias. Caldicott said there would be demands for Southern Rhodesia's secession if the RF won the election. The same demands would be made in Northern Rhodesia if an African nationalist government took power there.

Butler, however, stoutly maintained that he was not granting a general right of secession, but Robinson, somewhat acidly, remarked that he seemed only concerned with the views of the new Governments and not with those of the Federal Government, even though it had permanent responsibilities for many of the functions of the territories. Butler replied that there would have to be a new Rhodesian association and that many of the Federal functions would have to revert to the territories. Yet his Government could not pledge itself to any form of this association until the new Governments were in being, because they might be totally opposed to it. He felt that there was no hurry to settle the form of the association, and his Government had no desire to separate the two Rhodesias. The case of Nyasaland had been different because there had been a pledge to honour secession. He drew no retort, and the meeting ended.[82]

On the morrow, 11 December, they discussed the financial impact on the Federation through the probable loss of confidence which would be caused by Butler's statement. Butler explained that he would say that Nyasaland

[82] *Ibid.*, 20/3, ff. 139–140, Minutes of a Meeting with Butler, 10 December 1962.

would accept liability for its full share of the public debt and for the compensation of the Federal civil servants. However, Caldicott thought that mention should also be made of liabilities to the statutory bodies such as the Power Board, the Federal Broadcasting Corporation and the Central Bank. He said that there were political as well as financial considerations because, for instance, Nyasaland had to be prevented from using its broadcasting system against the Federation.

All three Federal Ministers warned that they would face strong public reaction if the Federal Government was expected to continue to finance Nyasaland after the announcement had been made, but before secession actually took place. Butler thought this would have to be part of the debt to be borne by Nyasaland. However, the Federal Ministers were dissatisfied with the statement that Nyasaland would bear an appropriate proportion of the public debt, because it was not creditworthy. They insisted that Britain should indicate that she would underwrite the liability, to calm the creditors' fears. They added that the creditworthiness of the Rhodesias would also be affected by the announcement, but Butler believed the reverse, that the Federation would be more attractive to the investor without the liability of Nyasaland. The British Government, he quickly added, aware of its obligations, would not allow Nyasaland to go bankrupt.

Whittome, a British official, said that the Federal Government had not been able to raise an external loan since 1959. This was confirmed by Dr A. G. Irvine of the Federal Treasury, but he pointed out that there had been considerable success in the securing of internal loans. Caldicott added that, as Minister of Finance, he had to find £7 000 000 in loan repayments in 1963. In reply, Butler assured him of his sympathy. After Robinson had insisted that the statement had to mention that the public debt would be underwritten by Britain, Butler agreed to consider it, along with a clear definition of Nyasaland's liabilities. Greenfield then spoke of the difficulties of recruiting civil servants, when it was clear that the Federation would be dissolved.[83]

After the meeting, the Federal Ministers and Robinson went to the office of the Lord Chancellor, Lord Dilhorne, where he and the Attorney-General, Sir John Hobson, expressed their eagerness to hear Greenfield on the 1957 Convention. Dilhorne pointed out that he had written an opinion on this subject in 1960 which was accepted by his predecessor, Lord Kilmuir. The opinion briefly was that, as a matter of law, the British Parliament was competent to remove Nyasaland from the Federation without the Federal Government's consent. Greenfield said he had never disputed this power, except in that the Convention, which was "a gentleman's agreement", inhibited the British Parliament from taking that action, unless it chose to ignore the Convention. They then argued at length as to whether the Convention was a written record of part of a wider convention, or whether it was a clarification of doubts raised over Article 29(7). The latter was Dilhorne's contention. He believed that the Federal Government was not competent to provide for the secession of one of its constituent parts, that the Convention was limited to matters within the scope of the Federal Government, and that

[83] *Ibid.*, ff. 131–134, Minutes of a Meeting with Butler, 11 December 1962.

British legislation on subjects outside the sphere of the Federal Parliament would not breach the Federal Constitution.

Greenfield disagreed that secession lay outside the Federal scope and, if it did, he would argue that then, equally, the British Government was not competent to act because legislation for secession would repeal every Federal law. Dilhorne did not believe they would be repealed, as their geographic area of translation would merely be truncated. Greenfield then pointed out that Butler had ruled that a similarly-worded convention prevented the British Government from repealing the Southern Rhodesian Constitution, but Dilhorne would not accept the analogy. He maintained that there would only be an analogy if the matter in question fell within Federal competence.

To Greenfield it was absurd that the British Government was inhibited by the Convention from dealing with minor matters, when it could destroy the Federation. Dilhorne denied any absurdity because, he maintained, it was inherent in the Constitution that Britain had delegated certain powers to the Federation and had said it would not interfere in their operation. The British Parliament, however, had reserved the right to recover them. Greenfield, however, obstinately insisted that *Halsbury's Laws of England* had revealed that there was a wider convention when describing that which applied to Southern Rhodesia. The effect was that, when a country became self-governing, its constitution could not be removed without its consent. Furthermore, there had been pledges given in 1953 by the British Ministers on which Lord Malvern had relied when accepting and endorsing the White Paper on the Federation.

Dilhorne dismissed this argument as irrelevant and contended that, if all the parties had claimed that the Federation could only be dissolved when they all consented, something would have been said about it in the Federal Constitutional Order in Council. Moreover, the Constitution said nothing about it being unalterable. Still unwilling to give way, Greenfield continued to maintain that Malvern had relied on the requirement of the consent of all parties before he had accepted the Federation. Dilhorne asked for a written exposition of Greenfield's case and that public dispute should be avoided. Greenfield agreed to comply with both requests, but warned of his Government's bitterness over what it considered to be the broken pledges and the proposed British course of action, which spelt disaster for everything it had tried to build over the past nine years.[84] Barrow telegraphed Welensky that no progress was being made, and Welensky responded by putting in train his arrangements for the wide publication of his speech on Butler's announcement, including its exposure in the British Press.

Welensky's continued campaigning for the UFP in the elections in both Rhodesias also occupied his time. In addition, he was becoming increasingly concerned over a build-up of UN forces in Katanga, fearing a third offensive against Tshombe.[85]

After a further meeting with the Federal Ministers in London on 11 December, the British agreed to produce a draft joint statement. However, when it appeared the next day, the Federal Ministers rejected it because it

[84] *Ibid.*, FGC(1), 33/62, Minutes of a Meeting with Lord Dilhorne, 11 December 1962.
[85] *Ibid.*, 24/152, ff. 121–122, Welensky to Joelson, 11 December 1962.

lacked a specific pledge on the continuation of the Federation. Butler stated that he did not want to prejudice the British position in any way, and proposed that they meet again to consider a further draft. Accordingly, the British Government produced a statement accepting the view of the MCP on secession and expressing the desire of the British Government to find an acceptable solution to the overall Federal problem which would retain the advantages of the current association. To achieve this, it would convene a conference to devise the formula. It had decided to accept in principle that Nyasaland could secede, and on that basis the negotiations would be conducted. It would ensure that the financial problems of Nyasaland's secession would be minimised, and detailed negotiations on this subject with the Federal and Nyasaland Governments were necessary before secession could be given effect. The Nyasaland Government would bear fully its commitments and liabilities, including those relating to the national debt and the re-deployment of civil servants. The British Government acknowledged the widespread desire for an early settlement to remove the uncertainty, and declared that, to achieve it, Butler would visit the Federation in January to devise an agreed, practical and durable solution for the future of the Governments concerned. Full account had to be taken of the close links which had developed between the territories and, in particular, those between the Rhodesias.[86]

This was telegraphed to Welensky but he immediately rejected it as dishonouring the firm and specific pledges given at the end of the Federal Conference in 1953. He told Barrow that he regarded these pledges as binding on all the contracting parties.

Welensky's rejection meant that when the Federal Ministers met Butler in the late afternoon they were in a troublesome mood. They declared that it was fundamental to state that Nyasaland's withdrawal did not mean the termination of the constitutional relationship between the Rhodesias. Butler understood their feelings but said he was anxious to avoid making a specific pledge on this.[87]

The next day, they held another short meeting at which Barrow bitterly criticised the pledge given to Banda by Sandys and the greater importance given to it than to the pledges of 1953. Butler could understand this depth of feeling but excused himself by saying that he had inherited the situation created by Sandys. He believed it was unfortunate that Sandys's verbal undertaking had been recorded.[88]

Barrow informed Welensky immediately of his failure to divert Butler, while Robinson transmitted a verdict of the Bank of England and the British Treasury that the secession of Nyasaland would not impair the basic economic strength of the rest of the Federation because of its agricultural, mineral and other resources.[89]

[86] *Ibid.*, 20/3, f. 138, Text of a proposed statement by Butler on Nyasaland, 12 December 1962; FGC(1), 33/62, Minutes of a Meeting with Butler, 11.30 a.m., 12 December 1962.
[87] *Ibid.*, 20/3, f. 135, Welensky to Barrow, 12 December 1962; FGC(1), 33/62, Minutes of a Meeting with Butler, 5 p.m., 12 December 1962.
[88] *Ibid.*, FGC(1), 33/62, Minutes of a Meeting with Butler, 13 December 1962.
[89] *Ibid.*, 32/63, f. 21b, Robinson to Welensky, 13 December 1962.

On 14 December, Barrow telephoned Welensky to say that, on the previous evening, Lords Boyd, Chandos and Salisbury had seen Butler and that Boyd had reported that Butler had appeared shaken when they declared they would confirm in the Lords that they had given the pledges to which Welensky had referred. That morning, Barrow had been told by Butler that if the British Government was attacked in Parliament it would defend itself. Butler knew that Welensky was proposing to publish a White Paper on the pledges, but thought it would be a grave error, and appealed to Barrow to persuade Welensky to respect the confidential nature of the (ten-year-old) documents in which the pledges were recorded. Butler argued that he did not propose to use confidential information himself, but Barrow said he was not sure what Welensky intended. However, Butler was most anxious that there should be no breaches of faith between the Governments through the publication of confidential documents, even though he would allow anyone who had been present, such as Lord Malvern, to state their views freely.

When told this by Barrow, Welensky's reaction was that he was certainly going to produce documentary evidence. Barrow asked him if Lord Malvern would attend the Lords debate and Welensky said that he would, but that his journey had to be kept secret. Welensky was shocked that Butler should think that the Federal Government should keep quiet and that a half promise to Banda should be honoured, while a full promise given to the Governments should not be disclosed. (Joelson was to add that he understood that Butler had never heard of the pledges until the Federal Ministers referred to them.)[90]

The Federal ministerial mission ended with a telephone call from Robinson to Welensky to say that they had seen the final version of the British statement. In releasing it to them, Butler had warned that, if it became obvious that the Convention and the legal position were in dispute, he might add a paragraph giving the British view. Furthermore, if there were any unforeseen developments before delivery, he reserved his right to deal with them in his statement, though he would first telegraph his intentions to Welensky. The date of release was now 19 December and presumably had been changed to coincide with the Lord's debate, rather than precede it.[91]

In the by-elections in Northern Rhodesia on 12 December the UFP gained three more seats, with two Europeans and one African being returned. The ANC secured two seats, for a European and an African. UNIP gained none. Five seats remained empty because the African voters in each constituency rejected the UFP and, likewise, the Europeans UNIP. The final composition of the House was 16 UFP, 14 UNIP and seven ANC Members. The UFP was thus in a position to form the Government if Nkumbula could be persuaded to join a coalition.

Southern Rhodesia's turn came on 14 December and the electorate ousted the UFP and replaced it with the RF. The latter gained 35 upper roll seats to the UFP's 14 upper and 15 lower roll seats. The RF is reputed to have been

[90] *Ibid.*, 20/3, ff. 124–127, Telephone conversation between Welensky and Barrow, 14 December 1962; FGC(1), 34/62, Minutes of a Meeting with Butler, 14 December 1962; 24/152, f. 120, Joelson to Welensky, 14 December 1962.

[91] *Ibid.*, 32/63, f. 22, Robinson to Welensky, 14 December 1962.

considerably surprised and somewhat unprepared for its success. Welensky believed that the electorate had rejected Whitehead rather than his Party, and Whitehead had not helped his cause by a last-minute prediction that his Cabinet would soon be composed of a majority of Africans. The electorate had also criticised his soft handling of the African nationalists.[92]

By 15 December, Welensky knew there would be an African nationalist coalition in Northern Rhodesia which meant that he was faced by three pro-secessionist territorial Governments even though Field, the new Southern Rhodesian Prime Minister, declared that he was not opposed to the Federation's existence. Welensky commented to Lord Colyton that it had been necessary for Field to say this because "Macleod has, I think, achieved that [the dissolution of the Federation]". He held little hope for the Federation because Kaunda and Nkumbula had already decided to introduce a motion calling for secession. Saddened, he was nonetheless determined to carry on as if nothing had happened. He ascribed as much blame for the Rhodesian Front's victory to Butler's leaks on Nyasaland's secession as he did to Whitehead's comments on the probability of an African government in Southern Rhodesia.[93]

Welensky made similar comments to his other correspondents, declaring that he had "never struck such racialism and such hatreds as developed in this particular battle". It had also paralleled the election of 1958 when the voters had expressed their opinion of Todd, rather than of the UFP. Welensky had soon discovered in the campaign that the mere mention of Whitehead's name would bring a howl of protest. The lack of support for the Federation by the Southern Rhodesian division of the UFP had counted, he said, because it was not missed by the electorate who knew that a house divided against itself could not stand. He had realised that Whitehead had misjudged the pace at which the Europeans would accept change, and he had pleaded with him to move nearer the centre and wait to be re-elected before speaking of and effecting the necessary reforms. However, Whitehead was so buoyed up by his success at the UN, and was so confident, that he rejected all advice.[94] Welensky did not add that had the Africans (who qualified) registered and exercised their vote, the RF might not have won.

With the situation so radically changed, Robinson warned Welensky that pressure could be expected on Butler to consider the Labour Party's line that Britain should interfere in Southern Rhodesia to introduce African majority rule as soon as possible, and that the independence of the northern territories would also be effected when practicable. Robinson had also gathered that Welensky would be virtually ignored, while Britain tried to deal with the pressure from the UN and that she might well hand the problem to the UN for solution. Robinson revealed that Lords Boyd and Colyton were deeply disappointed with the Southern Rhodesian result and that he was urging them not to slacken in their determination to apply pressure on Butler. Lord Salisbury, at least, intended to claim that British policies were responsible for

[92] *Ibid.*, 25/86, f. 1, Welensky to H. J. Millar, 17 December 1962; 24/13, ff. 1–3, Welensky to Mrs L. Easton, 18 December 1962.

[93] *Ibid.*, 43/*Colyton*, f. 47, Welensky to Colyton, 15 December 1962.

[94] *Ibid.*, 25/86, f. 1, Welensky to H. J. Millar, 17 December 1962.

the RF victory. Yet Robinson wanted Butler to welcome Field's election in a friendly fashion to prevent him from being driven into the arms of his extremists who would not find it difficult to embrace *apartheid.* It was imperative, he felt, that Butler should consult the four Governments on the new situation before taking the unilateral action which he intended to do on 19 December.[95]

Welensky did not entirely accept Robinson's advice when he wrote to Butler on 17 December. He confessed that the Southern Rhodesian election had placed him in a very difficult situation because it was widely interpreted as meaning that the break-up of the Federation was imminent. This compelled him to defend himself, he said, and he would have to make it clear that his advice had been consistently ignored by the British Government. He would have to say that he had been forced to watch an accelerating abandonment of principles and undertakings as a result of pressure from extreme African nationalism. He doubted if much could be saved of the Federation, but felt that he owed an explanation to those who had trusted him. He regretted having to do this because he had hoped to avoid an open clash with the British Government, but the circumstances differed so dramatically from the solid confidence of 1953 and 1957 that he had to account for the contrast.[96]

After he had written this, his Government issued its White Paper which recounted the negotiations with Butler and warned of the consequences for Nyasaland of secession. Then, on Wednesday afternoon, 19 December, Welensky informed the Federal Assembly that Butler would, within hours, announce the acceptance of the British Government of the secession of Nyasaland in principle. He acknowledged that, after the Press leaks of the past three weeks, no one would be surprised, and noted that Butler, in the Commons on 3 December, had said that one of the most comforting features of his advisory committee's report was the agreement of the MCP Ministers to take measures to deal with some of the economic consequences of secession. This, he said, was more than a hint to anyone of normal intelligence, and thus he had taken care in his recent speeches not to hide the certainty that secession would be granted before the end of the year. The British decision had, nevertheless, profoundly shocked him, particularly as he could recall the high resolve of the British Ministers in 1953 that the Federation should endure. He and Malvern had never doubted the solemnity of the undertakings of that date. The statements of Lords Swinton and Chandos, which he quoted, showed that the Federation was considered permanent and that it could not be liquidated without the consent of the four Governments. This proved that the British Government would soon have "ratted on us", destroying by "an act of treachery" something it had built.

Welensky described the events relating to the 1957 Accord and then the Monckton Commission and its negotiations. He and his Government, he said, would not accept that principles and ideals, which were laudable in 1953, should be undesirable eight years later. Basic values had not changed, but expediency had won the day, and Pan-Africanism had brought a degeneration in standards in so much of Africa. If Nyasaland had to be excised

[95] *Ibid.*, 32/28, f. 44, Robinson to Welensky, 16 December 1962.
[96] *Ibid.*, 20/3, f. 120, Welensky to Butler, 17 December 1962.

from the Federation, it should have been done by agreement and in a way which would protect the interests of the people of that territory.

Welensky maintained that it was clear that, ignoring the fine achievements of the Federation, the British Government was progressively withdrawing, despite its declarations to the contrary, and was being governed by expediency rather than principle. There was ample evidence, he said, of how often the Federal Ministers had been deliberately misled by their British counterparts who had not scrupled to employ methods which were the antithesis of what the British Government had stood for once. Yet the British Ministers would not admit that there had been any change in policy and would claim that their belief in the Federation was untarnished.

Welensky announced that Greenfield would deal with the subject of the 1957 Convention, and believed he would demonstrate that it was binding and that the British Ministers, if they were honourable men, would find themselves unable to allow Nyasaland to secede without Federal consent. It was necessary to emphasise that the sole responsibility for that day's decision lay with the British Government. To prove this, he recounted how his Government had not been consulted on the decision and, indeed, had only been informed of it after it had been made. Butler had hinted in the Commons on 8 May at the course he would follow when he noted the mandate on which Banda's MCP had been elected. Welensky said he had immediately pointed out to him that this was tantamount to acceptance of the principle of secession, but Butler had replied that the ramifications of the issue would be examined first. Thereafter, Butler had kept the results of that examination to himself. He had also promised to consult him fully before taking any decision, but had not. In saying this, Welensky quoted the record of the meeting of 14 May. Butler had done all this when he had known for a year that he would reluctantly accept the secession of Nyasaland if the British Government would give reasonable undertakings on the future of the Rhodesias, on the public debt, and on the rights of the minorities. If these had been given, Federal consent would have been forthcoming in terms of the Convention under which Britain could not interfere in the affairs of the self-governing territories of the Commonwealth.

Welensky said he did not want to sound bitter but felt impelled to remark on the change in public morality in the past decade. He had protested to Butler about his intentions on 7 November, but had only secured a postponement. In the last week, Barrow had discovered that Butler would not defer his announcement until he had seen Welensky, despite the total Federal rejection of the British Government's contention that it could act unilaterally. The consequence for Nyasaland would be disastrous, and thus he would go on fighting the British decision, as well as demanding compensation for those Nyasalanders who did not support the MCP.

Welensky confessed that the Southern Rhodesian election result had changed his plans. Had the UFP won, he would have notified the British Government that the Federal Government had no intention of allowing it to break or weaken the close ties between the Rhodesias. He would now have to discover the Southern Rhodesian Government's intentions. His Government had found in its dealings with the British Government that there was little honour left, that Britain had lost the will to govern and was careless of the fate of the Federal inhabitants, including British kith and kin. He acknowledged that there were those who believed his resignation would improve matters, but he would prefer to allow the House to express its verdict through a free vote.[97] As Welensky sat down, Alport stalked out of the Strangers' Gallery to refute in a Press conference, with Butler's permission, Welensky's charges. By doing this he believed that he gained greater publicity than Welensky, at the cost of almost destroying their relationship.[98]

Then Greenfield defended, as promised, the Federal view of the Convention. As he did, Butler, in the Commons, ignoring a last minute plea by Robinson for a postponement until January,[99] delivered his statement. He claimed his Government wished to find an acceptable solution in Central Africa which would retain the advantages of the association between the territories. It also acknowledged the desire of the MCP to secede. Because of the widespread wish for early decisions to give new impetus to progress and development, Butler announced he would soon visit the Federation to negotiate with the Governments. He accepted Nyasaland's withdrawal in principle, but maintained that it did not automatically destroy the current territorial relationship. The Nyasaland Government, he said, was alive to the serious financial implications of secession and would minimise them. Detailed negotiations with the Federal Government were needed to settle many of the intricacies, but Nyasaland's withdrawal should not affect the economic strength of the rest of the Federation. Finally, Butler promised that his Government intended to assist in maintaining confidence in the area.

Predictably, Healey welcomed the decision but called on Butler to acknowledge the overwhelming Northern Rhodesian desire to secede. He said he was also anxious that Butler's action should not imply independence for Southern Rhodesia while that territory rejected African majority rule. The Government had to withhold independence until all the Governments represented the majority of the population. Butler hastily confirmed that he had no plans to grant independence to any of the territories.

R. H. Turton, of the Conservative Party, asked if there had been a clear assurance on 19 January 1953 that the Federal structure could not be changed without the consent of the four Governments. If this were so, he wished to know why Britain was acting unilaterally. Butler replied that he was aware of the exchanges of 1953 which had hitherto not been published because they were confidential. However, he said, Britain had retained an inalienable right to act in these matters and, in any case, he had tried to obtain Federal consent since May, but had failed. In difficult circumstances, his Government had decided to do its duty for Nyasaland. He believed that future consultations would be more productive because of the initiative he was taking.

Grimmond asked if the British Government still accepted responsibility

[97] *The Issue of Nyasaland's Secession*, C. Fed. 231 (Salisbury, 19 December 1962); Fed R & N *Debates* (Salisbury), Vol. 19, Col. 2033, 19 December 1962; in January 1963, the Federal Government distributed a paper on the pledges to British MPs and editors. — *Federation and Nyasaland: The British Government's Broken Pledges and the Consequences* (Salisbury, January 1963).
[98] Alport, *The Sudden Assignment*, *op. cit.*, p. 224.
[99] Welensky Papers, 32/63, f. 26, Robinson to Butler, 19 December 1962.

for the political development of Southern Rhodesia. Butler confirmed that it did, and that it aimed to find the happiest, most durable and acceptable association of the territories. He believed that, since the decision had been taken, there was a greater chance of preserving ties with Nyasaland as well as those between the Rhodesias. Healey wanted an assurance that Butler would restore contact between the European minority and the African majority in Southern Rhodesia, but Butler replied that he had only met Field once and thus could not guarantee anything.[100]

Butler acknowledges that he escaped lightly in the Commons but that he was roasted in the Lords.[101] There, Lords Salisbury, Chandos, Boyd, Colyton, Milverton and Malvern thundered against the decision and confirmed the validity of the pledges. They declared that British actions had driven Welensky and Whitehead into the wilderness despite their unflinching stand for non-racialism. These Lords maintained that the vote in Southern Rhodesia was not a rejection of the UFP, but against interference in the territory's internal affairs. Malvern proclaimed that, had he known that the pledges could be repudiated, he would not have agreed to federation. He and the others provoked a long-winded exposition from Dilhorne on the 1957 Convention.[102]

The Federal debate continued on 20 December with Barrow and others denouncing bitterly the British betrayal. Savanhu, however, chose that moment to accuse the Federal Government of seeking only to maintain white supremacy. Replying, Welensky noted Butler's statements on seeking Federal agreement, since May, which implied continual and intensive consultation. He refuted this because he believed that there was a great difference between discussion and formal consultation. There had been no consultation on Nyasaland's secession, and the discussions of the last week had come six weeks after the decision had been taken. He was astonished by Butler's assertions because, when he saw him in September, he had not yet received the report of his advisory committee and could not say what it would contain or how it would affect the Federation. Thereafter, Butler had remained silent until 3 November, Welensky said, when Alport informed him that the decision had been taken. No effort was ever made to get him to agree to the announcement, and it shocked him that a Secretary of State could make such an outrageous claim in his own Parliament.

Welensky challenged the British Government to substantiate its claim on the consultation. He denounced as "totally irresponsible and wholly untrue" a claim that any differences between him and the British Government stemmed from his advocacy of amalgamation before 1953. The truth was that in 1952 he had accepted that amalgamation was impossible and had set himself the goal of federation. He had not raised the subject of amalgamation since then and, indeed, he and Greenfield had signed an agreement on its impossibility in 1957.

Welensky declared that Dilhorne's comments only deepened his distrust because, like Butler, Dilhorne knew of the pledges of 1953 but preferred to

[100] House of Commons *Hansard* (London), Vol. 669, Col. 1266 f., 19 December 1962.
[101] Butler, *The Art of the Possible*, *op. cit.*, p. 223.
[102] House of Lords *Hansard* (London), Vol. 245, Col. 1146 f., 19 December 1962.

discard them in favour of one given to Banda. In so doing, Dilhorne had ignored the disclosures of Lords Salisbury and Chandos, but had taken him, Welensky, to task for revealing the contents of confidential documents, and had stressed the special and unique confidential nature of the Commonwealth's exchange of views. As Dilhorne had thus indulged in cant, Welensky asked what value there was in such exchanges if the Governments could not rely on the British pledges. He despised the British effort to conceal the pledges, and noted that none of the current British Ministers could contradict Lords Malvern, Chandos and Salisbury, who were present in 1953. Lord Boyd had confirmed the pledges when he signed the Accord of 1957.

Welensky said the British Government should accept the record and reconsider the wisdom of its course. He confessed that he found it difficult to restrain himself when he read Dilhorne's thesis that, if the convention of non-interference were to apply, it should have been written into the Federal Constitution. It amazed him that a Lord Chancellor could claim that a convention lacked validity unless it was written into a country's constitution. He needed to be reminded that Britain herself lacked a constitution into which conventions could be written. Dilhorne had also questioned the veracity of the pledges, and had added that controversy over alleged breaches of conventions and pledges would not assist in solving Central Africa's future. The Federal Government had, in fact, always accepted Britain's sovereignty, even though it insisted on the sanctity of the pledges and conventions. All that the Lord Chancellor had really implied was an utter disregard for morality and honour and a willingness to condone the breaching of a convention when expediency demanded it.

Welensky noted that, in a televised interview on the previous evening, Butler had doubted that he would use force to resist the British decision, especially as the three territories had Governments which were not of his choosing. However, Welensky said, Butler was forgetting that defence was a Federal function and that all units were under Federal command (and thus Welensky had the means to take action). In any case, Welensky felt, all Butler was doing was to exploit, in its literal sense, his use of the word "fight". The Federal Assembly, Welensky declared, had to understand that, if it decided that he should remain the Prime Minister, his policy would remain unchanged. He would resist anything which he considered endangered the future prosperity of the Federation and its people. Nonetheless, he said he had made it clear to Butler in September that he did not foresee any circumstances in which his Government would use force against Britain. Butler had responded with a like prediction which was indeed a welcome change in British thinking because, as the House might know, in early 1962 the British Government had certainly intended using force against the Federation. The Federal Government would still not contemplate using force, but it had to reserve the right to make what dispositions it could to prevent any attempt to foist the will of the British Government upon the Federation.

Welensky said he was "tired of being the villain of the piece". The British Government was totally responsible for the formation of the Federation but it had never rushed to its defence. All burdens were left to be carried by him and he was sick of it. He was most concerned about the fate of the Nyasaland

Africans who had supported the Federation, and promised them that he would do all he could to ensure their protection.[103]

Alport immediately and publicly denied the existence of the military confrontation in 1962 but was forcefully corrected by Caldicott. On 21 December, the Federal Assembly thanked Welensky for his tireless efforts to preserve the Federation, and assured him of its support for whatever action was necessary to maintain political and economic links between the two Rhodesias. It warned the peoples of the Rhodesias of the fateful consequences of a break-up, and appealed to them to stand behind their Parliament in its determination to resist further interference in their affairs.[104]

On the previous day, Butler had refused a request from Healey to table in the Commons a full account of the pledges, because they were confidential. He also would not say if he would take the matter further but, in fact, he ordered the preparation of a White Paper to counter that of the Federal Government.[105]

Welensky thanked the Lords concerned and Joelson for their support but acknowledged that the Federation was doomed, even though Butler still had to negotiate the manner of its demise.[106] Macmillan had already reached the same conclusion ten days previously, writing in his diary that, though his Government would work to preserve a relationship between the Rhodesias, it could not pledge itself to a precise form. He felt: "It's all been very sad. The Federation *was* a good idea. But it has been wrecked by two things. *(a)* The 'wind of change' which has swept through Africa with unexpected force (unexpected, at least, ten years ago). *(b)* The policies of Huggins . . . and secondly of Welensky, which have made the Federation in the minds of Africans a symbol of white domination. Poor Sir Edgar has been the victim."[107]

Two weeks later, although he regretted the "retrograde and reactionary" vote which had ousted Whitehead, Macmillan welcomed the simplification of the situation which Butler faced because the Federation was rejected by all three territories. However, he could see the danger of the white being driven into extremism, which could include Southern Rhodesia joining South Africa, because multi-racialism had failed. He made no mention of his own responsibility for the course which events had followed. He claimed to understand Welensky's accusations of treachery, but dismissed them as unjustifiable when it was clear that the end was nigh.[108]

The end was certainly at hand, but the Federal Government still had to endure British procrastination over the continuance of the relationship between the Rhodesias before the dissolution process was begun. The Federation had a year left in which to die painfully.

[103] Fed R & N *Debates* (Salisbury), Vol. 19, Col. 2085 f., 20 December 1962.
[104] Welensky Papers, 24/152, ff. 112–115, Welensky to Joelson, 24 December 1962; Fed R & N *Debates* (Salisbury), Vol. 19, Col. 2191 f., 21 December 1962.
[105] House of Commons *Hansard* (London), Vol. 669, Col. 1441, 20 December 1962.
[106] Welensky Papers, 24/152, ff. 118–119, Welensky to Joelson, 20 December 1962; 32/63, f. 27, Welensky to Boyd, 21 December 1962; 43/*Colyton*, f. 49, Welensky to Colyton, 24 December 1962.
[107] H. Macmillan, *At the End of the Day* (London, 1973), p. 323.
[108] *Ibid.*, p. 324.

CHAPTER THIRTY-FIVE

The Eleventh Hour

The Federal Cabinet's Last Bid to save the Federation, December 1962–February 1963

IN the face of the inevitable recrimination, Butler would continue to maintain that Nyasaland was different from the other territories and, therefore, need not be a precedent for Northern Rhodesia's secession. He would undertake a somewhat futile visit to the Federation in an apparent search for a solution. The Federal Government would respond with a last concerted effort to save the Federation, but it knew that it was hopeless.

There was a month to go before Butler arrived in the Federation and, not unnaturally, Welensky spent much of it bitterly reflecting on the actions of the British Government and on Whitehead's rejection of his advice. He did not, however, spare himself as he wondered at his own naïvety. He concluded, angrily, that Alport was responsible for many of the British beliefs, including the accusation that he was the cause of the trouble and that he still wanted to amalgamate the Rhodesias. However, he hoped that Alport would not be withdrawn because he was a "tremendous" asset to him by being the most disliked British High Commissioner. Certainly, the Federal Cabinet felt strongly about him, and Welensky found that Alport had misled Butler into believing that the Federal Government would accept the decision on Nyasaland calmly. He also did not forgive Butler, and commented repeatedly on the lack of consultation. He resented the British censure on the confidential exchanges, when scant respect had been paid to the 1957 Convention.[1]

Sharing Welensky's views, Robinson wrote to Butler, on 27 December roundly condemning his actions. He recalled that Butler had led him to believe, in April, that a fair and just approach would be adopted by declaring that he (Butler) would inform Banda that there would be no unilateral secession. Since then Butler had complained frequently about his inheritance,

[1] Welensky Papers, 27/69, f. 35, Welensky to M. H. Blackwood, 21 December 1962; 43/*Colyton*, f. 49, Welensky to Lord Colyton, 24 December 1962; 32/28, f. 43, Welensky to Robinson, 24 December 1962; 24/152, ff. 112–115, Welensky to Joelson, 24 December 1962.

almost rejecting his collective responsibility for the mistakes of his colleagues. This had seemed strange, but Robinson had thought that Butler was trying to infer that he would not follow Macleod's plan of handing over to the African majority, whatever the cost. After all, before he took over, Butler had criticised Maudling for acting too quickly without a full knowledge of the problems, and had convinced Robinson that past policies would be abandoned.

Robinson told Butler that it was pertinent to describe Macmillan as the architect of those policies, and Macleod as the willing assistant. Macleod had once informed him that the British political relationship with Africa would be firmer once the political links had been abandoned and economic ties created to restore fully the British influence. This remark had been made before neo-colonialism was condemned by Moscow, Cairo and Accra. However, Robinson said that Macmillan and Macleod had avowed that they would not bow to extremism and would support the Federation, but had done nothing. Sir Michael Blundell of Kenya had told Robinson that Macleod was correct in believing that, if the Europeans conceded political power, it would be an act of great statesmanship which would fully meet the demands of African nationalism. It would result in the non-African communities being made welcome to stay and their skills being fully employed by the African nationalists in building a nation. However, later, in his farewell speech to the Kenyan Parliament, Blundell had admitted the complete failure of the experiment which left Kenya torn by racial and tribal differences. Despite this experience, Robinson noted that the British Government would impose the same solution on Rhodesia.

Robinson found that Butler had not only inherited policies, but had been more successful in their implementation by lulling the Europeans into a false sense of security. The Europeans and the moderate Africans had trusted him, only to discover that the British aim was unchanged. In creating this trust, Butler had avoided the threatened collision. Robinson confessed that he had believed that Butler would reject domination by either race and would promote partnership by seeking to remove discrimination. On the contrary, while his predecessors had believed that the Federation would be destroyed by a process of erosion, once Northern Rhodesia had an African nationalist majority in its legislature, Butler had advocated direct action to accomplish the same aim. He had exploited Welensky's request for direct British involvement, but not in the manner intended, and now excused himself by claiming that he had been forced to implement Sandys's unauthorised promise, thereby ignoring the pledges of 1953.

Butler had said that the concession on secession of 19 December would placate Nyasaland and produce a more constructive attitude, and thus Robinson asked what the British planned to do next. He wondered if a few common services would be retained in exchange for a Rhodesian subsidy for Nyasaland of £6 000 000 p.a. in order to relieve the British Government of any financial responsibility. Butler had asked him to influence the Federal Government to be constructive during his visit, while professing friendship for him and regard for Welensky. Yet his policies endangered Welensky's life's work. Butler had often talked about the "schizophrenic Banda" and about Kaunda's bad manners and how "dim" he was. He had spoken with contempt about

Nkumbula. He was obviously dismayed by the victory of the Rhodesian Front and had said that Nkomo was not equipped to take over in Southern Rhodesia. Yet he aimed at obtaining power for all these men. Despite Robinson's warnings, British policies had produced the reaction which had returned Field. The moderates, like Welensky, tens of thousands of others and himself, were seeing the destruction of all in which they believed. The only hope left lay in a determined attempt to negotiate a Northern and Southern Rhodesian association based on a constitutional link and supported by massive financial backing. Robinson noted, however, that Butler had admitted that he lacked the power to implement such an association and, although he had favoured it, he would still allow the Pan-Africanists to dictate his policy. It could not be argued that the Europeans of Southern Rhodesia wanted the Federation to end. All they had demonstrated was that they were afraid. Robinson urged Butler to exploit the desire of the moderates to co-operate in finding a constructive solution. If he would not comply, then he should reveal his true intentions so that the Federal Government could make its preparations accordingly.

Such was Robinson's mood that he asked that he should no longer be used to convey informal protests from Butler to Welensky, and suggested that Alport be used instead. Nonetheless, he still urged Butler to make a positive gesture to show that he did not favour African extremism. Robinson said he had found writing this letter difficult, but had deduced, from Butler's courteous but unusual action in telegraphing Christmas greetings to him, what his real intentions were. He still could not believe that Butler would wish to be remembered as the final architect of the tragedy of the Rhodesias and pleaded with him to persuade his colleagues to abandon their current and dangerous policies because he alone had the strength and status within the Conservative Party to alter the course of events.[2]

Butler promptly summoned Robinson to express great concern that Robinson had mentioned his references to Banda, Kaunda and Nkumbula, and at the implied threat that the Federal Government was making its preparations. He wondered if Robinson was referring to Welensky's statement on 19 December on the use of force. Robinson replied that Welensky was a constitutionalist, but that, if the British Government decided to use force, as it had threatened to do in 1961, it would be met by force. Butler was sorry that Robinson felt so deeply about matters and claimed that the past few weeks had also been most painful for him.

Robinson asked him to declare that the British aim was to preserve the constitutional relationship of the Rhodesias. He should do so even if he could not give a pledge thereon, because there was a great difference between allowing the situation to erode, and then accepting whatever territorial demands were made, and a deliberate attempt at preservation. Butler was happy to do this and promised to discuss it with his Cabinet and give the undertaking to Welensky during his visit.

Because Nkumbula's ANC commanded a degree of support, and as the Northern Rhodesian Europeans supported neither African nationalist Party,

[2] *Ibid.*, 23/22, ff. 39–43, Robinson to Butler, 27 December 1962.

Robinson thought that Kaunda should be told that the territory's current Constitution would endure for some time. It should also be clear that any changes should be compatible with the concept of partnership and should provide places for Europeans in the Legislative and Executive Councils to ensure multi-racial government. Butler ignored this and commented instead that the Northern Rhodesian industrialists were ready to work with an African majority government. He referred to Sir Ronald Prain, but Robinson explained that Prain had supported the Federation until 1958, and then had emulated the American principals of his mining organisation, the Rhodesian Selection Trust, by transferring support to the emergent African Parties. The Anglo American Corporation and the British South Africa Company, however, remained firm supporters of the Federation. Butler did not argue and said next that he wished to meet Field and his colleagues because Alport had reported that it seemed their policies were still fluid. He added that Alport would be retiring soon and that their special relationship arose from Alport being a great friend of his late brother. Finally, as the Governor-General, Lord Dalhousie, was also retiring, they discussed a successor, agreeing that there was danger in appointing someone who was totally ignorant of the area.[3]

Recrimination was not all that preoccupied Welensky because he was watching Field formulate his policies and attempt to woo the African nationalists. Thus Welensky enjoyed the almost immediate rebuffing of Field by Kaunda, who threatened to raise a tariff barrier if Nkomo were not promptly released from restriction. The Press, however, quickly pointed out the emptiness of the threat because Nkomo was due to be released in the New Year and because it would be a year or more before Kaunda could erect any such barriers.[4]

Katanga also offered distraction because, after months of fruitless negotiation, the UN had built up its forces and would win a third round of fighting. On 19 July the first hint of this intention had come when the *New York Times* discovered a three-phase UN operation against Katanga. The first phase was to seal off the southern boundaries to prevent the arrival of mercenaries. The second was to deny Katanga the means of production, and the third was to meet the inevitable Katangese reaction. The next day, 20 July, the US State Department had warned publicly that it would support every means short of force to unify the Congo. It denounced Tshombe's intransigence and his "organised violence".

Welensky had reacted by expressing grave concern at the threat of sanctions and by refuting the charges against Katanga. Nevertheless, he had continued to urge Tshombe to seek reconciliation, but U Thant, by describing Tshombe and his Government as "a bunch of clowns", had made reconciliation unlikely. The Congolese Central Government had provoked Katanga by severing all communications with it, thereby surprising the UN and the United States. The crisis had deepened on 24 August when Tshombe was given ten days in which to accept a plan of U Thant to share equally Katanga's wealth and revenue with the Congolese Central Government and to effect the reunification of the Congo Army. Failure to comply would bring a trade ban and, if

[3] *Ibid.*, 23/22, ff. 35–38, Minutes of a Meeting with Butler, January 1963.
[4] *Ibid.*, 32/28, f. 45, Welensky to Robinson, 31 December 1962.

that failed to achieve anything, the UN Command had been ordered to take all steps which it considered necessary.[5]

The British Government had enlisted Welensky's help, and consequently Tshombe had complied. Commissions had begun to work out the details of the reunification and when they failed, the US Government had pressed Adoula towards a military solution. Congolese and Katangese troops clashed in northern Katanga while the UN had begun to strengthen its forces.[6]

In late November, U Thant had declared that economic sanctions would be applied, and had prompted Welensky to remind the British Government of its promise not to be party to these. It had replied that it had not changed its mind, but that Tshombe had to be told that sanctions would be applied. A week later, Welensky had warned of the possibility of violence and of the danger that the Katangese Government might destroy the mines, dams and other irreplaceable installations. Simultaneously, he had pressed Tshombe to continue his efforts to find a peaceful solution. A US military mission had visited Elizabethville and shortly afterwards the bulk of the UN forces had concentrated there.

On 28 December, Tshombe was ordered to remove his troops from Elizabethville, and an attempt was made to arrest him. An attack was launched by the UN, and this time it took only two days to effect at last the collapse of the Katanga regime. Tshombe fled to the Federation, announcing from Welensky's official residence that his men would fight to the bitter end. Knowing the odds against Tshombe, Welensky advised him to seek reconciliation, but was rebuffed.[7] In the event, Tshombe had no choice but to surrender on 15 January to the Congolese Central Government and the UN. So closed a chapter which had served, as far as the Federal Government was concerned, to embitter relations with the British Government in particular and with the West in general. It occasioned a deep trauma in Rhodesian politics and made quite unacceptable the prospect of UN mediation there in any dispute or circumstances.

When Welensky thanked Robinson for his efforts with Butler, he declared that the British aim in the last 18 months had been to remove him because he appeared to be "a stumbling block". Whitehead had also once been thus depicted, and Welensky could recall Sandys saying that Whitehead had to go, thus making him realise that his turn was next. Describing local events, Welensky said that Field was beginning to learn the facts of life, particularly from the Federal Treasury, and that, as Gaunt and Harper favoured joining South Africa, Field faced divisions within his own team. However, Welensky was pleased that Field had insisted on being a party to any talks on Nyasaland. It seemed that Kaunda was now prepared to negotiate with Field, but had

[5] Sir Roy Welensky, *Welensky's 4 000 Days* (London, 1964), pp. 260–261; Welensky Papers, 42/67, f. 7, Welensky to Tshombe, 25 July 1962.

[6] Welensky Papers, 20/13, f. 115, Robinson to Welensky, 23 August 1962; f. 114, Home to Welensky, 23 August 1962; f. 113, Alport to Welensky, 23 August 1962; f. 111, Welensky to Home, August 1962; 43/*Millin*, Welensky to S. G. Millin, 30 August 1962.

[7] *Ibid.*, 20/13, f. 73, Welensky to Robinson, 1 December 1962; f. 72, Home to Welensky, 3 December 1962; f. 65, Welensky to Robinson, 11 December 1962; 32/28, f. 45, Welensky to Robinson, 31 December 1962.

told an acquaintance of Welensky that he wanted a complete political divorce from Southern Rhodesia. It was clear that Kaunda and his supporters would co-operate only with an African or pro-African Government in Southern Rhodesia.

Welensky was expecting Butler to court Field in order "to gang up" on the Federal Government after having done so with Whitehead who, in October, had committed himself extensively to Nyasaland's secession. Welensky was interested to hear that Butler had, on 16 December, informed Robinson that he would negotiate separately with Northern Rhodesia, and thus it was logical that he might be tempted to do the same with Southern Rhodesia. The situation was worsened by the Federal relationship with Alport, which was rendering contact with the northern Governments almost impossible. Welensky said he had considered declaring Alport to be *persona non grata* if his attitude did not change.

He was also troubled by the weakness of the Southern Rhodesian division of the UFP and by its prospects, while Whitehead remained its leader. The division was, of course, facing the rampant Rhodesian Front in Parliament with a mixed team of 14 European and 15 African MPs.[8]

When *The Times* attributed the apparent failure of the Federation to him, Welensky wrote to its reporter, Roy Lewis, protesting that he could hardly be blamed for the anti-Federal attitude of the two initial northern Governors, Benson and Colby, and for the decision to leave the daily affairs of the Africans to the territories. The removal of the colour bar had been a territorial, and not a Federal, responsibility, he said. Shots had only been fired on territorial orders, and the British Government, when blaming him, conveniently chose to forget that it had not only forced the inclusion of Nyasaland but had taken the final decision to found the Federation. It seemed incredible that the Lord Chancellor should consider his revelation of confidential documents as being more serious a crime than the breaking of pledges between Governments. It left him wondering if he had not outlived his usefulness because his standards differed from those currently being applied.[9]

In an interview on the BBC on 11 January, Welensky also rued his failure to confront Macmillan publicly over the terms of reference of the Monckton Commission. He felt that he should have ignored Macmillan when he pleaded with him not to break the tradition of confidence regarding inter-governmental exchanges in the Commonwealth.[10]

In the New Year, Field continued to seek to improve his relationship with the northern territories, visiting Banda to speak on the future of Southern Rhodesian exports to Nyasaland. The Federal Government had begun to prepare for Butler's visit and, in the first week of January, decided that Field should be informed of its strategy. This was to use, as a beginning, Butler's declaration of May 1962 which favoured the existing relationship between the Rhodesias. However, having accomplished Nyasaland's secession, Butler might have changed his mind and, because the problems of maintaining the relationship were so formidable, he might delay settling the issue. As this

[8] *Ibid.*, 32/28, f. 45, Welensky to Robinson, 31 December 1962.
[9] *Ibid.*, 29/27, f. 23, Welensky to R. Lewis, 29 December 1962.
[10] *Ibid.*, 32/76, f. 1, BBC Interview, 11 January 1963.

would not serve its interests, the Federal Government felt that he had to be forced to grasp the nettle.[11]

Predictably, a wide range of advice was forthcoming from within the Federal ranks. Lewanika pleaded that Barotseland and the pro-Federal Africans should not be betrayed into the hands of the African nationalists. Instead, all links should be preserved and Northern Rhodesia should be divided into four separate states. J. A. Clark believed that the Rhodesian Front would only want an economic association between the territories and wished to convert Field from this because, if Butler succeeded in dismantling the Federation, Southern Rhodesia would have to shoulder a heavy financial burden. Moreover, if Field assisted Butler, he would help to establish an independent African nationalist state, Northern Rhodesia, on Southern Rhodesia's borders, with representation at the UN, an army, and contact with the Communists. Clark felt that an economic agreement was insufficient because, while Southern Rhodesia needed the northern market, Northern Rhodesia was free to trade with anyone, and it would be difficult for Southern Rhodesia to compete with countries such as Japan. Furthermore, Kaunda would be subjected to strong internal and external pressure to make Southern Rhodesia's position as difficult as possible. The loss of vital markets would have a detrimental effect on Southern Rhodesia's economy, and the position would only be aggravated if Kaunda decided to refuse to co-operate with regard to the generation of power at Kariba. With its ability to borrow drastically affected, and burdened with a heavy portion of the Federal public debt, the presence of a militant Pan-Africanist government on the border might force Southern Rhodesia to spend heavily on defence, to the detriment of everything else.[12]

The Ministry of External Affairs provided a list of subjects for discussion which, aside from issues such as the northern bills of rights, included events in the Congo and relations with the Portuguese. The Ministry of Health worried about the effects of disintegration and, with his usual thoroughness, Evans contributed a memorandum. He advised that, as the world would not condone forceful resistance by the Federal Government to secession, Nyasaland's withdrawal would have to be accepted. This would show the Federal Government to be highly responsible and recover for it some prestige. It would still be able to make a strong stand in principle on the past British assurances, pledges and conventions. Its position could be enhanced by emphasising that it had always honoured its obligations to Nyasaland, and by striving to ensure protection of the interests of the people of that territory. Insistence on a British guarantee of Nyasaland's portion of the public debt might prevent further dissolution because the British Government might be reluctant to set a precedent for the other two territories. Similar action on the subject of Federal civil service pensions and compensation for loss of office might be an equal deterrent.

Evans believed that Nyasaland's withdrawal had to be considered separately, and that the existing Rhodesian relationship had to be the starting

[11] *Ibid.*, FGC(63), 1st Meeting, Restricted Annexure, Federal Cabinet, 7 January 1963.
[12] *Ibid.*, 23/22, ff. 97–101, G. M. Lewanika to Welensky, 7 January 1963; f. 105, J. A. Clark to Welensky, 10 January 1963.

point for discussions. The Federal Government would have to deal with an African Government in Northern Rhodesia, but that Government had a strong Opposition and the delicate balance of power made drastic changes in policy unlikely, even though the coalition would seize any opportunity to declare its opposition to the Federation. Currently there was the threat of a Northern Rhodesian motion demanding secession, but the British Government was likely to block it because of the uproar over the concession to Nyasaland. Evans thought that the "unholy" nature of the alliance of UNIP and the ANC should be exploited, with much being made of the intention of the former to swallow the latter. The Southern Rhodesian position also seemed crucial because, while the RF was not actively opposed to the Federation, it would not defend it. Thus he advised his Government to seek to win the support of the moderate Africans by emphasising the virtues of partnership, and to persuade the territorial Governments to embrace it. An attack should be mounted on the British Government for forsaking partnership through its failure to honour the pledges and through its encouragement of racial paramountcy. The economic argument should be used to support the Federation, and large extracts from the Conference of 1953 should be quoted to demonstrate the necessity for a political association to ensure economic and social development. Simultaneously, Evans suggested that much should be made of Federal achievements and future plans.[13]

Greenfield wanted to ensure that Butler compelled the Northern Rhodesian official Members to vote against any motion advocating secession. He believed, therefore, that Butler should be reminded of Maudling's promise that the real power lay in the Governor's hands. He should also be warned of the repercussions in Barotseland and elsewhere. In fact, he had to be persuaded to commit himself categorically to endeavouring to maintain the Rhodesian ties. Because the British Government never told the Federal Government more than it thought good for it, Greenfield argued that Butler should be pressed to state his intentions clearly. He should also be asked for details of the proposed union of the Rhodesias which he had discussed with Whitehead. It was necessary to know the method by which Nyasaland would secede and how the public debt would be apportioned and the common services continued. The future relationship between Northern Rhodesia and Barotseland had to be discussed. The defence of the Federation at the UN would have to be considered, and Greenfield suggested that the British UN spokesmen should visit the Federation.[14]

Greenfield proposed close collaboration with Field, Whitehead, Roberts and Blackwood, as they were all due to meet Butler. He did not expect Butler to have any definite plans, although he would have decided that the Federation could not continue. It could be assumed that he would advance Northern Rhodesia, under Kaunda, to independence within a year, and that he would favour economic and political links, but, if they could not be secured, he would allow the Federation to disintegrate, albeit in an orderly fashion. While the northern territories would receive independence, Southern

[13] *Ibid.*, ff. 45–50, K. H. Towsey to Welensky, 21 January 1963; ff. 2–5, Ministry of Health's Memorandum, 18 January 1963; ff. 71–76, Evans's Memorandum, 17 January 1963.
[14] *Ibid.*, 23/22, ff. 95 & 78–81, Greenfield to Welensky, 15 & 17 January 1963.

Rhodesia would not, until there was adult suffrage. Not wishing to hurry, Butler could be expected to delay the disintegration to search for a solution and to allow Kaunda to gain experience, while the Europeans became used to the idea of an African take-over. Butler would not be particularly concerned if the Federal economy were affected by his tactics, but the British Government was not anxious to spend money and would prefer that Southern Rhodesia subsidise Nyasaland in return for markets.

Greenfield predicted that Butler would pretend to favour closer association, but would refuse to make a stand against African nationalism. It was clear that the Federal Government was the main obstacle, and that thus he would try to isolate it from the Southern Rhodesian Government. Indeed, Greenfield knew that Alport was already making overtures to Field. Butler might suggest a conference, and might succeed, by suggesting a joint working party, in overcoming Field's refusal to attend unless definite proposals were formulated. Field might also be tempted to put forward a "half-baked" scheme which was currently being proposed by H. Reedman of the RF and until recently of the UFP. Thus the first priority was to ensure that the Federal Government was not isolated and, therefore, a close alliance with Southern Rhodesia was necessary to prevent Butler claiming that none of the territories wanted to be associated and that the Federal Government was merely trying to preserve its position. Field appeared willing to co-operate, but he had to be confided in fully lest he be offended. The Federal Government should also convince him that it was being realistic and that he would face disaster if the links with Northern Rhodesia were broken, even though the prospects were poor of maintaining them, in the light of British reluctance to oppose Kaunda. It had to be shown that British support was being sought for a new approach. Field might co-operate in planning that approach if a joint Federal-Southern Rhodesian working party were suggested.

Until the working party had found the solution, Greenfield believed that Butler had to understand that, while the Federal and Southern Rhodesian Governments saw Nyasaland's secession as unavoidable, they were determined to preserve the association of the Rhodesias and would insist that real political power be retained in the hands of a central government whose members were not committed to black domination, and who would guarantee a secure future for the Europeans. An apportionment commission on the public debt would be demanded, as well as arrangements for the Federal civil servants who were working in Nyasaland. Banda would be offered some of the army, but none of the air force. There had to be discussions on the future of the currency, the establishment of a common market, and on the supply of labour. The Federal and Southern Rhodesian Governments should insist on a timetable for the excision of Nyasaland and on a settlement of the questions of citizenship, of compensation for Europeans leaving Nyasaland, and of the future of European education.[15]

Welensky accepted Greenfield's advice, but they were both disturbed when Wall, their hitherto doughty supporter, wrote on 4 January pronouncing the Federation to be dead and urging concentration on efforts to obtain

[15] *Ibid.*, ff. 109–114, Greenfield's Memorandum, January 1963.

independence for Southern Rhodesia. Greenfield commented that Butler had told him in London that Southern Rhodesia would be the last British territory in Africa to achieve independence, and only when the majority of voters were black. Thus Greenfield suggested that Welensky warn Field of this, as it was clear that he would have to take unilateral action to obtain independence.[16]

It is not clear if Welensky complied, but he certainly informed Wall of what Butler had said, while confessing that he should have confronted Macmillan over Monckton, thereby preventing the secession recommendation. Curiously, Wall replied urging Welensky to accept that Butler was his most powerful friend in Britain because he was determined to preserve economic, if not political links, between the territories, while guaranteeing the independence of Southern Rhodesia. Wall believed it was paramount to secure Southern Rhodesia's independence soon, and certainly before the next British general election. He thought it would be politically disastrous for Macmillan if the Federation were to be destroyed at the same time as the European in Southern Rhodesia was betrayed. Thus he thought Macmillan and Welensky shared the same aim, if for different reasons.[17]

Elizabeth Owen, chairman of the East and Central Africa Group of the Conservative Party, also described the Federation as dead and called for a strong, independent Southern Rhodesia. Welensky, in reply, sought to dampen such hopes of a reasonable outcome to the dissolution of the Federation.[18]

At that moment, Tshombe had fled from Katanga, and the Federal Cabinet was considerably irritated to receive a protest from the Acting Governor of Northern Rhodesia, R. E. Luyt (later Sir Richard), on behalf of some of his Ministers who objected to Tshombe staying briefly on their soil. Alport also protested, but was ignored by Welensky who instructed the Federal Army to protect Tshombe, and the RRAF to fly him to Kolwezi.[19]

On 21 January, the day before the first meeting with Butler, the Federal Cabinet reviewed its objectives and decided that the existing relationship between the Rhodesias should be preserved. It did not favour attending a conference on the future of the Federation and the territories, nor did it want a new constitution to be devised. It felt that, if the current Federal Constitution were to survive, the secession of Nyasaland would have to be negotiated separately and not as part of an overall settlement. Hope was found in the British underestimation of the difficulties flowing from Nyasaland's secession, and it was felt that they might well have second thoughts on severing the bonds between the Rhodesias. There were indications that the current Constitution might survive because the British officials were thinking of excising Nyasaland by amending the Federal Act and the relevant Order in Council. However, it was not clear if Butler approved of this idea and if he would do so after he had heard the opinions which would be expressed to him in Lusaka.

[16] *Ibid.*, 43/*Wall*, Major P. Wall to Welensky, 4 January 1963; Greenfield to Welensky, 10 January 1963.

[17] *Ibid.*, Welensky to Wall, 11 January 1963; Wall to Welensky, 14 January 1963.

[18] *Ibid.*, 32/44, f. 1, E. Owen to Welensky, 16 January 1963; f. 2, Welensky to E. Owen, 22 January 1963.

[19] *Ibid.*, FGC(1), 2/63, Federal Cabinet Memorandum, 11 January 1963; 24/152, ff. 103–106, Welensky to Joelson, 12 January 1963.

The Federal Cabinet felt that the initiative on timing should be wrenched from the British Government because the absence of a timetable was creating difficulties for the civil service and the Federal Assembly. It thought that it might be advantageous to indicate that Federal services could only be maintained in Nyasaland for a specific period. Yet it might be inopportune to appear to be forcing the British hand, because satisfactory guarantees for the future had still to be secured, even though it was unlikely that the British Government would allow the rights of Federal stockholders to be prejudiced. It was more important to secure the British agreement to underwrite the apportionment of the public debt. The Cabinet decided to demand, on the date of secession, a guarantee of the full reimbursement of any Federal loans expended in Nyasaland after 19 December 1962.

Welensky and Greenfield met Field and Clifford Dupont that day, only to hear them say they could not reveal their plans before they met Butler, making it clear, therefore, that if he offered them independence and at a price which was not too high, they would accept it and abandon the Federation.[20]

Butler says he was hoping to demonstrate that the demands for the dissolution of the Federation came from the territories and not from his Government. He has also revealed that he had decided not to set up a commission or an interim government as advised by Alport and Sir Roger Stevens, because thereby the relations between the Federal and territorial Governments would only deteriorate. Thus, at his first meeting with Welensky and the senior Federal Ministers, he said that he was seeking ways of preserving some of the links between the territories, adding that his Government would meet its obligations fully.

As Alport and the minutes show, this did not spare Butler a torrent of recrimination. Attacked on the breaking of the pledges, he did not say that a White Paper would be published shortly to answer the Federal case, but replied that, as he might have to make a public statement, he wished to reserve his position. Nevertheless, he still maintained that nothing could ever limit the British power to act. Referring to the minutes of the 1953 Conference, Greenfield rejected this interpretation and declared that the pledges and the 1957 Convention did curb the power of the British Parliament. Butler was unconvinced, but regretted that the pledges could not be reconciled with current realities. He rejected the charge that his policy for the northern territories was the antithesis of partnership, because the secession of Nyasaland was inevitable and, until it was accepted, the MCP Ministers would not adopt a constructive approach.

Welensky and Caldicott accepted the purely legal theory, but maintained that the moral obligation conferred by the pledges and the Convention was being ignored. Butler replied that he had to balance that obligation with Britain's duty as protector. He could not accept that any of the four Governments had been given a veto in 1953. Barrow thought that the choice had been between the pledges and the promise given to Banda, and that expediency had won the day. Butler, however, maintained that the issue was more complex, with many factors, including the maintenance of law and order and

[20] *Ibid.*, FGC(63), 3rd Meeting, Restricted Annexure, Federal Cabinet, 21 January 1963.

the need to break the deadlock to procure a constructive solution. Caldicott, belittling this, thought that the Northern Rhodesian Africans were being encouraged to follow the same path as Nyasaland. Butler replied that this was inevitable and that the situation was unlikely to have been prejudiced by the decision on Nyasaland.

When Welensky spoke of the depth of the mistrust of British intentions, Butler would only repeat that he had inherited the position in which he found himself. He wanted the Federal opinion on continued association, which he favoured, though he would not make any promises he could not fulfil. Welensky, however, preferred first to describe the shock which Alport had given him in early November by announcing the intention on secession, after Butler had said nothing about it to him in London. In all prior negotiations, Butler had given assurances on consultation because he recognised how important the issue of secession was to the Federal Government. Furthermore, he had given no indication that Nyasaland would not be part of the overall Federal solution which he had led the Federal Government to believe he was seeking. Indeed, on 14 May, Butler had said that the current relationship could be the basis for negotiation, but then had abandoned it, gravely prejudicing the Federal position.

In return, Butler denounced the publication of the confidential correspondence and defended his record on the continual exchanges between London and Salisbury. In addition, he recalled receiving the Federal Ministers and postponing the secession announcement at their request. He had certainly indicated that Nyasaland would be dealt with separately. Greenfield interjected that the damage occasioned by the announcement was the widespread conclusion that, thereby, the Federation was destroyed. Butler denied this and expressed an earnest hope that something could be preserved, as the relationship between the Rhodesias was still intact. He would henceforth explore the nature of all future links. Welensky insisted that these be political as well as economic, but doubted British sincerity because recent history proved that the British Government was committed to transfer power to racialists pledged to destroy the Federation. He wondered how Butler would receive the recently publicised request for a new Northern Rhodesian constitution. Butler replied that he had not yet decided on this, but that experience was needed in working the territory's current Constitution.

Welensky was determined not to let Butler escape yet, and pointed out the anomaly that he was expected to be a supplicant, even though the Federation had been created by a British Act. His Government had discharged its duties conscientiously, yet would be abandoned, even though the British Government had consistently failed to give it the support and encouragement which it had the right to expect.

Butler, however, felt that it was rather unjust to blame his Government for everything, because it did not wish to destroy the Federation, but had to recognise the powerful forces which had emerged in the past decade, and to consider the wishes of the territories. He wanted to preserve the links but could not do so unaided, and had to have the goodwill and co-operation of all the Governments. He suggested that the mechanics of secession should be devised by a party of Federal and territorial officials under a British chairman and that the date of secession should be withheld until all problems had been considered. Greenfield, concerned about the Federal financial support for Nyasaland after secession, wondered if the working party should suggest alternative courses of action. However, Butler merely replied that he hoped that the Federal services would be maintained at their current level until the date of secession. As Federal Minister of Finance, Caldicott would not hear of this and would not provide anything more than that for which Nyasaland could pay. He thought that the difficulty could be overcome by the British underwriting the Nyasaland portion of the public debt and by guaranteeing that any Federal money expended in Nyasaland between 19 December 1962 and the date of secession would be refunded.

Butler hoped that the Federal Government would be more generous because Welensky had always indicated that it would be. He was sure it would not want to appear vindictive. Barrow reminded him that he had promised in the Commons that Nyasaland would shoulder its share of the public debt and would have the support of the British Government. Butler replied that his Government would be generous. He suggested the appointment of a commission on the public debt which would collect the amounts apportioned to the territories and pay out the stock-holders.

Welensky feared that Butler would bow to African nationalist pressure in Northern Rhodesia and ruin everything. Unless reassured, he warned, his Government could not be generous in circumstances for which it was not responsible. He provoked Alport to retort that, as suppliers of Federal revenue, the Rhodesias would expect statesmanship and that, in any case, Southern Rhodesia was anxious to retain its markets in Nyasaland. Welensky disagreed, because the demands for development were such that the Rhodesias would welcome any extra money.

This argument proved to Butler the necessity for the working party and he hoped for Federal support though he could not supply the *quid pro quo* which was being sought. He again promised to strive to preserve the Rhodesian association and trusted that his good faith with regard to secession would be accepted. Greenfield suggested that the working party should examine everything pertinent and that the members should seek directives from their Governments as the work progressed. The meeting agreed that the working party could not have executive powers and that matters of dispute should be referred to the Governments.

Evans, however, thought that certain fundamentals had to be resolved first, mentioning the British guarantees on Nyasaland's share of the public debt, a portion of the pensions, and the cost of compensating the Federal civil servants. Assurance was needed, he said, that the Federal African employees in Nyasaland would not be victimised. Caldicott still would not spend Federal money in Nyasaland without an undertaking on repayment at secession, because of increasing difficulties in raising loans locally and abroad. Welensky was only prepared to allow his officials to examine the terms of reference of the working party. He demanded the date of secession because it would affect the staffing of the Federal departments in Nyasaland. However, Butler could not comply but promised to keep him fully informed.

Welensky then asked about the likely attitude of the Governor and his officials if the Northern Rhodesian African nationalists introduced their motion calling for secession. He believed that the Governor should adopt the pro-Federal attitude of the British Government. Butler claimed not to have considered the matter, but promised to discuss it in Lusaka. The Federal Ministers then remarked on a report that, before the by-elections had produced a European Member who supported the ANC, the Governor had considered nominating an additional Member to the Executive Council to enable the coalition to satisfy the requirements for the composition of the Government. Reassurance was sought because the British Government had said that the power to nominate would only be used in emergencies, and the failure to return two European Members of the African nationalist Parties was hardly an emergency, when it was incumbent on those Parties to attract Europeans. It was essential that the power to nominate should not be abused.

Butler, ignoring him, merely promised again to endeavour to retain the closest possible links. He had, nonetheless, no illusions about the difficulties. He needed the co-operation of the Governments because there were strong elements at work in Africa which could not be ignored. Furthermore, the British Parliament would not sanction the use of force to preserve the links.

Welensky thanked Butler for being frank and expressed appreciation for his difficulties but asked him to remember that the Federal Government had responsibilities to its electorate who had to live with the consequences of the British decisions. The British Government, by showing no resolution in governing the northern territories, had to bear some responsibility for what was happening. He still believed that the British could influence the course of events in those territories by grasping the nettle.[21]

Although no record has been seen, it is clear from Welensky's correspondence that there was a further meeting with Butler at which the Federal Government indicated it would accept changes in the Federal Assembly because they were an inevitable consequence of Nyasaland's withdrawal. African domination of the Assembly was rejected and Butler was reminded that this Parliament was primarily concerned with the affairs of the Europeans. However, an increase in African membership was accepted as well as the return of some functions to the territories, although — lest there be anarchy — defence, finance, customs, immigration, transport and external affairs would have to remain Federal. Health and education would be relinquished with reluctance. Butler was also informed that no one could see how the Federation could be dissolved and then successfully resuscitated. Furthermore, the Federal Government would not contemplate any reform until the current position was clarified.[22]

The correspondence reveals that Butler was sufficiently shaken by the meetings with the Federal Cabinet to ask Field if Welensky would use force to preserve his position. Field, perfectly correctly, doubted that he would, and afterwards informed Welensky that he had told Butler that he would do nothing to prevent the continuance of the association between the Rhodesias

[21] *Ibid.*, FGC 19, f. 1, Minutes of a Meeting with Butler, 22 January 1963; Lord Butler, *The Art of the Possible: The Memoirs of Lord Butler* (London, 1973), p. 224; Lord Alport, *The Sudden Assignment* (London, 1965), p. 231.

[22] Welensky Papers, 32/17, f. 12, Welensky to Roberts, 23 January 1963.

but thought that Kaunda would allow only economic ties. Field pleaded in vain with Welensky to accept economic ties only as inevitable, prompting Welensky to deduce, accurately, that there would be no support forthcoming from Field who always had been anti-Federal.

Welensky summed up somewhat bitterly: "A man is drowning and Field is on the bank. He is not going to do anything to assist the drowning man and he is certainly not going to drown him because that isn't necessary, it is going to happen in any case."[23] However, when Field discovered that Welensky was going to retire from politics, he urged him to reconsider and enter Southern Rhodesian politics.

Welensky told Lord Salisbury that the meeting with Butler was strained and blamed Alport for fanning the flames. He believed that Alport was unhappy because he sensed the dislike of all sections of the Federal community. Alport has partly confirmed this by revealing that he was forced to take his telephone off the hook at night to avoid being awakened by abusive calls. Butler, quickly sensing the tension, had talked of removing Alport before July, when he was due to retire. Welensky asked that any replacement should be a professional diplomat because of the behaviour of Alport and his staff. An example of this was a public attack on Welensky by Alport's information officer.[24]

Welensky claimed that Butler had been so shaken by Caldicott's refusal to subsidise Nyasaland that it was "the first time I've seen the unflappable show any signs of flap".[25]

Even after the meeting, Welensky remained convinced that, if only the British would show some resolution, something could be saved. However, he knew that this was unlikely because Kaunda wanted total power and Field was unwilling to be associated with him. Nevertheless, he proposed to fight on against the odds because, if nothing else, he had to live with his conscience.

Butler had departed for the northern territories when the Federal Cabinet reviewed the position on 28 January. A remark by Nkumbula, that Butler would not refuse the coalition Government if it demanded secession, was noted, but a reaction from Butler had not yet been received. The Federal Cabinet was divided over the working party because some Ministers suspected that it might be a device to allow the MCP Ministers to avoid involvement in the exercise of apportioning the public debt and the responsibilities for the Federal civil servants. After the Cabinet meeting, the Federal officials rejected as impractical a British paper on the working party.[26]

Of the advice which Welensky received, the most dramatic was from Mrs S. G. Millin, the historian, who demanded that he proclaim the Federation independent while Butler was still in Salisbury. The Speaker of the Federal Assembly, T. I. F. Wilson, added that the Assembly should declare as *ultra vires* any unilateral British Act excising Nyasaland from the Federation. The

[23] *Ibid.*, 24/152, Welensky to F. S. Joelson, 24 January 1963.

[24] *Ibid.*, 43/*Salisbury*, Welensky to Lord Salisbury, 25 January 1963; Alport, *The Sudden Assignment*, *op. cit.*, p. 229.

[25] Welensky Papers, 43/*Salisbury*, Welensky to Salisbury, 25 January 1963.

[26] *Ibid.*, FGC(63), 4th Meeting, Restricted Annexure, Federal Cabinet, 28 January 1963; 32/89, f. 1, Evans to Welensky, 28 January 1963.

result could be awkward, he said, because either Banda or the British Army would then have to extricate Nyasaland.[27]

The Secretary to the Federal Treasury, H. M. McDowell, disliked the idea of the working party because it might bog down on the mass of detail and take years to resolve the issue. He preferred to set a date for secession in the near future, for instance on 1 July 1963, and for Nyasaland to set up the necessary mechanism. The Federal Government, ever helpful, he said, would provide all the services required, including advice on the new machinery of government, but would be reimbursed for them. The indefatigable Evans disagreed and wanted a working party, because planning was necessary and it was illogical to grant secession before all the machinery was ready. The fixing of the date was undesirable because it might be impossible to determine all the crucial requirements in time. The Federal position could be weakened, he said, as the British might side with the Nyasaland Government if secession were already a fact. Evans found tactical advantages in deferring the act of severance for as long as possible, provided that the accusation of deliberate delaying tactics could be avoided. As the Nyasaland Government greatly desired secession, it was likely to be reasonable, but if it secured the act of secession first, the British and Federal Governments would lose any hold over it. If the date were fixed arbitrarily, Banda could call the tune and ignore Federal claims. The situation could become impossible and the Federal officers providing the services could be subjected to slights and insults without redress. If there were any expensive or inconvenient services, which the Nyasaland Government was not ready or willing to provide, there would be no inducement to reach a settlement thereon.

Evans urged his Government to secure the initiative so that it could dictate the course of events. Therefore it could not adopt a passive role. There had to be a framework for an orderly hand-over as great Federal interests were at stake. To deal with these through *ad hoc* working parties, after the date of secession had been set, would mean that there would have to be a multiplicity of those parties working in unfavourable conditions and without central direction. Evans thought that what McDowell really sought to ensure was that no revenue from the Rhodesias was spent in Nyasaland after a certain date, ignoring the possibility that the Federal Government, through its weak position, might incur financial obligations which would be even more disadvantageous to the Rhodesias. The political consequences could be disastrous because the Northern Rhodesian African nationalists might be spurred to set the same seal on their political ambition.

Provided the British Government guaranteed the cost of the Federal services after a certain date, possibly 1 July 1963, Evans found great advantage in delaying secession to discover the attitude of the two new Rhodesian Governments towards the maintenance of links, as well as allowing the strengthening of the existing bond through new capital projects, such as a nitrogen factory. There was no point in surrendering all the bargaining counters just to ensure that Federal revenue was not wasted. In any case, the Federal Government needed time to make arrangements for Nyasaland's

[27] *Ibid.*, 43/*Millin*, S. G. Millin to Welensky, 29 January 1963; 31/87, f. 27, T. I. F. Wilson to Welensky, 29 January 1963.

secession and erect new customs posts and the like. McDowell's proposal could provoke Banda to demand the withdrawal of Federal services in order to replace them with services provided by America or the Soviet Bloc, which would be very embarrassing. The fixing of an arbitrary date would be ill-received by the world and would bring the Federal Government into disrepute. On the other hand, participation in a working party would show that the Federal Government was highly responsible and was acting constructively in the secession exercise.[28]

The Welensky Papers give only three glimpses of Butler on his tour of the northern territories. On 25 January, he met the Barotse National Government to hear it demand the return of Barotseland to separate status, because it did not want to be subjected to local rule once Northern Rhodesia achieved independence. In any case, it argued, experience had taught it to value its monarchical government. The possibility of secession after Northern Rhodesia was independent seemed remote and, it felt, might provoke intervention by the UN. The Barotse had also noticed that the British Government was contemplating granting independence to the High Commission Territories in South Africa. Butler courteously replied that he valued Barotseland's loyalty but that he was not contemplating any immediate changes to Northern Rhodesia's Constitution because it was so new. He had only just received Hudson's report on Barotseland but he suggested that separation would cause difficulties in economics, administration and defence. He proposed to discuss Barotseland's future in July or August but suggested that the Litunga and his Government could strengthen their position by separating their judiciary from the executive, by appointing a new Prime Minister, by holding more democratic elections, by publishing a development plan, and by securing the secondment of professional and technical officers. He advised strongly against isolating Barotseland from the rest of the world, but the Litunga remained adamant that his country should not be subordinated to an African nationalist Government in Northern Rhodesia. He promised, however, to improve his Government.[29]

From Nyasaland, J. R. Ness, of the Settlers and Residents Association, and Blackwood gave accounts of their meetings with Butler. Ness attacked Butler for appeasing extremism, but Butler "tried to quibble". Ness warned that Federal citizens, proud of the record of partnership, would not live under a black dictatorship and would become stateless. Butler could understand them not wanting to become Malawi citizens, but hoped that they would become British citizens for convenience. Ness scorned this offer because, after the Kenyan experience, he doubted if Britain would protect her citizens. Appearing hurt, Butler replied that it was a delicate matter which required legal opinion on the extent of British responsibility.

In his meeting with Butler and Jones, Blackwood discovered from Butler that the separation of Nyasaland would not be completed by 6 July 1963 to coincide, as Banda wished, with the anniversary of his return to Nyasaland. The end of 1963 or early 1964, Blackwood understood, was considered more

[28] *Ibid.*, 32/63, f. 36, Evans to Welensky, 29 January 1963.

[29] *Ibid.*, 33/58, f. 1A, Report of a Meeting between Butler and the Barotse National Government, 25 January 1963.

likely. Independence would follow, but not before Easter 1964. Blackwood gathered that the financial settlement was unresolved because the Federal Government was demanding £40 000 000, and Nyasaland was offering £20 000 000. Nyasaland intended to exchange Federal for British currency and to replace the Federal officers in the Nyasaland units of the army with British officers. However, Banda had no desire to integrate European education with African, but would do so with Asian education. In future the individual would receive the level of health service for which he could pay. No difficulties were anticipated with staffing, as teachers would be seconded from Hampshire, and Jones was confident that doctors could be attracted to Nyasaland. Jones was obviously not concerned about the fate of the posts and telegraph service.

Banda was considering asking the Italian airline, Alitalia, to run an air service, but Blackwood had convinced Butler that the idea was ludicrous and that Central African Airways had to continue to serve Nyasaland. Blackwood suggested that the British Government should grant £1 000 000 to develop a railway line to Ncala on the Moçambique coast and Butler showed signs of interest. Jones thought that the return of customs to Nyasaland would earn it £1 000 000 in revenue, but Blackwood doubted that it would because of the current economic decline.

Having assured Blackwood that the British would assist in drafting the bill of rights, Butler said that Banda was likely to accept five reserved seats for Europeans and Jones confirmed that he would. Banda did not appear to be intending to co-operate with the working party on secession.

After Butler had spoken on the problem of external representation, Blackwood and his Party enlightened him on the problems regarding freehold land and the invasion of squatters, mentioning the inability of the police to prosecute and the offer by the Nyasaland Government of £1 per acre to those who wished to sell. Chipembere was about to be released from gaol, and Jones indicated that the former's uncle, Archdeacon Chipembere, would resign his seat for him and that he would be appointed a Minister if he fought the by-election before the next session.

After discussion on citizenship and other such matters, Butler revealed that progress was being made in the negotiations with the Federal Government on the working party. He also said that he had told Kaunda that there could be no new Northern Rhodesian constitution for the present, but Blackwood gathered that Butler would separate the two Rhodesias if that were the wish of the Northern Rhodesian African nationalists.[30]

At a Press conference, Blackwood announced that his Party would retain its Federal links for as long as possible because it was in the best interests of Nyasaland. At that moment, the coalition in Northern Rhodesia seemed threatened as Nkumbula declared that it would not survive unless Kaunda controlled the violent elements of UNIP. In Nyasaland, on 1 February, Banda was sworn in as the first Prime Minister, having triumphantly excluded any Federal Government representatives from the ceremony. Before returning to Salisbury two days earlier, Butler had welcomed Banda's appointment

[30] *Ibid.*, 38/63, f. 50, J. R. Ness to Welensky, 29 January 1963; 32/63, f. 37, Report of a Meeting between Butler and Blackwood, 30 January 1963.

and had predicted that full self-government would be achieved in April. Thereafter, he had said he would consider the question of independence.[31]

Welensky knew that the second round of the negotiations with Butler would be crucial, but thought that Butler would be distracted by the news that de Gaulle had finally blocked Britain's entry into the Common Market and that he would not wish to add further Federal problems to Macmillan's burden.[32] He was correct because, on 31 January, Butler opened the negotiations by asking for constructive ideas and saying that no decision had been taken yet on the Federation's future. His enabling bill, he said, would only effect Nyasaland's secession, and the order in council, to amend the Federal Constitution, would follow later. However, he warned that it might be necessary to legislate for the total dissolution of the Federation.

Greenfield stressed the importance of the mechanics of the exercise because, if the legislation were confined to Nyasaland, the Federal public service could be preserved. If it embraced Northern Rhodesia, it meant dissolution. Butler would say no more because he wanted to consider carefully the possibilities of preserving some form of association. His uncertainty led Greenfield to suggest that it was too early to appoint a working party, but Butler reminded him that Alport had discussed the matter with Federal officials in his absence and that he had made a public announcement that it would be constituted.

The Federal Ministers offered to assist in drafting the British legislation to effect Nyasaland's secession, and Butler agreed they might if they understood that ultimately any decisions would be made by his Government alone. He was not optimistic about any future association because Field and the Northern Rhodesians had indicated to him that not even an economic one was possible. Barrow warned that, as there was no place for the Federal Government in an economic association, it could not be expected to advance any suggestions on the future. Welensky thought that, in any event, suggestions from the Federal Government would be condemned out of hand by the African nationalists. He reiterated that an economic union without political ties would be valueless.

Butler replied that the Federal Government had to do what it thought right, but that he was sure that an economic association was possible and he wanted the Federal views thereon before making a decision. He then described his meeting with the Litunga of Barotseland and Banda's comment to him that Nyasaland would not negotiate with the other territories until it had seceded. Banda had promised, however, to keep in close contact with the British Government on the fate of the Nyasaland migrant workers and on the possible customs union and other matters. He had agreed to reassure Nyasalanders on freehold title.

Welensky suggested 1 July 1963 as a date for secession because, he said, Banda wanted an early date and because the Federal Assembly was unlikely to vote funds for Nyasaland in excess of its contribution to Federal revenues. Welensky expected the British to supply the difference to maintain the

[31] *Ibid.*, f. 37, Blackwood to Welensky, 30 January 1963; *Northern News*, 30 January 1963; *The Rhodesia Herald*, 31 January 1963.

[32] Welensky Papers, 32/63, f. 38, Welensky to Blackwood, 30 January 1963.

services in Nyasaland at current standards. Caldicott confirmed that the Federal Treasury thought it was unreasonable to continue to spend at the current rate after the end of June. It was only realistic, and not vindictive, he said, to expect the British to find the difference. Butler could not commit the British Treasury but promised to consult his Government and Jones forthwith, even though this was a matter for the working party. Caldicott disagreed and maintained that a decision was needed as soon as possible so that he could frame his budget for 1963/64.

Butler claimed to have tried to sell to the Northern Rhodesian African nationalists the benefits of the Federation and the continued economic and political association of the Rhodesias. Alport added that the Federal Government should match this effort, and drew from Welensky a lengthy retort on how his Government had been left to face vicious attacks alone. For example, action by the Federal Army in support of the territorial Governments had been depicted as illustrating repression by the Federal Government. The British Ministers had not only failed to correct this, but had played down their responsibility for the situations which required military action. Welensky and his colleagues had tried to meet the African nationalists but had been rebuffed and had concluded that the minds of the latter were closed.

Butler appreciated the Federal difficulties but reminded the Federal Cabinet that he had problems of his own, even though he neither wished to impose a solution nor to destroy the Federation. Against the immense achievements of the Federation, he had to balance the considerable volume of criticism and dislike of it. Therefore the Federal Government should set out what it thought it could achieve so that his Government could give it due consideration.[33]

Before the meeting with Butler on the next day, the Federal Government produced a spate of memoranda covering the timetable for secession and the working party. It was thought that the working party could be accepted if it was served by two Federal and two Nyasaland representatives under a British chairman. The Federal departments would provide assistance, and the chairman of the Public Services Commission would be associated with any discussion on the civil servants. The working party should ensure a minimum disruption of services. It should make arrangements for the continued employment of those civil servants who wished to serve Nyasaland, and for just compensation for those who did not. The compensation would be underwritten by the British Government. Such a guarantee would also extend to the public debt and the moveable assets of the Federal Government. The legislation to be produced would be written in collaboration with the Federal Government. Other memoranda dealt with freedom of movement, reciprocal enforcement of judgments, and the common services which could be continued if the Nyasaland Government so wished. There was comment on the future of citizenship and the protection of minorities.[34]

Caldicott provided detailed assessments by the Treasury of the greatest

[33] *Ibid.*, FGC 19/1, f. 12, Minutes of a Meeting with Butler, 31 January 1963.

[34] *Ibid.*, f. 62, Memorandum on Secession — Timetable, 31 January 1963; f. 37, Proposed Working Party, 31 January 1963; f. 39, Mutuality between Nyasaland and Rhodesia, 31 January 1963; f. 40, Common Services, 31 January 1963.

difficulties to be faced, but acknowledged that many of these would fall away as it seemed that the British Government might accept secession on 1 July. The Treasury did not advise unilateral termination of services in Nyasaland because of the financial loss which would occur.[35]

On 1 February Butler faced a series of meetings. The first was at 9 a.m. with Welensky, Caldicott, McDowell and Dr A. G. Irvine of the Federal Central Bank. They laid before him the Treasury estimates for the period from 1 January 1963 to 30 June 1964. In this, £9 600 000 was required for loan redemption, and £3 300 000 for development plan expenditure which required further borrowing. The current deficit was £6 300 000, which meant that the total the Federal Government would have to find was £19 200 000. The cash in hand of £1 800 000 reduced this figure to £17 400 000 which was required by 30 June 1964. The revenue in 1962/3 from Nyasaland was £3 998 000, while expenditure had amounted to £9 272 000. Thus the deficit which the British Government would have to meet was £5 274 000. A Federal loan of £3 000 000 was about to be raised, but the prospect for any others was bleak because of the British decision on secession. It was impossible to maintain expenditure at the current level unless the Federal Government was reimbursed. There was, however, no desire to make the Nyasalanders suffer and the Federal Government would do what it could in the transitional period.

Butler confessed that he had not known that the position was so serious, but he suspected that the Federal Government would have had to face such a situation even if Nyasaland had not been allowed to secede. He asked how these figures would be affected by the withdrawal, but McDowell found it difficult to answer except in the case of borrowing because it was clear that loans could have been raised if it were not for the decision on secession. Furthermore, he would have recommended meeting some of the deficit with treasury bills, but the current uncertainty ruled them out.

Butler claimed that the Federal Central Bank and the Bank of England were not so perturbed about the Federal credit-worthiness and did not think that the situation was radically affected by the decision on Nyasaland. McDowell then recalled that a year previously the International Bank had declared that, because of the uncertainty, it could not consider loans without dispatching a quasi-political mission to examine the probability of any loan achieving its economic objective. Welensky pointed to current heavy withdrawals from the Post Office Savings Bank which, for the first time, was suffering a net reduction in its assets. The Nyasaland Government was encouraging withdrawals in order to sell its bonds but, in fact, had attracted only £20 000 of the £250 000 withdrawn.

Butler acknowledged that the Bank of England lacked these details. Nevertheless, he thought that the Federal Constitution bound the Federal Government to continue to supply and finance its services. He had told Banda that it would take from nine to twelve months to effect secession and he expected the Federal services to be maintained until then.

However, Welensky continued to assert that the British Government would

[35] *Ibid.*, 32/63, f. 44, Caldicott to Welensky, 1 February 1963, with enclosed memorandum.

have to pay for the services as a consequence of its unilateral decision on secession. He found little incentive for the Rhodesian taxpayer to subsidise these services. Butler was adamant that the financial support was a Federal responsibility. Caldicott supported Welensky and claimed that the only constitutional obligation was to pay Nyasaland six per cent of income tax revenue. One of Butler's officials countered by saying that Nyasaland would be forced to raise revenue in the Federal field to maintain these services, but Caldicott was confident that the Constitution forbad this.

Alport warned that, if the Federal civil servants were withdrawn before secession, their compensation and pensions would become entirely the Federal Government's responsibility. Welensky replied that most of the European civil servants wanted to be withdrawn and re-deployed elsewhere because they were facing personal attacks. What worried him was the fate of the African civil servants because the MCP had told them that there would be no place for them. Many were already seeking employment in the Rhodesias. He exonerated his Government from responsibility for any run-down because the British Government had taken the decision and had to face the consequences.

Butler felt that, if the constitutional link were severed on 1 July, not only would much be left unresolved, but it would be extremely damaging to the credit of the Federal Government if it were known that services were being reduced through Federal inability to support them. Welensky obstinately maintained that the Federation's credit was already damaged. He had repeatedly stressed that Nyasaland would face insuperable difficulties if it lost the Federal subsidy, but had been ignored by Banda. Consequently, the Nyasaland Government had produced a taxation plan which would have made even the British taxpayer squirm.

Butler was aware of the realities and of the Federal arguments, but had to consult his Government before he could choose a date for secession. He remained anxious that the Federal services should continue after 1 July until the date of secession. However, Caldicott would not co-operate without a British reimbursement. He was sure that Banda would not want to endure the tragic consequences of a collapse of the services.

McDowell recalled that it had taken years to centralise the services and, even now, some were still run on an agency basis by the Nyasaland Government. He thought that the reverse process could be difficult, and Caldicott added that it would demand goodwill from both sides when, currently, there was practically no official contact as the Nyasaland Government had decided not to co-operate with the Federal Government. Thus he argued that Banda had to be induced to change his attitude. Alport and M. D. Tennant, Secretary at the Central African Office, insisted that these were matters for the working party which had to provide a full picture before the British Government could select a date for secession. Caldicott, however, insisted that the decision on secession had absolved the Federal Government from any financial responsibility. He felt that Banda would have to decide how he would cope and whether he needed Federal assistance.[36]

[36] *Ibid.*, FGC 19/1, f. 17, Minutes of a Meeting, 9 a.m., 1 February 1963.

Butler promised to impart his new knowledge to the British Treasury and then went to meet Goldberg, the Federal Minister of Health, and Clark, the Federal Minister of Commerce. Goldberg told him of the difficulties experienced by his Ministry since the decision on secession. The African staff had experienced many forms of pressure, including physical assault and, as the Europeans wanted to leave immediately, the level of services could not be maintained after the end of June. He thought that the British Government would have to step into the breach, but Butler doubted that it would, and asked that the services be maintained until secession. Goldberg replied that the working conditions would render this impossible. Clark confirmed this because already the officials of his Ministry had to meet the Nyasaland officials surreptitiously in their homes. On the continued association between the Rhodesias, Clark warned that Northern Rhodesia would be most vulnerable because its economy was solely based on copper. Kaunda had claimed that he would diversify the economy, but the size of the internal market would allow only small-scale industrialisation. As Southern Rhodesia would lose its markets, because of the pathological hatred of the African nationalists, it was imperative to retain the political ties. Butler thought that Southern Rhodesia would keep her Nyasaland market, but asked Clark for a paper on the subject.[37]

At 11 a.m., Butler and Alport met Welensky, Barrow, Caldicott and Greenfield again. Tabling a memorandum on what should be preserved of the constitutional relationship, Welensky demanded the retention of the political ties and suggested that the Federal Government be retained to administer external affairs, defence, immigration, citizenship, customs, banking, currency, income tax, transport, power and non-African education. The Federal Assembly would be elected on a qualified franchise which would ensure the substantial representation of all races. A dual roll similar to those employed by the territories would be used.

Welensky warned that the memorandum had to be kept confidential because such was the mood in the Federation and abroad that, if publicised, it would not be considered fairly. He maintained, as always, that economic links would not suffice to avert the disastrous consequences of the demise of the current Federation. The African nationalists in Northern Rhodesia, he predicted, would combine with Field to destroy the Federation but, thereafter, would work to bring down Field's Government to replace it with African majority rule. The aims of Northern and Southern Rhodesia were so irreconcilable that a lasting economic association was impossible, and the failure of the Central African Council was an illustration of the need for political ties. Welensky said he would rename the truncated Federation "Rhodesia", and insisted that it had to be made a dominion. Greenfield emphasised the importance of non-African education remaining Federal because, otherwise, the Europeans, unwilling to accept lower standards for their children, would emigrate *en masse*. He reminded Butler that even the liberal Whitehead had never suggested the integration of education below school certificate level and that Banda also did not intend to integrate European and African education.

[37] *Ibid.*, f. 24, Minutes of a Meeting, 10.15 a.m., 1 February 1963.

Butler was unconvinced because it would be difficult to persuade the territories that they could not control such a nation-building service. Caldicott interjected to say that Greenfield was only being practical because the European would demand that standards were maintained or would emigrate.

Butler noticed in the memorandum that the Federal Government wanted to retain income tax and warned that he had been told in Lusaka that Northern Rhodesian revenue would not be spent beyond its borders. Caldicott, however, found great advantage in having a central taxing authority and suggested that the division of the proceeds could be decided by a fiscal commission. He hoped that Butler did not think that the current Northern Rhodesian contribution to the Federal exchequer was out of proportion to that of Southern Rhodesia. He said that the copper mines were the greatest Federal asset but, in fact, Southern Rhodesia produced more revenue, and since 1954 had contributed £244 000 000, in contrast to Northern Rhodesia's £173 000 000. Welensky agreed that the vulnerability of the Northern Rhodesian copper economy was the greatest argument for federation.

Butler asked if the territories should raise their own defence forces, but Barrow replied that it would be too costly and would impair local defence and that of the Commonwealth. Welensky agreed that standards had to be maintained because, after the withdrawal of the British forces from East Africa, there would be none south of Aden, despite Katanga and other issues causing concern.

Butler wondered if a central legislature elected by the territorial Governments had been considered, but Welensky dismissed this as unworkable because Northern Rhodesia was becoming an African state, and Southern Rhodesia was pursuing the goal of white supremacy. Butler sought Federal opinions on further Northern Rhodesian constitutional changes, but Welensky hoped there would be none until experience there had been gained in working the current Constitution. He accepted that there was a case for some advancement towards self-government in Northern Rhodesia because of the lack of provision for any, but felt that full internal self-government should be part of a package deal. Butler was grateful for this opinion because he had faced demands in Northern Rhodesia for an immediate constitutional conference as well as for the appointment of a commission to study the possibility of future economic, but not political, links with Southern Rhodesia. Field had told him that he did not want anything more than economic ties. Butler had refused the conference but could see advantages in inter-governmental discussions between the two Rhodesias which could frame the new association while being informal and excluding both Opposition Parties. Northern Rhodesia favoured these discussions, he said, and Southern Rhodesia would accept them if there were no striking of political attitudes. Welensky thought that all would agree on the Federation's dissolution but that nothing constructive would be achieved because he knew that the Southern Rhodesian Government contained anti-Federal elements and that Field was delaying action in the hope that the Federation would be destroyed by another Government, rather than his. Caldicott added that Field had no mandate to secede, as secession had not been a major issue in the recent Southern Rhodesian election. If it had been, the Rhodesian Front would not have won.

Nevertheless, Butler wondered if the ground should not be cleared by discussions between the Rhodesian Governments. He urged that, once this was accomplished, the Federal Government could participate, but Welensky would not hear of the existence of the Federation being thus ignored and declared that it was improper to exclude his Government at any stage. Greenfield said that the Northern Rhodesian African nationalists were dividing and ruling, using Southern Rhodesia to break up the Federation before turning on the former to ensure that it gained an extremist African government. They intended to foment discord and strife, and it was difficult to believe that the British Government would condone their actions. Butler promised that it would not, but warned that force would not be used to implement policy. He thought that a mass exodus of whites would be a tragedy and assured the Federal Ministers that he was seeking a solution that would maintain confidence and credit and encourage private enterprise to continue to invest in the area.

Greenfield concluded that the whites could expect little help from the British Government because it was unwilling to resist pressure from the African nationalists and to preserve the Federation. The dissolution of the Federation would only encourage a large number of whites to leave. Alport interjected that the views of the Southern Rhodesian Government could not be ignored, but Greenfield replied that it was inexperienced and had an imperfect knowledge of the consequences for Southern Rhodesia of the dissolution. He believed that Britain was failing in its duty as protecting power by handing over the inhabitants of the protectorates (Northern Rhodesia and Nyasaland) to immature racial extremists.

Welensky thought it was because the UFP held the largest number of seats that Kaunda sought a constitutional change so that he might head a one-party government. He knew that Kaunda could not abide criticism from any quarter and did not relish having to rely on the coalition with the ANC. Welensky proposed to clarify the position with Field, but hoped that the British Government would consider the Federal Government's scheme, outlined in the memorandum, before contemplating any changes. Butler promised to examine it carefully.

Greenfield still wanted to know the fate of the Federation as soon as possible and to discuss the working party. Welensky suggested, for complete impartiality, a Commonwealth chairman, but Butler rejected this because not only was the working party a British responsibility, but progress had to be guaranteed. D. Watson (later Sir Duncan) of Butler's delegation added that the working party should not be dictated to, but Greenfield argued that it would have to consider the compensation of the civil servants whose livelihood had been ruined by the decision on secession.

Butler closed by promising consultation on the terms of reference of the working party and to consider compelling the Nyasaland Government to employ the African Federal civil servants, 1 500 of whom were serving on pensionable terms.[38]

Afterwards, at a joint meeting of the Federal and Southern Rhodesian

[38] *Ibid.*, f. 27, Minutes of a Meeting, 11 a.m., 1 February 1963.

Cabinets, Field welcomed the Federal proposals. Finally, before leaving for London, Butler warned Welensky that he would be publishing a White Paper to answer his charges on the pledges, but Welensky's reply is not recorded.[39]

Although Welensky described the negotiations privately as very difficult, because Butler had contributed nothing apart from the appointment of the working party, he took care to correct the Press's belief that he and Butler had merely quarrelled, claiming that the talks had been forceful but cordial. The value of the visit, he said, was that each had learned something of the other's problems. He recognised the British preoccupation with the Common Market, with Britain's defence, unemployment and other problems, and, though not wishing to add to them, he had indicated that the current uncertainty in Central Africa could not continue. As the worst step that could be taken would be to destroy the Federation, he had urged building on the existing foundation. He accepted the need for radical change, although he objected to the British unilateral action on secession. He did not propose to dwell on the past and stoically promised to do the best he could with what remained.[40]

At his departure, Butler indicated to the Press that he was hopeful of unravelling the tangled problem of Central Africa. He intended to seek the support of everyone, including his Cabinet, he said, for a new arrangement whereby the three territories could live in accord despite the secession of Nyasaland and the probable withdrawal of Northern Rhodesia. His first step, he explained, would be to appoint a working party to examine the consequences of secession. Although Butler was more modest in his claims, the *Sunday Times* believed that he had enjoyed a diplomatic triumph over the Federal Government. Political observers, thinking erroneously that Welensky had remained silent, were surprised that he had not taken the opportunity to deliver a counter-blast.[41]

Welensky, of course, had made his feelings quite clear and had few illusions left. He was tired of British procrastination but, in fact, did not have long to wait to hear the fate of the Federation.

[39] *Ibid.*, 32/38, f. 47, Welensky to Robinson, 2 February 1963; 43/*Millin*, Welensky to Millin, 3 February 1963.
[40] *Ibid.*, 32/38, f. 47, Welensky to Robinson, 2 February 1963; 32/63, f. 42, Welensky's Statement, 1 February 1963.
[41] *Observer*, 3 February 1963; Welensky Papers, 32/63, f. 49, Article in the *Sunday Times*, by Ronald Legge, 3 February 1963.

CHAPTER THIRTY-SIX

The Death Blow

The British Decision to allow Northern Rhodesia to secede, February–March 1963

THE working party to devise the mechanics of Nyasaland's secession would be appointed. Federal and territorial delegations would go to London to search for a formula for a new inter-territorial association. However, Welensky had predicted that the British Government would not be prepared to disappoint the African nationalists, and was proved right as it would yield to their pressure for the secession of Northern Rhodesia. It did so before any real negotiations were conducted and thus gave the Federation its quietus.

If, in late January, Butler believed that he could preserve something of the relationship between the Rhodesias, Colin Legum of the *Observer* rightly thought that he entertained this belief at a time when the situation in Central Africa was filled with uncertainties and tensions. Legum commented on the severity of new Southern Rhodesian legislation, referring to the introduction of a mandatory death sentence for petrol bombing, irrespective of whether it was aimed at persons or property, and to 20-year prison sentences for the possession of offensive weapons, as well as wide powers of search without warrants. However, he failed to observe that Field had released the African nationalist detainees. Nonetheless, Legum's comments on the final days of the negotiations in Salisbury were so accurate that Welensky wondered how much Butler had told him. When questioned by Robinson in London, Butler testily maintained that he was not responsible for what a journalist wrote. Legum also failed to comment on Banda's first statement as Prime Minister that independence for Nyasaland would be insufficient when the Africans in Northern and Southern Rhodesia were not free from the racial domination which he hated.[1]

Legum ignored an incident at Salisbury Airport when Kaunda was returning from Blantyre on the morning of 2 February and had to wait for the

[1] *Observer*, 3 February 1963; Welensky Papers, 32/63, W. S. Parker to Robinson, 5 February 1963; f. 49, Robinson to Parker, 7 February 1963; *The Rhodesia Herald*, 2 February 1963.

evening connecting flight to Lusaka. With him were Simon Kapwepwe and Reuben Kamanga, both of whom were prohibited immigrants like himself in Southern Rhodesia. However, as they were all Ministers of the Crown, Kaunda assumed that they could travel into the city but he was told by the police that he could only do so if he furnished details of where he was going. Nkomo, who had come out to meet him, advised him to refuse. After sleeping on a bench, Kaunda told the Press of his humiliation but vowed that it would not affect his actions because he had more important objectives for his country.[2]

The Southern Rhodesian Government promptly and publicly apologised and declared that it was amending the Inter-Territorial Movement of Persons (Control) Act. It claimed it was merely unfortunate that Kaunda had arrived unannounced before the amendment was through, and noted that, in the past, Kaunda had given details of his movements and had been allowed to leave the airport. It knew that Nkomo had intervened, and regretted that he should have tried to make a racial issue out of a routine procedure which he knew was about to be amended. Despite the apology, Nkumbula, on behalf of Kaunda, threatened to declare the Southern Rhodesian Cabinet prohibited immigrants in Northern Rhodesia.[3]

Welensky informed Lords Avon and Salisbury and others that Butler, after a difficult time, had left a troubled man, worried by the prospect of a debate in the Lords on Britain's broken pledges, by the evident lack of short cuts to any overall solution, and by the knowledge that any decision which he took would be painful for many people. Welensky said he had endeavoured to put "some backbone" into Butler to convince him that only the British Government could play the honest broker because all the other parties were too prejudiced to produce an acceptable compromise. It was Welensky's fear that the British would "walk out" on their kith and kin, as they had in Kenya, after first procrastinating so as to weaken the Federal economy to prevent his Government making a stand. Butler, he said, was also trying to divide him and Field, but with little success so far. Welensky believed that Butler's spokesmen would argue in the Lords that the pledges related mainly to financial affairs and to the encouragement of investment. However, he advised, this argument was quite incorrect. Butler had received a plan for the future of the Federation, but Welensky did not expect him to do much to promote it. He revealed that Butler had secured support from many quarters for a purely economic association, but not from Field, and had been disappointed. Welensky thought that Butler was being unrealistic because Kaunda could only be stringing him along as he (Kaunda) was the current chairman of the Pan-African Freedom Movement of East, Central and Southern Africa and really believed that Field's Government was totally unacceptable and had to be destroyed. He also related that Butler would not order the Northern Rhodesian official Members in the Legislative Council to vote against secession but merely wished them to abstain.[4]

[2] *The Sunday Mail*, 3 February 1963.
[3] *The Rhodesia Herald*, 4 February 1963; *Central African Mail*, 5 February 1963.
[4] Welensky Papers, 27/95, f. 8, Welensky to Lord Avon, 3 February 1963; 43/*Salisbury*, Welensky to Lord Salisbury, 3 February 1963.

On 4 February Welensky apprised his Cabinet fully of the meetings with Butler. Consequently, the Cabinet decided that, amongst other matters, pressure should be applied on Butler to consider the fate of the civil servants in Nyasaland.

The next day, having been briefed by Butler, Robinson had much to report to Welensky. In particular, he had learned that the only constructive suggestion from the Northern Rhodesian African nationalists was the examination of the possibility of a Rhodesian economic association. Butler thought this might be practicable if Field supported it, but knew that a purely economic arrangement would mean the demise of the Federal Government. Butler revealed also that, with great reluctance, he was going to release his interpretation (the White Paper) of the pledges.[5]

Robinson said he had spoken to the pro-Federal MPs, Turton, Wall, Stephen Hastings and Victor Goodhew but, as Wall had already informed Welensky, they believed that the Federation could not survive and thus were anxious for its early dissolution with a simultaneous grant of independence for Southern Rhodesia. They feared any delay because it would reduce the likelihood of Conservative Party support for Southern Rhodesia because a group, led by Humphrey Berkley, opposing a hand-over to the whites, was gaining support.[6]

Although Wall wrote for the second time to Welensky to persuade him to accept the inevitable, he would not. Simultaneously, he was seeking, through van Eeden, to correct an impression amongst a young and restless element in the Northern Rhodesian division of the UFP that the Federal Cabinet was lethargic and defeatist in outlook. He told van Eeden that he suspected that the pressure to which he was being subjected, to accept the loss of the northern territories, was inspired by the British Government.[7]

Welensky's optimism about retaining the ties between the Rhodesias had not yet entirely evaporated because, on 9 February, when he could have been forgiven for taking the bleakest view, he informed Graylin that the difficulties of unravelling the two territories were almost insurmountable. He believed this because Butler had already met severe problems regarding Nyasaland and, without trying to minimise them, they appeared to be negligible when compared with the Rhodesian interdependency. Consequently there was a glimmer of hope that the Rhodesias would not be separated. Be that as it may, Welensky was not in a magnanimous mood and revealed to Graylin that he would make life difficult for Butler. Welensky proposed to arrange to have Butler asked publicly if Monckton had known of the pledges of 1953, even though he (Welensky) knew that Monckton had been informed of them and had ignored their existence.

On 12 February Welensky informed Wall that Field must have disappointed Butler by announcing that Southern Rhodesia would not initiate the destruction of the Federation, because it was clear that Butler had hoped

[5] *Ibid.*, FGC(63), 5th Meeting, Restricted Annexure, Federal Cabinet, 4 February 1963; 20/3, ff. 96–98, Robinson to Welensky, 5 February 1963.

[6] *Ibid.*, 20/3, ff. 99–102, Robinson to Welensky, 5 February 1963.

[7] *Ibid.*, 43/*Wall*, Major P. Wall to Welensky, 6 February 1963; 20/3, f. 95, Welensky to Robinson, 7 February 1963; 31/17, f. 14, Welensky to G. van Eeden, 7 February 1963.

that Field would join those who wanted only an economic association. Wall seemed to think that the northern territories had to sanction the survival of the Federation, but Welensky reminded him that Britain had acted for them in 1953. All that was needed was courage when dealing with Kaunda who, in any case, rode an unsteady horse. Welensky claimed that he would accept the modification of the Federation but would never agree to start all over again. He said that Butler was wisely seeking agreement on an agenda for a conference. However, Welensky believed that the task was impossible because each side was so fully committed to its course.[8]

Although the Federal Speaker warned that he would refuse to summon the Assembly to commit suicide, three days later Welensky informed Butler that he accepted the working party provided it had reasonable terms of reference. Explaining his acceptance to Robinson, Welensky stressed that this did not mean that he no longer considered that the decision on secession had violated the Convention or the pledges or that it would not be disastrous for the Nyasalanders. However, as the decision was irrevocable, he said he was forced to accept it and had to see that it was properly effected. He informed Robinson that Butler's new feeling of urgency arose from pressure from Banda, the Federal refusal to vote supplies for Nyasaland after 30 June, and the desire to withdraw the Federal civil servants as quickly as possible. Robinson had commented that Butler thought that political ties between the Rhodesias could not survive. Welensky said he had gained the same impression and knew also that, although Butler was concentrating on an economic association, he had no ideas on its form and, for the moment, intended to remove Nyasaland and leave the Rhodesias federally linked.

Welensky informed Robinson that he had told Butler it would be disastrous to wait for the dissolution of the Federation before taking a decision on a new association. Butler had disagreed because it was possible that, before anything else might be arranged, intense pressure from the Rhodesias for the dissolution might be irresistible. Indeed, Welensky said, as if to confirm Butler's assertion Field had recently indicated that he would press for dissolution unless a long-term political union between the Rhodesias was guaranteed. (This is an apparent contradiction of what Butler had revealed to the Federal Cabinet on 1 February in saying that Field had told him that he wanted nothing more than economic links.) However, Welensky added, Field had also repeated that he would do nothing to cause the break-up. Welensky confessed that the Federal Government had to evince a co-operative attitude towards Butler's idea of convening a conference to discuss the future of the Rhodesias, otherwise he might hold it without Federal participation. Welensky said he remained willing to consider changes, but still did not think that any purely economic arrangement could survive. Nonetheless, he promised to do everything possible to preserve the Rhodesian ties because breaking them invited disaster. Consequently, he asked Robinson to inform his supporters in the Lords not to press for a conference on the future of the Rhodesias because, despite the harmful uncertainty, it would be better first to discover how the difficulties of extricating Nyasaland affected the British attitude to-

[8] *Ibid.*, 32/100, f. 2, Welensky to J. Graylin, 9 February 1963; 43/*Wall*, Welensky to Wall, 12 February 1963.

wards the problem. He said he would ostensibly welcome such a conference for the reasons he had given. Believing that it would be better to modify the Federation than to destroy it and then attempt to re-form it, he would reveal a new policy shortly, and hoped to use Voice and Vision and his British friends in promoting it.[9]

The next day, 13 February, the British Government released its White Paper, rebutting the charges of bad faith. It contained the confidential verbatim minutes of 19 January 1953 which revealed the discussion on the Federal Review and whether it would impair the financial credit of the Federation. Eastwood had provoked this, the White Paper noted, by questioning whether this provision was a loophole for secession or voluntary liquidation. Consequently, Lyttelton and Swinton had declared that the four Governments would have to agree to the amendment or liquidation of the Constitution. Greenfield had accepted that the Constitution could not be upset without British intervention and that Britain, having created the Federation, could end it. However, he had pointed out they were not discussing the exercise of that power but what could be done at the Review.

As this was so, the White Paper maintained that statements made at the 1953 Conference could not be construed as pledges by British Ministers that no changes would be made in the Federation without the consent of the four Governments, even at the Review. It claimed, erroneously, that until 1962 there was no suggestion that any pledge had been made, forgetting Welensky's arguments in 1959 and 1960 over the Monckton Commission in which he had drawn attention to the pledges. It proclaimed that the Federal and territorial Governments would not have been allowed to have a permanent veto, which would have given each of them the right to demand the perpetuation of the Federation despite the desires of the others. In addition, nothing had been written into the Constitution relating to any pledge and none of the public documents had referred to pledges. If any pledge had been given, there was no reason for secrecy when, for example, the pledges on the protected status had been embodied in the Constitution. The Federal Government had argued that the omission of mention of the right of secession, and Swinton's confirmation thereof, proved the permanence of the Federation. However, the British Government maintained that the omission did not exclude secession in any circumstances because, although it had desired a stable and lasting form of federation, it had been unable to guarantee its permanency. Moreover, the establishment of the Federation had not reduced British responsibilities for the inhabitants of Nyasaland. Later, in changed circumstances, the White Paper observed, the majority of these people had desired secession, and Britain was bound to take notice, particularly when nothing which had been said in 1953 precluded action to satisfy them.[10]

Nevertheless, *The Times,* quoting the comments of Lyttelton (Lord Chandos), Swinton and Greenfield in 1953, concluded that the White Paper

[9] *Ibid.*, 32/63, f. 51a, T. I. F. Wilson to Welensky, 11 February 1963; 20/3, ff. 85–88, Welensky to Robinson, 12 February 1963.

[10] *The Federation of Rhodesia and Nyasaland: Commentary on Statements relating to the establishment of the Federation and their bearing on the withdrawal of Nyasaland,* Command 1948 (London, February 1963).

was fallacious because the pledges could not be denied as Lyttelton had said: "Nothing can liquidate the Constitution unless all four are agreed on it", and had repeated the statement twice. The newspaper reported that, after Swinton had talked about British Parliaments going off their heads, Lyttleton had added the most telling phrase: "Nothing [*sic*, Nobody] is safe from the Sovereign Government repudiating its obligations. In this case, there would have to be four people to do it."[11]

Joelson, in his *East Africa and Rhodesia,* called the White Paper tendentious and denounced it as contemptible when it was read in conjunction with the Federal White Paper. He called the rejection of the pledges "astonishing", and recalled not only the 1957 Convention but also Macmillan's statement in Salisbury in 1960 that the tearing up of the Federal Constitution would be an act of treachery.[12]

By 16 February Welensky had not yet seen the British White Paper, but Greenfield had told him that it was a "miserable affair" because it ignored Welensky's efforts in twice drawing Macmillan's attention to the pledges and, in 1962, apprising Butler of them. To counter it, Evans suggested that Malvern should speak in the Lords debate, but Welensky preferred to leave the defence to Robinson, Lord Salisbury, *et al.* K. M. Goodenough, the former Southern Rhodesian High Commissioner in London, assisted by recalling in *The Daily Telegraph* on 15 February that he had attended all the Federal Conferences and had heard Stockil raise the question of secession, only to be silenced almost immediately by the British constitutional advisers and all the delegates.[13]

Two days earlier, on 14 February, Robinson had addressed the Conservative Commonwealth Council and had commented that the Northern Rhodesian Legislative Council, with the official Members abstaining, had just endorsed a call for secession, by 21 votes to 15. He had added that Field had refused to take the initiative to break up the Federation, although he sought an early decision. Robinson had said that Welensky had proclaimed his willingness to consider radical changes. The tragedy was that the British Government had no real policy, and Robinson had appealed to it to examine the probable catastrophic effects of the secession of Northern Rhodesia. He had called on his audience to persuade Butler to take advantage of what still existed to secure agreement on the Federation's future.[14]

Field partly betrayed Robinson that day by calling for a "clean break". This was welcomed as "realistic" by Kaunda in the Northern Rhodesian legislature where he demanded a new constitution for Northern Rhodesia which would incorporate universal suffrage, with the protection of minorities. He would retain the whites, not for their skills, but because they were human beings. He wished that Field's realism would extend to Southern Rhodesian internal policies.[15]

[11] *The Times*, 14 February 1963.

[12] *East Africa and Rhodesia*, 14 February 1963.

[13] Welensky Papers, 25/152, ff. 87–89, Welensky to Joelson, 16 February 1963; 32/63, f. 54, Evans to Welensky, 16 February 1963; f. 55, Welensky to Evans, 16 February 1963.

[14] *Ibid.*, 32/63, f. 72, Address by Sir Albert Robinson, 14 February 1963.

[15] *The Rhodesia Herald*, 15 February 1963.

Robinson also wrote to *The Times.* He cited Lord Malvern quoting, in the Southern Rhodesian Assembly on 30 September 1953, the British Government's confirmation to the British Council of Churches that the Federal Constitution could be amended by a two-thirds majority and a British act. Malvern had acknowledged that the British Parliament's power to legislate could not be limited but, as the scheme was accepted by the four Governments and the British Parliament, he had believed that "it would be in the foreseeable circumstances morally and politically indefensible for Parliament to enact amendments which have not been similarly agreed". Malvern had added that, once having granted a parliament to any dependent part of the Empire, the British Government would refrain from interfering in its domestic affairs.[16]

In the Lords on 18 February, Lord Listowel asked for the Government's proposals on the Federation and urged that Central Africa should be speedily brought into line with the rest of the Commonwealth. Then he turned to the pledges because, he said, the Government's honour was at stake and many Lords were present to discuss them. He quoted from the minutes of the 1953 Conference and concluded that Lyttelton had pledged Parliament, even though in law it could not be bound. He complimented Robinson on succeeding in *The Times* in destroying the contention that the pledges related only to the Federal Review. Therefore, he denounced the Government for keeping secret a pledge of such enormous importance, although it could not be blamed for breaking it. The dishonesty lay in not admitting that it had been broken when it could have been said that circumstances had changed. The attempt to deny it through the White Paper had only resulted in Britain being despised, as well as distrusted. As the precedent had been set, he urged that Kaunda be told that Northern Rhodesia could secede so that he could discuss future links between the territories.

Lord Ogmore agreed that a pledge had been given, but maintained that Parliament could not be bound by something about which it knew nothing. Lord Swinton, supporting the Government, claimed, like the White Paper, that there had been no references to the pledges until 1962. Indeed, he went further because he denied giving any pledges and said he had, in fact, explained that nothing could fetter Parliament. He recalled Greenfield confirming this when he responded: "The Lord giveth and the Lord taketh away." Referring to Robinson's letter in *The Times,* Swinton confirmed that he had written to the British Council of Churches in 1953, but drew attention to the point he had made to the Council that the commitment, on change having to be endorsed by the Federal and territorial Governments, depended on "foreseeable circumstances". He found further confirmation, that pledges had not been given, in the very necessity to have to include the Convention in the 1957 Declaration, because it had sought to limit the power of Parliament, but only in relation to the powers delegated to the Federal Government. Not understanding that the purpose of the 1957 Declaration was to ensure that Britain did not exercise her theory of sovereignty and legislate for the Federation against its will, Swinton said it was curious that, if the pledges had

[16] *The Times,* 15 February 1963.

existed, Welensky had not insisted that they be included in the Declaration. Instead, he noted, the Declaration had simply re-affirmed the position of 1953. Moreover, he believed that, if there had been pledges, they would have been ignored in the current circumstances.

In the Lords debate, two months earlier (19 December 1962), Lord Chandos had emphatically declared that the agreement of the four Governments was required to change the Federal Constitution and that the pledges on that had been given. However, he now chose to agree with Swinton that they had never contemplated that the four Governments would have a permanent veto, nor had they given pledges thereon. Feeling that Welensky had been betrayed by an act of policy and not by the breaking of a pledge, he decried the Government's failure to call a conference before taking such a step. If that had been done, and it had then been found that the Federation had to be buried, it could have been done decently "without the mourners being seen squabbling round the grave as they are now".

At least Lords Salisbury, Milverton and Colyton remained faithful to the Federal interpretation. Salisbury thought that the British Government had been unworthy in declaring that, if statements did not appear in public documents, they were not binding. The point of the whole argument, he said, was not the British Government's power to do what it had done, but that it had said that it would not do it. Whether pledges had been given or not, the British Ministers had made unequivocal statements which had encouraged the territorial Governments to join the Federation. He believed that the Federal Government, having already been betrayed, should not have to foot the bill. Lord Colyton dismissed as absurd the argument that the pledges had applied only to the Review and that they could no longer apply because it had been suspended. He claimed that there had been no doubt in the minds of those who had attended the Federal Conferences that the sanction of all the parties to the Federation was required for any structural change. They had realised that the Federation could be dissolved by a British act, but no one had suggested that it should be. Like Listowel, Colyton thought that the Government could have merely said that the situation had changed and that the only solution lay in secession. He denounced the Government for failing to support the Federation and for abandoning Southern Rhodesia when it had begun to liberalise its policies.

Nonetheless, the belief of Lord Dilhorne, the Lord Chancellor, in the veracity of the British White Paper remained unshaken. He argued that it was curious that Salisbury and Colyton had never revealed the pledges in Parliament, if they thought them so vital, when there was no justification for secrecy. He regretted that Welensky had not consulted Chandos and Swinton before publishing the confidential documents. He deemed it most unlikely that Welensky would have allowed the Federal Order in Council, containing Article 29(7), to go through without reference to the pledges.[17] However, it will be recalled that in 1953 even Greenfield, much to his subsequent regret, had allowed Article 29(7) to be introduced by the British legal draftsmen.

The Lords debate prompted Sir Raymond Stockil to inform the Press that

[17] House of Lords *Hansard* (London), Vol. 246, Col. 1156 f., 18 February 1963.

in 1953 he had tried unsuccessfully to secure the insertion of a secession clause into the Constitution, as the Conference had been determined to ensure that the Federation could not dissolve. The British Government, and Lord Swinton in particular, had agreed that the only way to guarantee this was to ensure that dissolution was only possible with the consent of the Governments concerned. Thanking Stockil, Welensky told him that he was not surprised by the comments of the Lords, but that they could not change the record which he was quite willing to display publicly. He said he was angry that Chandos should have backpedalled and that Swinton should have supported the Government.[18]

At that moment, Welensky was having to deal with the culmination of the unrest amongst the younger members of the UFP with which van Eeden was associated. They had decided that Welensky was hampered at this crucial moment by his more staid Ministers and wanted them replaced. They believed that the Cabinet was doing little to save the situation. Consequently, Greenfield briefed them on the current negotiations but only provoked one of them, Robert Burns, to claim angrily that he could take over the Party leadership. When he heard this, Welensky responded with customary vigour by suggesting a vote of confidence in the Parliamentary Caucus in his leadership and, knowing at heart that the Federation was finished, Burns and his cohorts did not pursue the matter. However, C. D. Burney advised Welensky to use these men to restore public and Party morale. It was necessary, he said, for the public to understand the consequences of the break-up, and for Field to realise that Southern Rhodesia could not stand alone. Van Eeden added that the Federal Ministers should go to Northern Rhodesia to placate the fears of politicians there.[19]

Welensky thanked Lords Salisbury and Colyton for their support, but forbore from public comment on the Lords debate. Instead, addressing the congress of the UFP's Nyasaland division, he dwelt on Federal history and revealed matters which had hitherto been hidden from the public, such as the commitment by Sandys to Banda. He believed that, in 1962, he had so embarrassed the British Government that it had decided to get rid of him, making him all the more determined to resist. He described the conflict over the Northern Rhodesian Constitution and maintained that, ever since, he had been walking a delicate tightrope, despite his 300 lbs of weight. He confessed to having been mistaken in placing his trust in the British Government. Lords Chandos, Home and Boyd had been men of honour, but the same could not be said of Macmillan and "that jackal Macleod" who had decided five years previously to abandon the Commonwealth as Britain was seeking to enter the Common Market. He had discovered that the "Winds of Change" speech was to have been delivered in South Africa by Butler a year before

[18] Welensky Papers, 32/63, f. 60A, Stockil's Press Conference, 19 February 1963; f. 61, Welensky to Sir Raymond Stockil, 19 February 1963.

[19] Author's interview with Mr Robert Burns; Welensky Papers, 32/63, f. 65, W. S. Parker to Private Secretary, Minister of Law, 19 February 1963, with postscript by Greenfield, 20 February 1963; f. 12, A. Anderson to Welensky, 19 February 1963; f. 13, Welensky to Anderson, 20 February 1963; f. 15, Anderson to Welensky, 22 February 1963; f. 75, Memorandum by C. D. Burney, 25 February 1963; 32/17, f. 27, van Eeden to Welensky, 27 February 1963.

Macmillan did so, but that the South African Prime Minister, Strydom, had become ill, and Butler's visit had been cancelled.

Welensky described Butler as tough and unyielding with a remarkably devious mind. The only occasion, he said, on which Butler had shown any emotion had been when he had informed Butler that the Federation would pay nothing for Nyasaland after 1 July. Welensky declared that his Government had done all it could to prevent the decision of 19 December 1962, because it was as much against its own interests as Nyasaland's. Then, he related, the Federal Government had argued that he who called the tune had to pay the piper. He knew that the Southern Rhodesian Government thought that it could come to terms with the British Government and Kaunda, ignoring his warnings that Kaunda would co-operate only as long as it suited him. Thereafter, Welensky predicted, as chairman of the Pan-African Freedom Movement of East, Central and Southern Africa, Kaunda would ruthlessly turn the screw on Southern Rhodesia.[20]

Simultaneously, Alport was informing the Bulawayo public that, while there was little hope for a political association, economic links could survive if Britain applied pressure on Nyasaland, and the mining companies persuaded Kaunda to co-operate. This effort, Alport believed, could be assisted by the Acting Governor of Northern Rhodesia, R. E. Luyt, who had great influence over Kaunda and had already made him more amenable.[21]

However, Robinson had seen Butler that day and had gathered that the British heart was not in the fight. Even so, Butler had indicated that he would hold preliminary talks in London with the Governments concerned. Robinson had promised that the Federal Government would participate if the basis for discussion was the *status quo* and if the British intended to preserve a constitutional relationship between the Rhodesias. Butler had rejected these conditions because he thought the best way to induce the parties to attend was to widen the basis of the discussion to the broad subject of the future relationship of the Rhodesias. Robinson, though, had demanded that Butler take a positive attitude and attempt to preserve the current constitutional relationship, in whatever form was practicable. However, Butler had only looked exasperated, and Robinson concluded that he was the sort of man who "smiles sweetly, but cuts your throat in the end".

Butler had informed Robinson that Sir George Curtis, the Chief Land Registrar, would chair the working party. Nevertheless, suspecting that the Federal wishes on the terms of reference would be ignored, Robinson had replied that it would be pointless to send Curtis out to the Federation until Welensky had approved the terms of reference. Butler had ignored this suggestion but reluctantly conceded British responsibility for paying for the services in Nyasaland after June. However, he wanted the working party to recommend this. Nevertheless, he would give no assurance on this despite Robinson's demands that his Government should know where it stood.[22]

[20] *Ibid.*, 43/*Salisbury*, Welensky to Lord Salisbury, 22 February 1963; 43/*Colyton*, Welensky to Lord Colyton, 22 February 1963; 32/34, f. 104, Address by Welensky, 20 February 1963.

[21] *Ibid.*, 35/23N, f. 19, J. M. Macdonald to Welensky, 20 February 1963.

[22] *Ibid.*, 20/3, ff. 78–84, Telephone conversation between Welensky and Robinson, 20 February 1963.

Welensky supported Robinson by asking Butler for the dates of the introduction of the Nyasaland Secession Bill and of the Nyasaland Government's take-over of Federal services, because they were vitally needed for the Federal budget. However, before asking this, he reiterated that the violation of the pledges and the 1957 Convention could not be regarded as a precedent for similar action with regard to Northern Rhodesia. Like Robinson, he warned that Federal participation in the working party turned on reasonable terms of reference. He recalled that despite his protests, Butler had allowed the Northern Rhodesian official Members to abstain rather than vote against secession, displaying again the lack of British support for the Federation. Butler had promised that, in abstaining, the official Members would indicate that the British Government did not consider itself bound by the views of the Legislative Council, but even this had not been done. On 4 February, Butler had been quoted in *The Times* as saying that the general view in the Federation was that a new form of association would be preferable, and Welensky wished to correct him because, apart from the African nationalists, there was a large body of opinion which preferred the current association but knew that it might not be preserved because of lack of British support. Welensky closed by trying again to convince Butler of the detrimental effects of the separation of the Rhodesias.[23]

On the next day, 21 February, Welensky met Field twice and gathered that he was beginning to favour a strong stand on the maintenance of both economic and political ties between the Rhodesias. Welensky was determined that, with a little courage, a solution could be found, and he impressed on Field that, as Southern Rhodesia was one of the two high-contracting parties to the Federation, Britain (the other) could not dissolve the Federation without Southern Rhodesian permission. He had also emphasised what the loss of the Northern Rhodesian market would mean to Southern Rhodesia, and Field had listened with friendly interest.[24]

Nevertheless, within two weeks of their meetings, a public campaign, launched by J. A. Clark, to warn the Southern Rhodesians of the dire consequences of dissolution, provoked Field to protest in his Parliament at such interference in the internal affairs of Southern Rhodesia by Federal Ministers. He claimed that they were deliberately trying to undermine his Government. His outburst was rejected by the Federal parliamentarians because they could not see why the truth should be hidden from the public.[25]

Prior to this, Welensky had noticed that only the Europeans of the UFP's Southern Rhodesian division had supported the Federation in their Parliament, and he asked Whitehead to ensure that the Africans did likewise. He did so, he said, because the British always listened to Africans. He thought they could argue that the complete break-up, which was being encouraged by Field, would lead to widespread unemployment, with the consequence that power would pass entirely into the hands of extremists.[26]

Field was not faring too well because, aside from appearing to waver on the

[23] *Ibid.*, ff. 75–77, Welensky to Butler, 20 February 1963.
[24] *Ibid.*, 32/17, f. 19, Welensky to G. van Eeden, 22 February 1963.
[25] *Ibid.*, 32/63, f. 89, Federal Government Press Statement, 6 March 1963.
[26] *Ibid.*, f. 79, Welensky to Whitehead, 27 February 1963.

issue of the survival of the Federation, his Minister of Justice, Dupont, introduced his new, draconian security legislation on 21 February and provoked a storm of protest at home and abroad. However, Dupont said he would allow Nkomo to form a new party provided it acted constitutionally. Be that as it may, Nkomo had already indicated that he would not replace the banned Zimbabwe African People's Union because the successive banning of their Parties had cost him and his colleagues so much. He also refused an invitation to meet Field. Dr S. C. Mundawarara, later Deputy Prime Minister in Bishop Muzorewa's Government, was then approached to lead a new party but refused because he believed that any truly African nationalist party would inevitably be banned. Furthermore, he claimed to have great respect for Nkomo as a leader and condemned the "Settler Government" for attempting to dictate what names Africans could give to their parties, what leaders they should have, and for what cause they would fight. Nonetheless, Field at least puzzled the *Manchester Guardian* by releasing detainees and cultivating good relationships with Africans.[27]

Not only did Welensky seem to be convincing Field, but on 23 February, Blackwood sent news that Banda might be more reasonable. They had met the previous day and Banda had indicated that he would welcome discussion with Barrow and Caldicott on the subject of power supplies. Banda had said that, as secession was conceded, there was no need for him to continue to be difficult, but Blackwood wondered if the absence from Nyasaland of "Malawi" Jones was responsible for this softening of attitude. Banda had good-humouredly accepted that Welensky might terminate Federal services in July, and agreed that Welensky should press Butler to ensure that Britain underwrote them. Banda had thought that Southern Rhodesia would have to pay something for a customs union, and Blackwood accepted that as fair. He had asked about the fate of the Federal civil servants and Banda had reassured him that he would need all the African civil servants. He had stated there would be no victimisation, although those who had offended local politicians might not be required. Blackwood had asked about the trespassers on freehold land and Banda said he had been asking them to move. Banda had thought that Butler was playing for time to see how Kaunda would fare. Blackwood had mentioned his meeting with Banda to Nyasaland's Acting Governor, R. S. Foster, to his evident displeasure. Indeed, Foster was appalled that any dates should be discussed, because the working party had to complete its work first. Blackwood concluded that the Federal Government should be wary of the Nyasaland officials for fear of sabotage. He disliked Foster's attitude and found it identical to that of Jones. Accordingly, Blackwood advised that Barrow arrange a meeting direct with Banda, to ensure it was not sabotaged.[28]

While Burns and other Northern Rhodesians considered the Federal Cabinet to be lethargic, in late February three of the Federal Ministers, Graylin, Duncan and Owen effectively answered them by producing for the Cabinet a comprehensive survey of policy and possibilities. They argued that,

[27] *The Rhodesia Herald*, 21 February 1963; *African Daily News*, 8 February 1963; *Manchester Guardian*, 23 February 1963.

[28] Welensky Papers, 32/63, f. 68, Report by Blackwood, 23 February 1963.

as long as Britain had the power to alter the Federal Constitution, permanency was impossible. While the British retained this power, the African nationalists would play up to the Commons to gain what they wanted. Thus Britain had to be persuaded to give up that power — by negotiation, unconstitutional action, or the threat of it — lest everything which had been built be destroyed and the association of the Rhodesias lost forever. The Federal control of finance and defence empowered the Federal Government to refuse to implement any British decision to dissolve the Federation. Such a course would be attended by various risks, such as intervention by the United Nations, but it could ensure that the British Government did not commit the folly of attempting the dissolution. Moreover, a confrontation with the British Government would bring the wavering Southern Rhodesians to defend the Federation.

Graylin, Duncan and Owen knew that the best form of association between the Rhodesias was one which was based on agreement, provided that constitutional change was impossible unless the Federal Government agreed. However, they believed that it was unlikely that the African leaders would agree to serve under a white Federal Prime Minister unless the British displayed some courage and applied pressure on them.

The alternative, the three Ministers said, was an economic association in which the Federal Government would have no role. This would only loosen the ties while giving greater power to the northern African nationalists. Kaunda would demand that he be represented at the UN and that he should be able to control anything which smacked of discrimination, such as separate education. He would want to control a fair part of the economy and share the management of the rest. Southern Rhodesia would want full independence, access to the northern markets, and an association which would protect white interests. The central authority of the association would have to control customs, finance and certain other services, as well as aspects of the association which could be used by one partner against the other, such as the armed services and broadcasting.

The problem, they said, was to create a semi-permanent commission entrusted with the making of policy, which would not fall under the influence of the African nationalists. An elected body would be prey to such influence, and the only alternative was a commission appointed equally by the Rhodesian Governments. Together they could choose the chairman, and each could have three members on the commission. It would be assisted by a council of ministers comprising the two Rhodesian prime ministers and their finance ministers, and by an assembly which would be essentially only a forum for debate. If this did not work, then nothing would. The aim would be the realisation of broad, and not party, objectives. The non-racial aspect could be ensured by prescribing that Northern Rhodesia should appoint a non-African commissioner and Southern Rhodesia a non-European one. Within the commission, rule would be by majority and thus the choice of the first chairman would be crucial. The necessary curb on the commission would be provided by the council of ministers.

Graylin, Duncan and Owen allocated £38 000 000 for the services which would be retained centrally. These were finance, economic affairs, defence, power, the public service, transport, meteorology, commerce and industry, law, broadcasting, tourism, archives and aspects of public works. The territories would take over external affairs, aspects of finance, roads, prisons, immigration, parks, information, education, health, agriculture and public works, all of which currently cost £31 000 000. The British Government would have to relinquish all its powers, and any constitutional changes would have to be sanctioned by both Rhodesian Governments. Neither territory would be able to destroy the association unilaterally, and the commission would have delaying powers to prevent anything from being done in anger.

They believed that Kaunda would be attracted to the idea because it would offer him certain and rapid achievement of independence. However, if he were to be persuaded, there could be no delay. Southern Rhodesia would be drawn by the prospect of the immediate independence which it would not otherwise obtain without greater African representation. There remained, however, great dangers of a breakdown through African rivalries, disenchantment in the civil service, and a European exodus because of the integration of education.

They argued that if, instead, the Federation simply dissolved, Pan-Africanism would claim a triumph and then concentrate on destroying Southern Rhodesia. These consequences were so unpleasant that the British Government could not be allowed to destroy the Federation. The correct solution was to maintain the Federation, but the British Government would not co-operate. The economy was running down and Britain would inevitably dissolve the Federation within two or three years. However, the struggle to maintain the Federation could be continued for the moment. When the British Government finally lost patience with the Federation, the proposed commission could be advanced as an alternative. If then there were no agreement, the Federal Government would have to act unconstitutionally, and, with the backing of the Europeans, it had a fair chance of success. Chaos might ensue, but it could be no worse than that which would attend the break-up of the Federation.[29]

Reviewing these ideas for Welensky, Greenfield thought that their authors had not understood that Britain had already decided on dissolution. The correct alternative was an economic link, which Field favoured, but Greenfield was tempted to hang on grimly in the hope that the excision of Nyasaland would prove so difficult that the cutting of the Rhodesian ties could not be contemplated. However, he knew that everything depended on Field and thus urged that no effort should be spared in wooing him. He thought, however, that it was necessary to have an alternative plan for implementation when the forces of division became too strong to resist. He doubted whether so many functions (as suggested in the commission proposal) should be retained when, for example, defence depended on loyalty to a regime, and he suggested that it would be better for Southern Rhodesia to be responsible for the air force and the white units of the army, even if it needed South African backing.[30]

However, when Welensky thanked Graylin, Duncan and Owen for their

[29] *Ibid.*, f. 98, Memorandum by Graylin, Duncan and Owen, "Future of the Rhodesias", (undated).
[30] *Ibid.*, f. 98, Greenfield's Comments, 27 February 1963.

efforts, events had overtaken their proposal.[31] In any case, any further consideration was interrupted by a debate in the Commons on 28 February in which Butler fastened on the statements of Swinton and Chandos with delight. He declared that it was of great significance that the two Secretaries of State who had participated in the 1953 discussions should have said that the pledges did not exist and that the Federation had been founded in the hope that it would endure but that they had never intended to fetter Parliament. He said that they had certainly not granted anyone a permanent veto and that the omission of a clause on secession did not imply a guarantee of permanence. The recent White Paper had proved that the creation of the Federation had not impaired Britain's responsibility for Nyasaland so that, when the people of that territory had wanted to secede, their wishes had to be granted.

Butler denied that he had failed to consult the Governments over secession. To the contrary, he claimed that he had discussed the matter fully with them since the beginning of his Ministry. He had not been able to give the firm assurance which had been demanded, on the continuation of the association between the Rhodesias, because of his obligation to Nyasaland. Dealing with other matters, he exonerated his Government from implication in the introduction of the mandatory death sentence in Southern Rhodesia because it was powerless to intervene. He revealed that Nkomo was free to indulge in political activity because recent charges laid against him under the Southern Rhodesian Law and Order (Maintenance) Act had yet to be heard.

Butler described his visit to the Federation and his decision that a working party should examine the consequences of secession. He maintained that his Government would seek an acceptable association of the territories to preserve the benefits of the Federation and acknowledged that an economic link was best supported by political ties. However, the attitude of the leaders, except for Field, made a political arrangement unlikely. The Northern Rhodesian elected Ministers had made it clear that they sought a promise that their Constitution would be reformed before they attended any conference which sought to devise a new association.

Healey dismissed Butler's speech as "a travel diary", because he had given no solution to the Federal problem. Like Listowel, Healey maintained that pledges had been given which were binding in common honour and decency. Wondering why they had been kept secret, he decided that the reason was that, otherwise, the British Parliament would have refused to found the Federation. Consequently, doubt had been thrown on all British pledges. What was more, the precedent had been set for Northern Rhodesia to be granted secession. It seemed absurd that the territorial Governments should have to negotiate with a doomed Federal Government and it was better to accept Field's advice to allow the territories to deal separately with each other. There should be no delay to deny the Federal Government any opportunity for the abuse of power. Indeed, the Federation should be dissolved immediately in case frustration led to terrorism. He felt that economic co-operation between the Rhodesias depended on the political advancement

[31] *Ibid.*, f. 99, Welensky to J. P. G. Duncan, 7 March 1963.

of the Africans in Southern Rhodesia, and believed that it would soon be painfully obvious to the Europeans that their economic survival depended on conceding that right. He had known Field in the British Army and knew that he would soon succeed in moving the Europeans in the direction in which Whitehead had tried to lead them.

Nevertheless, Healey abhorred the current security measures and demanded that Butler should declare that independence for Southern Rhodesia would be withheld until African majority rule had been introduced.

After Stonehouse, Wall and others had spoken on the pledges and other matters, the debate was closed by the Attorney-General, Sir John Hobson, who gave the, by now, standard exoneration of the attitude towards the pledges.[32] As Hobson had made two mistakes of fact, Greenfield wrote to him correcting, in particular, his statement that, until 1962, Welensky and Greenfield had never mentioned the pledges. Greenfield pointed out that they had been raised before then and Hobson agreed to issue a correction. However, a year would pass before he did so.[33] On 4 March Welensky commented on the Commons debate through the Press and Federal broadcasting services. He reported on the problems to be faced following Butler's visit and the British debates and denounced the decision on secession as wrong in essence and harmful to the interests of Nyasalanders. He was confident that history would confirm this. He announced that there would be a British act on secession and that Banda wanted it by 6 July. All parties were agreed that, if the decision on Nyasaland's secession were irrevocable, it was best that it should be implemented quickly. Butler had announced the appointment of a working party, and the Federal Government had agreed to serve on it if its terms of reference were acceptable. It would study in particular the apportionment of the public debt and the fate of the Federal civil servants. He did not feel that the Federal taxpayer should support Nyasaland, and thought the British Government should assume responsibility for the £5 000 000 so required.

Welensky acknowledged that, after the announcement of 19 December 1962, many people had concluded that the Federation was dead. Too many had presumed that the British Government would thereafter separate the Rhodesias and that the inhabitants would meekly submit. He was determined to resist, and quoted Butler's statement of 19 December that the constitutional arrangement between the Rhodesias was unaffected. Butler believed, he said, that the economic strength of the area would not be impaired by secession and that its basic minerals and agriculture provided a basis for an expanding economy. After all, on 10 July, Butler had urged people to invest in the Federation and surely would not have done so if he had intended its destruction. Welensky attached the greatest importance to these statements and said he had discussed the future relationship of the Rhodesias with Butler on his recent visit to the Federation. Butler had arrived without any plan but, since his return to London, had spoken of the possibility of discussions with the individual Governments, to be followed, perhaps, by a general conference.

Welensky said that, in the short history of the Federation, he had witnessed the sorry spectacle of the British Government retreating in the face of

[32] House of Commons *Hansard* (London), Vol. 672, Col. 1458 f., 28 February 1963.

[33] J. M. Greenfield, *Testimony of a Rhodesian Federal* (Bulawayo, 1978), pp. 216–217.

extreme African nationalism and the bowing to the threats of a relatively small minority, while ignoring the interests of the masses. The British Government had sacrificed the ideals of racial co-operation on which the Federation was founded and, by excising Nyasaland, had endangered the historic relationship between the Rhodesias, and the security of their people.

Welensky revealed that he had consistently asked about the re-arrangement of the Federation, arguing that it was the British Government's responsibility to propose a positive, durable plan for the future of all, because it had chosen to appease African nationalism. He was willing to co-operate but was aware of the machinations to get rid of him and of comments that there was no room for a Bismarck in Central Africa. He knew of the propaganda depicting him as an obstinate man blindly refusing to see reality and obstructing change. It was utterly untrue, he said, as he had often indicated to the British Government that he would consider even radical changes, but not the scrapping of everything to start again. He was fully aware of the Pan-African intention to destroy the Federation and that there were some in the Federal ranks who believed that, through the appeasement of African nationalism, economic links could be retained. However, he knew that, once the Federation had gone, Pan-Africanism would isolate Southern Rhodesia. The Zambezi River would become the defence line, and every effort would be made to apply trade boycotts and to stir up violence within Southern Rhodesia.

Welensky promised he would negotiate on any change, attend any conference, but would never be a party to the disintegration of the Rhodesias in pursuit of the illusion of economic links. He was not willing to weaken the defence forces, either because of a lack of finance or to appease African nationalists, because the result would be an increasing use of violence to gain domination. It was his duty to make everyone, including the British, aware of the consequence of disintegration. He was not an alarmist, but, as a realist, knew that the well-being of all was at stake in the current negotiations. He only wished that the British would stand by the Rhodesians as they had stood by the British in two world wars. This was a criticism of the British Government and not of its people because many of them had written expressing distaste for the Government's policy. Not only had pledges been broken, but the position of Southern Rhodesia, as a high-contracting party to federation, had been ignored.

Welensky said he was having a White Paper on the consequences of dissolution prepared and asked for support for further negotiations as it would be a mistake to refuse them when the British Government might yet be persuaded not to destroy the Federation. As defeatism was pointless, the Rhodesians had to show courage, grit and determination. As their cause was just, they would succeed.[34]

Before uttering these brave words, Welensky had met his Cabinet and had reported that Butler proposed to see the Southern and Northern Rhodesian and Federal Governments — in that order — in London. Field could not leave until 21 March, so Alport had suggested that the process begin on 24 March. Welensky had demanded that the talks should overlap, in order that

[34] Welensky Papers, 32/63, f. 84, Welensky's Broadcast, 4 March 1963.

the public should not think that his Government was being isolated. He had also warned that he would withdraw the Federal services from Nyasaland on 1 July. Thus he had demanded an early agreement on the financing of the services, if they would be maintained, because the Federal civil servants would soon have to be given the three months' notice to which they were entitled. To maintain the services at the current level, he was asking the British to provide £270 000 a month.

The mention of Alport provoked the Cabinet to decide to protest to Butler about the manner in which Alport had discharged his duties. Doubts were also cast on the ability of the Nyasaland Government to cope with the problems of secession as, despite a bewildering array of problems, it did not seem to be considering the hand-over exercise properly. However, Banda's reassurance that the Federal civil servants would not be victimised, and would be re-employed, was welcomed and care was to be taken not to force him to act in any way. Barrow had visited Nyasaland and said he had reassured the Federal officials that they would not be compulsorily transferred or seconded to the Nyasaland Government and that, if they wished, they would be employed in the Rhodesias. Abolition of office terms would only be offered when an officer could not be employed elsewhere. Barrow had hoped to discuss these matters with Banda, but the meeting had been cancelled and Blackwood suspected sabotage by the Nyasaland officials.[35]

Two days later, on 6 March, Butler formally invited the Governments to London for preparatory talks for a conference. The first to meet him would be the Southern Rhodesians on 21 March, followed by the Northern Rhodesians on 25 March, and the Federal Government on the next day. Robinson saw Butler immediately and reported to Welensky that the working party would only consider the problems of the secession of Nyasaland, including the amount of British subsidy. Butler asked that notices of transfer or otherwise for the Federal civil servants should be withheld until the working party had resolved the financial arrangements. He promised to ensure that, in London, the delegations talked to each other and not just to him.[36]

The criticism of Alport reached such proportions that Barrow informed Welensky that day that the senior Federal Ministers were offended by his lack of tact. Indeed, they were appalled that, when last they met him, on 27 February, he should have seen fit to lecture Welensky "in the most offensive manner". Caldicott and Greenfield reiterated that they found Alport unsuitable to represent Britain. Barrow agreed, and recalled Alport's "pompous" behaviour at Ndola at the time of the Hammarskjold crash. He had often wondered if Alport had conveyed to Butler the correct impressions of discussions and events in the Federation and if he had accurately transmitted Butler's views to Welensky. However, the Federal Ministers ignored these doubts and based their verdict on Alport's unsuitability on his "unfortunate personality". They believed that he had recently tried to play the territorial Governments against them, and had so overstepped the mark that he had destroyed his relationship with the Federal Government.[37]

[35] *Ibid.*, FGC(63), 8th Meeting, Restricted Annexure, Federal Cabinet, 4 March 1963.
[36] *Ibid.*, 33/21, f. 9a, Telephone conversation between Welensky and Robinson, 6 March 1963.
[37] *Ibid.*, f. 15, Barrow to Welensky, 6 March 1963. As British High Commissioner, Lord Alport had

Barrow wanted to protest to Butler about Alport but Welensky was more preoccupied with Field. He told Joelson how difficult it had been to avoid antagonising Field unnecessarily in his recent broadcast. Yet he had felt he had to warn the Southern Rhodesians of the consequences of the break-up. Field had not attacked him for this, but had not spared Clark. Although Field was popular in Britain, Welensky found him ineffectual and unable to support multi-racialism, because he had been elected to secure white supremacy.[38]

The same day, 9 March, Welensky sympathised with Blackwood over the sabotaging of Barrow's meeting with Banda. Instead, Barrow had seen Chipembere and Chiume and they had told him that they intended to be as difficult as possible. On the Southern Rhodesian issue, Welensky expressed the hope to Blackwood that Field would not allow the British to isolate him. He thought that Field realised that he would be taken "for a ride" because the British wanted to blame him for the failure to retain the Rhodesian political ties.[39]

Two days later Welensky and Field discussed Southern Rhodesia's position should the Federation be dissolved, as well as the fate of the Federal civil servants, and the talks in London. By that day, Butler had finally refused to subsidise the Federal services in Nyasaland and proposed that the working party should devise an orderly transfer. However, both he and Sir George Curtis had seemed to accept that the Federal Government would not subsidise Nyasaland after 30 June, and they had decided that the position of the Federal civil servants had thus to be examined urgently. Barrow had discussed this problem with the Nyasaland Government but had failed to come to an agreement because the latter demanded their compulsory secondment to the Nyasaland service.[40]

Via Robinson came a warning to Welensky from Lord Lambton that the British Government had irrevocably decided to dissolve the Federation. It intended to try to establish an economic relationship but would not be surprised if it failed. Lambton doubted that Southern Rhodesia would be granted independence at the dissolution because, although Macmillan and Butler might be prepared to consider independence, Macleod would ensure that they went no further by threatening to resign, confident of the support of the progressives and radicals in the Conservative Party. Macmillan had no stomach for a crisis but might replace Macleod as chairman of the Party with Selwyn Lloyd. Therefore, Lambton advised Welensky to "play it along" until April, when Cabinet changes were likely. Any move before then could

been in charge of the arrangements for the meeting between Hammarskjold and Tshombe. The reason for this was that Britain was responsible for persuading both men to meet. The Federal Government had merely provided a neutral venue at Ndola Airport. Presumably Barrow and others of the Federal Government had taken exception to the manner in which Alport had discharged his duties. Alport had also, in the previous year, introduced the innovation of the Conference of the northern Governors which met under his chairmanship. This replaced the heads of Governments meetings and isolated the Federal Government from the northern Governors. As Sir David Scott rightly notes (D. Scott, *Ambassador in Black and White: Thirty Years of Changing Africa* (London, 1981), pp. 91–92) this was much resented by Welensky and his Cabinet. — JRTW.

[38] Welensky Papers, 24/152, ff. 74–77, Welensky to F. S. Joelson, 9 March 1963.

[39] *Ibid.*, 32/63, f. 101, Welensky to Blackwood, 9 March 1963.

[40] *Ibid.*, FGC(63), 9th Meeting, Restricted Annexure, Federal Cabinet, 11 March 1963.

prompt Macleod to resign, at a moment when there was mounting criticism of Macmillan's Government.[41]

On 18 March, the Federal Cabinet asked Welensky to raise again with Butler the reimbursement for services in Nyasaland, because the doubt over it was delaying consideration of the Federal budget.[42] It did not comment on a report of a political rally in Northern Rhodesia at which Kaunda declared that he would not compromise on secession. He warned that, if secession were not granted, his Party would render it impossible for any Federal department to operate in Northern Rhodesia. He would not accept an economic association without secession and amendment of the Southern Rhodesian Constitution (to allow for African majority rule).[43]

Nkomo followed Kaunda's lead and, at a meeting with Butler in London on 21 March, demanded British intervention in Southern Rhodesia because a new Defence of the Constitution Bill threatened him with 20 years' imprisonment if he did not dismantle his Party's office in Tanganyika and discontinue all political discussion outside Southern Rhodesia. After claiming that thousands of people were being arrested in Southern Rhodesia and that the police were planting bombs in houses, he threatened not to return home unless Butler immediately convened a constitutional conference to provide Southern Rhodesia with both majority rule and independence. Butler replied that the long-standing Convention of 1923 forbade him from acting unilaterally in this matter. It sickened the Federal Cabinet to see how he relied on this Convention while discounting their identical Convention of 1957.[44]

Field arrived in London that day and declared that, while the Federation was doomed, he hoped to secure an alternative association which would include an economic relationship with Nyasaland. Welensky remained convinced that Butler was trying to isolate him by seeing Field and Kaunda first in the hope that Field would agree to the announcement of the secession of Northern Rhodesia. Welensky believed the objective was to be able to present him with a *fait accompli.* Field was aware of this tactic, and Welensky thought that, if the British promised Field independence for Southern Rhodesia, he would sanction the announcement. Welensky gathered that Field's aim was to put Southern Rhodesia out of the reach of the UN because the Committee of Twenty-Four was again demanding change. Although Welensky had no hope of holding the Rhodesias together, he knew that Field considered an economic association possible. However, he felt that Field had not realised that Kaunda was his sworn enemy and would only deal with him while they shared the common aim of destroying the Federation.[45]

The minutes of the meetings between Field and Butler have not been seen, but Macmillan provides a glimpse of them by describing a luncheon with the Southern Rhodesians on 22 March. Macmillan found Field sensible, tough but not conceited. Dupont, who was with them, seemed clever but un-

[41] *Ibid.*, 32/21, f. 43, Robinson to Welensky, 14 March 1963.
[42] *Ibid.*, FGC(63), 10th Meeting, Restricted Annexure, Federal Cabinet, 18 March 1963.
[43] *The Rhodesia Herald*, 18 March 1963.
[44] *Glasgow Herald*, 22 March 1963; *Northern News*, 22 March 1963.
[45] *Glasgow Herald*, 22 March 1963; Welensky Papers, 31/87, f. 20, Welensky to T. I. F. Wilson, 22 March 1963.

impressive. Field informed Macmillan that the Federation was doomed and that Welensky was unlikely to attempt a *coup d'état* — this possibility clearly continued to worry the British Government. Field thought that Welensky had lost even the support of the Europeans, but Macmillan warned him that Welensky might try to hold a referendum. If Welensky loaded the question, he said, he might win by a great majority and claim a success for himself and a defeat for Field. Field appeared sceptical (as well he might, as Welensky had not thought of such action) but rather alarmed. Field raised the question of the independence which his Southern Rhodesians wanted, foreseeing difficulties of acceptance into the Commonwealth. However, he felt that, if Southern Rhodesia were spurned, an economic and defence relationship with South Africa could be developed. He did not think that the secession of Northern Rhodesia would be vital. Macmillan replied that the dissolution of the Federation had to precede the granting of independence to the three territories. First to be settled also would be an economic or other association.[46]

Butler and Dupont record that, at their meetings, the Southern Rhodesians demanded independence but Butler would not consider it until the Land Apportionment Act had been repealed and a third of the parliamentary seats filled by Africans to prevent any tampering with the Constitution. He expected the qualifications of the upper roll to be lowered to broaden its membership. Field replied that he would not assist in the dissolution of the Federation unless Southern Rhodesia was independent on an equal footing with the other territories. Although Butler denies it, Dupont recalls hearing him assure Field that, if he co-operated and attended the dissolution conference, Southern Rhodesia would be granted independence. Later, Butler repeated this to Dupont who had been left behind in London to secure the promise in writing. Butler, however, would not provide it.[47]

On 25 March, it was the turn of Kaunda and Nkumbula to lunch with Macmillan and the latter has described it as "a very sticky luncheon", despite the presence of Butler, Dilhorne, Macleod and Sir Keith Joseph. Afterwards, they met Butler who sat at the head of a T-shaped table flanked by Hone and Luyt, and heard him explain again the difficulties and dangers of secession. After about 15 minutes, Kaunda interrupted him, politely warning that they had made up their minds and simply wished to know if secession would be allowed. Shaken considerably, Butler replied that the situation was more complex than that and urged consideration of his arguments. At what appeared to be a pre-arranged signal, the delegation stood up, apologised for the necessity of their action, but declared they could no longer listen. They proposed to await Butler's answer on secession at their hotel. They then left the room.

Remarking that this had never happened to him before, Butler asked Luyt, who was — and remains — a good friend of Kaunda, to catch the delegation before it left the building. Hurrying, Luyt found the delegates on the stairs

[46] H. Macmillan, *At the End of the Day* (London, 1973), p. 325.

[47] C. Dupont, *The Reluctant President* (Bulawayo, 1978), p. 130; Lord Butler, *The Art of the Possible: The Memoirs of Lord Butler* (London, 1973), p. 227. Greenfield doubts Dupont's version because he believes that Butler was far too astute to give any such promise and certainly would not have done so with a witness present. — The Hon. J. M. Greenfield to the Author, 22 January 1981.

and asked them to return because one did not walk out of a meeting with the Secretary of State. They politely declined but agreed not to say anything to the Press until Luyt had seen them again. They were as good as their word, and only after Luyt had spoken to them again did Kaunda and Nkumbula tell the Press how they had come to London expecting to be given the right to secede, only to be confronted with an agenda for further negotiations. They were adamant that the British Government had to allow secession before they would talk about anything else.[48]

Luncheon with Macmillan did not precede the Federal delegation's discussions with Butler. At their first meeting, on 26 March, they were told that the objective was to arrange a conference on the Rhodesian relationship and the possibility of retaining some links with Nyasaland. Butler said that he lacked fixed ideas but wanted to retain many features of the Federation. Field, he revealed, was prepared to attend such a conference because he believed that the current situation could not continue. Then he briefly described the walkout of the Northern Rhodesians. They would not attend the conference, he said, unless their demand for secession was conceded. However, he could not answer them until he had the Federal Government's views on the conference.

Welensky had seen Field in London and replied that he wished to study the proposed association because Field had indicated that dissolution would be contingent on the settlement of new relationships. Butler thought this was reasonable because he was seeking only the Federal terms for attendance and not the agenda of the conference. However, somewhat suspicious, Welensky then asked if the current purpose was to secure his agreement to the British Government giving the Northern Rhodesian delegation the right of veto on the holding of the conference unless it received the prior right of secession. Butler denied this but said the Northern Rhodesian position was serious. Welensky reiterated doggedly that he had come to discuss the agenda but was now being told that Northern Rhodesia would be given the prior right to secede and therefore he had been brought to London on false pretences. Butler, however, claimed that his Government had thought that Northern Rhodesia would agree to settle the new association first. Thus the current impasse was a totally new development in the past 24 hours.

Greenfield reminded Butler of the Federal view that the existing association should not first be demolished in the hope of building a new one. Butler hastily confirmed that it would survive until a new basis had been negotiated, but Greenfield and Welensky warned that, if Northern Rhodesia obtained the prior right to secede, the conference would be pointless because all British and Federal options would have been thrown away. Welensky felt that all that was needed was for the British to tell the Northern Rhodesians firmly that they could raise any matter at the conference. Otherwise, to allow one party to threaten trouble over a precondition was intolerable. If firmness were shown, the Northern Rhodesians would undoubtedly attend because they were anxious to demolish the Federation and reform the Northern Rhodesian Constitution.

[48] Macmillan, *At the End of the Day*, *op. cit.*, p. 326; Author's interview with Sir Richard Luyt.

Chad Chipunza, of the Federal delegation, commented bitterly that it was clear from its evasiveness and vacillation that the British Government was no longer interested in the fate of the Federation's inhabitants. Robinson asked how the British Government could allow a prior right to secede and yet maintain that anything could be discussed. He wondered why the other parties were not allowed to make such stipulations. Butler answered that he had only outlined the situation to see how it could be met. The Federal Government, after all, he said, had responsibilities in this matter because of its authority. Welensky replied that the major responsibility lay with the British Government and it would be an impossible situation if one party, which did not have responsible government, was allowed to make a commitment which bound all other parties. Lewanika attempted to correct Butler's impression that Kaunda and Nkumbula represented the wishes of all Africans, and reminded him that Kaunda had rejected any association with Southern Rhodesia until it was governed by Africans. Butler replied that, on the previous day, Kaunda had nonetheless indicated that, on certain conditions, he would meet the Southern Rhodesians. Welensky concluded that this meant that Field would assist Kaunda in breaking up the Federation. Butler agreed, but Welensky then claimed that Field did not want the dissolution until the new association was settled.

Greenfield asked for the British ideas on the association but warned that the Federal Government would not suggest anything because that was the duty of those who wished to destroy the Federation. Caldicott added that there were advantages in a British initiative because ideas advanced by one Central African government would be automatically rejected by the other. Robinson joined this chorus, saying that the Federal Government was entitled to know the broad aims of the British Government. He wondered if Britain intended to dissolve the Federation and withdraw from the area as quickly as possible, as her habit was always to capitulate in the face of threats.

Butler maintained that no association could endure unless based on consent, but he still favoured the closest links between the Rhodesias. Getting down to some detail, he said he would prefer that defence was dealt with centrally, but thought it unlikely. The conduct of external affairs was an even more difficult problem because of the divergent views of the Rhodesias. He doubted whether his Government could adopt a more forceful attitude towards Northern Rhodesia because it had no troops in the area. He asked for Welensky's views and received the reply that there was more at stake than holding the conference. It was more important to discover who was going to maintain law and order. Butler did not answer, but said that, if Northern Rhodesia rejected the conference, the Federal Government could not prevent it from announcing that it wished to secede. He asked what could be discussed at the conference and if Welensky would stipulate that the constitutional ties had to be retained. Welensky thereupon rejected any pre-conditions lest the situation become impossible. Caldicott thought that Kaunda's chairmanship of the Pan-African Freedom Movement of East, Central and Southern Africa could not be ignored and that clearly he was subjected to external pressures.

Greenfield maintained that experience had shown that appeasement did not encourage the African leaders to be more reasonable, but Butler pointed out that, on the contrary, Banda had been prepared to consider a future association once he had secured the date of Nyasaland's secession. The meeting closed with Welensky commenting that he had come to London in a reasonable mood, prepared to discuss the vital issues at stake, when he could have adopted an entirely passive attitude and merely watched the British Government attempt to implement its wishes.[49]

Although nothing was said in the minutes of this meeting, there was a complaint laid against Luyt for his obstructive behaviour as Acting Governor of Northern Rhodesia. Consequently, Butler summoned him to say that the Federal delegates had refused to negotiate until the charges they had laid were answered. Butler proposed to chair a meeting between them and Luyt. Considerably taken aback, Luyt retorted that this proposal reminded him of the headmaster settling disputes between the boys. He suggested that he should see Welensky. Butler concurred and Luyt telephoned Welensky who promptly agreed.[50] At the second meeting, in the afternoon, Butler and Welensky confirmed the arrangement with Luyt. Then the Federal complaints against the Northern Rhodesian Government were aired. Welensky criticised the officials for not correcting certain statements which blamed the Federal Government for matters which were entirely the responsibility of the Northern Rhodesian Government. Agreeing, the other Federal Ministers claimed that these had included personal attacks on Welensky. Butler explained that, despite Welensky's request that the officials should vote against the secession motion in the Legislative Council, he had hesitated because it could mean that the officials would oppose their elected colleagues. For that reason, he had instructed them to abstain. Nevertheless, he promised to review the situation with Hone and Luyt.

Welensky commented on Kaunda's threats and, in particular, one on 17 March that, if the language of peace and co-operation failed, the British Government would be held responsible. Kaunda had added that, if his delegation did not obtain its way in London, through non-co-operation, the Federal Government would be prevented from operating in Northern Rhodesia. Welensky decried as impossible the situation where Ministers of the Crown were allowed thus to threaten another of the Queen's Governments. In addition, he maintained that Kaunda, as chairman of the Pan-African Movement, was bent on the destruction of the Southern Rhodesian Constitution, all of which was incompatible with his oath of allegiance to the Queen.

Greenfield described these threats as direct violations of the Federal Constitution. As undertakings were given to the Barotse National Government against unconstitutional acts by the Northern Rhodesian Government, Greenfield argued that the same should be accorded to the Federal Government. Welensky felt that he could not be blamed if he deployed his forces to protect Federal installations, but Butler thought it would be awkward to use the Northern Rhodesian Police against Northern Rhodesia's principal Minister, Kaunda, if he instituted his threats against the Federal Government. Greenfield replied that the Federal Supreme Court could judge such action to be unconstitutional and force the Northern Rhodesian Police to act. Butler

[49] Welensky Papers, 20/3, ff. 61–67, Minutes of a Meeting with Butler, 26 March 1963.
[50] Author's interview with Sir Richard Luyt.

avowed that his Government would not tolerate a deterioration of law and order led by a Minister. He also recognised the right of the Federal Government to use force to maintain order, even if it could not use it to preserve the Federation. Welensky declared that the Northern Rhodesian Ministers had to realise their responsibilities, and thought that Greenfield should discuss this problem with Luyt.

Welensky's final complaint was that the balance of power achieved at the Northern Rhodesian election had been destroyed by Butler ordering the nomination of a woman (to represent women's interests), and Hone selecting one from Kaunda's Party. Welensky suggested an additional nomination of a member of the UFP to restore the balance. A British official, D. Watson, replied that the Governor was empowered to nominate one or two Members to represent interests neglected by the election. He said that Hone had thought that a woman was needed. However, Watson claimed to be unaware of her political affiliation. Concluding the meeting, Butler promised an investigation and said that he had not been properly briefed when he had endorsed the appointment.[51]

Welensky and his Ministers met Luyt but immediately excused themselves and left him with Greenfield and a list of complaints. During the following three hours, Luyt answered some of these but could not satisfy Greenfield on them all.[52]

On the same day, Nkomo addressed the UN Committee of Twenty-Four in New York, claiming he had given Butler a month, expiring the next day, 27 March, to indicate whether he would intervene in Southern Rhodesia to prevent disaster. He said that the only response from Butler had come a week before when he had admitted that the British Parliament could legislate for Southern Rhodesia despite the inhibition of the 40-year-old Convention. Nkomo had replied by warning that he would not accept any constitution which did not recognise African aspirations. He revealed he was currently out on bail of £100 for a political charge and that his appearance at the UN constituted a further offence. He faced a possible 20 years in gaol. He asked that the Security Council intervene in Southern Rhodesia, but the British delegate maintained that his Government could not interfere with the territory's internal affairs.[53]

On 28 March, with the assistance of Hone and Luyt, Butler and the British Cabinet reappraised the situation and decided that it had to concede secession to Northern Rhodesia. Butler found it galling that, in their haste to secure independence, Kaunda and Nkumbula cared so little for an association with their neighbours. He broke the news separately to the delegations the next day, 29 March.[54]

At the meeting with the Southern Rhodesian delegation, on 29 March, Field immediately raised the question of full independence for his country, while Butler responded by inviting the Southern Rhodesian Government to a conference in Rhodesia later in the year to determine the broad lines of an

[51] Welensky Papers, 20/3, ff. 56–60, Minutes of a Meeting with Butler, 26 March 1963.
[52] Author's interview with Sir Richard Luyt.
[53] *Northern News*, 27 March 1963.
[54] Butler, *The Art of the Possible*, *op. cit.*, p. 225.

association with Northern Rhodesia. Field replied that his Government would not attend unless it received a written undertaking that Southern Rhodesia would be granted its independence on the date which either Northern Rhodesia or Nyasaland was allowed to secede, whichever was first. Butler considered this reasonable, but warned he could not make an early decision on Southern Rhodesia's independence. However, he was ready to receive a formal application.

When writing his application, Field thought it unnecessary to enlarge on the strength of his claim beyond saying that, as Southern Rhodesia had successfully managed its affairs for 40 years, it could not be granted anything less than Nyasaland which would have only enjoyed self-government for less than a year by the time it was independent. Secondly, he felt that, while links with Britain remained, the impression would persist that the British Government had the right to interfere in Southern Rhodesia's internal affairs. Thus there would continue to be danger of encouragement, by external influences, of serious disorder to compel the British Government to intervene. Butler had reassured Field that Britain would not intervene but, nonetheless, Field believed that the impression would endure. Field closed his application by stating that he would leave Dupont in London to receive the written assurance for which he had asked.[55]

Looking grey, wan and ill, Butler met the Federal delegation in his office before they were to attend a luncheon which Macmillan was giving for all three delegations. Butler apologised for not having met them the previous day, but explained that the British Cabinet had sat into the evening planning what to do. He had decided to break the news to the delegations before saying anything to Parliament. If any statement were made, it would be on Monday, 1 April. However, he would hold a Press conference at 6 p.m. that evening and would furnish Welensky with an advance copy of his statement. He could say now that his Government thought that, to be constructive, policy had to be aimed at achieving a mutually-acceptable relationship between the territories. In the light of its discussions on an agenda for the conference, it had decided that any territory had to be allowed to secede but not before there had been discussion on the new relationship. Butler acknowledged the importance of this decision to Welensky but assured him that it had been considered carefully.[56] Welensky replied bleakly: "First Secretary, will you ask one of your officials to tell Mr Macmillan that neither I nor any member of my delegation will be able to go to his luncheon today. I don't want to be discourteous, but I cannot accept the hospitality of a man who has betrayed me and my country."[57]

A British official left to convey the message to Macmillan, while Butler sat silent, looking stricken. He averted his gaze as Welensky denounced the British Government's habit of always giving way to African nationalists and

[55] *Correspondence between Her Majesty's Government and the Government of Southern Rhodesia, April - June 1963*, Command 2073 (London, June 1963), p. 3.

[56] Sir Roy Welensky, *Welensky's 4 000 Days* (London, 1964), p. 359; Butler, *The Art of the Possible*, *op. cit.*, p. 225; Welensky Papers, 20/3, ff. 53–55, Minutes of a Meeting with Butler, 29 March 1963.

[57] Welensky, *4 000 Days*, *op. cit.*, p. 359.

for not giving him a chance to reveal the constructive proposals he had brought to London. He said he had not produced them because the discussion had never progressed beyond the secession of Northern Rhodesia.

Lewanika asked Butler if Barotseland would be allowed to secede but Butler replied that no decision had been taken on that subject. He did not satisfy Lewanika who declared that the wishes of the Barotse would be overlooked while the demands of the African nationalists were met. He said forcefully that Barotseland had no wish to be ruled by Kaunda or any other African nationalist and recalled that his father, on behalf of his people, had made the treaties with Britain and that the request for protection had come from the Barotse and had not been suggested by the British. Butler would only comment that he had asked the Litunga to make certain administrative reforms and to consider a development plan. The Litunga had agreed, but Butler said he had heard nothing more and, moreover, he could not envisage a future for Barotseland without economic and administrative ties with Northern Rhodesia. Welensky interjected to say bitterly that he could not understand why Butler did not just admit that Barotseland was being "sold down the river".

Welensky declared that he would hold a Press conference at 4.30 p.m. and asked to see Butler's statement before then. Butler thought it might not be ready, but Welensky said he would proceed without it. He warned that his future actions depended on what occurred when he returned to Salisbury. He saw himself henceforth as a free agent who could do as he saw fit. The British Government had decided to dissolve the Federation but he was still its Prime Minister and would act accordingly. Caldicott proclaimed that Welensky had been treated with great discourtesy, and Welensky agreed that he could not have been treated with greater discourtesy if he had been a leader of a municipal council. Then he and his delegation rose and left.[58]

Welensky held his Press conference and bluntly announced that he had been betrayed. He described how the British Government had succumbed to the threats of the African nationalists and had failed the Federation. However, he acknowledged the legal right of the British Government to ignore the pledges. He promised he would not act unconstitutionally but he would not co-operate in the demolition of the Federation unless the vital interests of the territories were secured. He thought that Southern Rhodesia should be granted independence and that any new constitution for Northern Rhodesia should protect European interests and the various regional African interests, including the special status of Barotseland. Finally, he could find no grounds for interference by the UN.[59]

Thereafter, Butler's office issued his statement conceding the right to secede to all the territories to facilitate a fruitful and constructive future. Accordingly, before secession, there would be discussion on the transitional arrangements and on the broad lines of a new relationship.[60]

However it might be cloaked, this British decision had finally killed the Federation. All that was left to do was to arrange a decent burial.

[58] Welensky Papers, 20/3, ff. 53–55, Minutes of a Meeting with Butler, 29 March 1963.

[59] *Glasgow Herald*, 30 March 1963.

[60] Welensky Papers, 33/21, f. 69, Statement issued by the Central African Office, 29 March 1963.

CHAPTER THIRTY-SEVEN

The Wasted Chance

The Abortive Attempt to secure Independence for Southern Rhodesia, March–June 1963

WITH his life's work destroyed, Welensky was sorely tempted to resign. However, he allowed himself to be dissuaded because he wished to secure independence for Southern Rhodesia as well as ensure that the Federal civil servants and others were adequately compensated.

After the British Cabinet's decision, to allow Northern Rhodesia to secede, had been taken on 28 March, Macmillan confided its ramifications to his diary. He wrote that the Northern Rhodesians wanted to secede and to attain their independence a year after the Federation had been dismembered. The Southern Rhodesians were likewise bent on independence and, he acknowledged, it was not surprising as they had enjoyed independence for 40 years in everything except defence and external affairs. (He was mistaken in excluding defence.) The 1923 Convention had forbidden British interference in the internal affairs with, he believed, the result of a lack of African representation, until Sandys forced Whitehead's hand. Macmillan knew that Welensky wanted the Federation to continue but "realises that the game is up". The result was that "Welensky and Field are playing a curious game". "Curious," Macmillan wrote, because Field was a reactionary who was determined "to keep the black man in order", unlike Welensky's friend, Whitehead, who wished to remove even the discrimination in respect of land.

Macmillan noticed that Field was undoing everything which Whitehead had accomplished but yet had, for the moment, achieved "a strange kind of alliance" with Kaunda and Banda because they wanted to end the Federation. However, a further complication was that "there is, now that the die is cast, likely to be an alliance between Welensky and Field". Field was demanding, not unreasonably, Macmillan acknowledged, independence for Southern Rhodesia. Welensky would support this, leaving the British Government in the difficult position of having no physical power to act in Southern Rhodesia despite its legal and moral position. Like so many of his countrymen brought up on Harriet Beecher Stowe, Macmillan could not refrain from describing the Southern Rhodesian situation as "a Government of several million Africans by 200 000 whites, among whom the planter interest predominates", evoking images of Spanish moss, decaying white stucco and sweet magnolias blossoming.

The question was whether Macmillan could give such a country, with such a constitution, formal independence and, presumably, financial help. He argued with himself: "If we do, we shall be blamed by all progressive and moderate opinion. If we do not, we shall do *no* benefit to the Africans and we shall force S.R. into the hands of S. Africa. This will mean a bloc of White power from the Cape to the Zambesi. Is this a good thing or not?"[1]

Macmillan was right because, with the Federation effectively dead, Welensky and his supporters immediately concentrated on securing independence for Southern Rhodesia. However, by 30 March, they had made no progress and Welensky found Field deeply troubled. They were co-operating well, but anything closer was inhibited by Welensky's UFP relationship with Whitehead.[2]

Lord Colyton warned Welensky that the British Government, having betrayed the Federation, might stall on the Southern Rhodesian demand for independence because of pressure from Northern Rhodesia, British domestic politics and the discussions on the future association of the territories. However, Butler was non-committal on this when announcing in the Commons on 1 April that Northern Rhodesia could secede. He merely said that a letter had been received from Field.[3]

While independence for Southern Rhodesia was the immediate Federal aim, much time was spent on recrimination and many hundreds of letters were written to Welensky condemning the British action. Austin Ferraz, editor of *The Sunday Mail*, was typical in his bitter resentment of the treatment meted out to Welensky by "the most despicable bunch of traitors ever to inflict themselves on the British scene". Their behaviour led Ferraz to believe that Southern Rhodesia was doomed if it compromised with them in the expectation of being left alone to run its own affairs. A stand for independence had to be made, he said, even if it led to fighting. If it were made, the tide would turn. Ferraz was sure that Macmillan believed that Southern Rhodesia would never go as far as that, and it was time to disillusion him.[4] Ferraz's comments indicate the roots which the idea of unilateral action had established and it would gather strength in the coming months.

Not only the British were blamed. Reporting on European feelings in Northern Rhodesia, L. E. V. Mahoney of the UFP found that many believed that Greenfield had so mesmerised Welensky with legal theories and hypothetical constitutional arguments that he had failed to take proper action in 1961 (by not using force to resist Macleod's intentions for Northern Rhodesia). This idea would survive and, in later years, when musing on the Federation

[1] H. Macmillan, *At the End of the Day* (London, 1973), p. 327.
[2] Welensky Papers, 20/3, ff. 48–52, Welensky to Barrow, 30 March 1963.
[3] *Ibid.*, 43/*Colyton*, f. 68, Lord Colyton to Welensky, 30 March 1963; House of Commons *Hansard* (London), Vol. 675, Col. 32 f., 1 April 1963.
[4] Welensky Papers, 43/*Ferraz*, f. 23, A. Ferraz to Welensky, 1 April 1963.

some of Welensky's acquaintances convinced themselves that Greenfield had gained an undue and undesirable influence over Welensky.[5] This, of course, is unfair to both men, and Welensky was certainly always master of his own mind and did not dance to Greenfield's tune. For example, when formulating the Federal franchise, Greenfield had proposed a single common voters' roll but Welensky had chosen a dual one. Greenfield was the lawyer in the team and was bound to be saddled with the formulation of the constitutional arguments. He was certainly not the racialist that some believed him to be. Indeed, he was, in fact, the chief protagonist of the policy of partnership and wrote many of the treatises on it. The memorandum presented by the UFP to the Monckton Commission is a good example. Those who criticise the Federal Government on the implementation of partnership forget how little it could do in this field as, for instance, it could not repeal Southern Rhodesia's Land Apportionment Act.

Welensky must have been somewhat mollified by messages such as one from Percy Mkudu which thanked him on behalf of the loyal Africans of Manicaland for his gallant fight. Heartening also was the news from London, on 2 April, that Butler was under pressure from 60 Conservatives to make Southern Rhodesia independent.[6]

The next day, Welensky reported to his Cabinet on what had happened in London. He said he believed that the British decision was a carefully considered act of deliberate policy and not one which had been dictated by the attitude of the Northern Rhodesian leaders. As the decision was irrevocable, Welensky felt that the Federal Government should adopt a positive and realistic attitude, and not merely act as a caretaker. He was particularly anxious to avoid embarrassing the territorial Governments, the Southern Rhodesian in particular. Thus it would be unwise to undertake anything which the territories might be unable or unwilling to shoulder after secession. His attitude, he explained, would be governed by the degree to which the British Government recognised its obligations and bore its burden of responsibility.

The Cabinet agreed that its members should adopt a uniform approach towards assisting Southern Rhodesia to obtain its independence. However, the issues were so complicated and held such potential that a conference, rather than *ad hoc* meetings with territorial Ministers, might be necessary. Also to be remembered was the responsibility of the Federal Government to the Federation's people. As independence was necessary, everything should be done to strengthen the Southern Rhodesian position. It was noted that Field had already demanded independence at the moment that either of the northern territories seceded or achieved independence. Obviously, secession would come first and clearly, to be independent, neither territory could be associated with the other. Thus, to assist, the Federal Government should do what it could to hasten the process of secession. Turning to the fate of Barotseland, it was believed that the British Government was ignoring Barotseland's special status within Northern Rhodesia and the Federal

[5] *Ibid.*, 32/17, f. 34, L. E. V. Mahoney to Welensky, 2 April 1963; Author's confidential interviews.
[6] Welensky Papers, 32/2, f. 72, P. Mkudu to Welensky, 2 April 1963; *Evening Standard*, 2 April 1963.

Cabinet thought that taking of the matter to the International Court should be considered.[7]

As usual, Welensky summed up for his private correspondents, stating forcefully that, despite appearances, the British Government had not capitulated to African nationalist pressure, but had taken a coldly calculated step. Condemning this as "stupid", he ascribed it partly to the need to appease the Commons. He said plainly that he would back Field fully in his bid for independence.[8]

While writing thus, he refused the first of many requests that year to contest a seat in the next British general election because he had no intention of leaving Rhodesia. He had to answer, too, criticism from the UFP's Northern Rhodesian division for tamely accepting Northern Rhodesia's secession and failing to "go down fighting".[9]

Simultaneously, in London, Robinson criticised Butler for saying in the Commons that the British Government had waited until all the Governments had been given an opportunity to express their views when, in fact, his Government had never had that opportunity. To confirm this, he quoted from the minutes of the meeting on 26 March, in which Butler had said that he had no proposition to put to the Federal Government but only wanted to outline the situation to see how it could be met. Welensky had then suggested that the Northern Rhodesians should be told that change would be postponed until a conference had been held at which any topic, including secession, could be discussed. Refusing to sanction any pre-conditions, Welensky had become angry when Butler had proposed that the Northern Rhodesians should be given a veto and Welensky had demanded that it should not be granted. Butler had not sought Federal views on the merits of secession and, Robinson said, the only matter discussed was whether or not Britain should satisfy the Northern Rhodesian demand before the conference.[10]

Welensky, on his part, likened Butler's consultation with him to that between Hitler and Dollfuss. He could not understand how Butler could dare to claim in the Commons that the Federal Government had been properly consulted.[11]

Butler replied to Robinson, denying that there had been any misunderstanding, because his Commons statement made it clear that action had been taken in the light of the views expressed. However, he was obviously anxious to re-establish a relationship with Robinson and telephoned him on 5 April to wish him a Happy Easter. Robinson was out. Lady Robinson received the greeting formally and did not reciprocate because she did not want to be hypocritical. Her honesty pleased Welensky and he thought that the British Government should be treated as coolly as possible.[12]

[7] Welensky Papers, FGC(63), 12th Meeting, Restricted Annexure, Federal Cabinet, 3 April 1963.
[8] *Ibid.*, 32/2, f. 81, Welensky to A. J. Lewin, 3 April 1963.
[9] *Ibid.*, f. 67, Welensky to H. J. Lewis, 3 April 1963; 35/26, f. 168, W. B. L. Wilson to Welensky, 4 April 1963.
[10] *Ibid.*, 32/28, f. 58B, Robinson to Butler, 4 April 1963.
[11] *Ibid.*, 43/*Fraser*, f. 10, Welensky to Sir Keith Fraser, 8 April 1963.
[12] *Ibid.*, 32/28, f. 58A, Butler to Robinson, 4 April 1963; f. 58, Robinson to Welensky, 5 April 1963; f. 59, Welensky to Robinson, 10 April 1963.

Robinson also urged Lords Boyd and Chandos to assist Southern Rhodesia to obtain its independence. Boyd agreed but warned that Southern Rhodesia would have to broaden its franchise. However, Robinson gathered that Boyd and Chandos would not do much to help. Welensky agreed with this assumption because he thought it unlikely that any Conservative would "buck" the Establishment and that, in the end, the Party whips would triumph. In any case, he believed that Butler could rely on the Labour Party "to humble the supporters of the Federation".[13]

Despite his opinion, Welensky nevertheless apprised Boyd fully of how Butler had dealt with him. He said he still could not understand why the decision had been taken and supposed that the British felt that the process of dissolution had to be accelerated. This was due, perhaps, to pressure from Washington and was certainly not a surrender to the "rather milk and water attitude of Kaunda" who had been willing to attend a conference provided secession was the first item on the agenda. It annoyed Welensky not to have been given an opportunity to present his scheme to preserve political and economic links between the Rhodesias. He thought that the Conservatives would lose the next general election, but was unconcerned because Harold Wilson could not treat him any worse.[14]

Welensky decided to tell the complete story of his dealings with Macmillan to the Federal Assembly on 8 April so that it could reach its own verdict. He related how he had begun to distrust Macmillan when they had negotiated the appointment of the Monckton Commission. He recounted the events since then, describing his experience as a most painful lesson in dishonesty and deceit. He unveiled for the first time the content of his exchanges with Macmillan over Monckton. What mystified him, Welensky said, was the refusal of the British Government simply to reveal that it had changed its policies. An example of the deceit was Sandys's promise to Banda on secession which had not been discovered for months. More remarkable was Macmillan's negotiations with a prisoner (Banda) in a Federal gaol behind the Federal Government's back. Such acts had been committed while he and his Federal Government bore the brunt of the attacks of the African nationalists. Consequently, the Federal Government had been falsely blamed for the shootings in the Gwembe Valley in 1958 (when Northern Rhodesian tribesmen refused to evacuate their land as the waters of Lake Kariba rose), in the Nyasaland riots in 1959, and for territorial security legislation.

Welensky said he was contemptuous of the British Government and saw the recent events in London as just another step in the implementation of British policy and not the consequence of pressure from Kaunda. It was not clear, he explained, if this policy was purely to liquidate British assets in Africa or if it was a product of the influence of Washington, but it was certainly not the result of fear of African nationalism. He had been willing to consider change, though he would not condone the idea of dissolving the Federation to re-build it. He had also made it plain to the British Government that he did not think there was any value in purely economic links. Nonethe-

[13] *Ibid.*, 32/64, f. 18, Robinson to Welensky, 5 April 1963; f. 19, Welensky to Robinson, 9 April 1963.

[14] *Ibid.*, 27/62, f. 12, Welensky to Lord Boyd, 8 April 1963.

less, he had not expected the British Government to care over much for the fate of the inhabitants of the Federation, but thought that it would worry about the interests of the British taxpayer and investor. In the event, Butler had refused to discuss anything until the issue of Northern Rhodesia's secession was resolved. Butler had not allowed the Federal Government to present its plan for the excision of Nyasaland and the continued association of the remaining two territories under the name "Rhodesia". Welensky explained that the Federal plan had provided that, after a short time, Northern Rhodesia would gain responsible government, and then both territories would be given the right to secede. If one territory chose this, the other would be made fully independent and the Federal Government's residual powers would be taken over by a commission. However, Butler had not waited for these details before deciding to surrender.

As his sole concern was for the Federal inhabitants, Welensky announced that he would publish a paper on the seriousness of the effects of dissolution. He dwelt again on British perfidy, the latest example of which was Butler's most recent claim to have fully consulted the Federal Government when, in fact, argument was not allowed before the decision was taken. This was how Hitler had treated Dollfuss. The same had happened over Nyasaland and, to prove it, Welensky recounted the events since September 1962.

He said it had been fruitless to point out to Butler that Kaunda currently chaired an organisation (the Pan-African Freedom Movement) committed to the overthrow of the Southern Rhodesian Government. Equally, it had been pointless to remind Butler of Kaunda's threats to render the Federal departments inoperable. The March issue of *Voice of UNIP* had carried the slogan, "Violence pays, Peace does not pay", but had meant nothing to Butler. The duplicity of the British, he asserted, was only made worse by Butler wasting Welensky's time, 24 hours before the decision was taken on Northern Rhodesia, by raising the questions of successors to the Governor-General and the High Commissioners.

Summing up, Welensky decided that Macmillan's Government would be recorded as one of the most effete known aside from its deceit. The lesson to be learnt was that the British Government was still disengaging from Africa, and the interests of the whites and moderate Africans would be ignored in a long-drawn-out appeasement which would put "Munich in the shade". Northern Rhodesia would secede as soon as possible, but the Federal Government would ensure an orderly transfer of powers, and nothing should be done to damage the economies of the territories. He said he had informed Butler that he regarded himself as a free agent and that he would strive to ensure that there were safeguards for Europeans in the territories, despite the British efforts to allow autocracies to entrench themselves. He would attempt to protect Barotseland and to secure the interests of the Federal civil servants. If adequate safeguards were not provided, his Government would not co-operate in the dissolution exercise.

Welensky rued the reversal of the economic clock but acknowledged his own failure which was one of the most bitter experiences of his life. He had done his best, he said, but it had not been good enough. His political life was henceforth to be circumscribed though he still had obligations to the civil service. Nevertheless, he believed that he had advanced the cause of partnership and of real progress in Central Africa. Others had undone these, but he had served the common man, and time would vindicate him. He would always make his experience available to others.[15]

When opening Parliament that day, and reading the Speech from Throne, Lord Dalhousie had also spoken of betrayal and earned himself the censure of his peers in Britain. He could, of course, have refused to read it. However, he did, and gained Greenfield's respect by reading it without faltering. Listening in the Strangers' Gallery, Alport appeared to Greenfield to be choking with rage. Commenting in the debate, Wightwick said he had never expected to hear a British Governor-General speak thus. He was not surprised, because the Federation had been "sold down the Zambesi". He believed that, if its negotiations were fruitless, Southern Rhodesia would simply have to assume that it also had the right to independence. M. Visagie said that Welensky's honesty was his Achilles heel, while Eastwood recounted how the British Government had prevented mention of secession in the Federal Constitution. The debate adjourned after he had said that the British Government no longer had the stamina to keep the torch of progress and freedom burning in Africa.[16]

With the fate of Southern Rhodesia uppermost in his mind, Welensky immediately transmitted information to Field from a close confidant of Nkomo that Butler had assured Nkomo that Southern Rhodesia would not get its independence without a level of African representation akin to that in Northern Rhodesia. Nkomo had thought that the next Southern Rhodesian Government would be black, because he had been told in New York that the United States determined British Colonial policy and, in London, Butler had confirmed that it did. Nkomo had gathered that South Africa was anxious not to have a black state on its borders. He also thought that a unilateral declaration of independence by Field would greatly improve the chances of African nationalist rule. He had claimed that the US Government had promised large sums to finance an African government in Southern Rhodesia. He had said there were plenty of firearms for his use in the country (a cache had already been found at Rusape) but he did not expect to have to use them if Britain kept her promises.

In terms of the ruling of the Pan-African Freedom Movement, Nkomo had indicated that he would sever trade links with South Africa and expel all foreign labour. He had been assured in New York that the United States needed more trading space and that Africa was the only continent left to exploit. He had been told that Northern Rhodesia would receive a generous American loan at 5½ per cent. He had proposed to resuscitate the Federation once Southern Rhodesia had black rule. A Labour Party group had reassured him that Britain would never allow Southern Rhodesia to join South Africa and he had warned that, if Southern Rhodesia took its independence uni-

[15] Fed R & N *Debates* (Salisbury), Vol. 20, Col. 11 f., 8 April 1963; *The Break-up: Effects and Consequences on the Two Rhodesias*, C. Fed. 246 (Salisbury, 26 June 1963).

[16] Welensky Papers, 24/152, ff. 61-63, Welensky to F. S. Joelson, 16 April 1963; the Hon. J. M. Greenfield to the Author, 8 January 1981; Fed R & N *Debates* (Salisbury), Vol. 20, Col. 57, 9 April 1963.

laterally, the Pan-African Freedom Movement would deploy its underground system which had already been formed. He had claimed that Butler and Kaunda were still discussing aspects of the Southern Rhodesian question in Britain, and had predicted a British election within six months. Nkomo had also discovered that Kaunda had known that he would be given the right to secede before he went to Britain. Finally, Nkomo had conceded that prolonged violence would lose him African support.[17]

Field's reply to Welensky has not been seen, but he showed Welensky a report written by Dupont on 3 April in London. Dupont had related that Butler, being pressed on the issue of Southern Rhodesian independence by the Conservatives, the United States and the UN, had tried to get him to agree to Southern Rhodesia becoming independent only when all the ends of the dissolution had been tied up. Dupont had concluded that Butler was stalling and that agreement on independence was most unlikely. Butler had said that Kaunda had been most friendly and had not even mentioned Southern Rhodesia. Kaunda had informed the Labour Party that economic links were essential but that a full economic relationship depended on Southern Rhodesia adopting a liberal franchise.[18]

On 9 April, Butler replied to Field's letter of 29 March, saying that his Government had considered carefully the application for independence. In accordance with its decision that no territory could be held in the Federation against its will, the British Government accepted in principle that Southern Rhodesia, like the other territories, would proceed through the normal processes to independence. Southern Rhodesia could not expect to be independent in the fullest sense of the word while it remained a member of the non-independent Federation. Field was reminded that, in granting the right to secede, the British Government had prescribed that there would be a conference before secession to settle the broad lines of a new relationship, as well as the transitional arrangements. It was the normal procedure for the British Government to convene such a conference to examine all the ramifications before self-governing dependencies were granted independence.

Butler noted that Field had reiterated that independence should be granted to his territory on the first date on which either northern territory was allowed to secede or to obtain its independence, and pointed out that the secession of one of the territories would not terminate Southern Rhodesia's membership of the Federation. However, he acknowledged that he and Field had discussed a limited form of independence while Southern Rhodesia remained a member of the Federation. Therefore, Butler reminded Field of the terms of the White Paper on Southern Rhodesia's 1961 Constitution (Command 1399) and, in particular, of the paragraph which acknowledged that the Constitution of 1923 conferred responsible government on Southern Rhodesia and that, since then, a convention had been established that the British Parliament would not legislate for Southern Rhodesia on matters which fell within the competence of the Southern Rhodesian Assembly, except with the agreement of the Southern Rhodesian Government. Reaffirming this position, Butler could not see how it could be improved, short

[17] Welensky Papers, 30/7, f. 5, Welensky to W. Field, 6 April 1963.
[18] *Ibid.*, 20/9A, f. 24, Dupont to Field, 3 April 1963.

of full independence. However, his Government would gladly review the matter if Field so wished. The British Government recognised the desire for independence as soon as practicable and therefore invited the closest Southern Rhodesian co-operation in carrying out the processes to which it referred.[19] Butler was indeed stalling.

Dupont brought this letter from London, having had a series of meetings with Butler at which he had explained that he would stay in London until he had written confirmation of Butler's oral assurance to Field in London on 22 March that Southern Rhodesia would gain its independence at the Federal dissolution. On 8 April Dupont had demanded to know the reason for the delay and had indicated that he would accept even an informal note. Not surprisingly, Butler had replied: "You cannot expect me to bind my Cabinet by an informal note." Dupont then had asked that the British Cabinet be recalled, but Butler had merely replied that his Government would grant Southern Rhodesia independence if its Government attended the conference on dissolution.

That evening Dupont had telephoned Field and, because he knew that they were being misled, advised him not to attend the conference. Field had said he had spoken to Butler earlier on the telephone and had received certain assurances and that Dupont should return because he was sending another Cabinet Minister, J. H. Howman, to relieve him. Dupont had agreed to return but proposed to resign if Field decided to yield. Field had told him not to be "silly" and had explained that, without formally committing the British Government, Butler had promised that a meeting would be held before the conference in which the terms of independence for Southern Rhodesia would be agreed.[20] (Dupont relates the foregoing in his memoirs but it is possible that he confuses some of the events of early April with those of early June. As will be seen, he was in London again in early June, and it was only then that Howman arrived there.)

Field issued a Press statement and published his letter of 29 March. Welensky concluded that Field was "going to be taken for a ride" if he fell for the clear intention of the British to delay the independence issue. If he did, he would see his hopes fade with every passing day. Welensky could say this because he had been taken through the same process.[21] He informed Robinson that Butler's reply to Field had been as "equivocal as ever". Field, he said, had gained nothing but might be tempted to "paint it up in colours which the country will swallow". Welensky proposed to contradict Butler and hoped that Field would join forces with him, but doubted that he would.[22]

Lord Salisbury, supporting Field totally, thought it was, in fact, preferable that Butler should have turned down the Southern Rhodesian application completely rather than hedge it with unacceptable terms. However, he urged Field and Welensky not to let matters stand for too long because the British Government would have them back "in the same mess". He pressed Welensky

[19] *Correspondence between Her Majesty's Government and the Government of Southern Rhodesia, April – June 1963*, Command 2073 (London, June 1963), pp. 4–5, Butler to Field, 9 April 1963.

[20] C. Dupont, *The Reluctant President* (Bulawayo, 1978), p. 131.

[21] Welensky Papers, 32/2, f. 301, Welensky to J. C. Coleman, 10 April 1963.

[22] *Ibid.*, 32/28, f. 59, Welensky to Robinson, 10 April 1963.

to reconsider his decision to retire from politics on the grounds that "we all need you".[23]

In the Commons on 10 April Butler countered Field's statement to the Press, and the publication of Field's letter of 29 March to him, by describing his exchanges with Field and publishing them in a White Paper. Joelson, in his *East Africa and Rhodesia*, declared it was now plain that Southern Rhodesia had been given the cruel choice of either defying the British Government and taking consequences, or of abandoning independence. He knew that Southern Rhodesian faith in the British Government had been destroyed.[24]

Welensky promptly informed Joelson that he was becoming increasingly nervous because Field wanted to "play it long" when time did not allow it. The lack of time, Welensky believed, suited Butler because time would allow the generation of pressure from the Afro-Asian bloc and the British left wing. Welensky intended to keep pressure on Field but he and Greenfield agreed that Field was a "weak reed". It certainly appeared that Field had not grasped how dangerous was the opposition to him.[25]

At this moment, the arrival of a South African Air Force delegation in Salisbury showed the degree of South African concern at the Federation's dissolution. The delegation claimed to be authorised by its Government to offer to assist Southern Rhodesia in every possible way to take over the Royal Rhodesian Air Force. If necessary, the SAAF could take over equipment which Southern Rhodesia could not afford to operate and maintain, and return it free of charge when finances improved. The South African Government was about to build an airstrip at Katima Mulilo in the Caprivi Strip but the delegation thought that, alternatively, a first-class strip could be built at Wankie. The South African Government was also keen to construct a railway line from Beit Bridge to Rutenga, to lessen Southern Rhodesia's strategic dependence on the line through Bechuanaland, and would provide all the finance required. It pleased the Federal Government that the delegation expressed surprise at the RRAF's efficiency and effectiveness.[26]

In the Federal Assembly the debate on the Address was continuing, MP after MP, both black and white, regretting the dissolution of the Federation. The African MPs maintained that Britain was taking notice only of the opinion of the African nationalists who did not represent the whole population. A white MP, Group-Captain E. T. H. Nelson, tried to move a motion of regret at the lack of mention of maintaining the Federation. A. J. Pillay suggested similar action but Greenfield explained that the die was cast. He praised Welensky for not considering the use of force or any other form of unconstitutional action. Nonetheless, he found it strange that the British Government should so vigorously support the unification of the Congo while it dissolved the Federation. He defended the Federal Government's record

[23] *Ibid.*, 43/*Salisbury*, Lord Salisbury to Welensky, 11 April 1963.

[24] *Ibid.*, 32/64, f. 21a, Robinson to Welensky, 20 April 1963; *Correspondence between Her Majesty's Government and the Government of Southern Rhodesia*, Command 2000 (London, April 1963); *East Africa and Rhodesia*, 11 April 1963.

[25] Welensky Papers, 24/152, ff. 61–63, Welensky to Joelson, 16 April 1963.

[26] *Ibid.*, 33/84, f. 1, R. A. F. Bentley to Welensky, 14 April 1963.

on the implementation of partnership, pointing to the franchise law which would give the House an African majority if the Africans so wished. With regard to the fate of Southern Rhodesia, Greenfield argued that, as a high-contracting party to the foundation of the Federation, it should at least be restored to its former position. He thought that a total dissolution might prove impossible and that the irreducible minimum constitutional relationship would have to be maintained by the two Rhodesias.[27]

A distraction from this mourning was the arrival of Nkomo in Dar-es-Salaam on 18 April to attempt to set up a government-in-exile in anticipation of the British Government giving Southern Rhodesia its independence. Two days later, the other leaders of the banned Zimbabwe African People's Union slipped out of the Federation to join Nkomo. However, almost immediately they divided into two factions: the first favoured the creation of a government-in-exile, while the second wished to see first what Field would do next.[28]

On 20 April Field replied to Butler's letter of 9 April. He dwelt on Southern Rhodesia's development for which, he said, the Europeans were principally responsible, although the burden was now being shared by all races. Mildly correcting Butler, he explained that Southern Rhodesia had never been a dependency and had financed its own development, taxed itself and paid its way. It had defended itself, and in addition had contributed men and money to the defence of Western civilisation. It had operated a democratic parliamentary form of government successfully and had a record which more than fulfilled the requirements for independence and which rendered unnecessary any need for a conference to deal specifically with the granting thereof. Butler had insisted on following the normal processes to independence but Field believed that his territory had already been through them.

Field noted that Butler had not guaranteed that Southern Rhodesia would be granted independence on the first date on which either of the two northern territories seceded or gained its independence, but instead had talked of the dissolution conference. The Southern Rhodesians recognised the desirability of discussions on the future inter-territorial relationship and on the transitional arrangements, but they could not accept that the unqualified recognition of Southern Rhodesia's right to independence had to await these discussions. The guarantee which Field sought had nothing to do with these discussions, particularly because events were dictating that they would be confined to the subject of economic ties. With the acceptance of the principle of secession, there was clearly no bar to any of the territories becoming independent.

Field dismissed Butler's argument that membership of the Federation precluded a territory from becoming independent, because the decision to dissolve the Federation had been taken. What the Southern Rhodesian Government sought was the unqualified recognition of its right to full independence as soon as the Federation was terminated either by secession or by the granting of independence to one of the other territories.

Field could not accept that the British Parliament had the right to legislate for the dissolution of the Federation and so, indirectly, for Southern Rho-

[27] Fed R & N *Debates* (Salisbury), Vol. 20, Col. 277 f., 16 April 1963.

[28] *Washington Post*, 18 April 1963; *The Rhodesia Herald*, 20 April 1963.

desia. Accordingly, he referred Butler to the Joint Declaration of 1957 and its Convention which in practice prevented the British Government from initiating any legislation to amend or repeal any Federal Act or deal with any matter included within the competence of the Federal Parliament, except at the Federal Government's request. To Field, this was as binding as the Southern Rhodesian Convention of 1923 to which Butler had referred.

Field found a contradiction in the acceptance of the principle of secession and the insistence on discussions on the future relationship before its implementation because no relationship was possible unless it was freely entered into by territories which had gained complete control of their affairs. Certainly no imposed solution would endure. Thus Field contended that the programme of events had to be settled immediately and not at the dissolution conference. Britain was obliged to take the next step, he said, which was obviously to recognise unambiguously and immediately Southern Rhodesia's absolute right to independence.

Returning to "the normal process" of independence, Field pointed out that it was irrelevant and inappropriate because self-governing Southern Rhodesia had never been a dependency. It had been self-sufficient in finance and had provided its own defence since 1923, until the Federation assumed those functions in 1953. In 1961, it had gained the right to legislate with extra-territorial effect. This would enhance its status when subjects like defence were returned on dissolution. The removal of Britain's reserved powers in 1961 had made Southern Rhodesia practically independent, and the powers of constitutional amendment, granted in 1961 together with the Convention, made it impossible for the British Government to make any further changes, short of granting independence. Thus the next step was to pass through the British Parliament an independence act to provide that, from an appointed day, the British Government would cease to have any responsibilities for Southern Rhodesia, and that no British Act would apply to it. A conference was unnecessary because the current Constitution contained ample safeguards against racial and other discrimination. Changes in the membership of the Legislative Assembly and to the franchise could not be prerequisites for independence because these issues had been settled in 1961. (However, Butler would shortly show Field how wrong he was in this assumption.)

Field repeated that agreement on independence had to be secured before the dissolution of the Federation could begin. This was essential because it would prevent interference in the internal affairs of Southern Rhodesia at any conference on the future relationship. Reiterating that, as a high-contracting party to the Federation, Southern Rhodesia's consent was required for any change in the original Federal concept, Field maintained that the secession of one member certainly terminated the Federation. In any case, the question was academic, he said, because it was clear that the Northern Rhodesians were bent on secession. Therefore it was the duty of the Southern Rhodesian Government to protect its interests, and it would not attend a conference on the future relationship unless it received a written and acceptable undertaking that Southern Rhodesia would gain its full independence on the first date that either northern territory seceded or obtained its independence. Immediately that was done, the closest co-operation would be forthcoming for the endeavour to find an acceptable and durable relationship between the territories and the British Government. It was unfortunate that the British proposals suggested nothing which would bring a speedy end to the political and economic uncertainty which was having such serious repercussions on the well-being and progress of all Southern Rhodesians. Even so, it appeared that the British wished to prolong the uncertainty for their own reasons, despite its detrimental effect on Central Africa. Accordingly, Field asked for an immediate reply.[29]

Butler was in no hurry and took twelve days to reply. In the meantime, Welensky informed Wall that Field had taken a firm line. He told his other correspondents that he was still convinced that Field would be taken for the same ride as he had been. Nevertheless, he was most anxious that Southern Rhodesia should be independent because he wanted it to negotiate a defensive alliance with South Africa and Portugal. He thought that Butler would continue to stall to allow opposition to Southern Rhodesia's independence to mount.[30]

Welensky decided to intervene. He informed Robinson, on 27 April, that he had thought of calling publicly for a conference without reference to Butler. He had decided against this because he needed British support to induce Kaunda to attend. Banda's presence was deemed to be desirable but not vital. He then informed Robinson that Britain would not allow Southern Rhodesia its independence while it was part of the Federation. He believed that the British Government wished to hold an "independence" conference to force Southern Rhodesia "to buy" its way out of its colonial status. He said that Field would have to accept that Nyasaland would be independent before Southern Rhodesia and he proposed to convince him on this.

Welensky asked Robinson to tell Butler that he had been considering ways of clearing the difficulties of holding the conference on the future association because action was necessary to deal with the serious economic and political deterioration. The Southern Rhodesian prerequisite was the undertaking that its independence be granted concurrently with that of the secession or independence of the northern territories. This effectively meant the granting of independence to Southern Rhodesia when Nyasaland seceded. He suggested, as a compromise, that the British Government should formally promise Southern Rhodesia independence at the final dissolution of the Federation, when the two Rhodesias parted company and when the two northern territories received their promises of early independence. If both sides agreed on this course, it would open the way for the conference to forge new links on the basis of the territories moving towards independence but agreeing to maintain the common services for the benefit of all. He did not want the conference to deal with the details of the dissolution but knew that, nevertheless, the five Governments would have to secure the rights of government employees of all kinds and of the Federal creditors and citizens, and other such matters,

[29] Command 2073, *op. cit.*, p. 6, Field to Butler, 20 April 1963. This letter was drafted by Greenfield at the request of the Southern Rhodesian Cabinet. — The Hon. J. M. Greenfield to the Author, 21 January 1981.

[30] Welensky Papers, 42/*Wall*, f. 38, Welensky to Wall, 22 April 1963; 43/*Connell*, Welensky to J. Connell, 23 April 1963.

including the special position of Barotseland. Welensky offered to call publicly for such a conference and for such an agenda.[31]

Simultaneously, Greenfield suggested to the Litunga that he should demand the secession of Barotseland from Northern Rhodesia when the latter became independent, on the grounds that he did not want to entrust his country's future to a Northern Rhodesia which Britain no longer controlled.[32]

Robinson delivered Welensky's message to Butler on 2 May, expressing doubts whether Field would agree to negotiate Southern Rhodesia's independence after the conference. He asked, therefore, if the British Government would discuss immediately the basis for Southern Rhodesian independence. Butler replied that the Commonwealth, including Australia, opposed independence for Southern Rhodesia. He added that the Labour Party, certain sections of the Conservative Party and, indeed, the world endorsed this attitude. Robinson ignored such a marshalling of forces and warned that Field would not co-operate because the British plan would rob him of any bargaining counters by settling everything before he began to negotiate on independence. Therefore, Robinson asked if the British Government would agree, in principle, to Southern Rhodesia becoming independent at the Federation's dissolution. As this would be a concession to Field and Welensky, Robinson argued that the British Government could then demand that the terms of independence be negotiated first. He believed this should be done immediately.

Butler, however, said he could not comment as all Southern Rhodesian matters were being dealt with by a Cabinet committee. He added that Whitehead had recently told Alport that if he had still been Prime Minister the independence issue could have been quickly resolved, though he appreciated Field's difficulties. By coincidence, Butler confided to Robinson, Alport had also suggested that Field might be helped by the British acceptance of Southern Rhodesian independence at the dissolution, provided that the terms were negotiated immediately. Refusing to comment further on Southern Rhodesia, Butler asked for Robinson's co-operation in making the dissolution orderly.

However, Robinson said he would only comply if Butler made it easy for everyone to co-operate by granting Southern Rhodesia's requests. Butler replied that he had no power to alter the Southern Rhodesian Constitution but that he believed this should be done to show the world that ultimately there would be representative government.[33]

On the same day that he saw Robinson, Butler wrote to Field, declaring that his letter of 20 April had received the closest attention. He acknowledged the achievements of Southern Rhodesia and its contribution to the defence of the Commonwealth. He had affirmed in his last letter, on 9 April, that his Government accepted that Southern Rhodesia would proceed through the normal processes to independence. There had been no suggestion of a conference on the principle of independence, but before independence was granted to any country, there were always matters of mutual interest to be

[31] *Ibid.*, 20/3, ff. 44–47, Welensky to Robinson, 27 April 1963.
[32] *Ibid.*, 32/20, f. 36, Greenfield to the Litunga, May 1963.
[33] *Ibid.*, 20/9A, f. 21, Minutes of a Meeting with Butler, 2 May 1963.

considered and discussed if the transfer of power were to be effected in an orderly manner.

Aside from these considerations, Butler noted that Field still underrated the constitutional difficulties of granting independence to Southern Rhodesia while the Federation existed. These applied to all territories because the Federation was not independent. In any case, Butler continued to believe that the Federation was not dissolved by his recognition of the right of any member to secede, and maintained that neither was it ended by a British act removing one of the members from it. The Federation would only cease to exist when British legislation dissolved it.

Butler denied that he had ignored the Joint Declaration of 1957 but believed that its Convention was limited to matters within the competence of the Federal legislature. He welcomed Field's acknowledgement of the desirability of a conference on the future association and claimed that the independence of Southern Rhodesia after the dissolution had no bearing on the establishment of economic links between the territories. He found it necessary, nevertheless, to reiterate that his Government still contended that a new and fruitful relationship would depend on holding a conference. It was also recognised that no solutions could be imposed if anything was to endure. He promised that the internal affairs of the territories would be excluded from the agenda and, in response to Field's contention that the conference had no relation to the granting of independence, he proposed to hold it in two stages. The first stage would consider the orderly dissolution, which was vital to Southern Rhodesia, because, until the date was set, it would not be known when that territory would cease to be a member of the Federation. The second stage would discuss the future association of the territories.

Butler said that, in the British view, the pace of progress towards independence depended on the Southern Rhodesian Government. If it would discuss matters which had to be dealt with before independence, there was no reason for a lengthy delay. If it co-operated, the British Government would undertake to enter into negotiations on independence not later than the date on which similar negotiations began for the independence of the northern territories.

Butler thought it was not unreasonable, nor incompatible with Southern Rhodesia's status as a self-governing colony, to ask it to participate in the discussions on the orderly dissolution and the orderly achievement of independence. He reassured Field that a conference similar to that in 1961 was not contemplated and neither was any unilateral action by Britain with regard to constitutional change. The Southern Rhodesian legislature would effect any amendments but his Government would like to discuss necessary changes. It agreed that there should not be any delay and promised that, once the Southern Rhodesian Government accepted, it would immediately seek Federal and Northern Rhodesian co-operation for the first stage of the conference. Butler said he looked forward to hearing from Field as to how progress could be made on these lines.[34]

Butler also wrote to Welensky that day, 2 May, praising his constructive

[34] *Ibid.*, 20/3, ff. 39–43, Butler to Field, 2 May 1963 (published in Command 2073, *op. cit.*, p. 11).

attitude and recounting what he had just told Field. He hoped that Field and Welensky would agree that he was making a sincere effort to deal with the realities while taking account of Southern Rhodesia's position. He was also prepared to consider if the northern territories needed any further assurance on their independence. He confessed that, while he had offered Field a two-stage conference, he still preferred to consider the dissolution and the future relationship together. His main concern was to convene the conference as quickly as possible. He asked Welensky for his views on an agenda and said that his attitude encouraged him to suggest the appointment of an official working party to prepare for the discussion on the Federal civil service and the public debt. He would provide a chairman to work with representatives from the four Governments.[35] In fact, later, Butler would repeat this suggestion and have it accepted, although eventually there were two working parties which dealt separately with the civil service and the public debt.

Butler was being harassed by the Federal Speaker, T. I. F. Wilson, and wrote to him on 7 May assuring him that the British Government had always publicly recognised the achievements and services of Welensky and his Ministers. Despite them, Butler said, the question was how the British Government could keep people in the Federation against their will. He stated that, after deep thought, the British Government had decided that a satisfactory relationship could only be built up in Central Africa by consent.[36]

Butler would not have convinced the pugnacious Wilson any more than he did Welensky who promptly rejected the official working party suggestion. Welensky told Joelson that he had expected the British Government to grasp eagerly Field's concession to allow for independence upon the Federation's dissolution, rather than at the date of the secession of any of the territories. Instead, he said, there had been the disappointing, but typical, reply that official working parties should be appointed. He explained that he had demanded that the Southern Rhodesian issue be settled first. Butler was under pressure from the African nationalists to get on with the dissolution and Welensky hoped that Field matched his own determination to resist until the Southern Rhodesian independence question was resolved. To Mrs S. G. Millin, Welensky added that he was saddened by the departure of Lord Dalhousie who was replaced by Sir Humphrey Gibbs, the Governor of Southern Rhodesia, who would act as Governor-General until the dissolution.[37]

On 9 May Field acknowledged to Butler the offer of the two-stage conference and recorded his pleasure at Butler's statement that there would be no need for a pre-independence conference and that all amendments could be effected by the Southern Rhodesian Assembly. However, it appeared to Field that Butler would prefer that the pre-independence negotiations should be conducted after the conference. He had offered only a promise that they would coincide with negotiations with the northern territories. Field would not wait until then and maintained that his application of 29 March, for

[35] Welensky Papers, 20/3, ff. 35–38, Butler to Welensky, 2 May 1963.

[36] *Ibid.*, 31/87, f. 15, Butler to T. I. F. Wilson, 7 May 1963.

[37] *Ibid.*, 24/152, ff. 58–60, Welensky to Joelson, 8 May 1963; 43/*Millin*, f. 11, Welensky to S. G. Millin, 9 May 1963.

independence on the date of secession or independence of either of the northern territories, had been entirely reasonable. To meet Butler's difficulties, he reminded him, he had suggested that, under certain circumstances, he would accept independence on the date of the dissolution of the Federation instead. His conditions were that the negotiations on independence would precede the dissolution conference. As there would be no constitutional conference on his independence requirements, the negotiations on independence need not delay the dissolution process. Thus he invited Butler and his advisers to visit him to negotiate the terms of independence. Once these were agreed, the conference on dissolution could begin immediately.

Field wanted to draw up a time-table to permit the Governments to plan. The Federal and Southern Rhodesian budgets were scheduled for late June and July and so he asked Butler to arrive on 27 May and convene the dissolution conference immediately after Whitsun at the Victoria Falls or in Livingstone. He believed that the goodwill engendered by the Anglo-Southern Rhodesian agreement on independence would do much to facilitate the work of the conference.[38]

Welensky also replied to Butler at that moment, saying that Field had shown him his latest dispatch. He thought that, by altering his claim to independence, Field was being reasonable and co-operative and was well within his rights in asking for a settlement before the dissolution conference. Welensky could not understand how a two-stage conference would solve Field's problem of securing an assurance of independence at the dissolution. He reminded Butler that, but for the Federation, Southern Rhodesia would have been independent. He believed that, indeed, Field would be failing his country if he did not insist on immediate independence because it could not be left in "a twilight state" after the dissolution. He warned that the current "log-jam" could not be broken unless Field's demands were met, and urged haste because other decisions had to be taken before working parties could begin.[39]

Welensky informed Lords Salisbury and Colyton that the British Government was using all its wiles to shift Field from his position. He acknowledged that Field had hardened his attitude but his weakness lay in the financial straits of Southern Rhodesia. Welensky believed, rightly, that, if nothing were done at that moment to achieve Southern Rhodesian independence, nothing would ever be done. In his view, the Commonwealth should be ignored. Britain would have to decide, when Southern Rhodesia became independent, whether to allow it to join the Commonwealth or whether Nkrumah, Nyerere and Kenyatta should leave. He thought that Macmillan was so "gutless" that he would choose to keep "those three great patriots". The choice for Southern Rhodesia was to seek South African and Portuguese support, and accordingly with Field's blessing, Welensky said he was going to visit South Africa to speak to its Prime Minister, H. F. Verwoerd. He knew, however, that South Africa would avoid political ties because they would bring with them 3 000 000 additional Africans. The advantage of independence for Southern Rhodesia would be that, at least, it could seek its own

[38] *Ibid.*, 20/9A, f. 16, Field to Butler, 9 May 1963.
[39] *Ibid.*, 20/3, ff. 32–33, Welensky to Butler, 9 May 1963.

friends. Welensky closed by revealing that, having demolished the Federation, Macmillan had curbed Butler by appointing a Cabinet committee to deal with the remaining problems.[40]

While Welensky and Field wrote thus, Robinson and J. A. Clark (who had flown to London) met Butler and reviewed the economic problems which Southern Rhodesia would face without firm links with Northern Rhodesia. Clark reminded Butler that many investors had put money into the Federation on the strength of the British and Federal assurances on its permanence as a political entity, and on there being a common market of the three territories. Butler ignored this but asked him to use his influence to ensure that Southern Rhodesia came to the conference to resolve the question of the future links. He added that Southern Rhodesia would only harm itself by delaying. Clark replied that everything depended on a British concession to Southern Rhodesia and on immediate negotiations on independence. However, Butler said he preferred to await Field's reply to his latest dispatch. He revealed that an enabling bill for Nyasaland's secession was being drafted, and that it was fairly certain that soon the British Government would acquire the power to deal with the future of the Federation. Butler hastened to assure Robinson that the Federal Government would be fully consulted on this legislation. (Consequently Robinson advised Welensky to write to Butler, noting this undertaking and asking to see the drafts as soon as they were ready in order to have adequate time to study them. Robinson, however, distrusted Butler and did not expect the time to be granted.)

The final point raised with Butler was a bid by Kaunda's UNIP to have the Federal representatives excluded from a forthcoming Commonwealth Trade Ministers' Conference. Butler promised to ensure that the chairman of the Conference resisted this.[41]

Victor Goodhew, the Conservative MP, had been applying pressure for Southern Rhodesia, but Butler informed him that, if the Africans did not receive an adequate outlet for their political aspirations, the Europeans would have to resort to repressive measures to protect their position. In such circumstances, he said, the mere existence of a white Government would not convince investors of the enduring stability of the territory.[42]

Butler replied to Field on 16 May, claiming that they were closer to an understanding because they had agreed that any amendments would be effected by the Southern Rhodesian Parliament and that the terms of independence should be negotiated. The British Government would allow independence to coincide with the dissolution of the Federation if a satisfactory solution to the independence negotiations had been achieved. Noting that Field wanted to negotiate immediately, Butler assured him of his sympathy but he believed that Field was as anxious as he to dispel the uncertainties surrounding the dissolution. He knew the Northern Rhodesian Government also desired a quick resolution and, he recalled, Welensky had said more than once that he hoped the orderly dissolution would be implemented speedily.

[40] *Ibid.*, 43/*Salisbury*, f. 55, Welensky to Salisbury, 9 May 1963; 43/*Colyton*, f. 70, Welensky to Colyton, 9 May 1963.

[41] *Ibid.*, FGC(1), 12/63, Robinson's Report on Clark's meeting with Butler, 9 May 1963.

[42] *Ibid.*, 35/19B, f. 165, Butler to V. Goodhew, 9 May 1963.

As the issues of dissolution and independence were so closely connected, Butler declared he was prepared to negotiate immediately, but preferred London as a venue.

He agreed that the date of the dissolution conference should be fixed, and suggested that invitations should be sent to the Governments concerned simultaneously with the announcement of the opening of the negotiations on Southern Rhodesia's independence. If the latter were not completed by the opening of the dissolution conference, Butler promised that they would be resumed at the earliest convenient date. He hoped that Field would accept this sincere proposal to resolve their difficulties.[43]

When they discussed this the next day, 17 May, Robinson urged Butler to adopt a helpful attitude towards Field and independence. Butler replied that, while Kaunda had agreed to attend the dissolution conference, even though he had been very unpleasant about the unrepresentative nature of the Southern Rhodesian Government, the danger remained that he might reconsider if, in the imminent negotiations with Field, Britain appeared to move closer to the Southern Rhodesian position on independence. In fact, he said, it was becoming increasingly difficult to accommodate the various demands without endangering relations with one or the other Government.

Digressing, Butler said that the British Treasury would meet Nyasaland's current commitments but had not yet decided on future aid. Reverting to the dissolution, he warned that his Government was determined to secure agreement thereon and would resort to other methods, on which he did not elaborate, if the Southern Rhodesian independence negotiations failed. He asked for full Federal Government co-operation as, otherwise, there could be great suffering especially among the civil servants.

Lords Colyton and Salisbury provided an insight into current British opinion but offered no cheer for Field because there seemed no chance of securing Southern Rhodesian independence without the exertion of considerable pressure. Salisbury knew that the British Government would have the support of the Labour and Liberal Parties, as well as of 40 Conservatives, if it wished to withhold independence. If it chose to grant it, a schism in Conservative ranks was certain. People were worrying that Southern Rhodesia might adopt *apartheid* and Salisbury proposed that Welensky make a statement rebutting this. Colyton had discovered that Macleod was controlling the Cabinet committee on Southern Rhodesian matters and believed that there had been a considerable clash within the Cabinet on Southern Rhodesia. Consequently, Macleod and Edward Boyle had threatened to resign unless independence was granted only if Southern Rhodesia adopted universal suffrage or at least had an African majority in Parliament. Colyton was anxious that the independence issue be settled before the British parliamentary summer recess and urged that Field should not agree to attend the dissolution conference before such settlement. While doing this, he suggested that Field should take action to disabuse the critics who would tar him with the *apartheid* brush.[44]

[43] Command 2073, *op. cit.*, p. 14, Butler to Field, 16 May 1963.

[44] Welensky Papers, 20/9A, f. 12, Minutes of a Meeting with Butler, 17 May 1963; 43/*Salisbury*, f. 57, Salisbury to Welensky, 16 May 1963; 43/*Colyton*, f. 71, Colyton to Welensky, 17 May 1963.

On 18 May Field agreed to go to London. Accepting that they were close to an understanding, he concurred that Butler could announce the opening of the independence negotiations and simultaneously issue invitations to the dissolution conference. He was confident that the independence question could be resolved before the conference but warned that agreement was indispensable to Southern Rhodesian co-operation in the dissolution process and that he could not compromise on this. He recognised that it might be impossible to settle everything before the conference, but believed there was sufficient time to agree upon the essentials. Otherwise, there was no point in attending the conference. He preferred, however, to believe that, with Butler's recognition of the pledges to which he was committed, they could reach agreement.

He proposed to arrive in London on 27 May and suggested that the dissolution conference should open on 10 June at the Victoria Falls or in Livingstone. Butler had referred to alternative solutions when answering questions in the Commons on the future association of the territories, and Field wished to be informed about them because, unless there was an initial plan, the conference could not progress.[45]

Butler thereupon announced in the Commons that the Governments of the Federation had agreed to the dissolution conference being held in the second half of June — which was not quite what Field had said. He revealed also that Field was coming to London to discuss the independence issue.[46]

At that moment, Welensky was in South Africa holding the meeting with Verwoerd which so alarmed the Anti-Apartheid Movement. Thus it was only on 25 May — on his return — that he commented, privately, on the Anglo-Southern Rhodesian quarrel. He had seen Field that morning and, thinking that he was being won over by Butler who was asking for concessions in return for independence, had warned him that it was the beginning of the end if he conceded anything. He urged him to stand firm, assuring him of his support. He proposed not to agree to go to the dissolution conference until he knew the outcome of Field's negotiations.

Kaunda had suggested the replacement of the Federal Government by a British commission, but Welensky told Joelson that it would be unacceptable to the Southern Rhodesians who had never been ruled by the British. In any case, he felt, it was unlikely that the British would want to meet the cost of the commission.[47]

On 27 May, while Field began his negotiations in London, Welensky reported to his Cabinet on his South African visit. As its Air Force delegation had indicated earlier, he said that the South African Government wished to build the Beitbridge-Rutenga railway link at a cost of £2 500 000 for purely strategic reasons. It proposed to adjust the rating so that the Rhodesia Railways would not lose financially by the diminution of the traffic on its Bechuanaland line. The South African Government was also prepared to assist Southern Rhodesia by allowing it to raise a £5 000 000 loan. The

[45] *Ibid.*, 20/9A, f. 10, Field to Butler, 18 May 1963 (published in Command 2073, *op. cit.*, p. 16).
[46] Welensky Papers, 20/3, f. 31, Butler's Statement, 21 May 1963.
[47] *Cape Times*, 21 May 1963; Welensky Papers, 24/152, ff. 53–55, Welensky to Joelson, 25 May 1963.

question of favouring Southern Rhodesian textiles was considered, but Verwoerd had warned that South Africa had obligations to its Bantustans in that direction. He would not entertain a political link with Southern Rhodesia, but had promised economic aid.[48]

Welensky's meeting with Verwoerd aroused the suspicions of their opponents. Kaunda warned that Welensky would succeed Field as the Southern Rhodesian Prime Minister and, with Verwoerd and Portugal's President, Dr A. de O. Salazar, would threaten the peace of Southern Africa. He believed that Welensky was using Federal finances to aid Southern Rhodesia and was seeking military and economic links with South Africa. He implored the UN to intervene forcibly lest Welensky, Verwoerd and Salazar make a last ditch stand in Southern Africa with consequences which he claimed would be worse than those of the French Revolution. This was not, however, Kaunda's total preoccupation because he also demanded a new constitution for Northern Rhodesia.[49]

Welensky and the Federal Cabinet knew nothing about Field's talks in London until 30 May. Kenneth Young believes that Field's hopes of achieving anything were not very high and that, in his heart, he knew he was being outmanoeuvred. Butler told him at the outset that the Commonwealth demanded the imposition of "one man, one vote". Field's retort was that, in the rest of Africa, this meant "one party, one dictator". Moreover, he asked which Commonwealth countries were actually demanding it. (Apparently he received no answer.)

Macmillan had not only ordered Butler to "give him nothing" but had insisted that he discover from Field what he intended to do to liberalise his regime. Accordingly, Butler made it plain that fundamental constitutional changes were required before independence could be granted. He insisted that Field had to appease the Afro-Asian bloc in some manner, and expected him to increase the number of B roll seats by eight to create a "blocking third", a reduction in the qualifications for the A roll, and the abolition of racial discrimination.[50]

The Federal Cabinet was told of these terms on 30 May by Robinson and concluded that agreement on them was most unlikely. Consequently, the Federal Ministers agreed that, unless Field was given an acceptable accommodation, the Federal and Southern Rhodesian Governments should adhere to their threat not to attend the dissolution conference. It was recognised that this refusal might encourage the British Government to appoint a special commissioner and invest him with the powers of the Federal Government. Attempts could also be expected to try the loyalty of Federal civil servants. However, it was clearly impractical to make such an appointment and already, the Cabinet noted, Field had indicated that his Government would resist it.

The possibility of Southern Rhodesia making some concessions was examined but it was decided that its franchise and Constitution should not be altered. This, the Cabinet knew, would not satisfy the British Ministers who wished to be able to say at the UN and elsewhere that soon Southern

[48] Welensky Papers, FGC(63), 18th Meeting, Restricted Annexure, Federal Cabinet, 27 May 1963.
[49] *Northern News*, 28 May 1963.
[50] K. Young, *Rhodesia and Independence: A Study of British Colonial Policy* (London, 1967), p. 80.

Rhodesia would have an African Government. The Federal Ministers did not expect their boycott of the conference to provoke drastic British action. The Federal powers could continue to be run down gradually in consultation with the territories until all of them were handed over, but the Federal Parliament could not legislate itself out of existence as this was the prerogative of the British Parliament. The British Government was committed to enabling legislation and, the Federal Ministers thought, Butler seemed to consider it important that he should soon be able to inform the Commons that he had secured the agreement of the Governments concerned on the provisions of the legislation. As everything depended on Field's negotiations, the Federal Cabinet decided to do nothing until the final outcome of them was known. It was crucial, it concluded, that the Federal and Southern Rhodesian Governments acted in concert.[51]

Joelson warned Welensky that day, 30 May, that the British Press was trying to weaken Field. However, he was standing firm and, in addition, was rejecting all Butler's blandishments. In reply, Welensky said he was kept in the picture by Field, but thought that the British price might be too high. Field was also being pressed by other means because a bomb of British origin was found in the OK Bazaars in the centre of Salisbury, timed to go off simultaneously with the opening of the Pan-African Conference in Addis Ababa. The Federal Government suspected it was the work of a trained saboteur as a number of Rhodesian Africans had already received such training in Ghana and Egypt.

Kaunda was not the only Northern Rhodesian anxious for a speedy dissolution, because some of the Federal MPs from Northern Rhodesia, including van Eeden and A. W. Anderson, the chief whip, demanded that their territory shortly receive its fair share of Federal assets. Anderson even resigned his office on 30 May in a gesture of resistance to what he considered to be excessive Southern Rhodesian claims to the Federal spoils. The Southern Rhodesian Treasury was also known to be anxious that no further time be wasted in case the Southern Rhodesian share was reduced through the delay. It was believed to be short of money and anxious to tap Federal resources.[52]

Field returned on 6 June, leaving Dupont behind to undergo medical treatment. If the Southern Rhodesians were expecting to be enlightened on their fate, Field was to disappoint them. In a terse, brief statement to his Parliament he said little more than that he had made no concessions, even though Australia, New Zealand and Canada had been brought into the argument to try to force his hand. He believed that, in fact, only an exodus of all Europeans would please the Commonwealth and "we are not prepared to appease them in these matters". In fairness to Field, his negotiations were not complete and it was too soon to make anything public. He had, however, a surprise in store for the Federal Cabinet.

A meeting with Welensky, Greenfield and Caldicott was arranged to plan a common strategy. The first to arrive was I. D. Smith, and then Field appeared and stunned the Federal Ministers by announcing without further ado that he

[51] Welensky Papers, FGC(63), 19th Meeting, Restricted Annexure, Federal Cabinet, 30 May 1963.
[52] *Ibid.*, 24/152, f. 52, Joelson to Welensky, 30 May 1963; ff. 50–51, Welensky to Joelson, 5 June 1963; 31/56, f. 5, G. van Eeden to Welensky, 4 June 1963; *The Rhodesia Herald*, 1 June 1963.

had informed the British High Commissioner that his Government would attend the conference.[53]

Welensky recalls that Field said that: "I have played this card of non-attendance at the Conference until the spots are worn off. We are going."[54]

The Federal Government and, indeed, Dupont, had always believed that the British Government could not hold the dissolution conference without Southern Rhodesia because it was the other high-contracting party to the Federation. Lord Butler has confirmed that this was true, but Field went on to justify his decision to the Federal Cabinet by saying he had reason to think that the British Government would hold the conference regardless of whether Southern Rhodesia attended or not. Consequently, he said, Southern Rhodesia would suffer from not being adequately represented. Not surprisingly, consternation followed Field's announcement but the Federal Ministers succeeded in suggesting a further meeting between Caldicott and Field. Caldicott was a Southern Rhodesian and was held in high esteem by his fellow countrymen and, thus, it was hoped that he could persuade Field to reverse his decision and not throw away his strongest card. In the event, the meeting yielded nothing.[55]

On Saturday, 8 June, J. H. Howman, the Southern Rhodesian Minister of Community Development, arrived in London, to address the Royal Commonwealth Society, and briefed Dupont and Robinson. He informed them that Field had met his Cabinet on his return (prior to meeting Welensky, Greenfield and Caldicott) and had startled it by declaring that the Southern Rhodesian Government would not boycott the conference. Harper had objected, but Field had ignored him, saying that he had reviewed the situation with Smith and had decided to attend. He did not say that Smith had, in fact, advised against attending.[56]

Field later informed Kenneth Young that his Cabinet had taken the decision and that he had conveyed it to Welensky on 12 June. However, on Monday, 10 June, Welensky had already informed one of his confidants of Field's decision and that it left him with little choice but to agree to the Federal Government's attendance at the conference. Gaunt, then a member of the Southern Rhodesian Cabinet, moreover, confirmed in correspondence with Welensky in October 1968 that Field had informed the Cabinet and the Parliamentary Caucus that the Federal Government had decided to attend the conference, thus rendering pointless his refusal to attend.[57]

This was the basis of the canard which was perpetuated thereafter by the Rhodesian Front of the Federal responsibility for selling the pass. Welensky, Caldicott and others have consistently denied that it was their Government which took this step. In 1964 Gaunt inspired an exchange of letters in the Press from a variety of correspondents in an attempt to provoke Field into confirming publicly that he had misled his Cabinet. The only result, Gaunt

[53] Young, *Rhodesia and Independence*, *op. cit.*, p. 81.
[54] *The Rhodesia Herald*, Article by Welensky, 15 April 1969.
[55] Dupont, *The Reluctant President*, *op. cit.*, p. 133.
[56] Author's interview with Sir Albert Robinson and the Hon. I. D. Smith.
[57] Young, *Rhodesia and Independence*, *op. cit.*, p. 81; Welensky Papers, 43/*Grenfell*, Welensky to H. St L. Grenfell, 10 June 1963; 43/*Gaunt*, J. Gaunt to Welensky, 2 October 1968.

claimed, was that Ian Dillon (the RF chief whip, under whose name Gaunt had been writing to the Press) received a furious telephone call from Field.[58]

On 10 June, still somewhat disbelieving, Robinson telephoned Field for confirmation and tried to urge him to reconsider. Field would not yield, even when Dupont took over the telephone to protest. He told Dupont that it was a *fait accompli* because he had already informed the British High Commissioner in Salisbury. Dupont then proposed to resign because his advice was being ignored, but Field dissuaded him. To buy time, in case something could be done, Robinson informed Dupont that he would seek an interview with Butler. He did so and was granted one with alacrity. Butler greeted him with the news that Field had decided to attend. Robinson claimed that there must have been some mistake, but Butler responded by literally dancing around the desk, waving a telex and appearing utterly elated. It was from the British High Commissioner in Salisbury.[59]

There was nothing that Robinson could do and he certainly did not feel like dancing because he, Welensky and others had no doubt that the Rhodesian Front had thrown away its only real opportunity to force the British hand on the matter of independence. Butler might well have felt triumphant because he knew that otherwise he could not hold the dissolution conference and because he had avoided the necessity of settling the Southern Rhodesian question on terms which he believed his Parliament and the Commonwealth would not accept.[60] With the last obstacle removed, the process of dissolution could begin.

[58] Welensky Papers, 43/*Gaunt*, Welensky to J. Gaunt, 11 October 1968; Gaunt to Welensky, 28 October 1968.
[59] Author's interview with Sir Albert Robinson.
[60] Author's interview with Lord Butler.

CHAPTER THIRTY-EIGHT

Dissolution

The Victoria Falls Conference, and the Final Months of the Federation, June–December 1963

HAVING gulled Field, Butler would tantalise him on the independence issue until, in late 1963, Sir Alec Douglas-Home, Macmillan's successor as Prime Minister, disbanded the Central African Office and handed its responsibilities to Sandys, the Secretary of State for the Colonies and Commonwealth Relations. However, Sandys displayed even less inclination to settle the Southern Rhodesian issue before it became a running sore. Field, of course, had lost the lever to force the British Government to do anything. The exercise of dismemberment would be almost as frustrating. The Dissolution Conference was held and hailed as a triumph for Butler. Thereafter, committees were appointed to effect the dissolution, but the British Government showed a marked disposition to let matters slide until the Federal Government had lost any influence with which to force acceptance of its ideas. This would apply particularly to the fate of the Federal civil servants.

Shortly after Robinson had made his last bid to divert Butler, Field wrote, on 13 June, to Butler to confirm his decision. He recalled Butler's request for an early answer on the question of attendance at the conference, but felt that he did not need reminding that this had depended on the outcome of the negotiations on independence. In fact, Field said he was most disappointed that his entirely reasonable request for his country's independence had thus far not met with a favourable response from the British Government. Field did not propose to discuss what they had covered in London but felt that Butler should know that the British proposals were unacceptable to his Government. Thus he said he would continue to press his just and reasonable claims for independence, and would hold Butler to his promise of 16 May to resume these discussions at the earliest possible moment. Nevertheless, his Government believed it had to avoid prolonging the uncertainty for both the Federal Government and its employees, as well as for the Southern Rhodesians. Consequently, it was inclined to review the matter of attending the conference. However, it felt entitled to ask for further information before finally agreeing to attend. He asserted that Butler had constantly promised that the conference would not be an identical farce to that of the Federal Review in 1960 when there was no agenda and no apparent plan. That experience, Field said, made him insist that there should be preparatory work, an agenda and some idea from the British Government as to how it would deal with the situation which it had precipitated by its decision to dissolve the Federation. He could not believe that the British Government had taken this decision without having thoroughly considered the consequent problems. Thus it was only fair to ask it for tentative views on subjects on which it had so far been silent. Field specifically referred to the disposition of the public debt and the civil and armed services. As Butler had said that he wished to introduce enabling legislation before the British summer recess, it could be assumed that his preparations were nearly complete and Field thought that the Governments should be given sight of the draft bill. He found that the date for the conference was unacceptable because he was reporting to his Parliament on 18 June on their negotiations. Furthermore, the Federal Assembly would meet on 26 June and the Federal budget was due the next day. As these dates could not be altered, the conference would have to begin on 28 June, which would mean the adjournment of the Federal Assembly, but the Federal Government was willing to comply. To discuss independence further and to take advantage of Butler's willingness to meet him again before the conference, Field invited him to Salisbury on 25 or 26 June.

Then Field repeated his demand that all the Governments should be shown the British plans for the dissolution so that it would be clear that the conference "will not degenerate into a forum for the ventilation of evanescent political theories". He also recalled Butler's assurance of 2 May that the conference would not discuss the internal affairs of any territory. Subject to these conditions and the production of an acceptable agenda, he promised that the Southern Rhodesian Government would consider further its acceptance of the invitation to the conference.[1]

Welensky, who was angry with Field and none too enamoured of his dispatch to Butler, wrote to Butler saying that the Federal Government would attend if the Southern Rhodesian Government did. He echoed Field on the necessity of preparing for the conference and suggested that knowledge of British intentions would assist the Federal Government in deciding whether it should attend. He preferred working parties but, if the conference was necessary, it should be short, formal and designed to launch the working parties to prepare the ground for political decisions. These parties could report directly to the Governments or to the resumed conference later in the year. Like Field, Welensky saw difficulties in meeting earlier than 28 June.[2]

Welensky promptly informed Verwoerd in Pretoria that Field had failed to

[1] Welensky Papers, 20/3, ff. 23–26, Field to Butler, 13 June 1963 (published in *Correspondence between Her Majesty's Government and the Government of Southern Rhodesia, April – May 1963*, Command 2073 (London, June 1963), p. 16).

[2] Welensky Papers, 24/152, ff. 47–48, Welensky to Joelson, 13 June 1963; 20/9A, f. 5, Welensky to Butler, 13 June 1963.

get anywhere on the independence issue and was being faced with further demands, with Sir Robert Menzies, the Prime Minister of Australia, being brought into the argument. Menzies had written to Field and the tone of his letter had surprised Welensky. Field had responded by sending Howman to see Menzies who was currently in London.[3]

Butler replied promptly to Field agreeing that discussions should begin as soon as possible. As for the preparations for the conference, Butler knew that the Acting High Commissioner, D. A. Scott, had already spoken to Field and had found no difficulties. Butler confirmed that the internal affairs of any territory would not be discussed. He had considered allowing the Governments to reveal their plans to each other in advance, but thought it should be done at the conference. With some reluctance he agreed to postpone the conference to 28 June and proposed to announce it on 18 June and that the venue would be the Victoria Falls. He acknowledged Field's invitation to visit Salisbury on 25 or 26 June, but felt duty bound, as chairman, to travel directly to the Victoria Falls. However, he said he would arrive at the Falls on 26 June and would gladly receive Field to discuss the broadening of the basis of representation in the Southern Rhodesian Legislative Assembly and the issue of "non-discrimination". He felt that Field should not concern himself over the draft of the order in council because its final form would depend on the conference's decisions. Finally, he reminded Field that they had agreed that he (Butler) would publish their correspondence on 18 June when he announced the decision to hold the conference.[4] This appeared as the White Paper, Command 2073.

Butler replied to Welensky saying that he could see no difficulties with the agenda and, indeed, enclosed a draft which covered the ordering of the business of the conference, the problems of the reversion of the Federal functions to the territories, of the public debt, the civil service and the apportionment of assets and liabilities. It also provided for discussion on the machinery required for the resolution of those problems and on the timetable of dissolution. He felt that all this was best done at the conference and promised to play a full part in resolving the questions. The machinery had to be established, but he believed that the conference would be brief. He agreed reluctantly to the opening on 28 June, but warned about the detrimental effects of delay.[5]

Welensky replied that, if asked, his Government would formulate proposals on its commitments for submission at the conference. However, it reserved the right to tell its creditors of its plans. The next day, 19 June, he asked Robinson to inform Butler that, as the main purpose of the conference was to examine the problems of the dissolution and to set up the appropriate machinery, the Federal Government thought that the heads of the delegations (himself, Field and Hone) should only attend the opening, leaving the remainder of the respective delegations to continue the conference. This would reduce the likelihood of the adoption of strong political attitudes. Welensky repeated his suggestion of working parties to report to a second conference

[3] *Ibid.*, 43/*Verwoerd*, f. 6, Welensky to H. F. Verwoerd, 13 June 1963.
[4] *Ibid.*, 20/9A, f. 3, Butler to Field, 14 June 1963 (published in Command 2073, *op. cit.*, p. 18).
[5] *Ibid.*, 20/3, f. 17, Butler to Welensky, 15 June 1963.

after six months. The matter of forging new links between the territories could be reserved for this conference, he said. The prospects for these links being forged would be improved if everyone, except for Butler, was denied any opportunity to pronounce on them until the problems of the dissolution had been thoroughly examined in a non-political atmosphere. Thus, particular issues, such as the public debt, should be omitted from the agenda. To facilitate matters, he proposed that he, Butler, Hone and Field should meet on 27 June to review the conduct of the conference.[6] Welensky reserved for Goldberg, the Federal Minister of Health, his real emotion when telling him that the conference would be held. He said that "the Supreme Architect is determined to fill my cup of bitterness right to the brim".[7]

Greenfield was anxious to plan their strategy with the Southern Rhodesian delegation before anything else happened because he had received the rough draft of the dissolution bill and regarded its terms as wide, general and dangerous. He told Welensky that he had sent copies to Field and Dupont and was having it legally examined. Scott had warned him that Butler wanted the bill to be discussed by the conference but had said he would not "toss it into the arena".[8]

On 21 June Butler assured Welensky that the business of the conference would be so organised as to discourage the striking of political attitudes. Nevertheless, he was convinced that it would be pointless if the major problems of the dissolution were not examined before going to working parties, because the latter would need guidance as to how to proceed. Decisions on points of principle were required if the machinery was to work effectively. Future links should also be discussed lest the prospects for future collaboration diminish rather than improve. He rejected, as impossible, the suggestion that the leaders of the delegations should withdraw after the opening of the conference. In any case, they might not agree to comply. However, he gladly accepted the preliminary meeting of the leaders and was looking forward to working with Welensky.[9]

Welensky can be forgiven if he did not share the last sentiment. He rejected the discussion of major problems, before they were submitted to the working parties, because there had been no time for preliminary study. The results could be very damaging and it would be necessary to adjourn the conference for days at a time while the studies were made. There would, of course, be no documents available for research at the Victoria Falls. If discussion on major problems had to be held, Welensky demanded that Butler produce a list of points of principle to be reviewed in order that the inconvenience and delay might be reduced. He doubted the wisdom of discussing future associations because any progress would depend solely on official working parties which, behind the scenes, might be able to convince the immature territorial Ministers of the necessity of putting economics before political slogans.[10]

[6] *Ibid.*, ff. 12–13, Welensky to Butler, 18 June 1963; ff. 10–11, Welensky to Robinson, 19 June 1963.
[7] *Ibid.*, 43/*Goldberg*, f. 13, Welensky to B. D. Goldberg, 19 June 1963.
[8] *Ibid.*, 23/25, f. 1, Greenfield to Welensky, 19 June 1963; f. 6, Proposed Provisions for Inclusion in the Enabling Bill, (undated).
[9] *Ibid.*, 20/3, ff. 7–9, Butler to Welensky, 21 June 1963.
[10] *Ibid.*, ff. 2–3, Welensky to Butler, 22 June 1963.

Quite naturally, Welensky left the details of the Federal approach to Greenfield and his staff but gave his correspondents some idea of his opinions. On 21 June, he informed Stuart Cloete, the novelist, of his fury at a UN resolution which denounced the situation in Southern Rhodesia as explosive when, in fact, it was peaceful in contrast to Northern Rhodesia where, in a week, eight people had been killed and 50 injured in conflicts between the two Parties in the coalition Government. However, he said, the current double standards had never ceased to annoy him, as had the practice of treating him as the junior at Commonwealth Conferences. He had always been placed at the end of the table, while Makarios and Nkrumah were lionised. To others, he described the further discussions between Field and Butler, but warned that there were few, if any, cards left to play after Field had discarded his best hand. He still wondered why Field had returned from Britain convinced that he had to attend the conference when it was clear that he ought to refuse because Butler could not hold the conference without Southern Rhodesia. Welensky thought, correctly, that Field would pay bitterly for faltering. It was most pertinent that Butler had said in the Commons that independence for Southern Rhodesia was dependent on the concessions which its Government was prepared to make. Such a statement was unbelievable to Welensky when the 1961 Constitution was less than a year old, and of British invention, despite Whitehead's boasts to the contrary. Welensky said he was very disturbed. He was also irritated by Butler's decision to play the conference virtually "off the cuff", with little preparation. A suspicion that Butler wanted the conference to be only a façade filled him with trepidation. He was, however, flattered by being offered the sponsorship of his sympathisers as a candidate for, by now, five seats in the next British general election. It must have given him some satisfaction to hear John Connell, the journalist and biographer, maintain that Sandys, Macleod and Butler had removed themselves from the running for the leadership of the Tory Party through their habit of lying easily, deviously and continually about Africa.[11]

Welensky disclosed some of his thoughts to the public on 26 June when he presented the Federal Assembly with a White Paper dealing with the consequences of dissolution. He emphasised that there was no desire to re-open the controversy and hoped that the research and labour put into this Paper would serve the forthcoming negotiations constructively. In the same spirit of co-operation, he said that he and his colleagues would attend the conference, aiming to achieve a quick but orderly dissolution which would pay due regard to the rights of the Federal judiciary, civil and armed services, as well as to those of the creditors.[12]

The White Paper called for the well-being of the inhabitants to be given priority in the dissolution. The British Government might have decided to kill the Federation, but there was no need for a complete destruction of the territories' economic association. Certainly, the benefits of the Federation ought to be safeguarded while political considerations, which did not relate to

[11] *Ibid.*, 27/10, f. 33, Welensky to S. Cloete, 21 June 1963; 43/*Wall*, f. 45, Welensky to Major P. Wall, 21 June 1963; 43/*Salisbury*, f. 59, Welensky to Lord Salisbury, 24 June 1963; 43/*Connell*, f. 21, J. Connell to Welensky, 26 June 1963.

[12] Fed R & N *Debates* (Salisbury), Vol. 20, Col. 418, 26 June 1963.

the economic well-being of the inhabitants, should be ignored. The Federal achievements included the creation of a common economy with markets, currency, taxation and a central bank. Only the creation of the Federal capital market had made it possible to raise money internally and externally for development projects like Kariba. Aside from the £28 000 000 raised locally and the £47 000 000 secured externally for Kariba, between 1954-62 the Federal Government had obtained £94 000 000 in medium- and long-term loans from the domestic capital market, and £66 000 000 from abroad. The resulting growth in revenue had allowed the expansion of the railways, of power and of the copper industry. The separation of Northern and Southern Rhodesia would destroy the common economy and sever the common services. Northern Rhodesia would suffer from the disruption of power and transport services as its alternative routes had limited carrying capacity, and the development of new ones would be costly. The loss of the common capital market would limit development. (All these predictions would later come true for Zambia.)

The White Paper maintained that Southern Rhodesia would lose its markets in Northern Rhodesia and the revenue from that territory's mineral traffic. The conditions in Northern Rhodesia did not favour large-scale industrial development (as Kaunda would discover in the coming years) and the effect of the re-location of head offices from Salisbury to Lusaka would have only a transient effect. Northern Rhodesia's internal market was too small and the distances for the haulage of raw materials were too great. A shortage of labour would produce a high-cost structure which inevitably would bring tariff protection and, in its wake, lower tax yields, returns, and a reduction in the capacity to expand. It was likely that Northern Rhodesia would experience balance of payments difficulties which would be aggravated by fluctuations in the copper price. The price had fallen in the previous three years and the value of Northern Rhodesian exports was less in 1962 than it was in 1956. If the power grid were interfered with, great damage could be done to each of the Rhodesias and particularly to the Copperbelt which was dependent on power produced on the southern bank of Kariba. It was possible that the Southern Rhodesian thermal stations could be rejuvenated, with the effect that the Kariba power station would fall into disuse. There was a very real danger that friction could result from inter-territorial claims to Kariba's resources.

The White Paper surveyed Federal functions. For example, the headquarters of the Rhodesia Railways was in Bulawayo and all maintenance was done there. However, the repair facilities were too large for Southern Rhodesia's purposes alone, while Northern Rhodesia had inadequate facilities and insufficient men to man a separate service. It had also to be remembered that, of the £99 000 000 invested in the Rhodesia Railways, Southern Rhodesia had provided £39 000 000, while Northern Rhodesia had found only £15 000 000. The Federal Government had supplied £32 000 000. The discharge of the obligations to the creditors would be difficult and burdensome and could not be recouped by operating separate railways. Furthermore, if the two future railways did not pursue a common policy, they could have a detrimental effect on the economies of the Rhodesias.

The break-up of civil aviation, meteorological and postal services, the White Paper pointed out, could have equally harmful effects. The expansion of trade and commerce in the Federal era had, of course, been the result of the general development of the railways, power and other factors such as the Federal trade missions. Great diversification had been achieved as 66,6 per cent of all exports in 1954 went to Britain and South Africa while, in 1962, only 54 per cent went to those two countries. The Northern Rhodesian market was very important to Southern Rhodesia because it absorbed 25 per cent of its direct sales.

The same arguments applied to agriculture and the agricultural services which the Federation had supplied. In 1960-61, the gross agricultural product of Southern Rhodesia was £57 400 000 and that of Northern Rhodesia £7 400 000. The loss of markets and of marketing expertise would gravely affect Northern Rhodesia.

The majority of the specialist health services were in Southern Rhodesia where its greater fee-paying population could sustain them, and Northern Rhodesia would be put to great expense to replace them, as well as providing its own training facilities. Southern Rhodesia would suffer from having to bear alone the cost of the level of services which the Federal Government had built up.

Dissolution would have particularly damaging effects on education because the Federal Government had trained 91 per cent of all recruits to the non-African teaching service while assisting in the training of Africans. It had borne the cost of the university which could well become bankrupt. After dissolution and division, the broadcasting facilities could be misused to provide hostile inter-territorial propaganda.

The defence burden, which Southern Rhodesia would inherit, could be crippling. The current cost was £8 755 714 and, if it could not be found, a most efficient and potent army and air force could be lost. Finally, the White Paper said that the Federal Government was proud of its achievements and pleaded, therefore, that the needs of the people be placed foremost in the forthcoming readjustment.[13]

Greenfield, Evans and the Federal Attorney-General, R. A. Yates, had been arguing with Scott, the Acting British High Commissioner, over the British intentions with regard to the enabling bill. The British proposed dissolution through an order in council, but, as has been seen, Greenfield thought that its wide terms held dangers because the British Government could then legislate in any manner it wished. In particular, the British Government would be able to legislate for matters which fell within the competence of the Southern Rhodesian Parliament and for matters which affected Southern Rhodesia but which fell within the responsibilities of the Federal Assembly. There was no suggestion by the British of obtaining the prior approval of the territorial Governments or legislatures. Danger for Southern Rhodesia lay, for example, in changes in the law affecting non-African education, or defence. Southern Rhodesia could try to insist that the order in council should have its prior approval, but the British Government

[13] *The Break-up: Effects and Consequences on the Two Rhodesias*, C. Fed. 246 (Salisbury, 26 June 1963).

was unlikely to agree because the same privilege would have to be granted to the northern territories. The Southern Rhodesian Government could always fall back on its 1923 Convention with Britain, Greenfield concluded, to force her to comply in this matter.[14]

The Barotse Government compiled a memorandum for the conference because, while it had always been consulted before, it had not been invited to it. It warned that it would demand to be reinstated as a separate state in terms of the Treaty of 1900 under which no one could settle its boundaries except with the permission of the Litunga and Council. Barotseland had honoured the Treaty and expected others to do the same. Once independent, it proposed to modernise its Constitution, hold early elections and then negotiate with the other territories on an equal footing.[15]

As promised, Butler met Field and Smith on the eve of the conference at the Victoria Falls. (Dupont had arrived with them, but was ill.) Butler, however, merely reiterated his demands for the reform of the franchise, the broadening of the legislature and the abolition of racial discrimination. Field, of course, had won his election on the basis of the retention of the Land Apportionment Act and was, therefore, in an impossible position. Moreover, Kaunda and Nkumbula were demanding the implementation of universal adult suffrage in Southern Rhodesia and it was feared that they would influence Butler not to concede anything. Nevertheless, Field decided finally to attend the conference because Butler promised that the independence question would be dealt with immediately and had added that he saw no difficulty in granting Southern Rhodesia its independence when the northern territories received theirs. At least this is what Field and Smith heard Butler say.[16]

Butler denies that he said anything like this and claims that Welensky supports him. It is true that Welensky said, in April 1969, that nothing was said in his presence about Southern Rhodesia's independence but that he understood that negotiations thereon would resume immediately the problems of dissolution had been solved. Yet, the day after the conference ended he informed Wall that Field had made no progress of any kind with Butler.[17]

Dupont was assured by Field and Smith that the promise had been given and they told Kenneth Young that Butler and Field had been alone when the statement was made. Consequently, Field had gone to find Smith to have the promise repeated to him. This done, they left Butler's room convinced that independence was assured. Smith turned at the door and irreverently wagged his finger at Butler and asked him not to go back on his word. Field later repeated this story to Lord Blake. If the promise were given, Field's mistake was, again, not to have ensured that it was written down. Smith had asked for

[14] Welensky Papers, 23/25, f. 1, D. A. Scott to Evans, 21 June 1963; FGC(63), 22nd Meeting, Restricted Annexure A, Federal Cabinet, 24 June 1963.

[15] *Ibid.*, 32/20, f. 39, Memorandum by the Barotse Government, 25 June 1963.

[16] C. Dupont, *The Reluctant President* (Bulawayo, 1978), p. 133; K. Young, *Rhodesia and Independence: A Study in British Colonial Policy* (London, 1967), p. 89; Author's interview with the Hon. I. D. Smith.

[17] Lord Butler, *The Art of the Possible: The Memoirs of Lord Butler* (London, 1973), p. 227; *The Rhodesia Herald*, 15 April 1969; Welensky Papers, 43/*Wall*, Welensky to Wall, 4 July 1963.

this to be done but Field thought it unnecessary after Butler had given his word.[18]

Kaunda did not believe that Field had secured anything and said so publicly during the Conference. He was sure that: "Only one thing is certain, Nkomo is going to rule",[19] and, throughout the subsequent years, Kaunda remained determined that he would.

On 28 June, in the conference room of the Victoria Falls Hotel, Butler welcomed the delegates and described their meeting as being of the highest significance for Central Africa. He regretted that the Conference could not have been held earlier, and urged the delegates to look forward, even though some of them might regret "the ending of a cherished vision". His Government acknowledged that the Conference represented the closing of a great venture which had the highest purposes and hopes and, as its objective, the social, economic and political progress of its inhabitants. He thought the Conference should retain this objective.

Butler found that the current uncertainty made dissolution extremely urgent and suggested that the Conference first study its problems so that the necessary machinery could be created. However, he believed that sight should not be lost of the possibilities of future collaboration. Indeed, his Government intended to promote some sort of association, particularly one which would ensure economic prosperity.

Butler suggested that, once the necessary machinery for the transfer of Federal functions was ready, the working parties should receive guidance on the views of the territorial Governments with regard to functions and services. Firstly, he suggested, that the subjects which were easy to transfer should be identified. He believed that the fiscal powers would present particular difficulties. There should be time at least for a cursory look at the future arrangements for defence. There would be problems over citizenship and over inter-territorial movement. Courts of appeal would be needed to replace the Federal Supreme Court, as would alternative employment for the Federal public service. To allay the fears of the public servants, the Conference would want their views on their absorption by the territorial services. There was also the question of their pension liabilities. The Conference had to devise a broad approach to the problem of the public debt, the distribution of Federal assets and the apportionment of Federal liabilities. An apportionment commission might be more appropriate than an inter-governmental working party. As the work of all working parties had to be co-ordinated, a general dissolution committee might be needed. A firm programme for the dissolution was required to eliminate any future argument.

Butler invited the views of the delegates, and Welensky spoke first. He stated that his delegation accepted that the decision on dissolution was irrevocable and thus came prepared to co-operate. He agreed that the uncertainty had to be ended, and therefore no time should be wasted over effecting the dissolution, but with the minimum of harm to the territories.

[18] Dupont, *The Reluctant President*, *op. cit.*, p. 134; Young, *Rhodesia and Independence*, *op. cit.*, p. 89; R. Blake, *A History of Rhodesia* (London, 1977), p. 350; Author's interview with the Hon. I. D. Smith.

[19] Welensky Papers, 33/108, Press Report, 1 July 1963.

There were three important issues, namely, the fate of the Federal public service, of the public debt, and of the defence of the area. The last, however, could be left until the territories knew what responsibilities they could undertake. He urged the immediate appointment of working parties with simple terms of reference. He considered that a general survey of problems was unnecessary.

Field had little to add to Welensky's statement. He said his delegation was willing to co-operate and sought a quick end to the uncertainty. He agreed that there should be no general survey and that the details could be safely left to the working parties. There might be issues which defied resolution, but he wished to settle them as soon as possible on a friendly basis.

Hone claimed that Northern Rhodesians of all races welcomed the Conference and hoped for a speedy dissolution. He proposed that the Conference should devise all the machinery and draw up the time-table. Most urgent of all was to return the fiscal powers to the territories. The absorption of the Federal civil servants was most important, and he revealed that his Government would employ as many as possible. Unlike Field and Welensky, he favoured a general survey.

Kaunda welcomed the co-operative spirit displayed by Welensky and Field, and thought that, if it pervaded the Conference, complete success was possible. He wished to allay the fears of the Federal civil servants and thus would endorse Hone's statement that his Government would absorb as many as possible, irrespective of race. He agreed on the urgency of the transfer of the fiscal powers and thought it was imperative to appoint a commission, under an impartial and independent chairman, to effect the dissolution.

Nkumbula was equally impressed with the friendly atmosphere at the Conference. He endorsed the call for swift action and supported the idea of a dissolution commission. The sole representative of the Nyasaland Government, H. S. Norman-Walker, declined to make a statement and encouraged Butler to attempt to terminate the session. Butler noted Welensky's suggestion of concentration on the problems of the civil service and the public debt, Field's rejection of the survey of general problems, and Northern Rhodesia's demand for the urgent study of fiscal matters. He proposed that the afternoon's session should concentrate on the practical problems. Welensky was provoked sufficiently to reiterate that he would not agree to a general survey. He wanted time to study Butler's speech. The secretary-general of the Conference, M. D. Tennant (who was Secretary at Butler's Central African Office), then outlined the arrangements which he had made, and a Press communiqué was drafted stating that it had been agreed that the aim of the Conference would be to ensure the orderly and speedy transfer of powers to the territorial Governments. Butler added a request to the delegates to treat the Press with caution.[20]

Under the skilful guidance of Butler, the Conference concluded its business in less than a week. It was not, however, without its alarums and excursions. When Kaunda demanded that a British commission should replace the Federal Government in the final phase, Welensky threatened to withdraw

[20] *Ibid.*, 23/25, ff. 64–68, Opening Statement by Butler, 28 June 1963.

from the Conference. Butler would not allow him to do so and Hone thereupon asked for a 30-minute adjournment to permit his African Ministers' tempers to cool.[21]

On 1 July, the Federal Government claimed that, since the British had taken the decision to dissolve the Federation, they should meet the Federal financial obligations. Butler refused to accept this as entirely true because his Government had been forced to recognise the political realities when two of the territories had indicated that they wished to secede. In reply, Welensky said that the current circumstances were no different from 1953, when the Federation had been imposed, because the opposition of the Africans then was just as apparent. The only difference was that the British Government had changed its mind and should be compelled to accept the liabilities of its action. Kaunda interjected that the very real difference between 1953 and 1963 was that, in 1953, there had been no effective voice for the Africans. He agreed with Butler that the British Government had been left with no choice but to accept the wishes of the inhabitants of the northern territories. Nkumbula agreed. The Federal delegates said nothing more, though they could have repeated what they had said so often about Britain's fostering of African nationalism while failing to give the Federation any support. Field confined himself to complaining that the British Government had failed to consult him on the decision to dissolve the Federation even though Southern Rhodesia had been a high-contracting party to its formation.[22]

Otherwise, Butler managed to avoid controversy, but events in Nyasaland brought moments of unease. There were unpleasant incidents involving the MCP's "Malawi Police", including an assault on the occupants of a car which drew out in front of Banda's vehicle. An Austrian man, a girl of 16 and a boy of eleven were beaten and the result was a storm of protest from the European population, including the civil servants. A telephone call to Welensky from the Federal Ministry of Health described the situation as explosive. A hundred civil servants cabled the British Government asking for the control of the police to be returned to Jones.[23] The situation brought a warning from Welensky which worried Butler as Welensky said that the Federal Government still possessed the power to intervene in Nyasaland to restore law and order. The European civil servants threatened to leave unless action were taken, but little was done by the Nyasaland authorities. In the aftermath, a law was passed which compelled all drivers of vehicles to pull off the road when Banda's car appeared.[24]

On 3 July, the delegates recorded their closing remarks. Field thanked Butler for the manner in which he had conducted the Conference. He believed that the co-operative attitude displayed by the Northern Rhodesian Government augured well for the future, and asked the Nyasaland representative to convey his best wishes to his Government. He also expressed admira-

[21] *Manchester Guardian*, 5 July 1963.

[22] Welensky Papers, 23/25, f. 142, Minutes of the 5th Session of the Victoria Falls Conference, 1 July 1963.

[23] *The Rhodesia Herald*, 2 July 1963; Welensky Papers, 33/104, f. 7, Telephone conversation between Welensky and the officials of the Federal Ministry of Health, 2 July 1963.

[24] *The Daily Telegraph*, 4 July 1963.

tion for the helpful attitude of the Federal delegation. Hone endorsed these remarks and commended Welensky for the approach which he had adopted. Welensky agreed that Butler was largely responsible for the Conference's success. Although, Welensky said, the Conference had been a painful experience, his Government was determined to play its part in the work ahead. Butler was grateful for the compliments paid to him and, in thanking everyone for their co-operation, wished to pay a special tribute to the Federal delegation. He hoped that the same spirit would endure in the future.[25]

In his memoirs Butler also praises Welensky's magnanimity, though he appears to regret that Welensky and his Ministers continued to refuse his hospitality and ate apart from him in the hotel dining room. He was grateful that Welensky found time to visit him privately in the evenings to discuss the affairs of the day. Welensky told him of his plans for his retirement but, perhaps, had the delicacy not to convey what a bitter experience it was to assist in the destruction of his work of 25 years. He did not spare his correspondents on this subject while describing Butler as a skilful chairman and an arch-compromiser. Welensky said that Butler had not endeared himself to him by offering him a seat in the Lords, and only the presence of Mrs Butler tempered his reply. It irritated him very much that the Press and others described Butler's achievement as a victory, because he could see no victory in destruction. Field also annoyed him by failing to support him, against the bitter opposition of Kaunda, when he sought compensation for the Federal Ministers.[26]

Welensky indicated publicly that he continued to blame Macmillan for the break-up of the Federation. He maintained that the British Conservative Government lacked moral fibre and had been in power for too long. Privately he said that Macmillan was so cynical that he believed that no one would catch him out. Macmillan, he asserted, had convinced the Press to condone his acts of double-crossing in which he had liquidated the Commonwealth, expelled South Africa from it, betrayed the whites in Africa, and thrown away millions of pounds of British capital. It seemed ironical to Welensky that, after all that, Macmillan had only been discredited by the Profumo affair (in which the British Minister of War, John Profumo, had attempted to conceal his liaison with Christine Keeler who, at the same time, had a like relationship with a Russian diplomat). Finally, Welensky said that "the Victoria Falls Conference, like the Ides of March, has come but not gone" because its effects would be far reaching.[27]

Butler lingered to discuss with Kaunda and Nkumbula a new, self-governing constitution for Northern Rhodesia and promised there would be no delay. Hone, however, doubted whether elections could be held before October. Kaunda took the opportunity to praise Butler publicly for his

[25] Welensky Papers, 23/25, ff. 174–175, Minutes of the 8th Session of the Victoria Falls Conference, 3 July 1963.

[26] Butler, *The Art of the Possible*, *op. cit.*, p. 230; Welensky Papers, 43/*Goldberg*, f. 25, Welensky to B. D. Goldberg, 5 July 1963; 27/110, f. 7, Welensky to Sir Keith Acutt, 5 July 1963; 29/60, f. 4, Welensky to R. Meier, 10 July 1963; 27/109, f. 14, Welensky to A. T. Adams, 11 July 1963.

[27] *The Daily Telegraph*, 4 July 1963; Welensky Papers, 43/*Connell*, f. 22, Welensky to J. Connell, 5 July 1963; 32/4, f. 11, Welensky to Pike, 4 July 1963.

achievements and Welensky for the dignity which he displayed in, what must have been for him, a sad moment. Kaunda believed he could co-operate with Field with what remained of the common services, namely the Rhodesia Railways, Central African Airways and Kariba power.[28]

The Report of the Conference was published on 10 June. It recorded that the delegates had agreed on a speedy and orderly transfer, but had recognised that certain complex problems could not be settled immediately and had set up means to deal with them. These problems included the Federal civil service, the public debt, inter-territorial collaboration, citizenship and the Federal Supreme Court.

The Report described the rejection of Kaunda's idea of replacing the Federal Government with a British commission. Instead, the Conference had agreed to the appointment of two committees. Committee A, the general committee, would be drawn from the four Governments under a British chairman and would plan the orderly and speedy transfer of the Federal functions and devise solutions to the problems of dissolution. It would make recommendations concerning the handling of Federal assets and liabilities. If necessary, it would suggest the appointment of an apportionment commission. It would appoint sub-committees and seek to reach agreement with the respective Governments. The Governments would each appoint a principal representative to the Committee and could nominate alternative representatives in accordance with the subjects being discussed. Committee B would deal with inter-territorial questions and would comprise representatives of the three territories under a British chairman who would be assisted by Federal officials. It would keep the Federal Government informed as to when it required it to act. The chairman of Committee A would co-ordinate the work of both Committees. If a territorial government was ready to take over a Federal service, there would be no delay.

The Conference had agreed that as many Federal civil servants as possible would be employed by the territorial Governments which would state as soon as possible what terms they could offer them. Machinery was also to be created to secure the discharge of the pension liabilities for Federal officers and their dependants. The Federal Government had, however, strenuously resisted the compulsory secondment which the Northern Rhodesian Government had sought. It was agreed that the Federal Public Service Association would be consulted on this.

The Report recalled the thesis of the Federal Government that, as the Federal debt would cripple development in the territories, Britain was responsible for Federal obligations. The Southern Rhodesian Government had agreed, though it was prepared to meet its fair share of the public debt. Northern Rhodesia wanted the question re-examined, but the British Government would not accept its liability and argued that the territories were also gaining Federal assets as well as debts. However, it would consider aid in accordance with its policy of assisting developing countries. The matter was referred to a committee.

Butler had suggested that inter-territorial collaboration was in the interests

[28] *Daily Mail*, 5 July 1963.

of common prosperity. He referred to a common market for goods and labour, common banking and credit facilities, and the use of the same currency. There were also the common services, like the railways, which could be maintained. He had suggested that a body be appointed to examine these matters. The Federal delegation had dismissed the whole subject as one for the territorial Governments, but the Northern Rhodesians were only interested in the arrangements for the railways, the airways and hydro-electric power. The Southern Rhodesians hoped that collaboration would go a little further.

The problem of tax collection was discussed and various schemes were left for examination by a committee. Broadly it was agreed that the fiscal powers would be transferred at an agreed, early date. Until then the Federal Government would finance any services which were transferred. Defence would revert to the position before 1953 when Southern Rhodesia controlled its own forces, and Britain those of the northern territories. The members of the forces would be given the privilege of declaring in which territory they would serve. Any unit's assets would remain with it, though their value would be brought into account in apportioning assets and liabilities. The most important result was that Southern Rhodesia would gain intact the European army units (the Rhodesian Light Infantry and the Special Air Service), as well as the Royal Rhodesian Air Force with all its equipment, except for a few transport aircraft which were given to Northern Rhodesia.

Federal citizens would remain British subjects and would become citizens of the territories to which they belonged. A new court of appeal to replace the Federal Supreme Court was a matter of negotiation between the territories. Lastly, the target date for the completion of the dissolution was set at 31 December 1963. The Committees would have to report by mid-September to give the Governments time to provide the necessary legislation.[29]

Delivering the Report to the Federal Assembly, Welensky made it clear that the onus henceforth lay with the territorial Governments to achieve the transfer of powers. His Government would do what it could to ensure that the breaking of links did as little damage as possible. He thought that the most trying days lay ahead for the territories because he knew that it was easy to destroy but difficult to construct.[30]

Butler described the results of the Conference to the Commons on 11 July when the Rhodesia and Nyasaland Bill had its second reading. In doing so, he paid tribute to Welensky's statesmanlike attitude. The achievements of the Federation were plain and he was sure that everyone wished to pay tribute to those who had made them possible. Arthur Bottomley, the Labour MP, thought that Welensky had greater faith in the Conservative Party than he should have. He hoped that the two Rhodesias would be able to retain and strengthen their inter-territorial links. He thought that current circumstances forbad the granting of the Southern Rhodesian claims for independence. James Griffiths declared that Welensky was "the biggest man Central Africa has produced". He and Arthur Creech Jones explained their policies towards the Federation, telling again why the Colonial Office civil servants had not

[29] Welensky Papers, 42/109, Report of the Conference, 10 July 1963 — published as *Report of the Central African Conference*, Command 2093 (London, 1963).

been allowed to advocate it. Victor Goodhew decried both the Bill and the arrogance of those who thought they knew better than the men on the spot. R. H. Turton worried about the fate of the Federal services and, consequently, the spread of disease.[31]

The third reading of the Bill was held on 15 July, and ten days later it was the turn of the Lords. They discussed first the fate of Barotseland and were assured by the Lord Chancellor that no changes would be made without full consultation and the agreement of the Litunga. The Lord Chancellor and Lord Listowel, of the Labour Party, examined the Bill's clauses. Listowel welcomed Butler's refusal to give Southern Rhodesia independence under its current Constitution and discounted the possibility that Southern Rhodesia would take it unilaterally. However, he still felt that the Government needed reminding that British interests in Africa, at the UN and elsewhere would depend on how it dealt with Southern Rhodesia. Even the fate of the Commonwealth hung in the balance.

Lord Salisbury was determined that the names of Malvern and Welensky would endure as men ahead of their time. He wanted assurance that the Federal civil servants would not be forced to take territorial employment at the pain of losing their compensation. He feared for the fate of civilisation and noticed that Listowel and his ilk in the Commons still seemed to be inspired by the pathetic, if passionate, belief that democracy had only to be introduced for all troubles to end. He believed fervently in democracy but feared the dictatorships which would be introduced in Northern Rhodesia and Nyasaland. Southern Rhodesia was different, he said, because it was ruled by an oligarchy, as Britain had been for 700 years, and it might suit Southern Rhodesia at its current state of development. He asked why so much attention had to be paid to the views of people outside Southern Rhodesia — the Afro-Asians, the UN and others. The only motive of the Afro-Asians was to expel the white man from Africa and this, he declared, was unacceptable. They did not care for democracy or free institutions. Salisbury implored the Government not to force the Southern Rhodesians to the point where they felt they had no option but to seek their own destiny. The haggling should cease and they should be given their independence without more ado. He declared: "If we do, I feel confident that, blood of our blood and bone of our bone, they will prove worthy of it."

Lord Colyton believed that, as Britain had decided to dissolve the Federation, she should foot the whole bill and not just Nyasaland's portion. He could not vote for the Bill because it betrayed 9 000 000 people. He, too, paid a warm tribute to Welensky, his courage and his integrity. Lord De La Warr argued cogently for Southern Rhodesian independence, while Lord Milverton blamed the situation on the "vacillating incoherence" of the Government's African policy. Nonetheless, the Bill passed into law.[32]

Welensky wrote to Salisbury and Colyton thanking them for their defence of the Federation. The Conference, he said, had been a melancholy occasion and he had been criticised for refusing British hospitality. He disliked the

[30] Fed R & N *Debates* (Salisbury), Vol. 20, Col. 489, 10 July 1963.
[31] House of Commons *Hansard* (London), Vol. 680, Col. 1427 f., 11 July 1963.
[32] House of Lords *Hansard* (London), Vol. 252, Col. 825 f., 25 July 1963.

appointment of Sir George Curtis as chairman of Committee A, but felt that he had to accept him to get the Committees under way. He was thankful at least that Butler had avoided a repetition of events in the Congo by keeping the bulk of the armed forces under Southern Rhodesian control. However, he was convinced that Field was being "taken for a ride" by Butler and thought Field's hour of disillusionment was at hand.[33]

His role in trying to apply pressure on Field encouraged Sir Robert Menzies to write to Welensky on Southern Rhodesia, arguing as a supporter of the Commonwealth. He warned that the chances of Southern Rhodesia joining the Commonwealth or the UN would be profoundly affected by the attitude of the new Commonwealth and the Afro-Asian bloc. He wanted to help because he felt it would be a tragedy if Southern Rhodesia was squeezed out. He had met Howman in London and was surprised to find that he thought Southern Rhodesia was already a member of the Commonwealth and that only the question of expulsion would arise. Howman, in his view, was mistaken as the Commonwealth was an association of independent countries and Southern Rhodesia was not independent. If Southern Rhodesia gained independence, Menzies said, it was probable that it would be refused membership and would, unfortunately, be driven closer to South Africa.

Menzies reported that Butler had told him of the conditions for independence which he had transmitted to Field. Menzies saw no difficulties over these because the Africans in the "blocking third" would not want to block progressive legislation, and it was unlikely that Field would introduce retrogressive legislation. Thus Menzies wanted Welensky to use his "powerful" influence to produce a compromise which would stop short of universal suffrage. This could be accepted by the new Commonwealth, and Southern Rhodesia might be recognised. Menzies aligned himself with the strong support for Southern Rhodesia which was apparent in the Commons and amongst the British public. He thought that some of the new Commonwealth countries might threaten to withdraw but that this was preferable to the exclusion of Southern Rhodesia.[34]

Welensky replied on 16 July that the average Rhodesian found it strange that Southern Rhodesia's promotion from a self-governing state to independence would mean expulsion from the Commonwealth, when that territory had remained loyal in the Boer and two World Wars. Field had to weigh against Butler's conditions the risks of placing power too soon in the hands of the majority. The blocking third only needed the addition of a sixth, derived from the lowering of the A roll qualifications, to become a blocking half. In addition Field, unlike Whitehead, stood little chance of winning seats among the blocking third. Welensky agreed that, if Field were to obtain independence legally, he would have to please the British Government. However, it was difficult to advise Field to make the concessions which Butler sought because they would mean his eclipse and a foot on the path towards government by the unfit. He had seen that Menzies had spoken in Australia about the need for Southern Rhodesia to progress to majority rule within measurable time

[33] Welensky Papers, 43/*Salisbury*, f. 63, Welensky to Salisbury, 27 July 1963; 43/*Colyton*, f. 76, Welensky to Colyton, 22 July 1963.
[34] *Ibid.*, 29/64, f. 17, Sir Robert Menzies to Welensky, 27 June 1963.

and warned that the Southern Rhodesian European regarded this as the Australian would a hand-over to the Aborigine.[35]

In his reply to Welensky, Menzies felt it was undeniable that the new members of the Commonwealth controlled the application for membership. For that reason alone, he sought the concessions. In fact, in London recently, he had indicated that he would disapprove of only the northern territories being accepted as Commonwealth members. He was saddened by Britain's loss of interest in the Commonwealth because she was seeking her salvation in Europe. He explained that the new members regarded the Commonwealth as a version of the UN and displayed an incurable itch to interfere in other people's affairs. This was the very issue of the South African debate. Nevertheless, he did not think that the preponderance of republics should weaken the allegiance to the Crown and felt that such matters were ones which "reactionary old Tories", like Welensky and himself, could usefully discuss. In a second letter, striving behind the scenes to keep the Commonwealth together with the Crown as the pivot, Menzies asked Welensky to attend a conference but did not seem to realise that Welensky would not be in power for much longer.[36]

During this exchange, the Federal Government was chastised in the Federal Assembly by Savanhu for its failures on partnership. Replying, Greenfield thought this attack only harmed race relations by its distortions. He denied emphatically that his Government had pursued white supremacy and pointed out that a chief feature of the recent British action was the betrayal of partnership.[37]

In fact, Greenfield, who, like Welensky, had refused a British honour (the membership of the Privy Council) was in a troublesome mood. Inspired by the continuing violent unrest in the northern territories, he was determined to bring it to general notice. He was particularly annoyed by the result of a protest meeting of civil servants with regard to the assault on the occupants of the car stopped by the "Malawi Police" in June. The Deputy Chief Secretary, P. Youens, had addressed the meeting and had claimed that the police were investigating the affair. He was immediately contradicted by Superintendent Alan Kerr, the officer-in-charge of Blantyre, who said that the Nyasaland Government would not allow the police to charge the culprits. Kerr was promptly dismissed from the Nyasaland Police. Welensky, reporting this to Butler, added that he had been told how a tour of Nyasaland by Chipembere had left a trail of blood. He had been informed that the police were no longer allowed to attend meetings of the MCP Ministers and could not interrogate the Malawi Youth.[38]

Welensky also fed this information to John Biggs-Davison (later Sir John), the Conservative MP, because Butler had led the Commons to believe that Nyasaland was perfectly peaceful. Greenfield issued a ministerial statement in the Federal Assembly on 30 July, on the erosion of the rule of law in Nyasaland, which highlighted several important changes that had taken place

[35] *Ibid.*, f. 12, Welensky to Menzies, 16 July 1963; f. 10, Menzies's Press Conference, 15 July 1963.
[36] *Ibid.*, f. 5, Menzies to Welensky, 27 July 1963.
[37] Fed R & N *Debates* (Salisbury), Vol. 20, Col. 784 f., 17 July 1963.
[38] Welensky Papers, 27/28, f. 17, Welensky to Butler, 29 July 1963.

since self-government and which adversely affected the administration of justice, the maintenance of law and order, and the preservation of personal liberty. There had also been ominous Nyasaland ministerial pronouncements on these issues which had caused widespread concern. He said he issued the statement because, while it still existed, the Federal Government could to a small extent protect some of those rights. After its demise, people would have to look to Britain. He felt that the British people and the rest of the civilised world should understand what was happening so that they could press the British Government to restore the rule of law while it still had the power. If nothing were done, the Bill of Rights would become a mockery.

Greenfield believed it was clear that the objective was to create a one-party state in Nyasaland and that no opposition would be brooked. He cited complaints of people who did not belong to the Malawi Congress Party and who might have been assaulted by the Party's agencies, such as the Youth League. He noted that, on 27 June, Banda had publicly spoken about his "boys in white" — the MCP's "Malawi Police" — showing any arrogant European how tough they were. Three days later the "boys" had assaulted the three Europeans who had failed to move their car off the road as Banda passed. Greenfield knew that the MCP's hatred for everything Federal had made Federal civil servants reluctant to accept transfer to the Nyasaland service.

Greenfield pointed to the woeful shortage of lawyers in Nyasaland, noting that the only qualified African had become the Minister of Justice. He criticised the current reform of the local courts which was designed to divorce them from the district administration. He disliked the use by the local courts of men who had just emerged from a three-month "crash course", and their practice of excluding legal representation. He knew that the European police were resigning in large numbers and thought it was appalling that such an erosion of law could take place in a British protectorate which was not yet completely self-governing. He claimed that the British Government could easily set matters right by insisting that the elected Ministers exercise their powers in a just and reasonable manner. However, he omitted to demand similar action in Northern Rhodesia where, on the Copperbelt, there had been an eightfold increase in crimes of violence. For maximum effect, this statement was subsequently published as a pamphlet.[39]

The publication by Greenfield of a second such pamphlet in October led Jones to induce him to withdraw it because it included inaccuracies. Jones was particularly annoyed that Greenfield did so grudgingly. Jones stoutly asserted that he would maintain the rule of law and believed that Greenfield was inspired by a sense of resentment at the dissolution of the Federation, for which he held Nyasaland responsible. Greenfield acknowledged, to Welensky, that he should have been completely sure of his facts, but did not regret it because he had put the Nyasaland Government on its mettle.[40]

[39] *Ibid.*, 27/71, f. 5, Welensky to J. Biggs-Davison, 22 July 1963; Fed R & N *Debates* (Salisbury), Vol. 20, Col. 1287 f., 30 July 1963; *Northern News*, 18 July 1963; J. M. Greenfield, *The Erosion of the Rule of Law in Nyasaland* (Salisbury, 1963).

[40] Welensky Papers, 28/29, f. 9, Sir Glyn Jones to Greenfield, 21 October 1963; f. 7, Greenfield to Welensky, 12 November 1963.

Welensky was inevitably spending time in reflection, telling Mrs S. G. Millin that his worst failing was his willingness to accept the word of men like Macmillan. His excuse was that he had previously dealt with men of integrity like Lord Boyd. He made similar comments to his physician, Professor Michael Gelfand, who was writing a biography of Malvern with L. H. Gann. However, he blamed the British Government for failing to support his Government and for appointing anti-Federal Governors like Colby and Benson. He declared that he and Malvern had believed in the Imperial mission and had been betrayed. He had never seriously considered a *coup d'état* in 1961 as he had only intended to resist British intervention.[41]

Field's lack of action on the independence issue was causing Welensky and his colleagues concern. In late July, some Federal MPs approached Field to see if he would consider Butler's proposals, but he refused them an interview because they supported Whitehead's ideas. He offered, however, to accept any of them into the ranks of the Rhodesian Front if they embraced its policy. He also said that he was tired of the constant claim that he differed from his Party.[42]

At the moment, at least, Field gained something from a split in the ranks of his African nationalist foes, with the Reverend Sithole and others hiving off from Nkomo to form the Zimbabwe African National Union. This led not only to inter-faction violence, but to Nkomo forming a new organisation called the People's Caretaker Council.

Lord Salisbury and Welensky were most anxious that Field should not just "dig his toes in" with regard to Butler, because his enemies would not stand still. In August, Butler declared that Field should provide a solution if he would not accept the British proposals. Welensky diagnosed this as the British practice of "counter-punching", at which Butler was particularly skilled.[43]

By August the dissolution exercise was also causing disquiet in Federal circles because the British and Southern Rhodesian Governments were trying to keep the compensation to the Federal civil servants to the minimum. Welensky had considered compensating the civil servants from Federal resources before the dissolution, but there were legal and constitutional difficulties, and territorial reprisals might follow. He therefore remained adamant that Britain, and not the local taxpayer, should meet the financial obligations. The British Government was determined to avoid this, but Welensky, knowing that Nyasaland would be independent in 1964 and Northern Rhodesia in 1965, also wanted proper arrangements made for the Federal creditors because he believed that they would not happily accept the assurances of the territorial Governments.[44]

There was a further disappointment for Welensky in August because

[41] *Ibid.*, 43/*Millin*/2, f. 66, Welensky to S. G. Millin, 15 July 1963; 28/64, f. 2, Welensky to M. Gelfand, 16 July 1963.

[42] *Ibid.*, 27/110, f. 5, Welensky to Sir Keith Acutt, 29 July 1963.

[43] *Ibid.*, 43/*Salisbury*, f. 63, Welensky to Salisbury, 27 July 1963; f. 68, Salisbury to Welensky, 7 August 1963; 35/21, f. 147, Welensky to K. M. Goodenough, 8 August 1963.

[44] *Ibid.*, 43/*Colyton*, f. 80, Welensky to Colyton, 6 August 1963; f. 87, Welensky to Colyton, 13 August 1963.

Kaunda's UNIP won all 25 seats in the Barotseland local elections after a 14 per cent poll. The negotiations for the reform of the Northern Rhodesian Constitution had been proceeding since the Dissolution Conference at a pace which Welensky called "indecent". It was agreed in early September that 65 out of the 75 seats in the legislature would be elected on the basis of universal suffrage. The Federal Ministers were particularly angry with Butler because he had reduced the European seats to ten after Kaunda had indicated that he would accept 15.

Hone incurred the wrath of Roberts and his cohorts by legislating by regulation that all existing voters would have to appear before the registering officer to register. It was estimated that at least 40 per cent of the Europeans would not bother to comply, but it was clear that the British Government did not want to offend Kaunda by resisting.[45]

Welensky was further irritated by Butler in early September when the Queen agreed that there should be a dissolution Honours List, but he refused to allow more than an extended New Year's List. Welensky tartly questioned the Secretary of State's right to ignore the Queen's wishes, and Butler gave way to the extent that he agreed that the two Lists should be released as one.[46]

Matters seemed to improve in mid-September when a tentative agreement was reached on the fate of the Federal civil servants. However, neither they nor Welensky were particularly pleased with it. Welensky and Field had resisted "the golden handshake" because they disapproved of it and also had rejected compulsory secondment. It was finally agreed that the civil servants would be permitted to choose the territory in which they wished to serve and would be compensated if thereafter they were made redundant.[47]

From the Rhodesian Front's congress on 21 September came the encouraging news that its hierarchy had resisted reactionary motions and Field had declared that he would keep the army and the Royal Rhodesian Air Force at full strength. However, the RF did re-introduce the requirement (which Whitehead had removed) that a birth certificate had to state the race of the child.[48]

When it was announced in October that Nyasaland would be granted independence on 6 July 1964, Dupont asked Greenfield to assist him in drafting a letter to Butler asking him to reiterate his terms for Southern Rhodesia's independence. Greenfield complied, but advised Field to wait until he regained control of external affairs and of the Royal Rhodesian Air Force at the dissolution. Dupont replied that Field wished to keep the pot boiling and was intending that Smith should discuss the issue on an impending visit to London in pursuit of financial aid.[49]

[45] *Ibid.*, 28/4, f. 9, Welensky to Lord Dalhousie, 30 August 1963; 27/62, f. 11, Welensky to Lord Boyd, 2 September 1963; 28/4, f. 5, Welensky to Dalhousie, 8 September 1963; 27/40, f. 9, C. D. Burney to Welensky, 18 September 1963.

[46] *Ibid.*, 28/4, f. 5, Welensky to Dalhousie, 8 September 1963.

[47] *Ibid.*, 43/*Colyton*, f. 84, Welensky to Lord Colyton, 21 September 1963; 24/152, ff. 21–23, Welensky to Joelson, 21 September 1963.

[48] *Ibid.*, 28/4, f. 3, Welensky to Dalhousie, 21 September 1963; 24/152, ff. 21–23, Welensky to Joelson, 21 September 1963.

[49] *Ibid.*, 28/79, f. 15, Greenfield to Welensky, 9 October 1963.

Greenfield also advised Welensky not to hold a debate on the Federal expenditure in the Rhodesias because it would become clear that much more had been spent in Southern Rhodesia. In his opinion, it was better to let sleeping dogs lie, although much of the development had been on improving communications (roads, etc.) to Northern Rhodesia.[50]

Welensky visited the United States where he addressed Press clubs and television audiences and met President John Kennedy and Senator Barry Goldwater. Kennedy found him "a great personality" whose directness of approach was "challenging and stimulating". Welensky was so well received that he regretted he had not gone there in early 1962. He believed he shook the Press by defending South Africa and Portugal. When Kennedy asked why he was critical of American policy, he answered him frankly. In Washington he saw all the ambassadors of the old Commonwealth and discovered that their Governments did not object to Southern Rhodesia's independence *per se* but that they were not prepared to quarrel with the Afro-Asian members of the Commonwealth. The Australian Government, for example, had a parliamentary majority of one and was dependent on Asia for markets and, to a certain extent, for protection. A crumb of comfort was that high-ranking Americans told him that the United States would not be a party to the use of force in Southern Rhodesia.[51]

Returning from the United States, Welensky met Butler in London to discuss Southern Rhodesian independence as well as to plead for generous treatment for any Federal civil servants who were made redundant. He informed Butler he believed that the old Commonwealth was anxious to have the Southern Rhodesian question resolved, provided the Commonwealth was not damaged in the process. The US Government was equally anxious to see a settlement. However, without giving reasons, Butler enquired if Field could stay his hand until January 1964. Welensky agreed it was possible that he might. He gathered that a British general election was expected in May 1964 and believed that the Labour Party would win it. Thus he thought that there would be serious difficulties thereafter if the independence issue had not been resolved by then.[52]

Wall, however, warned the Federal Government that independence would not be granted to Southern Rhodesia before the British general election because of its inevitable effect on Party politics as well as on the Commonwealth and the UN. He believed that, if anything were to be done before Nyasaland became independent, it would have to be through a Southern Rhodesian threat to take independence unilaterally. Once the British Government understood that this was serious, a negotiated settlement which was acceptable to the old, and some of the new, Commonwealth countries was possible.

Wall knew that a change in the leadership of the British Government was imminent and felt that it might favour Southern Rhodesia if no time was wasted. He believed that any new British Prime Minister would welcome the

[50] *Ibid.*, 32/11, f. 60, Greenfield to Welensky, 9 October 1963.

[51] *Ibid.*, 33/124, f. 86, O. B. Bennett to Welensky, 14 October 1963; 43/*Ferraz*, f. 37, Welensky to A. Ferraz, 16 October 1963; 29/21, f. 2, Welensky to R. Kriston, 4 November 1963.

[52] *Ibid.*, FGC(63), 33rd Meeting, Restricted Annexure, Federal Cabinet, 14 October 1963.

settlement of this intractable problem and would make every effort to secure it, if he realised that the issue had to be faced before the election.[53]

Wall had not written directly to Welensky, but he replied, on 16 October, saying that Smith would be in London shortly. Welensky passed Wall's opinion to Field, but before Field could respond, Macmillan resigned because of ill-health and was succeeded by Sir Alec Douglas-Home (Lord Home of late, who had renounced his peerage to serve in the Commons). Douglas-Home replaced himself with Butler at the Foreign Office and abolished the Central African Office. Sandys became responsible for both the Colonial and Commonwealth Relations Offices. Welensky promptly wrote to Butler regretting that he would not be the Minister responsible for the Federation until its dissolution. He claimed that, although he had never failed to criticise British policy, he had always recognised that Butler had inherited very little room in which to manoeuvre. He wished they could have worked together in happier circumstances.[54]

In the meantime, on 15 October, Greenfield had introduced the Dissolution Bill in the Federal Assembly amid bitter comments. The next day a motion was defeated which asked Britain to intervene and allocate the Canberra squadron and the Selous Scouts (the armoured car squadron) to Northern Rhodesia. Proposing the motion, Savanhu claimed that the donation of most of the RRAF and all the European army units to Southern Rhodesia was designed to preserve white supremacy. Barrow, as Minister of Defence, replied that this was mischievous and inaccurate as the position in 1953 was simply being restored.[55]

A week later, Barrow reported on further progress in the dissolution exercise. He claimed that the Committees had accomplished a great deal but that they had only just reported. The defence arrangements were complete and the only unit being disbanded was the Selous Scouts. Northern Rhodesia would receive four Dakotas and two Pembrokes, while Southern Rhodesia proposed to dispose of a number of aircraft when they came under its control. All members of the armed services were being offered re-employment or terminal benefits.[56]

The Zimbabwe African National Union chose to take a hand in the Southern Rhodesian issue by writing to all Commonwealth Prime Ministers urging them to press the British Government to convene an immediate Commonwealth conference so that Welensky could be present. ZANU was prepared to accept a multi-racial coalition for four to ten years, but after that would expect universal suffrage to be introduced.[57]

Welensky met Field to discuss the independence issue and Field acknowledged that he would have to make some concessions. Field revealed that his lawyers had indicated that the repeal of the Land Apportionment Act need

[53] *Ibid.*, 27/28, f. 9, Major P. Wall to O. B. Bennett, 11 October 1963.

[54] *Ibid.*, 43/*Wall*, f. 54, Welensky to Wall, 19 October 1963; 27/38, f. 12, Welensky to Butler, 23 October 1963.

[55] Fed R & N *Debates* (Salisbury), Vol. 20, Col. 1391 f., 15 October 1963; Col. 1484 f., 16 October 1963.

[56] *Ibid.*, Col. 1566 f., 21 October 1963.

[57] Welensky Papers, 33/117, f. 3, J. Pank to Welensky, 4 November 1963.

not mean that education had to be integrated. However, he said, one of his Cabinet, Lord Graham, would not countenance any concessions and would resign, and mystified Welensky by adding that he would then have to do likewise. In any case, Field declared that he could not contemplate reneging on any of his election promises. He did not propose to fight a general election and thought that, if he had to resign, Smith would replace him.

Welensky suspected that Field was concerned about his ill-health. Welensky was again under pressure to enter Southern Rhodesian politics but wanted to retire even though Field indicated that he would welcome his participation. Welensky was writing his memoirs and worried that he might queer Douglas-Home's pitch, as it seemed like "the dawn of a new day to see him in office after the dirty nights of the Macmillan regime". He felt that Southern Rhodesia might well assist the Commonwealth by acting as a catalyst, and believed that Field should not worry about rows in the Commonwealth as he had to secure independence even at the cost of Southern Rhodesia's membership. If Southern Rhodesia were treated as favourably as South Africa had been, with regard to the Commonwealth preferences, Welensky was not particularly concerned about its expulsion.[58]

In London, Smith was rebuffed by Sandys on the issues of financial aid and independence. As a result, Lord Salisbury warned Welensky not to expect any changes in the British attitude. He thought that the British Government believed that the granting of independence, without a far-reaching extension of the franchise, would destroy the Commonwealth. Smith saw current demands as meaning the introduction of an African Government within five years. The alternative was unilateral action by Southern Rhodesia as he could see no middle course. If the Labour Party were returned, the position would only be worse. He convinced Lord Salisbury that the Rhodesian Front had to begin seriously to consider its alternative plans.[59]

This prospect of unilateral action seemed all the more certain on 12 November when Harold Wilson demanded a pledge in the Commons that there would be no independence for Southern Rhodesia until it had a democratic constitution. Douglas-Home replied that this was implicit in an earlier statement by him and, although he liked Douglas-Home, Salisbury felt that "the bleak fact which Southern Rhodesia has to face" was that the new Government would not differ from that of Macmillan.[60]

Welensky concluded that the prospects of a negotiated settlement were fading fast and that Douglas-Home had only promoted a *laager* mentality in Southern Rhodesia at a time when internal unrest was beginning to worry the authorities, with sabotage attacks being made against the railways. Sandys deepened this impression by proposing in the Commons to consult the Commonwealth on the Southern Rhodesian issue. This aroused Welensky's contempt because it was a departure for Britain not to deal solely with Southern Rhodesia, in accordance with her responsibilities. It was plain to him that Sandys wanted to "pass the buck", and he warned Field that this

[58] *Ibid.*, 28/79, f. 12, Welensky to Greenfield, 4 November 1963; 43/*Salisbury*, f. 86, Welensky to Lord Salisbury, 12 November 1963.
[59] *Ibid.*, f. 89, Salisbury to Welensky, 7 November 1963.
[60] *Ibid.*, f. 37, Salisbury to Welensky, 13 November 1963.

was the beginning of the double-cross. Salisbury thought that this proposal was cynical in the extreme and attacked Sandys publicly, and warned Field that he would have to be ready to act soon.[61]

Malvern, however, advised the dignified dropping of the bid for independence. In his view, Field should indicate that Southern Rhodesia should continue just as it was, independent to all intents and purposes. Field asked Welensky again to enter Southern Rhodesian politics, but Welensky had no desire to serve under him or even in a government with him.[62]

In late November, Welensky visited London to take leave of the Queen as Federal Prime Minister. He lunched with her and took tea with the Queen Mother. He refused again any honours, but accepted a silver cigarette box from the Queen.[63] He discussed various matters in London, including the future of the University College of Rhodesia and Nyasaland (of which the Queen Mother was Chancellor). He was told that Sandys had made his comment, on consulting the Commonwealth about Southern Rhodesia's independence, without reference to his Cabinet. When meeting Sandys, Welensky was asked to convey to Field an invitation to a conference with Menzies, Lester Pearson, Canada's new Prime Minister, and Nyerere. Sandys proposed to take the chair at this conference but refused to say under what conditions he would grant Southern Rhodesia its independence, beyond indicating that Commonwealth acceptance was a prerequisite. (This was an attitude which would still be maintained in 1979.) Welensky, agreeing to transmit the message, informed Sandys that he did not favour a unilateral declaration of independence and that he thought Field should repeal the Land Apportionment Act, outlaw racial discrimination, and increase African representation, in anticipation of Harold Wilson becoming the new Prime Minister. Nevertheless, he did not believe that there was any chance of achieving independence through negotiation and was worried that, if Southern Rhodesia acted unilaterally, it would lose its Commonwealth trade preference. He gathered that Douglas-Home wanted to grasp the reins of Government more firmly before exposing the Conservative Party to an election. Thus it seemed that an election was unlikely before September 1964. It irritated Welensky that Sandys had not finally settled the future of the Federal civil servants, despite a visit of a deputation from their association. However, of some comfort was a statement by Maudling, as Chancellor of the Exchequer, that his Government would undermine confidence in its own financial affairs if it failed to provide security for the holders of Federal stock. It was clear, nevertheless, that he did not extend this promise to local investors.[64]

Welensky saw Butler and was amused by his acrimonious comments on Macmillan. Referring to the task assigned to the Duke of Edinburgh of

[61] *Ibid.*, 28/79, f. 10, Welensky to Greenfield, 13 November 1963; 43/*Colyton*, f. 95, Colyton to Sir Alec Douglas-Home, 17 November 1963; 43/*Salisbury*, f. 88, Welensky to Salisbury, 19 November 1963; f. 90, Salisbury to Welensky, 19 November 1963; *The Rhodesia Herald*, 28 November 1963.

[62] Welensky Papers, 24/152, ff. 9–12, Welensky to Joelson, 22 November 1963.

[63] *Ibid.*, 43/*Ferraz*, f. 40, Welensky to A. Ferraz, 7 December 1963.

[64] *Ibid.*, 43/*Salisbury*, f. 94, Welensky to Lord Salisbury, 7 December 1963; FGC(63), 38th Meeting, Minute 2, Federal Cabinet, 2 December 1963.

lowering the Union Jack in Kenya, he asked Butler if "there is no limit to the extent to which you people are prepared to degrade yourselves". He was answered by a shrug of Butler's shoulders.[65]

On Welensky's return, Field rejected the Commonwealth conference, and the Rhodesian Front appeared to lose interest in the achievement of independence, perhaps because it also feared the loss of the tobacco preferences.[66]

Welensky and his Government were becoming increasingly frustrated by the dissolution exercise because, as their power waned, the other Governments tended to ignore them. This frustration was reflected by Caldicott in the final session of the Federal Parliament on 10 December. He recalled that the Report of the Victoria Falls Conference had provided not only for the completion of the dissolution by the end of December, but for the full consultation of all the Governments on all decisions taken. Instead — as usual — the rough draft of the order in council had arrived from London on 1 December with a request for a reply within three days. It contained provisions which were very nearly in their final form but, nevertheless, were subjects of dispute. The issue of the public debt was an example. The Federal representatives on Committee A had submitted a minority report, and the Southern and Northern Rhodesians had registered their reservations. Then, while the draft of the order in council was being considered, a dispatch had arrived giving the British view on the apportionment of the Federal assets and liabilities and rejecting the minority report. The opinion of the Federal Government had not been sought and the British view had been formed entirely on that of their officials who had served on Committee A. Despite the divergent views of the Committee, there had been no interchange between the five Governments. Furthermore, the virtual rejection by the local stockholders of the treatment proposed for them had been ignored. The Federal Government had urgently asked the British Government to convene an immediate conference of the five Governments, but had received a refusal on 4 December.

Disturbed, Caldicott said that Welensky had sent a personal message to Douglas-Home drawing his attention to Paragraph 57 of the Victoria Falls Report which provided for a further conference in the event of disagreement. He had done so immediately, but Douglas-Home had replied only late on 7 December and had merely reiterated that the mind of his Government was made up and that nothing could be changed. Accordingly, the order in council would be laid before the British Parliament on 10 December.

Nonetheless, Caldicott reported, the Federal Cabinet had met on 7 December and had protested to Douglas-Home that there were still matters to be decided and asked for a reply by 9 December because the Federal Parliament would be prorogued the next day. Douglas-Home must have appreciated, therefore, that this was the last possible day for a report to the Federal Assembly. To cap everything, the Federal Government discovered that, while it had been ignored, the territorial Governments had been consulted. Caldicott asked the House to appreciate that the Federal Government had no further powers to act and that it had done what it could for the Federal

[65] *Ibid.*, 27/10, f. 3, Welensky to S. Cloete, 10 December 1963.
[66] *Ibid.*, 43/*Ferraz*, f. 40, Welensky to Ferraz, 7 December 1963.

stockholders and those whose interests it had tried to protect. His Government, therefore, Caldicott said, left it to others to judge whether the undertaking given at the Victoria Falls had been honoured by the British and territorial Governments. Responsibility now passed to those Governments, but the Federal Government expressed its regret to the stockholders.[67]

On the previous day, 9 December, at Salisbury's Glamis Stadium, the Federal Army, marching in review, had bid a moving farewell to Welensky, while the RRAF flew past in last salute. He acknowledged that the thunderous ovation of the crowd of 16 000 had done "something to soothe the aches of the past year".

The Army presented Welensky with a plough and the general public contributed £25 000. This was done because neither he nor his Cabinet would receive pensions as they had felt that it would have been immoral to have appropriated what remained of Federal funds for this purpose. It touched him deeply that all races had subscribed to the donation. Indeed, Africans who could not contribute a shilling had given in kind, including ducks for the small farm which he would be buying on the northern outskirts of Salisbury.[68]

Back in the Federal Assembly, after the farewell parade, Welensky introduced a motion affirming the loyalty of the House to the Queen and thanking the civil servants, servicemen, judges, the Speaker, the Acting Governor-General, clerks and officers of the Federal Parliament for their loyal and devoted service. He found this motion the most difficult of his career to present and took no pleasure in the dissolution. However, he promised to avoid recrimination in this, his last major speech in Parliament. He believed that everyone in the three territories faced the most critical period of their lives and that they would be radically affected by the decisions to be taken in the coming year. He reminded the British Government that it was clearly responsible for the compensation of the redundant civil servants and recalled that it had been urged to be generous by its own Parliament in June. Yet the British Government had ignored this pressure. He did not likewise censure the territorial Governments for their attitudes because of the great difficulties which they faced with regard to their own budgeting. Britain had evaded her responsibility, while the territorial Governments had done what they could to find employment for the displaced personnel.

Welensky paid tributes to the armed services, the Federal creditors and to Lord Dalhousie and paused to read a message of good wishes from him. Welensky thanked the electorate, and his own constituency of Broken Hill, in particular, for its support. He declared that he still believed that the Federation had been a noble concept and that it could have survived if it had been given a proper sense of historical perspective and a firmness of resolution which was unaffected by considerations of short-term advantage.

Surveying Africa, Welensky found it natural that the under-developed countries would wish to redress the balance in the standards of living, but it concerned him as to how this would be tackled in the three territories. Africa, he said, was proving to be an unattractive field for investment as loans and

[67] Fed R & N *Debates* (Salisbury), Vol. 20, Col.1677 f., 10 December 1963.

[68] Welensky Papers, 43/*Wall*, f. 58, Welensky to Wall, 12 December 1963; 43/*Ferraz*, f. 40, Welensky to Ferraz, 7 December 1963.

grants were frittered away. The freedom to starve had never seemed to him a democratic virtue. The West regarded its foreign aid commitments as being overstretched, and under-developed countries would have to help themselves, but it would be a laborious and painful process. South Africa and the Rhodesias had thriving economies and there were propitious conditions for economic growth which would close the gap between the haves and the have-nots. Everything naturally depended on politics and was a question of reconciling the legitimate interests and apprehensions of the most economically productive element in society with the reasonable aspirations of the majority.

The House, Welensky believed, should remember that it took Britain almost a hundred years after the 1832 Reform Bill to achieve universal suffrage. The local problem was greatly complicated by the race issue which would be the most explosive factor in international relations in the next decade, and would be aggravated by the Communists using it to turn the dark-skinned nations against the West. The task of the Communists had been easy in Africa, he declared, because they could convince the former colonial peoples that their economic backwardness was the result of the evil designs of their colonial masters. This had engendered hostility towards the white man and had poisoned the atmosphere in Southern Rhodesia where the situation was not a colonial one.

The task in Central Africa was to abolish racial distrust, and the Federal Government had chosen to do this through partnership, but were not the only ones "who were driving the train". The dissolution would make the problem of finding a solution even greater. The realisation of the ambition of the northern African had encouraged the Southern Rhodesian Africans and had consequently made the problem of reconciliation even more difficult. Not only had the danger of conflict to be avoided, but the economy could not prosper in a tense situation.

The basis of any solution had to be the Western democratic tradition because it was necessary for the growth of modern technological civilisation. It disgusted him that attempts should be made to depict the totalitarian regimes of Africa as possessing the basic attributes of democracy. The problem of political readjustments in Africa, he said, were all too often represented as the problem of prising the Europeans away from a rigid determination to retain political control forever. The European in Central Africa had given ample evidence of his willingness to share political power with the African and ultimately to allow him to dominate. The greatest responsibility for the reduction of political tension rested with the Africans as they had to restore European faith in the democratic ideals because it had been undermined by events elsewhere in Africa. The European had to show at the same time a determination to preserve standards and not privileges.

Welensky acknowledged that he had often been accused of damaging race relations by attacking African nationalist leaders, but the truth, he said, was that he had never sought to frustrate the Africans' legitimate aspirations. His motives had always been to protect all races from the consequences of capitulating to claims which were untimely and unrealistic. He asked the Southern Rhodesian Africans to have faith in the good intentions of the

Europeans because, if they did, they would be amply rewarded. In 1961, the Southern Rhodesian Europeans had demonstrated their good faith by endorsing the new Constitution under which the African would eventually dominate the voters' rolls. If matters went wrong in Southern Rhodesia, it would be the result of the Africans failing to grasp the opportunities for political self-expression which had been opened to them. Yet some African leaders were urging the rejection of any compromise and thereby endangered the prospects of reconciliation.

Welensky criticised the United Nations for failing to command respect and suggested that balloting should be introduced into its proceedings so that votes would be cast on the merits of a resolution and not on the prospect of the return of favours from the right quarter. Then he listed the achievements of the Federation and acknowledged that the territories would have made material advances without federation, but doubted if they would have achieved quite what they had. Many of the benefits would outlive the Federation, and the future of the territories was brighter because the Federation had brought about significant advances in human relationships and had helped to break down the legal and social barriers which had kept the races apart. These advances, he said, were set out in a White Paper which would appear that day, entitled the *Legacy of Progress.*[69]

Welensky sat down amid applause but was instantly criticised by Savanhu for thanking the Federal civil servants, servicemen, judiciary and the members of the statutory commissions when they had failed to implement partnership. The primary rights of the Africans had been betrayed, Savanhu said, and the only partnership which had been practised was of the "horse and rider" variety. The Europeans had shown no intention of sharing power and economic gain, and their talk about the maintenance of standards had really meant the exclusion of the non-European. Todd and Whitehead had been rejected because they had tried to do too much for Africans, and currently almost all the Europeans supported the Rhodesian Front. Thus Savanhu proposed an amendment that the foundation of the Federation had been misguided and ill-conceived and that it had been used by the Governments of Malvern and Welensky to entrench white political domination, economic privilege and social ostracism. He thanked Macmillan for dismantling the Federation. However, his amendment was ignored by the other speakers who only praised the Federal record.[70]

On the next day, 10 December, Sir Donald Macintyre moved a motion thanking Welensky for his services to the Federation and expressing gratitude to the public for subscribing to the fund for Welensky. Macintyre claimed that Welensky's two greatest deeds were the winning of the mineral rights in Northern Rhodesia for the people of the Federation, and the part he played in the foundation of the Federation itself. No blame could be attributed to him for its break-up because the Western Powers had decided to settle the fate of Africa for purely economic reasons. Turning to the gift which would be presented to Welensky, Macintyre announced that the target of £25 000 had

[69] Fed R & N *Debates* (Salisbury), Vol. 20, Col. 1627 f., 9 December 1963; *Legacy of Progress: Achievements of the Years of Federation 1953–1963*, C. Fed. 269 (Salisbury, 9 December 1963).
[70] Fed R & N *Debates* (Salisbury), Vol. 20, Col. 1647 f., 9 December 1963.

been reached and, in addition, he would receive a Land-Rover, a tractor and boreholes which would be drilled on his farm when he bought it. Macintyre then handed the cheque to Welensky.

After his old opponent, R. Williamson, had paid him the tribute of always being "a bonny fighter", Welensky remarked that he had been actively engaged in politics for more than a quarter of a century and that politics had given him some of his most poignant pleasures and some of his most bitter disappointments. The Federation had encountered two obstacles which had proved to be insurmountable. The first was its constitutional framework, and the second was the vesting of the ultimate authority in the British Government that enabled decisions to be taken in London which took account of international pressures and British party political considerations, rather than the genuine needs of the Federation and its people. The Federal Constitution had empowered its Government to make economic decisions, but the British Government had ultimate responsibility for the political advancement of the northern territories.

Hindsight showed, Welensky acknowledged, that economic and political advancement were indivisible and had to ride "in tandem" or nullify each other, producing frustration and then stagnation. He had been accused of being both naïve and Machiavellian but, he claimed, the truth was that he was straightforward and had expected good faith as well as honesty from those with whom he dealt. He had no bitterness, however, nor complaint. He had fought and lost because he had not understood that he was playing a game of chance. He had believed that the British Government would have honoured the spirit and intention of the agreement of 1953 and the pledges given then. He had never imagined that the British Government would have taken refuge in legalistic jargon or would have resorted to dishonest practices. He had learned too late that he was wrong and asked the House to believe that he was sincere and that he would never knowingly have misled the electorate to whom he was responsible.

Welensky thanked those who had contributed to his fund and said that he would use it to buy land to demonstrate his unscathed confidence in his country. Far from being frightened of change, he recognised its inevitability and believed that, out of the ashes, a new Rhodesia would be born in the same manner that war-torn Britain had risen Phoenix-like from the ashes of 1940. He thanked everyone, including his wife, for their support, and resumed his seat.

Immediately, the Acting Governor-General, Sir Humphrey Gibbs, read the speech of prorogation from the throne. In this, he detailed the Federation's major achievements. His Government had aimed to have a completely non-racial civil service, and by 1963 had achieved the position in which a third of the pensionable posts were held by non-Europeans. The number of hospital beds had been doubled to 21 000 and the range of health facilities had increased to the extent that the Federation could train all the necessary staff. The work on malaria and bilharzia control had attracted world-wide attention. Great strides had been made in education, and local teacher-training had been an outstanding success, while technical training had been revolutionised. Gibbs hoped that the dissolution would not retard the development of the

University. He noted that the armed services had been developed into a modern, balanced and flexible force capable of meeting all likely demands, including a contribution to the defence of the Commonwealth.

Gibbs stated that capital investment on a large scale had made a vital contribution to the development of the Federal economy and that its major impact was still to come. A firmly-based policy of selective protection and assistance had encouraged the establishment of new industries. The progress of the manufacturing industry was illustrated by the growth in its net contribution to the gross domestic product from £29 000 000 in 1954 to over £55 000 000 in 1962. Major efforts had been made to expand trade links and, despite a substantial fall in prices, the value of visible exports had risen by nearly 43 per cent to £210 000 000 between 1954 and 1962. The favourable trade balance had grown steadily to £77 000 000 by 1962, while the gross national product grew by over 35 per cent. There had been impressive development in the agricultural sphere, and seasonal shortages of basic commodities had disappeared. Indeed, there were regular surpluses for export. The tourist industry was bringing in £4 000 000 per year as a result of a ten-fold increase in the expenditure on tourist promotion.

Gibbs claimed that the most outstanding achievement was the development of power and, in particular, of Kariba. £28 000 000 had been spent on road construction, and the Rhodesia Railways had been modernised and augmented. The Rhodesia Railways had been the first to eliminate racial discrimination in the services it offered to the public and in the various categories of employment. Central African Airways had been developed into a modern and efficient airline. New airports had been constructed, while others had been modernised and given radar and radio navigational aids. The meteorological services had been improved, and the postal and telecommunications services had been modernised. Finally, the Ministry of Works had provided the Federal Government with buildings worth £30 000 000.

Gibbs concluded that, despite the stresses and strains, the economy remained sound. Based on the firm and growing foundations of agriculture and mining, a sure base had been provided for the future. The investment and development had meant that the structure of the economy was more mature, and progress had been made towards the vital stage when economic growth would become self-sustaining. The well-being of the economy of the area would be enhanced by close co-operation, and Gibbs prayed that the future governments of the territories would strengthen the common ties. He ended by wishing the territories and their people "Godspeed", and then exercised his power to prorogue the Federal Assembly, forever.[71]

Two days later there followed a Federal banquet which Lord Malvern attended. Then, on 17 December, Welensky held his last Cabinet meeting and expressed his gratitude to his Ministers for the loyalty and support which they had always given him. He hoped that they would always maintain close contact with him. Barrow, as Deputy Prime Minister, replied that it had been a privilege for them to serve him and conveyed to him their best wishes for the future.[72]

[71] *Ibid.*, Col. 1681 f., 10 December 1963.

[72] Welensky Papers, FGC(63), 39th Meeting, Minute 3, Federal Cabinet, 17 December 1963.

Welensky was as deeply touched by all these tributes and gestures as he was hurt by having to destroy his life's work. He spent the remainder of the month quietly watching events and reflecting on the past. He doubted Field's ability to act in any way on the independence issue, and continued to be angered by the callous British attitude towards the Federal stockholder because he could not believe that anyone who had invested in the Federation would be pleased to be given a percentage of Nyasaland stock, as had been done.

He was cheered, however, by a vigorous attack on the British Government in the Lords on 17 December by Lord Listowel and by the ever faithful Lords Salisbury, Colyton, Boyd, Milverton and the others. They decried the haste in which the dissolution legislation was being presented to them, just before the Christmas recess, and in the form of an order in council which could not be altered. They criticised the lack of information, the refusal to underwrite the Federal stock, and the lack of compensation for the Federal civil servants. Colyton called it "a shabby end to a shabby episode". The threat to vote against the Government was only averted by an explanation by Lord Carrington, the Minister without Portfolio, of the consequences of rejection. These included keeping the Federation in being against everyone's wishes and the re-opening of issues which had been settled by the four Governments.[73]

Welensky was angered that the British Government sent only a curt telegram of thanks, pinned to another message, to "people who had worked and tried to do so much". He concluded that this had been done because, as in Kenya, "our skins are white and that's no good on this continent". Just before Christmas he made his final visit to Broken Hill to be entertained by his constituents, who had voted for him for 25 years, and acted, for the last time, his annual traditional role as Father Christmas for the children. He found his constituents' farewell the saddest of all, but was cheered by the knowledge that only once in all the years had an opponent of his saved his deposit.[74]

In late December Macleod attacked Welensky and his handling of Federal affairs in the *Spectator*. This roused Welensky sufficiently to reply, publicly, that "even Mr Macleod is aware that lions and jackals don't hunt together".[75]

Welensky described Old Year's Day 1963 as "grim" — it was the last day of the Federation of Rhodesia and Nyasaland. That night Malvern, at least, observed his daily ritual of drinking a whisky and going to sleep. Welensky, a teetotaller, could only do the latter and wake up with the Federation finally gone.

[73] House of Lords *Hansard* (Salisbury), Vol. 254, Col. 112 f., 17 December 1963.

[74] Welensky Papers, 43/*Salisbury*, f. 97, Welensky to Salisbury, 23 December 1963; 43/*Lisson*, Welensky to J. Lisson, 27 December 1963.

[75] *Ibid.*, 43/*Colyton*, f. 101, Welensky to Lord Colyton, 31 December 1963.

Postscript

IN the months and years that followed, Welensky would reflect on his fate, but he did not change his belief that the Federation had been destroyed by the British Government's "loss of will to govern". This, he felt, had been produced by American anti-colonial pressure and by the British Government's decision in the second half of 1959 to liquidate its African possessions and, if needs be, to destroy the Commonwealth, because Britain's destiny lay in Europe. He believed this because Butler had told him that it had been intended in 1958 that he should travel to South Africa to deliver the "Winds of Change" speech. Butler had been prevented from complying by the illness and subsequent death of Strydom, the South African Prime Minister. Instead, Butler had visited his relatives, Sir Stephen and Lady Courtauld in Umtali, leaving Macmillan to make the speech in Cape Town in 1960. In addition, Macmillan's private secretary, Lord Egremont, informed Welensky that the decision to enter the Common Market had been taken at that time (1958).[1]

Welensky continued to resent the manner in which the Federal issue had been handled by the British Government. Of the British Ministers, he forgave only Butler. Writing to him on 3 January 1964, he told Butler that he recognised how difficult the task had been for him and said he was convinced that Macmillan had given it to him to break him politically.[2]

Although he sympathised with Field, particularly after he had been ousted from the Southern Rhodesian premiership in 1964, Welensky could not forgive him for throwing away the card of non-attendance at the Victoria Falls, and time has proved that it was a cardinal error. Welensky had warned Sandys in December 1963 that a unilateral declaration of independence was

[1] *Ibid.*, 43/*Salisbury*, f. 111, Welensky to Salisbury, 6 January 1965; Author's interview with Sir Roy Welensky.
[2] *Ibid.*, 27/38, f. 2, Welensky to Butler, 3 January 1964.

contemplated.[3] When he discovered positively that it was the intention of the Rhodesian Front to take it, he emerged reluctantly from his retirement, in September 1964, to fight the Arundel by-election, only to be narrowly defeated by Clifford Dupont in the most vicious electoral campaign yet seen in Southern Rhodesia.

The subsequent gamble, taken on 11 November 1965 by I. D. Smith, was something which Welensky never approved or condoned, believing that it only hastened the advent of premature majority rule. Malvern agreed with that verdict and, with his years of experience, was confident that the Southern Rhodesian Constitution rendered the British powerless to act. Thus UDI to Malvern was merely pointless and destructive. He was, of course, ignoring the possibility that those who took UDI wanted to discard the 1961 Constitution and preserve power in white hands.

Despite his disapproval of the unilateral action of the Rhodesian Front, Welensky, writing to Lord Salisbury in December 1969, could still not forgive the Conservatives for the "dirty, underhand way" in which they had denied Southern Rhodesia its independence in 1963.[4] The Conservatives would counter by arguing that, except on the terms which they had offered Field, they could not have granted independence to Southern Rhodesia and emerge unscathed in the world.

Southern Rhodesia, like the Federation, whatever its constitutional imperfections, had faced the historical inevitability inherent in the imbalance of the racial populations, but then the advocates of federation would argue that they had recognised this and had provided for it in their policies of partnership. However, Savanhu and others had claimed that these advocates were only paying lip-service to partnership while hoping to maintain white supremacy.

The fundamental defect of the Federation was, without doubt, the denial to the Federal Government of control of the day-to-day affairs of the African. This was the subject which had to be handled centrally, in whatever direction, if the territories were not to diverge down different paths. The denial of this control made it impossible to implement partnership as a common policy at all levels. It lost the Federal Government any chance of gaining the loyalty of the Africans in competition with rampant African nationalism. It also allowed the Colonial Office to pursue remorselessly its policy of African domination, leading to territorial independence, and, in the process, to undermine the Federation from the outset. This was a process which Lennox-Boyd condoned but which Macleod accelerated by at least ten years. The Federation obviously could not survive if its component parts became independent and assumed that thereafter they could secede. The British Government liked to believe that it was only being realistic, but a case could be made that its policy of appeasement merely strengthened African nationalism. As has been seen, it was a policy which sickened Welensky, particularly because it embraced the condonation of practices which it would not allow in Britain.

The British decision to withdraw from Africa was undoubtedly taken, but, lacking the ability or the will to administer the clean kill, Macmillan preferred to allow the Federation to sicken into decay. On the evidence, he lacked a

[3] *Ibid.*, 43/*Salisbury*/2, Welensky to Salisbury, 19 January 1967.

[4] *Ibid.*, Welensky to Salisbury, 3 December 1969.

clear plan but, nevertheless, seemed to hope that something could be saved. This was a practice to be continued, with regard to Rhodesia, by all successive British Governments, with devastating effects. The British Cabinets always demanded concessions from the Federal and territorial Governments in the hope of satisfying the aspirations of the African nationalists. They did not understand, or pretended not to understand, that the African nationalists never compromised, never accepted the half-measure, and would never come into the system until they were sure of victory.

There are those who doubt that the Federation was even an economic success and believe that all it had achieved could have been done separately by the territories on their own.[5] It was, perhaps, foolish of the British and territorial Governments to ignore African opinion in 1953, but at that time there was serious doubt that anything more than a tiny minority ever truly felt strongly about federation. Many Southern Rhodesians were convinced that the Federation had cost Southern Rhodesia its chance of becoming a dominion. However, that status was certainly never offered, and it appears most unlikely that the Attlee or subsequent Conservative Governments would have made the exception — in the atmosphere of the post-war colonial retreat — and have granted independence on terms which the European would have accepted. The history of Northern Rhodesia has merely underlined the economic argument advanced before 1953 on the necessity for closer association to cushion the effects of total dependence on the production of copper. In its life, the Federation certainly ameliorated the consequences of the periodic falls in the price of copper.

Had constitutional reform taken a path which could have enabled the Federation to survive, the aridity of the years which followed its demise undoubtedly would have not been experienced and the territories would have been better placed to meet the aspirations of their burgeoning populations. Instead, those populations had to endure the experiments in both black and white nationalism, with dire consequences. The Federation was ill-conceived but, recognising that it was, Malvern and Welensky had accepted it on the basis that half the loaf was better than none at all and that they would have time to rectify the defects when its success had won the allegiance of all.

Although the seeds of racial antagonism were sown before 1953 and began to bear bitter fruit in the Federal decade, the Federation's material achievements of economic growth, development, Kariba, the power grid and even the inheritance of jet aircraft when later none were available, as well as the well-trained army units, would be much appreciated in the days that followed. Of course, the story would have been very different if closer association had been effected before 1939 or, better still, before 1914. Malvern and Welensky, however, were never given the time or the opportunity to develop the Federation politically, and the unreformed Federal structure was not able to survive the divergent constitutional advancement of the territories.

[5] D. S. Pearson and W. L. Taylor, "Break-up: Some Economic Consequences in the Rhodesias and Nyasaland", *Phoenix Paper*, 4 (Salisbury, 1963).

Select Bibliography

A. Manuscript Collections

The Papers of Sir Roy Welensky (Bodleian Library, Oxford).
The Papers of the Hon. J. M. Greenfield (Afrika Instituut, Pretoria).
The Papers of Sir Malcolm Barrow (National Archives of Zimbabwe, Salisbury).
The Papers of Mrs. N. Pegrum (in private possession).
The Papers of Stanley Cooke (in private possession).
The Papers of the United Central Africa Association (National Archives of Zimbabwe, Salisbury).
The Papers of the Capricorn Africa Society (National Archives of Zimbabwe, Salisbury).
Manuscript of Rex Reynolds: Discussions with Lord Malvern with comments by Sir Ernest Guest (in Lord Blake's possession).
The Papers of Sir Herbert Stanley (Rhodes House, Oxford).

B. Printed Works

Addicott, G., "Left, Right and Centre: A Commentary of the Federal Election", *New Rhodesia* (Salisbury), Vol. 22, 11.12.53.
"Africanus", "A Central African Confederation", *Journal of the Royal African Society* (London, 1918), Vol. 18.
"Africanus", "Reconstruction in Central Africa", *Journal of the Royal African Society* (London, 1919), Vol. 19.
Africa Bureau, *Central Africa and the British Parliament: Background to the Constitution Amendment Bill, 1957* (London, 1957).
Africa Bureau, *Central Africa and the Franchise: An Examination of the Federal Electoral Bill, 1958* (London, 1958).
Allighan, G., *The Welensky Story* (London, 1962).
Alport, Lord, "Central Africa in the Sixties", *Commonwealth Journal* (London, 1963), Vol. 6.
Alport, Lord, *Sudden Assignment* (London, 1965).
American Committee on Africa, "The Federation of Rhodesia and Nyasaland: The Future of a Dilemma", *Africa Today Pamphlets : 4* (New York, 1959).
Amery, L. M. S., *My Political Life* (London, 1953).

Anon., "Man of the Moment: Lieutenant-Colonel Sir Stewart Gore-Browne", *Africa Bureau News* (London, 1962), Vol. 2, 5.
Anthony, L. F. G., *North of the Zambezi* (Lusaka, 1953).
Armitage, Sir Robert, "Nyasaland", F. S. Joelson (ed.), *Rhodesia and East Africa* (London, 1958).
Arrighi, G., *The Political Economy of Rhodesia* (The Hague, 1967).
Attlee, Lord, *As It Happened* (London, 1954).
Banda, H. K. and Nkumbula, H., *Federation in Central Africa* (London, 1951).
Banda, T. D. T., "Nyasaland and Federation", *Africa South* (Cape Town, January-March 1958), Vol. 2.
Barber, J., *Rhodesia: The Road to Rebellion* (London, 1967).
Barber, J., *South Africa's Foreign Policy 1945–1970* (London, 1973).
Barber, W. J., *The Economy of British Central Africa* (Stanford, 1961).
Barnes, J. A., *Politics in a Changing Society* (Oxford, 1954).
Baxter, G. H. and Jodgens, P. W., "The Constitutional Status of the Federation of Rhodesia and Nyasaland", *International Affairs* (London, October 1957).
Beadle, T. H. W., *The Present Situation in Southern Rhodesia* (London, 1949).
Beadle, Sir Hugh, "How we could succeed where Rhodes failed", *Rhodes Newsletter* (Grahamstown, 1971).
Bean, E. A., *Political Development in Southern Rhodesia, 1890–1953: a bibliography* (Cape Town, 1969).
Beetham, T. A., *A New Order in Africa* (London, 1960).
Beit, Sir Alfred and Lockhart, J. G., *The Will and the Way* (London, 1957).
Beloff, M., *Imperial Sunset* (London, 1969), Vol. 1.
Bengs, B-A., *The Ndola Accident* (Stockholm, 1966).
Bennet, G. (ed.), *The Concept of Empire* (London, 1953).
Benson, Sir Arthur, "Northern Rhodesia", F. S. Joelson (ed.), *Rhodesia and East Africa* (London, 1958).
Berger, E. L., *Labour, Race and Colonial Rule: The Copperbelt from 1924 to Independence* (Oxford, 1974).
Blake, Robert, *A History of Rhodesia* (London, 1977).
Biggs-Davison, J., "Rhodesia: the Realities", *British Commonwealth Union* (London, 1966).
Birkenhead, Lord, *Walter Monckton: The Life of Viscount Monckton of Brenchley* (London, 1969).
Brelsford, W. V. (ed.), *Handbook to the Federation of Rhodesia and Nyasaland* (London, 1960).
Brett, E. A., *Colonialism and Underdevelopment: The Politics of Economic Change, 1919–39* (New York, 1973).
Bourne, K. and Watt, D. C., *Studies in International History* (London, 1969).
Bowett, D. W., *United Nations Forces* (London, 1964).
Bowman, L., *Politics in Rhodesia: White Power in an African State* (London, 1974).
Bull, T., *Rhodesian Perspective* (London, 1967).
Burns, A. L. and Heathcote, N., *Peace-Keeping by U.N. Forces: From Suez to the Congo* (New York, 1963).
Burns, J. M., *Roosevelt the Soldier of Freedom 1940–5* (London, 1971).
Butler, Lord, *The Art of the Possible: The Memoirs of Lord Butler* (Aylesbury, 1971).
Brockway, F., *The Colonial Revolution* (New York, 1973).
Calder, R., *The Agony of the Congo* (London, 1961).
Caplan, G., *The Elites of Barotseland 1878–1969* (London, 1970).
Cary, R. and Mitchell, D., *African Nationalist Leaders in Rhodesia: Who's Who* (Bulawayo, 1977).
Chandos, Lord, *Memoirs* (London, 1962).
Chanock, M. L., *British Policy in Central Africa, 1908–26* (University of Cambridge, Ph.D. Thesis, 1968).
Chanock, M. L., *Unconsummated Union: Britain, Rhodesia and South Africa, 1900–45* (Manchester, 1977).
Chisiza, D. K., "Africa — What Lies Ahead", *Indian Council for Africa* (New Delhi, 1961).
Chisiza, D. K., "Realities of African Independence", *Africa Bureau* (London, 1961).
Chiume, M. W. K., "Nyasaland Speaks — An Appeal to the British People", *Union of Democratic Control and the Movement for Colonial Freedom* (London, 1959).

Clegg, E. M., "The Franchise in Rhodesia and Nyasaland", *International Affairs* (London, 1957).
Clegg, E. M., *Race and Politics: Partnership in the Federation of Rhodesia and Nyasaland* (London, 1960).
Clements, F., *The Struggle with the River God* (London, 1969).
Clements, F., *Rhodesia, The Course to Collision* (London, 1969).
Clutton-Brock, A. G., "Facing 1960 in Central Africa", *Africa Bureau* (London, 1959).
Clutton-Brock, A. G., *Dawn in Nyasaland* (London, 1959).
Cohen, Sir Andrew, *British Policy in Changing Africa* (London, 1959).
Collins, M. O., *Rhodesia: Its Natural Resources and Economic Development* (Salisbury, 1965).
Colvin, I., *The Rise and Fall of Moise Tshombe* (London, 1968).
Commonwealth Parliamentary Association, *The Federation of Rhodesia and Nyasaland: Report on a Visit* (London, 1958).
Constantine, S., *The Formulation of British Policy on Colonial Development, 1914–29* (University of Oxford, D. Phil. Thesis, 1974).
Cordier, A. W. and Foote, W. (eds.), *Public Papers of the Secretaries-General of the United Nations: Volume 5: 1960–61. Dag Hammarskjold* (New York, 1975).
Council of Europe, Africa 1961, *A Survey of political events during 1961* (Strasbourg, 1962).
Creighton, T. R. M., *Southern Rhodesia and the Central African Federation: The Anatomy of Partnership* (London, 1960).
Creighton, T. R. M., "The Future of the Federation", *Africa South* (Cape Town, April-June 1961), Vol. 5, 3.
Culwick, A. T., *Britannia Waives the Rules* (Pretoria, 1964).
Currie, D. P. (ed.), *Federalism and the New Nations of Africa* (Chicago, 1964).
Curtin, P. D. (ed.), *Imperialism: Selected Documents* (London, 1972).
Day, J., *International Nationalism: The extra-territorial relations of Southern Rhodesian African Nationalists* (London, 1967).
Day, J., "The Creation of Political Myths: African Nationalism in Southern Rhodesia", *Journal of Southern African Studies* (Oxford, October 1975), Vol. 2, 1.
Dayal, R., *Mission for Hammarskjold: The Congo Crisis* (London, 1976).
Davies, M., *Incorporation in the Union of South Africa or Self-Government: Southern Rhodesia's Choice, 1922* (Pretoria, 1965).
Davidson, B., *Report on Southern Africa* (London, 1952).
Davidson, J. W., *The Legislative Council of Northern Rhodesia* (London, 1948).
Debenham, F., *Nyasaland: The Land of the Lake* (London, 1955).
Denoon, D., *A Grand Illusion* (London, 1973).
Dickie, J. and Rake, A., *Who's Who in Africa* (London, 1973).
Dikshit, R., "The Failure of Federation in Central Africa: A Politico-Geographical Post-Mortem", *Professional Geographic, 1971*, Vol. 23, 3.
Dotson, F. and L. O., *The Indian Minority of Zambia, Rhodesia and Malawi* (New Haven, 1968).
Drew, J. D. C., "The Four Southern Rhodesian Referendums", *Occasional Papers of the National Archives of Rhodesia and Nyasaland* (Salisbury, 1963), Vol. 1, 1.
Dreyer, E., *The Federation Movement in British Central Africa* (University of Georgetown, Ph.D. Thesis, 1951).
Dugauquier, D. P., *Congo Cauldron* (London, 1961).
Dunn, C., *Central African Witness* (London, 1959).
Dupont, C., *The Reluctant President* (Bulawayo, 1978).
Emerson, R., *From Empire to Nation: The Rise of Self-Assertion of Asian and African Peoples* (Cambridge, 1960).
Epstein, A. L., *Politics in an Urban African Community* (London, 1958).
Epstein, H. M. (ed.), *Revolt in the Congo, 1960–64* (Manchester, 1958).
Fage, J. D., *The Achievement of Self-Government in Southern Rhodesia, 1898–1923* (University of Cambridge, Ph.D. Thesis, 1949).
Fage, J. D., *A History of Africa* (London, 1978).
Fisher, Sir Nigel, *Iain Macleod* (London, 1973).
Franck, T. M., *Race and Nationalism: The Struggle for Power in Rhodesia and Nyasaland* (London, 1960).
Franklin, H., *Unholy Wedlock: The Failure of the Central African Federation* (London, 1963).

Gale, W. D., *Heritage of Rhodes* (Oxford, 1953).
Gale, W. D., *The Years Between 1923–1973: Half a Century of Responsible Government in Rhodesia* (Salisbury, 1973).
Gann, L. H., *The Birth of a Plural Society* (Manchester, 1958).
Gann, L. H. and Duignan, P., *White Settlers in Tropical Africa* (London, 1960).
Gann, L. H., "The White Settler: A Changing Image", *Race* (London, 1961), Vol. 2, 2.
Gann, L. H., "The Southern Rhodesian Land Apportionment Act, 1930: An Essay in Imperial Trusteeship", *Occasional Papers of the National Archives of Rhodesia and Nyasaland* (Salisbury, 1963), Vol. 1, 1.
Gann, L. H., *A History of Northern Rhodesia, Early Days to 1953* (London, 1964).
Gann, L. H. and Gelfand, M., *Huggins of Rhodesia* (London, 1964).
Gann, L. H., *A History of Southern Rhodesia, Early Days to 1933* (London, 1965).
Gann, L. H. and Duignan, P., *Burden of Empire: An Appraisal of Western Colonialism in Africa South of the Sahara* (London, 1968).
Gann, L. H. and Duignan, P. (eds.), *Colonialism in Africa 1870–1960: Volume II: The History and Politics of Colonialism 1914–1960* (Cambridge, 1970).
Gann, L. H., *Central Africa: The Former British States* (Engelwood Cliffs, 1971).
Gavshon, A., *The Mysterious Death of Dag Hammarskjold* (London, 1962).
Gavshon, A., *The Last Days of Dag Hammarskjold* (New York, 1962).
Gelfand, M., *Northern Rhodesia in the Days of the Charter* (Oxford, 1961).
Gelfand, M. and Ritchken, J. (eds.), *Godfrey Martin Huggins, Viscount Malvern, 1883–1971* (Salisbury, 1972).
Gelfand, M., *A Non-Racial Island of Learning: A History of the University College of Rhodesia from its Inception to 1966* (Gwelo, 1978).
Gerard-Libois, J., *Katanga Secession* (London, 1966).
Gerold-Scheepers, T. H., "African Resistance in Rhodesia: A Concise Survey of Publications", *African Perspectives 1* (1976).
Gibbs, P., *Avalanche in Central Africa* (London, 1961).
Goldsworthy, D., *Colonial Issues in British Politics 1945–61* (Oxford, 1971).
Gore-Browne, Sir Stewart, "The Federated States of Rhodesia", *Journal of the Royal African Society* (London, 1937), Vol. 36, 2, 7.
Gore-Browne, Sir Stewart, "Amalgamation of the Rhodesias and Nyasaland", *Four Colonial Questions: How Should Britain Act? Fabian Society* (London, 1944).
Gore-Browne, Sir Stewart, *Current Problems in Northern Rhodesia* (London, 1946).
Gore-Browne, Sir Stewart, "Partition in Africa", *Manchester Guardian* (25 August, 1950).
Gore-Browne, Sir Stewart, "Central African Problems", *London Newsletter* (London, 30 December 1951).
Gore-Browne, Sir Stewart, "Partnership in Central Africa", *Manchester Guardian* (7 February 1952).
Gore-Browne, Sir Stewart, "African Aristotle Taken to Task", *African Weekly* (20 February 1952).
Gore-Browne, Sir Stewart, "Early History of the Movement for Federation", *Northern News* (26 April 1952).
Gore-Browne, Sir Stewart, "First Federation Conference at Victoria Falls", *Northern News* (29 April 1952).
Gore-Browne, Sir Stewart, "Sir Stewart Reaffirms his Faith in N. R. Partition", *Northern News* (1 May 1952).
Gore-Browne, Sir Stewart, "Central Africa — The Issue", *Manchester Guardian* (15 May 1952).
Gore-Browne, Sir Stewart, "New Draft Constitution will simplify Federation Issue", *Northern News* (24 June 1952).
Gore-Browne, Sir Stewart, "Will Federal Constitution's Safeguards for Africans Work?", *Northern News* (26 June 1952).
Gore-Browne, Sir Stewart, "Partition May Be Only Way Out of the Present Deadlock", *Northern News* (28 June 1952).
Gore-Browne, Sir Stewart, "Sir Stewart Gore-Browne Replies to Partition Critics", *Northern News* (16 August 1952).
Gore-Browne, Sir Stewart, "Alternatives to Central African Federation", *Manchester Guardian* (13 April 1953).

Gore-Browne, Sir Stewart, "Real Partnership the Only Key to the Riddle", *The Bulawayo Chronicle* (6 August 1954).
Gore-Browne, Sir Stewart, "Partnership or Partition", *Northern News* (21 December 1954).
Gore-Browne, Sir Stewart, "Partition May Yet Be the Only Answer", *Central African Examiner* (30 August 1958).
Gore-Browne, Sir Stewart, "The Political Game in Northern Rhodesia", *Central African Examiner* (7 November 1959).
Gore-Browne, Sir Stewart, "Note on Northern Rhodesia", *Dissent* (Salisbury, 7 July 1960), Vol. 20, 7, 9.
Gore-Browne, Sir Stewart, "Urgent: A Fair Franchise", *African Mail* (April 1961).
Gordon, K., *The U.N. in the Congo: A Quest for Peace* (New York, 1962).
Gray, R., *The Two Nations: Aspects of the Development of Race Relations in the Rhodesias and Nyasaland* (London, 1960).
Greaves, L. B., *Everyman's Concern: The Rhodesias and Nyasaland* (London, 1959).
Gregory, Sir Theodore, *Ernest Oppenheimer and the Economic Development of Southern Africa* (Cape Town, 1962).
Greenfield, J. M., *The Erosion of the Rule of Law in Nyasaland* (Salisbury, August 1963).
Greenfield, J. M., *Testimony of a Rhodesian Federal* (Bulawayo, 1978).
Griffiths, J., *Pages from Memory* (London, 1969).
Gupta, A., *Reporting Africa* (New Delhi, 1969).
Gupta, P. S., *Imperialism and the British Labour Movement, 1914–64* (London, 1975).
Hailey, Lord, *Note on the bearing of native policy of the proposed amalgamation of the Rhodesias and Nyasaland* (London, 1941).
Hailey, Lord, *Native Administration in the British African Territories II: Central Africa: Zanzibar, Nyasaland and Northern Rhodesia* (London, 1950).
Hailey, Lord, *An African Survey* (London, 1956).
Hailey, Lord, *The Republic of South Africa and the High Commission Territories* (Oxford, 1963).
Hall, R. S., *Kaunda: Founder of Zambia* (London, 1964).
Hall, R. S., *Zambia* (London, 1965).
Hancock, I. R., "Sane and Pragmatic Liberalism: The Action Group in Bulawayo, 1955–65", *Rhodesian History* (Salisbury, 1976), Vol. 7.
Hancock, I. R., "The Capricorn Africa Society in Southern Rhodesia", *Rhodesian History* (Salisbury, 1978), Vol. 9.
Hanna, A. J., *The Beginnings of Nyasaland and North Eastern Rhodesia, 1859–1895* (Oxford, 1956).
Hanna, A. J., *The Story of the Rhodesias and Nyasaland* (London, 1960).
Hartz, L., *The Founding of New Societies* (New York, 1964).
Hastings, S., "The United Nations in Katanga", *African Affairs* (London, July 1962), Vol. 61.
Hatch, J., *Two African Statesmen: Kaunda of Zambia and Nyerere of Tanzania* (London, 1976).
Haw, R. C., *Land Apportionment in Rhodesia* (Salisbury, 1965).
Hazlewood, A., "The Economics of Federation and Dissolution in Central Africa", A. Hazlewood (ed.), *African Integration and Disintegration* (Oxford, 1967).
Hazlewood, A. and Henderson, P. D., *Nyasaland: The Economics of Federation* (London, 1960).
Hempstone, S., *Rebels, Mercenaries and Dividends: The Katanga Story* (New York, 1962).
Hempstone, S., *Katanga Report* (London, 1962).
Henderson, I., "The Origins of Nationalism in East and Central Africa: The Zambian Case", *Journal of African History* (London, 1970), Vol. XI, 4.
Henderson, I., "Wage-Earners and Political Protest in Colonial Africa: The Case of the Copperbelt", *African Affairs* (London, 1973), Vol. 72, 287.
Henderson, I., "The Economic Origins of Decolonization in Zambia, 1940–45", *Rhodesian History* (Salisbury, 1974), Vol. 5.
Hennesy, M. N., *The Congo – a Brief History and Appraisal* (London, 1961).
Hetherwick, A., "Nyasaland Today and Tomorrow", *Journal of the Royal African Society* (London, 1917), Vol. 17.
Hinden, R., *No Cheer for Central Africa* (London, 1958).
Hirsch, M., *Focus on Southern Rhodesia* (Bulawayo, 1964).
Hirsch, M., *A Decade of Crisis: Ten Years of R.F. Rule* (Salisbury, 1973).
Hole, H. M., *The Making of Rhodesia* (London, 1926).

Hodgkin, T. H., *Nationalism in Colonial Africa* (London, 1956).
Hodgkin, T. H., *African Political Parties* (London, 1961).
Home, Lord, "Impressions of the Federation", F. S. Joelson (ed.), *Rhodesia and East Africa* (London, 1958).
Home, Lord, *The Way the Wind Blows: an Autobiography* (London, 1976).
Horrell, Muriel, "Days of Crisis in Rhodesia", *Fact Paper No 16: South African Institute of Race Relations* (Johannesburg, 1965).
Hoskyns, C., *The Congo since Independence* (London, 1965).
Howarth, D., *Shadow of the Dam* (London, 1961).
Huggins, G. M., "Amalgamate the Two Rhodesias", F. S. Joelson (ed.), *East Africa and Rhodesia* (London, 3 June 1937).
Huggins, G. M., "Southern Rhodesia and the Bledisloe Report", *African World* (1939), Vol. 148.
Huggins, G. M., *Statement on Native Policy in Southern Rhodesia* (Salisbury, 1941).
Huggins, G. M., "The Native Problem in Southern Rhodesia", *African World* (1942), Vol. 158.
Huggins, G. M., "President's Speech to (the United Party) Congress", *National Progress* (Salisbury, October 1949), Vol. 3, 5.
Huggins, G. M., "Presidential Address to (the United Party) Congress", *National Progress* (Salisbury, September 1950), Vol. 4, 10.
Huggins, G. M., "Partnership Policy in Southern Rhodesia", *National Progress* (Salisbury, 1951), Vol. 4, 12.
Huggins, G. M., "Keep the United Party Alive", *National Progress* (Salisbury, June 1951), Vol. 4, 12.
Huggins, G. M., "The Federal Scheme: An Evaluation", *National Progress* (Salisbury, July 1952), Vol. 5, 3.
Huggins, G. M., "The African's Place in the Federation of Rhodesia and Nyasaland", *Optima* (Johannesburg, June 1954), Vol. 4, 2.
Huggins, G. M., "Federation of Rhodesia and Nyasaland: The Case for Independence", *Rhodesian Graphic* (Salisbury, 1959).
Hummel, H. C., *A Political Biography of Sir Charles Coghlan* (University of London, Ph.D. Thesis, 1975).
Hunter, G., *The New Societies of Tropical Africa* (London, 1963).
Hyam, R., *The Failure of South African Expansionism, 1908–48* (London, 1972).
Ionescu, G. and Gellner, E. (eds.), *Populism, Its National Characteristics* (London, 1969).
Irvine, A. G., *The Balance of Payments of Rhodesia and Nyasaland* (London, 1969).
(Joelson, F. S.) *Intimidation in Central Africa: Vote Me or Else* (London, 1962).
Jones, A. Creech, *African Challenge: The Fallacy of Federation* (London, 1952).
Jones, G. B., *Britain and Nyasaland* (London, 1964).
Joyce, P., *Anatomy of a Rebel* (Salisbury, 1974).
Judd, P. (ed.) *African Independence* (New York, 1963).
Kanza, T., *Conflict in the Congo* (London, 1972).
Kaunda, K. D., "Rider and Horse in Northern Rhodesia", *Africa South* (Cape Town, July-September 1959), Vol. 3, 4.
Kaunda, K. D., *Zambia Shall Be Free* (London, 1962).
Kaunda, K. D., "Some Personal Reflections", *Africa's Freedom* (London, 1964).
Kaunda, K. D. and Morris, C., *Black Government* (Lusaka, 1960).
Kay, G., *Rhodesia, a Human Geography* (London, 1970).
Keatley, P., *The Politics of Partnership* (London, 1963).
Keighley, D. A., *Review in Central Africa* (London, 1960).
Kinloch, G. C., "Changing Black Reaction to White Domination", *Rhodesian History* (Salisbury, 1974), Vol. 5.
King, G., *U.N. in the Congo* (New York, 1962).
Kirk, T., "Politics and Violence in Rhodesia", *African Affairs* (London, 1975), Vol. 74.
Kirkman, W. P., *Unscrambling an Empire: a Critique of British Colonial Policy* (London, 1966).
Kirkwood, K., "British Central African Politics under Federation", *Annals of the American Academy* (Philadelphia, 1955), Vol. 289.
Kirkwood, K., *Britain and Africa* (London, 1965).
Koebnev, R. and Schmidt, H. D., *Imperialism: The Story and Significance of a Political World 1840–1960* (Cambridge, 1965).

Lake, A., *The "Tar-Baby" Option: American Policy Towards Southern Rhodesia* (New York, 1976).
Lash, J. P., *Dag Hammarskjold* (London, 1962).
Lee, M. E., *Politics and Pressure Groups in Southern Rhodesia, 1898–1923* (University of London, Ph.D. Thesis, 1975).
Lee, M. E., "An Analysis of the Rhodesian Referendum", *Rhodesian History* (Salisbury, 1977), Vol. 8.
Lefever, E. W., *Crisis in the Congo* (Washington, 1965).
Lefever, E. W., *Spear and Sceptre: Army, Police and Politics in Tropical Africa* (Washington, 1971).
Legum, C., *Congo Disaster* (London, 1961).
Legum, C., *Pan-Africanism, A Short Political Guide* (London, 1962).
Legum, C. (ed.), *Africa: A Handbook to the Continent* (New York, 1962).
Legum, C., *Pan-Africanism* (revised) (London, 1965).
LeMarchand, R., *Political Awakening in the Belgian Congo* (Los Angeles, 1964).
Lennox-Boyd, A., "The Secretary of State's Point of View", F. S. Joelson (ed.), *Rhodesia and East Africa* (London, 1958).
Lewanika, G., "The Problems of a Multi-Racial Society in Central Africa", *African Affairs* (London, October 1958), Vol. 57, 229.
Leys, C., *European Politics in Southern Rhodesia* (London, 1959).
Leys, C. and Pratt, C., *New Deal in Central Africa* (London, 1960).
Lloyd, P. C. (ed.), *The New Elites of Tropical Africa* (London, 1966).
Loney, M., *Rhodesia: White Racism and the Imperial Response* (London, 1975).
Louis, W. R., *Imperialism at Bay: The United States and the Decolonisation of the British Empire, 1941–45* (Oxford, 1977).
Loveday, A. F., *Three Stages of History in Rhodesia* (Cape Town, 1960).
Lucas Phillips, L. E., *The Vision Splendid* (London, 1960).
Lugard, Lord, *The Dual Mandate in British Tropical Africa* (Edinburgh, 1922).
Lumb, S. V., *A Short History of Central and Southern Africa* (Cambridge, 1962).
McAdam, A., "Rhodesia's Phantom Liberalism: Imperialism, Federation and Rebellion in British Central Africa", *African Perspectives* (1976), 1.
Macmillan, H., *Pointing the Way* (London, 1972).
Macmillan, H., *The End of the Day* (London, 1973).
Macmillan, W. M., *Africa Emergent* (London, 1949).
Macpherson, F., *Kenneth Kaunda of Zambia: The Times and the Man* (Lusaka, 1974).
Mair, L. P., *Native Policies in Africa* (London, 1936).
Mair, L. P., *The Nyasaland Election of 1961* (London, 1962).
Mansergh, P. N. S., *Survey of British Commonwealth Affairs: Problems of External Policy* (London, 1952).
Martelli, G., *Leopold to Lumumba* (London, 1962).
Mason, P., *The Birth of a Dilemma: The Conquest and Settlement of Rhodesia* (London, 1958).
Mason, P., *Year of Decision* (London, 1960).
Mason, P., "Prospects and Progress in the Federation of Rhodesia and Nyasaland", *African Affairs* (London, January 1962), Vol. 61, 242.
Matthews, D., *African Powderkeg* (1966).
Maudling, R., *Memoirs* (London, 1978).
Melady, T. P., *Profiles of African Leaders* (London, 1961).
Meredith, M., *The Past is Another Country: Rhodesia 1890–1979* (London, 1979).
Merriman, A. P., *Congo – Background of Conflict* (Evanston, 1961).
Miller, J. D. B., *Survey of Commonwealth Affairs: Problems of Expansion and Attrition, 1953–1969* (London, 1974).
Mlambo, E., *Rhodesia, the Struggle for a Birthright* (London, 1972).
Morris, C., *The Hour after Midnight* (London, 1961).
Morris, H. and Read, J., *Indirect Rule and the Search for Justice* (London, 1972).
Mtshali, B. V., *Rhodesia: Background to Conflict* (London, 1967).
Mufuka, K. N., "Britain and Amalgamation of the Rhodesias, 1937–1941", *Rhodesian History* (Salisbury, 1976), Vol. 7.
Mulford, D. C., *The Northern Rhodesian General Election* (London, 1964).

Mulford, D. C., *Zambia: The Politics of Independence, 1957–1964* (London, 1967).
Murray, D. J., *The Governmental System in Southern Rhodesia* (Oxford, 1970).
Nyangoni, C. and Nyandoro, G., *Zimbabwe Independence Movements Select Documents* (London, 1979).
O'Brien, C. C., *To Katanga and Back* (London, 1962).
O'Brien, C. C., *Conflicting Concepts of the United Nations* (Leeds, 1964).
Oliver, R. and Fage, J. D., *A Short History of Africa* (London, 1962).
Oppenheimer, H. F., *The Conditions for Progress in Africa* (Cape Town, 1960).
Pachai, B. (ed.), *An Early History of Malawi* (London, 1972).
Pachai, B., *Malawi: The History of the Nation* (London, 1973).
Packard, E. D., *Report of the Survey of the British South Africa Police* (Salisbury, 1962).
Padmore, G., *History of the Pan-African Congress* (London, 1963).
Palley, C., *The Constitutional History and Law of Southern Rhodesia 1888–1965* (Oxford, 1966).
Palmer, R., *Aspects of Rhodesian Land Policy* (Salisbury, 1968).
Palmer, R., "European Resistance to African Majority Rule: The Settlers' and Residents' Association of Nyasaland, 1960–63", *African Affairs* (London, 1973), Vol. 72, 287.
Palmer, R., *Land and Racial Domination in Rhodesia* (London, 1977).
Parkinson, Sir Cosmo, *The Colonial Office from Within* (London, 1945).
Passmore, G. C., *Local Government Legislation in Southern Rhodesia up to 30th September 1963* (Salisbury, 1966).
Pearson, D. S. and Taylor, W. L., "Break-Up: Some Economic Consequences for the Rhodesias and Nyasaland", *Phoenix Paper No 4* (Salisbury, June 1963).
Peck, A. J. A., *Rhodesia Accuses* (Salisbury, 1966).
Perham, M., *The Colonial Reckoning* (London, 1961).
Perham, M., *Colonial Sequence* (London, 1967).
Perrings, C., *Black Mineworkers in Central Africa* (London, 1979).
Pike, J. G., *Malawi: A Political and Economic History* (London, 1968).
Powdermaker, H., *Copper Town: Changing Africa: The Human Situation on the Rhodesian Copperbelt* (New York, 1961).
Pratt, R. C., "Federation in Central Africa: The 1960 Conference", *World Today* (London, January 1960), Vol. 16, 1.
Pratt, R. C., "Partnership and Consent: The Monckton Report Examined", *International Journal* (Toronto, 1960–61), Vol. 16.
Prescott, O. (ed.), *Constitutional Development in the Federation* (Lusaka, 1959).
Ranger, T. O., *Revolt in Southern Rhodesia* (London, 1967).
Ranger, T. O. (ed.), *Aspects of Central African History* (London, 1968).
Ranger, T. O., *The African Voice in Southern Rhodesia, 1868–1930* (London, 1970).
Raven, F., *Central Africa: Background to Argument* (London, 1960).
Rea, F. B. (ed.), *Southern Rhodesia — The Price of Freedom* (Que Que, 1964).
Reed, D., *The Battle for Rhodesia* (Cape Town, 1966).
Reid, J. L., *Land Apportionment in Southern Rhodesia* (Salisbury, 1962).
Rennie, Sir Gilbert, "First Year of Federation", *African Affairs* (London, 1955), Vol. 54.
Rennie, Sir Gilbert, "Power in the Federation", F. S. Joelson (ed.), *Rhodesia and East Africa* (London, 1958).
Richardson, K., *Freedom in the Congo* (London, 1962).
Rifkind, M. L., "Land Apportionment in Perspective", *Rhodesian History* (Salisbury, 1972), Vol. 3.
Rikhye, I. J., Harbottle, M. and Egge, B., *The Thin Blue Line: International Peace Keeping and its Future* (London, 1974).
Rhoodie, N. J., *Apartheid and Racial Partnership in Southern Africa* (Pretoria, 1969).
Roberts, A., *A History of Zambia* (London, 1976).
Robinson, A. E. P., "1961, The Year of Decision in Rhodesia and Nyasaland", *African Affairs* (London, July 1960), Vol. 60, 240.
Robinson, K. E., *The Dilemma of Trusteeship* (London, 1965).
Robinson, R., Gallagher, J. and Denny, A., *Africa and the Victorians* (London, 1961).
Rotberg, R. I., "The Federation Movement in British East and Central Africa, 1889–1953", *Journal of Commonwealth Political Studies, II* (Leicester, 1964).
Rotberg, R. I., *A Political History of Tropical Africa* (New York, 1965).

Rotberg, R. I., "Race Relations and Politics in Colonial Zambia: The Elwell Incident", *Race VII* (London, 1965).
Rotberg, R. I., *Christian Missionaries and the Creation of Northern Rhodesia, 1880–1924* (Princeton, 1965).
Rotberg, R. I., *The Rise of Nationalism in Central Africa: The Making of Malawi and Zambia, 1873–1964* (London, 1965).
Rotberg, R. I., *Black Heart: Gore-Browne and the Politics of Multiracial Zambia* (Los Angeles, 1977).
Saksena, K. P., "Hammarskjold and the Congo Crisis: A Review Article", *India Quarterly* (New Delhi, April–June 1978).
Samkange, S., *On Trial for My Country* (London, 1966).
Samkange, S., *The Origins of Rhodesia* (London, 1968).
Sampson, A., *Macmillan: A Study in Ambiguity* (London, 1967).
Sanger, C., *Central African Emergency* (London, 1960).
Sanger, C., "A Long Time Dying: Central African Federation", *Africa South in Exile* (London, October–December 1961), Vol. 6.
Schuyler, P., *Who Killed the Congo?* (New York, 1962).
Scott, I., *Tumbled House: The Congo at Independence* (London, 1969).
Scott, P. A., "Shire Valley Project", F. S. Joelson (ed.), *Rhodesia and East Africa* (London, 1958).
Segal, R., *Political Africa* (London, 1961).
Segal, R., *African Profiles* (London, 1962).
Shamuyarira, N., *Crisis in Rhodesia* (London, 1965).
Shepperson, G. and Price, T., *Independent African* (Edinburgh, 1958).
Shepperson, G., "Nyasaland and the Millenium", S. L. Thrupp (ed.), *Millenium Dreams in Action* (The Hague, 1962).
Shepperson, G., "External Factors in the Development of African Nationalism, with particular Reference to British Central Africa", *Historians in Tropical Africa* (Salisbury, 1962).
Short, P., *Banda* (London, 1974).
Short, R., *African Sunset* (London, 1973).
Sithole, N., *African Nationalism* (London, 1959).
Sithole, N., *In Defence of a Birthright* (Stockholm, 1975).
Sithole, N., *Roots of a Revolution: Scenes from Zimbabwe's Struggle* (Oxford, 1978).
Slade, R., *The Belgian Congo* (London, 1960).
Soreff, H. and Greig, I., *The Puppeteers* (London, 1965).
Southall, A. (ed.), *Social Change in Modern Africa* (London, 1961).
Spiro, H. J., *Politics in Africa* (Englewood Cliffs, 1962).
Spurling, B. G., *Reluctant Rebel* (Pretoria, 1966).
Stabler, J. B., "The British South Africa Company proposals for Amalgamation of the Rhodesias, 1915-17", *African Social Research*, 7 (Lusaka, June 1969).
Standing, T. G., *A Short History of Southern Rhodesia and Her Neighbours* (London, 1935).
Steele, M. C., *The Challenge of Rhodesia to European Liberal Thought, 1893-1953* (University of Edinburgh, M. Litt. Thesis, 1968).
Steele, M. C., "White Working-Class Disunity: The Southern Rhodesian Labour Party", *Rhodesian History* (Salisbury, 1970), Vol. 1.
Stirling, D., "The Capricorn Contact", *African Affairs* (London, 1957), Vol. 56, 224.
Stokes, E. T. and Brown, R., *The Zambesian Past* (Manchester, 1966).
Stonehouse, J., *Central Africa: After Monckton What Next* (London, 1960).
Stonehouse, J., *Prohibited Immigrant* (London, 1960).
Struelens, M., *The United Nations in the Congo* (Brussels, 1976).
Stumbles, A. R. W., *Some Recollections of a Rhodesian Speaker* (Bulawayo, 1980).
Sturgeon, G. N., *Notes on Amalgamation with Specific Reference to Native Labour* (Bulawayo, 1928).
Symonds, J., *Southern Rhodesia: Background to Crisis* (London, 1965).
Tangri, R. K., "The Rise of Nationalism in Colonial Africa: The Case of Colonial Malawi", Pachai, B., Smith, G. W. and Tangri, R. K. (eds.), *Malawi Past and Present: Studies in Local and Regional History* (Blantyre, 1968).

Tangri, R. K., *The Development of Modern African Politics and the Emergence of a Nationalist Movement in Colonial Malawi, 1891-1958* (University of Edinburgh, Ph.D. Thesis, 1970).
Taylor, A. R. and Dvorin, E. P., "Political Development in British Central Africa, 1890-1956: A Select Survey of the Literature and Background", *Race* (London, November 1959), Vol. 1.
Taylor, D., *The Rhodesian: The Life of Sir Roy Welensky* (London, 1955).
Taylor, D., *The British in Africa* (London, 1962).
Temple, M. and Sokoni, J., *Kaunda of Zambia* (Lusaka, 1964).
Thompson, C. H. and Woodruff, H. W., *Economic Development in Rhodesia and Nyasaland* (London, 1955).
Tindall, P. E. N., *A History of Central Africa* (London, 1968).
Todd, J., *Rhodesia* (London, 1966).
Tredgold, Sir Robert, *The Rhodesia that was my Life* (London, 1968).
United Nations, *Commission to Investigate Conditions and Circumstances resulting in the Death of the Secretary-General and Members of his Party* (New York, 1961).
United Nations, *The United Nations and the Congo — Some Salient Facts* (New York, 1963).
Urquhart, B., *Hammarskjold* (London, 1973).
Vambe, L. C., "As an African Sees the Federation", F. S. Joelson (ed.), *Rhodesia and East Africa* (London, 1958).
Vambe, L. C., *An Ill-Fated People* (London, 1972).
Vambe, L. C., *From Rhodesia to Zimbabwe* (London, 1976).
Van Eeden, G., *The Crime of being White* (Cape Town, 1965).
Van Velsen, J., *Trends in African Nationalism in Southern Rhodesia* (Leiden, 1966).
Venter, A. J., *Zambezi Salient: Conflict in Southern Africa* (Cape Town, 1974).
Voice and Vision, *Inside the New Africa: Portrait of the Federation of Rhodesia and Nyasaland* (London, 1960).
Von Horn, C., *Soldiering for Peace* (London, 1966).
Walker, A. A., *The Rhodesias and Nyasaland: A Guide to Official Publications* (Washington, 1965).
Walker, E. A., *A History of Southern Africa* (London, 1957).
Wallis, J. R. R., *One Man's Hand: The Story of Sir Charles Coghlan and the Liberalisation of Southern Rhodesia* (London, 1950).
Warhurst, P. R., *Rhodesia and her Neighbours, 1900-23* (University of Oxford, D. Phil. Thesis, 1970).
Weinberg, S., *An Outline of the Constitutional Law of the Federation of Rhodesia and Nyasaland* (Salisbury, 1959).
Welensky, R., *A Case for Amalgamation* (Bulawayo, 1944).
Welensky, Sir Roy, "Federation of Rhodesia and Nyasaland", F. S. Joelson (ed.), *Rhodesia and East Africa* (London, 1958).
Welensky, Sir Roy, *The Federation and the Commonwealth: Sir Roy Welenksy, Prime Minister of the Federation of Rhodesia and Nyasaland, speaks in London, November 8, 1961* (Salisbury, 1961).
Welensky, Sir Roy, *Welensky's 4 000 Days: The Life and Death of the Federation of Rhodesia and Nyasaland* (London, 1964).
Wetherell, H. I., "N. H. Wilson: Populism in Southern Rhodesian Politics", *Rhodesian History* (Salisbury, 1975), Vol. 6.
Wetherell, H. I., *The Rhodesias and Amalgamation: Settler Sub-Imperialism and the Imperial Response, 1914-48* (University of Rhodesia, Ph.D. Thesis, 1977).
Wetherell, H. I., "Britain and Rhodesian Expansionism: Imperial Collusion or Empirical Carelessness", *Rhodesian History* (Salisbury, 1977), Vol. 8.
Wetherell, H. I., "Settler Expansionism in Central Africa: The Imperial Response of 1931 and Subsequent Implications", *African Affairs* (London, 1979), Vol. 78, 311.
Wheare, K. C., *Federal Government* (London, 1963).
Wilding, N., *Parliamentary Papers of Rhodesia 1954-1970* (Salisbury, 1970).
Wilkinson, A. R., *Insurgency in Rhodesia 1957-1973: An Account and Assessment* (London, 1974).
Williams, T. D., *Malawi: The Politics of Despair* (Ithaca, 1979).
Willis, A. J., *An Introduction to the History of Central Africa* (London, 1973).
Willson, F. M. G. (ed.), *Source Book of Parliamentary Elections and Referenda in Southern Rhodesia, 1898-1962* (London, 1963).

Willson, F. M. G. and Passmore, G. C., *Catalogue of Parliamentary Papers of Southern Rhodesia, 1899-1953* (Salisbury, 1965).
Willson, F. M. G. and Passmore, G. C., *Southern Rhodesia: Holders of Office and Members of the Legislature, 1894-1964* (Salisbury, 1966).
Windrich, E., *The Rhodesian Problem* (London, 1975).
Windrich, E., *Britain and the Politics of Rhodesian Independence* (London, 1978).
Wood, A. St. J., *Northern Rhodesia: The Human Background* (London, 1961).
Wood, J. R. T., "Siting the Capital of the Central African Federation", Benyon, J. A., Cooke, C. W., Davenport, T. R. H., Hunt, K. S. (eds.), *Studies in Local History: Essays in Honour of Professor Winifred Maxwell* (Cape Town, 1976).
Wood, R., "A Recent Visit to Central Africa", *African Affairs* (London, January 1958), Vol. 57, 226.
Young, C. and Banda, H. K. (eds.), *Our African Way of Life* (London, 1964).
Young, C., *Politics in the Congo — Decolonisation and Independence* (London, 1965).
Young, K., *Rhodesia and Independence: A Study in British Colonial Policy* (London, 1967).

C. Official Publications

British Government Publications

Cmnd 1273 (1921) *First Report of the Committee appointed to consider certain questions relating to Rhodesia.*
Cmnd 1471 (1921) *Second Report of the Committee appointed to consider certain questions relating to Rhodesia.*
Cmnd 2387 (1925) *Report of the East African Commission.*
Cmnd 3234 (1929) *Report of the Commission on Closer Union in East and Central Africa.*
Cmnd 3574 (1930) *Statement of the Conclusion of His Majesty's Government in the United Kingdom as regards closer union in East Africa.*
Cmnd 3731 (1930) *Correspondence with regard to Native Policy in Northern Rhodesia.*
Cmnd 5009 (1935) *Report of a Commission appointed to enquire into Disturbances on the Copperbelt of Northern Rhodesia.*
Cmnd 5449 (1938-9) *Report of the Royal Commission on Rhodesia-Nyasaland.*
Cmnd 5929 (1939) *Report of the Rhodesia and Nyasaland Royal Commission.*
Cmnd 8233 (1951) *Report of the Conference on Closer Association in Central Africa.*
Cmnd 8234 (1951) *The Central African Territories: Historical, Geographical and Economic Survey.*
Cmnd 8235 (1951) *Comparative Survey of Central African Native Policies.*
Cmnd 8411 (1951) *Closer Association in Central Africa: Statement by H.M. Government.*
Cmnd 8573 (1952) *Draft Federal Scheme.*
Cmnd 8671 (1952) *Report of the Judicial Commission.*
Cmnd 8672 (1952) *Report of the Fiscal Commission.*
Cmnd 8673 (1952) *Report of the Civil Service Preparatory Commission.*
Cmnd 8753 (1953) *Report of the Conference on Federation.*
Cmnd 8754 (1953) *Federal Scheme prepared by a Conference held in London in January 1953.*
Cmnd 298 (1957) *Federation of Rhodesia and Nyasaland Constitutional Amendment Bill.*
Cmnd 362 (1958) *Federation of Rhodesia and Nyasaland Electoral Bill.*
Cmnd 530 (1958) *Proposals for Constitutional Change in Northern Rhodesia.*
Cmnd 707 (1959) *State of Emergency.*
Cmnd 814 (1959) *Report of the Nyasaland Commission of Enquiry.*
Cmnd 815 (1959) *Despatch from the Governor of Nyasaland commenting on the Devlin Commission's Report.*
Cmnd 1132 (1960) *Report of the Nyasaland Constitutional Conference.*
Cmnds 1148-1151 (1960) *Report of the Advisory Commission on the Review of the Constitution of the Federation.*
Cmnd 1291 (1961) *Report of Southern Rhodesia Constitutional Conference in Salisbury.*
Cmnd 1295 (1961) *Northern Rhodesia: Proposals for Constitutional Change.*

Cmnd 1301 (1961) *Northern Rhodesia: Statement by the Secretary of State for the Colonies on Proposals for Constitutional Change.*
Cmnds 1399-1400 (1961) *Southern Rhodesia Constitution Parts I and II.*
Cmnd 1423 (1961) *Northern Rhodesia: Proposals for Constitutional Change.*
Cmnd 1887 (1962) *Report of the Nyasaland Constitutional Conference.*
Cmnd 1948 (1963) *The Federation of Rhodesia and Nyasaland: Commentary on Statements Relating to the Establishment of the Federation and their Bearing on the Withdrawal of Nyasaland.*
Cmnd 2000 (1963) *Southern Rhodesia: Correspondence between Her Majesty's Government and the Government of Southern Rhodesia.*
Cmnd 2073 (1963) *Southern Rhodesian Correspondence, April-June 1963.*
Cmnd 2093 (1963) *Report of the Central Africa Conference.*
Cmnd 2807 (1965) *Southern Rhodesia: Documents relating to the negotiations between the United Kingdom and Southern Rhodesian Governments, November 1963-November 1965.*

Federal, Central African Council, Northern Rhodesian, Southern Rhodesian and Nyasaland Publications.

CSR 3 – 1930 *Correspondence relating to the Constitutional Position of Southern Rhodesia* (1936).
Report of the Commission appointed to Enquire into the Advancement of Africans in Industry (Dalgleish Report) (Lusaka, 1948).
PAC 1. Central African Council: Comparative Survey of Native Policy: Northern Rhodesia, Nyasaland and Southern Rhodesia, 5 February 1951.
Conference on Closer Association in Central Africa: Vol I and II.
Conference on Closer Association of Central African Territories, 18-21 September 1951.
Conference on the Proposed Federation of Southern Rhodesia, Northern Rhodesia and Nyasaland, Vols I-III, April-May 1952.
Conference on the Federation of Southern Rhodesia, Northern Rhodesia and Nyasaland, Vols I-III, January 1953.
Report of the Commission on Higher Education for Africans in Central Africa, Central African Council, 1953.
Central African Federation: The Franchise for Federal Elections in Rhodesia and Nyasaland (Salisbury, 1957).
Proposals for Constitutional Change in Northern Rhodesia (Lusaka, 1958).
Report of the Commission Appointed to Inquire into the Circumstances Leading up to and Surrounding the Recent Deaths and Injuries Caused by the Use of Firearms in the Gwembe District and Matters relating thereto (Lusaka, 1958).
Federal Information Department: *A Note on Dominion Status,* September 1958.
N. A. C. Ridley, *Northern Rhodesia: Report of an Inquiry into all the Circumstances which gave Rise to the Making of the Safeguard of Elections and Public Safety Regulations* (Lusaka, 20 July 1959).
CSR 27-59 *Beadle Tribunal (Review Tribunal (Preventive Detention Temporary Provisions) Act 1959) General Report* (Salisbury, 1959).
LASC *First Report of the Select Committee on the Resettlement of Natives* (Salisbury, 1959).
LASC *Second Report of the Select Committee on the Resettlement of Natives* (Salisbury, 1960).
An Account of the Disturbances in Northern Rhodesia July to October 1961 (Lusaka, 1961).
The Southworth Commission Report, 1960 (Zomba, 2 May 1960).
Report of the Delimitation Commission (Lusaka, 1962).
Southern Rhodesia Information Services: *Southern Rhodesian Africans Speak: Our Fight Against Hooliganism and Thuggery* (Salisbury, 1962).
SRG *Report on the Zimbabwe African People's Union* (Salisbury, 1962).
C. Fed. 231 *The Issue of Nyasaland's Secession* (Salisbury, 19 December 1962).
Federation and Nyasaland: The British Government's Broken Pledges and Consequences (Salisbury, 1962).
C. Fed. 246 *The Break-Up: Effects and Consequences on the Two Rhodesias* (Salisbury, 26 June 1963).
C. Fed. 255 *Financial Obligations of the Federal Government* (Salisbury, 10 July 1963).
C. Fed. 256 *Report of the Central Africa Conference held at the Victoria Falls Hotel, 28th June 1963-3rd July 1963* (Salisbury, 10 July 1963).

Report of the Commission of Inquiry into Unrest on the Copperbelt, July-August 1963 (Lusaka, 1963).
C. Fed. 269 *Legacy of Progress: Achievements of the Years of Federation 1953-1963* (Salisbury, 1963).
Report of the National Convention of Southern Rhodesia (Salisbury, 1960).

Index

Note: Within each entry, items are recorded alphabetically except in the case of a person's offices which are recorded chronologically.

GLOSSARY

ANC, NR	African National Congress, Northern Rhodesia
ANC, SR	African National Congress, Southern Rhodesia
BBC	British Broadcasting Corporation
CAC	Central African Council
CID	Criminal Investigation Department
DP	Dominion Party
GATT	General Agreement on Trades and Tariffs
MCP	Malawi Congress Party
NDP	National Democratic Party
NIBMAR	No Independence Before Majority Rule
NR	Northern Rhodesia
Ny.	Nyasaland
SR	Southern Rhodesia
UDI	Unilateral Declaration of Independence
UCAA	United Central Africa Association
UFP	United Federal Party
UNIP	United National Independence Party
UN	United Nations
URP	United Rhodesia Party
ZANC	Zambia African National Congress
ZANU	Zimbabwe African National Union
ZAPU	Zimbabwe African People's Union